Uses of Nouns

N = person, place, thing, idea

Noun - subject
someone or
something

object
receives the action
Ask whom or what
(comes after the verb

Object of preposition
of, on, for

The Writer's Craft

ANNOTATED TEACHER'S EDITION

SENIOR AUTHOR

SHERIDAN BLAU

University of California at Santa Barbara

CONSULTING AUTHOR

PETER ELBOW

University of Massachusetts at Amherst

SPECIAL CONTRIBUTING AUTHORS

Don Killgallon

Baltimore County Public Schools

Rebekah Caplan

Oakland Unified School District

SENIOR CONSULTANTS

Arthur Applebee

State University of New York at Albany

Judith Langer

State University of New York at Albany

McDougal, Littell & Company
Evanston, Illinois

New York • Dallas • Columbia, SC

ISBN 0-8123-7869-5

Box 1667, Evanston, Illinois 60204

Printed in the United States of America.

1 2 3 4 5 6 7 8 9 0–VJM–98 97 96 95 94 93

Contents of the Annotated Teacher's Edition

Excellence in Three Parts

***The Writer's Craft* presents a perfect blend of literature, writing, and grammar. But the real value of the series lies in its flexible approach to teaching. This flexibility results from a unique three-part arrangement.**

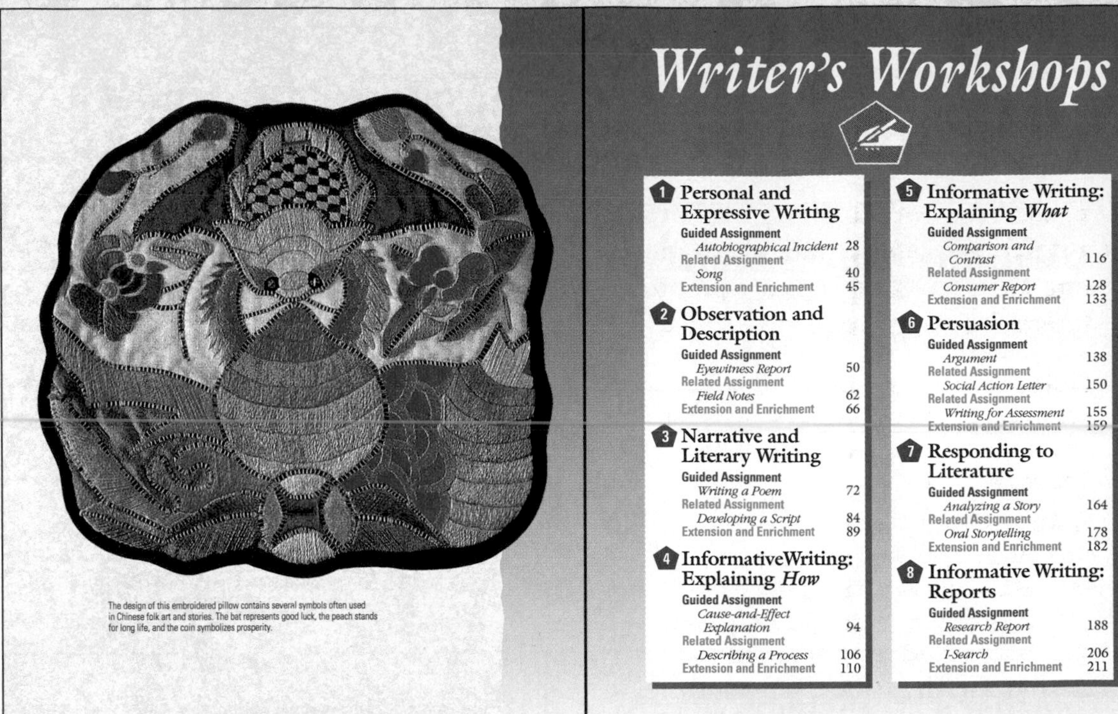

The design of this embroidered pillow contains several symbols often used in Chinese folk art and stories. The bat represents good luck, the peach stands for long life, and the coin symbolizes prosperity.

Writer's Workshops

The Writer's Workshops

Real-world writing experiences show students how writing can help them affect and make sense of their world. References to the two Handbooks help them solve any writing problems that arise.

This yarn drawing is an example of the artistry of the Huichol people, who live in a mountainous region of central Mexico. The deer, cow, cactus, and sun symbols commonly appear in Huichol textiles.

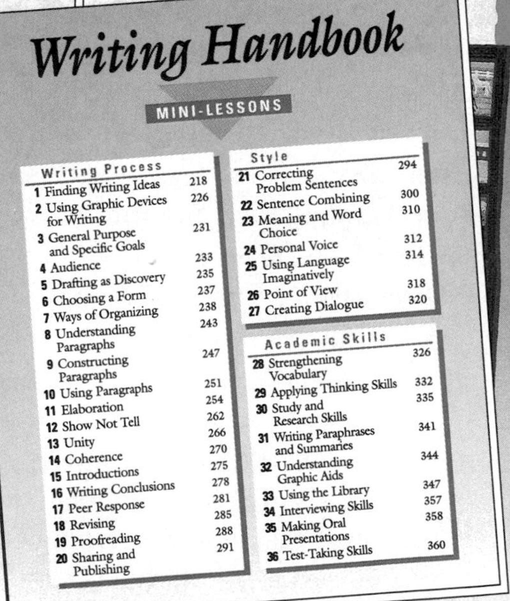

Writing Handbook

MINI-LESSONS

Grammar and Usage Handbook

MINI-LESSONS

The Writing Handbook

Mini-lessons on the writing process, style, and academic skills allow both teachers and students to find just the right help at just the right time.

The Grammar and Usage Handbook

Strong grammar instruction is taken out of isolation and presented in the context of drafting, revision, proofreading, and literature. Students apply their skills immediately after learning them.

Writer's Workshops

Each Writer's Workshop explores a writing mode or skill through one Guided Assignment and one Related Assignment.

Guided Assignments Hands-on activities provide in-depth suggestions and strategies for each stage of the writing process.

Related Assignments These streamlined writing experiences build on and extend the skills presented in the Guided Assignments by allowing students to problem solve within motivating, less traditional formats:

- Collage
- Children's Book
- Field Notes
- Graphics
- Commercials
- Oral History
- Song
- Script
- Magazine

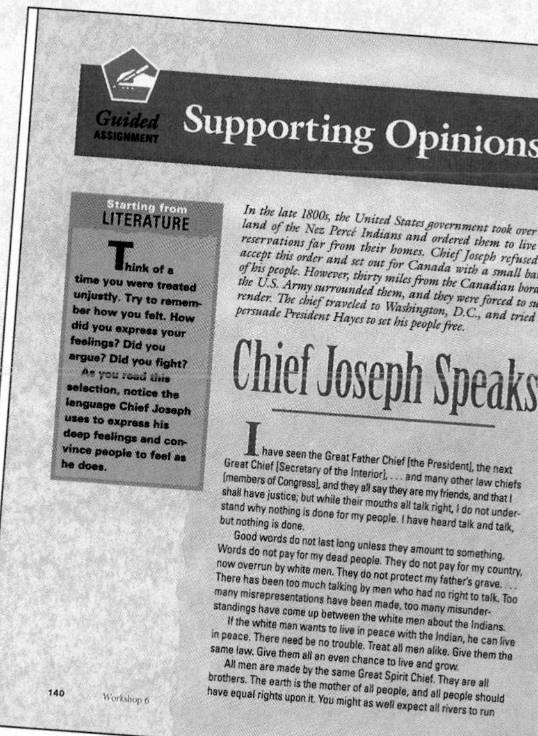

Guided ASSIGNMENT

Supporting Opinions

Starting from LITERATURE

Think of a time you were treated unjustly. Try to remember how you felt. How did you express your feelings? Did you argue? Did you fight?

As you read this selection, notice the language Chief Joseph uses to express his deep feelings and convince people to feel as he does.

In the late 1800s, the United States government took over the land of the Nez Percé Indians and ordered them to live on reservations far from their homes. Chief Joseph refused to accept this order and set out for Canada with a small band of his people. However, thirty miles from the Canadian border the U.S. Army surrounded them, and they were forced to surrender. The chief traveled to Washington, D.C., and tried to persuade President Hayes to set his people free.

Chief Joseph Speaks

I have seen the Great Father Chief [the President], the next Great Chief [Secretary of the Interior], . . . and many other law chiefs [members of Congress], and they all say they are my friends, and that I shall have justice; but while their mouths all talk right, I do not understand why nothing is done for my people. I have heard talk and talk, but nothing is done.

Good words do not last long unless they amount to something. Words do not pay for my dead people. They do not pay for my country, now overrun by white men. They do not protect my father's grave. . . . There has been too much talking by men who had no right to talk. Too many misrepresentations have been made, too many misunderstandings have come up between the white men about the Indians.

If the white man wants to live in peace with the Indian, he can live in peace. There need be no trouble. Treat all men alike. Give them the same law. Give them all an even chance to live and grow.

All men are made by the same Great Spirit Chief. They are all brothers. The earth is the mother of all people, and all people should have equal rights upon it. You might as well expect all rivers to run

140 Workshop 6

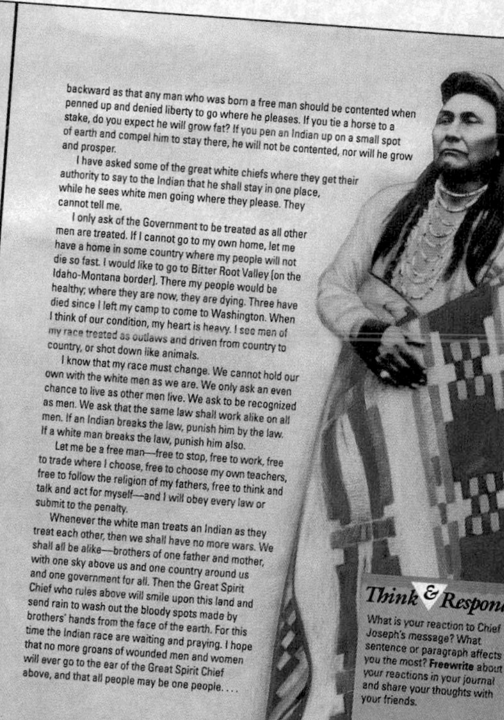

backward as that any man who was born a free man should be contented when penned up and denied liberty to go where he pleases. If you tie a horse to a stake, do you expect he will grow fat? If you pen an Indian up on a small spot of earth and compel him to stay there, he will not be contented, nor will he grow and prosper.

I have asked some of the great white chiefs where they get their authority to say to the Indian that he shall stay in one place, while he sees white men going where they please. They cannot tell me.

I only ask of the Government to be treated as all other men are treated. If I cannot go to my own home, let me have a home in some country where my people will not die so fast. I would like to go to Bitter Root Valley [on the Idaho-Montana border]. There my people would be healthy; where they are now, they are dying. Three have died since I left my camp to come to Washington. When I think of our condition, my heart is heavy. I see men of my race treated as outlaws and driven from country to country, or shot down like animals.

I know that my race must change. We cannot hold our own with the white men as we are. We only ask an even chance to live as other men live. We ask to be recognized as men. We ask that the same law shall work alike on all men. If an Indian breaks the law, punish him by the law. If a white man breaks the law, punish him also.

Let me be a free man—free to stop, free to work, free to trade where I choose, free to choose my own teachers, free to follow the religion of my fathers, free to think and talk and act for myself—and I will obey every law or submit to the penalty.

Whenever the white man treats an Indian as they treat each other, then we shall have no more wars. We shall all be alike—brothers of one father and mother, with one sky above us and one country around us and one government for all. Then the Great Spirit Chief who rules above will smile upon this land and send rain to wash out the bloody spots made by brothers' hands from the face of the earth. For this time the Indian race are waiting and praying. I hope that no more groans of wounded men and women will ever go to the ear of the Great Spirit Chief above, and that all people may be one people. . . .

Think & Respond

What is your reaction to Chief Joseph's message? What sentence or paragraph affects you the most? **Freewrite** about your reactions in your journal and share your thoughts with your friends.

Related ASSIGNMENT

Advertisement

Starting from ADVERTISING

With so many similar products on the market today, what makes you buy one brand rather than another? Sometimes you buy things because you're used to them or because your friends recommend them. Many times, though, you buy a product simply because you've seen a catchy ad for it. As you read this ad, notice how the writer used persuasive language to deliver the ad's message.

Think & Respond

What audience was the advertiser trying to reach? Do you think you would buy the cereal? Why? What words or pictures in the ad are most persuasive?

152 Workshop 6

Guided Assignment

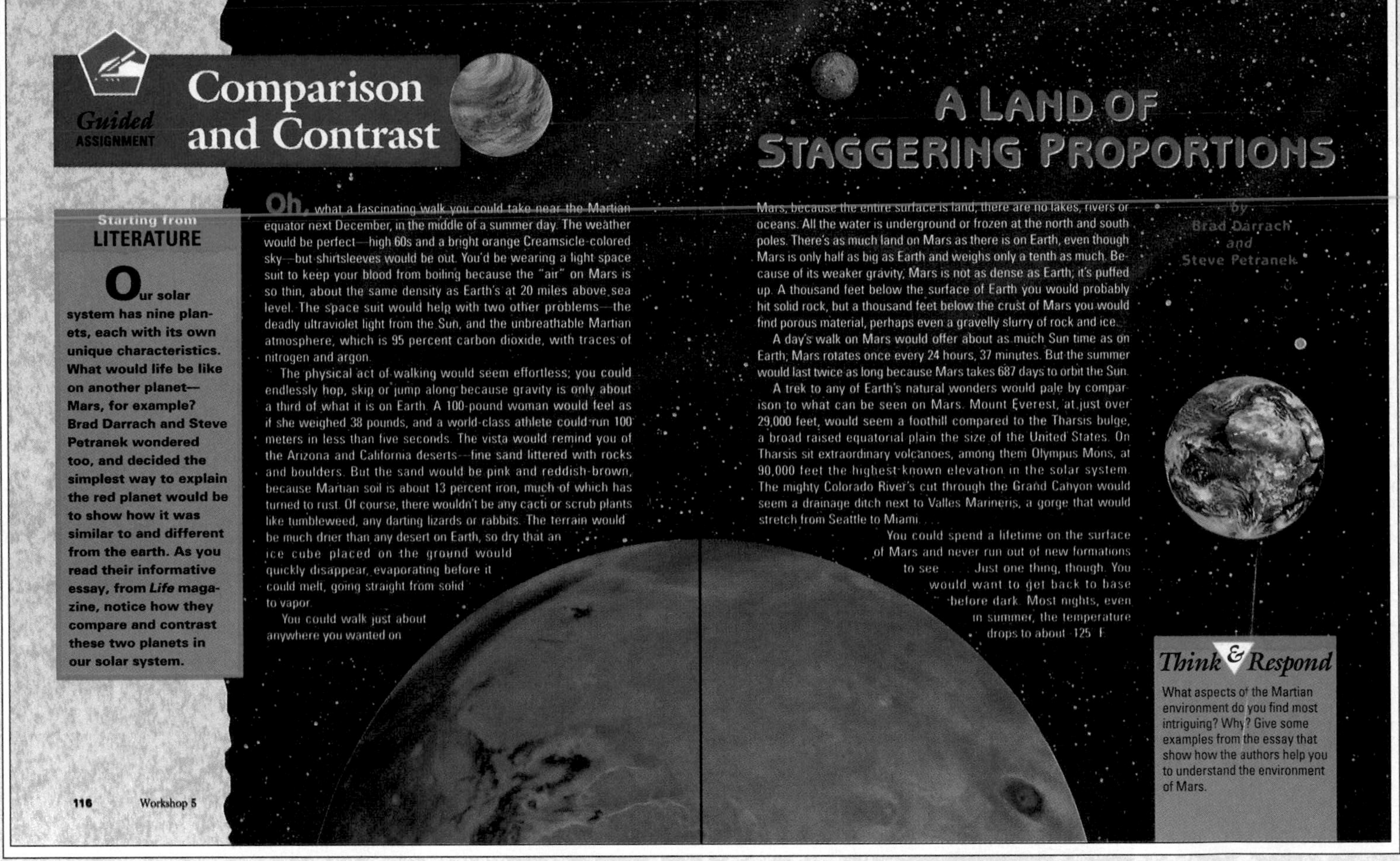

Guided ASSIGNMENT

Comparison and Contrast

Starting from LITERATURE

Our solar system has nine planets, each with its own unique characteristics. What would life be like on another planet—Mars, for example? Brad Darrach and Steve Petranek wondered too, and decided the simplest way to explain the red planet would be to show how it was similar to and different from the earth. As you read their informative essay, from *Life* magazine, notice how they compare and contrast these two planets in our solar system.

A LAND OF STAGGERING PROPORTIONS

by Brad Darrach and Steve Petranek

Oh, what a fascinating walk you could take near the Martian equator next December, in the middle of a summer day. The weather would be perfect—high 60s and a bright orange Creamsicle-colored sky—but shirtsleeves would be out. You'd be wearing a light space suit to keep your blood from boiling because the "air" on Mars is so thin, about the same density as Earth's at 20 miles above sea level. The space suit would help with two other problems—the deadly ultraviolet light from the Sun, and the unbreathable Martian atmosphere, which is 95 percent carbon dioxide, with traces of nitrogen and argon.

The physical act of walking would seem effortless; you could endlessly hop, skip or jump along because gravity is only about a third of what it is on Earth. A 100-pound woman would feel as if she weighed 38 pounds, and a world-class athlete could run 100 meters in less than five seconds. The vista would remind you of the Arizona and California deserts—fine sand littered with rocks and boulders. But the sand would be pink and reddish-brown, because Martian soil is about 13 percent iron, much of which has turned to rust. Of course, there wouldn't be any cacti or scrub plants like tumbleweed, any darting lizards or rabbits. The terrain would be much drier than any desert on Earth, so dry that an ice cube placed on the ground would quickly disappear, evaporating before it could melt, going straight from solid to vapor.

You could walk just about anywhere you wanted on Mars, because the entire surface is land; there are no lakes, rivers or oceans. All the water is underground or frozen at the north and south poles. There's as much land on Mars as there is on Earth, even though Mars is only half as big as Earth and weighs only a tenth as much. Because of its weaker gravity, Mars is not as dense as Earth; it's puffed up. A thousand feet below the surface of Earth you would probably hit solid rock, but a thousand feet below the crust of Mars you would find porous material, perhaps even a gravelly slurry of rock and ice.

A day's walk on Mars would offer about as much Sun time as on Earth; Mars rotates once every 24 hours, 37 minutes. But the summer would last twice as long because Mars takes 687 days to orbit the Sun.

A trek to any of Earth's natural wonders would pale by comparison to what can be seen on Mars. Mount Everest, at just over 29,000 feet, would seem a foothill compared to the Tharsis bulge, a broad raised equatorial plain the size of the United States. On Tharsis sit extraordinary volcanoes, among them Olympus Mons, at 90,000 feet the highest known elevation in the solar system. The mighty Colorado River's cut through the Grand Canyon would seem a drainage ditch next to Valles Marineris, a gorge that would stretch from Seattle to Miami. . . .

You could spend a lifetime on the surface of Mars and never run out of new formations to see. . . . Just one thing, though. You would want to get back to base before dark. Most nights, even in summer, the temperature drops to about -125° F.

Think & Respond

What aspects of the Martian environment do you find most intriguing? Why? Give some examples from the essay that show how the authors help you to understand the environment of Mars.

116 Workshop 5

Starting from Literature

The authors of *The Writer's Craft* believe that writing is an exciting journey of discovery where students explore ideas, examine options, problem solve, and share what they have done with others. Every assignment in each Writer's Workshop builds upon these ideas.

Literary and Professional Writing

Each Guided and Related Assignment begins with a model that focuses on a specific writing type or strategy. The introduction to the model presents the writing type to be covered, previews the literature, and sets a purpose for reading.

- **Models** cover a wide range of writing types, from traditional and contemporary literature, to newspaper and magazine articles, to consumer reports and TV scripts. Topics often lead to strong cross-curricular ties, and students gain a sense of how writing functions in the real world.
- **Think and Respond** questions allow students to respond to what they have read and prepare them to begin writing a piece of their own.

One Student's Writing

Have you ever dreamed about something for a long time and then had your dream come true? How did what you finally got compare to your fantasy? Rick Shen's dream came true when his mom announced the family was getting a dog. As you read Rick's essay, notice how his family's new pet compared to what he had in mind.

Thor!

The Wonder Dog?

By Rick Shen

When my mom announced at dinner one night that our family was finally getting a dog, I couldn't have been happier. I'd been listening to my friend Laura brag about her dog, Sam, forever. Sam's parents were national champions. Sam was faster than a Corvette. Sam could leap 10 feet in the air to catch a Frisbee. Sam brought the newspaper in every night. Listening to Laura, you'd think Sam did her math homework too. I decided my dog would do anything Sam could do, only better.

The next day, Mom brought Thor home from the animal shelter. I named him Thor even before I saw him because I remembered from English class that Thor is the Norse god of thunder, and I wanted my dog to be powerful and fast. Mom told us that Thor had been abandoned by his owners and had fallen off a bridge into the river. I guess I should have realized right then that he wasn't going to be the most coordinated dog in the world. But I didn't—at least not until Mom brought him in the front door. I looked at Thor and my heart sank. This was going to be my wonder dog? How was I ever going to face Laura and Sam?

You see, Sam is a golden retriever. Golden retrievers are sporting dogs. You can take them hunting, for companionship and to bring back any game birds you've brought down. Like all golden retrievers, Sam has long, silky, reddish-golden hair, a long tail, and a happy face. Sam always looks like she's smiling. Golden retrievers are great with little kids and make terrific pets.

Thor, on the other hand, is a dachshund, a hound. About all he has in common with Sam is that both dachshunds and golden retrievers are used for hunting. Instead of long, silky, golden hair, Thor has short, wiry, blackish-brown hair. His legs are about two inches long, and his stomach practically sits on the ground. Even with his head raised up, he can't be more than 12 inches tall. Thor looks sort of like a sausage with legs.

Dachshunds are also good with little kids, although when Thor howls I think a little kid would get scared. Thor howls because dachshunds don't bark exactly like other dogs do.

When I told Laura I had gotten a dog, she suggested we take our dogs to the park to play one Saturday morning. That's when I realized how else Thor was different from Sam.

Laura threw the Frisbee and Sam ran after it. At the last second Sam jumped up high and grabbed it out of the air. Now it was our turn. I threw the Frisbee and Thor ran underneath it. At the last second, it hit Thor in the head. He had tried to jump up, but dachshunds just weren't made for jumping.

Then Laura asked Sam to sit and shake her hand. Sam did both things easily. I told Thor to sit. Dachshunds don't sit like other dogs. Thor sort of leans over until the back part of his body flops on the ground. Then he tries to keep his front half steady. Shaking hands in this position isn't easy. We finally gave up. By the end of the afternoon, I think Thor was better friends with Sam than I was with Laura.

That was last year. By now I've grown to love Thor a lot. He'll never chase sports cars or catch Frisbees like Sam, although he has learned to shake hands. I guess people will always ask about his funny shape. And I don't let him get anywhere near the river. Thor will never be a wonder dog, but we've become really great buddies, and that's good enough for me.

Think & Respond

Respond as a Reader

- Do you think Rick's first impressions of Thor are understandable? Why?
- Did you ever dream big dreams for one of your own pets? Did your dreams come true?

Respond as a Writer

- How does Rick lead up to his comparison of golden retrievers and dachshunds?
- How does Rick organize his comparison and contrast?

Reading Student Writing

A student-written paper follows the opening model, demonstrating to students the importance of their own writing and the usefulness of the skills they will be learning.

Student Models

Each student model shows students the importance of becoming invested in their writing. A variety of publishing formats suggests the many ways writing can be shared.

- **Placement** of the complete model at the front of the lesson allows teachers to use the whole-to-part teaching strategy so successful with middle school students.
- **Think and Respond** questions focus on both reader response and on analyzing the writer's technique.

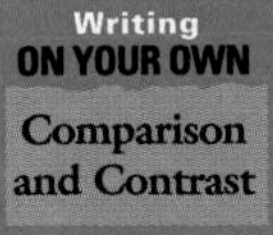

INVITATION TO *Write*

Like Brad Darrach and Steve Petranek, Rick Shen used comparison and contrast techniques as part of an informative essay. In both pieces of writing, the authors explained and described by showing how things are alike and different.

Write an informative essay that uses comparison and contrast to explain or describe something or someone.

PREWRITE AND EXPLORE

1. Look for comparisons and contrasts. When you compare and contrast persons or things, you try to find similarities and differences. What types of comparisons interest you? To find out, try some of the following activities.

Exploring Topics

- **One on one** Which team is better, the Chicago Bulls or the Los Angeles Lakers? What are the differences between laser discs and videocassettes? Which exercise gives you the best workout—cross-country skiing or tennis? Get together with some classmates and **brainstorm** to create a list of people, objects, and ideas you could compare and contrast, one on one. Make a list of the ideas you come up with.
- **Decisions, decisions** Personal decisions often involve comparison and contrast. Which summer camp will you attend? What clubs will you join at school? Which jeans will you buy? Recall decisions you have made in the past, or think about decisions you're facing now. **Freewrite** about one that involved comparing or contrasting two choices.

PROBLEM SOLVING

"How can I find a topic I care about?"

For additional suggestions for finding a writing topic, see

- Handbook 1, "Discovering Writing Ideas," pages 218–223

- **Time machine** If you could travel forward into the future or back to the past, what would be different? What would be the same? Choose a new lifetime and make a **chart** that shows what things are different and what things are the same.
- **Reading literature** Have any of your favorite stories or novels been made into movies? How are the two versions alike? How are they different? **Freewrite** about one such example.

What types of ideas have you gathered? Which one strikes you as the most interesting, unusual, or challenging? Choose one you'd like to explore in a comparison and contrast essay.

2. Investigate similarities and differences. To explore your topic, you need to find a way to sort out similarities and differences. One way is to figure out what features you want to compare and contrast. For example, if you were comparing compact discs and tapes, you might consider such features as sound quality, durability, and cost. Then you could make a chart to show how your two subjects measure up.

Another way is to make a Venn diagram. In the outer part of each circle, list what is different about each subject you are comparing. In the space where the circles overlap, list the similarities.

One Student's Process

Rick Shen used a Venn diagram to help him clearly see how Sam and Thor were alike and different.

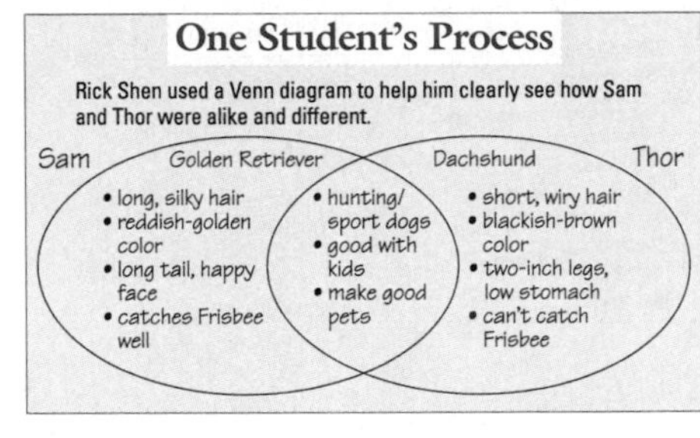

Moving to Writing

After discussing the model, your students are invited to write on their own. The detailed Guided Assignments lead students through each stage of the writing process, where they are presented with different strategies and encouraged to experiment, problem solve, and collaborate with others.

Writing on Your Own

A variety of features helps students make the transition from reading to writing.

- **Invitation to Write** refers to the professional and student models and describes the assignment students are to complete.
- **Exploring Topics** provides creative activities to help students find writing ideas they can care about.
- **Problem Solving** notes appear throughout the lesson and offer cross-references to the Handbooks. This provides you with ideas for mini-lessons and shows your students where they can look for additional help.
- **One Student's Process** follows a student writer through every stage of the assignment.

3. **Think about your purpose.** As you begin gathering details and ideas for your comparison, ask yourself, "What am I trying to accomplish with this comparison?" Do some freewriting about your purpose.

DRAFT AND DISCOVER

1. **Begin writing.** Start writing whatever part of your essay you feel most comfortable with. If you've thought of a great beginning, start there. If one similarity or difference stands out, write about it first. Don't worry about organization at this point.

Writer's Choice You don't have to limit your draft to the information in your charts, diagrams, or other prewriting notes. If new ideas occur to you as you write, include them in your draft.

2. **Organize information clearly.** At some point in your drafting process, you will want to begin organizing the information you're presenting. Here are two techniques you can try.

- **Feature by feature** Present a feature and explain how each subject is similar or different with regard to that feature. Darrach and Petranek organized their essay in this way.

  Feature I
  subject A
  subject B

  Feature II
  subject A
  subject B

- **Subject by subject** Present all the information about one subject first and then move on to the next subject, showing how it is similar or different. Rick Shen used this type of organization in the third and fourth para-graphs of his essay.

  Subject A
  feature I, feature II, feature III, fea
  Subject B
  feature I, feature II, feature III, fe

122 Workshop 5

3. **Write an intriguing introduction.** Start your essay with an introduction that makes the reader want to read on. Darrach and Petranek start by telling you that a midday walk on Mars would be fascinating. You read on to find out why and how. Rick Shen starts out with a story, telling you that his new dog will be better in every way than Laura's. You read on to find out if his prediction turns out to be true.

Paragraphs at Work When you write a comparison, you want to draw attention to the similarities and differences between the subjects. Your writing will be clear and easy to follow if you present only one subject or feature in each paragraph. Remember these tips.
- Begin a new paragraph for each subject or feature.
- Support the main idea of each paragraph with details or examples that illustrate specific similarities and differences.
- Delete any details that are not directly related to the main idea of the paragraph.

4. **Think about your draft.** Do you want to share your writing with a peer reader now, or should you make some changes first? The following questions can help you review your draft and get the help you need from your peers.

COMPUTER TIP

As you draft your writing, keep your prewriting notes visible on a split screen.

REVIEW YOUR WRITING

Questions for Yourself
- Have I accomplished what I set out to do with this comparison?
- Would my point be clearer if I organized my information differently?
- Have I forgotten to mention any important similarities or differences?

Questions for Your Peer Readers
- Why do you think I chose to compare these subjects?
- ... comparison helped you the most? ... about these

Peer Reader Comments

I didn't know any of this about golden retrievers.

What makes a dog's face happy?

You didn't tell me enough about Thor.

One Student's Process

Notice the comments Rick's peer readers made about this part of his first draft. What comments would you have made?

Sam is a golden retriever. Golden retrievers are sporting dogs. You can take them hunting, for companionship and to bring back any game birds you've brought down. Like all golden retrievers, Sam has golden hair, a long tail, and a happy face. Golden retrievers are real good with little kids and make great pets. Thor is a dachshund. Dachshunds are hounds who hunt by running along with their noses to the ground. Thor has blackish-brown hair.

Writer's Choice Would including a chart, drawing, or diagram help your readers understand your comparison more clearly?

REVISE YOUR WRITING

1. **Review your responses.** Your own reactions and the reactions of your peers can help you see how effectively your draft uses the techniques of comparison and contrast. Did you discover any places in your writing where you need to supply additional details or examples to explain a comparison or contrast more completely? Were your peer readers able to follow your explanation easily, or do you need to strengthen your organization? Would transitional words and phrases make your ideas flow more smoothly? At this point you can choose to make minor changes or completely rethink your essay.

124 Workshop 5

2. **Use transitions to point out similarities and differences.** Transitions can help you draw attention to points of comparison and contrast. Use such words and phrases as *both, also,* and *similarly* to draw attention to similarities. Use *but, instead,* and *on the other hand* to signal differences.

3. **Decide what changes you want to make.** You may want to make only minor changes, or you may want to strike out in an entirely new direction. Always keep in mind that the purpose of revision is to rethink what you have written. Making changes doesn't mean you've made mistakes—you've just found clearer, more interesting, more informative ways to express your ideas.

One Student's Process

After thinking about the peer responses he got and his own concerns, Rick made the following changes in his draft.

Sam is a golden retriever. Golden retrievers are sporting dogs. You can take them hunting, for companionship and to bring back any game birds you've brought down. Like all golden retrievers, Sam has ~~golden~~ long, silky, reddish- hair, a long tail, and a happy face. Sam always looks like she's smiling. Golden retrievers are real good with little kids and make great pets. ¶ Thor is a dachshund. Dachshunds are hounds who hunt by running along with their noses to the ground. Thor has short, wiry blackish-brown hair. His legs are about two inches long, and his stomach practically sits on the ground.

Comparison and Contrast

- **Drafting Strategies** and **Writer's Choice** options remind students that there are many ways to complete any piece of writing.
- **Writing Tips, Computer Tips,** and **Grammar Tips** provide helpful advice where students need it.
- **Paragraphs at Work** tailors tips on paragraphing to each specific type of writing.
- **Review questions** for both the writer and the peer reader make revision a rich, interactive process.
- **Revision in progress** shows peer response at work.

Standards for Evaluation

INFORMATIVE WRITING

Comparison and contrast writing

- introduces the subjects being compared in an interesting, intriguing manner
- discusses how the subjects being compared are similar and different
- organizes ideas logically, using feature-by-feature or subject-by-subject organization
- includes transitional words and phrases to make similarities and differences clear
- ends with a satisfying conclusion

LINKING GRAMMAR AND WRITING

Comparative and Superlative Forms

Whenever you use comparison and contrast, you will be comparing at least two subjects. Sometimes you may be working with more than two subjects. Depending on how many subjects you're comparing and contrasting, you will need to use different forms of adjectives and adverbs.

Use the **comparative** forms of adjectives and adverbs when you are comparing or contrasting two subjects.

Diamonds are <u>harder</u> than rubies.

Use the **superlative** forms of adjectives and adverbs when you are comparing or contrasting three or more subjects.

Diamonds are the <u>hardest</u> of all precious stones.

Rick Shen used the comparative form to compare Sam with a sports car.

Sam is <u>faster</u> than a Corvette.

Had Rick wanted to compare Sam with more than one other subject, he would have used the superlative form.

Of all the dogs in the park that day, Sam was <u>fastest</u>.

PROOFREAD

1. Proofread your work. Check your informative essay for errors in grammar, spelling, punctuation, and capitalization.

2. Make a clean copy of your paper. Use the Standards for Evaluation in the margin to make one final check of your writing. Then prepare a final copy of your informative essay.

PUBLISH AND PRESENT

- **Add graphics to your essay.** Photographs, drawings, and other visual aids can add interest to your informative essay.
- **Participate in a paper exchange.** Exchange essays with students in another class at your school or even at a different school. Attach a letter to the essay you've been asked to respond to, telling the writer what you liked about his or her work.
- **Make a bulletin board display.** Include a comparison and contrast chart about your subjects.

REFLECT ON YOUR WRITING

FOR YOUR **PORTFOLIO**

1. Add your writing to your portfolio. You have now written your own informative essay based on comparison and contrast. How did your writing experience go? Did you find this type of writing enjoyable? What was the most interesting or frustrating part of your writing experience? Write a brief note to yourself or your teacher that talks about your writing process. These questions may help you focus your thoughts.

- What did I learn about these subjects by comparing and contrasting them? Did anything surprise me?
- Was I surprised by any of the responses I got from my peer readers? Did I make any of the changes my peer readers suggested?
- Did I enjoy exploring comparisons and contrasts? Did this assignment give me any ideas for other comparisons I would like to investigate?
- Other than in an informative essay like Brad Darrach's and Steve Petravek's, in what other types of writing could I use comparison and contrast techniques?

2. Explore additional writing ideas. See the suggestions for writing a consumer report on pages 130–132, and Springboards on page 133.

Roller Rover (1987), William Wegman.

Related ASSIGNMENT

Consumer Report

Reading a CONSUMER REPORT

How do you decide what basketball shoe or blue jeans to buy? With so many brands to choose from, you have to be a smart consumer to get the most for your money. One way to spend your cash intelligently is to check out similar products in a consumer magazine. As you read this consumer report about frozen yogurt, think about the features of this warm-weather treat that the author focuses on. What other features would you have compared?

from *ZILLIONS*

WHY IS EVERYBODY EATING FROZEN YOGURT?

Why is frozen yogurt the fastest growing new food of the 1990's?

It's cold and sweet. Smooth and creamy. A lot like ice cream—but with a difference. Frozen yogurt has less fat and fewer calories. In these nutrition-conscious 90's, a healthier choice that tastes terrific is sure to find new fans.

Did we say *tastes terrific?* Whipping air and sugar into icy yogurt may not sound tempting to your taste buds. Isn't yogurt just sour milk? Doesn't it have a certain tang? It can't really compare to ice cream, can it? To find out, we asked 26 *Zillions* readers around the country to visit local frozen yogurt stores and check out some low-fat flavors.

What They Thought

Each member of the Yogurt Team tasted chocolate and one other flavor at three different stores. In all, they visited 80 stores and tried 160 samples. . . . Everyone found a favorite, and (surprise! surprise!) no one complained about this assignment. "Frozen yogurt doesn't taste as sour as I thought it would," said Adam. Cammie agreed: "I was really amazed at the similarity to ice cream."

The kids found the best samples were smooth (not icy), fairly sweet, with a gentle yogurt tang and good flavor.

- **Linking Grammar and Writing** and **Proofreading** strategies provide a springboard to language instruction.
- **Standards for Evaluation** shares assessment secrets with the students.
- **Publish and Present** suggestions make sure students have a real audience.
- **Reflect on Your Writing** encourages students to use a portfolio and to think about what they've learned.

Related Assignment

In this activity, students apply skills learned in the Guided Assignment. Here, the consumer report builds on skills presented in the compare-contrast assignment.

Writing Handbook

When do you want to teach your students about transitional devices? When they write a story? Before they explain a process? Perhaps you want to review the concept with each lesson. With the unique Writing Handbook, *you* decide what your students need to learn and when they need to learn it.

The Writing Handbook is divided into three sections, each with a wealth of mini-lessons:

Writing Process
Style
Academic Skills

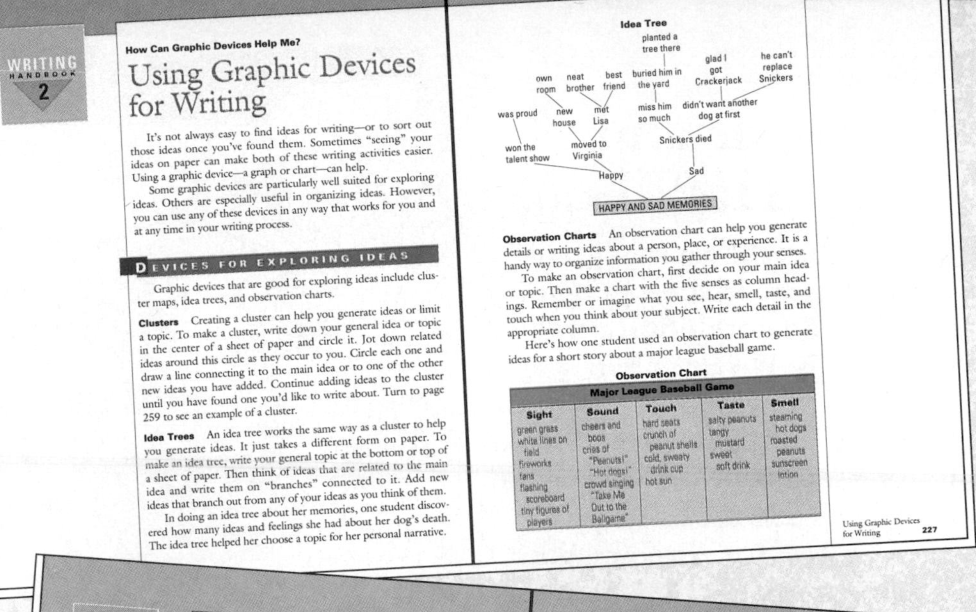

WRITING HANDBOOK 2

How Can Graphic Devices Help Me?

Using Graphic Devices for Writing

It's not always easy to find ideas for writing—or to sort out those ideas once you've found them. Sometimes "seeing" your ideas on paper can make both of these writing activities easier. Using a graphic device—a graph or chart—can help.

Some graphic devices are particularly well suited for exploring ideas. Others are especially useful in organizing ideas. However, you can use any of these devices in any way that works for you and at any time in your writing process.

DEVICES FOR EXPLORING IDEAS

Graphic devices that are good for exploring ideas include cluster maps, idea trees, and observation charts.

Clusters Creating a cluster can help you generate ideas or limit a topic. To make a cluster, write down your general idea or topic in the center of a sheet of paper and circle it. Jot down related ideas around this circle as they occur to you. Circle each one and draw a line connecting it to the main idea or to one of the other new ideas you have added. Continue adding ideas to the cluster until you have found one you'd like to write about. Turn to page 259 to see an example of a cluster.

Idea Trees An idea tree works the same way as a cluster to help you generate ideas. It just takes a different form on paper. To make an idea tree, write your general topic at the bottom or top of a sheet of paper. Then think of ideas that are related to the main idea and write them on "branches" connected to it. Add new ideas that branch out from any of your ideas as you think of them.

In doing an idea tree about her memories, one student discovered how many ideas and feelings she had about her dog's death. The idea tree helped her choose a topic for her personal narrative.

Idea Tree

Observation Charts An observation chart can help you generate details or writing ideas about a person, place, or experience. It is a handy way to organize information you gather through your senses.

To make an observation chart, first decide on your main idea or topic. Then make a chart with the five senses as column headings. Remember or imagine what you see, hear, smell, taste, and touch when you think about your subject. Write each detail in the appropriate column.

Here's how one student used an observation chart to generate ideas for a short story about a major league baseball game.

Observation Chart

Major League Baseball Game				
Sight	**Sound**	**Touch**	**Taste**	**Smell**
green grass white lines on field fireworks fans flashing scoreboard tiny figures of players	cheers and boos cries of "Peanuts!" "Hot dogs!" crowd singing "Take Me Out to the Ballgame"	hard seats crunch of peanut shells cold, sweaty drink cup hot sun	salty peanuts tangy mustard sweet soft drink	steaming hot dogs roasted peanuts sunscreen lotion

Using Graphic Devices for Writing 227

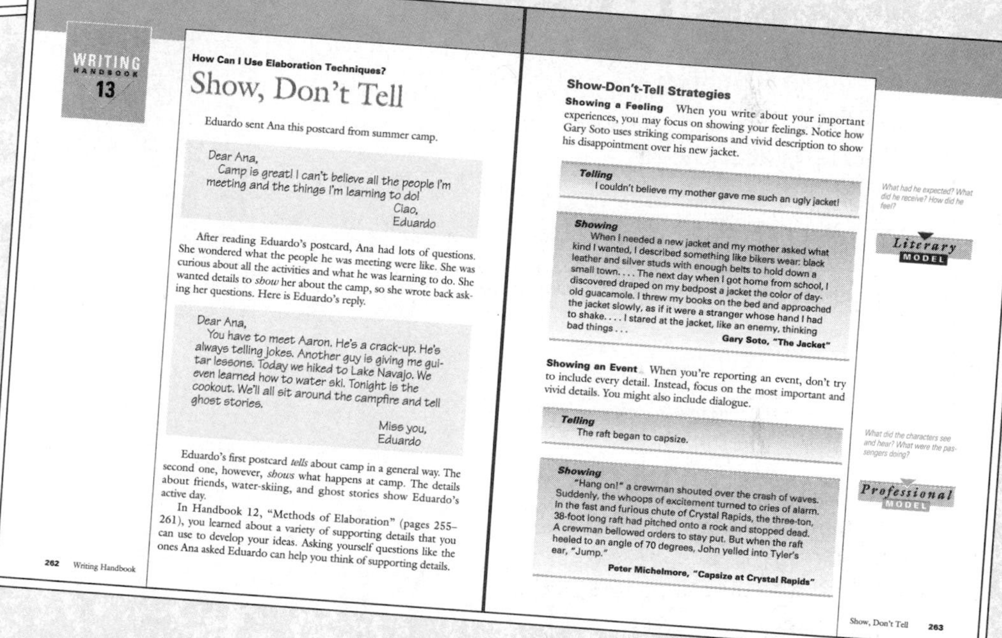

WRITING HANDBOOK 13

How Can I Use Elaboration Techniques?

Show, Don't Tell

Eduardo sent Ana this postcard from summer camp.

> Dear Ana,
> Camp is great! I can't believe all the people I'm meeting and the things I'm learning to do!
> Ciao,
> Eduardo

After reading Eduardo's postcard, Ana had lots of questions. She wondered what the people he was meeting were like. She was curious about all the activities and what he was learning to do. She wanted details to *show* her about the camp, so she wrote back asking her questions. Here is Eduardo's reply.

> Dear Ana,
> You have to meet Aaron. He's a crack-up. He's always telling jokes. Another guy is giving me guitar lessons. Today we hiked to Lake Navajo. We even learned how to water ski. Tonight is the cookout. We'll all sit around the campfire and tell ghost stories.
> Miss you,
> Eduardo

Eduardo's first postcard *tells* about camp in a general way. The second one, however, *shows* what happens at camp. The details about friends, water-skiing, and ghost stories show Eduardo's active day.

In Handbook 12, "Methods of Elaboration" (pages 255–261), you learned about a variety of supporting details that you can use to develop your ideas. Asking yourself questions like the ones Ana asked Eduardo can help you think of supporting details.

262 Writing Handbook

Show-Don't-Tell Strategies

Showing a Feeling When you write about your important experiences, you may focus on showing your feelings. Notice how Gary Soto uses striking comparisons and vivid description to show his disappointment over his new jacket.

Telling
I couldn't believe my mother gave me such an ugly jacket!

What had he expected? What did he receive? How did he feel?

Showing
When I needed a new jacket and my mother asked what kind I wanted, I described something like bikers wear: black leather and silver studs with enough belts to hold down a small town. . . . The next day when I got home from school, I discovered draped on my bedpost a jacket the color of day-old guacamole. I threw my books on the bed and approached the jacket slowly, as if it were a stranger whose hand I had to shake. . . . I stared at the jacket, like an enemy, thinking bad things . . .

Gary Soto, "The Jacket"

Literary MODEL

Showing an Event When you're reporting an event, don't try to include every detail. Instead, focus on the most important and vivid details. You might also include dialogue.

Telling
The raft began to capsize.

What did the characters see and hear? What were the passengers doing?

Showing
"Hang on!" a crewman shouted over the crash of waves. Suddenly, the whoops of excitement turned to cries of alarm. In the fast and furious chute of Crystal Rapids, the three-ton, 38-foot long raft had pitched onto a rock and stopped dead. A crewman bellowed orders to stay put. But when the raft heeled to an angle of 70 degrees, John yelled into Tyler's ear, "Jump."

Peter Michelmore, "Capsize at Crystal Rapids"

Professional MODEL

Show, Don't Tell 263

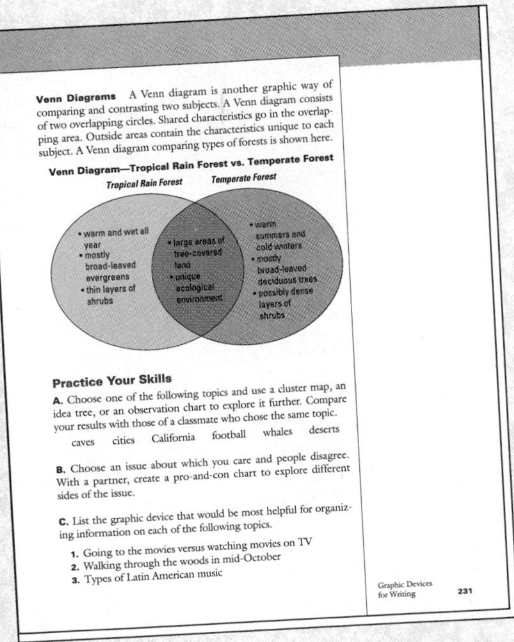

Venn Diagrams A Venn diagram is another graphic way of comparing and contrasting two subjects. A Venn diagram consists of two overlapping circles. Shared characteristics go in the overlapping area. Outside areas contain the characteristics unique to each subject. A Venn diagram comparing types of forests is shown here.

Venn Diagram—Tropical Rain Forest vs. Temperate Forest

Practice Your Skills

A. Choose one of the following topics and use a cluster map, an idea tree, or an observation chart to explore it further. Compare your results with those of a classmate who chose the same topic.

caves cities California football whales deserts

B. Choose an issue about which you care and people disagree. With a partner, create a pro-and-con chart to explore different sides of the issue.

C. List the graphic device that would be most helpful for organizing information on each of the following topics.

1. Going to the movies versus watching movies on TV
2. Walking through the woods in mid-October
3. Types of Latin American music

Graphic Devices for Writing 231

Use the cross-references in the Writer's Workshops to decide when to present lessons, or teach them whenever *you* see the need. You can also encourage your students to use the lessons independently as they problem solve their way through a piece of writing.

- **One key concept or skill** is the focus of each mini-lesson.
- **Charts and graphic devices** clarify difficult strategies and concepts.
- **Literary, professional, and student models** provide examples of different techniques and strategies.
- **Abundant practice** enables students to practice their new skills or hone abilities they already have.

Grammar and Usage Handbook

Research has shown that grammar and usage lessons, taught in isolation, do not improve student writing. *The Writer's Craft* solves this problem with its innovative Grammar and Usage Handbook. Every lesson provides instruction and practice in the context of drafting, revision, proofreading, and literature.

WHAT IS A NOUN?

A **noun** names a person, a place, a thing, or an idea.

All words may be classified into groups called **parts of speech.** A **noun** is the part of speech that names a person, place, thing, or an idea. You use nouns every day when you speak and write. Notice the nouns naming persons, places, and things that are printed on the game cards below.

Many nouns name things you can see.

Person	**Place**	**Thing**
stranger	orbit	short story
Edgar Allan Poe	Mars	half-moon
Agatha Christie	outer space	spyglass
water-skier	New Orleans	shadow

Some nouns name things you cannot see, such as ideas, feelings, and characteristics.

Idea	**Feeling**	**Characteristic**
justice	surprise	curiosity
fantasy	fear	courage
	suspense	imagination
	happiness	self-confidence

418 Grammar Handbo

Covering the Basics

Each lesson begins with clear teaching and a quick student check.

- **Thorough introductions to the concept** begin each lesson. Numerous charts and examples clarify the explanation.

POSSESSIVE NOUNS

A **possessive noun** shows who or what owns something.

The noun following a **possessive noun** may name a thing or a quality.

Thing	Yoki's raincoat	Bianca's umbrella
Quality	storm's fury	Bob's courage

Forming Possessives of Nouns

Type of Noun	Rule	Examples
Singular noun	Add an apostrophe and *s*.	Mr. Ross's plight tornado's path
Plural noun ending in *s*	Add an apostrophe.	the Rosses' home victims' losses
Plural noun not ending in *s*	Add an apostrophe and *s*.	children's fears women's boots

Writing **TIP**

Use the possessive forms to make phrases more concise.
Hurricane Andrew destroyed *homes of people.*
Hurricane Andrew destroyed *people's homes.*

Practice Your Skills

A. CONCEPT CHECK

Possessive Nouns In each sentence find the noun that should be possessive. Write the correct possessive form of that noun.

Writing Theme Storms

1. For years scientists gave hurricanes women names.
2. In 1978, however, scientists began giving hurricanes men names as well.
3. For example, the hurricane that slammed into South Carolina coast in 1989 was called Hugo.
4. The Caribbean islands were the first to feel Hugo fury.
5. This storm winds, waves, and rains caused widespread destruction.
6. The hurricane damaged homes, businesses, and merchants stores.
7. The destruction affected the islands tourist industry.
8. Worst of all, though, people lives were lost.
9. The Red Cross began relief efforts after the hurricane end.
10. Victims of the decade most costly storm also received aid from the government.

Using Nouns 425

- **Thematic exercises and examples** center around a subject that can be used as a springboard to writing.
- **Concept Checks** review the basic idea of the lesson in a simple format.

Applying in Context

A variety of creative exercises provides meaningful application of each concept:

- **Drafting** and **Revision Skills** exercises put the concept to work through such activities as sentence combining and elaboration.
- **Application in Literature** activities show the concept at work in professional writing.
- **Application in Writing** allows students to experiment with different formats while applying new skills.
- **Proofreading activities** provide opportunities to sharpen editing skills.
- **Writing Connections** tie the concept back to the Writer's Workshops.

B. REVISION SKILL

Using Adverbs There are many adverbs available for writers to use. Write the following paragraph, replacing the italicized adverbs with other adverbs that convey a similar meaning.

11When you think of mummies, do you think of the *very* old mummies of the ancient Egyptian Pharaohs? 12It was *once* thought that the Egyptian embalmers used mysterious methods and secret formulas to preserve the bodies *totally*. 13*Today* scientists know that it was the climate, which is *extremely* dry, that prevented the bodies f...

FOR MORE PRACTICE
See page 529.

B. APPLICATION IN LITERATURE

Recognizing Adjectives Notice how Ray Bradbury uses adjectives to create vivid, interesting images in the selection below. For each sentence in the paragraph, write the adjectives and the words they modify. Do not include articles. If there are no adjectives in the sentence, write *None.* You should find a total of twelve adjectives.

13They set foot upon the porch. 14Hollow echoes sounded from under the boards as they walked to the screen door. 15Inside they could see a bead curtain hung across the hall entry, and a crystal chandelier and a Maxfield Parrish painting on one wall over a comfortable Morris chair. . . . 16You could hear the tinkle of ice in a lemonade pitcher. 17In a distant kitchen, because of the heat of the day, someone was preparing a cold lunch.

Ray Bradbury,
The Martian Chronicles

C. APPLICATION IN WRITING

A Description Imagine that you are writing a script for a science fiction play. Write a brief description of the scene as the main character walks on stage. What does he or she see, hear, and feel? Use five of the adjectives listed below in your description.

shimmering	weird	immense
purple	American	cold
quiet	slimy	happy
	three	several

FOR MORE PRACTICE
See page 509.

B. PROOFREADING SKILL

Correct Comparative Forms Proofread and write the following paragraph, correcting errors in grammar, capitalization, punctuation, and spelling. Pay special attention to the use of comparative forms. (10 errors)

The United States has one of the most richest cooking traditions in the world. Santa Fe cooking is a cheif example. Its a blend of at least four traditions. The older tradition comes from Native Americans. Their more important contributions are the corn tortilla and chilies. Then the Spanish arrived they brought fruit from their homeland. Later, mexicans settled in the area, bringing New spices and sauces. People from other parts of the United States were the recenter arrivals. Together these cultures have made Santa Fe cooking among the wonderfullest anywhere.

FOR MORE PRACTICE
See page 510.

CHECK POINT
MIXED REVIEW • PAGES 496–503

Writing Theme
Dog-Sled Racing

Write the italicized adjectives in each sentence. Then label each adjective as either *Common* or *Proper.* Label any predicate adjectives *Predicate Adjective.* In addition, if an adjective is used in a comparison, label it as either *Comparative* or *Superlative.*

1In March 1925, a *serious* epidemic of diphtheria broke out in Nome, Alaska. 2The *winter* snows hampered rescue attempts. 3*Alaskan* dog-sled drivers loaded their sleds with medical supplies and mushed their teams from Anchorage to ... *Iditarod Trail* dog-sled

WRITING CONNECTIONS

Elaboration, Revision, and Proofreading

Revise the following draft of part of a report, using the directions given on this page. Then proofread for errors in grammar, capitalization, punctuation, and spelling. Pay particular attention to the use of adverbs.

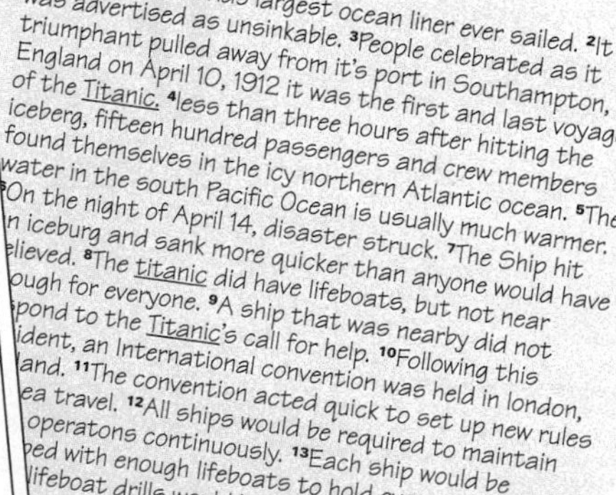

1Before the worlds largest ocean liner ever sailed. 2It was advertised as unsinkable. 3People celebrated as it triumphant pulled away from it's port in Southampton, England on April 10, 1912 it was the first and last voyage of the Titanic. 4less than three hours after hitting the iceberg, fifteen hundred passengers and crew members found themselves in the icy northern Atlantic ocean. 5The water in the south Pacific Ocean is usually much warmer. 6On the night of April 14, disaster struck. 7The Ship hit ...n iceburg and sank more quicker than anyone would have ...elieved. 8The titanic did have lifeboats, but not near ...ough for everyone. 9A ship that was nearby did not ...pond to the Titanic's call for help. 10Following this ...ident, an International convention was held in london, ...and. 11The convention acted quick to set up new rules ...ea travel. 12All ships would be required to maintain ... operatons continuously. 13Each ship would be ...ped with enough lifeboats to hold everyone on board. ...lifeboat drills would be conducted regular. 15A ... patrol was also organized too warn ships of ...s.

...nce 2, add an adverb to emphasize how unsinkable the ...

...e sentence that doesn't belong.

...ence 4 to a more logical position.

...owing clause ...

Informative Writing: Reports

Writing a report involves gathering information and presenting it in a clear and organized way. (See Workshop 8.) When you revise a report, make sure you have included all the facts your readers need to know in order to understand your topic. Look for ways you can use adverbs to add precision to your writing.

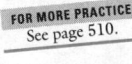

Special Features

Throughout the pupil's editions, special features provide opportunities for students to enjoy themselves as they learn.

- **Sketchbook** Sometimes funny, sometimes thought-provoking, the Sketchbooks let students experiment with "no-risk writing." A special "Show, Don't Tell" feature provides important practice with elaboration.
- **Sentence Composing** By imitating the sentences of professional writers, students develop their own more sophisticated style.
- **Springboards** Creative suggestions allow students to apply their writing skills across the curriculum.
- **On the Lightside** Your students will learn that language study can be fun.

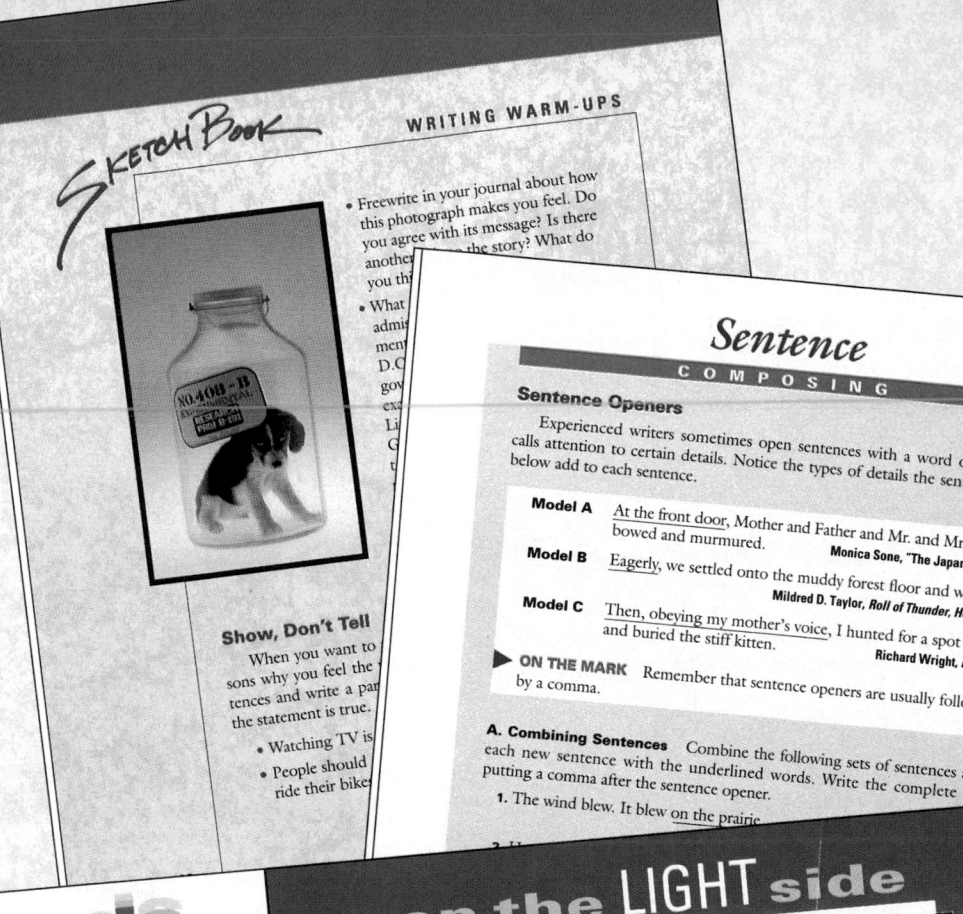

SKETCH BOOK
WRITING WARM-UPS
• Freewrite in your journal about how this photograph makes you feel. Do you agree with its message? Is there
NO. 408-B
EXPERIMENTAL
RESEARCH
Show, Don't Tell
When you want to
sons why you feel the
tences and write a par
the statement is true.
• Watching TV is
• People should
ride their bikes

Sentence COMPOSING

Sentence Openers

Experienced writers sometimes open sentences with a word or phrase that calls attention to certain details. Notice the types of details the sentence openers below add to each sentence.

Model A At the front door, Mother and Father and Mr. and Mrs. Matsui bowed and murmured. **Monica Sone, "The Japanese Touch"**

Model B Eagerly, we settled onto the muddy forest floor and waited. **Mildred D. Taylor, *Roll of Thunder, Hear My Cry***

Model C Then, obeying my mother's voice, I hunted for a spot of earth and buried the stiff kitten. **Richard Wright, *Black Boy***

▶ **ON THE MARK** Remember that sentence openers are usually followed by a comma.

A. Combining Sentences Combine the following sets of sentences and begin each new sentence with the underlined words. Write the complete sentence, putting a comma after the sentence opener.

1. The wind blew. It blew on the prairie.

Springboards
Science Think up an invention that the world needs. It could be something practical or something fanciful. Describe your invention, tell how it works, and explain how it will affect the world.
Literature Throughout history, people have thought up myths to explain strange natural events or remarkable human behavior. Write a myth of your own to explain an event or a behavior.
LOOK
History What if the South had won the Civil War? Imagine a different outcome to a well-known historical event. Then describe what your life would be like today as a result of that outcome.
Speaking and Listening
At what are you an expert? Explain one of your hobbies or skills in an oral presentation.
GEOGRAPHY
How has your community changed over the years? Why? Explain the effect one physical change has had on your community.

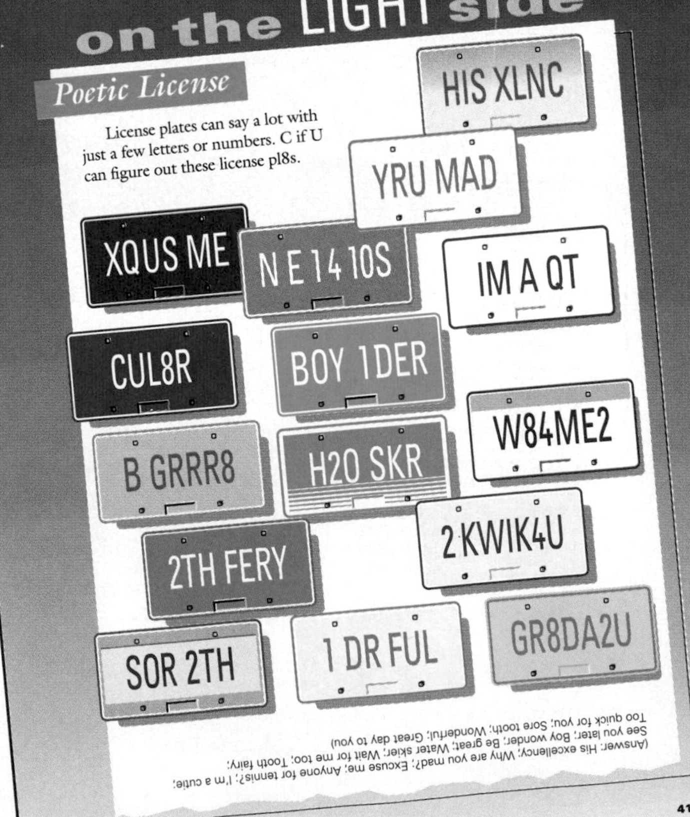

Review and Assessment

How can you check your students' progress? The Pupil's Edition and Teacher's Resource File for *The Writer's Craft* offer a wide variety of assessment tools.

Writing Assessment

- **Writing Prompts** Based on state assessments across the country, these prompts allow you to check students' writing progress. (Pupil book and Resource File)
- **Guides to Analytic and Holistic Scoring** Guidelines help you check achievement on any writing assignment. Models of student writing provide benchmarks to compare against. (Resource File)
- **Portfolio Assessment Suggestions** Guidelines in this Teacher's Edition and in the Resource File will help you use this effective evaluative technique.

Grammar and Usage Assessment

- **Checkpoints** These activities in the pupil book provide a mixed review after every two or three lessons.
- **Section Reviews** Cumulative activity sets allow you to evaluate student progress after every main Handbook section.
- **Skills Assessments** Structured like many state assessments, these appear throughout the handbooks and allow a mixed review of language concepts.
- **Pretests and Mastery Tests** The standardized format of these tests provides you with a quick way to evaluate student understanding. (Resource File)

Prompts for Persuasion

Imagine that your school has had a full program of extracurricular activities. Now, however, tax cuts have made it necessary to cut all but one of these activities. Write a speech to be given at a public hearing of the school board in which you tell which program you think should be saved. Remember that to convince the board members you will need to support your opinion with reasons and specific examples.

What's your pet peeve? Is it graffiti? Too many television commercials? Violence in movies? Write an editorial for your school newspaper. Clearly state what your gripe is and what you think should be done about it. Try to persuade your readers to accept your opinion.

One student will have the chance to work at a local television studio this summer. This student will be expected to answer phones, run errands, and do some library research. Above all, however, this person needs to be responsible, reliable, and eager to learn. Write an essay to convince the station managers that you are the ideal person for the job. Include specific incidents and examples to support your statements.

Your class has decided to stage a mock trial. The defendant is the villain from one of your favorite fairy tales. The lawyer for the defense is you. Choose the villain you would like to represent. This might be the wolf in *Little Red Riding Hood*, the stepmother in *Cinderella*, or any other character. Then write down what you will say in your final remarks to the jury. In this speech, you need to convince the jury to find your defendant "not guilty." Therefore, be sure to support your points with facts and examples and to answer important objections to your views.

6 *Persuasion*

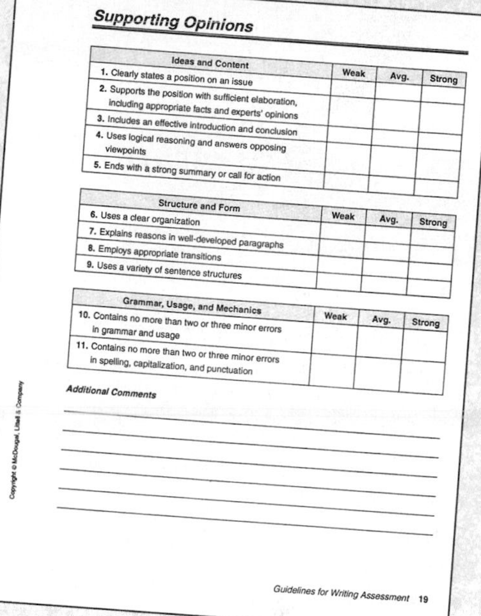

Supporting Opinions

Ideas and Content	Weak	Avg.	Strong
1. Clearly states a position on an issue			
2. Supports the position with sufficient elaboration, including appropriate facts and experts' opinions			
3. Includes an effective introduction and conclusion			
4. Uses logical reasoning and answers opposing viewpoints			
5. Ends with a strong summary or call for action			

Structure and Form	Weak	Avg.	Strong
6. Uses a clear organization			
7. Explains reasons in well-developed paragraphs			
8. Employs appropriate transitions			
9. Uses a variety of sentence structures			

Grammar, Usage, and Mechanics	Weak	Avg.	Strong
10. Contains no more than two or three minor errors in grammar and usage			
11. Contains no more than two or three minor errors in spelling, capitalization, and punctuation			

Additional Comments

Guidelines for Writing Assessment 19

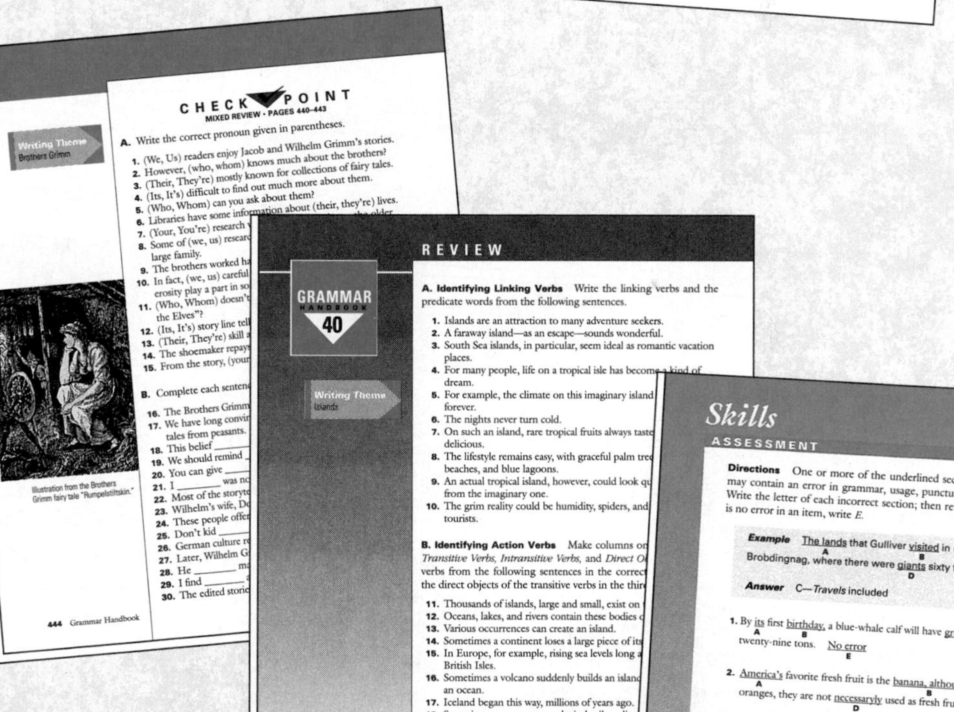

CHECKPOINT
MIXED REVIEW • PAGES 440–443

Writing Theme: Brothers Grimm

A. Write the correct pronoun given in parentheses.

1. (We, Us) readers enjoy Jacob and Wilhelm Grimm's stories.
2. However, (who, whom) knows much about the brothers?
3. (Their, They're) mostly known for collections of fairy tales.
4. (Its, It's) difficult to find out much more about them.
5. (Who, Whom) can you ask about them?

Illustration from the Brothers Grimm fairy tale "Rumpelstiltskin."

444 Grammar Handbook

REVIEW

GRAMMAR HANDBOOK 40

Writing Theme: Islands

A. Identifying Linking Verbs Write the linking verbs and the predicate words from the following sentences.

1. Islands are an attraction to many adventure seekers.
2. A faraway island—as an escape—sounds wonderful.
3. South Sea islands, in particular, seem ideal as romantic vacation places.

Skills

ASSESSMENT

PRETEST Grammar

Example The lands that Gulliver visited in *Gulliver's Travels* included Brobdingnag, where there were giants sixty feet tall. No error

Answer C—*Travels* included

370 Skills Assessment

NAME DATE SCORE Handbook 45 Pretest

Understanding Subject and Verb Agreement

Part 1 Identifying Singular and Plural Forms Below each sentence, identify the noun or verb that is singular. (4 points each)

1. The path through the woods stays cool even on hot days.
 ○ A. woods ○ B. stays ○ C. cool ○ D. days
2. Late in the day, the sun casts long shadows across the lawn.
 ○ A. in ○ B. casts ○ C. shadows ○ D. across
3. One of the boys on the corner was in my class last year.
 ○ A. boys ○ B. was ○ C. in ○ D. last

Below each sentence, identify the noun or verb that is plural. (4 points each)

4. Were the members of the team at the meeting last night?
 ○ A. Were ○ B. team ○ C. meeting ○ D. night
5. The old desks in this room need much repair work.
 ○ A. room ○ B. need ○ C. much ○ D. work
6. Some of the birds in our area are ready for the flight south.
 ○ A. our ○ B. are ○ C. ready ○ D. flight

Part 2 Making Subjects and Verbs Agree Choose the correct verb to complete each sentence. (4 points each)

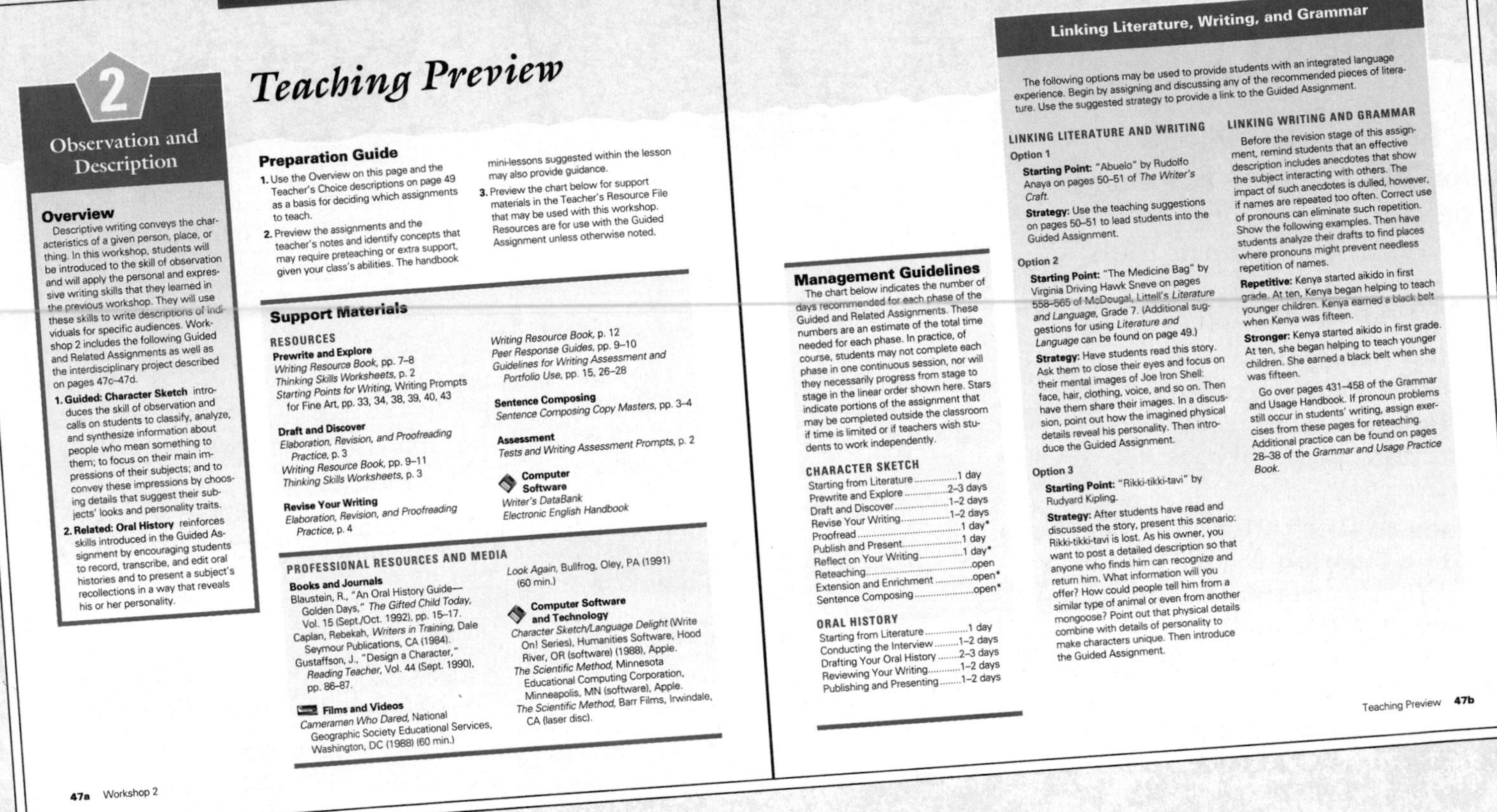

2

Observation and Description

Overview

Descriptive writing conveys the characteristics of a given person, place, or thing. In this workshop, students will be introduced to the skill of observation and will apply the personal and expressive writing skills that they learned in the previous workshop. They will use these skills to write descriptions of individuals for specific audiences. Workshop 2 includes the following Guided and Related Assignments as well as the interdisciplinary project described on pages 47c–47d.

1. **Guided: Character Sketch** introduces the skill of observation and calls on students to classify, analyze, and synthesize information about people who mean something to them; to focus on their main impressions of their subjects; and to convey these impressions by choosing details that suggest their subjects' looks and personality traits.
2. **Related: Oral History** reinforces skills introduced in the Guided Assignment by encouraging students to record, transcribe, and edit oral histories and to present a subject's recollections in a way that reveals his or her personality.

Teaching Preview

Preparation Guide

1. Use the Overview on this page and the Teacher's Choice descriptions on page 49 as a basis for deciding which assignments to teach.
2. Preview the assignments and the teacher's notes and identify concepts that may require preteaching or extra support, given your class's abilities. The handbook mini-lessons suggested within the lesson may also provide guidance.
3. Preview the chart below for support materials in the Teacher's Resource File that may be used with this workshop. Resources are for use with the Guided Assignment unless otherwise noted.

Support Materials

RESOURCES

Prewrite and Explore
Writing Resource Book, pp. 7–8
Thinking Skills Worksheets, p. 2
Starting Points for Writing, Writing Prompts for Fine Art, pp. 33, 34, 38, 39, 40, 43

Draft and Discover
Elaboration, Revision, and Proofreading Practice, p. 3
Writing Resource Book, pp. 9–11
Thinking Skills Worksheets, p. 3

Revise Your Writing
Elaboration, Revision, and Proofreading Practice, p. 4
Writing Resource Book, p. 12
Peer Response Guides, pp. 9–10
Guidelines for Writing Assessment and Portfolio Use, pp. 15, 26–28

Sentence Composing
Sentence Composing Copy Masters, pp. 3–4

Assessment
Tests and Writing Assessment Prompts, p. 2

Computer Software
Writer's DataBank
Electronic English Handbook

PROFESSIONAL RESOURCES AND MEDIA

Books and Journals
Blaustein, R., "An Oral History Guide—Golden Days," *The Gifted Child Today*, Vol. 15 (Sept./Oct. 1992), pp. 15–17.
Caplan, Rebekah, *Writers in Training*, Dale Seymour Publications, CA (1984).
Gustaffson, J., "Design a Character," *Reading Teacher*, Vol. 44 (Sept. 1990), pp. 86–87.

Films and Videos
Cameramen Who Dared, National Geographic Society Educational Services, Washington, DC (1988) (60 min.)
Look Again, Bullfrog, Oley, PA (1991) (60 min.)

Computer Software and Technology
Character Sketch/Language Delight (Write On! Series), Humanities Software, Hood River, OR (software) (1988), Apple.
The Scientific Method, Minnesota Educational Computing Corporation, Minneapolis, MN (software), Apple.
The Scientific Method, Barr Films, Irwindale, CA (laser disc).

47a Workshop 2

Management Guidelines

The chart below indicates the number of days recommended for each phase of the Guided and Related Assignments. These numbers are an estimate of the total time needed for each phase. In practice, of course, students may not complete each phase in one continuous session, nor will they necessarily progress from stage to stage in the linear order shown here. Stars indicate portions of the assignment that may be completed outside the classroom if time is limited or if teachers wish students to work independently.

CHARACTER SKETCH
Starting from Literature .... 1 day
Prewrite and Explore .... 2–3 days
Draft and Discover .... 1–2 days
Revise Your Writing .... 1–2 days
Proofread .... 1 day*
Publish and Present .... 1 day
Reflect on Your Writing .... 1 day*
Reteaching .... open
Extension and Enrichment .... open*
Sentence Composing .... open*

ORAL HISTORY
Starting from Literature .... 1 day
Conducting the Interview .... 1–2 days
Drafting Your Oral History .... 2–3 days
Reviewing Your Writing .... 1–2 days
Publishing and Presenting .... 1–2 days

Linking Literature, Writing, and Grammar

The following options may be used to provide students with an integrated language experience. Begin by assigning and discussing any of the recommended pieces of literature. Use the suggested strategy to provide a link to the Guided Assignment.

LINKING LITERATURE AND WRITING

Option 1

Starting Point: "Abuelo" by Rudolfo Anaya on pages 50–51 of *The Writer's Craft*.

Strategy: Use the teaching suggestions on pages 50–51 to lead students into the Guided Assignment.

Option 2

Starting Point: "The Medicine Bag" by Virginia Driving Hawk Sneve on pages 558–565 of McDougal, Littell's *Literature and Language*, Grade 7. (Additional suggestions for using *Literature and Language* can be found on page 49.)

Strategy: Have students read this story. Ask them to close their eyes and focus on their mental images of Joe Iron Shell: face, hair, clothing, voice, and so on. Then have them share their images. In a discussion, point out how the imagined physical details reveal his personality. Then introduce the Guided Assignment.

Option 3

Starting Point: "Rikki-tikki-tavi" by Rudyard Kipling.

Strategy: After students have read and discussed the story, present this scenario: Rikki-tikki-tavi is lost. As his owner, you want to post a detailed description so that anyone who finds him can recognize and return him. What information will you offer? How could people tell him from a similar type of animal or even from another mongoose? Point out that physical details combine with details of personality to make characters unique. Then introduce the Guided Assignment.

LINKING WRITING AND GRAMMAR

Before the revision stage of this assignment, remind students that an effective description includes anecdotes that show the subject interacting with others. The impact of such anecdotes is dulled, however, if names are repeated too often. Correct use of pronouns can eliminate such repetition. Show the following examples. Then have students analyze their drafts to find places where pronouns might prevent needless repetition of names.

Repetitive: Kenya started aikido in first grade. At ten, Kenya began helping to teach younger children. Kenya earned a black belt when Kenya was fifteen.

Stronger: Kenya started aikido in first grade. At ten, she began helping to teach younger children. She earned a black belt when she was fifteen.

Go over pages 431–458 of the Grammar and Usage Handbook. If pronoun problems still occur in students' writing, assign exercises from these pages for reteaching. Additional practice can be found on pages 28–38 of the *Grammar and Usage Practice Book*.

Teaching Preview **47b**

The Teacher's Edition

The Teacher's Edition of *The Writer's Craft* provides you with all the help you will need to prepare comprehensive, exciting lessons.

Teaching Preview

These pages appear before every Writer's Workshop and contain the following information:

- **Workshop Overview** Introduces the focus of the workshop and explains the relationships among the Guided and Related Assignments.
- **Preparation Guide** Guides your planning decisions and provides a chart of available support materials in the Teacher's Resource File, as well as lists of compatible computer software and other technology components.
- **Workshop Management Guidelines** Indicates recommended number of days for each part of the assignment, with suggestions for independent study.
- **Linking Literature, Writing, and Grammar** Presents three options for basing each writing assignment on literature and shows how to link any option with a grammar and usage mini-lesson.

A Nation of Immigrants

Overview

As students participate in this project, they will learn about immigration in both personal and historical terms. They will use their observation and description skills to write character sketches and oral histories of real or fictional immigrants and their families, helping others see the hopes and challenges immigrants have experienced.

Students will participate in the following activities:

- Investigate family backgrounds through interviews and research
- Research the history of immigration
- Develop character sketches and oral histories about immigrants and their families
- Invite parents and students to a presentation of immigrant histories
- Use language arts, social studies, science, math, and art skills to do research, develop and present materials, and analyze information

Preparation Guide

Tell students that the United States is often called a nation of immigrants because all of its people, with the exception of Native Americans, either have come here from other countries or are descendants of people who have done so during the past several hundred years. In this project students will have a chance to explore their individual family backgrounds and the experiences of immigrants throughout the nation's history.

Project File

Stage 1 Investigate Family Histories

1. Hold an initial discussion about immigration. Ask students to consider such topics as the reasons for immigration, the effects of immigration on the nation, and challenges faced by immigrants.
2. Have students investigate their families' histories through interviews with family members and historical research about their families' origins.
3. Have students write a brief family history or a description of the experiences of one person in the family.
4. Ask students to share, during informal class discussions, the information they discover.

TEAM TEACHING

The following activities may be used for team teaching or as extension and enrichment activities by the language arts teacher.

Language Arts Study interviewing skills. With partners, practice interview techniques (see *Resources, Stage 1).*

Social Studies Study the history of specific groups of people who have immigrated to the United States.

Math Create charts and graphs to show immigration trends over time, percentages of immigrants from different parts of the world, and settlement and work patterns.

TEACHING TIPS

- Invite parents and community members to speak to the class about their personal immigration experiences.
- Help students who do not have information about their family origins to explore the immigration experiences of friends or to identify people they can learn about in books.

Stage 2 Explore Immigration

1. Have students list key immigration periods —such as the 1600s to 1775, the 1820s to the 1870s, the 1880s to the 1920s (Ellis Island), and 1965 to the present—and identify the periods most relevant to their own family histories. Remind students that immigration declined dramatically during the Great Depression of the 1930s and during World War II but that they may still list this period if it is pertinent to their family history.
2. Have students form groups based on the time periods they wish to research, and have each group meet to brainstorm questions about immigration in their time period. Have each group assign members to research individual issues, such as where immigrants came from during the time period, why they came, and where they settled (see *Resources, Stage 2).*
3. Direct groups to use library research, personal interviews, and information from other students to find out about immigration in their time periods.

TEAM TEACHING

Science Learn about the role of environmental factors, such as disease and famine, in immigration.

Social Studies Learn about the role of economic factors, such as job opportunities and education, in immigration. Study immigration laws.

Language Arts Read stories about immigrants. Review interviewing techniques.

TEACHING TIPS

- Try to get students to investigate all the different time periods by encouraging them to think about possible multiple periods of immigration in their families.
- As an option, allow students to research specific immigrant groups—such as the Irish, the Italians, and the Chinese—rather than time periods.

Stage 3 Present Immigration Stories

1. Have each group create a character sketch of an immigrant, or a description of an immigrant family, who lived during the time period chosen by the group.
2. Have each group gather or create materials to illustrate the life of their individual or family. Such materials might include typical clothing, craft items, or artifacts related to customs or daily experiences.
3. Have each group make a presentation about their individual or family, using character sketches, oral histories, visual materials, music, skits, and role-playing to enhance the presentation.

TEAM TEACHING

Language Arts Study the techniques of writing character sketches, descriptions, and dialogue and of creating oral histories (see *Resources, Stage 3).*

Art Study folk-art traditions of various cultures. Create flags and other decorations to illustrate lives of immigrants.

Social Studies Study current issues in immigration. Learn about current immigration policy. As a follow-up activity, practice filling out a passport application form.

TEACHING TIPS

- If possible, invite a representative of the Immigration and Naturalization Service to speak to the class.
- Hold conferences with the groups to help them plan their character sketches and presentations. Help the groups divide the work evenly.
- Conduct both individual and group assessments.

Resources

STAGE 1

The Great Ancestor Hunt by Lila Perl offers suggestions students can use for exploring their family histories and creating family trees.

New Kids on the Block: Oral Histories of Immigrant Teens by Janet Bode gives first-person accounts of what it is like to move to the United States.

Roots by Alex Haley tells of his search for his African ancestors.

Breaking the Chains: African-American Slave Resistance by William Katz discusses the economic and historical forces behind the development of slavery.

Gift of Heritage (Mary Lou Productions) is a videotape that demonstrates how to create a family tree.

Trace Your Roots: A Step by Step Do-It-Yourself Workbook for Recording Your Family Tree by Grahame Hughes can help students create a family record.

The **local library** may have additional information on genealogical research.

The Writer's Craft, Grade 7, Handbook 34, "Interviewing Skills," page 357, provides guidelines for planning and conducting an interview.

STAGE 2

Information about and accounts of immigration from specific parts of the world are presented in the ***Coming to America*** series by Delacorte Press.

These videotapes present immigration from differing perspectives:

- ***The Immigrant Experience: The Long, Long Journey*** (Learning Corporation of America)
- ***America Becoming*** (PBS Video)
- ***Destination America*** (The Media Guild)
- ***The Golden Door*** (King Features Entertainment)

STAGE 3

The Immigration and Naturalization Service by Edward H. Dixon and Mark A. Galan provides information on current immigration issues.

Statistical Abstract of the United States, published yearly, has statistical information about immigration.

The Writer's Craft, Grade 7, Workshop 2, "Observation and Description," pages 49–61, teaches how to write a character sketch. The Related Assignment, "Oral History," pages 62–66, teaches how to create an oral history. Handbook 27, "Creating Dialogue," pages 320–322, can help students develop dialogue for their skits and role-playing. Handbook 35, "Making Oral Presentations," pages 358–359, has guidelines for practicing and presenting a talk.

Additional Projects

Weather Watch Have students study weather by learning about meteorology, by keeping detailed observations of weather, by reading weather-related literature, and by writing weather myths. Students can create their own weather instruments in the science lab. They might also develop travel materials that include weather information for various destinations.

A Day in the Life Have students make a record of a day in the life of their class, using photography, video and audio recordings, and artwork as well as writing.

Have students brainstorm to discover events and activities they want to show, including information about the school and about various class projects. Then have them consider the types of media they want to use and divide up the specific responsibilities for the project. Finally, ask them to make a multimedia presentation of their research.

Historical Newspaper Choose a historical period and set up the class as a newspaper staff to cover the events of one significant day during the time period. Students can prepare news stories, editorials, cartoons, advertisements, want ads, and other appropriate features.

Project File

Detailed suggestions for an exciting cross-curricular project follow each set of Preview pages and contain the following material:

- **Project Overview** Introduces the goals of the project and lists the key activities.
- **Guidelines for Implementation** Provides suggestions and management for implementing each stage of the project.
- **Team Teaching Suggestions** Shows the language arts teacher how to assign tasks among the disciplines or independently make connections to other subject areas.
- **Resources** Offers a wealth of print, video, and technological resources for each stage of the project.
- **Additional Projects** Presents capsulized summaries of other exciting cross-curricular projects.

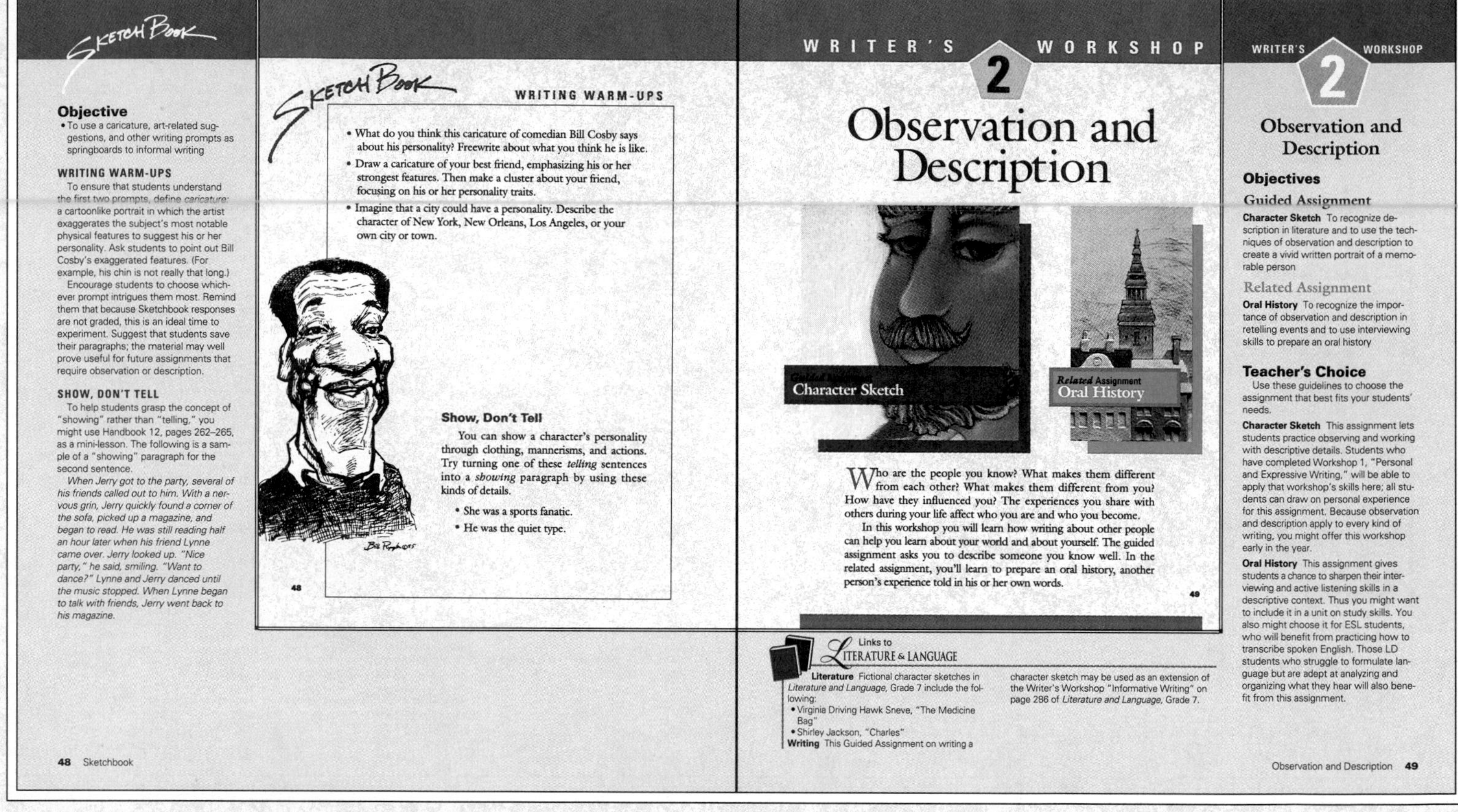

SKETCHBOOK

Objective

- To use a caricature, art-related suggestions, and other writing prompts as springboards to informal writing

WRITING WARM-UPS

To ensure that students understand the first two prompts, define *caricature:* a cartoonlike portrait in which the artist exaggerates the subject's most notable physical features to suggest his or her personality. Ask students to point out Bill Cosby's exaggerated features. (For example, his chin is not really that long.)

Encourage students to choose whichever prompt intrigues them most. Remind them that because Sketchbook responses are not graded, this is an ideal time to experiment. Suggest that students save their paragraphs; the material may well prove useful for future assignments that require observation or description.

SHOW, DON'T TELL

To help students grasp the concept of "showing" rather than "telling," you might use Handbook 12, pages 262–265, as a mini-lesson. The following is a sample of a "showing" paragraph for the second sentence.

When Jerry got to the party, several of his friends called out to him. With a nervous grin, Jerry quickly found a corner of the sofa, picked up a magazine, and began to read. He was still reading half an hour later when his friend Lynne came over. Jerry looked up. "Nice party," he said, smiling. "Want to dance?" Lynne and Jerry danced until the music stopped. When Lynne began to talk with friends, Jerry went back to his magazine.

SKETCHBOOK

WRITING WARM-UPS

- What do you think this caricature of comedian Bill Cosby says about his personality? Freewrite about what you think he is like.
- Draw a caricature of your best friend, emphasizing his or her strongest features. Then make a cluster about your friend, focusing on his or her personality traits.
- Imagine that a city could have a personality. Describe the character of New York, New Orleans, Los Angeles, or your own city or town.

Show, Don't Tell

You can show a character's personality through clothing, mannerisms, and actions. Try turning one of these *telling* sentences into a *showing* paragraph by using these kinds of details.

- She was a sports fanatic.
- He was the quiet type.

48

48 Sketchbook

WRITER'S WORKSHOP 2

Observation and Description

Character Sketch

Related Assignment Oral History

Who are the people you know? What makes them different from each other? What makes them different from you? How have they influenced you? The experiences you share with others during your life affect who you are and who you become.

In this workshop you will learn how writing about other people can help you learn about your world and about yourself. The guided assignment asks you to describe someone you know well. In the related assignment, you'll learn to prepare an oral history, another person's experience told in his or her own words.

49

Links to LITERATURE & LANGUAGE

Literature Fictional character sketches in *Literature and Language,* Grade 7 include the following:

- Virginia Driving Hawk Sneve, "The Medicine Bag"
- Shirley Jackson, "Charles"

Writing This Guided Assignment on writing a character sketch may be used as an extension of the Writer's Workshop "Informative Writing" on page 286 of *Literature and Language,* Grade 7.

WRITER'S WORKSHOP 2

Observation and Description

Objectives

Guided Assignment

Character Sketch To recognize description in literature and to use the techniques of observation and description to create a vivid written portrait of a memorable person

Related Assignment

Oral History To recognize the importance of observation and description in retelling events and to use interviewing skills to prepare an oral history

Teacher's Choice

Use these guidelines to choose the assignment that best fits your students' needs.

Character Sketch This assignment lets students practice observing and working with descriptive details. Students who have completed Workshop 1, "Personal and Expressive Writing," will be able to apply that workshop's skills here; all students can draw on personal experience for this assignment. Because observation and description apply to every kind of writing, you might offer this workshop early in the year.

Oral History This assignment gives students a chance to sharpen their interviewing and active listening skills in a descriptive context. Thus you might want to include it in a unit on study skills. You also might choose it for ESL students, who will benefit from practicing how to transcribe spoken English. Those LD students who struggle to formulate language but are adept at analyzing and organizing what they hear will also benefit from this assignment.

Observation and Description 49

Workshop Introduction

In the Pupil's Edition, this page allows both students and teachers to see—at a glance—the focus of the Workshop and the writing types they will be exploring. The Teacher's Edition provides this additional support:

- **Workshop Objectives** Lists general objectives for the Workshop as a whole.
- **Teacher's Choice** Helps the teacher choose assignments by describing each one, suggesting which students might benefit most, and recommending when it might best be taught.
- **Links to *Literature and Language*** Shows the teacher how to tie *The Writer's Craft* to McDougal, Littell's popular integrated language arts program.

Using The Models

Teacher notes accompany both the professional and student models to help introduce the characteristics of the writing that students will be working on.

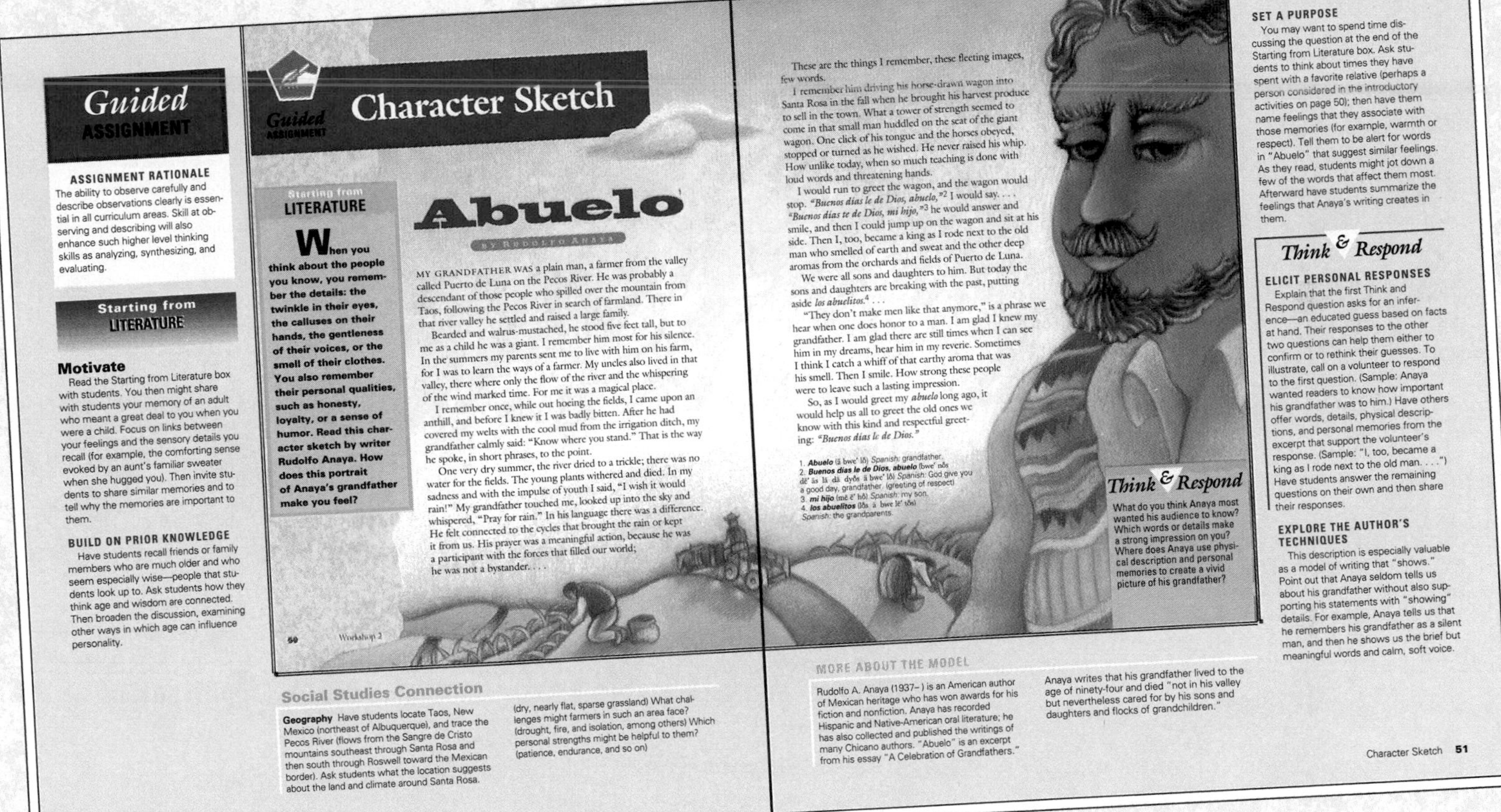

Guided **ASSIGNMENT**

ASSIGNMENT RATIONALE
The ability to observe carefully and describe observations clearly is essential in all curriculum areas. Skill at observing and describing will also enhance such higher level thinking skills as analyzing, synthesizing, and evaluating.

Starting from LITERATURE

Motivate
Read the Starting from Literature box with students. You then might share with students your memory of an adult who meant a great deal to you when you were a child. Focus on links between your feelings and the sensory details you recall (for example, the comforting sense evoked by an aunt's familiar sweater when she hugged you). Then invite students to share similar memories and to tell why the memories are important to them.

BUILD ON PRIOR KNOWLEDGE
Have students recall friends or family members who are much older and who seem especially wise—people that students look up to. Ask students how they think age and wisdom are connected. Then broaden the discussion, examining other ways in which age can influence personality.

Guided ASSIGNMENT **Character Sketch**

Starting from LITERATURE

When you think about the people you know, you remember the details: the twinkle in their eyes, the calluses on their hands, the gentleness of their voices, or the smell of their clothes. You also remember their personal qualities, such as honesty, loyalty, or a sense of humor. Read this character sketch by writer Rudolfo Anaya. How does this portrait of Anaya's grandfather make you feel?

Abuelo[1]

BY RUDOLFO ANAYA

MY GRANDFATHER WAS a plain man, a farmer from the valley called Puerto de Luna on the Pecos River. He was probably a descendant of those people who spilled over the mountain from Taos, following the Pecos River in search of farmland. There in that river valley he settled and raised a large family.

Bearded and walrus-mustached, he stood five feet tall, but to me as a child he was a giant. I remember him most for his silence. In the summers my parents sent me to live with him on his farm, for I was to learn the ways of a farmer. My uncles also lived in that valley, there where only the flow of the river and the whispering of the wind marked time. For me it was a magical place.

I remember once, while out hoeing the fields, I came upon an anthill, and before I knew it I was badly bitten. After he had covered my welts with the cool mud from the irrigation ditch, my grandfather calmly said: "Know where you stand." That is the way he spoke, in short phrases, to the point.

One very dry summer, the river dried to a trickle; there was no water for the fields. The young plants withered and died. In my sadness and with the impulse of youth I said, "I wish it would rain!" My grandfather touched me, looked up into the sky and whispered, "Pray for rain." In his language there was a difference. He felt connected to the cycles that brought the rain or kept it from us. His prayer was a meaningful action, because he was a participant with the forces that filled our world; he was not a bystander. . . .

50 Workshop 2

These are the things I remember, these fleeting images, few words.

I remember him driving his horse-drawn wagon into Santa Rosa in the fall when he brought his harvest produce to sell in the town. What a tower of strength seemed to come in that small man huddled on the seat of the giant wagon. One click of his tongue and the horses obeyed, stopped or turned as he wished. He never raised his whip. How unlike today, when so much teaching is done with loud words and threatening hands.

I would run to greet the wagon, and the wagon would stop. *"Buenos días le de Dios, abuelo,"*[2] I would say. . . . *"Buenos días te de Dios, mi hijo,"*[3] he would answer and smile, and then I could jump up on the wagon and sit at his side. Then I, too, became a king as I rode next to the old man who smelled of earth and sweat and the other deep aromas from the orchards and fields of Puerto de Luna.

We were all sons and daughters to him. But today the sons and daughters are breaking with the past, putting aside *los abuelitos.*[4] . . .

"They don't make men like that anymore," is a phrase we hear when one does honor to a man. I am glad I knew my grandfather. I am glad there are still times when I can see him in my dreams, hear him in my reverie. Sometimes I think I catch a whiff of that earthy aroma that was his smell. Then I smile. How strong these people were to leave such a lasting impression.

So, as I would greet my *abuelo* long ago, it would help us all to greet the old ones we know with this kind and respectful greeting: *"Buenos días le de Dios."*

1. **Abuelo** (ä bwe' lô) *Spanish:* grandfather.
2. **Buenos días le de Dios, abuelo** (bwe' nôs dē' äs lā dā dyôs ä bwe' lô) *Spanish:* God give you a good day, grandfather. (greeting of respect)
3. **mi hijo** (mē ē' hô) *Spanish:* my son.
4. **los abuelitos** (lôs ä bwe lē' tôs) *Spanish:* the grandparents.

Think & Respond

What do you think Anaya most wanted his audience to know? Which words or details make a strong impression on you? Where does Anaya use physical description and personal memories to create a vivid picture of his grandfather?

SET A PURPOSE
You may want to spend time discussing the question at the end of the Starting from Literature box. Ask students to think about times they have spent with a favorite relative (perhaps a person considered in the introductory activities on page 50); then have them name feelings that they associate with those memories (for example, warmth or respect). Tell them to be alert for words in "Abuelo" that suggest similar feelings. As they read, students might jot down a few of the words that affect them most. Afterward have students summarize the feelings that Anaya's writing creates in them.

Think & Respond

ELICIT PERSONAL RESPONSES
Explain that the first Think and Respond question asks for an inference—an educated guess based on facts at hand. Their responses to the other two questions can help them either to confirm or to rethink their guesses. To illustrate, call on a volunteer to respond to the first question. (Sample: Anaya wanted readers to know how important his grandfather was to him.) Have others offer words, details, physical descriptions, and personal memories from the excerpt that support the volunteer's response. (Sample: "I, too, became a king as I rode next to the old man. . . .") Have students answer the remaining questions on their own and then share their responses.

EXPLORE THE AUTHOR'S TECHNIQUES
This description is especially valuable as a model of writing that "shows." Point out that Anaya seldom tells us about his grandfather without also supporting his statements with "showing" details. For example, Anaya tells us that he remembers his grandfather as a silent man, and then he shows us the brief but meaningful words and calm, soft voice.

Social Studies Connection

Geography Have students locate Taos, New Mexico (northeast of Albuquerque), and trace the Pecos River (flows from the Sangre de Cristo mountains southeast through Santa Rosa and then south through Roswell toward the Mexican border). Ask students what the location suggests about the land and climate around Santa Rosa. (dry, nearly flat, sparse grassland) What challenges might farmers in such an area face? (drought, fire, and isolation, among others) Which personal strengths might be helpful to them? (patience, endurance, and so on)

MORE ABOUT THE MODEL

Rudolfo A. Anaya (1937–) is an American author of Mexican heritage who has won awards for his fiction and nonfiction. Anaya has recorded Hispanic and Native-American oral literature; he has also collected and published the writings of many Chicano authors. "Abuelo" is an excerpt from his essay "A Celebration of Grandfathers." Anaya writes that his grandfather lived to the age of ninety-four and died "not in his valley but nevertheless cared for by his sons and daughters and flocks of grandchildren."

50 Workshop 2

Character Sketch 51

- **Assignment Rationale** Explains the thinking behind the assignment and the reasons for its inclusion.
- **Motivate** Helps teachers prepare their students for reading the literature through ties to prior knowledge and setting a purpose.
- **Connections** Links to literature, science, social studies, and the fine arts.
- **More About the Model** Provides interesting background material or extended learning opportunities tied to the literature.
- **Think and Respond** Suggestions for eliciting personal responses and exploring the authors' techniques ensure that students will get the most from what they read.
- **Draw Conclusions** A summary after the student model encourages comparison of the two readings and helps students draw conclusions about the writing they will study.

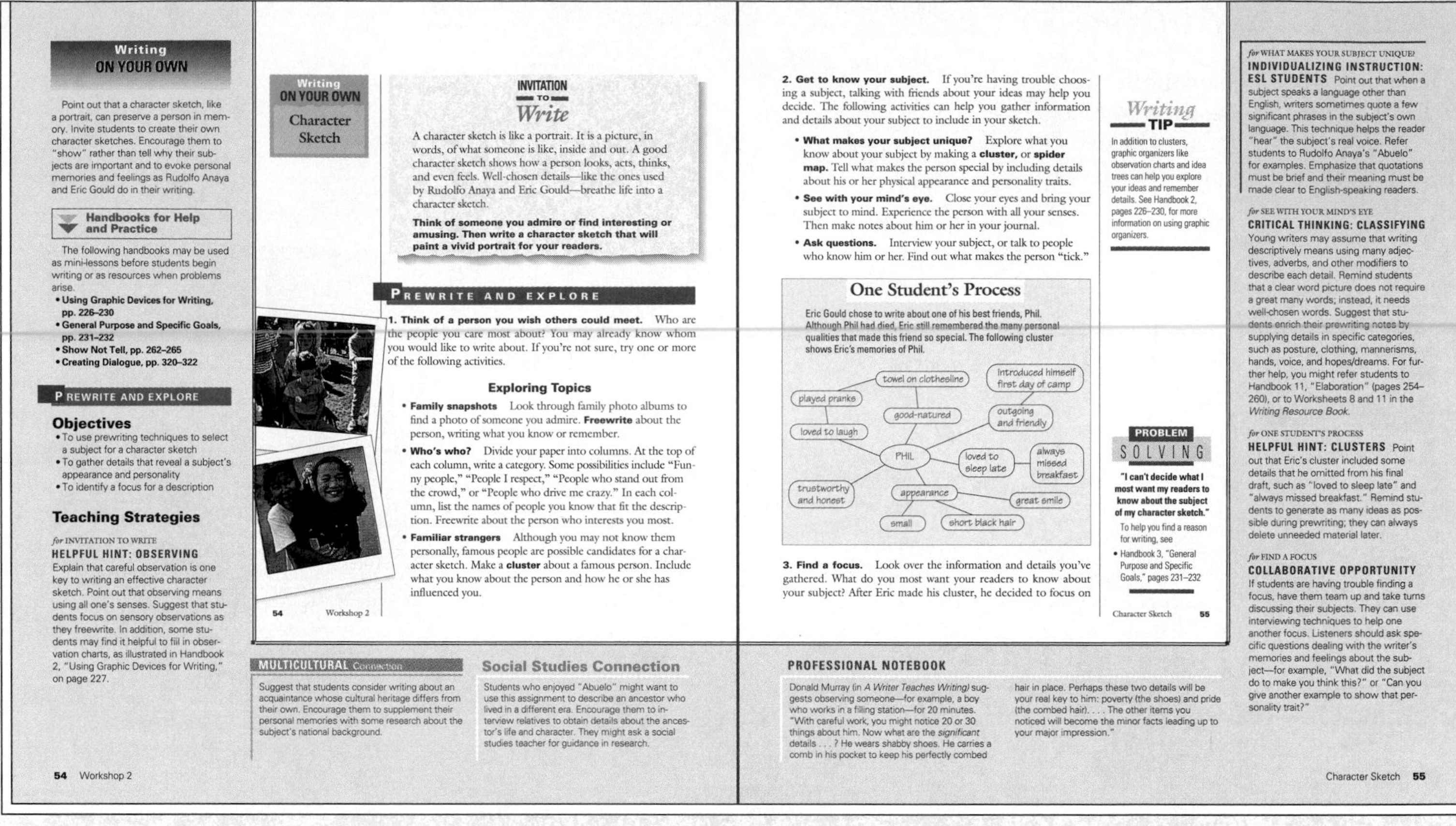

Writing ON YOUR OWN

Point out that a character sketch, like a portrait, can preserve a person in memory. Invite students to create their own character sketches. Encourage them to "show" rather than tell why their subjects are important and to evoke personal memories and feelings as Rudolfo Anaya and Eric Gould do in their writing.

Handbooks for Help and Practice

The following handbooks may be used as mini-lessons before students begin writing or as resources when problems arise.

- **Using Graphic Devices for Writing, pp. 226–230**
- **General Purpose and Specific Goals, pp. 231–232**
- **Show Not Tell, pp. 262–265**
- **Creating Dialogue, pp. 320–322**

PREWRITE AND EXPLORE

Objectives

- To use prewriting techniques to select a subject for a character sketch
- To gather details that reveal a subject's appearance and personality
- To identify a focus for a description

Teaching Strategies

for INVITATION TO WRITE
HELPFUL HINT: OBSERVING Explain that careful observation is one key to writing an effective character sketch. Point out that observing means using all one's senses. Suggest that students focus on sensory observations as they freewrite. In addition, some students may find it helpful to fill in observation charts, as illustrated in Handbook 2, "Using Graphic Devices for Writing," on page 227.

Writing ON YOUR OWN
Character Sketch

INVITATION TO *Write*

A character sketch is like a portrait. It is a picture, in words, of what someone is like, inside and out. A good character sketch shows how a person looks, acts, thinks, and even feels. Well-chosen details—like the ones used by Rudolfo Anaya and Eric Gould—breathe life into a character sketch.

Think of someone you admire or find interesting or amusing. Then write a character sketch that will paint a vivid portrait for your readers.

PREWRITE AND EXPLORE

1. Think of a person you wish others could meet. Who are the people you care most about? You may already know whom you would like to write about. If you're not sure, try one or more of the following activities.

Exploring Topics

- **Family snapshots** Look through family photo albums to find a photo of someone you admire. **Freewrite** about the person, writing what you know or remember.
- **Who's who?** Divide your paper into columns. At the top of each column, write a category. Some possibilities include "Funny people," "People I respect," "People who stand out from the crowd," or "People who drive me crazy." In each column, list the names of people you know that fit the description. Freewrite about the person who interests you most.
- **Familiar strangers** Although you may not know them personally, famous people are possible candidates for a character sketch. Make a **cluster** about a famous person. Include what you know about the person and how he or she has influenced you.

54 Workshop 2

2. Get to know your subject. If you're having trouble choosing a subject, talking with friends about your ideas may help you decide. The following activities can help you gather information and details about your subject to include in your sketch.

- **What makes your subject unique?** Explore what you know about your subject by making a **cluster,** or **spider map.** Tell what makes the person special by including details about his or her physical appearance and personality traits.
- **See with your mind's eye.** Close your eyes and bring your subject to mind. Experience the person with all your senses. Then make notes about him or her in your journal.
- **Ask questions.** Interview your subject, or talk to people who know him or her. Find out what makes the person "tick."

One Student's Process

Eric Gould chose to write about one of his best friends, Phil. Although Phil had died, Eric still remembered the many personal qualities that made this friend so special. The following cluster shows Eric's memories of Phil.

3. Find a focus. Look over the information and details you've gathered. What do you most want your readers to know about your subject? After Eric made his cluster, he decided to focus on

Writing TIP

In addition to clusters, graphic organizers like observation charts and idea trees can help you explore your ideas and remember details. See Handbook 2, pages 226–230, for more information on using graphic organizers.

PROBLEM SOLVING

"I can't decide what I most want my readers to know about the subject of my character sketch."

To help you find a reason for writing, see

- Handbook 3, "General Purpose and Specific Goals," pages 231–232

Character Sketch 55

for WHAT MAKES YOUR SUBJECT UNIQUE?
INDIVIDUALIZING INSTRUCTION: ESL STUDENTS Point out that when a subject speaks a language other than English, writers sometimes quote a few significant phrases in the subject's own language. This technique helps the reader "hear" the subject's real voice. Refer students to Rudolfo Anaya's "Abuelo" for examples. Emphasize that quotations must be brief and their meaning must be made clear to English-speaking readers.

for SEE WITH YOUR MIND'S EYE
CRITICAL THINKING: CLASSIFYING Young writers may assume that writing descriptively means using many adjectives, adverbs, and other modifiers to describe each detail. Remind students that a clear word picture does not require a great many words; instead, it needs well-chosen words. Suggest that students enrich their prewriting notes by supplying details in specific categories, such as posture, clothing, mannerisms, hands, voice, and hopes/dreams. For further help, you might refer students to Handbook 11, "Elaboration" (pages 254–260), or to Worksheets 8 and 11 in the *Writing Resource Book.*

for ONE STUDENT'S PROCESS
HELPFUL HINT: CLUSTERS Point out that Eric's cluster included some details that he omitted from his final draft, such as "loved to sleep late" and "always missed breakfast." Remind students to generate as many ideas as possible during prewriting; they can always delete unneeded material later.

for FIND A FOCUS
COLLABORATIVE OPPORTUNITY If students are having trouble finding a focus, have them team up and take turns discussing their subjects. They can use interviewing techniques to help one another focus. Listeners should ask specific questions dealing with the writer's memories and feelings about the subject—for example, "What did the subject do to make you think this?" or "Can you give another example to show that personality trait?"

MULTICULTURAL Connection

Suggest that students consider writing about an acquaintance whose cultural heritage differs from their own. Encourage them to supplement their personal memories with some research about the subject's national background.

Social Studies Connection

Students who enjoyed "Abuelo" might want to use this assignment to describe an ancestor who lived in a different era. Encourage them to interview relatives to obtain details about the ancestor's life and character. They might ask a social studies teacher for guidance in research.

PROFESSIONAL NOTEBOOK

Donald Murray (in *A Writer Teaches Writing*) suggests observing someone—for example, a boy who works in a filling station—for 20 minutes. "With careful work, you might notice 20 or 30 things about him. Now what are the *significant* details . . . ? He wears shabby shoes. He carries a comb in his pocket to keep his perfectly combed hair in place. Perhaps these two details will be your real key to him: poverty (the shoes) and pride (the combed hair). . . . The other items you noticed will become the minor facts leading up to your major impression."

54 Workshop 2

Character Sketch 55

Lesson Notes

The Teacher's Edition continues to help the teacher throughout the Workshop. Each lesson contains the following material:

- **Objectives** Specific goals for each part of the lesson.
- **Handbook Suggestions** Ideas for mini-lessons from the Handbooks.
- **Teaching Strategies** Point-of-use notes that truly make this one book for all students. Included are suggestions for

  Modeling Suggestions for making yourself a co-writer in the classroom

  Speaking and Listening Opportunities

  Critical Thinking

  Individualizing Instruction Tips for teaching LEP, LD, and students with different ability levels or learning styles

  Collaborative Opportunities

  Spot Checks

  Peer Response Suggestions

  Stumbling Blocks Potential problems and tips to avoid them

  Managing the Paper Load Ideas for cutting down on grading and review

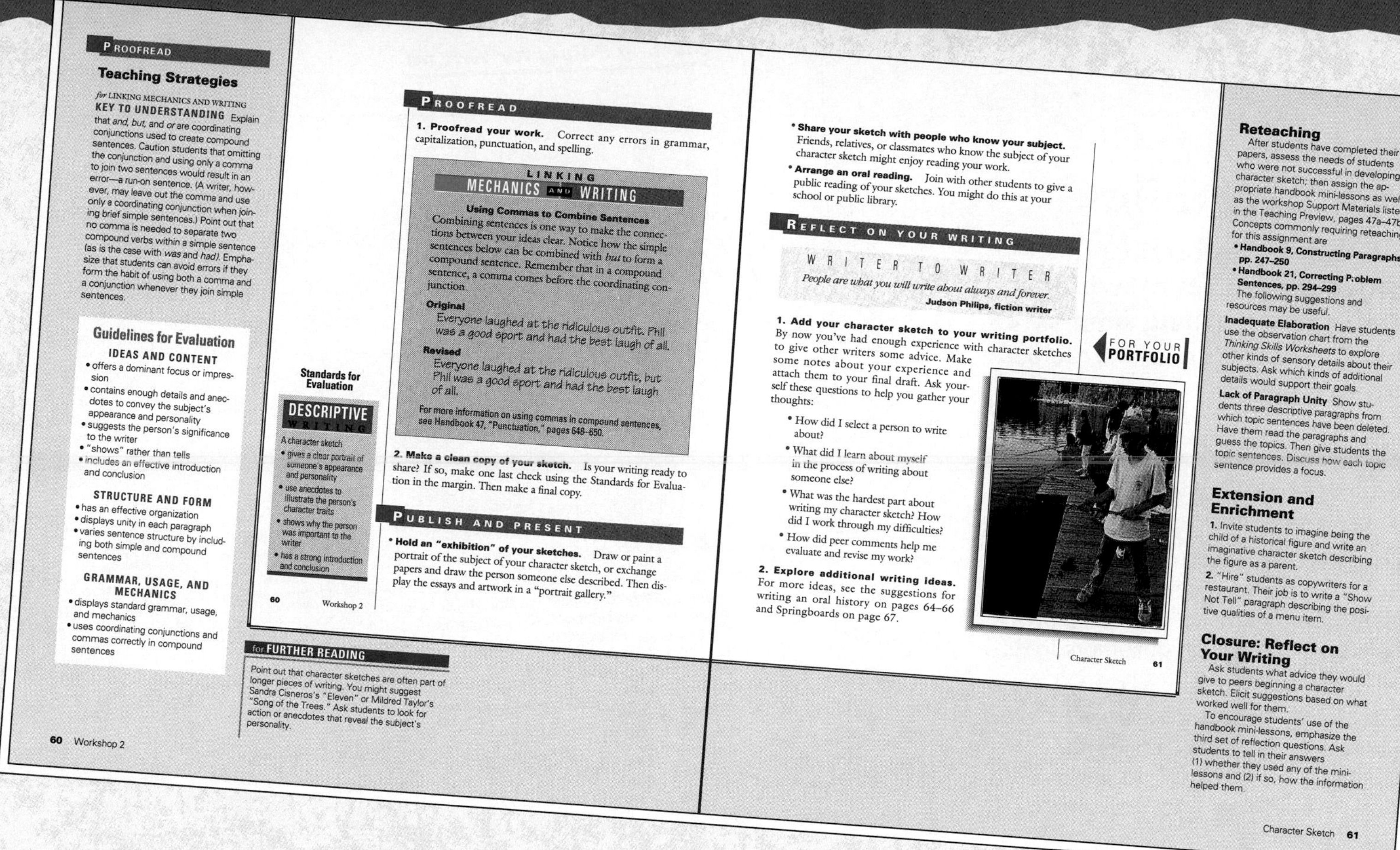

PROOFREAD

Teaching Strategies

for LINKING MECHANICS AND WRITING
KEY TO UNDERSTANDING Explain that *and, but,* and *or* are coordinating conjunctions used to create compound sentences. Caution students that omitting the conjunction and using only a comma to join two sentences would result in an error—a run-on sentence. (A writer, however, may leave out the comma and use only a coordinating conjunction when joining brief simple sentences.) Point out that no comma is needed to separate two compound verbs within a simple sentence (as is the case with *was* and *had*). Emphasize that students can avoid errors if they form the habit of using both a comma and a conjunction whenever they join simple sentences.

Guidelines for Evaluation

IDEAS AND CONTENT
- offers a dominant focus or impression
- contains enough details and anecdotes to convey the subject's appearance and personality
- suggests the person's significance to the writer
- "shows" rather than tells
- includes an effective introduction and conclusion

STRUCTURE AND FORM
- has an effective organization
- displays unity in each paragraph
- varies sentence structure by including both simple and compound sentences

GRAMMAR, USAGE, AND MECHANICS
- displays standard grammar, usage, and mechanics
- uses coordinating conjunctions and commas correctly in compound sentences

for FURTHER READING

Point out that character sketches are often part of longer pieces of writing. You might suggest Sandra Cisneros's "Eleven" or Mildred Taylor's "Song of the Trees." Ask students to look for action or anecdotes that reveal the subject's personality.

60 Workshop 2

PROOFREAD

1. Proofread your work. Correct any errors in grammar, capitalization, punctuation, and spelling.

LINKING MECHANICS AND WRITING

Using Commas to Combine Sentences

Combining sentences is one way to make the connections between your ideas clear. Notice how the simple sentences below can be combined with *but* to form a compound sentence. Remember that in a compound sentence, a comma comes before the coordinating conjunction.

Original
Everyone laughed at the ridiculous outfit. Phil was a good sport and had the best laugh of all.

Revised
Everyone laughed at the ridiculous outfit, but Phil was a good sport and had the best laugh of all.

For more information on using commas in compound sentences, see Handbook 47, "Punctuation," pages 648–650.

Standards for Evaluation

DESCRIPTIVE WRITING

A character sketch
- gives a clear portrait of someone's appearance and personality
- uses anecdotes to illustrate the person's character traits
- shows why the person was important to the writer
- has a strong introduction and conclusion

2. Make a clean copy of your sketch. Is your writing ready to share? If so, make one last check using the Standards for Evaluation in the margin. Then make a final copy.

PUBLISH AND PRESENT

- **Hold an "exhibition" of your sketches.** Draw or paint a portrait of the subject of your character sketch, or exchange papers and draw the person someone else described. Then display the essays and artwork in a "portrait gallery."

60 Workshop 2

- **Share your sketch with people who know your subject.** Friends, relatives, or classmates who know the subject of your character sketch might enjoy reading your work.
- **Arrange an oral reading.** Join with other students to give a public reading of your sketches. You might do this at your school or public library.

REFLECT ON YOUR WRITING

WRITER TO WRITER
People are what you will write about always and forever.
Judson Philips, fiction writer

1. Add your character sketch to your writing portfolio. By now you've had enough experience with character sketches to give other writers some advice. Make some notes about your experience and attach them to your final draft. Ask yourself these questions to help you gather your thoughts:
- How did I select a person to write about?
- What did I learn about myself in the process of writing about someone else?
- What was the hardest part about writing my character sketch? How did I work through my difficulties?
- How did peer comments help me evaluate and revise my work?

FOR YOUR PORTFOLIO

2. Explore additional writing ideas. For more ideas, see the suggestions for writing an oral history on pages 64–66 and Springboards on page 67.

Character Sketch 61

Reteaching

After students have completed their papers, assess the needs of students who were not successful in developing a character sketch; then assign the appropriate handbook mini-lessons as well as the workshop Support Materials listed in the Teaching Preview, pages 47a–47b. Concepts commonly requiring reteaching for this assignment are
- **Handbook 9, Constructing Paragraphs, pp. 247–250**
- **Handbook 21, Correcting Problem Sentences, pp. 294–299**

The following suggestions and resources may be useful.

Inadequate Elaboration Have students use the observation chart from the *Thinking Skills Worksheets* to explore other kinds of sensory details about their subjects. Ask which kinds of additional details would support their goals.

Lack of Paragraph Unity Show students three descriptive paragraphs from which topic sentences have been deleted. Have them read the paragraphs and guess the topics. Then give students the topic sentences. Discuss how each topic sentence provides a focus.

Extension and Enrichment

1. Invite students to imagine being the child of a historical figure and write an imaginative character sketch describing the figure as a parent.

2. "Hire" students as copywriters for a restaurant. Their job is to write a "Show Not Tell" paragraph describing the positive qualities of a menu item.

Closure: Reflect on Your Writing

Ask students what advice they would give to peers beginning a character sketch. Elicit suggestions based on what worked well for them.

To encourage students' use of the handbook mini-lessons, emphasize the third set of reflection questions. Ask students to tell in their answers (1) whether they used any of the mini-lessons and (2) if so, how the information helped them.

Character Sketch 61

- **Guidelines for Evaluation** Rubrics for evaluating student papers.
- **Reteaching Suggestions** Suggestions for providing additional instruction in areas where students were not successful.
- **Extension and Enrichment** Ideas for moving students beyond the assignment.
- **Reflect on Your Writing** Ideas that help students learn from each assignment and build writing portfolios.
- **For Further Reading** Other readings that are related to the model.

Other Features

Answer Keys Answers or suggested responses to all student activities.

Professional Notebook Quotes and suggestions from experts on teaching and the writing process.

Multicultural Connections Opportunities to broaden learning to include a variety of cultures.

Spice Box Motivating quotes and activities.

Teacher's Lounge Humor from the bulletin boards to you.

Teacher's Resource File

Motivation, reinforcement, creative approaches to writing, and practical teaching support are the hallmarks of the Teacher's Resource File.

Transparency Pack

A wealth of transparencies enhances all of your writing lessons.

- **Fine Art Transparencies** Classic and contemporary art reproductions offer springboards to writing. Worksheets provide writing prompts for a variety of modes.
- **Thinking Skills Transparencies** These graphic organizers can be used to help students find or develop ideas. Worksheets provide practice with each device.
- **Elaboration, Revision, and Proofreading Transparencies** Transparencies and worksheets give students extra experience with three key writing skills.

Guidelines for Writing Assessment and Portfolio Use

This booklet includes Evaluation Guidelines; models of strong, average, and weak student responses; and materials to aid in portfolio building.

Sentence Composing Copy Masters

These activities provide additional practice in composing sentences based on literary models.

McDougal, Littell

Starting Points for Writing

Another Vanishing Cowboy (1988), Stephen Rosser.

Stephen Rosser (1954–) is an Oklahoma arti... bright colors, bold shapes, and a playful style to... the horror movies and television programs he w... A movie character called the Invisible Man inspi... this "invisible" cowboy... realized that he was als... pearing from the West.

Copyright © McDougal, Littell & Company

McDougal, Littell

Thinking Skills

Problem-Solution Chart

Problem:	What	Choice: track team or community theater
	Why	Not enough time for both and homework

Possible Solutions	Results—Pros and Cons
1. Choose track	Pro Lots of friends on the team May get to go to regionals
	...e to earn money for ...ack shoes
	...o perform before ...le
	...ave to get a ride to ...ing practice ...nly lasts 4 weeks

Informative Writing: Explaining What

Elaboration

(1) When you sleep, something strange happens beneath your eyelids. (2) While your lids are closed, ...

Informative Writing: Explaining What

Elaboration

The following paragraph is from the beginning of a definition of *REM* sleep. Use the **Suggestions for Elaboration** to develop the paragraph further by adding information to sentences or by making up new sentences. You may find details and other ideas in the **Data Bank**. Write your paragraph on a separate sheet of paper.

First Draft

(1) When you sleep, something strange happens beneath your eyelids. **(2)** While your lids are closed, your eyeballs sometimes move. **(3)** The movement is a sign that you are in REM, or Rapid Eye Movement, sleep. **(4)** During REM sleep, other changes also take place in your body. **(5)** REM sleep occurs about every 90 minutes. **(6)** It's during REM sleep that you dream.

Data Bank

■ eyelids closed ■ eyeballs dart ■ move back and forth rapidly ■ as if watching fast game of tennis ■ occurs about every 90 minutes ■ takes up 25% of sleep time ■ heart rate and breathing often speed up or slow down ■ slight twitching of muscles ■ body seems paralyzed

Suggestions for Elaboration

- Elaborate on Sentence 2 by adding details and a comparison that shows how the eyeballs of a person in REM sleep move.
- Support Sentence 4 by adding examples of other changes that occur in the body during REM sleep.
- Following Sentence 5, add information telling how much of an average night is taken up with REM sleep.

Elaboration: Informative Writing/Explaining What 9

Writing from Personal Experience

Strong Response

A Perfect Bunt

I've always talked about giving people a chance, but I'd never tested my belief until one hot, dusty Saturday on the ballfield near my house. We were choosing up sides for the weekly softball team, and I was one of the captains. I noticed a new kid, Raul. He was short and skinny. Let Daryl choose him for his team, I thought. I want to win!

I chose Luiza, who was fast as a sprinter, Rob, who had a powerful arm, and five others. Soon it was down to Raul and Loren. I wanted Loren, but I stopped before calling her name. Should I give the new kid a chance?

My palms sweated as I thought. Raul *might* lose the game for us. I had to decide quickly, though. "Raul!" I shouted, swallowing hard. "You catch."

Raul struck out twice before the ninth inning. Then we ...

The introduction establishes the setting and personal nature of this narrative; it encourages the reader to continue.

Specific details help show the writer's feelings.

Paragraphs a... used effective... to present dialogue and show the next scene in the narrative.

Subject–Verb Splits: Phrases

Put a phrase between subject and verb to add details about the subject and give variety to your sentences. Here are examples of phrases as S–V splits.

Model A The other six, two brothers and four sisters, lived with their parents in a spacious house at 426 Twenty-Ninth Street, in Oakland.
Frank B. Gilbreth, Jr., and Ernestine Gilbreth Carey, *Cheaper by the Dozen*

Model B The boy, regaining his balance, dragged Sounder off the porch and to the corner of the cabin.
William H. Armstrong, *Sounder*

Model C Johnny, trained in a silver shop to do such work, made a bullet mold.
Esther Forbes, *Johnny Tremain*

A. Combining Sentences At the caret (^) in the first sentence, insert the underlined part of the second sentence as an S–V split. Add commas.

1. Mafuto ^ heard a scornful laugh. He was standing tense in the shadows.
Armstrong Sperry, *Call It Courage*

2. The voice of a different frog ^ croaked from the nearest bank. This voice was hoarser and not so deep.
Natalie Babbitt, *Tuck Everlasting*

3. A long table ^ took up almost the whole dining room. The table was loaded with food.
Norma Fox Mazer, "I, Hungry Hannah Cassandra Glen . . ."

4. Mr. Lema ^ greeted me and assigned me a desk. He was the sixth grade teacher.
Francisco Jiménez, "The Circuit"

Peer Response Guides

Students are given prompts to guide them through peer response sessions for each Guided Assignment.

Writing Resource Book

Practice and reteaching exercises are provided for each section of the Workshop as well as the Writing Handbook.

Grammar and Usage Practice Book

A variety of practice and reteaching exercises reinforces concepts taught in every Grammar Handbook section.

Spelling and Vocabulary Booklet

Ten spelling lessons and thirty-six vocabulary lessons improve student writing through a variety of activities and word lists based on current spelling research as well as SAT and ACT examinations.

Tests and Writing Assessment Prompts

This complete testing and assessment package offers Pretests and Mastery Tests for all grammar, usage, and mechanics concepts.

Writing Prompts for Assessment are provided for each Guided Assignment in the text to help prepare students for evaluation situations.

Classroom Technology

The *Writer's DataBank* software provides a data base and useful strategies that can be used during the writing process. A *Grammar Test Generator* allows teachers to create varied, comprehensive tests and practice sheets.

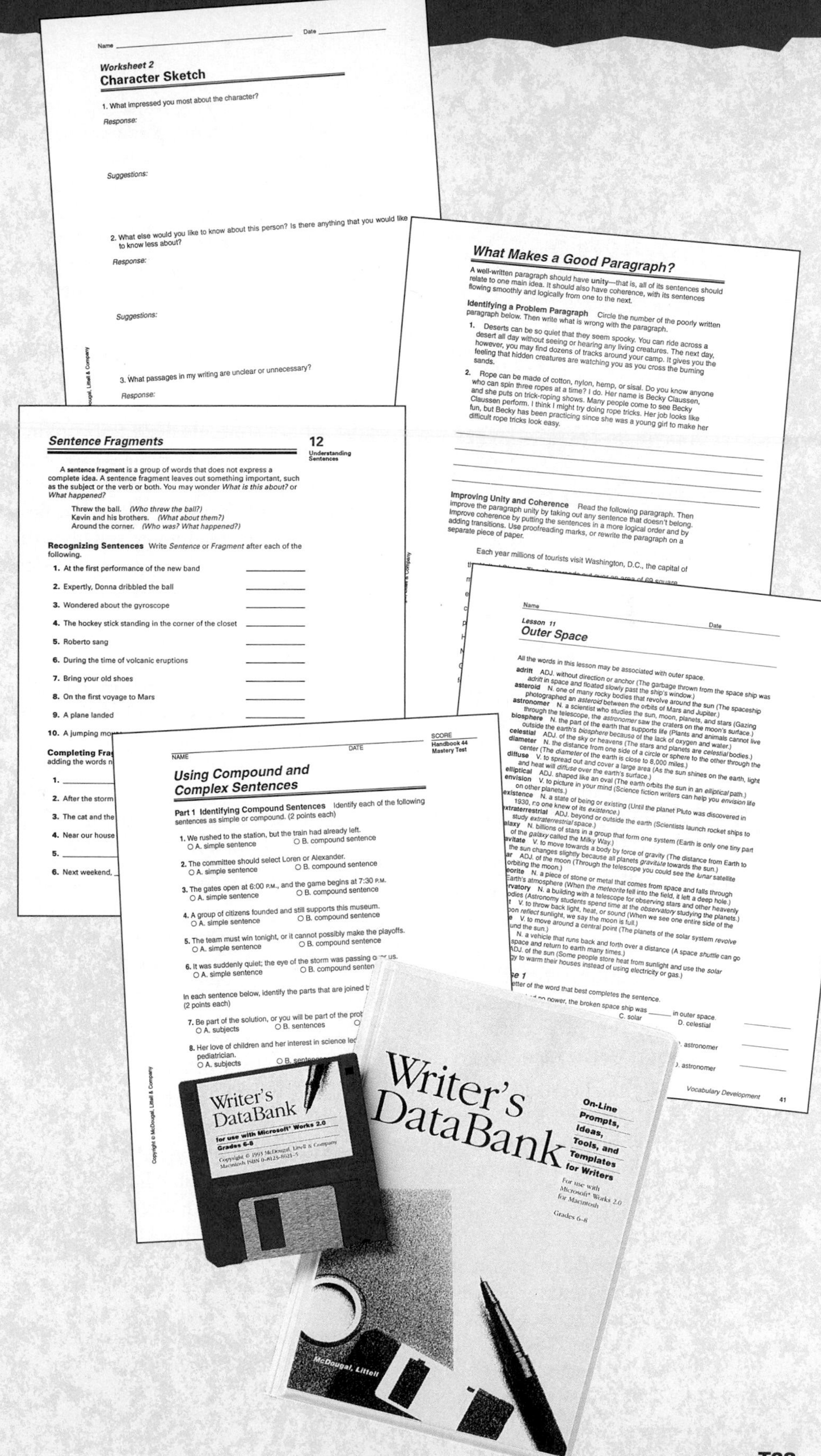

What makes my students different?

Teaching Young Adolescents: The Middle Years

Author:

Susan Hynds, Associate Professor and Director of English Education, Syracuse University, Syracuse, New York

Middle school students are, indeed, *in the middle* of childhood and young adulthood. But rather than living in some nether world between the two, they seem to be straddling them. Sometimes they tip more to the side of childhood, at other times to the side of young adulthood. That very quality is what makes them a delight to teach on one day, and an exercise in hair-pulling exasperation the next.

Physically, socially, intellectually, and emotionally, young adolescents seem more different from each other and seem to change more dramatically in four short years than children of almost any age. For example . . .

Physically . . .

Middle school students have three main characteristics: energy, energy, and energy! Just stand in a middle school hallway at the change of classes and feel the vibrating chaos as hundreds of spirited young bodies stream from classrooms, banging their lockers, flying up stairways, screaming at their peers and streaming past their teachers. But this seemingly endless reservoir of energy is fluctuating and unpredictable. The same students who were just screaming and hitting each other in the hallways can be seen a few minutes later, lounging in their desks in a near-catatonic state the minute classes begin again.

Because they always seem poised on the brink of hyperactivity or boredom, middle school students need to be invited to read about, write about, and explore topics that are personally meaningful and easily related to their own worlds in some way. They also need language activities that allow them to get up out of their desks, to switch intellectual gears, and to interact with other students.

Socially . . .

There is no question that middle school students are very social creatures. Often, it's only through the support of their peers that they discover and develop their own personal identities. Their social identities, like their moods, are in a perpetual and dramatic state of flux.

To move from the safe, self-contained classroom of the elementary school to the middle school with its changes of classes and teachers makes young adolescents needy of little touches that say they are cared about and part of a classroom family. If you are a middle school teacher, you know how often you seem to be dispensing paper clips, pencils, hall passes, hugs, and bandaids.

Young adolescents need to belong in another way as well. The friends of elementary school are often quickly forgotten, but middle school students are beginning to forge the bonds of friendships that can last a lifetime. At the same time, they are beginning to think of themselves as members of a society. They are curious about how issues of race, gender, poverty, and crime touch their own lives or neighborhoods. They are also becoming aware of social and cultural differences. For this reason, they need to be presented with situations that allow them to explore a variety of human relationships and cultural perspectives. Teachers need to invite them to write and talk about these perspectives with others, and to capitalize on their irrepressibly social natures.

Intellectually . . .

For many years, it was assumed that students between the ages of ten and fourteen were beginning to move from what Piaget called "concrete operations" into what he called "formal operations"—basically, that they could think abstractly about themselves and the world. For that reason, many instructional materials for junior high school students were geared to lead students up through the ranks from concrete to more abstract levels of thinking.

Today, we know that most middle school students—indeed, many high school students, and even adults—have not yet moved fully into formal operational thinking in the purest sense of that term. This doesn't mean that middle school learners can't think abstractly. It means that they need teachers who can help them make concrete connections between abstract ideas and their own personal worlds.

A middle school student writing about one of the Greek myths might remark: "He's just a male chauvinist!" or "She's just stupid!" They don't typically gravitate to more abstract comments like: "Greed is a common human characteristic," or "People should follow the spirit and not the letter of the law." Because young adolescents often believe that all eyes are on them, it's hard for them to look past their own viewpoints.

This doesn't mean that middle school learners can't think abstractly about people and events; it means that they need to be invited to think beyond themselves. They need to be challenged with statements like, "Tell me all the reasons that

you believe this solution is a good one," or "Does this historical event remind you of anything in today's world?" or "How could your experience be turned into a story with meaning for everyone?" They need to be led back and forth from the world of concrete, personal experience, into the realm of imagining, speculating, and hypothesizing.

Emotionally . . .

Middle school students are intense! Perhaps because life seems so intense for them, middle school students have a powerful need to be recognized, listened to. They need to have opportunities to perform, to be at center stage, and to express their feelings and concerns. A wide range of writing and speaking activities—journals, songs, scripts, opinion pieces, discussion groups, and storytelling—are all excellent ways for students to sort through and share all of the new emotions they are experiencing.

At the same time, because they are so intense, they have a very strong need for routine. This does not mean a need for boring drill and practice exercises, but for comfortable rituals which invite them to take risks and be creative. They need little routines that say "we are a classroom family, and we do things this way in *our* room." Providing predictable structures for portfolio conferences and writers' and readers' workshops will give students this sense of safety and comfort.

The Nineties: Harsh Realities

Unfortunately, there are many issues that may not have faced us in the days when we went to junior high school. We are beginning to see some of the effects of parental substance abuse, sexual abuse, and domestic violence on the intellectual and emotional capacities of young adolescents. These problems of abuse and neglect know no racial, ethnic, or socioeconomic lines. They are as present in suburbs as they are in cities.

There is also a great deal of media openness which treats virginity as a social disease, which promotes materialism, and makes a life of crime seem like a glamorous occupation. On top of this, young adolescents are reaching puberty earlier than their cohorts did at the turn of the century, and, perhaps regrettably, many of them are experimenting with issues and experiences that once were considered beyond the realm of children their age.

Finally, as productive members of society, middle school students are, quite literally, useless. Years ago, young people worked on farms or in the village when they weren't in school. They were an integral part of the larger social community. Today, although they might be loved, they aren't needed for much of anything. And so, they often become consumers of junk food, video games, or other kinds of mindless diversion.

Teachers need to realize that the teaching of literature and writing can provide a way for students to deal with sensitive or personal issues that may have no other outlet. They need to offer a range of topics for writing and discussion so that students who are uncomfortable with certain subjects can maintain a comfortable distance, while others can be free to explore those topics. Teachers also need to help young adolescents to feel integral and involved in their community and the larger world.

The Writer's Craft invites young adolescents to explore a whole array of personally meaningful topics and issues through a variety of different formats, both written and oral. A host of language activities invites students to work collaboratively or individually, moving beyond their own perspectives and considering the viewpoints of others. Best of all, *The Writer's Craft* invites you to create a sense of classroom community and to give your middle school students the self-confidence to become more involved in the world beyond the walls of school.

Related Reading

George, P. S.; Stevenson, C.; Thomason, J; & Beane, J. (1992). *The middle school and beyond*. Alexandria, VA: Association for Supervision and Curriculum Development.

Hester, J. P. & Hester, P. J (1983). Brain research and the middle school curriculum. *Middle School Journal 15* (1), pp. 4–7.

Johnson, J. H. & Markle, G. C. (1986). *What research says to the middle level practitioner.* Columbus, OH: National Middle School Association.

Lawrence, V. (1988). The teacher in the middle school. *Early Adolescence Magazine, 2* (3), pp. 19–21.

Silvern, S. B. (1990). Connecting classroom practice and research. *Journal of Research in Childhood Education, 5* (1), pp. 85–86.

Wiles, J. & Bondi, J. (1986). *Making middle schools work.* Alexandria, VA: Association for Supervision and Curriculum Development.

Is there a better way to teach writing?

Philosophy and Rationale

Authors:

Peter Elbow, Professor of English, University of Massachusetts at Amherst

Sheridan Blau, Senior Lecturer in English and Education, University of California at Santa Barbara

Teachers are constantly bombarded with confident pronouncements from experts and textbooks about the teaching of writing. But tidy theories don't usually hold up in the complex realities of the middle school classroom. This book, therefore, is based on the classroom experience of many teachers teaching in many different circumstances: experiences of success and of frustration and of puzzlement.

The truth is, writing is not a body of theoretical knowledge or precepts. Writing, rather, is a body of practices and strategies and activities—above all, a *craft*. Therefore if we truly want to teach writing, we must engage students in the activities of craftspersons. We must ask them to be writers and see themselves as writers. The premise of the book, then, is that we can and should treat our students as writers—putting strong faith in them yet also making strong demands on them.

The best way to explain what this book is about is to list some of the important things we know about writers:

Writers are not all alike. Therefore, there is no single "writing process" or lock step set of procedures that works for all writers or is appropriate for all students. Indeed, even the same person needs different processes on different occasions and for different kinds of writing. *The Writer's Craft* is based on the premise that students are no more like each other than other writers are, and that it is counterproductive to try to impose one alleged "writing process" on all students for all writing.

Writers make choices. Since writers are *not* alike, it follows, then, that they encounter different problems as they work and employ different strategies. Therefore this book is not organized in a linear fashion where every student follows the same path. Rather, it assumes that students will blaze their own trails. As each assignment is presented in the book, students are given numerous important but necessary decisions to make. (For example, "Do you want to start out by making an outline before you have done any writing, or wait until you've explored your ideas on paper or written a discovery draft? Good writers proceed in both ways.") Some assignments offer a great deal of guidance to the student and others offer very little. In short, the assignments as a whole follow a coherent path, yet there are many opportunities for choice.

Writers learn to write by writing. This book, therefore, does not require a lot of reading *about* writing. Instead it constantly invites the student to write: to write often, in many different forms and contexts, and for different audiences.

Writers learn by reflecting. Writers think about what they do. They observe themselves, learn from practice, think about the choices they make. They talk to others who are engaged in the same business, sharing problems and successes, and comparing the writing choices each of them made. So this book asks students to look not only at *what* they write but at *how* they write, to reflect for themselves on the complicated vagaries of their own writing processes, and to talk with other students and with teachers about how things went.

Writers learn by reading. Thus the book puts a big emphasis on reading the writing of others: the writing of fellow students in the class, the writing of well-known published writers, and some writing by students in other parts of the country (which is included in the book). The readings by published writers in the wider world are not just literary pieces: they also represent a wide range of other types of writing—from magazine articles to scripts to workaday on-the-job writing. The book reprints these writings as chances for students to see what other writers have done: not as pieces to revere—to put under glass like paintings in a museum—but rather as opportunities for students to come at them as fellow writers and questioners. Always, throughout the book, the question is, "Let's see: what choices was the writer making here?"

There is a community of writers. A few writers may squirrel themselves away from others and write entirely on their own, but, as the last two points above illustrate, most writers have important connections with other writers and with a larger community. The teachers behind this book have consciously emphasized this connected model of the writer. The book asks students to work with the smaller community of other writers in the class: to talk about writing and compare notes and drafts and discuss the writing process and give responses to each other. And it also asks students to work with and see themselves as part of the larger community of writers and readers in the world.

Writers must care about what they write. If they just do exercises, if they just find ideas and transmit them *like telegraph operators,* they will have no personal investment in what they write. This book shows students how to find writing ideas that matter to them. It encourages them to take responsibility for what they write, take ownership, take pride.

Writers have a lot to say. Because students are young and inexperienced—because they sometimes even tell us, "I have nothing to write about"—it is tempting to think of them as empty vessels that must be filled. But the teachers behind this book have found that their best teaching comes when they emphasize not what students *don't* know and can't do, but what they *do* know and can do. When we build on the considerable knowledge and language skills that students already have, they learn new things much faster. Experienced writers trust their own thinking, and students, too, must be given some confidence in themselves to function at their best.

Good writers explore and discover as they write. The book helps students to learn how to start from what they *don't* know as well as from what they do know—and then write their way to understanding. In short, writing is thinking, not just recording what is already worked out in some book or in one's mind. To write is to observe, to analyze, to solve problems, to make decisions. This book gives students continual practice in various forms of thinking.

Writers should experiment. The teachers behind this book made a conscious choice to push for a variety of writing experiences. Students should write in diverse modes. They should push at the edges of their experience and develop skills that come from trying various kinds of writing—from narratives to essays to oral histories to songs to visual collages. And not all writing need be earnest and heavy. Writers and students need low-stakes writing, too, in order to learn to take some of the risks and have some of the fun that is necessary if a writer is to develop. So while the book asks that most major assignments go through multiple drafts and be carefully revised, it also asks students in the "Sketchbook" and journal sections to make quick sketches and learn to play with writing.

Teachers have a unique opportunity with this program. The perspective that writing is a craft, and that students learn most from writing, provides teachers with an exciting role. Instead of feeling compelled to lecture or provide ready-made advice that fits all students and all situations, a teacher can instead be a coach, guide, responder, and nudger—one who will encourage those students who are too timid or fearful, and yes, push those who need a push.

How do I set up my classroom?

Establishing a Writing Workshop Classroom

Author:
Linda Lewis, Writing Specialist,
Ft. Worth Independent School District

How can a teacher organize a classroom for effective writing instruction? Perhaps predictably, there is no one best way. Outstanding writing classrooms take many different forms, each reflecting the preferences and personalities of the teacher and students who form that particular writing community. All effective classrooms, however, provide a caring, supportive environment that encourages even the most reluctant students to grow as writers. This environment is based on certain expectations:

- Everyone writes.
- Everyone shares.
- Everyone responds.

If these expectations are met, a key goal is achieved:

- Everyone succeeds.

Creating a Favorable Atmosphere

An effective writing classroom is actually a social place—an interactive community of writers. In such a classroom, the students are responsible for their own growth as writers; however, they are equally responsible for the learning and development of others.

Establishing expectations The teacher's approach to writing can have a tremendous impact on the classroom. Therefore, the following attitudes should be evident in every day's activities.

- **Writing is a meaningful activity.** To help students realize that writing has purpose, they should be encouraged to read as much as possible and to become aware of the power of the written word. Magazine excerpts, speeches, scripts, and newspaper articles are all excellent vehicles for making this point. To reinforce this understanding, the students' own writing must be done for real purposes and real audiences. *The Writer's Craft* can be used to give students opportunities to apply their skills in activities as diverse as oral histories and children's books.
- **Everyone can write.** The basic assumption that underlies an effective writing classroom is that everyone has both something to say and the basic tools with which to say it. Even reluctant writers should be engaged in producing whole texts, not just sentences or paragraphs. The teacher can reinforce this expectation by emphasizing and evaluating not only the student's final writing product, but also his or her individual process and progress.
- **Writing involves sharing and responding.** The purpose of almost all writing is communication. Therefore, students should be encouraged to share their writing at every stage of the writing process and to solicit the types of responses that they need from their peers. See pages T32–T35 for more information on peer response and collaborative learning.

Setting up the classroom The arrangement and content of the classroom itself can dynamically reinforce and enhance the feeling of a writing community.

- **The furniture** Student desks or tables can be arranged in many different configurations to facilitate various aspects of the writing activity. For example, some teachers prefer to have the class carry out individual and large-group activities with desks in traditional rows, rearranging them in clusters for collaborative work or peer-response sessions and in a large circle for sharing finished work. Others designate specific areas of the room for various writing activities, perhaps providing an editing corner, a conference table, tables for group response activities, and an area with student desks for private writing.
- **Displays of illustrative materials** Writing—by the students, the teacher, and professional writers—should be profusely displayed in the classroom, and changed as the teacher or students discover exciting new models. Several drafts of a given piece of writing, quotations by published authors about their writing process and products, and favorite writing samples can be included in these displays. A special motivational display, for example, could include brief autobiographical blurbs and pictures that students compile for their hypothetical future books.
- **Reference sources** In addition to providing an appropriate arrangement of furniture and motivational displays, an effective writing classroom should include a reference area stocked with various dictionaries, thesauruses, handbooks, and other reference books. Some teachers also provide files of writing done by students in previous classes.

Roles of Teacher and Students

To promote the individual and collaborative goals of effective writing instruction, both the teacher and the students must be aware of the different roles they can play in the classroom.

The teacher's roles There is no one writing process that will work for all students in all writing situations. Therefore, an effective writing teacher is a co-writer, collaborator, coach, and facilitator, rather than a lecturer.

- **The teacher as co-writer and collaborator** Probably one of the best ways for a teacher to advance the expectations of a writing classroom is to become a writer along with the students. In sharing not only finished writing products, but also work in progress, the teacher can instruct students through direct involvement and interaction.
- **The teacher as coach and facilitator** In addition to writing with students, the teacher can facilitate their learning in many ways. For example, during exploratory activities the teacher can help students find topics in which they can become invested; during drafting, support and problem solve with individual students as needed; and during revision, provide guidance and individual or small-group instruction. Providing time for one-on-one conferences is an excellent way of providing this kind of help while encouraging young writers to grow.

The students' roles Like the teacher, the students in an interactive writing classroom play many different roles.

- **The student as writer** It is important that students view themselves as writers with ideas to communicate to others, not as students completing an assignment for the teacher. The kinds of "real world" writing assignments included in *The Writer's Craft* can help create this attitude in the classroom. So can the use of peer response groups and an emphasis on other actual audiences. Probably the most important way to make students feel like writers, however, is to *treat* them as writers, to respect their ability as craftspersons and encourage them to analyze writing problems, explore options, and experiment with techniques.
- **The student as collaborator** In a writing workshop classroom, students are encouraged to share work in progress, help each other problem solve, and contribute ideas to the work of peers, if asked. Students who are not used to such an arrangement may at first have difficulty with this more open approach to writing, and should be allowed to work independently. However, teachers can encourage interaction by having writers work with single partners initially, and then combine to form groups as they become conversant and comfortable with sharing.
- **The student as responder** Student writing improves dramatically when students share their writing with each other. (See Peer Sharing and Peer Response on pages T32–T33.) There are several specific ways that teachers can help students become effective peer responders: (1) have students evaluate "training papers" by students from other classes before addressing the writing of classmates, (2) have them role-play successful and unsuccessful response groups and critique the interactions, and (3) model appropriate comments using transparencies such as those available in the Teacher's Resource File.

Ensuring Success

The success of a writing classroom depends largely on three factors: (1) clarity of goals, (2) commitment to working toward them, and (3) criteria for assessing progress and achievement. The teacher who is able to establish a favorable atmosphere for writing, and clear goals for writers as described above, is well on the way to success. Developing concrete standards of evaluation and making students aware of them is another important factor.

Standards of evaluation Students are more apt to become successful writers if they understand the specific criteria by which their writing will be judged before they undertake an assignment. The Standards for Evaluation in the Guided Assignments, as well as *Guidelines for Writing Assessment and Portfolio Use* in the Teacher's Resource File, can help students become familiar with and learn to identify the qualities of good writing and develop strategies for effecting them as they write.

Using portfolios In addition, students should be encouraged to reflect on their writing process as they complete each piece and to save selected works in a portfolio. They should also examine these writing portfolios from time to time and note their consistent strengths and weaknesses as well as specific aspects of their development as writers.

A writing workshop classroom can be a lively and stimulating place. And when it is successful, the teacher's expectations and those of the students become reality: everyone writes, everyone shares, everyone responds, and everyone succeeds.

How can I combine literature, writing, and grammar?

Integrating the Language Arts

Authors:

Arthur N. Applebee, Professor of Education, State University of New York at Albany

Judith A. Langer, Professor of Education, State University of New York at Albany

The English language arts curriculum has always been compartmentalized into a variety of special topics, including literature, writing, and grammar. Thought of as separate subjects, they have competed for time and attention in the classroom and in instructional materials. In this view, if we give more time to writing, then we must give less time to literature or grammar. This compartmentalization reflects a "building block" approach to student learning, implying that the various aspects of the language arts can be taught separately and yet still be put together by the student into some meaningful whole. This approach lends itself well to neatly organized segments of curriculum planning, presented in elaborate scope-and-sequence charts meant to coordinate the teaching of particular skills within each particular segment of the English curriculum.

Yet this building block approach does not fit very well with the ways in which human beings learn and use language. Rather than learning skills in isolation, we learn them best in the context of experiences. Young children learn to talk because they want to communicate their needs and share their interests with those around them. Older students similarly learn to read and write most effectively when they are reading, writing, and talking about things that interest and matter to them—and when they have a purpose for reading and writing about these things. An integrated approach to the language arts is much more effective in promoting "higher literacy" in students than the building block approach.

The Workshops in *The Writer's Craft* reflect the importance of an integrated approach to student language learning, and offer a variety of ways in which teachers can foster the integration of writing with literature and grammar. Some general suggestions follow.

Integrating Writing with Literature

The primary emphasis in many English classrooms is on the teaching of literature. The following suggestions provide ideas for integrating literature with the kinds of writing activities suggested in *The Writer's Craft:*

1. Let students think through writing. Use the students' responses to the literature—their developing understandings and interpretations—as the prompt for a writing activity. As students discuss and debate their responses, the motivation and opportunity to work out their ideas in writing can develop naturally out of their discussions. This is particularly true with the selections in McDougal, Littell's *Literature and Language* series, which places a similar emphasis on a process-oriented approach to the teaching of English language arts.

2. Use literary selections as springboards. The literature students read may suggest similar situations they want to explore, or concepts they want to analyze, or it may prompt them to create their own contribution to a particular genre. *The Writer's Craft* and *Literature and Language* were carefully planned to allow just this kind of interaction. The Writer's Workshops in the two series were built around the same scope and sequence, and a special "Links" feature in both Teacher's Editions suggests how to structure lessons that tie literature selections to the Writer's Workshops.

3. Use selections as both literature models and as examples of how other writers have gone about the craft of writing. Students can profitably spend some time discussing their responses to the selections, sorting out their differing evaluations and interpretations, before examining the ways in which the selections have been shaped and crafted.

4. Let students explore their understandings of and reactions to other students' writing. Examples of student work can be discussed in the same ways that you discuss published selections. If drafts are available, student work may be particularly useful in highlighting the choices a writer makes and the effects those choices have on readers. The Workshops in *The Writer's Craft* contain a variety of activities to help integrate students' writing with the literature they are reading.

Integrating Grammar Instruction

Students gain effective control of the conventions of written English when they are given many opportunities to use them in the context of their own writing. Isolated exercises in punctuating dialogue, for example, are likely to mean very little to students; learning how to punctuate dialogue because they want to incorporate it into a narrative of their own is much more likely to lead to long-term learning. To integrate grammar with writing and literature:

1. Encourage students to examine unusual features of the literature they read. With them, discuss how those features influence their reactions. For example, students may become aware of the effect of short, simple sentences in reading a folk tale by Virginia Hamilton, or alternatively of the more complex syntax characteristics in a novel by Madeleine L'Engle.

2. Emphasize specific writing conventions that may help while students are drafting or revising particular types of writing. Information about how to punctuate dialogue is likely to be particularly relevant when writing a story or reporting on an interview, for example. Information about formal versus informal usage is likely to be most relevant in writing to unknown or distant audiences.

3. Use opportunities for publication to provide instruction in grammar and usage tailored to individual students. Problems with the conventions of written English are usually highly individualized. In any given class, one student may have trouble with pronoun referents, another with managing verb tense, and still another with semicolons. Instruction to deal with such problems will be most effective as each student is revising a work to share with others. At that point, they will usually have a fairly clear idea of what they want to say, and are likely to be ready for help in saying it as clearly and effectively as they can. The mini-lessons in the Grammar and Usage Handbook are particularly useful in this context.

4. Let students teach one another. Some of the most effective instruction in grammar can come from peer responses to student writing. Because different students have different strengths, they can provide very effective help in "polishing" one another's drafts for publication—and the process of explaining the suggestions they make will strengthen each student's understanding of effective grammar and usage. For example, student pairs can help by reading each other's work and marking a "check" on any portion of the paper that doesn't "sound right" to them. The "check" can highlight questions about spelling, mechanics, grammar, or word choice and can signal useful places the writer can rethink when polishing the piece.

Each of the Workshops in *The Writer's Craft* highlights one or another aspect of grammar and usage in the context of the particular types of writing that students are being asked to do. Rather than isolated skill and drill, this grammar content is designed to highlight the relationship between knowledge of the conventions of language and the craft of writing. Each Workshop encourages students to experiment with language to make their own writing more effective.

The Language Arts Trio: Literature, Writing, and Grammar

Approached in these ways as interrelated segments of larger activities, the language arts "building blocks" can be taught just as systematically as the old scope-and-sequence charts implied—but much more effectively. When teachers integrate literature, writing, and grammar in their instructional program, the language arts will build upon and support each other. Instead of completing isolated lessons that assume the students will later be able to transfer the separate language arts skills to real literacy situations, students will learn language skills in complete and meaning-laden contexts in the first place. Thus, students' reading, writing, and language skills will develop in concert, in ways both students and their teachers recognize as meaningful, purposeful, and useful.

Is there a way to get students more involved?

Peer Sharing and Peer Response

Author:

Peter Elbow, Professor of English, University of Massachusetts at Amherst

Paul Goodman once said, "If we learned to speak the way we learn to write, there'd be lots more people who can't speak." Why? Because in many classrooms the context for writing is inexorable: the student writes, the teacher grades, and the teacher is the only audience. Imagine what speaking would be like if we spoke only to one person, and if every time we ever spoke, we were evaluated. Is this really the best way for students to learn to write? Does this diet of nothing but teacher grades and "corrected" papers really provide students with the nourishment they need to be better writers? And do tall stacks of papers only for teachers' eyes make for sane writing teachers?

There is another alternative: peers as audience and peers as responders. Peers are not a substitute for teachers as audience and responders, but a supplement or addition. Classmates are not asked to evaluate or correct each other's papers but rather to do what they are best at: to function as an audience, and provide an honest account of how they understand the text, how they reacted, and what was going on in their minds as they read. More and more teachers are finding peer responding a crucially helpful strand in their teaching.

Why Use Peer Response?

The use of peer response groups helps teachers to create a powerful change in their classrooms. Why is peer response so effective?

Students need audiences. One of the greatest weaknesses in student writing is a lack of awareness and connection with audience. When students write only for the teacher (which usually means for a grade), they often fall into certain bad habits—treating writing as an empty school exercise, and attempting simply to just "get it right" or "give teachers what they want." Yet surprisingly, students often care less about what they turn in to teachers than they do about what they read to or share with each other. They often hand writing to teachers that they don't really believe in.

When students write for their peers, however, they become very concerned about what they say and how they say it. In fact, the most powerful thing about the regular use of peer sharing and response groups is that students naturally and easily begin to learn that writing is not so much a matter of "figuring out what the teacher wants" but rather of discovering what they themselves have to say and then seeing whether they have gotten it across effectively to readers.

Just as this textbook tries to teach students that not everyone writes in the same way, so too does it teach students that not everyone reads in the same way. Peer response introduces students to the complex but ultimately empowering truth that the same text often produces different responses in different readers. The writer is then left in the position of having to evaluate those different responses and make writerly decisions about how to revise.

Teachers need relief. Another powerful reason teachers are making more and more use of peer response groups is brutally practical: the paper load for teachers.

Students don't learn to write well unless they write a great deal—which means writing more papers than teachers have time to read carefully and comment on. Peer sharing and response groups provide a way to increase the amount of writing that students do while assuring them of a response. For even though students may not be skilled at providing evaluation and advice, they are excellent at providing the one thing that writers need most—*an audience.*

Types of Response

Most students have never written words that they didn't turn in to a teacher for evaluation and criticism. Yet limiting feedback to this kind of response can cripple students' writing. Student writing almost always takes a big turn for the better when this traditional audience-relation is balanced by use of the other relationships described below. Indeed, this variety of types is crucial, for it provides the ideal "balanced audience diet" that students need—a balance among different relations to readers.

Private writing Students need opportunities to write privately—to do some writing that they don't show to anyone. This provides a crucial foundation of safety and comfort in writing and an arena for risk-taking.

Pure sharing Students need opportunities to share their writing with readers—but sometimes just for the sake of sharing with no response at all. This increases the risk ("going public"), and yet still provides a strong degree of safety since there is no feedback. The emphasis is placed on *communicating* rather than *feedback.* Sharing heightens the social dimension of writing, and there is also an enormous amount of extremely efficient learning that goes on, especially when the sharing is oral. Nothing teaches us so much about writing as the feel of our own sentences in our mouths and the sound of them in our ears. The process also gives students experience in working in groups before having to learn feedback techniques.

Limited feedback Students sometimes need opportunities to share writing and get responses—but not get criticism. By holding off the question of "how good is the writing?" students discover what is probably the most useful kind of feedback—learning how readers *understand* their words. Limited feedback, therefore, involves more risk, more feedback, and more learning. But because there is no criticism or advice, students find it a rewarding way to share, and can listen nondefensively to responses from readers.

Full feedback By working in peer groups in the two ways previously described, students heighten their reading and responding skills. Now they are ready to give and receive responses to the more demanding writerly questions like these: "What worked well and not so well? What suggestions do you have?"

This textbook provides a rich range of specific suggestions, prompts, and examples to enable students to learn how to become good peer responders to each other. By taking advantage of these techniques, students will find an audience, their teacher will gain time to teach, and writing will remain the exciting exchange of ideas and opinions it should always be.

Is there a way to get students more involved?

Collaborative and Cooperative Learning

Learning to use one's knowledge in collaboration with others is essential for success in and out of school. Consequently, group learning is becoming central to classrooms across the curriculum.

Collaborative learning is defined as any group activity that asks students to work together on a task. Advocates of collaborative learning assert that it motivates students to learn, improves social skills, and promotes self-esteem in students of all abilities. The students work together, and the teacher focuses on the different groups, carefully listening, watching, suggesting, and being prepared to work through any problems that naturally arise in the context of group work.

In **cooperative learning,** a more structured type of collaborative work, the success of one individual is linked to that of others. Each group member is responsible for helping other members to learn and for contributing a piece to a whole. Cooperative learning might be used, for example, if students were directed to stage a play, create an advertising campaign, complete a complex report, or produce a book of oral histories. Each student is held accountable for his or her own contributions and each student's mastery is assessed.

Getting Started

Divide the class into groups. Group students of differing abilities or talents together; pay particular attention to students with special needs: ESL and LD students, for example. Assure all students that creativity, problem-solving abilities, listening skills, empathy, and writing skills share equal importance in group work. Also, remind students that while they are responsible for their own learning, they are also responsible for helping others in the group to learn. Students should work together in an atmosphere of care, acceptance, trust, and support. Competition has no role in collaborative learning.

The size of groups depends on the purpose of the collaborative effort. Small groups of two or three students each are most appropriate when students are sharing personal writing and will benefit most from the individual attention one or two peers can offer. Larger groups of no more than six members can be effective too, particularly if the assignment is large or complex.

Specify objectives and purpose. Set clear, specific goals and objectives for each collaborative learning session. Also make sure students understand on what criteria they will be assessed.

Provide a structure. Assign specific responsibilities to students working in groups, or have the students do so themselves. For example, students working in a discussion group can take on specific roles, such as facilitator or discussion leader, recorder, reporter, and materials manager. If students are working cooperatively on a larger project, such as a research report, the assignment itself may be divided into parts and assigned; each student is responsible for completing his or her share of the work and for helping to join the pieces into a cohesive whole.

Monitor progress and achievement. The teacher's role during cooperative learning is that of facilitator or consultant. As group members work together, the teacher should circulate among them, mentally noting behavior and participation for future performance assessment. If necessary, the teacher should enter a group to clear up any misunderstandings or to ask questions that will direct students' thinking. If more than one group is having difficulty, the teacher may interrupt to reteach or clarify a point with the entire class.

Address assessment. Certain informal collaborative situations, such as peer response, require no evaluation procedure. Some situations, however, require assessment and grading to keep students

Author:

David Wallace, Researcher with the Center for the Study of Writing at Carnegie-Mellon University accountable for successful group process, for their own learning, and for that of other group members. Options for using grades to reward students for group learning include

- averaging individual scores within each group;
- giving a single score to all group members who have worked cooperatively on a single product;
- giving individual scores plus bonus points for successful group performance and the development of social skills.

Students should share in the assessment process by evaluating their own performance and that of their group. Students may judge that they've been successful if they have met the designated goals of the collaborative learning session. In evaluating group process, they might consider such questions as, "Did I feel supported? challenged? confronted? Were feelings hurt or were ideas shared and feedback given in an encouraging, supportive way? How might we improve the process next time?" Teachers and students should discuss what works and what doesn't work in group process and brainstorm together on ways of improving collaborative learning skills.

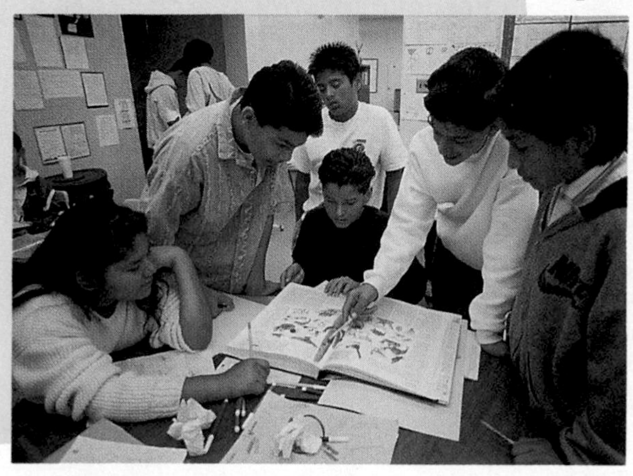

Ideas for Collaborative Learning

The Writer's Craft encourages students to work together in groups to explore concepts and ideas, problem solve, brainstorm, and collaborate during all phases of the writing process. The collaborative learning activities that follow can be effectively adapted for use in the English classroom.

Collaborative planning While students working alone during the planning stage rarely go beyond deciding what information to include in their texts, students planning in pairs or small groups consider the full range of writing variables and keep them in mind throughout the writing process. Developed at the Center for the Study of Writing at Berkeley and Carnegie-Mellon University under co-director Linda Flower, collaborative planning helps students learn to monitor their own learning about writing.

Before students begin to draft a writing assignment, divide the class into pairs or groups of three; have them take turns in the roles of writer and partner, talking through their writing ideas. While the writer talks about his or her ideas for content, audience, purpose, and form, partners help the writer by acting as a sounding board, listening carefully, asking for clarification or elaboration, and suggesting alternatives.

Jigsaw projects Students may choose to work collaboratively on any large or complex project, dividing the assignment into "pieces" and assigning each student to a piece. Students creating a video, for example, could divide the project into such "pieces" as research, scriptwriting, direction, and production. Students would then work together to meld the pieces into a coherent whole.

Learning partners After presenting new information on a topic or giving an assignment to the entire class, have students review the material out loud with a peer, using their notes as necessary to summarize or explain. For example, students could meet in small groups after grammar instruction. They could take turns paraphrasing the new rules out loud, presenting examples of the concept at work, or finding examples in their reading. The whole group can then complete or review the answers to the practice activities together, make necessary corrections, and submit a single set of answers for grading.

Research groups Students may conduct research on a topic and pool information into a written or oral report. Students will need to divide the workload equally, with each person responsible for researching a particular aspect of their outline. Students will join the pieces of information into a cohesive whole; one grade can be assigned to the entire group.

Team teaching Teachers from different subject areas may work together to develop theme-based projects that can lead to student learning and involvement across the curriculum. Because of their scope, such projects are ideal for collaborative learning activities. The Project Files preceding each Workshop in this Teacher's Edition provide detailed guidelines for this type of project. If team teaching is not utilized in a particular school, the projects can still be executed within the language arts classroom.

Are tests the only way to check progress?

Assessment and Response to Student Writing

Traditionally, much of the work in the teaching of writing has occurred in the process of responding to and assessing what students write. Teachers have given students topics to write about, and then have spent a great deal of time marking the papers that result—giving grades, making suggestions for ways the writing could have been improved, and correcting errors.

Such an approach is exhausting for teachers—the paperload quickly becomes overwhelming—and discouraging for students—whose papers "bleed" with the teachers' red penciling. Such an approach also works against what we know about the writing process. When students write about topics that have substance and depth, we can expect their work to be characterized by growth and change over time. They will try out and abandon ideas. They will reorganize sections. This is the "normal" state of affairs among the best of writers, and characterizes the *process* of crafting a text.

Response and Assessment

For students to engage in the kinds of thoughtful exploration described above, evaluation—judgments about how well the work has been done—needs to be separated from response—reactions to the paper and ideas for further development that come from an interested reader. This is because evaluation, although well-intentioned, can become too much a focus of ongoing instruction, and therefore inhibiting to students; it teaches them not to take risks, not to try new forms, not to draft and redraft, but to concentrate on letter-perfect work that says little and goes nowhere.

Response is the critical feature in writing instruction; it helps students know what works, what doesn't, and how to go about improving what they have written. The ideal writing environment invites students to engage in exploratory writing and offers response to work-in-process. Evaluation and grades are postponed until later.

Providing Effective Response

Teachers can use a number of strategies to ensure that students receive sufficient and helpful response to their work. The most powerful is the use of peer readers and peer response groups (see pages T32–T33). The following suggestions should also be kept in mind:

1) Limit the amount of writing to which you, the teacher, respond. Writers need frequent responses from interested readers, but that does not mean that the teacher needs to read everything that is written. Instead students may be asked to share with each other initial brainstorming about a topic, to reflect upon one another's notes and journals, and to respond to early drafts.

These early drafts and explorations have served their purpose once they have been discussed with an interested reader or mined for the nuggets that will become part of later drafts. Therefore, there is no reason for the teacher to read them, too: indeed, the teacher can become a bottleneck and may inadvertently turn students back toward thoughts already abandoned.

2) Respond to work in progress as a collaborator rather than an evaluator. Teachers can, of course, be very helpful while students are working on their drafts. They can show new ways to solve writing problems, suggest other issues to consider, and offer their own responses as readers about what parts are clear, what parts are interesting, and what parts fail to convince. These kinds of responses are instructional in the best sense: the teacher's suggestions about work in progress can become part of the developing writer's repertoire of strategies and models, available for use in other contexts.

Authors:

Arthur N. Applebee, Professor of Education, State University of New York at Albany

Judith A. Langer, Professor of Education, State University of New York at Albany

Exploring Assessment

Reader response is certainly the most productive way to respond to student writing, but evaluation is, of course, necessary. Report cards demand grades, and students want to know how they are doing. But there are a number of ways in which evaluation can be managed so it supports rather than subverts the processes of teaching and learning.

Choose criteria carefully. Since writing should be considered a process for exploring ideas and sharing them with others, it follows that conventions of writing should be treated as part of this process rather than as the focus of instruction. It is easy, however, for both writers and teacher to get bogged down in usage and mechanics.

Therefore, to prevent both writers and evaluators from losing track of the key issues of writing, it is important to have clear, consistent standards about what "writing well" will mean in your class. If "writing well" is to mean exploring ideas and experimenting with ways to share them effectively, then students who try to do this should be rewarded with higher grades—even if their experiments lead them to make mistakes. A new and difficult task, completed with some uncertainty, may reflect much more growth in writing achievement than a simple task completed with little thought and no "error."

Use a variety of evaluation methods. In recent years, teachers have developed a number of different ways to formalize their evaluations of student writing. Most of these have been used in the context of large-group assessment, where the concern is with how well students are doing *relative to* one another or to some external criterion. Using such procedures (for example, general impression [or holistic] scoring, analytic scoring, or primary trait scoring) is generally inappropriate within a classroom when used in a formal sense, but can be extremely helpful when used informally to guide teachers' and students' mutual understandings of the goals of the writing task. These methods, however, should be used sparingly and combined with more flexible techniques such as peer response and portfolio assessment.

For those occasions when holistic or analytic evaluations are desired, the Writer's Workshops in *The Writer's Craft* include specific criteria for evaluation of various types of writing, as does the booklet *Guidelines for Writing Assessment and Portfolio Use* in the Teacher's Resource File. Underlying these criteria are a few broad questions that can be used in assessing how well the writing succeeds:

- Is the writer's purpose clear? Has it caught my interest?
- Is there enough detail for me to accept or reject what the writer has said?
- Does the writing carry me through clearly from beginning to end, or are there places where I get lost or miss the point?
- Do the drafts indicate the student is learning to use the responses of readers effectively, or are successive drafts little more than neater versions of the same text?
- Has the writer taken care in the final draft to avoid distracting, careless errors in presentation?

Using Portfolios

Writers vary in how well they write from topic to topic and day to day. Again, this is normal and natural, but we often forget about it when judging how well a writer writes. To offer a well-grounded evaluation of a student's writing skills, we need to examine a broad sample of that student's work.

Portfolios of student work offer one of the best vehicles for classroom-based assessment for two reasons: 1) They typically contain a variety of different samples of student work, and 2) they make it easy to separate evaluation from the process of instruction. Evaluation can be based on the diverse samples of work in the portfolio rather than on the day-to-day progress of an individual piece of classroom work.

Portfolios take almost as many forms as there are teachers and can be tailored to virtually any classroom situation. The major options involve the form that portfolios take, what is included in them, and how they are evaluated.

continued

Portfolio Options

Form. Portfolios are a cumulative collection of the work students have done. The most popular forms include

- a traditional "writing folder" in which students keep their work
- a bound notebook with separate sections kept for work in progress and final drafts
- a looseleaf notebook in which students keep their drafts and revisions
- a published collection of carefully selected and hand-bound work

Content. Portfolios provide an ideal way to illustrate how a student's work has developed over time, and will give students, parents, administrators, and other teachers a much stronger sense of what students can do. Portfolios may contain

- everything a student writes for a particular class
- a selection of "best work" representing the diverse kinds of writing that a student has done
- selections chosen to represent each of the types of writing a student has done during a grading period
- a diverse collection of a student's performance including drawings and illustrations, tape recordings or videotapes of group work, and readings or dramatic presentations of the student's writing
- drafts and revisions
- a selection of finished work, chosen by the student, the teacher, or the student and teacher working together

Students can also be encouraged to reflect further upon their own progress as writers, providing an introductory essay summarizing their work as they see it in the portfolio. Like the reflective activities included at the end of each workshop in this textbook, such reflection can help students become aware of and take control over their own growth as writers.

Evaluating Content. Just as teachers vary in the form and content of the portfolios they ask their students to build, they also vary in how they use portfolios to determine students' grades.

An approach that many teachers have found to be particularly effective is to base grade a selection of work from the portfolio— chosen to reflect the range of types of writing that students have done during the grading period. Students can be asked to select the pieces to be graded, making the choice themselves or in conjunction with the teacher. With this approach, they should be given guidelines for what to choose: a narrative, an expository piece, and a persuasive essay, perhaps, plus an additional piece of their own choosing. The particular guidelines should reflect the goals and assignments in the writing program during the grading period.

The ability to choose works to be graded —rather than being graded on everything—can be a powerful motivational device as well. Many teachers give their students the opportunity to work further on the selections they want to have graded. Returning to these writings at a later point, students often recognize for themselves ways to make their writing more effective, and may reshape them substantially before offering them for evaluation.

The students' own impressions of their work should not be left out of the evaluation process. Young writers should be encouraged to comment on each piece added to their portfolios and to comment on their progress over time. Forms and guidelines in *Guidelines for Writing Assessment and Portfolio Use* in the Teacher's Resource File can help both students and teachers complete effective evaluations of finished pieces.

Weaning students from excessive evaluation. Many teachers who are new to such a workshop approach—postponing evaluation rather than interjecting it into the writing process—worry that students want quicker grades. If they aren't graded, will they do the work? One transitional device that works well in many classrooms is to give points when students have completed each separate part of the work. Everyone who completes a first draft, for example, might get a point, with another for doing a revision. These points can be totaled across the marking period to become part of the final grade.

If evaluation is separated from instruction, if criteria for evaluation are kept consistent with those stressed during instruction, and if response becomes a responsibility shared with students as well as the teacher, assessment can become an effective complement to the process of learning to write.

How do I meet the needs of different students?

Teaching Writing to Language-Minority Students

Author:

Marguerite Calderone, Associate Professor of Education in Psychology, University of Texas, El Paso

Increases in the immigrant population during the past two decades have dramatically transformed the cultural makeup of many American classrooms. Not since the great wave of immigrations around the turn of the last century have English teachers in American schools been so challenged to meet the special language needs of their students.

Few veteran English teachers are likely to feel professionally prepared to operate successfully in a multicultural, multilingual classroom. What follows here are some strategies for teaching writing to language-minority students—strategies that research has shown are especially effective with non-English speaking students but which are equally applicable to all students.

Developing Prior Knowledge

The more experience a writer has with the concepts and terms associated with a topic for writing, the easier it will be to write about that topic. Similarly, the more knowledge a teacher has of the culture and background of minority students, the easier it will be to adapt teaching strategies and writing assignments to meet their needs.

Hold class discussions. Clarify cultural references and provide general information to the entire class. Encourage language-minority students to comment on similarities to and differences from their own cultures.

Explore teaching alternatives. The use of visual aids and hands-on experiences are effective strategies for building prior knowledge and student confidence.

Encourage students to write about their native customs, holidays, geography, and foods. Such topics will be more comfortable for language-minority students. Additionally, the felt-pride from sharing their native culture will act as strong motivation for writing.

Provide opportunities for reading popular American magazines and newspapers. These activities will familiarize language-minority students with American people, places, and events. Television, movies, theater, and similar cultural activities will have the same impact.

Developing Vocabulary and Genre Knowledge

Mastering English vocabulary and patterns of discourse is essential to building writing proficiency among language-minority students. Students who are asked to write about a school or government election, for example, must be familiar with the terms and concepts of the subject, such as *parties, platform, campaign, run-off, running mate,* and so on. Ideally, preteaching vocabulary would become a regular part of each assignment.

Similarly, students who are asked to write a mock political campaign speech will feel entirely unable to do so unless they know what one looks and sounds like. All students should be given the opportunity to read a number of models of whatever type of writing they are being asked to produce.

Peer Interaction

Through group discussion, students with limited-English proficiency can build a repertoire of concepts, phrases, and rhetorical strategies by trial-and-error, questioning, and modeling. Whenever possible, divide the class into small discussion groups. Each group should include at least one language-minority student. Establish a protocol that requires all students to speak within the group. In this way language-minority students will be exposed to vocabulary and rhetorical strategies they can model and be encouraged to try out their developing English proficiency.

Writing in the Primary Language

There is strong research evidence showing that limited-English proficiency students in American schools can make significant progress toward literacy in English by reading and writing for some time in their primary language, making the transition to writing exclusively in English as they acquire English fluency. Allowing students to write in their primary language during the early stages of English acquisition offers the following advantages:

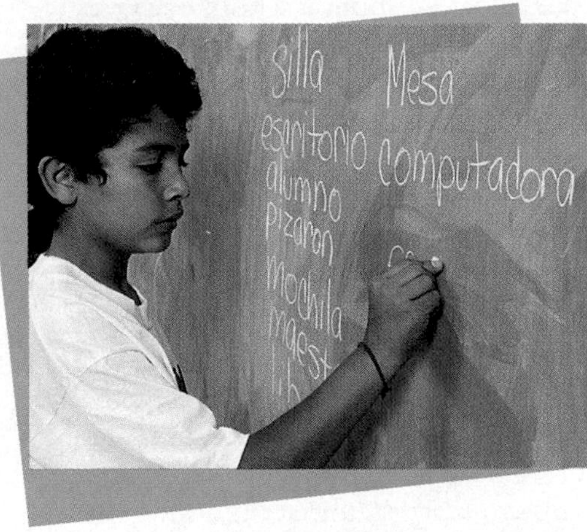

- It establishes a firm basis for acquiring universal reading and writing skills that are easily transferred from one language to another.
- It promotes success, enhances self-esteem, and builds students' confidence in their abilities as readers and writers.
- It enables students to function at the highest levels of their cognitive abilities, unhampered by their limited-English proficiency.

How can writing in languages other than English become a realistic instructional strategy in classes where teachers don't speak the primary language or languages of their non-English speaking students? Following are some strategies for implementing this instructional strategy:

- Encourage students to write in their primary language whenever they encounter a particularly demanding or complex writing assignment. This will enable them to clarify their thinking about the topic even if no one else can read what they've written.
- Have students write in their primary language only during the prewriting stage. Allowing them to focus their topic, generate ideas, and organize their material in a familiar language will lead to enhanced comprehension and increased motivation.
- Seek out individuals fluent in the student's primary language to act as responders. Such individuals might be teacher aides, parents, or classmates who speak the student's primary language but who are also fluent in English. Of course, if there are several students who share the same primary language, they can act as peer reviewers for one another.
- Invite students to translate their own primary language essays. Such translations should not be treated as final drafts, however, but as rough draft translations produced for the benefit of the teacher. Teachers who receive these translations can respond to the ideas contained in the translated essay rather than on problems in English language usage.

Additional Strategies

Following are some additional strategies for working with language-minority students:

- Preview the assignment to spot potential areas of difficulty—with cultural concepts, language requirements, research needs, and so on. Provide preteaching as necessary.
- Read aloud difficult parts of the assignment or lesson, allowing time for questions and clarification.
- Precede writing activities with similar oral activities to allow students to separate the task of clarifying ideas from that of translating them into written form.
- Provide guided practice, especially with prewriting and revising techniques.

Increased, individualized feedback and monitoring will enhance student comprehension and offer support—both of which lead to more successful writing experiences.

References

Calderone, M.; Tinajero, J.; & Hertz-Lazarowitz, R. (1990). "Effective Transition into English Reading Through CIRC." Baltimore, MD: Center for Research on Effective Education for Disadvantaged Students, Johns Hopkins University.

California State Department of Education (1981). *Schooling and Language Minority Students: A Theoretical Framework.* California State University, Los Angeles, EDAC.

Cummins, J. (1986). *Empowering Minority Students.* Sacramento, CA: California Association for Bi-Lingual Education.

Damon, W. (1984). "Peer Education: The Untapped Potential." *Journal of Applied Development Psychology:* 5, 331–343.

Stevens, R. J.; Madden, N. A.; Slavin, R. E.; & Farnish, A. M. (1987). "Cooperative Integrated Reading and Composition (CIRC)." Baltimore, MD: Center for Research on Elementary and Middle Schools, John Hopkins University.

How do I meet the needs of different students?

Addressing Different Learning Styles

People of all ages perceive and process information in different ways. A familiarity with learning styles can help educators develop teaching strategies to meet the needs of all students in the classroom.

The Types of Learners

Research on left- and right-brain functions has led to a variety of theories about preferred learning styles. The left brain is thought to be the center for analytical, logical, verbal, sequential, and convergent thinking, while the right brain is thought to be the center for emotion and visual, spatial, creative, experiential, and divergent cognitive styles. Left-brain students, who have traditionally been rewarded by the educational system, tend to excel in such school subjects as reading, mathematics, and computer programming. Right-brain dominant students tend to excel in art, dance, music, and geometry.

In addition to left/right-brain classification, students are often categorized according to three learning styles: visual, auditory, and kinesthetic.

Visual learners best comprehend and retain information presented in the form of graphs, charts, diagrams, and other visual images, such as fine art and photographs. Often, they benefit from a multimedia approach to learning.

Auditory learners, like visual learners, often benefit from a multimedia approach to learning. They need not only to read it and see it, but to hear it and discuss it.

Kinesthetic learners process information through tactile sensations, learning from activities that enable them to work with their hands or create meaning through movement and physical expression.

Harvard psychologist Howard Gardner has taken the analysis of learning styles and left- and right-brain dominance to yet another level in his theory of multiple intelligences.

The Seven Types of Intelligence

Linguistic	Verbal excellence, reading and writing skills
Logical-Mathematical	Conceptual, logical, abstract thinking
Spatial	Interest in visual images and pictures; designing, building, and inventing
Musical	Sensitivity to rhythm, singing, moving to and playing music
Bodily-Kinesthetic	Communicating with body language; processing information through bodily sensations
Interpersonal	Organizing, communicating, socializing, understanding others
Intrapersonal	Preferring to work alone and being independent, private, and self-motivated

Everyone has multiple intelligences and different styles of learning. However teachers, who tend to be left-brain oriented and strong in linguistic and logical-mathematical intelligences, often teach primarily in the modes most comfortable for them. They may therefore be unconsciously leaving a number of students out of the learning process. Yet how can any teacher adequately address the bewildering array of learning styles that may be present in any one classroom?

With its integrated approach to the development of writing, *The Writer's Craft* helps solve this problem by providing students with opportunities to work in a variety of learning modes. Teachers need only encourage students to take advantage of various learning strategies to maximize their intellectual and creative potential.

Applications in *The Writer's Craft*

Teacher's notes throughout the text point out the following learning opportunities:

Fine Art and Illustrations The art program throughout *The Writer's Craft* provides visual or spatial learners with an engaging and entertaining way into the material. Invite students to consider how the art enhances and reflects concepts in the text, and use the illustrations as springboards to creative writing.

Workshops and Related Assignments At each grade level, Workshops and Related Assignments include a broad range of activities, not all of which are writing based. Visual and spatial learners, for example, will particularly enjoy creating collages, graphic aids, and picture books. Auditory and musical learners will especially like creating videos, writing lyrics, and making oral presentations.

Exploratory Activities Workshops begin with a wide range of Exploratory Activities, providing students with options for entering writing assignments comfortably and naturally. The teacher can encourage students to experiment with the options until they find those that work best.

Graphic Organizers Graphic devices such as clusters, idea trees, flow charts, and pie graphs can be a tremendous boon to visual and kinesthetic students who learn from the physical act of writing ideas, organizing them spatially, and seeing and making the connections among them. Left-brain dominant students can organize their information with time lines, charts, and analysis frames.

Publishing Options The wide variety of publishing options offered throughout the Workshops allows students to tailor their work to their own learning styles. In different assignments, for example, students may be encouraged to include photographs or drawings, build models, incorporate music, or use videotapes, recordings, slides, or photos in a multimedia presentation.

Collaborative and Independent Learning Auditory and interpersonal learners may enjoy working collaboratively to brainstorm solutions to problems, discuss ideas, and share their writing. (See pages T34–T35.) Peer response sessions are also ideal for these kinds of learners. However, each lesson is so complete that the intrapersonal, or solitary, learner can succeed with little help from others.

Special Help with Learning Disabilities

Learning disabled students typically have average or above-average potential; however, specific areas of deficiency (which vary from student to student) make the processing of information and the acquisition of skills more difficult.

Students with learning disabilities often display some or all of the following characteristics:

- Low reading level
- Low motivation
- Difficulty organizing work or ideas
- Poor memory
- Difficulty sequencing and processing information
- Difficulty following directions and completing assignments
- Difficulty thinking, reasoning, and generalizing
- Hyperactivity and distractibility
- Poor fine-motor coordination and handwriting

It is essential to remember that learning disabilities are often physiologically based and beyond the student's control. What can appear to be inattentiveness or an uncooperative attitude may, in fact, reflect an inability to learn through conventional channels.

Whenever possible, teachers should provide opportunities for LD students to process information in their own preferred learning style. This approach will allow them to maximize their intellectual and creative potential in school. The following general strategies, along with any of the alternative strategies described in the section on learning styles, will help students get the most from classroom experiences:

- Seat students toward the front of the classroom where there are no obstructions to seeing or hearing.
- Present essential directions or material from the text both orally and in writing.
- Supply visual aids whenever possible to reinforce material from the text.
- To help students compensate for poor short- and long-term memory, repeat important ideas frequently and begin each lesson with a summary of material covered the previous day.
- When giving an assignment, model sample problems on the board, breaking the process down into clearly ordered steps.
- Encourage collaborative learning. Carefully monitor sessions to make sure they take place in an atmosphere of care, empathy, and support.
- Occasionally pair students according to ability for special peer-review sessions. For example, pair an LD student who has difficulties with sequencing and ordering events with a student who is particularly strong in those areas.

I've got a computer . . . Now what?

Teaching English in the Electronic Age

Author:

Dawn Rodrigues, Associate Professor of English, Colorado State University

New technology brings exciting changes to the curriculum. In the English classroom, the most visible of these changes has been the arrival of the computer, with all of its attendant software. The sheer volume of available material has proven to be occasionally intimidating, but teachers *can* take control of the technology by selectively integrating computer programs and strategies into their teaching.

Benefits of the Computer

Although research on the use of the computer in English classrooms is still somewhat limited, many studies have revealed some significant benefits of using a word processor:

- Students enjoy composing on a computer, tending to write more and work harder at their writing.
- Students do not resist revision, since changes can be more easily executed.
- Collaboration among students increases.

Computers have also proven to be especially helpful with low-ability students or those with handicaps and learning disabilities. First, the actual *physical* act of writing becomes easier, and the process as a whole becomes less intimidating—when words on a screen can be instantly deleted, writing anxiety diminishes.

Second, the process of using the computer forces special-needs students to focus more directly on their task. Finally, the clean, printed text eliminates some students' embarrassment over poor handwriting—for the first time in their lives, they can be proud of their writing.

New Strategies for Writing Instruction

With the increasing availability of computers, teachers can recommend that students use composing and collaborative strategies that were not possible before. Many of these strategies, such as invisible writing, listmaking, and the development of a writer's file, can be found in *The Writer's Craft* in the feature labeled Computer Tip. Some other strategies follow:

- Students can leave gaps in their paper where they need to add material or where they want to invite response from others. Notes such as the following, to themselves or their peer readers, can provide the cues:

CAN YOU HELP ME THINK OF A BETTER EXAMPLE HERE? or MAYBE THIS WOULD WORK AS THE INTRO—TRY LATER.

- Students can work on portions of the draft that they are most comfortable with, and then electronically paste the pieces together as their ideas take shape.
- Teachers and peer readers can read drafts on screen and leave notes to the writer at the appropriate points.

Making It Work

Making students comfortable with computers does not require that the entire class meet regularly in a lab. At many schools, a teacher can reserve a computer lab on occasion for the entire class. On those days, the teacher can introduce valuable computer-writing techniques, such as the use of an "alternate screen" to store outlines or notes while composing in the other window.

Spell-checkers, on-line thesauruses, and specialized software programs such as McDougal, Littell's *Electronic English Handbook* or *Writer's DataBank* can also be introduced. If a lab is not available, the teacher can occasionally bring a computer into the classroom to demonstrate various techniques.

No matter how the computer is used, however, it is important to remember that not all students adapt to word processing in the same way. Therefore, the teacher must be prepared to provide plenty of individual instruction. For example, freed from the restrictions of pen and paper, some students may overwrite. These individuals must be shown how to evaluate content and delete unnecessary material. Other students may have trouble adapting pen-and-paper planning or revision to the screen. These writers could be encouraged to use printouts in combination with composing on screen until they become more comfortable with the computer.

Conclusion

Computers, when used creatively, can be a powerful addition to a writing class. The computer has the amazing ability to transform itself into whatever the teacher or writer wants it to be—a magic slate for writing, an electronic window to an audience, or an endless resource for ideas and strategies. It allows teachers to create an almost unlimited set of instructional techniques and a chance to re-envision writing instruction.

Assignment Chart

Concept Development in *The Writer's Craft*

Varied, real-life writing assignments grow more sophisticated as your students do and provide opportunities for writing across the curriculum. **Guided Assignments** are listed in bold, followed by Related Assignments in each strand below.

Writing Strands	Grade 6	Grade 7	Grade 8
Personal and Expressive Writing	• **Writing from Your Journal** • Friendly Letter	• **Writing from Personal Experience** • Collage	• **Autobiographical Incident** • Song
Observation and Description	• **Describing People and Places** • Cultures and Customs	• **Character Sketch** • Oral History	• **Eyewitness Report** • Field Notes
Narrative and Literary Writing	• **Personal Narrative** • Writing a Poem	• **Short Story** • Children's Book	• **Writing a Poem** • Developing a Script
Informative Writing: Explaining *How*	• **Directions** • Explaining with Graphics	• **Problems and Solutions** • Group Discussion	• **Cause-and-Effect Explanation** • Describing a Process
Informative Writing: Explaining *What*		• **Informing and Defining** • Comparison and Contrast	• **Comparison and Contrast** • Consumer Report
Persuasion	• **Sharing an Opinion** • Public Opinion Survey • Writing for Assessment	• **Supporting Opinions** • Advertisement • Writing for Assessment	• **Argument** • Social Action Letter • Writing for Assessment
Responding to Literature	• **Personal Response** • Book Review	• **Interpreting Poetry** • Focusing on Media	• **Analyzing a Story** • Oral Storytelling
Informative Writing: Reports	• **Report of Information** • Family History	• **Multimedia Report** • Feature Article	• **Research Report** • I-Search

The Writer's Craft

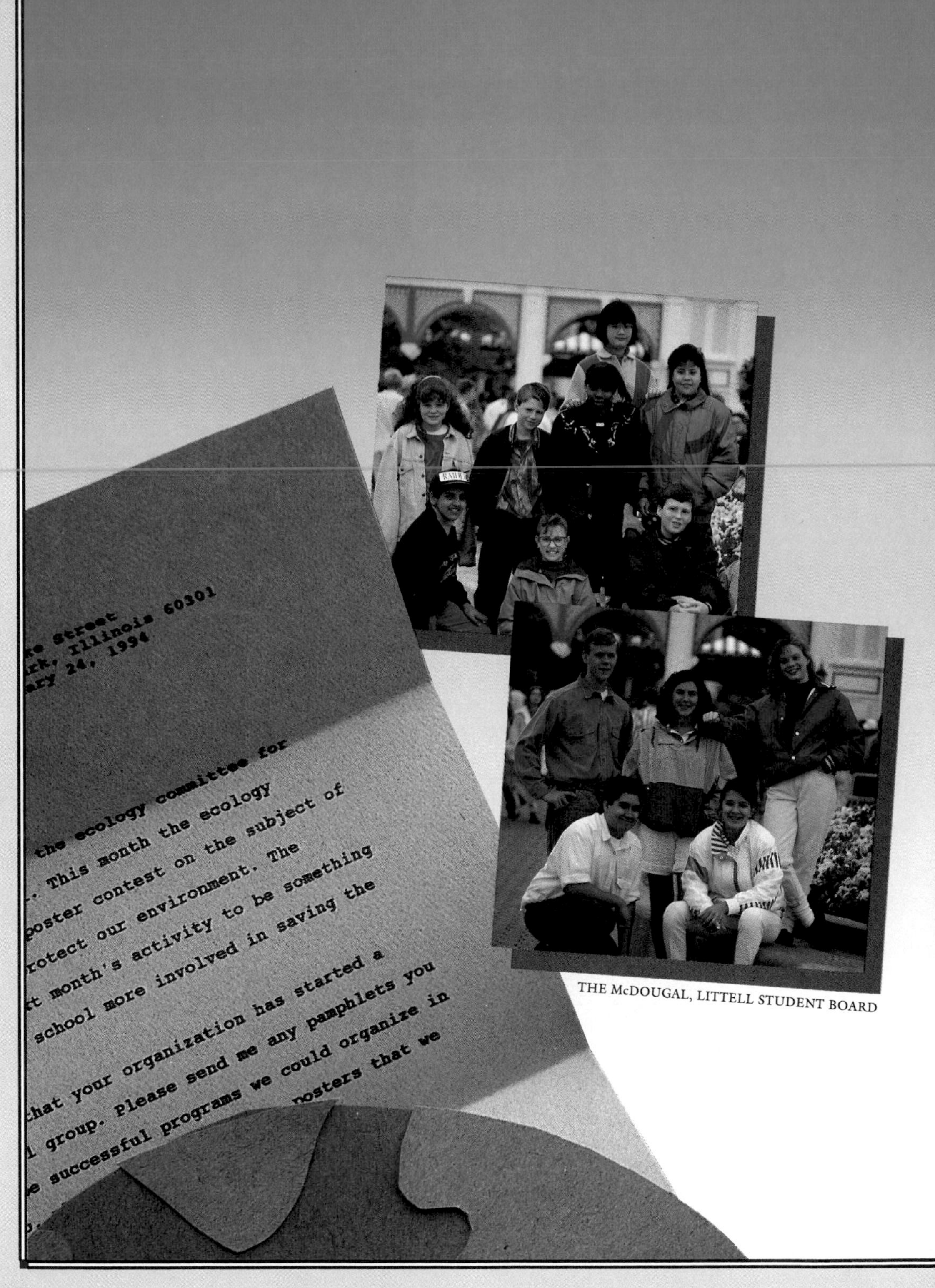
ke Street
rk, Illinois 60301
ary 24, 1994
the ecology committee for
. This month the ecology
poster contest on the subject of
rotect our environment. The
t month's activity to be something
school more involved in saving the
hat your organization has started a
l group. Please send me any pamphlets you
e successful programs we could organize in
posters that we

THE McDOUGAL, LITTELL STUDENT BOARD

The Writer's Craft

SENIOR AUTHOR
SHERIDAN BLAU
University of California at Santa Barbara

CONSULTING AUTHOR
PETER ELBOW
University of Massachusetts at Amherst

SPECIAL CONTRIBUTING AUTHORS
Don Killgallon
Baltimore County Public Schools

Rebekah Caplan
Oakland Unified School District

SENIOR CONSULTANTS
Arthur Applebee
State University of New York at Albany

Judith Langer
State University of New York at Albany

McDougal, Littell & Company
Evanston, Illinois

New York • Dallas • Columbia, SC

SENIOR AUTHOR

Sheridan Blau, Senior Lecturer in English and Education and former Director of Composition, University of California at Santa Barbara; Director, South Coast Writing Project; Director, Literature Institute for Teachers

The Senior Author, in collaboration with the Consulting Author, helped establish the theoretical framework of the program and the pedagogical design of the Workshop prototype. In addition, he guided the development of the spiral of writing assignments, served as author of the literary Workshops, and reviewed completed Writer's Workshops to ensure consistency with current research and the philosophy of the series.

CONSULTING AUTHOR

Peter Elbow, Professor of English, University of Massachusetts at Amherst; Fellow, Bard Center for Writing and Thinking

The Consulting Author, in collaboration with the Senior Author, helped establish the theoretical framework for the series and the pedagogical design of the Writer's Workshops. He also reviewed Writer's Workshops and designated Writing Handbook lessons for consistency with current research and the philosophy of the series.

SPECIAL CONTRIBUTING AUTHORS

Don Killgallon, English Chairman, Educational Consultant, Baltimore County Public Schools. Mr. Killgallon conceptualized, designed, and wrote all of the features on sentence composing.

Rebekah Caplan, Coordinator, English Language Arts K-12, Oakland Unified School District, Oakland, CA; Teacher-Consultant, Bay Area Writing Project, University of California at Berkeley. Ms. Caplan developed the strategy of "Show, Don't Tell," first introduced in the book *Writers in Training,* published by Dale Seymour Publications. She also wrote the Handbook lessons and Sketchbook features for this series that deal with that concept.

SENIOR CONSULTANTS

These consultants reviewed the completed prototype to ensure consistency with current research and continuity within the series.

Arthur N. Applebee, Professor of Education, State University of New York at Albany; Director, Center for the Learning and Teaching of Literature; Senior Fellow, Center for Writing and Literacy

Judith A. Langer, Professor of Education, State University of New York at Albany; Co-director, Center for the Learning and Teaching of Literature; Senior Fellow, Center for Writing and Literacy

MULTICULTURAL ADVISORS

The multicultural advisors reviewed the literary selections for appropriate content and made suggestions for teaching lessons in a multicultural classroom.

Andrea B. Bermúdez, Professor of Multicultural Education; Director, Research Center for Language and Culture, University of Houston—Clear Lake

Alice A. Kawazoe, Director of Curriculum and Staff Development, Oakland Unified School District, Oakland, CA

Sandra Mehojah, Project Coordinator, Office of Indian Education, Omaha Public Schools, Omaha, NE

Alexs D. Pate, Writer, Consultant, Lecturer, Macalester College and the University of Minnesota

STUDENT CONTRIBUTORS

The following students contributed their writing.

Amity Baca, Denver, CO; Mousumi Behari, Aurora, CO; Mark Blatchford, Grand Rapids, MI; Regina Bly, Atco, NJ; Chakkarin Burudpakdee, Clementon, NJ; Stacy Smith, Kenosha, WI; Rene Froehmer, Clovis, CA; Matthew D. Jackson, Clarksville, TN; Ashley Kuhlman, Lansing, MI; Jamie Lentz, Hamilton, OH; Annie Maxwell, Santa Barbara, CA; Jim McConnell, York, PA; Utica Miller, Evanston, IL; David Norr, Evanston, IL; Nina Ramundo, Hamilton, OH; Trang Phan, York, PA; Luziris Pineda, Houston, TX; Tiffany Shue, York, PA; Jennica Thuet, Las Vegas, NV; Brook Volle, Las Vegas, NV; Jennifer Wilson, Mount Clemens, MI

The following students reviewed selections to assess their appeal.

Meghan Dwyer, Chicago, IL; Jason Greer, Evanston, IL; DeDe Heuerman, Effingham, IL; Adam Hooks, Mason, IL; Lucy Luevano, Chicago, IL; David Moo, Gurnee, IL; Katie Schnepf, Barrington, IL

TEACHER CONSULTANTS

The following teachers served as advisors on the development of the Workshop prototype and/or reviewed completed Workshops.

Wanda Bamberg, Aldine Independent School District, Houston, TX

Karen Bollinger, Tower Heights Middle School, Centerville, OH

Barbara Ann Boulden, Issaquah Middle School, Issaquah, WA

Loutish Burns, M. Lamar High School, Houston, TX

Christine Bustle, Elmbrook Middle School, Elm Grove, WI

Denise M. Campbell, Eaglecrest School, Cherry Creek School District, Aurora, CO

Cheryl Cherry, Haven Middle School, Evanston, IL

Gracie Garza, L.B.J. Junior High School, Pharr, TX

Patricia Fitzsimmons Hunter, John F. Kennedy Middle School, Springfield, MA

Mary F. La Lane, Driftwood Middle School, Hollywood, FL

Barbara Lang, South Junior High School, Arlington Heights, IL

Harry Laub, Newark Board of Education, Newark, NJ

Sister Loretta Josepha, S.C., Sts. Peter and Paul School, Bronx, NY

Jacqueline McWilliams, Carnegie School, Chicago, IL

Joanna Martin, Thompson Junior High School, St. Charles, IL

Karen Perry, Kennedy Junior High School, Lisle, IL

Patricia A. Richardson, Resident Teacher-Trainer, Harold A. Wilson Professional Development School, Newark, NJ

Pauline Sahakian, Clovis Unified School District, Clovis, CA

Elaine Sherman, Curriculum Director, Clark County, Las Vegas, NV

Richard Wagner, Language Arts Curriculum Coordinator, Paradise Valley School District, Phoenix, AZ

Beth Yeager, McKinley Elementary School, Santa Barbara, CA

ISBN 0-8123-7868-7

Box 1667, Evanston, Illinois 60204

2 3 4 5 6 7 8 9 10 – VJM – 98 97 96 95 94 93

Table of Contents

OVERVIEW

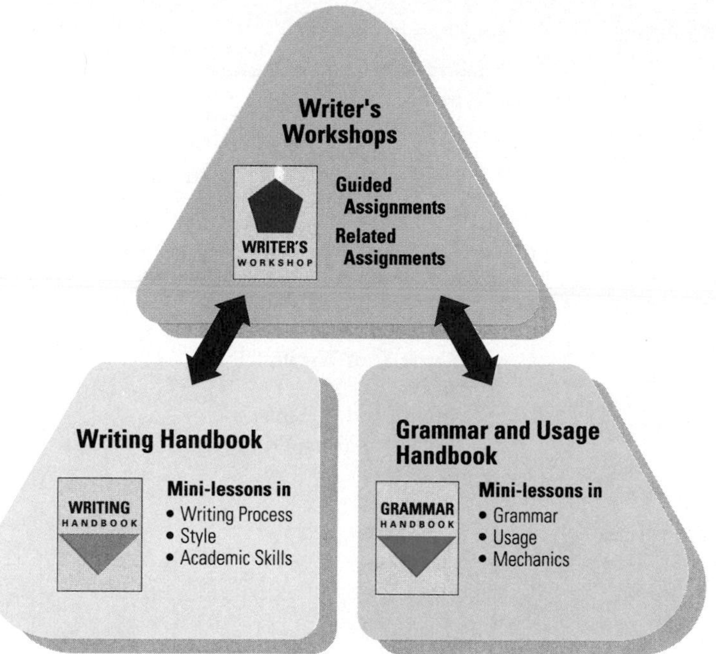

You are special. You think and act in ways that are uniquely your own. This book recognizes the fact that you are an individual. On every page you will be encouraged to discover techniques best suited to your own personal writing style. Just as important, you will learn to think your way through every writing task.

In each of the Writer's Workshops, you will experiment with ideas and approaches as you are guided through a complete piece of writing. Cross-references to the Handbooks will allow you to find additional help when you need it. Then, as you write, you will discover what you think about yourself—and about the world around you.

Getting Ready presents the philosophy of *The Writer's Craft* and introduces the concept of a community of writers to students.

Getting Started explains that the writing process is flexible and recursive, not static and linear.

Using This Book relates the sections of this text to the writing process.

The **Discovery Workshop** guides students in using the writing process.

Starting Points

For more in-depth treatment of each stage of the writing process, see the Writing Handbook Mini-lessons on pages 215–375.

Writer's Workshops

WRITER'S WORKSHOP 1

Personal and Expressive Writing

In each **Writer's Workshop,** students learn to write by writing, not by reading about writing.

In each Writer's Workshop, students have the opportunity to explore a particular type of writing in two different assignments.

The **Guided Assignments** in each workshop provide information about types of writing and offer detailed guidance in completing the stages of the writing process.

The **Related Assignments** give students an opportunity to apply skills learned in the Guided Assignments. The streamlined format challenges students to make independent writing decisions.

Assignments such as "Song" build oral language skills and allow students with different learning styles to shine.

Each workshop begins with a **Sketchbook,** which allows students to try out writing ideas in a no-risk atmosphere.

Each Guided Assignment follows the progress of one student through the stages of the writing process.

Strategies for writing are presented throughout the stages of the writing process.

Assignments such as "Field Notes" invite students to apply their writing skills to other areas of the curriculum.

The **Sentence Composing** activities help students to add variety and sophistication to their writing by having them analyze and imitate the sentence structure of professional writers.

WRITER'S WORKSHOP 2

Observation and Description

viii

WRITER'S WORKSHOP 3

Narrative and Literary Writing

Each Guided Assignment begins with literature or other professional writing; this model is followed by a student piece, to encourage all student writers.

Each Guided Assignment suggests a variety of exploratory activities to aid students in choosing a topic meaningful to them.

The Related Assignment, "Developing a Script," builds collaborative skills and promotes attitudes of cooperation and respect for the ideas of others.

Additional writing opportunities are found in the **Springboards** activities in every Writer's Workshop.

Assignments such as "Cause and Effect" build and reinforce critical thinking skills.

Students are exposed to multiple drafting and revising strategies, so that they can choose the ones most effective for a particular piece of writing.

Paragraphs at Work suggests appropriate paragraphing strategies for each type of writing.

Standards for Evaluation provides students with a checklist of criteria for each writing type, so that they can determine how well their pieces meet the criteria.

Reflect on Your Writing offers portfolio activities and other opportunities for students to grow as writers.

WRITER'S WORKSHOP 4

Informative Writing: Explaining *How*

x

WRITER'S WORKSHOP 5

Informative Writing: Explaining *What*

Assignments such as "Comparison and Contrast" equip students for success in courses across the curriculum.

Students find solutions to their writing questions through various drafting and revising strategies.

Questions for both the writer and peer readers are included to foster self-assessment and peer response.

Publish and Present suggests several ways for students to share what they have written with varied audiences.

Assignments such as "Consumer Report" emphasize the importance of the media and take writing beyond the classroom.

Assignments such as "Argument" enhance critical thinking skills as students examine both sides of a controversial issue and then take a stand.

Each Workshop assignment encourages students to shape the writing process to fit their topic and style.

Linking Grammar and Writing shows the connections between effective writing and the use of standard grammar and usage.

Assignments such as "Writing a Social Action Letter" demonstrate that writing is a real-world activity.

"Writing for Assessment" helps students gain success across the curriculum by having them both analyze assessment prompts and practice responses.

WRITER'S WORKSHOP 6

Persuasion

WRITER'S WORKSHOP 7

Responding to Literature

Students write a response to a short story in which they analyze a literary element.

Linking Mechanics and Writing shows the connections between effective writing and the use of standard capitalization and punctuation.

"Oral Storytelling" emphasizes the importance of effective oral communication skills.

On the Lightside offers unusual facts and offbeat and humorous reflections about our language.

WRITER'S WORKSHOP 8

Informative Writing: Reports

The "Research Report" gives students the opportunity to gather, organize, synthesize, and document material for a formal report.

The model, a well-developed and annotated report, shows how one student responded to the assignment.

Practical tips guide students in the efficient use of library resources.

Examples of standard MLA style are included.

The "I-Search," a nontraditional report format, is also explored.

Writing Handbook

MINI-LESSONS

Sketchbook

WRITING PROCESS

The **Writing Handbook** provides extra support for students. Because the handbook is cross-referenced in the Writer's Workshops, teachers can present mini-lessons to the class or to individual students at appropriate times.

Handbooks 1–21 contain detailed information on the writing process and may be used for preteaching or to help students solve problems during the composing process.

The mini-lessons include activities for both practice and reinforcement.

Students discover graphic devices as tools to find topics, sort ideas, and organize information.

Models from literature and professional and student writers illustrate various writing concepts.

Handbooks 9 and 10 cover paragraph skills in depth, and Handbook 11 extends these skills to cover longer pieces of writing.

Handbook 12 includes many strategies for elaboration.

Showing, not telling, is emphasized in Handbook 13, with specific strategies provided for developing writing.

Handbook 18 contains practical approaches to peer response.

Handbooks 22–29 enable each student to develop his or her own writing style.

The variety and rhythm of sentences are demonstrated in Handbooks 23 and 24.

Handbook 27, "Using Poetic Devices," is a strong companion to Writer's Workshop 3, "Poetry."

Handbooks 30–38 cover academic skills essential to classroom success.

Critical thinking skills are the cornerstone of effective writing and are particularly useful with Writer's Workshop 6, "Argument."

Handbook 35 familiarizes students with library organization and important reference works.

Critical listening and observing skills are introduced in Handbook 37 and are used throughout the workshops.

Grammar and Usage Handbook

MINI-LESSONS

The **Grammar and Usage Handbook** presents a series of grammar mini-lessons within the context of writing.

The **Skills Assessment** pages, which include a pretest, a post-test, and four proficiency tests, provide instruments to measure student learning.

Each handbook provides various types of exercises: Concept Checks; Drafting, Revision, and Proofreading activities; Applications in Literature; and Applications in Writing.

Students integrate grammar and writing skills as they elaborate upon, revise, and proofread a draft in **Writing Connections.** Each Writing Connection is related to skills introduced in one of the workshops.

Handbook exercises focus on different themes; these themes can become springboards to a writing assignment.

Checkpoints provide a review of concepts and are found after every few mini-lessons.

Additional Practice and **Review** can be used for a variety of purposes: as a refresher, for a review, for more practice, or to check student mastery.

A standardized test format, often seen on state assessment examinations, is used for the "Skills Assessments."

Resources most commonly used by writers are found in the **Appendix.**

The **Glossary for Writers** contains definitions of important writing terms.

ART NOTE The Makah live on Cape Flattery at the northwestern tip of the Olympic Peninsula in Washington state. Here, the Pacific Ocean meets the Strait of Juan de Fuca, marking the American-Canadian border.

All Makah families have welcome drums, which they use to welcome visiting clans. The Makah are proud of their hospitality and boast that a visitor will never go hungry.

These four drums were painted by two modern artists, and their decorations have special meaning. To the Makah people, the bear is the animal most closely related to humans because bears can stand on two legs. Bears are often represented in Makah family crests and stories.

The raven, or *Klookshood* ("wide at the waist"), is a trickster hero in Native American myths and legends. To the Makah people, the raven also represents gluttony. The raven overeats, trying to stuff itself to bursting. (Ask whether students can find the salmon eggs and stylized feathers on this drum.)

The other two drums depict a welcoming host and a whale, a symbol for the Makah not only of bravery but also of strength and vitality.

You might ask students to think about a circular design for their own welcome drum. What animal or symbol has special meaning for them? Encourage students to draw or paint their designs.

(Clockwise from top left) "Mother Bear and Cub," Greg Colfax; "Welcome Drum," Spencer McCarty; "Raven Eating Salmon Eggs" and "Whale," Greg Colfax. The Makah are a Native American people of northwestern Washington. Colorful storytelling drums play an important part in their culture. Makah stories often tell about the figures represented such as the whale, a symbol of bravery, or the raven, a symbol of trickery.

Starting Points

Suppose you were asked to list your favorite activities. What would you include? Would listening to music, playing a sport, or watching TV make your list? Would you include talking on the phone, going to the movies, or taking care of a pet? Would *writing* appear on your list of favorite things to do? If not, you're not alone.

Many people don't write unless they have to. They would rather speak with another person face-to-face or talk on the telephone. For some people—and perhaps for you too—writing is difficult and boring, something to avoid as much as possible.

Writing doesn't have to be that way, however. Writing can be exciting, satisfying, even fun! This book can help you find the fun in writing. Perhaps one day soon, writing *will* appear on your list of favorite pastimes.

Starting Points

The purpose of this chapter is to aid teachers in creating a classroom atmosphere in which students will want to write and will have an increased chance at success in writing. The Starting Points chapter includes the four sections described below.

- **Getting Ready** provides motivation to students and emphasizes writing as discovery and as a source of personal satisfaction. It also introduces students to freewriting, writing for oneself, and writing with others.
- **Getting Started** gives students an overview of the stages of the writing process. This section provides explanations and examples of the kinds of activities that characterize each stage, while stressing that the process is not linear but recursive.
- **Using This Book** offers students an overview of the textbook. It describes the content of the Writer's Workshops and the handbooks and also explains the use of writing folders and portfolios.
- The **Discovery Workshop** invites students to experience the joy of discovery in writing, as they complete an open-ended assignment. Students learn that the content of writing can shape its form as they experiment with the stages of the writing process.

Getting Ready

After students have read this motivational section, remind them that they probably do their best writing when they are writing about something that interests them. Many students probably have used journals in the past, and this is a good time to suggest that they keep one during this school year. Explain that a journal is a place in which they can explore their feelings, their ideas, their hopes, their frustrations, or anything else that they see or hear that interests them. Sometimes what they have written in their journals can give them writing ideas.

Getting Ready

WHY WRITE?

Try to remember what you were like two or three years ago. What did you like to do after school? What were you interested in? Who were your friends?

Now think about who you are today. How is your life different than it was back then? What has changed? Has anything stayed the same? Is making and keeping friends as easy as it was? Maybe you have more independence. How does that feel?

You're not the only one growing and changing—so are your family, your school, your neighborhood, and the rest of the world. Do you find that you're more concerned about what's going on in the world than you were a few years ago? Does what you see interest you, or excite you, or worry you? What can you do to make sense of it all?

You may be surprised to learn that the writing you do for yourself and the writing you plan to share with others are terrific ways to make sense of your past and your present—to sort through your feelings and your ideas. The process of writing can help you discover more about who you are, what you think, and why you think the way you do.

MAKING WRITING MEANINGFUL

WRITER TO WRITER

I often use writing to contact my emotions.

Mousumi Behari, student, Aurora, Colorado

Take a few minutes to think about what writing means to you. Perhaps your teachers have told you what a powerful tool writing can be. Have you ever experienced that power? Has your writing ever made someone laugh or cry? Has it ever persuaded someone to do something or to feel the same way you do?

Perhaps you've read about how rewarding it can be to write for yourself. Have you ever used writing to help you "contact your emotions," understand how you feel, or figure something out? If your answer was *yes* to any of these questions, then this book will help you go on using writing as a tool for discovery. If writing has been dry and boring for you up until now, however, then get ready—you'll soon discover how to make your own writing important to you.

Make It Your Own

Writing is more rewarding when you focus on topics and issues you think really matter. When you explore what is important to you, you may find that your ideas—and your words—will flow faster than you can write or type them.

Even when you're writing for school, you can find a way to care about each topic you explore. You might even be able to turn a topic you don't particularly care about into one you do. As you'll see in the Discovery Workshop that follows, every topic can be looked at and written about from many different angles. Your writing will always be unique because no one else sees things in quite the same way you do.

Freewrite

What's the best way to discover what's on your mind or what you care most about? Freewriting is a simple but very useful writing technique that allows you to explore your thinking. When you freewrite, you just start writing and keep on writing, even when you're not sure you have anything to say. Start anywhere and let one idea flow into the next. Don't stop to worry about how you sound or whether you've remembered all your commas. Like a doodle that turns into an amazing design, your freewriting can start small and turn into something special and unique as you write.

FREEWRITING

Sometimes students are reluctant to try freewriting. Assure them that their freewriting is for their eyes only. To help get them started, assign the following exercise:

Invite students to write for three minutes about whatever comes into their minds. Tell them not to erase or stop to make corrections. If they can't think of anything more to say, they can repeat the last word until they think of another idea.

After three minutes, tell students to read what they have written and to underline the parts that they particularly like. Suggest that they save their freewriting because they might want to use some of the ideas in future writing assignments.

Focused freewriting is a kind of freewriting that can help you discover what you think about something. Instead of writing about anything that comes to mind, however, you begin with a specific subject and go from there. If your subject is allergies, for example, you might freewrite what you know about them, then write about what you don't know. What do you want to know? What do you need to find out? Freewrite the answers, and you're on your way.

Write for Yourself

Have you ever wanted to say something but no one was there to listen? Do you have a secret you could never tell anyone but that you still want to express? When you write for yourself, you can explore your innermost thoughts and feelings without worrying about what someone else will think or say. Private writing is for your eyes only, so feel free to take risks and write about anything that's on your mind. Even if you're writing something you want to share with others, you can keep early drafts private. Take chances when you write for yourself—you have nothing to lose!

Write with Others

Most writers—including novelists, journalists, poets, songwriters, and technical writers—think of themselves as part of a community of writers. They read and respond to each other's work, offer advice and encouragement, and share frustration and inspiration.

You too belong to a community of writers—when you work with your peers on writing projects, when you write for yourself, and when you publish or present your writing to a wider audience.

Even though there will be times when you'll want to write on your own and keep your writing strictly private, at other times it can be fun and helpful to show your writing to other people. In *The Writer's Craft,* you'll be encouraged not only to share the final products of your writing but also to share your writing process with your peers at several steps along the way.

4 Starting Points

Getting Started

UNDERSTANDING THE WRITING PROCESS

When you write to a friend, do you plan your letter first, or do you just sit down and start writing? Do you read the letter over for spelling and punctuation when you're finished? Now think about a school assignment. Do you write a report the same way?

Writing is a process, a group of related activities that you can use in any order or way that is helpful. The following activities are all part of the writing process:

- prewriting and exploring
- drafting and discovering
- sharing and getting responses
- revising
- proofreading
- publishing and presenting
- reflecting on your writing

The way you write will depend on what and why you're writing. In some situations, you might ask someone else what they think of your topic before you begin to explore it for yourself on paper. Sometimes, you might need to repeat a prewriting activity. Revising your writing may mean changing the form of your work. You can create and re-create your own writing process each time you write.

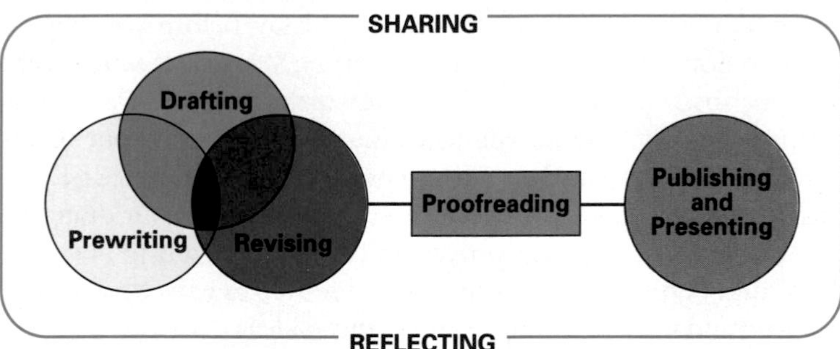

Getting Started

As you read this page with students, focus on the diagram. Point out that the prewriting, drafting, and revising stages are shown as overlapping circles because they are not three steps that follow one after the other in a neat pattern.

Explain that the next few pages describe each stage of the writing process. Students will have an opportunity to try out what they learn, in the Discovery Workshop on pages 11–23.

PREWRITE AND EXPLORE

Encourage students to share favorite strategies for finding writing ideas. Remind them that a wide range of activities, including thinking, can be prewriting strategies.

Direct students' attention to the Writer to Writer quotations. Explain that they will see similar quotations throughout the book; these quotations are thoughts and suggestions about writing from other student writers, as well as from professionals.

DRAFT AND DISCOVER

Remind students that *draft* is another word for *write.* Tell students that when they are drafting, they are putting their ideas on paper in sentences and paragraphs.

PREWRITE AND EXPLORE

WRITER TO WRITER

What I like about writing is that there is no limit to expanding your imagination.

Luziris Pineda, student, Houston, Texas

Think of prewriting as exploring what you already know and discovering what you need to find out. At this stage you may also gather material that you may or may not use later in your writing.

To help you explore ideas, you might try a variety of prewriting activities, such as freewriting, talking to friends, reading, or even drawing pictures. Handbooks 1–5, pages 218–235, will help you learn more about prewriting. Remember that this is a time to experiment, so let your imagination roam as far and wide as it will go.

DRAFT AND DISCOVER

WRITER TO WRITER

When you write, write to please yourself.

Matthew D. Jackson, student, Clarksville, Tennessee

Drafting is a stage of discovery where you put your thoughts on paper and see where they lead. Let your thinking be your guide, but allow your ideas to develop and change as you write.

When you draft, don't worry about whether or not you're saying exactly what you thought you would say before you began. You also don't need to worry about getting your ideas in the right order or about choosing just the right words. Like a dancer who is creating a dance, a writer will take a number of steps in one direction and then turn and try the steps in a different order. If you spend too much time trying to perfect every detail, your draft will go nowhere fast. The very process of drafting, of writing out your ideas, may surprise you and help you discover exactly what you're thinking and how you might express those ideas.

After you've completed a first draft, set it aside for a while. Then review your draft and think about how it strikes you. Do you like what you read? Your writing may look like a complete mess, but that's OK—you're not done yet.

At this stage, you might want to go back and work on your draft some more, clarifying your ideas or adding more information. However, you may wish to share your writing with others first. Hearing what your writing sounds like and finding out how it strikes others early in your writing process can help you see what in your draft is working and what is not. The responses of other students—peer readers—can help you get even closer to what *you* want to say. Handbooks 6–18, pages 236–286, give you the specific help you'll need as you draft.

REVISE YOUR WRITING

WRITER TO WRITER

Sometimes you just can't get everything in your head on that little piece of lined paper.

Mark Blatchford, student, Grand Rapids, Michigan

Your first drafts are almost never what you want your finished piece of writing to be. That's because it's nearly impossible to get all of what you wanted to say onto your paper the first time around. Revising is a stage of thought and change. It is much more than making corrections—touching things up and fixing mistakes. When you revise, you have a chance to rethink and rearrange what you have written. Revising may mean replacing ideas. It may even mean creating a whole new draft. See Handbook 19, pages 287–289, for more information about revising and making your writing as good as it can be.

REVISE YOUR WRITING

Assure students that writers often draft and revise a number of times as they work on a piece of writing. Often writers might draft and revise and then draft and revise again, as their ideas become more focused.

PROOFREAD

Proofreading is the stage where you correct errors in grammar, capitalization, spelling, and punctuation and get your writing ready for your teacher, your classmates, or a wider audience. Use the symbols in the box on page 20 to help you mark changes in your draft. After you've proofread your writing, you can make a final copy. Handbook 20, pages 290–292, contains more information about proofreading.

PUBLISH AND PRESENT

Although you may have shared your writing process with peer readers, now is the time to share your finished piece with a larger audience. You may choose to present your work orally, to display it on a bulletin board in your classroom or in a school corridor, or to submit it for publication in a class, school, or community newspaper or magazine. Handbook 21, page 293, has more information about how to share and publish your writing.

REFLECT ON YOUR WRITING

When you have finished a piece of writing, take some time to think about your writing process. Reflecting on your writing experience can help you gain new insights about writing and about yourself. You may want to ask yourself questions like these.

- What new things did I learn about myself—and about my subject—through writing?
- Which parts of the writing process were easiest for me? Which parts were most difficult?
- What was the biggest problem I faced as I wrote? How did I solve it?
- What have I learned that I can apply to my future writing?

Your reflections may take the form of a journal entry or a note to your fellow writers or your teacher. Attach your reflections to your writing, and add your work to your writing portfolio.

8 Starting Points

Using This Book

You have seen how writing is a process of discovery. You discover what you want to say and the best way to say it in each writing situation. Since there is no "right" way to complete a piece of writing, *The Writer's Craft* shows you what your choices are and offers directions and suggestions so you can choose what's best for you each time you write.

The Writer's Craft has three sections: Writer's Workshops, a Writing Handbook, and a Grammar and Usage Handbook.

WRITER'S WORKSHOPS

Each Writer's Workshop focuses on a specific kind of writing. You'll explore each writing type in a guided assignment, in a related assignment, and through additional writing opportunities.

Guided Assignments

In each guided assignment, you'll have the opportunity to write on your own and to discover writing strategies that will help you achieve your goals and create something uniquely your own. You'll also see how a professional writer and another student approached the same kind of writing activity. As you work through each guided assignment, you can turn to the Handbooks for assistance or practice with certain skills.

Related Assignments

A related assignment follows each guided assignment and helps you build on the skills you've developed. While the guided assignment offers detailed writing options, the related assignment gives you greater freedom to explore independently and to solve your own writing problems.

Additional Writing Opportunities

Throughout *The Writer's Craft,* you will find feature pages that provide further opportunities for you to practice your writing skills. **Sketchbooks** give you a chance to be creative and try out writing

Using This Book

Point out that pages 9 and 10 provide a guide to what is included in this textbook. Discuss the relationships among the various parts of the textbook.

ideas just for fun. **Springboards** offer suggestions for applying writing skills to other subjects, such as science, art, or history. Finally, **Sentence Composing** activities give you the chance to develop your writing style by studying and imitating sentences written by professional writers.

HANDBOOKS

The Writing Handbook and the Grammar and Usage Handbook give you the help you need when you need it most. These Handbooks contain mini-lessons that allow you to develop new skills or give you extra practice with skills you already have.

The **Writing Handbook** lessons cover the writing process, writing techniques and style, and skills you need to succeed in school. The **Grammar and Usage Handbook** lessons cover the essentials of good grammar, usage, and mechanics.

Throughout the Workshops, **Problem Solving** notes direct you to particular Handbooks for help and explanation. You'll also want to explore the Handbooks on your own, especially when you need to find answers to questions that arise as you write.

USING WRITING FOLDERS AND PORTFOLIOS

FOR YOUR **PORTFOLIO**

As you work on a piece of writing, keep all your drafts and notes in a writing folder. You may need to go back to your prewriting notes or an earlier draft to get more ideas or to check how your thinking has progressed.

You may wish to put the finished piece in a portfolio, just as an artist does. Your portfolio might contain the pieces you're proudest of, and it might also include your reflections—your thoughts and feelings about each piece.

Now that you've read about the writing process and about how *The Writer's Craft* is organized, you're ready to discover what writing can mean to you. In the Discovery Workshop that follows, you'll see how *The Writer's Craft* can be your guide to writing something special, something uniquely your own.

10 Starting Points

Discovery Workshop

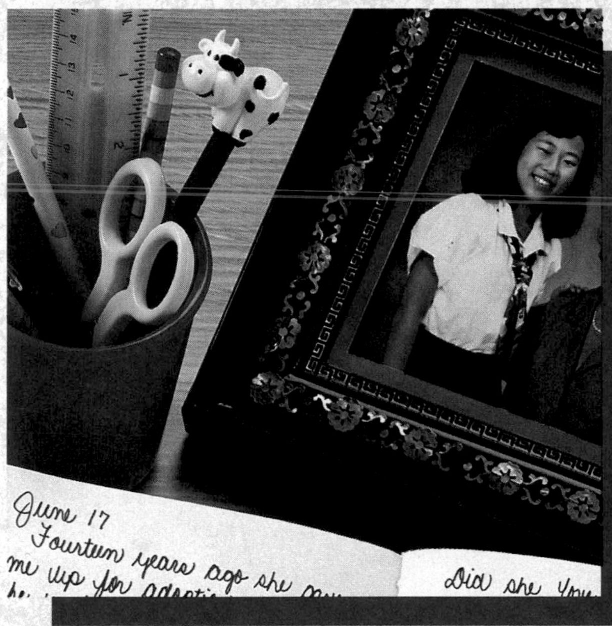
June 17
Fourteen years ago she

Each Writer's Workshop in *The Writer's Craft* tells you what form your writing will take—for example, an autobiographical incident, a report, or a poem. Sometimes, though, writers have no idea where their writing will lead. They begin with what's important to them—an incident (a friend moves away), a feeling (jealousy), or an issue (racism). They write to explore what they think.

The Discovery Workshop will give you a chance to see what this kind of writing surprise feels like. You'll write about something that matters to you and gain a better understanding of how your own writing process works. You'll also see how you can use this book to help you grow as a writer and accomplish your writing goals.

STARTING POINTS

Discovery Workshop

The Discovery Workshop is somewhat different from the other workshops in this text. Although all the workshops allow students to choose their own topics, only the Discovery Workshop leaves open the form of the writing that students are asked to create.

Author Peter Elbow explains: "The Discovery Workshop comes at the beginning for a reason. It provides a writing framework in which a student can start with anything that's on his or her mind, explore the issue, and watch it evolve, so that content ultimately leads to form. Learning to let content determine form gives students important skills that they'll use in many other writing situations—in this book, in other classes, at work, in life."

As students complete this assignment, they also discover the richness of variables that the writing process offers. More importantly, they learn that writing can have personal meaning, as they begin to identify their own writing goals. Thus the Discovery Workshop provides students with a strong foundation, so that they approach writing tasks with flexibility and confidence. This foundation can extend beyond the classroom, making students lifelong writers.

A Student Model begins the Discovery Workshop. Since this workshop centers on the process of writing, rather than on one form, the Student Model is actually several "discovery" drafts on the same subject. Teaching suggestions offer ways to use the model as a springboard to students' own writing.

The Discovery Workshop also provides students with a chance to see you, their teacher, as a fellow writer. If at all possible, write along with students during this workshop. Share your experiences and responses with students and encourage them to share theirs.

Guided ASSIGNMENT

Starting from LITERATURE

Motivate

Ask students about the writing they do outside of school. What types of writing do they do? Why do they write? If no one mentions writing as a way to sort out feelings or to solve a problem, you might want to mention this use. Perhaps you might describe a time when you used writing to solve a problem.

BUILD ON PRIOR KNOWLEDGE

The topic of these Student Models is a sensitive one: adoptions. Invite students to share what they know from the news media about adoptions. Students might want to discuss such issues as the emphasis on not revealing the identity of birth parents or the budding trend toward "open" adoptions. You might want to point out that the child, the birth parents, and the adoptive parents all have rights, and these rights have to be respected.

Many states now have registries in which both the adopted person and the birth parents can indicate their wish to contact each other. If both parties agree, once the adopted child is an adult, contact can be established.

SET A PURPOSE

Before students read Starting from Literature, ask them to identify some of the forms of writing on these two pages (report, poem, journal entry, short story, letter). Explain that the same student wrote all of these pieces as she struggled to deal with an important issue in her life. Remind students that as they read, they should think about how the pieces are similar and how they are different.

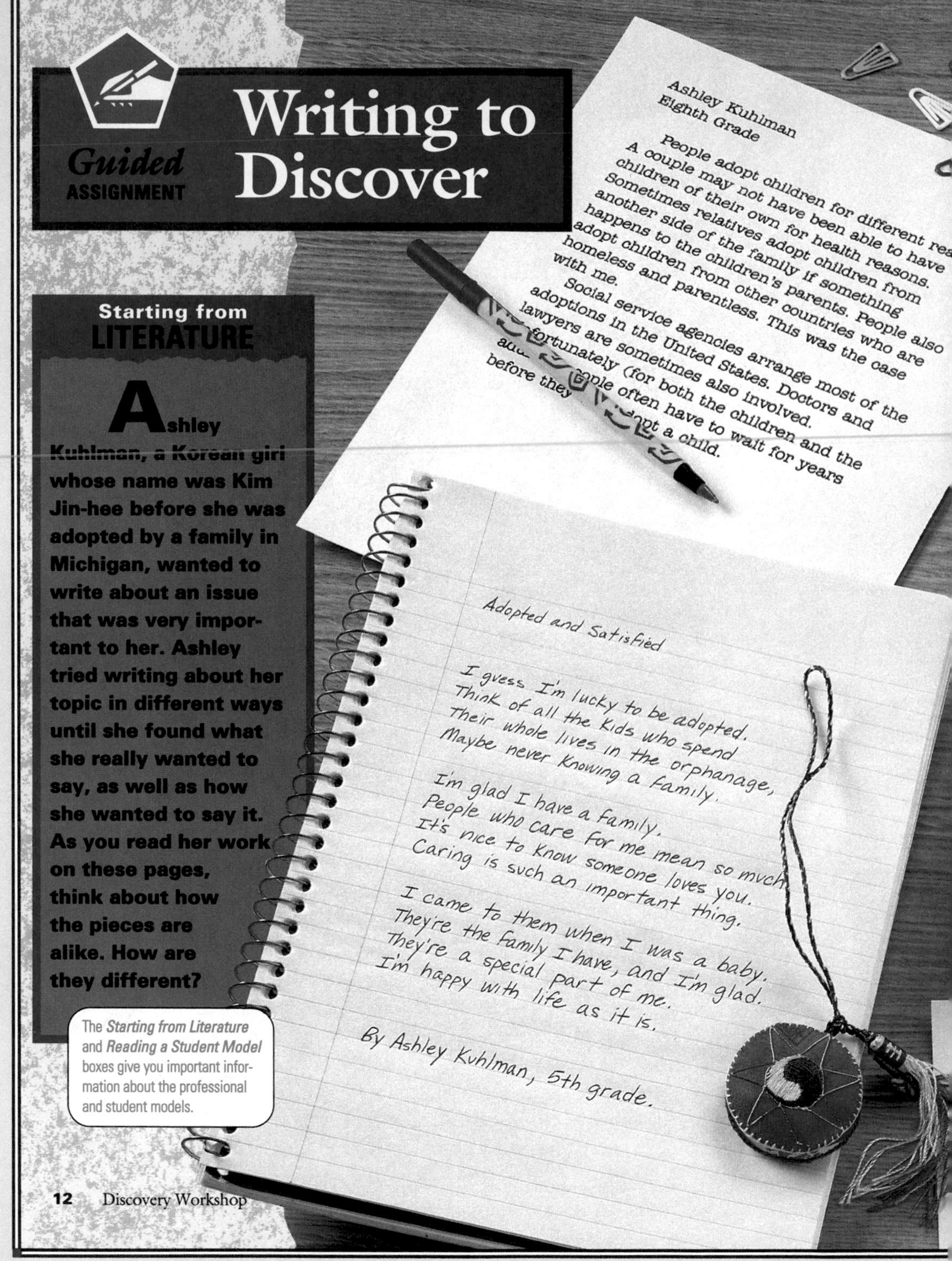

Guided ASSIGNMENT

Writing to Discover

Starting from LITERATURE

Ashley Kuhlman, a Korean girl whose name was Kim Jin-hee before she was adopted by a family in Michigan, wanted to write about an issue that was very important to her. Ashley tried writing about her topic in different ways until she found what she really wanted to say, as well as how she wanted to say it. As you read her work on these pages, think about how the pieces are alike. How are they different?

Ashley Kuhlman
Eighth Grade

People adopt children for different rea
A couple may not have been able to have children of their own for health reasons. Sometimes relatives adopt children from another side of the family if something happens to the children's parents. People also adopt children from other countries who are homeless and parentless. This was the case with me.

Social service agencies arrange most of the adoptions in the United States. Doctors and lawyers are sometimes also involved. ...fortunately (for both the children and the ...ople often have to wait for years before they ...opt a child.

Adopted and Satisfied

I guess I'm lucky to be adopted.
Think of all the kids who spend
Their whole lives in the orphanage,
Maybe never knowing a family.

I'm glad I have a family.
People who care for me mean so much.
It's nice to know someone loves you.
Caring is such an important thing.

I came to them when I was a baby.
They're the family I have, and I'm glad.
They're a special part of me.
I'm happy with life as it is.

By Ashley Kuhlman, 5th grade.

The *Starting from Literature* and *Reading a Student Model* boxes give you important information about the professional and student models.

12 Discovery Workshop

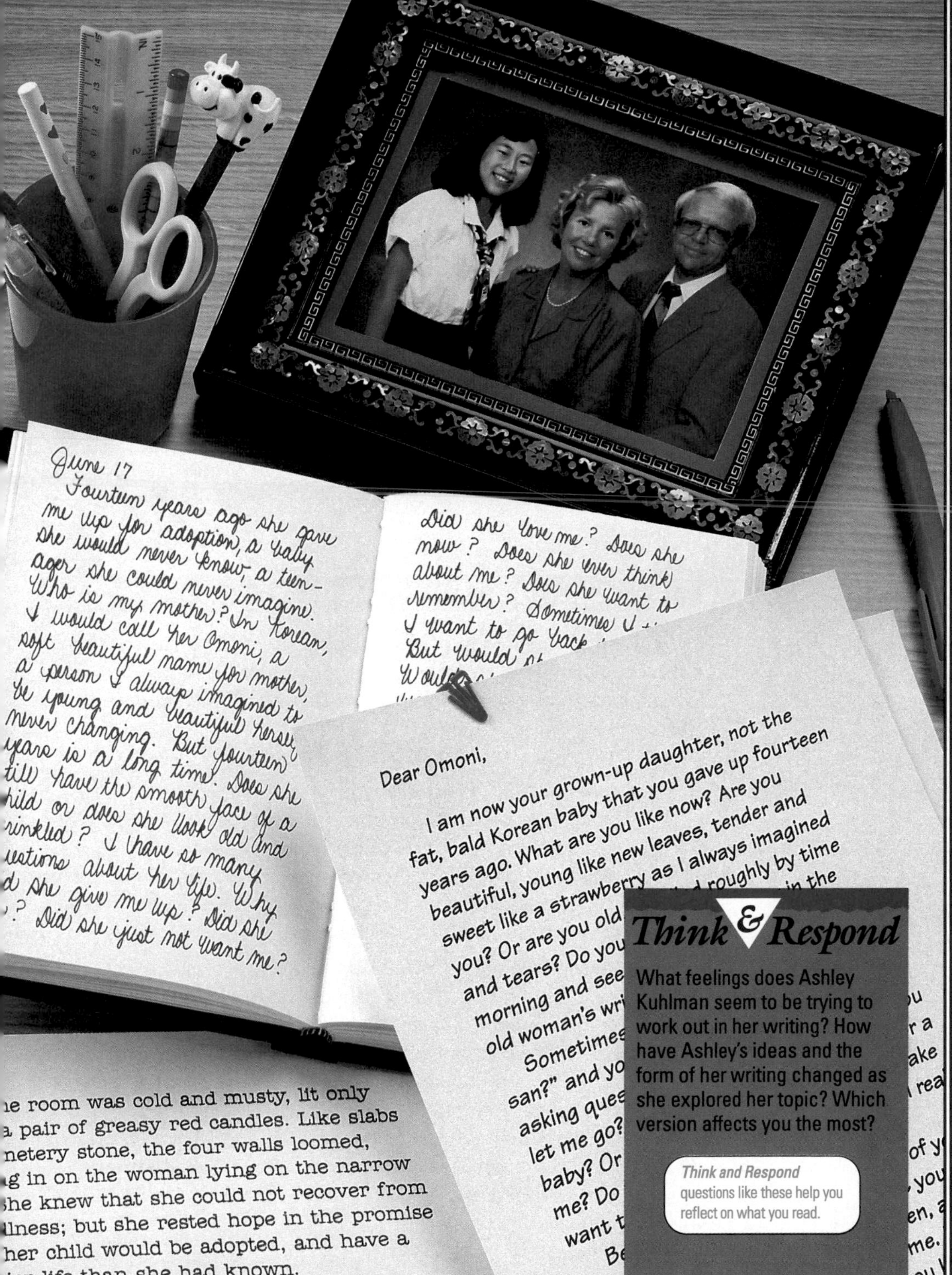
June 17
Fourteen years ago she gave me up for adoption, a baby she would never know, a teen-ager she could never imagine. Who is my mother? In Korean, I would call her Omoni, a soft beautiful name for mother, a person I always imagined to be young and beautiful herself, never changing.
Did she love me? Does she about me? Does she ever think
Dear Omoni,
I am now your grown-up daughter, not the fat, bald Korean baby that you gave up fourteen years ago. What are you like now? Are you beautiful, young like new leaves, tender and sweet like a strawberry as I always imagined
the room was cold and musty, lit only
a pair of greasy red candles. Like slabs
Think & Respond
What feelings does Ashley Kuhlman seem to be trying to work out in her writing? How have Ashley's ideas and the form of her writing changed as she explored her topic? Which version affects you the most?
Think and Respond questions like these help you reflect on what you read.

Think & Respond

ELICIT PERSONAL RESPONSES

Have students share the similarities and differences they noticed in the models. (Students should mention specific details about audience, form, and content.)

As students respond to the first question, elicit information about Ashley's story so that students understand why she needed to work out her feelings about being adopted. (The story is true; Ashley, an infant, was left at an orphanage in Korea; she was adopted by a couple in the United States and has no information about her birth parents; she has not been to Korea, so does not have first-hand knowledge of her heritage.)

In answering the second question, students should note that Ashley wrote the poem while in fifth grade, and at that time, her emphasis was on being grateful that she had loving adoptive parents. The other pieces were written in eighth grade, and the emphasis has shifted to wanting to know about her birth mother.

In responding to the final question, students should explain why a particular version affected them.

Writing ON YOUR OWN

The Invitation to Write creates a bridge between the model and the writing assignment. Therefore, you might remind students that Ashley chose a topic that she had been dealing with over a period of several years; by trying various forms of writing, she kept discovering more and more about herself and her ideas. Point out that like Ashley, students are invited to choose topics that are meaningful to them and to try several forms of writing as they explore and discover what they want to say.

PREWRITE AND EXPLORE

Objectives

- To use prewriting techniques to discover and explore a topic
- To identify several possible writing forms

Teaching Strategies

GENERAL NOTE

KEY TO UNDERSTANDING Explain that just as Ashley struggled to figure out how she felt about being adopted, students also have ideas and feelings that are important but may be hard to bring into focus. Tell students that the more they write, and the more forms of writing they try, the clearer their thoughts will become. For that reason, students might wish to try all the suggestions in this workshop.

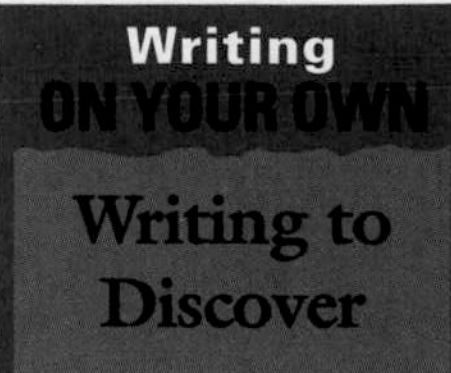

INVITATION TO *Write*

Ashley Kuhlman's writing process was one of exploration and discovery; she learned what she wanted to say by trying out different ways of saying it. In this workshop, you too will have the chance to explore your ideas in writing—without requirements or restrictions. You will write simply to discover what you want to say and how you can say it best.

Explore some ideas that really matter to you, ideas that you care about. Then begin writing to see where your ideas lead you and what form they take.

Here is an invitation especially for you! It asks you to find a topic you're interested in and to put your thoughts and feelings about it into writing.

PREWRITE AND EXPLORE

1. Find an idea to explore. The best writing ideas come from events, memories, or feelings that are important to you. Try these activities to find an idea or incident that makes you *want* to write.

Discover and explore exciting writing ideas by trying one or more of the activities described in this section.

Exploring Topics

- **Freewriting** What's on your mind? Is there a particular incident or conversation that you can't seem to forget? What people or issues are you thinking about? Make a list of possible topics for writing, then do some freewriting about one or two of them and see what you have to say. Begin anywhere you want and let each idea flow into the next.
- **Instant replay** Rewind the events of the last few days in your mind. Did anything happen that took you by surprise or that made you feel particularly happy, disappointed, or confused? Did you have any conversations that you wished afterwards had never happened—or that you wished had happened a lot sooner? Get together with some of your friends and talk about what's happened lately and what's on your mind right now. Together you may find ideas you want to explore in writing.

2. Share your ideas. After you come up with some writing ideas, you may wish to discuss them with others. Listen carefully—one of your classmate's ideas may spark a memory, lead you to a new topic, or help you look at your idea from a new perspective.

One Student's Process

Ashley Kuhlman talked to her friends about their family histories. The conversation turned to adoption when Ashley spoke of her family's past. After the conversation, Ashley did some freewriting to help her clear her mind and sort through her feelings.

Talked to Nora, Greg, and Amanda today—about our parents, grandparents, how we came to live in Lansing, etc. We talked about my family too. They all knew I was adopted, and they asked the same questions I get all the time— how does it feel? (fine) Do you talk to your parents about it? (yes) Would you want to meet your mother if you knew where to find her? (I don't know.) I wrote a poem in 5th grade about being adopted. I should try to find that—it really said a lot about how I felt then and still do feel about my family, my real family here in Lansing. That question about meeting my mother is tough. It's weird to think that somewhere out there is a person who was once your mother—that a stranger might be thinking about you sometimes. Does my other mother think about me? I wonder if she thinks about me as much as I think about her.

In *One Student's Process*, you'll follow the thinking, writing, and revising done by student writers just like you. Your own writing process may be similar—or it may be very different.

3. Imagine possibilities. Think about what kind of writing you might work on. Do you, for example, see the beginnings of a short story in your freewriting? Perhaps you think a poem or song lyrics would best express your feelings or experiences. Maybe you want to share your ideas in a letter to a friend. It's all right if you're not sure you'll continue with a choice you make now. Remember, you are free to change your mind about your topic or your form at any time during your writing process.

Problem Solving features help you find answers to your writing questions. When you feel stuck, these features will direct you to the Writing Handbook and to the Grammar and Usage Handbook for help.

PROBLEM SOLVING

"I'm not sure what form I want my writing to take later on. What are my options?"

For more information about various writing forms, see

- Handbook 7, "Forms of Writing," page 238

for ONE STUDENT'S PROCESS

KEY TO UNDERSTANDING This feature provides examples of student work at various stages of the writing process. As you discuss the feature, remind students that they can try techniques other than the one illustrated.

Teaching notes for this feature often provide ways to link the example to the work of your students. For example, you might point out that Ashley freewrites only a few sentences about each thought, then moves on to a new idea without starting a new paragraph. Be sure students understand that jumping from one idea to another is fine in freewriting. Among their many thoughts, writers can usually find several that they would like to expand upon.

Objectives

- To write successive drafts, focusing on the same subject but using different writing forms
- To identify personal writing goals

Teaching Strategies

GENERAL NOTE

HELPFUL HINT Since this is the Discovery Workshop, stress the *discover* in Draft and Discover. Although in later workshops students will probably stick closely to their prewriting, suggest that this time they put it aside after they have looked it over. Encourage them to begin drafting and to expect surprises as they record their emerging ideas.

GENERAL NOTE

KEY TO UNDERSTANDING As students work through the Draft and Discover section, be sure they notice that Ashley tried three approaches to her subject—a report, a short story, and a letter. Students should recognize that each draft deepened Ashley's understanding of her subject and its importance to her. Encourage students to try several forms of writing as Ashley did.

for ONE STUDENT'S PROCESS

KEY TO UNDERSTANDING Point out that in her first draft, Ashley didn't worry about putting her ideas in a logical order or about having included a sentence not clearly related to the rest of the paragraph ("This was the case with me."). Emphasize that a draft needn't be anywhere close to perfect. There will always be time for making changes during the revision stage.

DRAFT AND DISCOVER

In this section, you'll find plenty of suggestions for getting your ideas down on paper.

1. Start writing. Try drafting one of the writing ideas you came up with during prewriting. Remember, drafting can be an adventure in which you uncover unexpected ideas. You don't need to know where you'll go with your writing when you begin. Just trust that your writing will lead you to a place you'll want to explore further.

One Student's Process

Ashley reread her freewriting and thought she might like to write an informative report about adoption. She had done some reading on the topic, and she knew she could include her own experiences.

People adopt children for different reasons. A couple may not have been able to have children of their own for health reasons. Sometimes relatives adopt children from another side of the family if something happens to the children's parents. People also adopt children from other countries who are homeless and parentless. This was the case with me.

Social service agencies arrange most of the adoptions in the United States. Doctors and lawyers are sometimes also involved. Unfortunately (for both the children and the adults), people often have to wait for years before they can adopt a child.

Margin notes like these offer writing and grammar tips and suggestions for using computers when you write.

TIP

Some people like to write with music playing in the background; others need absolute quiet. Find the working style that's best for you.

2. Write some more. As you continue to write, you may find your words flowing faster and faster. Don't stop if the writing is going well. If you do pause to review your writing, ask yourself some of these questions. Your answers may help guide you.

- What do I want this piece of writing to accomplish?
- Do I like the direction I'm going in?
- Am I saying what I want to say? What else do I want to say?
- What's the best part of what I've written so far? Will my readers think my draft is interesting or meaningful?
- Do I like the form I'm using? Should I try a different form?

PROFESSIONAL NOTEBOOK

Advice from the Authors Share this suggestion from Peter Elbow to help students experiment with a variety of forms: "Try it as a dialogue, a poem, or a TV show. Try it as a letter from someone on Mars or as a six-year-old kid might write. Trying out different forms and different voices strengthens your own writing voice."

Writer's Choice What form has your writing taken so far? Does it feel right? Ask yourself if another form would better suit your ideas. For example, would a personal narrative work better for you than a report?

You can tailor the writing process to suit yourself each time you write. The *Writer's Choice* feature gives you options and allows you to select what's right for you.

One Student's Process

Ashley was frustrated with the draft of her report on adoption. She wasn't saying what was really on her mind. What she really kept thinking about was her birth mother and what might have happened to her. She thought the short story format would better suit this topic, so she invented this story about her birth.

The room was cold and musty, lit only with a pair of greasy red candles. Like slabs of cemetery stone, the four walls loomed, closing in on the woman lying on the narrow cot. She knew that she could not recover from her illness; but she rested hope in the promise that her child would be adopted, and have a happier life than she had known.

A baby's cry spread through the dark room, and a sigh escaped the woman's lips. An old woman, her only friend, cradled the baby girl in one wrinkled arm, and the dying woman breathed her last, supported by the old woman's other arm.

3. Find your focus. Has your drafting led you to some conclusions about your personal goals, your content, or your organization? Jot down some responses to these questions.

Personal Goals

- Will this writing be for my eyes only or will I share it?
- If I share it, what effect do I want this piece to have?
- What do I want to learn from this writing experience?

Content and Development

- Have I gotten to the heart of what I want to say?

Form and Organization

- Are my ideas in an order that makes sense?
- Has my draft led me to a specific form of writing?

Keep the answers to these questions in mind as you work on your draft. See Handbook 12, "Methods of Elaboration," pages 255–261, for more information on how to develop your ideas.

for ONE STUDENT'S PROCESS

KEY TO UNDERSTANDING You might ask students what they think the short story form accomplished for Ashley that the report form did not. (Sample: Ashley could deal with feelings in the short story; in the report, she provided information.)

for FIND YOUR FOCUS

KEY TO UNDERSTANDING Tell students that in this workshop, they are learning how to recognize their own writing goals, how to choose their own audience, and how to develop a form and an organization for what they want to say. Explain that the questions in the text can help them learn these skills.

for CONTENT AND DEVELOPMENT

KEY TO UNDERSTANDING Be sure students recognize that a sense of personal satisfaction will let them know when they have arrived at the heart of a topic. This means that they may not be completely satisfied with their writing, but that they will feel enthusiastic about what they are saying and interested in the way the writing is developing.

for DECIDE ABOUT FEEDBACK

KEY TO UNDERSTANDING: PEER RESPONSE Each workshop invites students to seek peer responses before revising. However, writers retain authority over their drafts by specifying the kinds of things they want peers to respond to. Most Guided Assignments offer students two sets of appropriate questions. (See page 35 for an example.) For more information about how to give and receive peer response, refer students to Handbook 18, pages 284–286, and to pages 681–682 in the Appendix.

for ONE STUDENT'S PROCESS

HELPFUL HINT Point out that Ashley's peer reader proposed a form (a letter) that seemed especially suitable for the content of Ashley's writing. Tell students to look for a form that the content of their writing suggests.

"How can readers help?"

For information about peer response, see

- Handbook 18, "Peer Response," pages 284–286

4. Decide about feedback. Sometimes you don't want anyone's opinion but your own. At other times, you may want to see how others respond to your writing. Are you ready to share your draft with peers? You may simply want to read your draft aloud to them to hear how it sounds. On the other hand, you may want someone to read your draft closely and offer reactions and suggestions. Try asking your peer readers questions like these:

- What do you think my piece is really about?
- Which parts did you like best? How did it make you feel?
- What do you want to know more about?

One Student's Process

Peer Reader Comments show you the responses and suggestions that one student gave to another.

Peer Reader Comments

After writing the beginning of her story, Ashley found that she was still thinking about her friends' question: Would she want to meet the mother who gave birth to her? Ashley knew that going ahead with her short story wouldn't bring her any closer to the answer. She did some more writing and then shared it with a close friend whose responses appear in the margin.

Fourteen years ago she gave me up for adoption, a baby she would never know, a teenager she could never imagine. Who is my mother? In Korean, I would call her Omoni, a soft beautiful name for mother, a person I always imagined to be young and beautiful herself, never changing. But fourteen years is a long time. Does she still have the smooth face of a child or does she look old and wrinkled? I have so many questions about her life. Why did she give me up? Did she die? Did she just not want me? Did she love me? Does she now? Does she ever think about me? Does she want to remember? Sometimes I think I want to go back to her. But would she want me? Would she take my love? I want to know the answers, but then again, maybe I don't.

> I'd be asking myself this question too.

> I like this line about Omoni.

> So many questions only Omoni could answer. . . . What if you tried writing her a letter?

> I know what you mean—you want to know and not know at the same time.

REVISE YOUR WRITING

1. Consider your readers' comments. How did your draft strike your readers? What can you learn from their responses? Think about what your readers said—and what you yourself think about your draft—and decide what changes you want to make. Remember that this is your writing, and whether or not you take the advice of others is completely up to you.

2. Think about your goals. Have you said what you most wanted to say when you began? Have your writing goals changed now that you've written a draft? Check to see if you need to add more information to make your writing clear and complete.

3. Check your organization. You might want to read your draft aloud to see if your writing flows smoothly from beginning to end. Is anything out of place?

In this section, you'll learn strategies for reworking your writing and making it as good as it can be.

COMPUTER TIP

Make a copy of your original document on your disk. Then, experiment with your organization by moving blocks of copy around. You'll always be able to return to the original.

One Student's Process

Ashley thought her friend's suggestion to write a letter was a great one. Here is a piece of her next draft and some changes she made by hand. She would make even more changes later.

Dear Omoni,

I am now your grown-up daughter, not the baby you gave up fourteen years ago. What are you like now? Are you beautiful, young [like new leaves], tender and sweet [like a strawberry] as I always imagined you? Do you look in the mirror [mirror → mirror, "e" corrected to "o"] in the morning and see a [smooth] child['s face] or an old woman['s wrinkles]?

Sometimes I talk to you, asking questions about your life. Why did you let me go? Did you die? Did you not plan for a baby? Or did you just plain not want to take me? Do you love me [at all]? ~~Do I even want to know?~~ [I don't think I really want to find out.]

REVISE YOUR WRITING

Objective

- To evaluate and revise a draft

Teaching Strategies

for CONSIDER YOUR READERS' COMMENTS

KEY TO UNDERSTANDING: PEER RESPONSE Note that writers are advised that they don't have to make all—or any—changes that peers suggest.

for ONE STUDENT'S PROCESS

HELPFUL HINT After students have noted the changes that Ashley made in this section, have them study her final draft on pages 22–23. Ask them to identify the kinds of changes that Ashley made. (She added new details, substituted specific terms for vague ones, and deleted some parts.) Point out that students can make these and other types of changes as they revise.

Writing to Discover 19

PROOFREAD

Teaching Strategies

GENERAL NOTE

KEY TO UNDERSTANDING This section introduces students to proofreading. In other Guided Assignments, a feature titled Linking Grammar and Writing (or Linking Mechanics and Writing) appears in this section. These features focus on grammar and mechanics that are appropriate for each writing assignment, and they include cross-references to the *Grammar and Usage Handbook.* See pages 38 and 80 for examples.

for PROOFREADING CHECKLIST

HELPFUL HINT Students should note the location of this proofreading chart and checklist so that they can refer to them when they proofread future assignments. Strategies for proofreading also appear in Handbook 20, pages 290–292.

PROOFREAD

Before you prepare a final copy of your writing, check for errors in grammar, capitalization, punctuation, and spelling. These errors can distract your readers and make your writing hard to follow. Ask yourself the questions in the Proofreading Checklist below, and mark corrections on your draft using the proofreading symbols shown.

Proofreading Checklist

Step 1: Check the forms of words.

- Did I use correct verb tenses?
- Did I use any adjectives where I should have used adverbs?
- Did I use *-er/-est* and *more/most* correctly in comparisons?
- Did I use all forms of *be* and other irregular verbs correctly?
- Did I use the correct forms of pronouns?

Step 2: Check sentence structure and agreement.

- Are there any run-on sentences or sentence fragments?
- Do all verbs agree with their subjects?
- Do all pronouns agree with their antecedents?
- Did I keep all verb tenses consistent?

Step 3: Check capitalization, punctuation, and spelling.

- Did I use the correct form for every plural noun?
- Did I capitalize the first word of each sentence?
- Did I capitalize all proper nouns and proper adjectives?
- Is any punctuation mark missing or not needed?
- Did I spell all words, including possessive forms, correctly?

Proofreading Symbols

Symbol	Meaning	Symbol	Meaning
∧	Add letters or words.	/	Make a capital letter lowercase.
⊙	Add a period.	¶	Begin a new paragraph.
≡	Capitalize a letter.	∼	Switch the positions of letters or words.
⁀‿	Close up space.	— or ℓ	Take out letters or words.
∧,	Add a comma.		

PUBLISH AND PRESENT

You can share your writing with other people—your classmates, your teacher, or even a public audience outside of school—in a variety of ways. Here are a few of your options.

- **Give an oral reading.** Get together with a small group of your classmates and take turns reading your works aloud. After each piece is read, discuss the thoughts and feelings the writing inspired.
- **Make a poster for your classroom or school hallway.** Try illustrating your writing with drawings, photos, or pictures from magazines. You might even assemble a collage to go with your writing. Display your work on a bulletin board.
- **Send it off.** Submit your writing to your school or community newspaper, to a magazine, or to a writing contest.

Each workshop suggests a variety of ideas for sharing your writing with a wide audience.

REFLECT ON YOUR WRITING

You can learn a lot about yourself as a writer by reflecting on your writing process. As you look back over your prewriting notes and your drafts, you can see changes in your thinking and patterns in your writing.

You'll have the opportunity to reflect on what you've learned about writing and about yourself after you've completed each piece of writing.

Take some time to think about the writing you just completed. You may wish to do some freewriting or write a note and attach it to your final draft. The following questions can help you get started. Then attach your reflections to your finished piece and put your work in your portfolio.

- How did I discover my topic? How did I know it was what I wanted to focus on?
- What surprised me most about this piece of writing?
- Did I share my drafts with others? How did I feel about their responses? Did I make any changes they suggested? Why?
- How do I feel about the final piece?
- What part do I like best? What, if anything, would I change?
- Did I write differently from the way I usually write? How? Why?

GENERAL NOTE

ASSESSMENT You might consider marking students' papers on a credit/no credit basis, since this assignment is exploratory and personal in nature. For all of the other Guided Assignments, evaluation standards appear in the student book in the margin of the Proofreading section or the Publish and Present section, accompanied by assessment guidelines in the teacher's edition. (For an example, see page 38.)

Closure: Reflect on Your Writing

This section directs students to write briefly about their experiences with the assignment and to add their reflections to their portfolios. The purpose of the suggestions in this section is to increase each student's awareness of his or her own writing process and to focus students' attention on their growth as writers. Suggest that they choose one or two questions and write a thoughtful response.

One Student's WRITING

The final draft of Ashley Kuhlman's (Kim Jin-hee's) letter appears on these pages. Ask students to comment on why Ashley chose to sign her letter with her Korean name first. Be sure that students recognize that this was a conscious decision on Ashley's part, only one of many decisions that a writer must make.

Have students compare Ashley's final draft with the journal entry on page 13. How did Ashley's feelings intensify toward her mother, between that entry and her final draft? (She was not so sure she wanted the answers to her questions or even if she truly wanted to meet her mother.) Which parts of the final draft did students find most effective?

As students discuss their responses, help them to recognize that the writing process involves much more than sitting down, immediately writing a paper, and then correcting errors in grammar, capitalization, and punctuation. Ashley went through a long process—from being grateful to her adoptive parents, to thinking she wanted to be with her birth mother, to recognizing finally that perhaps she did not want to know her after all. Along the way, Ashley grew both as a person and as a writer.

One Student's Writing

Dear Omoni,

I am now your grown-up daughter, not the fat, bald Korean baby that you gave up fourteen years ago. What are you like now? Are you beautiful, young like new leaves, tender and sweet like a strawberry as I always imagined you? Or are you old, handled roughly by time and tears? Do you look in the mirror in the morning and see a smooth child's face or an old woman's wrinkles?

Sometimes I miss you, I call out, "Omoni-san?" and you don't come. But I talk to you, asking questions about your life. Why did you let me go? Did you die? Did you not plan for a baby? Or did you just plain not want to take me? Do you love me at all? I don't think I really want to find out.

Because I don't want my dreams of you to be shattered. I want to believe that you were poor, or already had several children, and most of all that you did want to keep me. Maybe I'm fooling myself, but if I am—if you know I am—keep it to yourself. I don't want to hear it.

Omoni, do you remember me? Do you want to? I want to wrap my love around you. I want to come back to you like a pigeon goes home. But do you want my love, would you take it? And do I want to be tied to you?

Do I want to know you and belong to you? Or will I be happier depending on myself? You see, I think we'd both be expecting too much of each other—you'd be expecting an innocent child, I an angel who can do no wrong. I think I'd rather keep my illusions of you and let you keep yours.

I used to dream that one day we would get a <u>very long</u> distance call, and it would be you. And we would talk, and I used to think this is what you'd say:

"Hello, Jin-hee. I'm sorry if you wondered about me and never got any answers. I had to finish school and get a good job before I could come back for you. Then I spent years trying to trace you. But now everything is fine. Will you come back and live with us?"

Yes, Omoni, I would always say. And so we'd live happily ever after. But, Omoni, I was a child then. I was the innocent child that you probably want me to be, and you were the cherry blossoms at Halla and Paektu. I do not believe in the innocence of spring anymore. I am too old for a child's fantasies. And . . . I guess . . . Omoni, you do not make the same magic in my heart.

Your daughter,

Kim Jin-hee

Ashley Kuhlman

Writing to Discover 23

ART NOTE You might point out on a map the mountainous Sichuan Province in south-central China, where this embroidered pillow was made. Fine embroidery has been a highly developed art form there since about 1000 B.C.

This pillow, embroidered by an ordinary citizen, shows four Chinese good-luck symbols. Ask students whether they can find the bat, which stands for luck (see the eyes and face in the upper center, and the wings decorated with flowers); the peach, for long life (in the center, just below the bat's eyes); and the coin, for prosperity (below the peach at the very bottom center). To the lower left of the peach is a citrus fruit called a Buddha's hand, which symbolizes wealth because it is said to look like a hand grasping money.

Explain that the Chinese words for *bat* and *luck* have the same pronunciation: *fu.* Since the bat is one of the Chinese symbols of good luck, the two words are linked by both sound and meaning. *Wu Fu* means both "five bats" and "five blessings." The standard five blessings the Chinese wish for are long life, health, wealth, love of virtue, and a natural death.

You might ask students to identify their own "five blessings"—five wishes for a good life. Then discuss students' reasons for choosing these particular blessings. You might also discuss the ways in which students' chosen blessings are similar to and different from those of the Chinese.

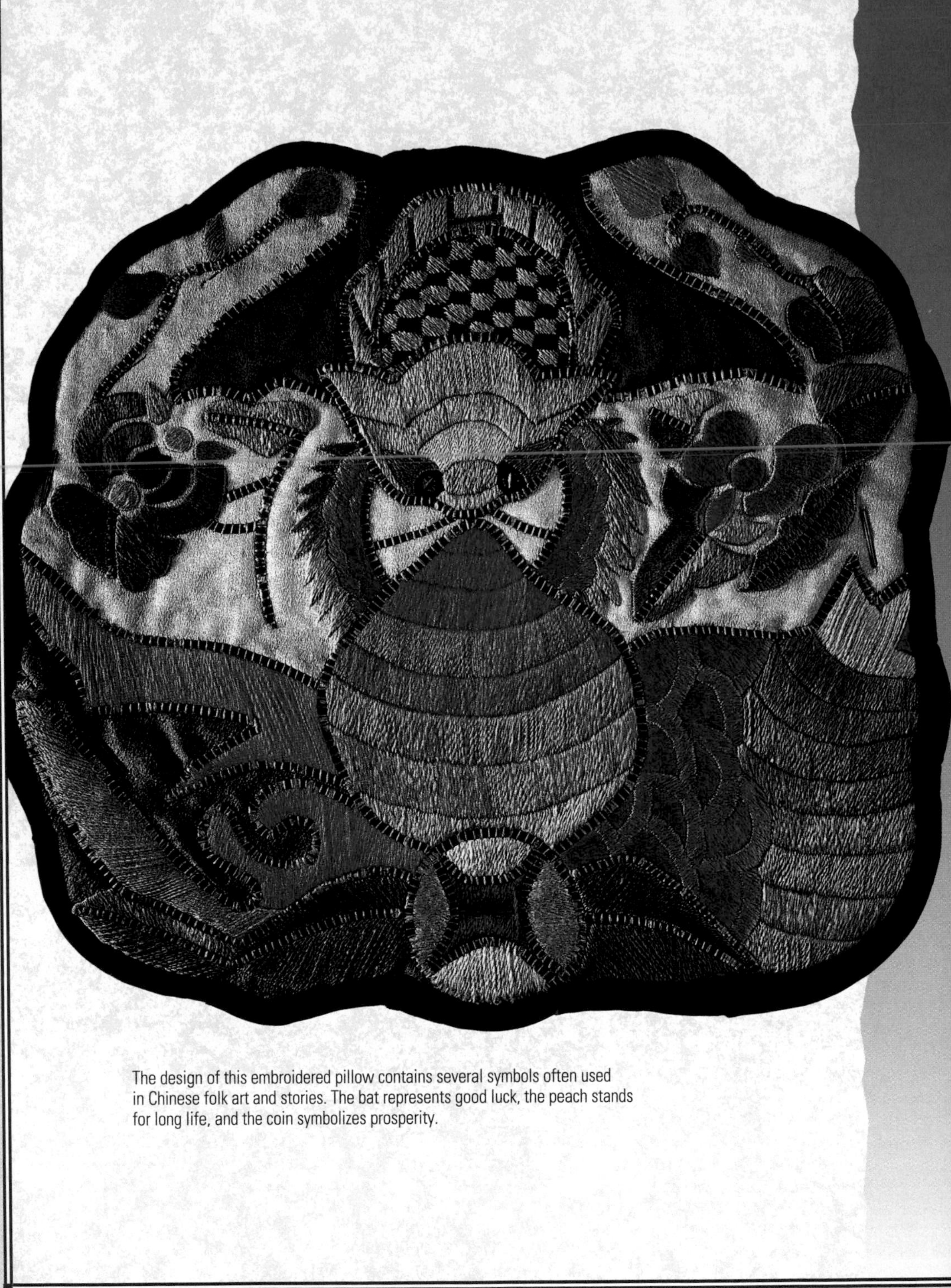

The design of this embroidered pillow contains several symbols often used in Chinese folk art and stories. The bat represents good luck, the peach stands for long life, and the coin symbolizes prosperity.

Writer's Workshops

Writer's Workshops

Personal and Expressive Writing

Overview

Personal and expressive writing conveys the significance of a writer's ideas, thoughts, and feelings. In this workshop, students will be introduced to the basic skills of narration and description as they recount a special autobiographical incident. They will also work with figurative language and sound devices to express personal ideas and feelings in song lyrics. Workshop 1 includes the following Guided and Related Assignments, as well as the interdisciplinary project described on pages 25c–25d.

1. **Guided: Autobiographical Incident** introduces the skills of personal writing in a narrative context. As students choose an incident and write about it in a way that shows its significance to them, they recognize their personal writing voice, identify a focus, select details, and present events in chronological order.
2. **Related: Song** reinforces skills introduced in the Guided Assignment. Students compose song lyrics that tell a story or express feelings or ideas. The assignment allows students the option of following the structure offered by a melody and lets them apply the skills of personal writing while working with figurative language, repetition, and other sound devices.

Teaching Preview

Preparation Guide

1. Use the Overview on this page and the Teacher's Choice descriptions on page 27 as a basis for deciding which assignments to teach.
2. Preview the assignments and the teacher's notes and identify concepts that may require preteaching or extra support, given your class's abilities. The handbook mini-lessons suggested within the lesson may also provide guidance.
3. Preview the chart below for support materials in the Teacher's Resource File that may be used with this Workshop. Resources are for use with the Guided Assignment unless otherwise noted.

Support Materials

RESOURCES

Prewrite and Explore
Writing Resource Book, pp. 1–3
Thinking Skills Worksheets, pp. 1–2
Starting Points for Writing, Writing Prompts for Fine Art, pp. 29–31, 35, 38, 42

Draft and Discover
Elaboration, Revision, and Proofreading Practice, p. 1
Writing Resource Book, pp. 4–5
Thinking Skills Worksheet, p. 7

Revise Your Writing
Elaboration, Revision, and Proofreading Practice, p. 2
Writing Resource Book, p. 6
Peer Response Guides, pp. 9–10
Guidelines for Writing Assessment and Portfolio Use, pp. 14, 23–25

Sentence Composing
Sentence Composing Copy Masters, pp. 1–2

Assessment
Tests and Writing Assessment Prompts, p. 1

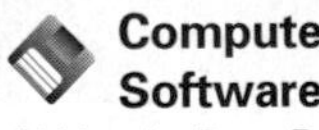
Computer Software
Writer's DataBank
Electronic English Handbook

PROFESSIONAL RESOURCES AND MEDIA

Books and Journals
Hamann, L. S., and others, "Making Connections: The Power of Autobiographical Writing Before Reading," *Journal of Reading,* Vol. 35 (September 1991), pp. 24–28
Lyons, Mary E., *Letters from a Slave Girl: The Story of Harriet Jacobs,* Charles Scribner's Sons (1992)
Uchida, Yoshiko, *The Invisible Thread,* Messner (1992)

Films and Videos
A Certain Age (Smithsonian World Series), PBS Video, Alexandria, VA (1991) (60 min.)
Runaway (WonderWorks), Public Media Video, Chicago (1992) (58 min.)
Tuskegee Airmen, Carousel, New York (1992) (23 min.)

Audiocassette
The Land I Lost, American Audio Prose Library, Columbia, MO (1986)

Computer Software and Technology
All About Me, Creative Pursuits/SoftKat, Chatsworth, CA (1992) (software for use with The Children's Writing & Publishing Center), Apple family; Macintosh; PC

Linking Literature, Writing, and Grammar

The following options may be used to provide students with an integrated language experience. Begin by assigning and discussing any of the recommended pieces of literature. Use the suggested strategy to provide a link to the Guided Assignment.

LINKING LITERATURE AND WRITING

Option 1

Starting Point: "Papa Was an American" by Leo Buscaglia on pages 28–29 of *The Writer's Craft.*

Strategy: Use the teaching suggestions on pages 28–29 to lead students into the Guided Assignment.

Option 2

Starting Point: *Once Upon a Time When We Were Colored* by Clifton Taulbert on pages 47–52 of McDougal, Littell's *Literature and Language,* Grade 8. (Additional suggestions for using *Literature and Language* can be found on page 27.)

Strategy: Have students read the selection to find out who Clifton Taulbert is. Ask students to discuss why this autobiographical incident is significant to Taulbert. Use a summary of the discussion to introduce students to the Guided Assignment.

Option 3

Starting Point: *The Diary of Anne Frank,* as dramatized by Frances Goodrich and Albert Hackett.

Strategy: Have students read the drama. Ask them which of Anne's feelings they can identify with and what insights they gained. How did writing in her diary probably help Anne? Discuss the various benefits—for both readers and writers—of writing about personal experiences, thoughts, and feelings. Use the discussion to lead students into the Guided Assignment.

LINKING WRITING AND GRAMMAR

Before the revising and proofreading stages of this assignment, tell students that in personal writing, as in other kinds of writing, unnecessary repetition can slow action and make writing dull. Point out that using pronouns is one way to avoid repeating nouns unnecessarily. Write these examples on the board and discuss them with students.

Repetitive: I saw Joel start across the stream, holding on to the thin willow branches. The stream was flowing deeper and faster since the rains had swollen the stream. Within seconds, the stream had swept Joel's feet out from under Joel.

Stronger: I saw Joel start across the stream, holding on to the thin willow branches. The stream was flowing deeper and faster since the rains had swollen *it.* Within seconds, *it* had swept *his* feet out from under *him.*

Have students find places in their writing where pronouns might be used to eliminate the weak repetition of nouns.

Go over pages 435–469 of the Grammar and Usage Handbook. If pronoun problems still occur in students' writing, assign exercises from these pages for reteaching. Additional practice can be found in the *Grammar and Usage Practice Book* on pages 23–36.

Management Guidelines

The chart below indicates the number of days recommended for each phase of the Guided and Related Assignments. These numbers are an estimate of the total time needed for each phase. In practice, of course, students may not complete each phase in one continuous session, nor will they necessarily progress from stage to stage in the linear order shown here. Stars indicate portions of the assignment that may be completed outside the classroom if time is limited or if teachers wish students to work independently.

AUTOBIOGRAPHICAL INCIDENT

Starting from Literature................1 day
Prewrite and Explore................2–3 days*
Draft and Discover....................1–2 days*
Revise Your Writing.................1–2 days*
Proofread.....................................1 day*
Publish and Present......................1 day
Reflect on Your Writing................1 day*
Reteaching.....................................open
Extension and Enrichment ....open*
Sentence Composing.....................open*

SONG

Appreciating a Song ....1 day
Exploring Your World................1–2 days*
Drafting Your Song...................1–2 days*
Reviewing Your Writing............1–2 days*
Publishing and Presenting........1–2 days

They're the Greatest: Celebrating Your Heroes

Overview

As students complete the following project, they will determine the traits of a hero and then do research to prepare a presentation about a personal hero for a Heroes Day celebration. They will practice group problem-solving skills and will use skills from various curriculum areas to develop a presentation that has personal meaning for them.

Students will participate in the following small-group activities:

- Discuss the qualities that they most admire in others
- Identify personal heroes and arrive at a consensus about one hero for their group to introduce to the class
- Use research to explore the hero's life and accomplishments
- Plan and give a Heroes Day presentation introducing the hero
- Use language arts, science, social studies, math, art, and music skills to do research, interpret findings, and develop materials

Preparation Guide

Ask students to name some people they admire and to tell why. Encourage them to include real-life heroes, such as parents or teachers or people who have overcome disabilities, as well as heroes from novels, myths, and folklore. Stress that a hero can be male or female.

Tell students that during this project they will learn about a hero of their choice. They will explore the meaning of *hero* and think about what the choice of a hero says about themselves and our society.

Project File

Stage 1 Decide What Makes a Hero

1. Have students brainstorm to list their personal heroes.
2. Divide the class into groups. Ask students to study the list of heroes and then to freewrite or cluster to create a list of traits they consider heroic. Encourage students to develop their own definitions of the word *hero*. Have them discuss their definitions in their groups.
3. Have each group choose one hero as the focus of their project.
4. Have students use group problem-solving techniques to resolve any conflicts (see *Resources, Stage 1*).

TEAM TEACHING

The following activities may be used for team teaching or for enrichment and extension activities by the language arts teacher.

Science Discuss scientific discoveries that have helped humankind, such as the Salk polio vaccine or penicillin. Are the scientists who made these discoveries heroes? Find out about the scientists and their contributions.

Social Studies Identify heroes from history as well as famous modern figures. Identify contemporary people who may not be famous but who are heroic.

Math Investigate popularity indexes such as Gallup polls or Nielsen ratings. Learn how researchers convert raw numbers into statistics.

TEACHING TIPS

- Show films or videos about real-life heroes (see *Resources, Stage 1*).
- As the groups work, remind students to use interpersonal communication skills.
- Hold conferences with the groups to help them focus their choices.

Stage 2 Investigate a Hero

1. Direct each group's members to work cooperatively to get an overview of their hero's life and accomplishments from books, encyclopedias, newspapers, magazines, and other library materials.
2. Ask students in each group to form interview teams. Have each team interview someone who can shed additional light on the group's hero. For example, students focusing on Jonas Salk might interview a science teacher, a physician, and older relatives or friends who remember polio epidemics before the development of Salk's vaccine.
3. Instruct group members to compile their findings and then discuss and categorize the information they have found.

TEAM TEACHING

Language Arts Study research skills and interviewing skills (see *Resources, Stage 2*).

Social Studies Learn about the place and time in which the hero lived. If the hero is contemporary, learn about political events that have influenced his or her life.

Science Learn about scientific principles related to the hero's contribution.

Art Find and bring to class paintings about the hero.

Music Find songs or other musical works written about the hero.

TEACHING TIPS

- Schedule a library tour to familiarize students with reference resources.
- Invite a biographer to speak to the class about information sources and information-gathering techniques.

Stage 3
Celebrate a Hero

1. Have each group plan a presentation to share information about their hero and to show how they feel about him or her.
2. Instruct groups to create materials for their presentations. These may include students' personal writings about their heroes, either to be read aloud or to be displayed. Other materials might be taped or live songs, costumes, posters, models, photographs, drawings, and videos. Encourage students to play the roles of their heroes as part of the presentation.
3. Hold a Heroes Day at which the group presentations are given. Consider asking other classes and any local heroes who are being celebrated to attend.
4. Invite students to reflect on their experiences with the project by writing their thoughts in their journals.

TEAM TEACHING

Music Choose or compose songs about the heroes. Select and prepare appropriate music to accompany the group's presentation.

Science Build and label models illustrating inventions or discoveries.

Art Develop visuals to accompany the presentation (see *Resources, Stage 3*).

Language Arts Review techniques of personal writing. Learn about poetic devices for songs (see *Resources, Stage 3*).

TEACHING TIPS

- Share your assessment criteria with students as they begin their plans.
- Assess groups as well as individuals.
- Encourage students to use still or video cameras, tape recorders, and personal writing to create a record of the Heroes Day presentations.

Resources

STAGE 1

The Achievers (Lerner), a series of short biographical books, profiles winners who started small or overcame adversity.

One Fine Day (Ishtar Films), a brief video/film with study guide, available through the National Women's History Project, introduces numerous heroic American women of the 1700s, 1800s, and 1900s.

Black Americans: Political Leaders, Educators, and Scientists (Afro-Am Distributing Co.) provides a video survey of the achievements of Shirley Chisholm, Thurgood Marshall, and others.

Ballad of an Unsung Hero (Cinewest), a thirty minute video, chronicles the life of the Hispanic-American activist Pedro J. Gonzales.

Making Waves with Creative Problem Solving by Vaune Ainsworth-Land and Norma Fletcher teaches group problem-solving skills.

STAGE 2

Daniel Boone by Laurie Lawlor, ***Frederick Douglass and the Fight for Freedom*** by Douglas T. Miller, and ***The Story of Sacajawea, Guide to Lewis and Clark*** by Della Rowland detail the lives of three early American heroes.

The magazine ***Cable in the Classroom*** indexes current biographical programs on educational channels. Some of these programs are also available on videotape.

Cobblestone and ***Calliope,*** history magazines for young people, devote some issues to famous historical figures.

The Writer's Craft, Grade 8, Handbook 32, "Study and Research Skills," pages 340–345, and Handbook 35, "Making Use of the Library," pages 352–361, teach research skills. Handbook 36, "Interviewing Skills," page 362, offers guidelines for interviewers.

STAGE 3

The Writer's Craft, Grade 8, Workshop 1, "Personal and Expressive Writing," pages 26–44, teaches techniques of personal writing, including the writing of songs. Handbook 27, "Using Poetic Devices," pages 318–321, teaches about figurative language and sound devices.

Kidpix (Broderbund), software for Apple, IBM, or Macintosh, helps students create illustrations and graphics.

Posterworks is Macintosh software that lets students make posters and other visuals of up to 100 square feet.

Additional Projects

Those Were the Days Invite students to re-create an era of American history. Suggest that they research everyday life, political events, scientific knowledge, and technological devices of the period. Then encourage them to fabricate diaries, letters, and other personal writings that reflect the era. Ask them to present their work by transforming the classroom for a day. Have them plan displays, foods, costumes, skits, and readings.

Ways of Seeing Divide the class into groups, and have each group study a specific movement in art. Suggest that the groups examine portraits that typify the movements. Encourage students to write personal responses to the portraits, expressing the feelings and ideas that the portraits suggest to them. Their responses might range from in-depth descriptions to stories and poems. Have them present illustrated readings.

Who's Tops? Propose that students take a poll to determine what political, sports, entertainment, and historical figures other eighth graders admire and why. Have students devise questions, conduct the poll, tabulate responses, and analyze results. Invite them to create an article telling the story of their poll and sharing their thoughts and feelings about the results. Show them how to submit the article to the school or local newspaper.

Objective

- To use a quotation, art, and other writing prompts as springboards to informal writing

WRITING WARM-UPS

Encourage students to respond freely and informally to at least one of the Sketchbook prompts. Students may begin by discussing their reactions to the E.E. Cummings quotation and then freewriting in their journals. Remind them that their responses will not be graded and may provide them with useful material for other personal writing assignments.

SHOW, DON'T TELL

To help students grasp the concept of "showing" rather than "telling," you might use Handbook 13, "Show, Don't Tell," on pages 262–267 as a mini-lesson. The following is an example of a showing paragraph for the second sentence:

I've spent summers in Wisconsin with my dad ever since I was six. In the evenings, we cook out and then roast marshmallows over the backyard barbecue. On Saturday mornings he plays basketball with his friends. I play too or else goof around with their kids. But last summer, Junior Theater offered me the lead in Androcles and the Lion. *It would mean staying with my mom instead of going to Wisconsin. I love acting. But I love my dad too. I only had a week to decide. Every night that week, I woke up in the middle of the night with a stomachache.*

To be nobody-but-yourself—in a world which is doing its best, night and day, to make you everybody else—means to fight the hardest battle which any human being can fight; and never stop fighting.

E. E. Cummings
A POET'S ADVICE TO STUDENTS

- What is special about you? What makes you who you are? Jot down some of your thoughts.
- Think about something you did that made you proud. Write about the experience.

Show, Don't Tell

When you write about personal experiences, you re-create the events so that readers feel what you felt. By using examples and details, or anecdotes and descriptions, you show what happened rather than just tell about it. Turn one of the *telling* sentences below into a *showing* paragraph.

- It was one of the best moments of my life.
- I had to make a difficult decision.

Personal and Expressive Writing

Guided Assignment
Autobiographical Incident

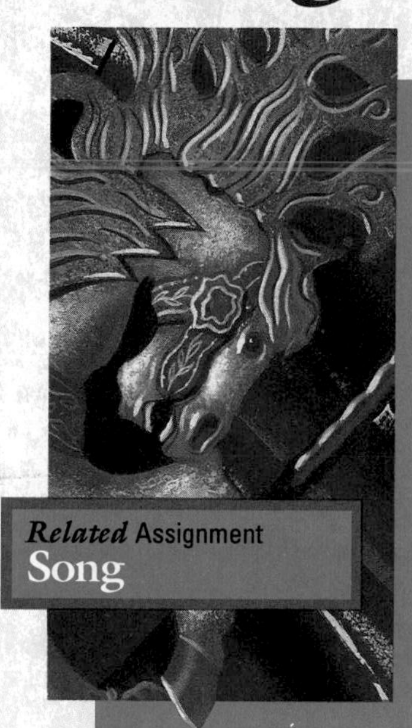

Related Assignment
Song

Autobiograpical writing is special. Only you can see the world through your eyes. Only you know what it's like to be you. In personal and expressive writing, you draw upon your own thoughts, memories, and feelings to create something no one else in the world could have produced.

This workshop will give you a chance to do this special kind of writing. It will guide you in describing an incident out of your own life. In the related assignment, you'll be able to capture a special feeling or insight and put it into a song.

Links to LITERATURE & LANGUAGE

Literature For more examples of autobiographical writing, see the following selections in *Literature and Language,* Grade 8:

- Clifton Taulbert from *Once Upon a Time When We were Colored*
- Dave Barry, "Memories of Dating"
- Julia Alvarez, "Dusting"

Writing This guided assignment may be used as an extension of the Writer's Workshop "Personal Writing: Humorous Memoir," in *Literature and Language,* Grade 8.

WRITER'S 1 WORKSHOP

Personal and Expressive Writing

Objectives

Guided Assignment

Autobiographical Incident To respond to autobiographical writing and to write a personal narrative recounting a meaningful incident in the writer's life

Related Assignment

Song To write a song lyric that expresses personal ideas, insights, or feelings

Teacher's Choice

Use the following guidelines to choose the assignment that best suits students' needs.

Autobiographical Incident All students will draw on their own experiences for this assignment, which offers a chance to write an informal personal narrative. If students have completed the Discovery Workshop, they will strengthen their understanding of the writing process by completing the assignment; if not, the assignment itself can serve as an introduction to the process. In addition, the assignment provides guided instruction in focusing, which students will use in most other kinds of writing. For these reasons, you may wish to offer this workshop early in the year.

Song This assignment gives students a chance to express their thoughts and feelings in a poetic and musical context. ESL students and some LD students may find this assignment more approachable than a prose narrative. Students can draw on personal experience both for subject matter and for format. You might include this assignment in a unit on fine arts and music or collaborate with a music teacher or local professional musician in its presentation.

Guided ASSIGNMENT

ASSIGNMENT RATIONALE

In narrating an autobiographical incident, students identify and strengthen their personal writing voices, creating the foundation for further development of writing abilities. Students also work with such critical thinking skills as sequencing, forming generalizations, and selecting supporting details.

Starting from LITERATURE

Motivate

On the chalkboard write the heading *Turning Points.* Ask students for examples of turning points in a person's life (such as starting school or moving to another town) or in their own lives if they feel comfortable sharing such information. Prompt, if necessary, by sharing a turning point in your life. Then read the Starting from Literature box with students.

BUILD ON PRIOR KNOWLEDGE

Have students recall times when they didn't fit in—perhaps when they were "new kids" in a school or an activity group. Ask volunteers to share memories and feelings. Point out that dealing with the feeling of being different from others can bring one's own identity into clearer focus.

Guided ASSIGNMENT

Autobiographical Incident

Starting from LITERATURE

Have you ever felt as if you didn't quite fit in? Growing up can be difficult, as you discover who you are—and who you're not. Leo F. Buscaglia learned an important part of this lesson when he was just about your age. This experience had such an impact on him that he wrote about it years later. As you read this excerpt from his autobiography, try to put yourself in his place. What feelings would you have had? How would you have acted?

from

PAPA WAS AN AMERICAN

by **LEO F. BUSCAGLIA**

AS I ENTERED JUNIOR HIGH, Papa and Mama, whom I had loved without question, suddenly became an embarrassment. Why couldn't they be like other parents? Why didn't they speak without accents? Why couldn't I take peanut-butter-and-jelly sandwiches in my school lunches, rather than calamari? (Yuck, the other kids said, he eats squid legs!) There seemed no escape from the painful stigma I felt in being Italian, the son of Tulio and Rosa. "Buscaglia"—even my name became a source of distress.

One day, as I left school, I found myself surrounded by a group of boys. "Dirty dago!" they shouted. "Your mom's a garlic licker. . . . Go back where you came from!"

It seemed an eternity before I was released from the circle of pushes, punches, and taunts. I wasn't really certain what the epithets meant, but I felt their sting. Humiliated and in tears, I broke free and dashed home. I locked myself in the bathroom, but I couldn't stop the tears. What had happened seemed so wrong, yet I felt helpless to do anything about it.

Papa knocked on the door. "What's the matter?" he asked. "What is it?"

I unlatched the door, and he took me in his arms. Then he sat on the edge of the bathtub with me. "Now tell," he said.

When I finished the story, I waited. I guess I expected Papa to immediately set off in search of the bullies or at least find their parents and demand retribution. But Papa didn't move.

MORE ABOUT THE MODEL

Author Note Leo F. Buscaglia (1924–), educator and author, was born into a close-knit family of Italian immigrants in Los Angeles, where his parents owned a restaurant. The model is taken from his 1989 memoir *Papa, My Father: A Celebration of Dads.* Buscaglia has said, "I realized after [my father] died . . . that as close as I was to him and as much as I loved him, he really died a stranger to me. . . . Should I have considered asking him more of the questions that really pertained to him? Then he might not have died a comparative stranger. That for me was the great lesson of writing this book."

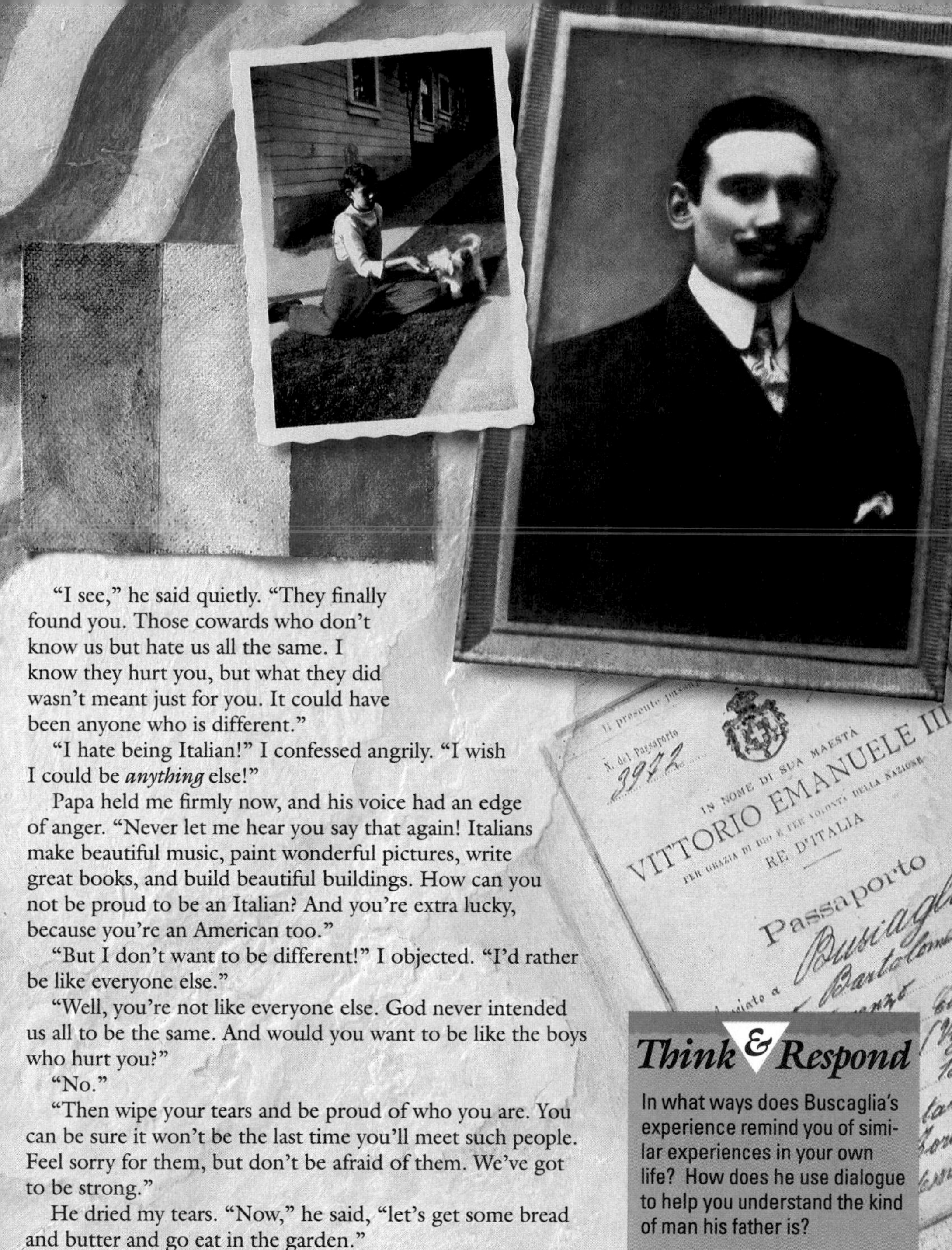

"I see," he said quietly. "They finally found you. Those cowards who don't know us but hate us all the same. I know they hurt you, but what they did wasn't meant just for you. It could have been anyone who is different."

"I hate being Italian!" I confessed angrily. "I wish I could be *anything* else!"

Papa held me firmly now, and his voice had an edge of anger. "Never let me hear you say that again! Italians make beautiful music, paint wonderful pictures, write great books, and build beautiful buildings. How can you not be proud to be an Italian? And you're extra lucky, because you're an American too."

"But I don't want to be different!" I objected. "I'd rather be like everyone else."

"Well, you're not like everyone else. God never intended us all to be the same. And would you want to be like the boys who hurt you?"

"No."

"Then wipe your tears and be proud of who you are. You can be sure it won't be the last time you'll meet such people. Feel sorry for them, but don't be afraid of them. We've got to be strong."

He dried my tears. "Now," he said, "let's get some bread and butter and go eat in the garden."

Think & Respond

In what ways does Buscaglia's experience remind you of similar experiences in your own life? How does he use dialogue to help you understand the kind of man his father is?

SET A PURPOSE Direct students to the purpose-setting statement and questions at the end of the Starting from Literature box. You might then ask a student to read Buscaglia's first paragraph aloud. Ask the class to respond. Explain that calamari is squid, an Italian delicacy. Ask students what they might do if others teased them about their lunches. Have them read the rest of the model on their own. Suggest that they stop periodically and ask themselves "How would I handle this?"; "What would I do?"

Think & Respond

ELICIT PERSONAL RESPONSES

As students consider the first Think & Respond question, point out that the details of their experiences need not be the same as Buscaglia's. The similarity may lie in the emotions the experience aroused or in its importance to the student. Have students freewrite responses to that question. For the second question, ask students to supply adjectives that describe Buscaglia's father. (Sample: warm, strong, wise) Then ask which of his words show these traits. (Sample: wise—". . . what they did wasn't meant just for you. It could have been anyone who is different.")

EXPLORE THE AUTHOR'S TECHNIQUE

You might have students speculate about what the incident in the model meant to Buscaglia. (Samples: It helped him see who he was; it helped him feel proud of himself and of his heritage.) Ask where Buscaglia tells us the incident's meaning. (He doesn't.) Then ask how he shows the incident's meaning. (First, he portrays himself as tearful, humiliated, and angry at being Italian; then he portrays himself as realizing that he wouldn't want to be like the boys who attacked him for being different.)

MULTICULTURAL Connection

Call students' attention to Tulio Buscaglia's assertion that "Italians make beautiful music, paint wonderful pictures, write great books, and build beautiful buildings." Urge them to search social studies texts and other references for examples of each accomplishment. (Samples: the Colosseum, the *Mona Lisa, The Divine Comedy, Rigoletto)*

turning point
details
dialogue

Reading a STUDENT MODEL

Both Leo Buscaglia and Brook Volle learned important lessons from experiences with an "in" group—Buscaglia from being excluded, and Volle from reaching out to include someone new. Brook's autobiographical incident is the final draft of the piece that students see in process on the workshop pages that follow.

Motivate

Point out that school isn't the only place where people learn. Ask students to think about "life lessons" that are learned outside of school—for example, principles about getting along with others that we learn from our reading, from the media, and especially from our own experience. Encourage students to give examples and to comment on any "life lessons" that they have found particularly practical.

BUILD ON PRIOR KNOWLEDGE

On the chalkboard write the adage "You can't judge a book by its cover." Ask students how this saying might apply to people. Encourage students to offer examples of times when they have judged someone (or have themselves been judged) on the basis of appearance or first impressions. Did their judgments turn out to be right, wrong, or a little of both? How did they learn what the person was really like?

SET A PURPOSE

Go over the Reading a Student Model box with the class. Explain that on the first page of this model, the writer describes her expectations; on the second page, she shows what really happened. Have students pause at the end of the first page and notice some of Brook's expectations about Jorgina. As they read the second page, have them decide which expectations proved true and which did not.

One Student's Writing

Reading a STUDENT MODEL

Sometimes people turn out to be different from what we expect before we meet them. That's what happened to Brook Volle, a student at Harold J. Brinley Junior High School. Brook wrote about an experience she had during the preceding summer. Notice how things don't go the way she expects them to—and how making a new friend changes the way she thinks about others.

A Lesson Learned Well

Brook Volle

It was a Wednesday night in mid-June when I first met Jorgina. My youth group was having an activity to prepare us for camp. My leader started calling out names for the tent assignments.

Just as I thought my name would never be called, I heard it, along with Kari's, Cynthia's, and Jorgina's. I didn't know Kari very well, but I knew I could probably get along with her. Cynthia I knew was very quiet and shy. Then there was Jorgina. Wasn't she the new girl all the boys were drooling over?

At that moment I glanced up at the door and saw a girl who was probably no older than myself. She reminded me of a princess in a fairy tale. I immediately assumed she was Jorgina—perfect in every way. Not one hair on her head was out of place. Her face looked like that of a porcelain doll. Her clothes were immaculate. Her whole appearance made me think of a future Miss Universe.

"How am I going to spend a whole week in the mountains with a girl who will probably faint every time she cracks a nail?" I questioned myself.

Our leader brought Jorgina over to our group.

"Girls, this is Jorgina Jorgenson. She just moved to Las Vegas from a small town in Utah. I'm sure you'll all become good friends," my leader exclaimed with a false smile.

"Hi ya, girls," Jorgina said with too much enthusiasm. We all just stared at her like she was an alien invading our private space. "So, what's it like in Las Vegas?" she asked nervously.

"It's ok," I commented, trying to avoid eye contact. "What's it like where you came from?" I asked.

30 Workshop 1

for FURTHER READING

Story to Read Students who enjoyed Brook Volle's insights about prejudging others may also enjoy Langston Hughes's short story "Thank You, Ma'am." In it, a boy learns that an older woman is more than she appears to be and gains a new view of himself as well.

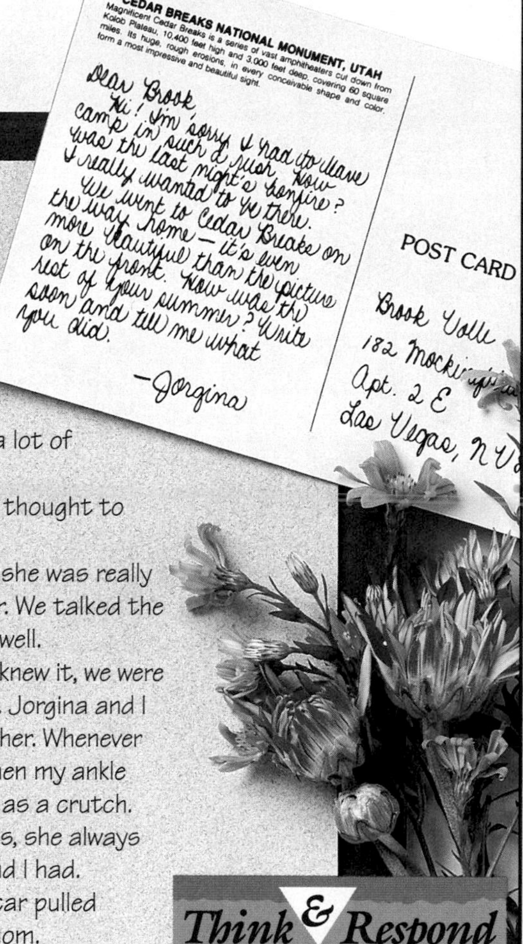

CEDAR BREAKS NATIONAL MONUMENT, UTAH
Magnificent Cedar Breaks is a series of vast amphitheaters cut down from Kolob Plateau, 10,400 feet high and 3,000 feet deep, covering 60 square miles. Its huge, rough erosions, in every conceivable shape and color, form a most impressive and beautiful sight.

Dear Brook,
Hi! I'm sorry I had to leave camp in such a rush. How was the last night's bonfire? I really wanted to be there. We went to Cedar Breaks on the way home — it's even more beautiful than the picture on the front. How was the rest of your summer? Write soon and tell me what you did.

—Jorgina

POST CARD

Brook Volle
182 Mocking
Apt. 2 E
Las Vegas, NV

"It's just great!" she said with a smile. "I lived on a farm. We had a river and a pond in our back yard!"

"What did you do for entertainment?" I questioned. I was more interested in her than I had hoped to be.

"Oh, we would always go exploring through the woods. Plus, there was a mall. I also spent a lot of time at gymnastics," she replied.

"So maybe she's not such a snob after all," I thought to myself.

I decided to give her a chance to prove what she was really like instead of just making judgments about her. We talked the rest of the evening, and I got to know her quite well.

The next two weeks slipped by, and before we knew it, we were in camp at Beaver High Adventure Base in Utah. Jorgina and I became very trusting and dependent on each other. Whenever she had a problem, I tried to help her solve it. When my ankle started to give me problems, she let me use her as a crutch. When I wanted to go tromping through the woods, she always came with me. She quickly became the best friend I had.

On the last day of camp, tragedy struck. A car pulled into our campsite, and out stepped Jorgina's mom.

"Jorgina," she said, "you need to get your stuff, 'cause we're movin' back home tonight."

I went with Jorgina to our tent and helped her pack. Then we said our goodbyes and she left.

We still keep in touch, and every once in a while, she comes to visit. Jorgina made a great impression on my life and taught me a very important lesson. Because of her I've promised myself never again to judge people because of their appearance.

Think & Respond

Respond as a Reader

▸ How would you have first reacted to Jorgina?

▸ Why do you think Brook's feelings changed?

Respond as a Writer

▸ What descriptive details help you understand Brook's initial reaction?

▸ How does she show the reader her own changes in attitude?

Think & Respond

RESPOND AS A READER

▶ You might let the class respond orally to the first question. Boys' responses may be very different from girls'. Use the differences to help students see that Think & Respond questions seldom call for one "right" answer. In fact, responses should reflect students' individuality.

▶ For the second question, suggest that students use freewriting. Direct them to focus first on their impressions of Brook's interests and values. Then have them speculate about what changed her feelings toward Jorgina.

RESPOND AS A WRITER

▶ Students should notice the following descriptions of Jorgina on the first page of the model: paragraph 2, lines 5–6; all of paragraph 3; all of paragraph 7. They also should note details that Brook uses to show her own personality: paragraph 2, lines 2–3; all of paragraph 4; paragraph 7, line 2; all of paragraph 8.

▶ For the second question, suggest that students freewrite to sum up the changes in Brook's feelings. Then have them skim the second page of the model for parts that show how Brook ended up feeling about Jorgina.

Draw Conclusions

To make sure students understand this introduction to personal and expressive writing, challenge them to list the characteristics they have noticed in both models. Responses may include:

- tells the story of an experience important to the writer
- shows what the experience means to the writer
- uses specific details to establish setting and character
- may make use of dialogue

Writing ON YOUR OWN

Point out that students tell about autobiographical incidents every day—for example, when telling friends what happened at home. Invite students to choose a memorable incident to write about. Urge them to use specific details and dialogue to show how the event became meaningful, as Buscaglia and Volle have done.

Handbooks for Help and Practice

The following handbooks may be used as mini-lessons before students begin writing or as resources when problems arise.

- **Discovering Writing Ideas, pp. 218–223**
- **Writing Dialogue, pp. 324–327**

PREWRITE AND EXPLORE

Objectives

- To use prewriting techniques to select a topic for an autobiographical incident
- To gather details for a first-person narrative

Teaching Strategies

for LOOK FOR AN INCIDENT

HELPFUL HINT Students may remember incidents that evoked strong feelings but may not completely understand their significance. Encourage them to begin making notes even without that understanding; the meaning may reveal itself during students' prewriting explorations. If they still are not satisfied with their insights but have enough material to begin drafting, encourage them to do so—at that point the fragments of meaning may come together.

Writing ON YOUR OWN
Autobiographical Incident

INVITATION TO Write

Leo F. Buscaglia and Brook Volle both had experiences that changed the way they think. Both writers gained a greater understanding of themselves and of their experiences after writing about them.

Write about an incident in your life that stands out in your memory or has special meaning for you. Help your readers understand why you wanted to write about the experience.

PREWRITE AND EXPLORE

1. Look for an incident. Look back through your life for a special moment. It might be funny or frightening, sad or embarrassing—maybe something you learned from. It could be moving into a new neighborhood, feeling close to a grandparent, or losing a pet. Here are strategies for finding a special memory to write about.

Exploring Topics

- **Categories** Jot down terms like "summertime," "holidays," "accidents," "moving," "grandparents," and "pets." Maybe, like Leo Buscaglia, you'll find a term like "Papa" that brings back a powerful memory. **Brainstorm** to find memories that you associate with these terms.
- **Snapshots** Browse through personal or family photo albums. Try freewriting about the pictures to see where your thoughts lead. Use a **cluster diagram** to follow up on any promising topics.
- **Famous firsts** Do you remember your first bicycle, ice skates, or skateboard or your first teacher, friend, or pet? How about your first job, your first painful loss, your first vacation, or your first dance? Choose one and **freewrite** about it.

PROBLEM SOLVING

"How can I find an incident to write about?"

For help finding ideas, see

- Sketchbook, page 26
- Springboards, page 45
- Handbook 1, "Discovering Writing Ideas," pages 218–223

Science Connection

You might use excerpts from accounts by scientists and naturalists such as *Through a Window: My Thirty Years with the Chimpanzees of Gambe,* by Jane Goodall, *King Solomon's Ring,* by Konrad Lorenz, or *Never Cry Wolf,* by Farley Mowat to point out that experiences with the natural world can be deeply meaningful. Suggest that students interested in ecology, animal behavior, biology, or astronomy consider writing about experiences related to those interests. They might, for example, write about gaining a key insight or observing an unusual phenomenon.

One Student's Process

Brook Volle started with the idea of summer and used a clustering technique to look for memories and associations of summer. Her cluster looked like this:

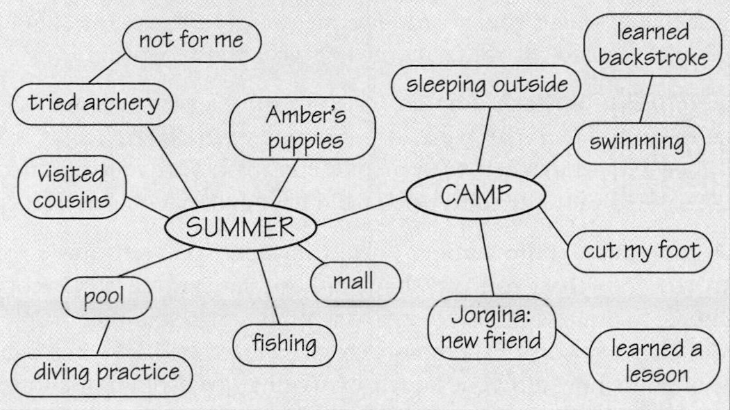

2. Select an idea and begin exploring it. Try one or more of the following ideas to help get you started.

- **Sharing with others** Jot down four or five incidents that stand out in your memory as special—even if you don't know why. Then briefly describe each of them to a small group of classmates. Which incident seems most important, powerful, or puzzling—something the others would like to know more about?
- **Jumping in** If you like, just begin writing about the experience. Go back to it in your mind and start at whatever point seems most interesting. As you write, look for meaning in the incident, the reason you care about it.
- **Mental snapshot** Imagine a snapshot of the most important moment of your experience. Hold that picture in your mind and quickly make some notes. What do you see—what people, objects, scenery? What do you smell and hear? How are you feeling, physically and emotionally? What is the story you can't see, the story behind the snapshot? Try to capture on paper as many sensory details as you can.

COMPUTER TIP

If you tend to slow down during freewriting, always correcting what you write, try writing at a computer with the screen turned off. Turn it on sometimes to see what you've written.

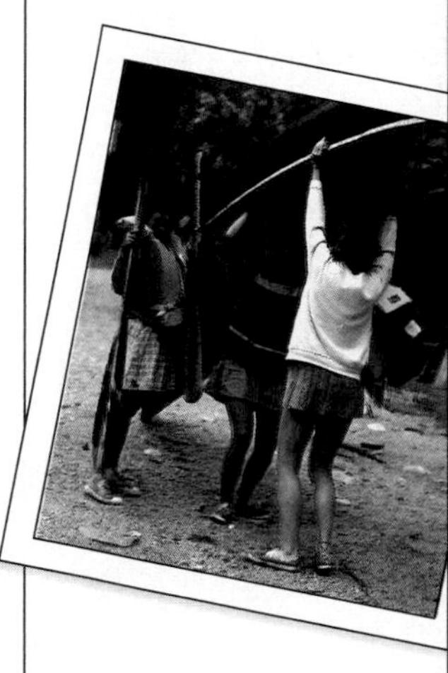

SPICE BOX

Improvisation is an exciting way for students to explore their topics. Call on volunteers to use body movements and facial expressions to improvise incidents similar to the following:

- the first time they learned to ride a bicycle
- the day they got a pet puppy or kitten
- the time they burned a batch of cookies while baking

As students do these improvisations, point out that they may gain insights that will enliven the writing of their autobiographical incident.

for ONE STUDENT'S PROCESS

KEY TO UNDERSTANDING Explain that Brook began by clustering what the word *summer* brought to mind. She then chose the idea she felt most interested in *(camp)* and made another cluster around it. Point out that many of the ideas in the second cluster are more specific than those in the first. (For example, "cut my foot" is one incident, whereas "fishing" covers many; "Jorgina: new friend" focuses on one person, whereas "visited cousins" refers to several.) Suggest that students try a second cluster or freewriting to narrow a broad subject to a more specific topic.

for SELECT AN IDEA . . .

COLLABORATIVE OPPORTUNITY If students are having trouble thinking of incidents to write about, suggest that they work in small groups. Give them several "titles," such as "My Proudest Day," "My Most Embarrassing Moment," or "A Lesson I'll Never Forget." Have students take turns selecting a title and telling a true story that it calls to mind. Hearing their classmates' memories may trigger more memories of their own.

for MENTAL SNAPSHOT

INDIVIDUALIZING INSTRUCTION: VISUAL LEARNERS You might suggest that rather than work from a "mental snapshot," students actually sketch one or more scenes from their experiences. Emphasize that the act of drawing and the sketch itself can help them recall details of the experience, its setting, and their feelings.

GENERAL NOTE

MANAGING THE PAPER LOAD To save time later, confer briefly with students during prewriting. Be sure that students have chosen one incident rather than a series of events and that they are generating enough details to support a draft. For those who need more specifics, you might provide additional help by assigning page 3 on observation from the Thinking Skills Worksheets.

DRAFT AND DISCOVER

Objectives

- To draft an autobiographical incident, choosing details that show rather than tell
- To create unified narrative paragraphs
- To respond to one's own draft and to that of a peer

Teaching Strategies

for BEGIN DRAFTING

INDIVIDUALIZING INSTRUCTION: ESL STUDENTS Some ESL students may find that they are stopping to grope for English terms. Suggest that they simply leave a blank and go on. Explain that during revision they can check dictionaries, consult you, or ask peers about the terms they need. To increase their working vocabularies, students should list the new terms and write their definitions in English in small "personal dictionary" notebooks.

Writing **TIP**

Try to grab your readers' interest at the start, perhaps with a bit of action or dialogue.

DRAFT AND DISCOVER

1. Begin drafting. Try focusing on that mental snapshot of the event you chose to write about, and start there. As you write, you may discover things you hadn't remembered earlier. That's fine—just follow where your words and memories lead. You can always go back later to change or reorganize what you've written.

Writer's Choice Is your story a very personal one? You may wish to tell about your experience as if it happened to someone else instead of to you. If so, use the third person and have a narrator tell the story.

2. Include specific details. Your incident will seem more real to your readers if you can show, rather than just tell, your story. Brook doesn't say that Jorgina was pretty. She says that Jorgina was "the new girl all the boys were drooling over." Leo Buscaglia shows just how different he felt by writing, "Why couldn't I take peanut-butter-and-jelly sandwiches in my school lunches, rather than calamari? (Yuck, the other kids said, he eats squid legs!)"

Paragraphs at Work In autobiographical writing, a paragraph might not need a topic sentence. Make sure, however, that all the sentences in a paragraph contribute to a main idea or focus. Look, for example, at Brook's third paragraph. All of its details have the same focus: Jorgina's hair, face, and clothes; fairy-tale princess; Miss Universe. The reader gets a unified impression of Jorgina as Brook saw her. Remember these tips.

- Not every paragraph has a topic sentence.
- Every paragraph should have a single main idea or focus.

3. Conclude your draft. How do you know when to stop writing? You can end after you've fully described what happened, or you can summarize what you learned or tell why the incident is important to you.

4. Reflect on your writing. Decide whether you'd like to show your draft to a reader now or work on it some more first. If you do want to make changes at this time, read over the questions for yourself under "Review Your Writing."

REVIEW YOUR WRITING

Questions for Yourself

- What part of this incident do I care most about?
- What details can I add so that I show instead of tell?
- How have I made clear where and when the events took place?
- Have I shown why the experience is important to me?
- Is my order of events clear? Does the piece make sense from beginning to end?

Questions for Your Peer Readers

- How did you react to the experience I wrote about?
- What parts helped you really feel or understand what I was describing?
- What would you like to know more about?
- Which passages seemed most memorable or striking?

One Student's Process

Here is part of Brook's first draft. She asked a classmate to read it and offer some reactions. How would you have responded?

My leader said she knew we would all become good friends, but I wasn't sure she meant it. When Jorgina said hi, we all just stared at her like she was an alien invading our private space. Finally she asked us what Las Vegas is like.

"It's ok," I commented, trying to avoid eye contact. She looked so neat and clean. I was wondering if she had a ton of friends at home and if she would fit in here. I asked her what it was like where she came from.

"It's just great," she said with a smile. "I lived on a farm. We had a river and a pond in our back yard!"

Peer Reader Comments

Why weren't you sure?

I like the alien part. What was Jorgina really saying and doing?

The eye contact part works for me—really shows your feelings.

This really gets across an idea of her personality.

for QUESTIONS FOR YOURSELF

CRITICAL THINKING: EVALUATING Suggest that students reflect on whether the significance of the incident has become clearer to them or perhaps even changed during drafting. If necessary, they can rework their drafts to reveal any new insight. Remind them that they can add details to make key events more vivid and they can condense less important parts of their narrative.

for QUESTIONS FOR YOUR PEER READERS

PEER RESPONSE Suggest that peer reviewers read the draft at least twice before responding to the Questions for Your Peer Readers. Tell writers that they may add their own questions to the list; for example, "What do you think this experience meant to me?"

for ONE STUDENT'S PROCESS

KEY TO UNDERSTANDING Point out that Brook's classmate asked specific questions and commented on specific words and phrases rather than making such general remarks as "This is a good draft." Invite students to offer specific responses to Brook's draft.

TEACHER'S LOUNGE

"Teacher burnout."

REVISE YOUR WRITING

Objectives

- To evaluate responses to a draft of personal writing and to revise a draft with those responses in mind
- To use chronological order to organize a narrative

Teaching Strategies

for REVIEW THE RESPONSES . . .

HELPFUL HINT: REVISING Discuss ways in which students might use their peer responses. For example, if a peer couldn't picture what the writer was describing, the writer might add dialogue, details showing setting, or other descriptive details. If a peer misunderstood the incident's significance, the writer might add details showing his or her feelings. Stress, however, that peer comments are only suggestions. Writers make the final decisions.

for CHECK YOUR ORGANIZATION

CRITICAL THINKING: SEQUENCING Discuss the model storyboard, having students compare it to the student model on pages 30–31. Encourage students to use this technique to check the narrative sequence in their drafts.

As student need or interest dictates, you might have students consider how transitions can strengthen narrative sequence. You can use Handbook 15, "Coherence", on pages 273–277 for this purpose.

for CHECK YOUR ORGANIZATION

INDIVIDUALIZING INSTRUCTION: ADVANCED STUDENTS Encourage these students to try using flashbacks or flashforwards. For example, students might open with a vivid scene from the end of the incident and then go back to tell how this scene came about. Alternatively, they might pause in the narration and jump ahead to the present. Emphasize that the careful use of transitions will keep readers oriented during these leaps in time. (See note above.)

REVISE YOUR WRITING

Writing TIP

You may want to use a flashback, pausing in your story to tell about an earlier event.

1. Review the responses of your readers. Look over the responses to the questions you asked yourself and your peer readers. Remember that you get to decide which changes you would like to make.

2. Check your organization. Whether you start your story at the beginning, the middle, or the end, you'll need to make clear the order of the events. Brook tells her story in chronological order—that is, she begins on the Wednesday night she first met Jorgina, and she winds up in the present.

Making a time line or storyboard may help you plan the sequence of events in your story. Here is a storyboard for Brook's autobiographical incident.

hi!
1.
MEET JORGINA — THINK SHE MIGHT BE A SNOB
SHE'S NOT SO BAD
2.
BEGIN TO LIKE HER
3.
SHARE CAMP EXPERIENCES
4.
BECOME GOOD FRIENDS
bye.
5.
JORGINA LEAVES
?
6.
LEARN NOT TO PREJUDGE

Grammar Connection

Some students' incidents may involve characters whose speech reflects a specific cultural background and distinctive features in grammar, usage, and mechanics. Encourage these students to catch the flavor of dialects and other speech patterns as they write dialogue. For example, Brook uses interjections such as "Hi ya," and "So," to capture her own speech habits as well as Jorgina's. She uses nonstandard spellings such as "'cause" and "movin'" to recreate the pronunciation used by Jorgina's mother.

One Student's Process

Brook considered her classmate's reactions. She decided to add details to make the behavior of the characters clearer and to help readers see and experience what happened. She made even more changes later.

¶"Hi ya, girls," Jorgina said with too much enthusiasm.

~~My leader said she knew we would~~ "I'm sure you'll all become good friends," my leader exclaimed with a false smile. ~~but I wasn't sure she meant it.~~ ~~When Jorgina said hi,~~ We all just stared at her like she was an alien invading our private space. ~~Finally she asked us what~~ "So, what's it like in Las Vegas?" she asked nervously. ~~is like.~~

"It's ok," I commented, trying to avoid eye contact. She looked so neat and clean. I was wondering if she had a ton of friends at home and if she would fit in here. I asked, ~~her~~ "What's it ~~was~~ like where ~~she~~ you came from?"

"It's just great," she said with a smile. "I lived on a farm. We had a river and a pond in our back yard!"

¶ "What did you do for entertainment?" I questioned. I was more interested in her than I had hoped to be. "So maybe she's not such a snob after all," I thought to myself.

for ONE STUDENT'S PROCESS

HELPFUL HINT You might have students locate places where Brook replaced "telling" words with "showing" details. (Samples: "my leader exclaimed with a false smile"; "'So what's it like in Las Vegas?' she asked nervously.")

for ONE STUDENT'S PROCESS

SPEAKING AND LISTENING Point out that Brook added several pieces of dialogue to her draft. Remind students again that dialogue can be an effective way to show rather than tell. You might pair students who are using dialogue and have them take turns reading their dialogue sections aloud to each other. This activity can help writers locate places where slight changes might make dialogue sound more natural.

for ONE STUDENT'S PROCESS

CRITICAL THINKING: ANALYZING With students, compare this revision to the final draft on pages 30–31. Ask them to speculate about why Brook omitted the sentences "She looked so neat and clean. I was wondering if she had a ton of friends at home and if she would fit in here" from her final draft. If students seem at a loss, ask whether the sentences repeat ideas that Brook expressed elsewhere. (Both repeat ideas that Brook stated or suggested in paragraph 3 of the final draft.) Help students to see that the unnecessary repetition of ideas can weaken a draft, just as the unnecessary repetition of words can.

GENERAL NOTE

MANAGING THE PAPER LOAD Before students begin their final revisions, invite them, on a voluntary basis, to have you check their work for clear chronological order. If necessary, suggest rearranging paragraphs or inserting transitions to clarify the sequence of events. Suggesting these changes now can save time when you evaluate final revisions.

PROOFREAD

Teaching Strategies

for LINKING MECHANICS AND WRITING

HELPFUL HINT Suggest that if students are unsure about whether the second part of a divided quotation should begin with a capitalized word, they should write out the quotation without the dividing phrase. Demonstrate with the model sentence from the text; on the chalkboard write, "She said, 'Jorgina, you need to get your stuff 'cause we're moving back home tonight.'" Students will see that capitalizing "you" would be incorrect.

Guidelines for Evaluation

IDEAS AND CONTENT

- recounts a personal experience accurately
- shows the meaning of the experience to the writer
- includes enough descriptive details to make setting and characters clear
- has an effective introduction and satisfying conclusion

STRUCTURE AND FORM

- displays clear chronological order of events
- presents a single focus in each paragraph

GRAMMAR, USAGE, AND MECHANICS

- displays standard spelling, usage, and mechanics
- punctuates dialogue correctly

GENERAL NOTE

ASSESSMENT Consider using primary trait scoring for this assignment. Because the assignment stresses the importance of personal insights and specific detail, you might make content the primary trait, awarding high content scores to papers that include sufficient showing details to recount the incident vividly and to show its meaning for the writer.

Standards for Evaluation

PERSONAL WRITING

An autobiographical incident

- explores an experience important to the writer and shows why it was important
- draws the reader in at the beginning and concludes in a satisfying way
- makes the setting clear—where things happen
- gives a good sense of time, place, and character through vivid sensory details and possibly dialogue
- helps readers follow the order of events in time

PROOFREAD

1. Proofread your work. Check your work for errors in grammar, capitalization, punctuation, and spelling.

LINKING MECHANICS AND WRITING

Punctuating Dialogue

If you divide a quotation with a phrase such as "he said," don't capitalize the first word of the second part unless it begins a new sentence. Any comma or period at the end of a quotation goes inside the closing quotation marks. Notice how Brook followed these rules.

Original

"Jorgina," she said, "You need to get your stuff 'cause we're movin' back home tonight."

Revised

"Jorgina," she said, "you need to get your stuff 'cause we're movin' back home tonight."

For more information about punctuating dialogue, see Handbook 49, "Punctuation," pages 651, 664, and 665.

2. Make a clean copy of your writing. Are you satisfied with your work? Give your piece a final check, using the Standards for Evaluation listed in the margin. Make any additional changes you feel are necessary and make a final copy.

PUBLISH AND PRESENT

- **Share your experience.** Send your writing to friends, relatives, or other people involved in your experience. Ask for responses.
- **Have a readers' theater.** In a performance for the class, different class members can read or act out their stories.

- **Publish your story.** Print your class's stories in a class magazine or submit them to a schoolwide literary magazine.
- **Display your story.** Make a class bulletin-board display, including any drawings or photographs that could illustrate the stories.

REFLECT ON YOUR WRITING

WRITER TO WRITER

Good writers write to find out about themselves.

Gloria Steinem, writer

FOR YOUR **PORTFOLIO**

1. Add your writing to your portfolio. Now that you have written about an autobiographical incident and have read two others, think about your writing process. Jot down answers to some or all of the following questions, and attach your answers to your piece when it goes into your portfolio.

- How did I decide what to write about?
- What kinds of changes did I make after my first draft?
- What could I learn about myself from my story?
- What did I most enjoy about this assignment? What didn't I like?
- What writing techniques from my own piece or from the autobiographical incidents I read did I especially like? Which ones could I try again in another piece of writing?

2. Explore additional writing ideas. See the suggestions for writing a song on pages 42–44 and Springboards on page 45.

Reteaching

After students have completed their papers, assess the needs of students who were not successful in developing an autobiographical incident; then assign the appropriate handbook mini-lessons as well as the workshop Support Materials listed in the Teaching Preview, pages 25a–25b. Concepts commonly requiring reteaching for this assignment are listed below.

- **Handbook 12, Methods of Elaboration, pp. 255–261**
- **Handbook 26, Developing a Personal Voice, pp. 316–317**

The following suggestions and resources may also be useful.

Irrelevant Details Use pages 1–4 from the Elaboration, Revision, and Proofreading Transparency Pack to show students how to identify and delete (or replace) irrelevant details.

Flat Introductions In students' literature texts, point out first-person narrative openers with strong action or vivid description. Group students and have them find other examples of engaging introductions.

Extension and Enrichment

1. Give students the following scenario: You are now seventy-five years old. Look back on your life; then write about the day you attained a cherished dream.

2. Suggest that students take the point of view of a fly outside the window and narrate, in detail, one event that happened in class this week.

Closure: Reflect on Your Writing

Ask whether students are familiar with the process of reflecting on their writing. If they are, have them choose two questions to respond to. If they are not, explain that the questions are intended to help them learn about themselves as writers. Model typical answers. Then suggest that students choose only one of the questions.

Related ASSIGNMENT

Appreciating a SONG

Objectives

- To respond to and analyze a song lyric
- To create a song lyric that expresses the writer's ideas, thoughts, or feelings

Motivate

Song lyrics have meaning by themselves, but they come to life when joined with a melody. If at all possible, therefore, play a recording of Joni Mitchell's "The Circle Game" for students. Then have students share their general responses to it. Ask, for example:

How does it make you feel?
Which lines and phrases do you like or dislike?
What do you think the song is about?

BUILD ON PRIOR KNOWLEDGE

Point out that popular songs can carry messages that affect listeners deeply. You might mention a song whose lyrics affected you when you were growing up. Then ask students to tell about songs that have meaning for them.

SET A PURPOSE

As you read Appreciating a Song with students, you might create a class list of popular songs that do each of the things mentioned. As students suggest examples, tell them to observe how some songs do more than one thing. Then direct students' attention to the purpose-setting questions. Tell them to decide, as they read, whether "The Circle Game" does one, several, or all of the things mentioned. Have students read the song silently; then ask volunteers to read it aloud.

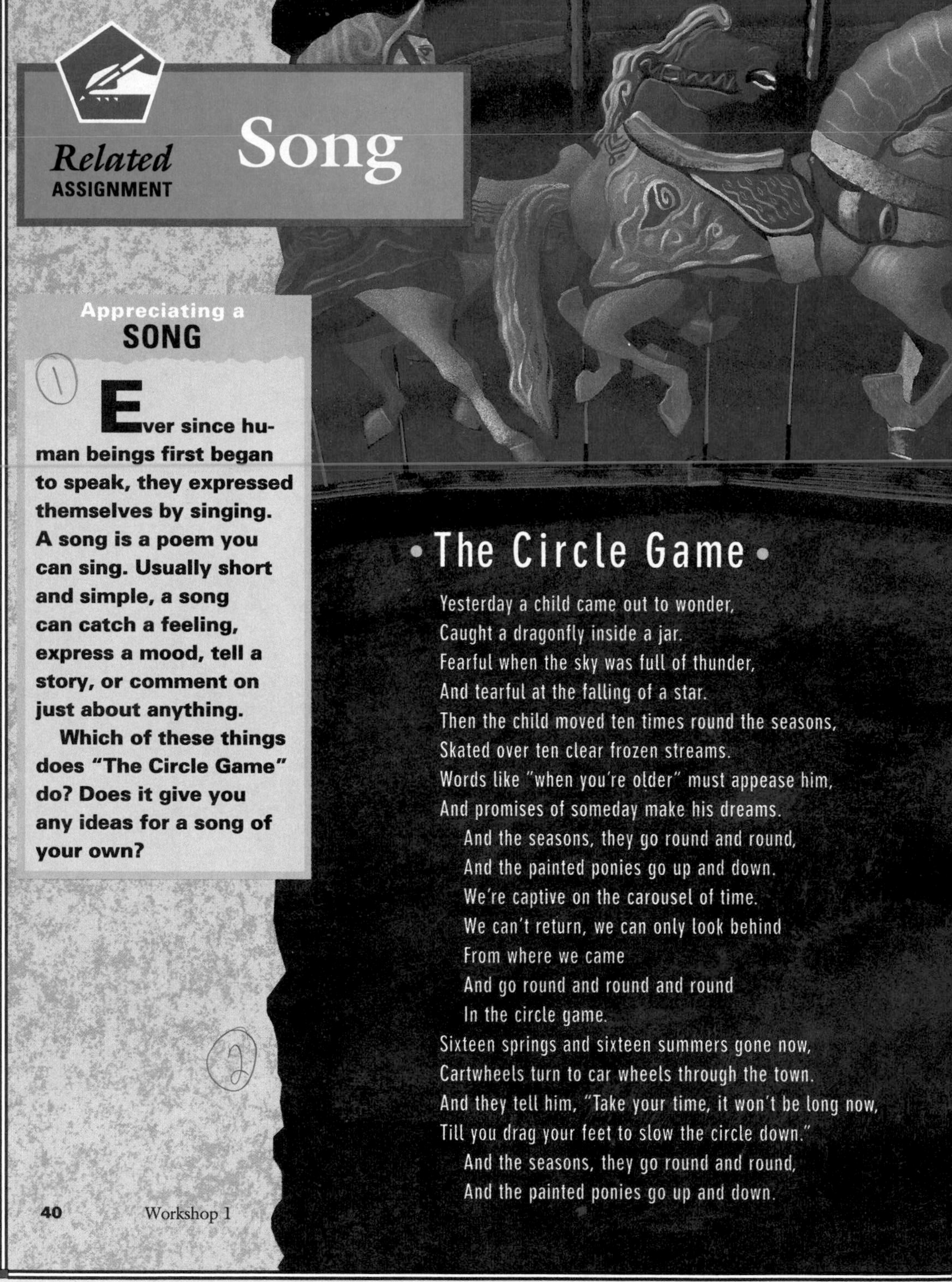

Related ASSIGNMENT

Song

Appreciating a SONG

Ever since human beings first began to speak, they expressed themselves by singing. A song is a poem you can sing. Usually short and simple, a song can catch a feeling, express a mood, tell a story, or comment on just about anything.

Which of these things does "The Circle Game" do? Does it give you any ideas for a song of your own?

• The Circle Game •

Yesterday a child came out to wonder,
Caught a dragonfly inside a jar.
Fearful when the sky was full of thunder,
And tearful at the falling of a star.
Then the child moved ten times round the seasons,
Skated over ten clear frozen streams.
Words like "when you're older" must appease him,
And promises of someday make his dreams.
And the seasons, they go round and round,
And the painted ponies go up and down.
We're captive on the carousel of time.
We can't return, we can only look behind
From where we came
And go round and round and round
In the circle game.
Sixteen springs and sixteen summers gone now,
Cartwheels turn to car wheels through the town.
And they tell him, "Take your time, it won't be long now,
Till you drag your feet to slow the circle down."
And the seasons, they go round and round,
And the painted ponies go up and down.

40 Workshop 1

Literature Connection

Author Note Joni Mitchell (1943–), award-winning songwriter and singer, was born in Fort MacLeod, Alberta, and raised in Saskatoon, Saskatchewan. As a child, she taught herself guitar from a Pete Seeger instruction book. Her songs include "Both Sides Now," "Big Yellow Taxi," and "Woodstock," which celebrates the famous 1969 rock music festival. "The Circle Game" first appeared on her 1970 album *Ladies of the Canyon*. An accomplished artist who creates her own album covers, Mitchell compares songwriting to "going into a trance." To write a song, she says, "I sit down with a melody and reminisce."

We're captive on the carousel of time.
We can't return, we can only look behind
From where we came
And go round and round and round
In the circle game.
So the years spin by and now the boy is twenty,
Though his dreams have lost some grandeur coming true.
There'll be new dreams, maybe better dreams, and plenty,
Before the last revolving year is through.
And the seasons, they go round and round,
And the painted ponies go up and down,
We're captive on the carousel of time.
We can't return, we can only look behind
From where we came
And go round and round and round
In the circle game.

—Joni Mitchell

Think & Respond

What does the child seem to want as he grows up? Why does the image of a carousel, or merry-go-round, seem appropriate? How does Joni Mitchell use verses to organize the ideas in her song?

Think & Respond

ELICIT PERSONAL RESPONSES

You might begin by asking students to **describe** the images the song leaves in their minds. Then guide the class in answering the Think & Respond questions orally. Suggest that they scan the song for references to the boy's dreams and to the advice he gets from others. By rereading these lines, they can infer what he wants (to be mature and independent).

To help the class explore the second question, ask, "How is a carousel ride like a lifetime, according to the song?"

For the third question, point out that the indented sections are a chorus, separating and drawing conclusions about the verses. Have students sum up the events or ideas in each verse. Help them to see that the verses tell a story in chronological order.

EXPLORE THE AUTHOR'S TECHNIQUES

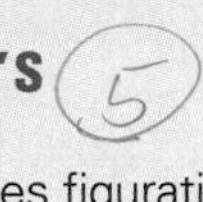

Point out how Mitchell uses figurative language to express her central idea; then tell students that they can use figurative language to make their own songs memorable. Explain that in figurative language, one thing is likened to another; for example, Mitchell refers to "the carousel of time." Ask students to locate other examples of figurative language in the song. (Samples: "moved ten times round the seasons"; "cartwheels turn to car wheels"; "drag your feet to slow the circle down")

Explain that Mitchell also uses repetition for emphasis and that students can use this technique in their songs as well. Point out her repetition of key words *(round, dreams)* and key images (circles and cycles). Ask students to identify examples of circle imagery. (Samples: carousel, cartwheels, car wheels, the cycle of seasons, years that spin and revolve)

for FURTHER READING

Poems to Read Encourage students to savor the musical qualities of the language as they read narrative poems, folk songs, and ballads, such as "Paul Revere's Ride," "The Big Rock Candy Mountain," and "The Ballad of John Henry." Even if students choose to write a reflective lyric rather than a narrative one, their exposure to works such as these may start them thinking about techniques they would like to use in their own writing.

Writing ON YOUR OWN

Emphasize that a good song need not be complicated; some of the most enduring songs are simple, capturing one feeling or idea. You might play songs that illustrate this, such as Taj Mahal's version of Elizabeth Cotton's "Freight Train," Paul Simon's "El Condor Pasa," or Bob Marley's "Hold On Till Tomorrow." Then invite students to create their own songs.

Handbooks for Help and Practice

The following handbooks may be used as mini-lessons before students begin writing or as resources when problems arise.

- **Meaning and Word Choice, pp. 314–315**
- **Using Poetic Devices, pp. 318–321**

Teaching Strategies

for CAPTURE A MOOD OR A FEELING

INDIVIDUALIZING INSTRUCTION: LD STUDENTS Those students who need a great deal of structure may benefit from choosing a melody before searching for song ideas. The mood of the melody can generate ideas for the lyrics, and the structure imposed by the melody can suggest phrasing. Urge students to choose melodies to which they respond strongly. You might suggest folk tunes or "golden oldies," and guide students in verbalizing their feelings. Point out that many developing songwriters begin in this way.

for READ AND LISTEN TO SONGS

COLLABORATIVE OPPORTUNITY Provide tape players and have students bring in tapes of favorite songs. After checking the tapes for appropriateness, group students and have them play and discuss their choices. Encourage them to listen for the way rhythm or beat affects lyrics. This collaborative discussion may spark ideas for students' own songs.

Writing ON YOUR OWN

Song

INVITATION TO *Write*

A song can deal with very basic feelings, very ordinary experiences. Joni Mitchell uses the image of a revolving carousel to symbolize the passage of time as a child grows to adulthood.

Write the words for a song that expresses a feeling or idea, tells a story, or describes a scene.

EXPLORING YOUR WORLD

1. Capture a mood or a feeling. Your own song could spring from feelings of sadness, jealousy, anger, love, confusion, or wonder. Try to remember specific occasions when you felt any of these feelings powerfully. A **cluster** may generate usable details about feelings you want to explore further.

2. Read and listen to songs. You may get inspired by reading other song lyrics or listening to songs. Look for interesting lines, clever rhymes or rhythms, powerful images, and effective use of repetition.

3. Listen to language. Carry around a notebook so that you can jot down interesting language you come across—from books, movies, TV shows, even everyday conversation. A popular phrase, for example, might give you a line for a song.

Writer's Choice You can simply write the lyrics for a song, but you may want to compose a musical accompaniment. If you put your lyrics to music, you might choose to write the words first and then find a suitable melody, or you might write words to go with an already-written melody.

Social Studies Connection

Many events and movements in American history have been recorded in songs, from "Yankee Doodle" (about the American Revolution) to "We Shall Overcome" and Joni Mitchell's "Woodstock." You might play some of these songs for students and suggest that they try writing songs about historical events that interest them.

MULTICULTURAL Connection

Invite students to write new lyrics for the melodies of songs from their own cultural backgrounds. Alternatively, proverbs or stories from students' individual cultural traditions might supply the basis for song lyrics.

DRAFTING YOUR SONG

1. Start with a line or a phrase. Look for a line, perhaps from your freewriting, that has a ring to it, that feels good to your ear. Joni Mitchell, for example, might have started with a line like "the seasons, they go round and round."

2. Develop an idea. Try to hit on one main idea for your song. This might grow out of your catchy line, or it could be a feeling, a simple statement, or a very short story. Each verse could then carry the story forward or present a different example.

3. Use figurative language. Like other poems, songs often suggest much in few words. They do this by using vivid images and imaginative comparisons. "The Circle Game," for example, compares the passage of time to the movement of a carousel. A boy who has lived ten years—ten winters—has "skated over ten clear frozen streams."

4. Consider rhyme and repetition. Remember, however, that rhyming is optional in poetry and song. Don't let a search for rhymes distract you from thinking about what you want to say. Forced rhyming can make your song sound more like a jingle. You can use inexact rhymes, like "seasons" and "appease him." You may want to repeat key lines or phrases. Many songs, like "The Circle Game," benefit from a repeated refrain, or chorus.

PROBLEM SOLVING

"How can I use similes and metaphors?"

To learn more about figurative language, see

- Handbook 27, "Using Poetic Devices," pages 318–321

Writing TIP

You can use a rhyming dictionary to get ideas for rhymes.

for DEVELOP AN IDEA

CRITICAL THINKING: GENERALIZING
Tell students to read over their prewriting notes and to sum up, in one sentence, the main idea or feeling they want to convey. Explain that this generalizing can guide them in choosing details from their notes to use in their drafts.

for USE FIGURATIVE LANGUAGE

HELPFUL HINT To reinforce the concepts of metaphor and simile (outlined in Handbook 27), group students and give them "starters," such as "The wind was like . . ." or "His laughter was. . . ." Encourage students to supply several endings, reflecting varying moods, for each starter. Then suggest that each student try to generate one original metaphor or simile to use in his or her song.

for CONSIDER RHYME AND REPETITION

INDIVIDUALIZING INSTRUCTION: ESL STUDENTS Because rhyming is extremely difficult for students who are acquiring a second language, suggest that students work with native English speakers when composing their lyrics. You also might encourage students to rely on the techniques of repetition and inexact ("slant") rhyme.

GENERAL NOTE

HELPFUL HINT: TITLE Before students begin to review and revise their songs, have them check to see that each song has a single focus. You might ask students what titles they would choose for their songs; struggling over a title may indicate an unclear focus.

SPICE BOX

Point out that the best figurative language features comparisons that are unusual. Tell students that some similes and metaphors are so old and tired that they have become clichés, but that writers who are "metaphor medics" can revive them. To illustrate, list (or have students list) simile and metaphor clichés such as "smooth as silk," "sweet as pie," and so on. Then group students. Challenge each group to choose a cliché and to come up with original comparisons to replace the outworn one. Model imaginative examples such as "smooth as a new car's paint job" or "sweet as a purple popsicle."

for READ YOUR SONG LYRICS ALOUD

KEY TO UNDERSTANDING: DICTION The need for "singability" adds a dimension to a songwriter's word choices. You might offer this example to the class: Suppose a songwriter wanted to say that she felt as if she could fly. Words like *ascend* and *flutter* might look good on paper, but they are hard to sing and hard to understand when heard. *Soar* is singable, but will listeners know that it is *soar* instead of *sore?* Generally, words with strong vowels "sing" well, especially at the ends of lines. Joni Mitchell's songs are especially rich in "singability." Point to examples in "The Circle Game," such as the words ending each line of the refrain *(round, down, time, behind, came, round, game).*

for LOOK AT YOUR SONG'S FORM

PEER RESPONSE To help students structure their songs effectively, encourage them to work with peer readers. Students might ask such questions as the following: What is the main idea of each verse? If there is a refrain or chorus, what does it say that the verses do not? Does the thought progress from verse to verse in a logical way, a way that makes the overall main idea clear?

Guidelines for Evaluation

AN EFFECTIVE SONG LYRIC

- reveals the thoughts, feelings, or ideas of the writer
- is unified by one main idea, feeling, or story line
- consists of verses (perhaps with a refrain or chorus) organized in a logical sequence
- uses devices such as figurative language, repetition, and rhyme to express meaning
- follows enough conventions of grammar, usage, and mechanics to make the meaning clear

REVIEWING YOUR WRITING

1. Read your song lyrics aloud. Listen to their rhythm. Do the lyrics sound as if they could be sung? Do you like the sound of the words? Does a tune suggest itself to you? If so, try to sing your song into a tape recorder or pick it out on a guitar, piano, or other instrument.

2. Look at your song's form. Verses of a song are like the paragraphs of a story. Your song may have just one verse; more likely it will have two or three, perhaps divided by a refrain.

3. Share your song lyrics. In a spirit of fun and good will, read or sing your song to friends, and listen to their songs. Share useful comments.

PROBLEM SOLVING

"How can I find better words to make my ideas clear?"

For help in choosing the right words, see

- Handbook 25, "Meaning and Word Choice," pages 314–315

Grammar TIP

For song lyrics, you may decide not to capitalize the first word of each line or not to punctuate normally. You might use contractions that are normal in speech, like "Hey, good lookin'."

PUBLISHING AND PRESENTING

- **Have a concert.** Perform your song for your class or for a larger group in your school.
- **Record your song.** Make an audiocassette recording of your song. If you have a video camera, you may want to produce a music video, designing specific visuals to go with your song.
- **Publish a songbook.** Collect the song lyrics your class wrote and publish them in a book, with or without musical notation.

PROFESSIONAL NOTEBOOK

Songwriter Sheila Davis, who has written several books about her craft, offers this advice and encouragement to developing songwriters: "In addition to thinking independently, being curious, and writing from your own reality, finding your voice requires emotional grit. It takes courage to put your thoughts on paper—to let the world see how your mind works. Because, ultimately, writing means to expose yourself. But to risk exposure is exactly what every first-rate writer has been brave enough to do."

Springboards

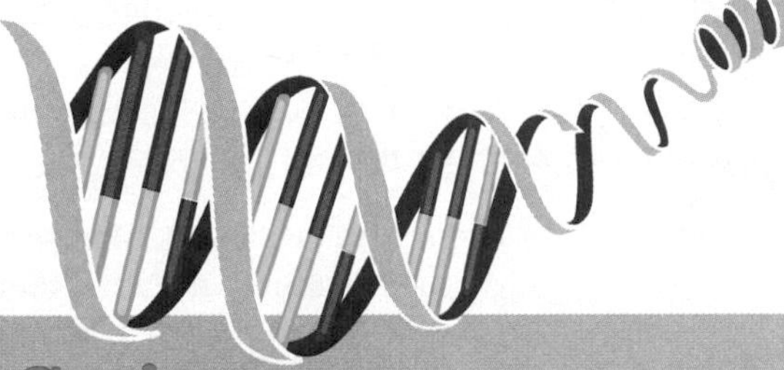

Literature Write about a milestone in the life of a literary character or your favorite author. You might compose your story in the form of a journal entry written by the character, trying to capture his or her individual voice.

Science Present a news bulletin about an important scientific breakthrough, such as the discovery of antibiotics or of the structure of the DNA molecule. If you prefer, write a diary entry as if you were the scientist who made the discovery. You may choose to fictionalize your account, setting your news bulletin in the future.

SPEAKING AND LISTENING Tape-record interviews with members of your family about important incidents in their lives. You could ask about their memories of historic events or scientific discoveries or about their experiences in coming to this country.

Art Make a painting, sculpture, or drawing to convey an important event in your life. Your piece may be representational or abstract, but it should express the mood and significance of the event.

History Become a historical figure and narrate an important event from your life, stressing the significance of the incident. For example, you could present the March on Washington as told by Dr. Martin Luther King, Jr. You could also choose someone who was not famous—for example, a pilgrim sailing to America.

Teaching Strategies

for SCIENCE

HELPFUL HINT: SHOW, DON'T TELL Students who enjoy science fiction may enjoy responding to this prompt by writing about a future discovery. Encourage them to generate "showing" details by filling in an observation chart about the imagined discovery.

for HISTORY

HELPFUL HINT: PERSONAL WRITING You might give students the option of adopting the character of an imaginary person their own age who lived during an earlier time in American history—perhaps a member of a family that settled Jamestown or a young citizen of Vicksburg during the Civil War. As that character, students can write a brief series of journal entries describing daily life, a historical event, or both.

Imitating Sentences

Objectives

- To recognize varied sentence patterns
- To imitate sentence patterns, using correct punctuation

Teaching Strategies

KEY TO UNDERSTANDING
Introductory elements are words and phrases that come before the subject and predicate. Interrupters are words or phrases that break the flow of thought in a sentence. An appositive is a word or phrase that (usually) follows a noun and renames or identifies it. Each of these sentence elements should be set off by commas. For more about these sentence elements and for practice exercises, refer students to pages 646–650 of Handbook 49, "Punctuation."

KEY TO UNDERSTANDING: SENTENCE PATTERNS Be sure students understand that they are looking not for similar wording but for similar patterns. Give the following illustration: A sentence beginning with a prepositional phrase such as "Behind the trees" can be imitated by a sentence beginning with a different prepositional phrase: "Under the porch," "Above the clouds," and so on.

Additional Resource

Sentence Composing Copy Masters, pp. 1–2

Sentence

COMPOSING

Imitating Sentences

Professional writers vary their sentences to add richness and interest to their writing. By imitating their sentences, you can learn new ways to compose, structure, and punctuate your own writing. Notice how the writer of the following description varies the rhythm of each sentence.

Model A In her attic bedroom, Margaret Murry, wrapped in an old patchwork quilt, sat on the foot of her bed and watched the trees tossing in the frenzied lashing of the wind.

Model B Behind the trees, clouds scudded frantically across the sky.

Model C Every few moments, the moon ripped through them, creating wraithlike shadows that raced along the ground.

Madeleine L'Engle, *A Wrinkle in Time*

ON THE MARK Use commas to set off introductory elements, interrupters, and appositives.

A. Chunking Sentence Parts People read and write sentences in meaningful "chunks." By dividing sentences into parts, or chunks, you can see how together the parts express a complete thought. Choose the sentence in each pair below that is divided into meaningful chunks. Explain how each chunk relates to those around it.

1. **a.** In her attic / bedroom, Margaret Murry, / wrapped in an old / patchwork quilt, / sat on the foot of her bed / and watched the trees / tossing in / the frenzied lashing of the wind.
   b. In her attic bedroom, / Margaret Murry, / wrapped in an old patchwork quilt, / sat on the foot of her bed / and watched the trees / tossing in the frenzied lashing of the wind.

2. **a.** Behind the trees, / clouds scudded frantically / across the sky.
   b. Behind / the trees, clouds / scudded frantically across the sky.

3. **a.** Every / few moments, the / moon ripped through them, creating wraithlike shadows that / raced along the ground.
   b. Every few moments, / the moon ripped through them, / creating wraithlike shadows / that raced along the ground.

B. Identifying Imitations Find the sentences in each pair below that can be divided into chunks that match the structure of the chunks in the models.

1. Choose the sentence that imitates Model A.
   a. Prancing around the ring and led by Mrs. Jackson, the toy poodle resembled a miniature giraffe with cotton balls on its feet and a sneering look on its face that, in a person, would have seemed conceited.
   b. After his escape, the fox, tired from his race across the field, stood in the mouth of the hole and observed the dogs sniffing the ground for a scent.
2. Choose the sentence that imitates Model B.
   a. In the morning, blackbirds cackled annoyingly in the trees.
   b. An expert swimmer, Albert had no trouble getting a summer job.
3. Choose the sentence that imitates Model C.
   a. Each Thursday, Mr. Samuels went to the mall, meeting several friends who strolled there with him.
   b. Feeling somewhat anxious, Janie was practicing her hardest piece, a composition that had to be played very fast.

C. Unscrambling and Imitating Sentences Unscramble the sentence chunks below to create sentences that match a model on page 46. Then write correctly punctuated sentences that imitate each model.

1. Write sentences that imitate Model A.
   played at the highest possible volume / and sent the chaperones scurrying for the controls of the stereo / the music / reverberated against the walls of the cafeteria / during the dance
2. Write sentences that imitate Model B.
   Joon sketched quickly / on his drawing board / with his pencil
3. Write sentences that imitate Model C.
   creating a wave / that spread around the stadium / during the baseball game / the fans raised their arms.

Grammar Refresher See Handbook 44, "Using Prepositions, Conjunctions, and Interjections," pages 540–541, for more on prepositional phrases, and Handbook 47, "Using Verbals," pages 599–601, for more on participial phrases.

Answer Key

A. Chunking Sentence Parts

1. **b** Sample explanation: One chunk tells whom the sentence is about; two others tell what she did; the rest add descriptive details.
2. **a** Sample explanation: The middle chunk is the core sentence.
3. **b** Sample explanation: Chunks 1, 3, and 4 describe chunk 2.

B. Identifying Imitations

1. b
2. a
3. a

C. Unscrambling and Imitating Sentences

Unscrambled sentences are shown below.

1. During the dance, the music, played at the highest possible volume, reverberated against the walls of the cafeteria and sent the chaperones scurrying for the controls of the stereo.
2. With his pencil, Joon sketched quickly on his drawing board.
   or
   On his drawing board, Joon sketched quickly with his pencil.
3. During the baseball game, the fans raised their arms, creating a wave that spread around the stadium.

2

Observation and Description

Overview

In descriptive writing, students use their powers of observation and vivid language to share their perceptions with readers. In this workshop, students apply and extend the skills of personal and expressive writing from the previous workshop to help them develop ways to present events to readers. Workshop 2 includes the following Guided and Related Assignments as well as the interdisciplinary project described on page 47c–47d.

1. **Guided: Eyewitness Report** invites students to use their personal experience as they identify a noteworthy event, choose details that bring the event to life, and relate the event in language that shows, rather than tells, as they describe the experience to an audience.
2. **Related: Field Notes** calls on students to use observational and descriptive skills from the Guided Assignment to study a subject in the natural world and to record their reactions, impressions, and feelings.

Teaching Preview

Preparation Guide

1. Use the Overview on this page and the Teacher's Choice descriptions on page 49 as a basis for deciding which assignments to teach.
2. Preview the assignments and the teacher's notes and identify concepts that may require preteaching or extra support, given your class's abilities. The handbook mini-lessons suggested within the lesson may also provide guidance.
3. Preview the chart below for support materials in the Teacher's Resource File that may be used with this Workshop. Resources are for use with the Guided Assignment unless otherwise noted.

Support Materials

RESOURCES

Prewrite and Explore
Writing Resource Book, pp. 7–9
Thinking Skills Worksheet, p. 3
Starting Points for Writing, Writing Prompts for Fine Art, pp. 31–32, 34, 36–38

Draft and Discover
Elaboration, Revision, and Proofreading Practice, p. 3
Writing Resource Book, pp. 10–11
Thinking Skills Worksheet, p. 7

Revise Your Writing
Elaboration, Revision, and Proofreading Practice, p. 4
Writing Resource Book, p. 12
Peer Response Guides, pp. 11–12
Guidelines for Writing Assessment and Portfolio Use, pp. 15, 26–28

Sentence Composing
Sentence Composing Copy Masters, pp. 3–4

Assessment
Tests and Writing Assessment Prompts, p. 2

Computer Software
Writer's DataBank
Electronic English Handbook

PROFESSIONAL RESOURCES AND MEDIA

Books and Journals
Calkins, Lucy, "Heads Up: Write What You See," *Language Arts* 55, No. 3, 7th March 1978, p. 355
Elbow, Peter, and Belanoff, Pat, "Experience into Words: Description," *A Community of Writers,* Random House (1989), pp. 78–87
Parks, Rosa, and Haskins, Jim, *Rosa Parks: My Story,* Dial (1992)

Films and Videos
Johnstown Flood, University of Pittsburgh Press/CUP Services, Ithaca, NY (1990) (26 min.)
Logan Challenge, Mystic Fire Video, Cooper Station, NY (1992) (58 min.)
When the Bay Area Quakes, University of California Extension Center, Berkeley, CA (1991) (20 min.)

Computer Software and Technology
Ace Reporter Deluxe, Mindplay, Danvers, MA (software), Apple II, Apple 3.5, PC
You Be the Reporter, Educational Activities, Freeport, NY (laser disc)

Linking Literature, Writing, and Grammar

The following options may be used to provide students with an integrated language experience. Begin by assigning and discussing any of the recommended pieces of literature. Use the suggested strategy to provide a link to the Guided Assignment.

LINKING LITERATURE AND WRITING

Option 1

Starting Point: "Amid the Rubble" by Deborah Sontag on pages 50–51 of *The Writer's Craft.*

Strategy: Use the teaching suggestions on pages 50–51 to lead students into the Guided Assignment.

Option 2

Starting Point: *Survive the Savage Sea* by Dougal Robertson on pages 619–629 of McDougal, Littell's *Literature and Language,* Grade 8. (Additional suggestions for using *Literature and Language* can be found on page 49.)

Strategy: Have students read this nonfiction piece to find a second eyewitness account imbedded within the main narrative. How are observational skills used in each? How do the two reports differ? In which do students feel more excitement? Why? Have students consider why the author includes a report from someone else. Use the discussion to introduce students to the Guided Assignment.

Option 3

Starting Point: "Barbara Frietchie" by John Greenleaf Whittier.

Strategy: Read the poem aloud. Point out that this poem is about an incident during the Civil War. Discuss the techniques Whittier uses to make students feel they are there, witnessing the march of General Lee and his army. Then introduce the Guided Assignment.

LINKING WRITING AND GRAMMAR

As students draft and revise their pieces, tell them that the use of verbals can make descriptions concise and vivid for readers. Review the use of verbals with them. Write these examples on the board and have students identify the verbals in the second sentence.

Wordy: An alligator was startled by the boat's engine, and so it lifted its long snout out of the water and then it bared its sharp teeth.

Concise: An alligator, *startled* by the boat's engine, lifted its long snout out of the water, *baring* its sharp teeth.

Remind students to check their writing for places where verbals can help make their writing more concise and vivid. Go over pages 595–610 of the Grammar and Usage Handbook. If students still have difficulty in using verbals, assign exercises from these pages for reteaching. Additional practice can be found in the *Grammar and Usage Practice Book* on pages 99–108.

Management Guidelines

The chart below indicates the number of days recommended for each phase of the Guided and Related Assignments. These numbers are an estimate of the total time needed for each phase. In practice, of course, students may not complete each phase in one continuous session, nor will they necessarily progress from stage to stage in the linear order shown here. Stars indicate portions of the assignment that may be completed outside the classroom if time is limited or if teachers wish students to work independently.

EYEWITNESS REPORT

Starting from Literature ....1 day
Prewrite and Explore ....2 days*
Draft and Discover ....1–2 days*
Revise Your Writing ....1–2 days*
Proofread ....1 day*
Publish and Present ....1 day
Reflect on Your Writing ....1 day*
Reteaching ....open
Extension and Enrichment ....open*
Sentence Composing ....open*

FIELD NOTES

Starting from Literature ....1 day
Finding a Subject ....1–2 days*
Reviewing Your Field Notes .....1–2 days*
Sharing Your Field Notes ....1 day

Extra! Read All About It: Creating a Newspaper

Overview

As students work through this project, they will gain a deeper understanding of a historical period of their choice. They will also learn about the parts of a newspaper, and they will draw on skills from many areas of the curriculum to create and publish an issue of a newspaper.

Students will participate in the following activities:

- Choose a key event and a time period to investigate
- Use research skills to compile information about the event and the time period
- Study the sections, features, and organization of newspapers
- Plan and publish one issue of a newspaper, reflecting the event and period they have researched
- Use language arts, science, social studies, math, and art skills to complete their research and develop materials

Preparation Guide

Point out to students that a newspaper is like a slice of history: it shows everything from world political events to the price of shoes. Students should understand that such newspaper features as eyewitness reports, want ads, and advertisements reflect everyday life as well as major events.

Tell students that this project will let them use skills of descriptive writing to create a newspaper that informs its readers about a major event and time period of the past.

Project File

Stage 1 Focus on History

1. Have students brainstorm about the periods of history that intrigue them.
2. Direct students to skim social studies texts and other sources, such as back issues of newspapers and periodicals, to find major events in these periods of history. Have them think about an interesting lead story for a class newspaper (see *Resources, Stage 1*).
3. Hold a class discussion to identify ideas for the lead story. List students' ideas on the board and conduct a decision-making session to select a lead story from the list.

TEAM TEACHING

The following activities may be used for team teaching or as enrichment and extension activities by the language arts teacher.

Language Arts Read memoirs, journals, and other first-person material from periods of special interest.

Science Read about science milestones, such as the Apollo moon landing and the first organ transplants.

Social Studies Study historically significant events, such as the founding of Jamestown or the 1929 stock-market crash.

TEACHING TIPS

- Invite a journalist to speak to the class about his or her experiences witnessing and reporting events.
- Schedule a library tour focusing on resources for history research and on the use of microfilm readers.
- If your students have difficulty reaching a consensus on a topic for the lead story, use group problem-solving strategies to help them reach a decision (see *Resources, Stage 1*).

Stage 2 Gather Information

1. Have students bring in and examine current newspapers to determine the kinds of articles and features they want their class newspaper to have.
   Possibilities include the following:
   - world, national, and local news
   - business news and sports news
   - editorials and letters to the editor
   - advice columns and essays
   - arts and entertainment
   - restaurant and movie reviews
   - foods and family life
   - want ads

   Have students form groups to work on the various sections of their newspaper.
2. Direct groups to begin their research, concentrating on information needed for their sections (see *Resources, Stage 2*).
3. Suggest that in addition to using library resources, students interview either someone who witnessed key events of the period or an expert on the period.

TEAM TEACHING

Art View art or photos of the period (see *Resources, Stage 2*).

Music Listen to popular songs of the period. What do the lyrics reveal about people and issues of that time?

Science Explore the scientific knowledge of the period. Learn scientific principles related to the event selected for the lead article.

Social Studies Learn what was going on in the nation and in the world and what daily life was like when the lead event occurred.

Language Arts Discover how newspapers are organized. Study the reporting styles used during the period.

TEACHING TIPS

- Show videos or films of eyewitness news reports (see *Resources, Stage 2*). Discuss the kinds of details included.

- Take a field trip to a museum whose collection relates to the topic of the lead article or to the time period.
- Teach note-taking techniques. Remind students to record sources of quotations and facts (see *Resources, Stage 2*).

Stage 3 Create and Publish the Newspaper

1. Direct the groups to plan the articles, features, and layout of their sections. Have the editors of each section confer to organize the newspaper.
2. Have students write articles, create graphics, paste up their sections, and compile the sections to form the newspaper.
3. If possible, have students make copies of their newspaper and distribute the copies to other classes.

TEAM TEACHING

Social Studies Plan advertisements reflecting daily life of the period.

Math Make graphs and tables to present the statistics mentioned in articles.

Art Take photos to illustrate articles. Sketch cartoons and illustrations. Create page layouts, using computers, photos, and drawings (see *Resources, Stage 3*).

Language Arts Review techniques of descriptive writing. Learn to incorporate quotations, to check accuracy, and to sort out facts and opinions (see *Resources, Stage 3*).

TEACHING TIPS

- Arrange for students to use cameras, computers, publishing software, and photocopying equipment (see *Resources, Stage 3*).
- Visit a newspaper office. Plan for students to tour various departments.
- Invite a newspaper editor to speak to the class about news writing.

Resources

STAGE 1

The ***New York Times*** dates back to 1851; the ***Chicago Tribune,*** to 1847. Most public libraries have back issues of these and other major newspapers on microfilm for viewing and photocopying.

The **Timelines** series (Crestwood House) includes books summarizing major events, as well as fads and fashions, of each decade from the 1900s through the 1980s.

Where in America's Past Is Carmen Sandiego? (Broderbund), a computer game, can help students recall major events in American history.

Making Waves with Creative Problem Solving by Vaune Ainsworth-Land and Norma Fletcher teaches group problem-solving skills.

STAGE 2

The **Women in American Life** series (National Women's History Project) includes five 15-to-25-minute videos showing daily life from 1861 to 1977.

The video ***Catastrophe*** (Embassy) combines newsreel footage and eyewitness accounts of the crash of the *Hindenburg,* the sinking of the *Andrea Doria,* and seven other disasters.

National Geographic World and ***Cricket*** magazines include articles on events related to science and history.

The National Gallery of Art and ***The National Gallery of Art: A Videodisc Companion*** (The Voyager Company) include photos of more than 1,500 artworks.

The Writer's Craft, Grade 8, Workshop 8, "Informative Writing: Reports," pages 197–198, teaches note taking. Handbook 33, "Writing Paraphrases and Summaries," pages 346–348, teaches summarizing and paraphrasing.

STAGE 3

The Writer's Craft, Grade 8, Workshop 2, "Observation and Description," pages 48–61, teaches the writing of eyewitness reports. Handbook 12, "Methods of Elaboration," pages 255–261, demonstrates the use of quotations.

News or Not? by Ann E. Weiss explores such news-writing issues as fact versus opinion, accuracy, bias, and audience.

Hot off the Press: Getting the News into Print by Ruth Crisman provides useful background, tracing the process of producing modern newspapers.

Pagemaker (Aldus), computer software, lets students create newspaper layouts.

Additional Projects

Eyes on Ecology To demonstrate the use of observation and description in earth sciences, propose that students set up a recycling program. Start by having them learn about the need to conserve resources and about methods of conservation. Ask students to observe and describe recycling measures already in place at their home and school. Then ask them to observe and describe further opportunities for recycling. Guide them as they plan, set up, and publicize a recycling program.

Student Historians Invite students to use observation and descriptive writing while working as local archivists. Have students use data from written records and notes of interviews with longtime residents to compile descriptions of your area's past. They can also use observation and interviews to create descriptions of life in various parts of your area today. Encourage students to donate their work to a local historical society or library.

Calculating the Future Have students use observations of current trends, along with math skills, to predict conditions in your community fifty years from now. During this project students can confer with city planners and use population and growth databases, such as those available from *Newsweek.* The project can culminate in a Future Fair, featuring graphs and illustrations showing your community's future.

Objective

- To use an illustration and suggested writing prompts as springboards to informal writing

WRITING WARM-UPS

Encourage students to respond freely to at least one of the Sketchbook prompts. Students may begin by discussing their ideas in small groups and then freewriting in their journals. Remind them that their responses will not be graded and may provide them with useful material for other descriptive assignments.

SHOW, DON'T TELL

To help students grasp the concept of showing rather than telling, you might use Handbook 13, pages 262–266, as a mini-lesson.

The following are samples of showing sentences for the prompts:

Harris just stole the ball! There are fifteen seconds left! Can she make a basket and break the tie before the buzzer sounds? . . . Swish! Yes! We win!

A huge tree had crashed through our roof, live power lines lay in a tangle on the ground, and overturned cars littered the ditches.

Sketch Book

WRITING WARM-UPS

- You're in your room. You hear a roar. You look out the window. Something strange is happening to the house across the street! Describe what you see.
- Describe the most amazing thing you ever saw.

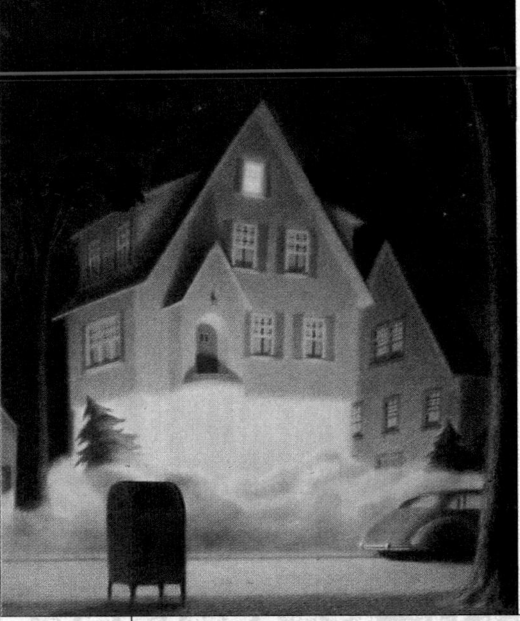

THE HOUSE ON MAPLE STREET

It was a perfect lift-off.

Show, Don't Tell

You can use facts, details, even dialogue to re-create an event you've witnessed. Rewrite the *telling* sentences below to capture a reader's interest and *show* what is happening.

- Our player scored the winning point.
- The storm caused a great deal of damage.

Observation and Description

Guided Assignment
Eyewitness Report

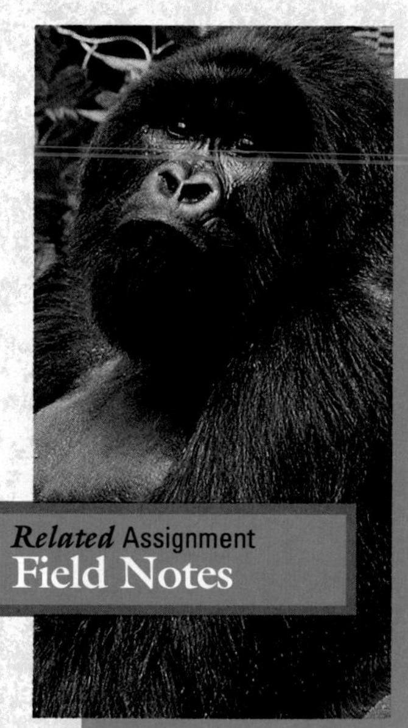

Related Assignment
Field Notes

When you're on a vacation, you can take snapshots of sights you want to remember—a violet-orange sunset, a funny street performer, a misty coast. However, how do you capture a moment in time or a special event?

In this workshop you will use your powers of observation and description to vividly re-create an event in an eyewitness report. Then, in a related assignment, you will have a chance to use the same skills to capture observations and thoughts in the form of field notes about a subject of personal interest to you.

Links to LITERATURE & LANGUAGE

Literature For more examples of writing that contains eyewitness reports, see *Literature and Language*, Grade 8:

- Dougal Robertson, *Survive the Savage Sea*
- Theodore Waldeck, "Battle by the Breadfruit Tree"
- Rogelio R. Gomez, "Foul Shots"

Observation and Description

Objectives

Guided Assignment

Eyewitness Report To respond to and analyze an eyewitness report written by a journalist and to create an eyewitness report that uses sensory details, dialogue, and action verbs

Related Assignment

Field Notes To respond to and analyze field notes by professional writers and to create field notes that summarize and draw conclusions from first-hand observations

Teacher's Choice

Use the following guidelines to choose the assignment that best suits students' needs.

Eyewitness Report This assignment will sharpen students' observational skills and their ability to describe events accurately and vividly. Because these skills are essential to most types of writing, you may want to offer this workshop early in the year, perhaps in conjunction with a current events unit in social studies. Students interested in journalism will especially enjoy writing this report.

Field Notes This assignment allows students to use their powers of observation and description to study a subject in the natural world. You might want to offer this assignment when your students are involved in a science unit on plant or animal life.

Guided ASSIGNMENT

ASSIGNMENT RATIONALE

The ability to make detailed observations and to report those observations accurately and vividly is important in many learning situations across the curriculum and in many fields of work, such as science, business, and journalism. This assignment helps students analyze and interpret their observations and judge the relative importance of various details in order to make a strong impression in writing.

Starting from LITERATURE

Motivate

Invite students to discuss the work of a news or sports reporter whose work they really enjoy, either on TV or in a newspaper. Ask whether students have ever considered a career in news or sports reporting. Then ask what qualities they think a good reporter needs. (Samples: Curiosity, courage, determination, the ability to draw people out, the ability to observe carefully and describe accurately)

BUILD ON PRIOR KNOWLEDGE

Ask students to share what they remember about Hurricane Andrew, the storm that hit southern Florida in 1992. Students may be able to share personal experiences or memories of what they saw on TV or in the newspapers. Point out that TV reporters have vivid pictures to help them tell their stories, whereas newspaper reporters, for the most part, must create mental pictures with the words they use.

Guided ASSIGNMENT Eyewitness Report

Starting from LITERATURE

Have you ever felt as if you had experienced an event in history just by reading about it? The main goal of an eyewitness report is to give you that kind of experience. Eyewitness reporters strive to bring events to life through print.

In this 1992 eyewitness report, journalist Deborah Sontag takes you to Florida's coast to show how survivors of Hurricane Andrew coped with the destruction caused by the storm. As you read her account, notice the words, phrases, and images that help you to feel as though you were there.

50 Workshop 2

MORE ABOUT THE MODEL

Hurricane Andrew occurred in late August 1992. It roared across the Bahamas and Florida, then swept into Louisiana with winds of up to 164 miles per hour. The hurricane killed 33 people and destroyed at least 63,000 homes in Florida alone, leaving approximately 300,000 people homeless. Andrew caused about $30 million in damages and has been judged to be the costliest natural disaster in the history of the United States.

from *The New York Times*

AMID THE RUBBLE

by Deborah Sontag

The night Hurricane Andrew hit the Florida coast, Ronald Bruscia, 46, Pamela Jones, 41, and Pamela's son, Scott, 13, had huddled around candles in the bathroom with a mattress propped against the door. Listening to the wind tear off sections of the r[illegible]ve them, the three promised themselves that if they came through that night alive, they would stop leading selfish lives. Five days later, journalist Deborah Sontag spent twenty-four hours with these three survivors. The following is her report.

It was ninety-two degrees at noon Saturday, the fifth day after Hurricane Andrew. Ronald Bruscia maneuvered his van around mounds of brush and tangles of fallen power line. Shards of glass flew from his shattered windshield as he drove toward a friend's house that had collapsed during the storm.

The friend had offered fifty gallons of gasoline in exchange for help in moving, and Mr. Bruscia was eager for the trade. . . .

[He] swerved around pretzels of metal railing and bumped over downed wires that, the radio kept warning, could still be live.

Mr. Bruscia screeched to a halt as a hog waddled across the street.

"That pig just blew into the neighborhood during the storm," he said. . . .

1 P.M. [Later,] Mr. Bruscia and Ms. Jones, heading home with their gasoline, saw a Federal Express truck making a delivery to a house without walls.

"What the . . . ?" Mr. Bruscia started to say, before he realized and leapt out of the van.

"Ice!" Ms. Jones cried. "They're delivering ice, God bless them. Ice is gold." . . .

2:30 P.M. The storm clouds darkened. Mr. Bruscia and his neighbors clambered on and off their makeshift roofs, trying to secure the new plywood, the tar paper, and the plastic sheeting with extra nails.

Relatively speaking, the families on Martinique Drive were lucky. The storm only took half their roofs, most of their ceilings, all of their windows, and an entire bedroom here and there. They had no belongings, but for the most part, they still had their walls. . . .

5 P.M. The family unloaded charcoal, bottled water, cans of chili, and other goods that Mr. Bruscia's sister had driven down from Orlando.

Ms. Jones had salvaged a large bell from their boat, and she rang and rang it to let the neighbors know provisions had arrived. "I was about ready to give up this morning, but now I feel better," she said.

Thunder rumbled. "Uh oh, maybe not," she said. . . .

Gnats and mosquitoes swirled in the gusting winds as the rain started falling in sheets.

"About this moment is where you have people finally going over the edge," Mr. Bruscia said. "Not me, though. I spent enough years living on that edge to know how to cling on real tight."

Think & Respond

What was your reaction to this report? Consider the impression it made on you. Then look for sensory details and bits of dialogue that helped to create this impression.

SET A PURPOSE

To help students focus on the purpose-setting statement at the end of the Starting from Literature box, remind them to notice words and phrases that paint a picture in their minds as they read.

Think & Respond

ELICIT PERSONAL RESPONSES

Have students consider the questions in the Think & Respond box. To help them share their reactions, ask, "Did the report make you feel sorry for the survivors? Did it make you admire them? Did you feel shocked or surprised by what people went through? Did you want to help them in some way?"

EXPLORE THE AUTHOR'S TECHNIQUES

To help students use the excerpt as a model for writing, review the techniques that Deborah Sontag uses to create a vivid impression of the effects of the storm and the ways in which people responded to it. She uses vivid sensory details, such as "Shards of glass flew from his shattered windshield" and "Gnats and mosquitoes swirled in the gusting winds. . . ." She also includes survivors' own words, such as "That pig just blew into the neighborhood," "Ice is gold," and "About this moment is where you have people finally going over the edge."

for FURTHER READING

Students might compare the techniques used by Deborah Sontag with those used by other reporters who covered Hurricane Andrew. For example, have them check news magazines, such as *Time* and *Newsweek,* for the week of September 7, 1992, for more eyewitness accounts of the storm.

Reading a STUDENT MODEL

Reporter Deborah Sontag wrote an eyewitness report about a disaster of national interest, but good reports can be written about local events that might never be reported in a national newspaper. This student model is an eyewitness account of a type of dramatic event that many teenagers are likely to have witnessed—a fight. It is the final draft of the piece that students will see in process on the workshop pages that follow.

Motivate

Have students imagine that they are reporters covering school events for the local newspaper. What recent events in school do they consider newsworthy? Could they write interesting eyewitness accounts of the events?

BUILD ON PRIOR KNOWLEDGE

Ask students whether they have ever witnessed a fight at your school. What details about the fight stand out in their minds? How did students watching the fight react?

SET A PURPOSE

Encourage students to try to picture the scene and "hear" the dialogue in their minds as they read. Have students ask themselves, "Which words make me feel that I am watching the fight?"

One Student's Writing

Reading a STUDENT MODEL

Have you ever, in a letter or a conversation, tried to share something exciting or strange you witnessed? How did you go about it? Were you successful?

As you read Rene Froehmer's eyewitness account, decide whether she achieves her goal of vividly recreating a fight that she witnessed.

Fight
by Rene Froehmer

As the two teen boys began yelling, everybody in the area, including me, knew that a fight was going to occur. They were in each other's face, yelling rude remarks.

"So, do you wanna fight?" the smaller boy said. "Come on!"

The other guy wouldn't budge. He knew that if he started the fight, he wouldn't be at this school for long.

Finally, the smaller boy couldn't wait any longer. He hit his enemy on the shoulder of his white T-shirt. The second boy reacted quickly to this, as if it had happened to him many times before.

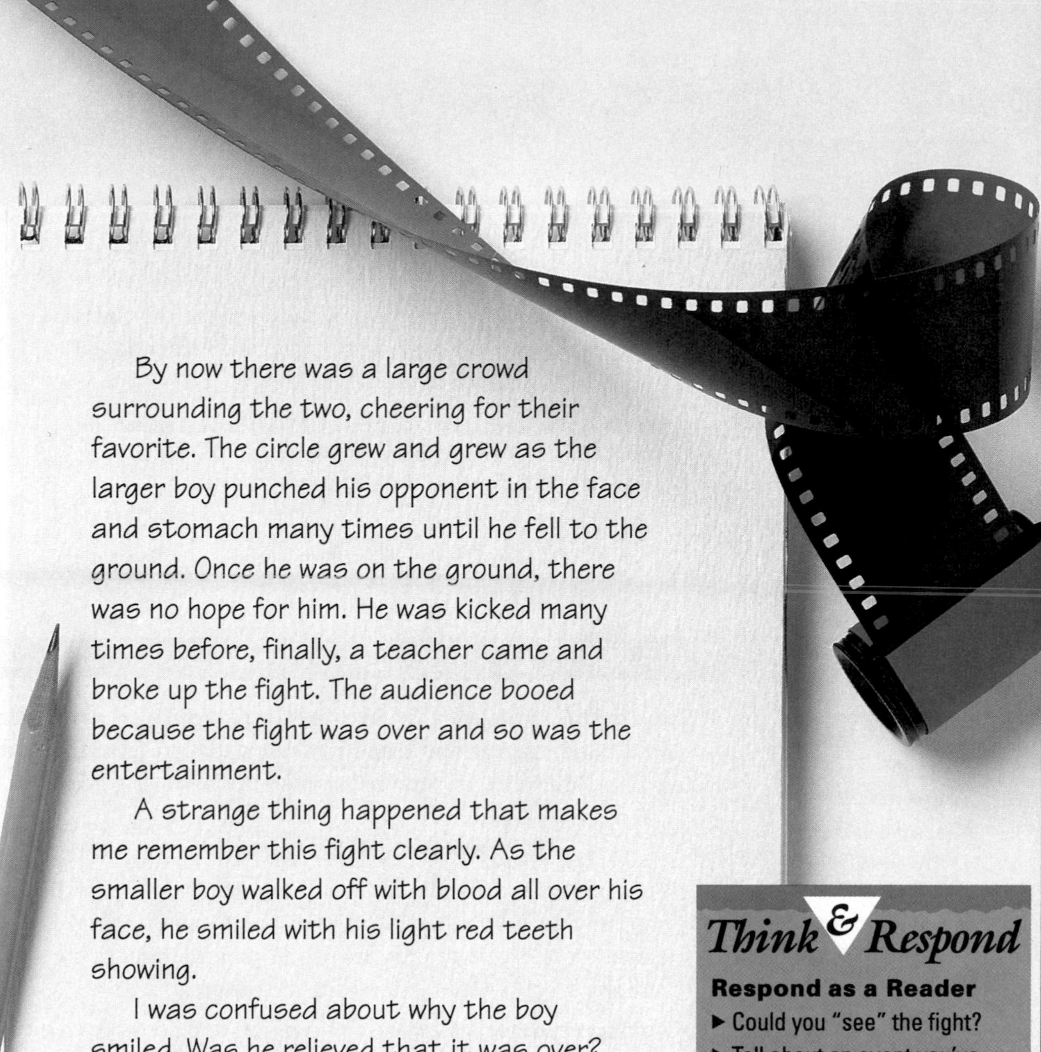

By now there was a large crowd surrounding the two, cheering for their favorite. The circle grew and grew as the larger boy punched his opponent in the face and stomach many times until he fell to the ground. Once he was on the ground, there was no hope for him. He was kicked many times before, finally, a teacher came and broke up the fight. The audience booed because the fight was over and so was the entertainment.

A strange thing happened that makes me remember this fight clearly. As the smaller boy walked off with blood all over his face, he smiled with his light red teeth showing.

I was confused about why the boy smiled. Was he relieved that it was over? Was he pleased that he'd gotten the bigger kid in trouble? Was he just trying to look as if he wasn't hurt? I don't know.

All I do know is that I definitely will not forget that fight and that boy's weird smile.

Think & Respond

Respond as a Reader

▶ Could you "see" the fight?

▶ Tell about an event you've witnessed that made as strong an impression on you as this fight made on Rene Froehmer.

Respond as a Writer

▶ What words and phrases does Rene use to create excitement and tension at the beginning of this account?

▶ What detail of this account stands out the most for you? Why do you think you remember that one best?

Think & Respond

RESPOND AS A READER

▶ Have students point out vivid descriptions and dialogue that helped give them a sense of "being there."

▶ Encourage students to talk about dramatic events—other than fights—in which a crowd gathered or in which they felt torn between staying to watch and walking away.

RESPOND AS A WRITER

▶ Phrases used to create tension and excitement include "knew that a fight was going to occur," "in each other's face, yelling rude remarks," "'Come on!'" and "wouldn't budge."

▶ Accept all responses and have students give their reasons. Students might mention the detail of the smaller boy with bloodied teeth walking away with a smile. It is a vivid, dramatic image that will probably create a strong impression. The image is also emphasized by the writer, who, at the end of her report, wonders about the meaning of the boy's smile.

Draw Conclusions

To make sure students understand this introduction to eyewitness reports, challenge them to list the characteristics they have noted thus far. Responses may include:

- vivid sensory details
- dialogue from participants in the event
- a clear focus or impression of the event
- an easy-to-follow order of presentation

Writing ON YOUR OWN

Point out to students that they give eyewitness reports all the time—whenever someone asks, "What happened?" Stress the importance of sensory details and dialogue in an eyewitness report; encourage students to use these elements in their own writing.

Handbooks for Help and Practice

The following handbooks may be used as mini-lessons before students begin writing or as resources when problems arise.

- **Graphic Devices for Writing, pp. 227–231**
- **Show, Don't Tell, pp. 262–267**
- **Introductions, pp. 278–280**
- **Conclusions, pp. 281–283**
- **Critical Listening and Observing, pp. 363–366**

PREWRITE AND EXPLORE

Objectives

- To use prewriting techniques to select a topic for an eyewitness report
- To observe and record details
- To choose a focus for the report

Teaching Strategies

for EXPLORING TOPICS

COOPERATIVE LEARNING Have a group of students cover a sporting event or a concert. Assign different aspects to different reporters. For a concert, students might cover the crowds, the performance, audience reaction, and so on. Have each group compile and present its report.

for OBSERVE AND RECORD DETAILS . . .

CRITICAL THINKING: CLASSIFYING Students can use the Observation Chart on page 3 of the Thinking Skills Worksheets to organize details.

Writing ON YOUR OWN

Eyewitness Report

INVITATION TO *Write*

Eyewitness reports, like Deborah Sontag's story about the survivors of Hurricane Andrew and Rene Froehmer's account of a fight, make it possible for events to touch our lives.

Write an eyewitness account of an interesting or special event that you experienced. Try to make your readers feel as if they were there.

PREWRITE AND EXPLORE

1. Be on the lookout for interesting events. Any event observed with interest and attention can make an engaging subject. To find an event, try one or more of the following activities.

Exploring Topics

- **School scout** Situations worth reporting can be found right in your own school. Pay attention to what goes on around you as you sit in homeroom, the cafeteria, or the auditorium and while you're outside on break.
- **Roving reporter** See what's going on at places like video arcades, roller rinks, bowling alleys, shopping malls, and parks.
- **News hound** Newspapers and local magazines can tip you off to many local happenings, from concerts to political gatherings and sports events. Pick one or two to attend.

2. Observe and record details, impressions, and dialogue. Good reporters rely on more than just their memories. They take detailed notes on the scene. When you're at an event, record *all* your sense impressions—not just sight and hearing—to gather as many details as possible and get an overall impression. You might **list,** make a **sketch,** or create an **observation chart.**

Transparency

PROBLEM SOLVING

"What's the best way to write down what I observe?"

To find out more about ways to record what you observe, see

- Handbook 3, "Graphic Devices for Writing," pages 227–231
- Handbook 32, section on "Taking Notes," page 341
- Handbook 37, "Critical Listening and Observing," pages 363–366

Also note as precisely as possible any comments or bits of conversation that seem meaningful. A bit of dialogue can be even more memorable than a collection of sensory details. For instance, think about the power of this quotation from Deborah Sontag's report: "They're delivering ice, God bless them. Ice is gold."

3. Pick a topic. Is there one event or some strong image that keeps coming to mind? If so, perhaps your topic has already chosen you. If not, you may want to try freewriting about events you've witnessed to see which one interests you most. You may not be able to pick a topic until after you have drafted for a while.

4. Look for a focus. What had the biggest impact on you? This could be a sound, an image, a bit of dialogue, a key event, or even a general impression. Make this the focus of your account. In other words, when you write your account, make sure that this thing comes across to your readers just as strongly as it did to you. If you can't find a focus now, try drafting for a while. Also bear in mind that as you draft, your focus may change.

One Student's Process

While scouting around her school for events, Rene Froehmer witnessed a fight. Since her thoughts kept returning to this fight, she chose it as her topic. Then, after reviewing her notes on the event, Rene decided to focus on the fact that the bigger kid didn't want to fight, but the smaller one did.

<u>Fight</u>

in each other's face
lots of yelling
fists clenched
big kid doesn't want to fight, but smaller one does—why?
✔ smaller kid shoves first
big kid is suddenly all over him
✔ Has he fought before?
✔ Was he kicked out of other schools for fighting?
✔ Was he afraid he'd be kicked out of our school?
crowd forms circle
cheering
teacher breaks it up
blood all over smaller kid's face, but he's smiling
big kid is hauled to office

Grammar TIP

If you use direct quotations in your report, be sure to use quotation marks correctly. For help, see Handbook 49, "Punctuation," pages 664–665.

for PICK A TOPIC

INDIVIDUALIZING INSTRUCTION: BASIC STUDENTS If students have trouble getting started, remind them of events that the class as a whole witnessed. Suggest that students brainstorm in small groups to help them recall details about the event.

for LOOK FOR A FOCUS

MODELING To help students learn to trust their own impressions, tell about an event you witnessed with a friend or family member and how the two of you recalled different aspects of it. Stress that the impressions of the writer are what counts in an eyewitness report.

for ONE STUDENT'S PROCESS

CRITICAL THINKING: MAKING INFERENCES Have students notice that Rene's notes contain unanswered questions about the boys in the fight and the details of the scene. Ask how she might have gotten answers to these questions (by interviewing the boys). Encourage students to include in their notes comments or questions about people's motives.

Art Connection

Students covering a local news event who are interested in photography might take pictures of key people and events. Afterward they can evaluate the details captured in the pictures and determine what should be explained in words. Encourage students to include a photo layout in the final copy of their reports.

DRAFT AND DISCOVER

Objectives

- To draft an eyewitness report
- To respond to one's own draft and to that of a peer

Teaching Strategies

for BEGIN WRITING

INDIVIDUALIZING INSTRUCTION: AUDITORY LEARNERS These students may wish to begin drafting what they remember hearing at the event. For example, they might begin by writing the most memorable dialogue and then filling in other details.

for THINK ABOUT YOUR GOALS

KEY TO UNDERSTANDING: FOCUS Remind students that their reports should focus on the one impression that struck them most dramatically and that they want readers to remember. Point out that the focus of the Student Model on pages 52–53 comes at the end. Unlike Rene, however, students may choose to open their reports with the most memorable element or to make it a recurring image throughout.

for GIVE YOUR ACCOUNT A SHAPE . . .

CRITICAL THINKING: ANALYZING Help students analyze the structure of the Student Model on pages 52–53. The first three paragraphs, before the fight begins, are the opening. The next two paragraphs, which describe the fight, make up the middle. The last three paragraphs, which focus on the image of the smaller boy's weird smile, make up the ending.

Writer's Choice Some writers prefer to draft carefully; others take a more adventuresome approach. You can select details from your notes now to create a plan for drafting or just see which details come to mind as you put ideas on paper.

DRAFT AND DISCOVER

1. Begin writing. You can start by writing about any part of the event that interests you. For example, you might begin by writing about the moment of greatest excitement, by relating your first impressions of the scene, or by describing an image that keeps coming to mind. Then work your way backward or forward from this material to fill out the rest of your account.

2. Think about your goals. Your main goal should be to get your readers to feel as if they were in the center of the action. A second goal is to give your account a clear and vivid focus.

Rene Froehmer thought she wanted to focus on the fact that the bigger boy didn't want to fight but the smaller boy did. As she drafted, however, she realized that what kept coming to mind was the odd fact that the bloodied smaller boy had smiled. So she switched her focus to the strange smile.

3. Work with your draft. Try using different details in different drafts of your account to see which ones best help you to accomplish your goals. Notice the details Deborah Sontag selects to show how people were working together cooperatively.

> The storm clouds darkened. Mr. Bruscia and his neighbors clambered on and off their makeshift roofs, trying to secure the new plywood, the tar paper, and the plastic sheeting with extra nails.

4. Give your account a shape, and check your organization. Look at your report as a whole. Does it have a strong opening, a well-developed middle, and an ending that effectively brings your account to a close? Have you organized your details sensibly and linked them with transitions where necessary?

PROBLEM SOLVING

"How do I write a strong beginning and an effective ending?"

For information on ways to begin and end compositions, see

- Handbook 16, "Introductions," pages 278–280
- Handbook 17, "Conclusions," pages 281–283

Grammar Connection

Remind students to use quotation marks only when citing a speaker's exact words. If students cannot recall those words, they can paraphrase them in an indirect quotation without quotation marks.

TEACHER'S LOUNGE

"One of the main tasks of the school teacher is to take a roomful of live wires and see that they're grounded."

from *Educator's Lifetime Library*

5. Take a break. Once you've finished your first draft, put it aside for a few hours or even a few days. Then use the following questions to help you and your readers review this draft.

REVIEW YOUR WRITING

Questions for Yourself

- What have I done to help readers feel as if they were actually at the scene themselves? What more could I do?
- Does the image or moment I focused on come across clearly?
- What did I discover about this event by writing about it?

Questions for Your Peer Readers

- What words and phrases helped you to feel that you were at the scene?
- What parts did you have trouble "seeing"?
- What was missing? What do you want to know more about?
- What images, moments, and ideas do you recall most vividly?
- Was the account easy to read and understand? What, if anything, is unclear?
- What could I do to make my report flow more smoothly and naturally?

One Student's Process

Here is part of Rene's first draft. Read it and then review the peer comments. What comments, if any, would you add?

As the two teen boys began yelling, everybody in the area knew that a fight was going to occur. I was on my way over to a friend's house, but when I heard the yelling, I stopped to watch. They were in each other's face, yelling rude remarks. But I got the impression that the smaller kid wanted to fight more than the other one did. Finally, the smaller boy couldn't wait any longer and hit his enemy.

Grammar TIP

Using the present tense helps your readers feel that the story is unfolding as they're reading about it. If you use the present tense, don't suddenly switch to the past tense or the future tense. Such switches can confuse your readers.

Peer Reader Comments

I like the way you get right into the action.

What were they yelling?

What makes you think this? Where did he hit him? I need more details to picture this clearly.

for REVIEW YOUR WRITING

SPEAKING AND LISTENING To help students get a fresh perspective on their report, have them read it aloud into a tape recorder and play it back several times, evaluating a different element of their work each time they listen.

for ONE STUDENT'S PROCESS

PEER RESPONSE Point out that the peer reader asked questions about unclear parts of Rene's draft. Encourage peer readers in your class to do likewise; point out that sometimes, asking questions is more helpful to the writer than giving specific advice.

for ONE STUDENT'S PROCESS

CRITICAL THINKING: EVALUATING Point out the peer reader's comment about Rene's opening. Ask students whether they liked the opening as much as the peer reader did. Then ask what other openings Rene could have used. Encourage students to try two or three different kinds of openings in their reports and to choose the best one for the final draft.

Grammar Connection

To demonstrate the effect of using the present tense in an eyewitness report, have a volunteer read aloud the opening paragraph of One Student's Process on this page, replacing past-tense verbs with present-tense ones. Have students discuss the difference in effect, then vote on which version they prefer.

Revise Your Writing

Objectives

- To evaluate responses to a draft of an eyewitness report and to revise a draft with those responses in mind
- To evaluate the effectiveness of the opening and closing of an eyewitness report
- To evaluate the structure of a draft, paragraph by paragraph

for SHOW, DON'T TELL

HELPFUL HINT One way for writers to discover additional sensory details is to return mentally to the scene of the event being described. They can replay the scene in their minds, looking for details that they may have overlooked. Point out the vivid words *swerved, screeched,* and *waddled* in the excerpts from the model. Encourage students to use a thesaurus to find vivid words with which to replace words in their draft that do not paint a vivid picture.

for CHECK YOUR OPENING AND CLOSING

HELPFUL HINT As an alternative to ending their reports with a sensory image, students might close with a strong quotation or piece of dialogue that reinforces their focus. Point out how Deborah Sontag closed her report with a quote that emphasized both the desperation and the determination of the survivors.

Revise Your Writing

1. Review your responses and goals. Look at your peer responses as well as your own notes and goals. Then decide which changes you might want to make.

2. Show, don't tell. In the body of your composition, look for general statements or conclusions. Think about replacing them with the sensory details and quotations from which you drew these conclusions in the first place.

PROBLEM SOLVING

"How can I 'show' rather than 'tell' a story?"

For more information on showing instead of telling, see

- Handbook 13, "Show, Don't Tell," pages 262–267

Deborah Sontag could have just told her readers that the hurricane victims were still struggling to survive. Instead, she uses sensory details and quotations to show these people dealing with their hardships.

> [He] swerved around pretzels of metal railing and bumped over downed wires that, the radio kept warning, could still be live.
>
> Mr. Bruscia screeched to a halt as a hog waddled across the street.
>
> "That pig just blew into the neighborhood during the storm," he said.

3. Check your opening and closing. Your beginning should interest your readers in your account. Your ending should leave them with something to think about.

If your opening and closing still need work, sensory details might help you to improve them. Sensory details can help your readers understand what something or someone looks, smells, tastes, feels, and sounds like. For example, Rene Froehmer first involves readers in the fight with descriptive statements such as, "They were in each other's face, yelling rude remarks." Likewise, she uses sensory details to create a vivid closing image of a bloodied young boy smiling with "light red teeth."

PROFESSIONAL NOTEBOOK

Advice from the Author In *Writing with Power,* Peter Elbow gives this tip to enliven students' reports:

"Direct all your efforts into experiencing—or re-experiencing—what you are writing about. . . . Be there. See it. *Participate* in whatever you are writing about and then just let the words come of their own accord."

Paragraphs at Work Each paragraph in an eyewitness report should convey a single main idea or impression. When you revise your account, check the content of your paragraphs.

- Make sure that each paragraph conveys only one main idea or impression.
- Make sure that the sentences in each paragraph contain enough sensory details to develop one idea or impression adequately.
- Eliminate details that don't belong, or move them to other paragraphs where they do belong.

One Student's Process

After thinking about her peer readers' comments and questions, Rene decided to take out unnecessary information and add specific dialogue and details. Notice how her changes affected one part of her draft.

¶ The other guy wouldn't budge. He knew that if he started the fight, he wouldn't be at this school for long.

As the two teen boys began yelling, everybody in the area, including me, knew that a fight was going to occur. ~~I was on my way over to a friend's house, but when I heard the yelling, I stopped to watch.~~ They were in each other's face, yelling rude remarks. ¶ "So do you wanna fight?" the smaller boy said. "Come on!" ~~But I got the impression that the smaller kid wanted to fight more than the other one did.~~

¶ Finally, the smaller boy couldn't wait any longer. He ~~and~~ hit his enemy on the shoulder of his white T-shirt. The second boy reacted quickly to this, as if it had happened to him many times before.

Writing TIP

Think about what your audience needs to know to understand the event you've witnessed. Then provide them with that background information.

for PARAGRAPHS AT WORK

HELPFUL HINT After students have read the instruction about paragraphing, use One Student's Process on this page to illustrate some of the principles mentioned. For example, ask why Rene deleted the sentence about being on her way to a friend's house. (Sample: It did not contribute to the main idea or impression of the paragraph, which focused on suspense caused by the feeling that the fight could begin at any moment.)

Then ask why Rene decided to start a new paragraph with the sentence beginning "Finally, the smaller boy . . ." (to signal that the fight was about to begin). Finally, ask why Rene decided to add two sentences after this sentence (to provide sensory details that would help develop the scene).

GENERAL NOTE

MANAGING THE PAPER LOAD At this point you may want to walk around the room and spot-check students' opening paragraphs to make sure they convey a single main idea or impression. Point out details that could be eliminated or added to the body of the report to support and illustrate the main idea.

for ONE STUDENT'S PROCESS

CRITICAL THINKING: EVALUATING Have students reread the Peer Reader Comments on page 57. Ask why Rene added the smaller boy's dialogue. (Her peer reader wanted to know what the two boys were yelling.) Then ask why Rene added the descriptive details about how the fight started. (Her peer reader could not clearly picture the fight.)

MULTICULTURAL Connection

Many communities have festivals to celebrate the harvest of local fruits and vegetables. As a way of learning about other cultures, send a team of interested students to cover one of these fairs or markets in a nearby area. Ask students to gather information about the event and its traditional purpose and meaning for the community. Suggest that they interview people and take photographs. On their return students can write an eyewitness report to be published in the school or local newspaper.

for LINKING GRAMMAR AND WRITING

INDIVIDUALIZING INSTRUCTION: ESL STUDENTS Because of their limited English vocabularies, some ESL students may need help with choosing precise and descriptive action verbs, as they work to improve their eyewitness reports. Pair each of these students with a native English speaker. The two students can work together to identify vivid verbs in a thesaurus or dictionary.

PROOFREAD

Guidelines for Evaluation

IDEAS AND CONTENT

- focuses on one main image or impression of the event
- uses sensory details and dialogue to re-create the event
- gives background information, if needed, to help readers understand the event
- has a strong opening and closing

STRUCTURE AND FORM

- presents details in a logical order
- has a clear beginning, middle, and end
- has well-developed paragraphs, each conveying one main idea or impression
- uses appropriate transitions

GRAMMAR, USAGE, AND MECHANICS

- displays standard grammar, usage, and mechanics
- uses vivid action verbs
- uses verb tenses correctly
- punctuates quotations correctly

COMPUTER TIP

If you write *there* when you should have written *their,* a computer spelling checker will not identify *there* as an error. So in addition to using a spelling checker, always look over your writing yourself to make sure you have used words correctly. To check your word choices, see "Using the Right Word" on pages 688–691.

LINKING GRAMMAR AND WRITING

Action Verbs

An action verb tells that something is happening, has happened, or will happen. A linking verb, on the other hand, simply states that something exists, or it links a subject with a word that describes or renames it. To help readers feel as if they were actually at the scene of an event, look for ways to use action verbs rather than linking verbs. Notice how an action verb can improve a sentence.

The wind was on her face.
The wind cooled her face.

Now compare these two versions of a sentence from "Amid the Rubble." Which one would you say conveys a more powerful image?

Version 1

Gnats and mosquitoes appeared in the gusting winds as the rain started falling in sheets.

Version 2

Gnats and mosquitoes swirled in the gusting winds as the rain started falling in sheets.

Standards for Evaluation

DESCRIPTIVE WRITING

An eyewitness report

- uses sensory details, dialogue, and action verbs to show what was observed, bringing the event to life
- has a clear focus
- provides readers with the information they need to understand the event
- presents details in a sensible order that is easy to follow

PROOFREAD

1. Proofread your work. Correct any errors in grammar, usage, and mechanics.

2. Make a clean copy of your account. Is your eyewitness report ready to publish? Give it a final once-over, using the Standards for Evaluation shown in the margin. Then make a clean final copy.

PUBLISH AND PRESENT

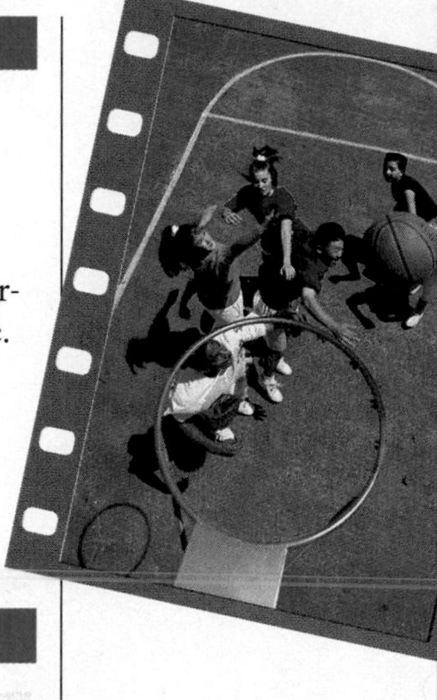

- **Publish your report in a school or local newspaper.** Newspapers often publish community-interest stories. Submit your report for publication. Include a suggested headline and any photographs you may have of the event.
- **Arrange an oral reading.** Read your account to a group interested in the event you witnessed. Share any photos you may have.
- **Create a "News of the Week" bulletin board display.** Mount your eyewitness account on a current events bulletin board. Then, as you and your classmates write new eyewitness reports, replace the "old news" with "new news."

REFLECT ON YOUR WRITING

WRITER TO WRITER

There aren't even phrases in the languages for half the things happening just on the block where I live, not yet anyhow.

Toni Cade Bambara, novelist, short story writer, and editor

1. Add your report to your portfolio. While the eyewitness report is still fresh in your mind, you might want to write some notes to yourself about your writing process. Answering the following questions can help you get started. Attach your notes to your final draft before putting your draft in your portfolio.

- How did I find an event for my report?
- In what ways was the process of writing an eyewitness account different from writing other kinds of narratives?
- What writing techniques were particularly useful to me?
- Were my peer readers' responses helpful? Why or why not?
- What would I do differently next time?

2. Explore additional writing ideas. See the suggestions for writing field notes on pages 64–65 and Springboards on page 66.

Reteaching

After students have completed their papers, assess the needs of students who were not successful in developing an effective eyewitness report; then assign the appropriate handbook minilessons as well as the Workshop Support Materials listed in the Teaching Preview, pages 47a–47b.

Concepts commonly requiring reteaching for this assignment are

- **Handbook 13, Show, Don't Tell, pp. 262–267**
- **Handbook 16, Introductions, pp. 278–280**
- **Handbook 17, Conclusions, pp. 281–283**

The following suggestions and resources may also be useful.

Confusing Sequence of Events Have students use the Sequence Chain on page 7 of the Thinking Skills Worksheets to practice ordering a sequence of events.

Extension and Enrichment

Have students imagine how a TV news reporter would cover a typical day in students' lives. Have them write mock eyewitness reports describing the events of their day.

Closure: Reflect on Your Writing

Direct students to the third reflection question, "What writing techniques were particularly useful to me?" Ask them to describe specifically the prewriting strategies they used. Did they create a cluster or a list? Which prewriting techniques would they want to try again?

Related ASSIGNMENT

Starting from LITERATURE

Objectives

- To respond to and analyze field notes
- To create field notes based on observations of the natural world

Motivate

Before directing students to the Starting from Literature box, have them freewrite a description of an interesting animal, then share their descriptions orally in a small group.

BUILD ON PRIOR KNOWLEDGE

After students have shared their descriptions, ask how easy or difficult it was to write about the animal and what might have made the task easier. (Sample: Having the animal or a picture of it in front of them) Then ask students whether they have ever seen TV documentaries in which scientists recorded observations of animals in their natural environment. (Students may recall *National Geographic* and other TV specials.) Tell them that such recorded observations are called field notes.

SET A PURPOSE

After students read the opening question in the Starting from Literature box, ask whether any animals they described in the Motivate activity were observed in their natural environment and if so, how students managed not to frighten them away. As students read the field notes, have them pay attention to the techniques Adams uses to observe his subjects and record his feelings about them.

Related ASSIGNMENT

Field Notes

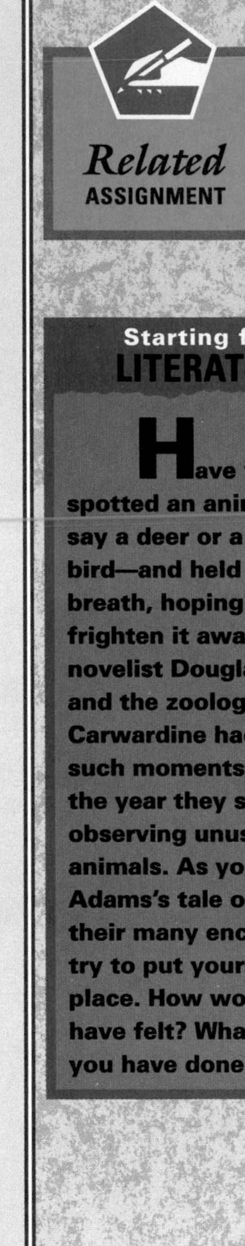

Starting from LITERATURE

Have you ever spotted an animal—say a deer or a strange bird—and held your breath, hoping not to frighten it away? The novelist Douglas Adams and the zoologist Mark Carwardine had many such moments during the year they spent observing unusual animals. As you read Adams's tale of one of their many encounters, try to put yourself in his place. How would you have felt? What would you have done?

from

LAST CHANCE TO SEE

by Douglas Adams and Mark Carwardine

JUST AS WE WERE ABOUT TO GIVE UP and go back, we tried one more turning, and suddenly the forest seemed to be thick with gorillas. A few feet above us, a female was lounging in a tree, idly stripping the bark off a twig with her teeth. She noticed us but was not interested. Two babies were cavorting recklessly ten feet from the ground in a very slender tree, and a young male was chugging through the undergrowth nearby on the lookout for food. We stared at the two babies in astounded fascination at the wonderful wild abandon with which they were hurling themselves around each other and the

62 Workshop 2

for FURTHER READING

To give students a sense of the variety of styles writers use to describe the natural world, you might read aloud passages from "Green Gulch" by Loren Eiseley, "Animal Craftsmen" by Bruce Brooks, *Pilgrim at Tinker Creek* by Annie Dillard, or *The Way to Rainy Mountain* by N. Scott Momaday.

MORE ABOUT THE MODEL

Author Note Douglas Adams was born in England in 1952. He is the author of the popular science fiction series *The Hitchhiker's Guide to the Galaxy* and has written for the TV series *Dr. Who.* Mark Carwardine is a zoologist, writer, and photographer, who has worked for the World Wildlife Fund.

terrible meagerness of the tree in which they had elected to do it. It was hard to believe the tree could support them, and indeed it couldn't. They suddenly came crashing down through it, having completely misunderstood the law of gravity, and slunk off sheepishly into the undergrowth.

We followed, encountering one gorilla after another until at last we came across another silverback lying on his side beneath a bush, with his long arm folded up over his head, scratching his opposite ear while he watched a couple of leaves doing not very much. It was instantly clear what he was doing. He was contemplating life. He was hanging out. It was quite obvious. Or rather, the temptation to find it quite obvious was absolutely overwhelming. . . .

I crept closer to the silverback, slowly and quietly on my hands and knees, till I was about eighteen inches away from him. He glanced around at me unconcernedly, as if I was just someone who had walked into the room, and continued his contemplations. I guessed that the animal was probably about the same height as me—over six feet tall—but I would think about twice as heavy. Mostly muscle, with soft grey-black skin hanging quite loosely on his front, covered in coarse black hair.

As I moved again, he shifted himself away from me, just about six inches, as if I had sat slightly too close to him on a sofa and he was grumpily making a bit more room. Then he lay on his front with his chin on his fist, idly scratching his cheek with his other hand. I sat as quiet and still as I could. . . .

After a quiet interval had passed, I carefully pulled the pink writing paper out of my bag and started to make the notes that I'm writing from at the moment. This seemed to interest him a little more. I suppose he had simply never seen pink writing paper before. His eyes followed as my hand squiggled across the paper, and after a while he reached out and touched first the paper and then the top of my ballpoint pen—not to take it away from me, or even to interrupt me, just to see what it was and what it felt like. I felt very moved by this and had a foolish impulse to want to show him my camera as well.

Think & Respond

Discuss with classmates your reactions to Douglas Adams's account. What parts were most exciting? Why? Do you think you might have reacted the way Adams did? List some of the details you think probably came straight from Adams's notes. What do you notice about these details you listed?

Think & Respond

ELICIT PERSONAL RESPONSES

After students read the excerpt, have them discuss the questions in the Think & Respond box.

Students' answers will vary. They might call most exciting either the moment when Adams crept to within eighteen inches of the silverback (adult male), or the moment when the gorilla reached out and touched Adams's pen. Some students may say they would have used more caution in approaching so powerful an animal. Details that probably came directly from the authors' notes include "female . . . stripping the bark off a twig. . . . two babies . . . cavorting . . . ten feet from the ground. . . . silverback . . . over six feet tall. . . Mostly muscle . . . soft grey-black skin hanging quite loosely on his front," and so on. Students should notice how specific these details of size, age, sex, location, and movement are and how they are based on the writer's direct observations.

EXPLORE THE AUTHORS' TECHNIQUES

Discuss the specific details and the vivid action verbs (such as *lounging, cavorting, chugging, hurling, crashing,* and *slunk)* used to describe the gorillas. Also, point out that Adams and Carwardine compare the behavior of the gorillas to that of humans and that they present their notes as a humorous adventure, complete with a suspenseful plot. Be sure students understand that these literary characteristics are not necessary components of field notes but definitely add interest to the authors' presentation of what they observed.

MORE ABOUT THE MODEL

Writer Douglas Adams and naturalist Mark Carwardine met in 1985 when a magazine editor assigned them to find and report on a rare animal called the aye-aye. When Adams learned from Carwardine of the many animal species that were becoming extinct, the two undertook a ten-month adventure around the world in search of endangered animals. Their quest to see the Komodo dragon of Indonesia, the white rhino of Zaire, the river dolphin of China, and other fascinating creatures is recounted in their book *Last Chance to See.*

Writing ON YOUR OWN

Tell students that Douglas Adams is a writer of humorous novels and that the tone and purpose of these field notes reflect this fact. Encourage them to write field notes that reflect their own interests and writing styles.

Handbooks for Help and Practice

The following handbook may be used as a mini-lesson before students begin writing or as a resource when problems arise.

- **Critical Listening and Observing, pp. 363–366**

Teaching Strategies

for DECIDE ON A PURPOSE

HELPFUL HINT Have students save their field notes for later use in the Guided Assignments for Workshops 4 or 5.

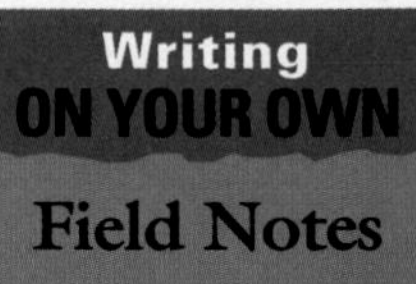

Writing ON YOUR OWN

Field Notes

INVITATION TO *Write*

Field notes used to be thought of as strictly a scientist's way of recording observations made in the natural world—that is, "the field." Today, however, writers in many professions have discovered the benefits of taking field notes.

Think of something in the natural world that you find interesting or want to learn more about. Observe it and write field notes in which you record your observations, thoughts, and feelings.

FINDING A SUBJECT

1. Think of subjects of interest that can be observed. For ideas, complete each of the following sentence starters four or five times.

- I want to know more about . . .
- I'm really fascinated by animals like . . .
- Why do people . . .

2. Pick a subject. Freewrite on a few subjects, and then choose the one that interests you most.

3. Decide on a purpose. Do you want to learn more about your subject? Are you hoping to see the effects or results of something? Will you compare it with another subject?

4. Observe your subject. Plan a suitable observation period. For instance, if you've arranged to observe a snake, you may want to see how it behaves before and after a feeding.

5. Record the data you obtain from all your senses. Be alert to the sounds things make, their colors under various conditions, and any smells they give off. Also record when events occur. Take notes on any important measurements such as distance, height, or weight. Draw sketches or diagrams if they would be useful.

Writing TIP

Try creating the kind of three-column chart many scientists use. Label the left-hand column "Time," the center column "Actions and Details Observed," and the right-hand column "Personal Reactions, Impressions, and Comments." Then fill in each column with appropriate information.

Science Connection

You may want to work with your students' science teacher to coordinate this assignment with a particular field-observation assignment in the science curriculum. You and the science teacher may want to team-teach a lesson on appropriate techniques of observation and note-taking in the field.

Math Connection

You may want to have students convert any measurements to metric units or to compute percentages of growth or change in organisms over time. Work with a math or science teacher to coordinate the quantifying aspects of the field notes.

REVIEWING YOUR FIELD NOTES

1. Notice what is important. In your notes, look for the following:

- **Patterns of events or other details** For instance, does your subject change color whenever it hears a loud noise?
- **Especially exciting, interesting, odd, or funny details** Adams includes an amusing incident involving two baby gorillas playing on a slender tree.
- **Details that make a strong impression on you**
- **Strong reactions or feelings** "I felt very moved by this," Adams writes, "and had a foolish impulse to want to show him my camera as well."
- **Conclusions you draw from your observations** For example, "It was instantly clear what he [the silverback gorilla] was doing. He was contemplating life. He was hanging out."
- **Examples that support your conclusions**

2. Write a summary. In your summary, you might cover the important details you observed and comment on them, discuss your impressions of the subject, or draw conclusions.

Writer's Choice If your subject is likely to be unfamiliar to most people, you may want to compare it to something people commonly recognize. Similes, metaphors, and other poetic devices are especially good for making such comparisons.

SHARING YOUR FIELD NOTES

- **Publish a report or present your findings to a group.** Pick a focus for your report and decide what goals you want to accomplish. Include sketches, photographs, lists, and any other kinds of data you gathered "in the field."
- **Create a display.** Use diagrams, sketches, photographs, or objects related to your subject to create a display for your classroom, school, or local library.

PROBLEM SOLVING

"How do I draw conclusions or make generalizations from my notes?"

For help in drawing conclusions and making generalizations, see

- Handbook 31, "Critical Thinking and Writing," pages 337–339

Guidelines for Evaluation

EFFECTIVE FIELD NOTES

- contain precise, vivid details and objective data based on careful observation
- highlight especially interesting or unusual details
- may include the observer's impressions, reactions, and feelings
- include a summary with commentary or conclusions about the subject

for WRITE A SUMMARY

CRITICAL THINKING:DRAWING CONCLUSIONS As students draw conclusions, caution them against the pitfalls of overgeneralization. In addition, you may remind them to use with caution words such as *all, never,* and *always.* For instance, a generalization such as "All silverbacks are friendly" cannot be justified by these field notes and is probably a false conclusion. Suggest that students use the Drawing Conclusions chart on page 10 of the Thinking Skills Worksheets to help them draw sound conclusions.

GENERAL NOTE

MANAGING THE PAPER LOAD You may want to share evaluation responsibilities for this assignment with a science or math teacher. You can comment on the vividness and clarity of the details and examples, while the subject-area teachers evaluate the accuracy of the details, the soundness of the conclusions, and the correctness of the computations.

Springboards

Teaching Strategies

for MEDIA

COOPERATIVE LEARNING If possible, send out pairs of "eyewitness news" reporters to find newsworthy stories in your school or town. One student in each pair can operate the video camera while the other can narrate an eyewitness account and interview witnesses.

for LITERATURE

CRITICAL THINKING: CLASSIFYING Before students start writing their diary entries, suggest that they classify the situation, using the following categories: what the character witnessed, why it was important, what the character said and felt at the time.

for THEATER

HELPFUL HINT Students interested in adapting their eyewitness reports into scripts may want to consult Workshop 3, Related Assignment: Developing a Script, on pages 84–88.

Springboards

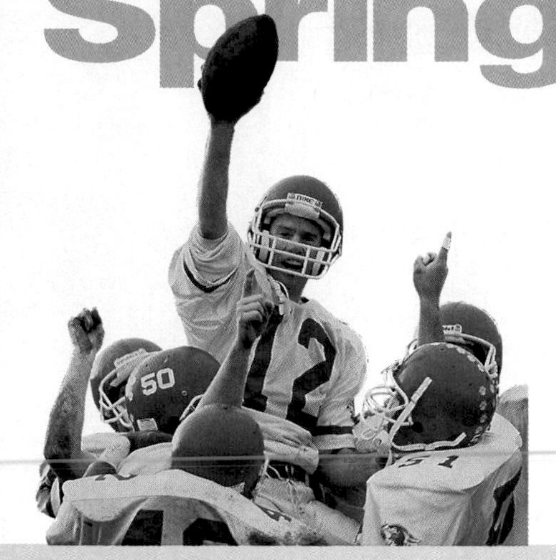

Science Go into the field—be it kitchen, zoo, or back yard—and write field notes on something you observe. Then use your notes to create a report in which you present your information as if it were new, groundbreaking material. In your conclusion, explain why your readers (scientists) should be excited about your discoveries.

MEDIA Write and present an on-the-scene news report about an event you witnessed. Try to include photographs or a videotape, statements from other witnesses and people who were involved, and documents or other items that might shed light on what happened.

Art Create a drawing, painting, collage, sculpture, or other type of artwork to show your impression of an event you observed. Title your piece and add to it a brief written explanation of what it shows.

Literature Imagine that you're a character from literature who witnessed an important event. Write an entry for this character's diary. For example, what might Angie Lowe or Cochise from Louis L'Amour's story "The Gift of Cochise" have written after their first meeting? Include the character's comments, thoughts, and feelings.

THEATER Collaborate with a group of classmates to script a reenactment of an event you witnessed. Feel free to include a narrator to provide background information and commentary. Then perform your reenactment.

After the Alaskan Oil Spill,
Sigrid Holmwood, Age 11

Who Flang That Ball?

A reporter is interviewing Infield Ingersoll, a former shortstop known for his colorful language.

"Well," he said, "it was the day us Wombats plew the Pink Sox . . . "

"Plew the Pink Sox?" I interrupted. "Don't you mean *played?"*

Infield's look changed to disappointment. "Slay, slew. Play, plew. What's the matter with that?"

"Slay is an irregular verb," I pointed out. . . .

He paused belligerently, and then went on. "What I'm tryin' to do is easify the languish. I make all regular verbs irregular. Once they're all irregular, then it's just the same like they're all regular.

That way I don't gotta stop and think."

He had something there. "Go on with your story," I said.

"Well, it was the top of the fifth, when this Sox batter wang out a high pop fly. I raught for it."

"Raught?"

"Past tense of verb to reach. Teach, taught. Reach,—"

"Sorry," I said. "Go ahead."

"Anyhow I raught for it, only the sun blound me."

"You mean blinded?"

"Look," Infield said patiently, "you wouldn't say a pitcher winded up, would you? So, there I was, blound by the sun, and the ball just nuck the tip of my glove—that's nick, nuck; same congregation as stick, stuck. But luckily I caught it just as it skam the top of my shoe."

"Skam? Could that be the past tense of *to skim?"*

"Yeah, yeah, same as swim, swam. . . . Well, just then the umpire cell, 'Safe!' Naturally I was surprose. Because I caught that fly, only the ump cell the runner safe."

"Cell is to *call* as *fell* is to *fall,* I surpose?" I inquired.

"Right. . . . so I yold at him, 'Robber! That decision smold!' "

W. F. Miksch

on the LIGHT side

Ask a student who is gifted in oral interpretation to read this humorous piece aloud. Afterward, students can discuss their own frustrations with verb tenses and perhaps invent irregular verb forms of their own.

Compound Subjects and Compound Verbs

Objectives

- To identify compound subjects and compound verbs in sentences
- To compose sentences with compound subjects and compound verbs and to punctuate them correctly

Teaching Strategies

GENERAL NOTE

KEY TO UNDERSTANDING To demonstrate the comparative effectiveness of sentences with compound subjects and compound verbs, write the following multi-sentence version of Model C on the board:

Johnny stretched out on his back. I stretched out on my back. He looked at the stars. I looked at them too.

Ask students how this version differs from the model. Be sure they see that the series of short sentences can be repetitious and monotonous.

Sentence

COMPOSING

Compound Subjects and Compound Verbs

You can add information to your sentences by including more than one subject or verb. You can also use compound subjects and compound verbs to add rhythm and variety to your sentences. Notice how the compound subjects and compound verbs in the sentences below make each sentence more complete.

Model A Jewels,[S] pins,[S] and brooches[S] glittered in her tangle of weedy hair. *(compound subject)* **Lloyd Alexander, "The Foundling"**

Model B Mrs. Jones stopped,[V] jerked[V] him around in front of her, put[V] a half nelson about his neck, and continued[V] to drag him up the street. *(compound verb)* **Langston Hughes, "Thank You, M'am"**

Model C Johnny[S] and I[S] stretched[V] out on our backs and looked[V] at the stars. *(compound subject and compound verb)* **S. E. Hinton, *The Outsiders***

▶ **ON THE MARK** Place a comma after every item except the last item in a series of three or more subjects or verbs. Do not use a comma with two subjects or two verbs.

A. Combining Sentences Make a new sentence by replacing the italicized part in the first sentence with the detailed information underlined in the second sentence. Eliminate any words in the second sentence that are not underlined. The new sentence will contain a compound subject or verb. Punctuate correctly.

1. He *did several things.* He stood up and eased his shoulders, turned his feet in their ankle sockets, rubbed the back of his neck. **Harper Lee, *To Kill a Mockingbird***
2. *We* were seated at the dining-room table having lunch. We were Daddy, Mama, Doodle, and I. **James Hurst, "The Scarlet Ibis"**
3. He *performed several jobs.* He sorted the new crates, stacked the canned goods, and lugged the filthy garbage pails out back. **Robert Lipsyte, *The Contender***

B. Unscrambling and Imitating Sentences Unscramble each set of sentence chunks below to create a sentence that matches one of the models on page 68. Then write a correctly punctuated sentence of your own that imitates each model. Be sure each of your sentences contains a compound subject or compound verb.

1. Write sentences that imitate Model A.
   on the ferry boat / traveled across the bay / cars, trucks, and vans
2. Write sentences that imitate Model B.
   turned himself around in the middle of his flight / lifted the ball above his head / the star player / and proceeded to jam it through the hoop / leaped
3. Write sentences that imitate Model C.
   and landed on the air mattress / the firefighter and the cat / leaped down from the roof

C. Expanding Sentences Use your imagination to expand the parts of sentences given below by adding compound subjects or compound verbs in the places indicated. Be sure to use commas to separate the items in each series.

1. Mr. Jamison picked up his briefcase, *(add two more actions that he did)*.
   Mildred D. Taylor, *Roll of Thunder, Hear My Cry*
2. In her room, Jane locked the door against the sound of the playing children, *(add two more actions that Jane did)*.
   Mary Elizabeth Vroman, "See How They Run"
3. The insects buzzed, *(add four more sounds that the insects made)* as the air grew warmer in the sunset. **Richard Adams, *Watership Down***
4. There was a pontoon bridge across the river, and *(add five things crossing the bridge)* were crossing it.
   Ernest Hemingway, "Old Man at the Bridge"
5. Every muscle, *(add two more things)* was tired, dead tired.
   Jack London, *The Call of the Wild*

Grammar Refresher To learn more about compound subjects and verbs, see Handbook 39, "The Sentence and Its Parts," pages 403–405.

Additional Resource

Sentence Composing Copy Masters, pp. 3-4

Answer Key

A. Combining Sentences

1. He stood up and eased his shoulders, turned his feet in their ankle sockets, rubbed the back of his neck.
2. Daddy, Mama, Doodle, and I were seated at the dining-room table having lunch.
3. He sorted the new crates, stacked the canned goods, and lugged the filthy garbage pails out back.

B. Unscrambling and Imitating Sentences

Unscrambled sentences are given. Imitative sentences will vary but should follow the same pattern.

1. Cars, trucks, and vans traveled across the bay on the ferry boat.
2. The star player leaped, turned himself around in the middle of his flight, lifted the ball above his head, and proceeded to jam it through the hoop.
3. The firefighter and the cat leaped down from the roof and landed on the air mattress.

C. Expanding Sentences

Answers will vary. Authors' sentences are given.

1. Mr. Jamison picked up his briefcase, ran his fingers through his graying hair, and met Papa's eyes.
   Mildred D. Taylor, *Roll of Thunder, Hear My Cry*
2. In her room, Jane locked the door against the sound of the playing children, put her head on the desk, and cried.
   Mary Elizabeth Vroman, "See How They Run"
3. The insects buzzed, whined, hummed, stridulated and droned as the air grew warmer in the sunset.
   Richard Adams, *Watership Down*
4. There was a pontoon bridge across the river, and carts, trucks, and men, women, and children were crossing it.
   Ernest Hemingway, "Old Man at the Bridge"
5. Every muscle, every fiber, every cell was tired, dead tired.
   Jack London, *The Call of the Wild*

3

Narrative and Literary Writing

Overview

Literary writing provides a means of self-expression and entertains an audience. In this workshop, students will apply skills learned in previous workshops on expressive and descriptive writing to complete assignments with two different literary forms: poetry and drama. Workshop 3 includes the following Guided and Related Assignments as well as the interdisciplinary project described on pages 69c–69d.

1. **Guided: Writing a Poem** invites students to express their emotions and experiences through carefully selected sensory words and figurative language. It encourages students to use words powerfully and economically and to consider the sounds of language, as well as the arrangement of words on a page.
2. **Related: Developing a Script** calls on students to dramatize a scene from fiction or from personal experience. Students use speaking and listening skills, as well as their imaginations to create realistic dialogue. They also write stage directions based on how they visualize the action of their scene.

Teaching Preview

Preparation Guide

1. Use the Overview on this page and the Teacher's Choice descriptions on page 71 as a basis for deciding which assignments to teach.
2. Preview the assignments and the teacher's notes and identify concepts that may require preteaching or extra support, given your class's abilities. The handbook mini-lessons suggested within the lesson may also provide guidance.
3. Preview the chart below for support materials in the Teacher's Resource File that may be used with this Workshop. Resources are for use with the Guided Assignment unless otherwise noted.

Support Materials

RESOURCES

Prewrite and Explore
Writing Resource Book, pp. 13–14
Thinking Skills Worksheets, pp. 3, 5
Starting Points for Writing, Writing Prompts for Fine Art, pp. 29–30, 36, 39–40, 42

Draft and Discover
Elaboration, Revision, and Proofreading Practice, p. 5
Writing Resource Book, pp. 15–16

Revise Your Writing
Elaboration, Revision, and Proofreading Practice, p. 6
Writing Resource Book, p. 17
Peer Response Guides, pp. 13–14
Guidelines for Writing Assessment and Portfolio Use, pp. 16, 29–31

Sentence Composing
Sentence Composing Copy Masters, pp. 5–6

Assessment
Tests and Writing Assessment Prompts, p. 3

Computer Software
Writer's DataBank
Electronic English Handbook

PROFESSIONAL RESOURCES AND MEDIA

Books and Journals
Connell, Marjorie, "Click: Poets at Work in the Middle School," *English Journal*, Vol. 79 (November 1990), pp. 30–31
Livingston, Myra Cohn, *Poem-Making: Ways to Begin Writing Poetry*, HarperCollins (1991)
Nye, Naomi Shihab, ed., *This Same Sky: A Collection of Poems from Around the World*, Four Winds (1992)

Films and Videos
Math . . . Who Needs It? Instructional Video, Lincoln, NE (1992) (58 min.)
Mutzmag, An Appalachian Folktale, Davenport Films, Delaplane, VA (1992) (53 min.)
3 Minutes from Broadway, Chip Taylor Communications, Derry, NH (1992) (29 min.)

Computer Software and Technology
"Author! Author!"—Play Writing, Mindplay, Danvers, MA (software) Apple II
Poetry Express, Mindscape/SVE, Chicago, IL (software), Apple II
Writing Adventure, DLM/SoftKat, Chatsworth, CA (software), Apple II

Linking Literature, Writing, and Grammar

The following options may be used to provide students with an integrated language experience. Begin by assigning and discussing any of the recommended pieces of literature. Use the suggested strategy to provide a link to the Guided Assignment.

LINKING LITERATURE AND WRITING

Option 1

Starting Point: "Celebration" by Alonzo Lopez, "the drum" by Nikki Giovanni, and "The Base Stealer" by Robert Francis on pages 72–73 of *The Writer's Craft.*

Strategy: Use the teaching suggestions on pages 72–73 to lead students into the Guided Assignment.

Option 2

Starting Point: "Watching Gymnasts" by Robert Francis on page 162 of McDougal, Littell's *Literature and Language,* Grade 8. (Additional suggestions for using *Literature and Language* can be found on page 71.)

Strategy: Read the poem aloud. Have students listen and try to visualize the actions of the gymnasts. Afterward, have them list words, phrases, and comparisons that helped them see, hear, and feel the gymnasts in action. Then introduce the Guided Assignment.

Option 3

Starting Point: "For My Sister Molly Who in the Fifties" by Alice Walker

Strategy: Have student volunteers read each stanza of the poem aloud. Then ask students to describe the feelings the speaker of the poem seems to have for her sister Molly. What details in the poem reveal her feelings? Can students think of a special relative or friend they would like to pay tribute to in a poem? Use the discussion to introduce the Guided Assignment.

LINKING WRITING AND GRAMMAR

As students work on the drafting or revision stages of this assignment, tell them that using modifiers is one way to add sensory details to their poems. However, caution them not to pad their writing with unnecessary modifiers. Write these examples on the board.

Helpful Modifier: *Gladly,* he agreed to help. (Ask students to replace the adverb with one that creates a different impression.)

Unnecessary Modifier: The racing cars *quickly* flew by. (Point out that the verb *flew* is enough to suggest quickness.

Have students check their poems for unnecessary modifiers. Go over pages 506–513 of the Grammar and Usage Handbook. If students need more help with modifiers, assign the exercises on those pages for reteaching. Additional practice can be found in the *Grammar and Usage Practice Book* on pages 57–59.

Management Guidelines

The chart below indicates the number of days recommended for each phase of the Guided and Related Assignments. These numbers are an estimate of the total time needed for each phase. In practice, of course, students may not complete each phase in one continuous session, nor will they necessarily progress from stage to stage in the linear order shown here. Stars indicate portions of the assignment that may be completed outside the classroom if time is limited or if teachers wish students to work independently.

WRITING A POEM

Starting from Literature	1 day
Prewrite and Explore	1–2 days*
Draft and Discover	1–2 days
Revise Your Writing	1–2 days*
Proofread	1 day*
Publish and Present	1 day
Reflect on Your Writing	1 day*
Reteaching	open
Extension and Enrichment	open*
Sentence Composing	open*

DEVELOPING A SCRIPT

Starting from Literature	1 day
Thinking about Your Scene	1–2 days*
Drafting Your Script	1–2 days
Reviewing Your Script	1 day
Publishing and Presenting	1–2 days

Project File

Shining Through the Ages: Stories of the Moon and Stars

Overview

Students participating in this project will study the roles that the moon and the stars have played in human cultures. They will study in depth one aspect of the relationship human beings have had with the moon and the stars. They will then present their findings, using a variety of presentation techniques. Finally, students will create their own myths, poems, or stories based on their experience.

Students will participate in the following activities:

- Gather information about the moon and the stars from literature and history
- Research scientific knowledge about the moon and the stars
- View artists' depictions of the moon and the stars
- Use language arts, science, math, social studies, and art skills to stage group presentations and to write and share their own moon and star myths, stories, and poems

Preparation Guide

Tell students that ever since prehistoric times, people have watched the moon and the stars and wondered about them. Suggest that the history of humankind is full of songs, myths, art, and scientific theories that deal with the moon and the stars.

Point out that during this project students will become experts on specific aspects of the moon and the stars and will make a multimedia presentation of their findings to the class. They will also write their own myths, stories, and poems based on what they discover.

Stage 1
Explore the Skies

1. In a class discussion, encourage students to list facts they know about the moon and the stars, such as their composition, location, and dimensions.

2. Suggest that besides simply being distant objects, the moon and the stars are sources of inspiration and wonder. Brainstorm with the class about the many ways people have been involved with these celestial bodies. Possible ideas include songs and nursery rhymes, myths and legends, navigation, calendars, and space travel (see *Resources, Stage 1*).

3. Have volunteers offer specific examples of how people have written about or studied the moon and the stars, such as the song "Blue Moon," legends about the man in the moon, and the Apollo space program. List the examples on the board.

TEAM TEACHING

The following activities may be used for team teaching or as enrichment and extension activities by the language arts teacher.

Science Investigate the study of astronomy. Examine the makeup of the moon and the stars, identify specific stars and their locations, and study the phases of the moon and the moon's relation to events on the earth.

Social Studies Learn about moon and star deities of various cultures. Study astrology and learn about planting cycles and religious rituals related to moon and star cycles (see *Resources, Stage 1*).

Math Discover how ancient cultures used the moon and the stars to calculate time and distance. Learn how an astrolabe works.

Language Arts Read moon and star tales from various cultures (see *Resources, Stage 1*).

Art View artworks showing moon, star, and sky deities of various cultures.

TEACHING TIPS

- Suggest that students examine a library catalog or a periodical index under the broad categories of "Moon" and "Star" to explore the wide range of material available.
- Invite a storyteller to visit and tell moon and star myths and legends (see *Resources, Stage 1*).

Stage 2
Focus on the Moon and the Stars

1. Divide the class into small groups,and have each group choose a topic relating to the moon and the stars and research it in depth. Groups might choose topics such as the following:
- myths and legends
- uses in navigation, agriculture, and timekeeping
- science fiction tales
- depictions in music and art
- space exploration

2. Have the members of each group share their findings, with one another.

3. Tell each group to decide how best to present their information to the rest of the class. Encourage them to produce multimedia presentations that include art, models, music, and other aids.

4. Direct the groups to stage their presentations for the class.

TEAM TEACHING

Science Study the Apollo moon missions, space probes, and other missions into space (see *Resources, Stage 2*).

Math Calculate and graph cosmic distances and time periods, and express them in terms of more familiar and conceivable distances and processes.

Social Studies Examine the importance of the moon and the stars in various cultures, past and present.

Music Choose and record music for presentations.

Art Prepare drawings, photographs, and other visuals for presentations.

TEACHING TIPS

- Encourage students to use nontraditional sources of information. For example, a group studying stellar astronomy might visit a local college's observatory, or one studying space travel might contact NASA.
- Schedule a field trip to a planetarium.
- Show a videotape of the 1969 *Apollo 11* moon landing.

Stage 3 Reflect and Write

1. Encourage students to freewrite to discover what aspects of the moon and the stars they care most about.
2. Direct students to write compositions about the moon and the stars. Possible forms their writing might take include:
   - science fiction or historical fiction
   - dramatic scenes or radio scripts
   - tall tales, myths, legends, or hero tales
   - epic, narrative, or lyric poems
3. Collect the finished compositions for a class book about the moon and the stars.

TEAM TEACHING

Language Arts Review techniques of narrative and literary writing. Study the uses of point of view and dialogue (see *Resources, Stage 3*).

TEACHING TIPS

- Propose that students interested in writing drama collaborate to write and put on a play.
- Take the class to hear a poetry reading or see a live drama. Alternatively, show videotapes of poetry readings and plays (see *Resources, Stage 3*).
- Remind students to do further research, if needed, as they work on their writing.

Resources

STAGE 1

The Classical Companion by Charles F. Baker III and Rosalie Baker is a teachers' resource with reproducible pages, covering myths of Rome, Greece, Persia, Carthage, Gaul, and Egypt.

Odyssey is an astronomy magazine for young people.

In ***The Glorious Constellations: History and Mythology,*** Giuseppe Maria Sesti discusses many constellations and the Milky Way and presents associated lore from various cultures, along with 672 illustrations.

For a listing of storytellers in your area, contact the **National Association for the Preservation and Perpetuation of Storytelling,** P.O. Box 309, Jonesborough, TN 37659.

STAGE 2

Articles in ***Calliope,*** a world-history magazine for students, and ***Faces,*** an anthropology magazine, explore cultural traditions of the past and the present.

In her book ***In the Beginning,*** Virginia Hamilton retells creation stories from many cultures, including tales of the creation of the sun, moon, and stars.

Exploring the Sky: One Hundred Projects for Beginning Astronomers by Richard Moeschl offers a hands-on approach to astronomy.

Whitney's Star Finder by Charles A. Whitney covers 1990–1995 and includes a "star finder wheel."

Small Worlds: Exploring the Sixty Moons of Our Solar System by Joseph W. Kelch includes Voyager photos of the moons of Uranus and Neptune.

Bright Stars, Red Giants, and White Dwarfs by Melvin Berger explores the life cycles of the sun and other stars.

NASA has produced videotapes of all sixteen Apollo missions, including **Apollo 11: *Man's First Moon Landing*** and ***The Flight of* Apollo 11.**

STAGE 3

The Writer's Craft, Grade 8, Workshop 3, "Narrative and Literary Writing," pages 70–88, teaches the writing of poems and scripts. Handbook 28, "Point of View," pages 322–323, and Handbook 29, "Writing Dialogue," pages 324–327, offer tips for writing fiction and drama.

Poetry for People Who Hate Poetry (Steffens Shed Poetry Films) features videotaped readings by Roger Steffens of works by poets ranging from William Shakespeare to E. E. Cummings.

Additional Projects

Another World Have groups of students invent an imaginary planet. Students should use social studies and science skills to describe the planet's location, climate, geography, life forms, and history. Students can create stories, poems, diaries, maps, models, and illustrations to convey information about the planet and its life forms. To present the project, students can create props and sets to convert the classroom into a part of their imaginary planet.

Great Moments Propose that students create a series of literary writings that bring great moments of the past to life for younger children. During the course of this project, students can target a specific group of younger children, research turning points and milestones in history and the sciences, create and illustrate their writings, and present their writings in person to the younger group. Presentations may take the form of one-on-one readings, a Readers Theater, or other types of performances and should include appropriate music, costumes, and props to help bring the era to life.

Creative Filmmaking To demonstrate how words and visual images can be blended to create "visual literature," have students make films or videotapes of their own literary writings or of their favorite literature. Direct them to go beyond illustrating the writings; encourage them, instead, to combine verbal and visual elements to create new versions of the original works.

SKETCHBOOK

Objective

- To use humorous verse and suggested writing prompts as springboards to informal writing

WRITING WARM-UPS

Encourage students to respond freely and informally to at least one of the Sketchbook prompts. They may begin by discussing their reactions in small groups and then freewriting in their journals. Remind students that their responses will not be graded and may provide them with useful material for other assignments.

SHOW, DON'T TELL

Encourage students to picture in their minds a gloomy day or a happy child before they write. Sample lines of poetry might be

Thick clouds hung over the bare, colorless trees.

Bouncing up and down,/The child squealed with joy.

5 verses
1 each on
-taste
-smell
-touch
-sound
-sight

SKETCHBOOK

WRITING WARM-UPS

The local groceries are all out of broccoli,
Loccoli.
Roy Blount, Jr., "SONG AGAINST BROCCOLI"

I wish that I
Were up to my knees
In my mother's mac-
Aroni and cheese.
Roy Blount, Jr., "SONG TO MY MOTHER'S MACARONI AND CHEESE"

Parsley
Is gharsley.
Ogden Nash, "FURTHER REFLECTION ON PARSLEY"

- Write a love note to your favorite food. You can use poetry or prose.
- Describe in ten or fewer words the best thing you've seen lately.
- Roy Blount, Jr., and Ogden Nash made up the words "loccoli" and "gharsley" to describe their feelings. What words can you make up to describe people, places, or things you like or dislike?

Show, Don't Tell

Poetry creates pictures or feelings for a reader with carefully chosen sensory words and images. Turn each *telling* sentence into a *showing* line of poetry by using more vivid words.

- The day was gloomy.
- The child jumped for joy.

70

Narrative and Literary Writing

Guided Assignment
Writing a Poem

Related Assignment
Developing a Script

Even without knowing it, you've probably written some kind of poetry. You may have played with the sounds of words or the pictures they create. Perhaps you've written a valentine or put some rap lyrics together. Your everyday life is full of material for poetry. This workshop will help you to turn some of your own thoughts and experiences into poems. In the related assignment you'll do a different kind of literary writing as you create a dramatic scene through dialogue—characters speaking and interacting with one another.

WRITER'S 3 WORKSHOP

Narrative and Literary Writing

Objectives

Guided Assignment

Writing a Poem To respond to poetry and to create a poem that reflects the writer's ideas, experiences, or emotions

Related Assignment

Developing a Script To analyze a film script and to create a script for a dramatic scene

Teacher's Choice

Use the following guidelines to choose the assignment that best suits students' needs.

Writing a Poem This assignment will help students express a single idea or feeling in a few carefully chosen images. Because it requires the skillful use of sensory detail, it is a natural follow-up to Workshop 2 in which students practice the skills of observation and description.

Developing a Script This assignment will appeal to all students who enjoy theater, television, and film.

Links to Literature & Language

Literature For more examples of vivid poetry that captures the beauty and excitement of sports, see the following in *Literature and Language,* Grade 8:

- Robert Francis, "Watching Gymnasts"
- Shiro Murano, "Pole Vault"
- Maxine W. Kumin, "400-Meter Freestyle"

Nikki Giovanni also wrote the poem "The World Is Not a Pleasant Place to Be," in *Literature and Language,* Grade 8.

Guided ASSIGNMENT

ASSIGNMENT RATIONALE

Writing poetry enables students to express their ideas and emotions directly and powerfully by using vivid language and sensory details. Poetry writing encourages students to focus on a single idea or emotion, to use words economically, and to consider the sounds of language as well as the arrangement of words on the page.

Starting from LITERATURE

Motivate

After students have read the Starting from Literature box, have them discuss their ideas and feelings about poetry. First, have them attempt a definition of poetry. Then have them describe experiences of listening to or reading poetry.

BUILD ON PRIOR KNOWLEDGE

To prepare students for reading "The Base Stealer," ask baseball fans to explain the purpose and importance of stealing a base. Have them explain how a base is stolen. Then have them describe base-stealing feats they have achieved or observed. (How does it feel to steal a base or to watch someone else do so?)

Depending on the interests of your students, you may wish to begin with one of the other poems.

SET A PURPOSE

To help students focus on the purpose-setting statement at the end of the Starting from Literature box, encourage them to picture in their minds the scenes the poets describe and to notice the particular words they chose to express what they saw, heard, thought, and felt.

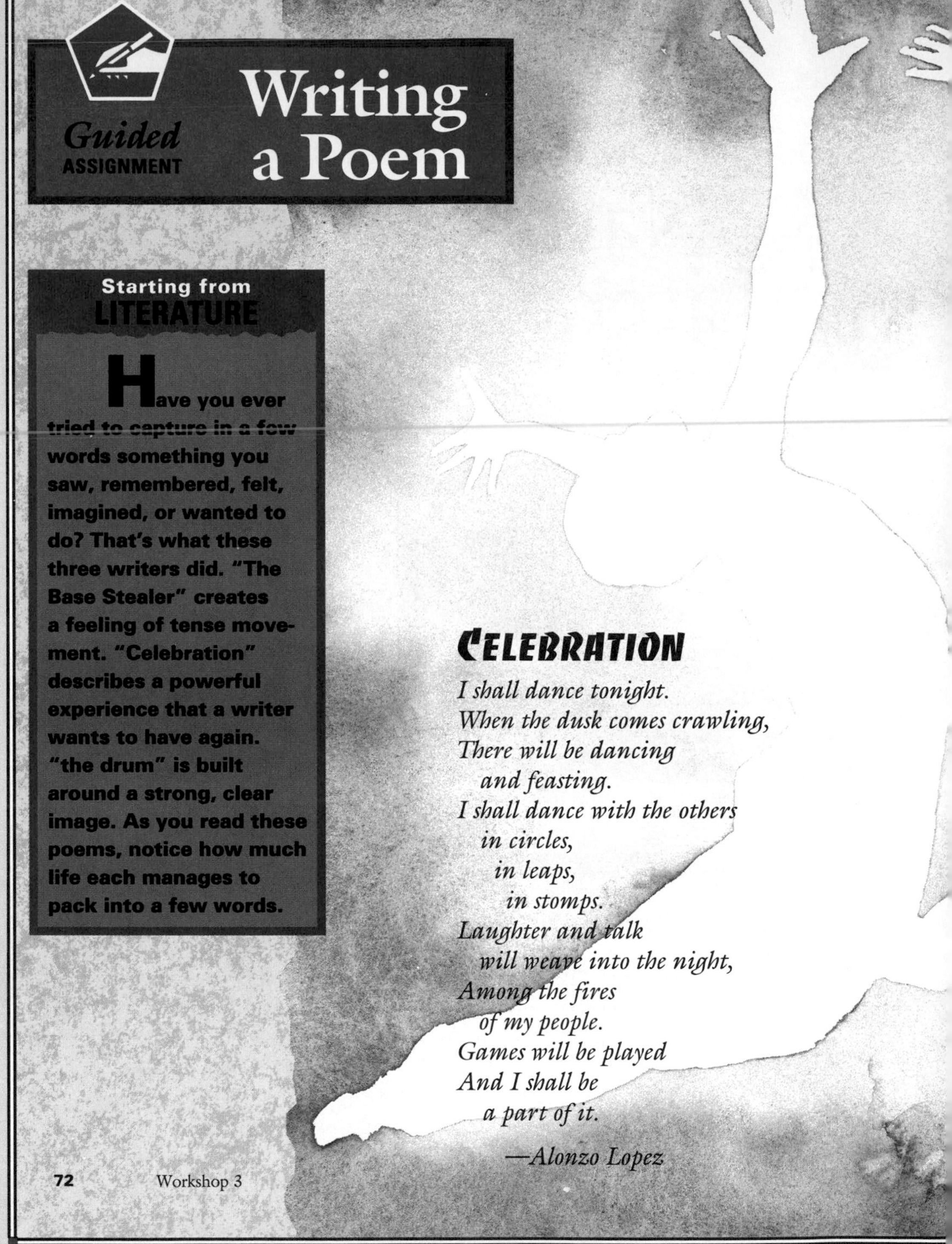

Guided ASSIGNMENT

Writing a Poem

Starting from LITERATURE

Have you ever tried to capture in a few words something you saw, remembered, felt, imagined, or wanted to do? That's what these three writers did. "The Base Stealer" creates a feeling of tense movement. "Celebration" describes a powerful experience that a writer wants to have again. "the drum" is built around a strong, clear image. As you read these poems, notice how much life each manages to pack into a few words.

CELEBRATION

I shall dance tonight.
When the dusk comes crawling,
There will be dancing
and feasting.
I shall dance with the others
in circles,
in leaps,
in stomps.
Laughter and talk
will weave into the night,
Among the fires
of my people.
Games will be played
And I shall be
a part of it.

—Alonzo Lopez

MORE ABOUT THE MODEL

Author Notes Robert Francis (1901–1987) grew up in rural Pennsylvania. Early in his career, Francis created quiet, thoughtful poems; but the poems in his 1960 book *The Orb Weaver,* from which "The Base Stealer" is taken, focus on colorful action, such as wrestling, swimming, and playing baseball.

Nikki Giovanni was born in Tennessee in 1943. With vivid imagery, her poems express a strong, individual point of view. Giovanni has recorded several albums of her poetry.

Alonzo Lopez, a Papago Indian, was born in Arizona. His poetry has appeared in several anthologies, including *The Whispering Wind.*

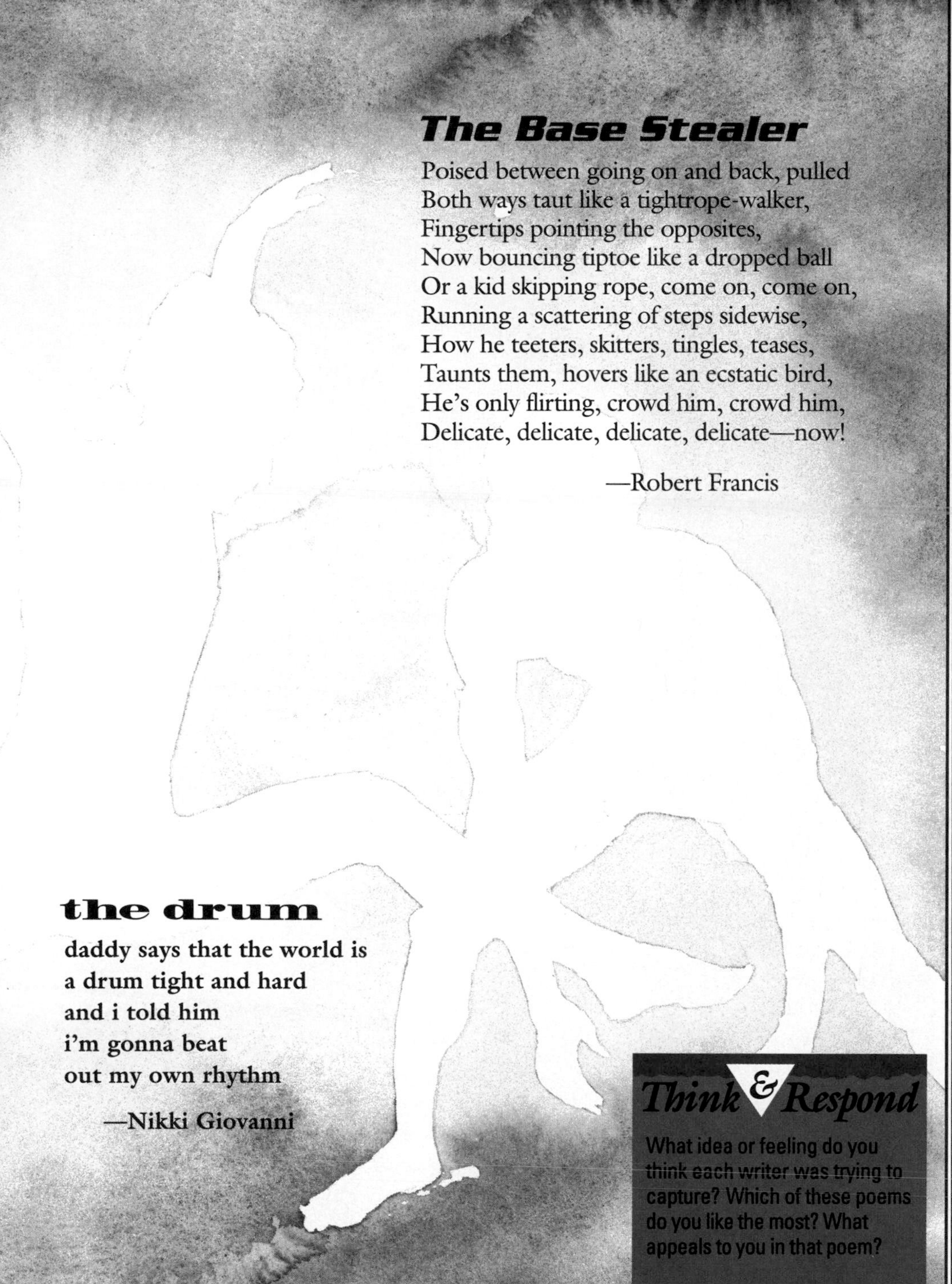

The Base Stealer

Poised between going on and back, pulled
Both ways taut like a tightrope-walker,
Fingertips pointing the opposites,
Now bouncing tiptoe like a dropped ball
Or a kid skipping rope, come on, come on,
Running a scattering of steps sidewise,
How he teeters, skitters, tingles, teases,
Taunts them, hovers like an ecstatic bird,
He's only flirting, crowd him, crowd him,
Delicate, delicate, delicate, delicate—now!

—Robert Francis

the drum

daddy says that the world is
a drum tight and hard
and i told him
i'm gonna beat
out my own rhythm

—Nikki Giovanni

Think & Respond

What idea or feeling do you think each writer was trying to capture? Which of these poems do you like the most? What appeals to you in that poem?

Think & Respond

ELICIT PERSONAL RESPONSES

Have students consider the questions in the Think & Respond box. Encourage them to share their responses freely. Stress that people's responses to poetry are very personal and can vary widely.

Students might say that "Celebration" captures the joy of belonging, that "The Base Stealer" conveys the suspense of a sporting event, and that "the drum" expresses a young person's determination to express her individuality.

Students will prefer different poems for a variety of reasons, including subject matter, imagery, rhythm, original comparisons, or other matters of style or of voice.

EXPLORE THE AUTHORS' TECHNIQUES

To help students use the poems as models for their own writing, point out that each poet focuses on a single feeling, idea, or event and that each uses sensory language and strong comparisons to create vivid pictures in the reader's mind. In "The Base Stealer," for example, the runner is compared to a tightrope walker, a dropped ball, a kid skipping rope, and an ecstatic bird. In "the drum," living in the world is compared to beating a drum. In "Celebration," the dusk is personified as "crawling."

Reading STUDENT MODELS

Like the three poems by well-known poets on pages 72–73, each of the three student poems uses a few carefully chosen words to focus on an emotion, experience, or idea. Taken together, the six poems convey the broad range of subject matter that can inspire poetry. "The Teddy Bear" is the final draft of the poem that students will see in process in the workshop pages that follow.

Motivate

After students have read the material in the box, remind them that poems can be based on actual events or on imaginary ones and can express many moods. Encourage students to share moments from their everyday lives that might provide material for a poem: for example, the death of a pet, a happy experience with friends or family, or a daydream.

BUILD ON PRIOR KNOWLEDGE

Ask students whether all poems rhyme. Have them recall poems they have read that rhyme and ones that do not; discuss with them characteristics of poetry other than rhyme—such as compactness, rhythm, and vivid words. Tell students to look for examples of these characteristics in the poems they are about to read.

SET A PURPOSE

Encourage students to notice their reactions to each poem as they read and to think about how each poem developed from a "seed" idea—such as a familiar object, a painful experience, or a "what-if" game—to a full-grown poem.

One Student's Writing

Reading STUDENT MODELS

Everyone's life contains both good and bad times, sudden whims or memories, moments of grief or laughter or surprise. Any of those moments could become the seed of a poem. Read these poems, all written by eighth graders. Note that Tiffany Shue builds a little story around something familiar, a teddy bear. In "A Life Is Gone," Jim McConnell uses sense images to work through some difficult emotions about the death of his brother. Trang Phan plays a "what-if" game to create "Creatures from Outer Space."

The Teddy Bear

There was a little teddy bear,
who belonged to a girl I knew,
that was loved so much,
the fur started falling off of it.
Pretty soon its right eye fell off.
That did not stop the girl
from taking the bear everywhere she went.
Now, twenty-five years later,
she still has that bear.
She also has two girls of her own.
One girl reminds me
very much of her mother.
That little girl has a teddy bear,
that also is showing much wear.
And travels too.

Tiffany Shue

Creatures from Outer Space

This unknown planet contains creatures
different from our own.

Like dogs with no fur,
Tigers that don't roar.
Cats without whiskers,
And eagles that don't soar.

Like woodpeckers that don't peck,
Lions with no mane.
Zebras without stripes,
And kittens that aren't tame.

Like hyenas that don't laugh,
Squirrels that hate nuts.
Birds with no beaks,
And lambs that give haircuts.

Like cheetahs that run slow,
Ladybugs that are men.
Flamingos that are blue,
And giraffes that live in dens.

Like roosters that don't crow,
Tortoises that beat the hare.
Owls that don't give a hoot,
And wooly mammoths that are bare.

Where is this place?
And where do we look to find?
Oh, I don't know.
Maybe in our minds!

Trang Phan

A Life Is Gone

It is cold.
The trees rustle
as the wind nips
my face.

A child's lonely cry
known only to one.
He lies motionless
and can not be seen.

A face hidden
from the world.
It is cold.
It is so cold.

Jim McConnell

Think & Respond

Respond as a Reader

▶ What favorite toy or object of yours comes to mind as you read "The Teddy Bear"?

▶ What was your first reaction to "A Life Is Gone"?

▶ Could you create any other creatures from outer space?

Respond as a Writer

▶ How did the writer link the ending of "The Teddy Bear" to the rest of the poem?

▶ How does a sense of cold contribute to the feeling of "A Life Is Gone"?

▶ What effect does rhyme have in "Creatures from Outer Space"?

Think & Respond

RESPOND AS A READER

▶ Students may wish to freewrite and then share in small groups their feelings about their favorite childhood toys.

▶ Most students will describe their reaction as one of sadness or desolation. Some students may prefer to reflect on the poem in their journals.

▶ Students might wish to form small groups and brainstorm ideas for imaginary creatures.

RESPOND AS A WRITER

▶ The writer compares the little girl's teddy bear to the one mentioned in the poem's opening lines; both bears are well-loved and go with their owners from place to place.

▶ The coldness of the weather mirrors the loss of the physical and emotional warmth of a relationship.

▶ Students might say that rhyme gives the poem a funny, playful feeling.

Draw Conclusions

To make sure students understand this introduction to poetry, challenge them to list the characteristics they have noted thus far. Responses may include:

- focus on a single feeling, experience, or idea
- sensory language
- original comparisons
- a few carefully chosen words

Writing ON YOUR OWN

Remind students that each poet expresses a memorable experience or feeling by means of sensory language and comparisons. By doing so, they are able to convey a strong impression of their subject in only a few words. Encourage students to keep these techniques in mind as they write.

Handbooks for Help and Practice

The following handbooks may be used as mini-lessons before students begin writing or as resources when problems arise.

- **Discovering Writing Ideas, pp. 218–223**
- **Meaning and Word Choice, pp. 314–315**
- **Using Poetic Devices, pp. 318–321**

PREWRITE AND EXPLORE

Objectives

- To use prewriting techniques to select a topic for a poem
- To record observations, using sensory details
- To explore a topic by freewriting

Teaching Strategies

for MEMORIES

INDIVIDUALIZING INSTRUCTION: VISUAL LEARNERS These students may find recalling memories and emotions easier if they bring in photo albums and describe to a partner the events and people shown in the photos and how they felt about them at the time.

for THE WORLD AROUND YOU

COLLABORATIVE OPPORTUNITY If students have gone on a class trip recently, have them work in groups to brainstorm impressions and sense memories of the place they visited. You might want to plan a trip to a park or nature center and have students work in groups to record or sketch their observations.

Each of the six poems you have read grew out of something seen, remembered, imagined, or strongly felt. The writers found that poetry was the best way to express their ideas.

Now write a poem that expresses something you have experienced, felt, or thought about in your own life.

PREWRITE AND EXPLORE

1. Let ideas come from anywhere. Anything can trigger a poem. It might be something you see, read, laugh at, remember, worry over, or wonder about. The starting point for your poem might be a bit of language: a phrase, something someone said, words that stick in your mind. A dream you had, if put into words, might become a poem. The following activities may help you to discover a "poetic moment."

Exploring Topics

- **Memories** What images or experiences from your past often come back to you? These might be pleasant memories, such as a birthday party or a peaceful summer day. The images also could be difficult ones, such as a death, a disappointment, or a fight. Try writing "I remember" at the top of a sheet of paper. Then keep writing, listing whatever comes to mind.
- **The world around you** Be alert to scenes and sounds, emotions, episodes between people in your everyday life. You may be in the cafeteria, in class, at a party, at a sports or religious event, or outdoors in a park. Carry a small notebook to **sketch** or **freewrite** about what you see, hear, smell, and feel.

PROBLEM SOLVING

"I still can't find an idea."

For help in discovering the right idea for your poem, see

- Sketchbook, page 70
- Springboards, page 89
- Handbook 1, "Discovering Writing Ideas," pages 218–223

SPICE BOX

Students might enjoy this game suggested by Peter Elbow in *Writing with Power:* "Writing group-poems can be a good way of pooling imagination. There's the familiar party-game approach where each person writes just one line. (You can have each person write knowing all the previous lines, or else have each person know only the preceding line, or else play with everyone blind to *all* other lines.) These games often provide a kind of loosening up, randomness, even hilarity. They usually increase everyone's verbal and imagistic resources."

- **Reading literature** Read as many different kinds of poetry as you can. You could even launch your poem with a line borrowed from someone else's poem. It becomes yours as you change it to fit your needs.

2. Discover your poem. Read over your notes. Underline words, feelings, and ideas that seem to stand out. Look for connections between some of the things you underlined. Jotting down these connections on a new piece of paper might give you the beginning of a poem. If you start two or three poems, one will gradually emerge as the one you want to work on more.

3. Explore your ideas. The key is to write as much as you can about your subject or subjects. Keep jotting words, phrases, and ideas around the lines you have already written. Freewriting is another good way to explore your subject. Try drawing a picture of your subject and then freewriting about what you have drawn.

One Student's Process

Tiffany Shue loved her big sister but wasn't sure how to write about her in a poem. She began freewriting and then underlined what seemed to mean the most to her.

My big sister, I love her so much. She always took care of me, she was my hero, she was so grown up in high school and still had time for me, <u>but she was really a shy person deep inside. She slept with her old teddy, she took it on overnights.</u> I understood, I had stuffed animals too. She's married now, but I still love my big sister, and the girls too, my littlest niece especially, she looks just like my sister and even talks like her, their baby pictures are just alike. <u>She even has a teddy too, it kind of reminds me of the other one. She brought it last time they came over. My mom and dad even noticed.</u>

for READING LITERATURE

INDIVIDUALIZING INSTRUCTION: BASIC STUDENTS These students may especially appreciate being given a line or two from a famous poem to help them start their own work. Possibilities include lines from Robert Frost's "Nothing Gold Can Stay," Emily Dickinson's "I'm Nobody! Who are you?," Langston Hughes's "The Dream Keeper," and Nikki Giovanni's "The World Is Not a Pleasant Place to Be." (All of these works appear in *Literature and Language,* Grade 8.)

for DISCOVER YOUR POEM

MODELING Set aside ten or fifteen minutes of class time for students to complete steps 2 and 3. As they do so, you might explore your own ideas for a poem, freewriting and then underlining ideas that strike you. At the end of the exploring period, share your ideas with students and encourage them to share theirs.

for ONE STUDENT'S PROCESS

KEY TO UNDERSTANDING Point out that Tiffany could have chosen to underline "she was my hero" or "their baby pictures are just alike" and could have written equally interesting poems, focusing on those themes and images, instead of concentrating on the image of the teddy bear.

MULTICULTURAL Connection

Read aloud poems from different cultures and encourage students to use the poems as models. For example, you might read Japanese haiku, traditional British ballads, traditional African poetry, or Native-American poetry. Resources include *More Cricket Songs,* edited by Harry Behn (haiku), The *Viking Book of Folk Ballads of the English-Speaking World,* edited by Albert B. Friedman, *Poems from Africa,* edited by Samuel Allen, *Harper's Anthology of 20th Century Native American Poetry,* edited by Duane Niatum, and *The Gift Outright,* edited by Helen Plotz (poems on diverse American experiences).

DRAFT AND DISCOVER

Objectives

- To draft a poem
- To respond to one's own draft and that of a peer

Teaching Strategies

for BEGIN SHAPING YOUR POEM

HELPFUL HINT Have students study the line lengths and stanza patterns of the student and professional poems on pages 72-75. Discuss how the form of each poem is suited to the ideas and emotions it expresses. Students may enjoy creating shaped poems in which the pattern of the lines on the page forms a picture of the subject. (See Maxine Kumin's "400-Meter Freestyle" in *Literature and Language,* Grade 8.)

for PLAY WITH IMAGES

CRITICAL THINKING: MAKING COMPARISONS To help students write comparisons, teach the mini-lesson on figurative language in Handbook 27, "Using Poetic Devices." Set aside a corner of the chalkboard as a Comparison Exchange. Here, students can ask for suggestions from classmates. For example, a student might write, "The fresh snowfall was like ____," and a classmate could fill in the blank.

for LISTEN TO THE SOUNDS

INDIVIDUALIZING INSTRUCTION: ESL STUDENTS Encourage students to write in their first language because they are more aware of its rhythms and idioms. If possible, pair an ESL student with a bilingual student to work on an English translation.

for WRITER'S CHOICE

INDIVIDUALIZING INSTRUCTION: ADVANCED STUDENTS Challenge these students to create a poem with a specific rhyme scheme and meter. Suggest that they browse through poetry anthologies for models.

COMPUTER TIP

With a word processor you can easily try out different ways of arranging lines or stanzas. You can also copy any line or refrain that you want to repeat.

DRAFT AND DISCOVER

1. Begin shaping your poem. You may already have many of the words you'll use. Try rearranging them. Experiment with different line lengths. Think about ways of grouping ideas and dividing your material into smaller units, as Trang Phan did with a stanza for each group of creatures. Aim for economy: cut out words you don't need. Remember that most poetry is tightly focused, often concentrating on a single idea or feeling.

2. Play with images. An image is a mental picture that appeals to any of the senses. For example, in "The Base Stealer," several images help to give a picture of the jumpy, waiting runner: a tightrope-walker, a dropped ball, a kid skipping rope, an ecstatic bird. Take advantage of any imaginative comparisons like these that come into your mind.

3. Listen to the sounds. Most poetry is meant for the ear. Read your poem aloud as you write it. Listen to the vowels, the consonants, and the rhythms. Listen for words that sound like what they mean. In "The Base Stealer," lively verbs—"teeters, skitters, tingles, teases"—all sound like something nervous, bouncy, quivery. In "A Life Is Gone," the repeated sound of "cold" increases the feeling of loneliness and grief.

Writer's Choice Do you want to write your poem in free verse, or do you want your poem to rhyme and have a regular beat? If you want to use rhyme, be careful not to fall into too much of a singsong pattern. Poetry thrives on playful and imaginative use of language, but it doesn't have to rhyme.

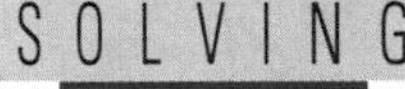

PROBLEM SOLVING

"I can't get my poem to say what I want it to."

For tips on word choice, see

- Handbook 25, "Meaning and Word Choice," pages 314–315

4. Think about your draft. If possible, put your poem aside for a few hours or even a day or two. Then test it on your ear by reading it aloud. Does it seem to express what you meant to say? If not, don't be too critical yet. You may decide to stop working on this poem and work on a different one. When you're satisfied with your poem, you may want to read or show what you've written to classmates and see how they respond. The questions on the next page can help you review your work.

SPICE BOX

Students can have fun exploring language—making comparisons, finding synonyms, learning definitions, and creating rhymes—by experimenting with "Inky Pinkies." To play, give one of the following definitions and have students supply two rhyming words that together yield the same meaning.

- pretending to be very surprised *(mock shock)*
- all the players shouting *(team scream)*
- a tune that goes on and on *(long song)*
- a search for a visitor *(guest quest)*

Have students make up their own "Inky Pinkies" to share with the class.

REVIEW YOUR WRITING

Questions for Yourself

- What main feeling, idea, or experience do I want to convey in my poem?
- Do any words or lines seem unnecessary to the meaning or impact of my poem?
- What parts of the poem feel most right for me?

Questions for Your Peer Readers

- What feeling, idea, or experience does my poem create for you?
- Which words, lines, or sections of my poem interest you or stand out the most?
- Which line or part of my poem is most important to you? Why?
- Which parts of my poem puzzle you?

One Student's Process

Here is Tiffany's first draft, with her friends' comments on the side. What would some of your comments have been?

Two Girls

When I was little,
My big sister always took care of me.
She was already a teenager, but she was shy.
When she slept over with girlfriends,
she always took her old teddy bear,
that was so worn out
the fur started falling off of it.
My big sister is a mother now,
with girls of her own.
One girl reminds me
Very much of her mother.
She even has a teddy bear too,
just like her mother.

Peer Reader Comments

I wonder what the first lines have to do with the rest of the poem.

I like the teddy bear. It makes me remember when I was little.

They both had teddy bears. Maybe you could use that idea more.

for QUESTIONS FOR YOURSELF

CRITICAL THINKING: JUDGING As students judge which words or lines should be kept in their poems and which should be left out, remind them that lines of poetry do not have to form complete sentences and that fragments are frequently used. Point out, in the student poems on page 75, examples of fragments, such as "A face hidden/from the world" in "A Life Is Gone" and "Maybe in our minds!" from "Creatures from Outer Space." Encourage student poets to be free and playful in their use of language, paying attention to sound and rhythm as well as to sense and meaning.

for QUESTIONS FOR YOUR PEER READERS

PEER RESPONSE Have peer readers read the partner's poem aloud so that the writer can hear how the poem sounds as interpreted by someone else. This reading may offer the writer clues as to which parts of the poem work and which do not.

GENERAL NOTE

ASSESSMENT: SPOT CHECK Students who are completing the first drafts of their poems may wish to share them with you for some feedback or advice. Point out any vivid images, original comparisons, or striking sound effects you see. You'll get an idea of how well students are mastering the techniques of poetry, and you'll boost students' confidence in their abilities at the same time.

for ONE STUDENT'S PROCESS

CRITICAL THINKING: EXPRESSING PERSONAL OPINIONS Ask students whether they agree with the peer reader's comment about the teddy bear. In what way would the image of the teddy bear bring together the writer's impressions of her sister and her sister's daughter? What does the teddy bear seem to represent? What other comments would students like to make about this draft of a poem?

PROFESSIONAL NOTEBOOK

As students draft, share these ideas from *Sleeping on the Wing* by Kenneth Koch and Kate Farrell:

"There isn't a right answer when you write a poem. To create something means to make something that wasn't there before, so how can there be a right answer? Try writing down the first thing that comes into your mind and whatever else comes after that, even if it's not connected."

REVISE YOUR WRITING

Objectives

- To evaluate the responses to a draft of a poem and to revise a draft
- To evaluate a poem's structure and line length
- To effectively use vivid, specific modifiers

Teaching Strategies

for REVIEW YOUR READERS' COMMENTS

HELPFUL HINT As students evaluate responses to their first draft, encourage them to write at least two different new drafts, each creating a different effect. Have them choose the draft they like best.

for LINKING GRAMMAR AND WRITING

KEY TO UNDERSTANDING Point out the importance of specific modifiers in the professional models on pages 72–73. For example, the effect of Nikki Giovanni's poem depends on a father's and a daughter's contrasting views of the same image—the world as a drum. The modifiers *tight* and *hard* suggest that the father sees the world as a difficult place, whereas the daughter sees it as a challenging surface on which she can make her own unique music. Also point out the sensory impact of the modifiers *taut* and *sidewise* in "The Base Stealer," and, especially, of the repeated adjective *delicate* in the last line of that poem.

PROBLEM SOLVING

"My words don't seem as exciting as my idea does."

For new ways to express your ideas, see

- Handbook 27, "Using Poetic Devices," pages 318–321

REVISE YOUR WRITING

1. Review your readers' comments. Review the comments and think about whether you want to change your poem. If your readers didn't like your favorite part, should you still keep it? That's your choice. After all, you're the poet here.

2. Think about how your poem looks on the page. Look for a natural place to begin each line. Longer lines may produce an effect like conversation. Shorter lines may create more emphasis. In "Creatures from Outer Space," the lines fall into a regular pattern and a capital letter begins each line. In "Celebration," short lines seem right: "in circles,/ in leaps,/ in stomps." Check books of poetry to see how other poems look.

LINKING GRAMMAR AND WRITING

Effective Modifiers

Adjectives and adverbs, if carefully chosen, can add detail, affect the mood, and make your images stand out. Notice the revisions involving modifiers in the second stanza of "A Life Is Gone."

Original	Revised
A child's cry known only to one. He lies there and can not be seen	A child's lonely cry known only to one. He lies motionless and can not be seen.

The adjective *lonely,* in the first line, helps to set a somber mood. It also echoes with *only* in the second line. The adverb *motionless,* in the third line, stresses a feeling of desolation.

For more information on modifiers, see Handbook 43, "Using Modifiers," pages 506–507 and 511–513.

3. Check your words once more. Are your words as specific as possible? Do they call up the picture you want?

One Student's Process

After reading her classmates' comments, Tiffany decided to focus on the teddy bears that belonged to her sister and her niece. With this new focus, she added some details and crossed out others. Then she realized she needed a different title.

~~Two Girls~~ The Teddy Bear

~~When I was little,~~
There was a little teddy bear,
~~My big sister always took care of me.~~
who belonged to a girl I knew,
~~She was already a teenager, but she was shy.~~

~~When she slept over with girlfriends,~~

~~she always took her old teddy bear,~~

that was ~~so worn out~~ loved so much,

the fur started falling off of it.

~~My big sister is a mother now,~~

~~with~~ she also has two girls of her own.

One girl reminds me

~~V~~very much of her mother.

~~She even~~ That little girl has a teddy bear ~~too,~~,

~~just like her mother.~~

that also is showing much wear.
And travels too.

Pretty soon its right eye fell off.
That did not stop the girl
from taking the bear everywhere she went.
Now, twenty-five years later,
she still has that bear.

COMPUTER TIP

Working on a word processor, you can experiment with various line lengths and stanza breaks. Some programs will help you to make a poem into different shapes.

for ONE STUDENT'S PROCESS

CRITICAL THINKING: ANALYZING

To analyze the changes made at this stage of the revision process, ask students who or what was the focus of the poem's original first two lines (the writer). Who or what is the focus of the revised lines? (the teddy bear) What effect does adding the detail about the bear's eye falling off have? (Sample: The detail helps readers to visualize the worn and well-loved toy.) What reason might Tiffany have had for adding the words "that also is showing much wear. And travels too."? (Sample: She wanted to strengthen the feeling of connection between mother and daughter.)

GENERAL NOTE

MANAGING THE PAPER LOAD

Instead of responding to students' work in writing at this point, you might schedule conferences in which students explain the central focus of their poems, read them aloud to you, and receive your comments on how well they are maintaining their focus.

PROFESSIONAL NOTEBOOK

Advice from the Authors In *Writing with Power,* Peter Elbow advises writers not to *explain* too much when they are revising their poetry: "Sometimes it's hard to resist over-clarifying or over-stating your meaning when you revise. . . . If you can cut away what isn't needed, but leave the best original words with juice, that is often the best way to revise."

for PARAGRAPHS AT WORK

CRITICAL THINKING: ANALYZING

Have students analyze the stanzaic structures of the student and professional poems on pages 72–75. Ask them to suggest why each poem was written in only one stanza. (Each focuses on one feeling, idea, or scene without breaking the mood or changing the focus.) Then ask them to suggest why the writer of "A Life Is Gone" broke his poem into three stanzas. (Sample: The first focuses on the cold weather and the solitary speaker; the second, on the buried child; the third returns to the theme of cold, but in a larger context.)

PROOFREAD

Teaching Strategies

for PROOFREAD YOUR POEM

HELPFUL HINT Point out patterns of capitalization and punctuation in the professional poems. Have students discuss the effects of there being no capital letters in "the drum," or of the punctuation that makes "The Base Stealer" one long sentence. Have them analyze their own poems and the effects of the patterns of capitalization and punctuation in those poems.

Guidelines for Evaluation

IDEAS AND CONTENT

- focuses on an idea, feeling, or experience
- uses a few carefully chosen words
- uses vivid images
- may include figurative language
- may include poetic sound effects

STRUCTURE AND FORM

- may use lines of varying lengths
- may use stanza breaks to show changes in mood, images, or emphasis

GRAMMAR, USAGE, AND MECHANICS

- may include nonstandard grammar and mechanics for expressive purposes

Paragraphs at Work Poems don't have paragraphs, but they may have groups of lines, or stanzas. The "Creatures" poem is an example. Stanzas can work like paragraphs by introducing new ideas in a poem. You may want to start a new stanza at the following points:

- when the feeling in your poem changes
- when you describe a new image
- when you want to emphasize something

PROOFREAD

1. Proofread your poem. Check your grammar, spelling, punctuation, and capitalization. It is often useful to punctuate poetry as if it were prose, unless you have some reason not to. The same is true of capitalization, unless you decide to start each line with a capital. Poetry does not always follow formal grammar. In "A Life Is Gone," for example, notice that "A face hidden / from the world" is a sentence fragment.

2. Make a clean copy of your poem. Are you ready to prepare your poem for publication? If so, the Standards for Evaluation can help. After making final changes, you can write out a clean copy.

Standards for Evaluation

LITERARY WRITING

A poem

- usually centers around a particular idea, feeling, story, or experience
- often creates specific, concrete images
- usually produces part of its effect with the sounds of its words
- uses few words, all chosen with great care

PUBLISH AND PRESENT

- **Present a poetry reading.** Join with a group of friends and classmates to read poems aloud for other students. You might choose appropriate musical accompaniment, either live or recorded, for each poem.
- **Create an anthology.** Arrange your poems by theme or type to form a class poetry anthology. Find a way to present them by using fine handwriting or by using a word processor.
- **Submit poems for publication.** Your teacher can help you send your poems to your school or local newspaper or to a literary magazine.
- **Make poetry posters.** Combine artwork and poetry in colorful posters you can hang in the school hallways.

TEACHER'S LOUNGE

Teacher Lorraine Mund writes, ". . . I am very strict about grammar and punctuation. One day as we read the works of a modern poet, a young woman seemed puzzled. 'How come he uses capital letters in the middle of the sentence and misspells some of the words?' she asked.

"'That's called *poetic license,*' I explained.

"'Oh,' she replied. 'How can I apply for one?'"

from *Reader's Digest,* June 1992

- **Find imaginative presentations.** Write poems in fancy handwriting and frame them. Put poems on greeting cards or T-shirts, or stitch them on samplers. Turn poems into illustrated children's books or into songs.

REFLECT ON YOUR WRITING

WRITER TO WRITER

Remember to be alive to everything, not just to what you're feeling, but also to your pets, to flowers, to what you are reading.

May Sarton, poet

1. Write an introduction to your poem. Before you add your poem to your portfolio, write an introduction for it, telling readers about the poem and about your experience in writing it. In this introduction, reflect on some of the following questions.

- Where did my poem come from? How did I decide what to write about and how to get started?
- How would I compare writing a poem to doing other kinds of writing? Did my poem surprise me in any way?
- In what ways did my readers help—or not help—me in writing this poem?
- What was I trying to accomplish with this poem? How well do I think I have accomplished it?
- What parts of my poem am I now the most and the least satisfied with?
- Would I like to write more poetry?

2. Explore other writing ideas. See the suggestions in Springboards on page 89.

Reteaching

Assess the needs of students who were not successful in developing an effective poem; then assign the appropriate handbook mini-lessons, along with the appropriate support material for this assignment. Concepts commonly requiring reteaching for this assignment are:

- **Handbook 25, Meaning and Word Choice, pp. 314–315**
- **Handbook 27, Using Poetic Devices, pp. 318–321**

The following suggestions and resources may also be helpful.

Weak Imagery Display photographs of striking scenes from nature or of colorful celebrations. Have students imagine they are at the scene. Have them record what they see, hear, taste, touch, and smell, using the Observation Chart in the *Thinking Skills Worksheets,* page 3. For additional instruction on creating imagery, assign "Experimenting with Poetic Images and Sounds," page 15, in the Writing Resource Book.

Extension and Enrichment

1. Have students write poems to be used in greeting cards to honor family and friends on special occasions. Have them design the cards and print their poems inside.

2. Have students compose poems in honor of a person, a holiday, or an important event in the school, community, or country. Select poems and readers for oral presentations at a school assembly.

Closure: Reflect on Your Writing

Students may focus their reflections on comparing poetry-writing with earlier assignments: an autobiographical incident and an eyewitness report. Which type of writing did they enjoy most? Could the subjects of their earlier assignments also be subjects for poems?

Related ASSIGNMENT

Starting from LITERATURE

Objectives

- To respond to and analyze scenes from a script
- To write, revise, and perform a script for a dramatic scene

Motivate

Have students make lists of their five favorite movies, and ask them to pick a favorite scene from each movie. Call on volunteers to describe a movie scene they chose and to tell why they think it worked so well. Was it because of the actors? the special effects? the dialogue? List students' responses on the board. Afterward, summarize characteristics of successful movie scenes.

BUILD ON PRIOR KNOWLEDGE

Ask whether students have ever read a play or script. Besides dialogue, what other kind of writing does a script contain? Ask students: What is the purpose of stage directions in a play or script? (They describe the way actors move or speak. They can also describe setting, lighting, and sound effects.)

SET A PURPOSE

Ask whether any students have seen the movie *Stand and Deliver*. Have them give a summary of the plot and their evaluation of the movie. Then ask students to notice, as they read the script, how the dialogue and stage directions convey the characters of Mr. Escalante and Pancho and what kind of relationship the teacher and student have.

Related ASSIGNMENT Developing a Script

Starting from LITERATURE

Shakespeare wrote, "All the world's a stage." He also knew that putting actors on a stage is one of the best ways to tell a story. For that reason, drama is at least as old as the ancient Greeks and as up-to-date as tonight's TV shows.

The script for the movie *Stand and Deliver* was written by Ramon Menendez and Tom Musca. The film is about Jaime Escalante, a high school math teacher who dares to believe his students can learn more than anyone expects them to. In the following scenes he asks students to commit themselves to doing extra work.

PRODUCTION

from *Stand and Deliver*

SCENE 36 | TAKE 4

by RAMON MENENDEZ and TOM MUSCA

[Escalante classroom interior—day. The beginning of the second year. The classroom is . . . upbeat looking . . . colorful. Posters with success as the theme decorate the walls. Escalante stands at the door as the students march in. He hands each of them a piece of paper. . . . Javier reads the piece of paper he was handed.]

JAVIER: Oh, come on! Contracts? You mean you can't trust us by now?

ESCALANTE: For those of you making the commitment you will be preparing yourself for the Advanced Placement Test. Make sure you have one, make sure it's signed before you come to class tomorrow.

ANA: We have to come here an hour before school, take your class two periods and stay until five?

ESCALANTE: Believe it or don't.

Links to LITERATURE & LANGUAGE

Literature For more scripts, see *Literature and Language*, Grade 8:

- Walter A. Hackett, *The Million-Pound Bank Note* (Mark Twain)
- Adele Thane, *Rip Van Winkle* (Washington Irving)
- Christopher Sergel, *The Kid Nobody Could Handle* (Kurt Vonnegut, Jr.)
- Frances Goodrich and Albert Hackett, *The Diary of Anne Frank* (Anne Frank)

PANCHO: Saturdays? We gotta come on Saturdays? And no vacations?

ESCALANTE: Yep. Pass the A.P. exam and you get college credit.

CLAUDIA: Big deal.

LUPE: Kimo,[1] we're seniors. This is our year to slack off. *[The students get up and begin to file out. . . .*

(Next day) Escalante stands by the door collecting signed contracts from the students as they enter.]

ESCALANTE: Thank you very much. You don't got it signed, you don't get a ticket to watch the show. Thank you, Mr. Kung Fu. Good morning, good morning. Mr. Blue Eyes, thank you very much. Elizabeth, my tailor! Sophia, my Loren. Hey, get a haircut. One more time I gotta tell you. Thank you very much. *[Pancho hands in his contract.]* Hey! You didn't. . . . *[Escalante pushes past some students to Pancho.]* Get out of the way. *[to Pancho]* Here. You didn't sign it.

PANCHO: Come on, Kimo. I gotta put school on hold.

ESCALANTE: Go back until you sign it.

PANCHO: My uncle offered me a job operating a forklift Saturdays and Sundays. I'll be making time and a half.

ESCALANTE: So what?

PANCHO: Two years in the union and I'll be making more than you.

• • •

[Pancho's car, interior—night. Escalante is at the wheel.]

PANCHO: Kimo, I don't want to let you down, but the money I'll be making will buy me a new Trans Am.

ESCALANTE: No one cruises through life, Pancho. Wouldn't you rather be designing these things than repairing them? You can't even do that if they got fuel injections. *[He downshifts roughly.]*

PANCHO: Kimo, you're gonna strip my gears, man.

[Escalante speeds up and begins to really play at the gear shift.]

ESCALANTE: What's the big problem?

PANCHO: Orale,[2] Kimo.

ESCALANTE: Don't panic, Johnny. Just watch out for the other guy. Right or left?

[Escalante speeds up. A fork in the road.]

PANCHO: Where are we going?!

ESCALANTE: Right or left?

PANCHO: Go right! Go right!

ESCALANTE: *[Escalante veers right at the last moment. He speeds up and comes to a screeching halt in front of a sign that reads "Dead End."]* All you see is the turn. You don't see the road ahead.

1. **Kimo** nickname.
2. **orale** (ō rä' lā) *Spanish:* come on.

How would you react to this teacher? How does he seem to motivate his students? How does the dialogue help shape your impression of each character? How do the stage directions add to the story?

Think & Respond

ELICIT PERSONAL RESPONSES

Have students discuss whether they would like to be students in Mr. Escalante's class. Would they sign the contract?

To focus attention on how well the dialogue is used for characterization, ask volunteers to read the scenes aloud, with feeling. Then have students describe the characters whose lines they read and point out clues in the dialogue that help reveal the characters' personalities.

Have students find stage directions that give clues to Mr. Escalante's character and stage directions that help them visualize the action or create suspense.

EXPLORE THE AUTHORS' TECHNIQUES

Make sure students understand that brackets and italics are used in a script to signal stage directions, and that names in all capital letters are used to signal speakers.

After the discussion of the Think & Respond questions, have students summarize their opinions of the authors' techniques by writing brief reviews of the scenes. Their reviews should focus on how well the authors used dialogue and stage directions to reveal character, help readers visualize the action, and create suspense. Have them cite examples from the script. (Sample: The stage directions for the scene in the car helped me visualize the scene and made me wonder how far Mr. Escalante would go to make his point. Dialogue such as "No one cruises through life, Pancho. Wouldn't you rather be designing these things than repairing them?" showed that Mr. Escalante cared about Pancho's future and wanted Pancho to set high goals for himself.)

MORE ABOUT THE MODEL

The movie *Stand and Deliver* is based on the teaching career of Jaime Escalante. A native of Bolivia, he began teaching in 1974 in an East Los Angeles high school where drugs and gangs were serious problems. Using humor and discipline, he was able to work with kids who could barely add and to teach them calculus.

Literature Connection

Students may adapt stories or diaries for their scripts; help them understand the process by bringing in Irving's story "Rip Van Winkle" for them to compare with the scripted version in *Literature and Language,* Grade 8. Point out how narrative descriptions become stage directions, and conversations become dialogue.

Writing ON YOUR OWN

Remind students how the realistic dialogue and stage directions in the script for *Stand and Deliver* brought the characters to life for the audience.

Handbooks for Help and Practice

The following handbooks may be used as mini-lessons before students begin writing or as resources when problems arise.

- **Audience, pp. 234–235**
- **Writing Dialogue, pp. 324–327**

Teaching Strategies

for THINK ABOUT POSSIBLE STORIES

COLLABORATIVE OPPORTUNITY
You might encourage groups of students to work together on a script. Instead of freewriting, they can brainstorm ideas and improvise dialogue.

for LOOK FOR A STORY TO ADAPT

INDIVIDUALIZING INSTRUCTION: BASIC STUDENTS These students might begin by adapting a short story they have already read. Suggest that they pick up dialogue as is and look for descriptive details of setting and character that they can use in their stage directions. Students might also adapt a story from their own portfolios.

for CHOOSE A TYPE OF PRESENTATION

SPEAKING AND LISTENING
Borrow tapes of old radio plays from a library and play them for the class. Have students listen and analyze how dialogue, narration, sound effects, and music work together to create the desired effect for a listening audience.

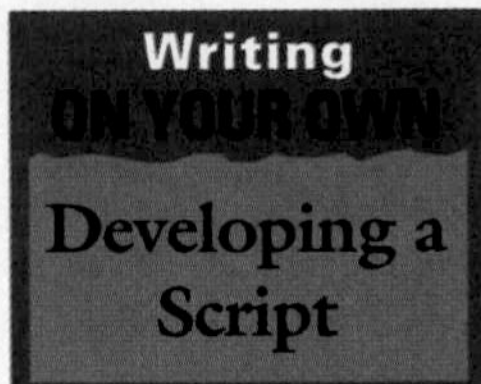

The script you have just read presents two brief scenes that are part of a longer story. It uses stage directions as well as actors' dialogue to indicate how the scenes could be performed for an audience.

Now write a script for a dramatic scene. You may make up the events or take them from your life or from a story you have read.

THINKING ABOUT YOUR SCENE

1. Think about possible stories. List moments in your life when you experienced or witnessed something memorable. Also think about family stories. Imagine the center of this memory or story. What happened, and where? Who said what to whom, and why? What was the result? Try freewriting to produce a dramatic scene from this material.

2. Look for a story to adapt. You may not want to make up your own scene. In that case, choose one from a short story, novel, legend, religious story, or historical event that you are familiar with. Look for a moment in the story where the characters face some challenge or learn an important lesson. Choose a short scene with a single, clear event.

3. Choose a type of presentation. Scenes for the stage, for film (movies or TV), or for radio all have advantages. A radio script allows you to travel widely through time and space because your listeners can use their imaginations freely. Scripts for film and stage can make use of strong visual effects like gestures and costumes. Think about what you want to accomplish in your script; then make your choice.

PROBLEM SOLVING

"I don't know how to decide what kind of scene makes a good script."

To get an idea of the kind of scene that works well as a script, skim library books containing one-act plays.

MULTICULTURAL Connection

Encourage students to make a dramatic adaptation of a folk tale, legend, fable, tall tale, or other story from their own cultures. They might also adapt a tale from another culture by transforming the characters, setting, and dialogue to fit their own background. (Unit Six of *Literature and Language*, Grade 8, contains folk tales from the Americas.)

. **Plan your script.** Imagine how your scene might look if per- ›rmed, or how it would sound on radio or tape. Think about the ıain effect you want to create for the audience. If you are adapt- ıg a story, decide whether you will need to add anything to the riginal. Consider how you will open and close your scene.

ƆRAFTING YOUR SCRIPT

. **Set the scene.** The first part of your script will include brief age directions in order to identify the characters, set, and props r to describe these to a listening audience.

. **Get your characters talking.** In drama, good dialogue is early everything. It should sound natural while always carrying ıe story forward. The first lines your actors speak should "grab" ›ur audience, giving an idea of the characters and setting and ferring to earlier events if necessary.

. **Present a dramatic action.** After your scene begins, the dia- ›gue should begin to reveal some central problem or conflict nong the characters and show how that problem develops. on't worry if you find yourself writing dialogue that wasn't part f the original story, or even adding a new event or character. You ın do whatever seems best for your script.

. **Look for an effective nding.** Your ending might ıow the action building to a imax or coming to an end. might show a problem eing solved or a conflict eing settled. If there is no lution to the problem, you ın show how the characters act to that fact. Even if the ıd of your scene is not the ıd of the story, your audi- ıce should feel that some- ing has happened.

Edward James Olmos plays math teacher Jaime Escalante in the film *Stand and Deliver.*

Writing TIP

A radio script can have a narrator, who introduces setting and characters. Sound effects and back-ground music can be used to set the mood.

PROBLEM SOLVING

"I'm not used to writing dialogue."

For tips on effective dia-logue, see

- Handbook 29, "Writing Dialogue," pages 324–327

for SET THE SCENE

KEY TO UNDERSTANDING Have students turn back to the model script on pages 84–85 to see how to use stage directions to set a scene. Have them note that the first set of directions indicates where and when the action is set. The classroom props reveal something about the character of Mr. Escalante (he wants to motivate his students to succeed). The final two sentences of the directions describe the action that gets the scene in motion.

for GET YOUR CHARACTERS TALKING

HELPFUL HINT Point out to students that in good dialogue, each character has a distinctive style of speaking that reflects the person's age, personality, background, and attitudes. Before students begin writing, encourage them to recall their earlier readings and discussions of scenes from the play and to look at the brief reviews they wrote to discover characters' personality traits that could be expressed through dialogue. For example, how would a shy person ask for a favor? How would a proud person admit a mistake?

for PRESENT A DRAMATIC ACTION

CRITICAL THINKING: ANALYZING Have students analyze the dramatic structure of the model on pages 84–85 for clues as to how to build a scene. Ask what conflict the first exchange of dialogue reveals, with what character the teacher develops a particularly strong conflict, and how this conflict reaches a high point of tension and suspense. Have students discuss the ending of the scene and predict whether and how the conflict will be resolved. Encourage students to find ways to build and release tension in the scenes they write.

SPICE BOX

Give pairs of student volunteers some high-interest situations; ask them to improvise dialogue and create characters in a spontaneous performance for the class. Possible situations: a conflict between siblings; a misunderstanding between a store clerk and a customer.

Art Connection

Students interested in art and design may enjoy browsing through books on set design and costuming in the contemporary theater. They may want to submit a few sketches with their scripts, showing how the scenes and actors would look on stage.

Guidelines for Evaluation

AN EFFECTIVE SCRIPT

- uses dialogue that reveals character and advances the plot
- includes stage directions that establish the setting, describe the action, and give clues to character
- presents a central problem or conflict

for TRY OUT A PERFORMANCE

PEER RESPONSE Tell students that even professionally-staged plays have previews, tryouts in which audience response is gauged and changes are made before the play officially opens. If students are writing their plays in groups, have each group perform their work-in-progress for the class. Classmates can act as reviewers, filling out response cards in which they evaluate the believability and interest of dialogue and the level of dramatic tension in the plot. Have each group weigh classmates' responses and decide what changes, if any, to make in their script.

for PERFORM YOUR SCENE WITH CLASSMATES

INDIVIDUALIZING INSTRUCTION: LEARNING STYLES Developing and presenting the script as a group project can benefit students with a variety of learning styles. For example, independent learners can contribute by researching period details or other important information about the production; visual and auditory learners will enjoy set designing and voice coaching; kinesthetic learners will be drawn to the performance aspect of the project, and social learners will welcome interaction from the group.

REVIEWING YOUR SCRIPT

1. Put yourself in the place of the audience. Now read over your script, imagining you are not familiar with the story it is based on. Ask yourself these questions:

- Does the script tell the story I want it to tell?
- Have I captured the sound of real speech?
- Would an audience find the scene interesting, even without knowing the whole story?
- Do I give the audience enough information about the background, setting, and characters so that they can follow the story?

2. Try out a performance. Probably the best way to shape a script is to try it out on an audience. Plays are often revised during rehearsals and even during the first performances. You might have friends read your script aloud so that you can decide which parts seem most, or least, effective.

PUBLISHING AND PRESENTING

- **Perform your scene with classmates.** You can select actors, a stage designer, a props manager, a costumer, musicians, and any other assistants you need. Remember that some skits can be performed very effectively with few props and no scenery. Your audience may be members of your class or of another class.
- **Videotape your scene.** You might show it to your classmates, friends, or family.
- **Tape your script as a radio drama.** Find creative ways to get the sound effects or music you need. Play your tape for classmates.
- **Present your script as a dramatic reading.** Select some helpers and plan a Reader's Theater presentation with appropriate costumes and props. You can perform it for your class or for others.

Lou Diamond Phillips rehearses during the filming of *Stand and Deliver.*

PROFESSIONAL NOTEBOOK

Playwright Arthur Miller's advice on writing good plays may help students as they review their scripts: "We have to remember that, maybe more than any other art, the play . . . is a set of *relationships.* There really are no characters in plays; there are *relationships.*"

Ask students what they think Miller might have meant. As they review their scripts, they should consider how dialogue shows how people feel about one another and how one character's actions and attitudes affect those of the other characters.

Springboards

Music Find a poem or script that would benefit from musical accompaniment. Write or perform this music, or choose appropriate recorded music for the performance.

MEDIA Write a newspaper review of a TV program, a radio show, a movie, or a play that you felt strongly about—or rewrite the ending of the story.

History Write a poem or a radio drama about a character from history or a famous historical event. The character could be the speaker in a poem or the narrator of a radio story.

Speaking and Listening Choose a scene from a play, a scene to be performed by two or three actors. Prepare a performance of this scene for the class.

89

Springboards

Teaching Strategies

for MEDIA

CRITICAL THINKING: ANALYZING AND EVALUATING Before students write their reviews, have them study published reviews from magazines or newspapers. Have them note features that reviewers commonly evaluate, including dialogue, plot, suspense, characterization, actors' performances, directing, camera angles, and so on.

for HISTORY

HELPFUL HINT If students choose to write a narrative poem about a historical event, have them first study a professional model such as Longfellow's "Paul Revere's Ride."

for SPEAKING AND LISTENING

HELPFUL HINT Provide resources to help students find appropriate scenes to perform. Sources include *Plays: The Drama Magazine for Young People; 50 Great Scenes for Student Actors,* edited by Lewy Olfson; and *24 Favorite One-Act Plays,* edited by Bennett Cerf and Van H. Cartmell.

Words in a Series

Objectives

- To recognize how words in a series enrich sentences
- To combine sentences by using words in a series and punctuating correctly
- To implement the techniques of professional writers through sentence imitation and expansion

Teaching Strategies

STUMBLING BLOCK: USING COMMAS In Model B, students may wonder why there is a comma after *water lilies,* the last item in the series, even though the instruction in On the Mark tells them to use a comma after every item in a series except the last. Point out that this comma serves to separate the two independent clauses of a compound sentence. To refresh students' memories about this use of commas, refer them to page 642.

In Model C, point out that the comma after *Cheerful and willing* is used to set off an introductory element, not to punctuate items in a series. To refresh students' memories about this use of commas, refer them to page 646. No comma is used after *Cheerful* because there are only two adjectives connected by *and.* Commas are used to separate a series of three or more items.

Answer Key

A. Combining Sentences

1. The chin was now clean, polished, soft.
2. She finished her breakfast and then went for her coat and hood, her school books, and her satchel.
3. He was more than a tough, long, rawboned boy.
4. I hated the tests, the raised hopes, and failed expectations.
5. Full and smooth, the light lay like gold rind over the turf, the furze, the yew bushes, and the few wind-stunted thorn trees.

Sentence COMPOSING

Words in a Series

Good writers sometimes use nouns or adjectives in a series to add smoothness and detail to their sentences. Notice how the words in a series make the sentences below more vivid.

Model A It was a day something like right now, *dry, hot, and dusty.*
Ernest Gaines, *The Autobiography of Miss Jane Pittman*

Model B I would gather *wildflowers, wild violets, honeysuckle, yellow jasmine, snakeflowers, and water lilies,* and with wire grass we'd weave them into *necklaces and crowns.*
James Hurst, "The Scarlet Ibis"

Model C *Cheerful and willing,* he went about every task with eagerness and good grace. **Lloyd Alexander, "The Foundling"**

▶ **ON THE MARK** In a series of three or more nouns or adjectives, use a comma after every item except the last one.

A. Combining Sentences Make a new sentence by putting the underlined parts into the first sentence as a series. Decide where the series fits best. Write the complete sentence, putting commas between items in the series.

1. The chin was now clean. It was also polished, soft.
Hernando Téllez, "Lather and Nothing Else"
2. She finished her breakfast and then went for her coat and hood. She also got her school books and her satchel. **Daphne du Maurier, *The Birds***
3. He was more than a tough boy. He was also more than a long, rawboned boy. **Carl Sandburg, *Abraham Lincoln: The Prairie Years***
4. I hated the tests. I also hated the raised hopes and failed expectations.
Amy Tan, *The Joy Luck Club*
5. The light lay like gold rind over the turf. The light was full and smooth. It also lay over the furze, yew bushes, and the few wind-stunted thorn trees.
Richard Adams, *Watership Down*

Additional Resource

Sentence Composing, pp. 5-6

B. Unscrambling and Imitating Sentences Unscramble each set of sentence chunks below to create a sentence that matches the structure of one of the models on page 90. Then write a correctly punctuated sentence of your own that imitates each model. Be sure each of your sentences contains a series.

1. Write sentences that imitate Model A.
   cold, melting, and delicious / a lot like an ice-cream cone / it was a treat
2. Write sentences that imitate Model B.
   novels, short stories, plays, newspaper articles, essays, and magazines, / Becky would read / she'd remember their contents for years and years / and with her photographic memory
3. Write sentences that imitate Model C.
   the runner headed toward the finish line / tired and aching / with determination and persistence

C. Expanding Sentences Become a partner with a professional writer. Use your imagination to expand the parts of sentences given below by adding a series of nouns or adjectives where indicated. Be sure to use commas to separate the items in each series.

1. The house was silent, *(add two more adjectives describing the house).*
   Cynthia Voigt, *Homecoming*
2. My mother's voice was like a cool dark room in summer—*(add three adjectives describing the mother's voice).* **Eugenia Collier, "Marigolds"**
3. He loved his vegetable plot, *(add two more things he loved).*
   Lloyd Alexander, "Coll and His White Pig"
4. There was a camera store, a newsstand, *(add three other kinds of stores),* and several other shops including a shoeshine stand tended by a boy of about Slake's age. **Felice Holman, *Slake's Limbo***
5. On the dashboard in front of him, Brian saw dials, switches, *(add three more things Brian saw)* that were wiggling and flickering. . . . **Gary Paulsen, *Hatchet***

Grammar Refresher For more on punctuating series of nouns and adjectives, see Handbook 49, "Punctuation," pages 644–645.

B. Unscrambling and Imitating Sentences

Unscrambled sentences are given. Imitative sentences will vary but should follow the same pattern.

1. It was a treat a lot like an ice-cream cone: cold, melting, and delicious.
2. Becky would read novels, short stories, plays, newspaper articles, essays, and magazines: and with her photographic memory she'd remember their contents for years and years.
3. Tired and aching, the runner headed toward the finish line with determination and persistence.

C. Expanding Sentences

Answers will vary. Authors' sentences are given.

1. The house was silent, vacant, neglected.
   Cynthia Voigt, *Homecoming*
2. My mother's voice was like a cool dark room in summer—peaceful, soothing, quiet.
   Eugenia Collier, "Marigolds"
3. He loved his vegetable plot, his apple orchard, and, above all, his white pig, Hen Wen.
   Lloyd Alexander, "Coll and His White Pig"
4. There was a camera store, a newsstand, a florist, a jewelry shop, a shop that repaired watches, and several other shops including a shoeshine stand tended by a boy of about Slake's age.
   Felice Holman, *Slake's Limbo*
5. On the dashboard in front of him, Brian saw dials, switches, meters, knobs, levers, cranks, lights, handles that were wiggling and flickering. . . .
   Gary Paulsen, *Hatchet*

HELPFUL HINT Note that the authors' sentences for items 1 and 2 do not use the word *and* between the adjectives listed in a series. The use of the word *and* in such a series of adjectives is often optional. Leaving out the word may be a deliberate choice and part of the author's distinctive style and voice. Give students credit for combining the sentences correctly using the word *and,* even if the author did not.

Informative Writing: Explaining *How*

Overview

Informative writing, also called expository writing, is based on facts. In this workshop, students use their narrative and descriptive writing skills to explain a relationship or process in factual detail. Workshop 4 includes the following Guided and Related Assignments as well as the interdisciplinary project described on pages 91c–91d.

1. **Guided: Cause-and-Effect Explanation** asks students to explain the relationship between events. Students choose a suitable topic, determine a purpose, offer a reasonable explanation of the causal relationship, and use facts and examples to support the explanation.
2. **Related: Describing a Process** invites students to use the skills of informative writing and chronological order to explain how to do something, how something works, or how something happens.

Teaching Preview

Preparation Guide

1. Use the Overview on this page and the Teacher's Choice descriptions on page 93 as a basis for deciding which assignments to teach.
2. Preview the assignments and the teacher's notes and identify concepts that may require preteaching or extra support, given your class's abilities. The handbook mini-lessons suggested within the lesson may also provide guidance.
3. Preview the chart below for support materials in the Teacher's Resource File that may be used with this Workshop. Resources are for use with the Guided Assignment unless otherwise noted.

Support Materials

RESOURCES

Prewrite and Explore
Writing Resource Book, pp. 18–19
Thinking Skills Worksheets, pp. 7–8
Starting Points for Writing, Writing Prompts for Fine Art, pp. 31–34, 41, 43

Draft and Discover
Elaboration, Revision, and Proofreading Practice, p. 7
Writing Resource Book, pp. 20–22

Revise Your Writing
Elaboration, Revision, and Proofreading Practice, p. 8
Writing Resource Book, pp. 23–24
Peer Response Guides, pp. 15–16
Guidelines for Writing Assessment and Portfolio Use, pp. 17, 32–34

Sentence Composing
Sentence Composing Copy Masters, pp. 7–8

Assessment
Tests and Writing Assessment Prompts, p. 4

Computer Software
Writer's DataBank
Electronic English Handbook

PROFESSIONAL RESOURCES AND MEDIA

Books and Journals
Beattie, Owen, and Geiger, John, *Buried in Ice: The Mystery of a Lost Arctic Expedition,* Scholastic (1992)
Reeves, Nicholas, and Froman, Nan, *Into the Mummy's Tomb,* Scholastic/Madison Press (1992)
Tchudi, Stephen, and Huerta, Margie, *Teaching Writing in the Content Areas,* National Education Association (1983)

Films and Videos
Chicano Park, Cinema Guild, New York (1990)
Danger at the Beach, PBS Video, Alexandria, VA (1992) (58 min.)
Meet a Working Sculptor: Martine Vaugel, SRA, Blacklick, OH (1993)
Sugaring Time, American School Publishers, New York (1984)

Computer Software and Technology
Bake & Taste: Following Directions, Mindplay, Danvers, MA (software), Apple II, Apple 3.5, PC, PC 3.5
Junior High Writing: Writing to Explain, Mindplay, Danvers, MA (software), Apple II family, PC/MS–DOS

Linking Literature, Writing, and Grammar

The following options may be used to provide students with an integrated language experience. Begin by assigning and discussing any of the recommended pieces of literature. Use the suggested strategy to provide a link to the Guided Assignment.

LINKING LITERATURE AND WRITING

Option 1

Starting Point: "Krakatoa: The Greatest of Them All" by Margaret Poynter on pages 94–95 of *The Writer's Craft.*

Strategy: Use the teaching suggestions on pages 94–95 to lead students into the Guided Assignment.

Option 2

Starting Point: *Harriet Tubman: Conductor on the Underground Railroad* by Ann Petry on pages 176–185 of McDougal, Littell's *Literature and Language,* Grade 8. (Additional suggestions for using *Literature and Language* can be found on page 93.)

Strategy: Have students read the selection about the escape of slaves. Tell them that an escape attempt results in a chase,which is an example of a cause—the escape—and an effect—the chase. Suggest that they jot down other examples of cause-and-effect relationships as they read the story. After students have finished the selection, discuss these examples to lead them into the Guided Assignment.

Option 3

Starting Point: "Casey at the Bat" by Ernest Lawrence Thayer.

Strategy: Read the poem aloud. Have students use a sequence chart to note the many changes in the feelings of the fans during the poem. Discuss what causes each change. Then introduce the Guided Assignment.

LINKING WRITING AND GRAMMAR

Before the drafting and revision stages of this assignment, remind students that the relationship between ideas should be clear to readers. Point out that a complex sentence often clarifies the cause-and-effect relationship. The subordinate conjunctions *because* and *since* can be used to connect ideas. Write these examples on the board.

Less Clear: I didn't have my key. I couldn't lend it to my brother.

More Clear: *Since* I didn't have my key, I couldn't lend it to my brother.

Have students check their writing for places where the use of a complex sentence would make the cause-and-effect relationship between ideas clearer. Go over pages 560–573 of the Grammar and Usage Handbook. If problems in subordination still appear in student papers, assign the exercises on these pages for reteaching. Additional practice can be found in the *Grammar and Usage Practice Book* on pages 81–91.

Management Guidelines

The chart below indicates the number of days recommended for each phase of the Guided and Related Assignments. These numbers are an estimate of the total time needed for each phase. In practice, of course, students may not complete each phase in one continuous session, nor will they necessarily progress from stage to stage in the linear order shown here. Stars indicate portions of the assignment that may be completed outside the classroom if time is limited or if teachers wish students to work independently.

CAUSE-AND-EFFECT EXPLANATION

Starting from Literature ....1 day
Prewrite and Explore ....2 days*
Draft and Discover ....2–3 days*
Revise Your Writing......................1 day*
Proofread ....1 day*
Publish and Present......................1 day
Reflect on Your Writing ....1 day
Reteaching......................................open
Extension and Enrichment ....open*
Sentence Composing ....open*

DESCRIBING A PROCESS

Starting from Literature ....1 day
Planning Your Explanation............1 day*
Drafting Your Explanation.............1 day*
Reviewing Your Writing ....1 day*
Publishing and Presenting............1 day

Project File

Earthquakes and Volcanoes: Looking at Causes and Effects

Overview

Students participating in this project will study earthquakes and volcanoes in the contexts of history, science, mythology, and art. The project will culminate in multimedia exhibits and demonstrations, showing causes and effects of specific earthquakes and volcanic eruptions and presenting the results of research into topics such as earthquake prediction and seismic measurement.

Students will participate in the following activities:

- Research causes of earthquakes and volcanoes
- Research scientific and cultural issues involving earthquakes and volcanoes
- Gather information about the effects of major earthquakes and volcanic eruptions throughout history
- Create an exhibit center for presentations about earthquakes and volcanoes
- Use language arts, science, math, social studies, and art skills to complete their research and to develop and present exhibits.

Preparation Guide

Tell students that earthquakes and volcanoes are among the most spectacular phenomena in nature—and among the most destructive. Point out that because of new knowledge about the causes and the long-term effects of earthquakes and volcanic eruptions, people today can protect themselves against these disasters to some extent.

Explain that during this project students will learn about causes and effects of earthquakes and volcanoes and will create exhibits and demonstrations to share their findings.

Stage 1 Gather Information

1. Brainstorm with students to help them discover what they already know about earthquakes and volcanoes and what aspects of the topic they would like to know more about. They may list some of the following:
   - eruptions of specific volcanoes, such as Vesuvius or Mount St. Helens
   - specific earthquakes, such as those in San Francisco in 1906 and 1991
   - earthquake prediction
   - the "rim of fire"
   - earthquakes and volcanoes in literature
   - theories of plate tectonics
   - the development of the Richter scale
2. Have students read and discuss stories and articles about earthquakes and volcanoes.
3. Direct students to gather dates and locations of, and other general data about, major earthquakes and volcanic eruptions of the past (see *Resources, Stage 1*).

TEAM TEACHING

The following activities may be used for team teaching or as enrichment and extension activities by the language arts teacher.

Social Studies Learn about the excavations of Pompeii and Herculaneum and the history of Mount Vesuvius (see *Resources, Stage 1*).

Science Discuss major classifications of volcanoes and earthquakes. Study fault zones and the Pacific "ring of fire" volcano belt (see *Resources, Stage 1*). Identify any faults or volcanic landforms in your area.

Math Learn about earthquake measurement on the Richter scale.

Language Arts Read myths and folklore about volcanoes (see *Resources, Stage 1*).

TEACHING TIPS

- Designate one area of the classroom as an exhibit and data center. Provide folders and areas for storage of oversize materials.
- Plan a library tour, paying special attention to geology source materials.
- Show videos of recent earthquakes and eruptions (see *Resources, Stage 1*).

Stage 2 Choose a Focus and Do Research

1. Have students choose topics from their list of possibilities to research further.
2. If students have chosen to focus on a single event, direct them to research specific details of the eruption or earthquake they have chosen, such as the magnitude and duration of the event and the kinds and amount of damage it caused.
3. Encourage students to study both short-term and long-term effects of the occurrences they have chosen.
4. Students researching general topics should be sure to examine recent scientific studies as well as the history of their topics.

TEAM TEACHING

Science Explain the causes of eruptions and earthquakes. Research tidal waves and the atmospheric effects of volcanic eruptions. Cite and explain scientific efforts at prediction (see *Resources, Stage 2*).

Social Studies Explain historical events related to earthquakes or eruptions. Trace cultural aftereffects. Provide examples of individuals' experiences.

Language Arts Read eyewitness accounts of earthquakes and eruptions. Study interviewing skills (see *Resources, Stage 2*).

TEACHING TIPS

- Offer students the option of working in groups to research their topics.
- Suggest that students interview people who have experienced earthquakes or witnessed volcanic eruptions.
- Visit a museum of natural history or science.

Stage 3
Write and Present Case Histories

1. Direct students to write case histories of volcanic eruptions or earthquakes they have studied. Remind them to describe the causes and effects of the events.
2. Students investigating topics such as earthquake prediction should list the questions they have researched and the answers they have found.
3. Have students plan and stage exhibits and presentations of their case histories and their other research.
4. Have students consider using any of the following for their exhibits:
   - charts, graphs, and time lines
   - drawings, paintings, photos, and posters
   - audiotapes of sound effects
   - walk-through exhibits featuring special effects
   - dioramas and cross-sectional models
   - process demonstrations

TEAM TEACHING

Language Arts Review techniques for writing about processes and their causes and effects. Also discuss how to differentiate between facts and theories (see *Resources, Stage 3*).

Art Create visuals for presentations.

Math Present charts of the heights of famous volcanoes and the magnitudes of well-known earthquakes.

Science Create models and devise demonstrations to accompany exhibits.

TEACHING TIPS

- Tell students that quotations from myths and folklore can be effective introductions and conclusions for their writing.
- Suggest that students with related topics collaborate on multimedia presentations.

Resources

STAGE 1

Volcano! The Eruption of Mt. St. Helens (ABC News), a thirty-minute video, shows news footage of the 1980 eruption and its aftermath.

Hawaiian Legends of Volcanoes by William Westervelt recounts tales of the goddess Pele and other volcano lore.

Pompeii: Nightmare at Midday by Kathryn Long Humphrey re-creates daily life in ancient Pompeii and the events of the eruption that buried the city.

Volcanoes and Earthquakes by Zuza Vrbova (in Troll Associates' Our Planet series) offers a basic introduction, with color illustrations on each page and a high-interest fact file.

Historical Catastrophes: Earthquakes by B. W. Cutchen and W. R. Brown examines earthquakes in legend and folklore and surveys major temblors from the 1755 Lisbon earthquake through the 1964 Alaska quake.

STAGE 2

Volcanoes: The Fiery Mountains and ***Earthquakes: Looking for Answers,*** both by Margaret Poynter, explore causes, effects, and catastrophic occurrences through history.

Earthquake by John Gabriel Navarra of Chicago's Museum of Science and Industry examines plate tectonics; disturbances along faults, trenches, and sutures; and earthquake prediction.

The Writer's Craft, Grade 8, Handbook 36, "Interviewing Skills," on page 362, offers useful tips on conducting interviews.

Collier's magazine for May 5, 1906, contains the novelist Jack London's eyewitness account of the San Francisco earthquake; ***Dragonwings,*** a historical novel by Laurence Yep, offers another perspective on the 1906 San Francisco earthquake.

STAGE 3

The Writer's Craft, Grade 8, Workshop 4, "Informative Writing: Explaining *How,*" pages 92–109, teaches how to write about causes and effects and about processes. Handbook 37, "Critical Listening and Observing," pages 363–366, discusses how to distinguish between facts and opinions.

Kidpix (Broderbund) and **Posterworks** (S. H. Pierce & Co.) are programs that allow students to use computers to create illustrations and posters.

Timeliner and **Mactimeliner** (Tom Snyder Productions) are software that students can use to make timelines.

Using Charts and Graphs: One Thousand Ideas for Visual Persuasion by J. White offers ways to use graphics in presentations.

Additional Projects

Social Activism Have students choose community problems they care about and identify the causes of these problems. Then propose that students choose one problem and plan a course of action to alleviate it. For example, students might organize a monthly neighborhood cleanup day, set up a child-care service or referral center, or create an after-school activity program for people their age. During the project, students should observe and record the effects of their efforts. Afterwards, they can write reports summing up the causes of the problem and the stages and effects of their project.

By the Numbers "Hire" students as "consultants" to study the relationship between school attendance and standardized-test scores in your district or city. Have students consider the ways they will obtain the data on attendance and test scores. Tell them to make lists of school officials they might interview and to determine whether they wish to compare data from several different years. Propose that they use research and surveys to identify other factors that might affect test scores. Direct them to create reports, graphs, and charts to present and explain their findings.

SKETCH BOOK

Objective

- To use illustrations and writing prompts as springboards to informal writing

WRITING WARM-UPS

Encourage students to respond freely and informally to at least one of the Sketchbook prompts. Students may begin by freewriting in their journals. Remind them that their responses will not be graded and may provide them with useful material for other writing assignments.

SHOW, DON'T TELL

The following is a sample of a "showing" paragraph for the third prompt.

The ads just say "Brand X." There are no other words. They all show people doing exciting things. One teenager on a skateboard whizzes around a curve and jumps an obstacle. A very young woman is working to help tornado victims. A glamorous-looking model is rushing through a busy foreign airport. They're all getting big smiles from other people—and, of course, each is wearing Brand X jeans. Since this ad campaign first aired, just about everyone in our school has begun to wear Brand X jeans. Even the principal was wearing them on Field Day.

SKETCH BOOK

WRITING WARM-UPS

- What if pigs could fly? What if the earth were flat? What if . . . ? Ask yourself a "what if" question, and then try to answer it.
- What would you like to change about yourself? How would your life be different if you made the change?
- What lessons have you learned? Write about an experience that taught you a lesson.

Show, Don't Tell

When you show how one event influences another event, you use facts, examples, and personal experiences to prove your point. Turn one of the *telling* sentences below into a *showing* passage, using examples that illustrate your point.

- Something made her change.
- Movies can start a trend.
- Creative advertising can really sell a product.

Informative Writing: Explaining *How*

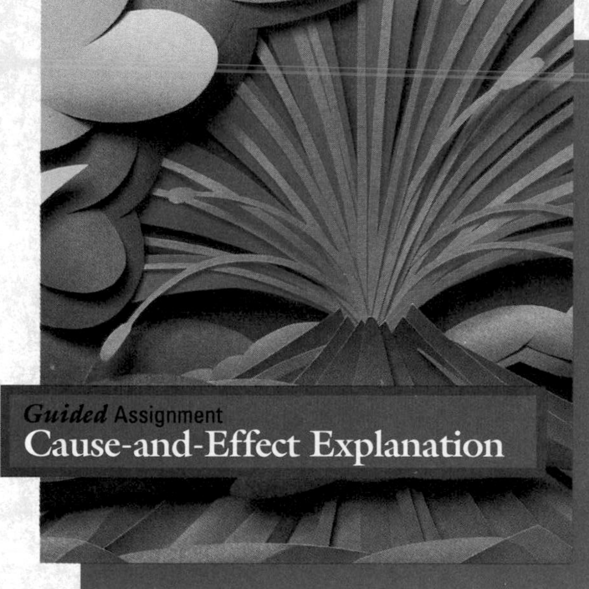

Guided Assignment
Cause-and-Effect Explanation

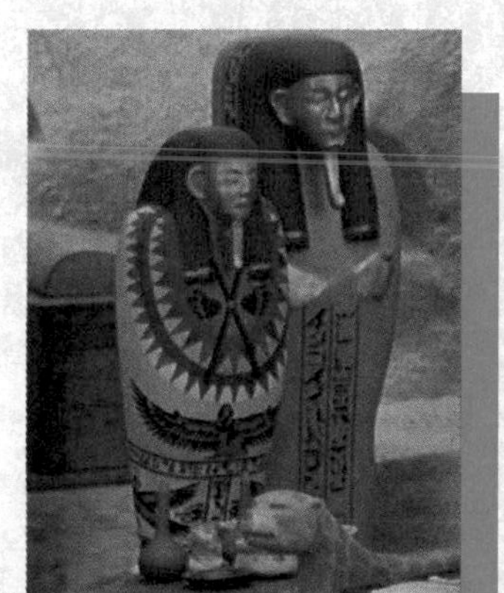

Related Assignment
Describing a Process

A song on the radio makes you think of a friend. You wonder how your life will change if your family moves to another city. You try to figure out why your muscles are sore and then remember that you cleaned the garage over the weekend. Cause-and-effect relationships are everywhere.

In this workshop, you'll learn how to explain cause-and-effect relationships. You'll also learn how to describe a process. What's more, as you write about relationships and processes, you'll probably come to understand them better than ever before.

Informative Writing: Explaining *How*

Objectives

Guided Assignment

Cause-and-Effect Explanation To write an explanation of a cause-and-effect relationship

Related Assignment

Describing a Process To write a step-by-step explanation of a process

Teacher's Choice

Use the following guidelines to choose the assignment that best suits students' needs.

Cause-and-Effect Explanation This assignment guides students in explaining causes and effects that are of interest or importance to them. For this assignment, students will draw on skills of narrative and descriptive writing and will be introduced to informative writing techniques. Therefore, you might assign this workshop after students have gained experience with descriptive and narrative writing.

Describing a Process In contrast to the guided assignment, which invites students to choose among several ways of organizing informative writing, this assignment provides practice in using chronological order.

Links to Literature & Language

Literature For more examples of writing with cause-and-effect elements, see the following selections in *Literature and Language,* Grade 8:

- Ann Petry, from *Harriet Tubman: Conductor on the Underground Railroad*
- Dougal Robertson, from *Survive the Savage Sea*
- Edgar Allan Poe, "The Tell-Tale Heart"

Guided ASSIGNMENT

ASSIGNMENT RATIONALE

When students write explanations of causes and effects, they build communication and reasoning skills useful in their science, math, and social studies courses, as well as in language arts. This assignment helps students explore relationships between causes and effects and to study chains of events, seeking causal connections. As they do so, they develop key critical thinking skills of analyzing, predicting, and drawing conclusions. They also learn to detect flaws in reasoning.

Starting from LITERATURE

Motivate

Share an experience you have had during a natural disaster, such as a tornado, hurricane, blizzard, earthquake, or fire. Emphasize any cause-and-effect sequences that occurred. For instance, you might discuss how the gale winds of a particular storm knocked down electrical wires and left your home without electricity. Then read Starting from Literature with students.

BUILD ON PRIOR KNOWLEDGE

Ask what students know about volcanoes—for example, how volcanoes form, what happens during an eruption, and what effects eruptions can have. Then ask where Indonesia is. Have students locate this island nation on a map (south of Malaysia). Guide students in finding Indonesia's Sunda Strait, between Java and Sumatra.

Guided ASSIGNMENT

Cause and Effect

Starting from LITERATURE

Did you realize that just the sound of a volcano exploding can shatter windows for hundreds of miles around? Did you know that a volcanic eruption can create a tidal wave?

In this article, journalist Margaret Poynter describes the chain of destructive events triggered by three volcanoes erupting at the same time. As you read her account, notice the images and similes she uses to help you vividly picture the effects of this triple blast.

from

KRAKATOA THE GREATEST OF THEM ALL

by Margaret Poynter

Krakatoa was a small island made up of three volcanoes—Perbuwatan, Danan, and Rakata—in the Sunda Strait of Indonesia. . . . On August 26, 1883, Krakatoa's three volcanoes began to erupt, the noise shaking houses a hundred miles away. Steam rose to a height of seven miles, and dust fell as far as three hundred miles from the island.

By the end of the day, Krakatoa was hidden by clouds of smoke and ash. Loud explosions occurred almost every ten minutes, and stones were tossed high into the air as lightning flashed through the inky black sky. The only other light came from a shower of glowing mud that looked like thousands of fireflies. It covered the ships in the area that were trapped by the mass of floating volcanic rock.

Meanwhile, more openings appeared on the slopes of the volcanoes, and hundreds of gallons of water rushed through them. The plug in the main vent still held firm, and the internal pressures grew. At dawn the next day, the sides of the island started to burst open, and the first of four huge explosions was heard. An hour later came a second; then there was silence for over three hours.

At 10:02 that morning, a gigantic explosion occurred, making the loudest noise ever reported by human beings! The sound waves cracked windows and walls for two hundred miles around. In Burma, fifteen hundred miles away, the noise sounded

MORE ABOUT THE MODEL

Most of Krakatoa sank into an underground magma chamber, creating a 900-foot-deep ocean basin next to the part of one mountain (Rakata) left standing. Plant and animal life on the island was obliterated; regrowth did not start for five years. By 1950, a new volcanic cone had risen 360 feet above sea level.

Author Note Margaret Poynter (1927–) has written nonfiction books on subjects from earthquakes to space exploration. Interested students might enjoy Poynter's *Volcanoes: The Fiery Mountains.*

like gunfire at sea. A man on an island in the Indian Ocean east of Africa heard the noise from Krakatoa four hours later. The sound waves had traveled three thousand miles!

The eruption caused a cloud of dust to rise fifty miles into the air, and at least five cubic miles of rock and dirt were blown out of the inside of the volcano. Since there wasn't enough rock left to support it, the peak collapsed into the crater of the volcano, carrying two-thirds of the island with it. . . .

The ocean had been greatly disturbed by all the activity, and tidal waves, or *tsunamis* (tsoo-nah-mees), were formed. The largest, created by the 10:02 explosion and the island's collapse, rushed away from Krakatoa at a top speed of 350 miles per hour. As the huge wave approached land, it grew stronger and higher. A wall of water as high as a ten-story building crashed down on the coast of Java. Within minutes it destroyed three hundred villages, and parts of Sumatra were covered with eighty feet of water. . . .

For many months after the eruption, the Indonesian sea was full of floating rocks. The pillar of dust was caught up in the winds of the upper atmosphere, where it orbited the earth for several years! The dust was so thick that it formed a wall between the earth and the sun for two years. The average temperature of the earth dropped almost one degree. Strange blood-red sunsets were seen in many places. The sun appeared to be green or blue, and sometimes the moon seemed to be wearing a green halo.

Several years passed before the last of the dust fell back to earth. By that time, a bit of Krakatoa had been left in every part of the world.

Think & Respond

Which of the effects Poynter describes surprised or impressed you most? What did you learn from Poynter's article that you hadn't known before? Now look at how she organizes the effects she presents. How does this organization help you to understand what happened?

SET A PURPOSE

Direct students to the purpose-setting statement at the end of the Starting from Literature box. Remind them that an image is a word-picture and that a simile is a comparison using "like" or "as." Suggest that students go back after their first reading and jot down images and similes that seem most vivid to them.

Think & Respond

ELICIT PERSONAL RESPONSES

Ask students to respond orally to the first Think & Respond question. Encourage them to offer multiple responses and to explain why certain things impressed them more than others did. Have students **freewrite** responses to the second question.

EXPLORE THE AUTHOR'S TECHNIQUES

As students consider the final Think & Respond question, explain that cause-and-effect writing can move from cause to effect or from effect to cause, often following the order of events in time. Lead students to see that effects of the eruption become, in turn, causes of other events and that Poynter uses time order to keep the complicated chain of events clear.

Point out that Poynter also keeps the chain of events clear by using words and phrases related to time as transitions between paragraphs. (For example, she cites an exact date—August 26, 1883—in paragraph 1, and she uses time-related words, phrases, and clauses to open paragraphs 2, 3, 4, 7, and 8.) Have students locate other references to time (paragraph 2: *every ten minutes;* paragraph 3: *still, At dawn the next day, An hour later,* and *then, for over three hours;* paragraph 4: *four hours later).*

Social Studies Connection

History contains many chains of events that offer possible writing topics. Suggest that students explore causes and effects of events (such as the meeting of the First Continental Congress), of confrontations (such as the battle of Bunker Hill), or of movements (such as westward expansion).

Reading a STUDENT MODEL

Margaret Poynter writes about a geological phenomenon that is literally earth-shattering; Steve Ginensky writes about a social phenomenon that is shattering in a different sense. Both writers use striking details to achieve their purposes. Steve's informative writing is the final draft of the piece that students will see in process on the workshop pages that follow.

Motivate

Point out that even major changes often go unnoticed for a long time because their original causes seem minor and the effects occur gradually. You might name the hole in the earth's ozone layer as an example. The causes—chlorofluorocarbons—built up slowly in the atmosphere for decades. The change went unnoticed until the hole appeared and long-term health effects became apparent.

BUILD ON PRIOR KNOWLEDGE

Your students' knowledge of gang activities may come only from television or news magazines; or, like Steve Ginensky's, it may come from personal experience. Ask students to share their feelings or questions about youth gangs and their activities.

SET A PURPOSE

Go over Reading a Student Model with the class. As students read, have them notice how the topic sentence in each paragraph relates to the introduction and pertains to Steve's main point. Each topic sentence lists one of the things lost as a result of gangs.

One Student's Writing

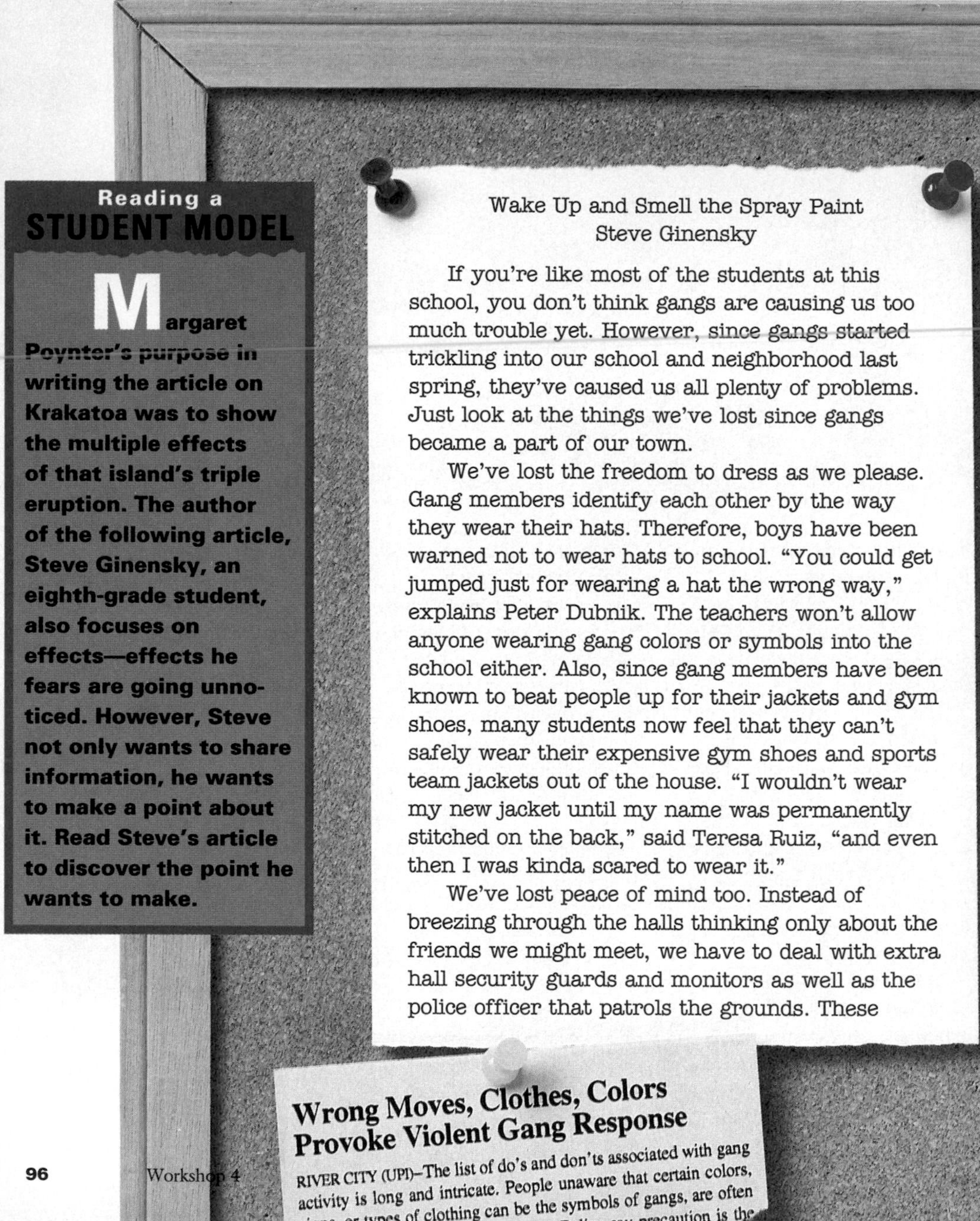

Reading a STUDENT MODEL

Margaret Poynter's purpose in writing the article on Krakatoa was to show the multiple effects of that island's triple eruption. The author of the following article, Steve Ginensky, an eighth-grade student, also focuses on effects—effects he fears are going unnoticed. However, Steve not only wants to share information, he wants to make a point about it. Read Steve's article to discover the point he wants to make.

Wake Up and Smell the Spray Paint
Steve Ginensky

If you're like most of the students at this school, you don't think gangs are causing us too much trouble yet. However, since gangs started trickling into our school and neighborhood last spring, they've caused us all plenty of problems. Just look at the things we've lost since gangs became a part of our town.

We've lost the freedom to dress as we please. Gang members identify each other by the way they wear their hats. Therefore, boys have been warned not to wear hats to school. "You could get jumped just for wearing a hat the wrong way," explains Peter Dubnik. The teachers won't allow anyone wearing gang colors or symbols into the school either. Also, since gang members have been known to beat people up for their jackets and gym shoes, many students now feel that they can't safely wear their expensive gym shoes and sports team jackets out of the house. "I wouldn't wear my new jacket until my name was permanently stitched on the back," said Teresa Ruiz, "and even then I was kinda scared to wear it."

We've lost peace of mind too. Instead of breezing through the halls thinking only about the friends we might meet, we have to deal with extra hall security guards and monitors as well as the police officer that patrols the grounds. These

Wrong Moves, Clothes, Colors Provoke Violent Gang Response
RIVER CITY (UPI)–The list of do's and don'ts associated with gang activity is long and intricate. People unaware that certain colors, signs, or types of clothing can be the symbols of gangs, are often

Grammar Connection

Point out that Steve uses many personal pronouns to emphasize the personal feelings that are part of his explanation—for example, "If *you*'re like most of the students . . ." (paragraph 1); "*We*'ve also lost *our* feelings of trust in each other" (paragraph 4). Ask how Steve's writing would change if he minimized his use of personal pronouns—for example, if his opening sentence read, "Most students at this school don't think gangs are causing too much trouble yet." (It would be less direct, more formal.) Have students consider whether personal pronouns will help them achieve the tone they want in their writing.

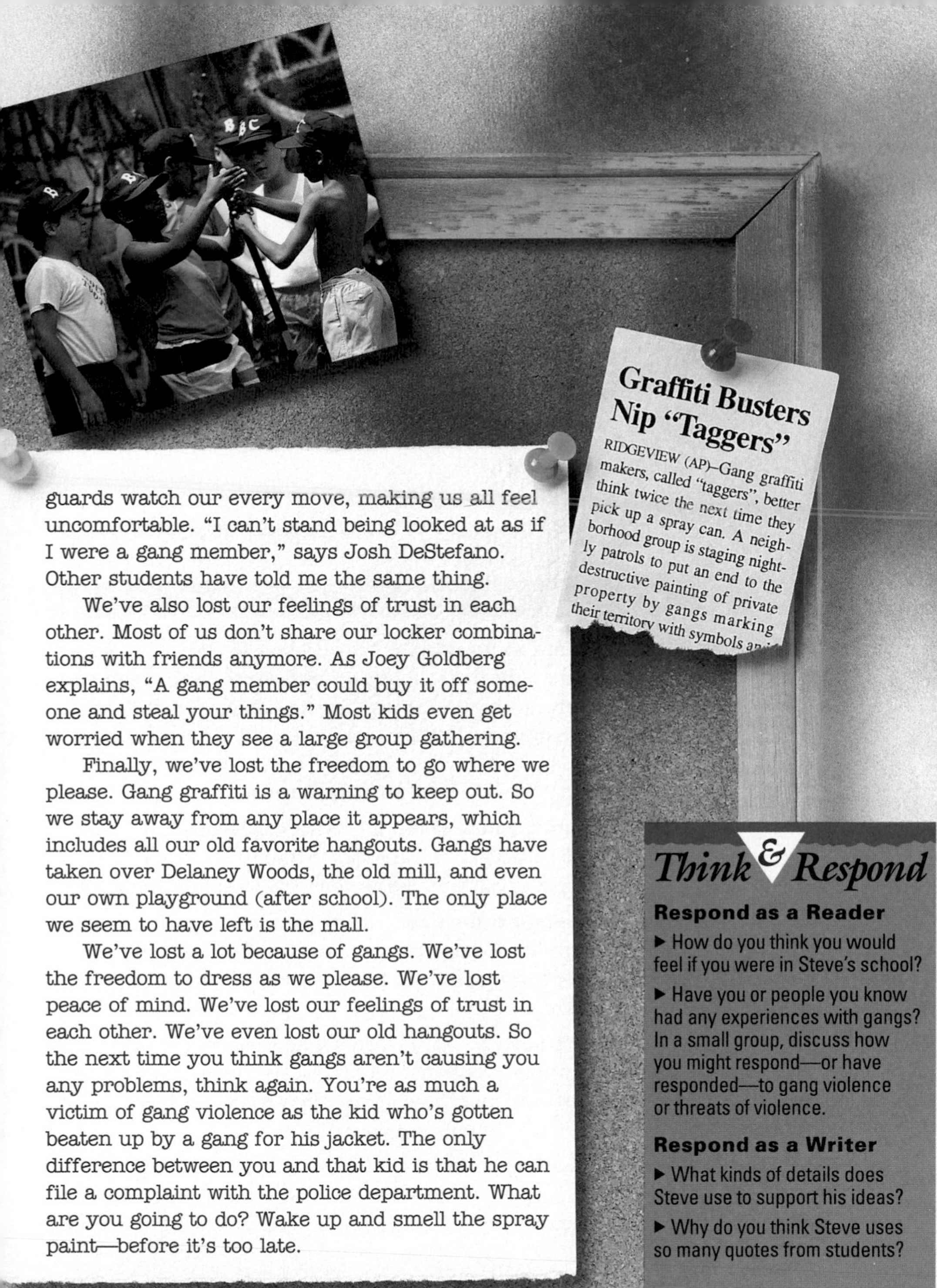

guards watch our every move, making us all feel uncomfortable. "I can't stand being looked at as if I were a gang member," says Josh DeStefano. Other students have told me the same thing.

We've also lost our feelings of trust in each other. Most of us don't share our locker combinations with friends anymore. As Joey Goldberg explains, "A gang member could buy it off someone and steal your things." Most kids even get worried when they see a large group gathering.

Finally, we've lost the freedom to go where we please. Gang graffiti is a warning to keep out. So we stay away from any place it appears, which includes all our old favorite hangouts. Gangs have taken over Delaney Woods, the old mill, and even our own playground (after school). The only place we seem to have left is the mall.

We've lost a lot because of gangs. We've lost the freedom to dress as we please. We've lost peace of mind. We've lost our feelings of trust in each other. We've even lost our old hangouts. So the next time you think gangs aren't causing you any problems, think again. You're as much a victim of gang violence as the kid who's gotten beaten up by a gang for his jacket. The only difference between you and that kid is that he can file a complaint with the police department. What are you going to do? Wake up and smell the spray paint—before it's too late.

Graffiti Busters Nip "Taggers"

RIDGEVIEW (AP)–Gang graffiti makers, called "taggers", better think twice the next time they pick up a spray can. A neighborhood group is staging nightly patrols to put an end to the destructive painting of private property by gangs marking their territory with symbols an

Think & Respond

Respond as a Reader

▶ How do you think you would feel if you were in Steve's school?

▶ Have you or people you know had any experiences with gangs? In a small group, discuss how you might respond—or have responded—to gang violence or threats of violence.

Respond as a Writer

▶ What kinds of details does Steve use to support his ideas?

▶ Why do you think Steve uses so many quotes from students?

Think & Respond

RESPOND AS A READER

▶ You might have students freewrite responses to the first question. Encourage them to respond to effects Steve cites regarding clothing, locker combinations, security guards, and police protection.

▶ For the second question, have students form small discussion groups. After the discussion, have one member of each group report to the class on points that the group raised.

RESPOND AS A WRITER

▶ Students responding to the first question should notice some or all of the following kinds of details: quotations (paragraphs 2, 3, and 4), facts (paragraphs 2, 3, and 5), feelings (paragraphs 2, 3, 4, and 6), and examples and anecdotes (paragraphs 2, 4, and 5).

▶ Encourage students to discuss the second question. (Sample: It shows that he's not the only one who considers gangs a problem; quotations show people's feelings rather than just tell about them.)

Draw Conclusions

To make sure students understand this introduction to informative writing that explains *how,* have them list, as a class, the characteristics they have noticed in both models. Responses may include comments such as these:

- focuses on reasonable explanations of causes and effects
- includes several kinds of showing details—including images, similes, facts, quotations, examples, and anecdotes—to support the main idea
- uses words and phrases that make cause-and-effect connections clear
- has an organization that fits the writer's purpose

SPICE BOX

To give students practice in thinking about causes and effects, bring in several worn or broken items—a sprung umbrella, a flashlight that barely flickers, a smashed toy car, a chipped cup, a sweater with a hole in the elbow, and so on. "Hire" students as detectives; each student should examine the items carefully and make up a brief explanation of how one of the items came to be in that condition. Have students orally share their "theories."

Writing ON YOUR OWN

Remind students that both the Professional Model and the Student Model explain causes and effects by using facts, examples, quotations, and other vivid details. As students begin to choose a cause-and-effect relationship that has meaning for them, remind them that they, like Margaret Poynter and Steve Ginensky, can use several kinds of details to demonstrate the exact relationships among events.

Handbooks for Help and Practice

The following handbooks may be used as mini-lessons before students begin writing or as resources when problems arise.

- **Types of Organization, pp. 239–243**
- **Paragraphs in Longer Writing, pp. 252–254**
- **Methods of Elaboration, pp. 255–261**
- **Show, Don't Tell, pp. 262–267**

PREWRITE AND EXPLORE

Objectives

- To use prewriting techniques to select a topic for an informative essay on a cause-and-effect relationship
- To gather specific details for a cause-and-effect explanation

Teaching Strategies

for EXPLORING TOPICS

INDIVIDUALIZING INSTRUCTION: SOCIAL LEARNERS Students may wish to explore writing ideas in pairs or in groups of three. Together they can brainstorm a list of "What if?" questions, hypothesize about the answers, and share research responsibilities as they track down causes and effects.

Writing ON YOUR OWN

Cause-and-Effect Explanation

INVITATION TO *Write*

Cause-and-effect explanations like Margaret Poynter's article about Krakatoa and Steve Ginensky's piece about the effects of gangs make people aware of important relationships between events.

Now explain a cause-and-effect relationship that you think is important or interesting.

PREWRITE AND EXPLORE

1. Take time to wonder. Why do people crack their knuckles? How did the light bulb change people's lives? Find something that sparks your curiosity by freewriting to come up with "why" and "how" questions, or by engaging in some of the activities below.

Exploring Topics

- **Capturing your questions** What might happen if I change schools? What causes tornadoes to form? Record what you wonder about as you go through your day. Then share your notes.
- **Peeking into the past** How has the computer influenced modern life? What were the causes of the French Revolution? Browse through history books to find inventions and events that interest you.
- **What's news?** Look through newspapers and magazines to find current events and recent discoveries that concern or interest you. **List** these items. Then predict or speculate about their effects on you and your future.
- **"Ah ha!" experiences** Have you figured something out about people or events? Do you have a theory or an idea you're eager to explore? Jot down your theories, ideas, and speculations.

Science Connection

Point out that every time we ask "Why?" we probe causes and effects. The existence of black holes, for example, was discovered when astrophysicists Stephen Hawking and Roger Penrose wondered why light and other radiation seemed to disappear into apparently empty areas of the universe. Suggest that students skim their journals for mention of natural phenomena that they wonder about. Such questions can lead to topics for informative writing about causes and effects.

2. Begin exploring. Once you have several topics, freewrite, research, or brainstorm to answer any of these questions: "What happened?" "What might happen?" and "What caused it?"

After you've explored for a while, choose the topic you'd most like to explain to others. Begin to examine it more closely.

3. Gather information. If you need to know more about your topic, conduct library research or interviews, or do experiments.

4. Notice relationships. As you try to see the connections among your details, keep the following points in mind.

- One cause can have more than one effect.
- One effect may have many causes.
- In a true cause-and-effect relationship, one event doesn't only happen later than another. Instead, the second event actually happens *because* the first event occurred.

5. Sort out your details. Try drawing a cause-and-effect chart. Start with one cause and work forward, noting its effects. Or, begin with an effect and work backward, noting its causes. Add details that support your ideas and, if possible, a conclusion.

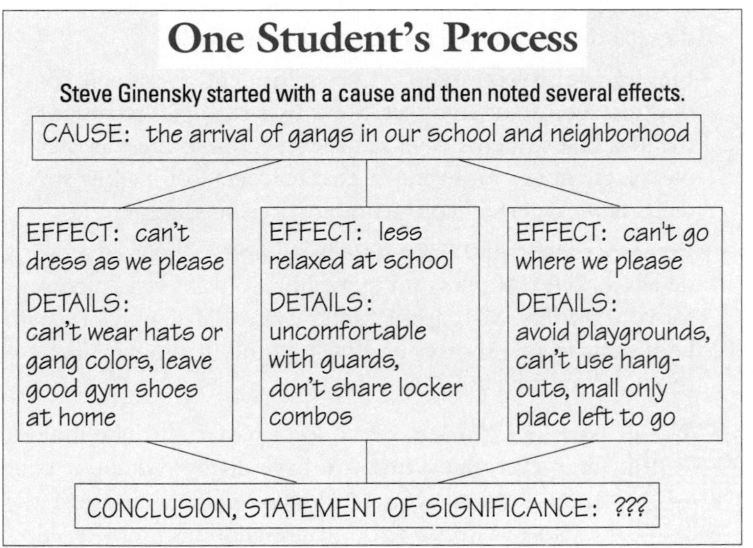

One Student's Process
Steve Ginensky started with a cause and then noted several effects.
CAUSE: the arrival of gangs in our school and neighborhood
EFFECT: can't dress as we please
DETAILS: can't wear hats or gang colors, leave good gym shoes at home
EFFECT: less relaxed at school
DETAILS: uncomfortable with guards, don't share locker combos
EFFECT: can't go where we please
DETAILS: avoid playgrounds, can't use hang-outs, mall only place left to go
CONCLUSION, STATEMENT OF SIGNIFICANCE: ???

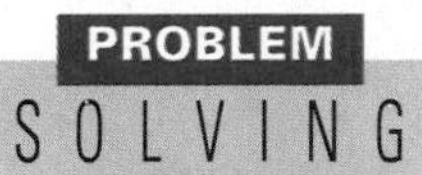

"Have I described a true cause-and-effect relationship?"

For help in checking your reasoning, see

- Handbook 31, "Critical Thinking and Writing," pages 337–339

for GATHER INFORMATION

COLLABORATIVE OPPORTUNITY
If some students choose to explain the causes of historical events, you might suggest that they choose related events. Offer them the option of working collaboratively, sharing research tasks as they gather information.

for NOTICE RELATIONSHIPS

CRITICAL THINKING: DRAWING CONCLUSIONS Explain that a common error in reasoning happens when people assume that an event occurring before a second event must have caused the second event. Example: Because a chill is often the first symptom of the fever accompanying a cold, people have long thought that chills cause colds. Repeated studies show, however, that there is no cause-and-effect connection. Urge students to check assumptions about causes and effects carefully.

for ONE STUDENT'S PROCESS

KEY TO UNDERSTANDING Explain that Steve's chart didn't have to be limited to three effects. Cause-and-effect charts can list as many causes and effects as necessary. You might show students the blank cause-and-effect chart from the Thinking Skills Worksheets and discuss how they can modify it to fit their needs. For example, they could put an effect in the top box and show causes in the other boxes.

Be sure students understand that each effect Steve lists can be seen as the cause of something else. Ask students to supply the next links in the cause-and-effect chain. (Sample: Being unable to go where they please causes students to congregate at the mall.)

GENERAL NOTE

MANAGING THE PAPER LOAD If students' prewriting includes charts or other graphics, spot-check these to make sure that students have enough information to support their main ideas and that their reasoning is sound.

TEACHER'S LOUNGE

"But, Mr. Barnes, this is heaven! You don't have to prepare a plan book, have bus duty or attend staff meetings!"

DRAFT AND DISCOVER

Objectives

- To draft an explanation of a cause-and-effect relationship, choosing details that show rather than tell
- To respond to one's own draft and to that of a peer

Teaching Strategies

for START WRITING

HELPFUL HINT Encourage students to consider long-term causes and effects as well as immediate ones. For example, in her last two paragraphs, Margaret Poynter mentions effects that occurred years after the eruption of Krakatoa. Challenge students to speculate about even longer-term effects of the eruption—such as its possible contribution to a greenhouse effect, or the social and cultural consequences of the tidal wave that struck Java. Then urge students to try out this kind of long-range thinking in their own explanations.

for ELABORATE ON IDEAS

HELPFUL HINT: QUOTATIONS Some students may want to elaborate on their ideas by using quotations, as in Steve Ginensky's model. Have them reexamine it to see how to incorporate quotations smoothly. For more examples and for punctuation tips, refer students to pages 664–668 of Handbook 49.

DRAFT AND DISCOVER

1. Start writing. Focus on whatever is clearest to you, then work backward or forward as you figure things out. Also, as you draft, feel free to explore additional causes or effects.

2. Be on the lookout for your purpose and goals. As Steve explored the effects of gangs, he realized that he and his friends had been overlooking lots of changes in their lives. He became concerned about these changes and the fact that no one was noticing them. So he decided his purpose for writing would be to point out these gang-related changes. His personal goal would be to wake his friends up "by shaking them up," as he put it.

As you write, think about your purpose and goals. Do you simply want to describe certain causes or effects? Do you want to persuade your readers to think or act in a certain way? What feelings or thoughts do you want your readers to get from your writing?

3. Elaborate on ideas. Is there more you can say? Try showing what you mean by adding some of the following details.

- **Facts and statistics** Include startling or impressive facts and statistics. For instance, "The sound waves cracked windows and walls for two hundred miles around."
- **Incidents and examples** Use an incident or example to illustrate a cause or an effect. Steve uses examples to support the idea that students have lost the freedom to dress as they please. He notes, for instance, that teachers won't allow students to wear certain color combinations to school.
- **Sensory details and figurative language** Use vivid sensory details as well as similes and metaphors to paint vivid pictures for your readers. Margaret Poynter writes, "The only other light came from a shower of glowing mud that looked like thousands of fireflies."

Writer's Choice You don't have to include in your draft everything that you have discovered about your topic. Instead, you can focus on explaining just the causes or effects of your cause-and-effect relationship.

"How can I do a better job of showing instead of telling?"

For help in showing instead of telling, see

- Handbook 13, "Show, Don't Tell," pages 262–267

Writing TIP

Dialogue and anecdotes can help bring to life a cause-and-effect explanation. They can also help your readers to feel personally touched by the causes or effects you are describing.

PROFESSIONAL NOTEBOOK

Arlene Silberman (in *Growing Up Writing*) describes the beliefs and teaching methods of instructor Terry Moher: "'One idea per conference while students are immersed in the process of writing is more helpful . . . than ten ideas on a piece that is already completed.'" Silberman also notes that Moher "relies on the technique of repeating what she understands a student to have said. 'Is this what you meant,' she asks, 'or am I interpreting what you wrote incorrectly?' Brief as [Moher's] questions sometimes are, she helps students sharpen their thinking, yet she divides her limited time so as to reach everyone."

4. Organize your material. Here are three good ways to organize cause-and-effect writing:

- **Cause to effect** Start by describing the causes. Then move on to the effects. Steve, for example, first identifies a single cause and then describes several effects.
- **Effect to cause** Begin by telling what happened. Then explain or speculate on why it happened. If what happened is especially exciting or interesting, describing it first is a good way to grab your reader's attention.
- **Chronological order** If, like Margaret Poynter, you are describing a series of causes and effects in which each effect also acts as a cause, you may want to present each event in the order it occurs or might occur.

5. Examine your draft. Use the following questions to help you and your peer readers review your draft.

REVIEW YOUR WRITING

Questions for Yourself

- Are there any other possible causes or effects I might want to include?
- Have I emphasized the most important causes and effects?
- Have I shown clear connections between causes and effects?
- Have I explained my ideas with facts, incidents, and anecdotes?

Questions for Your Peer Readers

- Why do you think I wrote this essay?
- Do the connections I've made between causes and effects seem reasonable? Which connections are the strongest, or most reasonable? Which are weakest?
- Have I left out any causes or effects? If so, what are they?
- What questions do you have? What would you like to know more about?

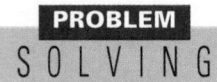

PROBLEM SOLVING

"How do I organize my material?"

For help with cause-and-effect organization, see

- Handbook 8, "Types of Organization," pages 239–243

COMPUTER TIP

You can experiment with different ways of organizing the details in cause-and-effect writing by using the block move (cut and paste) command.

for ORGANIZE YOUR MATERIAL

INDIVIDUALIZING INSTRUCTION: LD STUDENTS Some students may have particular difficulty understanding sequence of events. You may wish to confer briefly with these students as they begin writing, to ensure that they have accurately sequenced their cause-and-effect relationships. You might guide them in developing a flow chart to show the relationships.

for REVIEW YOUR WRITING

HELPFUL HINT Remind students that they need not ask peers to comment on their drafts if they do not yet feel ready. If students using the Questions for Yourself are unsure about how to show connections between causes and effects, refer them to Handbook 15, "Coherence," pages 273–277, for lists of transitions and for examples of other ways to show connections.

for ONE STUDENT'S PROCESS

KEY TO UNDERSTANDING Remind students of Steve's goal—to wake up his friends "by shaking them up." Ask students which sentence in Steve's concluding paragraph shakes them up most. Then direct them to the peer comments in the margin; invite them to offer more suggestions that might help Steve achieve his goal.

REVISE YOUR WRITING

Objectives

- To evaluate responses to a draft and to revise with those responses in mind
- To use appropriate transitions to indicate cause-and-effect relationships

Teaching Strategies

for HAVE YOU STAYED ON TRACK?

INDIVIDUALIZING INSTRUCTION: BASIC STUDENTS Students who made an outline or used a cause-and-effect chart during prewriting should look again at those graphic devices to be sure they have included all the points they had wanted to use.

for PARAGRAPHS AT WORK

HELPFUL HINT Explain that transitions can be helpful not only in topic sentences, but also within paragraphs. You might have students locate one-word transitions in Steve's final draft on pages 96–97 and in the Professional Model on pages 94–95.

Peer Reader Comments

The beginning of this paragraph doesn't seem as strong as the end.

You sound really frustrated. Why?

I like the last sentence.

One Student's Process

Here is the conclusion of Steve's first draft. Read it and then look at the peer comments. What comments, if any, would you add?

We've lost a lot because of gangs. We've lost the freedom to dress as we please, peace of mind, trust in each other, and even our old hangouts. Why doesn't anyone else besides me see these things? Is being beaten up for your jacket or gym shoes the only kind of effect of gangs you guys can recognize? Why won't anybody wake up and smell the spray paint?

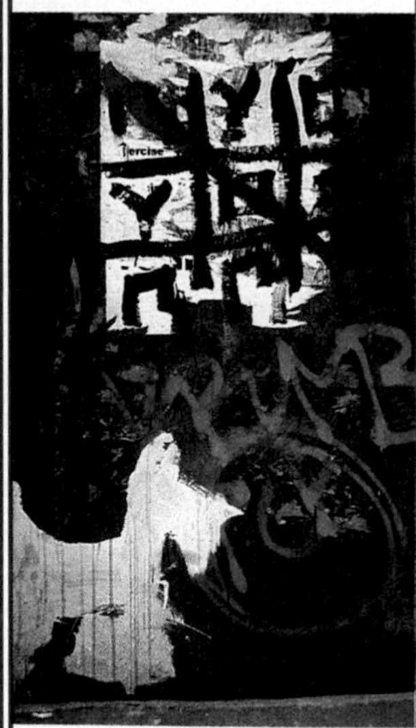

REVISE YOUR WRITING

1. Review your responses. Read your peer responses as well as your own notes to pinpoint the strengths and weaknesses of your writing. Then decide which changes you might want to make.

2. Have you stayed on track? You may have discovered new causes or effects as you drafted. If so, now is the time to ask yourself if they belong in your composition.

3. Check your organization and add transitions. If your cause-and-effect relationships are unclear, try organizing your details differently. Adding transitions can also help make relationships clearer.

Paragraphs at Work In a cause-and-effect explanation, you can help readers understand the relationships between causes and effects by focusing on only one major cause or effect in each paragraph. In addition, remember the following tips.

- Transitions in your topic sentence can help you clarify cause-and-effect relationships.
- All the details in your paragraph should help develop the major cause or effect that is the focus of that paragraph.

4. Think again about your purpose and goals. Did your peer readers understand your purpose for writing? One way to help your purpose come across clearly is to state it in your introduction. Also remember that your purpose and goals may change as you draft.

5. Review your conclusion. In your conclusion, you may simply want to restate or summarize your main ideas. However, you can also comment on these ideas, make a proposal, or call your readers to action.

After reviewing his peer readers' comments, Steve realized that his conclusion wasn't helping him get his message across. So he decided to rewrite the ending to get his readers to realize he wanted them to take some action.

One Student's Process

Read Steve's revised conclusion to see his changes.

We've lost a lot because of gangs. We've lost the freedom to dress as we please, [⊙ We've lost] peace of mind, [⊙ We've lost our feelings of] trust in each other, ~~and~~ [⊙ We've lost] even our old hangouts. ~~Why doesn't anyone else besides me see these things? Is being beaten up for your jacket or gym shoes the only kind of effect of gangs you guys can recognize? Why won't anybody~~ wake up and smell the spray paint[—before it's too late.]

So the next time you think gangs aren't causing you any problems, think again. You're as much a victim of gang violence as the kid who's gotten beaten up by a gang for his jacket. The only difference between you and that kid is that he can file a complaint with the police department. What are you going to do?

PROBLEM SOLVING

"How do I know when to paragraph in a longer piece of writing?"

For more help with paragraphing in longer pieces of writing, see

- Handbook 11, "Paragraphs in Longer Writing," pages 252–254

for REVIEW YOUR CONCLUSION

HELPFUL HINT Remind students that an effective conclusion often contains a memorable image or statement. For example, Margaret Poynter's last sentence creates a memorable image, summing up the far-reaching effects of Krakatoa's eruption: ". . . a bit of Krakatoa had been left in every part of the world." Steve's call to action, "Wake up and smell the spray paint—before it's too late," is a clever wrap-up that readers will remember.

for ONE STUDENT'S PROCESS

HELPFUL HINT Point out that Steve strengthened the first part of his paragraph by breaking his awkward second sentence into a series of three sentences and using *parallelism,* the repetition of key words ("We've lost . . ."). Students will have an opportunity to practice using parallelism in the Sentence Composing exercises on pages 112–113.

MULTICULTURAL Connection

As students revise their explanations, point out that many fables and folk tales illustrate cause-and-effect relationships. You might have students give examples from their own cultural backgrounds, explaining the cause-and-effect relationships. Suggest that a summary of an appropriate story from students' cultural heritages might help create a striking introduction or a memorable conclusion.

PROOFREAD

Teaching Strategies

for LINKING MECHANICS AND WRITING

STUMBLING BLOCK Explain that the transition words *because* and *since* are never directly followed by a comma. These words are always used as part of a phrase or clause ("because of gangs", "since gangs started trickling in"). When used as an introductory element, the whole word group is usually followed by a comma.

Example: Since gang violence has increased, guards must patrol our school.

Guidelines for Evaluation

IDEAS AND CONTENT

- explains a true cause-and-effect relationship
- includes several kinds of specific details to make the relationship and its significance clear
- demonstrates a clear purpose and goals
- has an effective conclusion

STRUCTURE AND FORM

- displays a clear and reasonable organization
- contains unified, well-developed paragraphs
- uses transitions to show cause-and-effect relationships

GRAMMAR, USAGE, AND MECHANICS

- displays standard grammar, usage, and mechanics
- correctly punctuates transition words and phrases

GENERAL NOTE

ASSESSMENT Because this may be students' first attempt at informative writing, you may wish to consider holistic scoring as a means of assessment.

Writing TIP

The words *effect* and *affect* are often confused. To use them correctly, remember that an ***e**ffect* is an **e**nd result and ***a**ffect* means to **a**ct on.

Standards for Evaluation

INFORMATIVE WRITING

A cause-and-effect explanation

- focuses on a true cause-and-effect relationship
- offers reasonable explanations of cause-and-effect relationships
- shows clear connections between causes and effects
- presents causes and effects in a sensible order
- uses facts, examples, and other details to illustrate each cause and effect

PROOFREAD

1. Proofread your work. Correct any errors in grammar, capitalization, usage, and spelling.

2. Make a clean copy of your paper. Use the Standards for Evaluation in the margin to check your paper one last time. Then make a clean final copy.

LINKING MECHANICS AND WRITING

Punctuating Transition Words and Phrases

Transition words and phrases can help you to make the connections between causes and effects clear. When you begin a sentence with a transition word or phrase, set off that word or phrase with a comma.

Original

Gang members identify each other by the way they wear their hats. Boys have been warned not to wear hats to school.

Revised

Gang members identify each other by the way they wear their hats. Therefore, boys have been warned not to wear hats to school.

For more information on punctuating sentences with introductory elements, see Handbook 49, "Punctuation," page 646.

PUBLISH AND PRESENT

- **Arrange an oral presentation.** Share your explanation with a group that might be interested in understanding the cause-and-effect relationship you have described. If possible, consider demonstrating the cause-and-effect relationship to this group as part of your presentation.

- **Create a book-on-tape.** Record your explanation along with those of your classmates to form a book-on-tape. Make this "book" available at the learning center in your school.
- **Make a cause-and-effect chart.** Use your prewriting chart and notes as well as your final paper to prepare a poster-sized cause-and-effect chart that explains your cause-and-effect relationship. Then display your poster alongside others on a bulletin board.

REFLECT ON YOUR WRITING

WRITER TO WRITER

Have something to say, and say it as clearly as you can.

Matthew Arnold, poet and critic

FOR YOUR **PORTFOLIO**

1. Add your explanation to your portfolio. Now that you have written about a cause-and-effect relationship, what are your thoughts about this type of informative writing? Write down your reactions and attach your notes to your final draft. Answering the following questions may help you to focus your thoughts.

- What did I learn about finding ideas for cause-and-effect writing?
- What did I discover as I started writing about my cause-and-effect relationship? Did it seem simpler or more complicated once I began exploring it?
- How did I organize my details? Why? Did I make any changes in my organization during revision? If so, why?
- What was the most difficult part about writing this explanation? What techniques helped me with this part?
- Were my peers' responses helpful? Why or why not?
- If I were to rewrite my paper again, what would I change?

2. Explore additional writing ideas. See the suggestions for describing a process on pages 108–109 and Springboards on page 110.

Reteaching

After students have completed their papers, assess the needs of students who were not successful in developing an effective cause-and-effect explanation; then assign the appropriate handbook mini-lessons, along with the Workshop Support Materials listed in the Teaching Preview, pages 91a–91b. Concepts commonly requiring reteaching for this assignment are:

- **Handbook 10, Developing Paragraphs, pp. 248–251**
- **Handbook 11, Paragraphs in Longer Writing, pp. 252–254**
- **Handbook 15, Coherence, pp. 273–277**

The following suggestions and resources also may be useful.

Unclear Causal Links Assign the Showing Cause and Effect section of Handbook 13, page 264, and the Cause-and-Effect Order section of Handbook 8, page 241, as mini-lessons. If students need additional help, assign page 21, "Showing Causes and Effects," in the Writing Resource Book.

Weak Conclusions Bring in examples (from magazines or anthologies) of causal explanations with strong conclusions. Pair students and have them brainstorm memorable statements to enliven each other's conclusions.

Extension and Enrichment

1. On the board, write, "If I inherited a million dollars . . ." Have students write an explanation of how the money might affect their lives six months, five years, and twenty years from now.

2. Invite students to choose a desired effect, such as improved grades or less friction with a sibling. Then have them write about how they might bring about the effect they chose.

Closure: Reflect on Your Writing

Open a general discussion about the writing assignment that students have just completed. Ask questions such as: What surprised you most as you worked on this assignment? and What advice would you give someone just starting the assignment?

Related ASSIGNMENT

Starting from LITERATURE

Objectives

- To respond to and analyze an explanation of a process
- To use prewriting techniques to identify and explore a process
- To write a vivid and clearly organized process explanation

Motivate

Tell students that our need to know how things work is so strong that we often make up explanations for processes we don't understand. For example, some young children assume that televisions have miniature performers inside. Ask students to share "how-it-works" explanations that they devised in early childhood or have heard children make up.

BUILD ON PRIOR KNOWLEDGE

Ask: When you hear the term *ancient Egyptians,* what mental pictures do you see? Let students share what they know about ancient Egypt. Lead them to a discussion of mummies. Then ask questions like: What do you know about how mummies were made? What do you still want to know?

SET A PURPOSE

After reading and discussing Starting from Literature, call students' attention to the purpose-setting statement at the end. List on the board students' guesses about the kinds of information, other than steps in the mummification process, that the article might contain. Invite students to read the article and see how many of their guesses were on target.

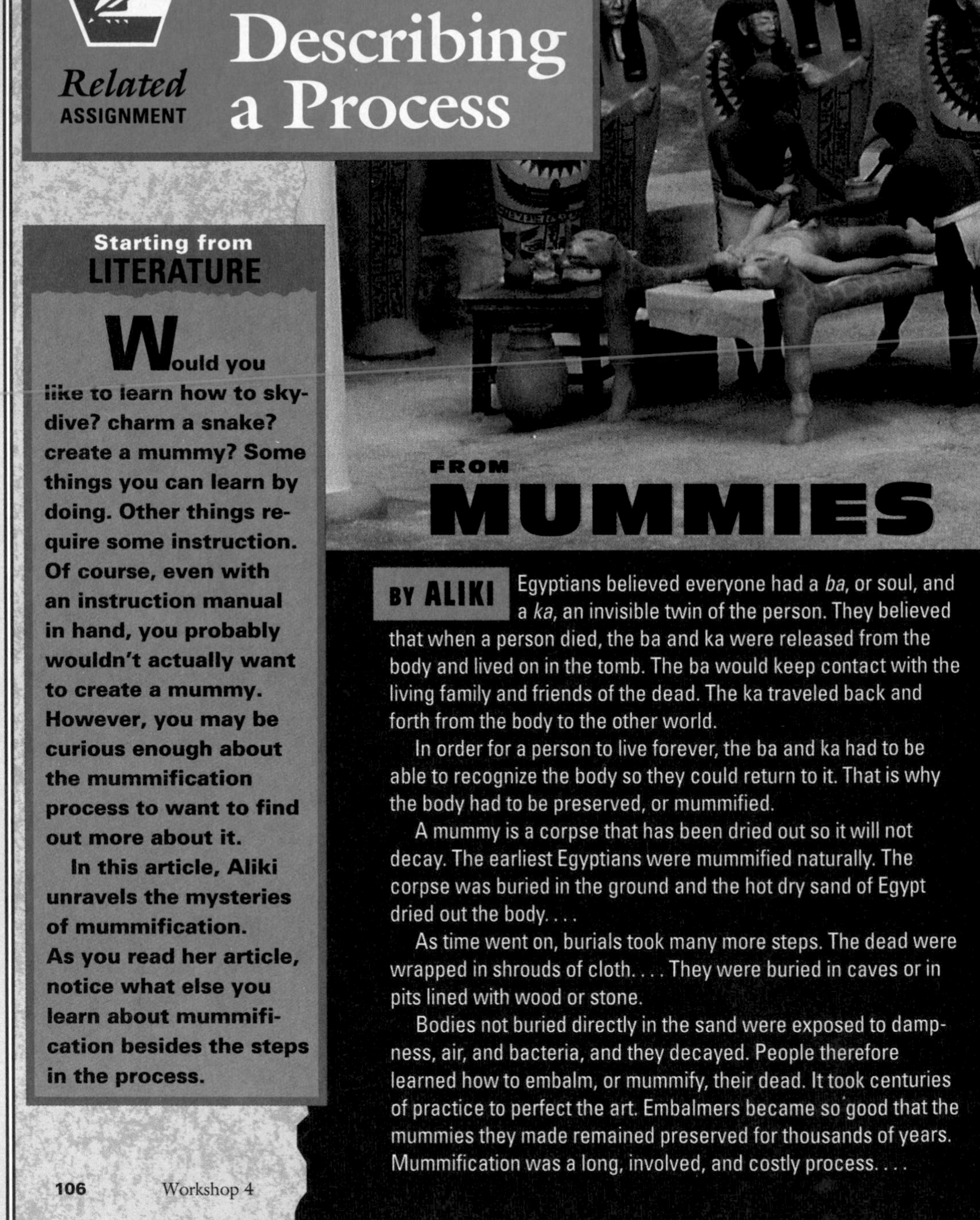

Related ASSIGNMENT Describing a Process

Starting from LITERATURE

Would you like to learn how to skydive? charm a snake? create a mummy? Some things you can learn by doing. Other things require some instruction. Of course, even with an instruction manual in hand, you probably wouldn't actually want to create a mummy. However, you may be curious enough about the mummification process to want to find out more about it.

In this article, Aliki unravels the mysteries of mummification. As you read her article, notice what else you learn about mummification besides the steps in the process.

FROM MUMMIES

BY ALIKI

Egyptians believed everyone had a *ba*, or soul, and a *ka*, an invisible twin of the person. They believed that when a person died, the ba and ka were released from the body and lived on in the tomb. The ba would keep contact with the living family and friends of the dead. The ka traveled back and forth from the body to the other world.

In order for a person to live forever, the ba and ka had to be able to recognize the body so they could return to it. That is why the body had to be preserved, or mummified.

A mummy is a corpse that has been dried out so it will not decay. The earliest Egyptians were mummified naturally. The corpse was buried in the ground and the hot dry sand of Egypt dried out the body. . . .

As time went on, burials took many more steps. The dead were wrapped in shrouds of cloth. . . . They were buried in caves or in pits lined with wood or stone.

Bodies not buried directly in the sand were exposed to dampness, air, and bacteria, and they decayed. People therefore learned how to embalm, or mummify, their dead. It took centuries of practice to perfect the art. Embalmers became so good that the mummies they made remained preserved for thousands of years. Mummification was a long, involved, and costly process. . . .

MORE ABOUT THE MODEL

Author Note American author and artist Aliki (Aliki Brandenberg) (1929–) has won many awards for her fiction and nonfiction for young people. She explains, "Nonfiction needs fascination with a subject (often one I know very little about), an overabundance of research, and time to assimilate. The pleasure of these books (science, biography, history) is writing complicated facts as clearly and simply as possible, so readers (and I) who know nothing about a subject, learn a great deal by the time we are finished. I find humor indispensable for making information palatable and fresh. The most fascinating subject is dreary without it."

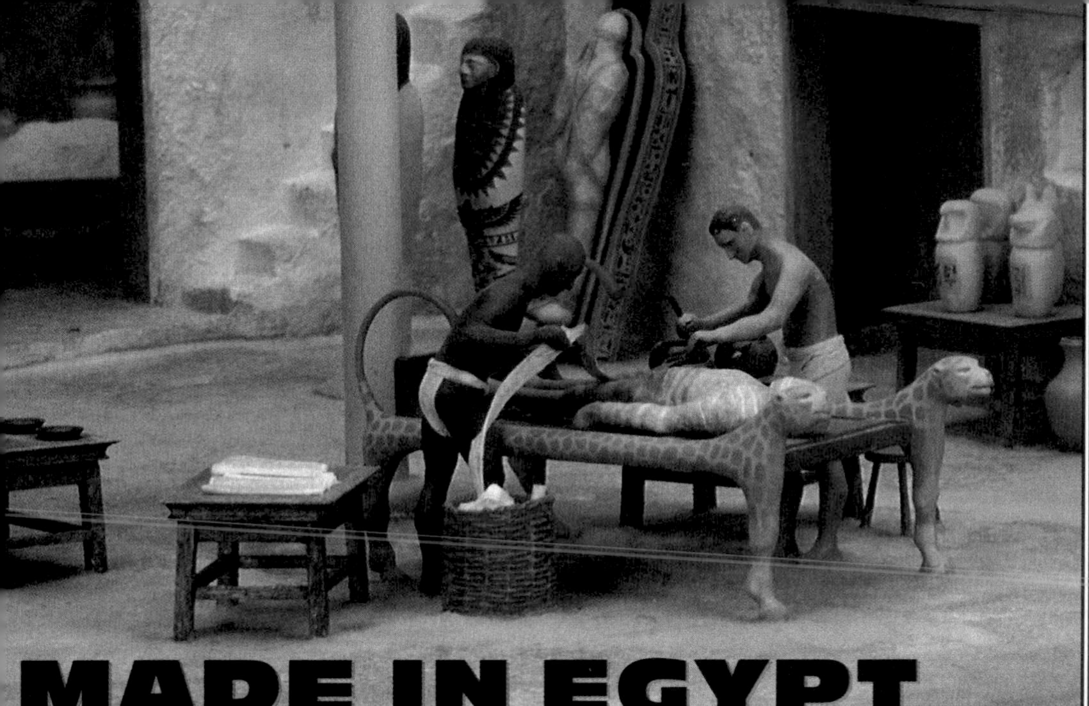

MADE IN EGYPT

The embalmers first took out the inner organs. They removed the brain through the nose with metal hooks. Then they made a slit in the left side of the body. They took out the liver, lungs, stomach, and intestines through this slit. Each of the organs was embalmed in a chemical called natron. It was put in its own container called a canopic jar. The heart was left in place. The embalmers later used stuffing to shape the thorax and stomach cavity.

In some cases, small bundles of natron wrapped in linen were stuffed inside the body. The outside was covered with natron too. The chemical dried out the body the same way the sand had done.

Then the body was carefully bound with long, narrow strips of linen. Fingers, toes, arms, and legs were wrapped separately. Sometimes, linen shrouds were placed between the layers of binding. Every few layers were glued together with resin.

[Small figurines of gods] were tucked in between the mummy's wrappings. Jewelry items such as rings, bracelets and necklaces were also placed between the layers of wrappings.

In some cases, the bound head was covered with a portrait mask. If anything happened to the mummy, the ba and ka would still be able to recognize it. The mask, too, was bound. Then the body was wrapped in a shroud and given a last coat of resin. The mummy was finished. . . .

Think & Respond

What surprised or impressed you about this process? Discuss your thoughts and reactions with your classmates. Then look back over the article to see how Aliki interests her audience in the mummification process. Notice, also, how Aliki helps her audience to understand unfamiliar terms.

Think & Respond

ELICIT PERSONAL RESPONSES

Have students share and discuss their answers to the first Think & Respond question. For the next question, ask what made these parts interesting to them. (If students say they like the "grossness," point out that Aliki's use of specific terms makes these parts vivid. More sample responses: She gives reasons for mummification; she explains the history of the process.) Finally, have the class define the terms *ba, ka, natron,* and *canopic jar.* Then ask how Aliki shows the meaning of each. (She uses appositives and synonyms.)

EXPLORE THE AUTHOR'S TECHNIQUES

To help students use Aliki's article as a model for writing, point out that the first page of the article gives background information and that the second page explains the steps in the mummification process. Have students go over the second page and list the steps. Explain that Aliki uses words showing time order to help readers understand the process. Have students find examples (paragraph 6: *first, then, later;* paragraph 8: *then, sometimes;* paragraph 10: *then, last).* Point out, as well, that Aliki uses words showing spatial order. Offer these examples from paragraph 6: *inner, through the nose, in the left side, through this slit, in its own container, in place.* Have students find other examples in paragraphs 7–10.

Links to LITERATURE & LANGUAGE

Literature For more literature with a strong "process" element, see *Literature and Language,* Grade 8:
- Daniel Keyes, "Flowers for Algernon"
- Mark Twain, "The Million-Pound Bank Note"
- Robert Silverberg, "Pompeii"
- Delia Ephron, "How to Die of Embarrassment"

Writing This related assignment may be used as an extension of the Writer's Workshop "Informative Writing: Explaining a Process" on page 227 of *Literature and Language,* Grade 8.

Writing ON YOUR OWN

Point out that any set of instructions outlines the steps in a process. Explain that Aliki's writing goes beyond that—it makes the process vivid by showing both how it works and why it works the way it does. Then invite students to create their own "showing" explanation of a process.

Handbooks for Help and Practice

The following handbooks may be used as mini-lessons before students begin writing or as resources when problems arise.

- **Effective Paragraphs, pp. 244–247**
- **Meaning and Word Choice, pp. 314–315**

Teaching Strategies

for PLANNING YOUR EXPLANATION

INDIVIDUALIZING INSTRUCTION: LD STUDENTS If you have students who are challenged by sequencing, encourage them to describe an activity they can physically perform. Have them "walk through" the activity, taking numbered notes about what they do first, second, and so on. Then have them flesh out their notes with background information and descriptive details.

for INVESTIGATE THE PROCESS

CRITICAL THINKING: MAKING COMPARISONS Suggest that students ask themselves how the processes they have chosen are similar to and different from other related processes. For example, Aliki compares intentional mummification to the natural mummification that occurred when bodies were simply buried in sand.

Writing ON YOUR OWN
Describing a Process

INVITATION TO Write

Aliki makes the complicated process of embalming easy to follow by explaining it in a step-by-step way. By breaking a process down into its steps, you, too, can help others to understand it. In fact, you'll probably come to understand it better yourself.

Now write a description of a process in which you tell how to do something, how something works, or how something happens.

PLANNING YOUR EXPLANATION

1. Ask "I wonder how" questions. Have you ever wondered how to develop a photograph, how Velcro works, or how a caterpillar changes into a butterfly? List several "I wonder how" questions. As you list, think about processes that explain the workings of everyday items around your house, events in nature, and recent inventions or technology. Then choose a process that interests you.

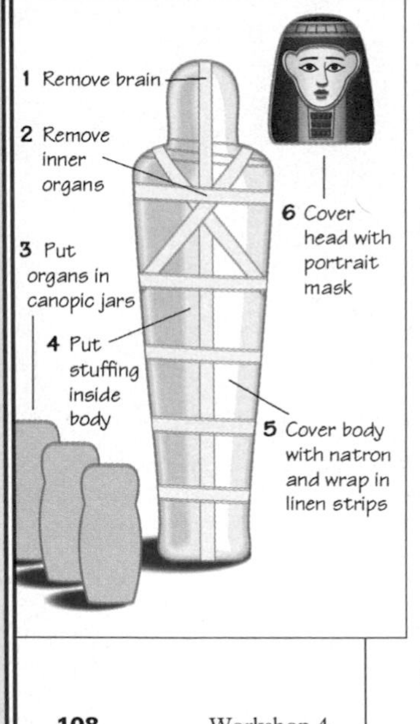
1 Remove brain
2 Remove inner organs
3 Put organs in canopic jars
4 Put stuffing inside body
5 Cover body with natron and wrap in linen strips
6 Cover head with portrait mask

2. Investigate the process. If the process is something you can do yourself, give it a try, or watch someone else do it. Take notes on what happens so you can describe the process carefully step by step. If the process is something you can't do or watch, try finding information in the library or interviewing an expert.

3. Map out the steps. Once you understand how the process works, arrange the steps in chronological order—the order in which they happen. To do this, you may want to create a timeline, flow chart, or even some sort of diagram such as the one in the margin showing the basic steps in the mummification process. You may want to include such a chart or a diagram with your final written explanation.

PROFESSIONAL NOTEBOOK

These categories from David Skwire *(Writing with a Thesis)* may steer students toward topic ideas: "A 'how-it-works' paper explains the functioning of anything from an electric toothbrush to the system for ratifying a new constitutional amendment. A 'how-it-*was*-done' paper might trace the process by which Stonehenge or the Pyramids were built. . . . A 'how-*not*-to-do-it' paper might trace the process by which the writer did everything wrong in reshingling the roof or buying a used car."

DRAFTING YOUR EXPLANATION

1. Start your draft. Describe the process in the order that it is done or takes place. You may want to begin by writing about whatever you know best and then fill in the rest of the steps.

2. Think about your reasons for explaining this process. Why did you choose to write about this process? Point out what is unusual or interesting about the process or how it might be useful.

3. Consider the needs of your audience. Provide background information, definitions of terms, and lists of needed materials. Also use sensory details and examples to make your process clear.

REVIEWING YOUR WRITING

1. Ask a classmate to read your work. Have a peer reader identify any terms you need to define or any spots in your draft where steps seem to be missing or unclear. If you have explained how to do something, you may want to see if your reader can actually perform the process from your written instructions.

2. Check your organization. For help in checking your organization, ask yourself the following questions:

- Do I identify my process in my introduction?
- Does each paragraph cover only one main step in the process?
- Are the steps in their proper order?
- Would adding transitions make the order of my steps clearer?

PUBLISHING AND PRESENTING

- **Present an oral report in person or on videotape.** Consider using illustrations, photographs, or other props. If possible, you might even demonstrate the process.
- **Create a class booklet.** Group the explanations by their subject matter. Add a table of contents, title page, and cover. Then lend the booklet to the school or local library.

PROBLEM SOLVING

"How do I present the steps in my process?"

For help in presenting the steps in your process, see

- Handbook 9, "Effective Paragraphs," pages 244–247

Grammar TIP

As much as possible, use precise nouns. For example, don't say *container* if you mean *thermos.*

for ASK A CLASSMATE . . .

PEER RESPONSE Suggest that writers ask peers: Are the steps in my process clear? Do you know if I've left any steps out? Students may want to revise their writing in accordance with the suggestions of their peers.

Guidelines for Evaluation

AN EFFECTIVE EXPLANATION OF A PROCESS

- explains the steps in a process that is interesting to the writer
- provides descriptive details, reasons, and background information about the process
- presents the steps in a logical order
- defines unfamiliar terms
- displays appropriate grammar, usage, and mechanics

GENERAL NOTE

ASSESSMENT If you choose to score students' grammar and mechanics, you might focus on the effective and correct use of conjunctive adverbs, phrases, and clauses as transitions.

MULTICULTURAL Connection

Some students may enjoy explaining how to prepare a food unique to their cultural heritage. Remind them to use vivid descriptions and background information, as Aliki does, so that their writing becomes more than a mere recipe. For example, students might observe or interview adults in their family for specific details about the history of the particular dish or information about how the recipe was passed from generation to generation.

Teaching Strategies

for LITERATURE

HELPFUL HINT You might give students the option of writing myths explaining the "origins" of commonly used items such as blow-dryers, pocket calculators, shoelaces, or table napkins. Encourage students to create appropriate mythic characters (such as heroes and monsters) as part of their explanations.

for SPEAKING AND LISTENING

COLLABORATIVE OPPORTUNITY As students prepare their oral presentations, suggest that they have a partner test the effectiveness of the explanation by trying to perform the skill. This activity will show presenters where they need to revise in order to make their explanations thorough and clear.

Springboards

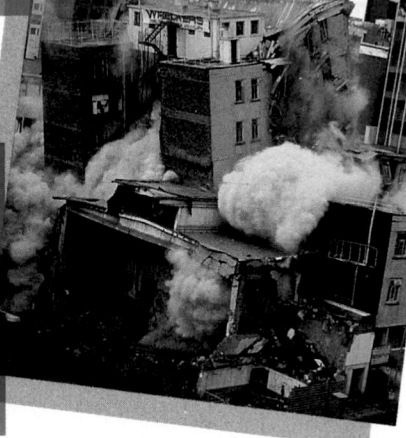

Science Think up an invention that the world needs. It could be something practical or something fanciful. Describe your invention, tell how it works, and explain how it will affect the world.

Literature Throughout history, people have thought up myths to explain strange natural events or remarkable human behavior. Write a myth of your own to explain an event or a behavior.

History What if the South had won the Civil War? Imagine a different outcome to a well-known historical event. Then describe what your life would be like today as a result of that outcome.

Speaking and Listening At what are you an expert? Explain one of your hobbies or skills in an oral presentation.

GEOGRAPHY How has your community changed over the years? Why? Explain the effect one physical change has had on your community.

110

Send Out for a Sniglet

What do you call those little squares in a waffle? How about *squaffles?* This word is an example of a "sniglet"—a word that doesn't appear in the dictionary, but perhaps should. Here are some other familiar things with new names. You might try making up sniglets of your own.

bobble gesture (bah′bol jes′cher) n. The classroom activity of not knowing an answer but raising one's hand after determining a sufficient number of other people have also raised their hands, thus reducing the likelihood of actually being called on.

erdu (uhr′dew) n. The leftover accumulation of rubber particles after erasing a mistake on a test paper.

gazinta (gah zin′tah) n. Mathematical symbol for division; also the sound uttered when dividing out loud. (Example: "Four *gazinta* eight twice.")

grackles (grak′elz) n. The wrinkles that appear on the body after staying in water too long.

gyroped (jy′roh ped) n. a kid who cannot resist spinning around on a diner stool.

hangle n. A cluster of coat hangers.

laminites (lam′in itz) n. Those strange people who show up in the photo sections of brand-new wallets.

mittsquinter n. A ballplayer who looks into his glove after missing the ball, as if, somehow, the cause of the error lies there.

Rich Hall and Friends

on the LIGHT side

You might remind students that many English words are blends, crafted in the same way as *squaffle:* for example, *smash* (smack + crash), *flare* (flame + glare), *telethon* (television + marathon), and *popsicle* (lollipop + icicle).

TEACHER'S LOUNGE

More "sniglets" from Rich Hall and Friends:

brattled (brat′ uld) adj. The unsettling feeling, at a stoplight, that the busload of kids that just pulled up beside you is making fun of you.

optortionist (op tor′ shun ist) n. The kid in school who can turn his eyelids inside out.

spirobits (spy′ ro bits) n. The frayed bits of left-behind paper in a spiral notebook.

beavo (bee′ vo) n. A pencil with teeth marks all over it.

B+ stampede (bee′ plus stam peed) n. The attempt by half the classroom to claim the paper with no name on it.

Series of Sentence Parts

Objectives

- To recognize parallelism in sentences
- To imitate sentences that use parallelism
- To expand sentences using parallelism

Additional Resource

Sentence Composing, pp. 7–8

Answer Key

A. Combining Sentences

1. He galloped with the herd that day, across the plain, down to the river, up into the hills.
2. He went everywhere the slightest hope drove him, to the police station, to the newspapers to post a reward, to the cab companies.
3. Rising out of the grass, wreathing the tree trunks and hanging from their branches, climbing up the walls and spreading over them with long garlands that fell in cascades, the roses came alive day by day, hour by hour.

B. Unscrambling and Imitating Sentences

Students' imitations will vary but should follow the patterns of the sentences given. Sample unscrambled sentences are shown below.

1. We marveled at the coziness of the campsite, the stillness of the evening, the fragrant smell of the pine needles, the brightness of the stars.

Sentence

COMPOSING

Series of Sentence Parts

A series of similar sentence parts can add detail and power to writing. The repetition of similar sentence parts and similar words (*-ness* words in Model A, the word *cursing* in Model B, and the word *because* in Model C) adds emphasis and rhythm to the sentences below. This device is called **parallelism.**

Model A She grieved over the shabbiness of her apartment, the dinginess of the walls, the worn-out appearance of the chairs, the ugliness of the draperies. **Guy de Maupassant, "The Necklace"**

Model B His teeth chattered, and he began to gibber to himself, cursing the day, cursing himself, cursing everybody.
Liam O'Flaherty, "The Sniper"

Model C As I continued my delivery, I began to chuckle small bits of contentment to myself because Mr. Brewer had invited me to his shop for haircuts, because the gringo customer had smiled at me, and because now all the gringos of the town would know me and maybe accept me.
Daniel Garza, "Everybody Knows Tobie"

▶ **ON THE MARK** Use commas to separate sentence parts used in a series.

A. Combining Sentences Make a new sentence by putting the underlined series of the second sentence into the first sentence at the caret (^). Write the complete sentence, putting commas between the sentence parts in the series.

1. He galloped with the herd that day, ^ . He galloped across the plain, down to the river, up into the hills. **Julius Lester, "The Man Who Was a Horse"**
2. He went everywhere the slightest hope drove him, ^ . He went to the police station, to the newspapers to post a reward, to the cab companies.
Guy de Maupassant, "The Necklace"
3. ^ The roses came alive day by day, hour by hour. They were rising out of the grass, wreathing the tree trunks and hanging from their branches, climbing up the walls and spreading over them with long garlands that fell in cascades.
Frances Hodgson Burnett, *The Secret Garden*

B. Unscrambling and Imitating Sentences Unscramble each set of sentence chunks below to create a sentence that matches the structure of the models on page 112. Then write a correctly punctuated sentence of your own that imitates each model. Be sure each of your sentences contains a series.

1. Write sentences that imitate model A.
   the coziness of the campsite / we marveled at / the stillness of the evening / the fragrant smell of the pine needles / the brightness of the stars
2. Write sentences that imitate model B.
   praising the entire school / praising the students / and he began to speak to the assembly / praising the teachers / the principal stood
3. Write sentences that imitate model C.
   as I did my chores / and after all the clothes in the hamper would be washed and dried / after I had put the dishes from the dishwasher into the cabinet / I began to make my plans for what I would do / after I had shopped for dinner

C. Expanding Sentences Follow the directions in parentheses to add sentence parts that are parallel in structure to the underlined portion of each sentence. Be sure to use commas to separate the items in each series.

1. It was a guy's room with all his stuff, <u>a hockey stick,</u> *(add two other sentence parts that begin with* a *and tell what he had in his room).*
   Richard Peck, *Voices After Midnight*
2. I'd be chugging along through the fall and the winter, <u>enjoying school during the week,</u> *(add three other sentence parts that begin with* enjoying *and tell other things this person liked to do).* **Robert Lipsyte, *One Fat Summer***
3. The day had been one of the unbearable ones, <u>when every sound had set her teeth on edge like chalk creaking on a chalkboard,</u> *(add one more sentence part that begins with* when *and gives a reason the day had been unbearable).*
   Dorothy Canfield Fisher, "The Apprentice"

Grammar Refresher Verbal phrases are often used in series. To learn more about verbals and verbal phrases, see Handbook 47, "Using Verbals," pages 596–605.

2. The principal stood, and he began to speak to the assembly, praising the students, praising the teachers, praising the entire school.
3. As I did my chores, I began to make my plans for what I would do after I had put the dishes from the dishwasher into the cabinet, after I had shopped for dinner, and after all the clothes in the hamper would be washed and maybe dried.

C. Expanding Sentences

Students' expanded sentences will vary. Authors' original sentences are given below.

1. It was a guy's room with all his stuff, a hockey stick, a pair of high-topped leather shoes, and a collection of sports cards.
   Richard Peck, *Voices After Midnight*
2. I'd be chugging along through the fall and the winter, enjoying school during the week, enjoying weekends and holidays at Rumson Lake, enjoying walking alone in the snow or reading in front of the fireplace or kidding around with Joanie, and then spring would come.
   Robert Lipsyte, *One Fat Summer*
3. The day had been one of the unbearable ones, when every sound had set her teeth on edge like chalk creaking on a chalkboard, when every word her father or mother said to her or did not say to her seemed an intentional injustice.
   Dorothy Canfield Fisher, "The Apprentice"

GRAMMAR REFRESHER Parallelism can involve the use of several sentences following the same pattern, or it can involve the use of parallel structures within a sentence. These structures may include single words, phrases (as in model sentences A and B), or clauses (as in model sentence C). All parallel structures within a sentence should be separated by serial commas. For more information on the use of serial commas, refer students to pages 644–645 in Handbook 49, Punctuation.

Informative Writing: Explaining *What*

Overview

Informative writing can take many forms but is always based on factual material. In this workshop, students extend their informative writing skills from the previous workshop and use their descriptive writing skills to explain similarities and differences. Workshop 5 includes the following Guided and Related Assignments, as well as the interdisciplinary project described on pages 113c–113d.

1. **Guided: Comparison and Contrast** invites students to choose two people, objects, or ideas to investigate their similarities and differences; and to use a logical pattern of organization to present an explanation.
2. **Related: Consumer Report** calls on students to use the skills of comparison and contrast from the Guided Assignment to inform readers about a consumer product and to make recommendations.

Teaching Preview

Preparation Guide

1. Use the Overview on this page and the Teacher's Choice descriptions on page 115 as a basis for deciding which assignments to teach.
2. Preview the assignments and the teacher's notes and identify concepts that may require preteaching or extra support, given your class's abilities. The handbook mini-lessons suggested within the lesson may also provide guidance.
3. Preview the chart below for support materials in the Teacher's Resource File that may be used with this Workshop. Resources are for use with the Guided Assignment unless otherwise noted.

Support Materials

RESOURCES

Prewrite and Explore
Writing Resource Book, pp. 25–27
Thinking Skills Worksheets, pp. 2, 9
Starting Points for Writing, Writing Prompts for Fine Art, pp. 29, 32–35, 43

Draft and Discover
Elaboration, Revision, and Proofreading Practice, p. 9
Writing Resource Book, p. 28

Revise Your Writing
Elaboration, Revision, and Proofreading Practice, p. 10
Writing Resource Book, p. 29
Peer Response Guides, pp. 17–18
Guidelines for Writing Assessment and Portfolio Use, pp. 18, 35–37

Sentence Composing
Sentence Composing Copy Masters, pp. 9–10

Assessment
Tests and Writing Assessment Prompts, p. 5

Computer Software
Writer's DataBank
Electronic English Handbook

PROFESSIONAL RESOURCES AND MEDIA

Books and Journals
Berck, Judith, *No Place to Be: Voices of Homeless Children,* Houghton Mifflin (1992)
Caplan, Rebekah, "Structuring Through Comparison and Contrast," *Writers in Training,* Dale Seymour Publications (1984), pp. 55–78
Soto, Gary, *Baseball in April,* Harcourt Brace Jovanovich (1990)

Films and Videos
Buy Me That! A Kid's Survival Guide to TV Advertising, Films, Inc., Chicago, IL (1990) (28 min.)
50 Simple Things Kids Can Do to Save the Earth, Churchill, Los Angeles (1992) (44 min.)
The No-Guitar Blues, Phoenix/BFA, New York (1992) (27 min.)

Computer Software and Technology
"And If Re-elected," Focus Media, Hicksville, NY (software), Apple II
Decisions, Decisions: On the Campaign Trail, Tom Snyder Productions, Cambridge, MA (software), Apple II, PC, Macintosh

Linking Literature, Writing, and Grammar

The following options may be used to provide students with an integrated language experience. Begin by assigning and discussing any of the recommended pieces of literature. Use the suggested strategy to provide a link to the Guided Assignment.

LINKING LITERATURE AND WRITING

Option 1

Starting Point: "A Land of Staggering Proportions" by Brad Darrach and Steve Petranek on pages 116–117 of *The Writer's Craft.*

Strategy: Use the teaching suggestions on pages 116–117 to lead students into the Guided Assignment.

Option 2

Starting Point: *Flowers for Algernon* by Daniel Keyes on pages 267–292 of McDougal, Littell's *Literature and Language,* Grade 8 (Additional suggestions for using *Literature and Language* can be found on page 115.)

Strategy: Have students read the story. Encourage them to take notes about the changes that they see in Charlie. How does Charlie's behavior after the operation compare with that before? How does his behavior after the operation compare with his behavior at the end of the story? After students have made the comparison, introduce the Guided Assignment.

Option 3

Starting Point: *Where the Red Fern Grows* by Wilson Rawls.

Strategy: Suggest that students think about how the two dogs, Old Dan and Little Ann, compare. Then make a chart that lists each dog's characteristics. (Old Dan—brave, headstrong, powerful; Little Ann—small, intelligent, sensitive, a good tracker) Use the discussion to lead students into the Guided Assignment.

LINKING WRITING AND GRAMMAR

Before students revise their writing, remind them that in writing that compares and contrasts, the relationship between ideas should be clear and easy to understand. One way to make this relationship clear is through the use of compound sentences. The coordinating conjunction *and* is often used to signal a similarity; the coordinating conjunction *but* signals a difference. Write the following sentences on the board.

Less Clear: Roller skates were invented in the 1700s. Roller blades are a phenomenon of the present decade.

More Clear: Roller skates were invented in the 1700s, but roller blades are a phenomenon of the present decade.

Have students look for instances in their own writing in which the use of a compound sentence can make the relationship between ideas clearer. Go over pages 556–559 of the Grammar and Usage Handbook. If problems in using compound sentences still appear in student papers, assign the exercises on those pages for reteaching. Additional practice can be found in the *Grammar and Usage Practice Book* on pages 79–80.

Management Guidelines

The chart below indicates the number of days recommended for each phase of the Guided and Related Assignments. These numbers are an estimate of the total time needed for each phase. In practice, of course, students may not complete each phase in one continuous session, nor will they necessarily progress from stage to stage in the linear order shown here. Stars indicate portions of the assignment that may be completed outside the classroom if time is limited or if teachers wish students to work independently.

COMPARISON AND CONTRAST

Starting from Literature ....1 day
Prewrite and Explore ....1–2 days*
Draft and Discover ....2–3 days*
Revise Your Writing..................1–2 days*
Proofread ....1 day*
Publish and Present......................1 day*
Reflect on Your Writing ....1 day
Reteaching......................................open
Extension and Enrichment. ....open*
Sentence Composing ....open*

CONSUMER REPORT

Reading a Consumer Report........1 day
Planning Your Consumer Report ....2 days*
Writing Your Consumer Report....2 days*
Reviewing Your Report ....1 day*
Sharing Your Report. ....1 day

Project File

Popular Culture: Then and Now

Overview

Students will work in groups to complete this project. Each group will choose a decade of the twentieth century and will study the popular culture of that decade. Groups will then present their findings, and each group will, through writing and a panel discussion, compare and contrast its decade with that of another group in the class.

Students will participate in the following activities:

- Study trends in the popular culture of various decades of the twentieth century
- Give presentations of their findings
- Create informative essays that compare and contrast the fads and trends of two decades
- Use a panel-discussion format to present their writings

Preparation Guide

Invite students to recall TV shows, clothing, cars, and toys that were popular when they were in kindergarten. Explain that these are all parts of popular culture.

Tell students that during this project they will work in groups to explore the popular culture of earlier decades. They will create presentations featuring what they discover, and in writing and in panel discussions, each group will compare and contrast the popular culture of their decade with that of another decade.

Stage 1
Choose a Decade and Gather Information

1. Have the class brainstorm about popular culture. What is popular culture? What are its elements?
2. Divide the class into small groups. Ask each group to list all the events and trends they can find for each decade of the twentieth century. Each group should use their list to choose a decade to study in depth.
3. Direct the groups to select the aspects of popular culture they want to research—music, toys, foods, fashions, entertainment, technology, and so forth.
4. Have students in each group research their decade (see *Resources, Stage 1*). Encourage them to interview older family members and acquaintances about the decade they chose.

TEAM TEACHING

The following activities may be used for team teaching or as enrichment and extension activities by the language arts teacher.

Science Learn about scientific advances, such as heavier-than-air flight or lasers, that launched new trends (see *Resources, Stage 1*).

Social Studies Study historical events and movements of the time (for example, the Great Depression, World War II, or the civil rights movement). Consider their relationships to the decade's trends. Learn about daily life during the decade (see *Resources, Stage 1*).

Math Compile and graph data about how long fads and trends lasted, which age groups they appealed to, and what percentages of the total population were involved.

Language Arts Study interviewing skills (see *Resources, Stage 1*). Read popular literature of the decade.

Art Learn about art, decoration, and clothing trends of the decade.

Music Investigate the popular music of the time.

TEACHING TIPS

- Invite speakers to share their memories of being in eighth grade during earlier decades.
- Suggest that students examine family photo albums and memorabilia, as well as back issues of magazines such as *Life, Look,* and *The Saturday Evening Post.*

Stage 2
Give Presentations

1. Have each group plan and stage a presentation about the trends in popular culture during their chosen decade.
2. Encourage groups to use skits, illustrated talks, and hands-on demonstrations with commentaries to present their materials.
3. Remind the groups to provide information about events in politics and in the arts and sciences that affected trends.
4. Tell students to take notes on each presentation for use during Stage 3.

TEAM TEACHING

Social Studies Create time lines, maps, and other aids to show major world and national events that influenced the popular culture of the decade.

Language Arts Study techniques of public speaking.

Art Create drawings or models of products and fashions.

Music Record or rehearse music for the presentation.

TEACHING TIPS

- Make videos showing life in earlier decades available to students (see *Resources, Stage 2*).
- Propose that students wear costumes, display items, play music, and offer samples of popular foods from their decades when presenting their talks.

- Suggest that students search thrift stores for clothing, household items, toys, and magazines from past decades.

Stage 3 Compare and Contrast Findings

1. Tell each group to select one aspect of popular culture (such as fashions or music). Have them use this aspect as a basis for comparing their decade with another group's decade.
2. Direct each group to collaborate in writing about the similarities and differences they discover.
3. Have pairs of groups form panels to present and discuss their writings.

TEAM TEACHING

Language Arts Review the use of comparison-and-contrast techniques in writing (see *Resources, Stage 3*). Compare the popular literature of the two decades.

Math Compile statistics on differences in the two decades being compared.

Science Show how differences in life in the two decades were based on differences in technology. For example, how did entertainment change after the development of television?

Social Studies Examine political changes that occurred between the two decades.

Art Compare and contrast the art and fashions of the two decades.

TEACHING TIPS

- Remind students to compare and contrast general trends as well as specific fads.
- Encourage students to support their ideas with specifics from the presentations.
- Go over group discussion techniques (see *Resources, Stage 3*).
- Invite American history classes to listen to the panel discussions.

Resources

STAGE 1

Each of the books in the **Timelines** series looks at the fads, fashions, and major events of one decade from the 1900s to the 1980s. The volumes covering earlier decades are by Gail Stewart; the others are by Jane Duden.

The **Fashions of a Decade** series surveys fashions in the light of contemporary culture, politics, and technology. Its volumes include *The 1920s* and *The 1970s* by Jacqueline Herald, *The 1940s* and *The 1950s* by Patricia Baker, *The 1930s* by Maria Constantino, *The 1960s* by Yvonne Connikie, and *The 1980s* by Vicky Carnegy.

Back issues of ***Cobblestone*** magazine focus on fabulous fads, toys of the past, popular music from the 1950s on, American clothing, automobiles, cartoons, comics, and the funnies. Back issues of ***Odyssey*** magazine include articles on famous recent discoveries, spinoff technology from the space program, and robots.

How to Tape Instant Oral Biographies by William Zimmerman offers tips on interviewing, on using video cameras and tape recorders, and more.

What Did You Do in the War, Grandma? by the students of South Kingstown High School presents twenty-six firsthand accounts of life during the World War II era.

STAGE 2

The **Women in American Life** video series, from the National Women's History Project, includes four videos spanning the years 1880–1977, with photos and film footage showing changes in daily life.

Public libraries may have out-of-print cookbooks that are sources of recipes from earlier decades.

STAGE 3

The Writer's Craft, Grade 8, Workshop 5, "Informative Writing: Explaining *What,*" pages 114–132, teaches writing a comparison-and-contrast essay.

Making Waves with Creative Problem Solving by Vaune Ainsworth-Land and Norma Fletcher teaches group discussion and problem-solving skills.

Additional Projects

Comparing Ecosystems Propose that students study ecosystems inhabited by endangered species. Direct them to compare and contrast the characteristics of each ecosystem with its characteristics at a specified time in the past (fifty years ago or one hundred years ago, for example). Suggest that students use charts, graphs, and photos or other illustrations to present their findings.

Comparative Literature Invite students to compare and contrast two favorite novels. Direct them to research the time periods when the works were written and the histories and backgrounds of the authors. Have students use this information, as well as their observations about literary elements such as plot and theme, to develop their comparisons. Students can include paintings, drawings, or collages to illustrate their writings.

Adding It Up Propose that students prepare consumer reports comparing and contrasting brands of a heavily advertised grooming product, such as shampoo, soap, or toothpaste. Reports should compare prices per ounce, ingredients, and other data. In addition, ask students to conduct polls to determine the products' popularity and degree of user satisfaction. Have students create graphs and tables to accompany their reports.

SKETCH BOOK

Objective

- To use an excerpt and writing prompts as springboards to informal writing

WRITING WARM-UPS

Encourage students to respond freely and informally to at least one of the Sketchbook prompts. Students may begin by discussing their reactions in small groups and then freewriting in their journals. Remind them that their responses will not be graded and may provide them with useful material for other informative writing assignments.

SHOW, DON'T TELL

The following is a sample of a showing paragraph for the first prompt:

Have you ever tried to explain to your parents why you want to spend Saturday afternoon at the mall? I have, but they don't understand. To them, a mall is a place to shop. To me, it's a place to see my friends and to hang out. For example, last Saturday my parents and I went to the mall. Mom bought a pair of shoes, and Dad got some pants. We weren't there an hour, and they wanted to go! Gosh! It was still early; my friends were just getting there. I told Mom and Dad to leave me and I'd catch a ride later, but Mom wanted to wait and help me find what I needed. Well, of course I didn't need anything. I just wanted to be there. Try explaining that to a parent, though. They just don't understand.

SKETCH BOOK

WRITING WARM-UPS

> *It all started when Gilbert's older cousin Raymundo brought over* The Karate Kid *on video. Never before had a message been so clear, never had Gilbert seen his life on TV. As he sat in the dark with a box of Cracker Jacks in his lap, he knew that he, Gilbert Sanchez, a fifth-grader at John Burroughs Elementary, was the Karate Kid. Like the kid on the screen, he was pushed around by bullies. He too was a polite kid who did his homework and kept to himself. And, like the kid in the movie, Gilbert wanted to be strong enough to handle anyone who tried to mess with him.*
>
> Gary Soto, "THE KARATE KID"

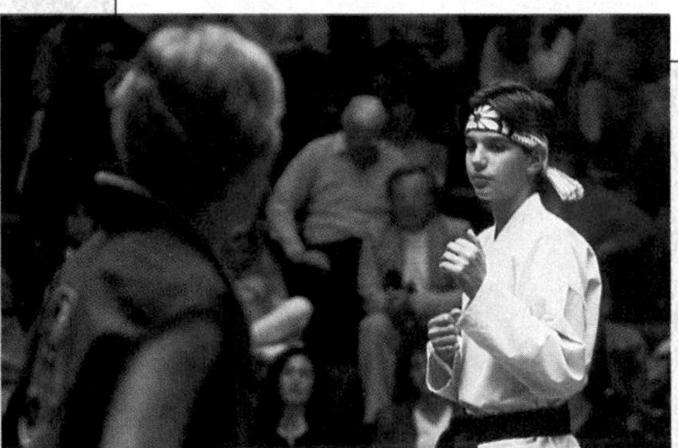

- Have you ever compared yourself to someone in a movie or to someone famous? Write about the similarities you discovered.
- In what ways are you like your best friend? How are you different?

Show, Don't Tell

When you compare and contrast two subjects, you show how the subjects are alike and different. Turn one of the following *telling* sentences into a *showing* paragraph.

- Our parents' generation is different than our generation.
- The present can be like the past.

Informative Writing: Explaining *What*

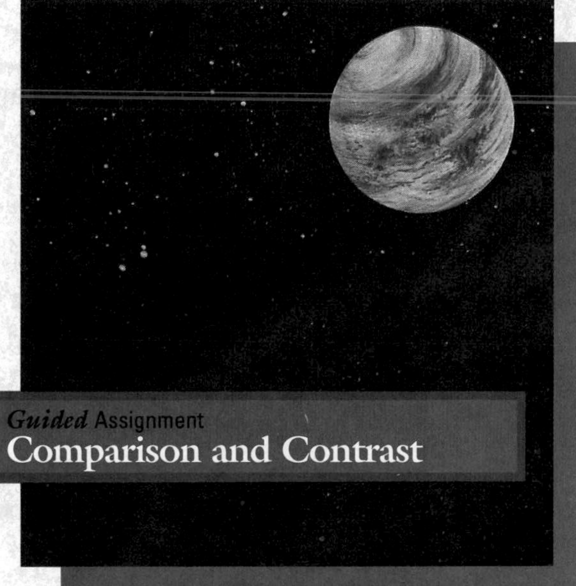

Guided Assignment
Comparison and Contrast

Related Assignment
Consumer Report

Have you ever told a friend that some unusual food "tastes just like chicken, only . . . you know . . . different"? Have you ever known twins who looked very much alike but had quite different personalities? The world is filled with such interesting similarities and differences.

In this workshop you will have the opportunity to explain or describe something or someone through comparison and contrast. In a related assignment, you will create a consumer report.

WRITER'S 5 WORKSHOP

Informative Writing: Explaining *What*

Objectives

Guided Assignment

Comparison and Contrast To recognize the techniques of comparison and contrast in literature and to create a piece of informative writing that explains or describes something through comparison and contrast

Related Assignment

Consumer Report To analyze and contrast techniques used in a consumer report and to create an informative consumer report, using those techniques

Teacher's Choice

Use the following guidelines to choose the assignment that best suits students' needs.

Comparison and Contrast This assignment will benefit most students by giving them a chance to practice comparing and contrasting. Comparing and contrasting are important aspects of analyzing and evaluating, are essential for understanding figurative language, and can provide a means for structuring informative writing. You will probably want to offer this workshop after students have had experience with writing a simple description.

Consumer Report This assignment will help students grasp the practical application of comparing and contrasting in clarifying ideas and information.

Links to LITERATURE & LANGUAGE

Literature For more examples of writing that contains elements of comparison and contrast, see *Literature and Language*, Grade 8:
- Daniel Keyes, "Flowers for Algernon"
- Julia Alvarez, "Dusting"
- Nancy Masterson Sakamoto, "Conversational Ballgames"

Writing This guided assignment may be used as an extension of the Writer's Workshop, "Writing About Literature: Characters in Contrast," on page 572 in *Literature and Language*, Grade 8.

Guided ASSIGNMENT

ASSIGNMENT RATIONALE

The ability to see similarities and differences helps students relate the new to the known and to make judgments about information that is presented to them. The ability to organize information by comparison and contrast also provides students with a valuable method of presenting information to others.

Starting from LITERATURE

Motivate

After students have read Starting from Literature, you might elicit their ideas of what life on another planet might be like. Ask them to speculate about the climate and living things that might be found there. Then ask whether people's ideas of life on other planets are modeled on life forms on Earth, and why. Does comparing something unfamiliar to something familiar help make the unfamiliar seem accessible?

BUILD ON PRIOR KNOWLEDGE

Ask students to identify the sources of our scientific knowledge of outer space. Ask, for example, "How have space probes of Mars, as with *Viking 1* and *2,* helped increase our knowledge? What do scientists hope to learn from them?" (Sample: Scientists hope to learn more about our solar system and the greater universe; they want to know more about the elements that make up the planets and how the planets were formed; they are searching for life forms.)

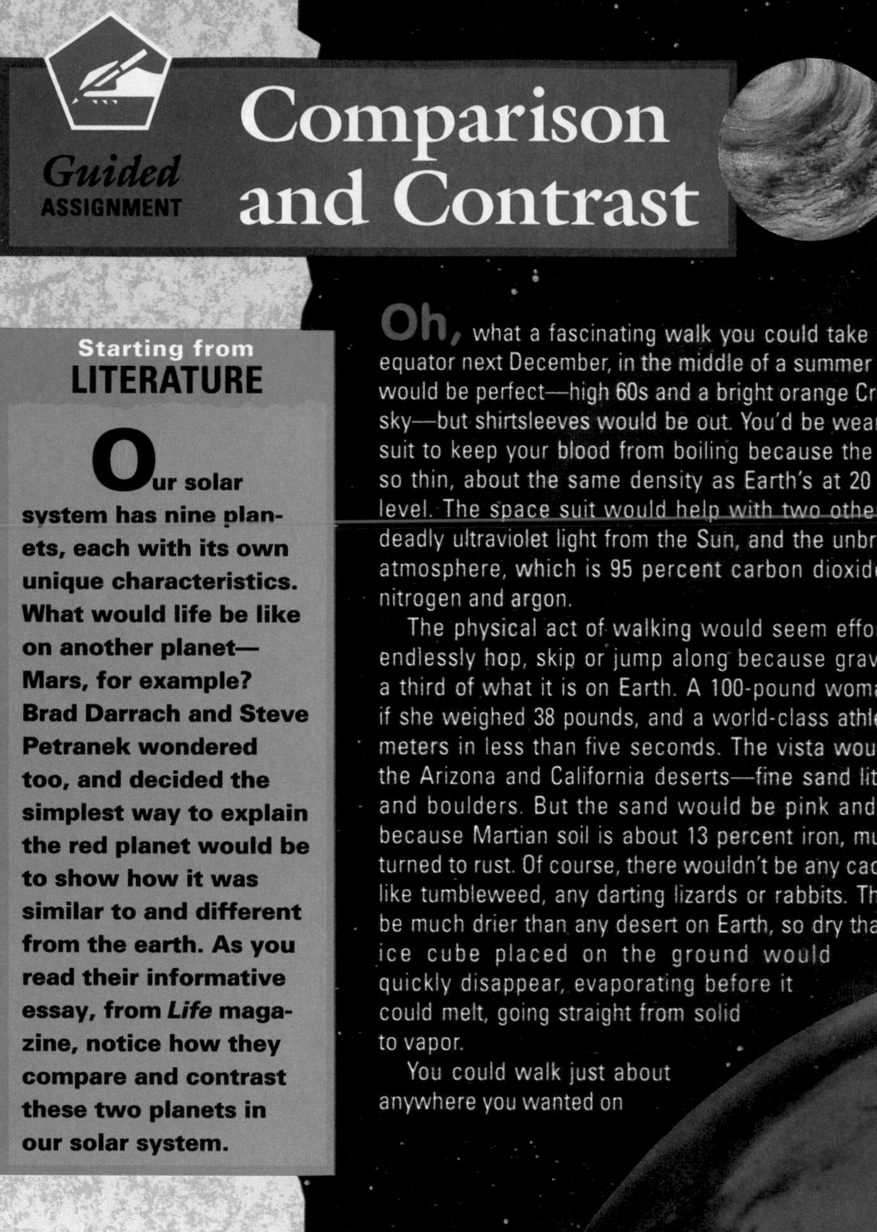

Guided ASSIGNMENT Comparison and Contrast

Starting from LITERATURE

Our solar system has nine planets, each with its own unique characteristics. What would life be like on another planet—Mars, for example? Brad Darrach and Steve Petranek wondered too, and decided the simplest way to explain the red planet would be to show how it was similar to and different from the earth. As you read their informative essay, from *Life* magazine, notice how they compare and contrast these two planets in our solar system.

Oh, what a fascinating walk you could take near the Martian equator next December, in the middle of a summer day. The weather would be perfect—high 60s and a bright orange Creamsicle-colored sky—but shirtsleeves would be out. You'd be wearing a light space suit to keep your blood from boiling because the "air" on Mars is so thin, about the same density as Earth's at 20 miles above sea level. The space suit would help with two other problems—the deadly ultraviolet light from the Sun, and the unbreathable Martian atmosphere, which is 95 percent carbon dioxide, with traces of nitrogen and argon.

The physical act of walking would seem effortless; you could endlessly hop, skip or jump along because gravity is only about a third of what it is on Earth. A 100-pound woman would feel as if she weighed 38 pounds, and a world-class athlete could run 100 meters in less than five seconds. The vista would remind you of the Arizona and California deserts—fine sand littered with rocks and boulders. But the sand would be pink and reddish-brown, because Martian soil is about 13 percent iron, much of which has turned to rust. Of course, there wouldn't be any cacti or scrub plants like tumbleweed, any darting lizards or rabbits. The terrain would be much drier than any desert on Earth, so dry that an ice cube placed on the ground would quickly disappear, evaporating before it could melt, going straight from solid to vapor.

You could walk just about anywhere you wanted on

116 Workshop 5

Science Connection

You might point out that the comparison/contrast structure lends itself to writing about science topics. Encourage students to use it in their science reports. A report on African wildlife, for example, might compare lions to domestic cats. A report on tropical storms might compare them to ordinary rainstorms.

A LAND OF STAGGERING PROPORTIONS

by
Brad Darrach
and
Steve Petranek

Mars, because the entire surface is land; there are no lakes, rivers or oceans. All the water is underground or frozen at the north and south poles. There's as much land on Mars as there is on Earth, even though Mars is only half as big as Earth and weighs only a tenth as much. Because of its weaker gravity, Mars is not as dense as Earth; it's puffed up. A thousand feet below the surface of Earth you would probably hit solid rock, but a thousand feet below the crust of Mars you would find porous material, perhaps even a gravelly slurry of rock and ice.

A day's walk on Mars would offer about as much Sun time as on Earth; Mars rotates once every 24 hours, 37 minutes. But the summer would last twice as long because Mars takes 687 days to orbit the Sun.

A trek to any of Earth's natural wonders would pale by comparison to what can be seen on Mars. Mount Everest, at just over 29,000 feet, would seem a foothill compared to the Tharsis bulge, a broad raised equatorial plain the size of the United States. On Tharsis sit extraordinary volcanoes, among them Olympus Mons, at 90,000 feet the highest known elevation in the solar system. The mighty Colorado River's cut through the Grand Canyon would seem a drainage ditch next to Valles Marineris, a gorge that would stretch from Seattle to Miami. . . .

You could spend a lifetime on the surface of Mars and never run out of new formations to see . . . . Just one thing, though. You would want to get back to base before dark. Most nights, even in summer, the temperature drops to about -125° F.

Think & Respond

What aspects of the Martian environment do you find most intriguing? Why? Give some examples from the essay that show how the authors help you to understand the environment of Mars.

SET A PURPOSE

To help students focus on the purpose-setting statement at the end of the Starting from Literature box, ask them to list some characteristics of the planet Earth. (Samples: air, water, oceans, continents, mountains, deserts, plants and animals, a 365-day year) As they read the article, invite them to look for information about Mars that they can compare with the characteristics they have listed for Earth.

Think & Respond

ELICIT PERSONAL RESPONSES

Ask students to freewrite for a few minutes in response to the questions in the Think and Respond box. Then ask volunteers to state their reactions.

EXPLORE THE AUTHOR'S TECHNIQUES

Point out how Darrach and Petranek explain facts that are unusual and unfamiliar by comparing and contrasting them with facts with which readers are familiar. For example, they compare Mars's sky to an orange Creamsicle, suggesting a contrast with Earth's blue sky (paragraph 1). They contrast a woman's weight on Mars to her weight on Earth, and they point out the differences in terrain (paragraph 2). Reading about the various similarities and differences gives readers a vivid picture of a world they might otherwise be unable to imagine.

for FURTHER READING

Books to Read Students interested in other planets might enjoy the following books:

- any book in Isaac Asimov's Library of the Universe series
- any book in Seymour Simon's series on the planets (each book titled according to the planet studied)
- Patricia Lauber, *Journey to the Planets*
- Franklyn Mansfield Branley, *Mysteries of the Planets*
- Jeanne Bendick, *The Planets: Neighbors in Space*

Reading a STUDENT MODEL

Brad Darrach and Steve Petranek's informative article presents scientific facts, but any factual subject—serious or humorous—can become a topic for informative writing. The student model shows how one writer uses comparison and contrast to share his experience with dogs. It is the final draft of the piece that students will see in process on the workshop pages that follow.

Motivate

When it comes to getting students thinking about dogs, you will not have to say much—almost everyone enjoys talking about dogs. You might want to guide the discussion with questions such as the following:

- What kind of dog would be the perfect pet?
- What's the silliest-looking dog you've ever seen? the most handsome?
- What can dogs be trained to do?

BUILD ON PRIOR KNOWLEDGE

Ask students what they know about the characteristics of some breeds. For example, how is a German shepherd different from a cocker spaniel? Why choose one kind of dog over another? (Samples: size, temperament, intelligence, exercise needs, trainability, cost, and hunting or retrieving skills)

SET A PURPOSE

Direct students to the purpose-setting statement at the end of the Reading a Student Model box. Suggest that they look for words and phrases that signal comparisons—for example, "Thor, on the other hand" (paragraph 4), and "Dachshunds don't sit like other dogs" (paragraph 7).

One Student's Writing

Reading a STUDENT MODEL

Have you ever dreamed about something for a long time and then had your dream come true? How did what you finally got compare to your fantasy? Rick Shen's dream came true when his mom announced the family was getting a dog. As you read Rick's essay, notice how his family's new pet compared to what he had in mind.

Thor! The Wonder Dog?

By Rick Shen

When my mom announced at dinner one night that our family was finally getting a dog, I couldn't have been happier. I'd been listening to my friend Laura brag about her dog, Sam, forever. Sam's parents were national champions. Sam was faster than a Corvette. Sam could leap 10 feet in the air to catch a Frisbee. Sam brought the newspaper in every night. Listening to Laura, you'd think Sam did her math homework too. I decided my dog would do anything Sam could do, only better.

The next day, Mom brought Thor home from the animal shelter. I named him Thor even before I saw him because I remembered from English class that Thor is the Norse god of thunder, and I wanted my dog to be powerful and fast. Mom told us that Thor had been abandoned by his owners and had fallen off a bridge into the river. I guess I should have realized right then that he wasn't going to be the most coordinated dog in the world. But I didn't—at least not until Mom brought him in the front door. I looked at Thor and my heart sank. This was going to be my wonder dog? How was I ever going to face Laura and Sam?

You see, Sam is a golden retriever. Golden retrievers are sporting dogs. You can take them hunting, for companionship and to bring back any game birds you've brought down. Like all golden retrievers, Sam has long, silky, reddish-golden hair, a long tail, and a happy face. Sam always looks like she's smiling. Golden retrievers are great with little kids and make terrific pets.

Thor, on the other hand, is a dachshund, a hound. About all he has in common with Sam is that both dachshunds and golden retrievers are used for hunting. Instead of long, silky, golden hair, Thor has short, wiry, blackish-brown hair. His legs are about two inches long, and his stomach practically sits on the ground. Even with his head

Grammar Connection

Point out that Rick Shen uses comparative and superlative forms in his essay. Ask students to identify some of these words in the student model and tell what is being compared. (paragraph 1: *happier*—Rick's feelings about getting a dog; *faster*—Sam and a car; *better*—what his dog would do; paragraph 2: *most coordinated*—Thor and all other dogs; paragraph 7: *better*—Thor's friendship with Sam) Encourage students to think about how they could use comparative and superlative forms in their own writing.

raised up, he can't be more than 12 inches tall. Thor looks sort of like a sausage with legs. Dachshunds are also good with little kids, although when Thor howls I think a little kid would get scared. Thor howls because dachshunds don't bark exactly like other dogs do.

When I told Laura I had gotten a dog, she suggested we take our dogs to the park to play one Saturday morning. That's when I realized how else Thor was different from Sam.

Laura threw the Frisbee and Sam ran after it. At the last second Sam jumped up high and grabbed it out of the air. Now it was our turn. I threw the Frisbee and Thor ran underneath it. At the last second, it hit Thor in the head. He had tried to jump up, but dachshunds just weren't made for jumping.

Then Laura asked Sam to sit and shake her hand. Sam did both things easily. I told Thor to sit. Dachshunds don't sit like other dogs. Thor sort of leans over until the back part of his body flops on the ground. Then he tries to keep his front half steady. Shaking hands in this position isn't easy. We finally gave up. By the end of the afternoon, I think Thor was better friends with Sam than I was with Laura.

That was last year. By now I've grown to love Thor a lot. He'll never chase sports cars or catch Frisbees like Sam, although he has learned to shake hands. I guess people will always ask about his funny shape. And I don't let him get anywhere near the river. Thor will never be a wonder dog, but we've become really great buddies, and that's good enough for me.

Think & Respond

Respond as a Reader

- Do you think Rick's first impressions of Thor are understandable? Why?
- Did you ever dream big dreams for one of your own pets? Did your dreams come true?

Respond as a Writer

- How does Rick lead up to his comparison of golden retrievers and dachshunds?
- How does Rick organize his comparison and contrast?

Think & Respond

RESPOND AS A READER

▶ Before students respond to the first question, point out the exaggeration used in describing Sam ("faster than a Corvette," "leap 10 feet," "did her math homework"). When students respond to the first Think & Respond question, they will understand that Rick wanted a dog like Sam, only better; he wanted it so badly that he set an unrealistic standard for Thor.

▶ Encourage students to share dreams they have had for their pets, such as that the pet would win a show prize or save someone from a burning building.

RESPOND AS A WRITER

▶ Students should note that Rick describes all the things Sam can do and tells of his dream of having a dog that will outdo Sam.

▶ Students will observe that Rick describes Sam and then Thor. The pattern is followed throughout the composition.

Draw Conclusions

To make sure students understand this introduction to comparison and contrast writing, challenge them to list the characteristics they have noted thus far. Responses may include the following:

- an interesting introduction
- showing of similarities and differences in an order that makes sense
- choice of details that support one main point of the piece

Social Studies Connection

Social Awareness Point out to students that Thor was adopted from a shelter after having been abandoned by his original owners (paragraph 2). Some students may wish to research the problem of abandoned pets in their area. They might contact the local animal shelter or Humane Society for information. Suggest that when students begin their own writing, they consider comparing an ideal program for protecting unwanted pets and the available facilities in their community.

Writing ON YOUR OWN

Remind students that they probably use comparing and contrasting whenever they explain or describe something. In this guided assignment, they will use comparison and contrast to inform others about a topic of their choice. Remind students of how Brad Darrach and Steve Petranek used comparison and contrast writing to help readers understand an unusual environment, and of how Rick Shen used this technique to describe his personal feelings about his pet. Encourage students to try the same techniques.

Handbooks for Help and Practice

The following handbooks may be used as mini-lessons before students begin writing or as resources when problems arise.

- **Discovering Writing Ideas, pp. 218–223**
- **Types of Organization, pp. 239–243**

PREWRITE AND EXPLORE

Objectives

- To use prewriting techniques to find topics for a comparison-contrast piece
- To investigate similarities and differences in topics

Teaching Strategies

for EXPLORING TOPICS

HELPFUL HINT If students have trouble with choosing a pair of things to compare and contrast, suggest that they think of one topic that particularly interests them—a hobby, sport, career, animal, place, event, or anything else. You might then set aside time to help them think of something with which to compare that topic.

Writing ON YOUR OWN

Comparison and Contrast

INVITATION TO *Write*

Like Brad Darrach and Steve Petranek, Rick Shen used comparison and contrast techniques as part of an informative essay. In both pieces of writing, the authors explained and described by showing how things are alike and different.

Write an informative essay that uses comparison and contrast to explain or describe something or someone.

PREWRITE AND EXPLORE

1. Look for comparisons and contrasts. When you compare and contrast persons or things, you try to find similarities and differences. What types of comparisons interest you? To find out, try some of the following activities.

Exploring Topics

- **One on one** Which team is better, the Chicago Bulls or the Los Angeles Lakers? What are the differences between laser discs and videocassettes? Which exercise gives you the best workout—cross-country skiing or tennis? Get together with some classmates and **brainstorm** to create a list of people, objects, and ideas you could compare and contrast, one on one. Make a list of the ideas you come up with.
- **Decisions, decisions** Personal decisions often involve comparison and contrast. Which summer camp will you attend? What clubs will you join at school? Which jeans will you buy? Recall decisions you have made in the past, or think about decisions you're facing now. **Freewrite** about one that involved comparing or contrasting two choices.

PROBLEM SOLVING

"How can I find a topic I care about?"

For additional suggestions for finding a writing topic, see

- Handbook 1, "Discovering Writing Ideas," pages 218–223

MULTICULTURAL Connection

Encourage students to explore their individual cultural backgrounds for topics to compare and contrast. In some cultures—those of Indonesia, Japan, and China, for example—crickets and other insects are often kept as pets. Students might compare these types of pets with those common in the United States.

- **Time machine** If you could travel forward into the future or back to the past, what would be different? What would be the same? Choose a new lifetime and make a **chart** that shows what things are different and what things are the same.
- **Reading literature** Have any of your favorite stories or novels been made into movies? How are the two versions alike? How are they different? **Freewrite** about one such example.

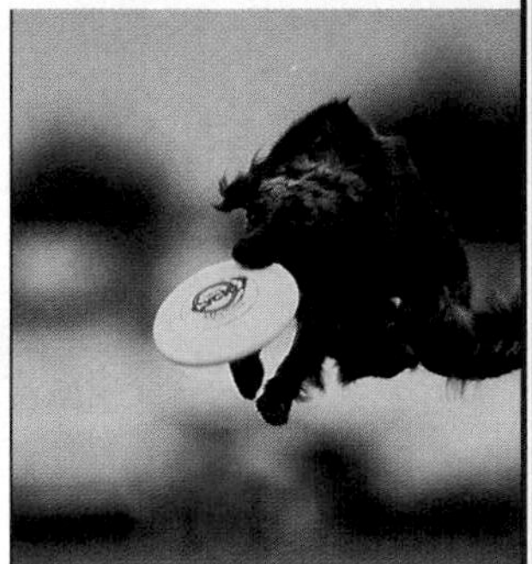

What types of ideas have you gathered? Which one strikes you as the most interesting, unusual, or challenging? Choose one you'd like to explore in a comparison and contrast essay.

2. Investigate similarities and differences. To explore your topic, you need to find a way to sort out similarities and differences. One way is to figure out what features you want to compare and contrast. For example, if you were comparing compact discs and tapes, you might consider such features as sound quality, durability, and cost. Then you could make a chart to show how your two subjects measure up.

Another way is to make a Venn diagram. In the outer part of each circle, list what is different about each subject you are comparing. In the space where the circles overlap, list the similarities.

One Student's Process

Rick Shen used a Venn diagram to help him clearly see how Sam and Thor were alike and different.

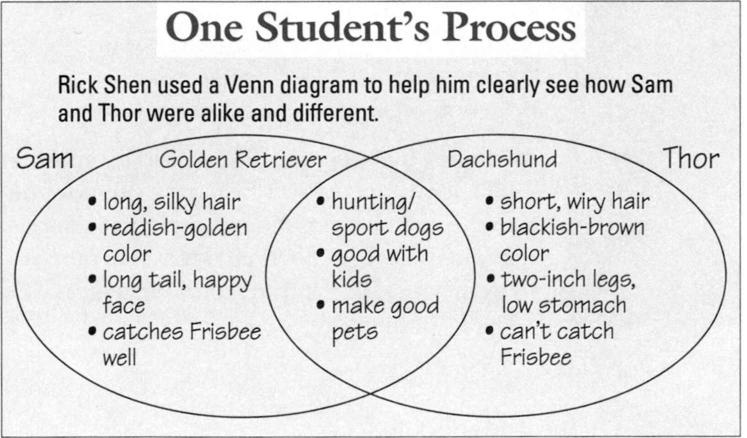

for EXPLORING TOPICS

INDIVIDUALIZING INSTRUCTION: ADVANCED STUDENTS Point out to your advanced students that more than two subjects can be the topic of a comparison and contrast essay. You might challenge these students to select three people or things to compare.

for INVESTIGATE SIMILARITIES . . .

MODELING If you are writing with students, you may wish to model the use of a comparison-contrast chart. Develop your chart on the board or use an overhead projector, thinking aloud as you analyze your topic to identify similar and contrasting features. After completing your model, you may wish to give students the option of using the comparison-contrast chart on page 9 of the Thinking Skills Worksheets to organize their work.

for ONE STUDENT'S PROCESS

HELPFUL HINT: GRAPHIC DEVICES Review with students the features of the Venn diagram to be sure that they understand the significance of the overlapping circles. You might suggest that when they make a diagram of their own, they label the overlapping part of the diagram "Both." *Writing Resource Book,* page 26, "Exploring a Topic," gives students more practice using Venn diagrams.

GENERAL NOTE

PEER RESPONSE When students feel they have collected enough material to begin drafting, pair them with other students who have reached the same stage for a brief peer review. Have students explain their subjects to their peers and answer questions about what facts and details will be included.

for THINK ABOUT YOUR PURPOSE

HELPFUL HINT Tell students that Darrach and Petranek's purpose in "A Land of Staggering Proportions" was to explain the environment of Mars by using clear, familiar comparisons. Urge students to formulate a one- or two-sentence purpose statement for their comparisons before drafting and to refer to it often as they work.

DRAFT AND DISCOVER

Objectives

- To draft a piece of informative writing, using a comparison-contrast structure
- To respond to one's own draft and to that of a peer

Teaching Strategies

for BEGIN WRITING

INDIVIDUALIZING INSTRUCTION: BASIC STUDENTS You may wish to meet with these students before they begin drafting. Make sure they have well-developed charts or lists of relevant features to compare and contrast. Also check that they have a well-focused statement of purpose.

for BEGIN WRITING

HELPFUL HINT: AUDIENCE Before students begin writing, urge them to consider their audience. Have them write answers to these questions:

- Who is my audience?
- What does my audience know about this subject?
- Which comparisons and examples will help my audience understand my subject best?

for ORGANIZE INFORMATION CLEARLY

HELPFUL HINT: ORGANIZING For an example of feature-by-feature organization, have students look at paragraph 5 of Darrach and Petranek's article and describe how the authors arranged their details. (Sample: Feature I: mountains; subject A, Earth [Mount Everest]; subject B, Mars [the Tharsis bulge]. Feature II: canyons, etc.) If students need further instruction, direct them to the *Writing Resource Book,* page 69, "Comparison and Contrast Order."

3. Think about your purpose. As you begin gathering details and ideas for your comparison, ask yourself, "What am I trying to accomplish with this comparison?" Do some freewriting about your purpose.

DRAFT AND DISCOVER

1. Begin writing. Start writing whatever part of your essay you feel most comfortable with. If you've thought of a great beginning, start there. If one similarity or difference stands out, write about it first. Don't worry about organization at this point.

Writer's Choice You don't have to limit your draft to the information in your charts, diagrams, or other prewriting notes. If new ideas occur to you as you write, include them in your draft.

2. Organize information clearly. At some point in your drafting process, you will want to begin organizing the information you're presenting. Here are two techniques you can try.

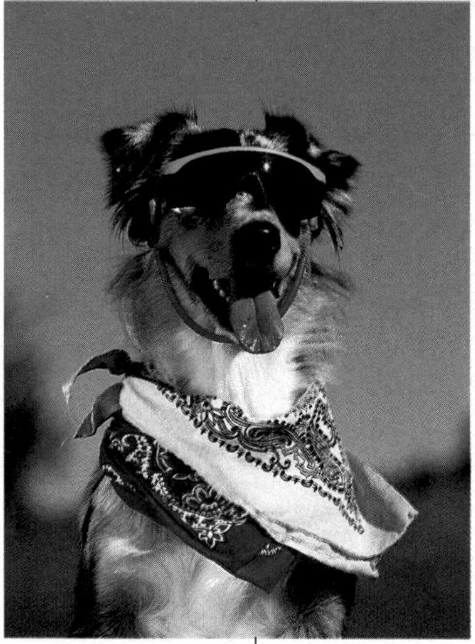

- **Feature by feature** Present a feature and explain how each subject is similar or different with regard to that feature. Darrach and Petranek organized their essay in this way.

Feature I	Feature II
subject A	subject A
subject B	subject B

- **Subject by subject** Present all the information about one subject first and then move on to the next subject, showing how it is similar or different. Rick Shen used this type of organization in the third and fourth paragraphs of his essay.

Subject A
  feature I, feature II, feature III, feature IV
Subject B
  feature I, feature II, feature III, feature IV

3. Write an intriguing introduction. Start your essay with an introduction that makes the reader want to read on. Darrach and Petranek start by telling you that a midday walk on Mars would be fascinating. You read on to find out why and how. Rick Shen starts out with a story, telling you that his new dog will be better in every way than Laura's. You read on to find out if his prediction turns out to be true.

Paragraphs at Work When you write a comparison, you want to draw attention to the similarities and differences between the subjects. Your writing will be clear and easy to follow if you present only one subject or feature in each paragraph. Remember these tips.

- Begin a new paragraph for each subject or feature.
- Support the main idea of each paragraph with details or examples that illustrate specific similarities and differences.
- Delete any details that are not directly related to the main idea of the paragraph.

4. Think about your draft. Do you want to share your writing with a peer reader now, or should you make some changes first? The following questions can help you review your draft and get the help you need from your peers.

REVIEW YOUR WRITING

Questions for Yourself

- Have I accomplished what I set out to do with this comparison?
- Would my point be clearer if I organized my information differently?
- Have I forgotten to mention any important similarities or differences?

Questions for Your Peer Readers

- Why do you think I chose to compare these subjects?
- Which points of comparison helped you the most?
- Is there anything else you'd like to know about these subjects?

GENERAL NOTE

INDIVIDUALIZING INSTRUCTION: VISUAL LEARNERS Suggest that these students sketch the two things they are comparing. Encourage them to refer to these sketches as they draft. Students can elaborate on their sketches as necessary to get more ideas for writing.

for PARAGRAPHS AT WORK

HELPFUL HINT: MAIN IDEA/ DETAILS You might direct students' attention to paragraph 5 of Darrach and Petranek's article and paragraphs 3 and 4 of Rick Shen's essay as examples of particularly well-focused paragraphs. Ask students to identify the main idea of each paragraph and to note how the details support it.

for THINK ABOUT YOUR DRAFT

HELPFUL HINT: ELABORATION Remind students that their writing should show, not just tell, how the things they are comparing and contrasting are alike and different. You might ask them to select from the student model on pages 118–119 words and phrases that they think show particularly well. (Samples: "silky, reddish-golden hair," "stomach practically sits on the ground," "a sausage with legs.") Students who need more help might benefit from *Writing Resource Book,* page 28, "Using Details to Show Comparisons and Contrasts."

PROFESSIONAL NOTEBOOK

"The student writer should be taught to work on leads," advises Donald M. Murray. "It is the lead which establishes his tone and his hold over his subject." The lead also "informs and entices" the reader.

Murray recommends that students be sent on "lead-hunting expeditions" to collect gems like this one (from Ray Bradbury's *Dandelion Wine):* "Late that night, going home from the show with his mother and father and his brother Tom, Douglas saw the tennis shoes in the bright store window. He glanced quickly away, but his ankles were seized, his feet suspended, then rushed. The earth spun. . . ."

for ONE STUDENT'S PROCESS

PEER RESPONSE Have volunteers give additional peer comments on Rick's draft. (Samples: I'd like to know if dachshunds make good pets. Why do golden retrievers make great pets? What does a dachshund hunt?) Point out that the peer reader commented only on Rick's use of details. Remind students that other concerns can be raised at this point too—but that considering the number and choice of details is a good way to start.

REVISE YOUR WRITING

Objectives

- To evaluate responses to a draft of informative writing and to revise a draft with those responses in mind
- To use transitions to show similarities and differences

for REVISE YOUR WRITING

MODELING If you have chosen to write with your students, you might distribute copies of your first draft and solicit written responses to it. Share some of these with the class and talk about how you plan to revise your draft in light the comments it received.

for REVISE YOUR WRITING

MANAGEMENT TIP Students are more likely to request help if you move around the room as they revise. Remind them, as well, to use all the other resources available to them—for example, prewriting notes, peer comments, textbooks, dictionaries, and other reference works.

One Student's Process

Notice the comments Rick's peer readers made about this part of his first draft. What comments would you have made?

Sam is a golden retriever. Golden retrievers are sporting dogs. You can take them hunting, for companionship and to bring back any game birds you've brought down. Like all golden retrievers, Sam has golden hair, a long tail, and a happy face. Golden retrievers are real good with little kids and make great pets. Thor is a dachshund. Dachshunds are hounds who hunt by running along with their noses to the ground. Thor has blackish-brown hair.

Peer Reader Comments

I didn't know any of this about golden retrievers.

What makes a dog's face happy?

You didn't tell me enough about Thor.

Writer's Choice Would including a chart, drawing, or diagram help your readers understand your comparison more clearly?

REVISE YOUR WRITING

1. Review your responses. Your own reactions and the reactions of your peers can help you see how effectively your draft uses the techniques of comparison and contrast. Did you discover any places in your writing where you need to supply additional details or examples to explain a comparison or contrast more completely? Were your peer readers able to follow your explanation easily, or do you need to strengthen your organization? Would transitional words and phrases make your ideas flow more smoothly? At this point you can choose to make minor changes or completely rethink your essay.

SPICE BOX

Challenge students to a game that taps their thinking and speaking skills and fosters creativity. Invite them to respond to the following questions by saying, "I am more like a ______ because. . . ."

Are you more like a sports car or a station wagon?
Are you more like a rose or a geranium?
Are you more like a sneaker or a loafer?
Are you more like a muffin or a cupcake?
Are you more like the sun or the moon?
Are you more like a mountain or a river?

Encourage students to think of other pairs.

2. Use transitions to point out similarities and differences. Transitions can help you draw attention to points of comparison and contrast. Use such words and phrases as *both, also,* and *similarly* to draw attention to similarities. Use *but, instead,* and *on the other hand* to signal differences.

3. Decide what changes you want to make. You may want to make only minor changes, or you may want to strike out in an entirely new direction. Always keep in mind that the purpose of revision is to rethink what you have written. Making changes doesn't mean you've made mistakes—you've just found clearer, more interesting, more informative ways to express your ideas.

One Student's Process

After thinking about the peer responses he got and his own concerns, Rick made the following changes in his draft.

Sam is a golden retriever. Golden retrievers are sporting dogs. You can take them hunting, for companionship and to bring back any game birds you've brought down. Like all golden retrievers, Sam has [long, silky, reddish-] golden hair, a long tail, and a happy face. [Sam always looks like she's smiling.] Golden retrievers are real good with little kids and make great pets. ¶ Thor is a dachshund. Dachshunds are hounds who hunt by running along with their noses to the ground. Thor has [short, wiry] blackish-brown hair. [His legs are about two inches long, and his stomach practically sits on the ground.]

for USE TRANSITIONS . . .

INDIVIDUALIZING INSTRUCTION: BASIC STUDENTS Brainstorm with students to identify other words and phrases that signal comparison and contrast. (Samples: comparison—*like, the same as, similar to, just as;* contrast—*in contrast, different from, less than, more than, better, worse, instead of, unlike)* Encourage students to use a variety of signal words in their essays.

for ONE STUDENT'S PROCESS

CRITICAL THINKING: ANALYZING Have students compare Rick's new draft with his previous draft. How did he take the comments of his peer readers into account? (He added information about Sam, particularly what makes her look "happy," and expanded the information about Thor and placed it in a new paragraph.) If students do not know how to respond to the comments of their peer readers, suggest that they talk over the comments with those readers before revising their drafts.

for LINKING GRAMMAR AND WRITING

HELPFUL HINT: COMPARATIVE AND SUPERLATIVE FORMS Ask students to look back at the Student Model and describe Thor and Sam in original sentences, using the comparative form. (Samples: Thor looks *funnier* than Sam. Sam is *bigger* than Thor.) Then challenge them to compose sentences using the superlative form, perhaps by comparing Sam and Thor to their own pets or to other breeds of dogs.

PROOFREAD

Teaching Strategies

Guidelines for Evaluation

IDEAS AND CONTENT

- compares and contrasts subjects clearly
- demonstrates a clear sense of purpose
- opens with an attention-getting introduction
- ends with an effective conclusion

STRUCTURE AND FORM

- organizes ideas logically, using either a feature-by-feature or a subject-by-subject format
- links ideas with appropriate transitions
- devotes one paragraph to each main idea

GRAMMAR, USAGE, AND MECHANICS

- displays standard grammar, usage, and mechanics
- uses comparative and superlative forms of adjectives and adverbs correctly

GENERAL NOTE

MANAGING THE PAPER LOAD
Have students use the Standards for Evaluation on the pupil page to evaluate their essays. You may also wish to comment only on content and organization rather than on grammar or mechanics.

Standards for Evaluation

INFORMATIVE

Comparison and contrast writing

- introduces the subjects being compared in an interesting, intriguing manner
- discusses how the subjects being compared are similar and different
- organizes ideas logically, using feature-by-feature or subject-by-subject organization
- includes transitional words and phrases to make similarities and differences clear
- ends with a satisfying conclusion

LINKING GRAMMAR AND WRITING

Comparative and Superlative Forms

Whenever you use comparison and contrast, you will be comparing at least two subjects. Sometimes you may be working with more than two subjects. Depending on how many subjects you're comparing and contrasting, you will need to use different forms of adjectives and adverbs.

Use the **comparative** forms of adjectives and adverbs when you are comparing or contrasting two subjects.

Diamonds are <u>harder</u> than rubies.

Use the **superlative** forms of adjectives and adverbs when you are comparing or contrasting three or more subjects.

Diamonds are the <u>hardest</u> of all precious stones.

Rick Shen used the comparative form to compare Sam with a sports car.

Sam is <u>faster</u> than a Corvette.

Had Rick wanted to compare Sam with more than one other subject, he would have used the superlative form.

Of all the dogs in the park that day, Sam was <u>fastest</u>.

PROOFREAD

1. Proofread your work. Check your informative essay for errors in grammar, spelling, punctuation, and capitalization.

2. Make a clean copy of your paper. Use the Standards for Evaluation in the margin to make one final check of your writing. Then prepare a final copy of your informative essay.

PUBLISH AND PRESENT

- **Add graphics to your essay.** Photographs, drawings, and other visual aids can add interest to your informative essay.
- **Participate in a paper exchange.** Exchange essays with students in another class at your school or even at a different school. Attach a letter to the essay you've been asked to respond to, telling the writer what you liked about his or her work.
- **Make a bulletin board display.** Include a comparison and contrast chart about your subjects.

REFLECT ON YOUR WRITING

1. Add your writing to your portfolio. You have now written your own informative essay based on comparison and contrast. How did your writing experience go? Did you find this type of writing enjoyable? What was the most interesting or frustrating part of your writing experience? Write a brief note to yourself or your teacher that talks about your writing process. These questions may help you focus your thoughts.

- What did I learn about these subjects by comparing and contrasting them? Did anything surprise me?
- Was I surprised by any of the responses I got from my peer readers? Did I make any of the changes my peer readers suggested?
- Did I enjoy exploring comparisons and contrasts? Did this assignment give me any ideas for other comparisons I would like to investigate?
- Other than in an informative essay like Brad Darrach's and Steve Petranek's, in what other types of writing could I use comparison and contrast techniques?

2. Explore additional writing ideas. See the suggestions for writing a consumer report on pages 130–132, and Springboards on page 133.

Roller Rover (1987), William Wegman.

ART NOTE

Students may be interested to know that William Wegman's humorous photographs of his pet Weimaraners have made him world famous. His dog portraits are recognized for their playfulness and sense of the absurd.

You might wish to work with students to generate some comparison and contrast comments on the board. Students could compare the look on the dog's face to the silly situation it's in; alternatively, they might compare this dog's modeling career with the life of an ordinary dog. Accept both serious and humorous comments of comparison.

Reteaching

After students have completed their papers, assess the needs of students who have not been successful in developing an effective informative piece using comparison and contrast; assign the appropriate handbook mini-lessons as well as the Workshop Support Materials listed in the Teaching Preview, pages 113a-113b. Concepts commonly requiring reteaching for this assignment are:

- **Handbook 8, Types of Organization, pp. 239–243**
- **Handbook 9, Effective Paragraphs, pp. 244–247**

The following suggestions and resources may also be useful.

Lack of clear comparison and contrast Urge students to make a chart of comparison-contrast details used in their papers. Explain that for every detail about item A, there should be a similar kind of detail about item B.

Weak detail To sharpen their observation skills, students should independently examine a pair of objects, such as two magazine covers, and list similarities and differences. Then have them share their observations.

Extension and Enrichment

1. Explain that comparison and contrast writing is useful for political issues. Have students identify an issue and write a letter to the editor, using comparison and contrast.
2. Ask students to write a poem based on an unusual comparison.

Closure: Reflect on Your Writing

As an alternative to the questions in Reflect on Your Writing, have students use a Venn diagram (page 121) to compare and contrast this piece of writing with another piece in their portfolio. Points of comparison might be the strategies used in writing or the topics themselves.

Related ASSIGNMENT

Reading a CONSUMER REPORT

Objectives

- To respond to and analyze a consumer report
- To choose a product, set standards for it, and gather information for a consumer report
- To draft, revise, and share a consumer report

Motivate

Ask students whether they have ever been disappointed in something they bought because of its poor quality. Encourage a few students to tell about their experiences.

BUILD ON PRIOR KNOWLEDGE

Referring to one or two of the students' experiences with poor products, ask how the experiences might have been avoided. Guide students in developing a list of sources for reliable information about products. (Samples: friends who have tried various brands of a product; recommendations from experts; magazines such as *Zillions, Consumer Reports,* or *Consumer Digest)* Guide students in understanding that the most useful information results from comparing a large number of similar products.

SET A PURPOSE

Advise students to be critical in judging the information presented in the report. They might ask themselves the following questions:

Are the conclusions based on sound evidence?

How do the results compare with my own experiences with frozen yogurt?

What else would I like to know about this product?

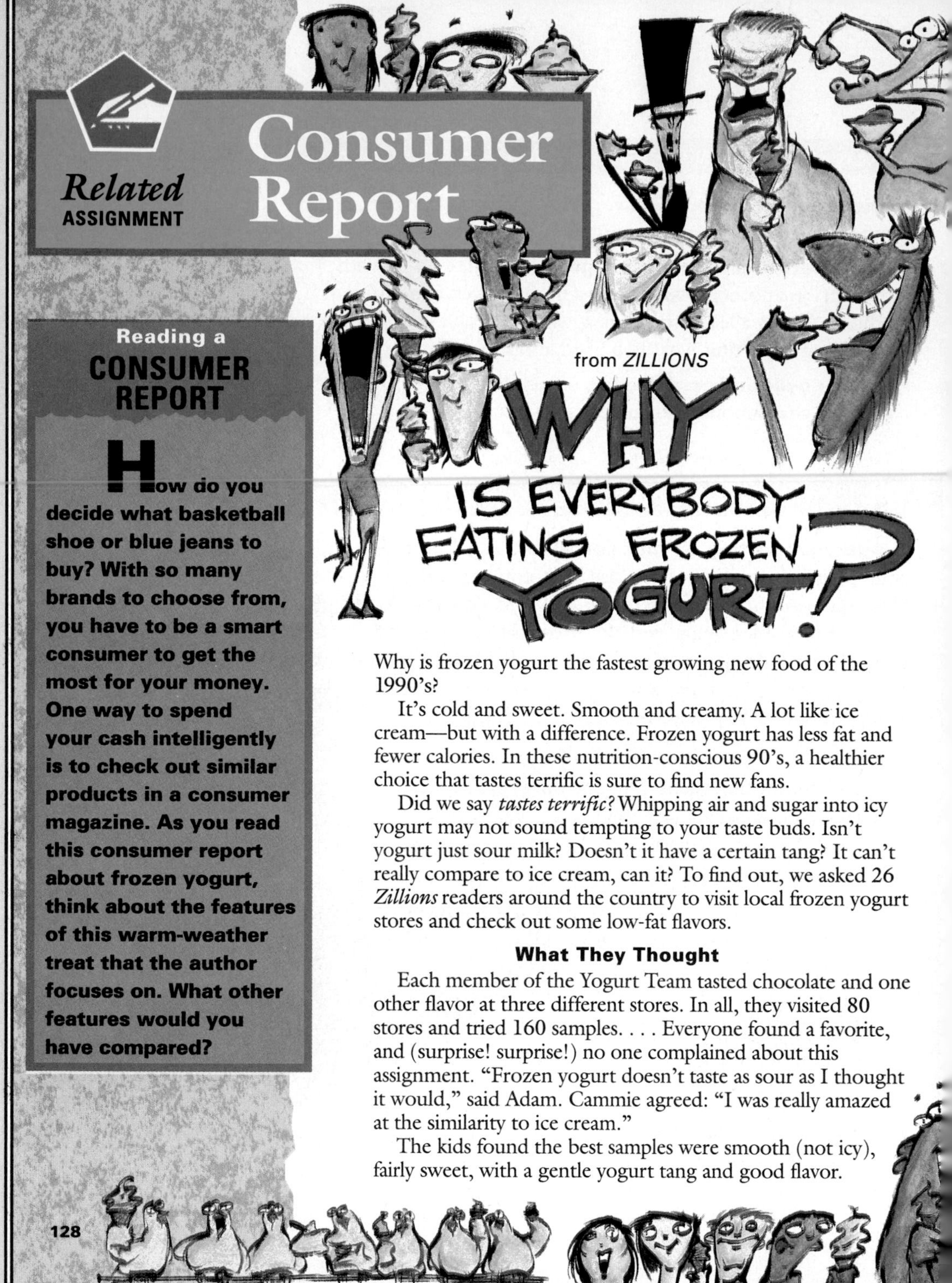

Related ASSIGNMENT Consumer Report

Reading a CONSUMER REPORT

How do you decide what basketball shoe or blue jeans to buy? With so many brands to choose from, you have to be a smart consumer to get the most for your money. One way to spend your cash intelligently is to check out similar products in a consumer magazine. As you read this consumer report about frozen yogurt, think about the features of this warm-weather treat that the author focuses on. What other features would you have compared?

from *ZILLIONS*

WHY IS EVERYBODY EATING FROZEN YOGURT?

Why is frozen yogurt the fastest growing new food of the 1990's?

It's cold and sweet. Smooth and creamy. A lot like ice cream—but with a difference. Frozen yogurt has less fat and fewer calories. In these nutrition-conscious 90's, a healthier choice that tastes terrific is sure to find new fans.

Did we say *tastes terrific?* Whipping air and sugar into icy yogurt may not sound tempting to your taste buds. Isn't yogurt just sour milk? Doesn't it have a certain tang? It can't really compare to ice cream, can it? To find out, we asked 26 *Zillions* readers around the country to visit local frozen yogurt stores and check out some low-fat flavors.

What They Thought

Each member of the Yogurt Team tasted chocolate and one other flavor at three different stores. In all, they visited 80 stores and tried 160 samples. . . . Everyone found a favorite, and (surprise! surprise!) no one complained about this assignment. "Frozen yogurt doesn't taste as sour as I thought it would," said Adam. Cammie agreed: "I was really amazed at the similarity to ice cream."

The kids found the best samples were smooth (not icy), fairly sweet, with a gentle yogurt tang and good flavor.

for FURTHER READING

Novel to Read As a result of this assignment, some students may become interested in consumer affairs. You might direct these students to Judie Angell's novel *A Word from Our Sponsor,* a humorous, thoughtful story of a twelve-year-old's introduction to consumer activism.

Even the richest frozen yogurts don't pack the flavor punch of fine ice cream, but the worst ones "tasted like cardboard," said Sarah. . . .

Why Switch?

Okay, it tastes good. So does ice cream. Why would you want to trade your old favorite for a swirl of yogurt? Because of two things you don't want lots of: calories and fat. . . .

Premium ice creams . . . are made with more cream and have less air whipped into them than regular ice creams. . . . That makes them *much* higher in fat and calories than frozen yogurt. Doctors say Americans should cut down on fat. Eating too much can lead to health problems, like heart disease.

Our testers found that switching to frozen yogurt is a delicious way to drop some fat, even for kids who don't choose snacks for nutrition reasons.

ICE CREAM VS. FROZEN YOGURT

Premium Ice Cream	330 calories	20 grams of fat
Regular Ice Cream	180 calories	9 grams of fat
Frozen Yogurt	150 calories	3 grams of fat

If you drown your treat in M&Ms, coconut, sprinkles, nuts, syrup, and such, the calories (fifty for a tablespoon of nuts) will climb. So will the cost of your order. Most stores dish up a hefty swirl of yogurt, but "it's not cheap," complained Michael. Our testers paid between $1 and $1.50 for a plain "small" portion. An 80-cent cone was the only real bargain. Most other stores offer an inexpensive kiddie cup that might satisfy many kids.

Frozen Assets

So the heat has hit and you're willing to give frozen yogurt a try. What should you order? Some kids liked the chocolate, but Esther recommends "sticking to unusual flavors. Classic flavors aren't quite as rich." Most testers especially enjoyed flavors like peach, raspberry, lime cooler, and peanut butter fudge.

No matter what flavor you pick, you may find you agree with Brian: "I never thought of going into a frozen-yogurt store before. But now that I've tried it, I'll definitely go back!"

Think & Respond

What else do you want to know about frozen yogurt that this report doesn't tell you? Why do you think the author presented the information about fat and calories as a chart? Do you think the quotations from the taste-testers are convincing? Why or why not?

Think & Respond

ELICIT PERSONAL RESPONSES

You might have students quickly jot down three things they learned about frozen yogurt and their own reactions to the idea of eating it. Then direct their attention to the first question in the Think & Respond box and ask what else they would like to know. (Samples: Are even 3 grams of fat a lot? How do the amounts of other nutrients, such as calcium and protein, in ice cream compare to the amounts in yogurt?) In response to the second question, students may note that a chart format allows quick comparison of important facts. For the third question, have students consider the audience for this piece. You might ask, "Why, in your view, has the magazine provided quotations from its readers, rather than from nutritionists?" (Samples: The facts are clear—but in a matter of opinion, a peer's comments mean the most; the magazine is appealing to its audience.)

EXPLORE THE AUTHOR'S TECHNIQUES

After students have discussed the Think & Respond questions, work with them to develop a list of the various kinds of factual information in the consumer report. The completed list should look something like this:

- results of a survey
- quotations from survey participants
- indirect quotations from an authoritative source
- notes about possible objections to a product
- a chart of statistical information
- price information

Encourage students to consider all of these possibilities as they create their own consumer reports.

MULTICULTURAL Connection

Yogurt, a traditional food in the Middle East and in Mediterranean countries such as Turkey and Greece, is an ethnic food that has become popular in the United States. As students consider products for their consumer reports, you might encourage them to look for other currently popular products that originated outside the United States.

Writing ON YOUR OWN

Point out that the writers of this report used two kinds of support—concrete facts (of various kinds) and testimonials of consumers. Suggest to students that as they write their own consumer reports, they try combining facts with the personal opinions of consumers to make their reports lively and convincing.

Handbooks for Help and Practice

The following handbooks may be used as mini-lessons before students begin writing or as resources when problems arise.

- **Graphic Devices for Writing, pp. 227–231**
- **Audience, pp. 234–235**
- **Creating Graphic Aids, pp. 349–351**

Teaching Strategies

for CHOOSE A PRODUCT

INDIVIDUALIZING INSTRUCTION: KINESTHETIC LEARNERS Suggest that students who learn best by physical activity and touch select products they can handle, such as articles of clothing, small electronic devices, or tools. Encourage them to carry out their own evaluations or tests on these products.

for SET YOUR STANDARDS

HELPFUL HINT: GRAPHIC DEVICES To give students ideas for setting up their ratings charts, you might want to provide them with examples from a consumer magazine, such as *Zillions* or *Consumer Reports,* that uses charts to compare product features.

Writing ON YOUR OWN
Consumer Report

INVITATION TO *Write*

As a consumer you are faced with a wide variety of products—so many, in fact, that making an intelligent choice can be difficult. Comparing products in an organized way, such as by creating a consumer report, can help you—and your readers—make wise decisions.

Write a consumer report to help people decide which brand, model, or type of product they should buy.

PLANNING YOUR CONSUMER REPORT

1. Choose a product. Have you purchased something lately that you were dissatisfied with? Are you thinking of buying something in the near future, but you're not sure which brand or model really suits your needs? How could you have made a better choice last time and make the right choice this time? Discuss these questions with classmates, and brainstorm a list of products you'd like to investigate. Which product would you like to report on?

2. Set your standards. Before you can evaluate a product, you have to decide what you expect from it. For example, if you were evaluating different brands of frozen yogurt, you might look for such features as delicious taste, good nutritional value, low fat and calories, and a reasonable price.

Make a list of the features you think your product should have. Then arrange those features in a chart you can use to present your evaluation of each individual brand.

3. Gather information. Now it's time to find out how the individual brands of the product you've chosen to evaluate measure up. On the next page are some evaluation techniques you can try.

PROBLEM SOLVING

"How can I present information visually?"

For more information on using charts and graphs, see

- Handbook 34, "Creating Graphic Aids," pages 349–351

- **Read product labels.** Labels often include useful information that can help you better understand the product's features.
- **Try out the product.** The best way to check out a product is to wear it, taste it, use it, ride it—in other words, try it out.
- **Take a survey.** Talk to people who use the product you're investigating. Why do they like or dislike it? What are its best or worst features?

Record your findings on your chart. In addition, write down what people have to say about the product. You may want to include their quotations in your final report.

Writing TIP

Studying advertisements for your product can help you identify important features.

WRITING YOUR CONSUMER REPORT

1. Start writing. Your chart and notes tell you what you discovered about your subject. What, however, will you *say* about your findings? Do some freewriting about your product evaluation. Did your findings surprise you in any way? Do you have any recommendations you want to make?

2. Shape your report. There are many ways to present a consumer report. However, you will want to include these elements:

- **Introduction** Tell your readers what product you are evaluating and the purpose of your evaluation. Are you rating individual brands? Are you judging how useful the product is?
- **Explanation of your method** Tell your readers about the standards you used and how you went about your evaluation.
- **Your findings** Present your evaluations, plus any reactions or personal opinions you think are useful. You might choose to write about each brand in turn, telling how it measured up to your standards. Another option is to present each of your standards in turn, explaining how the individual brands rate.
- **Conclusion** You might want to summarize the information, recommend one brand, or even recommend that people not buy this product at all.

GENERAL NOTE

COOPERATIVE LEARNING Offer students the option of working in a group to gather information about a product or service (for example, local pizza parlors or hair salons) and produce a comprehensive study. Tasks would include taking and interpreting a survey, creating charts and graphs, organizing and editing information, and designing and illustrating the report.

for SHAPE YOUR REPORT

CRITICAL THINKING: EVALUATING If students are overwhelmed by large amounts of product information, you might suggest that they begin by prioritizing the features of the product they want to evaluate. Students might decide to assess only three or four of the most important features of the product. They can then rate the product for each feature before coming up with an overall evaluation.

for SHAPE YOUR REPORT

ASSESSMENT: SPOT CHECK As students are drafting their reports, ask them to label each part—purpose, standards/methods, findings, and recommendations—in the margin of their papers. Check to see that the parts are there and help students as necessary.

Guidelines for Evaluation

AN EFFECTIVE CONSUMER REPORT

- states the purpose in the introduction
- explains the standards and methods of evaluation that were applied
- evaluates a product by comparing and contrasting brands or models
- contains accurate factual information
- ends with a summary or recommendation

for REVIEWING YOUR REPORT

PEER RESPONSE Suggest that when students have produced a first draft of their consumer report, they ask a peer reviewer to read and comment on it. Students might ask their peers three questions:

Which details seemed most convincing?

What else would you like to know?

What about the report did you like best?

for REVIEWING YOUR REPORT

HELPFUL HINT: USING QUOTATIONS Remind students that when they use direct quotations, they must quote their sources accurately and set the quotations off with quotation marks. You may wish to review the correct use of quotation marks with students, or you might refer them to Handbook 49, pages 651 and 664–668.

Writer's Choice Do you want to develop a rating system for judging individual brands? For example, you could give each brand a certain number of stars or a letter grade depending on how well it measures up to your standards.

REVIEWING YOUR REPORT

1. Size up your audience. Your goal is to help consumers like yourself make intelligent product decisions, so think about what your readers need to know. Have you given them enough background information about the product? Are there any special terms or concepts you should define?

2. Check your accuracy. In order to be useful, your information must be reliable. Check to make sure you spelled brand names correctly and listed prices, ingredients, and other details accurately.

SHARING YOUR REPORT

- **Create a consumer magazine.** Make copies of the magazine available to the rest of the school.
- **Submit your report to your school or community newspaper.** You might suggest that the newspaper consider running a regular column of consumer reports.
- **Give a demonstration.** Bring samples of the products you evaluated to class and show how they measure up to each other.
- **Hold a consumer conference.** Present and discuss the consumer reports as a group.

Springboards

MEDIA Imagine you work for the advertising agency that just won the account for your favorite product. Create an advertisement or commercial that compares and contrasts the product with its main competitor.

Music Many songs have been recorded by more than one artist. Choose such a song, and compare and contrast the versions by different musicians or musical groups.

Speaking and Listening What if you could have helped elect Abraham Lincoln or Thomas Jefferson or any other President? Choose a presidential candidate (from the present or the past) and write a campaign speech comparing your candidate with his opponent.

Colored Campbell's Soup Can (1965), Andy Warhol

Science We take for granted many inventions that have made our lives easier. What if the telephone, the automobile, or the computer had never been invented? Choose an invention, and then compare and contrast what life would be like if it didn't exist.

Teaching Strategies

GENERAL NOTE

COLLABORATIVE OPPORTUNITY
Encourage students to organize themselves into small groups according to the prompt they are interested in exploring. As a group, have students brainstorm for ideas to compare and contrast. Remind students that during brainstorming, they should allow their imaginations free rein to explore even the most unusual ideas.

for MUSIC

INDIVIDUALIZING INSTRUCTION: AUDITORY LEARNERS You might suggest that these students develop a tape-recorded informative essay. Their audio essay should include excerpts of the songs that demonstrate points of comparison and contrast. Remind students that their audio essays should conform to guidelines for a written essay: an intriguing introduction, clear organization, and a strong conclusion.

ART NOTE

The Campbell's soup can was a typical subject for Andy Warhol (1930?–1987), a filmmaker and painter who was a leader of the pop art movement in the United States during the 1960s. Pop artists used common, everyday objects as the basis of their subject matter or style. Working on three-foot high canvases, Warhol painted some soup cans with the familiar red and white label. Others labels were painted in shades of purple, green, or pink.

Adding Sentence Parts

Objectives

- To combine sentences by creating sentence openers, S-V splits, and sentence closers
- To compose and correctly punctuate sentences that include sentence openers, S-V splits, and sentence closers
- To expand sentences by adding sentence parts

for ON THE MARK

HELPFUL HINT: PUNCTUATING SENTENCE PARTS To reinforce the use of commas with sentence openers, interrupters, and closers, you might ask volunteers to read the model sentences aloud. Call attention to the natural pauses that occur. Point out that natural pauses often signal comma placement. If students need more practice, direct them to relevant portions of Commas That Set Off Special Elements, pages 646–650.

Additional Resource

Sentence Composing Copy Masters, pp. 9–10

Answer Key

A. Combining Sentences

1. Curled up near the chimney of a building two houses away from his, Benno can see that the sun has moved way over to the river, and it is beginning to get cold.
2. I didn't own a suit, but I had a sport coat, and I got a pair of leather penny loafers for the occasion, unsneakering my feet.

Sentence

COMPOSING

Adding Sentence Parts

You can make your sentences more informative by adding sentence parts at the beginning of sentences (sentence openers), between the subject and the verb (S-V splits), or at the end of a sentence (sentence closers). Read the sentences below without the underlined sentence parts. Then notice how the underlined parts make each sentence more interesting and complete.

Model A, Sentence Opener When we were about a hundred yards from the foot of the mountain, we stopped and sat on a bench.
William Pene du Bois, *The Twenty-One Balloons*

Model B, S-V Split John (S), the oldest of the children left at the home place, sat (V) at the end of the table facing his mother.
Irene Hunt, *Across Five Aprils*

Model C, Sentence Closer Rachel is sitting in the library during seventh period, writing in her notebook.
Norma Fox Mazer, *After the Rain*

▶ **ON THE MARK** Use commas to set off sentence openers, closers, and S-V splits from the rest of the sentence.

A. Combining Sentences Make a new sentence by putting the underlined part of the second sentence into the first sentence in the position indicated *(sentence opener, closer, or S-V split)*. Write the complete sentence, using commas to set off the addition from the rest of the sentence.

1. Benno can see that the sun has moved way over to the river, and it is beginning to get cold. He sees this as he lies curled up near the chimney of a building two houses away from his. *(sentence opener)*
Felice Holman, *Secret City, U.S.A.*

2. I didn't own a suit, but I had a sport coat, and I got a pair of leather penny loafers for the occasion. The new shoes led to unsneakering my feet. *(sentence closer)* **Richard Peck, *Remembering the Good Times***

3. Charlie Bond sat facing them. He was a pleasant-faced youth of twenty. *(S-V split)* **Oliver La Farge, "The Little Stone Man"**

B. Unscrambling and Imitating Sentences Unscramble each set of sentence chunks below to create a sentence that matches the structure of one of the models on page 134. Then write a correctly punctuated sentence of your own that imitates each model. Be sure each of your sentences contains a sentence opener, S-V split, or sentence closer.

1. Write sentences that imitate Model A.
   we lay on our blankets / when we were only little kids / and napped / in the first grade of elementary school
2. Write sentences that imitate Model B.
   nominated for most unusual behavior / playing his imaginary harmonica / Weird Walter / the looniest of the kids / stood on the bleachers
3. Write sentences that imitate Model C.
   dreaming of supper / was dozing in his doghouse during the storm / Snoopy

C. Expanding Sentences Use your imagination to add sentence openers, S-V splits, and sentence closers to the sentences below. Follow the directions in parentheses.

1. The heat hit my face like a steamy towel, and I gasped for air. *(Add a sentence opener that begins with* when *and tells why it was so hot.)*
   Robert Lipsyte, *One Fat Summer*
2. The black stallion raised his head and whistled when he saw him. *(Add a S-V split that begins with an* -ing *word and describes the stallion.)*
   Walter Farley, *The Black Stallion*
3. The stray dogs had a pen out back. *(Add a sentence closer that begins with* a *and describes the pen for the dogs.)* **Gary Paulsen, *The Monument***

Grammar Refresher Sentence openers, S-V splits, or sentence closers are often subordinate clauses. To learn more about subordinate clauses, see Handbook 45, "Using Compound and Complex Sentences," pages 560–570.

3. Charlie Bond, a pleasant-faced youth of twenty, sat facing them.

B. Unscrambling and Imitating Sentences

Unscrambled sentences are given. Imitative sentences will vary but should follow the same pattern.

1. When we were only little kids in the first grade of elementary school, we lay on our blankets and napped.
2. Weird Walter, the looniest of the kids nominated for most unusual behavior, stood on the bleachers playing his imaginary harmonica.
3. Snoopy was dozing in his doghouse during the storm, dreaming of supper.

C. Expanding Sentences

Answers will vary. Authors' sentences are given.

1. When I turned and walked into the sun, the heat hit my face like a steamy towel, and I gasped for air.
   Robert Lipsyte, *One Fat Summer*
2. The black stallion, standing beside the spring, raised his head and whistled when he saw him.
   Walter Farley, *The Black Stallion*
3. The stray dogs had a pen out back, a chain-link concrete pen.
   Gary Paulsen, *The Monument*

6

Persuasion

Overview

Persuasive writing convinces readers that they should agree with the beliefs or feelings of the writer. At times, persuasive writing goes one step further by not only asking for the audience's agreement, but also issuing a call to action. In this workshop, students apply the skills of informative, descriptive, and narrative writing studied in the previous workshops as they develop their opinions. Workshop 6 includes the following Guided and Related Assignments as well as the interdisciplinary project described on pages 135c–135d.

1. **Guided: Argument** asks students to present both sides of an issue fairly and to support each side with appropriate evidence, so that readers can make up their own minds.
2. **Related: Social Action Letter** invites students to use the skills developed in the Guided Assignment to take a firm stand on an issue and to call on readers to take action.
3. **Related: Writing for Assessment** calls on students to use persuasive writing to respond to prompts similar to those found on standardized writing tests.

Teaching Preview

Preparation Guide

1. Use the Overview on this page and the Teacher's Choice descriptions on page 137 as a basis for deciding which assignments to teach.
2. Preview the assignments and the teacher's notes and identify concepts that may require preteaching or extra support, given your class's abilities. The handbook mini-lessons suggested within the lesson may also provide guidance.
3. Preview the chart below for support materials in the Teacher's Resource File that may be used with this Workshop. Resources are for use with the Guided Assignment unless otherwise noted.

Support Materials

RESOURCES

Prewrite and Explore

Writing Resource Book, pp. 30–32
Thinking Skills Worksheets, pp. 6, 8
Starting Points for Writing, Writing Prompts for Fine Art, pp. 35–36, 39–41, 44

Draft and Discover

Elaboration, Revision, and Proofreading Practice, p. 11
Writing Resource Book, pp. 33–34

Revise Your Writing

Elaboration, Revision, and Proofreading Practice, p. 12
Writing Resource Book, pp. 35–36
Peer Response Guides, pp. 19–20

Guidelines for Writing Assessment and Portfolio Use, pp. 19, 38–40

Sentence Composing

Sentence Composing Copy Masters, pp. 11–12

Assessment

Tests and Writing Assessment Prompts, p. 6
Writing Resource Book, pp. 37–38

Computer Software

Writer's DataBank
Electronic English Handbook

PROFESSIONAL RESOURCES AND MEDIA

Books and Journals

Elbow, Peter, and Belanoff, Pat, "Persuasion," *A Community of Writers,* Random House (1989), pp. 217–240
McKissack, Patricia C., and McKissack, Fredrick, *Sojourner Truth: Ain't I a Woman?* Scholastic (1992)
Murphy, Jim, *The Long Road to Gettysburg,* Clarion (1992)

Films and Videos

Last Breeze of Summer, Carousel, New York (1992) (30 min.)
T. J.'s Rights, Film Ideas, Northbrook, IL (1992) (18 min.)

Computer Software and Technology

Audubon Wildlife Adventures: Grizzly Bears, Top Ten Software/SoftKat, Chatsworth, CA (software), Apple II, Apple IIGS, PC: PC 3.5
Decisions, Decisions: Prejudice, Tom Snyder Productions, Watertown, MA (software), Macintosh, Apple, MS—DOS
Reading Realities: Real Life Issues, Teacher Support Software Chatsworth, CA (software), Apple II

Linking Literature, Writing, and Grammar

The following options may be used to provide students with an integrated language experience. Begin by assigning and discussing any of the recommended pieces of literature. Use the suggested strategy to provide a link to the Guided Assignment.

LINKING LITERATURE AND WRITING

Option 1

Starting Point: "Privacy and Teens" by Lauren Tarshis on pages 138–139 of *The Writer's Craft.*

Strategy: Use the teaching suggestions on pages 138–139 to lead students into the Guided Assignment.

Option 2

Starting Point: "Where the Rainbow Ends" by Richard Rive on page 377 of McDougal, Littell's *Literature and Language,* Grade 8. (Additional suggestions for using *Literature and Language* can be found on page 137.)

Strategy: Have students read the selection to discover what Rive suggests (a place where the world can sing together, united). What evidence does he use to show that his idea is reasonable? (no such thing as a black tune or a white tune) How does he show that he recognizes an opposing view? (He admits it's a difficult tune to learn.) Use the discussion to lead into the Guided Assignment.

Option 3

Starting Point: "Harlem Night Song" by Langston Hughes.

Strategy: Read the poem aloud. Then have students list the five reasons that Hughes gives for roaming the night together and singing. Which reason do students think is the most powerful? (I love you.) Encourage students to comment on the suitability of this appeal to the emotions. Then introduce the Guided Assignment.

LINKING WRITING AND GRAMMAR

Before students begin to draft their arguments, remind them that persuasive writing is most effective when sentences are clear and direct. One technique that helps make sentences direct is the use of active rather than passive verb forms, wherever active voice is the more appropriate choice. Put these examples on the board to illustrate the difference.

Less Clear: It has been known by doctors for some time that colds are not caused by either cold weather or wet hair.

More Clear: Doctors have known for some time that neither cold weather nor wet hair causes colds.

When students revise their work, remind them to look for and replace sentences in which active voice would be more effective than passive. Go over pages 489–491 of the Grammar and Usage Handbook. If problems with voice still appear in student papers, assign the exercises on those pages. Additional practice can be found in the *Grammar and Usage Practice Book* on page 51.

Management Guidelines

The chart below indicates the number of days recommended for each phase of the Guided and Related Assignments. These numbers are an estimate of the total time needed for each phase. In practice, of course, students may not complete each phase in one continuous session, nor will they necessarily progress from stage to stage in the linear order shown here. Stars indicate portions of the assignment that may be completed outside the classroom if time is limited or if teachers wish students to work independently.

ARGUMENT

Starting from Literature................1 day
Prewrite and Explore....................2 days*
Draft and Discover....................2–3 days*
Revise Your Writing..................1–2 days*
Proofread......................................1 day*
Publish and Present......................1 day
Reflect on Your Writing................1 day*
Reteaching......................................open
Extension and Enrichment. ....open*
Sentence Composing......................open*

SOCIAL ACTION LETTER

Reading a Social Action Letter .....1 day
Discovering and Exploring........1–2 days*
Planning and Drafting ....2 days*
Reviewing Your Letter ....1 day*
Publishing and Presenting............1 day

WRITING FOR ASSESSMENT

Starting from a Prompt.................1 day*
Analyzing, Planning, and
Drafting...................................1 day
Reviewing Your Response...........1 day

Project File

You Be the Judge: A Mock Trial

Overview

Students participating in this project will apply principles of argumentation and will gain a deeper understanding of the judicial system as they choose a person involved in a conflict—a literary character, a living person, or a person from history—and conduct a mock trial. They will present opposing arguments, evaluate them, and render a verdict.

Students will participate in the following activities:

- Review standard courtroom procedures
- Choose a character to be tried
- Research and write arguments for the prosecution and the defense
- Plan, assume roles for, and conduct a mock trial
- Use language arts, science, social studies, math, and art skills to complete their research and present the trial

Preparation Guide

Tell students that an understanding of the persuasive techniques used in trials can help them to defend their own rights and the rights of others. Point out that although courtroom procedures may seem complex, these procedures are based on clear reasoning.

Tell students that during this project they will become more familiar with courtroom procedures. They will develop persuasive materials and use them to plan and conduct a mock trial.

Stage 1
Study Courtroom Procedures and Choose a Character

1. Have students examine the roles of jury-trial participants. Encourage students to explore the roles of plaintiffs, defendants, witnesses, and jurors and the duties of attorneys and their assistants, judges, bailiffs, and other officers of the court (see *Resources, Stage 1*).
2. Invite students to choose a controversial character—contemporary, literary, or historical—to be tried. Possible characters include the following:
   - a sports hero who is being denied induction into the Hall of Fame because he gambled on sporting events
   - a school librarian who refuses to remove *Huckleberry Finn* from the shelves after the community has voted to ban the book
   - a fictional character, such as Robin Hood or Zorro, who opposes authority
   - a character from a work such as *To Kill a Mockingbird* or "The Tell-Tale Heart"
   - an American patriot who destroyed tea during the Boston Tea Party
3. Direct students to decide whether they will try a case in which the government prosecutes their character or one in which another character sues their character.

TEAM TEACHING

The following activities may be used for team teaching or as enrichment and extension activities by the language arts teacher.

Social Studies Study the organization of federal, state, and local judicial systems.

Language Arts Skim novels, stories, and plays that involve controversies or that show characters in strong conflicts. Read literature involving trials. Examine media coverage of recently publicized trials.

TEACHING TIPS

- Schedule a field trip to a local court.
- Show films or videos of trials.
- Invite a judge or an attorney to speak to the class about his or her duties.

Stage 2
Prepare Arguments

1. Divide the class into two groups to collaborate on arguments for the prosecution and the defense.
2. Direct group members to share the tasks of researching facts and events for evidence, choosing techniques of persuasion, and planning arguments.
3. Remind groups to prepare strong opening and closing statements.
4. Have groups create detailed written outlines of their arguments.

TEAM TEACHING

Social Studies Learn basic legal terminology. Research historical figures chosen for the trial. Research political or historical events that affect the case.

Language Arts Review techniques for writing arguments. Learn about appeals to emotion, appeals to reason, and logical fallacies. Learn to prepare outlines (see *Resources, Stage 2*).

Science Research scientific procedures useful in the case, such as how to date materials or how to verify the authenticity of objects.

Art Create sketches and diagrams needed as evidence.

TEACHING TIPS

- Suggest that students interview experts to learn about terminology, laws, and precedents that apply to their case.
- Remind students to anticipate opposing arguments and to counter them.
- Encourage students to watch television programs involving trials and to evaluate what they see.

Stage 3
Conduct the Trial

1. Have each student select a role to play in the upcoming trial.
2. Have students plan and prepare for the trial according to standard legal practices: conferences between attorneys and clients, planning sessions for attorney teams, jury selection, the judge's preliminary procedures, and so on.
3. Direct students to conduct the trial, and have the jury render a verdict.
4. Have students discuss and reflect on their experiences during the project and write their reflections in a class file.

TEAM TEACHING

Social Studies Establish and follow standard legal procedures.

Math Study the formulas used for sentencing and parole. Calculate time served under various sentencing options.

Language Arts Study techniques of public speaking, debate, and critical listening (see *Resources, Stage 3*).

TEACHING TIPS

- To be sure all students have roles, create teams of attorneys for the prosecution and defense, and designate jury alternates.
- Set aside several days for the trial, the jury deliberations, and the rendering of the verdict.
- Arrange for students to videotape each segment of the trial and to review previous sessions in preparation for each day's session.
- Have attorney teams pause before the concluding session to make final revisions in closing arguments.

Resources

STAGE 1

The Great Monkey Trial by Tom McGowen examines the Scopes trial, tracing the ten-day trial itself and considering the history of the dispute and the effects of the outcome.

To Kill a Mockingbird by Harper Lee includes realistic trial sequences.

Trial by Jury by Jo Kolanda and Judge Patricia Curley describes court procedures and includes a glossary.

Legal Careers and the Legal System by William Fry and Roy Hoopes describes what lawyers do and how the legal system works.

Public Defender: Lawyer for the People by Joan Hewett follows a Los Angeles public defender, Janice Fukai, through a week of work.

STAGE 2

The Writer's Craft, Grade 8, Workshop 6, "Persuasion," pages 136–149, teaches the writing of arguments. Handbook 31, "Critical Thinking and Writing," pages 337–339, covers appeals to emotion, appeals to reason, and logical fallacies. The Appendix, page 683, teaches outlining.

For videos of trials and commentaries broadcast on educational television, contact the **Court TV Video Library** in New York City.

You Be the Judge by Sidney B. Carroll outlines thirteen classic American legal cases, dating from 1773 to 1962, for the reader to decide. (Resolutions and explanations are included.)

STAGE 3

The Writer's Craft, Grade 8, Handbook 37, "Critical Listening and Observing," pages 363–366, teaches listening skills.

Video Power: A Complete Guide to Writing, Planning, and Shooting Video by Tom Shachtman and Harriet Shelare includes instructions for using a video camera to record events.

How to Make a Speech, a McGraw-Hill video narrated by Steve Allen, offers fundamentals of writing and delivering effective oral presentations.

Additional Projects

Evaluating the Media Have students choose and explore a question about the media, such as, Do children's cartoons contain harmful levels of violence? During this project students should target specific media, devise research-based criteria, and develop and conduct surveys of various age groups to determine viewpoints on the issue. In presenting their findings, they can set forth arguments for and against each point of view.

Solving Science Mysteries Direct students to investigate science-related mysteries, such as the Bermuda Triangle and the disappearance of the dinosaurs. Propose that students formulate scientific theories to explain the mysteries. Direct them to use persuasion to write speeches supporting their theories. The project will culminate when students present their speeches, utilizing illustrations, slides, videos, and other visual aids.

Whodunits in History Invite student teams to write their own unsolved murder mysteries, using research to create accurate historical settings and realistic characters and events. Then tell teams to trade mysteries. Direct teams to read the mysteries, to use group problem-solving techniques to decide which character is probably guilty, and to prepare arguments in support of their decisions. Encourage them to research historical facts and data to support their arguments.

SKETCH BOOK

Objective

- To use pictures of campaign buttons and suggested writing prompts as springboards to informal writing

WRITING WARM-UPS

Encourage students to respond freely and informally to at least one of the Sketchbook prompts. They may begin by discussing their reactions in small groups and then freewriting in their journals. Remind students that their responses will not be graded and may provide them with useful material for other persuasive assignments.

SHOW, DON'T TELL

The following is a sample of a showing paragraph for the pro side of the uniform argument.

Imagine never again going to your closet in the morning and sighing, "What shall I wear today?" Imagine never again having to worry about whether you have the latest style in jackets or the "in" athletic shoes. This could happen if our school adopts uniforms.

SKETCH BOOK

WRITING WARM-UPS

- Who gets your vote? Give some convincing reasons to support the candidate you choose. Be original; be daring; have fun!
- What's your pet peeve? Jot down some of your thoughts.
- Tell the story of an argument you had recently. Who was right? Who won?

Show, Don't Tell

When you present both sides of an issue, show your readers all the important arguments, both pro and con. Use the following *telling* sentence to write two *showing* paragraphs, one paragraph for each side of the argument.

- All students should wear uniforms to school.

Persuasion

Guided Assignment
Argument

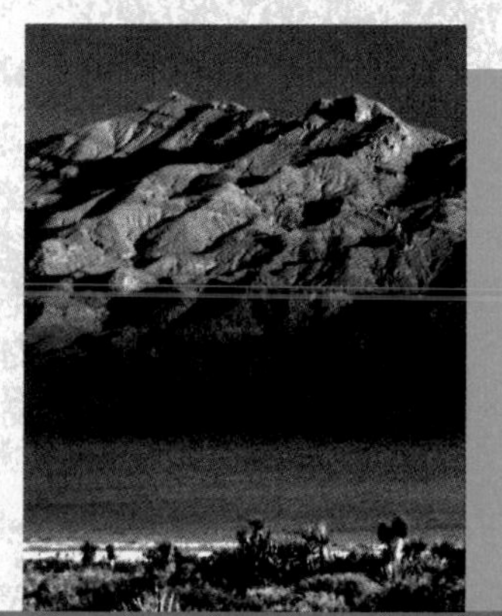

Related Assignment
Social Action Letter

Related Assignment
Writing for Assessment

Persuasive writing allows you to use the power of language to educate and influence people and to help others understand how *you* see the world. In this workshop you will have the chance to argue both sides of an issue of your choice. In one related assignment you will be able to present your views in a social action letter to an official who can help make those ideas a reality. In another assignment, you will learn how to present your ideas effectively and persuasively in a writing assessment situation.

Links to LITERATURE & LANGUAGE

Literature For more examples of writing that contains persuasive elements, see Grade 8 *Literature and Language:*

- William Tsuchida, from *Wear It Proudly*
- Nancy Masterson Sakamoto, "Conversational Ballgames"
- Bob Greene, "Baseball and the Facts of Life"

Writing This guided assignment may be used as an extension of the Writer's Workshop, "Persuasive Writing: Editorial," on page 423 in *Literature and Language,* Grade 8.

WRITER'S 6 WORKSHOP

Persuasion

Objectives

Guided Assignment

Argument To recognize persuasion in literature and to create a piece of writing that presents both sides of an argument, supporting each side with evidence

Related Assignments

Social Action Letter To analyze a letter that takes a stand on an issue and to create a social action letter

Writing for Assessment To analyze sample essay-test questions and to write a response to a writing assessment prompt

Teacher's Choice

Use the following guidelines to choose the assignment that best suits students' needs.

Argument This assignment gives students an opportunity to look at both sides of an issue and then present each side fairly. Because strong arguments make use of facts, statistics, and examples as evidence, an understanding of these types of details would be helpful.

Social Action Letter This persuasive letter presents one side of an issue and ends with a call to action. This assignment is particularly interesting to those students who feel strongly about a cause. Such students are often very vocal about their opinions and want to persuade others to adopt their point of view.

Writing for Assessment Before students can respond to an essay question, they have to analyze the prompt. This assignment helps students respond to the kind of writing found on many state tests.

Guided ASSIGNMENT

ASSIGNMENT RATIONALE

Knowing how to argue effectively is a skill that helps people get what they want. People who can defend their views may also gain self-confidence as they do so. This assignment helps students to examine both sides of an issue and to choose evidence that will effectively support a position.

Starting from LITERATURE

Motivate

Ask students how they react when someone says to them, "My favorite ballplayer is better than your favorite player." How would they prove that their favorite is a better player? (Sample: Use facts and statistics from games.) Have students read Starting from Literature and share their experiences in answer to the opening question. Then ask them to suggest how presenting an argument can be like defending their favorite ballplayer. (Sample: Both activities involve supporting an opinion with facts and other evidence.)

BUILD ON PRIOR KNOWLEDGE

Invite students to share their opinions on, and knowledge of, controversial school issues. (Samples: longer school days, cafeteria menus, year-round schooling) Urge students to listen carefully to the differing opinions and arguments expressed on these issues. Remind them that there are usually sound reasons to support either side of a controversial question.

Guided ASSIGNMENT Argument

Starting from LITERATURE

Have you ever felt strongly about an issue but changed your mind when someone made a good case for the other side? Most important issues have more than one side. The one you agree with often depends on how convincing the speaker's or writer's arguments are. As you read this article notice the arguments that Lauren Tarshis gives to support each position.

by Lauren Tarshis

PRIVACY AND TEENS

from Scholastic Update

IT WAS LUNCHTIME at Miami Southridge High School, and Tara McClary and a group of her friends were relaxing before afternoon classes . . . when a school security guard rounded them up and ushered them to the school office. "We didn't know what was going on," she says.

What was going on, she soon learned, was a drug search. Since Tara wasn't into drugs and had never been in trouble at school, the idea of a drug search didn't particularly concern her.

Paul Cooper, the assistant principal who led the search, didn't find any drugs that afternoon. But while sifting through the contents of Tara's purse, he discovered

MORE ABOUT THE MODEL

Lauren Tarshis reports that Tara's father based his argument on the Fourth Amendment. Students should know what the Fourth Amendment states: "The right of the people to be secure in their persons, houses, papers, and effects, against unreasonable searches and seizures, shall not be violated, and no warrants shall issue, but upon probable cause, supported by oath or affirmation, and particularly describing the place to be searched, and the persons or things to be seized."

You may want to define difficult words and concepts in the amendment and open up a discussion about it.

another type of contraband: six unsigned and unauthorized hall passes. Tara insisted that she had found the passes crumpled up on a classroom floor. But Cooper slapped her with a five-day suspension.

[Tara's father] was angry at Cooper and the school administration for what he claims is a serious violation of his daughter's Fourth Amendment rights, which protect Americans from unreasonable searches and seizures.

The Fourth Amendment is key to Americans' right to privacy. It states that government officials (like the police) cannot conduct a search without "probable cause"—good reason to suspect they'll find something illegal.

[On the other hand,] law enforcement officials and many school administrators say that the Fourth Amendment can interfere with their ability to preserve order and student safety.

They point to increased violence in schools, particularly in cities. Tara's school, for instance, is located in a particularly rough section of Miami. The school doesn't have a crime problem. But the surroundings are infamous for drug traffic. And there have been a number of shootings on or close to school property. Cooper and other Southridge administrators insist that student searches are vital to keeping the peace at Southridge. "Would you want your kids in a school where there might be weapons?" he asks.

[Others], like former Supreme Court Justice William Brennan, insist that young people deserve full Fourth Amendment coverage, particularly in school. "Schools cannot expect their students to learn the lessons of good citizenship when the school authorities themselves disregard the fundamental principles underpinning our constitutional freedoms," Brennan once wrote.

Legal experts on both sides of the student-rights issue agree that the courts need to set down more specific guidelines about student searches. They say that many rights violations occur because administrators don't know when a search crosses constitutional boundaries.

Tara and her father are hoping that her case will help clarify the constitutional rights of students.

Think & Respond

Which do you think is more important—students' privacy or their safety? Which of Lauren Tarshis's arguments influenced your thinking?

SET A PURPOSE

Ask students to identify the purpose-setting statement in Starting from Literature (the last sentence). Then write the title of the selection on the board and divide the space under the title into two columns, labeled *Pro* and *Con.* Invite students to jot down notes appropriate to each column as they read.

Think & Respond

ELICIT PERSONAL RESPONSES

After students have read the selection, have them respond to the first question in the Think & Respond box by **voting.** Invite students who have opposing opinions to **discuss** their points of view. Have them **write** the argument that most influenced them under *Pro* or *Con* on the graphic organizer on the board.

EXPLORE THE AUTHOR'S TECHNIQUES

A good essay begins with an attention-getting introduction and ends with a strong conclusion. Lauren Tarshis gets the reader's attention by beginning with a story about a teenager named Tara. She proceeds from this case study to the main issue, privacy versus safety, and presents arguments for both sides. Invite students to speculate about why Lauren concludes her essay the way she does. (Sample: to remind the reader that this is not a dry legal issue; it is one that involves a real teenager—Tara)

Reading a STUDENT MODEL

Lauren Tarshis wrote about the right to privacy—an issue important to both teenagers and adults. This student, Utica Norr, writes about another issue that evokes strong feelings in teenagers and adults. This student model is the final draft of the work in process you will see on the workshop pages that follow.

Motivate

To help students focus on the beginning sentences of Reading a Student Model, you might share with them an issue that you debated with your own parents when you were about their age. (For example, you might have argued with your parents about a curfew or chores.) Then invite students to share their own issues and experiences.

BUILD ON PRIOR KNOWLEDGE

Discuss the general process you went through to reach a compromise with your parents. Then ask students who also have reached agreements with their parents or with other persons to describe the process they went through. In the discussion, point out the importance of stating one's own view and explaining its merit, of listening to the other person's explanation of his or her position, and of choosing a course of action that takes both viewpoints into account.

SET A PURPOSE

In this piece the student writer presents both sides of the issue of how to react to explicit lyrics in popular music. To assist students in recognizing Utica's arguments, suggest they look for the words *one side, the other side,* and *both sides.* These words make the organization of her essay clear.

One Student's Writing

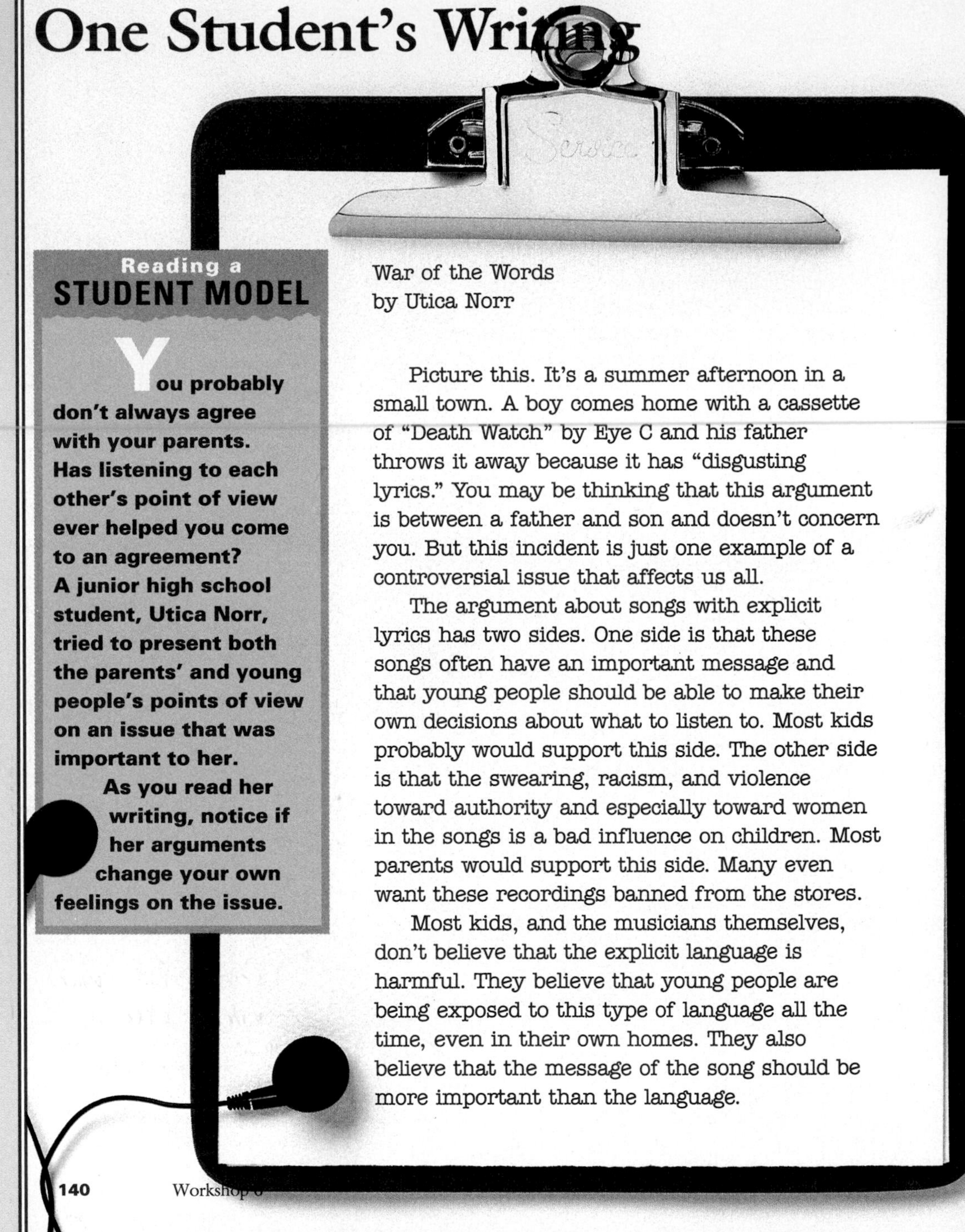

Reading a STUDENT MODEL

You probably don't always agree with your parents. Has listening to each other's point of view ever helped you come to an agreement? A junior high school student, Utica Norr, tried to present both the parents' and young people's points of view on an issue that was important to her.

As you read her writing, notice if her arguments change your own feelings on the issue.

War of the Words
by Utica Norr

Picture this. It's a summer afternoon in a small town. A boy comes home with a cassette of "Death Watch" by Eye C and his father throws it away because it has "disgusting lyrics." You may be thinking that this argument is between a father and son and doesn't concern you. But this incident is just one example of a controversial issue that affects us all.

The argument about songs with explicit lyrics has two sides. One side is that these songs often have an important message and that young people should be able to make their own decisions about what to listen to. Most kids probably would support this side. The other side is that the swearing, racism, and violence toward authority and especially toward women in the songs is a bad influence on children. Most parents would support this side. Many even want these recordings banned from the stores.

Most kids, and the musicians themselves, don't believe that the explicit language is harmful. They believe that young people are being exposed to this type of language all the time, even in their own homes. They also believe that the message of the song should be more important than the language.

Music Connection

Interview Students sometimes think that theirs is the first generation to run afoul of their parents' taste in music. Suggest that they interview their parents or other adults who can tell them about *their* parents' reaction to rock 'n' roll in the 1950s or to the "British invasion" in the 1960s. To understand parents' reactions, students might like to contrast music from these two eras with music from the 1940s.

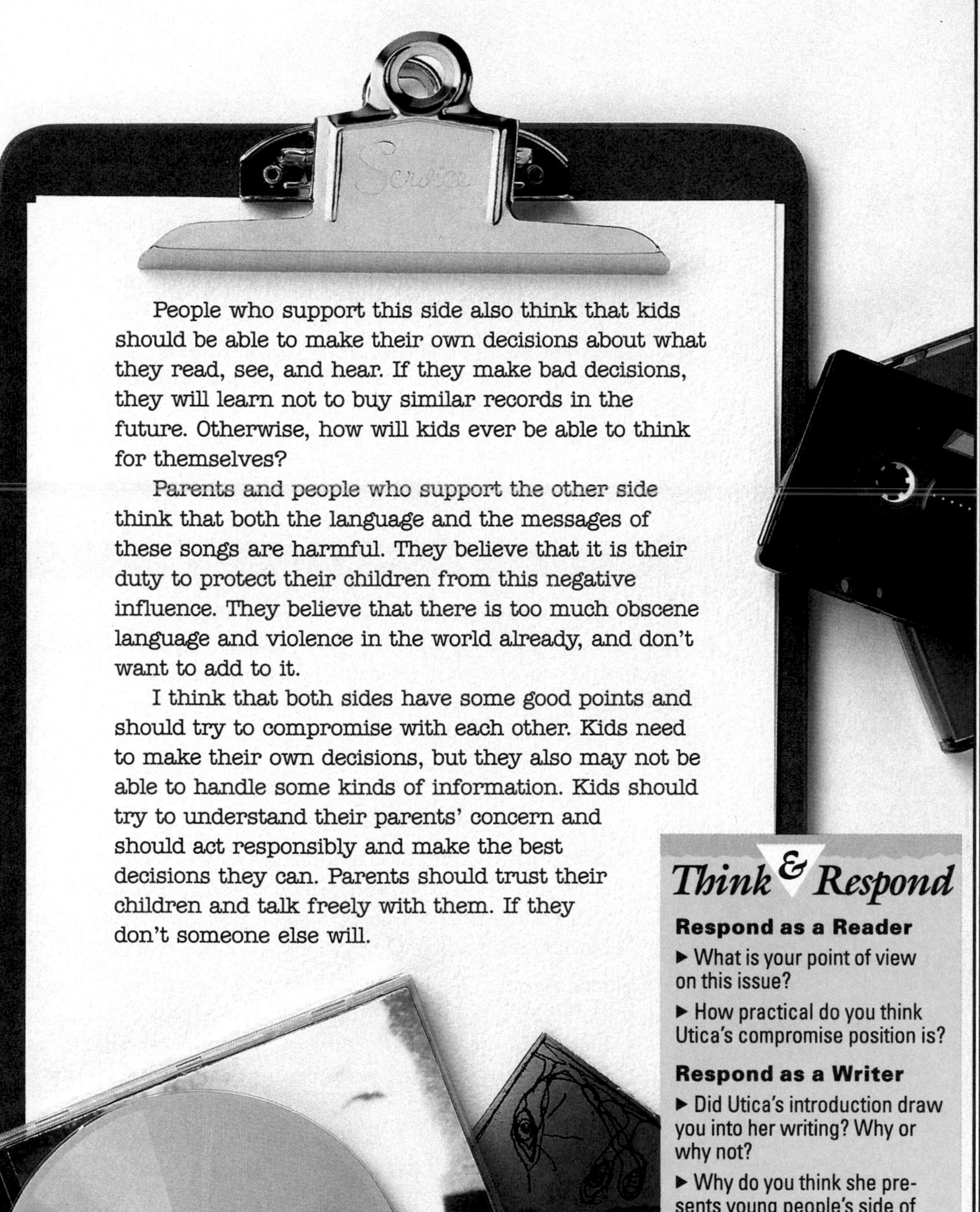

People who support this side also think that kids should be able to make their own decisions about what they read, see, and hear. If they make bad decisions, they will learn not to buy similar records in the future. Otherwise, how will kids ever be able to think for themselves?

Parents and people who support the other side think that both the language and the messages of these songs are harmful. They believe that it is their duty to protect their children from this negative influence. They believe that there is too much obscene language and violence in the world already, and don't want to add to it.

I think that both sides have some good points and should try to compromise with each other. Kids need to make their own decisions, but they also may not be able to handle some kinds of information. Kids should try to understand their parents' concern and should act responsibly and make the best decisions they can. Parents should trust their children and talk freely with them. If they don't someone else will.

Think & Respond

Respond as a Reader

▸ What is your point of view on this issue?

▸ How practical do you think Utica's compromise position is?

Respond as a Writer

▸ Did Utica's introduction draw you into her writing? Why or why not?

▸ Why do you think she presents young people's side of this issue first?

Think & Respond

RESPOND AS A READER

▶ Students might consider why they buy particular CDs or tapes. How important are the lyrics to them? What other factors are involved in making their selections?

▶ Invite a volunteer to restate Utica's compromise position. (Students should be allowed to make their own decisions after they have discussed the issue with their parents and taken into account the parents' concerns.) As you discuss the practicality of the position, stress the word *compromise;* Utica's position certainly will not be practical unless *both* sides are willing to be flexible.

RESPOND AS A WRITER

▶ Students who were drawn into the essay by the introduction might mention that Utica described a scene involving someone their own age and an issue of importance to them.

▶ The author presents the young people's side first because she herself is young and expects her audience to be young also. She supports this side and hopes her audience will too.

Draw Conclusions

Have students list whatever characteristics of persuasive writing they have noted thus far. Responses may include the following:

- clear statement of the topic
- fair and accurate presentation of both sides of the issue
- evidence to support the writer's opinion
- strong introduction and conclusion

MULTICULTURAL Connection

When students think of music from a culture other than their own, they probably think the only difference in the music is the language in which the lyrics are expressed. The differences, however, go much deeper than language. Encourage students to bring in recordings of music that represents their cultural background. Then ask them to discuss the type of music, the instruments, and the occasions on which the music is played. Do young people in other cultures face similar conflicts about music with their parents?

Writing ON YOUR OWN

Remind students that persuasion is an art or skill that people use frequently; then invite them to create their own persuasive piece. As they write, students should recall how Lauren Tarshis and Utica Norr presented both sides fairly and supported their arguments with evidence.

Handbooks for Help and Practice

The following handbooks may be used as mini-lessons before students begin writing or as resources when problems arise.

- **Methods of Elaboration, pp. 255–261**
- **Introductions, pp. 278–280**
- **Conclusions, pp. 281–283**
- **Making Use of the Library, pp. 352–361**
- **Interviewing Skills, p. 362**

PREWRITE AND EXPLORE

Objectives

- To use prewriting techniques to select a controversial topic for a persuasive piece
- To identify a purpose and audience
- To gather evidence for both sides of the issue

Teaching Strategies

for EXPLORING TOPICS

INDIVIDUALIZING INSTRUCTION: SOCIAL LEARNERS Brainstorming with a partner or with a small group to come up with controversial topics and to gather evidence will help students who learn best from interacting with others. Encourage divergent thinking and remind students to reserve judgment during brainstorming.

Writing ON YOUR OWN

Argument

INVITATION TO *Write*

Lauren Tarshis and Utica Norr each explored an issue that was important to her. Both writers persuasively present two sides of a controversial issue. As a result, readers are able to draw their own conclusions.

Examine a controversial issue that interests, concerns, or angers you and write an argument that presents both sides of the issue.

PREWRITE AND EXPLORE

1. Identify a controversial issue. What subject in the news or in your personal life do you and your friends or parents disagree on? Should people who don't recycle be fined? Should community service be a requirement for graduation from high school? The following activities can help you discover an issue you feel strongly about.

Exploring Topics

- **Power play** What if you had the power to change anything you wanted? How would you change your life, your school, the world? **Freewrite** about how people might argue against your ideas and how you would help them see your point of view.
- **Media march** Tune in on important current issues by watching or listening to news or talk shows. Read the editorials and the letters to the editor in your local newspapers. What issues make you want to voice your opinion? **Brainstorm** various sides of these issues with friends.
- **Reading literature** Stories and plays often explore controversial issues. Make a **list** of some issues dealt with in your favorite literary works.

Social Studies Connection

Community Affairs Sometimes students find it easier to get involved in issues close to home, such as the need for a traffic light, stop sign, or better-equipped recreation area. Have students talk with their parents and friends about local concerns. Then have them brainstorm to develop a list of possible topics.

2. Look at your issue from both sides. Once you identify an issue that you want to explore, examine it from all sides. It's important to understand your issue thoroughly. The following activities can help you investigate your issue.

- **Research your issue** Learn what other people think about your subject. You can locate recent magazine articles by using the *Readers' Guide to Periodical Literature* or your library's computerized index. Conducting interviews or taking opinion polls is another way to gather information.
- **Debate your issue** Hold an informal debate or discussion about your subject with a few friends. Have each person take a different position and present arguments to support it. Challenge or offer additional support for each other's statements to make the strongest possible case for each side.

3. Sort your information. Listing the ideas you have gathered about your issue in a chart may help you organize them. Divide a piece of paper in half. In one column list the arguments that support one side of the issue; in the other column list the arguments for the opposing side.

One Student's Process

Utica Norr had been arguing with her parents about the lyrics of a song that she liked. She decided that writing about the issue might help her clarify her own position and understand her parents' point of view better. She made the following chart to organize her ideas.

What I believe	What my parents believe
Songs often have serious messages.	These songs are a bad influence on kids.
Language is not as important as the message.	Kids need to be protected.
Kids hear bad language all the time anyway.	There's enough violence in the world already.
Kids should make their own decisions about what they hear.	Offensive songs should be banned from the stores.

PROBLEM SOLVING

"How can I find support for both sides of my issue?"

To help you find sources of information, see

- Handbook 35, "Making Use of the Library," pages 352–361
- Handbook 36, "Interviewing Skills," page 362

for LOOK AT YOUR ISSUE . . .

KEY TO UNDERSTANDING: TOPIC
Students might need a reminder that a topic for this assignment has to be an issue on which there are at least two reasonable positions. For example, it would be hard to argue *against* eating healthful foods; therefore, a noncontroversial subject such as this would not be a good topic for this assignment.

for LOOK AT YOUR ISSUE . . .

MODELING Give students a brief demonstration about how *you* would examine an issue from both sides. For example, if you chose the issue of adding a period to the school day, you might start by saying: "An additional period could allow students to take a course that is fun, but opponents of this proposal might say that students can have all the fun they want after school. An additional period could allow students to have a study hall, but opponents might say that most students waste their time in study halls."

for SORT YOUR INFORMATION

INDIVIDUALIZING INSTRUCTION: ADVANCED STUDENTS Encourage four students to choose the same topic. Have two students research the *pro* side of the issue and two research the *con* side. Allow students to pool their research for the paper. Later, have them use the research to stage a formal debate for the class.

for ONE STUDENT'S PROCESS

HELPFUL HINT: GRAPHIC DEVICES Point out Utica Norr's balanced presentation of the points in her chart. She is in favor of kids making their own decisions, but she presents the other side fairly.

for ONE STUDENT'S PROCESS

MANAGING THE PAPER LOAD
Check students' lists to be sure that they have chosen an appropriate topic and that they have at least the beginnings of *pro* and *con* arguments. Creating workable lists should make it easier for students to write their persuasive pieces and for you to grade them.

DRAFT AND DISCOVER

Objectives

- To draft a persuasive piece of writing
- To respond to one's own draft and to that of a peer

Teaching Strategies

for START WRITING

STUMBLING BLOCK Audience may be a more important concern in persuasive writing than in any other kind of writing. When writers do not know who the audience is, they cannot infer what kinds of objections the audience might raise. Before students begin drafting, therefore, suggest that they write at the top of their papers whom they expect their audience to be.

for TYPES OF SUPPORT . . .

CRITICAL THINKING: EVALUATING Invite students to study the chart. Discuss questions such as the following: Which kinds of support seem to be the strongest? (facts, statistics) the weakest? (opinions) Why are opinions weak support? (They express personal feelings and can't be proved.)

for TYPES OF SUPPORT . . .

INDIVIDUALIZING INSTRUCTION: VISUAL LEARNERS Encourage these students to use a chart or other graphic device to assess the types of evidence they have gathered to support their arguments.

for SIDE BY SIDE

INDIVIDUALIZING INSTRUCTION: LD STUDENTS Students who have difficulty with organization might do better with a side-by-side approach, which would allow them to present all the evidence for one side of the issue before dealing with the other. Suggest that they cover the second column of their chart as they write about the first side of the issue. When they are ready to write about the other side, they should cover the first column.

Writer's Choice You don't have to continue with a subject just because it's the one you started exploring. If you lose interest in your topic, find another one that interests you more.

DRAFT AND DISCOVER

1. Start writing. You can begin writing any part of your argument that you are comfortable with and have ideas about. At some point you will need to clearly state your issue and its two sides. Some writers find that setting down that statement when they begin writing helps them to focus as they draft.

PROBLEM SOLVING

"What kinds of information can I use to support my arguments?"

For help in developing your writing ideas, see

- Handbook 12, "Methods of Elaboration," pages 255–261

2. Support both sides of the issue. The statements you make about each side of your issue must be backed up by solid evidence. Try to present each side fairly and support it as well as you can. Here are some kinds of evidence you can use.

Types of Support for Arguments

	Definition	Example
Facts	Statements that can be proved	"Death Watch" by Eye C was the best-selling single in 1992.
Statistics	Facts that involve numbers	Over two million copies of the single have been sold.
Incidents and examples	Events or specific cases that illustrate a point	Tim's dad threw away Tim's copy of "Death Watch."
Opinions	Personal feelings or beliefs	Tim's dad thinks the song has disgusting lyrics, but I don't agree.

3. Organize your arguments. You can organize your writing in two basic ways—point by point or side by side.

- **Point by point** Discuss one point from each side of the issue, then the next point from each side, then the next, until you have covered all the points you want to make.
- **Side by side** Discuss all the points on one side of the issue first, then all the points on the other side.

For example, notice that Utica used the side-by-side organization. First she presented all the arguments on the young people's side and then all those on the parents' side.

4. Think about your draft. Are you ready for some feedback, or do you want to continue to work independently? If you want, get the reactions of some friends. Try answering these questions.

REVIEW YOUR WRITING

Questions for Yourself
- What is most important to me about this issue?
- How can I state the argument more clearly?
- What reasons matter most to me?
- Have I presented both sides fairly?

Questions for Your Peer Readers
- What part of my argument seems strongest to you?
- What do you want to know more about?
- What don't you understand about the issue or about my arguments?

One Student's Process

Utica understood the young people's point of view on song lyrics very well, so that's where she began her draft. She wasn't sure how others would react, though, so she decided to ask some classmates for their comments.

Most kids don't believe that the explicit language is harmful. My friend had to ask her older brother what some of the words meant. They also believe that the message of the song should be more important than the language. Also, young people should be able to make their own decisions about what they read, see, and hear. If they make bad decisions, they can learn from their mistakes. Otherwise, how will kids ever be able to think for themselves?

COMPUTER TIP

As you draft your writing, keep your prewriting notes visible on a split screen.

Peer Reader Comments

I think this is your strongest argument.

Don't forget people who think the message is just as bad as the language.

I don't get it. What do they learn from buying offensive music?

for THINK ABOUT YOUR DRAFT

SPEAKING AND LISTENING
Sometimes, before asking for a response from others, writers find it helpful to read aloud to themselves what they have written. When they do not have to consider someone else's response at the same time, students often can hear what doesn't "sound" right in their own draft.

for REVIEW YOUR WRITING

COLLABORATIVE OPPORTUNITY
Encourage students to meet in groups of three or four for feedback. Sometimes what is being said by one student will provoke an unexpected response from another student. When this happens, peer response becomes almost like brainstorming in prewriting, and the results are often more helpful to the writer than the response of only one reader.

for REVIEW YOUR WRITING

PEER RESPONSE Sometimes writers think that their topic is self-evident when, in fact, they haven't stated the issue clearly. Before peer readers answer the questions, suggest that they finish this statement about the writer's piece: "I think you are arguing whether or not ________." If readers cannot finish the statement accurately, the writer can conclude that he or she has not stated the issue clearly.

for ONE STUDENT'S PROCESS

CRITICAL THINKING: ANALYZING
Ask students what other comments they would make about this portion of Utica's draft if she were one of their classmates. (Sample: "I found the sentence about the friend and the older brother confusing. How does it fit in?")

Grammar Connection

In One Student's Process, Utica uses the verbs *read, see,* and *hear* together. Point out this series of words in sentence 4 and ask how the writer separated these words (with commas). Have students refer to the final draft on pages 140–141 to find another example of words in a series (p. 140, paragraph 2: *swearing, racism, and violence toward authority).* You might want to mention that some writers omit a comma before *and* (or another coordinating conjunction in a series), but that a comma is usually preferred, to prevent confusion.

REVISE YOUR WRITING

Objectives

- To evaluate the responses to a persuasive draft and to revise a draft with those responses in mind
- To analyze logical reasoning in a draft
- To evaluate the introduction and conclusion of a draft

Teaching Strategies

for CHECK YOUR REASONING

CRITICAL THINKING: RECOGNIZING LOGICAL FALLACIES Alert students to the hazard of logical fallacies. For example, students who want to use someone's opinion as support for an argument should be sure that the person is an authority. To illustrate, ask students what is wrong with the following statement: "My mathematics teacher says that professional athletes should not be allowed to compete in the Olympics." (Being a mathematics teacher does not make someone an expert on Olympic competitions.) For more information about errors in reasoning, refer students to Handbook 31, pages 337–339.

for PARAGRAPHS AT WORK

CRITICAL THINKING: ANALYZING Each of Utica's paragraphs has a topic sentence. Refer students to pages 140–141 and ask them to identify these sentences. (The topic sentence is the first sentence of each paragraph, except for the first paragraph; in the first paragraph, it is the final sentence.) Invite students to explain the purpose of each paragraph. (The first two paragraphs are introductory, the next two give the young people's side, the fifth paragraph gives the parents' side, and the sixth paragraph is the conclusion.) Encourage students to review their own work for proper paragraphing.

for DECIDE WHICH CHANGES . . .

PEER RESPONSE If students are uncertain about some of the changes they have made, encourage them to share, with a peer or with you, what they have done. Specifically, if they have made a change in response to what another student said, they might want to get a reaction from that student.

REVISE YOUR WRITING

1. Review your responses. Reread your writing and think about your own reactions and your peer readers' responses. How can you strengthen your arguments and the way you present them?

2. Put yourself in your reader's place. Who will be reading your writing? Think about your audience's interests and experience and make sure you have given them enough background information to understand the issue. Remember to define any words that may be unfamiliar to readers.

3. Check your reasoning. Review your writing to see if your explanation of the issue is logical. Have you drawn conclusions based on evidence you've provided? If you state your own opinions, make sure you support them with sufficient facts and examples.

4. Make sure your introduction and conclusion are strong. The beginning and ending of your writing are often the things that stick in readers' minds. Your introduction should make people want to keep reading. A question, surprising fact, or anecdote is a good way to create interest. Your conclusion might summarize the two sides of the issue, restate your position on the issue, invite readers to make up their own minds, or call for some action.

Notice how Utica draws readers into her writing by relating an interesting anecdote. She ends by offering her solution, one that both young people and their parents might support.

Paragraphs at Work In presenting an argument, it is usually a good idea to start a new paragraph for each side or point you present. Also, stating in a topic sentence what each paragraph is about can help readers follow your argument easily. Remember these points.

- You could present each side or point of the argument in a separate paragraph.
- You may want to begin each paragraph with a topic sentence that states the subject of the paragraph.

5. Decide which changes you want to make. Remember that this is *your* work, and you alone decide how to revise it.

PROBLEM SOLVING

"How can I improve my introduction and conclusion?"

For help beginning and ending your writing, see

- Handbook 16, "Introductions," pages 278–280
- Handbook 17, "Conclusions," pages 281–283

Writing TIP

Use transitional words and phrases—for example, *however, nevertheless, on the other hand,* and *in contrast*—to show when you are shifting to another part of your argument.

SPICE BOX

Advertisements sometimes make use of logical fallacies. Consider, for example, the implication that everyone—the "in" group—is buying a product; endorsements by celebrities who are not experts in the field; statements that a product has more or less of some ingredient (more or less than what?); and price comparisons of dissimilar products. All of these approaches use fallacious reasoning.

Bring in some magazine advertisements, or some descriptions of commercials, that illustrate errors in reasoning. Have students discuss how the advertisements use unsound reasoning.

One Student's Process

After thinking about her peer readers' comments and her own reactions to her draft, Utica made the following changes to her draft.

Most kids [, and the musicians themselves,] don't believe that the explicit language is harmful. ~~My friend had to ask her older brother what some of the words meant.~~ [They believe that young people are being exposed to this type of language all the time, even in their own homes.] They also believe that the message of the song should be more important than the language. ~~Also,~~

¶ [People who support this side think that kids] ~~young people~~ should be able to make their own decisions about what they read, see, and hear. If they make bad decisions, they ~~can~~ [will] learn ~~from their mistakes~~ [not to buy similar records in the future]. Otherwise, how will kids ever be able to think for themselves?

for ILLUSTRATION

COLLABORATIVE OPPORTUNITY Invite small groups of students to discuss the meaning of the illustration and its relationship to Utica's draft. (The figures stand for "see no evil, hear no evil, speak no evil." It is appropriate because it touches on the idea that students "should be able to make their own decisions about what they read, see, and hear." It also may illustrate the view that young people should not read, talk about, or listen to so-called evil lyrics.)

for ONE STUDENT'S PROCESS

CRITICAL THINKING: DRAWING CONCLUSIONS How to revise a draft is up to the individual. Ask students to suggest why Utica revised the sentence that begins "If they make. . . ." (A peer reader had asked what students learn from buying offensive music. Utica made the sentence more specific.)

GENERAL NOTE

INDIVIDUALIZING INSTRUCTION: BASIC STUDENTS These students might have difficulty in making their writing flow from one idea to the next. Suggest that they underline transition words and use Handbook 15, pages 273–276, to help themselves clarify relationships among ideas.

PROOFREAD

Teaching Strategies

for LINKING GRAMMAR AND WRITING

HELPFUL HINT: CONNOTATION

To help students understand the connotative power of words, write the word *odor* on the board. Have students brainstorm nouns that are synonyms for *odor.* (Samples: *smell, stench, aroma, stink, scent*) Then have students classify the nouns according to neutral, positive, or negative connotations. (Answers may vary, but students probably will say, neutral: *odor, smell;* positive: *aroma, scent;* negative: *stench, stink.*) If students are having difficulty in classifying the words, suggest that they use each in a sentence.

for LINKING GRAMMAR AND WRITING

INDIVIDUALIZING INSTRUCTION: ESL STUDENTS The loaded adjectives often used in persuasive writing can create a problem for ESL students, who are not always aware of the connotations of English words. Pair ESL students with native English speakers to help them determine the best choice when connotation is an issue.

Guidelines for Evaluation

IDEAS AND CONTENT

- states the issue clearly
- presents both sides fairly
- uses logical evidence to support the writer's view
- shows an awareness of the emotional power of word choices

STRUCTURE AND FORM

- has an attention-getting introduction and a strong conclusion
- uses paragraphs effectively

GRAMMAR, USAGE, AND MECHANICS

- displays standard grammar, usage, spelling, and mechanics
- uses commas to separate words in a series

PROOFREAD

1. Proofread your work. Errors in grammar, capitalization, punctuation, and spelling can confuse readers and weaken the impact of your argument. Double-check your writing for accuracy.

LINKING GRAMMAR AND WRITING

Avoiding Loaded Adjectives

Adjectives are powerful words, and they can sway readers to one side or the other of an argument. For example, saying someone is "brave" would be a compliment, while calling the same person "foolhardy," "rash," or "reckless" would be an insult. When choosing adjectives, pay attention to their **connotations,** the emotional associations people make with words.

Notice how Utica replaced a loaded adjective with a more neutral one when she revised her writing.

Original

One side is that these songs often have an incredible message and that young people should be able to make their own decisions.

Revised

One side is that these songs often have an important message and that young people should be able to make their own decisions.

For more information on the connotations of words and using adjectives correctly, see Handbook 25, "Meaning and Word Choice," pages 314–315 and Handbook 43, "Using Modifiers," pages 505–533.

2. Make a clean copy of your work. Are you satisfied with your writing now? If so, do a final check of the content using the Standards for Evaluation shown in the margin and decide if you want to make any additional changes. Then make a final copy.

Standards for Evaluation

PERSUASIVE WRITING

An argument

- describes the issue clearly
- supports the writer's position with good evidence
- treats both sides fairly
- has a logical organization
- uses appropriate language for the audience
- concludes strongly with a summary of the issue, the writer's position, or a call for action

PROFESSIONAL NOTEBOOK

Advice from the Authors Sometimes students think that once they have revised a piece, they are finished with the writing process. They believe that fine-tuning their language is unnecessary. Of this stage Peter Elbow says: "You have a newly written draft that says what you want to say in the right order. Nevertheless it is liable to be imprecise, wordy, and awkward. You need to stop being the writer and read over your draft with the fresh eyes of a reader. The best way is to put it aside for a while and then to read it over out loud."

Peter Elbow, *Writing with Power*

PUBLISH AND PRESENT

- **Submit your argument as a letter to the editor.** Share your ideas with a general audience by submitting your writing to your local or school newspaper for publication.
- **Present your argument as a pamphlet.** Design and produce a pamphlet based on your writing. Distribute it to an organization that is interested in your issue.
- **Stage a debate.** Working with a friend, choose a controversial issue you both care about and stage a debate for your class. Then hold a class discussion in which students vote for one side of the argument, explaining the reasons for their choices.

Warning:
This Album May Contain
EXPLICIT LYRICS
Parental Supervision
Is Advised

REFLECT ON YOUR WRITING

FOR YOUR PORTFOLIO

1. Add your writing to your portfolio. Now that you have read two arguments and written one of your own, think about what you have learned. Write a paragraph or two that focuses on your writing process and attach it to your final piece. The following questions may help you focus your thinking.

- How did I decide on which issue to write about?
- What did I learn about myself or about my beliefs as I explored this issue?
- What was hardest for me about doing this kind of writing? What was easiest?
- Did I fairly present the side of the issue I don't agree with?
- What comments from my peers were most helpful? What kinds of help would I ask for next time?
- What did I learn about writing that I could use in completing other writing assignments?

2. Explore additional writing ideas. See the suggestions for writing a social action letter on pages 152–154 and Springboards on page 159.

Reteaching

Assess the needs of students who were not successful in developing an effective argument; then assign the appropriate handbook mini-lessons, as well as the Workshop Support Materials listed in the Teaching Preview, pages 135a–135b. Concepts commonly requiring reteaching for this assignment are:

- **Handbook 12, Methods of Elaboration, pp. 255–261**
- **Handbook 17, Conclusions, pp. 281–283**

The following suggestions and resources also may be useful.

One-Sided Presentation Have students work in pairs on the Writing Resource Book "Examining Both Sides of an Issue," on page 32. Have each student take turns generating facts, opinions, examples, reasons, and so on to support one side of the issue. Encourage students to keep an open mind and think creatively about both positions.

Lack of Evidence Have students work in a small group on "Persuasion: Elaboration," page 11, of the Elaboration, Revision, and Proofreading Practice copymasters. Students can work together to add details to support the issue in the paragraph.

Extension and Enrichment

1. Supply this scenario: You have just developed a new kind of shoe for middle and junior high school students. Create an advertisement that will persuade young people to buy the shoes.
2. Have students imagine that their families are going to buy a car. The adults want a four-door sedan; the students want a sports car. Have students argue for the sports car, taking into account the adults' position.

Closure: Reflect on Your Writing

After students have written about their writing process, suggest that they go back and look at some of the other responses in their portfolios. Encourage them to think about the answers to these questions: How was this response different from their previous responses? In what ways was it the same? What kind of writing have they enjoyed the most?

Related ASSIGNMENT

Reading a SOCIAL ACTION LETTER

Objectives

- To respond to and analyze a social action letter
- To choose a topic, identify an audience, and determine a form for a social action letter
- To draft, revise, and send a social action letter

Motivate

Before students begin reading, ask them how they would respond to the following situation: A local restaurant often has a surplus of food. This surplus consists of vegetables and fruits that look less than fresh after three or four days but are still fresh enough to eat. It also consists of day-old rolls and bread. Every evening at 10:30, a truck pulls up to the back door of the restaurant, and the leftover food is transported to the city dump. (Students probably will mention that this is a waste of food; they may suggest that the food could be used to feed hungry people.)

BUILD ON PRIOR KNOWLEDGE

Invite students to share what they know about disposal of hazardous waste. Has their community faced an emergency related to such materials? How would students feel if part of their area had been selected as a disposal site?

SET A PURPOSE

After students read Reading a Social Action Letter, remind them that in the Guided Assignment, they studied what makes a good argument. As they read Jennica's letter, have them evaluate her arguments.

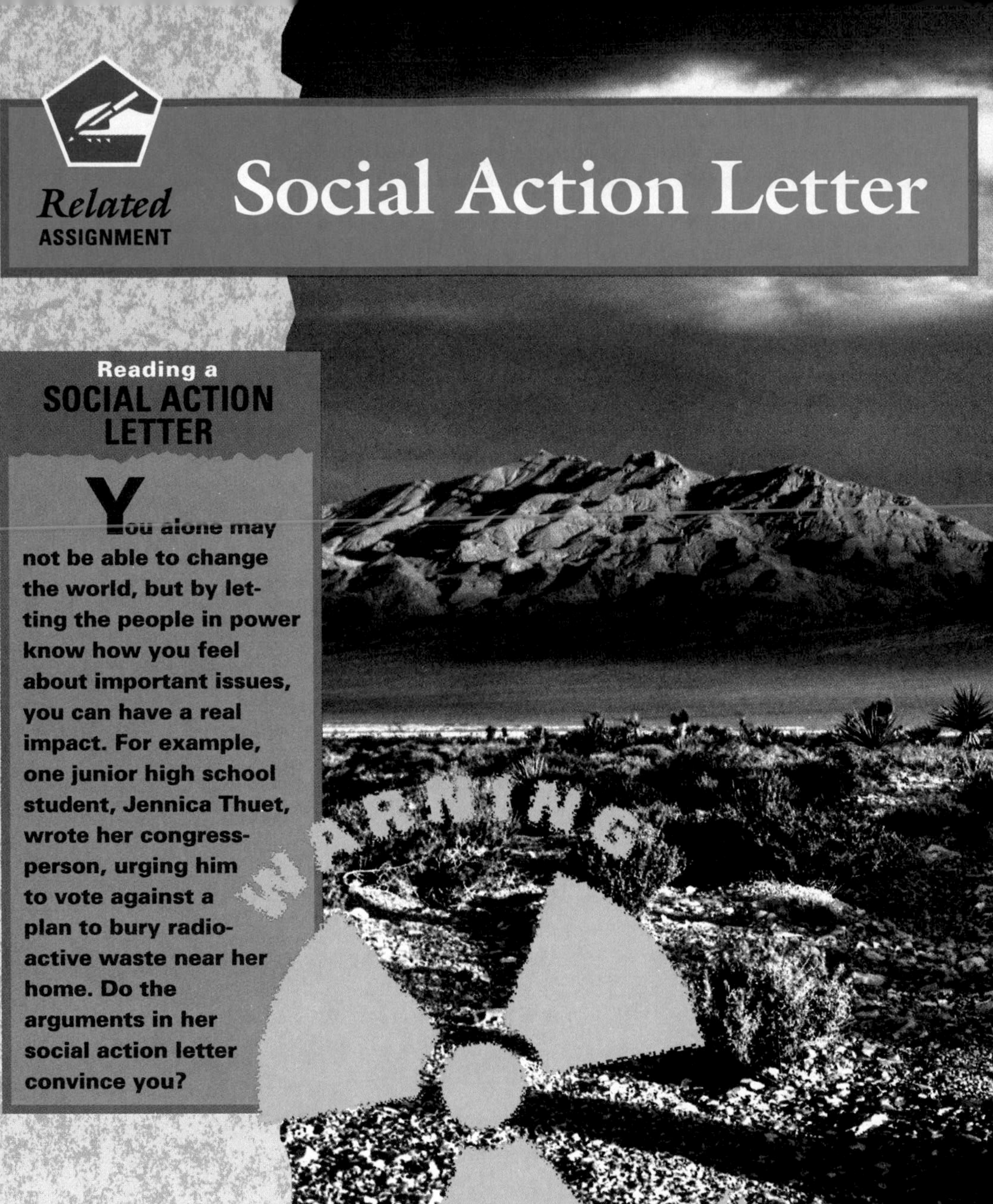

Related ASSIGNMENT

Social Action Letter

Reading a SOCIAL ACTION LETTER

You alone may not be able to change the world, but by letting the people in power know how you feel about important issues, you can have a real impact. For example, one junior high school student, Jennica Thuet, wrote her congressperson, urging him to vote against a plan to bury radioactive waste near her home. Do the arguments in her social action letter convince you?

150 Workshop 6

for FURTHER READING

Book to Read To write a social action letter, students must take a stand on an issue. One book that might help them clarify their beliefs and feelings is *Ethics* by Susan Neiburg Terkel. The author aims her book at middle- and high-school students, encouraging them to make up their own minds about important issues.

MULTICULTURAL Connection

Encourage students to identify issues that are important to their culture and to think about responding to one of these in a social action letter. Some of these issues might include land disputes involving Native Americans, restrictions on immigration, or busing to achieve integration.

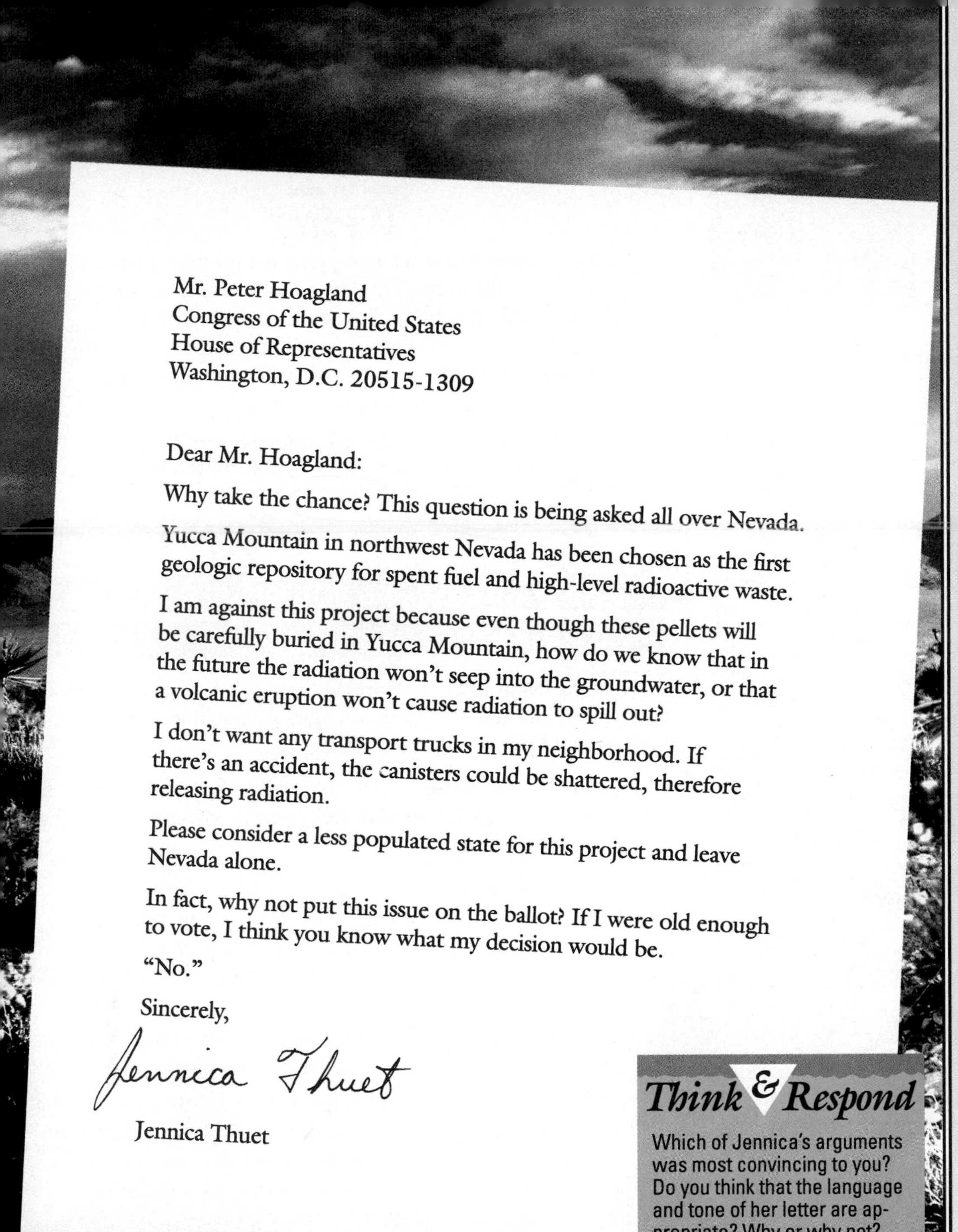

Mr. Peter Hoagland
Congress of the United States
House of Representatives
Washington, D.C. 20515-1309

Dear Mr. Hoagland:

Why take the chance? This question is being asked all over Nevada.

Yucca Mountain in northwest Nevada has been chosen as the first geologic repository for spent fuel and high-level radioactive waste.

I am against this project because even though these pellets will be carefully buried in Yucca Mountain, how do we know that in the future the radiation won't seep into the groundwater, or that a volcanic eruption won't cause radiation to spill out?

I don't want any transport trucks in my neighborhood. If there's an accident, the canisters could be shattered, therefore releasing radiation.

Please consider a less populated state for this project and leave Nevada alone.

In fact, why not put this issue on the ballot? If I were old enough to vote, I think you know what my decision would be.

"No."

Sincerely,

Jennica Thuet

Jennica Thuet

Think & Respond

Which of Jennica's arguments was most convincing to you? Do you think that the language and tone of her letter are appropriate? Why or why not?

Think & Respond

ELICIT PERSONAL RESPONSES

Because the issue of how to dispose of hazardous waste is often in the news, suggest that students freewrite their personal response before discussing the issue. Then focus attention on the first question in the Think & Respond box. Have students **explain** what makes the chosen argument convincing. You might also suggest that students **speculate** about why Jennica addressed her letter to a member of Congress rather than to the President or to a newspaper editor. (A representative is interested in state issues and has the power to fight for them.)

EXPLORE THE AUTHOR'S TECHNIQUES

The second question addresses language and tone. Students should note that the language is appropriate for Jennica's audience. Because she is writing to a government official, she does not simplify the language, and she uses the appropriate terms ("first geologic repository for spent fuel and high-level radioactive waste"). Her tone is straightforward, bordering on conversational. She uses contractions as in a conversation.

Some students may object to the contractions and say that the tone should be more formal—a valid point. Jennica apparently believed, however, that she could get her representative's attention by "talking" as someone her age would. Remind students that they may want to make decisions about the language they will use and the tone they will take, before they begin to write.

Writing ON YOUR OWN

Review the strong points of Jennica's letter (an attention-getting opening sentence; a firm stand supported by examples). Suggest that students use these same techniques as they write their social action letters.

Handbooks for Help and Practice

The following handbooks may be used as mini-lessons before students begin writing or as resources when problems arise.

- **Meaning and Word Choice, pp. 314–315**
- **Developing a Personal Voice, pp. 316–317**

Teaching Strategies

for STOP, LOOK, AND LISTEN

HELPFUL HINT: TOPIC Some students may have difficulty in selecting a topic because they don't like to get involved or to draw attention to themselves. They find it scary to take a public stand on an issue. Assure these students that people in high positions are used to getting mail. If students still are not convinced, suggest that they choose a topic—and thus an audience—that is less "scary," perhaps an issue in the classroom.

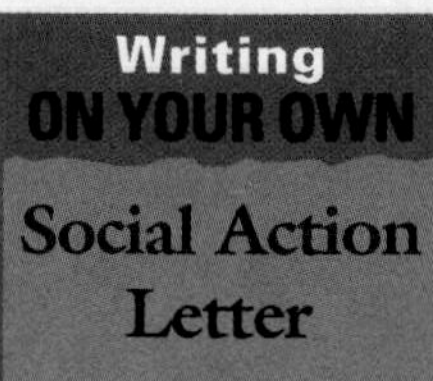

Jennica Thuet wrote a letter to her congressional representative to try to prevent the mountains near her home from becoming a dumping ground for radioactive waste. Writing gives you power. With well-chosen words directed to the right people, you, too, can help bring about changes in your world.

Choose an issue that is important to you. Write a social action letter to a public official stating your concern and calling for action.

DISCOVERING AND EXPLORING YOUR ISSUE

1. Find an issue that matters to you. What social issues do you care deeply about? You might start by thinking of events that have touched your own life.

2. Stop, look, and listen. The advice that helped you cross the street safely as a child can also help you discover an issue that demands social action.

- **Stop** and think about social action organizations you have heard about—Greenpeace or Students Against Drunk Driving, for example. You might brainstorm as a class to come up with a list of these groups. Then check the library or write to each group for more information.
- **Look** in the newspaper for articles about issues that concern you. Write your reactions to them in your journal.
- **Listen** to your friends and family talk about events that had a major impact on their lives. Share your own experiences, too. Did someone's child get lead poisoning from eating peeling paint? Was someone's life saved by using a seat belt? Try freewriting about one of these issues.

Science Connection

Advances in scientific knowledge often lead to new controversies. For example, although measles vaccines are a highly effective means of preventing the childhood disease, researchers have discovered that young women who were vaccinated as children do not pass on a strong immunity to their infants, and that more infants are getting measles. Another example is that rock salt is used on icy roads, but researchers have discovered that the chemical seeps into the ground, polluting wells and reservoirs. Discuss these and other science-related topics to help students find an issue to write about.

3. Explore your issue. Try these techniques.

- **Loop it.** Freewrite for five minutes about your issue. Pick out the most important thought or feeling in that writing. Use that idea as the basis for another freewriting loop, and so on. Keep looping until you have enough ideas to work with.
- **Talk it over.** Discuss your issue in a small group. Take notes during the discussion and, later, freewrite about your ideas.

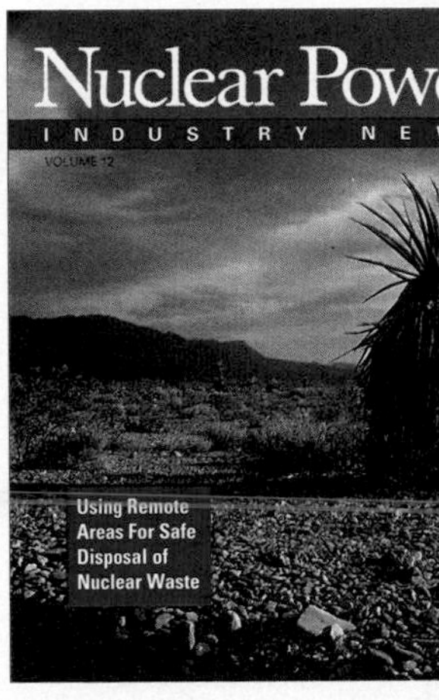

PLANNING AND DRAFTING YOUR LETTER

1. Think about your audience. A social action letter expresses your personal feelings and calls for action. To be effective, however, it must be addressed to the person or group with authority to act on the issue. The following chart should help you direct your letter to the appropriate people.

Social Action Letter

Audience	Type of Issue	Form of Letter
Government or corporate officials	Laws or business policies (a factory dumps harmful wastes into a river)	Business letter to an individual
Citizens of your community	Community activities (a neighborhood watch program may prevent crime)	Open letter or petition
Family and friends	Family or neighborhood concerns (an empty lot can become a playground)	Personal letter or flyer

Writer's Choice Do you want to get together with other students and write a letter collaboratively? You could also write the letter on your own and ask others to join you in signing it. The choice is yours.

2. Start writing. Once you have some ideas about your issue, begin putting them down on paper. You may already have some freewriting or prewriting notes that can help get you started. Don't worry if you still have questions about your issue—your opinions may still be valid.

for EXPLORE YOUR ISSUE

INDIVIDUALIZING INSTRUCTION: ESL STUDENTS ESL students may find freewriting laborious because they cannot think fast enough in English. Invite these students to tape their thoughts in their first languages. As they play back their thoughts, they can choose the ideas they wish to develop in English.

for THINK ABOUT YOUR AUDIENCE

CRITICAL THINKING: ANALYZING
Once students have reviewed the chart on the pupil page, have them discuss the tone and language that is usually appropriate for use with each group (government official: formal, use of sophisticated vocabulary; citizens: informal, use of local jargon; friends: conversational tone and language). Remind students that they, as writers, have to make their own decisions and might have a good reason for choosing a different tone, as Jennica did.

for WRITER'S CHOICE

COLLABORATIVE OPPORTUNITY
An open letter makes a good small-group project. You can broaden the project by suggesting that each student in the group express in a different way the ideas the group has generated. (One student might write an open letter, another student might write a skit based on the group's ideas, and a third student might create a storyboard or poster.) Alternatively, you can suggest that students figure out a general format in which they can present many related pieces. For example, they might present an hour of television around one issue, complete with skits that dramatize the various points of view, news breaks, and station editorials.

for START WRITING

HELPFUL HINT Before students begin writing, remind them that they not only need to express an opinion, they also need to tell their audience—an audience with the power to change things—what action to take.

TEACHER'S LOUNGE

"I look at the clock. Time to begin.

"'Back. Back, I say!' I brandish an imaginary sword over the students clustered around my desk. They laugh and scatter toward their assigned seats. 'Everyone take a seat, please.' A commanding appearance belies my own inner feeling of disorientation. I stand before the assembled class and look out over their expectant faces. Four silent questions form in my mind: Which class is this? What am I supposed to teach them? Where am I? When can *I* go to the bathroom?"

James Nehring, *"Why Do We Gotta Do This Stuff, Mr. Nehring?"*

for REVIEWING YOUR LETTER

ASSESSMENT: SPOT CHECK Before students ask for peer or teacher response, suggest that they attach to their papers a note with one or two questions they would like answered about their draft. This note can help direct both you and other students to areas of the paper that may need strengthening before the student writes the final draft.

for PROOFREAD YOUR LETTER

PEER RESPONSE Because, in many cases, these letters will be mailed to people outside the school system, you might suggest that students ask for a second peer response after revising. This time students should read each other's letters as editors, focusing on the proper format of a letter and on other mechanical details.

Guidelines for Evaluation

AN EFFECTIVE SOCIAL ACTION LETTER

- is directed to an appropriate audience
- takes a strong stand on an issue
- supports the position with facts or examples
- uses language and tone effectively
- proposes a course of action
- follows the format and conventions of a letter

for PUBLISHING AND PRESENTING . . .

HELPFUL HINT Some students may have written to a government or corporate official for whom they do not have an address. Direct these students to the school or local library. The librarian or media specialist will show them which reference materials contain the addresses they need.

3. Support your statements. Be sure to support your position on the issue with convincing evidence. Presenting facts, statistics, and the opinions of experts can help persuade people to take the action you recommend.

Reviewing Your Letter

1. Reread your draft. Look over your writing to be sure you have included all the important points you want to make. Your letter should clearly state the issue and your position on it. You might want to ask several classmates to respond to your work and to offer additional arguments you could use to support your case.

2. Focus on the action. Your letter should tell the addressee exactly what action you want him or her to take on your issue. Notice how Jennica ended her letter with a call to action—and a very personal reason why her congressperson might want to comply.

3. Proofread your letter. Factual or grammatical errors in your letter can prevent people from taking it seriously. Before making a clean copy, be sure that your facts, grammar, capitalization, punctuation, and spelling are correct. Also check to be sure you have addressed the appropriate person or organization and that you have the correct mailing address.

PROBLEM SOLVING

"How do I set up my letter?"

For correct letter format, see

- Appendix, page 684

Publishing and Presenting Your Letter

- **Mail it.** If you've written to a government or corporate official, just drop your letter in the mail. Be sure to include your return address and to keep a copy for yourself.
- **Display it.** If you've written an open letter to your school or community, display it on a poster. Create an eye-catching layout and headings for your letter. Use colors and illustrations or photographs to enhance the content.
- **Read it aloud.** If you've written an open letter to friends or people in the community, read it aloud at an informal gathering.

PROFESSIONAL NOTEBOOK

Patricia Grabill of Leo Junior/Senior High School in Indiana tells what happened when her students mailed out social action letters: "Several students told me that they did not expect a response because no one cared what they thought. They were not old enough to vote, they did not have any money, and they did not have any prestige. . . . I believe that people who write well have power, and I told them that. . . .

"The response was overwhelming. Of the thirty-seven students who wrote letters, only seven of them received no response."

English Journal, "Writing the *Real* Persuasion"

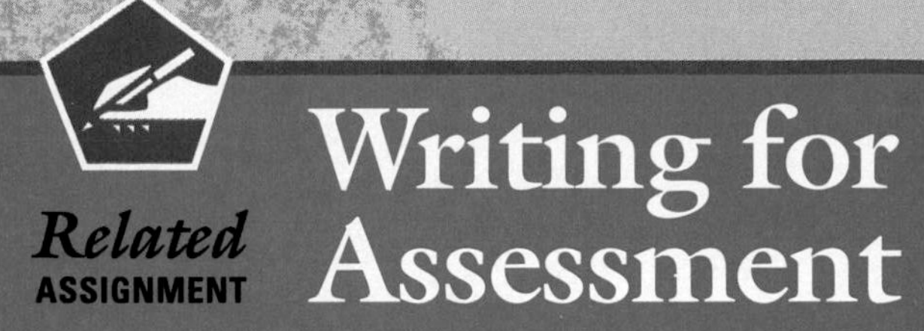

Related ASSIGNMENT

Writing for Assessment

Tests. Nobody likes them, but everybody has to take them. Knowing what to expect on a test, however, can help you do your best. There are basically two types of tests. In one type, you are asked to write an essay to show your knowledge of a school subject, like history or science. In the other type of test, a *writing assessment,* you must write to express your own thoughts or feelings.

Look at the two essay-test questions and two prompts for a writing assessment on this page. What key words tell you what you are expected to do?

- ***Health*** In a short composition, explain the health risks of smoking. Include facts and examples that show the risks to both smokers and the people around them.

- ***English*** Choose a character from *The Red Pony* who changes in some important way during the story. Write at least three paragraphs describing the causes of the change and its effects on the character.

- ***Writing Assessment*** Imagine that the magazine *Awesome Audio* has asked readers to submit statements endorsing their favorite piece of audio equipment. Write a letter to the editor describing your favorite piece of equipment and tell why it is important to you.

- ***Writing Assessment*** Imagine that your city has a new law that all bicycle riders must wear helmets. Supporters say that the law will reduce injuries. Others say that helmets are costly and confining. Write an editorial for your local newspaper expressing your opinion on this issue.

Literature Connection

Teachers generally ask essay questions to elicit specific facts about a subject area, but occasionally a teacher will give a more open-ended prompt. Interested students might enjoy responding to these literature prompts:

- Imagine that the author of a book you enjoy is thinking about changing the setting. Help the author choose a new setting for the story. Explain how the new setting affects one of the characters.
- Imagine that the main character of a story you like is running for class president. Write a speech in support of the candidate.

Related ASSIGNMENT

Starting from QUESTIONS AND PROMPTS

Objectives

- To interpret an essay question that calls for knowledge of a school subject, and an essay prompt that asks for opinions and beliefs
- To plan, write, and revise an essay response to a prompt that asks for opinions and beliefs

Motivate

Ask students whether they usually feel confident when they are about to take a test. Ask them which they prefer to take: a test that has one-word answers or a test that has essay questions. As students respond, tell them that they will learn some strategies that will make taking essay tests easier.

BUILD ON PRIOR KNOWLEDGE

Invite students to share examples of essay questions that they remember from tests in other subject areas. Ask them to explain what they thought made each question easy or hard to answer. Discuss what makes answering an essay question difficult. (Samples: Focusing on what is being asked, thinking of specific details, and worrying about time)

SET A PURPOSE

Have students read the boxed introduction to find out about the two basic kinds of writing tests: essay and writing assessment. Then ask a volunteer to describe the sample Writing Assessment prompts. (Ask the writer to express both thoughts and feelings on a matter of opinion.)

Writing ON YOUR OWN

Tell students that the writing assessment examples on the preceding page are the types of prompts they are likely to see on standardized tests. In this assignment they will learn how to write effective responses to such a prompt.

Handbooks for Help and Practice

The following handbooks may be used as mini-lessons before students begin writing or as resources when problems arise.

- **Effective Paragraphs, pp. 244–247**
- **Coherence, pp. 273–277**
- **Critical Thinking and Writing, pp. 337–339**

Teaching Strategies

for IDENTIFY THE IMPORTANT INFORMATION

CRITICAL THINKING: GENERALIZING Have students compare the Health and English questions with Writing Assessment prompts. What generalization can students make about the audience for each type of writing prompt? (Sample: The audience for essay tests on school subjects is usually the teacher; the audience for writing on a standardized test is often stated or implied in the prompt.)

for LOOK FOR KEY WORDS

HELPFUL HINT Students sometimes have difficulty with essay questions because they don't know how to analyze the prompt. Have students study the chart and then apply the information about the key words and strategies to the topics on the preceding page. (Health: key word—*explain;* English: key words—*causes, effects;* Writing Assessment 1: *endorsing, describing;* Writing Assessment 2: *expressing your opinion)*

Writing

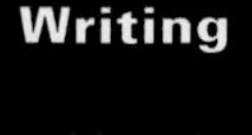

INVITATION TO Write

Test taking can make you panic—or it can be your chance to shine. Knowing how to analyze test questions and learning how to respond to them can help you relax and do your best on any type of test.

Following the directions in the fourth prompt on page 155, express your views in an editorial.

ANALYZING THE PROMPT

1. Identify the important information. Writing prompts tell you what you are being asked to do on the test. As you read a prompt, look especially for these three pieces of information:

- what you'll write about—topic
- whom you'll write for—audience
- the form your writing will take—format

2. Look for key words. Prompts also include key words that suggest the best writing strategies to use. Some of these words and strategies are shown below.

Key Words	Strategy
Describe, define	Identify main qualities; give specific facts or sensory details about each.
Narrate, tell how, trace the steps, describe the process	Tell sequence of events or steps in a process in chronological order.
Explain, analyze, compare, contrast, show causes and effects	Present the main points of a topic. Develop each point with facts, examples, or other specific details.
Persuade, convince, give reasons, express your opinion	State your point of view and support it with facts, examples or anecdotes.

SPICE BOX

To help students think quickly, form them into small groups. Then give students a statement such as "CDs are better than cassettes" or "Ice skating is superior to roller skating." Have students generate reasons to support the statement. The first group to generate five solid reasons will be the winner.

Social Studies Connection

Time Line Remind students that the chart is meant to be a guide and does not contain all the strategies they might use to develop a prompt. For example, historical questions often involve tracing a series of events. A logical strategy to use in such a case is a time line.

PLANNING YOUR RESPONSE

1. Budget your time. For example, on a thirty-minute writing test, you might prewrite for ten minutes, draft for fifteen minutes, and revise and proofread during the last five minutes.

2. Do some prewriting. A list, cluster, or quick freewriting can help you gather your thoughts. Keep in mind the strategy suggested by the prompt. For example, if you need to write a description, list the subject's characteristics and note sensory details.

3. Organize your thoughts. Make an informal outline or numbered list of your main ideas.

One Student's Process

Clifford Merrill decided to respond to the third writing prompt. He analyzed the prompt, then planned his response.

Topic: Favorite audio equipment; Audience: Audio magazine readers; Form: Letter to editor; Strategy: Describe equipment, tell what it means to me and why.

1. General statement—My tape player's the best.
2. Descriptive details
3. Uses—a) relaxing after school b) listening with friends, sharing new music.

DRAFTING YOUR RESPONSE

1. Jump right in. Get to the point immediately. You might begin with a one- or two-sentence summary of your answer. Then cover the points in your prewriting list or outline. Be sure to include specific details, facts, or examples about each point.

2. Stick to the point. Cover each of your main ideas in a separate paragraph and make sure that every sentence in the paragraph relates to that idea. Use transitional words between paragraphs to link your ideas.

PROBLEM SOLVING

"What is the most logical order in which to present my ideas?"

For help in organizing your response logically, see

- Handbook 15, "Coherence," pages 273–277

GENERAL NOTE

CRITICAL THINKING: COMPARING AND CONTRASTING Although both a workshop assignment and a writing prompt on a test have the same end product—a finished piece of writing—there are many differences in the ways in which students go about creating them. Invite students to compare the two processes. (Workshop assignment: Students usually can choose their own topics; take time for careful planning, drafting, and revising of their papers; and get feedback from others along the way. Writing prompt on a test: A topic is usually assigned, a strict time limit is enforced, and no collaboration is permitted.)

for DO SOME PREWRITING

INDIVIDUALIZING INSTRUCTION: SOCIAL LEARNERS These students may find this type of assignment particularly frustrating because they enjoy working in a group situation. As students plan their response, circulate through the classroom, paying particular attention to the effectiveness of the individual planning strategies of these students.

for ONE STUDENT'S PROCESS

HELPFUL HINT: ORGANIZING TECHNIQUES Clifford Merrill's outline is easy to follow, and it contains the important points he wants to make. Students might want to follow his format. Which headings would they need to change, and why? ("Descriptive details" and "Uses," because an editorial requires opinions and supporting evidence)

for JUMP RIGHT IN

HELPFUL HINT: THESIS Tell students that a strong essay usually has a statement of the writer's purpose in the introductory paragraph. Likewise, somewhere in the introduction to an editorial, the writer usually takes a position on an issue. Urge students to state their position on bicycle helmets early in their written responses.

PROFESSIONAL NOTEBOOK

Advice from the Authors Most students think of outlining as a prewriting activity. In *Practical Ideas for Teaching Writing as a Process,* Sheridan Blau offers this suggestion:

"Most of the revising and editing tricks that experienced teachers are fond of showing to their students also entail metaprocessing. One such trick is to have students outline drafts of their essays after they finish them. From such an outline students can gain new perspectives on the structure of their essays—on the relative emphasis they have given to main and subordinate points and on the progression of their arguments."

for REVIEWING YOUR RESPONSE

HELPFUL HINT Because peer response is not possible in a true testing situation, you might want students to do their own reviewing. Suggest that students compare their outline or list with their draft to see whether they included all the points they wanted to cover.

GENERAL NOTE

MANAGING THE PAPER LOAD In a true testing situation, the content and development of a response are usually considered more important than the mechanics—unless errors in mechanics interfere with the paper as a whole. Therefore, you might want to grade these papers holistically.

Guidelines for Evaluation

AN EFFECTIVE EDITORIAL

- takes a strong stand on an issue
- supports the position with facts or examples
- uses a separate paragraph to introduce and support each point
- use language and a tone appropriate for the audience
- concludes with a summary or restatement of the main idea
- follows the conventions of grammar, punctuation, and spelling

GENERAL NOTE

ASSESSMENT Give students periodic practice in writing from prompts. For additional prompts, see "Writing Prompts" in the Tests and Writing Assessment Prompts booklet in the Teacher's Resource File. Encourage students to date their samples and keep them in their writing folders. By comparing the length and quality of each student's responses, you and the students will have an indicator of growing ability to elaborate.

3. Write a strong conclusion. You might summarize the points you have made or restate your main idea in a different way.

REVIEWING YOUR RESPONSE

1. Reread the prompt. Have you answered the questions fully? Make any changes between the lines or in the margins.

2. Proofread your work. Check your grammar, capitalization, punctuation, and spelling and correct any errors.

One Student's Process

Here's how Clifford's test paper looked when he had finished.

To the Editor, Awesome Audio magazine:

You can stop looking right now. No piece of audio equipment can beat my tape player.

It's not really much to look at. It has the basics—a handle, a row of buttons, an earphone jack, a microphone, and a cassette holder. It also has powerful speakers despite their compact size.

Looks mean very little to me, however. It's the music it plays that's more important. I listen to tapes every day after school and on the weekends with my friends. We trade tapes and record new ones, telling jokes or stories. The player is portable, so it goes where I go. That's why my tape player means so much to me.

Sincerely,

Clifford Merrill

Grammar Connection

Students sometimes confuse possessive pronouns and contractions. Point out that Clifford originally used the possessive pronoun *its* when he meant *it's* or *it is* (paragraph 3, line 1). Other confusing pairs are *your/you're* and *their/they're.*

Refer students who have difficulty with this skill to Handbook 41, "Possessive Pronouns and Contractions," pages 445–446.

Springboards

Literature

Think of a character in a short story, poem, or novel who chooses between two different courses of action. Explain why you agree or disagree with the character's choice.

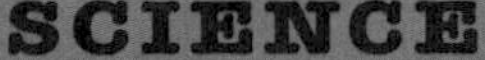

SCIENCE

Some scientists now believe that we cannot save all endangered plant and animal species because we don't have the money or the technology. Write an editorial that either sides with the scientists or proposes a different approach.

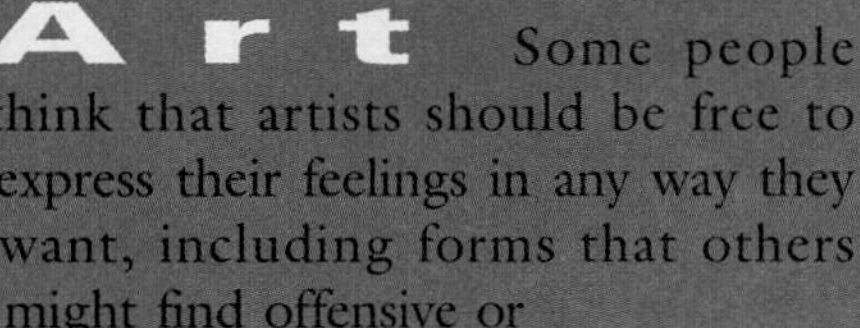

Art

Some people think that artists should be free to express their feelings in any way they want, including forms that others might find offensive or immoral. Write a letter to a local art museum asking the director to either include or exclude such artwork from the museum's collection.

MEDIA

Think about a controversial movie you have heard about. Write a letter to a friend that explains both sides of the controversey.

Springboards

Teaching Strategies

for ART

HELPFUL HINT Remind students that to respond to this issue, they will need to incorporate what they learned when they wrote their social action letter: that is, they must state their position, back it up with evidence, and end with a call to action.

for MEDIA

INDIVIDUALIZING INSTRUCTION: SOCIAL LEARNERS These students might like to do a variation on the media topic. Encourage those students who have seen the same movie to discuss the film to determine an audience for whom it is appropriate, as well as one for whom it is inappropriate. Suggest that students write a letter to each audience, explaining the reasons for their choice.

Adding Lists

Objectives

- To add information, in the form of lists, to sentences
- To use a colon to separate a list from the rest of the sentence

for MODELS

CRITICAL THINKING: ANALYZING

Ask students to analyze why each list in the models works well. (Each item in the list in Model A is a noun; each item in the list in Model B begins with a past-tense verb; each item in the list in Model C is a prepositional phrase beginning with the word *from*.) Note that these lists are examples of parallel structure. Encourage students to use parallel structure when they compose their sentences in Exercises B and C.

for ON THE MARK

STUMBLING BLOCK: COLON

Students sometimes believe that any list in a sentence should be preceded by a colon. This is not the case. What comes before a colon must be a complete sentence in itself; otherwise, no colon is needed.

Additional Resource

Sentence Composing Copy Masters, pp. 11–12

Answer Key

A. Combining Sentences

1. Animals took shape: yellow giraffes, blue lions, pink antelopes, lilac panthers cavorting in crystal substance.
2. The mountains were miles away from the house of the family, and sometimes they were altogether hidden by weather: clouds, rain, or wind alive with dust.
3. When I went inside, there was the new milliner, seated at a table littered with things: feathers, bird wings, satin bows, stiff tape, bolts of velvet, linen, silk, and so on, and several life-sized dummy heads.

Sentence COMPOSING

Adding Lists

Good writers sometimes add information or an explanation to sentences in the form of lists. Notice how the repetition of similar words or sentence parts in the underlined lists adds clarity, detail, and rhythm to the sentence.

Model A I advocate the establishment of shrines in recognition of baseball greats: Ty Cobb, Tris Speaker, Shoeless Joe Jackson, Ruth, Gehrig, Mantle, Mays, DiMaggio, and a few dozen others.
W. P. Kinsella, *Shoeless Joe*

Model B They began to ransack the floor: pulled suitcases and boxes off shelves, tore clothes off hooks in the closets, pulled beds away from walls.
James Thurber, "The Night the Ghost Got In"

Model C He showed him the different methods of propagation: from seed, from cuttings, or from layering.
John Christopher, *The Guardians*

▶ **ON THE MARK** Use a colon to separate a list from the rest of the sentence. Use commas to separate the items in the list.

A. Combining Sentences Make a new sentence by putting the underlined list of the second sentence into the first sentence. Write the complete sentence, putting a colon before the list.

1. Animals took shape. The shapes were of yellow giraffes, blue lions, pink antelopes, lilac panthers cavorting in crystal substance.
Ray Bradbury, "There Will Come Soft Rains"
2. The mountains were miles away from the house of the family, and sometimes they were altogether hidden by weather. The weather consisted of clouds, rain, or wind alive with dust.
Paul Horgan, "To the Mountains"
3. When I went inside, there was the new milliner, seated at a table littered with things. The things were feathers, bird wings, satin bows, stiff tape, bolts of velvet, linen, silk, and so on, and several life-sized dummy heads.
Olive Ann Burns, *Cold Sassy Tree*

B. Unscrambling and Imitating Sentences Unscramble each set of sentence chunks below to create a sentence that matches the structure of one of the models on page 160. Then write a correctly punctuated sentence of your own that imitates each model. Be sure each of your sentences contains a list separated from the rest of the sentence by a colon.

1. Unscramble the chunks to match the structure of model A.
   recommends the enjoyment / our music appreciation teacher / rock, classical, reggae, new age, opera, jazz, blues, rap, and a couple of others / of many forms of music
2. Unscramble the chunks to match the structure of model B.
   wrapped dishes and glasses in paper / placed refrigerated foods safely in a picnic chest / they started to pack their belongings / stacked books in piles on the floor
3. Unscramble the chunks to match the structure of model C.
   by adding / the writing teacher / by changing / and by deleting / taught the class practical ways to revise

C. Expanding Sentences Use your imagination to add a list to the end of each sentence below. Be sure to answer the question in parentheses and to use commas to separate the items in each series.

1. I was faced with two choices: *(What were they?)* **Mark Mathabane, *Kaffir Boy***
2. When I stepped out into the bright sunlight from the darkness of the movie house, I had only two things on my mind: *(What were the two things?)*
   S. E. Hinton, *The Outsiders*
3. The men in the seat were tired and angry and sad for they had got eighteen dollars for every movable thing from the farm: *(What things from the farm did they sell?)* **John Steinbeck, *The Grapes of Wrath***
4. She had come to San Francisco in 1949 after losing everything in China: *(What things had she lost?)* **Amy Tan, *The Joy Luck Club***

Grammar Refresher For more on using colons to introduce lists, see Handbook 49, "Punctuation," pages 657–658.

B. Unscrambling and Imitating Sentences

Unscrambled sentences are given. Imitative sentences will vary but should follow the same pattern.

1. Our music appreciation teacher recommends the enjoyment of many forms of music: rock, classical, reggae, new age, opera, jazz, blues, rap, and a couple of others.
2. They started to pack their belongings: wrapped dishes and glasses in paper, placed refrigerated foods safely in a picnic chest, stacked books in piles on the floor.
3. The writing teacher taught the class practical ways to revise: by adding, by changing, and by deleting.

C. Expanding Sentences

Answers will vary. Authors' sentences are given. Added elements are in bold type.

1. I was faced with two choices**: starve or beg.**
   Mark Mathabane, *Kaffir Boy*
2. When I stepped out into the bright sunlight from the darkness of the movie house, I had only two things on my mind: **Paul Newman and a ride home.**
   S. E. Hinton, *The Outsiders*
3. The men in the seat were tired and angry and sad for they had got eighteen dollars for every movable thing from the farm: **the horses, the wagon, the implements, and all the furniture from the house.**
   John Steinbeck, *The Grapes of Wrath*
4. She had come to San Francisco in 1949 after losing everything in China: **her mother and father, her family home, her first husband, and two daughters, twin baby girls.**
   Amy Tan, *The Joy Luck Club*

Responding to Literature

Overview

When students respond to literature, they offer their opinions and analyses of a literary work. In this workshop, students draw on the skills of informative and persuasive writing from previous workshops as they offer their written and oral interpretations of literature. Workshop 7 includes the following Guided and Related Assignments as well as the interdisciplinary project described on pages 161c–161d.

1. **Guided: Analyzing a Story** calls on students to choose a meaningful short story, to explore their reactions to it, and to focus on one literary element of the story for interpretation. Students cite evidence from the story to support their interpretations.
2. **Related: Oral Storytelling** invites students to retell a story for a targeted audience. To retell a story convincingly, students draw on the interpretive skills they acquired in the Guided Assignment and practice effective delivery techniques.

Teaching Preview

Preparation Guide

1. Use the Overview on this page and the Teacher's Choice descriptions on page 163 as a basis for deciding which assignments to teach.
2. Preview the assignments and the teacher's notes and identify concepts that may require preteaching or extra support, given your class's abilities. The handbook mini-lessons suggested within the lesson may also provide guidance.
3. Preview the chart below for support materials in the Teacher's Resource File that may be used with this Workshop. Resources are for use with the Guided Assignment unless otherwise noted.

Support Materials

RESOURCES

Prewrite and Explore
Writing Resource Book, pp. 39–41
Thinking Skills Worksheet, p. 5
Starting Points for Writing, Writing Prompts for Fine Art, pp. 30, 33, 37–38, 42, 44

Draft and Discover
Elaboration, Revision, and Proofreading Practice, p. 13
Writing Resource Book, p. 42
Thinking Skills Worksheet, p. 6

Revise Your Writing
Elaboration, Revision, and Proofreading Practice, p. 14
Writing Resource Book, p. 43
Peer Response Guides, pp. 21–22
Guidelines for Writing Assessment and Portfolio Use, pp. 20, 41–43

Sentence Composing
Sentence Composing Copy Masters, pp. 13–14

Computer Software
Writer's DataBank
Electronic English Handbook

PROFESSIONAL RESOURCES AND MEDIA

Books and Journals
Blau, Sheridan, *Building Bridges Between Literary Theory and the Teaching of Literature,* National Research Center on Literature and Learning (1993)
Warawa, Bonnie, "Write Me the Story: Responding to Literature Through Storytelling," *English Journal,* Vol. 78 (February 1989), pp. 48–50

Films and Videos
Telling Whoppers: The Fine Art of Storytelling, Cheshire, Denver, CO (1990) (23 min.)

Filmstrips
How to Read a Book and Live to Tell About It, Cheshire, Denver, Co (1990) (25 min.)
Three Short Stories, Nystrom/Eye Gate Media, Chicago, IL (1991)
Storytelling in North America, National Geographic, Washington, DC (1992) (18 min.)

Computer Software and Technology
What Is a Short Story? "The Necklace", Encyclopedia Britannica, Chicago (laser disc)

Linking Literature, Writing, and Grammar

The following options may be used to provide students with an integrated language experience. Begin by assigning and discussing any of the recommended pieces of literature. Use the suggested strategy to provide a link to the Guided Assignment.

LINKING LITERATURE AND WRITING

Option 1

Starting Point: "Dancing for Poppa" by Pat MacEnulty on pages 164–167 of *The Writer's Craft.*

Strategy: Use the teaching suggestions on pages 164–167 to lead students into the Guided Assignment.

Option 2

Starting Point: "Stop the Sun" by Gary Paulsen on pages 17–24 of McDougal, Littell's *Literature and Language,* Grade 8.

Strategy: Have students read the short story. Discuss the significance of these words of Terry's father: "Nobody was there but me and some other dead people, and they can't talk because they couldn't stop the morning." After students have given their interpretations, summarize their analyses. Tell students that in this Guided Assignment, they will have the opportunity to analyze some aspect of a short story.

Option 3

Starting Point: "A Retrieved Reformation" by O. Henry.

Strategy: Have students read the short story. Briefly discuss Jimmy Valentine's/Ralph Spencer's actions. What is the significance of Jimmy Valentine's name? (The name *Valentine* shows he was probably always a romantic person.) How does the title predict the story's conclusion? (Jimmy's reformation was almost snatched away from him by Ben Price; but instead, Price let him go for saving the little girl's life.) Then introduce the Guided Assignment.

LINKING WRITING AND GRAMMAR

In writing a literary analysis, students will often quote an author's exact words and then interpret what the author means. Before students revise their pieces, remind them that the author's words should be put in the context of a complete sentence. Write the following sentences on the board.

Incorrect: The author uses phrases that keep reappearing. "A white dove on the roof." "A gold coin uncovered in the garden." Symbols for peace and prosperity.

Correct: The author uses "a white dove on the roof" and "a gold coin uncovered in the garden" as symbols of peace and prosperity.

Have students check for complete sentences in their writing. Go over pages 381–388 of the Grammar and Usage Handbook. If problems with sentence structure still appear in student writing, assign the exercises on these pages for reteaching. Additional practice can be found in the *Grammar and Usage Practice Book* on pages 1–4.

Management Guidelines

The chart below indicates the number of days recommended for each phase of the Guided and Related Assignments. These numbers are an estimate of the total time needed for each phase. In practice, of course, students may not complete each phase in one continuous session, nor will they necessarily progress from stage to stage in the linear order shown here. Stars indicate portions of the assignment that may be completed outside the classroom if time is limited or if teachers wish students to work independently.

ANALYZING A STORY

Starting from Literature	1 day
Prewrite and Explore	2–3 days*
Draft and Discover	2–3 days*
Revise Your Writing	1–2 days*
Proofread	1 day*
Publish and Present	1 day
Reflect on Your Writing	1 day*
Reteaching	open
Extension and Enrichment.	open*
Sentence Composing	open*

ORAL STORYTELLING

Starting from Literature	1 day
Choosing a Story	1 day*
Practicing Your Story	2 days*
Publishing and Presenting	1–2 days

Staging a Folk Fair: Traditions Old and New

Overview

During this project students will develop an increased awareness of the varied forms and functions of oral literature as they explore folk literature and other aspects of folk culture from around the world and then plan and present a folk festival.

Students will participate in the following activities:

- Explore the characteristics of folk literature and folk culture
- Research the folk literature and related traditions of a specific culture
- Stage a folk fair featuring folk literature and traditions
- Use language arts, science, social studies, music, and art skills to complete their research and present the folk fair.

Preparation Guide

Explain to students that folk culture—in the form of literature, music, foods, entertainment, and other traditions—is tremendously varied. Point out that some aspects of folk culture, such as folk literature, continue to evolve today in forms ranging from children's rhymes and jingles to urban legends and songs.

Tell students that in this project they will agree on a definition of folk culture, investigate the traditions of a specific culture, and stage a folk fair in which they share what they have discovered.

Project File

Stage 1 Develop an Overview and Choose a Focus

1. Lead a class discussion about cultural traditions students have encountered. Have them list these traditions, dividing them into categories such as the following:
   - stories and rhymes
   - foods and recipes
   - arts and crafts
   - toys and games
   - music and musical instruments
   - holidays
   - clothing and textiles
   - work and tools
   - health and medicine
2. Have students interview family members and friends to hear about their experiences with specific folk traditions and to find additional examples to add to the list. (see *Resources, Stage 1*).
3. Have students read folk tales and listen to folk songs from various cultures. Hold a class discussion about the songs and stories.
4. Divide the class into groups and have each group choose a folk culture as a focus for in-depth investigation.

TEAM TEACHING

The following activities may be used for team teaching or as enrichment and extension activities by the language arts teacher.

Social Studies Explore specific customs, such as weddings and harvest celebrations, in various cultures.

Language Arts Study the forms and uses of oral literature in various cultures.

Science Survey science-related folk customs, such as methods of weather prediction and alternative medical practices.

Art Explore the varieties of folk art.

Music Listen to folk music from various traditions.

TEACHING TIPS

- Help each group to limit their topic by focusing on a specific time period or a specific tradition within the chosen culture.
- Suggest that interested students explore the folk traditions of their own families' cultures.
- Show films or videos of traditional celebrations in other countries.
- Invite a storyteller to recount folk tales of various times and places, including modern urban legends (see *Resources, Stage 1*).
- Visit a museum of natural history.

Stage 2 Research Folk Literature and Traditions

1. Direct students to use library materials and other sources to research folk traditions of the cultures they have chosen (see *Resources, Stage 2*).
2. Suggest that students conduct interviews to record stories, songs, and other oral literature of their chosen cultures.

TEAM TEACHING

Social Studies Learn about folk traditions in daily life.

Language Arts Read or listen to folk tales, legends, songs, and proverbs. Learn how, when, and where they were recorded.

Science Research the techniques and effectiveness of folk medicine. Study links between folk medicine and modern medicine.

Art Watch a folk artist or artisan at work.

Music Learn about music and instruments unique to specific folk traditions.

TEACHING TIPS

- Plan a panel discussion in which exchange students or Peace Corps volunteers discuss the roles of folk traditions in specific cultures and the importance of respecting cultural traditions.

- Have students read transcripts of interviews dealing with folk traditions to prepare them for conducting interviews (see *Resources, Stage 2*). Encourage them to review telephone courtesy, list their questions, and practice with peers before contacting people for interviews.
- Take the class to visit a museum or gallery that displays folk art and crafts or to a folk music performance.

Stage 3
Plan and Stage a Folk Fair

1. Direct each group to choose one or more folk traditions from their chosen culture to present at the fair.
2. Instruct students to plan presentations in which they recite, chant, or sing folk literature; display illustrations or samples of traditional clothing, foods, and crafts; and re-create ceremonies and games.
3. Encourage students to publicize the folk fair throughout the school and to present it at a time when students from other classes can attend.

TEAM TEACHING

Art Create signs, banners, flags, and posters to publicize and decorate the fair.

Music Choose and record, or prepare to perform, music to accompany the presentations.

Language Arts Review oral storytelling techniques (see *Resources, Stage 3*).

Social Studies Ensure that the presentations and displays are accurate and are respectful of all cultures.

TEACHING TIPS

- Arrange for students to have access to audiovisual equipment.
- Have students recruit parents or friends to help set up booths and other structures.
- Propose that students invite people they interviewed to attend the folk fair.

Resources

STAGE 1

Virginia Hamilton's ***The Dark Way: Stories from the Spirit World*** is a collection of folk tales from many cultures; her ***In the Beginning: Creation Myths from Around the World*** includes myths, legends, and background information.

For a listing of storytellers in your area, contact the **National Association for the Preservation and Perpetuation of Storytelling,** P.O. Box 309, Jonesborough, TN 37659.

Faces and ***Calliope,*** an anthropology magazine and a world-history magazine for young people, focus on world cultures and folk traditions of the past and the present.

In the **public library,** books about holiday traditions around the world are shelved under Dewey decimal number 393.

STAGE 2

Sorrow's Kitchen: The Life and Folklore of Zora Neale Hurston by Mary E. Lyons combines a biography of the pioneering African-American folklorist with samples of her work.

Folk-tale collections from specific cultures include ***Earthmaker's Tales: North American Indian Stories About Earth Happenings,*** retold by Gretchen Will Mayo; ***Yiddish Folktakes,*** edited by Beatrice S. Weinreich; ***Fairy Tales of Ireland,*** retold by the poet William Butler Yeats; ***The Rainbow People*** by Laurence Yep; ***Folk Tales from the Soviet Union,*** five volumes compiled by R. Babloyan and M. Shumskaya; ***A Treasury of Turkish Folktales for Children*** by Barbara K. Walker; and ***Akavak, Tikta'liktak,*** and ***The White Archer*** by James Houston, retellings of Inuit legends.

The **Foxfire** series, edited by Eliot Wigginton, records vanishing folk traditions of the American South, including stories, photos, diagrams, and transcripts of interviews.

STAGE 3

The Writer's Craft, Grade 8, Workshop 7, "Responding to Literature," pages 178–181, teaches oral storytelling techniques.

The Art of Storytelling: Tall Tales (Society for Visual Education) is a video that introduces students to basic storytelling techniques, using the tall tales "Pecos Bill" and "Annie Christmas."

Additional Projects

The Play's the Thing Propose that students dramatize a favorite story and stage their drama for parents and other students. Tell students to examine their reasons for including certain characters and scenes and not others. Encourage them to discuss their interpretations of the story as they script it, assign parts, create sets and costumes, and rehearse. Students should also publicize the play and write programs that include a brief introduction explaining why they chose the story and scripted it as they did.

Science Tales Have students read nature literature and then explore the links between one literary work of their choice and current ecological issues. Encourage them to use their own thoughts and responses, as well as research, to examine how the literary work relates to issues such as deforestation and pollution and how it might be used to support or to discourage environmental preservation efforts. Have each student present his or her ideas to classmates as part of an oral literary review.

Sketch Book

Objective

- To use a sculpture and writing prompts as springboards to informal writing

WRITING WARM-UPS

Encourage students to respond freely and informally to at least one of the Sketchbook prompts. Students may begin by discussing their reactions in small groups and then freewriting in their journals. Remind students that their responses will not be graded and may provide them with useful material for other writing assignments.

SHOW, DON'T TELL

The following is a sample of a showing paragraph for the first prompt:

When I read "A Mother in Mannville" by Marjorie Kinnan Rawlings, I was moved by Jerry's wish for a mother, a wish so strong that he invented one. I identified with Jerry because sometimes I too imagine a different relationship with my mother. Because I have five sisters and two brothers, my mother rarely has a moment to give just to me—and that makes me feel almost motherless. So sometimes I, like Jerry, daydream. I imagine that I am my mother's only child. She's always there whenever I need her. She comes to all my soccer games and afterward tells me how well I played.

Sketch Book

WRITING WARM-UPS

- Write down the first two thoughts that come to mind after seeing this piece of sculpture. Freewrite about one of your thoughts.
- Does anything puzzle you or confuse you about this sculpture? Explore your reactions to it.
- Create a work of art—drawing, collage, or sculpture—and share it with a friend. Write about your friend's reaction.

Show, Don't Tell

When you respond to a piece of writing, try to show the connections the selection has to you and to things in your own life. Turn one of the *telling* sentences below into a *showing* paragraph, using examples to support your feelings.

- The story impressed me.
- What that person did made me mad.

Responding to Literature

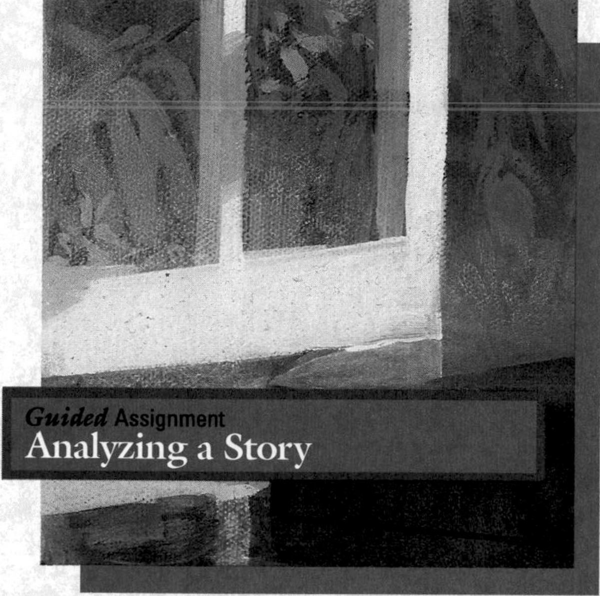

Guided Assignment
Analyzing a Story

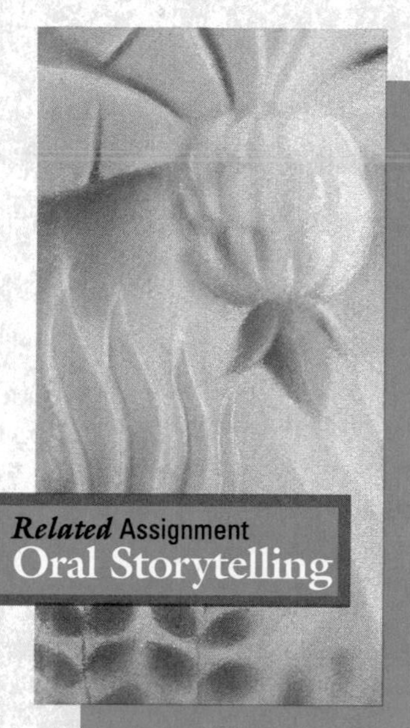

Related Assignment
Oral Storytelling

Part of the fun of reading a good book or watching a movie comes afterwards when you can talk it over with friends. You might compare notes, argue about a character, or complain about the ending.

What you've really been doing is analyzing the work—figuring out what you think about it. Analysis is a good way to understand and enjoy something more. This workshop will help you learn how to analyze a literary work. In the related assignment you can bring the meaning of a story to life by retelling it orally.

WRITER'S 7 WORKSHOP

Responding to Literature

Objectives

Guided Assignment

Analyzing a Story To recognize a literary analysis and to respond to a story by writing an analysis of some aspect of it

Related Assignment

Oral Storytelling To read a story and retell it orally

Teacher's Choice

Use the following guidelines to choose the assignment that best suits students' needs.

Analyzing a Story This assignment will benefit most students by helping them to think critically about literature. You may prefer to assign this workshop near the end of the school year because it draws on the expository writing skill of analysis. Alternatively, you may want to teach this assignment while students are reading and responding to a particularly challenging literature selection.

Oral Storytelling This assignment is especially suited to those students who like to perform for an audience, as well as to those who prefer speaking to writing. You might combine this assignment with the study of folk literature.

Guided ASSIGNMENT

ASSIGNMENT RATIONALE

Writing literary analyses can help students become more thoughtful and insightful readers. As students progress through high school and beyond, the ability to write analytically and with insight becomes increasingly important. This assignment will help students find a focus for an analysis; it also provides an opportunity to practice such high-level thinking skills as drawing conclusions, evaluating, and synthesizing.

Starting from LITERATURE

Motivate

Ask students whether they have ever felt pressured to do something they did not want to do, such as learn to play a sport or musical instrument. Have volunteers share a few experiences.

BUILD ON PRIOR KNOWLEDGE

Ask students whether any of them have ever taken ballet lessons or other dance lessons. Ask, "What does it take to be a good ballet dancer?" (a certain amount of natural ability and a great deal of practice) "What other activities demand these same things?" (playing a sport, playing a musical instrument, learning a trade, and so on) Have students briefly discuss how they feel about parents or other adults who lead young people to take dance or music lessons or to participate in a particular sport.

Guided ASSIGNMENT

Analyzing a Story

Starting from LITERATURE

A short story can affect readers in many different ways. As you read a story, you might be fascinated by how the events unfold. Your friend, on the other hand, might notice one character in particular. A third person might wonder about the story's message. All of you might find parts you don't totally understand. As you read this excerpt from the short story "Dancing for Poppa," be aware of your reactions —what you are thinking, feeling, wondering, or noticing about the story.

"Dancing for Poppa" explores a young person's reaction to the death of a family member. After her grandfather's funeral, Connie remembers his love for her and his desire for her to become a ballerina. It was Poppa who bought Connie's first pair of pink ballet slippers, drove her to dance class, and proudly applauded her first recital solo. Connie is struggling with some difficult decisions about what she wants and what others expect of her.

from

Dancing for Poppa

by
Pat MacEnulty

✦

Poppa always thought I would be a ballerina. And I guess I did, too, until I was about fourteen and realized that even though I was quite good, I wasn't good enough to be a star for a major ballet company, and I didn't want to be in a company if I was just going to be a member of the corps. I had been a star in Miss Bell's senior class, and that had spoiled me for anything but the spotlight.

For the first five years, I had been a mainstay of the back row, but I started coming to the school and practicing by myself early in the mornings and one day, Miss Bell asked me to

Links to LITERATURE & LANGUAGE

Literature Pat MacEnulty's "Dancing for Poppa" appears in its entirety in *Literature and Language*, Grade 8. For other examples of short stories in *Literature and Language*, Grade 8, see the following:

- Gary Paulsen, "Stop the Sun"
- Lensey Namioka, "The Inn of Lost Time"

Writing This guided assignment may be used as an extension of the Writer's Workshop "Writing About Literature: Critic's Corner Review," page 479, or "Writing About Literature: Characters in Contrast," page 572, in *Literature and Language*, Grade 8.

SET A PURPOSE

Have students read the Starting from Literature box. Remind them that people often have different reasons for reading. Sometimes people read for information; at other times they read for entertainment, hoping to lose themselves in an exciting story. Suggest that as students read this selection, they pay attention to the plot of the story and to their feelings about the main character and the decision she makes.

for FURTHER READING

"Dancing for Poppa" is a short story that focuses on character development. If students like this story, they might also enjoy Toni Cade Bambara's "Raymond's Run" or Isaac Bashevis Singer's "The Day I Got Lost." Students might want to select one of these stories for a literary analysis.

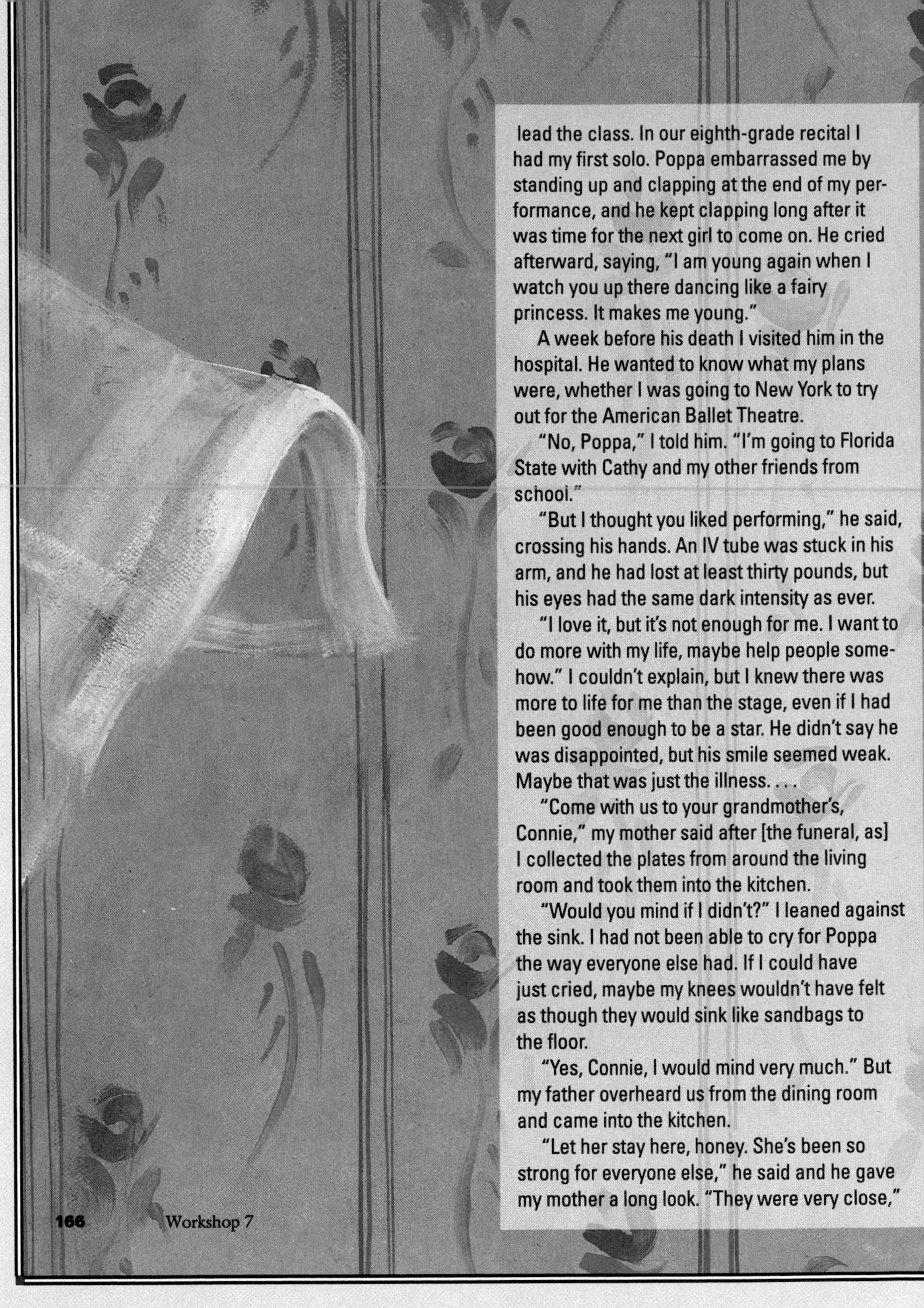

lead the class. In our eighth-grade recital I had my first solo. Poppa embarrassed me by standing up and clapping at the end of my performance, and he kept clapping long after it was time for the next girl to come on. He cried afterward, saying, "I am young again when I watch you up there dancing like a fairy princess. It makes me young."

A week before his death I visited him in the hospital. He wanted to know what my plans were, whether I was going to New York to try out for the American Ballet Theatre.

"No, Poppa," I told him. "I'm going to Florida State with Cathy and my other friends from school."

"But I thought you liked performing," he said, crossing his hands. An IV tube was stuck in his arm, and he had lost at least thirty pounds, but his eyes had the same dark intensity as ever.

"I love it, but it's not enough for me. I want to do more with my life, maybe help people somehow." I couldn't explain, but I knew there was more to life for me than the stage, even if I had been good enough to be a star. He didn't say he was disappointed, but his smile seemed weak. Maybe that was just the illness. . . .

"Come with us to your grandmother's, Connie," my mother said after [the funeral, as] I collected the plates from around the living room and took them into the kitchen.

"Would you mind if I didn't?" I leaned against the sink. I had not been able to cry for Poppa the way everyone else had. If I could have just cried, maybe my knees wouldn't have felt as though they would sink like sandbags to the floor.

"Yes, Connie, I would mind very much." But my father overheard us from the dining room and came into the kitchen.

"Let her stay here, honey. She's been so strong for everyone else," he said and he gave my mother a long look. "They were very close," he added in a voice so soft he must have thought I couldn't hear him. . . .

Soon the house was quiet except for the running water as I rinsed off the dishes before loading them into the dishwasher. . . . The house was back to normal, as if Poppa had never died, as if he would come in any moment and say, "How's my princess?"

I sat in the living room on the couch where earlier Aunt Lynn and Aunt Maryjane had been discussing Poppa's will. He had left enough to take care of Grandma and a few tokens for members of the family. He had left me a framed photograph of the Degas statue the *Little Ballerina*, which sat on the coffee table next to the catalog from the college where I had been accepted.

I opened the catalog. . . . When I came to the page of dance classes, I stopped a moment to daydream. I imagined being on stage, felt the warmth of the lights and the tightness of the costume with its sequins and straps. I looked back at the catalog and noticed something I hadn't seen before. Just below the list of dance courses was a section of dance-therapy classes. I had never even heard of dance therapy, but it made sense. I turned to the course descriptions and found that there was even a major for dance therapy.

"Dance makes people happy," Poppa had said one Christmas after a family dinner. "Even a little baby knows how to dance. Before she can walk or talk, she'll start bouncing when she hears music." . . .

He was right. Dancing had always made me happy. And watching me dance had always made Poppa happy. It occurred to me that perhaps Poppa didn't want me to cry for him. Maybe he just wanted me to be happy. . . .

I walked to my bedroom and found my toe shoes hanging by their laces in the closet. I stuffed some fresh lamb's wool in the toes, pulled on my tights and leotard, and went back into the living room. We had a recording of *Swan Lake*, and I lowered it onto the turntable. The music started, soft and sad. Instead of dancing the traditional version, I made up my own steps. My arm swung above my head and I rose up on my toe and stretched my leg out in an arabesque. My leg rose higher and straighter than it ever had before. Then I brought my foot to my knee. My body had a life of its own as I twirled. It seemed that I twirled in slow motion and that sitting on the couch, Poppa was shouting and clapping, "Bravo!" My torso stretched taller than ever and I could pirouette three times in one continuous spiral. Every movement was perfect. I played side one and then side two and then I started over again. I danced until, with bleeding toes, I landed in a lake of dreams.

The next morning my mother woke me up and said, "Hey, you slept in your ballet clothes. Might as well get up. You've only got a couple of weeks left until summer vacation is over. Better enjoy every minute of it."

She opened the window before she left. I rolled over in my bed and inhaled the last notes of my childhood. Outside a breeze danced through the leaves of a chinaberry tree, and it sounded like distant applause.

Think & Respond

How did the story make you feel? How do you feel about the way Connie resolves her problem? Does anything about the story puzzle or confuse you? How would you describe this story to someone else? Share your ideas with other readers of the story.

Think & Respond

ELICIT PERSONAL RESPONSES

Have students **freewrite** a response to how the story made them feel; ask volunteers to share their responses. Then have students **discuss** the other questions in the Think & Respond box. As students identify parts of the story that confused or puzzled them, list those parts on the board and save them, so that students can refer to them after having read the student analysis on pages 168–169.

EXPLORE THE AUTHOR'S TECHNIQUES

Point out that "Dancing for Poppa" is written from a first-person point of view—the main character narrates the story. Note that this point of view draws readers into the story and helps them identify with the main character because they learn her thoughts and feelings directly. Note also how the author organizes the story chronologically: The main character begins the story by telling about the past, then shifts the story to the present.

Music Connection

Suggest that students who are interested in classical music find out what *Swan Lake* is about and why it was an appropriate choice for Connie's dance. If possible, you might play a recording of the music for the class and have students freewrite a response to it.

Art Connection

The story "Dancing for Poppa" mentions a statue of a ballerina by Edgar Degas. See the Art Note about Degas on page 172 and refer students to the painting on the pupil page.

Reading a STUDENT MODEL

Pat MacEnulty's short story deals with the conflict a young girl feels between what she wants for herself and what her grandfather wanted for her. The Student Model shows Annie Maxwell's analysis of this short story. It is the final draft of the piece students will see in process on the workshop pages that follow.

Motivate

Sometimes students mistakenly believe that teachers have all the answers in interpreting literature. Share with them lines from a poem or short story that you found particularly difficult to interpret. Explain the process you went through to find a meaning that seemed "right" to you.

BUILD ON PRIOR KNOWLEDGE

Ask students to describe book reports they have written in the past. Have them discuss what they included in the reports and how they structured them. Then have students speculate as to how an analysis might be similar to or different from a book report.

SET A PURPOSE

Have students read the Reading a Student Model box. Suggest that they prepare to read the model by reviewing their list of parts of "Dancing for Poppa" that puzzled them (see the Elicit Personal Responses note on page 167). Have them plan to compare their notes with the problems that Annie Maxwell identifies. (Annie had problems with two sentences: "I inhaled the last notes of my childhood" and "Outside a breeze danced through the leaves of a chinaberry tree and it sounded like distant applause.")

One Student's Writing

Reading a STUDENT MODEL

When Annie Maxwell read "Dancing for Poppa," she was confused by its ending. She decided to write a literary analysis of the story to see if she could understand the story better. As you read her analysis, notice the problems she identified. Then consider how she went about finding meaning in the story.

Applause for Connie
By Annie Maxwell

Many young people are faced with a dilemma when it comes to choosing a career. This, I think, is the main message of Pat MacEnulty's "Dancing for Poppa." In this touching short story the main character, Connie, is faced with the problem of deciding her future. She must consider her goals, but she also wants to be sensitive to the desires of her family. Connie is mainly concerned about the wishes of "Poppa," who is her grandfather, her friend, and "the one who knows her dreams."

Throughout the story, Connie does not know what to do with her life. Her family wants her to attend college, but her beloved Poppa wants her to become a ballerina. She realizes the importance of Poppa's hopes for her even more when he dies; she feels that she desperately needs to express her gratitude to her deceased grandfather. After all, she didn't even know she liked dancing until Poppa gave her her first ballet shoes.

Toward the end of the story, Connie discovers a possible compromise. She can major in dance therapy. That way she can go to college and still dance. At this point I thought Connie's struggle had been resolved and drawn to a logical conclusion. Then I read the ending for the first time, and I was confused. It seemed to hold out the possibility of Connie following another path. In particular, I had problems with two statements.

I was puzzled by the sentence "I inhaled the last notes of my childhood," but I quickly decided that it refers to Connie leaving childhood and its hobbies. She's going on to study dance therapy in college—going on to becoming an adult. I had more trouble though with the final sentence: "Outside a breeze danced through the leaves of a chinaberry tree and it sounded like distant applause." Does the breeze represent Poppa and show that now his spirit is free because Connie has made her decision, or does it represent Connie's final dance for Poppa? Does the distant applause stand for more applause to come for Connie because she will become a ballerina, or is it a sign of approval for her decision to go into dance therapy?

After studying these lines, I decided they are meant to show that through Connie's decision to pursue a career that includes ballet, she has resolved her conflict. The ending proves that not only is Connie satisfied with her choice, but also that Poppa's wishes are fulfilled. What convinced me most of all was the description near the end of the story of Connie's final performance for Poppa. She dances the best ever, and she imagines Poppa sitting on the couch clapping for her, congratulating her on her decision and her dancing. (Earlier, Connie had not been able to cry for her grandfather. This dance is her way of crying.)

I feel satisfied that Connie was happy and was going to continue with dance through dance therapy. The breeze in the end represents this last dance and the distant applause is the reassurance of Connie's first happiness as an adult.

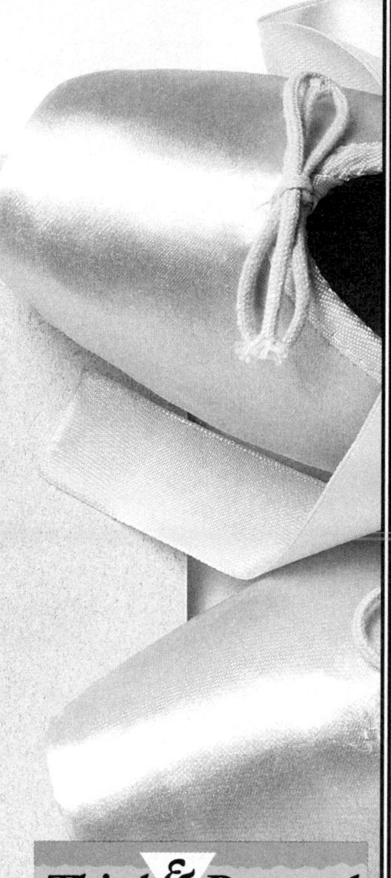

Think & Respond

Respond as a Reader

▶ What do you think you would do if you were faced with a decision similar to Connie's?

▶ Can you think of a time when you were torn between what you wanted to do and what your family wanted you to do?

Respond as a Writer

▶ How does Annie help the reader to understand the background of the problem she will discuss?

▶ How does Annie support her interpretation of the ending?

Think & Respond

RESPOND AS A READER

▶ In discussing the first question, encourage students to imagine an actual situation for themselves. For example, what might their parents or another adult like them to do with their lives? Although students' responses will vary, many students will say that they want to be true to themselves in making a career decision.

▶ Encourage volunteers to relate a time when they faced such a similar conflict. Discuss questions such as the following: What happened? How did they resolve the conflict? Looking back, do they believe they resolved it in the best possible way? Why or why not?

RESPOND AS A WRITER

▶ Students should note that Annie gives a brief summary of the story. Point out that the summary makes the analysis understandable even to someone who might not have read the story.

▶ Annie supports her interpretation by using evidence from the story—the description of Connie's final dance for Poppa.

Draw Conclusions

Ask students to identify the characteristics they have noted in a literary analysis. Responses may include

- a brief summary of the story
- an identification of one key feature or problem to be analyzed
- a personal interpretation of the problem or feature
- evidence from the story to support the interpretation

Writing ON YOUR OWN

Remind students that writing an analysis of a work of literature can help them—and others—to understand it. Students should remember to support their interpretations with evidence from the story, as Annie Maxwell did.

Handbooks for Help and Practice

The following handbooks may be used as mini-lessons before students begin writing or as resources when problems arise.

- **Methods of Elaboration, pp. 255–261**
- **Writing Paraphrases and Summaries, pp. 346–348**

PREWRITE AND EXPLORE

Objectives

- To use prewriting techniques to choose a topic for a literary analysis
- To identify a focus for a literary analysis

Teaching Strategies

for TEXT RENDERING

HELPFUL HINT To help students get the most out of this brainstorming activity, suggest that they take notes or use a cassette recorder. When students are ready to write their analyses, they can refer to the group's ideas.

Writing ON YOUR OWN

Analyzing a Story

INVITATION TO *Write*

Annie Maxwell chose to write about the ending of "Dancing for Poppa" in order to sort out—to analyze—her reactions to the story. By doing so she found a deeper meaning to the story. Writing an analysis is a good way to appreciate a literary work and come to understand it better.

Choose a short story and write an essay in which you analyze some part of it.

PREWRITE AND EXPLORE

1. Find a story. Think about a story—or even a novel or play—that you found challenging, liked or disliked strongly, or were unable to forget. For short stories, you might consider "Dancing for Poppa," "The Dinner Party" by Mona Gardner, or "A Cap for Steve" by Morley Callaghan. To help you make your choice, try one or more of the following activities.

Exploring Topics

- **First impressions** You can **freewrite** about your initial reactions—the kinds of things you might tell a friend who had just asked you about the story.
- **Text rendering** A good way to dig into a story is to meet with classmates who also have read it. Each person reads aloud whatever lines or phrases seem particularly important, interesting, or troubling. Some passages might get called out more than once. This process often gives you unexpected ideas about the story.

After you've explored your choices, choose the story you are most interested in. Think about ideas that you'd like to follow up.

History Connection

Works of literature often reflect the period of time in which the author lived. Students who are especially interested in history might like to choose an appropriate story and explore how historical context had affected it and how people might have felt about the story at the time.

2. Reread and record. Read the story again. This time, jot down what you notice, think, feel, or wonder about. For example:

- Questions you have about characters, actions, or setting
- Lines that interest, puzzle, amuse, or anger you
- Ideas you agree with, want to argue about, or remember
- Memories, thoughts, or feelings triggered by your reading

A double entry journal is a good tool for recording and exploring reactions to important or confusing lines or passages. Write the lines from the story in one column and your reactions in a second column.

One Student's Process

Annie found certain passages troubling. She created this double-entry journal to explore the meaning of those key passages. The notes from her first reading are shown in blue. As she reread the story, she added new thoughts.

Quotes from story	Ideas
"I rolled over in my bed and inhaled the last notes of my childhood."	• What does this have to do with anything? • Is she leaving the hobbies of childhood behind? • Is she becoming an adult, going into dance therapy?
"Outside a breeze danced through the leaves of a chinaberry tree and it sounded like distant applause."	• Does this mean she's going into ballet after all? • Does the breeze represent Poppa—his spirit free now and her mind at rest? • Or does it represent her last dance for Poppa? • The applause could be a sign of approval for her decision to study dance therapy.

COMPUTER TIP

You might want to create your reading journal on a computer. You could create one file for memorable quotations, one for questions, and one for comments.

GENERAL NOTE

STUMBLING BLOCK Sometimes students struggle with literary analyses because they lack confidence in their own interpretations and believe that there must be one "right" response. Assure them that you are interested in their ideas and will respect any interpretation, as long as it is well supported by evidence from the text.

for ONE STUDENT'S PROCESS

HELPFUL HINT Suggest that students leave extra space between entries in their double-entry journals so that they can record new ideas during rereadings of the text. When students reread their journal entries, they might highlight those ideas they particularly like and want to use in their drafts.

GENERAL NOTE

PERSONAL TOUCH If you are working on this assignment along with your students, explain which methods you are using to explore your ideas. Share any freewriting, journal entries, or graphic organizers you created to help yourself make sense of your topic.

for EXPLORE YOUR REACTIONS

INDIVIDUALIZING INSTRUCTIONS: AUDITORY LEARNERS Pair these students with some who are good oral readers. Listening to the story, rather than rereading it, enables auditory learners to respond to what they hear.

DRAFT AND DISCOVER

Objectives

- To draft a literary analysis
- To respond to one's own draft and to that of a peer

Writer's Choice You might want to make notes on a photocopy of the work you are analyzing. You can also highlight or underline important passages.

3. Explore your reactions. Read the story one more time, and keep taking notes. See if your understanding changes as you read the story again.

Detail of *The Ballerina* (1875–1877), Edgar Degas.

4. Find a focus. An analysis is more than a summary. It often means looking at a work from a certain angle—examining a particular feature, noticing how one element of a story helps make the story more effective or interesting. Look through your journal and mark any entries that seem especially interesting or thought provoking. You could focus on any of the following:

- **Plot** Are the events believable, predictable, surprising?
- **Theme** Does the story teach an idea you agree with? Why do you agree or disagree?
- **Character** Do the characters act in ways that fit their personalities? Are the characters presented as stereotypes?
- **Confusing elements** Where does the story confuse you? You could explore parts that puzzle you and look for solutions.

DRAFT AND DISCOVER

1. State your focus in a sentence. Then freewrite to discover more about what you think. Consider what details you could use to explain your ideas. Don't worry if your thoughts seem disorganized, or even contradictory. You can sort out your ideas—or even change your mind—once you get something on paper.

2. Begin organizing your draft. Most literary analyses follow this general pattern:

Introduction Give the title, the author of your story, and enough background for readers to understand the story. Explain the focus of your analysis. Show why you found the subject interesting.

PROBLEM SOLVING

"How can I tell my readers about the story as briefly as possible?"

For help writing a summary, see

- Handbook 33, "Writing Paraphrases and Summaries," pages 346–348

ART NOTE

Edgar Degas (1834–1917), a French impressionist painter and sculptor, often portrayed people in scenes from everyday life. He was also interested in theater. *The Ballerina* is one of many of his portrayals of scenes from the ballet. Degas painted pictures not only of performances but also of dancing classes, rehearsals, and backstage scenes.

SPICE BOX

As part of the prewriting process, students might imitate TV critics who analyze and recommend movies. Using the questions in **Find a focus,** a pair of student-critics who have read the same story should express their feelings and reactions to the work. To sum up their opinions, students can give the thumbs-up or thumbs-down signal.

Body Present your analysis. Show—don't just tell—what you think about your subject. Explain the steps in your reasoning. Refer specifically to the story, and use quotations to support your argument. Summarize where necessary. Like Annie, you may want to explore a topic or problem that puzzles you. Notice some of the various ways to organize analyses.

Organizing the Body

Analyzing a Problem Passage	Analyzing a Character	Analyzing Themes or Ideas
• Show where the problem part fits into the whole story. • Explain any problems you had understanding the passage. • Explore some possible meanings or interpretations, possibly picking the best and explaining why it is the best.	• Show what the character is like at the beginning. • Show how the character changes. • Show how the character is different at the end.	• Summarize the story. • State what you think the theme is and what you think it means. • Agree or disagree with the theme or idea and give your reasons.

Closing Summarize important points, and state your feelings about the story or conclusions you have reached.

3. Think about your draft. After you've put your analysis aside for a while, read it again with fresh eyes. The following questions can help you and your peers respond to your draft.

REVIEW YOUR WRITING

Questions for Yourself

- What is the focus of my essay?
- How do my details support this focus?
- How have I shown that this topic interested me?
- What additional information do my readers need?

Questions for Your Peer Readers

- What title would you give my essay? Tell me in your own words what you think it is about.
- What part of my essay is most important or interesting?
- How does my essay give you a better or different understanding of the story?

Teaching Strategies

for ORGANIZING THE BODY

MODELING Help students see that each of the three columns of the chart can serve as an informal outline for an analysis. Briefly model one of these organizing structures for students. For example, you might write on the board:

Analyzing a Problem Passage

I. Identify the problem passage and show how it fits into the story.
   a. problem passage—"Outside a breeze danced through the leaves of a chinaberry tree, and it sounded like distant applause."
   b. how it fits—It is the last sentence of the story in which Connie agonized about whether to become a ballerina, as her grandfather had wished.

II. Explain the problem with the passage.
   a. The passage is open to many interpretations
   b. Applause is usually associated with two things: (1) performances and (2) approval

III. Explore possible meanings; pick the best and give your reasons.
   a. Possible interpretations—Has Connie decided to perform as a ballerina, or does Connie feel at peace about becoming a dance therapist?
   b. My interpretation—The applause is Grandfather's sign of approval.
   c. Reasons—Connie seems languid and calm in the morning. The breeze dancing through the trees is happy imagery.

If students need more practice in organizing a literary analysis, refer them to "Planning a Literary Analysis," Writing Resource Book, page 41.

for QUESTIONS FOR YOUR PEER READERS

PEER RESPONSE Remind peer readers to use "I" statements in responding: "I think a good title would be. . . .," rather than "You should title your essay. . . ." This reminds the writer that a peer reader's statements are one person's opinions while final decisions belong to the writer.

for ONE STUDENT'S PROCESS

CRITICAL THINKING: ANALYZING One of the peer reader's comments is "I still don't understand how the ending proves this." Ask students why the peer reader said that. (Annie says that the ending proves it, but she doesn't offer any evidence to show it.)

REVISE YOUR WRITING

Objectives

- To evaluate the responses to a literary analysis and to revise a draft with those responses in mind
- To evaluate the supporting details in a draft
- To evaluate the logical flow of paragraphs in a draft

Teaching Strategies

for REVIEW YOUR RESPONSES

ASSESSMENT:SPOT CHECK Sometimes students like a "second opinion" on their own responses or on a peer's. Circulate through the classroom and encourage students to ask you about any changes they are not certain they should make.

for PARAGRAPHS AT WORK

HELPFUL HINT Refer students to the organizing chart on page 173. Point out that besides a paragraph for each point, strong analysis needs an introduction that states what the paper will be about and a conclusion that summarizes the analysis.

One Student's Process

In this part of Annie's first draft, she thought about possible meanings of the breeze mentioned at the end of the story. Afterwards, she asked her peers to react to her interpretation.

So does the breeze represent Poppa and show that his spirit is free because Connie has made her decision, or does it represent Connie's final dance for Poppa. Does the distant applause of the wind stand for more applause to come because she will become a ballerina, or is it a sign of approval for her decision to go into dance therapy. After reading and studying these lines, I decided they are meant to show that she has resolved her conflict. The ending proves that not only is Connie satisfied with her choice, but also that Poppa's wishes are fulfilled.

Peer Reader Comments

These are interesting ideas. I hadn't thought of them.

I still don't understand how the ending proves this.

REVISE YOUR WRITING

1. Review your responses. Think about how you answered your own questions. How did the responses from your peer readers help you see your writing differently?

2. Look over your argument. Have you supported your analysis with enough well-chosen details, such as reasons, examples, and quotations from the story?

Paragraphs at Work In a literary analysis, paragraphs need to flow logically. For example, look on page 173 at the suggested method of organization for analyzing a problem passage. This list could serve as an outline for a brief analysis of a passage. Each of the points could be covered in a paragraph. So remember these tips.

- Consider an outline like one of those on page 173.
- Write a paragraph for each point in the outline.
- Support each main idea with specific details.

PROBLEM SOLVING

"Have I given enough reasons to explain my interpretation?"

For help with elaborating on ideas, see

- Handbook 12, "Methods of Elaboration," pages 255–261

3. Decide what changes you want to make. While it's helpful to consider the responses of your readers, you need to trust yourself most of all.

One Student's Process

After reviewing her peers' comments, Annie decided she needed to present more evidence to back up her interpretation of the ending.

through Connie's decision to pursue a career that includes ballet,

~~So~~ does the breeze represent Poppa and show that his spirit is free because Connie has made her decision, or does it represent Connie's final dance for Poppa? Does the distant applause ~~of the wind~~ stand for more applause to come because she will become a ballerina, or is it a sign of approval for her decision to go into dance therapy? ¶ After reading and studying these lines, I decided they are meant to show that she has resolved her conflict. The ending proves that not only is Connie satisfied with her choice, but also that Poppa's wishes are fulfilled.

What convinced me most of all was the description near the end of the story of Connie's final performance for Poppa. She dances the best ever, and she imagines Poppa sitting on the couch clapping for her, congratulating her on her decision and her dancing. (Earlier, Connie had not been able to cry for her grandfather. This dance is her way of crying.)

Writing TIP

Remember to include details from the story that will help you show, not tell, how you reached your conclusion.

Grammar TIP

To show the relationship between two contrasting ideas you are explaining, try combining the two ideas with the conjunction *or* or *but.* Remember to use a comma.

for ONE STUDENT'S PROCESS

CRITICAL THINKING: DRAWING CONCLUSIONS Refer students to the text that Annie added to the bottom of her paper. Ask them how they know that Annie considers this explanation her best evidence for her interpretation. (She uses the words *most of all.)* Point out that writers often give their strongest evidence last. Ask students why many writers use that order. (Samples: They like to build up to the most powerful argument; readers are likely to remember what comes at the end.)

Grammar Connection

Sometimes students confuse compound sentences with simple sentences that have compound predicates. In the first instance, a comma is needed before the conjunction; in the second, no comma is used. As you discuss the Grammar Tip, you might use these sentences to illustrate the difference:

Compound Sentence: The batter hit a hard line drive past the pitcher's mound, and the runner advanced to third.

Compound Predicate: The batter hit a hard line drive and ran all the way to second base.

If students need additional help, refer them to Grammar Handbook 45, pages 556–559.

PROOFREAD

Teaching Strategies

for LINKING MECHANICS AND WRITING

HELPFUL HINT: CAPITALIZING

Although many students know that all the important words in a title should be capitalized, some students mistakenly believe that all short words, or words of only two letters, should not be capitalized. Explain to students that the words that are not capitalized in a title are the articles *a, an,* and *the,* as well as prepositions and conjunctions of fewer than five letters (unless one of these is the first word in the title). The words *it* and *is* are not articles, prepositions, or conjunctions; therefore, they should be capitalized.

Guidelines for Evaluation

IDEAS AND CONTENT

- gives a summary of the work that includes the title, author, and important parts of the plot
- analyzes one feature or element of the story
- uses evidence from the story to support the analysis
- suggests the personal impact of the story

STRUCTURE AND FORM

- begins with an introduction that states the focus
- has a logical organization
- ends with a conclusion that summarizes the analysis

GRAMMAR, USAGE AND MECHANICS

- displays standard grammar, usage, and mechanics
- punctuates quotations correctly
- capitalizes and punctuates titles correctly

Grammar TIP

Remember to use quotation marks when you quote lines exactly. When you put a passage in your own words, do not use quotation marks.

Standards for Evaluation

INTERPRETIVE WRITING

A story analysis

- identifies the author and title and briefly summarizes the work
- shows why the writer found the subject interesting
- clearly focuses on one feature of the work
- presents an interpretation of that feature
- supports the interpretation with reasons, examples, quotations, or other evidence

PROOFREAD

1. Proofread your writing. Look for errors in grammar and spelling. Be sure you have used quotation marks correctly. Also, since you will be referring to a novel, short story, or play, be especially careful in the handling of punctuation and capitalization of titles.

LINKING MECHANICS AND WRITING

Writing Titles

When you write titles, the first and last words and all other important words should be capitalized. The titles of poems, short stories, and songs should be enclosed in quotation marks. The titles of books, plays, magazines, very long poems, and motion pictures are normally set in italics. You can indicate italics by underlining.

Example

Pat MacEnulty, the author of "Dancing for Poppa," is also the fiction editor for Sun Dog magazine.

For more information on correct punctuation of titles, see Handbook 49, "Punctuation," pages 666–667.

2. Make a clean copy of your analysis. Did you accomplish what you wanted to with your analysis? Read it over one more time as you think about the Standards for Evaluation shown in the margin. If you are ready for publication, make a final copy.

PUBLISH AND PRESENT

- **Hold a reading.** Read your essay aloud to a small group of classmates who have read the same work. You might want to discuss similarities and differences in your analyses. Then share at least one essay from each group with the whole class.

- **Post your analysis.** Make a bulletin board display that groups together analyses written about the same work.
- **Publish a class collection.** Share the collection with other classes.

Reflect on Your Writing

WRITER TO WRITER

If one cannot enjoy reading a book over and over again, there is no use in reading it at all.

Oscar Wilde, playwright and poet

1. Add your analysis to your portfolio. Now that you've read Annie's analysis and written one of your own, summarize what you learned in a brief introductory note for your paper. Consider how you put together this essay, how peer responses may have helped, and what you think of your analysis now that you've written it. Some of these questions may help you focus your thinking.

- What was the hardest part of writing my analysis? Is there any way to make it easier next time?
- What did I enjoy most or find easiest to do?
- What part of my essay do I like best, and what would I like a reader to appreciate most?
- If I were to write it again, how would I change this essay?

2. Explore additional literary ideas. See the suggestions for oral storytelling on pages 180–181 and Springboards on page 182.

At age 100, arthritis sufferer Clare Willi stays limber thanks to dance therapy.

Reteaching

After students have completed their papers, assess the needs of students who were not successful in developing an effective literary analysis. Assign the appropriate handbook mini-lessons as well as the Workshop Support Materials listed in the Teaching Preview, pages 161a–161b. Concepts commonly requiring reteaching for this assignment are:

- **Handbook 12, Methods of Elaboration, pp. 255–261**
- **Handbook 33, Writing Paraphrases and Summaries, pp. 346–348**

The following suggestions and resources also may be useful.

Weak Character Analysis To help students focus on how a character changes and why, suggest that they make a time line or storyboard of the character's actions and behavior throughout the story. Refer students to page 36 for an example of a storyboard that they could adapt to their purposes.

Mechanics and Usage: Quotations If students failed to cite passages from the text correctly, refer them to Handbook 47, pages 664–665. For more reinforcement, assign the quotation exercises in the Grammar and Usage Practice Book, pages 134–137.

Extension and Enrichment

1. Have students choose a poem to analyze. Encourage them to prepare an oral reading of the poem along with their presentation of the analysis.

2. Suggest that students choose a scientific discovery or invention from the last thirty years and analyze how it has changed people's lives. Some examples include the microwave oven, the portable telephone, and the VCR.

Closure: Reflect on Your Writing

Encourage students to include, in an introductory note to their essays, the answer to at least one of the questions.

Related ASSIGNMENT

Starting from LITERATURE

Objectives

- To read a story and analyze its appropriateness for reading aloud
- To determine an effective manner for reading a story aloud
- To practice and present a story orally

Motivate

From the library, select a story on tape that would appeal to your students. Play the beginning and ask students to pay attention to how the storyteller makes the story come alive for listeners. After playing the tape, ask students to comment on the storyteller's techniques.

BUILD ON PRIOR KNOWLEDGE

Ask students what kinds of stories they liked to listen to when they were younger; then ask what kinds of stories are meant to be read aloud. (Possible responses: ghost stories, fables, myths, legends) Ask why they liked these stories. Encourage comments not only on the content or kinds of stories but also on the way in which the stories were told or read.

SET A PURPOSE

Tell students that folktales are stories that have been told and retold from generation to generation; some of these tales, like the African tale "Why Monkeys Live in Trees," explain why something in nature occurs as it does. As students read the story, they might imagine how it would sound if it were read aloud.

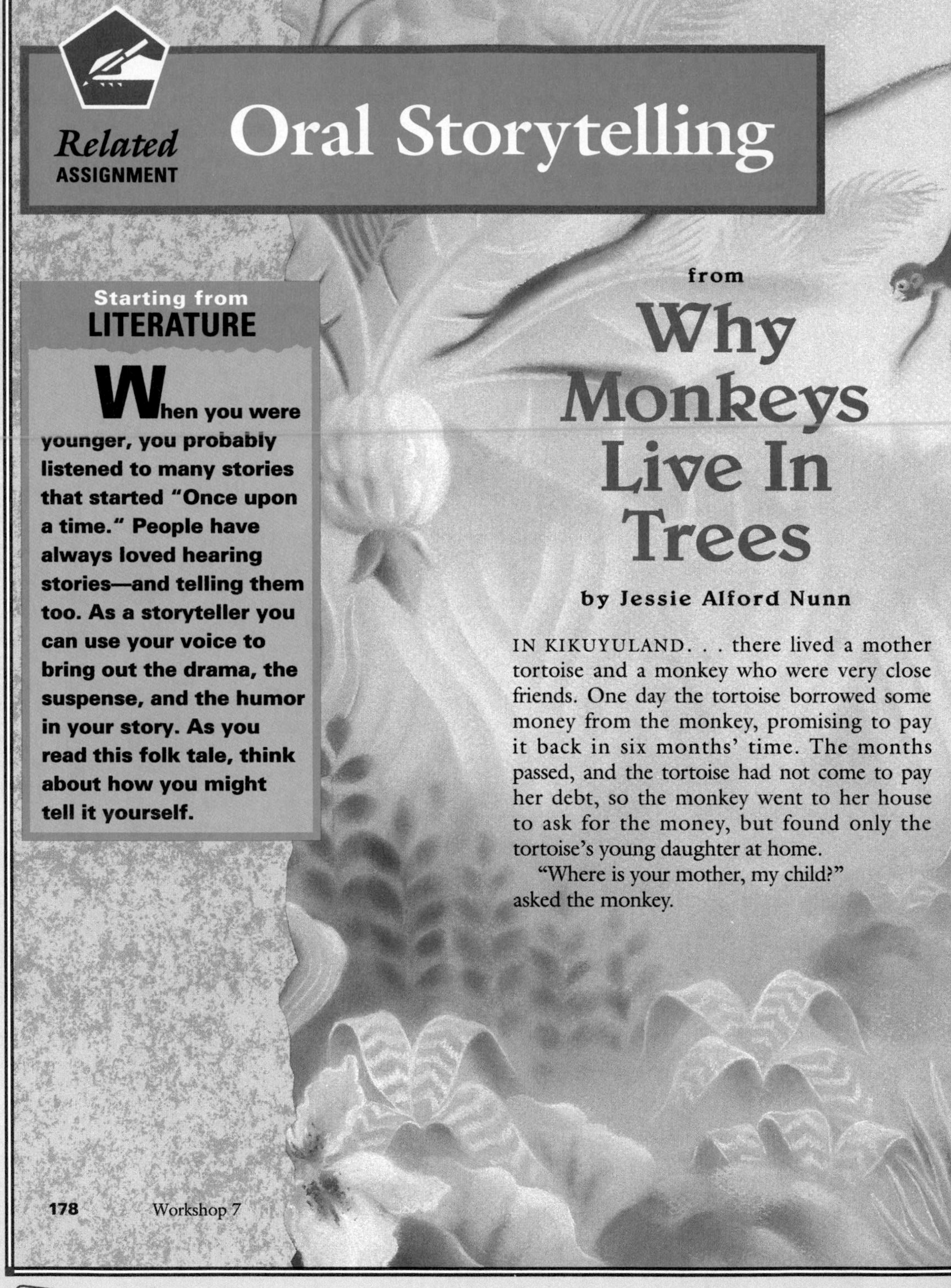

Related
ASSIGNMENT
Oral Storytelling
Starting from
LITERATURE
When you were younger, you probably listened to many stories that started "Once upon a time." People have always loved hearing stories—and telling them too. As a storyteller you can use your voice to bring out the drama, the suspense, and the humor in your story. As you read this folk tale, think about how you might tell it yourself.
from
Why Monkeys Live In Trees
by Jessie Alford Nunn
IN KIKUYULAND. . . there lived a mother tortoise and a monkey who were very close friends. One day the tortoise borrowed some money from the monkey, promising to pay it back in six months' time. The months passed, and the tortoise had not come to pay her debt, so the monkey went to her house to ask for the money, but found only the tortoise's young daughter at home.
"Where is your mother, my child?" asked the monkey.
178 Workshop 7

Links to LITERATURE & LANGUAGE

Literature For more examples of folk literature suitable for oral storytelling, see Unit 6: "Themes in Folklore from the Americas" in *Literature and Language,* Grade 8. This unit includes tales from North America, Central America, and South America.

"Alas, I do not know," the little one replied sadly. "Indeed, it has been six months since I last saw her."

Every day the monkey went to the tortoise's house, but every day the answer was the same. . . .

Now the wily tortoise was at home all the time, but she lay very still behind the house, and being the very color of *murram* (earth), escaped detection by the monkey.

At last, however, she became tired of hiding. . . .

"The next time he comes," she told her child, "simply turn me upside-down, and he will think I am a grinding stone."

So the following day, when the monkey appeared, the daughter quickly turned her mother upside-down and began to grind millet on the bottom of her shell. Exasperated at the thought of yet another fruitless visit, the monkey became furious. Enraged, he picked up the grinding stone and hurled it as far as possible into the thick bush. . . .

Not at all hurt by this treatment because of the protection provided by her hard shell, the mother tortoise calmly picked herself up and strolled nonchalantly back into her house.

"Good afternoon, friend," she said pleasantly to the monkey. "I am sorry to have been away so long. Have you come to collect the money I borrowed from you?"

"Yes, I have," growled the monkey. "Oblige me by giving it to me right away."

"Why certainly, my dear friend," replied the tortoise in a sweet voice. "It is stored right here in the grinding stone."

"In the grinding stone?" screeched the monkey.

"Yes, indeed. . . . But I don't see my favorite grinding stone. Where can it be?"

With much chagrin, the monkey had to confess that he had just thrown the stone into the thick bush.

"Ah, well," returned the tortoise blithely, "don't worry; just go out and search for the grinding stone, and when you find it, you'll have your money."

So the monkey went into the bush but he could see nothing. Up the branches into the trees he scampered, looking and worrying. . . . All the other monkeys came around to ask what he was doing, and he persuaded them to help him search. Soon the trees were alive with monkeys hunting, running up and down in the swinging branches from first dawn to lantern dark.

At this very moment, if you go into the forest and look into the trees, you will find the entire monkey family swinging from branch to branch and tree to tree, still hunting and searching for the grinding stone that holds the money.

Think & Respond

What qualities make this a good story to read aloud? What tone of voice would you use to tell it? How would you make each character sound different? Does this story remind you of any stories you would like to tell?

Think & Respond

ELICIT PERSONAL RESPONSES

Have students discuss answers to the first question in the Think & Respond box. Then discuss the tone of the story (humorous) and the appropriate inflection for each character. (Sample answers: child—innocent; monkey—angry; mother—sly) Ask students why this story might be more effective when read aloud. (The traits of the characters can be emphasized through oral interpretation.) Encourage students to jot down in their writing folders the titles of stories they recall that might be especially suited to oral storytelling.

EXPLORE THE AUTHOR'S TECHNIQUES

To help students choose appropriate stories for oral storytelling, point out some of the features that make this story especially suitable: (1) provides clues to speech patterns and tone of voice, (2) contains dialogue, which adds to the ease of telling and adds interest to the presentation, (3) features animals that possess human qualities and characteristics, and (4) contains suspense and an interesting plot twist.

SPICE BOX

To get students in the mood for storytelling, have them create a "chain" story. You can begin by relating a story starter, such as the following: "I'll never forget that night. I was baby-sitting for my little brother. We were eating popcorn while we watched his favorite monster movie, *The Anteater Eats California.* Just as the anteater was about to bite off another chunk of the Golden Gate Bridge, we heard a loud crash in the basement." Then go around the classroom, having each student add the next few details to the story. The last student will conclude the story.

Writing ON YOUR OWN

Invite students to find a story to tell. They may wish to look for a story that shares some of the same qualities as "Why Monkeys Live in Trees" so that they can bring it to life through vocal inflection and gestures.

Handbooks for Help and Practice

The following handbooks may be used as mini-lessons before students begin writing or as resources when problems arise.

- **Introductions, pp. 278–280**
- **Critical Listening and Observing, pp. 363–366**

Teaching Strategies

for FIND A STORY TO TELL

PERSONAL TOUCH Share with students a story that is meaningful to you in some way. It might be a story that your family used to tell when you were young, a story you like to tell your children, or a story a teacher once read to you in class. As time permits, tell the story, incorporating the techniques on page 181 and thus modeling them for students.

for USE YOUR VOICE . . .

HELPFUL HINT Tell students that practicing is one way to calm "butterflies" about presenting in front of a group. One way in which students can become more comfortable with how they look is by practicing in front of a mirror at home, coordinating their words with gestures and facial expressions. If students have access to a video camera, they could record their performances to see how they might improve.

Writing ON YOUR OWN
Oral Storytelling

INVITATION TO *Write*

Oral storytelling is a way you can entertain listeners with your own interpretation of a story. You can make any story come alive by using your voice in different ways when you tell the story.

Choose a story you would like to tell and tell it in a way that will entertain your listeners.

CHOOSING A STORY

1. Find a story to tell. You may wish to retell "Why Monkeys Live in Trees." You could also look through collections of folk tales, myths, and legends. Here are some other possibilities:

- scary stories
- stories from camp
- urban folklore
- holiday stories
- family tales or legends
- stories you make up

2. Reread the story. Think about what makes the story a good one to tell. Is it the suspense, the interesting characters, or the humor? If the story is long, you might choose one key part to tell.

Writing TIP

It's a good idea to put marks and notes to yourself on a photocopy of the story. These will remind you which words to emphasize or how to read certain passages.

PRACTICING YOUR STORY

1. Use your voice for different effects. You want your listeners to experience the story through your voice as well as through the author's words. Try using a tape recorder to practice your presentation. By playing back the tape you can evaluate your performance. Think about ways you can vary your presentation and bring out the special features of the story when you read it aloud. Look at the suggestions on the following page.

MULTICULTURAL Connection

Encourage students to choose folk tales, myths, or legends from their cultural heritage. Some students might be interested in comparing common threads among stories from different cultures.

- **Pitch** Help your listeners identify characters by using high pitch for some characters, low for others.
- **Volume** Consider where a loud or forceful tone will be best and where speaking more softly is more effective. Volume can be used to create mood or for emphasis.
- **Pace** Speed up your speaking when the action heats up; slow down to increase suspense. Pause for dramatic effect.
- **Dialect** Let your characters speak in dialect where appropriate—if you think you can do this convincingly.
- **Gestures** Facial expressions and effective gestures can help you put your story across.

2. Try out different approaches. A good way to practice is to work with someone else. Try using different approaches and commenting on each other's presentations. See which effects work best.

3. Prepare an introduction. Think about what your listeners need to know about the story. Do you need to give any background about the story or its author? Are there any words or ideas you should explain beforehand? You also might want to explain why you chose to tell this story. For example, does it have some special meaning for you, or is there a particular message you want to convey?

Writer's Choice You could make your reading a multimedia presentation by adding music, props, costumes, or other special effects.

PUBLISHING AND PRESENTING

- **Hold a round robin.** Get together with other class members and take turns telling your stories.
- **Be a storyteller.** Make arrangements to tell your story to a group that would be interested in it. You might choose another class, a group of younger children, or a family gathering.
- **Make a recording.** Use a tape recorder to record your tale. You might want to add music or other special effects.

for PITCH, VOLUME, PACE . . .

INDIVIDUALIZING INSTRUCTION: AUDITORY LEARNERS Some students may be especially aware of the importance of pitch, inflection, volume, and pace. Encourage them to demonstrate how certain changes in voice can create suspense or indicate mood or character.

for DIALECT

STUMBLING BLOCK Effective use of dialect can be a bit tricky, and if not handled well, offensive. You could explain the difference between an *inflection* (voice pitch, emphasis, and so on) and an *accent* (saying words incorrectly); too often, an accent is incorrectly (and offensively) attributed in an attempt to reproduce an inflection. You might want to check with students who are using dialect to see that the dialect adds flavor to the story and is not offensive. Help students to revise their stories if necessary.

for TRY OUT DIFFERENT APPROACHES

COOPERATIVE LEARNING Some students might like to work together to present a story. Each student can take a particular role. For example, one student might be the narrator and other students might take the parts of the characters.

GENERAL NOTE

INDIVIDUALIZING INSTRUCTION: LEP STUDENTS Telling a story might be difficult for students who have limited proficiency in English. These students need encouragement, so fostering a supportive atmosphere in class is important. You might also pair these students with those whose English language abilities are strong.

Guidelines for Evaluation

AN EFFECTIVE ORAL STORYTELLING

- presents a short, interesting story or meaningful segment of a story
- includes introductory information as appropriate
- interprets the story through the use of voice and gesture

Teaching Strategies

for CURRENT EVENTS

MANAGEMENT TIP For students who choose this activity, have available several issues of *Time* or *Newsweek* so that students can see how these newsmagazines present information.

for HISTORY

COOPERATIVE LEARNING The History Springboard might be extended into a group activity with a different role for each student. For example, one student might act as Lincoln giving the speech; a second student might speak as a politician responding to the speech; a third student might act as a reporter analyzing the speech; and a fourth student might speak as a parent of a soldier who died at Gettysburg.

Springboards

Media You and one of your classmates have been chosen as the Roger Ebert and Gene Siskel of your school. Choose a classmate and then choose a movie to review. In front of the class, share your reviews and then comment on the similarities and differences in your analyses.

CURRENT EVENTS *Time* magazine has chosen you to analyze an important issue facing teenagers today. Choose an issue and then write your analysis of it.

History What if you had been on hand when President Abraham Lincoln gave the Gettysburg Address? How would you have responded to it? Choose an important historical speech and write an analysis of it.

Art What do you see when you look at a painting or a sculpture? Choose a work of art and write an analysis of it.

SPEAKING & LISTENING Choose a scene from a story or play you like. Then, with some of your classmates, act out the scene for the rest of the class.

182

Cucaracha (1948), Alexander Calder.

ART NOTE

This sculpture is one of many animal designs by American artist Alexander Calder (1898–1976). Calder crafted both mobiles and stabiles (stationary sculptures that look like mobiles).

You might want to ask a student who knows Spanish to share the meaning of *cucaracha* with the class (cockroach). Encourage interested students to use *Cucaracha* for the Art Springboard.

on the LIGHT side

Private? No!

So you don't think punctuation makes a difference? Which of these signs is more inviting?

Private No Swimming Allowed	Private? No. Swimming Allowed.

Willard Espy, who writes interesting books about language, came up with this demonstration of what a small change in punctuation will do. Here are some of his other examples:

The butler stood by the door and called the guests' names as they arrived.
The butler stood by the door and called the guests names as they arrived.

The murderer protested his innocence. An hour after, he was put to death.
The murderer protested his innocence an hour after he was put to death.

I'm sorry you can't come with us.
I'm sorry. You can't come with us.

The escaping convict dropped, a bullet in his leg.
The escaping convict dropped a bullet in his leg.

Go slow—children.
Go slow, children.

A clever dog knows its master.
A clever dog knows it's master.

Do not break your bread or roll in your soup.
Do not break your bread, or roll in your soup.

on the LIGHT side

Discuss how the meanings of the examples are changed by the changes in punctuation. Students should recognize that some of the sentences become humorous, as in the case of the murderer's protesting his innocence *after* he was put to death.

Challenge students to come up with their own pairs of sentences in which the punctuation changes the meaning.

Adding Extensions

Objectives

- To combine sentences by using a dash before extensions
- To imitate the structure of sentences with extensions
- To expand sentences by adding extensions

Teaching Strategies

for ON THE MARK

HELPFUL HINT Some students might ask about using dashes within a sentence. Explain that a pair of dashes is used when an extension occurs within a sentence. Provide this example:

The student came to class at 9:30—an hour late—and sat down at his desk without saying a word.

Additional Resource

Sentence Composing Copy Masters, pp. 13–14

Sentence

COMPOSING

Adding Extensions

Effective writers occasionally use a dash to signal an extension or afterthought at the end of a sentence—like a P.S. at the end of a letter. Using a dash allows you to add information that is related to the idea in a sentence but is not essential.

Model A It was just the most beautiful thing to have a really and truly best friend—a friend that you could enjoy.

Rosa Guy, The Friends

Model B There, on the farther side of the clearing, dark, heavy forms were making a silent advance—a sea of thick, powerful black bodies with short bristles, small black snouts, and long yellowish tusks. **Tom Gill, "Jungle Wars"**

Model C My mother had trouble persuading me to carry one because I was a lady, but I now realized that a handkerchief was an invaluable tool for a counter-spy—to erase fingerprints, and so forth. **Katherine Patterson, *Jacob Have I Loved***

▶ **ON THE MARK** Use a dash to separate nonessential material from the rest of the sentence. Place a period at the end of the extension or afterthought.

A. Combining Sentences Make a new sentence by putting the underlined part of the second sentence into the first sentence as an extension or afterthought. Write the complete sentence, putting a dash before the extension or afterthought.

1. At the time I thought the blame for my unhappiness had to be fixed. The blame had to be fixed on Caroline, on my grandmother, on my mother, even on myself. **Katherine Patterson, *Jacob Have I Loved***
2. With rattlesnake speed, Maniac snatched the book back. He snatched it back except for one page, which stayed, ripped, in Mars Bar's hand. **Jerry Spinelli, *Maniac Magee***
3. Each morning she would get up at six, and walk all the way from Thirteenth Avenue to First Avenue. The walk was a distance of about two miles to and fro. **Mark Mathabane, *Kaffir Boy***

B. Unscrambling and Imitating Sentences Unscramble each set of sentence chunks below to create a sentence that matches the structure of one of the models on page 184. Write a correctly punctuated sentence of your own that imitates each model and contains an extension or afterthought.

1. Write sentences that imitate Model A.
   a toothache that Jeremy couldn't stand / to get a really nasty and throbbing toothache / it certainly was a terrible time
2. Write sentences that imitate Model B.
   now, toward the goal line of the visitors / a fullback with strong, punishing long strides / fast, powerful Klemsky was running the ball / in black jersey, battered silver helmet, and grass-stained silver pants
3. Write sentences that imitate Model C.
   but Sally finally agreed that a big dog would be the best pet for her / the pet store owner had difficulty convincing Sally to buy a big dog / to watch the house and everything else / since Sally was so tiny

C. Expanding Sentences Use your imagination to add an extension to the end of each sentence. Be sure each extension answers the question in parentheses.

1. There Trufflehunter called at the mouth of a little hole in a green bank, and out popped the last thing Caspian expected—*(What popped out?)*
   C. S. Lewis, *Prince Caspian*
2. All was well until one day they met a thunderstorm—*(What was the thunderstorm like?)* **J.R.R. Tolkien, *The Hobbit***
3. When Slake sat down to dine in the evening, his dinner awaited him in his shirt pocket—*(What was his dinner?)* **Felice Holman, *Slake's Limbo***
4. I was halfway across the dump area when I saw something I didn't like—*(What did you see?)* **Stephen King, "The Body"**

Grammar Refresher Extensions and afterthoughts are often sentence fragments that do not by themselves express a complete thought. To learn more about sentences and fragments, see Handbook 39, "The Sentence and Its Parts," pages 382–383.

Answer Key

A. Combining Sentences

1. At the time I thought the blame for my unhappiness had to be fixed—on Caroline, on my grandmother, on my mother, even on myself.
2. With rattlesnake speed, Maniac snatched the book back—except for one page, which stayed, ripped, in Mars Bar's hand.
3. Each morning she would get up at six, and walk all the way from Thirteenth Avenue to First Avenue—a distance of about two miles to and fro.

B. Unscrambling and Imitating Sentences

Unscrambled sentences are shown below. Imitative sentences will vary but should follow the same pattern.

1. It certainly was a terrible time to get a really nasty and throbbing toothache—a toothache that Jeremy couldn't stand.
2. Now, toward the goal line of the visitors, fast, powerful Klemsky was running the ball—a fullback with strong, punishing long strides in black jersey, battered silver helmet, and grass-stained silver pants.
3. The pet store owner had difficulty convincing Sally to buy a big dog since Sally was so tiny, but Sally finally agreed that a big dog would be the best pet for her—to watch the house and everything else.

C. Expanding Sentences

Answers will vary. Author's sentences are given below. Added copy is in bold type.

1. There Trufflehunter called at the mouth of a little hole in a green bank, and out popped the last thing Caspian expected—**a Talking Mouse.**
   C. S. Lewis, *Prince Caspian*
2. All was well until one day they met a thunderstorm—**more than a thunderstorm, a thunder-battle.**
   J. R. R. Tolkien, *The Hobbit*
3. When Slake sat down to dine in the evening, his dinner awaited him in his shirt pocket—**the second half of his lunch sandwich.**
   Felice Holman, *Slake's Limbo*
4. I was halfway across the dump area when I saw something I didn't like—**Milo Pressman's port-holed '56 Buick was parked behind his tarpaper shack.**
   Stephen King, "The Body"

8

Informative Writing: Reports

Overview

Informative writing is writing that explains or informs. Most often, the writer of an informative piece does research to expand on his or her ideas and knowledge. In this workshop, students research a topic and use their informative and analytical writing skills, developed in previous workshops, to share what they know in an extended piece of writing. Workshop 8 includes the following Guided and Related Assignments as well as the interdisciplinary project described on pages 185c–185d.

1. **Guided: Research Report** invites students to choose a topic of interest, to use various sources to research the topic, to take notes from more than one source, to document the information, and to present the information in a well-organized report.
2. **Related: I-Search** asks students to use their knowledge of report writing from the Guided Assignment to write a personally meaningful report. In this type of report, students include not only the results of their research but also the process of the research itself.

Teaching Preview

Preparation Guide

1. Use the Overview on this page and the Teacher's Choice descriptions on page 187 as a basis for deciding which assignments to teach.
2. Preview the assignments and the teacher's notes and identify concepts that may require preteaching or extra support, given your class's abilities. The handbook mini-lessons suggested within the lesson may also provide guidance.
3. Preview the chart below for support materials in the Teacher's Resource File that may be used with this Workshop. Resources are for use with the Guided Assignment unless otherwise noted.

Support Materials

RESOURCES

Prewrite and Explore

Writing Resource Book, pp. 44–49
Thinking Skills Worksheets, pp. 1, 4
Starting Points for Writing, Writing Prompts for Fine Art, pp. 37, 39–41, 43–44

Draft and Discover

Elaboration, Revision, and Proofreading Practice, pp. 15–17
Writing Resource Book, pp. 50–51

Revise Your Writing

Elaboration, Revision, and Proofreading Practice, p. 18
Writing Resource Book, p. 52
Peer Response Guides, pp. 23–24
Guidelines for Writing Assessment and Portfolio Use, pp. 21, 44–46

Sentence Composing

Sentence Composing Copy Masters, pp. 15–16

Computer Software

Writer's DataBank
Electronic English Handbook

PROFESSIONAL RESOURCES AND MEDIA

Books and Journals

Cudd, E. T., "Magazine Report Frames," *Reading Teacher,* Vol. 45 (October 1991), pp. 160–162
Freedman, Russell, *An Indian Winter,* Holiday (1992)
Kirby, Dan, and Liner, Tom, "Expository Writing," *Inside Out: Developmental Strategies for Teaching Writing,* Boynton/Cook (1988)

Films and Videos

Africa on the Move, Bullfrog, Oley, PA (1992) (55 min.)
The Massachusetts 54th Colored Infantry (American Experience Series), PBS, Alexandria, VA (1991) (60 min.)
The Panamanian Way of Life, Aims, Chatsworth, CA (1992) (24 min.)

Computer Software and Technology

Dr. Peter Owen's Research Paper Writer, Tom Snyder Productions, Cambridge, MA (software), MAC
Homework Helper: Writing, Queue, Fairfield, CT (software), Apple II, PC

Linking Literature, Writing, and Grammar

The following options may be used to provide students with an integrated language experience. Begin by assigning and discussing any of the recommended pieces of literature. Use the suggested strategy to provide a link to the Guided Assignment.

LINKING LITERATURE AND WRITING

Option 1

Starting Point: "Respecting the Heritage of the Mound Builders" by Tom Witosky, student, on pages 188–193 of *The Writer's Craft.*

Strategy: Use the teaching suggestions on pages 188–193 to lead students into the Guided Assignment.

Option 2

Starting Point: "Tracee" by Robert Lipsyte on pages 155–162 of McDougal, Littell's *Literature and Language,* Grade 8. (Additional suggestions for using *Literature and Language* can be found on page 187.)

Strategy: Have students read the story about Tracee Talavera, a young gymnast. Ask students what they think Lipsyte's purpose was in writing this selection (to show that the life of an aspiring Olympic competitor is very hard). Why does Lipsyte focus on Tracee, rather than on young gymnasts in general? (The life of a real young girl captures the audience's interest better than would a list of facts about gymnasts.) Summarize the discussion and introduce the Guided Assignment.

Option 3

Starting Point: "Roberto Clemente: A Bittersweet Memoir" by Jerry Izenberg.

Strategy: Have students read the selection. Discuss what students learned about the late baseball star. What else would they like to know about Clemente? Use the discussion to lead into the Guided Assignment.

LINKING WRITING AND GRAMMAR

Before students revise their reports, remind them that a strong report follows the conventions of standard written English. A verb agrees with its subject, not with any words that come between the subject and verb. Write the following sentences on the board.

Incorrect: The White House, the scene of many political demonstrations, have a fascinating history.

Correct: The White House, the scene of many political demonstrations, has a fascinating history.

Have students check their papers for problems in subject-verb agreement. Go over pages 577–592 in the Grammar and Usage Handbook. If problems in agreement still appear in student papers, assign the exercises on these pages for reteaching. Additional practice can be found in the *Grammar and Usage Practice Book* on pages 92–98.

Management Guidelines

The chart below indicates the number of days recommended for each phase of the Guided and Related Assignments. These numbers are an estimate of the total time needed for each phase. In practice, of course, students may not complete each phase in one continuous session, nor will they necessarily progress from stage to stage in the linear order shown here. Stars indicate portions of the assignment that may be completed outside the classroom if time is limited or if teachers wish students to work independently.

RESEARCH REPORT

Reading a Student Model	1 day
Prewrite and Explore	1 week*
Research Your Topic	1 week*
Draft and Discover	1–2 weeks*
Revise Your Writing	1 week*
Proofread	1–2 days*
Publish and Present	1 day
Reflect on Your Writing	1 day
Reteaching	open
Extension and Enrichment	open*
Sentence Composing	open*

I-SEARCH

Starting from Literature	1 day
Researching Your Report	1–2 weeks*
Writing Your Report	1–2 weeks*
Reviewing Your Writing	1 week*
Publishing and Presenting	1 day

The Rain Forest: Exploring a Vanishing Treasure

Overview

Students engaged in this project will research and prepare reports about the world's rain forests. In doing so, they will gain insights into the relationships among the earth's ecosystems and into the complex issues involved in efforts to preserve rain forests. Students will also organize and synthesize content material from various curriculum areas to extend their learning beyond the classroom.

Students will participate in the following activities:

- Develop and share an overview of rain forests and of contemporary issues related to rain forests
- Select topics related to rain forests and research them in depth
- Prepare research reports
- Create and stage presentations featuring their reports and showing what they have learned

Preparation Guide

Tell students that rain forests are disappearing at the rate of one and a half acres per second, twenty-four hours a day, and that biologists see rain forest destruction as our most serious environmental problem.

Explain that during this project students will use research skills to study rain forests in depth and that they will present their findings in formats that will help to increase people's understanding of the issues and problems related to the preservation of rain forests.

Project File

Stage 1 Identify Topics

1. Divide the class into four groups. Assign each group one of the following questions: (1) What is a rain forest? (2) Where are the world's rain forests and who lives in them? (3) Why do some people want to cut down rain forests? (4) Why do some people want to preserve rain forests?
2. Have students survey general resources for specific answers to their questions. Tell them to record facts they find and to note their sources.
3. Direct groups to report their findings orally to the class and to file their notes in a class fact file.
4. After groups have shared their findings, invite each student to select a topic involving rain forests as a focus for research.

TEAM TEACHING

The following activities may be used for team teaching or as enrichment and extension activities by the language arts teacher.

Science Learn about the climatic and biological conditions that produce rain forests. Learn about the layers of a rain forest (see *Resources, Stage 1*).

Social Studies Locate the world's rain forests on maps: Learn about important products from rain forests and about groups of people who inhabit rain forests.

Math Calculate rates of rain forest destruction in various areas and during various time periods.

Language Arts Review techniques for making source cards, previewing sources, and taking notes (see *Resources, Stage 1*).

TEACHING TIPS

- Show slides of rain forest plants and animals and play an audiotape of rain forest sounds.
- Designate an area for the class fact file.
- Suggest that each student narrow his or her topic by focusing on an aspect of the rain forest in a specific country.
- Allow students interested in similar topics to work together in small groups.

Stage 2 Explore and Research Topics

1. Direct students to explore their topics by using prewriting techniques and then to begin research (see *Resources, Stage 2*).
2. Encourage students to expand their research beyond books by referring to periodical articles, audiotapes, films, videos, and television documentaries and by interviewing experts (see *Resources, Stage 2*).
3. Tell students to search for visual materials (photos and illustrations) as well as written materials. Tell them to take careful notes about the facts and images that interest them most.

TEAM TEACHING

Science Study rain forest ecosystems and their contribution to the global ecosystem. Learn about areas where rain forests have been destroyed, and examine the consequences of such destruction. Study medicinal uses of rain forest plants (see *Resources, Stage 2*).

Social Studies Learn about lifestyles of rain forest peoples. Explore the conflicting needs of native peoples, national economies, and the global community. Learn about efforts to save rain forests (see *Resources, Stage 2*).

Language Arts Review research skills.

Art View artworks inspired by rain forests. Examine crafts of native peoples.

TEACHING TIPS

- Remind students to use the class fact file for locating source materials.
- Schedule a field trip to a zoo or a botanic garden displaying rain forest organisms.

Stage 3
Write and Present Reports

1. Direct students to write reports based on their research (see *Resources, Stage 3*).
2. Tell students to plan presentations of their reports. Suggest that the presentations include original poems, songs, or short stories or that they involve more than one medium.
3. Have students videotape their presentations and donate the videotapes to a public library or to an organization working to preserve rain forests (see *Resources, Stage 3*).

TEAM TEACHING

Language Arts Review techniques of writing and revising research reports (see *Resources, Stage 3*).

Math Devise charts and graphs to display the numerical data found.

Social Studies Show how proposals to preserve rain forests can take into account the needs both of native peoples and of national economies.

Science Prepare experiments to demonstrate the ways rain forests function in the earth's ecosystem.

Art Create illustrations or models to accompany presentations.

TEACHING TIPS

- Make video equipment available for presentations.
- Arrange for students to stage their presentations for members of a local environmental group, such as the Sierra Club or the Nature Conservancy.

Resources

STAGE 1

The Writer's Craft, Grade 8, Workshop 8, "Informative Writing: Reports," pages 196–199, provides instruction in previewing sources, making source cards, and taking notes.

Tropical Rain Forests Around the World by Elaine Landau, with color photos on each page, provides maps and a general introduction to rain forests.

Forests and ***Weather,*** both by David Lambert, include material about rain forests and contain fact files.

STAGE 2

The Writer's Craft, Grade 8, Handbook 32, "Study and Research Skills," pages 340–345, offers tips for note taking and active reading. Handbook 33, "Writing Paraphrases and Summaries," pages 346–348, gives guidance on specific note-taking skills. Handbook 35, "Making Use of the Library," pages 352–361, teaches students how to locate and use library sources.

Tropical Rainforests: An Endangered Environment by James D. Nations explores rain forest issues in detail, including chapters on medicines and other rain forest products and on native peoples, and provides information on rain forest preservation.

Back issues of ***Faces, Odyssey,*** and ***National Geographic*** magazines carry numerous illustrated articles about rain forests and the peoples who inhabit them.

Lobo of the Tasaday by John Nance and ***The Tasaday Controversy: Assessing the Evidence,*** edited by Thomas N. Headland, offer two conflicting views of rain forest dwellers of the Philippines.

Saving the Earth: A Citizen's Guide to Environmental Action by Will Steger and ***The Green Lifestyle Handbook: 1001 Ways to Heal the Earth,*** edited by Jeremy Rifkin, include suggestions for measures that can help to preserve rain forests.

STAGE 3

The Writer's Craft, Grade 8, Workshop 8, "Informative Writing: Reports," pages 186–205, presents techniques for drafting, revising, and documenting sources in a research report.

Students might donate videotapes of their presentations to the **Rainforest Action Network,** 450 Sansome St., Suite 700, San Francisco, CA 94111, or to the **World Wildlife Fund,** 1250 Twenty-fourth Street NW, Washington, DC 20037.

Additional Projects

Wildlife Rescue Propose that students start a program to aid animals native to your area. Students might organize an assistance program for injured wildlife, or they might work to protect and rehabilitate local habitats. Students should use research skills to learn about local wildlife's needs and habitats. They can also write pamphlets describing the goals of their program to solicit community support.

Art Works! Invite students to set up and staff a mobile art exhibit. Direct them to survey art available on loan from local libraries and museums, to pick suitable works for local preschools or convalescent homes, and to take the art "on tour." Students should use research skills to learn background information about the artworks, to learn techniques of art appreciation, and to plan art-related activities, tailoring presentations to audiences' interests and needs.

Music Power Have students identify a community issue of concern to them, research the issue, and create a music video or an audiotape that presents their findings and explains their concerns. Direct students to enlist the help of community groups in producing the presentation and to ask local television or radio stations to donate air time.

Objective

- To use art and suggested writing prompts as springboards to informal writing

WRITING WARM-UPS

Encourage students to respond freely and informally to at least one of the sketchbook prompts. They may begin by discussing their reactions in small groups and then freewriting in their journals. Remind students that their responses will not be graded and may provide them with useful material for other informative writing assignments.

SHOW, DON'T TELL

The following is a sample of a showing paragraph for the second prompt:

News programs today provide more entertainment than information. The lead story on the news often features the latest celebrity gossip, and important political stories are often told with brief sound bites rather than in-depth reporting. Even during the sports segment, viewers are entertained with bloopers and blunders on the playing field.

Sketch Book

WRITING WARM-UPS

Desert Metropolis, Robert McCall.

- Where do you think people will live in the future? Write down some of your thoughts.
- What have you wondered about recently? What puzzles you? Make a list of things that you would like to know more about.
- If you could meet any person in history, who would it be? Explain why you would like to meet the person you picked.

Show, Don't Tell

When you write a report, you can show your knowledge by using concrete details. Your sources of information—such as books, eyewitness accounts, and interviews—can help you find the facts and examples you need. Add examples to one of the *telling* sentences below, turning the statement into a *showing* paragraph.

- Technology changes quickly.
- News programs today provide more entertainment than information.

ART NOTE

Desert Metropolis is part of a series depicting gravity-free "floating cities" of the future, as imagined by artist Robert McCall. Unlike many futurists, McCall is optimistic. He says, "I see people building more beautiful cities and more wonderful environments for themselves to live in." McCall's work is admired for its convincing detail that conveys his daring vision of the future.

Informative Writing: Reports

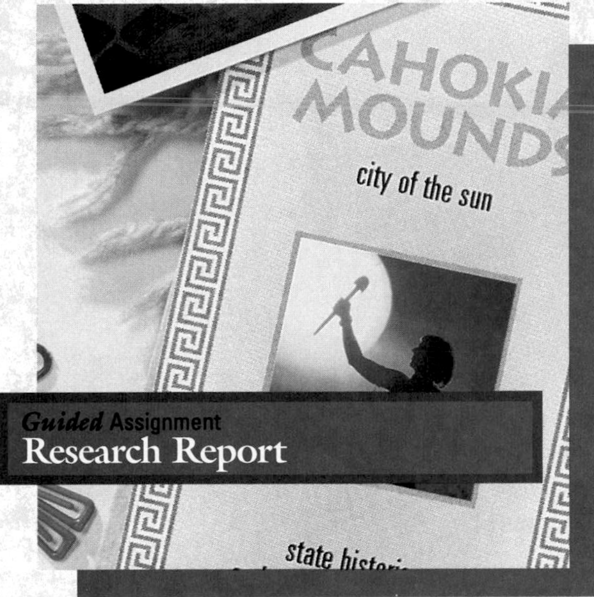

Guided Assignment
Research Report

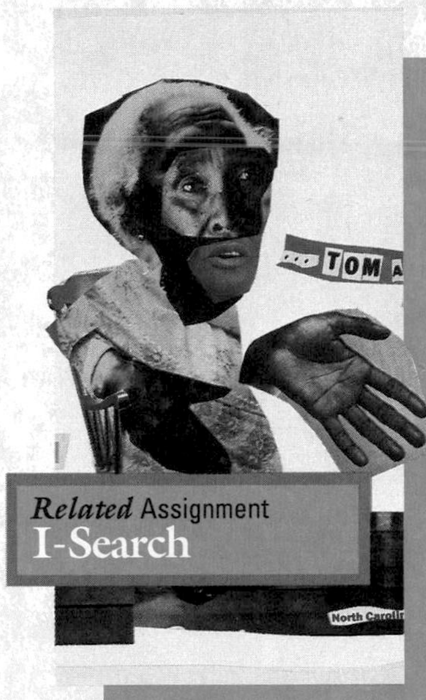

Related Assignment
I-Search

What is a research report? It is more than library books and magazine articles, more than note cards and outlines and getting all your facts right. Writing a research report is about questions and answers, about *your* questions and *your* answers. It's about discovery—finding a subject you're curious about, uncovering information in a variety of places, and then sharing what you've discovered with others.

In this workshop, you'll have the opportunity to research subjects you're curious about and to report on what you learn.

WRITER'S WORKSHOP 8

Informative Writing: Reports

Objectives

Guided Assignment

Research Report To respond to a research report and to create a report on a topic of interest to the writer, using information from several sources

Related Assignment

I-Search To respond to a report that has a strong personal focus and to write a report on a topic of personal significance

Teacher's Choice

Use the following guidelines to choose the assignment that best suits students' needs.

Research Report This assignment offers students step-by-step guidance in choosing a topic, researching and note taking, organizing a report, and crediting sources. Because report writing calls on students to synthesize many skills, you will probably want to assign it late in the year, after students have had experience with shorter pieces of expository writing in Workshops 4, 5, and 6.

I-Search This assignment will benefit students who prefer to do a report with a strong personal focus. You might offer it as an alternative to the Guided Assignment, especially if students completed a formal report in another subject area earlier in the year.

Links to Literature & Language

Literature For more examples of writing that contains research elements, see *Literature and Language,* Grade 8.
- Robert Lipsyte, "Tracee"
- Ann Petry, from *Harriet Tubman: Conductor on the Underground Railroad*
- Hazel Shelton Abernethy, "The Home Front: 1941–1945"
- Robert Silverberg, "Pompeii"

Writing This guided assignment may be used as an extension of the Writer's Workshop "Informative Writing: Research Report" on page 633 in *Literature and Language,* Grade 8.

Guided ASSIGNMENT

ASSIGNMENT RATIONALE

The ability to write effective research reports is fundamental to academic success in high school and college and to success in many job fields. This assignment provides a step-by-step guide to choosing a topic, gathering and recording information, and writing a report based on research. It also offers practice in combining many high-level thinking skills.

Reading a STUDENT MODEL

This student model shows how a research report addresses a topic of current concern and reflects a writer's personal interests. It is the final draft of the report shown in progress on the workshop pages that follow.

Motivate

Begin the discussion of research reports by describing your own interest in a particular topic, and then tell how you proceeded to get more information on the subject. For example, describe a TV documentary you watched, cite two or three questions the show raised in your mind, and then share a library book or magazine article you discovered that helped you answer your questions.

Now have students summarize newsmagazine articles, TV news reports, or documentaries that interested them recently. Make a list of the topics they mention.

Guided ASSIGNMENT Research Report

Reading a STUDENT MODEL

Do you ever hear reports on TV or radio that leave you with unanswered questions? Do you ever wish you could find answers to those questions yourself—if you only had the time? When you write a research report, you take the time. You ask questions, look for answers, and write up your findings to share with others.

Tom Witosky's social studies report reflects his interest in his Native American ancestry. As you read, think about how Tom combines what he learns about history with an issue that is important today.

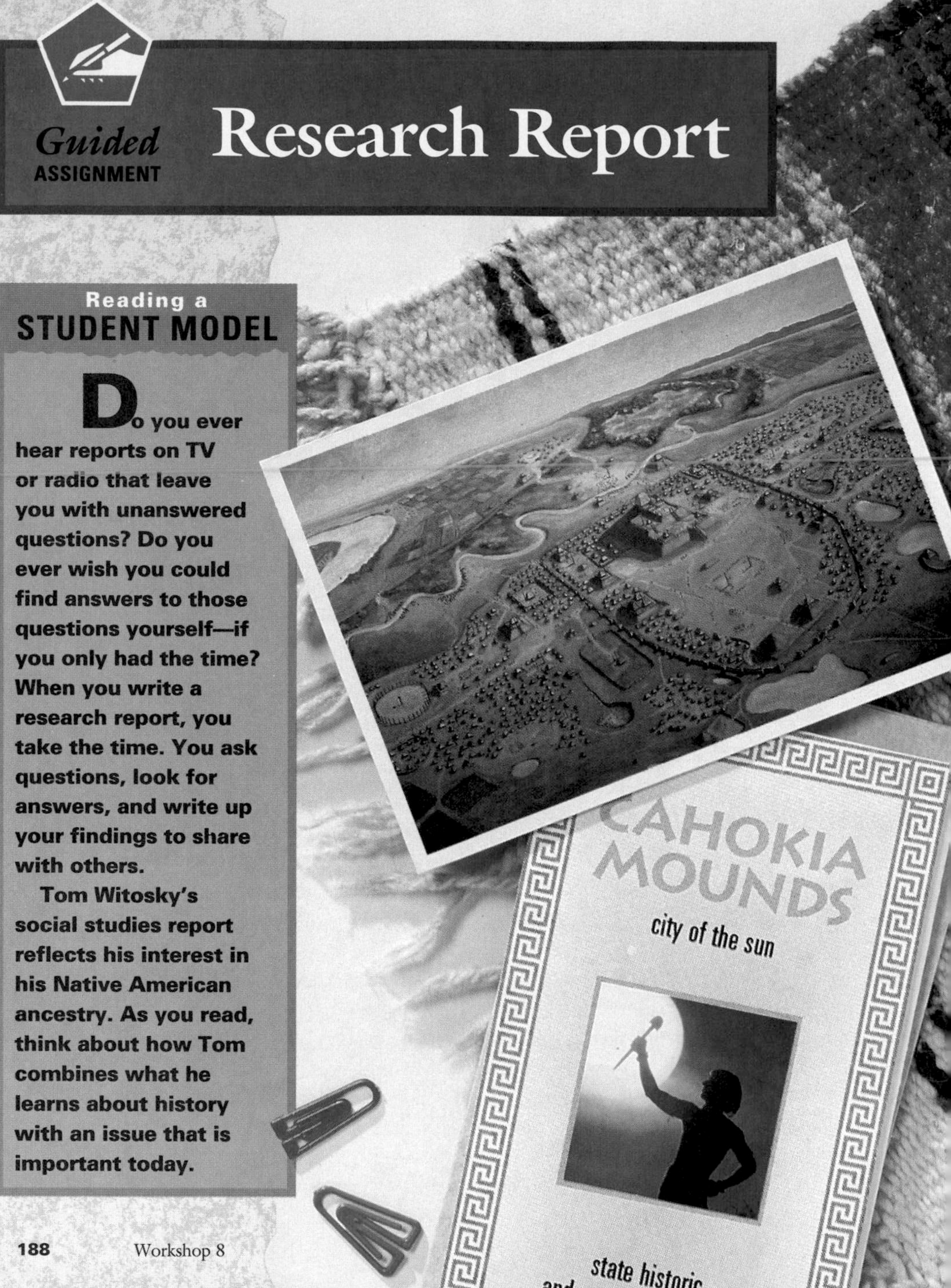

188 Workshop 8

MULTICULTURAL Connection

The Cahokia Mounds of Illinois were made by the people of the Mississippian culture. The Mississippian people raised livestock and grew crops. They lived in densely populated river towns. Each town had a central plaza for ceremonies. The mounds were grouped around the plaza. Not much more is known about the lives of the mound builders because they did not leave written records behind. Ask students to consider how, without written records, we gain knowledge of ancient civilizations.

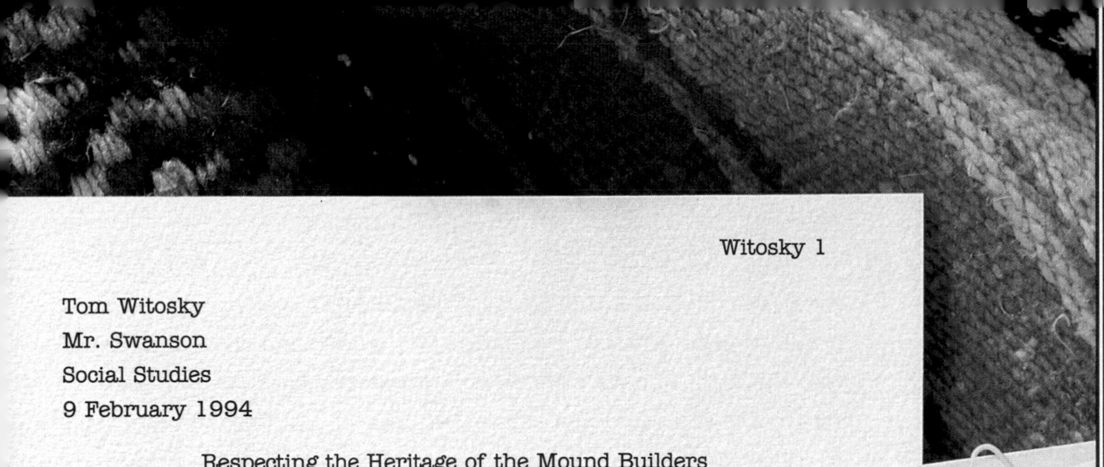

Witosky 1

Tom Witosky
Mr. Swanson
Social Studies
9 February 1994

Respecting the Heritage of the Mound Builders

Hundreds or even thousands of years from now, what will happen to our remains? Will our graves become tourist attractions for future generations?

That may seem impossible, but it is not. In fact, it has happened to ancient cultures of American Indians called mound builders. In many places around the country, the mounds have been excavated. Some of the mounds were burial sites, and people's remains have been displayed on the site of the mound or are stored and studied in museums around the country. As a result of protests by modern American Indian groups, the displays have been closed and museums have returned some of the remains to the Indian groups that claim them. The controversy over respect for the dead and for Native American heritage versus the historical importance of the mounds continues today.

To understand the controversy, we need to first understand the mounds themselves and the people who built them. The term "mound builders" is used to describe several different groups of early North American Indians. Between about 1000 B.C. and A.D. 1500, they built mounds of earth as burial places and sites for temples. Tens of thousands of mounds were built in river valleys in the Midwest, the South, and parts of the East.

There were three main groups of mound builders. One major

Monk's Mound—Cahokia

BUILD ON PRIOR KNOWLEDGE

Ask students whether they have heard or read any recent news about concerns of Native Americans. Students may mention legal struggles in several states over land and water rights, or attempts to preserve Native American culture. If any such reports have appeared in your local newspaper recently, bring them in, pass them around the class, and discuss the issues at hand.

Then ask whether students have seen museum exhibits of American Indian artifacts or remains. Invite them to share their reactions to the exhibits. Did they learn something about the people who created the artifacts? How did they feel if they found themselves viewing the bones of human beings? Tell students that exhibits that display artifacts from burial grounds are very controversial today and that the report in the Student Model will help them understand why.

SET A PURPOSE

Have a volunteer read aloud the first two paragraphs of the Student Model. Point out that the paragraphs describe a contemporary controversy. Then read aloud the first sentence of the third paragraph and ask students what connection the writer is making. (The writer is connecting the present and the past.) Have students read the rest of the report to find out what part the past has played in the present-day controversy.

MULTICULTURAL Connection

Students might be inspired by this report to research burial practices or attitudes toward ancestors in a variety of cultures and time periods. For example, individuals or small groups might investigate ancient Egyptian burial customs, the Mexican Day of the Dead festivities, the history of All Hallow's Eve and All Saints' Day in Catholic cultures, or the importance of ancestors in Asian cultures. Students might be particularly interested in exploring and sharing attitudes toward ancestors in their own ethnic groups.

Teaching Strategies

The following annotations explore matters of style and organization in the Student Model. Use these annotations as necessary as students work on their own reports.

for . . . GROUP WAS THE ADENA CULTURE

The writer presents the mound-building groups in chronological order, beginning with the earliest group.

for ANOTHER MAJOR GROUP . . .

The writer describes the achievements of the Hopewell to show how the mound builders changed over time.

for THE THIRD MAJOR GROUP . . .

The source of this remarkable claim about Monk's Mound is credited correctly.

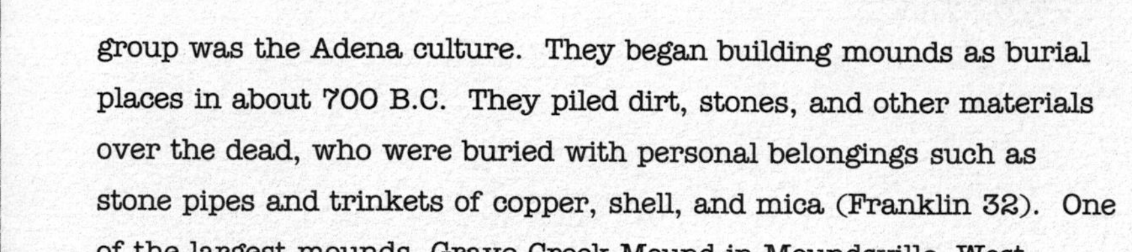

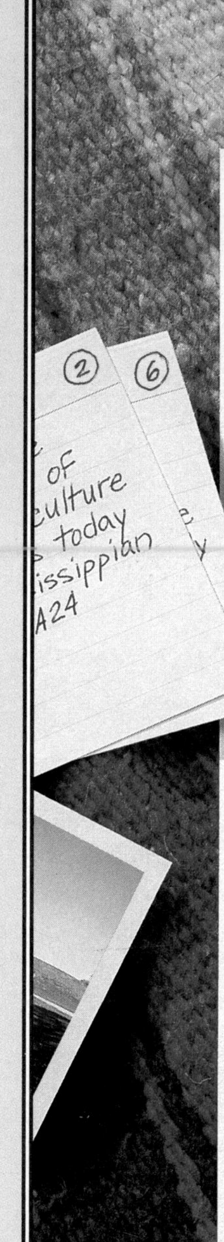

Witosky 2

group was the Adena culture. They began building mounds as burial places in about 700 B.C. They piled dirt, stones, and other materials over the dead, who were buried with personal belongings such as stone pipes and trinkets of copper, shell, and mica (Franklin 32). One of the largest mounds, Grave Creek Mound in Moundsville, West Virginia, is 70 feet high. The Adena also made some mounds shaped like animals. The most famous is the Great Serpent Mound near Hillsboro, Ohio. It is shaped like a huge snake and is about one quarter of a mile long (Snow).

Another major group of mound builders was the Hopewell culture. Between 100 B.C. and A.D. 500, they built mounds that were more elaborate than the Adena's. Some were circular or octagonal. Hopewell mounds were often surrounded by miles of earthen walls. Pearl necklaces, obsidian blades, and birds and fish made of beaten copper were buried inside the mounds. Paula Franklin says that "the objects found inside with the burials are of great beauty and superb workmanship. . . . The Hopewell people were the finest Indian metal workers in North America" (33).

The third major group was the Mississippian culture. It lasted from about A.D. 700 to the 1700s. The Mississippians made some of the most complicated mounds. Some were burial places, but others were bases for temples. These were large, flat-topped mounds similar to pyramids. One of them, called Monk's Mound in Cahokia, Illinois, is 100 feet high, 1,000 feet long, and 700 feet wide. It is considered the largest man-made earthen structure in the world (Franklin 33).

Eventually, the native peoples stopped building mounds, and their cultures died out. No one is sure why. Possible reasons are

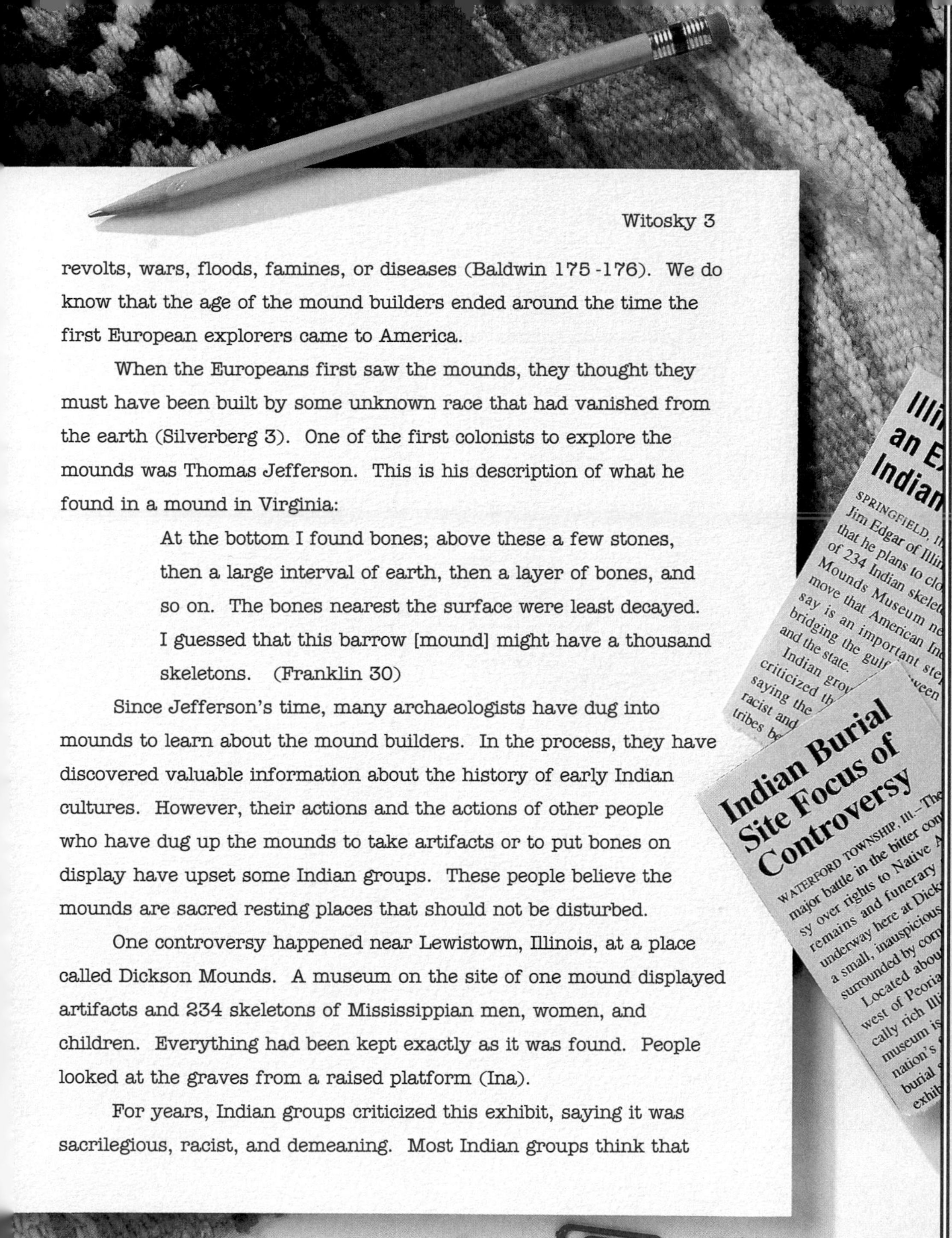

Witosky 3

revolts, wars, floods, famines, or diseases (Baldwin 175-176). We do know that the age of the mound builders ended around the time the first European explorers came to America.

When the Europeans first saw the mounds, they thought they must have been built by some unknown race that had vanished from the earth (Silverberg 3). One of the first colonists to explore the mounds was Thomas Jefferson. This is his description of what he found in a mound in Virginia:

> At the bottom I found bones; above these a few stones, then a large interval of earth, then a layer of bones, and so on. The bones nearest the surface were least decayed. I guessed that this barrow [mound] might have a thousand skeletons. (Franklin 30)

Since Jefferson's time, many archaeologists have dug into mounds to learn about the mound builders. In the process, they have discovered valuable information about the history of early Indian cultures. However, their actions and the actions of other people who have dug up the mounds to take artifacts or to put bones on display have upset some Indian groups. These people believe the mounds are sacred resting places that should not be disturbed.

One controversy happened near Lewistown, Illinois, at a place called Dickson Mounds. A museum on the site of one mound displayed artifacts and 234 skeletons of Mississippian men, women, and children. Everything had been kept exactly as it was found. People looked at the graves from a raised platform (Ina).

For years, Indian groups criticized this exhibit, saying it was sacrilegious, racist, and demeaning. Most Indian groups think that

for AT THE BOTTOM I FOUND BONES . . .

This quotation from the archaeological writings of Thomas Jefferson reconfirms the massive scale of the mounds. Since the quotation is longer than four typed lines, it is correctly set off from the text and indented ten spaces from the left margin.

for SINCE JEFFERSON'S TIME . . .

Note the writer's use of transitions. *Since* indicates chronological order. *However* develops the controversy introduced in the second paragraph of the report.

for FOR YEARS, INDIAN GROUPS . . .

By summarizing the arguments against excavating the mounds and by quoting an expert on Indian treaty rights, the writer is considering both sides of the issue.

Social Studies Connection

Encourage students to collect newspaper and newsmagazine articles about controversial issues that Native Americans are trying to resolve with the U.S. government or with officials of other public institutions. Have students debate the pros and cons of one or more of the issues.

for . . . SOMEONE'S SOUL CANNOT . . .

The quotation from James Yellowbank is a poignant appeal to respect the religious traditions of Native American peoples.

for ON THE OTHER HAND . . .

Note the use of the transitional phrase "On the other hand" to signal a return to the arguments of the archaeologists.

for TODAY, THE CONTROVERSY CONTINUES

This conclusion sums up the positions of both sides clearly and concisely.

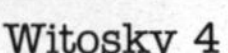

Witosky 4

someone's soul cannot rest if his or her bones are uncovered and shown in a public display ("Illinois"). James Yellowbank of the Indian Treaty Rights Committee said, "These people are American Indians and entitled to rest in peace regardless of whether they died 10 years ago or 10,000 years ago" (Culloton). He also said, "We want them reburied properly and left alone" ("Illinois").

On the other hand, museum displays teach people about the past. Archaeologists study the artifacts they uncover and use them to understand history. Willard Boyd, president of Chicago's Field Museum of Natural History, said, "We clearly believe it is appropriate to have remains in the collections for purposes of continuing research. We can learn more and more from them as techniques of research [improve]" (Wilson).

Complaints have caused museums and the U.S. government to change the way they handle bones and artifacts. Museums such as the Smithsonian Institution and the Field Museum have agreed to remove remains from display and return them to groups that can prove that they are descendants. Congress passed the Indian Graves Protection and Repatriation Act in 1990, which gives Indian groups a say in the handling of remains (Ina). The Dickson Mounds Museum is still open, but the exhibit of the burial excavation has been sealed off and closed to the public.

Today, the controversy continues. Modern Indian groups are still fighting for recognition and due respect for their sacred sites. Even so, our understanding of other cultures and of our own history has been enhanced by the research that has been done on the historic mound sites.

192 Workshop 8

Witosky 5

Works Cited

Baldwin, Gordon C. America's Buried Past. New York: Putnam's, 1962.

Culloton, Dan. "House Panel Foils Burial Site Closing." Chicago Tribune 21 Mar. 1991, sec. 2: 2.

Franklin, Paula Angle. Indians of North America. New York: McKay, 1979.

"Illinois to Shut an Exhibit of Indian Skeletons." New York Times 29 Nov. 1991: A30.

Ina, Lauren. "Indian Burial Site Focus of Controversy." Washington Post 10 Nov. 1991: A24.

Silverberg, Robert. Mound Builders of Ancient America. Greenwich: New York Graphic Society, 1968.

Snow, Dean. "Mound Builders." The World Book Encyclopedia. 1990 ed.

Wilson, Terry. "Protesters Assail Dickson Mounds." Chicago Tribune 4 Jan. 1991, sec. 1: 3.

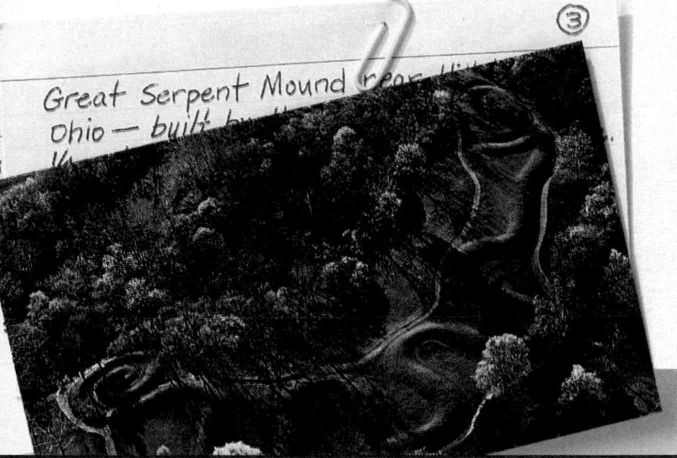

Think & Respond

Respond as a Reader

▶ What did you learn about the mound builders that you didn't know before?

▶ What do you think about the Dickson Mounds controversy? Should museum displays like this one stay open?

Respond as a Writer

▶ What does Tom do to get you interested in his report?

▶ Find three different kinds of details Tom uses to support his ideas.

Think & Respond

RESPOND AS A READER

▶ To help students discuss what they learned about the mound builders, write the cue words *who, what, where, why, when, how* on the board. Invite students to give responses that answer each question. Accept any fact from the report.

▶ Accept student opinions that are based on personal beliefs, as well as opinions based on factual details in the report.

RESPOND AS A WRITER

▶ Students may point out that Tom opens his report with a question that dramatically personalizes the issue of making human remains a tourist attraction.

▶ Students may mention the facts about each group of mound builders, an example of a controversial museum display, and quotations from experts.

Draw Conclusions

To make sure students understand this introduction to research reports, challenge them to list the characteristics they have noted thus far. Responses may include:

- an interesting introduction
- facts, examples, and quotations from several sources to support the main ideas
- credit given to sources of quotes and ideas in text and in a final Works Cited list
- information presented in logical order and with appropriate transitions

for FURTHER READING

The book *Native American Testimony: A Chronicle of Indian-White Relations from Prophecy to the Present, 1492–1992,* edited by Peter Nobokov, contains primary sources spanning five hundred years. In these sources, Native Americans express their views of the effects of European settlement of the New World.

Writing ON YOUR OWN

Tell students that one of the reasons for the success of Tom Witosky's report was his choice of a topic: one that was important to him and that he wanted to learn more about. Suggest that students choose a topic that they will enjoy researching. Remind them that Tom used facts, examples, and quotations from a variety of sources; encourage them to do likewise.

Handbooks for Help and Practice

The following handbooks may be used as mini-lessons before students begin writing or as resources when problems arise.

- **Focusing a Topic, pp. 224–226**
- **Types of Organization, pp. 239–243**
- **Study and Research Skills, pp. 340–345**
- **Writing Paraphrases and Summaries, pp. 346–348**
- **Making Use of the Library, pp. 352–361**
- **Interviewing Skills, p. 362**

PREWRITE AND EXPLORE

Objectives

- To use prewriting techniques to select a topic for a research report
- To focus a topic so that it is neither too broad nor too narrow
- To identify a purpose and establish goals for writing a report
- To brainstorm questions about the topic to guide research

Writing ON YOUR OWN
Research Report

INVITATION TO Write

As Tom Witosky investigated the burial mounds of his Native American ancestors, he found a way to connect what he had learned about the past to a recent controversy. Writing a report means learning about an interesting subject and sharing what you learn with others.

Choose a subject that interests you and research it in several sources. Then write a short research report that tells what you have learned.

PREWRITE AND EXPLORE

1. Find a subject you'd like to investigate. Consider your interests—both in and out of school—and think about subjects you've been wanting to learn more about. Has something been in the news lately that intrigues you? Do you have a special hobby? Has a concept in one of your classes caught your interest? Try one or more of these activities to help you find a subject.

Exploring Topics

- **From A to Z** At your library, browse through books and magazines, flip through some volumes of an encyclopedia, or scan a computer index. What catches your eye? Make a **list** of subjects you would like to know more about.
- **From the familiar to the strange** What's familiar to you may be unfamiliar to someone else. What—or whom—do you know that others don't? Make a **chart** listing names of people, places, or things you know a bit about. For example, you might include figures in history, cultural traditions and customs, or places you've lived or visited. Then make some notes about one or two items in your chart. What do you already know? What do you want to find out?

This falcon-shaped copper cutout from the Hopewell culture dates back to the Middle Woodland period (200 B.C.–A.D. 1). Likenesses of birds such as this one often played an important part in Hopewell funeral ceremonies.

ART NOTE

Hopewell artisans worked with copper, silver, iron, gold, and mica. Materials from the Rockies, the Gulf of Mexico, and the Atlantic were found at the Midwestern sites of the Hopewell, leading archaeologists to conclude that trade was widespread. Ask: What could future scholars tell about our culture if items from your room were dug up in the year 3000?

MULTICULTURAL Connection

Encourage students to research issues that are of concern to their own religious or ethnic communities. This type of activity will be especially suitable for many ESL students, who can conduct research in their first language, interviewing people and reading newspapers and other publications.

- **From the mystery files** The world is full of mysteries, puzzles that have yet to be solved. Is there a Loch Ness monster? Does Bigfoot exist? What is a black hole? Who—or what—made England's crop circles? What is the purpose of Stonehenge? Make a list of unanswered questions and **freewrite** about the ones that interest you most.

Ceremonial deer mask made from carved cedar and shells, found at the Spiro Mound site near Spiro, Oklahoma.

2. Suit yourself. Teachers in different subject areas may ask you to write research reports. Try to find ways you can tailor your writing to your own interests. For example, if you are assigned a science report on outer space, and if astronomy is your hobby, you could focus on theories about distant galaxies. If you have an interest in science fiction, you could write about futuristic space stations or about the prospect of life on other planets.

3. Check out your ideas. You may wish to talk to classmates about your topic possibilities. A friend may help you find a fresh angle on an idea, suggest other topics, or mention possible resources.

Writer's Choice Do you want to share your expertise with others by choosing a topic you already know quite a bit about? Would you rather increase your own knowledge by tackling something that is totally new to you? The choice is yours.

4. Find a focus. The hardest part of choosing a report topic is finding a focus. If your topic is too broad, there will be too much information to cover in a short report. If your topic is too narrow, you won't be able to find enough information. Doing some reading on your general topic can help you find a focus that's right for you.

For example, you might have trouble writing a short research report on the topic of computers. The subject is too broad. If you read a few articles about new applications for computers, however, you might come across the subtopic "computers in architecture." This idea might be just the right size for your purposes.

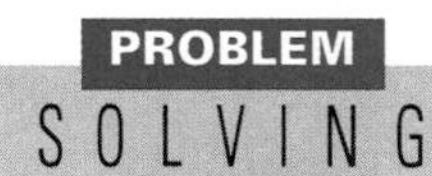

"How can I find a focus for my report?"

To learn how to make your topic the right size, see

- Handbook 2, "Focusing a Topic," pages 224–226

Teaching Strategies

for SUIT YOURSELF

HELPFUL HINT If your students have been assigned a research report by a teacher in another subject area, you may want to team-teach this workshop or consult with the other teacher about timing, acceptable topics, and style of crediting sources. Your school librarian can help by setting aside books and periodicals on the general topics that the reports must cover. You might want to display some of these sources in your classroom and have the class brainstorm interesting angles on the general topic.

for CHECK OUT YOUR IDEAS

PEER RESPONSE Students should tell their classmates what feedback they would like as they explore possible topics. Writers who prefer that peers simply listen to them think out loud at this point should say so. Writers may also want to ask their peers for specific advice about assessing the potential of two or more topic possibilities.

for FIND A FOCUS

ASSESSMENT: SPOT CHECK
Because this step is crucial to the success of students' final reports, you may want to do the mini-lesson "Focusing a Topic," pages 224–226, and then have students submit a brief description of their focused topics to you. Schedule teacher or peer conferences for students who are having trouble finding a focus.

ART NOTE

Scholars believe that dancers may have worn masks like this one in ceremonies conducted to ensure the success of hunters. The Spiro Mound is thought to have been an important ceremonial center where different groups of mound builders held meetings.

Social Studies Connection

Students might enjoy researching such report topics as the training of archaeologists and anthropologists or the techniques they use. How do these scholars base hypotheses about ancient cultures on artifacts such as the ones shown in this workshop? How does the lack of written records affect their work?

for ONE STUDENT'S PROCESS

KEY TO UNDERSTANDING Have students notice which parts of the cluster are linked by connecting lines, and ask why Tom connected these items. (The ideas are related.) Ask why identifying related ideas before beginning research would be helpful. (It helps the writer focus the topic.)

for EXAMINE YOUR PURPOSE AND GOALS

HELPFUL HINT Tell students that many reporters do their best research and writing on stories that relate to their own lives. Students who select highly personal topics may want to try the I-Search approach presented in the Related Assignment on page 206.

RESEARCH YOUR TOPIC

Objectives

- To identify, record, and preview possible sources of information
- To take notes on index cards, paraphrasing source material and marking direct quotes
- To focus research on main points

Teaching Strategies

for LOOK FOR SOURCES

INDIVIDUALIZING INSTRUCTION: BASIC STUDENTS Some students may feel overwhelmed by the variety of materials available in the library. You might pair these students with students who are familiar with the library and know how to find relevant source material. Before beginning, the more experienced partner can share his or her most successful techniques for locating and evaluating information.

One Student's Process

Tom Witosky's social studies class was asked to write a report on some aspect of Native American culture. After talking to an uncle who works for the Native American Rights Fund in Colorado, Tom decided to write a report on a contemporary Native American concern. He explored possible topics in this cluster and decided to write about burial mound excavations.

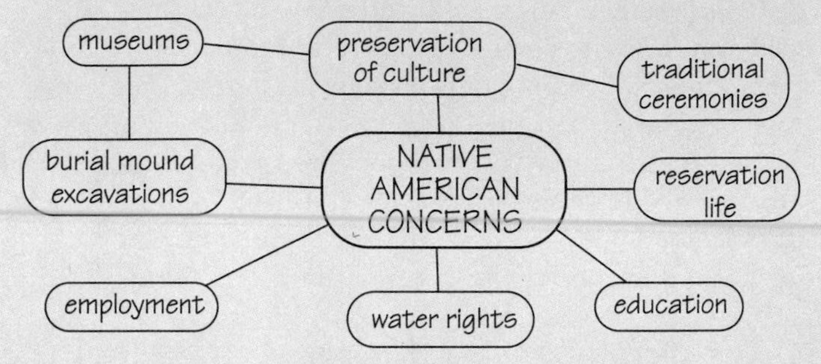

5. Examine your purpose and goals. Is there a point you want to make about your subject? Is there something specific you want to learn? Even if you are completing an assignment for your teacher, think about what *you* want to get out of the project. Finding a goal—a reason to care—early in your writing process will help you research and write your report. Keep in mind, though, that your reasons for writing may change as you work.

6. What do you want to find out? Before you begin your research, jot down a list of questions about your topic. These questions can guide your search for information. Cross out questions as you find answers to them and add new questions as you learn more about your topic.

Writing TIP

Many of your sources will mention other books or articles on the same topic that could be key to your research. Check the book or article's bibliography, and watch for in-text references to other sources.

RESEARCH YOUR TOPIC

1. Look for sources. Begin investigating your topic by looking for sources in your school or local public library. Handbook 35, "Making Use of the Library," pages 352–361, can help you make

PROFESSIONAL NOTEBOOK

In *On Writing Well,* William Zinsser says: "Ultimately every writer must follow the path that feels most comfortable. For most people who are learning to write, that path is nonfiction. It enables them to write about what they know or can observe or can find out. This is especially true of young people—they will write far more willingly about experiences that touch their own lives because that's what interests them. Motivation is at the heart of writing. If nonfiction is where you do your best writing, or your best teaching of writing, don't be buffaloed into the notion that it's an inferior species."

the most of your library's resources. You might also try exploring unconventional sources of information, so think creatively. Can government agencies or your local chamber of commerce help? Are there experts you could interview?

2. Make a written record of the sources you might use. It's too early to tell which sources you'll actually use when you write your report. However, you should still create a source card for each book or article you think might be useful. Write down the publication information from your sources, using a separate index card for each source. Here are a few of the source cards Tom made as he conducted his research.

Be sure to give each source card a number, as shown on these samples. Numbered source cards can help you in two ways. First, when you take notes, you can refer to the source of the information by number instead of writing down the title or author over and over again. Second, your source cards will help you assemble your Works Cited list, an alphabetized list of the sources you actually used in writing the report.

3. Preview your sources. Before you begin taking notes from a source, check to see if it answers any of your questions. Look over the book's table of contents and the index to find the sections that apply to your specific topic. If you're skimming an article, read the title and any headings that are in bold type. Handbook 32, "Study and Research Skills," pages 340–345, can help you make the most of the time you spend with your sources.

Source Card for Book

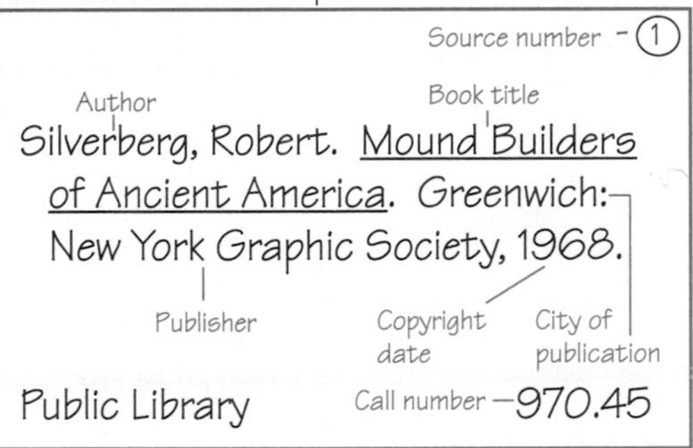

Source Card for Newspaper or Magazine Article

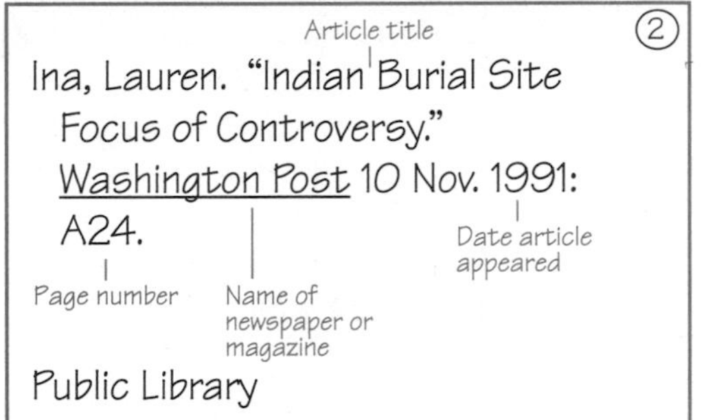

Source Card for Encyclopedia Entry

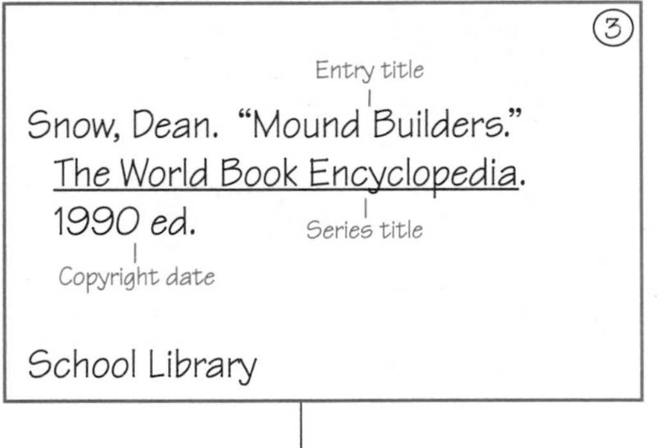

GENERAL NOTE

HELPFUL HINT Share with students these additional sources of information. Many phone books have blue pages with listings of government agencies. Another helpful source is *The New York Public Library Book of How and Where to Look It Up*, containing alphabetized lists of subjects, the titles of the best reference books, government sources, telephone sources (including toll-free 800 numbers), and electronic databases on each subject.

for MAKE A WRITTEN RECORD . . .

STUMBLING BLOCK Some students find creating source cards a frustrating experience. Have each student bring in note cards and the titles of five potential sources of information. Have students work in collaborative groups to create source cards. Go to each group to spot-check cards for common errors or the omission of key information. Tell students that following the correct style shown on the sample source cards will make the creation of their Works Cited list a simple task.

for MAKE A WRITTEN RECORD . . .

CRITICAL THINKING: MAKING COMPARISONS Before students make source cards, have them note similarities and differences among cards for books, articles, and encyclopedia entries shown on this page. (Sample: Book cards have city of publication, name of publisher, and library call number; newspaper cards have the section and the number of the page on which the article appears.)

for PREVIEW YOUR SOURCES

INDIVIDUALIZING INSTRUCTION: BASIC STUDENTS These students will benefit by taking time to practice the study and research skills covered in Handbook 32 on pages 340–345. You may need to show some students individually how to locate information by looking for topic-related key words in indexes and tables of contents and by skimming chapter heads and subheads. Students should apply these skills to their research.

Science Connection

Students researching health or science topics may find the following resources helpful: National Cancer Institute Cancer Information Service, 800–4–CANCER (also offers free publications); National Clearinghouse for Alcohol and Drug Information, 800–729–6686; Environmental Protection Agency Public Information Center, 202–382–2080; Smithsonian National Air and Space Museum Library, 202–357–3133. Encourage students to call these sources for up-to-date information on their topics.

for TAKE NOTES . . .

MODELING Many students are uncertain about which information in their source material is important enough to write on note cards. To model the thinking process involved, choose a research report topic and a magazine article on the subject. Then tell your students how you would decide which facts, anecdotes, and statistics from the article are important enough to record. You may wish to assign "Taking Notes from Sources" on page 47 of the Writing Resource Book.

for USE YOUR OWN WORDS

INDIVIDUALIZING INSTRUCTION: LEP STUDENTS These students may have difficulty paraphrasing and summarizing information when they take notes. You may wish to assign Handbook 33, "Writing Paraphrases and Summaries," pages 346–348. You may also want to meet with these students in a small group and have them work together to paraphrase and summarize selected sections of articles. If necessary, encourage them to paraphrase or summarize aloud before trying a written version.

for USE YOUR OWN WORDS

CRITICAL THINKING: MAKING INFERENCES Have students notice the page numbers written at the end of each note. Ask students why it is important to include these page numbers. (They will be used later to credit sources in the text; they can also be used to check the accuracy of quotations and paraphrases.)

PROBLEM SOLVING

"How can I take notes and use source material in my writing?"

For information on how to use sources, see

- Handbook 33, "Paraphrases and Summaries," pages 346–348

4. Take notes from your sources. Take notes on another set of index cards. Include the facts, anecdotes, or statistics that you think will later be useful in your writing. Use a new card for each piece of information. That way, you can move the cards around, organizing and reorganizing your ideas and information when you're ready to write a draft.

5. Use your own words. To help you understand what you read, record important information in your own words. Rewriting information can help you uncover what you don't understand or what else you need to find out about. However, if you come across statements you think are particularly interesting or well said, copy them word for word and enclose them in quotation marks.

Tom Witosky found several newspaper articles that discussed a controversial exhibit of a burial excavation at the Dickson Mounds Museum in Illinois. He recorded information from each article on several note cards. Here are two of them.

Source card number — (2)

About a thousand years ago, the Mississippian people built some of the mounds in Illinois. Their culture died out—but Indian groups today protest the display of Mississippian skeletons and artifacts. p. A24 — Page number from source

Note written in Tom's own words

(6)

Beliefs: Souls can't rest if their bones are uncovered and shown in a public display. James Yellowbank of the Indian Treaty Rights Committee said, "We want them reburied properly and left alone." p. A30

Quotation copied word for word

Writing TIP

If you later discover that a source doesn't contain the information you need, throw away the source card and return the book or magazine to the library. Make new source cards as you conduct more research.

6. Begin to focus your research. As you gather information and take notes, your report should begin to take shape in your mind. Try making a list of the main points you think you'll want to cover, then sort your note cards into groups under each of those points. Do you think you have enough information on each point? If not, do some more research to uncover what you need.

One Student's Process

Tom's list of main points turned into a preliminary outline for his report. He knew he'd probably make some changes in the organization of the parts of his report once he started drafting. This is what his early outline looked like.

1. Introduction
2. Excavating mounds
   —Dickson Mounds example
3. Different points of view
4. Conclusion

DRAFT AND DISCOVER

1. Start writing. Use your rough, preliminary outline and your notes to help get you started. Do you have a lot of note cards for one particular section of your report? You might begin there, drafting the part of your report you've learned the most about. As you write, keep yourself open to new ideas and insights. Does your explanation of the topic raise new questions in your mind? Does it suggest another focus that might be more interesting to you? You may want to do additional research and rework your outline as you strike out in new directions.

2. Think about organization. What's the best way to organize your ideas? There's no one right way to organize a research report; many possibilities are open to you. For example, you might want to use chronological order for any historical material or biographical information in your report. You might use order of importance or order of familiarity for other sections. Once you start drafting and see how your ideas fit together, you'll be able to judge which organizational techniques will work best for your topic and for the information you want to present.

COMPUTER TIP

If you write your paper on a word processor, set your file to double space the entire paper. Set your tabs at five spaces and ten spaces from a one-inch left margin. Each new paragraph should be indented five spaces, and long quotations set off separately should be indented ten spaces.

PROBLEM SOLVING

"How can I organize my draft?"

For more information on organizing ideas, see

• Handbook 8, "Types of Organization," pages 239–243

for ONE STUDENT'S PROCESS

HELPFUL HINT Have students turn to Tom's report on pages 189–193. Ask them to try to match sections of the report with headings in the preliminary outline. Did Tom write about each heading? (yes) What main points did he include in the report that he did not list in the preliminary outline? (facts on the history of mound-building cultures) Why did Tom add these facts? (to provide background information)

DRAFT AND DISCOVER

Objectives

- To draft a research report
- To credit sources used in a report
- To respond to one's own draft and to that of a peer

Teaching Strategies

for START WRITING

PEER RESPONSE Because writing a research report will probably be the longest, most complex writing project students will be undertaking, you might want to schedule ten minutes at the beginning of each class for pairs of writers and peer readers to review their progress, discuss problems, and offer feedback. Encourage writers to keep their minds open, to change focus if necessary, and to do additional research.

for THINK ABOUT ORGANIZATION

CRITICAL THINKING: JUDGING Depending on the subject matter of their reports, students may find cause-effect or problem-solution organizational techniques useful. You may want to review the informative writing skills learned in Workshops 4 and 5 and direct students to appropriate graphic aids in the Thinking Skills Worksheets.

for ONE STUDENT'S PROCESS

CRITICAL THINKING: INFERRING SEQUENCE Ask students why Tom listed the Adena culture first in his outline. (It was the earliest.) On what evidence did they base their answer? (the date 700 B.C.) Tell students that as they work with information from various sources, they will sometimes have to infer which events came before others.

for WRITER'S CHOICE

INDIVIDUALIZING INSTRUCTION: BASIC STUDENTS These students may need help with outlining. Schedule teacher conferences to review their outlines, asking questions about what kinds of information they plan to include in each section. Indicate areas that may require further research or elaboration. For a quick review of outlining, you might assign these students "Creating an Outline" on page 49 of the Writing Resource Book.

for WRITE AN INTRODUCTION . . .

KEY TO UNDERSTANDING: THESIS STATEMENT Point out that in addition to stating the main idea, a thesis statement can clue readers in to the organization of the report. Have students reread the opening two paragraphs of the Student Model on page 189. Ask students to identify the thesis statement (the last sentence of the second paragraph) and ask what it suggests about the organization of the report. (Tom states the main point of his report, hints that there will be historical information about the mounds, and suggests that he will discuss contemporary attitudes on both sides of the controversy.)

One Student's Process

Tom started drafting the part of his report he knew the most about: the controversial Dickson Mounds Museum exhibit. He realized, though, that he would need to provide background information on the history of the mounds and the people who built them. Tom did more research, then revised his outline. Notice the chronological order in the outline's first section.

The Mound Builders

Introduction

I. Mound Builders—three cultures
  A. Adena (700 B.C.)
  B. Hopewell (100 B.C.)
  C. Mississippian (A.D. 700–1700)

II. Discovery of the Mounds
  A. Thomas Jefferson
  B. Archaeologists

III. Controversial Displays
  A. Dickson Mounds
    1. Indians' ideas
    2. Archaeologists' ideas
  B. Museums
  C. Result of conflict

Conclusion

PROBLEM SOLVING

"I need to make a formal outline, but I'm not sure how."

For help creating a formal outline for your writing, see

• Appendix, page 683

Writer's Choice Some writers like to create formal outlines that include headings and subheadings for every section of their writing. Others prefer to make a rough outline, listing only key words for the report's main sections. Use the approach that works for you or that meets your class requirements.

3. Write an introduction and a conclusion. Your opening paragraph should draw readers into your report and clearly state your topic. For example, you might begin with a thought-provoking question, as Tom Witosky did. You could also open with an interesting fact about your topic or tell a brief anecdote. Your introduction should also include a **thesis statement** that tells the main idea or overall purpose of your report.

PROFESSIONAL NOTEBOOK

Writer and teacher William Zinsser emphasizes the importance of a good introduction in this quote from his book *On Writing Well:* "The most important sentence in any article is the first one. If it doesn't induce the reader to proceed to the second sentence, your article is dead. And if the second sentence doesn't induce him to continue to the third, it's equally dead. Of such a progression of sentences . . . a writer constructs . . . the 'lead.'" Here is one of Zinsser's favorite leads: "I've often wondered what goes into a hot dog. Now I know and I wish I didn't." Have students share their own favorite leads.

Your closing paragraph might summarize your main points, make a prediction, propose an action, or draw a conclusion.

4. Give credit where credit is due. You don't need to credit either your own ideas or information that is considered common knowledge and can be found in several sources. (It is considered common knowledge, for example, that many mound-building groups lived near rivers.) However, you do need to give credit when you use someone else's ideas, facts, or information—even when you put that information in your own words. You must also give credit to the source of direct quotations.

There are several ways to credit your sources, so check with your teacher to see which method he or she prefers. You can use these Modern Language Association guidelines—as Tom did—to help you credit sources correctly.

Mississippian mound builders made this head-shaped pottery bottle. The vessel, which stands six inches high and is equally as wide, is painted with ochre, an earth-tone pigment. The bottle could be hung or carried by stringing leather straps through the holes in the ears.

Guidelines for Crediting Sources in Text

- **Work by one author** Put the author's last name and the page number in parentheses: (Silverberg 3). If the author's name is mentioned in the sentence, put only the page number in parentheses: (3).
- **Work by more than one author** Put the authors' last names and the page number in parentheses: (Erdoes and Ortiz 87). If a source has more than three authors, give the first author's last name followed by *et al.*, and the page number: (Milner et al. 21).
- **Work with no author listed** Give the title or a shortened version and the page number: ("Ancient" 30).
- **One of two or more works by the same author** Give the author's last name, the title or a shortened version, and the page number: (Silverberg, The Old Ones 145).

5. Think about your draft. Look back over your work and decide if you want to make changes now or first see what people think of your draft. The questions on the following page can help you and your readers review your draft.

for GIVE CREDIT . . .

KEY TO UNDERSTANDING Tell students that it is especially important to credit information or ideas that some readers might question or want to know more about. For example, in the Student Model, Tom credits sources for the claims that the Hopewell people were the finest metalworkers of North America and that Monk's Mound is the largest man-made earthen structure in the world. (See page 190.) He also credits the newspaper articles that cover current controversies over Native American burial sites. Have students check their own drafts to see whether they have credited all facts and ideas that are not common knowledge.

for GIVE CREDIT . . .

HELPFUL HINT To avoid causing confusion and frustration among students, work with teachers in other subject areas to agree on a consistent system for crediting sources in research reports.

for GUIDELINES FOR CREDITING . . .

MODELING Gather several source materials from your students and demonstrate how to credit them. Try to choose a sampling that represents the variations mentioned in the chart. If students need additional practice, assign "Crediting Sources in Text" on page 51 of the Writing Resource Book.

for REVIEW YOUR WRITING

INDIVIDUALIZING INSTRUCTION: VISUAL/KINESTHETIC LEARNERS These students may find it easier to analyze the organization of their reports if they physically rearrange the sections by cutting and pasting them in different positions. Suggest that they make several copies of their drafts and experiment with different arrangements.

for ONE STUDENT'S PROCESS

PEER RESPONSE Students should note that the peer reader's questions show the writer where he needs to add more information.

REVISE YOUR WRITING

Objectives

- To evaluate responses to a research report draft and to revise with those responses in mind
- To find and correct examples of plagiarism and inaccuracy
- To create a Works Cited list for the report

Teaching Strategies

for REVISE YOUR WRITING

INDIVIDUALIZING INSTRUCTION: ESL STUDENTS Because ESL students have limited English vocabularies, they may find themselves unintentionally plagiarizing. Make certain they understand why using others' words or ideas without giving credit is unacceptable. Work with these students individually, or pair them with English-proficient students or adult volunteers who can help them credit their sources and express their own ideas in English.

REVIEW YOUR WRITING

Questions for Yourself

- Have I answered all my questions about my topic? Did I find good sources, or should I look for more information?
- Is my report clearly organized? Does it flow smoothly from beginning to end, or are there parts I should rearrange?

Questions for Your Peer Readers

- What would you say is the main point of my report?
- Do you now know more than you did about my topic?
- Which parts seemed confusing or out of place?

Peer Reader Comments

I didn't know anything about the history of the mounds—it's really interesting. When did the Hopewell people build their mounds?

What was buried there? Can you give some details?

This doesn't sound like you. Did you forget to cite your source?

One Student's Process

Tom showed his draft to a friend whose comments appear in the margin. How would you have responded?

Another major group of mound builders was the Hopewell culture. They built mounds that were more elaborate than the Adena's. Some were circular or octagonal. Hopewell mounds were often surrounded by miles of earthen walls. All kinds of artifacts were buried inside the mounds. The objects found inside with the burials are of great beauty and workmanship. The Hopewell people were the finest Indian metalworkers in North America.

REVISE YOUR WRITING

1. Review your responses. Your reactions and those of your peers should help you see if your writing is on target. You may find it helpful to revise your outline before you write another draft. Check to see if you've **plagiarized,** or used the words or ideas of others without giving credit. Check your notes and either add a citation or use an exact quotation from one of your sources instead.

Paragraphs at Work Each heading in your outline should be discussed in one or more separate paragraphs.

- Discuss one aspect of your topic in each new paragraph.
- Write a topic sentence for each paragraph.
- Include in each paragraph only those details and examples that support the paragraph's main idea.

2. Confirm the facts. Accuracy is essential in a report. Make sure the dates, statistics, names, and other facts are correct and that you have properly credited your sources.

3. Create a Works Cited list and attach it to your report. A Works Cited list is an alphabetized list of only those sources you cited in the text of your report. Here are models to help you write and punctuate the entries in your list.

Book—One author

Silverberg, Robert. Mound Builders of Ancient America. Greenwich: New York Graphic Society, 1968.

Book—Two or more authors

Erdoes, Richard, and Alfonso Ortiz, eds. American Indian Myths and Legends. New York: Pantheon, 1984.

Book—No author given

The Times Atlas of the World. Rev. ed. London: Times, 1984.

Newspaper or Magazine Article—Author given

Ina, Lauren. "Indian Burial Site Focus of Controversy." Washington Post 10 Nov. 1991: A24.

Newspaper or Magazine Article—No author given

"Illinois to Shut an Exhibit of Indian Skeletons." New York Times 29 Nov. 1991: A30.

Article from Encyclopedia or Other Reference Work

Snow, Dean. "Mound Builders." The World Book Encyclopedia. 1990 ed.

Interview

Boyd, Willard. Telephone interview. 15 Nov. 1992.

Writing **TIP**

When you make your Works Cited list, use the source cards you made as you conducted research. They should contain all the publication information you need.

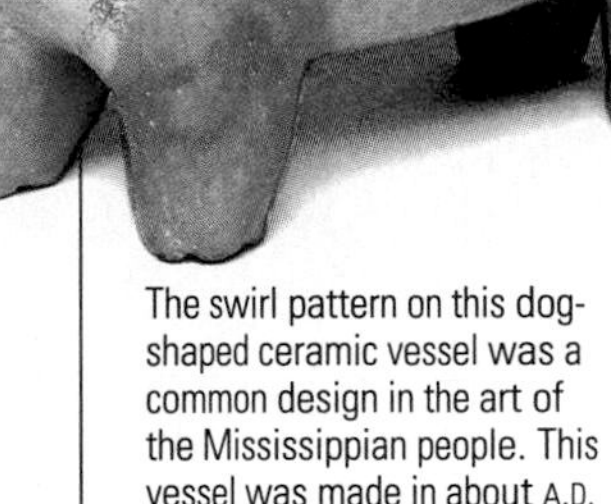

The swirl pattern on this dog-shaped ceramic vessel was a common design in the art of the Mississippian people. This vessel was made in about A.D. 1500.

for PARAGRAPHS AT WORK

CRITICAL THINKING: ANALYZING

Point out Tom Witosky's use of paragraphs in the Student Model on pages 189–193. Tom devotes a separate paragraph to each of the three mound-building cultures. He uses a new paragraph for each main idea and his topic sentences often fall at the beginning of his paragraphs.

for CONFIRM THE FACTS

HELPFUL HINT Suggest that students spot-check the accuracy of one or two facts or quotes on each page of their report, going back to their note cards or to their original sources. If they find many errors, they should recheck every credited fact and quotation.

for CREATE A WORKS CITED LIST. . .

KEY TO UNDERSTANDING

Students should notice that the format of the entries in the Works Cited list is the same as the one they used for their source cards. Have students examine Tom Witosky's Works Cited list on page 193 and note that works with authors named are alphabetized by author, whereas a work with no author given is alphabetized by title.

GENERAL NOTE

MANAGING THE PAPER LOAD

Your final assessment of students' reports should focus on how well they state and support their main ideas. If you have been checking and evaluating focused topics, source cards, note cards, and outlines as students were writing their reports, and if you scheduled teacher conferences for students who needed help, you already have a good idea of how students are progressing.

ART NOTE

Mississippian artisans used techniques such as engraving, embossing, carving, and molding to decorate the objects they made. Encourage interested students to research and report on these techniques.

for ONE STUDENT'S PROCESS

PEER RESPONSE Point out how Tom answered his peer reader's questions as he revised his paragraph. He added facts and examples, and he gave proper credit to his source.

PROOFREAD

Teaching Strategies

for LINKING MECHANICS AND WRITING

HELPFUL HINT Explain the use of ellipsis points in One Student's Process. Help students see that when material is left out between sentences, the three ellipsis points are added after the period that ends the sentence. When material is left out *within* a sentence, only three points are used.

Guidelines for Evaluation

IDEAS AND CONTENT

- has an attention-getting introduction that includes a thesis statement
- supports main ideas with facts and examples from several sources
- has a strong conclusion

STRUCTURE AND FORM

- has a logical organization
- credits sources consistently
- includes a Works Cited list

GRAMMAR, USAGE, AND MECHANICS

- displays standard grammar, usage, spelling, and mechanics
- punctuates quotations correctly
- uses ellipsis points correctly in quotations to show where words have been left out

This two-thousand-year-old Adena figurine stands eight inches high. The Adena inhabited areas of what is now Ohio.

One Student's Process

Tom added details and quotations to support his points.

Another major group of mound builders was the Hopewell culture. [Between 100 B.C. and A.D. 500,] They built mounds that were more elaborate than the Adena's. Some were circular or octagonal. Hopewell mounds were often surrounded by miles of earthen walls. ~~All kinds of artifacts~~ [Pearl necklaces, obsidian blades, and birds and fish made of beaten copper] were buried inside the mounds. [Paula Franklin says that "]The objects found inside with the burials are of great beauty and [superb] workmanship. [. . .] The Hopewell people were the finest Indian metal workers in North America." (33).

PROOFREAD

1. Proofread your work. Carefully reread your report, looking for mistakes in grammar, spelling, usage, and mechanics.

LINKING MECHANICS AND WRITING

Using Quotations and In-text Citations

- Copy quoted passages word for word.
- Use ellipses (. . .) in your quotation to show where you've left out material.
- Follow the guidelines on page 201 for crediting sources.

ART NOTE

Some scholars believe that the arts and crafts of the mound builders of North America were influenced by those of the Indians of Mexico and Central America in the same time period, but other scholars disagree. Students might enjoy researching representations of human and animal figures from ancient Mexico and comparing and contrasting them with those depicted in this assignment.

2. Make a final copy. Review the Standards for Evaluation in the margin. Have you met the requirements of the assignment? Make any necessary changes and neatly write or print out a clean copy.

PUBLISH AND PRESENT

- **Present your report to another class.** If your report deals with a topic in another subject area, such as science or social studies, give an oral presentation in that class.
- **Create a class encyclopedia.** Gather reports and arrange them alphabetically or by subject.
- **Turn your written report into a multimedia presentation.** Bring in photographs, illustrations, or maps related to your topic. You could also play an audiotape of a piece of music or a recording of an interview you conducted during your research.

REFLECT ON YOUR WRITING

WRITER TO WRITER

The element of discovery takes place, in nonfiction, not during the writing but during the research.

Joan Didion, novelist and essayist

Add your writing to your portfolio. First, write the story of your research and attach it to your finished piece. These questions may help you focus your thoughts.

- How did you find your topic? Did you change your topic once you began your research? Why or why not?
- Were you surprised by what you learned about your topic?
- How did you find your information? Did you wish you had more information as you drafted your report? Did you have too much?
- In what other writing situations could you use research skills?

Standards for Evaluation

INFORMATIVE WRITING

A research report

- has an interesting introduction that clearly states the topic and the purpose
- contains facts and details to support main ideas
- presents information in a logical order
- uses information from multiple sources
- gives credit for the ideas and facts of others
- ends with a strong conclusion
- includes a Works Cited list

Reteaching

Assess the needs of students who were not successful in developing an effective research report; then assign the appropriate handbook mini-lessons, as well as the Workshop Support Materials listed on page 184a. Concepts commonly requiring reteaching for this assignment are:

- **Handbook 2, Focusing a Topic, pp. 224–226**
- **Handbook 33, Writing Paraphrases and Summaries, pp. 346–348**

The following suggestions and resources may also be useful.

Weak Thesis Statements Remind students that a thesis statement should state the main idea of a report. Encourage students to read the "Strong" model for the research report in the Guidelines for Writing Assessment and Portfolio Use Booklet and identify its thesis statement. Then ask: How does this sentence sum up the purpose of the report?

Poor Paraphrasing and Summarizing Have students practice by writing paraphrases and summaries of selected paragraphs in news articles.

Extension and Enrichment

1. If students have written on topics that are currently in the news, start a research update bulletin board. Have students revise their reports to incorporate the new information.

2. Encourage students to start their own lending library of materials on their favorite subjects.

Closure: Reflect on Your Writing

As students reflect on their writing, you may want to have them summarize in a paragraph or two the writing skills they used in doing their reports: researching, outlining, note taking, and so on. Ask them to think of other classes or situations in which they could use these skills.

Related ASSIGNMENT

Starting from LITERATURE

Objectives

- To respond to an I-Search report
- To choose a topic of personal importance, determine a purpose for writing, and research a topic
- To draft, revise, and present an I-Search report

Motivate

Ask students to share stories they have heard about relatives or family friends of long ago. Do they think the stories are true? Have they ever been curious to find out more? Point out that some of the most fascinating research reports grow out of a strong personal curiosity about a subject.

BUILD ON PRIOR KNOWLEDGE

Ask how many students have seen the TV mini-series *Roots* or *Queen.* Have students summarize the story line of each. Then explain that the TV series were based on Alex Haley's books chronicling the lives of his ancestors—in Africa, in the United States as slaves, and finally as free men and women. Ask whether students know how Alex Haley came to write about his ancestors. Tell students that the account they will read tells how his search for his roots began.

SET A PURPOSE

After students have read the material in the Starting from Literature box, put on the board a chart with the following headings: *Reasons for His Research, Research Techniques, What He Learned About Himself.* Suggest that students look for information that might fall under each heading as they read.

Related ASSIGNMENT I-Search

Starting from LITERATURE

I-Search reports, like research reports, present information gathered from a variety of sources. An I-Search, however, has a personal focus. Why do you want to know more about your topic? How are you finding out what you need to know? What are you discovering about yourself along the way?

Read author Alex Haley's story of his search for information about his family history. He later incorporated what he learned into his autobiographical book *Roots.* How do you think he would answer the questions above?

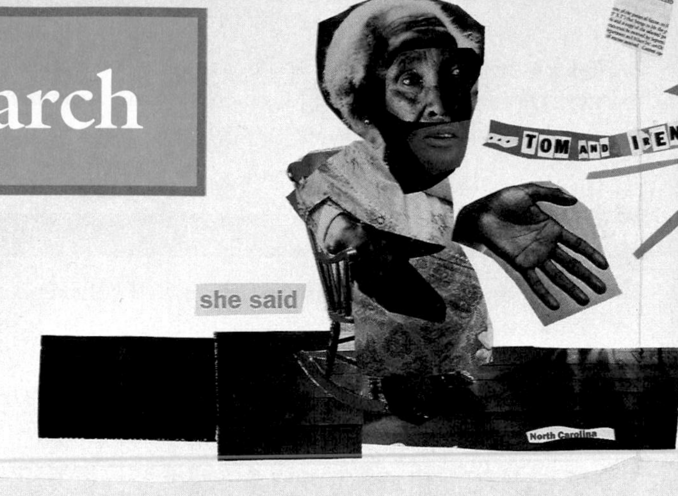

from THE NEW YORK TIMES

My Furthest-Back Person

by ALEX HALEY

One Saturday in 1965 I happened to be walking past the National Archives building in Washington. Across the interim years I had thought of Grandma's old stories—otherwise I can't think what diverted me up the Archives' steps. And when a main reading-room desk attendant asked if he could help me, I wouldn't have dreamed of admitting to him some curiosity hanging on from boyhood about my slave forebears. I kind of bumbled that I was interested in census records of Alamance County, North Carolina, just after the Civil War.

The microfilm rolls were delivered, and I turned them through the machine with a building sense of intrigue, viewing in different census takers' penmanship an endless parade of names. After about a dozen microfilmed rolls, I was beginning to tire, when in utter

Links to LITERATURE & LANGUAGE

Literature For more nonfiction writing about roots and identity, see the following selections in *Literature and Language,* Grade 8:

- Clifton Taulbert, from *Once Upon a Time When We Were Colored*
- Janet Bode, "Von"
- William Tsuchida, from *Wear It Proudly*

astonishment I looked upon the names of Grandma's parents: Tom Murray, Irene Murray . . . older sisters of Grandma's as well—every one of them a name that I'd heard countless times on her front porch.

It wasn't that I hadn't believed Grandma. You just *didn't* not believe my Grandma. It was simply so uncanny actually seeing those names in print and in official U.S. government records.

During the next several months I was back in Washington whenever possible, in the Archives, the Library of Congress, the Daughters of the American Revolution Library. . . . In one source or another during 1966 I was able to document at least the highlights of the cherished family story. I would have given anything to have told Grandma, but, sadly, in 1949 she had gone. So I went and told the only survivor of those Henning front-porch storytellers: Cousin Georgia Anderson, now in her eighties in Kansas City, Kansas. Wrinkled, bent, not well herself, she was so overjoyed, repeating to me the old stories and sounds; they were like Henning echoes: "Yeah, boy, that African say his name was *'Kin-tay';* he say the banjo was *'ko,'* an' the river *'Kamby Bolong,'* an' he was off choppin' some wood to make his drum when they grabbed 'im!" Cousin Georgia grew so excited we had to stop her, calm her down, "You go 'head, boy! Your grandma an' all of 'em—they up there watching what you do!" . . .

I was on a jet returning to New York when a thought hit me. Those strange, unknown-tongue sounds, always part of our family's old story . . . they were obviously bits of our original African *"Kin-tay's"* native tongue. What specific tongue? Could I somehow find out?

Back in New York, I began making visits to the United Nations Headquarters lobby; it wasn't hard to spot Africans. I'd stop any I could, asking if my bits of phonetic sounds held any meaning for them. A couple of dozen Africans quickly looked at me, listened, and took off—understandably dubious about some Tennessean's accent alleging "African" sounds.

Think & Respond

Discuss Alex Haley's essay with your classmates. How did Haley present the details of his research process along with information about his family history? What do you know of your own family history? How could you find additional information?

Think & Respond

ELICIT PERSONAL RESPONSES

To start a discussion about the first question in the Think & Respond box, ask students whether the piece reminded them in any way of a mystery story. Lead them into a discussion of the storylike aspects of the selection.

For the last two questions, be sensitive to the feelings of any students in your class for whom questions of family history and identity are emotionally difficult. Have students who are interested in researching their own or someone else's family history scan the piece to remind themselves of the kinds of sources Haley used in his search. Encourage them to pursue additional sources of information that might be available to them.

EXPLORE THE AUTHOR'S TECHNIQUES

Alex Haley makes his strong personal involvement in his research evident from the first paragraph. He uses narrative techniques, such as plot, dialogue, and suspense, to help readers share the excitement of his personal search for his roots.

for FURTHER READING

Students may enjoy hearing excerpts from Alex Haley's book *Roots* read aloud. For example, you or a volunteer might read about Kunta Kinte's kidnapping by slave traders in Africa or about the lives of Tom and Irene Murray, Haley's great-grandparents, whose names he found in the census records.

Writing ON YOUR OWN

Ask students how Alex Haley's account differs from other research reports they have read. (He was personally involved in his topic; his report included the story of his search; he included dialogue and other storytelling techniques.) Encourage them to use similar techniques to personalize their reports.

Handbooks for Help and Practice

The following handbooks may be used as mini-lessons before students begin writing or as resources when problems arise.

- **Discovering Writing Ideas, pp. 218–223**
- **General Purpose and Personal Goals, pp. 232–233**
- **Study and Research Skills, pp. 340–345**
- **Making Use of the Library, pp. 352–361**

Teaching Strategies

for THINK ABOUT YOUR PURPOSE

PERSONAL TOUCH Share with students some personal research you have done and your purpose for doing it. For example, you may have begun interviewing aging relatives to increase your awareness of family history, or you may have begun researching the safety of incinerators because you were worried about plans to build one in your town.

for RESEARCH YOUR TOPIC

HELPFUL HINT Suggest that students begin a KWL chart (see page 342) about their topics. Have them make columns with the following heads: *What I KNOW, What I WANT to Know, What I LEARNED.* Have them fill in the first two columns before they begin their research, then gradually fill in the last column as they gather information.

Writing ON YOUR OWN

I-Search

INVITATION TO *Write*

The stories Alex Haley grew up hearing on his grandmother's front porch inspired him to research his family history. An I-Search records the research process from a very personal point of view. Writing an I-Search is a chance to explore a subject you care about and to share your research with others.

Research a topic that is personally important to you. Then write an I-Search report that tells about the topic and your experiences finding out about it.

RESEARCHING YOUR I-SEARCH REPORT

PROBLEM SOLVING

"How can I find a topic I care about?"

For more information about finding ideas to suit your purpose, see

- Handbook 1, "Discovering Writing Ideas," pages 218–223
- Handbook 4, "General Purpose and Personal Goals," pages 232–233

1. Find a topic. Since an I-Search paper is a personal research report, you'll want to choose a topic you feel strongly about. If you're not sure what you want to research, try listing your personal goals or interests, or just start asking yourself "I wonder why" questions. You might also check your journal to see what's been on your mind lately. Then choose the topic you care about most.

2. Think about your purpose. Make some notes in your journal about why this topic is important to you. For example, are you interested in flying because you'd like to become a pilot? Do you want to learn more about dyslexia because you or someone you know is affected by it? Getting a clear idea of why you want to write about your topic can help you focus your research.

3. Research your topic. You should go about your research in the same way that you would for any other research paper. Gather information from a variety of sources and keep track of your own reactions to what you learn. For example, if you discover that some of your first ideas about your topic weren't true, make some notes about how your new understanding affects you.

MULTICULTURAL Connection

Students may want to research how and why their ancestors or present family members came to the United States. Why did relatives or family friends settle within a certain geographic area? Students can conduct interviews with friends or family members, or use resources such as *How to Find Your Family Roots* by Timothy Field Beard.

You may want to have a special "Searching for Our Roots" day in which students present their findings.

Keep track of your research process. Are you solving a mystery, where each clue leads you on a search for additional clues? Are you discouraged because you cannot find information easily or because you discover there are no clear answers to some of your questions? Write down your thoughts and reactions as you conduct your research.

Writing TIP

You might try charting your progress and discoveries on a time line or story line as you research.

WRITING YOUR REPORT

1. Set the stage. You might begin with an explanation of why it's important for you to learn more about your topic. A brief anecdote or story that explains why you care about the topic is one way to start. You might also show what you already know or think is true about your topic and what else you need to find out.

2. Tell your story. If you'd like, write your paper as a personal narrative. Show the steps of your research, reporting the information you gather and your reactions to the experience. Since an I-Search paper is a personal research report, your reactions are just as important as the facts you gathered. Remember that an I-Search paper can have a more personal and informal tone than other research reports.

Writing TIP

You don't need to recount every single step of your research. Focus on the key steps, the ones where you learned important information or had significant personal reactions.

3. Wrap it up. The conclusion to your I-Search should sum up what this personal research experience meant to you. Did your investigation back up your original ideas? Did you come to a new understanding or appreciation of your topic? How did your attitudes or ideas about the topic change? What advice do you have for other people who might be interested in researching this topic further? Remember that your personal reaction to the experience is what counts.

for FIRST WRITING TIP

HELPFUL HINT Students may choose to keep a special I-Search diary or learning log (see page 342) to record the ups and downs of their research process. Allow a few minutes at the end of each class period for students to record their thoughts.

for SET THE STAGE

CRITICAL THINKING: EVALUATING If students have problems with their introductions, remind them that Alex Haley began his report with an anecdote, or telling of an incident. Have them reread the opening paragraph on page 206 and evaluate how effective the anecdote is. They might also evaluate the model anecdote on page 280 in Handbook 16, "Introductions."

for TELL YOUR STORY

LISTENING AND VIEWING To provide further exposure to the use of the personal narrative form, you might also show students a videotape of the film *Lorenzo's Oil,* about a mother and father who researched their son's rare illness and in the process helped discover a treatment for it.

for WRAP IT UP

INDIVIDUALIZING INSTRUCTION: BASIC STUDENTS If students have problems drafting their conclusions, schedule teacher conferences with them to review their KWL charts, I-Search diaries, time lines, or learning logs. Have students orally tell what they have learned about their topics and describe how their newly acquired knowledge helped change their ideas or attitudes. Then ask questions to help them focus their conclusions.

PROFESSIONAL NOTEBOOK

"To write in their own voices about things that count in their lives is surely the basic step for students learning to write," says Ken Macrorie in *Practical Ideas for Teaching Writing as a Process.* He recommends the I-Search paper. "Something you *need* to find out in your life, however small or large, should be the ruling passion," he writes. "Where there is no genuine need or itch to know, the search will be half-hearted or desultory and the paper vague and *Engfishy.*" All students can make an I-Search by asking themselves these questions: 1. What did I want to know? 2. How did I find out about it? 3. What did I learn? 4. What will I do with this information?

Guidelines for Evaluation

AN EFFECTIVE I-SEARCH REPORT

- conveys the writer's strong personal interest in the topic
- presents information from several sources
- includes an account of the writer's research experiences
- concludes with the writer's personal reactions and observations

for REVIEWING YOUR WRITING

PEER RESPONSE Peer readers may wish to write their responses in a personal letter to the writer, telling which parts of the report they found most moving, interesting, or surprising.

for CHECK FOR ACCURACY

HELPFUL HINT Refer students to the Guidelines for Crediting Sources in Text on page 201 and to the models for a Works Cited list on page 203. Provide help with less common sources of information, such as unpublished letters or documents.

GENERAL NOTE

MANAGING THE PAPER LOAD You might evaluate students' I-Search reports in terms of key elements such as (1) significance of the topic to the writer, (2) variety of information and range of sources, and (3) understanding of the research-as-discovery process.

for PUBLISHING AND PRESENTING

HELPFUL HINT: PORTFOLIO You may wish to do a collective "Showcase Portfolio" of students' I-Search papers. Have students decide on a pattern of organization and prepare a table of contents. Make more than one copy; keep one volume in your classroom and give the rest to the school library.

REVIEWING YOUR WRITING

1. Reread your draft. You chose this topic because it had a special meaning to you. Does that meaning come through in your report? Check to see if you need to do more to explain why you care about this topic. Also check to make sure you have covered the topic thoroughly, explaining what you have learned.

2. Share your report. An I-Search report has two goals—to provide information and to explain the experiences you had while gathering that information. Ask your classmates whether your paper meets both goals. Is there anything else your readers want to know?

3. Check for accuracy. Like any other research report, an I-Search report should contain facts that are accurate. Double-check statistics, dates, and other details. Also be sure you have given proper credit to your sources. Then revise your report using your own reactions and any thoughts from your peers you want to respond to. Proofread your final draft carefully.

PUBLISHING AND PRESENTING

- **Hold an "I-Search Day."** Classmates can share their reports orally.
- **Submit your paper to a school or community newspaper.** Your paper could make an interesting feature story.
- **Share your findings.** If a person or group of people would benefit from hearing about your experience, distribute copies of your report or share it orally.

Math Connection

If any students used statistics in their reports, encourage them to have a math teacher or an advanced math student judge whether the statistics were interpreted correctly.

Health Connection

If many students in your class wrote on subjects relating to health, nutrition, exercise, and medical treatments, encourage them to present their findings at a Health Fair for your class or for the entire school. Alternatively, students can compile their reports into a class *Encyclopedia of Health.*

Springboards

Speaking and Listening

Imagine you are a television reporter on the scene for a major event in world history. You can choose an event from the past several years, such as the Persian Gulf War, or an event much earlier, such as the signing of the Declaration of Independence. Work with others to prepare an in-depth report for the evening news.

Sports

Trace the history of your favorite sport. How and where did it begin? How have the rules and equipment changed over time? What other cultures have similar games?

MUSIC What kind of music do you enjoy most? Check into the origins of your favorite music and explore how it has developed.

Geography Choose a place you would like to visit—an exotic, distant land or a historic site in your state—and find out all you can about it. Then write a travel brochure for the place, describing its main attractions. Illustrate your brochure with maps, photos, or drawings of your own.

Teaching Strategies

for SPEAKING AND LISTENING

COOPERATIVE LEARNING You might wish to have students work in groups and assume such roles as researcher, reporter, participant in the event, dialogue recorder, and camera operator (if students wish to videotape their reports). Suggest that students research an event and then role-play the parts of the participants to come up with dialogue. Student recorders can write down the dialogue; then the group can edit it for the final presentation.

for SPORTS

HELPFUL HINT A good place to begin researching sports is *The Browser's Book of Beginnings* by Charles Panati.

for GEOGRAPHY

CRITICAL THINKING: EVALUATING As part of their research, students can call or write travel agencies and chambers of commerce for information. When they receive professional brochures, students should evaluate which are most successful and why. Then they can apply to their own brochures some of the successful techniques they have identified in the professional ones.

Reviewing Sentence Composing Skills

Objectives

- To identify several methods of adding details, emphasis, and variety to sentences
- To compose correctly formed and punctuated sentences by using a variety of sentence composing skills

GENERAL NOTE

HELPFUL HINT Before students try Exercise A, ask volunteers to write examples of sentences illustrating each of the composing skills listed in the exercise. If students do not remember a specific skill, reteach the technique, using the appropriate lesson in the ancillary Sentence Composing Copy Masters. For additional review, use Handbook 23, "Sentence Variety," pages 302–303, or Handbook 24, "Sentence Combining," pages 304–313, as mini-lessons.

Sentence

COMPOSING

Reviewing Sentence Composing Skills

In the preceding Sentence Composing exercises, you studied several ways professional writers add detail, emphasis, and variety to their writing. These methods include using compound subjects and verbs, series of words, series of sentence parts, sentence openers, sentence closers, lists, and extensions.

A. Identifying Sentence Composing Skills The sentences below are from *Across Five Aprils,* a novel about the Civil War by Irene Hunt. Each sentence illustrates one of the sentence composing skills you have studied. For each sentence, write the letter identifying the skill illustrated in the underlined part.

a. compound subject
b. compound verb
c. series of words
d. series of sentence parts
e. sentence opener
f. S-V split
g. sentence closer
h. sentence with a list (colon)
i. sentence with extension (dash)

1. She had borne twelve children, four of whom were dead—perhaps five, for the oldest son had not been heard from since he left for the gold fields of California twelve years before.
2. A cupboard of heavy walnut put together with wooden pegs stood near the fireplace and held dishes, food, and cooking utensils.
3. When the barn was burned to a pile of glowing coals, the men asked Jethro to draw water from the stock well to throw around the edges of the coals.
4. McClellan, the most promising young officer in his class at West Point, was the general who either didn't move at all or moved ineffectually.
5. He looked at the faces around him, and they spun in a strange mist of color: black eyes and blue eyes, gray hair and gold and black, pink cheeks and pale ones and weather-beaten brown ones.
6. Ellen, the two young women, and Jethro stood in the yard and watched silently.

7. The sun was getting low by the time he reached the ruins of what had been the county's first schoolhouse, a landmark known as the eight-mile point north of Newton.

8. The restaurant was warm and clean, full of the fragrance of roasting meat, freshly baked wheat-flour bread, and strong, rich coffee.

9. He lay with his face close to the earth, clutching the fresh spring grass with both hands.

10. He picked up Tom's letter, read it again, smoothed it carefully, and returned it to the envelope.

11. Jethro, understanding the situation more fully now that he was older, wondered at his father's intervention that afternoon.

12. They say, too, that hundreds of people climbed up on rooftops to watch the flight—as if it were a circus of some kind.

B. Matching and Imitating Sentences Each sentence below can be divided into chunks that resemble the chunks in one of the sentences in Exercise A. Write the number of the sentence in Exercise A that each sentence imitates. Then write your own imitation.

1. Janine sat with her feet up to the fire, stretching her damp, chilled toes with growing contentment.

2. Michele had invited ten friends, nine of whom were coming—perhaps ten, since one friend had not called back before Michele went to the store for refreshments fifteen minutes ago.

3. Thom, the unpredictable new member of the cross-country team at Jefferson School, was the runner who either led from the start or lagged behind.

4. When the beach was deserted after sunny afternoons in the summer, the beachcomber used his metal detector to find items beneath the sand to sell at the recycling center in town.

5. The cellar was humid and dank, full of the smell of rotting wood, long-neglected furniture, and damp, mildewed cloth.

Additional Resource

Sentence Composing Copy Masters, pp. 15–16

Answer Key

A. Identifying Sentence Composing Skills

1. i	**5.** h	**9.** g
2. c	**6.** a	**10.** b
3. e	**7.** g	**11.** f
4. f	**8.** c	**12.** i

B. Matching and Imitating Sentences

Matching models from Exercise A are given. Imitative sentences will vary but should follow the same pattern.

1. 9
2. 1
3. 4
4. 3
5. 8

ART NOTE As a folk art, quilting dates back to ancient times. The earliest example is a quilted garment on an Egyptian carved figure from 3400 B.C. Quilting has also been a valued art in America since colonial times. Fabric was scarce in colonial America, so quilters artfully pieced scraps from discarded clothing into intricate designs. In the nineteenth century, quilts made to honor weddings and funerals were popular. Over the years, anonymous women worked for thousands of hours to create beautiful quilts, some of which hang in art museums today.

Faith Ringgold (b. 1930), an African American who grew up in the Sugar Hill section of Harlem and still lives there, creates quilt series that tell stories. This quilt, *The Wedding: Lover's Quilt #1,* is the first in a three-part continuous story about a couple's life. The second quilt in the trilogy is *Sleeping: Lover's Quilt #2;* the third is *The Funeral: Lover's Quilt #3.* Down the middle of each quilt, Addy, the bride and narrator, recounts the blessings, accidents, and mistakes in the couple's lives. On the last quilt, we discover that Addy has died.

Ask students to describe what this quilt shows. (Sample: the bride's family on the right; the groom's on the left; the bridal party with probably the honor attendant next to the bride; the flower girl in front of this maid or matron; and the ring bearer on the other side of the bride) Ask what mood the quilt evokes. Then ask students to identify what important events or people they would show in a quilt that tells their life story.

The Wedding: Lover's Quilt #1 (1986), Faith Ringgold. This African-American folk artist pieced together images and text in three quilts that tell the story of a couple's life. In this quilt, the couple is shown at their wedding.

Literature Connection

Students will enjoy reading or hearing read aloud Alice Walker's short story "Everyday Use." The story is about an African-American mother, her two daughters, and two hand-stitched quilts made many years before. The mother must decide which of her very different daughters will inherit these prized quilts.

The story deals with family conflicts, values, and attitudes toward the African-American heritage. Faith Ringgold knows and admires Alice Walker's writings about the experiences of African-American women.

Writing Handbook

MINI-LESSONS

Writing Process

Style

Academic Skills

MINI-LESSONS

Writing Handbook

The mini-lessons in this handbook may be used for a variety of purposes.

Preteaching—to introduce specific concepts and skills before beginning a Guided or Related Assignment
Reference—to provide extra help and practice as students problem-solve their way through a piece of writing
Reteaching—to remedy specific problems in student writing

To match mini-lessons to an assignment, see "Handbooks for Help and Practice" in the teaching notes for the Writer's Workshops, and handbook cross-references on the pupil page.

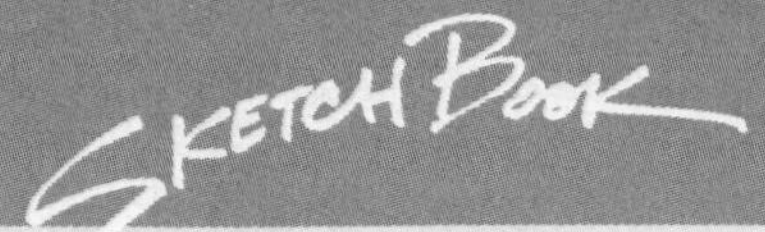

Objective

- To use writing prompts and a comic strip as springboards to informal writing

WRITING WARM-UPS

Advise students that these Sketchbook activities will not be graded; rather, students should use them to help explore ideas, to experiment with various writing forms, and to think about themselves as writers. Students may respond to one or more of the prompts through writing, through class or small-group discussion, or through art.

You might use the discussion of the comic strip to emphasize the importance of a journal as a personal record-keeper or to encourage students to begin keeping a writing journal if they have not already done so.

Sketch Book

WRITING WARM-UPS

Calvin and Hobbes

by Bill Watterson

- What important thoughts do *you* have? Jot down some ideas that are on your mind.
- Draw a picture that shows what you are feeling or thinking about right now.
- How do you figure things out? Describe how you made a recent decision.

216

Writing Process

WRITING
HANDBOOKS

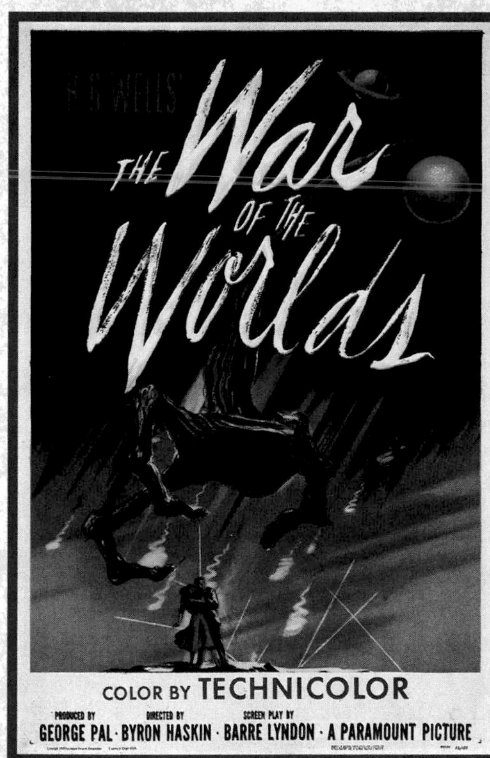

Where do you think the idea for this movie came from? It could have started with a writer doodling on a piece of paper—perhaps drawing Martians invading Indianapolis.

Writing isn't just a matter of putting words down on paper. It's a process of figuring out what you're thinking and how you want to express your thoughts. The handbooks that follow can help you explore, write, and polish your ideas.

Writing Process

INTRODUCING THE HANDBOOKS

Use the poster for *The War of the Worlds* to start students talking about the thought that goes into developing a film project. (Be prepared to answer the question on the pupil page—namely, that the 1953 film was based on H. G. Wells's 1898 novel by the same name.)

If applying the same thought and planning to their writing projects worries students, point out that these handbooks will help them express their ideas plainly. Remind them how much they enjoy seeing the movies that result from filmmakers' thinking. In much the same way, students will enjoy seeing the results of their—and their peers'—thinking in writing.

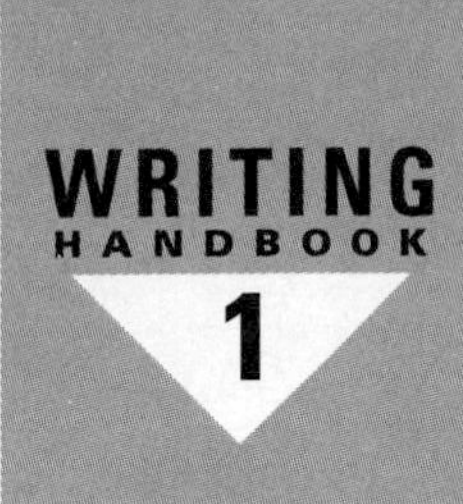

Discovering Writing Ideas

Objective

- To learn and apply personal, sharing, writing, and graphic techniques for generating writing ideas

Related Mini-Lessons

For information on topics related to discovering writing ideas, see the following mini-lessons:

- **Focusing a Topic, pp. 224–226**
- **Graphic Devices for Writing, pp. 227–231**

Motivate

Have students imagine that they work for a nationally known magazine. The next issue must be finished in two days, and a one-page story has just been pulled for further research. If students had to fill that page, what would they do? Discuss their strategies for finding ideas, noting several on the board. Then offer an overview of this handbook by comparing students' suggestions with the techniques indicated in the various lesson heads.

Teaching Strategies

for PERSONAL TECHNIQUES

PERSONAL TOUCH You may wish to share an excerpt from a recent piece of your own writing, following up by telling students how you got the idea for that piece. Whenever possible, use your personal writing experiences to illustrate specific techniques presented in this handbook.

WRITING HANDBOOK 1

How Do I Find a Topic?

Discovering Writing Ideas

Where do writing ideas come from? They can come from just about anywhere—observations, experiences, memories, conversations, dreams, or imaginings. The writer Alice Walker got the idea for her book *The Color Purple* from a remark her sister made. Maya Angelou's book *I Know Why the Caged Bird Sings* is based on her memories of growing up in the South during the 1930s. The idea for Roald Dahl's book *Charlie and the Chocolate Factory* came from a note in a journal: "What about a chocolate factory that makes fantastic and marvelous things—with a crazy man running it?"

Like Walker, Angelou, and Dahl, you are constantly surrounded by good writing ideas. All you have to do is start looking. The techniques presented in this handbook can help you find a topic you really care about. Try them out and use the ones that work for you.

PERSONAL TECHNIQUES

One of the best places to look for writing ideas is inside yourself. You can begin by exploring your own memories, interests, and imagination.

Do you remember learning to ride a bicycle? a trip to visit your grandmother? your twelfth birthday? Your life is full of experiences that can yield good writing ideas. To help jog your memory, try any of the following techniques:

- **Look** through your journal, family photo albums, and scrapbooks. List people, places, and things that have been important to you.
- **Recall** significant events. A time line might help you remember events from different periods of your life.

PROFESSIONAL NOTEBOOK

Advice from the Authors In *Writing with Power,* Peter Elbow recommends open-ended writing, or looping, as a way of finding ideas. To begin this process, write for several minutes (without stopping) about whatever interests you. Then pause and find the main point in what you've written. Write that idea in one sentence and then use the sentence as the starting point for a new burst of writing. Repeat the cycle "till you get to the piece of writing that is in you that wants to get written." The process "is most useful if you sense you have something useful to write but don't quite know what it is."

- **Talk** to a friend or family member about incidents from your childhood or experiences you've shared.

Taking Stock of Your Interests What do you most like to do? Watch horror movies? Study the sky through a telescope? Play soccer? Your own interests can be a good source of writing ideas. Questions like the ones below can help you identify your interests:

- What books and magazines do I like to read?
- What is my favorite sport?
- What kinds of television programs do I like?
- What do I do in my free time?
- What would I like to learn more about?
- Who are my heroes?

WRITER TO WRITER

You'd be surprised to know how many everyday things will trigger a great idea. I always keep a piece of paper handy—you never know when that great idea will come!

Jennifer Wilson, student, Mount Clemens, Michigan

Responding to Triggers Sometimes just a word or a picture can set your thoughts in motion. Simply focus on a word or image—the first one that comes to mind or one that you find in your journal. Then jot down ideas and questions that occur to you as you think about it.

Nighthawks (1942), Edward Hopper.

Answering Reporters' Questions When reporters gather information for a news story, they ask basic questions beginning with *who, what, where, when, why,* and *how.* These questions can help you find ideas for writing, too. Suppose your social studies teacher has assigned a paper on the Civil War. You might ask questions like the ones on the next page to help you identify a topic:

GENERAL NOTE

HELPFUL HINT The writing prompts in the Tests and Writing Assessment Prompts in the Teacher's Resource File provide a wealth of topic ideas. The prompts for the workshops on Personal and Expressive Writing and on Narrative and Literary Writing will be especially helpful for students who are looking for ideas for creative writing.

GENERAL NOTE

STUMBLING BLOCK Sometimes writers struggle so hard to find ideas that they become blocked. The best strategy then is to set the task aside for a while and focus on something else, preferably something relaxing. Writers often find that ideas come spontaneously when they take breaks between rounds of concentrated thinking.

for RESPONDING TO TRIGGERS

INDIVIDUALIZING INSTRUCTION: VISUAL LEARNERS Students whose primary learning style is visual may be very successful in using "trigger" words to discover ideas. These students tend to have active imaginations and are able to visualize ideas and images and "see" associations among them. In addition to having them search their journals for ideas, provide them with a list of words—for example, *fire, danger, party, football,* and *mystery*—that can stimulate an emotional response or association.

LEP STUDENTS The "idea" stage of writing is one in which LEP students sometimes can flower because it rewards imagination and does not require language mastery. Point out to these students that memories and subjects often can be summed up in just a few words.

ART NOTE

Edward Hopper (1882–1967) was one of the greatest American realistic painters of his time. Born in Nyack, New York, he worked as a commercial illustrator before becoming a successful painter in his forties. In *Nighthawks,* perhaps his most famous painting, students can discover Hopper's characteristic portrayal of bleak scenes from the lives of lonely, ordinary people. This painting makes an excellent trigger for story ideas. Invite students to ask questions about the lives of the people in the painting. (Samples: Who are they? What are they thinking?)

for ASKING CREATIVE QUESTIONS

CRITICAL THINKING: INFERRING AND SYNTHESIZING Point out that "What if?" questions can result in real-life inventions as well as in writing ideas. Ask students to identify these real-life examples from the list of questions on page 220: the mattress filled with water (a waterbed), a surfboard used as a water ski (a sailboard), a television and a telephone combined (a picturephone). Then discuss how one of the creative questions might be turned into a writing idea. (Sample: What if people lived underwater? Write a short story about a scientist who lives with her family in an underwater life station in the ocean.) Encourage students to brainstorm other creative questions.

- Who were the leaders of the Union and of the Confederacy?
- What were some of the consequences of the war?
- Where were the major battles fought?
- When did the war begin?
- Why was the war fought?
- How did average soldiers feel about the war?

Asking Creative Questions In the movie *Big,* the actor Tom Hanks plays a young boy who, incredibly, grows up overnight. The idea for that movie probably came from asking the question "What if?" Asking that question can help you come up with writing ideas that are just as original. Even questions that seem ridiculous can lead to promising writing ideas. Here are some examples:

- What if I changed a familiar object in some way? (What if a mattress were filled with water?)
- What if I used a familiar object in a new way? (What if a surfboard were used as a water ski?)
- What if I put two things together in a new way? (What if a television and a telephone were combined?)
- What if a person had never existed or an event had never happened? (What if television had not been invented?)
- What if relationships between people or things were changed? (What if your cat kept you as a pet?)
- What if things happened differently? (What if people got younger instead of older? What if people lived underwater?)

What if . . . ?

Literature Connection

As the pupil page suggests, "What if?" questions are the springboards for much science fiction. A classic example is Daniel Keyes's "Flowers for Algernon" on page 267 of *Literature and Language,* Grade 8. Have students suggest at least one "What if?" question on which that story is based. (Samples: What if it were possible to increase a person's intelligence? What if someone I knew suddenly became very important? What if a person who had great power [in this case, Charlie's enhanced intellect] felt that power slipping away?)

Gleaning Just as some people collect baseball cards, you can collect ideas by gleaning, or gathering, ideas from the world around you. Whenever you come across something that intrigues you—something you see, hear, read, or experience—jot down your thoughts, feelings, and observations in your journal. When you need a writing idea, just look through your collection.

SHARING TECHNIQUES

When you're searching for ideas, you might also try getting a little help from your friends. Working with other people is often more effective than working alone.

Brainstorming One way to come up with a lot of ideas quickly is to brainstorm. Get together with a few friends or classmates. Choose someone to record the group's ideas on the chalkboard or on a large sheet of paper. Pick a topic and then try to come up with as many ideas as fast as you can. Don't stop to comment on any of the ideas. One person's ideas may spark other ideas, like a chain reaction. After about five or ten minutes, review your list for potential writing ideas.

Here are the results of a brief brainstorming session in which students began with the topic *oceans:*

oceans	Pacific	dolphins	submarines
waves	Atlantic	shipwrecks	*Alvin* submersible
tides	salt water	coral reefs	Jacques Cousteau
sharks	tidal waves	whales	scuba diving

Discussion Although brainstorming can help you generate ideas quickly, a discussion can help you explore a topic in more depth. Here are some guidelines for holding a discussion:

- Agree on a general topic for discussion.
- Give each person a chance to speak and to ask questions about or to react to what others have said.
- Listen carefully and respectfully to what others have to say.

Afterwards, jot down notes about the discussion and ideas you would like to develop in a piece of writing.

for BRAINSTORMING

COLLABORATIVE OPPORTUNITY

Consider holding a brainstorming contest in which small groups try to add as many ideas as they can to the *oceans* list within a five-minute period. Alternatively, give students a new topic, such as *cars.*

for DISCUSSION

HELPFUL HINT To demonstrate how topics can be developed through discussion, have small groups choose a topic they have brainstormed and discuss ways to turn it into a specific writing project. Encourage students to think of a variety of forms of writing. For instance, one topic on the subject of dolphins might be "a research article on how dolphins communicate" and another might be "a poem about the beauty of dolphins."

TEACHER'S LOUNGE

OH NO! NOT AGAIN! I CAN'T THINK OF A THING TO WRITE!
IT COULD BE ANOTHER CASE OF WRITER'S BLOCK...
BUT MOST LIKELY IT'S A MUCH MORE WIDESPREAD AFFLICTION...
BRAIN CRAMP.

Discovering Writing Ideas 221

for FREEWRITING

USING THE MODEL Have a volunteer read the Student Model aloud. Ask the class to identify the topics generated by the freewriting (climate, gold rush, forty-ninth state, oil, conflict between Eskimos and oil companies). Then have students freewrite on a similar topic, perhaps your own state. Ask volunteers to share their freewriting and to identify ideas they might explore further.

GENERAL NOTE

HELPFUL HINT Many teachers find it helpful to keep a file of possible writing topics that students can draw from or add to throughout the year. A covered cardboard box on a shelf in a corner of your room can do nicely. Some teachers prefer a more formal file folder, and others allow students to write ideas on small pieces of paper and tack them to a reserved section of a bulletin board. Maintain a single topic pool for all your classes in a single grade.

WRITING TECHNIQUES

Your pen or pencil can also lead you to new ideas. Just putting your thoughts on paper can help get them flowing.

Freewriting The only rule in freewriting is "Keep writing." To begin, set a time limit, say five minutes. Pick a topic or start by writing down the first words that come into your head. If you get stuck, keep writing the same words over and over until a new thought occurs to you. Don't worry about grammar, spelling, punctuation, or logic, and don't stop to read what you've written. Just keep writing. When the time is up, read through your freewriting. Circle any ideas you'd like to explore further. You can even do more freewriting to develop one of those ideas.

Here's how one student used freewriting to come up with a topic for a social studies report on Alaska:

Student MODEL

Alaska. What do I know about it? Lots of snow and ice. Ice and snow, snow and ice. Cold. Gold. Forty-niners. It's the forty-ninth state. The Gold Rush. Somewhere I read about a new gold rush for liquid gold—oil. There's some kind of battle between Eskimos who hunt caribou for food and the oil companies. They want to drill wells where the caribou herds migrate. I wonder what's going to happen. Maybe I could write about that.

Listing Like brainstorming, listing is a good way to generate writing ideas quickly. First pick a topic. Then start listing all the related ideas that occur to you. Don't stop to judge your ideas—just get as many thoughts down as fast as you can.

Using a Journal Sometimes the best ideas occur to you when you're not even looking for them. That's why many writers regularly record their observations, thoughts, and feelings in a journal. You can do the same. Your journal is just for you. You can use it to explore your ideas, sort out your feelings, record your experiences, and dream about the future. You can also use it to keep clippings of newspaper and magazine articles, quotes, cartoons, photographs, and anything else that interests you.

When you need a writing idea, thumb through your journal and see what catches your eye. Then use one of the techniques presented in this handbook to explore the idea further.

GRAPHIC TECHNIQUES

Sometimes "seeing" your ideas in graphic form can help you clarify them. For help with using graphic devices, see Handbook 3, "Graphic Devices for Writing," pages 227–231.

Practice Your Skills

A. Choose one of the topics below or study the photograph on this page. Then use two of the following techniques to generate writing ideas: recalling, answering reporters' questions, asking creative questions, or gleaning. Compare the results of the two techniques. Which technique worked better for you?

rain	winning	sports
mountains	spiders	careers
honesty	change	
music videos	high school	

Little Sparrows (1969), Jill Freedman.

B. In a small group, choose one of the topics below and use brainstorming or discussion to develop writing ideas.

adventure	travel	freedom
frustration	Mars	amusement parks
grandparents	animals	
winter	discovery	

C. Look through your journal, or use freewriting, listing, or a graphic device, to come up with writing ideas on one of the following topics.

making decisions	friendship	racism
sharing	disappointments	popularity
writing	volunteering	
telephones	disease	

for GRAPHIC TECHNIQUES

INDIVIDUALIZING INSTRUCTION: VISUAL LEARNERS Invite one or more volunteers to create a graphic device that presents all the idea-generating techniques discussed in this handbook. You might wish to post the results on a bulletin board for permanent reference.

for PRACTICE YOUR SKILLS

ASSESSMENT Assessment should be informal and ungraded. Emphasize that students should use this opportunity to try out techniques that are new to them.

Additional Resources

Writing Resource Book, pp. 53–54
Thinking Skills Transparency Pack
Thinking Skills Worksheets, pp. 1, 4, 5
Fine Art Transparency Pack
Tests and Writing Assessment Prompts, pp. 1–7

Answers to Practice Your Skills

A. Answers will vary. Students should show an understanding of the two techniques they chose.

B. Answers will vary. Each group should submit a single list of writing ideas.

C. Answers will vary. Students should submit a list of writing ideas and any notes or drawings that show their thinking processes.

ART NOTE

Jill Freedman (1939–) is a self-taught American photographer who has also been a musician. She is known for her deep involvement with her subjects. In a series of books, she has portrayed human beings in such highly specific settings as a circus, a police beat, and a poor people's march. Ask students to look at the photograph and discuss how photographers find ideas for pictures. Encourage them to make comparisons between ideas for photography subjects and writing ideas.

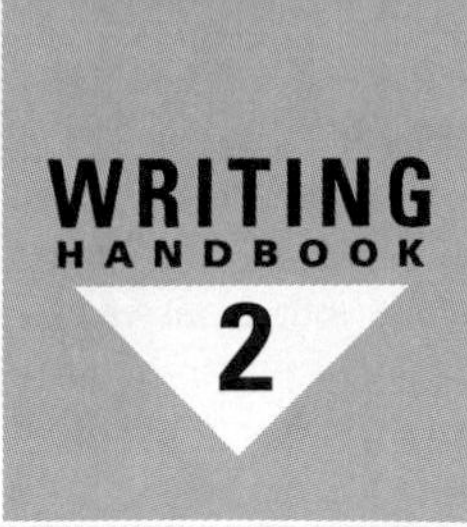

Focusing a Topic

Objective

- To use the strategies of questioning, looping, graphic devices, and brainstorming to focus a topic

Related Mini-Lessons

For more information related to focusing a writing topic, see the following mini-lessons:

- **Discovering Writing Ideas, pp. 218–223**
- **Graphic Devices for Writing, pp. 227–231**

Motivate

Write these headings on the board: *Music, Fashion, Sports.* Ask students why these might be difficult topics to write about. (They're too broad.) Then ask them whether they've ever had the experience, after thinking of a topic, of discovering that it was either too broad or too narrow. Ask how students overcame that problem. Encourage them to share their personal strategies. Inform them that this handbook will introduce them to techniques of making topics more specific.

Teaching Strategies

for QUESTIONING

INDIVIDUALIZING INSTRUCTION: ADVANCED STUDENTS Have students imagine that they are magazine editors. Have them search copies of their favorite magazines for articles that especially interest them, think of at least two new topics for future articles, and focus these topics by using the technique of questioning.

WRITING HANDBOOK 2

How Do I Make My Topic the Right Size?

Focusing a Topic

As any photographer will tell you, there is more than one way to focus on a scene. Sometimes a sweeping, overall view works best. At other times a close-up is more effective. The same is true of writing. Part of choosing a writing topic is bringing the ideas into focus by giving them sharpness and clarity. Many of the techniques for finding a topic discussed in Handbook 1 can also help you focus a topic.

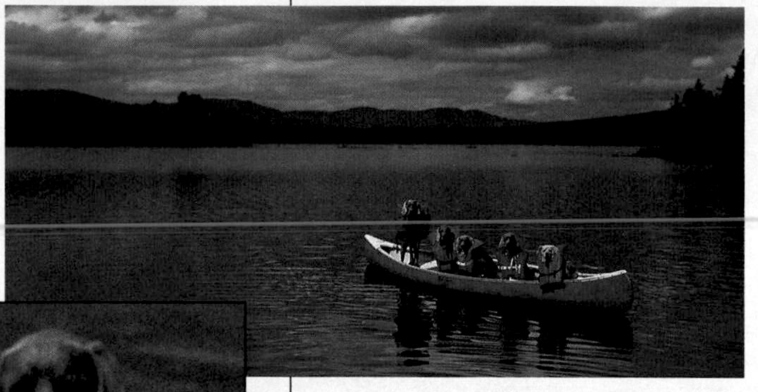

Loon Lake, Maine, (1990), William Wegman.

QUESTIONING

Asking questions about a topic is a good way to find a focus. Suppose that your social studies teacher has assigned a two-page paper on Mexico. That topic is too broad to cover in two pages, so you might begin to narrow it by asking questions that begin with *who, what, where, when, why,* and *how.*

- Who are some famous Mexican artists?
- What are some major events in Mexican history?
- When did Mexico gain its independence from Spain?
- Why did the United States and Mexico fight a war?
- How has the geography of Mexico affected its history?

If your topic is too narrow, you can also use questioning to expand it. For example, suppose that you are writing a four-page report on space exploration. After watching a science program on television, you become interested in pictures of the United States taken from the Landsat satellites. There is not enough nontechnical

ART NOTE

William Wegman (1943–) is a photographer and video artist known for his wry sense of humor. Many of his photographs and videotapes feature his dog, Man Ray—named for a great surrealistic photographer of the 1920s who was also known for *his* sense of humor. Wegman often dressed Man Ray (the dog) in funny costumes or put him in weird photographic situations, as in "Loon Lake, Maine." When the dog died in 1982, Wegman published a book of color photos of him, called *Man's Best Friend.* (Note the pun on "Man" in the title.) Invite students to share their reactions to this photograph.

information on this topic for a four-page report. However, you can ask questions such as these to find a broader topic:

- Who invented the Landsat satellites?
- What are some other kinds of artificial satellites?
- Where are satellites like Landsat built and launched?
- When was the first artificial satellite put into orbit?
- Why are artificial satellites useful?
- How have Landsat images been used?

LOOPING

Another way to limit or expand a topic is to use looping. This is a special kind of freewriting. (See Handbook 1, "Discovering Writing Ideas," pages 218–223.) First, choose a writing topic. Then freewrite about it for five minutes without stopping. When the time is up, read through what you have written and look for a possible focus for your writing. State that focus in a sentence and use it as a starting point for more freewriting.

You may need to repeat this looping process several times before finding a topic that's just the right size. For example, after freewriting three loops on the topics "sleep," "napping," and "relaxation," one student discovered her writing topic—"hypnosis."

USING GRAPHIC DEVICES

Graphic devices such as clusters and idea trees can also help you focus a topic. (See Handbook 3, "Graphic Devices for Writing," pages 227–231, for examples of these graphics.) As you use a cluster or an idea tree to limit a broad topic, try to think of specific parts of the larger topic. Then think of even narrower ideas associated with each of those parts. That way, the ideas will get more focused as you move farther from the center.

For example, one student made the cluster on the next page to narrow the topic "new technology" so that it could be covered in a five-page report.

GENERAL NOTE

INDIVIDUALIZING INSTRUCTION: BASIC STUDENTS Some students may have trouble recognizing why the topics *Mexico* and *Landsat satellites* need refocusing. Point out that sometimes it is hard to see the difficulty in any topic until one begins doing research and then finds either too much or not enough information. Point out, for example, that there may be dozens of books about Mexico in a given library's catalog but not a single book devoted exclusively to Landsat satellites. Ask, "Do you think a library might have at least one book about artificial satellites in general?" (yes) Point out that the questions on the pupil page help to broaden the topic by speaking of artificial satellites in general.

for LOOPING

HELPFUL HINT To give students practice in looping, suggest a broad topic, such as *sports* or *animals*. Have students perform the looping process through three five-minute cycles and then decide on a focused topic. Encourage volunteers to share their responses.

for USING GRAPHIC DEVICES

MODELING Because a full discussion of graphic devices appears in Handbook 3, you may want to introduce the class to idea trees and clusters through a demonstration. Have students suggest a topic for you to develop. Think out loud as you begin to develop it through a chalkboard sketch; then invite their ideas and add them to the chalkboard graphic. After each graphic has been completed, have volunteers identify possible focused writing topics.

for CLUSTER

USING THE MODEL As students examine the model cluster, point out how the topics become narrower as they branch out from the center topic. Invite students to suggest other topics that could have been added to the cluster. Finally, ask students which topics are focused enough to write about. (Possible answers: high-definition TV, virtual reality games, 3-D movies, 3-D cameras, laser discs, video phones)

for BRAINSTORMING

CRITICAL THINKING: MAKING COMPARISONS Ask students how clusters and brainstorming are similar and different. (Some students may feel that a cluster is simply the visual equivalent of brainstorming, but point out that clusters show the relationship among ideas, whereas brainstorming notes do not.)

Additional Resources

Writing Resource Book, p. 55
Thinking Skills Transparency Pack
Thinking Skills Worksheets

Answers to Practice Your Skills

Strategies and topics will vary. Sample answers are shown below.

1. *Dr. Martin Luther King, Jr.*
   Strategy: idea tree; Narrower topic: Dr. King's role in the 1963 March on Washington
   Strategy: looping; Broader topic: the civil rights movement of the 1950s and 1960s
2. *The moon*
   Strategy: questioning; Narrower topic: the craters of the moon
   Strategy: cluster; Broader topic: the solar system
3. *Science fiction*
   Strategy: questioning; Narrower topic: a work by Ursula K. Le Guin
   Strategy: cluster; Broader topic: popular fiction
4. *Sports played on ice*
   Strategy: questioning; Narrower topic: how to play ice hockey
   Strategy: brainstorming; Broader topic: winter sports

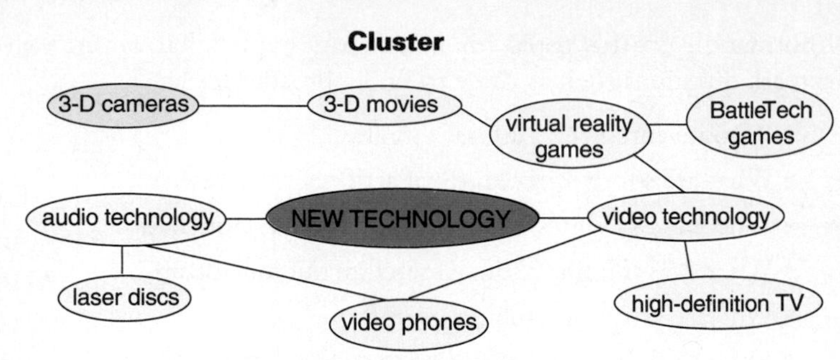

BRAINSTORMING

W R I T E R   T O   W R I T E R

Start with a brainstorm or a single idea. You could get a whole page of thoughts from one word.

Stacy Smith, student, Kenosha, Wisconsin

Brainstorming can not only help you find writing topics but also help you take the next step and focus your topic. You can brainstorm alone, with a partner, or in a small group. First pick a topic. Then jot down all the related ideas that you or other people suggest. Don't stop to discuss or criticize the ideas. Just keep writing them down. At the end of the session, you will probably have found a topic that is just the right size for your writing project.

In addition to brainstorming, techniques such as listing and questioning can help you expand your topic if its focus is too narrow. (See Handbook 1, "Discovering Writing Ideas," pages 218–223.)

Practice Your Skills

For each topic listed below, use one of the strategies presented in this handbook to find one topic that is narrower and one that is broader in focus. Tell which strategy you used to find each topic.

Dr. Martin Luther King, Jr.	science fiction
the moon	sports played on ice

When Can I Use a Graphic Organizer?

Graphic Devices for Writing

When people want to make sure that they've gotten their message across, they often say, "Do you see what I mean?" Seeing is an important part of understanding. Sometimes putting your thoughts in visual form—in a graph or a chart—can help you both develop and organize your writing ideas.

GRAPHICS TO DEVELOP IDEAS

Some graphic devices that are especially helpful in exploring and developing ideas are clusters, idea trees, observation charts, and pro-and-con charts.

Clusters A cluster can help you explore a general idea to see how its parts are related. To make a cluster, write the general topic in the center of your paper and circle it. Write down related ideas as you think of them. Circle each of these ideas and draw lines connecting them to the main topic or to related ideas. (Look on the opposite page for an example of a cluster.)

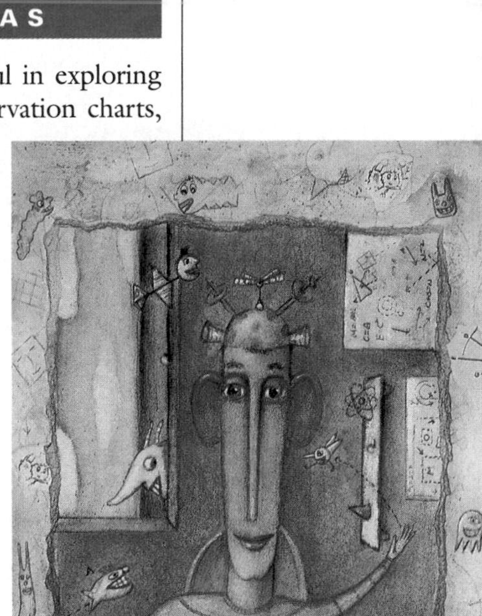

Idea Trees An idea tree is especially useful for breaking down a general topic into its parts. Start by writing the general topic at the bottom or top of your paper. Then think about subtopics that are related to that topic. List these on "branches" growing out of the main topic. Keep dividing each new topic into subtopics until you have generated enough ideas or have found a topic to write about. One student used the idea tree on the next page to find an aspect of bats that she wanted to write about—how they navigate in the dark by echolocation.

Graphic Devices for Writing

Objective

- To identify and use clusters, idea trees, observation charts, and pro-and-con charts to explore and develop writing ideas
- To identify and use idea-and-details charts, classification frames, compare-and-contrast charts, and Venn diagrams for help in organizing ideas for writing

Related Mini-Lessons

For information on topics related to using graphic devices for writing, see the following mini-lessons.

- **Discovering Writing Ideas, pp. 218–223**
- **Focusing a Topic, pp. 224–226**
- **Methods of Elaboration, pp. 255–261**

Motivate

Display a copy of the newspaper *USA Today*. Point out the many graphic devices used to organize and illustrate ideas. Explain that students can use graphic devices to develop and organize their own ideas.

Teaching Strategies

for CLUSTERS

COLLABORATIVE OPPORTUNITY

To help students understand how to use a cluster to develop writing ideas, draw their attention to the sample cluster on page 226. Ask a volunteer to choose from the cluster a topic to develop further; write this topic on the board. Ask other volunteers to generate related ideas and link them to the central topic or to one another. After the cluster is completed, briefly discuss how students might use the cluster for a writing project.

SPICE BOX

Students might enjoy playing "Cluster Quest," in which classmates try to guess the central topic of a cluster from the related ideas. Form the class into small groups. Have each group choose a topic and make a cluster. Then ask each group in turn to read the related ideas from their cluster, one by one. After each related idea is read, allow time for the class to try to guess the original (central) topic.

for IDEA TREE

HELPFUL HINT Have students study the example of an idea tree and then create another idea tree on the chosen subject, echolocation. Ask volunteers to think of subtopics and write them on the board. (Examples include *how it works, advantages,* and *other animals that use it.)* Lead students to see how an idea tree might be used to develop and organize writing ideas as well as to discover a topic.

for OBSERVATION CHART

COOPERATIVE LEARNING Have students work in groups of five to create observation charts on a shared experience, such as a school dance or a Saturday afternoon at a shopping mall. Suggest that each student in a group contribute the sensory impressions for one sense.

Idea Tree

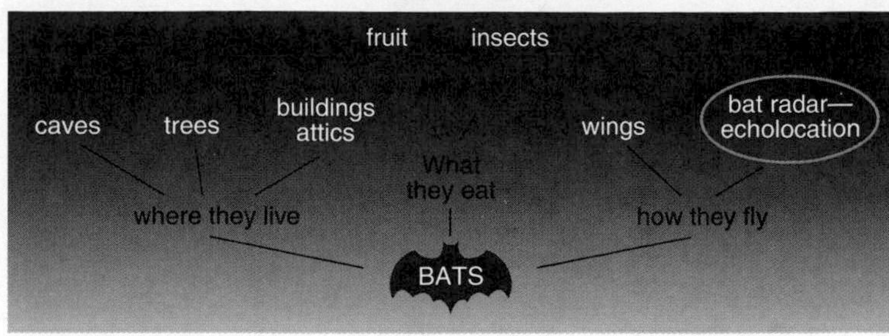

Observation Charts A good way to come up with details for descriptive writing is to use an observation chart. First, think of a person, place, thing, or experience you want to write about. Then list the five senses as column headings. Try to recall or imagine details about your topic, focusing on each sense in turn.

After you've finished, look over your list for vivid images and unexpected observations. These may be good starting points for writing. For example, after making the following observation chart, one student decided to write a story about a camping trip from the point of view of his feet.

Observation Chart

Camping Trip				
Sight	**Sound**	**Touch**	**Taste**	**Smell**
moose grazing brother's footprints in mud light filtering through trees brilliant stars	crunch of dry leaves and twigs underfoot crackle of campfire	rough fir tree bark icy water of stream on feet warm mud between toes painful blisters	sweet and salty trail mix bitter berries	wood smoke pine needles wildflowers dirty socks

Pro-and-Con Charts When you're trying to develop material for persuasive writing, you need to evaluate the advantages and disadvantages of an idea. A pro-and-con chart can help you. First, divide a sheet of paper into two columns. Then list the advantages, or pros, of your idea in one column and the disadvantages, or cons, in the other.

For example, one student who wanted to start a paper-recycling program at her school decided to write a letter to the student council. She used the following pro-and-con chart to explore the advantages and disadvantages of her idea.

Pro-and-Con Chart

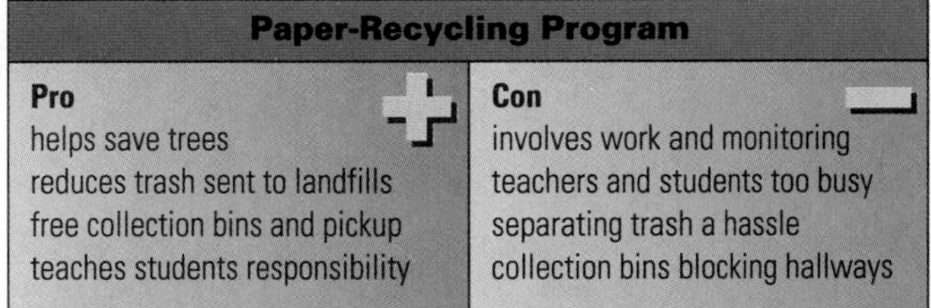

Paper-Recycling Program	
Pro	**Con**
helps save trees	involves work and monitoring
reduces trash sent to landfills	teachers and students too busy
free collection bins and pickup	separating trash a hassle
teaches students responsibility	collection bins blocking hallways

GRAPHICS TO ORGANIZE IDEAS

Once you have generated and developed your ideas, you can also use graphics to help you organize your writing and visualize its structure. Devices that are particularly helpful include idea-and-details charts, classification frames, compare-and-contrast charts, and Venn diagrams.

Idea-and-Details Charts If you have trouble separating main ideas and supporting details, try using an idea-and-details chart. You can rank the details by numbering them in order of their importance. Some writers use this graphic instead of an outline.

Idea Chart—"Smart" TVs

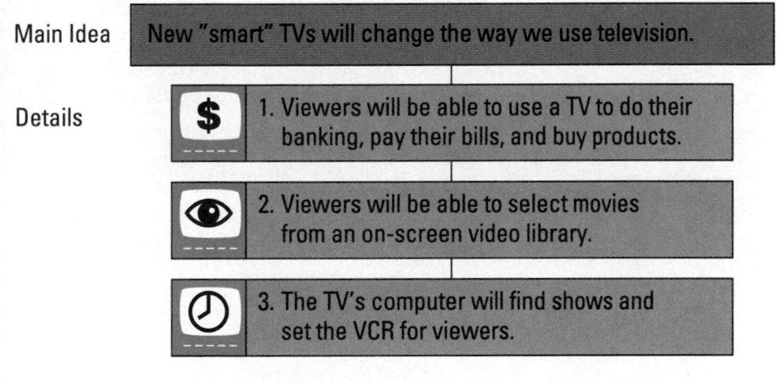
Main Idea
New "smart" TVs will change the way we use television.
Details
$
1. Viewers will be able to use a TV to do their banking, pay their bills, and buy products.
2. Viewers will be able to select movies from an on-screen video library.
3. The TV's computer will find shows and set the VCR for viewers.

for PRO-AND-CON CHART

KEY TO UNDERSTANDING Help students see the usefulness of the sample pro-and-con chart by discussing how the arguments it lists might become part of the proposed letter to the student council. For example, ask, "How would you order the 'pro' arguments if you were writing the letter?" (Answers will vary, but most students would place either the first or fourth argument in a prominent position.) "How might you use the 'con' arguments?" (Sample: You might defend your position against one or more of them.)

for GRAPHICS TO ORGANIZE IDEAS

INDIVIDUALIZING INSTRUCTION: ESL STUDENTS Graphic organizers are especially helpful for ESL students because the students can represent their ideas in a few words, without much concern about grammar and writing style.

for IDEA-AND-DETAILS CHARTS

CRITICAL THINKING: MAKING COMPARISONS Have students discuss the similarities and differences between an idea-and-detail chart and an outline. Ask which device students would prefer to use and why.

for CLASSIFICATION FRAMES

ASSESSMENT: SPOT CHECK To make sure that students understand that a classification frame can be used to group ideas into categories, ask whether they would create a classification frame to organize details on each of the following topics:

- how to prepare bread dough (no)
- the relationships among various types of stars and planets (yes)
- the disadvantages of using TV in the classroom (probably not)
- divisions of the human nervous system (yes)

for COMPARE-AND-CONTRAST CHARTS

HELPFUL HINT When students create their own compare-and-contrast charts, suggest that they color-code the items to distinguish similarities and differences. Note that the sample chart contains only differences but that charts on other subjects might contain both similarities and differences.

Classification Frames When you write, you may need to break an idea down into its parts or group several ideas in categories and consider how they are related. A classification frame can help you picture these relationships.

For example, one student was having trouble organizing a report on the martial arts. He knew that all of the styles could be used for exercise and for self-defense, but he didn't know how to group them. While making a classification frame, he found that the styles fell into two groups, depending on body contact.

Classification Frame

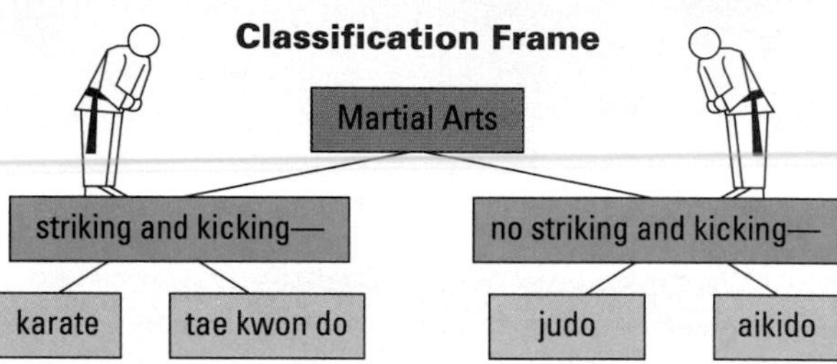

Compare-and-Contrast Charts A compare-and-contrast chart can help you clearly see the similarities and differences between two or more subjects. You can then use the chart to help you organize your writing by either subject or characteristic. Here is a compare-and-contrast chart that a student used in preparing a science report on forests.

Compare-and-Contrast Chart

Characteristics	Subjects Being Compared: Tropical rain forest	Temperate forest
Location	near the equator	eastern North America, western Europe, eastern Asia
Climate	warm and wet all year	warm summers and cold winters
Types of trees	mostly broad-leaved evergreens	mostly broad-leaved deciduous
Shrubs	thin layers	possibly dense layers

Science Connection

Point out the importance of classification in science and suggest that students might use classification frames when writing about certain scientific subjects. For example, all living things are classified according to shared characteristics.

Venn Diagrams A Venn diagram is another graphic way of comparing and contrasting two subjects. A Venn diagram consists of two overlapping circles. Shared characteristics go in the overlapping area. Outside areas contain the characteristics unique to each subject. A Venn diagram comparing types of forests is shown here.

Venn Diagram—Tropical Rain Forest vs. Temperate Forest

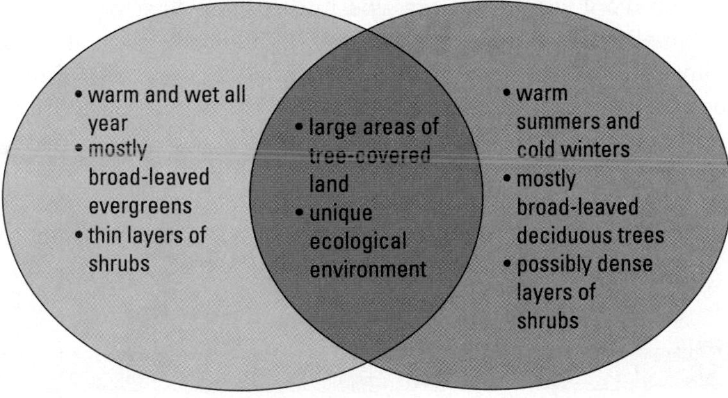

Practice Your Skills

A. Choose one of the following topics and use a cluster map, an idea tree, or an observation chart to explore it further. Compare your results with those of a classmate who chose the same topic.

caves cities California football whales deserts

B. Choose an issue about which you care and people disagree. With a partner, create a pro-and-con chart to explore different sides of the issue.

C. List the graphic device that would be most helpful for organizing information on each of the following topics.

1. Going to the movies versus watching movies on TV
2. Walking through the woods in mid-October
3. Types of Latin American music

for VENN DIAGRAMS

CRITICAL THINKING: MAKING COMPARISONS Ask students to compare the Venn diagram on forests with the compare-and-contrast chart on the same subject. (Students should note that the Venn diagram includes similarities, but the compare-and-contrast chart does not.) Point out that the use of a Venn diagram forces the writer to think about what two subjects have in common, as well as about how they differ.

Additional Resources

Writing Resource Book, pp. 56–57
Thinking Skills Transparency Pack
Thinking Skills Worksheets

Answers to Practice Your Skills

A. Answers will vary. The basic structure of students' graphic devices should match the examples given in the text.

B. Answers will vary. The basic structure of students' charts should match the pro-and-con chart on page 229.

C. Answers will vary. Possible answers are shown below.

1. Venn diagram or compare-and-contrast chart
2. Idea-and-details chart
3. Classification frame

MULTICULTURAL Connection

Students from different cultural backgrounds might work together in pairs to create Venn diagrams comparing the observance of a shared holiday—such as New Year's Day or a harvest celebration—in the two cultures.

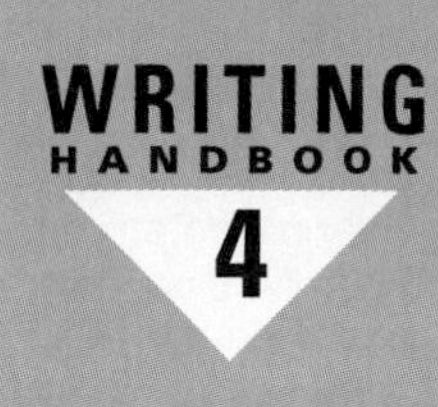

General Purpose and Personal Goals

Objectives

- To recognize the different purposes and personal goals that writers attempt to fulfill
- To identify a purpose and personal goals for a piece of writing

Related Mini-Lessons

For information on topics related to identifying a purpose and personal goals for writing, see the following mini-lessons.

- **Audience, pp. 234–235**
- **Meaning and Word Choice, pp. 314–315**
- **Developing a Personal Voice, pp. 316–317**

Teaching Strategies

for PURPOSE

PERSONAL TOUCH You might share with students examples of writing you have done for different purposes. Examples might include personal letters, class tests or instructions, grant proposals, and so on.

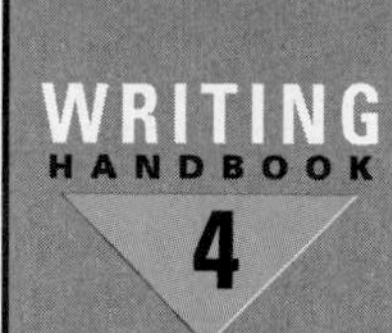

What Is My Purpose for Writing?

General Purpose and Personal Goals

Imagine that you are directing a skit for a class performance. As you work with the actors, you must decide what you want to accomplish. Do you want to make your audience laugh? Do you want to force them to think? Do you hope they will do a little of both? At some time during your writing process, you must ask yourself similar questions:

- What is my **purpose,** or general reason for writing?
- What are my **personal goals,** or things I want my writing to accomplish for myself and my readers?

PURPOSE

There are hundreds of reasons for writing. These purposes generally fall into four categories: **to express yourself, to entertain, to inform,** and **to persuade.** For example, after arguing with your best friend, you may write in your journal the apology you couldn't say to her face. You might write a card to someone who needs cheering up. Sometimes you may have two or even more purposes for writing. For example, you might write to inform your classmates about your favorite rock group and to persuade them to listen to the group's music.

Sometimes you know your purpose before you begin writing or can state it after doing some freewriting or brainstorming. Often, though, you discover your purpose as you write. You may even find your purpose changing as you continue to draft and revise. To help clarify your purpose for writing, ask yourself questions like the ones below:

- Why did I choose to write about this topic?
- What effect do I want my writing to have on my readers?

Literature Connection

Memoir to Read Have students read the excerpt from Clifton Taulbert's *Once Upon a Time When We Were Colored* on page 47 of *Literature and Language,*Grade 8. Invite students to jot down in their journals brief statements of what they think Taulbert's general purpose and personal goals were, in writing about his childhood experiences of discrimination. Then encourage them to discuss their ideas on the subject.

Personal Goals

Your personal goals are the specific things you want to achieve with this piece of writing. These goals might involve ways the writing can help you understand an idea, or they might simply focus on the impression you want to make. Asking yourself questions such as the following can help you identify your personal goals:

- What aspects of this topic mean the most to me?
- What specific feelings or thoughts do I want my readers to get from this piece of writing?

For example, imagine you are writing a story for your school newspaper about a recent basketball game. Your purpose might be to inform your classmates about the game. However, one of your several personal goals might be to point out the contributions of a player you think the coaches and fans don't really appreciate. In another piece of writing, your purpose might be to persuade readers to visit Mammoth Cave in Kentucky. A personal goal, however, could be to re-create the sense of wonder you felt inside the cave.

Writing TIP

Freewriting can help you clarify your personal connection with your topic.

Practice Your Skills

A. Choose a piece of writing from your portfolio, or think of a topic you want to explore in a future piece of writing. Then state your purpose and your personal goals for that writing.

B. The purpose of the following paragraph is to provide information. Rewrite the paragraph to persuade readers that some television programs are more worthwhile than others. As you think about this topic, list your personal goals for writing. Include specific examples of television programs in your new paragraph.

> What is the first thing many students do when they get home from school? After raiding the refrigerator, they turn on the TV. They have a variety of television programs to choose from. These programs include sitcoms, soap operas, talk shows, sports programs, travelogues, newscasts, variety shows, cartoons, educational shows, science and nature programs, and full-length movies.

Caricature of Rocky and Bullwinkle, © 1992 Ward Productions, Inc.

for PERSONAL GOALS

STUMBLING BLOCK If students have difficulty in finding a personal goal for writing, encourage them to ask themselves questions about the topic as they prepare to write. Some questions might include: What impact does this topic have on my life? What do I want to learn by exploring this topic?

In answering these and similar questions, students will find writing easier and more enjoyable.

for PRACTICE YOUR SKILLS

INDIVIDUALIZING INSTRUCTION: LEP STUDENTS Some students may have difficulty in rewriting this paragraph because of their limited vocabulary. Improve their comprehension of the initial paragraph by defining unfamiliar words and expressions. Then show them how to use a program guide to identify specific programs and classify them according to the categories listed. Finally, encourage students to explain why their favorite shows are more worthwhile than others.

Answers to Practice Your Skills

A. Answers will vary. Good statements of purpose and goals, however, will include such words as *to express, to entertain, to inform,* or *to persuade;* and goals will be specific, rather than general. Students' purposes and goals should be appropriate for the topics they choose.

B. Answers will vary. Students should submit a rewritten paragraph and a list of personal goals. A student model is shown below.

Some people think watching TV is bad for kids, but it's important to remember that TV has some good effects too. For one thing, TV takes us to places and events all over the world. It gives us the best seats for important sports events like the Winter Olympics, and it shows us how people live in such faraway places as China and the Amazon jungle. In addition, TV brings art, music, and plays into our living rooms. It gives us the opportunity to watch a performance by the Dance Theater of Harlem, a concert by Bruce Springsteen, or a play by Shakespeare. We can learn a lot from TV too. Science programs like *Nova,* nature programs like *Living Wild,* and the evening news are great ways to learn about our world.

Additional Resource

Writing Resource Book, p. 58

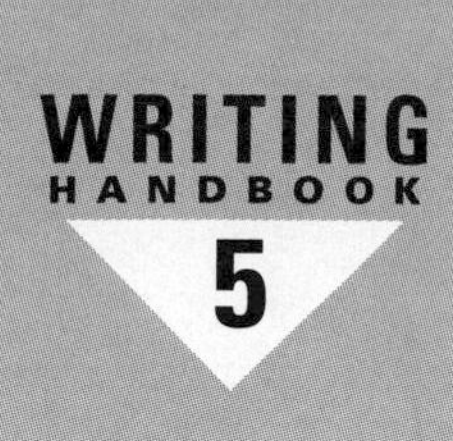

Audience

Objectives

- To recognize the importance of identifying the audience for a piece of writing
- To explore how knowledge of the audience affects the way a writer presents material

Related Mini-Lessons

For information on topics related to identifying an audience for writing, see the following mini-lessons.

- **General Purpose and Personal Goals, pp. 232–233**
- **Sharing and Publishing, p. 293**
- **Meaning and Word Choice, pp. 314–315**

Motivate

Write the following movie ratings system on the board:

G	General admission
PG	Parental guidance suggested
PG-13	Parental guidance for those under 13
R	Parent or guardian must accompany those under 17
NC-17	No one under 17 admitted

Make sure students understand that a movie's rating indicates its appropriateness for the audience designated. Point out that just as filmmakers have to consider their audience as they work, writers must think about who will be reading their writing.

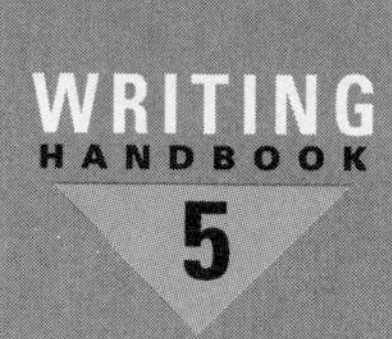

Who Is My Audience?

Audience

If a tree falls when there's no one around to hear it, does it make any sound? People have argued about that question for centuries and still don't know the answer. One thing we *do* know, though, is that wherever people are, there's almost always someone else around to hear them. We live, work, play, and talk with other people. When we write, we write to other people.

IDENTIFYING YOUR AUDIENCE

WRITER TO WRITER

My favorite audience is teenagers. Because I am one, I can relate to them.

Mousumi Behari, student, Aurora, Colorado

Sometimes your audience is chosen for you. For example, the audience for the writing you do at school is usually your teacher and classmates. At other times, however, you decide who your readers will be. If you want to write a short story about a baby sitter, you might choose to write for parents and other adults or for people your age. Even if you choose not to share your writing with anyone else, you still have an audience—yourself.

Knowing who will read your writing can help you decide on your purpose and personal goals. It can also help you choose what kinds of details, language, sentences, and tone to use. As you think about your readers, ask yourself the following questions:

- How much do they already know about my topic?
- What will they be most interested in?
- What will they agree with? disagree with?
- What kind of language can I use to help them understand what I am saying?

Writing TIP

You can make even the most difficult ideas understandable in your writing. Just be sure to use language and examples that are familiar to your readers.

Literature Connection

Play to Read Mark Twain originally wrote his story "The Million-Pound Bank Note" as fiction. Walter A. Hackett then adapted it as a radio play. Have students read the radio play on page 209 of *Literature and Language,* Grade 8. Challenge them to find aspects—such as the frequent narrative speeches and the absence of stage directions — that are specifically tailored to a radio audience.

One student wrote a report on humpback whales for her science class. When her younger brother started asking questions about it, she decided to rewrite the report for children her brother's age. Notice how each piece of writing is appropriate for its audience.

Middle-School Audience

The most unusual thing about a humpback whale is the way it behaves. One of its playful behaviors is called tail slapping. A humpback stands on its head and slaps the water with its flukes. The most spectacular humpback behavior is called breaching. A whale jumps out of the water, arches over, and lands on its side or back.

Student
MODEL

Third-Grade Audience

Like you and your friends, a humpback whale loves to play. One of its favorite games is tail slapping. The whale stands on its head and slaps the water with the side of its tail. The water splashes and crashes. Breaching is the most exciting game to watch. The whale shoots out of the water and straight up into the air. Then it turns over and lands on its side or back with a huge splash.

Practice Your Skills

Rewrite the following paragraph, adjusting tone, sentence length, and word choice so that it appeals to third graders.

About 63 million years ago, coinciding very closely with the disappearance of the dinosaurs, the world went through a great change of climate. It got colder. This may very well have killed the dinosaurs. While it is true that a big body keeps its heat for a long time, it is also true that it takes a very long time to regain it once it is lost. . . . A series of bitterly cold nights could have drained a big dinosaur of its heat beyond all recovery. With its body badly chilled, it might not be able to summon sufficient energy to move its huge bulk and browse. So a steady cooling of the climate . . . may well have led to the death of the large herbivores.

David Attenborough, *The Living Planet*

Teaching Strategies

for STUDENT MODELS

USING THE MODEL Have students compare the vocabulary, sentence length, and tone of the two student models. Ask volunteers to find words in the first model that do not appear in the second *(unusual, behaviors, flukes, spectacular, arches)*. Then ask them to compare the sentence length in the two models. (Sentences are shorter in the second model.) Finally, discuss with students the difference in tone of the two pieces. Encourage them to notice the friendlier, more casual tone of the second piece.

for STUDENT MODELS

INDIVIDUALIZING INSTRUCTION: AUDITORY LEARNERS Because these learners have good auditory discrimination, they may be more successful in adjusting their writing to different audiences if they are given an opportunity to hear the two student models read aloud and to discuss how the language, sentence structure, and tone change for the third-grade audience.

Additional Resource

Writing Resource Book, pp. 59–60

Answers to Practice Your Skills

Revisions will vary. A sample revision is shown below.

Try to imagine what the earth was like a long time ago—sixty-three million years ago. Human beings didn't exist back then. Dinosaurs did, but they were slowly disappearing. Maybe they were dying because the earth had gotten colder. Imagine that you were a big dinosaur living on the cold earth. It would take you a long time to warm up your huge body. If the weather stayed cold night after night, you might not be able to warm up at all. Your body would get weaker, and you would not be strong enough to move around and look for food. After a while, you would get weaker and weaker and soon you would die. Maybe this is why the dinosaurs disappeared so many years ago.

SPICE BOX

Students can have fun changing famous quotations to suit various audiences. Write well-known quotes on slips of paper and put them in a bowl. Have students write (on separate slips of paper) descriptions of audiences and put those in another bowl. Each student can pick a quotation and an audience and then, if necessary, rewrite the quote so that it is appropriate for the audience.

Drafting to Learn

Objectives

- To recognize different approaches to drafting
- To analyze one's own drafting processes

Related Mini-Lessons

For information on topics related to drafting, see the following mini-lessons.

- **General Purpose and Personal Goals, pp. 232–233**
- **Developing a Personal Voice, pp. 316–317**

Teaching Strategies

for ADVENTURESOME DRAFTING

COLLABORATIVE OPPORTUNITY

Have the class try some group adventuresome drafting by orally creating a round-robin story. Begin the story with an opening sentence, such as "On a hill above a small town stood a dark mansion, empty for decades." One by one, have each student in class contribute a sentence to the story. Encourage students to let their ideas flow freely as they offer their sentences.

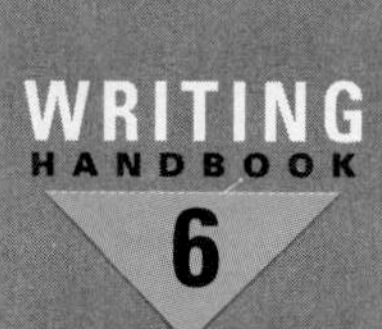

How Do I Draft My Writing?

Drafting to Learn

WRITER TO WRITER

I learn more about myself by putting my innermost feelings on paper.

Regina Bly, student, Atco, New Jersey

Like Regina, many writers have learned that drafting, or trying out their ideas on paper, can help them discover what they think and feel.

HOW TO APPROACH DRAFTING

The most important thing to remember about drafting is that there is no right way to do it. Sometimes you might want to be adventuresome and just dive right into your writing. At other times, you might want to proceed more carefully, planning what you want to say beforehand. Feel free to try different methods and use the one that works best for you and your writing project.

Adventuresome Drafting

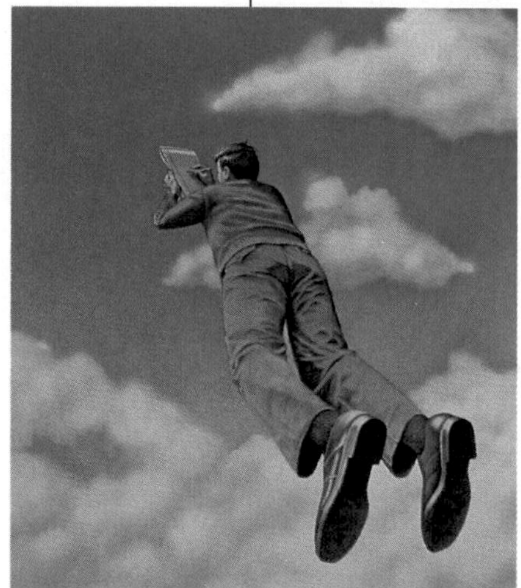

When you draft in an adventuresome way, you just begin writing. You can start with the beginning, the middle, or the end—any part you have ideas about. You don't even need to know what your writing will eventually be about. Just write freely, letting one idea spark the next and following wherever your ideas lead. Adventuresome drafting works particularly well for writing that does not require much research or planning. For example, this kind of drafting can help you discover your opinions for a movie review, the ending of a short story, or the lyrics for a song.

Careful Drafting

Like some writers, you may prefer a more careful approach. Think through a writing plan or make an outline before you begin drafting. Then follow your plan as you write, developing your ideas and filling in details as you go. Because you will already have thought through your ideas, you will be able to concentrate on **bridge building**—exploring and showing the connections between ideas. Careful drafting is a good way to develop reports, business letters, and other kinds of formal writing.

TIP

If you're not sure which kind of drafting to use, try mixing both approaches. Begin with a general plan, but explore new ideas and directions as they occur to you.

WHEN TO STOP DRAFTING

Since drafting is the process of trying out ideas on paper, keep writing until you are satisfied with your ideas. You may need to make many drafts—changing direction or even starting over—before you're ready to revise and polish your writing.

Once you have produced a draft you feel good about, take a break and reread what you have written. Note your own and your peer readers' reactions and write in the margins any specific ideas you have for improving your draft. Then set the draft aside for a few hours or a day. This break will help you see your writing more objectively and revise it more effectively.

Practice Your Skills

Choose from your portfolio a piece of writing that you especially like, and think about the writing process you went through. Then write a letter to yourself or your teacher, answering questions such as the following. Attach the letter to your writing and return it to your portfolio.

- Did I use an adventuresome or a careful approach in drafting this writing?
- What discoveries did I make during drafting?
- How many drafts did I write before I was satisfied that my ideas were clear and complete?
- What would I do differently in drafting a similar piece of writing?

GENERAL NOTE

INDIVIDUALIZING INSTRUCTION: LD STUDENTS Some LD students may have difficulty with the physical act of writing. Encourage these students to speak into a cassette recorder to create their drafts.

for WHEN TO STOP DRAFTING

PEER RESPONSE Emphasize that peer response to a draft should focus on overall content and meaning, not on spelling, grammar, or mechanics. Peer readers should assume that writers intend to correct technical mistakes during the proofreading process.

for PRACTICE YOUR SKILLS

MANAGING THE PAPER LOAD Inform students that the Practice Your Skills assignment will not be graded. Explain that the purpose of the activity is to help them gain insight into their personal writing process. Rather than reading students' letters, you might hold a short class discussion focusing on what they discovered by analyzing their writing process.

Additional Resource

Writing Resource Book, p. 61

Answers to Practice Your Skills

Each student's letter will be unique. Students' responses to these questions or to any they make up, however, should show thoughtful consideration of their writing processes.

PROFESSIONAL NOTEBOOK

Share this quotation about drafting by June Gould, the author of *The Writer in All of Us:*

"I plan my writing journeys the way I plan a trip. I decide . . . where my major stops will be, but I leave myself the freedom to discover alternate routes, interesting byways, and further paths within the . . . parameters of my story."

Forms of Writing

Objectives

- To recognize various forms of writing
- To identify suitable forms of writing for different topics

Related Mini-Lessons

For information on topics related to forms of writing, see the following mini-lesson.

- **General Purpose and Personal Goals, pp. 232–233**

Teaching Strategies

for FORMS OF WRITING

INDIVIDUALIZING INSTRUCTION: ESL STUDENTS Some forms of writing that are common in American culture may be unfamiliar to some ESL students. As much as possible, provide examples of the forms of writing listed in the table.

Additional Resource

Writing Resource Book, p. 62

Answers to Practice Your Skills

Answers may vary. Possible answers are shown below.

- instructions, poster, report
- autobiography, friendly letter, journal entry, short story
- journal entry, poem, autobiography, friendly letter
- letter to the editor, speech

WRITING HANDBOOK 7

What Writing Forms Can I Choose?

Forms of Writing

One very creative man asked his girlfriend to marry him by painting his proposal on a large billboard near her office. She said yes! She might have married him anyway, but the unusual form of his proposal certainly helped get his message across.

Unlike this marriage proposal, most writing takes a form more typically suited to its topic and audience. For example, you probably wouldn't write instructions on how to pop popcorn in the form of a poem. This doesn't mean, however, that you shouldn't experiment with surprising and creative forms. That's part of what makes writing fun.

Forms of Writing

A **form** of writing is a shape or structure that the writing takes. Which of the forms listed below have you used? The next time you do a piece of writing, try using a different form.

Forms of Writing

announcement	journal entry	poem
autobiography	letter to the editor	postcard
book review	limerick	poster
family history	movie review	report
friendly letter	news report	short story
instructions	play	speech

Practice Your Skills

Suggest a suitable form for writing about each of these topics.

- what to do during an earthquake
- an important event in your life
- your thoughts and feelings about your family
- the need to expand school-bus service

TEACHER'S LOUNGE

In "Here Come the Book Reports!" teacher Steven Wills describes his students' approaches to a familiar form of writing:

"At first glance, the long-awaited pile of papers looks inviting enough. Marlene has used her purple, lilac-scented pen for page one, and the brown, cinnamon ink for page two. I haven't checked the olfactory invitation to page three yet. I can overlook the hearts Donna uses to dot her *i*'s, knowing hers was in the right place. Steven's essay scares me, however. His pen has been possessed by a demon that has crawled upon his paper and died in a convulsive fit."

How Can I Structure My Writing?

Types of Organization

Do you ever feel lost as you make your way through a piece of writing? Like Snoopy, do you long for a landmark or a compass to help you find your way?

If a piece of writing presents ideas in an organized way, readers won't have to worry about where they are and where they are going. They can relax and follow the various guideposts the writer provides.

How should you organize your writing so it is easy for your readers to follow? There is no single right way. The answer depends on the type of writing you are doing. There also is no single right time in the writing process to think about organization. Some writers like to work out a structure before they write the first word. Others prefer to just start writing. These writers organize their material as they work on their revision. Use the method and type of organization that work for you and your particular piece of writing. This handbook describes several types of organization you can try.

WRITER TO WRITER

There are no right or wrong answers in writing.

Nina Ramundo, student, Hamilton, Ohio

MAIN IDEA AND SUPPORTING DETAILS

Many types of writing can be organized into main ideas and details that support those ideas. For example, in the paragraph on the next page, notice that in the first sentence Anne Frank states her main idea—she feels alone even though she is surrounded by family and many friends. She then provides details and examples that support her feeling of isolation.

PEANUTS reprinted by permission of UFS, Inc.

Types of Organization

Objectives

- To recognize and use different types of organization for writing
- To identify an appropriate type of organization for a group of details
- To use groups of details to write well-organized paragraphs

For information on topics related to types of organization, see the following mini-lessons.

- **Graphic Devices for Writing, pp. 227–231**
- **Developing Paragraphs, pp. 248–251**
- **Paragraphs in Longer Writing, pp. 252–254**
- **Coherence, pp. 273–277**

Motivate

Write these directions on the chalkboard:

To get to the Community Center, walk three blocks east from the school. Make a left before the stop sign. Be sure you've counted the blocks from the north corner of the school property. After you've made the left, you'll notice a golf course on your right. Walk past the golf course. The center is three storefronts past the service station. You'll come to the service station just after the golf course.

Ask students what is wrong with the directions. Point out that just as directions are confusing when they have not been ordered correctly, so writing is confusing when it has not been organized logically.

Teaching Strategies

GENERAL NOTES

INDIVIDUALIZING INSTRUCTION: VISUAL LEARNERS Some students learn best when they are given visual cues to accompany an explanation. When teaching organizational structures, create overhead transparencies of the Student Model and Literary Models in the text. Use a grease pencil to mark the transitions and other organizational devices in the paragraph.

for LITERARY MODEL

USING THE MODEL To make sure students understand organization by main idea and supporting details, ask volunteers to identify the details that support Anne Frank's main idea—she feels alone, even though she is surrounded by other people. (She has parents, a sister, thirty friends, aunts, uncles, and a good home; but her friends just joke with her and do not draw close.)

for STUDENT MODEL

ASSESSMENT: SPOT CHECK After discussing the organization of the model paragraph, invite students to work in pairs to create a list of five to ten items ordered by a certain quality or characteristic. For example, students can order eight mammals by size, or they can order the same eight mammals by the speed at which they move. Student pairs can read their lists aloud, and the rest of the class can try to guess the quality used to order the list.

Let me put it more clearly, since no one will believe that a girl of thirteen feels herself quite alone in the world, nor is it so. I have darling parents and a sister of sixteen. I know about thirty people whom one might call friends . . . . I have relations, aunts and uncles, who are darlings too, a good home, no—I don't seem to lack anything. But it's the same with all my friends, just fun and joking, nothing more. . . . We don't seem to be able to get any closer, that is the root of the trouble.

Anne Frank, *Anne Frank: The Diary of a Young Girl*

ORDER OF IMPORTANCE OR DEGREE

You might want to organize your ideas by order of importance or degree. You can use any quality that suits your subject, such as most to least useful or older to younger, for example. In the following introduction to a report about health, the writer starts with the most familiar disease and ends with the least familiar.

It's a battleground out there, and the worst part is that you can't even see the enemy. Every time you breathe or eat, thousands of invisible organisms—bacteria, viruses, and fungi—threaten your health. You have all probably lost the battle to the viruses that cause the common cold, mumps, or chicken pox. You may even know someone who had polio or scarlet fever. Hopefully, however, you'll never experience diseases like meningitis, elephantiasis, or breakbone fever.

CHRONOLOGICAL ORDER

In your writing, you often tell about events that happened over a period of time. Biographies, histories, and stories are usually told in chronological order—the order in which events took place. You can also use chronological order to explain a process, give

Literature Connection

Read this main idea/details paragraph: "How to Die of Embarrassment" by Delia Ephron.

"Pick up a piece of pizza and take a bite. Watch the mozzarella cheese stretch. Bite down harder. It is still stretching. Move the slice farther away from mouth. The strands are growing thinner and longer. You can see three . . . extending out of your mouth. They are hanging between the slice and your mouth like jump ropes. You do not know what to do. With the hand that is not holding the pizza, grab cheese with fingers, break off, and stuff ends in mouth. Chew, swallow, do not look at date, and begin again."

directions, or support an argument. Using transitional words and exact dates or other time references can help make the order of events clear.

At six-thirty the sky was still dark, the rain falling steadily. **An hour later:** rain. **Two hours later:** no change. I got up, washed, ate some fruit and cheese. I draped across the bunk and read, occasionally looking into the gray obscuring rain, listening to thunder (puts the sugar in the cane), watching Spanish moss (a relative of the pineapple) hang still in the trees like shredded, dingy bedsheets. **At ten-thirty** the rain dropped straight down as if from a faucet; I was able to leave the front windows half open. I didn't know then, but in April in coastal Louisiana you don't wait for the rain to stop unless you have all day and night. Which I did.

William Least Heat Moon, *Blue Highways*

Writing TIP

Transitional words that indicate chronological order include *first, immediately, last, later, meanwhile, next, soon,* and *then.*

CAUSE-AND-EFFECT ORDER

In various types of writing, you explain why something happened. For example, in a science paper, you might tell why the sky is blue. In a research report, you could show why the Soviet Union broke apart. In a story, you might want to suggest why a character acted in a certain way. An effective way to organize this type of writing is by using cause-and-effect order. In the following paragraph about football, notice how the writer uses the transitional words *because* and *so* to point out the cause and its effect.

Why are there fewer barefoot punters than place kickers? [The answer is] **because** punts are executed on the outside rather than the inside of the foot. If you kick a punt on the same spot as a place kick, the ball won't spiral properly. The outside of the foot is a little more susceptible to pain and injury than the inside of the foot, **so** there are fewer barefoot punters.

Cause

Effect

David Feldman, *Why Do Dogs Have Wet Noses? and Other Imponderables of Everyday Life*

for CAUSE-AND-EFFECT ORDER

CRITICAL THINKING: ANALYZING

To be sure students understand cause-and-effect organization, have volunteers complete these sentences after thinking of an effect for each cause.

1. Because the team's best pitcher was badly injured, ______________.
2. Because the earthquake struck at daybreak, ______________.
3. Because the electricity went out during the storm, ______________.
4. Because the students had studied hard for the test, ______________.

for FIRST PROFESSIONAL MODEL

SPEAKING AND LISTENING To impress on students how spatial order can help make a description clear, have them close their eyes and try to visualize the office as you read the model aloud. Then ask them to open their eyes, recall the room as they visualized it, and compare their descriptions.

for SECOND PROFESSIONAL MODEL

USING THE MODEL Point out that the writer uses a metaphor—comparing the *Titanic* to a layer cake—as a vehicle for classifying people on the ship. Note that the writer describes the cake from bottom to top. Ask a volunteer to draw a three-layer cake on the board and fill in the group or groups of people that make up each layer and the icing.

SPATIAL ORDER

To help your readers understand what something looks like, you might present the details in the way you see them. This is called **spatial order.** You can organize the details from near to far, top to bottom, or left to right, for example.

The writer of the following paragraph uses spatial order to describe the inside of a government office. Notice how she uses transitional words to make the description clear for readers.

Inside, the place was gray. There were rows of long benches like church pews facing each other across a middle aisle that led to a central desk. **Beyond** the benches and the desk, four hallways led off to a maze of partitioned offices. **In opposite corners,** huge fans hung from the ceiling, humming from side to side, blowing the heavy air for a breeze.

Paulette Childress White, "Getting the Facts of Life"

CLASSIFICATION

When you are writing about a number of ideas, consider classifying them into groups or categories. For example, in the following passage about the *Titanic,* a passenger ship that sank in 1912, the writer classifies people on the ship by social status.

In fact, the *Titanic* was a kind of floating layer cake, composed of a cross-section of the society of the day. **The bottom layer** was made up of the most lowly manual laborers toiling away in the heat and grime of the boiler rooms and engine rooms located just above the keel. **The next layer** consisted of steerage or third-class passengers—a polyglot mixture hoping to make a fresh start in the New World. **After that** came the middle classes—teachers, merchants, professionals of moderate means—in second class. **Then finally,** the icing on the cake: the rich and the titled.

Robert D. Ballard, *The Discovery of the* Titanic

SPICE BOX

To illustrate how spatial order can be used in interesting and unusual ways, show students the opening of one of these classic movies: *Vertigo,* or *North by Northwest* or *Citizen Kane.* Have them take notes on what they see from the camera's perspective. Tell them to watch for unusual angles or details. Then ask how these details of description are ordered—from near to far, top to bottom, or left to right, for example.

COMPARISON-AND-CONTRAST ORDER

An important part of classifying subjects is noting how they are the same and how they are different. You can compare and contrast two subjects by discussing the characteristics of one subject first and then those of the other subject. You can also discuss the characteristics one by one, first in one subject and then in the other. The following comparison is organized by characteristic.

Professional MODEL

Comparison

Contrast

> The washer-dryer [designed for a space station] uses 1.1 gallons of water to clean each pound of clothes—**compared with** a typical seven gallons per pound for Earth's current models—and uses 20 percent less energy than other machines. It holds seven pounds of clothes—about half the amount of a conventional machine—though it could be sized for larger loads. **Rather than** agitating clothing for cleaning, it extracts soil with a detergent solution.
>
> **Mariette DiChristina, "Appliances from Space"**

Practice Your Skills

Write the type of organization you would use to make each group of ideas into a paragraph. Then write a paragraph.

1. • ping-pong table in center of basement
   • gas furnace in far left corner
   • inside basement door—washer and dryer on left, rug and weights on right
   • stacks of boxes in far right corner and along back wall
2. • senses of humans: sight is most highly developed sense; senses of hearing and smell not as keen as in dogs
   • senses of dogs: smell is most highly developed sense; better sense of hearing than people; poorer sight than people
3. • Lee became angry with the coach.
   • Lee was late for soccer practice.
   • The coach made him sit out the next game.
   • Lee quit the soccer team.

for PROFESSIONAL MODEL

INDIVIDUALIZING INSTRUCTION: VISUAL LEARNERS To help visual learners "see" the organization of the model, create a comparison-and-contrast chart on the board and allow students to fill in the details from the paragraph. (See page 230 for an example of a comparison-and-contrast chart.) Use the subject headings *Space Station Washer-Dryer* and *Conventional Machine.* For characteristics, use these headings: *Amount of Water Used, Amount of Energy Used, Amount of Clothing Held,* and *Method of Operation.*

for PRACTICE YOUR SKILLS

INDIVIDUALIZING INSTRUCTION: VISUAL LEARNERS For the first group of ideas in Practice Your Skills, suggest that students use the details to sketch a layout of the basement before they begin writing. They then can use the layout to guide their writing.

Additional Resources

Writing Resource Book, pp. 63–67
Thinking Skills Transparency Pack
Thinking Skills Worksheets

Answers to Practice Your Skills

Answers may vary. Suggested answers are shown below, but other types of organization are acceptable if students can justify their use in the given situation.

1. Spatial order
2. Comparison-and-contrast order
3. Cause-and-effect order

Students' paragraphs will vary. Good paragraphs, however, will reflect an understanding of how to use the type of organization chosen. A sample paragraph for Exercise 1 is shown.

1. Spatial order

As he entered the basement, he saw a washer and dryer to the left of the door. Just to the right were a rug and a pile of weights. In the center of the basement was a Ping-Pong table. To his right, in the far corner, he saw stacks of boxes that extended along the back wall. In the far left corner, the gas furnace hummed.

Effective Paragraphs

Objectives

- To identify paragraphs that display unity and coherence
- To rewrite a paragraph to improve its unity or coherence
- To identify the purpose of a paragraph

Related Mini-Lessons

For information on topics related to effective paragraphs, see the following mini-lessons.

- **Types of Organization, pp. 239–243**
- **Developing Paragraphs, pp. 248–251**
- **Paragraphs in Longer Writing, pp. 252–254**
- **Achieving Unity, pp. 268–271**
- **Coherence, pp. 273–277**

Teaching Strategies

for WHAT IS A GOOD PARAGRAPH?

KEY TO UNDERSTANDING Some students may not immediately grasp the distinction between unity and coherence. Write these two definitions on the board: *Sentences stick to the main idea* and *Sentences are presented in a logical order.* Point out that the first definition tells about unity and the second tells about coherence.

for LITERARY MODEL

USING THE MODEL Ask a volunteer to read the paragraph aloud and identify the main idea. (The bunk room at camp looked like a jail.) Have other volunteers identify how the remaining sentences support the main idea. (They detail the bare and bleak appearance of the room.) Finally, emphasize that the sentences are logically ordered. They describe details as a person who is first seeing the room might notice them.

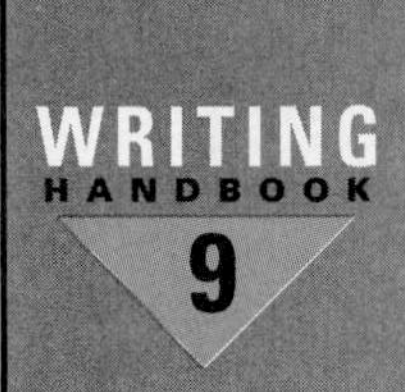

What Is a Good Paragraph?

Effective Paragraphs

You are listening to some musicians as they tune up and practice their riffs and scales. It's a strange jumble of noise—guitar, keyboard, bass, and percussion, each doing something different. Then a conductor brings the group together, and music begins. The separate players are now a group with a common goal.

Like the group of musicians, a **paragraph** is made up of individual parts that work together toward a common goal. Each sentence in a paragraph helps to develop an idea or accomplish a purpose. Paragraphs can be any size and can be used in many different ways. Usually, they are part of a longer piece of writing, such as a lab report or a story. Some writing, however, such as an essay-test response, may be only one paragraph long.

WHAT IS A GOOD PARAGRAPH?

No matter what their size and purpose, all good paragraphs have two things in common—unity and coherence. For a paragraph to have **unity,** each of its sentences must relate to the main idea of the paragraph. For a paragraph to have **coherence,** the sentences must be presented in an order that makes sense. (For more information on unity and coherence, see Handbooks 14 and 15, pages 268–277.)

Is the following passage a good paragraph?

I was assigned to Bunk 7, the Senior Girls. The inside of our bunk was like a long bedroom, with ten cots, five on each side, lined up against the walls. There were windows, but they had no glass, only screens and canvas shades that rolled down on the outside. The floors were raw planks that looked like they'd give you splinters regularly, and the walls were unfinished pine with exposed beams between the windows. A jail, I thought, must look a lot like this.

Ellen Conford, *Hail, Hail Camp Timberwood*

This is a good paragraph because all the sentences help describe the bunk room at a summer camp. They are also logically connected to one another—the paragraph moves from a general description of the room to the specific details.

Read the next paragraphs. Does each have unity and coherence?

> I gripped the bat and clenched my teeth. Now it was up to me. Sweat dripped down my face as I stared at my enemy—the pitcher on the mound. He just transferred to our school. I hadn't had a hit in five games and I had already struck out twice in this game. What had happened to my magic touch?

Are any sentences unrelated to the main idea?

The purpose of the paragraph above is to describe the batter's nervousness. The sentence about the pitcher transferring to the school does not help develop that idea. Therefore, the paragraph is not unified. Now read another paragraph.

> The land began to shudder and then just split open. The sidewalk was twisted like a rubber band and our thirty-foot-tall pine tree was tossed across the street the way someone would toss a matchstick. Suddenly, without warning, the earthquake struck. Miraculously, nobody was hurt. We sure were scared, though. We were having a picnic in the back yard on a beautiful summer afternoon.

Are any events out of order?

The paragraph is unified because all the sentences describe the experience of an earthquake. However, the events are not presented in an order that makes sense. Therefore, the paragraph is not coherent. The revised paragraph follows.

Notice how repositioning two sentences improves coherence.

> We were having a picnic in the back yard on a beautiful summer afternoon. Suddenly, without warning, the earthquake struck. The land began to shudder and then just split open. The sidewalk was twisted like a rubber band and our thirty-foot-tall pine tree was tossed across the street the way someone would toss a matchstick. Miraculously, nobody was hurt. We sure were scared, though.

GENERAL NOTE

INDIVIDUALIZING INSTRUCTION: BASIC STUDENTS If some students don't grasp the problems in the first two sample paragraphs on the pupil page, or if they don't see why the Student Model paragraph is an improvement, have them reread those paragraphs with a partner. Suggest that students turn each paragraph into a numbered list of sentences. In the first sample paragraph, point out the unrelated sentence by asking students to provide a one-word label for the subject of each sentence; in the second, have students number the sentences in chronological order.

for THE FIRST MODEL

STUMBLING BLOCK Many students may see nothing wrong with the first model because they are not used to judging writing critically, sentence by sentence. Because the sentence about the pitcher relates to the previous sentence, it may not strike them as being out of place in the paragraph. Ask students whether that sentence relates to the one that follows it, however. (It does not.) Read the paragraph aloud without that sentence to help students see the improvement.

for STUDENT MODEL

CRITICAL THINKING: SEQUENCING AND CONTRASTING Have a volunteer read aloud the revised Student Model. Then ask students to explain how the sentences in the paragraph are organized (by the order in which they happened in time). Ask why the previous paragraph—which presented the same information—was so confusing. (The events were not described in the order in which they happened.)

for PURPOSES OF PARAGRAPHS

KEY TO UNDERSTANDING Explain to students that in order to be effective, paragraphs must not only be unified and coherent; they must also achieve their purpose. For example, a paragraph that begins a composition might be unified and coherent without effectively introducing the main idea of the composition. You also might point out that a given paragraph may have more than one purpose (for example, a paragraph might describe or explain through comparison and contrast). One purpose, however, will be dominant.

for PURPOSES OF PARAGRAPHS

INDIVIDUALIZING INSTRUCTION: ADVANCED STUDENTS Ask a group of students to search through their literature anthologies to find examples of paragraphs that serve the purposes listed in the chart. Within the group, students can compare selections and come to agreement about the main purpose of each. Have the group share their examples orally with the rest of the class.

for PROFESSIONAL MODEL

USING THE MODEL After students read Macaulay's paragraph, ask them to explain in their own words how submersibles work. Then have them comment about how effective the paragraph is in explaining the idea.

for LITERARY MODEL

CRITICAL THINKING: SUMMARIZING After students read the Literary Model, have them state in one sentence how the author distinguishes the relationship with parents from a typical peer relationship. (Sample: You can choose your friends but not your parents.)

USES OF PARAGRAPHS

Paragraphs can serve many purposes. Some common purposes are listed below.

Purposes of Paragraphs

Introduce a piece of writing	Define
Tell a story	Show cause and effect
Describe	Connect two ideas
Compare and contrast	Persuade
Explain	Conclude a piece of writing

The main purpose of the following paragraph is to explain how submersibles—boats that can operate underwater—work.

Submersibles are designed for use at great depths. They need to be able to sink, to rise, and also to float underwater. They do this by altering their weight with a system of ballast tanks which can hold either air or water. If a craft's ballast tanks are flooded with water, the craft's weight increases. If the water is then expelled by compressed air, the weight decreases. By adjusting the amount of water in the tanks, the craft's weight and buoyancy can be precisely regulated.

David Macaulay, *The Way Things Work*

The following paragraph compares two kinds of relationships—relationships with parents and friendships with peers.

Sam stopped, bent down to tie his sneaker, and looked up at his oldest friend. He couldn't remember when he didn't know Benjy. It was a good thing, Sam was thinking, to be able to go back that far with somebody who wasn't a parent. You had no choice with parents, and they had no choice with you. You're stuck with each other. But if he and Benjy didn't choose, and didn't keep choosing, to like each other, there'd be no reason for them to keep going home from school together and hanging out with each other on the weekends.

Nat Hentoff, *This School Is Driving Me Crazy*

Practice Your Skills

A. Indicate whether each of the following paragraphs displays unity and coherence. If necessary, rewrite the paragraph to correct the problem.

1. First Officer Thims took a deep breath and punched in the coordinates for the next destination on the ship's computer. This was his third, uneventful year as navigator for the *Fantasy,* an interstellar cruise ship. Each year the ship carried vacationers to all the popular galactic ports of call—the red sand beaches of Io, the underground pyramids of Mars, and the golf courses on Pluto. He had once gotten a hole in one on the thirteenth hole because the force of gravity was only a fraction of Earth's.

2. As a young man, Ernest Hemingway worked in Europe as a newspaper correspondent. He also wrote short stories. Unfortunately, the suitcase was stolen from a train platform. All but two of the many stories Hemingway had started were lost. One year he and his wife were getting ready to vacation in Switzerland. His wife carefully packed in a suitcase most of the stories he was working on. Hemingway wanted to work on the stories while he and his wife were away. Hemingway was crushed by the loss, but he kept writing.

B. Identify the purpose or purposes of each of the following paragraphs.

1. The members of the photography club need a darkroom, and we are asking for your support. Students need to learn more than reading, writing, and arithmetic at school. For example, student photographers can learn real-world skills if we can work in a darkroom. The photography club is willing to hold fund-raising events to raise the money needed for basic equipment and supplies. If the school will give us a room, we'll take care of the rest.

2. Dodging boulders the size of small cars, she steered the kayak down the river. The water roared, and the spray sparkled in the late afternoon sun as the kayak shot through the rapids. She felt as if she could touch the red canyon walls rising steeply on either side of her. The thin slice of dark blue sky was so far above her head that it made her dizzy to look at it.

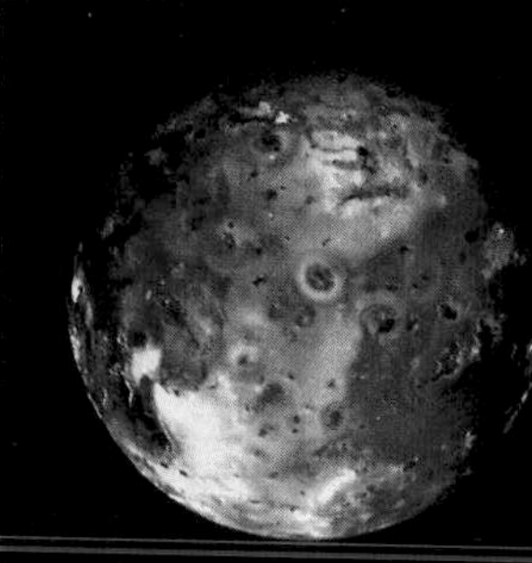

This computer-enhanced image shows Io, one of Jupiter's moons.

for PRACTICE YOUR SKILLS

INDIVIDUALIZING INSTRUCTION: SOCIAL LEARNERS These learners are good at group problem solving. Form the class into small groups and have students collaborate to identify the purpose(s) of the paragraphs in Exercise B.

Additional Resource

Writing Resource Book, pp. 70–71

Answers to Practice Your Skills

A.

1. The paragraph is coherent but not unified. Students should rewrite the paragraph, deleting the last sentence.
2. The paragraph is unified but not coherent. A possible revision is shown below.

As a young man, Ernest Hemingway worked in Europe as a newspaper correspondent. He also wrote short stories. One year he and his wife were getting ready to vacation in Switzerland. His wife carefully packed in a suitcase most of the stories he was working on. Hemingway wanted to work on the stories while he and his wife were away. Unfortunately, the suitcase was stolen from a train platform. All but two of the many stories Hemingway had started were lost. Hemingway was crushed by the loss, but he kept writing.

B.

1. The purpose of the paragraph is to make an argument and to persuade.
2. The paragraph describes a setting and tells a story.

for **FURTHER READING**

You might use Practice Your Skills, exercise A, as an opportunity to introduce your students to the writer Ernest Hemingway. His short novel *The Old Man and the Sea* or his story "A Day's Wait" may interest them.

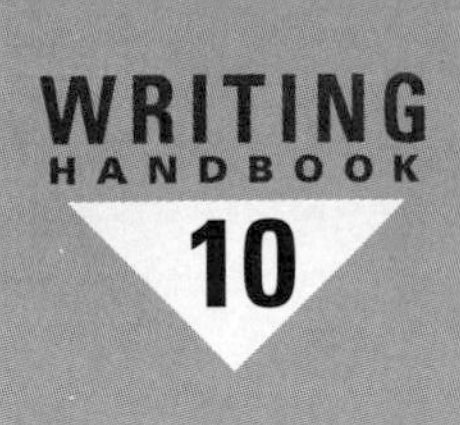

Developing Paragraphs

Objectives

- To write effective topic sentences
- To use various types of supporting details to develop paragraphs
- To present supporting details in a logical flow

Related Mini-Lessons

For information on topics related to developing paragraphs, see the following mini-lessons.

- **Effective Paragraphs, pp. 244–247**
- **Paragraphs in Longer Writing, pp. 252–254**
- **Methods of Elaboration, pp. 255–261**
- **Achieving Unity, pp. 268–271**
- **Coherence, pp. 273–277**

Teaching Strategies

for WRITING A TOPIC SENTENCE

KEY TO UNDERSTANDING Focus attention on the sample topic sentences. Ask students how sentences 2 and 3 differ from sentences 1 and 4. (Sentences 2 and 3 appeal to the imagination; they not only identify the topic but encourage the audience to envision it.) Ask volunteers to suggest ways to improve sentences 1 and 4, possibly by using a method described at the top of page 249. (Samples: With the right equipment and know-how, you can fix a flat bicycle tire in ten minutes. How would you like to sail across a rippling bay on a surfboard?)

WRITING HANDBOOK 10

How Do I Create a Paragraph?

Developing Paragraphs

Mosaics, such as this one below by Lupus, are made up of hundreds of pieces put together in precise patterns. To create a mosaic, the artist may first develop an overall design and then develop the details with the individual pieces.

Like a mosaic, a piece of writing is made up of smaller parts, or paragraphs. The process that writers go through in creating a piece of writing may be similar to the way an artist works. Often writers first think about the overall purpose of their writing and then work on individual paragraphs. Not all writers work this way, however. Some writers like to begin writing just to get their ideas on paper. Then they organize their material into paragraphs as they revise.

Untitled classical head (1991), Lupus.

WRITING A TOPIC SENTENCE

A **topic sentence** makes the main idea of a paragraph clear and tells readers what to expect from the paragraph. In addition, a good topic sentence can serve as a lead to catch the readers' attention and make them want to keep reading. However, as you will see later, not all paragraphs have a topic sentence.

Which of the following topic sentences would make you want to read the rest of a paragraph?

1. I am going to tell you how to fix a flat bicycle tire.
2. Imagine a computer that responds to the sound of your voice or reads even the most illegible handwriting.
3. The giant octopus has been called the "devilfish"—with good reason.
4. This paragraph is about windsurfing.

The second and third sentences probably caught your interest. What would you do to improve the first and fourth sentences?

Every paragraph is different, so no single kind of topic sentence—no matter how good it is—will work all the time.

Fortunately, however, there are several techniques you can choose from to write an effective topic sentence for any paragraph.

- **State an unusual fact or intriguing detail.**

  Mozart had an older sister who may have been just as talented as the famous composer, but she never got a chance to fully develop her genius—just because she was a girl.

- **Ask a question.**

  How can you make a healthy meal choice at a fast-food restaurant?

- **Give a command.**

  Try to remember what it was like to be four years old.

DEVELOPING YOUR MAIN IDEA

To write an effective paragraph, you need more than just a main idea. You need to support that idea with additional details, or **elaboration.**

The type of supporting details you use will depend on the main idea or purpose of your paragraph. Here are several types of details you can choose from.

Types of Supporting Details

Facts and statistics statements that can be proved

Sensory details words that appeal to the five senses

Incidents events that illustrate your main idea

Examples specific cases or instances that illustrate your main idea

Quotations the words of an expert or an authority

If the purpose of your paragraph is to describe a setting in a short story, you might use sensory details. On the other hand, if your purpose is to support an opinion, you might use facts and statistics. (For more information about elaboration, see Handbook 12, "Methods of Elaboration," pages 255–261.)

Grammar **TIP**

When using direct quotations, be sure to enclose the person's words in quotation marks.

for WRITING A TOPIC SENTENCE

HELPFUL HINT Remind students that a stated topic sentence does not have to be the first sentence of a paragraph—it can be in the middle or at the end of a paragraph. Tell them that even if the first sentence of a paragraph is not a topic sentence, it should be interesting enough to "hook" a reader. You might challenge students to use each of the three identified techniques—stating an unusual fact or intriguing detail, asking a question, and giving a command—as opening sentences for a paragraph they are currently writing.

for DEVELOPING YOUR MAIN IDEA

COLLABORATIVE OPPORTUNITY Form students into small groups and have them search through their literature anthology, magazines, and newspapers to find examples of paragraphs that contain the types of supporting details listed in the chart. Have each group share its examples with the rest of the class.

for PROFESSIONAL MODEL

USING THE MODEL Read the model aloud to students, or ask a volunteer to do so. Suggest that students try to visualize the scene as the paragraph is read. Then write the names of the five senses on the board and ask students to identify words or phrases that appeal to the different senses. They should be able to find examples for every sense except taste.

INDIVIDUALIZING INSTRUCTION: BASIC STUDENTS To help students understand the concept of an implied topic sentence, list the following details from the Professional Model on the chalkboard:

- caverns plunge and snake and twist
- impenetrable darkness
- black velvet
- silence is absolute
- like this in outer space

Discuss the connotations of each phrase and the cumulative effect of all the phrases. Then work with the group to create a topic sentence for this paragraph. (Sample: I found the underground caverns and passages of the Lechuguilla Cave to be as black and silent as outer space.)

for LITERARY MODEL

USING THE MODEL Point out that the Literary Model demonstrates how a paragraph in a narrative might be developed, by recounting events in the order they happened. Emphasize how the paragraph focuses on one set of actions—coming into the dock and mooring the boat. Ask students to repeat the sequence of events in their own words.

Notice the many sensory details the writer used in elaborating the following paragraph.

Sensory details

I sit on my air mattress and wait to stop sweating. Fifty miles of caverns plunge and snake and twist away from me in every direction, passages of impenetrable darkness, like damp black velvet pressing against my face. The disk of light from my helmet lamp sweeps across the walls of the tunnel as I turn my head. The surface is white, glittering with gypsum crystals, and crystals loosened by my body heat snow gently onto my hands. The air smells clean and wet, like fresh laundry, and the silence is absolute. It must be like this in outer space, I think, but I am a thousand feet underground.

Tim Cahill, "The Splendors of Lechuguilla Cave"

Logical Flow of Details Notice that the paragraph above does not have a topic sentence. In many paragraphs—especially in paragraphs that relate events or that tell a story—the main idea is not stated directly; it is only implied. This type of paragraph will have unity and coherence if the sentences all relate to the purpose of the paragraph and if the supporting details flow in a sensible way from one another.

Like the paragraph above, the following paragraph does not have a topic sentence. However, the paragraph is unified because all the sentences relate to its purpose—describing the setting and action in a story. The paragraph is coherent because the details are presented in a way the reader can follow—the order in which they happened.

They were silent the rest of the way back to their grandmother's dock. The two children climbed out there. Dicey took the line and tied it around one post. Then she sat on the edge of the dock and held the boat steady with her feet while her grandmother lifted the motor up and rocked it into a resting position inside the boat. The metal propeller blades dripped water into the bay like sullen raindrops.

Cynthia Voigt, *Homecoming*

SPICE BOX

To develop students' awareness of sensory details, write the five senses—sight, sound, taste, smell, and touch—on slips of paper and place them in one bag. In a second bag, place slips naming five familiar settings—a beach, a supermarket checkout counter, the school cafeteria, a snowy forest, a city park.

Call on each student to choose one slip from each bag. Tell them to write sensory details or impressions that they could have in the setting, using the sense they have chosen. Ask them to write as many as possible in one minute. Call on volunteers to read their lists aloud, setting by setting.

ORGANIZING YOUR PARAGRAPH

Whether or not a paragraph has a topic sentence, details must be presented in a sensible order. The type of order you choose will depend upon the purpose of your paragraph. For more information on ways of organizing the details in a paragraph, see Handbook 8, "Types of Organization," pages 239–243.

Practice Your Skills

A. Decide which of the following topic sentences are weak. Then revise them to make them stronger.

1. This is a story about a cat.
2. Who do you see when you look in the mirror?
3. Prairie-dog towns are so well organized that they even have their own security systems.
4. One kind of summer job you can try is starting your own business.
5. My topic is the Australian outback.

Prairie dogs on "sentry duty" watch for danger.

B. Read the following paragraph. Rearrange the sentences to present the details in a logical order.

"What is your destination?" Instead of finding the rough draft of her English composition, Anna found herself staring at a message blinking insistently on the screen. OK, thought Anna, I'll play along. It had seemed like any other afternoon, until Anna turned on her computer to do her homework. She thought for a moment and then typed in the words "the moon." As she watched the screen, something very strange happened. Maybe this was some new computer game of her brother's.

C. Write a paragraph about each of the following topics. Vary the types of topic sentences and elaboration you use. Remember that not every paragraph needs a topic sentence.

- a place you like to visit
- how something works
- an important incident in your life

Additional Resources

Writing Resource Book, pp. 72–73
Elaboration, Revision, and Proofreading Practice
Elaboration, Revision, and Proofreading Transparency Pack

Answers to Practice Your Skills

A. Topic sentences 1, 4, and 5 are weak. Revised sentences will vary, but they should be more interesting and specific than the original ones. Students might use one of the following techniques for writing topic sentences: (1) State an unusual fact or intriguing detail, (2) Ask a question, or (3) Give a command.
Sample revisions are shown below.

1. Jasper was the only one-eared cat I ever knew.
4. Try starting your own business!
5. If you look at a map of Australia, you'll see that almost all the towns hug the coast; after all, who would build a city in the lonely, waterless, blazing Australian outback?

B. It had seemed like any other afternoon, until Anna turned on her computer to do her homework. Instead of finding the rough draft of her English composition, Anna found herself staring at a message blinking insistently on the screen. "What is your destination?" OK, thought Anna, I'll play along. Maybe this was some new computer game of her brother's. She thought for a moment and then typed in the words "the moon." As she watched the screen, something very strange happened.

C. Paragraphs will vary. Paragraphs may or may not have a topic sentence, but each paragraph should focus on one main idea or event. Each paragraph should be developed with supporting details, such as facts and statistics, sensory details, incidents, examples, or quotations. These details should be presented in a logical order.

Paragraphs in Longer Writing

Objectives

- To recognize the need for paragraphing in a piece of writing
- To apply guidelines for paragraphing

Related Mini-Lessons

For more information relating to paragraphing, see the following mini-lessons.

- **Effective Paragraphs, pp. 244–247**
- **Developing Paragraphs, pp. 248–251**
- **Methods of Elaboration, pp. 255–261**
- **Achieving Unity, pp. 268–271**
- **Coherence, pp. 273–277**

Teaching Strategies

for GUIDELINES FOR PARAGRAPHING

KEY TO UNDERSTANDING As you discuss the guidelines, note that a new paragraph is necessary whenever there is a shift or change in the writing. Point out to students that the first three bulleted items contain the word *change*—a change in topic, setting, action, or speaker. Encourage them to use this principle when they are paragraphing their next writing assignment.

How Do I Use Paragraphs?

Paragraphs in Longer Writing

Imagine that you're driving in an unfamiliar place at night. It's so dark that you can barely see the side of the road. There are no landmarks, no signs to tell you where you are, and no place to rest. You realize with a sinking feeling that you're lost!

That's what it might feel like to read a book without paragraphs. In writing, paragraphs are like the signs along a road. They signal the reader: Pay attention! New idea here! Paragraph indents also break up the page, giving readers' eyes a rest and helping them keep track of where they are on the page.

WHEN SHOULD I PARAGRAPH?

Few writers know exactly how many and what kinds of paragraphs they will write when they begin drafting. Some writers try out different idea groupings and create paragraphs as they draft. Other writers just get everything on paper during drafting and wait to group ideas into paragraphs when they revise their writing. Here are some suggestions to help you paragraph your writing.

Guidelines for Paragraphing

Begin a new paragraph when
- a new idea is introduced or the topic changes
- there is a major change in setting or action
- the speaker in a dialogue changes

Make sure your paragraphs include
- only one main idea
- adequate elaboration
- no unrelated details
- a logical order of presentation

PROFESSIONAL NOTEBOOK

In his book *On Writing Well,* William Zinsser gives this advice about paragraphing:

"Keep your paragraphs short, especially if you're writing for a newspaper or a magazine that sets its type in a narrow width. . . .

"Short paragraphs put air around what you write and make it look inviting, whereas one long chunk of type can discourage the reader from even starting to read."

Invite students to search a newspaper for a paragraph of more than three sentences. It may take some looking to find one!

In the following passage, notice how Helen Keller begins a new paragraph to introduce a new idea—that people who can see don't really use that gift.

I have often thought it would be a blessing if each human being were stricken blind and deaf for a few days at some time during his or her early adult life. Darkness would make people more appreciative of sight; silence would teach them the joys of sound.

Now and then I have tested my seeing friends to discover what they see. Recently I was visited by a very good friend who had just returned from a long walk in the woods, and I asked her what she had observed. "Nothing in particular," she replied. I might have been incredulous had I not been accustomed to such responses, for long ago I became convinced that the seeing see little.

Helen Keller, "The Seeing See Little"

Toshio Mori begins a new paragraph each time the speaker changes in the following dialogue between the owner of a flower shop and a sales clerk.

Mr. Sasaki ran excitedly to the front. "Teruo! She forgot to pay!"

Teruo stopped the boss on the way out. "Wait, Mr. Sasaki," he said. "I gave it to her."

"What!" the boss cried indignantly.

"She came in just to look around and see the flowers. She likes pretty roses. Don't you think she's wonderful?"

"What's the matter with you?" the boss said. "Are you crazy? What did she buy?"

"Nothing, I tell you," Teruo said. "I gave it to her because she admired it, and she's pretty enough to deserve beautiful things, and I liked her."

"You're fired! Get out!" Mr. Sasaki spluttered. "Don't come back to the store again."

Toshio Mori, "Say It with Flowers"

Room in Brooklyn (1932), Edward Hopper.

for FIRST LITERARY MODEL

USING THE MODEL Invite student comments on Keller's conclusion that "the seeing see little." Remind them of the importance of sensory details in writing; suggest that students try to become more aware of such details to improve their writing.

for SECOND LITERARY MODEL

CRITICAL THINKING: MAKING COMPARISONS Tell students that the rule for beginning a new paragraph for each change of speaker did not always exist. Ask students to turn to Practice Your Skills on page 254 to see what writing without paragraphing looks like. Ask, "Why do you think the paragraphing guidelines we use today became popular?" (Sample: Many readers found that the lack of separate paragraphs made the writing hard to follow.)

ART NOTE

American painter Edward Hopper (1882–1967) focused his work on the isolation and loss of identity that people suffer in big cities. In *Room in Brooklyn,* Hopper shows a woman with her back to the viewer, making her seem as impersonal as the rows of brownstone buildings outside. The beauty of the flowers contrasts with the coldness of the scene. (Hopper's painting *Nighthawks* appears on page 219 of this textbook.)

for PRACTICE YOUR SKILLS

MANAGING THE PAPER LOAD
You might have students complete the Practice Your Skills activity in small groups, after which you could discuss suggested revisions with the entire class.

for PRACTICE YOUR SKILLS

INDIVIDUALIZING INSTRUCTION: BASIC STUDENTS These students may have difficulty in generating a set of revision instructions. Suggest that these students and any other students who so desire first write the revision of the passage, then go back over their improved versions to develop their revision instructions.

AUDITORY LEARNERS Because the primary mode of learning for these students involves speaking and listening, have them tape the piece of writing and play it back, listening for the cues that will help them to be effective editors.

Additional Resource

Writing Resource Book, p. 74

Answers to Practice Your Skills

Instructions for revising the passage may vary in wording. A suggested set of instructions is given below.

1. Delete sentences 1 and 2, beginning the passage with sentence 3.
2. Delete sentence 8.
3. Begin a new paragraph with sentence 12.
4. Delete sentence 15.
5. Sentences 19, 20, 21, followed by 16, form their own paragraph. Position this paragraph after Sentence 14.
6. Begin a new paragraph with Sentence 17.

Practice Your Skills

Act as peer editor for the following piece of writing, paying special attention to paragraph breaks, unity, and coherence. Write instructions for revising the passage. (For example, "Begin a new paragraph with sentence __." or "Delete sentence __.") Note that one paragraph should be repositioned.

Equipment such as this hydraulic lift helped to create remarkably realistic special effects in the film *Jaws.*

[1]In the movie *Jaws,* a giant shark gobbles up a fisherman. [2]In the movie *Who Framed Roger Rabbit?* an actor and a cartoon character race through the streets in a cartoon car. [3]Have you ever watched a movie with great special effects and wondered, "How did they do that?" [4]Surprisingly, special effects rely on just a few basic filmmaking techniques. [5]One of the secrets behind many special effects is a technique called stop-motion photography. [6]A filmmaker shoots the frames of a film one at a time and then combines them to make the action look continuous. [7]For example, stop-motion photography helped turn actor Lon Chaney, Jr., into a monster in the movie *The Wolf Man.* [8]Chaney was the son of a famous silent film star. [9]First the filmmaker shot a few frames of the actor. [10]Then the makeup crew added pieces of hair to Chaney's face and hands. [11]A few more frames were shot, and the process was repeated until Chaney had become a full-fledged werewolf. [12]Other special effects rely on the use of models and miniatures which can be photographed to look like live action. [13]The shark in *Jaws,* for example, was really three different mechanical models, each designed to be used in different scenes. [14]In the 1976 movie *King Kong,* the giant ape was actually a Styrofoam model just forty feet high. [15]The original King Kong movie was made in 1933. [16]Combining live action with animation like this can produce astonishing illusions. [17]The next time you watch a movie, you won't have to ask, "How did they do that?" [18]You'll know how. [19]Some of the most complex special effects involve a process called composite photography. [20]For instance, in the film *Who Framed Roger Rabbit?* the cartoon characters' actions were drawn and photographed on one piece of film—the live actors' movements on another. [21]The two pieces of film were then combined so that it looked as if the "Toons" and the humans were on screen together.

How Can I Develop My Ideas?

Methods of Elaboration

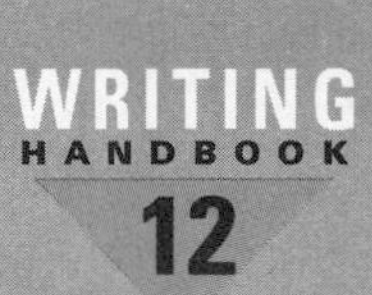

How many times have you said to someone you were talking to, "You know what I mean?" When you write, however, you don't have a chance to ask that question. Your writing should give readers enough specific details, or **elaboration,** so that they understand your ideas completely and aren't left with any unanswered questions.

TYPES OF ELABORATION

You can use many types of details to elaborate on your ideas. These details include facts, statistics, sensory details, incidents, examples, quotations, and graphic aids. The details you choose should fit your purpose, audience, and topic.

Facts and Statistics A statement that can be proved is a **fact.** An example of a fact is "Greg LeMond of the United States won the Tour de France bicycle race in 1986, 1989, and 1990." A **statistic** is a fact stated in numbers. "Cyclists in the Tour de France usually cover between 2,500 and 3,000 miles" is a statistic. You can find such statements in a sports encyclopedia.

Facts and statistics are especially useful in supporting opinions. For example, Mariolle and Shermer used facts and figures to show that U.S. women have dominated cycling for years.

Professional MODEL

In 1984, many TV viewers saw Americans Connie Carpenter Phinney and Rebecca Twigg win the gold and silver medals in the first cycling event ever held for women in the Olympics. (Fact) It was no accident. American women have been prominent in international cycling competition since 1969, when Audrey McElmury won the road race at the World Championships in Brno, Czechoslovakia. (Fact) She was the first American champion, male or female, in 57 years. (Statistic) Since 1945, Americans have won a total of 35 medals at the Worlds and 27 of them were won by women. (Statistic)

Elaine Mariolle and Michael Shermer, *The Woman Cyclist*

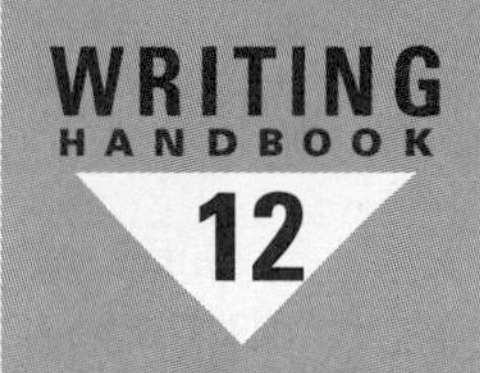

Methods of Elaboration

Objectives

- To identify types of elaboration
- To identify methods of generating details
- To elaborate on given ideas

Related Mini-Lessons

For information on topics related to methods of elaboration, see the following mini-lessons.

- **Graphic Devices for Writing, pp. 227–231**
- **Show, Don't Tell, pp. 262–267**
- **Creating Graphic Aids, pp. 349–351**

Teaching Strategies

for TYPES OF ELABORATION

INDIVIDUALIZING INSTRUCTION: ESL STUDENTS Because elaboration depends partly on precise and varied word choice, students for whom English is a second language are often at a disadvantage in writing. Suggest that they use a student thesaurus for help with their writing. You might also pair ESL students with native English speakers to discuss word choices and to consider both the denotations and the connotations of words.

for PROFESSIONAL MODEL

USING THE MODEL Have students locate the statistics in the excerpt (the years 1984, 1969, 1912 [57 years before 1969], and 1945; the number of medals [35 and 27]). Ask them where else they might find some of this information. (Sample: In newspapers and magazines) *for* SENSORY DETAILS

PERSONAL TOUCH From your own writing, share with students a paragraph that demonstrates the use of sensory details. Ask them to identify each sensory detail and the sense to which it appeals.

for FIRST PROFESSIONAL MODEL

SPEAKING AND LISTENING Have a volunteer read the model aloud while students close their eyes and try to imagine themselves in the scene. Then ask them to identify each sensory detail in the model and to name the sense to which that detail appeals. Note that writers base some descriptions primarily on the sense of sight, but that a description appealing to several senses creates a fuller, richer experience for the reader.

for SECOND PROFESSIONAL MODEL

USING THE MODEL Tell students that magazine and newspaper articles often use specific incidents to illustrate an important point. Show students that by putting the incident before the idea expressed in the final sentence, Dodson allows readers to draw the conclusion for themselves.

Sensory Details You can help readers experience what you are writing about by showing how something looks, sounds, smells, tastes, or feels. These sensory details can help you bring a description or narration to life. To find sensory details, try recalling, observing, or imagining. Then look for specific nouns and active verbs to describe these details.

In the following paragraph, notice how the writer uses sensory details of smell, sound, and sight to make readers feel as if they're standing right beside him as he tracks the gorilla.

Professional MODEL

Smell

Sound

Sight

The musty, somewhat sweet odor of gorilla hung in the air. Somewhere ahead and out of sight, a gorilla roared and roared again, *uuua-uuua!* an explosive, half-screaming sound that shattered the stillness of the forest and made the hairs on my neck rise. I took a few steps and stopped, listened, and moved again. The only sound was the buzzing of insects. Far below me white clouds crept up the slopes and fingered into the canyons. Then another roar, but farther away. I continued over a ridge, down and up again. Finally I saw them, on the opposite slope about two hundred feet away, some sitting on the ground, others in trees.

George B. Schaller, *The Year of the Gorilla*

Incidents Sometimes, describing a brief event, or **incident,** can help you explain an idea. In the following passage the writer uses an incident to show the importance of following the proper procedure.

Seek help. Just as police are trained to call for backup during emergencies, so the rest of us should guard against going it alone if help is available.

When fire was reported in an office building in Hartford, firefighters were startled to see how far the blaze had progressed by the time they arrived. Construction workers on the scene had tried to put the fire out themselves. "By the time they called the fire department," says [fire captain] Fred Crocker, "smoke was up to the third floor. It was amazing nobody died." Crocker points out that the proper sequence is to call for help first, and *then* try to handle the problem.

Reynolds Dodson, "Control Your Crisis"

Literature Connection

Share with students this passage from John Steinbeck's *The Pearl.* Have them identify sensory details and each sense that is appealed to.

"The roosters were crowing and the dawn was not far off. Smoke of the first fires seeped out through the walls of the brush houses, and the first smell of cooking corncakes was in the air. Already the dawn birds were scampering in the bushes. The weak moon was losing its light and the clouds thickened and curdled to the southward. The wind blew freshly into the estuary, a nervous, restless wind with the smell of storm on its breath, and there was change and uneasiness in the air."

When relating an incident, be sure to include enough details to support your idea and to leave out ones that might be confusing. Notice how Dodson described the fire by using sensory details and by quoting the firefighter's own words.

WRITER TO WRITER

"In your writing you want to have all of the what, when, where, how, *and* why.*"*

Jamie Lentz, student, Hamilton, Ohio

Examples Sometimes a "for instance," or **example,** can also help you elaborate on an idea. A well-chosen example often can be more effective than a whole page of explanation.

In the following paragraph, notice how the writer uses examples to show how Olympic track-and-field coach Bob Kersee gives his athletes the winning edge.

Example of new training developments

Example of Kersee's techniques

> Kersee is a keen student, staying abreast of all the latest training developments and scientific research. He knows all about weight training, diet, muscles, massage, and techniques for throwing, running, and jumping. He sees himself as a "detail" person. He carefully studies videotapes of his athletes' performances and watches for the smallest change in form or the tiniest adjustment. What he notices may add only an inch to a long jump or shave just hundredths of a second off a sprint, but at the highest levels of track and field, those differences can decide who wins and who finishes last.
>
> **Jay Jennings, "Jackie Joyner-Kersee and Bob Kersee: Track's Wedded Winners"**

Quotations Quoting people directly can be a powerful way to elaborate on and support your ideas. In choosing quotations to include in your writing, however, just as in choosing incidents, be sure that they make your point clearly. Also be sure to copy the words exactly and to credit the writer or speaker.

For example, the writer of the passage on the next page uses a quotation from an expert to support his statements about space junk.

for EXAMPLES

ASSESSMENT: SPOT CHECK To review techniques presented thus far, ask students to suggest how they might use facts and statistics, sensory details, or incidents to elaborate on the main idea of Jennings's paragraph. (Samples: Statistics might show a case in which Kersee's observations resulted in a measurable improvement; an incident might tell a story of a time when Kersee advised an athlete and both saw the results. Sensory details might appear in either case but could be especially appropriate in an incident.)

for QUOTATIONS

HELPFUL HINT Remind students that the second Professional Model on page 256, which demonstrates the use of an incident to elaborate on an idea, also contains a quotation. Stress that writers often combine several kinds of elaboration to support their main ideas.

for PROFESSIONAL MODEL

USING THE MODEL Point out that in many kinds of writing (especially in informative or persuasive writing), it is important to show that the speaker is an authority. Direct students' attention to the phrase "a radar specialist with the Jet Propulsion Laboratory in Pasadena," which identifies the expertise of the person quoted in the model.

Professional
MODEL

There's all sorts of junk whizzing around in Earth orbit, bits and pieces of spacecraft that nobody ever cleaned up. The military's early warning radar can spot the big pieces—those four inches long and up. . . . Researchers even know a lot about the tiny pieces, less than two-hundredths of an inch across. . . .

But between four inches and two-hundredths of an inch lies a lot of garbage about which little is known. "These things have a closing speed of ten miles per second," says Richard Goldstein, a radar specialist with the Jet Propulsion Laboratory in Pasadena. "That means that if you're ten miles away from a piece of debris, you have one second to duck."

"Looking for Trash," ***Discover***

Graphic Aids You've probably heard the expression, "A picture is worth a thousand words." That certainly can be true. So, if you have to present a large amount of information in a small space in your writing, consider using **graphic aids** such as maps, tables, and diagrams. For example, the following diagram shows a figure skater doing the complicated triple axel jump. Describing this movement in words would be very difficult and would take a great deal of space.

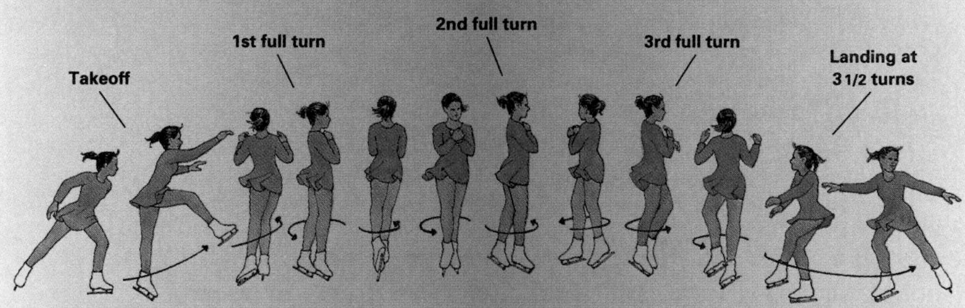
Counting the turns
A triple axel in figure skating is hard to follow because the motion is so rapid. The skater makes three and one-half turns in less than one second.
Takeoff
1st full turn
2nd full turn
3rd full turn
Landing at 3 1/2 turns

Presenting information graphically can also make the relationships between ideas clear. Notice that the bar graph on the next page shows at a glance how the distribution of Peace Corps volunteers changed from 1967 to 1992.

Science Connection

Point out that graphic aids might be especially useful in writing about a scientific subject. Suggest that students skim their science textbooks and note the many ways in which photographs, diagrams, and other graphic aids are used to convey information.

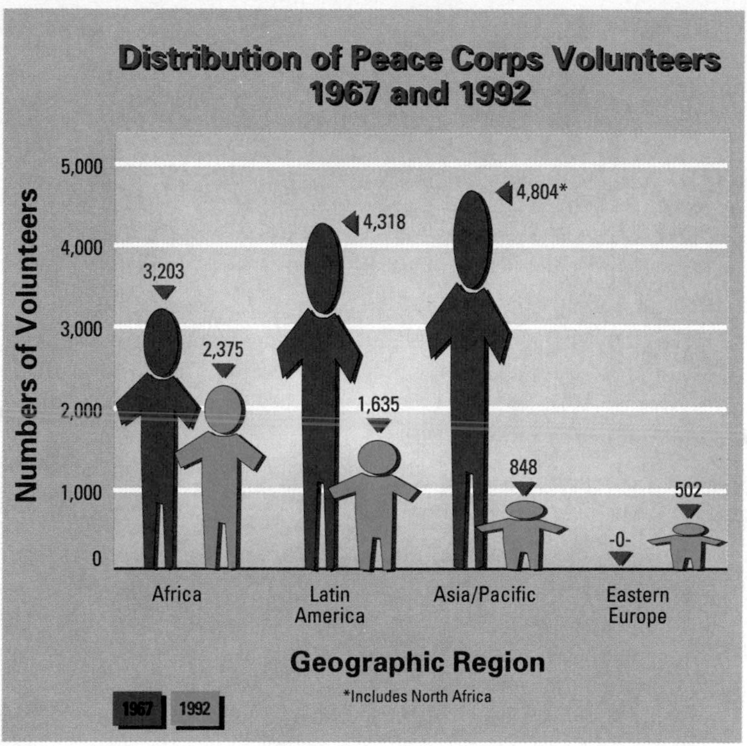

SOURCES OF ELABORATION

Even if you know what type of elaboration you need to develop your writing ideas, you still have to gather specific details. What sources or methods will best help you gather the information you need?

Questioning What do you know about your topic? Asking questions can help you find out. The answers to the questions are the details you can use to elaborate on your writing. The questions you can't answer can help direct your research. A student made the chart on the next page as she was working on a report about the guitarist Les Paul. Notice that she included reminders to herself in the chart.

for BAR GRAPH

CRITICAL THINKING: INTERPRETING To make sure that students can interpret the bar graph, ask them to summarize the changes that the bar graph shows. (The number of Peace Corps volunteers in each geographic region except Eastern Europe decreased between 1967 and 1992. The greatest decrease occurred in the Asia/Pacific region.)

for SOURCES OF ELABORATION

COOPERATIVE LEARNING Before discussing the methods for gathering details, you might make a class list of topics for which students would want to find information. (Students will probably see the practicality of the methods if they use the topics of upcoming reports or projects.) As each method is discussed, students can apply it to some or all of the topics on the list and determine whether that is a method any of them would want to use.

for QUESTIONING

HELPFUL HINT As you discuss the technique of questioning as a method of gathering details, refer students to the Writer to Writer tip on page 257. Note that questioning means asking and answering *who? what? when? where? why?* and *how?*

Links to LITERATURE & LANGUAGE

You might direct students to Hazel Shelton Abernethy's "The Home Front: 1941–1945" and to the excerpt from Dougal Robertson's *Survive the Savage Sea* on page 258 and page 619 of *Literature and Language,* Grade 8. Have students discuss how both authors use various types of elaboration to tell their stories.

for EXPLORING

MODELING Exploring techniques can be used both to discover a writing idea and to elaborate on it. For example, you might write the subject *Childhood Memories* on the board and use recalling to list ideas about the subject, such as *visiting the zoo* or *learning to ride a bike.* Then demonstrate how you would use recalling to generate details about the topic—for example, *cute baby elephant, tigers romping like kittens, sore feet at day's end,* and so on.

for RESEARCH

HELPFUL HINT Make a connection between the questioning and research methods by noting that before students begin library research, they should have a list of at least some of the questions to which they want to find answers.

for GRAPHIC DEVICES

INDIVIDUALIZING INSTRUCTION: ADVANCED STUDENTS You might ask these students to demonstrate for the class the use of the various graphic devices to generate details on a previously arranged topic.

Additional Resources

Writing Resource Book, pp. 75–79
Elaboration, Revision, and Proofreading Practice
Elaboration, Revision, and Proofreading Transparency Pack
Thinking Skills Worksheets
Thinking Skills Transparency Pack

Details About Les Paul

Who?	guitarist Les Paul
What?	helped develop modern electric guitar
When?	early 1950s? (FIND THE EXACT DATE!)
Where?	(DOESN'T MATTER)
Why?	wanted a different sound
How?	attached pickups below strings of an acoustic guitar

Exploring The same methods that are useful for exploring writing ideas can also be used to generate details that elaborate on those ideas. These methods, which are presented in Handbook 1, "Discovering Writing Ideas," pages 218–223, include recalling, brainstorming, freewriting, listing, and using a journal.

Research The library is a storehouse of many types of resource materials you can use to help you elaborate on your ideas. For more information about finding and evaluating library sources, see Handbook 35, "Making Use of the Library," pages 352–361.

People who have special knowledge about your topic can also be good sources of information. Before contacting an expert, make a list of questions you want to ask. Then arrange an interview and take good notes. Finally, double-check any answers that sound wrong. Even experts can make mistakes.

Graphic Devices Another good way to find details is to use graphic devices such as clustering, charting, and analysis frames. These devices can help you learn what you know and what you need to find out about a topic. (See Handbook 3, "Graphic Devices for Writing," pages 227–231.)

Practice Your Skills

A. Choose two of the following main ideas. Then elaborate each idea in a brief paragraph by following the suggestions in parentheses.

1. Airports are interesting places.
(*Suggestion:* Give examples. Include sensory details that describe what you see, hear, smell, taste, and touch.)

2. There is nothing spookier than a deserted street at night. (*Suggestion:* Give sensory details or tell about an incident. The incident can be real or made up.)
3. Changing a tire on a bicycle is easy if you know how. (*Suggestion:* Research the topic by watching someone change a tire or by doing it yourself. Draw a diagram or use another graphic aid to make your explanation clear.)
4. A pet's antics are amusing to watch. (*Suggestion:* Give examples or tell about an incident.)
5. _______ is the best team in the league. (*Suggestion:* Choose a team. Give facts or statistics from a recent newspaper or magazine article. Consider including a graphic aid.)
6. Our town has changed in the past thirty years. (*Suggestion:* Research the topic by interviewing older relatives or family friends. Include examples and a quotation from one of them.)
7. _______ was the most important day of my life. (*Suggestion:* Tell about an incident.)
8. The best video game is _______. (*Suggestion:* Use specific examples from the game.)

B. Imagine that you have to write about each main idea listed below. Name the method of generating details that will help you produce the most interesting and informative piece of writing. Then list the types of details you might use.

1. Different kinds of music fit different moods.
2. Certain species of whale are in danger of becoming extinct.
3. Soccer is the world's most popular sport.
4. Riding a bicycle in a large city can be dangerous.
5. Off in the distance, I heard a waterfall and a person shouting.
6. Athletic shoes are now made for every possible purpose.

Answers to Practice Your Skills

A. Students should develop their paragraphs with vivid examples and details based on the suggestions in parentheses. All answers will vary. An example of an elaborated paragraph is shown below.

1. The airport is a beehive of motion and activity during the day. The continuous buzz of conversation fills the terminals as people hurry from place to place, bags and babies in their arms. Static interrupts the stream of announcements made over the loudspeakers. The airport is never quiet, even after closing time. You can hear the steady *swish swish* of a janitor's mop as the sharp odor of ammonia fills the air.

B. Answers will vary. Possible responses are listed below.

1. Method: exploring, graphic devices
   Types of details: examples, sensory details, incidents
2. Method: research
   Types of details: facts/statistics, graphic aids
3. Method: questioning, research
   Types of details: facts/statistics, graphic aids
4. Method: graphic devices
   Types of details: examples, incidents, quotations
5. Method: questioning, exploring, graphic devices
   Types of details: sensory details
6. Method: questioning, exploring
   Types of details: facts/statistics, examples, quotations

Show, Don't Tell

Objectives

- To use a variety of show-don't-tell strategies to reveal feelings, events, cause and effect, comparisons and contrasts, and opinions
- To use "showing" strategies to avoid clichés and unnecessary language

Related Mini-Lessons

For information on topics related to using show-don't-tell strategies, see the following mini-lessons.

- **Methods of Elaboration, pp. 255–261**
- **Revising, pp. 287–289**
- **Meaning and Word Choice, pp. 314–315**

Motivate

On the board, write a dull "telling" sentence about a tourist attraction or historic site. For example, "Old Faithful, a geyser in Yellowstone National Park, is an unusual natural phenomenon." Then ask students what they think of this description. Would they envision the geyser's appearance? What additional questions do they have?

Teaching Strategies

for EDUARDO'S POSTCARDS

USING THE MODEL Have students list the questions Ana might have asked Eduardo and locate in Eduardo's reply details that answer them.

WRITING HANDBOOK 13

How Can I Use Elaboration Techniques?

Show, Don't Tell

Eduardo sent Ana this postcard from summer camp.

> Dear Ana,
> Camp is great! I can't believe all the people I'm meeting and the things I'm learning to do!
> Ciao,
> Eduardo

After reading Eduardo's postcard, Ana had lots of questions. She wondered what the people he was meeting were like. She was curious about all the activities and what he was learning to do. She wanted details to *show* her about the camp, so she wrote back asking her questions. Here is Eduardo's reply.

> Dear Ana,
> You have to meet Aaron. He's a crack-up. He's always telling jokes. Another guy is giving me guitar lessons. Today we hiked to Lake Navajo. We even learned how to water ski. Tonight is the cookout. We'll all sit around the campfire and tell ghost stories.
> Miss you,
> Eduardo

Eduardo's first postcard *tells* about camp in a general way. The second one, however, *shows* what happens at camp. The details about friends, water-skiing, and ghost stories show Eduardo's active day.

In Handbook 12, "Methods of Elaboration" (pages 255–261), you learned about a variety of supporting details that you can use to develop your ideas. Asking yourself questions like the ones Ana asked Eduardo can help you think of supporting details.

262 Writing Handbook

Show-Don't-Tell Strategies

Showing a Feeling When you write about your important experiences, you may focus on showing your feelings. Notice how Gary Soto uses striking comparisons and vivid description to show his disappointment over his new jacket.

What had he expected? What did he receive? How did he feel?

Telling
I couldn't believe my mother gave me such an ugly jacket!

Showing
When I needed a new jacket and my mother asked what kind I wanted, I described something like bikers wear: black leather and silver studs with enough belts to hold down a small town. . . . The next day when I got home from school, I discovered draped on my bedpost a jacket the color of day-old guacamole. I threw my books on the bed and approached the jacket slowly, as if it were a stranger whose hand I had to shake. . . . I stared at the jacket, like an enemy, thinking bad things . . .

Gary Soto, "The Jacket"

Showing an Event When you're reporting an event, don't try to include every detail. Instead, focus on the most important and vivid details. You might also include dialogue.

What did the characters see and hear? What were the passengers doing?

Telling
The raft began to capsize.

Showing
"Hang on!" a crewman shouted over the crash of waves. Suddenly, the whoops of excitement turned to cries of alarm. In the fast and furious chute of Crystal Rapids, the three-ton, 38-foot long raft had pitched onto a rock and stopped dead. A crewman bellowed orders to stay put. But when the raft heeled to an angle of 70 degrees, John yelled into Tyler's ear, "Jump."

Peter Michelmore, "Capsize at Crystal Rapids"

GENERAL NOTE

HELPFUL HINT: ELABORATION Briefly review the elaboration techniques presented in Handbook 12—facts and statistics, sensory details, incidents, examples, quotations, graphic aids. Ask students to suggest which ones Eduardo might have used to think of more details that would show Ana what his camp is like.

for SHOWING A FEELING

USING THE MODEL Ask students how the narrator felt about the jacket he wanted and about the jacket he received. How do they know? Have them point out the comparisons he makes and the examples of vivid descriptions that reveal the narrator's feelings. Explain that the writer uses figurative language to make the experience vivid. Point out use of metaphor (comparing the color of the jacket to day-old guacamole) and simile (comparing the jacket to a stranger).

for SHOWING AN EVENT

USING THE MODEL Ask students to tell which of the five senses Peter Michelmore appeals to in this passage from "Capsize at Crystal Rapids" (hearing). Have students point out details that appeal to this sense. (Samples: crash of waves; whoops of excitement; cries of alarm; bellowed; yelled) Point out that the brief dialogue in the scene serves to move the action along without distracting from the excitement of the event.

Literature Connection

Read aloud this excerpt from "Raymond's Run" by Toni Cade Bambara.

". . . And then I feel my weight coming back just behind my knees, then down to my feet, then into the earth, and the pistol shot explodes in my blood and I am off and weightless again, flying past the other runners, my arms pumping up and down, and the whole world is quiet except for the crunch as I zoom over the gravel in the track."

Have students identify the strategies that the author uses to show, rather than tell, about this character's experience in a track race.

for SHOWING CAUSE AND EFFECT

ASSESSMENT: SPOT CHECK After students have read the "telling" sentence and the "showing" paragraph, ask them to list the specific details the writer uses to prove that rope-jumping can improve a person's tennis game. To guide their responses, ask students to consider these questions: What physical skills does rope-jumping require? (Jumping on the balls of the feet; short, controlled steps; quick-footed movements) How are these skills helpful in tennis? (These skills help a player get to the ball.) How does the quotation by Greg Moran reinforce the cause-and-effect relationship? (This quotation from a qualified tennis professional recounts first-hand experiences.)

for SHOWING CAUSE AND EFFECT

USING THE MODEL Have students read the "telling" and "showing" passages carefully. Then have them answer the questions in the margin. Remind them that details that show cause and effect include first-hand observations, facts, examples, and expert opinions. Have volunteers tell which of these details answers the first question (facts, first-hand observations) and which answer the second question (expert opinion, first-hand observations, facts).

Showing Cause and Effect When you write about a situation and its results, use specific details to make each point clear. You might include first-hand observations, facts, examples, and expert opinions, for example. The telling sentence below states a connection between rope jumping and tennis. The showing paragraph, however, provides specific details and the experience of an expert to explain the cause-and-effect relationship.

How does rope jumping affect your skill? What does rope jumping do that helps you play a better game?

Telling

Rope jumping can improve your tennis game.

Showing

The big appeal for tennis players is that rope jumping mimics many movements you execute on the court. Tennis is played on the balls of the feet. You're constantly moving in short, controlled steps, much the way you move while jumping rope. Improve your jumping ability and you'll get to the ball quicker.

"One of the biggest problems tennis players have is being out of position," says Greg Moran, the head pro at the Four Seasons Racquet Club in Wilton, Conn., who has been jumping rope for ten years. "You need short steps to adjust to the ball. If I stop jumping rope for a while, I feel heavy-footed and slow on the court."

Susan Festa Fiske, "Jump To It"

Showing Comparisons and Contrasts When you compare or contrast two subjects, use the same set of details to show their similarities or differences. Notice how the following writer contrasts Saturday and Sunday. Each paragraph focuses on the same kinds of details in the same order, but each paints a sharply different picture. The concluding sentence neatly summarizes the contrasts of the two days.

What's the difference in the way each day feels? What do you do differently on each day?

Telling

Saturday feels different from Sunday.

PROFESSIONAL NOTEBOOK

From the Authors Rebekah Caplan offers a tip to help students understand why showing is necessary in writing: "I remind students that the storybooks they read as very young children are filled with colorful illustrations that show the events described on accompanying pages; the writer does not have to describe the lovely red barn with the carved wooden trim, for the picture next to the caption, 'The barn was beautiful,' reveals that idea. However, in more mature literature, drawings disappear from the pages, and the writer assumes the role of illustrator. Language must be the author's brush and palette."

Practical Ideas for Teaching Writing as a Process

Student MODEL

Showing

Without the help of an alarm clock, at 8:30 sharp Saturday morning, I wake up brimmed with energy and ready to take on any activity that floats my way. The sun is pouring bars of golden liquid in my window and the blue jays are singing merrily at the top of their musical voices. Anticipating a whole day to do whatever I want, I eagerly throw on my clothes and spring down the stairs. In a flash, I'm out the door and running.

On Sunday, though, my mother is shaking me and saying, "It's past 11:00. Get up, there's work to do." With a deep groan I open my eyes and am immediately blinded by the terrible glare of the sun beaming hot and stuffy directly on me. Very slowly I claw my way out of bed, and in a drained, limp state of semi-consciousness, stumble sheepishly down the stairs. Saturday was freedom; Sunday means mowing the lawn.

Showing an Opinion When writers argue for something they believe in, they use facts and examples to support their point of view. Using evidence based on research strengthens your argument. Notice how the writer in the model below supports one side of a controversial issue.

Telling

Animal research is good because it has produced major advances in medicine.

What medical advances have been made? What are different examples?

Professional MODEL

Showing

Anyone who has looked into the matter can scarcely deny that major advances in medicine have been achieved through basic research with animals. Among these are the development of virtually all modern vaccines against infectious diseases, the invention of surgical approaches to bone and joint injuries and eye disorders, the discovery of insulin and other hormones, and the testing of new drugs and antibiotics.

Frederick A. King, "Animals in Research: The Case for Experimentation"

for STUDENT MODEL

LINKING GRAMMAR AND WRITING Make sure students realize that the use of vivid and specific words—nouns, verbs, and adjectives—helps the writer contrast the feelings that he or she experiences on the two days. On Saturday, for example, the eager writer *springs* down the stairs, while on Sunday the same person *stumbles* down. On Saturday, the sun's "bars of golden liquid" reflect the writer's upbeat mood; on Sunday, however, the sun's "terrible glare," "beaming hot and stuffy," emphasizes that the writer feels oppressed. Ask students to name other specific nouns, verbs, and adjectives that help create an interesting contrast between the two days.

for SHOWING AN OPINION

INDIVIDUALIZING INSTRUCTION: BASIC STUDENTS Review with students that an opinion is a statement that cannot conclusively be proved true or untrue. An opinion is based on what seems true in one's own judgment, so writers who are attempting to persuade must convince their readers that their judgment is valid. Point out that a responsible reader does not accept a writer's opinion unless the writer provides enough compelling facts and examples to support the opinion. Have students answer the questions in the margin and decide for themselves whether the writer has offered enough support for his opinion.

TEACHER'S LOUNGE

This anecdote is from *Educator's Lifetime Library of Stories, Quotes, Anecdotes, Wit and Humor* by P. Susan Mamchak and Steven R. Mamchak.

"Jimmy," said the teacher, "your composition on milk was supposed to be two pages long, but this is only half a page. What happened?"

"Don't tell me," said Jimmy, "that you've never heard of evaporated milk?"

for SHOWING A CLICHÉ

HELPFUL HINT Have students select one of the clichéd phrases below and use fresh words and descriptive details, as in the Student Model, to show what the cliché means.

as hungry as a bear
as slow as molasses
as flat as a pancake
as proud as a peacock

for SHOWING A CLICHÉ

INDIVIDUALIZING INSTRUCTION: ESL STUDENTS Clichés and overused expressions may be new and confusing to ESL students. Help these students recognize clichés in their own and others' writing by pointing them out whenever appropriate and explaining the meaning of these figurative expressions.

for SHOWING AN IDEA IN A SINGLE SENTENCE

LINKING GRAMMAR AND WRITING Point out that Alice Walker has not developed the image of a happy baby by merely adding adjectives or adverbs. Elicit some of the specific verbs *(stroking, kneading)* and specific nouns *(thumb, forefinger)* that she uses to create a sharp image of contentment.

Other Show-Don't-Tell Strategies

Showing a Cliché A cliché is an overused expression, such as *She was as quiet as a mouse* or *I could hardly believe my eyes,* that has become meaningless and dull because it has been repeated over and over again. To avoid using a cliché, try to find fresh words or descriptive details that will show the meaning and add interest. Here is an example.

What made him such a model of health? Why did he seem so fit?

Telling
He was the picture of health.

Showing
He was off once more to play basketball, running full-speed, leaving the exercise room far behind. Dodging through the crowded corridors, leaping over benches, and sliding down banisters, in no time he found himself at the entrance to the basketball court.

Showing an Idea in a Single Sentence When writers strengthen their writing by showing instead of telling, they don't always develop whole paragraphs to add specific details and descriptions. Sometimes one or two sentences can be just as effective as an entire paragraph. In the excerpt below, Alice Walker uses only a single sentence to *show* instead of *tell* what the baby is doing in her mother's lap.

What gestures was the baby making? Why did she seem happy?

Telling
The baby was happy in her mother's lap.

Showing
Once in her mother's lap she rested content all the way home, sucking her thumb, stroking her nose with the forefinger of the same hand, and kneading a corner of her blanket with the three fingers that were left.

Alice Walker, *The Color Purple*

Practice Your Skills

A. Rewrite the following telling sentences to turn them into showing paragraphs. Use the writing strategies in parentheses.

1. It felt great to be alive. (Show your feelings through sensory details.)
2. The mood was somber. (Show the mood through a comparison.)
3. The game was a close one. (Show the suspense by focusing on a single moment.)
4. Students should (should not) be allowed to watch television as much as they want. (Show reasons to support your opinion.)
5. He was a new person after a week's vacation. (Show the different ways his vacation affected his outlook.)
6. The words *skinny* and *trim* suggest different meanings. (Show the contrast in meanings by giving specific examples.)
7. Athletic shoes can vary in price, depending on where you buy them. (Show facts and statistics to support this statement by researching local stores.)
8. Video games are too violent. (Support your opinion with descriptive details and specific examples.)
9. My two friends are as different as night and day. (Show this cliché.)
10. Cable television has changed viewing habits. (Show the effects of cable television by using facts and examples.)

B. Write a showing paragraph for each sentence.

1. We took a risk.
2. The sea is full of mystery.
3. The streets were crowded.
4. I could tell the book was going to be good.
5. Mothers can be different from fathers.
6. American diets are changing.
7. Homework is (is not) necessary to improve learning.
8. The grass is always greener on the other side of the fence.

C. Write a showing sentence (or two) for each telling sentence.

1. I was annoyed.
2. The speaker captured our attention.
3. Dogs are different from cats.
4. Exercise can improve health.

for PRACTICE YOUR SKILLS

MANAGING THE PAPER LOAD

Point out to students that the items in Exercise A correspond to the types of writing in the Writer's Workshops. If students are working on a cause-and-effect explanation, for instance, you might suggest that they select item 10. If they are writing an eyewitness report, you might assign them to write a showing paragraph for item 3. Students can share their paragraphs with a partner who can give them feedback on the effectiveness of their details. Partners can also work together to generate additional details that will strengthen their showing paragraphs.

Additional Resources

Writing Resource Book, pp. 80–82
Elaboration, Revision, and Proofreading Practice
Elaboration, Revision, and Proofreading Transparency Pack

Answers to Practice Your Skills

A. Answers will vary. Students should use the suggestions in parentheses and the strategies described in the handbook to write their paragraphs. Here is one example of a *showing* paragraph.

1. When we finally reached the lookout at the top of the mountain, my legs ached so much I thought they would collapse under me. I completely forgot the pain, though, when I looked down and saw the beautiful green valley below, dotted with wildflowers. A family of deer had gathered to drink from a stream. A smile spread across my face, and when I looked at my friend, he was smiling, too. There was nothing to say. All we could do was stand there with happy grins on our faces.

B. Answers will vary. Students' paragraphs will reflect a variety of show-don't-tell strategies.

C. Answers will vary. Students' sentences should include specific details and descriptions.

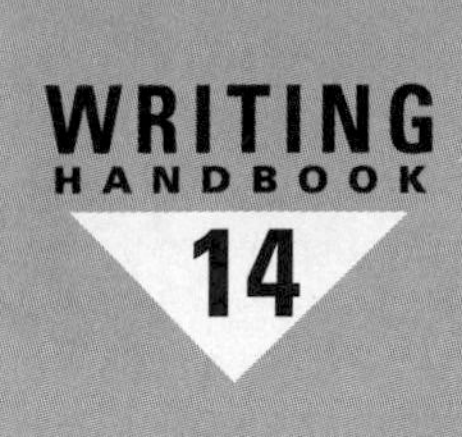

WRITING HANDBOOK 14

Achieving Unity

Objectives

- To understand the concept of unity in paragraphs and compositions
- To use a topic sentence to express the main idea of a paragraph
- To achieve unity in a written paragraph

Related Mini-Lessons

For information on topics related to achieving unity in writing, see the following mini-lessons:

- **Graphic Devices for Writing, pp. 227–231**
- **Types of Organization, pp. 239–243**
- **Developing Paragraphs, pp. 248–251**
- **Revising, pp. 287–289**

Teaching Strategies

GENERAL NOTE

INDIVIDUALIZING INSTRUCTION: BASIC STUDENTS To help students understand the meaning of *unity,* point out that it is related to the words *one* and *unit.* Ask students to identify the three sentences in the first model that are not in the second model. Encourage them to explain why the sentences were removed. Then have students find examples of unified paragraphs in magazines.

WRITING HANDBOOK 14

How Do I Make My Writing Unified?

Achieving Unity

You go to the mall to buy a new pair of jeans and come home with new shoes, a magazine, and two shirts. What happened? You got distracted by the shoe store, the bookstore, and the rack of shirts you had to pass on your way.

As you write, you can become just as distracted by fond memories, vivid details, and interesting ideas. However, if you include everything that interests you, your main idea may not come across very clearly. For example, read the following paragraph.

> What do the scent of seaweed and the aroma of an apple-spice mixture have in common? Both can relax you. Odors can also jog memories. The scent of seaweed makes me think of the beach. Researchers have found that people who sniffed the essence of seaweed became as much as 17 percent calmer than they had been beforehand. People who smelled an apple-spice fragrance were soothed in the same way. Sometimes people scent their homes with apple-spice fragrance.

That paragraph contains many interesting details. Yet the paragraph's main idea isn't very easy to follow. Notice how much more clearly the main idea comes across when the details unrelated to it are removed.

Student MODEL

> What do the scent of seaweed and the aroma of an apple-spice mixture have in common? Both can relax you. Researchers have found that people who sniffed the essence of seaweed became as much as 17 percent calmer than they had been beforehand. People who smelled an apple-spice fragrance were soothed in the same way.

A paragraph has **unity** if all of its sentences support the same main idea or purpose. A composition has unity if all of its paragraphs work together to achieve the same goal. It is usually much easier to grasp the main idea of a unified paragraph, such as the one you just read, than to grasp the main idea of a paragraph lacking in unity. Therefore, as a writer you should always try to give your paragraphs and compositions unity.

WAYS TO ACHIEVE UNITY

To achieve unity in a paragraph, do the following:

- Make sure that your paragraph focuses on one main idea.
- Check to be sure that all of the sentences in the paragraph relate to its main idea.
- Use a topic sentence if necessary.

Follow this advice to achieve unity in a composition:

- Start a new paragraph each time you begin a new idea.
- Make sure that all of the paragraphs in the composition help to achieve its goal.

Performers from the Cirque du Soleil use lights, costumes, movements, and music to create a unified aerial ballet.

Unity with Topic Sentences

A **topic sentence** states the main idea or purpose of a paragraph. Stating your main idea in a topic sentence can help you to stay focused on this main idea as you write and revise. In the following paragraph, the main idea is stated in a topic sentence, and the rest of the sentences help to develop this idea.

Literary MODEL

> Manuel was middle-aged, patient, and fatherly. He bent down on his haunches to talk to kids. He spoke softly and showed interest in what we had to say. He cooed "good" when we made catches, even routine ones.
>
> **Gary Soto, "Baseball in April"**

for WAYS TO ACHIEVE UNITY

HELPFUL HINT To encourage students to think about unity before they write a paragraph, suggest that they first jot down the main idea they intend to develop. After completing the draft, students can read aloud each sentence in the paragraph to check it against the main idea.

for UNITY WITH TOPIC SENTENCES

INDIVIDUALIZING INSTRUCTION: BASIC STUDENTS Explain that the *topic* of a paragraph is what the writing is all about. Point out that a topic can usually be stated in one or two words. Go on to review that a *topic sentence* in a paragraph contains the paragraph's main idea. Invite students to identify the topic sentence in the Literary Model on page 269 (the first sentence).

for UNITY WITH TOPIC SENTENCES

USING THE MODEL Call on students to explain how each of the supporting sentences develops the main idea that Manuel is middle-aged, patient, and fatherly. Also, ask volunteers to create supporting sentences of their own that might be included in this paragraph to develop the topic sentence further.

Science Connection

Call on students to analyze how the authors of their science textbook have used topic sentences. First, have students note the total number of paragraphs in a section or subsection of the text. Then ask them to determine which of the paragraphs contain topic sentences. (Remind them that not every paragraph has a stated topic sentence and that if there is one, it is not necessarily the first sentence in the paragraph.) Discuss with students the main ideas of each paragraph. Finally, ask volunteers to tell how topic sentences help readers focus on the important aspects of a scientific concept.

for UNITY WITHOUT TOPIC SENTENCES

CRITICAL THINKING: ANALYZING Ask students to look through newspaper or magazine articles to find a paragraph that does not have an explicit topic sentence. Have them analyze the paragraph to determine its topic and main idea. Then ask them to draft a topic sentence to include in the paragraph.

for NARRATING AN EVENT

USING THE MODEL Elicit that Michelle Hamilton's goal for this paragraph is to narrate a terrifying event—a canoeing accident in which she almost drowned. Then read the paragraph, stopping after each sentence for a volunteer to tell what detail or details in that sentence support the author's overall goal. Ask students to suggest why the author did not use a topic sentence for this paragraph. (Sample: A topic sentence might diminish the immediacy and horror of the scene.)

for DESCRIBING A CHARACTER

USING THE MODEL After students read the model from "The Medicine Bag," point out that the topic is Grandpa. Then ask students to suggest a topic sentence that tells what the author is saying about Grandpa in this paragraph. To guide students' response, you might point out that the paragraph is organized to compare and contrast. (Sample: Grandpa had taken special care with his appearance on this occasion.) Finally, ask students to suggest why the author chose not to include a topic sentence in this paragraph. (Sample: She wanted to reveal the change in Grandpa slowly to heighten its significance.)

Unity Without Topic Sentences

You do not always have to use a topic sentence to create unity in a paragraph. Instead, you can try the following method:

- Decide on an overall goal for the paragraph.
- Make sure that each sentence supports that goal.

You can use this approach in all kinds of writing. Some examples are given below.

Writing TIP

To create unity in a longer narrative, think of the main event as a series of separate incidents. Then develop each incident in a separate paragraph.

Narrating an Event If your overall goal in writing a paragraph is to capture an event, then make sure that each of your sentences helps to develop this event. For example, each sentence in the following paragraph helps the reader feel a young woman's terror.

> The canoe was thrown violently into the air, and I felt myself free-falling. The boat was gone. I had lost hold of my lifeline. The impact [of the mammoth wave] was so savage it forced the breath from my lungs. I felt myself spiraling down into a current of suffocating foam, buried in a turmoil of furious water. A powerful sucking force was swallowing me. All I could think was, *This is it, Michelle.*
>
> **Michelle Hamilton with Rachelle Hamilton, "Swept to Sea"**

Describing a Character If your overall goal in writing a paragraph is to describe a character, then make sure that all of your sentences tell something about that character. For example, each sentence in the following paragraph describes Grandpa.

> When we got to my house, Grandpa was sitting on the patio. He had on his red shirt, but today he also wore a fringed leather vest that was decorated with beads. Instead of his usual cowboy boots, he had solidly beaded moccasins on his feet that stuck out of his black trousers. Of course, he had his old black hat on—he was seldom without it. But it had been brushed, and the feather in the beaded headband was proudly erect, its tip a brighter white. His hair lay in silver strands over the red shirt collar.
>
> **Virginia Driving Hawk Sneve, "The Medicine Bag"**

Literature Connection

Read the opening paragraph from "The Tell-Tale Heart" by Edgar Allan Poe.

"True!—nervous—very, very dreadfully nervous I had been and am; but why *will* you say that I am mad? The disease had sharpened my senses—not destroyed—not dulled them. Above all was the sense of hearing acute. I heard all things in the heavens and in the earth. I heard many things in hell. How, then, am I mad?"

Have students discuss what all Poe's sentences in this paragraph suggest about the speaker. (Sample: Despite his claims, he does not seem at all sane.)

Practice Your Skills

A. Revise the following paragraph by eliminating those sentences that are unrelated to the main idea stated in its topic sentence.

What do fireflies and vampire bats have in common? They are both nocturnal, or active only at night. By day, fireflies hide. At night, however, they flash a greenish yellow light to find one another. My science teacher says that this blinking is like a mating call. He also says that female fireflies don't have any wings. On the other hand, all vampire bats have big blue-black wings. Vampire bats sleep all day. Then, on dark nights, they fly out in search of other mammals to prey upon. Vampire bats can puncture your skin and drink your blood.

B. Determine the overall goal of the following paragraph. Then revise the paragraph to give it unity by eliminating those sentences that fail to support this goal.

We began hiking into the canyon at high noon without water. There are supposed to be snakes and scorpions at the bottom of the canyon. At the top, mules were the only creatures we saw. Down we marched, the hot sun feeling good on our backs. Two hours later, the sun didn't feel so good. We were sweaty, sunburned, and thirsty. Aloe is supposed to be really good for treating sunburn. On my next hike, I intend to take along plenty of aloe and water. Soon our throats were as dry as the orange canyon dust, so we decided to turn around. That's when we panicked.

C. Create a unified paragraph about one of the following topics. You may use a topic sentence or just make sure that each sentence in your paragraph helps to achieve the same goal.

1. a scary event (getting lost, being chased by a dog)
2. a person who is special to you (friend, relative, teacher)
3. a fun or interesting place (carnival, museum, vacation spot)

Additional Resources

Writing Resource Book, p. 83
Elaboration, Revision, and Proofreading Practice
Elaboration, Revision, and Proofreading Transparency Pack
Guidelines for Writing Assessment and Portfolio Use

Answers to Practice Your Skills

A. Answers may vary. A possible revision is shown below.

What do fireflies and vampire bats have in common? They are both nocturnal, or active only at night. By day, fireflies hide. At night, however, they flash a greenish yellow light to find one another. Vampire bats sleep all day. Then, on dark nights, they fly out in search of other mammals to prey upon.

B. Answers may vary. A possible revision is shown below.

We began hiking into the canyon at high noon without water. Down we marched, the hot sun feeling good on our backs. Two hours later, the sun didn't feel so good. We were sweaty, sunburned, and thirsty. Soon our throats were as dry as the orange canyon dust, so we decided to turn around. That's when we panicked.

C. Answers will vary. A unified paragraph, however, will focus on a single main idea. All sentences in the paragraph should relate to the main idea.

When discussing this feature, call on volunteers to tell why each headline is humorous, or a "howler." For instance, "Juvenile Court to Try Shooting Defendant" was meant to convey the idea that a defendant charged with a shooting was going to trial in juvenile court. Because of the two meanings of *try*, however, the headline suggests the court will attempt to shoot the defendant.

Some students might enjoy drawing cartoons that illustrate the unintended and humorous meanings of the headlines. Other students might enjoy looking for additional headline howlers in their local newspaper.

on the LIGHT side

Headline Howlers

COLD WAVE LINKED TO TEMPERATURES
Daily Sun/Post (San Clemente, CA) 1/17/77

Food is Basic to Student Diet
Bridgeport (CT) Post 1/18/78

Fish and Game to Hold Annual Elections
Berkshire Courier (Great Barrington, MA)

Police Can't Stop Gambling
Detroit Free Press 7/1/75

THE FUTURE IS GETTING CLOSER
Post-Crescent (Appleton, WI)

Lead-lined Coffins Termed Health Risk
The Washington Post

JUVENILE COURT TO TRY SHOOTING DEFENDANT
Deseret News (Salt Lake City, UT)

Town OK's Animal Rule
The Asheville (SC) Citizen 3/2/77

Shut-Ins Can Grow Indoors With Lights
The Miami Herald 7/21/78

Robber Holds Up Albert's Hosiery
Buffalo Evening News 9/19/75

School Board Agrees to Discuss Education
Philadelphia Evening Bulletin 10/8/74

MILK DRINKERS TURN TO POWDER
Detroit Free Press

Man Eating Piranha Mistakenly Sold as Pet Fish
The Milwaukee Journal 7/16/76

272

How Can I Make My Ideas Easy to Follow?

Coherence

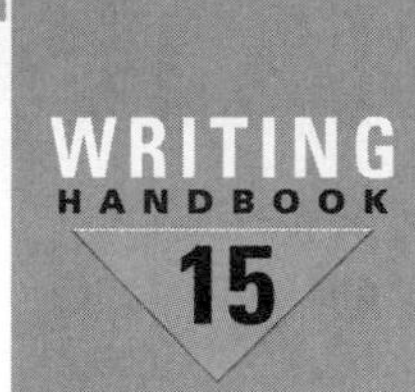

Imagine reading a recipe that first tells you to frost a cake and then tells you to bake it. The recipe would be pretty difficult to follow, and the resulting cake would be a mess. To make details easy to follow, you need to present them in a clear, sensible order. Keep these points in mind as you read the following paragraph.

> Since they were three years old, Judit, Zsuzsa, and Zsofia Polgar have been playing chess with amazing results. At fifteen, Judit became the youngest chess grandmaster ever. The sisters earn enough money from tournaments and appearances to support themselves and their parents. She is now sixteen and the top-ranked female chess player in the world. Judit was beating her father at the game by the age of five. She and her sisters dominated the women's Chess Olympiad when Judit was twelve.

Do you think the information in that paragraph is clear? To decide, compare the paragraph with this revision.

> Since they were three years old, Judit, Zsuzsa, and Zsofia Polgar have been playing chess with amazing results. **By the age of five,** Judit was beating her father at the game. **When Judit was twelve,** she and her sisters dominated the women's Chess Olympiad. **At fifteen,** Judit became the youngest chess grandmaster ever. **Today, at the age of sixteen,** Judit is the top-ranked female chess player in the world. **In addition,** the sisters **now** earn enough money from tournaments and appearances to support themselves and their parents.

The revised version of the paragraph is **coherent**—that is, all of its details flow logically from one to another. To ensure that your paragraphs are coherent, make sure your details are arranged in a sensible order. Then link your details with connecting words that help make their relationship clear.

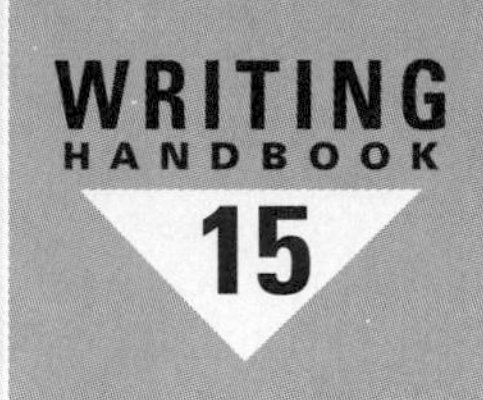

Coherence

Objectives

- To arrange details in a paragraph in coherent order
- To recognize and use transition words that show relationships between details
- To use synonyms to aid coherence and add interest to a paragraph

Related Mini-Lessons

For information on topics related to coherence, see the following mini-lessons.

- **Graphic Devices for Writing, pp. 227–231**
- **Types of Organization, pp. 239–243**
- **Developing Paragraphs, pp. 248–251**
- **Revising, pp. 287–289**

Motivate

Cut a short news story from a local paper into six or more pieces. Place the pieces in a box. Ask volunteers to each take one and read them aloud in random order. Elicit words to describe the result. (Samples: confused, incoherent) Ask the same volunteers to put the pieces in an order that makes sense and to read the result aloud. Elicit words to describe the reassembled story. (Samples: logical, coherent)

Teaching Strategies

for STUDENT MODEL

USING THE MODEL Invite students to tell why the second paragraph about the sisters is easier to follow. (The sentences are in chronological order.) Ask volunteers to explain the purpose of its boldfaced words and phrases. (They link the sentences by showing the time order.)

for USING WORDS THAT CLARIFY RELATIONSHIPS

KEY TO UNDERSTANDING Point out that *transition* comes from a Latin verb meaning "to go across." Students might be familiar with the word *transit* as used to describe bus and train transportation. Suggest that just as a bus or train gets a person from one place to another, a transition takes a reader smoothly from one sentence or detail to another. Have students look again at the boldfaced words and phrases in the Student Model on page 273 and explain how each connects one sentence to the next.

for TRANSITION WORDS AND PHRASES

SPEAKING AND LISTENING Challenge students to find in books and magazines paragraphs that illustrate the six methods of organization or logical relationships shown in the left-hand column of the chart. Have them read aloud to the class the paragraphs they find. Direct students to listen to each paragraph carefully, identify its method of organization, and jot down the words and phrases that serve as transitions.

for TRANSITION WORDS AND PHRASES

INDIVIDUALIZING INSTRUCTION: BASIC STUDENTS Briefly review the different types of organization, using Handbook 8, pages 239–243. Point out to students that they will be able to choose appropriate transitions once they have decided on the type of organization they want to use in a piece of writing.

ESL STUDENTS Students may find that the variety of transition words and phrases available in English is confusing. Encourage these students to refer to the chart and to experiment with various choices in their writing. Pair them with native English speakers who can serve as peer readers, responding to the transitions in the ESL students' writing.

USING WORDS THAT CLARIFY RELATIONSHIPS

The connecting words that show how details are related are called **transitions.** You can use transitions to point out relationships in time and space, to show order of importance, and to show cause-and-effect relationships. You can also use transitions to clarify whether details are similar or different. Look at the following list to become familiar with some of the many words and phrases that can serve as transitions.

Other World (1947), M. C. Escher. © 1947 M. C. Escher/Cordon Art–Baarn–Holland.

Transition Words and Phrases

Chronological Order	first second always then next	later soon before finally earlier	afterwards meanwhile eventually next week tomorrow
Spatial Order	in front behind next to nearest	lowest above below outside	underneath on the left on the right in the middle
Degree	mainly strongest weakest first	second third most important less important	equally important most significant least significant best
Comparison	similarly likewise in addition	like than as	neither . . . nor either . . . or by comparison
Contrast	however by contrast yet	but unlike instead	nevertheless as opposed to on the other hand
Cause and Effect	since because thus therefore	so due to as a consequence accordingly	for this reason if . . . then as a result owing to

ART NOTE

As students study *Other World* on page 274, explain that the Dutch artist M. C. Escher (1898–1972) is known for drawings of recognizable figures and settings in impossible spatial situations. Ask: From what three perspectives do we see this bird figure? (We see it from above, from below, and from the side.) Elicit why the print's spatial relationships seem incoherent. (We are used to looking at things from one perspective.) Point out that closer study reveals that Escher has used details to give the print its own logical coherence. For example, each flat surface in the print serves as a ceiling, a floor, and a wall.

Chronological Order Transitions that show relationships in time help make clear the order in which events occurred, as in the following paragraph.

Literary MODEL

> **Then** we sat on the big snowbank at the edge of the rink and just watched. It was cold **at first** even with my skating pants on, sitting on that hard heap of snow, but **pretty soon** I got warm all over. He threw a handful of snow at me and it fell in a little white shower on my hair and he leaned over to brush it off. I held my breath. The night stood still.
>
> **Maureen Daly, "Sixteen"**

Spatial Order Transitions such as those in the following paragraph help to point out where details are located in space.

> Tall trees grew **down in the canyon** and **leaned out over** a deep hole of clear water. **In the trees** nested hundreds of long-shanked herons, blue ones and white ones with black wing tips. . . . And **beneath them, down in the clear water,** yard-long catfish lay on the sandy bottom, waiting to gobble up any young birds that happened to fall out of the nests.
>
> **Fred Gipson, *Old Yeller***

Degree Transitions can help you to clarify relationships of degree of importance or any other quality. In the following paragraph, transitions rank clues by their degrees of reliability.

> Some people appear older than they actually are. The Carnival age-and-weight guesser Willy "the Jester" Stewart is seldom fooled, however. **Some of the best clues to people's ages,** according to Willy, come from their hands. If a girl is wearing a wedding ring, she's old enough to be married. **A less reliable clue** is braces. Nowadays people may get braces later in life. **The least certain sign of age** may be gray hair. "Gray hair is a fooler," says Willy.

Comparison and Contrast Transitions that introduce points of comparison help readers know when to look for similarities.

for CHRONOLOGICAL ORDER *and* SPATIAL ORDER

INDIVIDUALIZING INSTRUCTION: ADVANCED STUDENTS Invite students to create some original sentences to continue the action in the model paragraph by Maureen Daly. Urge them to use transition words and phrases to relate their sentences chronologically to what has already taken place. Similarly, students working in a small group might expand Fred Gipson's description of the water hole in the canyon and use spatial-order transitions to maintain the coherence of the paragraph.

for DEGREE

CRITICAL THINKING: SYNTHESIZING In the Student Model, transitions rank clues to a person's age by their degrees of reliability. Have students suggest other qualities that might be used to rank details or information (difficulty, usefulness, familiarity). Then ask students to describe a writing task in which they would rank the details by the degrees of one of the qualities mentioned.

PROFESSIONAL NOTEBOOK

Read and discuss this excerpt by William Strunk, Jr., coauthor of *The Elements of Style:*

"In general, remember that paragraphing calls for a good eye as well as a logical mind. Enormous blocks of print look formidable to a reader. . . . Moderation and a sense of order should be the main considerations. . . ."

for WRITER TO WRITER

HELPFUL HINT Discuss the quotation. Ask students to suggest some synonyms for *fluent* (smooth, flowing, eloquent), and have them explain how transitions help create fluent language (by eliminating awkward or confusing breaks between sentences; by making connections clear).

for STUDENT MODEL

HELPFUL HINT Point out that comparison-contrast paragraphs can focus on (1) comparing, or stating similarities; (2) contrasting, or stating differences; or (3) both comparing and contrasting. Ask students to tell which of these patterns the Student Model follows (pattern 3 compares and contrasts).

for CAUSE AND EFFECT

CRITICAL THINKING: ANALYZING Ask students to identify the two cause-and-effect relationships in the Professional Model. *(Cause 1:* The fluid in our bodies is not pulled toward our feet. *Effect 1:* More of this fluid stays in our faces and makes them a little fatter; *Cause 2:* In weightlessness, our spines are not compressed. *Effect 2:* We are about an inch taller while in orbit.)

for USING SYNONYMS

HELPFUL HINT Encourage students to make frequent use of a thesaurus to locate synonyms that would create coherence and variety in their writing. Emphasize the importance of distinguishing the subtle differences in meaning among a group of synonyms, then choosing the most suitable or accurate word for the context and purpose.

WRITER TO WRITER

Fluent language is very important to keep a reader's interest.

Chakkarin Burudpakdee, student, Clementon, New Jersey

Transitions that introduce contrasts signal readers to look for differences. Notice the use of transitions in the next paragraph.

Like mountain bikes, specially designed off-road wheelchairs have enabled thrill-seeking riders to blaze new trails over rocks and down steep mountainsides. **Both** types of all-terrain vehicles let riders whip around sharp corners and fly off jumps. **Unlike** its two-wheeled counterpart**, however,** an off-road wheelchair has four wheels, a low-slung seat, and disc brakes.

Cause and Effect To show that details are linked in a cause-and-effect relationship, use transitions such as *because* and *therefore.* Look at how transitions in the following passage connect weightlessness with some of its effects on appearance.

[When I'm weightless] I *look* a little different, though—all astronauts do. **Since** the fluid in our bodies is not pulled toward our feet as it is on Earth, more of this fluid stays in our faces and upper bodies. This makes our faces a little fatter and gives us puffy-looking cheeks. We are also about an inch taller while in orbit **because** in weightlessness our spines are not compressed.

Sally Ride with Susan Okie, *To Space and Back*

USING SYNONYMS

Sometimes writers weave sentences together with **synonyms**—different words with similar meanings. By linking your sentences with synonyms, you can avoid repetition and add variety as well as

Social Studies Connection

Ask students to review a chapter or unit of their social studies text. Ask them to find paragraphs that illustrate at least three of the types of organization described in this Handbook—chronological order, spatial order, degree, comparison and contrast, and cause and effect. Invite individuals to read paragraphs aloud. As they read, point out any transition words and phrases. Then ask the class to identify the method of organization.

information to your writing. For instance, notice how synonyms of *message* both strengthen the coherence of the following paragraph and add variety to its sentences.

Student MODEL

The principal got the **message** first. He passed the **news** to the teachers. However, a student must have overheard the teachers talking about the **announcement,** for by the afternoon everyone seemed to have the **information.** Of course, by then the **story** had become exaggerated. Still, there must be some truth to the **tale** I heard—and what I heard is that we're all going to be in a movie!

Practice Your Skills

Revise the following paragraphs to improve their coherence. Feel free to rearrange and combine sentences in addition to adding transitions.

1. If you don't want to get struck by lightning during a thunderstorm, this advice is for you. If you're stuck outside, sit or crouch down. Do this away from tall trees. Stay away from water and metal, because they are both good conductors of electricity. Head indoors when it starts raining. That's the best thing you can do.

2. Throughout the day, everybody's body changes in predictable ways. If you're like most people, your mind is most alert during a certain few hours. These are the late morning hours. On the other hand, sometime between 8:00 and 11:00 P.M., you begin to feel sleepy. Between 3:00 and 4:00 P.M., you regain your energy. In those late afternoon hours, athletic activities seem easier than at any other time of day. By comparison, early in the afternoon, your energy level tends to drop. Just before supper time, your senses of taste and smell become quite sharp. However, at the same time, so may your tongue. Five o'clock is prime time for arguments. Your eyesight is at its sharpest at a particular time of day too. That time of day is noon.

for PRACTICE YOUR SKILLS

MANAGING THE PAPER LOAD
Before students start to revise for coherence, have them identify the type of organization used in each paragraph. Then, as students work, move around the room, spot-checking the transitions used and providing help where necessary. When students have finished, call on volunteers to read their paragraphs aloud.

for PRACTICE YOUR SKILLS

INDIVIDUALIZING INSTRUCTION: LD STUDENTS Some students may have difficulty in rearranging the ideas in these paragraphs. Simplify the task by rewriting each sentence of the first paragraph on a strip of posterboard and encouraging students to try out different sequences. Once students are pleased with the basic sequence, you can work with them to add transitions, use synonyms, and combine sentences to improve coherence.

Additional Resource

Writing Resource Book, p. 84

Answers to Practice Your Skills

1. If you don't want to get struck by lightning during a thunderstorm, this advice is for you. The best thing you can do is to head indoors when it starts raining. However, if you're stuck outside, sit or crouch down away from tall trees. Finally, stay away from water and metal because they are both good conductors of electricity.
2. Throughout the day, everybody's body changes in predictable ways. If you're like most people, your mind is most alert during the late morning hours. At noon, your eyesight is at its sharpest. Early in the afternoon, your energy level tends to drop. Later, between 3:00 and 4:00 p.m., you regain your energy and find athletic activities easier than at any other time of day. Just before supper time, your senses of taste and smell become quite sharp. However, at the same time, so may your tongue, since five o'clock is prime time for arguments. Finally, sometime between 8:00 and 11:00 p.m., you begin to feel sleepy.

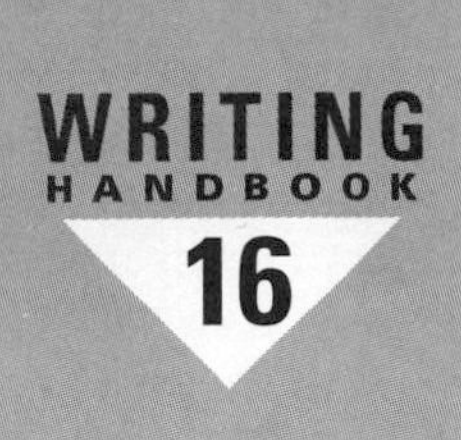

Introductions

Objectives

- To become familiar with various ways to introduce a piece of writing
- To create an effective introduction for a piece of writing

Related Mini-Lessons

For information on topics related to writing introductions, see the following mini-lessons.

- **Methods of Elaboration, pp. 255–261**
- **Meaning and Word Choice, pp. 314–315**

Motivate

Read to students Hemingway's introduction to "The Snows of Kilimanjaro."

> Kilimanjaro is a snow covered mountain 19,710 feet high, and is said to be the highest mountain in Africa. Its western summit is called the Masai "Ngàje Ngài," the House of God. Close to the western summit there is the dried and frozen carcass of a leopard. No one has explained what the leopard was seeking at that altitude.

Ask students what details captured their attention. (Samples: unusual facts, the mystery of the leopard) Discuss why this introduction makes them want to keep reading.

WRITING HANDBOOK 16

How Do I Introduce My Writing?

Introductions

WRITER TO WRITER

The hardest part [of writing] is deciding where to begin.

Amity Baca, student, Denver, Colorado

Amity Baca is not the only writer who has trouble getting started. Most people face that problem at one time or another. One way to get beyond the hurdle of putting down that first word is not to worry about beginning with an introduction. Just start writing any part of your piece that you have ideas about. As you write, your purpose or focus will become clearer. Then you will better know how to begin.

VARIETIES OF INTRODUCTIONS

An introduction has two purposes—to capture your audience's attention and to present the main idea of your writing. There are as many varieties of introductions as there are ways of saying hello. For example, you may say "Hi," "How ya doin'," "What's new?" or just "Hello," depending on the situation. Choosing an introduction is similar. Here are some approaches to try.

Sharing an Unusual Fact

Beginning your writing with a startling or interesting fact can make your audience want to keep reading. Why does the following introduction make you want to learn more about what trees have to say?

Professional MODEL

> Some gardeners talk to their plants. Scientists have learned that plants can "talk," too. During long periods without rain, trees make high-pitched sounds. The message: They're weak from thirst.
>
> ***National Geographic World,* "The Trees Are Talking"**

SPICE BOX

Newspapers and magazines use interesting facts in headlines to lure people to read further. These headlines act as introductions to the articles. Have each student find one unusual fact in a reputable newspaper or magazine and present it to the class as a headline written to capture the interest of a reader.

Presenting a Lively Description

A vivid description can capture your readers' imagination and welcome them into a whole new world. Notice how the following description almost makes you want to put your hands into your pockets to warm them.

> Winter came upon us like the sudden opening of a tomb. Almost overnight it seemed that the last multicolored banners of autumn leaves had been wrenched from the trees by the wind and built up in great moldering piles that smelled like plum cake when you kicked them. Then came the early-morning frost that turned the long grass white and crisp as biscuit, made your breath hang in pale cobwebs in front of you and nipped at your fingertips with the viciousness of a slamming door.
>
> **Gerald Durrell, *A Bevy of Beasts***

Asking a Question

Asking a question in your introduction can get your readers thinking about the answer your writing will provide. The following opening is an intriguing example.

> Do you eat like a bird and still gain weight? Believe it or not, you may be eating in your sleep.
>
> Sleepeating is an unusual but far-from-rare phenomenon, according to Neil Kavey, director of the Sleep Disorders Center at New York's Columbia Presbyterian Medical Center. Kavey recently wired up three people thought to be sleepeaters in a scientific attempt to show that they would try to eat in their sleep. Sure enough, they did.
>
> **Paul McCarthy, "Snacking in Your Sleep"**

Relating an Incident

An interesting or humorous story can draw readers into your writing by making them part of the action. The anecdote on the next page invites readers to share the real-life adventure of four children in a Costa Rican rain forest.

Teaching Strategies

for PROFESSIONAL MODEL

CRITICAL THINKING: PREDICTING Remind students that an introduction presents the main idea of a piece of writing. Have students identify the main idea of the Professional Model. (Sample: Plants can communicate.) Have volunteers predict what the rest of the piece is about. (Sample: studies of plant communication)

for LITERARY MODEL

USING THE MODEL Read aloud the paragraph from *A Bevy of Beasts* and allow students to enjoy the richness of Durrell's language. Draw attention to his use of descriptions that appeal to different senses. Then read the passage again, having volunteers identify the sense to which each descriptive statement appeals. (Samples: "multicolored banners"—sight; "moldering piles . . . like plum cake"—smell; "crisp as biscuit"—touch)

for PRESENTING A LIVELY DESCRIPTION

INDIVIDUALIZING INSTRUCTION: LEP STUDENTS For students learning English as a second language, the concept of "lively" language is an elusive one. Bring in a photograph of a familiar place and elicit from students descriptive words to list on the board. Afterward, help students distinguish the more "vivid" or "lively" words from words such as *nice, good,* and so on.

for PROFESSIONAL MODEL

USING THE MODEL Focusing on the first sentence in the model, point out how McCarthy uses the personal pronoun *you* to address the reader directly and, in so doing, draws the reader into the writing. Note also that McCarthy follows the lead question with an unusual fact, making his introduction even more intriguing.

Literature Connection

Read aloud this famous introduction to O. Henry's "The Gift of the Magi."

"One dollar and eighty-seven cents. That was all. And sixty cents of it was in pennies. Pennies saved one and two at a time by bulldozing the grocer and the vegetable man and the butcher until one's cheeks burned with the silent imputation of parsimony that such close dealing implied. Three times Della counted it. One dollar and eighty-seven cents. And the next day would be Christmas."

Discuss students' reactions to the introduction. Do they want to know what Della does about her problem?

for PROFESSIONAL MODELS

LINKING MECHANICS AND WRITING
Remind students that direct quotations must be enclosed in quotation marks. Draw attention to the punctuation of the dialogue in both models, noting also that commas go inside quotation marks.

for PRACTICE YOUR SKILLS

INDIVIDUALIZING INSTRUCTION: SOCIAL LEARNERS You might allow these students to work in a group to discuss possible techniques before they begin writing introductions for the Practice Your Skills activities.

Additional Practice

Writing Resource Book, p. 85

Answers to Practice Your Skills

A. Answers will vary. A strong introduction, however, will attract the reader's interest and suggest the writer's main idea.

B. Answers will vary. You may wish to have students explore their topics by means of brainstorming, clustering, or some other method before they begin to write.

The roar of a howler monkey boomed through the treetops. Down below, four kids stopped walking and looked up. But the jungle was too dark and thick with leaves for them to see anything. Henri tried to copy the monkey's call. But his yell sounded more like a small hoot than a howl.

"No question who's king of *this* jungle," Cynthia said with a little chuckle. **Chris Wille, "Kids Saved It!"**

Using Dialogue

Quoting people's own words can add interest to an introduction. The following dialogue introduces an article about a driving instructor in New York City.

Professional MODEL

"O.K., start the engine, put your foot on the brake, and put it in D for dumb," Bob Kousoulos said.

Ely Quezada, terror etched on her face, did as instructed.

"Now, remember, I don't know anything," Ms. Quezada said. **N. R. Kleinfield, "It's a Harrowing Drive on the Learning Curve"**

Practice Your Skills

A. Rewrite one of the following weak introductions, using a technique you learned in this handbook.

1. I'm going to tell you how to remember names better.
2. There's no more enjoyable activity than playing basketball. (or building model cars, or walking the dog, etc.)
3. My summer vacation was fun.

B. Choose a writing topic from the following list. Then write *two* different introductions for a piece of writing about that topic.

physical fitness	being different	training a pet
learning to cook	a favorite team's latest victory	allowances
skin care	chocolate	boys' sports and girls' sports
making friends	clothing styles	
household chores		

Music Connection

Many popular songs from earlier generations have introductions. Play one or two of these songs for the class. Some possibilities include "Night and Day," "One Dozen Roses," and "I Left My Heart in San Francisco." Discuss with students how each song's introduction works to grab the listener's attention and to introduce the main idea of the song. You also might point out that such introductions are rare in today's pop music. Have students discuss how their favorite songs are introduced. (Sample: A guitar riff introduces the feeling, rather than the main idea, of many songs.)

How Do I Conclude My Writing?

Conclusions

Think of how good it feels to fit the final piece into a jigsaw puzzle. The picture is complete and everything finally makes sense. In your writing, you can give readers that feeling of satisfaction by ending with a strong conclusion.

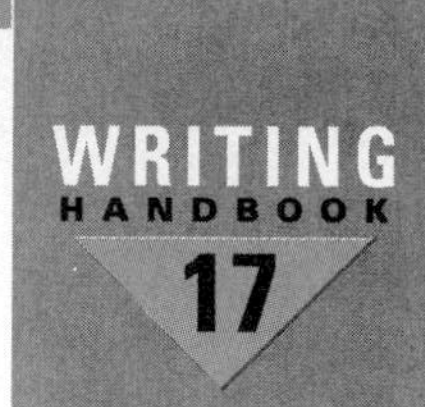

WRITING CONCLUSIONS

There are many ways to end a piece of writing. However, every conclusion should give readers a feeling of completeness. It should leave them with a strong final impression that supports your purpose for writing. It should not introduce new information or unrelated ideas. Here are some types of conclusions that you might try.

Restating the Main Idea

One way to complete your writing is to remind readers of the main points you've made. The following paragraph concludes an essay that presented guidelines for preparing vegetarian meals. Notice how the first sentence of the conclusion links it with what has gone before.

> Using these basic guidelines, it's relatively easy to plan well-balanced vegetarian meals that are low in fat, calories, and cholesterol, as well as high in carbohydrates and fiber. A vegetarian diet can be just as healthy, nutritious, and delicious as any other diet around.
>
> **Carol Bialkowski, "The Veg Edge"**

Asking a Question

Another good way to end your writing is to ask readers a question that sums up what you have told them and leaves them with something to think about. The conclusion shown on the next page does just that.

Science Connection

Explain to students that science writing often concludes by restating the main idea. Have students find in newspapers or magazines examples of science articles that end in this way. Invite them to share their examples with the class.

Conclusionss

Objectives

- To become familiar with a variety of ways to conclude a piece of writing
- To identify well-written conclusions and weak ones
- To write strong conclusions

Related Mini-Lessons

For information on topics related to writing conclusions, see the following mini-lessons.

- **Introductions, pp. 278–280**
- **Revising, pp. 287–289**
- **Meaning and Word Choice, pp. 314–315**

for WRITING CONCLUSIONS

PERSONAL TOUCH Tell students about a story ending that made a strong impression on you, something like the conclusion to Shirley Jackson's short story "Charles." Explain why the conclusion left such a strong impression. Ask volunteers to describe story endings they remember vividly and to explain what made them memorable.

for PROFESSIONAL MODEL

USING THE MODEL Have students identify the main idea in the Bialkowski piece. (Sample: A vegetarian diet can be both healthful and satisfying.) Ask, "What kind of information do you think came before this paragraph?" (Sample: Meal-planning guidelines, nutritional information, perhaps sample menus and recipes) "How can you tell?" (The words *healthy, nutritious,* and *delicious* are clues.)

for MAKING A RECOMMENDATION

HELPFUL HINT Stress to students that when they conclude a piece of writing by making a recommendation, they should be sure that the body of the piece provides information that makes the recommendation seem natural and reasonable. If possible, share with students a newspaper editorial that ends with a recommendation. Discuss how the body of the editorial builds to the recommendation.

for LITERARY MODEL

USING THE MODEL Read the Literary Model aloud to the class. Discuss what the writer means when she refers to the "wall" and the "bricks" between the mother and the narrator. Point out to students that this simple conclusion is a beginning as well—the beginning of a renewed relationship between the mother and the daughter.

With devotees such as [former Lakers basketball star Kareem] Abdul-Jabbar, it's no wonder hatha yoga has become a new fitness craze—it's even been dubbed "yogarobics." So even if you're not quite ready for chanting and not the least bit interested in perfecting the double lotus, you can still enjoy yoga. After all, what other exercise routine builds the mind as much as the body?

Emerald, "Yoga Yo' Body"

Making a Recommendation

When you are writing to persuade, you can use your conclusion to tell readers what you want them to do. The following paragraph concludes an article persuading people that they can get the jobs they want. It tells readers the simple steps for success.

From my standpoint, that's what it's all about. Prepare to win. Never stop learning. Believe in yourself, even when no one else does. Find a way to make a difference. Then go out and make your own tracks in the snow.

Harvey B. Mackay, "Get the Job You Want"

Ending with the Last Event

If you're telling a story—either real or imaginary—you can just end with the last thing that happens. The book *The Pig-Out Blues* tells the story of a young girl's struggle to get along with her mother and to accept herself. It ends with an important moment of understanding.

"I love the spread. It will be perfect for my room. Thank you." She squeezed my hand and started the motor.

"Now, if I were you," Mother said, "I'd do the whole bedroom in vivid colors."

"But I'm not you," I said quietly.

She nodded. Out of the wall that was between us came one brick at a time.

Jan Greenberg, *The Pig-Out Blues*

Literature Connection

Read aloud to the class the conclusion of "To Build a Fire" by Jack London. Discuss with students the impact of this last event.

". . . [T]he man remained silent. Later, the dog whined loudly. And still later it crept close to the man and caught the scent of death. This made the animal bristle and back away. A little longer it delayed, howling under the stars that leaped and danced and shone brightly in the cold sky. Then it turned and trotted up the trail in the direction of the camp it knew, where were the other food-providers and fire-providers."

Generalizing About Your Information

A good way to conclude many types of writing is to make a general statement that shows the overall importance of what you've said. The following paragraph concludes an article about the many roles a father can play in his children's lives. Notice that it clearly explains what all these roles have in common.

Despite all that mothers provide, children feel safe and protected with their fathers. Read into it whatever you want. Nothing can change the need for a dad.

Ralph Kinney Bennett, "What Kids Need Most in a Dad"

Practice Your Skills

A. Decide which of the following conclusions are well written and which are not. Rewrite any weak ones.

1. Together again after twenty years, mother and child walked down the dim corridor into the sunlight of a June morning. Their search for each other was over.
2. Well, that's all I have to tell you about why you should be concerned about the messy conditions in the town park. Please be neater and don't throw stuff in the bushes.
3. No matter which of the after-school clubs you decide to join, you will make new friends, take pride in your new skills, and have an enjoyable time. Club presidents will sign up new members next Tuesday afternoon. Join a club and be an active member of our school.
4. So that's why bike riders should wear safety helmets. I think wearing them is a good idea. Don't you? Furthermore, it would be a good idea for skateboarders to wear helmets too. I should have mentioned that before. Skateboarders can have just as many accidents as bike riders.

B. Choose from your portfolio a piece of writing that you want to revise. Use one of the techniques presented in this handbook to make your conclusion stronger.

GENERAL NOTE

INDIVIDUALIZING INSTRUCTION: LD STUDENTS Some LD students will find it difficult to determine the appropriateness of the "conclusions" in this handbook without additional context. Select short stories and nonfiction that students have read previously and discuss the effectiveness of the conclusions. Make sure students can identify the type of conclusion used in each selection.

Additional Resource

Writing Resource Book, p. 86

Answers to Practice Your Skills

A. Conclusions 1 and 3 are well written. Conclusions 2 and 4 are weak and should be rewritten. Conclusion 2 is too informal and not at all persuasive; conclusion 4 introduces new information.

Rewritten conclusions will vary. Sample conclusions are shown below.

2. The park in the center of town belongs to all of us, and everyone is responsible for it. Please do your share to keep the park clean. Don't litter! The next time you're passing through the park, pick up a piece of trash and put it in a garbage can. If we all do our part, we can make a difference.
4. Riding a bike without wearing a helmet is like walking on a high wire without a net below. There's a chance you'll reach your destination safe and sound; however, if you fall or are hit by a car, a pedestrian, or another biker when you're not wearing a helmet, you could be seriously injured or even killed. Isn't it better to be safe than to be sorry?

B. Answers will vary.

SPICE BOX

Fairy tales almost always end with the last event—but what if the last event were different? For example, Cinderella's feet could have swelled after a night of dancing. What if the glass slipper *didn't* fit? As a group storytelling activity, invite the class to pick a well-known fairy tale and orally revise its conclusion.

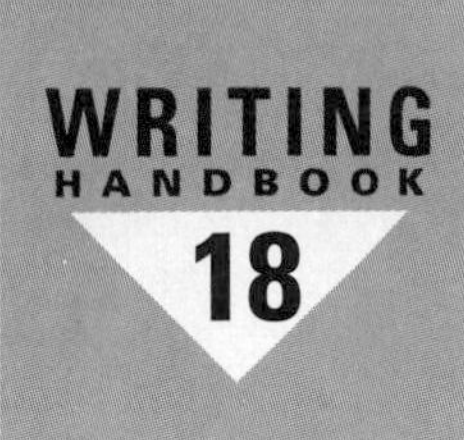

Peer Response

Objectives

- To understand guidelines for giving and receiving peer response
- To practice various peer-response techniques

Related Mini-Lessons

For information on topics related to peer response, see the following mini-lesson.

- Revising, pp. 287–289

Teaching Strategies

GENERAL NOTE

PERSONAL TOUCH To help create a class atmosphere in which students feel comfortable about asking one another for feedback, share with students a first draft of your own. Seek feedback from the class by asking specific questions about your draft. Students will find it helpful to see that your drafts are not perfect, either!

for USING PEER RESPONSE

HELPFUL HINT For the second guideline on seeking peer response, provide examples of questions that require only "yes" or "no" answers, such as the following: Do you like the story? Do you understand my main idea?

Note that page 286 provides examples of questions that will help a writer get specific information.

WRITING HANDBOOK 18

How Can Others Help Me Improve My Writing?

Peer Response

When you were a young child, you picked up crayons, pencils, or pens and scribbled on every scrap of paper you could find. Long before you knew how to form letters or draw objects, you were experimenting with putting ideas and feelings down on paper. Remember how good it felt when people responded to your early work, praising it and displaying it on the refrigerator door?

Sharing your work with others and hearing their responses can be as satisfying now as it ever was. It still feels good when people read your writing and tell you how much they like it. Praise, however, is just one aspect of **peer response**—the comments friends or classmates make about your writing. Working with others on your writing can help you discover new ideas, decide what else you want to say, and see how well you've communicated your ideas.

USING PEER RESPONSE

You can ask peer readers for help at any point in your writing process—from prewriting to final revision. For example, before you begin writing, you might ask your readers how much they know about your topic. Later, you might ask readers to listen to a first draft and tell you where they think you might be headed with your writing. As you revise, you can ask your readers if your organization makes sense or if there's anything else they would like to know. You can also read your draft to a friend without asking for any response at all. This gives you the opportunity to hear what you've written.

You can help your peer readers provide you with the most useful kinds of feedback by following these guidelines:

- Tell your readers where you are in your writing process. Are you still trying out ideas, or have you completed a draft?
- Ask questions that will help you get specific information about your writing—ones that require more than "yes" or "no" answers.

PROFESSIONAL NOTEBOOK

How can you prevent a peer reader from attempting to "fix" his or her partner's work? In *Write On: A Conference Approach to Writing,* Jo-Ann Parry and David Hornsby suggest that the solution begins in teacher-student conferences in which the teacher encourages the student to express ideas and find his or her own answers.

"As the tutors themselves have been through the process of learning skills within a conference situation, they are able to guide their 'student' through the same process and not simply supply the answers."

- Encourage your readers to be open and honest when they respond to your work. It's OK if you don't agree with them—you always get to decide which changes to make.

Just as you may ask others to read and respond to your writing, they may ask the same of you. Follow these guidelines when you act as a peer reader for someone else:

- Be respectful and considerate of the writer's feelings.
- Make sure you understand what kind of feedback the writer is looking for before you respond. If you are asked for help with organization, don't comment on word choice.
- Always use "I" statements. Saying "*I* like your ending" or "It would help *me* understand your point if you would . . ." reminds the writer that your impressions and advice may not be the same as someone else's.

TRYING RESPONSE TECHNIQUES

Four of the most useful peer-response techniques you can use are **pointing, summarizing, replying,** and **identifying problems.** Here is part of a piece of student writing. The writer's questions and the reader's answers on the next page show how these peer response techniques work.

Student **MODEL**

It was a perfect day for a bike ride, and Kim had borrowed her brother's new bike—a shiny red twelve-speed—to ride to a friend's house. Kim rode along Eleventh Avenue, where a new building was going up. She stopped to watch the construction and looked through a hole cut in the wooden fence surrounding the site. Huge bulldozers scooped up mounds of earth. Cranes, like giant mechanical birds, pecked at a pile of lumber.

Kim turned around to get the bike, but it was gone! She could hardly believe it. In the short time that she had stopped to watch the construction, someone had taken the bike. Her brother's bike. The one he had saved his money all year to buy.

GENERAL NOTE

STUMBLING BLOCK Some students may not recognize how the wording of their responses might be hurtful to a writer. To help students understand the importance of wording, ask volunteers to restate these inappropriate responses:

- You always start your sentences the same way. It's boring. (Sample: I'm wondering whether all these sentences need to start the same way.)
- I have no idea what's going on in the second half of the story. (Sample: I'm a little lost in this part of the story.)
- The character of Andrea was just plain silly. You didn't make her believable at all. (Sample: Maybe Andrea would seem more real to me if you. . . .)

for TRYING RESPONSE TECHNIQUES

USING THE MODEL A guided critique of this passage appears on page 286—but before students read it, encourage them to jot down their own thoughts about the piece. Have them note, at least, what they consider its strongest and weakest aspects. Then have them compare their responses to those on page 286.

for SUMMARIZING

CRITICAL THINKING: DRAWING CONCLUSIONS Ask students how the answers to the summarizing questions would help a writer. (The answers would let the writer know whether the piece of writing conveys what he or she intended.)

for REPLYING

HELPFUL HINT Tell students that the replying questions have been designed, in part, to help the writer find out how much more he or she needs to explain to the reader.

Additional Resources

Writing Resource Book, pp. 87–88
Peer Response Guides

Answers to Practice Your Skills

A. Answers will vary. Students should submit their lists of questions for peer readers. Good questions will follow the guidelines on pages 284–285.

B. Responses will vary. Examples of possible responses are shown below.

Pointing: I like your description of the sea animals. Specific words like *scramble* and *sway* really help me see this underwater world.

Summarizing: I think your main point is that creatures have adapted to life in unusual places, even at the bottom of the sea.

Replying: I once read about scientists who explored the deepest parts of the ocean in a submersible called *Alvin.* Would you want to include some information on their experiences?

Identifying Problems: I'm not sure what vents are. It would help me visualize the scene if you define *vents* when you first use the term.

TIP

When you're ready to share your ideas or your writing with others—no matter where you are in your writing process—ask for the kinds of feedback that will be most useful to you. The Peer Response Chart on pages 681–682 will help you identify how and when to ask others for advice.

Pointing "What parts of my draft do you particularly like or dislike? Which words or phrases stick out in your mind—for better or worse?"

> "I like your description of the construction site. I could really see the crane! I like the words *scooped* and *pecked.*"

Summarizing "What do you think I'm trying to say? What's my main idea?"

> "A girl borrows her brother's bike and someone steals it. Now she has to tell her brother about the loss. Is that your story's main idea?"

Replying "What do you know about my topic? Has anything like this ever happened to you? What else do you want to know?"

> "I once borrowed my sister's backpack and then lost it, so I know how Kim feels. I'd like to hear more about what's going on in Kim's mind. What's she going to tell her brother?"

Identifying Problems "Did you have any trouble with my writing? Where did you get lost or confused?"

> "Where was the bike when Kim looked through the fence? Wasn't she on it?"

Practice Your Skills

A. Choose a piece of writing from your portfolio and share it with others. Be sure to ask for the kind of feedback you want.

B. Imagine that the paragraph below is from the first draft of a friend's science report. Your friend is ready for peer response and asks you to point, summarize, reply, and identify problems in the writing. Write your responses to the questions on this page for each of these response techniques.

> Living things have found ways to survive in very unusual places. For example, colonies of giant mussels and clams live in total darkness along volcanic vents in the ocean floor. Ghostly white crabs scramble over the rocks. Enormous tube worms, some measuring ten feet, sway in the ocean's current. How can this underwater world survive without sunlight?

286 Writing Handbook

How Do I Evaluate and Improve My Draft?

Revising

Have you ever made a project out of clay? As you worked, you probably pinched and pulled the clay many ways before the form pleased you.

When you write, you also pinch and pull and reshape. When you revise, you may even end up starting over. Because you are rethinking your ideas, revision involves much more than simply copying your piece and adding a comma or two.

TYPES OF REVISION

The changes you make in your writing usually fall into two categories: revising for ideas and revising for form. When you add new ideas, develop old ones, or delete unrelated ideas, you are **revising for ideas.** When you change the organization and presentation of your ideas, you are **revising for form.** Use the following charts to identify and solve problems in your writing.

Revising for Ideas

Problem	Solution
• My opening isn't catchy enough to make the reader continue reading.	• Begin with an interesting fact, story, or quotation.
• I didn't present my most important idea early enough.	• State the main idea in a sentence near the beginning.
• The reader might need more information or details.	• Add more details in places that left you asking *who, what, where, when, how,* or *why.*
• Some ideas or details are unnecessary. Others distract from the main idea.	• Delete or move any idea that does not relate to the main idea.
• My conclusion doesn't tie my ideas together.	• Summarize the main idea and the supporting details.

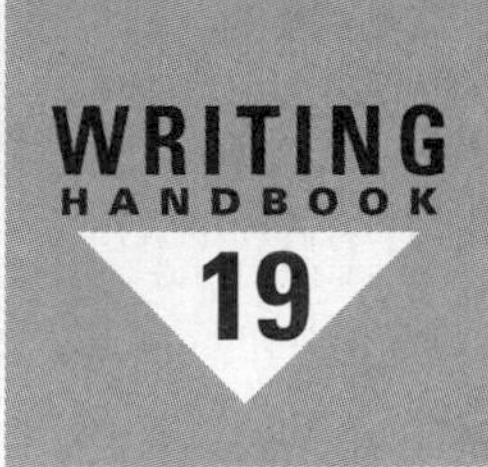

Revising

Objectives

- To recognize the difference between revising for ideas and revising for form
- To revise writing for ideas and for form

Related Mini-Lessons

For information on topics related to revising, see the following mini-lessons.

- **Methods of Elaboration, pp. 255–261**
- **Show, Don't Tell, pp. 262–267**
- **Achieving Unity, pp. 268–271**
- **Correcting Sentence Errors, pp. 296–301**
- **Meaning and Word Choice, pp. 314–315**

Teaching Strategies

for TYPES OF REVISION

HELPFUL HINT Advise students to read through their drafts several times. Each time they may notice and correct different problems in the piece of writing. In addition, suggest that students read their work aloud at least once as they revise; an oral/aural review may reveal strengths and weaknesses that they had not noticed before.

for TYPES OF REVISION

STUMBLING BLOCK Students should not become so intent on distinguishing between "ideas" revisions and "form" revisions that they lose sight of the goal of revising: to make writing vivid and clear. Encourage the use of the charts on pages 287 and 288 as a master revision checklist.

for REVISING FOR FORM AND LANGUAGE

HELPFUL HINT: TRANSITIONS Have students explain the relationship suggested by each of the transition words on the chart. *(Now, later, then,* and *next* show chronological order; *finally* and *therefore* suggest a conclusion; *therefore* also suggests an effect; *however* suggests an exception.) On pages 274–276, students can learn more about transitions.

for STUDENT MODEL

SPEAKING AND LISTENING To make sure that students see how the revisions improved the student draft, read the model aloud without the revisions. Then read the revised version aloud. Discuss each revision that was made and the reason for the change.

GENERAL NOTE

STUMBLING BLOCK If a writer does not have sufficient distance from a work to look at it objectively, revising can sometimes hurt rather than help the draft. Urge students to let their writing "sit" for a while before beginning to revise.

COMPUTER TIP

A word processor makes it easy for you to copy, move, or delete words, sentences, and blocks of text as you revise your writing.

Revising for Form and Language

Problem	Solution
• My readers can't tell where ideas begin and end.	• Start a new paragraph for each idea and for each change of speaker or setting.
• My ideas don't seem to be ordered logically.	• Check the order by jotting down each idea in a time line, a flow-chart, or an outline.
• My ideas don't flow smoothly from one sentence to another.	• Link the sentences, using transition words such as *now, later, then, next, finally, therefore,* and *however.*
• This idea or detail doesn't work well here.	• Move or delete details that aren't related to main idea.
• Another word might get my meaning across better.	• Use a dictionary or thesaurus to find alternative words that state more precisely what you want to say.

The passage below is from a writer's first draft. Notice the various revision strategies used to revise the draft.

Student MODEL

Loggerheads are the most common kind of sea turtle. They have thick, reddish brown shells and huge heads. ^The shape of their head gives them their name.^ They are ~~powerful~~ ^good^ swimmers and can travel more than forty miles a day. They live in tropical waters around the globe. Adults ^can^ weigh as much as 450 pounds. ¶ These ancient creatures are now in danger. ~~Green turtles are, too.~~ Each year ~~many~~ thousand^s of^ loggerheads drown in shrimp nets. Others choke on plastic trash ^floating in the sea^. Their nesting sites on beaches have been destroyed by homes and hotels. Loggerheads are now a threatened species.

Detail added

More accurate word

Moved sentence up to keep related details together

Begin a new paragraph for each new idea

Not related to the topic

Detail added

Practice Your Skills

A. Revise the passage below, making any changes in ideas or form you think are needed. Delete unrelated ideas or details.

Dolphins use sound in special ways. Bats do too. Dolphins have a special organ, called the melon, on their forehead. The fatty tissue in the melon lets dolphins focus sound waves into narrow beams. These sound waves are powerful enough to stun fish. The sound waves are also used to communicate. Dolphins are very intelligent in captivity. People are only now discovering how complex and varied dolphin "speech" is. Dolphins use squeaks and whistling noises to talk to one another. Some whistles are "names." Other whistles warn of danger and identify sources of food. The whistles let one dolphin tell other dolphins who it is and where it is. Many experiments are underway to learn more about it.

B. Select a piece of your writing you wish to review again or a piece of writing you are currently developing. Revise it for ideas and for form, using the charts to help you. Then discuss your revisions with one or more classmates. Explain why you made each change.

C. Revise the passage below. Make any changes in ideas or form you think are needed. Delete unrelated ideas or details.

Even today we have much to fear from the great power of natural forces. We don't have the knowledge yet to predict with total accuracy when volcanoes will go off. We have no control at all over the shifting of the giant plates of rock forming the crust of the earth. We also can't predict when earthquakes will occur. Our knowledge of weather is just as limited. On radar we can see a hurricane forming. We can't tell accurately if or where it will hit land until just before it does. Have you ever seen a hurricane? It's really something. We cannot prevent droughts or control the causes of major floods. We can make artificial snow, though. Scientists are hard at work trying to understand all these forces. Maybe within our lifetime they will find the answers.

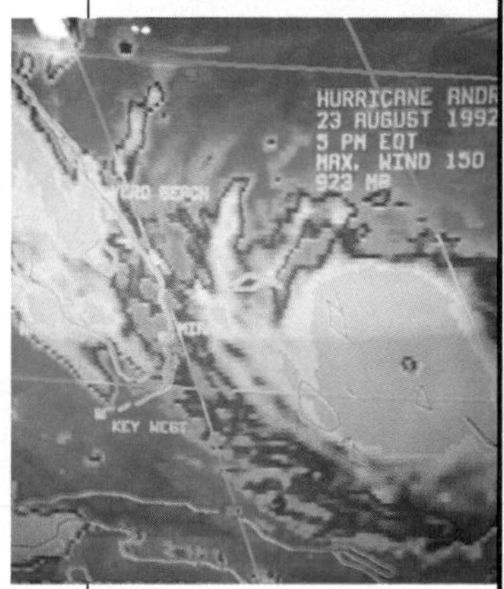

A satellite view of Hurricane Andrew as it passed over the Bahamas on its way to Florida on August 23, 1992.

for PRACTICE YOUR SKILLS

COOPERATIVE LEARNING You might allow students to work with partners or in small groups to complete Exercises A and C.

Answers to Practice Your Skills

A. Revisions may vary. In this sample, a paragraph break was added. Two unrelated sentences were deleted: "Bats do too" and "Dolphins are very intelligent in captivity." Italicized words and sentences were changed or moved.

Dolphins use sound in special ways. *They* have a special organ, called the melon, on their forehead. The fatty tissue in the melon lets dolphins focus sound waves into narrow beams. These sound waves are powerful enough to stun fish. The sound waves are also used to communicate.

Scientists are only now discovering how complex and varied dolphin "speech" is. Dolphins use squeaks and whistling noises to talk to one another. Some whistles are "names." *The whistles let one dolphin tell other dolphins who it is and where it is.* Other whistles warn of danger and identify sources of food. Many experiments are underway to learn more about *how dolphins communicate.*

B. Revised drafts will vary but should show changes in ideas, form, and language.

C. Revisions will vary. In this sample, two paragraph breaks were added. Three unrelated sentences were deleted: "Have you ever seen a hurricane? It's really something" and "We can make artificial snow, though." Italicized words and sentences were changed or moved.

Even today we have much to fear from the *tremendous* power of natural forces. We don't have the knowledge yet to predict with total accuracy when volcanoes will *erupt. We also can't predict when earthquakes will occur.* We have no control at all over the shifting of the giant plates of rock forming the crust of the earth.

Our knowledge of weather is just as limited. On radar we can see a hurricane forming. *However,* we can't tell accurately if or where it will hit land until just before it *happens.* We *also* cannot prevent droughts or control the causes of major floods.

Scientists are hard at work trying to understand all these forces. Maybe within our lifetime they will find the answers.

Additional Resources

Writing Resource Book, p. 89
Elaboration, Revision, and Proofreading Practice
Elaboration, Revision, and Proofreading Transparency Pack

Proofreading

Objectives

- To recognize and use strategies for proofreading
- To recognize proofreading symbols

Related Mini-Lessons

For information on topics related to proofreading, see the following mini-lesson.

- **Correcting Sentence Errors, pp. 296–301**

Motivate

Ask students if they have ever seen someone in a play, concert, dance program, or live TV show make a mistake. Point out that writing has the advantages of a taped production—writers, like TV editors, can check their presentation, eliminate any errors, and put it in top shape before sharing it with the public.

Teaching Strategies

for STRATEGIES FOR PROOFREADING

PEER RESPONSE Suggest that students ask a peer to proofread their writing after their own first proofreading. Point out that someone unfamiliar with the writing might be more likely to notice errors.

for PROOFREAD MORE THAN ONCE

HELPFUL HINT Suggest that students try reading their writing aloud. They will read more slowly and thus may spot errors they would otherwise miss. Alternatively, suggest that as they proofread, students slow down their reading speed by pointing to each word and punctuation mark with a finger or pencil.

WRITING HANDBOOK 20

How Can I Polish My Writing?

Proofreading

Before a space shuttle takes off from its launch pad at Cape Canaveral, technicians at mission control always perform a last-minute check of the shuttle's vital systems. The ship's computers must be operating correctly, fuel pressure must be at the right level, electrical systems must check out. The shuttle doesn't fly until all the status lights at mission control are green.

Before you present your writing to a public audience, you, too, should perform a last-minute check. You'll want to look for and correct run-on sentences, incorrect verb tenses, and errors in capitalization, punctuation, spelling, and pronoun usage. Don't let your writing "fly" until everything checks out properly.

STRATEGIES FOR PROOFREADING

The following proofreading strategies will help you to search for and correct errors in your writing:

Proofread more than once. Don't try to catch every possible error in just one proofreading session. Proofread your writing several times, perhaps looking for different kinds of mistakes each time. Put aside your writing between proofreadings. When you go back to it, you may see errors you didn't notice before.

Proofread for complete sentences and end punctuation. Look over your sentences. Is each one actually a sentence? Does it have a subject and a verb? Does it express just one complete thought? When you're satisfied that you've eliminated any fragments or run-ons, check your end punctuation. First decide whether each sentence makes a statement, asks a question, or expresses a strong feeling. Then be sure you've used the correct end punctuation for each type of sentence.

Proofread for initial capitals. Remember that every sentence should begin with a capital letter. Also, read carefully to identify proper names and be sure that they begin with capital letters.

PROFESSIONAL NOTEBOOK

In "Proofreading: The Skill We've Neglected to Teach," teacher Jan Madraso suggests limiting the focus of proofreading:

"[S]tudents need to be aware of their own weaknesses, those errors repeatedly pointed out by their readers and teachers (not just their English teachers). It is impractical to think that even the most motivated student would be able to proofread for all possible errors. I give students who have many areas of difficulty gentle guidance to help them choose only a few areas to focus on."

February 1993 *English Journal*

Proofread for commas within sentences. Notice where you pause naturally as you read your writing aloud. Such a pause may mean that a comma is needed.

Proofread for other punctuation. Be sure that you correctly used punctuation marks in abbreviations, dates, and addresses. For quotation marks, parentheses, and other punctuation marks used in pairs, be sure that you used both opening and closing marks.

Proofread for confusing words. Watch for such words as *your* and *you're, peace* and *piece,* and *accept* and *except* that are often misused and misspelled.

Proofread for spelling. Check the spelling of each word by reading your writing backwards, one word at a time. When you think a word may be misspelled, circle it. Then use a dictionary to check the spelling of all the circled words.

Proofreading Checklist

Step 1: Check the forms of words.

- Did I use correct verb tenses?
- Did I use any adjectives where I should have used adverbs?
- Did I use *-er/-est* and *more/most* correctly in comparisons?
- Did I use all forms of *be* and other irregular verbs correctly?
- Did I use the correct forms of pronouns?

Step 2: Check sentence structure and agreement.

- Are there any run-on sentences or sentence fragments?
- Do all verbs agree with their subjects?
- Do all pronouns agree with their antecedents?
- Did I keep all verb tenses consistent?

Step 3: Check capitalization, punctuation, and spelling.

- Did I use the correct form for every plural noun?
- Did I capitalize the first word of each sentence?
- Did I capitalize all proper nouns and proper adjectives?
- Is any punctuation mark missing or not needed?
- Did I spell all words, including possessive forms, correctly?

for PROOFREAD FOR SPELLING

HELPFUL HINT Suggest that students become aware of the words that they frequently misspell. You could recommend creating a personal list of spelling "demons." Then students, when proofreading for spelling, can focus especially on such words. You also might encourage students by sharing your own spelling weaknesses—those words that you always look up in a dictionary.

for PROOFREADING CHECKLIST

INDIVIDUALIZING INSTRUCTION: BASIC STUDENTS Scale down the Proofreading Checklist for basic students, suggesting that they focus on just one or two types of errors. For example, if you wish them to focus on verbs, suggest they use separate slips to check their writing for different factors:

Step 1: correct verb tenses and correct forms of the verb *to be* and other irregular verbs; Step 2: consistent verb tenses and agreement of subject and verb; Step 3: correct spelling of verb forms, especially those ending in *-ing* and *-ed.*

for PROOFREADING SYMBOLS

MODELING You might demonstrate the use of each proofreading symbol by using one set of transparencies from the Elaboration, Revision, and Proofreading Transparency Pack with the class as a whole.

for PRACTICE YOUR SKILLS

HELPFUL HINT Remind students to use the proofreading strategies and checklist on pages 290–291 as they complete the Practice Your Skills exercise.

Additional Resources

Writing Resource Book, p. 90
Elaboration, Revision, and Proofreading Practice, especially pp. 25–35
Elaboration, Revision, and Proofreading Transparency Pack

Answers to Practice Your Skills

Corrections are shown in boldface type.

The Call of the Wild is more than a book about a **dog. It's** a book about survival. The hero is a dog **named** Buck. Buck is **stolen** from his home in **California** and taken to the Arctic. The land is hostile. In the winter, the **temperature** can reach sixty-six degrees below zero. The dogs that pull the dog sled are hostile. They fight like **wolves.** Any dog that falls in a fight is **killed** by the pack. The dog trainers **are** hostile. They use clubs to make the **dogs** obey. **The** dogs that **don't** are killed. Buck survives **because** he is smart. He can adapt, and other dogs can't. **Buck's** primitive instincts take over.

Use these proofreading symbols to mark the changes you want to make in your draft.

Proofreading Symbols

Symbol	Meaning	Symbol	Meaning
∧	Add letters or words.	/	Make a capital letter lowercase.
⊙	Add a period.	¶	Begin a new paragraph.
≡	Capitalize a letter.	∼	Switch the positions of letters or words.
⁀	Close up space.	— or ℓ	Take out letters or words.
∧,	Add a comma.		

Notice how the symbols are used in the following passage.

> Beetles were eating Austrailla's cane sugar. So australians imported cane toads to eat the Beetles⊙ since the beeteles fly and the toad∧s don't,∧ the plan has worked not well. Now the people do'n't know how to get rid of the toads.

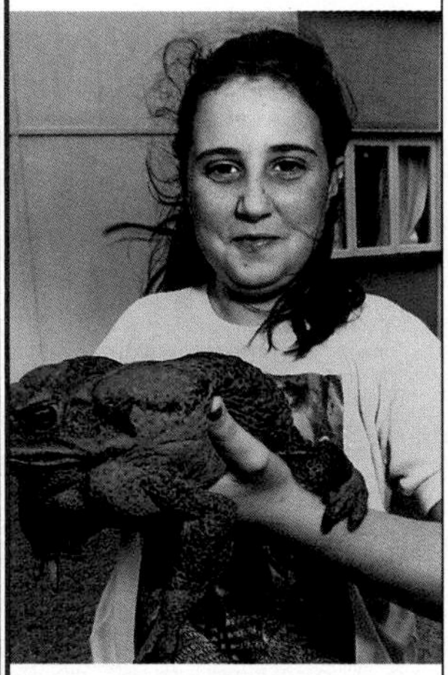

Possibly the world's largest cane toad, weighing in at almost four pounds, this specimen was found by Myrt and John Deambrogio in northeastern Australia.

Practice Your Skills

Proofread the passage below for mistakes in grammar, capitalization, punctuation, and spelling. Rewrite the passage correctly.

The Call of the Wild is more than a book about a dog it's a book about survival. The hero is a dog name Buck. Buck is stole from his home in california and taken to the Arctic. The land is hostile. In the winter, the temperture can reach sixty-six degrees below zero. The dogs that pull the dog sled are hostile. They fight like wolfs. Any dog that falls in a fight is kill by the pack. The dog trainers is hostile. They use clubs to make the dogs' obey. the dogs that dont are killed. Buck survives cuz he is smart. He can adapt, and other dogs can't. Bucks primitive instincts take over.

SPICE BOX

Point out how important checking commas is. Write these pairs of sentences and have students tell how the addition or removal of a comma changes the meaning.

Do not break your crackers, or roll in your soup.
Do not break your crackers or roll in your soup.
Shall I stick the stamps on myself?
Shall I stick the stamps on, myself?
The movie ended happily.
The movie ended, happily.

Challenge students to write an original sentence and then to change its meaning by adding or removing a comma.

How Can I Publish My Writing?

Sharing and Publishing

WRITING HANDBOOK 21

When you perform in a talent show, run in a race, or compete in a band contest, you are sharing your achievements by letting others see your accomplishments. But how do you share a poem or a story that you have written? You announce its completion. You publish it!

WAYS TO SHARE AND PUBLISH YOUR WRITING

When possible, share and publish your writing in a creative way. Here are a few suggestions.

Creative Publishing Ideas

- Present writing that is related to a special day or event over the school's public address system or at a school assembly.
- Include the finished product in a collection of your other writings. Add a cover, an acknowledgment page, and a table of contents. Then display the book in your classroom or elsewhere in the school.
- Work with friends and classmates to dramatize one of your scripts or to perform a song for other classes, for parents, or for interested community groups.
- Submit your writing to the school or community newspaper, to magazines that publish student writing, or to organizations that sponsor writing contests.
- Tape-record your writing, and illustrate the writing with transparencies. Then use an overhead projector to show the illustrations to the class as you play the tape.
- Read one of your short stories aloud to a class of younger students. Ask the students to illustrate parts of the story on a roll of paper. Display the finished product on a wall.

Sharing and Publishing

Objective

- To recognize creative ways of sharing writing with others

Related Mini-Lessons

For information on topics related to sharing and publishing, see the following mini-lessons.

- **Audience, pp. 234–235**
- **Forms of Writing, p. 238**

Motivate

If possible, invite a published author of young adult books to speak to the class. Have the writer describe what having writing published has taught him or her.

Teaching Strategies

for CREATIVE PUBLISHING IDEAS

HELPFUL HINT Note that many students may need to become accustomed to sharing their writing, first with a partner and then with a small group of peers, before they will feel comfortable presenting their work to a larger audience. Allow students to set their own goals and choose their own means of publishing their work.

for CREATIVE PUBLISHING IDEAS

INDIVIDUALIZING INSTRUCTION: KINESTHETIC LEARNERS Dramatizations enable kinesthetic learners to become physically involved in their learning process. Students who are encouraged to act out their finished stories or scripts are more likely to complete their writing assignments with enthusiasm.

Objective

- To use writing prompts and a photograph as springboards to informal writing

WRITING WARM-UPS

Remind students that these Sketchbook activities will not be graded. Students should have fun and feel free to experiment. Urge students to respond to at least one of the prompts and encourage them to share and save their responses.

Because all the prompts require students to think about the word *style,* you might have them freewrite or create a cluster about the word before beginning to write.

If students select the second prompt, make sure they realize that they must compare a pop singer with a classical singer. Ask students if they recognize the pop singer (Annie Lennox); point out that the classical artist is Kathleen Battle. If possible, play an example of each singer's work to help students contrast the two.

WRITING WARM-UPS

- What style of music is your favorite? Tell why you like it.
- If the singer on this page met the singer on the next page, what would they talk about? Write the dialogue of their conversation. Try to use words that show the personalities of both musicians.
- What can you tell about people by the way they dress?

Style

When a classical singer like Kathleen Battle learns a new piece, she starts with the written notes. She soon adds her own interpretation, however. Her personal style comes through.

You, too, have your own personal style. The way you talk, the way you dress, the way you act, and the way you think are all your own. So is the way you write. In these handbooks you will learn ways you can make your unique qualities come through in your writing.

Style

Objectives

- To correct run-on sentences, sentence fragments, and other errors in problem sentences
- To achieve sentence variety through sentence combining, the addition of phrases and clauses, and other methods
- To make appropriate word choices based on denotation, connotation, the audience, and the occasion
- To work toward developing a personal voice
- To use figurative language and sound devices
- To identify point of view
- To write dialogue

INTRODUCING THE HANDBOOKS

Have a volunteer describe the scene in the photograph. Ask students to point out details (such as costumes and facial expressions) that suggest the style of the music or of the singer.

Explain that the way in which a writer organizes sentences, as well as the words and phrases a writer uses to express ideas represent the writer's style. Point out that the styles of various writers can be as dramatically different as musical styles—or types of personality. Tell students that in the handbooks that follow, they will learn how to develop their own unique styles.

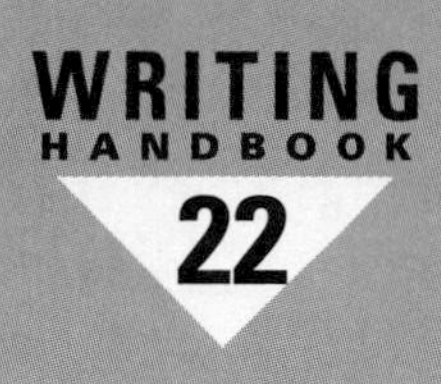

Correcting Sentence Errors

Objective

- To identify and revise sentence fragments, run-ons, stringy sentences, empty sentences, and padded sentences

Related Mini-Lessons

For more information relating to correcting problem sentences, see the following mini-lessons.

- **Revising, pp. 287–289**
- **Proofreading, pp. 290–292**
- **The Sentence and Its Parts, pp. 381–414**

Teaching Strategies

for CORRECTING SENTENCE FRAGMENTS

KEY TO UNDERSTANDING Point out that fragments are very common in speech. In the context of a conversation, the exchange of ideas is rapid, and complete sentences are often unnecessary. Also explain that when people are talking, incomplete sentences are easier to understand because the listener may be able to see the speaker's gestures and expressions and hear the intonations of the speaker's voice. In writing, these clues do not exist, so careful structuring of sentences is critical.

WRITING HANDBOOK 22

How Can I Create Strong Sentences?

Correcting Sentence Errors

What an experience! There were auditions. For a whole week. The best part was performing. Because we all wore costumes.

Talking with a friend about drama club, you would probably have no trouble understanding these words. Reading these words, however, might leave you confused about where thoughts begin and end. This handbook will help you identify and revise problem sentences so that you can communicate clearly and concisely.

REVISING SENTENCE FRAGMENTS AND RUN-ONS

Sentence fragments and run-ons interfere with a reader's understanding. A fragment leaves out a major part of a sentence. A run-on contains two or more sentences that should be separate.

Correcting Sentence Fragments

Do some of your sentences leave a reader asking *whom* or *what* the sentence is about or *what happened?* A **sentence fragment** does not express a complete thought. The subject, the verb, or sometimes both are missing. Often you can change a fragment into a complete thought by supplying the missing part.

Fragment For almost a week *(What happened?)*
Sentence For almost a week we rehearsed.

Other times you can join the fragment to an existing sentence.

Sentence The best part was performing.
Fragment Because we all wore costumes
Revised The best part was performing because we all wore costumes.

296 Writing Handbook

Rewriting Run-on Sentences

Watch for sentences that do not clearly show where one idea ends and the next one begins. A **run-on sentence** consists of two or more sentences written incorrectly as one. Run-ons may occur because the writer either used no end mark or used a comma instead of a period to end the first complete thought. One way to revise a run-on is to use the proper end mark after the first sentence and to capitalize the first letter of the next sentence.

Run-on Scottie raced up the court his defender closed in.
Revised Scottie raced up the court. His defender closed in.

Run-on The referee watched closely, Scottie took his time.
Revised The referee watched closely. Scottie took his time.

If the ideas are closely related, you may revise the run-on by joining the ideas with a semicolon.

Run-on Scottie faked a shot, his defender wasn't fooled.
Revised Scottie faked a shot; his defender wasn't fooled.

Grammar **TIP**

Remember that a comma is not strong enough to join two complete thoughts.

Practice Your Skills

A. Correct each sentence fragment in the following passage.

What's your hobby? Some people enjoy doing ceramics. Because it relaxes them. They enjoy watching the clay take shape. As their hands and fingers move. Other people are collectors. They collect things such as stamps. Baseball cards. Or comic books. Some people race remote-control cars. And airplanes. Whatever your hobby is. Invite a friend to join you.

B. Improve the following paragraphs. Revise each run-on sentence.

Why not visit a county fair this summer? County fairs are exciting city people in particular enjoy these festivals.

Teenagers show their farm animals in the livestock contest, everyone is nervous. Judges inspect each animal they award blue ribbons to the best.

Other activities are entertaining too. You're assured of some fun at the pig race, you can cheer your favorite logger in the lumberjack contest, don't miss out on the fun!

for REWRITING RUN-ON SENTENCES

CRITICAL THINKING: ANALYZING

Remind students that a run-on sentence contains two or more subject-verb pairs. Tell students that "Scottie raced" is one subject-verb combination in the first sample sentence. Ask students to identify the other pair ("defender closed"). Have students find the subject-verb pairs in the other two sample run-ons. Then emphasize that the best way to avoid writing run-ons is by identifying the subject-verb pairs in sentences and checking the punctuation between sentences.

for PRACTICE YOUR SKILLS

INDIVIDUALIZING INSTRUCTION: AUDITORY LEARNERS Auditory learners tend to be sensitive to the cadence and rhythm of language. Suggest that students record the sentences in Exercise B and then play back the tape, listening to identify where thoughts begin and end.

Answers to Practice Your Skills

A. Answers may vary. See typical answers below.

What's your hobby? Some people enjoy doing ceramics because it relaxes them. They enjoy watching the clay take shape as their hands and fingers move. Other people are collectors. They collect things such as stamps, baseball cards, or comic books. Some people race remote-control cars and airplanes. Whatever your hobby is, invite a friend to join you.

B. Answers may vary. See typical answers below.

Why not visit a county fair this summer? County fairs are exciting. City people in particular enjoy these festivals.

Teenagers show their farm animals in the livestock contest. Everyone is nervous. Judges inspect each animal; they award blue ribbons to the best.

Other activities are entertaining too. You're assured of some fun at the pig race. You can cheer your favorite logger in the lumberjack contest. Don't miss out on the fun!

for REVISING STRINGY SENTENCES

KEY TO UNDERSTANDING: USING *AND* Point out that the word *and* is used to connect related ideas that are of equal importance. When ideas that are not related or not equally important are connected with *and,* stringy sentences may result. Have students review a piece of their writing, circling every *and.* You may wish to have volunteers read aloud sample sentences containing two or more *and*s. As a class, discuss which ideas would be better linked with one of the other connecting words listed.

for REVISING STRINGY SENTENCES

CRITICAL THINKING: CLASSIFYING Point out that the words listed express types of relationships. Help students classify the words according to their function in a sentence. For example, *because* and *if* signal a cause-and-effect relationship; *when, after, then, next, later, soon,* and *until* show chronology or sequence.

Answers to Practice Your Skills

Answers may vary. Typical answers are shown below.

1. Greg's front tire has hit a bump, and he has lost control. The bike is swerving into the railing. Greg's chance to win the Tour de France is gone now.
2. The conductor looked angry as the woman searched nervously for the ticket. When she dumped out the entire contents of her purse, she found the crumpled stub.
3. Ada began to make the batter. When she went to get the eggs, she found she was one short. She would have to go to the store.

REVISING STRINGY SENTENCES

Do your sentences go on and on? A **stringy sentence** loosely connects two or more ideas with the word *and.*

Stringy The temperature fell below zero, and a water main under the street burst, and soon we had our own skating rink, and then a work crew turned the water off.

A reader may have difficulty sorting out the ideas and seeing the relationship between them. To revise the sentence begin by separating each of the ideas.

Separate ideas The temperature fell below zero.
A water main under the street burst.
Soon we had our own skating rink.
Then a work crew turned the water off.

Think about how ideas are related and combine them with words such as *because, when, after, before, if, then, next, later, soon, although, as,* and *until.* To clearly show the relationships, you can also rearrange and reword the other ideas or leave them separate.

Revised A water main under the street burst when the temperature fell below zero. Soon we had our own skating rink. Then a work crew turned the water off.

Practice Your Skills

Separate the ideas in each stringy sentence. Then recombine the closely related ideas and rearrange and reword as necessary.

1. Greg's front tire has hit a bump, and he has lost control, and the bike is swerving into the railing, and Greg's chance to win the Tour de France is gone now.
2. The woman searched nervously for the ticket, and the conductor looked angry, and she dumped out the entire contents of her purse, and she found the crumpled stub.
3. Ada began to make the batter, and she went to get the eggs, and she found she was one short, and she would have to go to the store.

SPICE BOX

Composing stringy sentences can be made into a storytelling game. Have each student in turn say a narrative sentence, ending it with the word *and.* The next student adds another sentence to the string, developing the narrative and again ending with *and.* You might want to record the game and play back the final sentence for students' amusement. Use this activity to point out how ridiculous stringy sentences can become.

4. The wind was blowing, and many garbage cans toppled over, and soon the whole block became covered with debris.
5. The doorbell rang, and I answered it, and a person in a delivery service uniform handed me a mysterious package.

REVISING EMPTY SENTENCES

Check that each of your sentences really contributes to the ideas you are expressing. An **empty sentence** either repeats an idea or makes a claim without giving enough supporting details.

Eliminating Repeated Ideas

If the words in different parts of a sentence or in several sentences have the same meaning, delete the repeated idea.

Repetitive Are you a procrastinator, and do you put things off until tomorrow? (A procrastinator is a person who puts things off. Delete the second clause.)

Revised Are you a procrastinator?

Sometimes you can combine sentences so that an idea is not repeated.

Repetitive The canoe trip began at the river's source and ended at the mouth. The canoeists paddled the whole river. Then they continued into Lake Erie. (You can delete the second sentence and combine the first and third sentences.)

Revised The canoe trip began at the river's source and continued to the river's mouth and into Lake Erie.

Adding Supporting Details

Watch for sentences that leave a reader asking *why?* Always support a claim with reasons, facts, or examples.

Unsupported Musicals are the best shows to see. (The sentence does not explain why they are the best.)

Revised Musicals are the best shows to see because the lyrics tell a story and the dances are fun to watch.

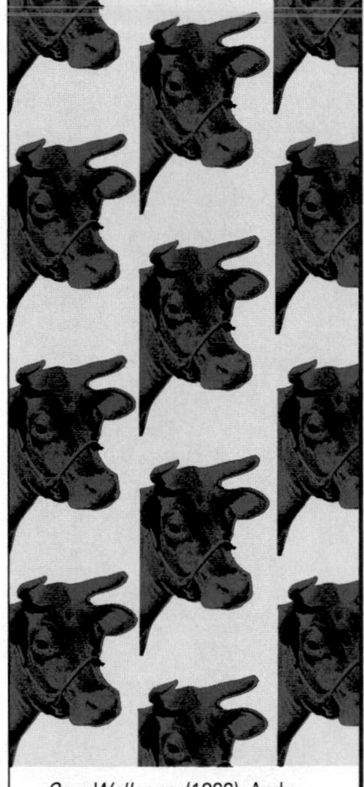

Cow Wallpaper (1966), Andy Warhol.

4. Because the wind was blowing, many garbage cans toppled over. Soon the whole block became covered with debris.
5. When the doorbell rang, I answered it. A person in a delivery service uniform handed me a mysterious package.

for REVISING EMPTY SENTENCES

KEY TO UNDERSTANDING Have volunteers read aloud the sample repetitive and unsupported sentences on this page. Ask: Are these sentences grammatically correct? (yes) Use students' responses to emphasize that while sentence fragments and run-ons are grammatically incorrect, empty sentences are not necessarily so; they simply repeat or fail to provide information.

for ADDING SUPPORTING DETAILS

HELPFUL HINT Remind students that whenever they add details to sentences, they should make relationships between ideas clear. Refer students to the list of connecting words on page 298. You might also refer them to Handbook 44, pages 543–544, for more information on the use of conjunctions.

ART NOTE

Andy Warhol (1930?–1987) was a member of the pop art movement of the 1960s. Pop artists often depicted everyday objects and frequently used commercial art techniques like silk screening, one of Warhol's favorite methods. Many of his most famous works consist of repeated images, such as tomato soup cans and soap pad boxes. Ask students to comment on the repeated image in *Cow Wallpaper.* What effect did it have on them?

Answers to Practice Your Skills

Answers may vary. Typical answers are shown below.

1. Many athletes have quick reflexes.
2. Swimming is good for you because it exercises all the major muscle groups without putting stress on the bones and joints.
3. Ten thousand people went to last night's open-air concert in the park, but everyone had to leave when the downpour started.
4. Correct
5. Correct
6. Richard shared a secret with me.

for REVISING PADDED SENTENCES

STUMBLING BLOCK Point out that padded sentences sometimes occur when students are writing to meet a required essay length. If students find themselves padding their writing for this reason, suggest that they take a break from drafting to brainstorm additional ideas about their topics.

Practice Your Skills

Revise the empty sentences below. Add details or delete repeated ideas as necessary. Write *Correct* if no revision is needed.

1. Many athletes have quick reflexes and they react fast.
2. Swimming is good for you.
3. Ten thousand people went to last night's concert in the park. The open-air concert was outdoors. Everyone had to leave when the downpour started.
4. I like baseball because you play it outdoors, you learn teamwork, you develop a number of athletic skills, and besides, you can pretend you're Hank Aaron.
5. The drama club is presenting the popular musical *The Wiz* in the school auditorium on Friday and Saturday evenings at eight o'clock.
6. Richard shared a secret with me. He told me something that he had never told anyone else before.

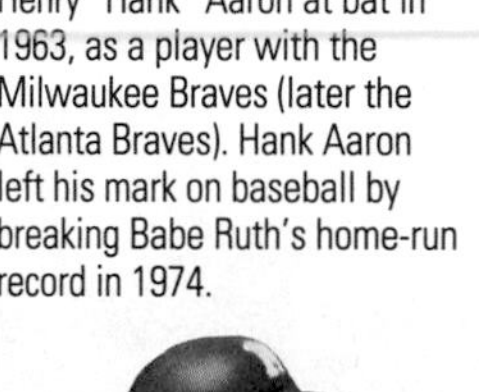

Henry "Hank" Aaron at bat in 1963, as a player with the Milwaukee Braves (later the Atlanta Braves). Hank Aaron left his mark on baseball by breaking Babe Ruth's home-run record in 1974.

REVISING PADDED SENTENCES

Are all the words in your sentence important to the meaning of the sentence? A **padded sentence** contains unnecessary words that make it difficult for a reader to follow the ideas. You can strengthen your writing by taking out the padding. Sometimes you can remove the padding by deleting the extra words that merely repeat an idea. Other times you can take out the padding by simplifying or reducing groups of words to shorten phrases.

Deleting Extra Words

Some expressions contain extra words that you can remove.

Padded Hank Aaron is famous on account of the fact that he hit 755 home runs during his career in major-league baseball. (The expression *on account of the fact that* contains words that don't add to the meaning of the sentence.)

Revised Hank Aaron is famous because he hit 755 home runs during his career in major-league baseball.

TEACHER'S LOUNGE

"Redundancies are the junk food of our language. . . . Indeed, in this day and age redundancies are multiplying by fits and starts and leaps and bounds. Rather than aiding and abetting these fattening snack-size doublets, let us find the ways and means to oppose them with all our vim and vigor and might and main. Lo and behold, perhaps one day they will be over and done with and we shall be free and clear of them."

Richard Lederer, *The Miracle of Language*

Ways to Remove Padding

Padded:		Better:
	because of the fact that	because, since
	in spite of the fact that	although
	call your attention to the fact that	remind you
	what I want is	I want
	what I want to say is	(Just say it!)
	what I mean is	(Just say it!)

To make your sentences clearer and less wordy, avoid the following padded expressions:

Expressions to Avoid

the point is	the reason is	being that
the thing is	it happens that	it would seem that

Reducing Groups of Words

Sentences that contain word groups beginning with *who is, which is,* or *that is* can be simplified by taking out those words.

Wordy I left my hat on the bench, which is near the snack bar.
Revised I left my hat on the bench near the snack bar.

Wordy The person who is behind the counter is my dad.
Revised The person behind the counter is my dad.

Practice Your Skills

Revise this passage by shortening the padded sentences.

Because of the fact that there was little snow that winter, the water levels in the reservoirs were low. What the town faced was a hot and waterless summer. The reason that young people were upset was because the town pool, which was a source of odd jobs for teenagers, had to be closed. Furthermore, people who were in town could not water lawns or wash cars. Let me point out that no one wanted a summer like that one again.

for WAYS TO REMOVE PADDING

SPEAKING AND LISTENING Point out that many expressions commonly used in informal spoken English are considered padding when used in writing. Ask students to listen for padded expressions in conversation and compile a list to share with the class.

Additional Resources

Writing Resource Book, pp. 91–94
Elaboration, Revision, and Proofreading Practice
Sentence Composing Copy Masters

Answers to Practice Your Skills

Answers will vary. A typical revision is shown below.

Because there was little snow that winter, the water levels in the reservoirs were low. The town faced a hot and waterless summer. Young people were upset because the town pool, a source of odd jobs for teenagers, had to be closed. Furthermore, people could not water lawns or wash cars. No one wanted a summer like that one again.

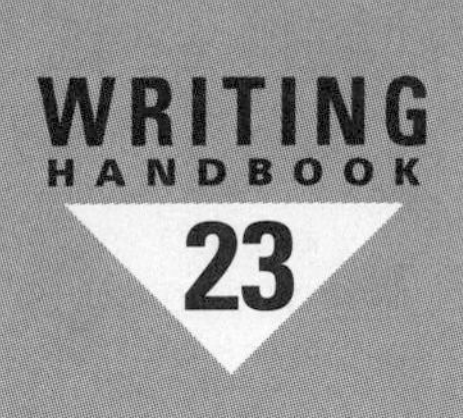

Sentence Variety

Objectives

- To identify simple, compound, and complex sentences
- To vary the length and structure of sentences
- To vary sentence beginnings

Related Mini-Lessons

For information on topics related to sentence variety, see the following mini-lessons.

- **Revising, pp. 287–289**
- **Correcting Sentence Errors, pp. 296–301**
- **Using Compound and Complex Sentences, pp. 555–575**

Motivate

Ask students to describe how they would feel if they lived in a community where everyone lived in identical houses, wore identical clothes, and drove identical cars. Then point out that likewise, passages of writing become monotonous and tedious when sentence after sentence follows the same pattern. Ask students to suggest ways in which they can vary the sentences they write.

Teaching Strategies

for UNDERSTANDING KINDS OF SENTENCES

LINKING GRAMMAR AND WRITING Have students identify the subject(s) and predicate(s) of the model simple and compound sentences. Also, ask them to identify the main and subordinate clauses of the complex sentence. Then invite students to create their own simple, compound, and complex sentences about the pictured musician and songwriter, Carlos Santana.

WRITING HANDBOOK 23

How Can I Vary My Sentences?

Sentence Variety

A composer uses a variety of tones, rhythms, melodies, and harmonies to create a pleasing arrangement of sounds. Similarly, you can vary sentence type and length as well as the way you begin and end sentences to add interest and impact to your writing.

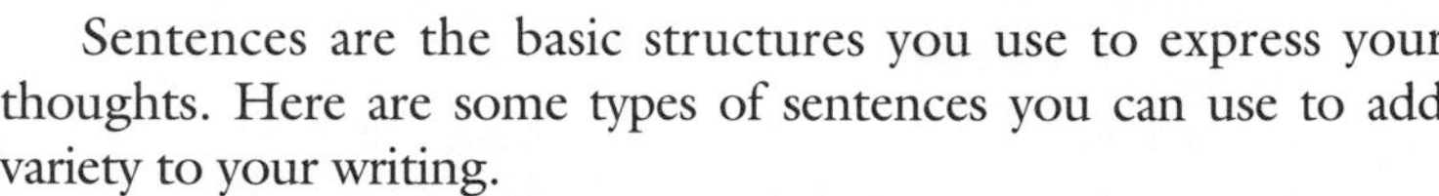

UNDERSTANDING KINDS OF SENTENCES

Sentences are the basic structures you use to express your thoughts. Here are some types of sentences you can use to add variety to your writing.

A **simple sentence** has only one subject and one predicate.

The lead guitarist ran onstage.

A **compound sentence** contains two or more simple sentences combined with a conjunction or a semicolon.

The lights flicked on, and the lead guitarist ran onstage.
The lights flicked on; the lead guitarist ran onstage.

A **complex sentence** has one main clause and one or more subordinate clauses.

Fans cheered when they saw their favorite guitarist.

(For more about compound and complex sentences, see Grammar Handbook 45, pages 556–561.)

Carlos Santana, musician and songwriter.

Varying Length and Structure

Change the rhythm of your writing by occasionally varying the types of sentences as well as the length of sentences you use.

Then it happened. The stage lights went out. The excited fans cheered continuously because they wanted an encore. The stage remained dark, however. The concert was over.

Varying Sentence Beginnings

Make your writing more interesting by beginning each sentence differently. Try using some of these sentence openers.

Opener	Sentence
Adverb	*Suddenly,* the amplifier went dead.
Prepositional phrase	*Within minutes,* a stagehand found a blown fuse.
Verb form (*-ing*)	*Hurrying,* the stagehand searched for a new fuse.
	Replacing the fuse solved the problem.
Verb form (*to*)	*To start* the concert, the group played its best-known hit.
Adverb clause	*When the music started,* the audience cheered loudly.

Practice Your Skills

A. Revise the paragraph below to improve sentence variety:

1. Join sentences 2 and 3 to form a compound sentence using *but.*
2. Join sentences 4 and 5 to form a complex sentence beginning with *when.*
3. Vary the beginnings of sentences 1, 6, 7, 8, and 9 by moving the underlined parts. Use commas as necessary.

[1]The microprocessor was developed <u>in 1971</u>. [2]The microprocessor is a tiny computer chip. [3]It has had a big effect on the computer industry. [4]Inventions such as video games appeared. [5]This happened when smaller computers became possible. [6]Video games became popular <u>quickly</u>.

[7]Video games are fun <u>because they have realistic graphics and interesting sound effects</u>. [8]A player must have good coordination and good reflexes <u>to win</u>. [9]A player's greatest challenge, <u>however,</u> is concentrating.

B. Choose a piece of writing from your writing portfolio. Use some of the strategies you learned in this handbook to improve sentence variety and to clarify your ideas.

for VARYING SENTENCE BEGINNINGS

KEY TO UNDERSTANDING: SENTENCE OPENERS Invite students to think of different openers that will change the meaning of each sentence on the chart. Get students started by offering *Gradually* and *Usually* as examples of adverb openers that change the meaning of the first sentence. Then have volunteers suggest two or three examples of each type of opener for each of the model sentences.

for PRACTICE YOUR SKILLS

MANAGING THE PAPER LOAD
You might suggest that students work in small groups to complete Exercise A. Then have different groups exchange and compare their work. Have students work on Exercise B individually.

Additional Resources

Writing Resource Book, p. 95
Elaboration, Revision, and Proofreading Practice
Sentence Composing Copy Masters

Answers to Practice Your Skills

A. Answers may vary. A sample revision is shown below.

In 1971 the microprocessor was developed. The microprocessor is a tiny computer chip, but it has had a big effect on the computer industry. When smaller computers became possible, inventions such as video games appeared. Quickly, video games became popular.

Because they have realistic graphics and interesting sound effects, video games are fun. To win, a player must have good coordination and good reflexes. However, a player's greatest challenge is concentrating.

B. Revisions will vary. Students should demonstrate an understanding of simple, compound, and complex sentences. Students should vary the length and structure of their sentences; some students might focus on varying their sentence beginnings.

Literature Connection

Read this passage from "Once Upon a Time When We Were Colored" by Clifton Taulbert.

"No sooner had she spoken than I jumped from bed and ran to get the wash pan so I could wash up before eating my breakfast. The smell of hot oil sausages and grits floated through the house and I could hardly wait. How lucky could I be—a trip to Hollandale with Uncle Cleve, *and* my favorite breakfast. The food went fast, and I found myself ready and waiting when Uncle Cleve came by. True to form, he was a little early."

Have students discuss how the sentences vary in length, structure, and beginnings.

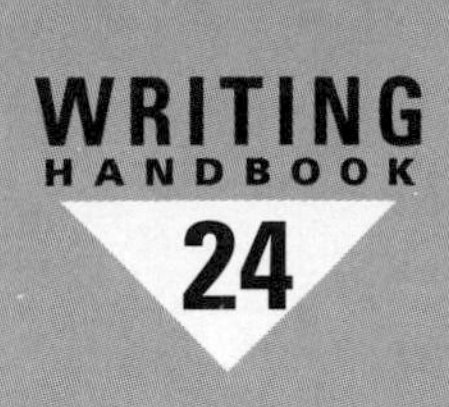

Sentence Combining

Objectives

- To combine sentences and sentence parts, using conjunctions
- To combine sentences by moving words and word groups
- To combine sentences, using *who, that,* or *which*

Related Mini-Lessons

For information on topics related to combining sentences, see the following mini-lessons.

- **Revising, pp. 287–289**
- **Correcting Sentence Errors, pp. 296–301**
- **Sentence Variety, pp. 302–303**

Motivate

Take a well-known passage and break it up into short, choppy sentences. For example:

I pledge allegiance. I pledge to the flag. It is the flag of the United States of America. I pledge to the republic of the United States. The flag stands for that republic.

After reading it aloud, have students discuss the advantages of combining short, choppy sentences into longer, more complicated ones.

Teaching Strategies

for USING COORDINATING CONJUNCTIONS

COOPERATIVE LEARNING Invite one student to say a simple sentence aloud. Then ask another student to make up an equally important, related sentence, combining it with the first by using a coordinating conjunction. Have the pair discuss how the ideas in the combined sentence are related.

WRITING HANDBOOK 24

How Can I Craft Better Sentences?

Sentence Combining

A stained-glass window may consist of thousands of pieces of glass of varying sizes, shapes, and colors. An artist arranges the pieces of glass to form interesting designs and pictures.

Likewise, the sentences you write may contain a variety of different details. You can arrange the words and phrases in a sentence to show how ideas are related and to make your writing more interesting.

COMBINING SENTENCES AND SENTENCE PARTS

Short sentences can work well for expressing single ideas. Sometimes, however, you may want to show that there is a connection between two or more ideas. You can use a conjunction to join words, groups of words, or sentences that are related.

Combining Related Sentences

There are a variety of possible relationships between ideas. You can use either a coordinating conjunction or a subordinating conjunction to join ideas, depending on the kind of relationship you wish to show.

Using Coordinating Conjunctions Two sentences of equal importance may contain similar ideas, contrasting ideas, or a choice between ideas. You may show the relationship between these complete thoughts by combining the sentences with a **coordinating conjunction,** such as *and, but,* or *or.*

Join sentences that are equally important and contain similar ideas with a comma and the word *and.*

Separate The cover of this book is torn.
Some of the pages are missing.

Combined The cover of this book is torn**, and** some of the pages are missing.

Use a comma and *but* to join sentences that present differing but equally important thoughts on the same topic.

Separate Few readers know the name Theodor S. Geisel. Many recognize this writer's pen name Dr. Seuss.
Combined Few readers know the name Theodor S. Geisel**,** **but** many recognize this writer's pen name Dr. Seuss.

When sentences offer a choice between equally important thoughts, combine the sentences with a comma and the word *or.*

Separate Is the library still open? Has it already closed?
Combined Is the library still open**,** **or** has it already closed?

Using Subordinating Conjunctions If the ideas in two sentences express relationships of time or cause, you can combine the sentences with a **subordinating conjunction,** such as *because, when, after, before, until, unless,* or *if.* A subordinating conjunction shows that the idea in the main sentence is more important than the idea that has been added. For more information on subordinating conjunctions, see Handbook 45, "Using Compound and Complex Sentences," pages 560–561.

Separate Kim will enjoy this book. She likes mysteries.
Combined Kim will enjoy this book **because** she likes mysteries.

When you begin a sentence with a subordinating conjunction, place a comma between the ideas.

Separate Ian mended the book. He put it on the shelf.
Combined **After** Ian mended the book**,** he put it on the shelf.

Combining Sentence Parts

Just as you can use *and, but,* or *or* to join complete sentences, you can use one of these conjunctions to join parts of two sentences that contain related ideas. However, do *not* place a comma before a coordinating conjunction that joins sentence parts. Delete repeated words or ideas. Study the examples shown on the next page.

TIP

Look for opportunities to combine sentences with subordinating conjunctions when you write about relationships such as cause and effect.

for USING SUBORDINATING CONJUNCTIONS

INDIVIDUALIZING INSTRUCTION: BASIC STUDENTS To make sure students understand relationships of time and cause, elicit or provide some examples:

After I ate breakfast, I went to work. (Time)

Because I have gained weight, my summer clothes do not fit. (Cause)

for USING SUBORDINATING CONJUNCTIONS

COLLABORATIVE OPPORTUNITY
Invite pairs of students to combine sentences by subordinating ideas. The first student says a simple sentence—for example, *Kim will be late for school.* The second student adds a subordinate idea to the sentence, using one of the subordinating conjunctions—for example, *If she misses the bus, Kim will be late for school.*

for USING SUBORDINATING CONJUNCTIONS

CRITICAL THINKING: ANALYZING
Call on volunteers to find in their writing portfolios paragraphs that use coordinating or subordinating conjunctions to combine sentences. Have students first read the paragraphs aloud. Then ask peers to identify the sentences combined with conjunctions.

for USING SUBORDINATING CONJUNCTIONS

HELPFUL HINT: COMMAS Ask students to consider why a comma is placed after a subordinate idea that begins a complex sentence. (The comma alerts the reader or speaker to pause between the subordinate idea and the main idea.) Explain that no comma is needed when a subordinate clause ends the sentence because a reader tends naturally to pause before a conjunction that appears midway through the sentence.

for SAMPLE SENTENCES

LINKING GRAMMAR AND WRITING Ask students to analyze the grammatical role of the sentence parts combined in these three pairs of sentences. The parts are related mainly by their role or function in the sentence.

for PRACTICE YOUR SKILLS

INDIVIDUALIZING INSTRUCTION: LEP STUDENTS One way to help students avoid repeating elements when combining sentences and sentence parts is by providing oral practice. (Use the items in Exercise A on page 7 of the Sentence Composing Copy Masters.)

AUDITORY LEARNERS Encourage students to read the combined sentences aloud, listening to the pacing and rhythm. You might allow them to complete the activities orally.

Answers to Practice Your Skills

A. Answers may vary slightly. Students should maintain the meaning of the original sentences. Possible answers are shown below.

1. In the past people could eat produce only in season, but now many fruits and vegetables are available year-round.
2. Airplanes deliver ripe raspberries in winter and fresh bananas every month of the year.
3. It's winter in the United States when it's summer in Australia.
4. The United States imports produce during the winter and exports produce during the summer.
5. Out-of-season produce is expensive because delivery costs are so high.
6. Do you prefer the way it was in the past or the way it is now?

B. Answers may vary. Possible answers are shown below.

[1] The steam whistle sounds, and the paddle wheel stops. [2] Passengers quickly step off the steamboat after it is tied to the pier. [3] They can't wait to see Mark Twain's boyhood home in Hannibal, Missouri, and the surrounding countryside. [4] Will the visitors join the fence-whitewashing contest, or will they tour the dark passages of the cave? [5] The tomboy contest would be interesting, but the frog-jumping contest might be more fun to watch. [6] Most visitors find these attractions especially interesting because they have read *Huckleberry Finn* or *Tom Sawyer.*

Separate	Photographers consider lighting. *They plan* composition.
Combined	Photographers consider lighting **and** composition.
Separate	The photo is very small. *It is* remarkably clear.
Combined	The photo is very small **but** remarkably clear.
Separate	Is this lens for all kinds of pictures? *Is this lens for* only close-ups?
Combined	Is this lens for all kinds of pictures **or** only close-ups?

Practice Your Skills

A. Use the word in parentheses to combine each pair of sentences. Drop repeated words and ideas. Add commas where necessary.

1. In the past people could eat produce only in season. Now many fruits and vegetables are available year-round. (*but*)
2. Airplanes deliver ripe raspberries in winter. They deliver fresh bananas every month of the year. (*and*)
3. It's winter in the United States. It's summer in Australia. (*when*)
4. The United States imports produce during the winter. The United States exports produce during the summer. (*and*)
5. Out-of-season produce is expensive. Delivery costs are so high. (*because*)
6. Do you prefer the way it was in the past? Do you prefer the way it is now? (*or*)

B. Combine each pair of sentences with *and, but, or, because,* or *after.* Delete repeated words and add commas where necessary.

[1]The steam whistle sounds. The paddle wheel stops. [2]Passengers quickly step off the steamboat. It is tied to the pier. [3]They can't wait to see Mark Twain's boyhood home in Hannibal, Missouri. They can't wait to see the surrounding countryside. [4]Will the visitors join the fence-whitewashing contest? Will they tour the dark passages of the cave? [5]The tomboy contest would be interesting. The frog-jumping contest might be more fun to watch. [6]Most visitors find these attractions especially interesting. They have read *Huckleberry Finn* or *Tom Sawyer.*

ADDING WORDS AND WORD GROUPS

Using conjunctions is one way to join related ideas. You can also combine sentences by moving details from one sentence to another. The newly formed sentence is often a tighter, more effective way of expressing the ideas.

Adding Single Words

Sometimes details in one sentence can contribute important information to another sentence. When the idea you want to add to the main sentence is only a single word from another sentence, move that key word to the main sentence and delete the remainder of the related sentence.

Separate This aquarium contains many colorful fish. *The fish are* tropical.
Combined This aquarium contains many colorful **tropical** fish.

Separate Special filters and a heater are necessary to maintain the correct environment. *These special filters are* charcoal. *The heater is* electric.
Combined Special **charcoal** filters and an **electric** heater are necessary to maintain the correct environment.

Sometimes you must add either a comma or the word *and* when you move an important detail into the main sentence.

Separate The Smithsonian has a zoo. *It is a* small *zoo. It is an* unusual *zoo. It is an* insect *zoo.*
Combined The Smithsonian has a **small, unusual insect** zoo.

Separate One cockroach sits in a display. *The display was* carefully prepared. *The display is* elaborate.
Combined One cockroach sits in a **carefully prepared and elaborate** display.

Wood sculptor Patrick Bremer relaxes with one of his creations, a six-foot-tall praying mantis. More insect sculptures greet visitors at the Smithsonian Institution's Insect Zoo, part of the Museum of Natural History.

for ADDING SINGLE WORDS

STUMBLING BLOCK Tell students to separate adjectives with a comma if each modifies the noun alone. For example:

It was a long, hot summer.

She was a talented, generous person.

No comma should be used, however, if the first adjective modifies the idea expressed by the combination of the second adjective and the noun. For example:

We saw an angry brown bear.

Typical bad habits include nail biting.

for ADDING SINGLE WORDS

COLLABORATIVE OPPORTUNITY
Have pairs of students role-play writer and editor. The writer creates three short, choppy sentences that repeat ideas. The second student, or editor, combines the sentences, using commas and the word *and* when necessary. Afterward have the pair discuss which versions they prefer.

Sentence Combining **307**

for ADDING *-Y* OR *-LY*

KEY TO UNDERSTANDING: SUFFIXES Review how a suffix consists of one or more syllables, is added to the end of a word, and changes the word's meaning and often its part of speech. Point out that the suffix *-y* means "showing" and is usually added to a noun to form an adjective. Ask volunteers to name other adjectives that are formed by adding *-y* to a noun. (Samples: *dirty, thirsty, airy, sandy)* Also, explain that the suffix *-ly,* which means "like," is usually added to adjectives to form adverbs. Elicit other examples of words with the *-ly* suffix *(kindly, sadly).*

for ADDING *-Y* OR *-LY*

HELPFUL HINT: WORD ORDER
Show students that placing the adverb at the beginning of a sentence tends to emphasize the adverb. Discuss how putting adverbs in other positions in a sentence affects meaning.

for ADDING *-Y* OR *-LY*

STUMBLING BLOCK Point out that using adjectives as adverbs without adding the *-ly* ending is a common error, as in *We trudged up the mountain slow and quiet.* Explain that in the separate sentence *We were slow, slow* is an adjective modifying *We.* However, when *slow* is added to the sentence *We trudged up the mountain,* it becomes an adverb modifying the verb *trudged* and answers the question *how.* Therefore, *slow* needs the *-ly* ending: *slowly.*

for ADDING *-ED* OR *-ING*

INDIVIDUALIZING INSTRUCTION: ESL STUDENTS You may need to review the spelling rules that apply when adding *-ed* and *-ing* to words. For example, a word ending in a consonant and *e,* such as *raise,* drops the *e* when *-ing* is added. Also, short words ending in a vowel and a consonant, such as *run,* double the final consonant before *-ing* is added. Ask students to find examples of words that follow these spelling patterns.

Adding Words That Change Form

Sometimes you must change the form of an important word before you add it to a main sentence.

Adding *-y* or *-ly* What word change was made in this example?

Separate Our guide led us along the trail.
The trail had rocks.
Combined Our guide led us along the **rocky** trail.

Words that end in *-ly* often fit in more than one place in the main sentence.

Separate We followed the guide. *We were* cautious.
Combined **Cautiously,** we followed the guide.
We **cautiously** followed the guide.
We followed the guide **cautiously.**

Separate We trudged up the mountain.
We were slow. *We were* quiet.
Combined **Slowly and quietly,** we trudged up the mountain.
We **slowly and quietly** trudged up the mountain.
We trudged up the mountain **slowly and quietly.**

Adding *-ed* or *-ing* Notice the changes in these examples.

Separate Our guide showed us a trail on the map.
The map had many details.
Combined Our guide showed us a trail on the **detailed** map.

Separate We inched closer to the mountaintop.
The mountaintop glistened.
Combined We inched closer to the **glistening** mountaintop.

Adding Groups of Words

You can also combine sentences by moving groups of words.

Separate Many people enjoy hot-air ballooning.
The people fly balloons over the countryside.
Combined Many people enjoy hot-air ballooning **over the countryside.**

Literature Connection

Point out that not all short sentences should be combined into longer or more complex structures. Short sentences are effective in expressing suspense, action, anger, or other emotions. As an example, read these lines from the play, *The Diary of Anne Frank* by Francis Goodrich and Albert Hackett.

Anne's Voice *You could not do this and you could not do that. They forced Father out of his business. We had to wear yellow stars. I had to turn in my bike. I couldn't go to a Dutch school any more.*

Discuss the impact of these short sentences. Have students find similar literary models.

Separate Balloonists meet at huge rallies.
They hold the rallies to compete with one another.

Combined Balloonists meet at huge rallies **to compete with one another.**

Before adding a group of words to a main sentence, you may need to change the ending of one word in the group.

Separate A propane burner heats the air in the bag. *The burner* rests inside the basket of the balloon.

Combined A propane burner **resting inside the basket of the balloon** heats the air in the bag.

Practice Your Skills

A. Combine the following sentences, deleting unnecessary words. You may need to change the forms of some words.

1. The teen club sponsored a trip to a local park. The trip was by bus. The trip was to an amusement park.
2. The club had rented a school bus. The bus was ancient. It was rickety.
3. We got off the bus. We were glad. The bus was uncomfortable.
4. We waited in a line at the Ferris wheel. We were patient. The line was long.
5. We watched the people riding the roller coaster. The people screamed. We were fearful.

B. Combine each sentence pair. Change word endings as necessary.

[1]The National Weather Service issued a warning. The warning was about a storm. [2]Rains had struck the towns. The rains were torrential. The towns were along the coast. [3]Now the storm was turning. Its turn was sudden. It was turning inland. [4]Winds and hail accompanied the rains. The winds raged. The hail pelted. [5]Many travelers were stranded. This happened when the airport closed. The closing was temporary. [6]The National Weather Service urged people to take precautions. The people live near the path of the storm. The service also urged people to evacuate the area.

for PRACTICE YOUR SKILLS

MANAGING THE PAPER LOAD

Call on students to complete the items in Exercise A orally. Have students identify which technique of those taught on pages 307–309 they used to combine the sentences. Make sure students realize that they must add a word or words from the less important sentence(s) to the main sentence in each item. Have students complete Exercise B independently.

Answers to Practice Your Skills

A. Answers may vary. Students should use conjunctions and commas correctly. Words that were changed in form should be spelled correctly, as shown in the examples below.

1. The teen club sponsored a bus trip to a local amusement park.
2. The club had rented an ancient, rickety school bus.
3. We gladly got off the uncomfortable bus.
4. We patiently waited in a long line at the Ferris wheel.
5. We fearfully watched the screaming people riding the roller coaster.

B. Answers may vary slightly. The revised passage should contain appropriate conjunctions and commas, and all words should be spelled correctly. Possible answers are shown below.

[1] The National Weather Service issued a storm warning. [2] Torrential rains had struck the towns along the coast. [3] Now the storm was suddenly turning inland. [4] Raging winds and pelting hail accompanied the rains. [5] Many travelers were stranded when the airport temporarily closed. [6] The National Weather Service urged people living near the path of the storm to take precautions and evacuate the area.

for WRITER TO WRITER

CRITICAL THINKING: INTERPRETING Ask a volunteer to read the quotation aloud. Tell the class that Anatole France (1844–1924) was a French writer and Nobel Prize winner known for his clear and elegant writing style. Be sure students understand that in the quote France is comparing writing to carpentry. Then ask a volunteer to explain why a carpenter usually planes wood (to shape and smooth it by shaving off bumps and other unwanted parts so two pieces of wood fit together smoothly). Ask students what France might have meant by "planing down your sentences" (eliminating unnecessary words so ideas fit together smoothly in sentences).

for COMBINING WITH *WHO* . . .

STUMBLING BLOCK The question of whether to use commas with essential and nonessential details often confuses students. If students have trouble in this area, suggest that they read the sentence aloud, with and without the added detail. Hearing the sentences might help them decide whether or not the added information is essential for understanding the sentence.

WRITER TO WRITER

You become a good writer just as you become a good joiner [carpenter]—by planing down your sentences.

Anatole France, novelist and critic

COMBINING WITH *WHO, THAT,* OR *WHICH*

Perhaps you have written two sentences that provide details about the same person, place, or thing. You can avoid repetition by combining such related sentences with *who, that,* or *which* or by using an appositive.

Using *Who*

When two sentences give details about a person, you can combine the sentences by using the word *who* to replace *he, she, they,* or another word that names the person.

Separate Runners seldom get muscle injuries. *They* stretch regularly.

Combined Runners **who stretch regularly** seldom get muscle injuries.

Notice in the combined sentence above that the added detail "who stretch regularly" is necessary for you to understand which runners are seldom injured. When an added detail is essential to the meaning of the sentence, do not set off the added words with commas.

Separate Laurence Yep has published many books.
Laurence Yep wrote *Dragonwings.*

Combined Laurence Yep**, who wrote *Dragonwings,*** has published many books.

In the combined sentence above, the added detail "who wrote *Dragonwings*" is not needed in order to understand the main idea of the sentence. The added words provide extra information about Laurence Yep, so they are set off with commas.

Literature Connection

Point out how Dave Barry uses *who* and *that* in this passage from "Memories of Dating."

". . . it's difficult to get a date with a girl who has never, technically, been asked. This is why you need Phil Grant. Phil was a friend of mine who had the ability to talk to girls. It was a mysterious superhuman power he had, comparable to X-ray vision. So, after several thousand hours of intense discussion and planning with me, Phil approached a girl he knew named Nancy, who approached a girl named Sandy, who was a direct personal friend of Judy's and who passed the word back to Phil via Nancy that Judy would be willing to go on a date with me."

Using *That* or *Which*

If the common element in related sentences is a place or a thing, use *that* or *which* to combine the sentences. The word *that* or *which* replaces the words that name the place or thing.

Use *that* when the added detail is an essential element that identifies or explains an idea in a main sentence. Do not set off such essential elements with commas.

Separate Workers in a field uncovered a steamboat. *The steamboat* had sunk in the Missouri River in 1856.

Combined Workers in a field uncovered a steamboat **that had sunk in the Missouri River in 1856.**

Use *which* when the added detail is a nonessential element that merely provides extra information about an idea in a main sentence. Use commas to set off nonessential elements.

Separate Poodles were once used as hunters and retrievers. *Poodles* now make smart and friendly house dogs.

Combined Poodles**, which now make smart and friendly house dogs,** were once used as hunters and retrievers.

Grammar **TIP**

Remember, information that is essential to the sentence is not set off with commas.

Using Appositives

Sometimes you can combine closely related sentences by using an appositive instead of the word *who, that,* or *which.* An **appositive** is a noun or phrase that explains one or more words in a sentence. Do not set off an appositive with commas if it adds an essential detail to the main idea of the sentence. Do use commas if the appositive adds extra information to the main idea.

Separate Spike Lee has made many films about social issues. *He* is an African-American director.

Appositive without Commas The African-American director **Spike Lee** has made many films about social issues.

Appositive with Commas Spike Lee**, an African-American director,** has made many films about social issues.

for USING APPOSITIVES

KEY TO UNDERSTANDING Explain that the word *appositive* comes from Latin words meaning "put near." An appositive is put near, or next to, the noun that it explains or renames. To help students distinguish between essential and nonessential appositives, suggest that they read a sentence without the appositive to see if it is clear and complete. Emphasize that only nonessential appositives are set off by commas.

for USING APPOSITIVES

INDIVIDUALIZING INSTRUCTION: ESL STUDENTS The use of appositives that are set off with commas can be a problem for ESL students if they mistakenly think the appositive and its antecedent are two separate ideas in a series, instead of two related elements. Provide these students with examples of appositives with commas and explain the close relationship between the appositives and the words they rename.

for PRACTICE YOUR SKILLS

MANAGING THE PAPER LOAD

You may wish to do Exercises A, B, and C orally with your class. Hearing the combined sentences will also reinforce students' understanding of sentence combining techniques.

Additional Resources

Writing Resource Book, pp. 96–98
Sentence Composing Copy Masters

Answers to Practice Your Skills

A. Answers may vary slightly. Students should use *who, which,* and *that* properly. Possible answers are shown below.

1. The pier on Main Street, which extends nearly a block into the ocean, draws a variety of visitors.
2. Some people, who spend a relaxing afternoon dangling a hook and line in the water, fish mostly for enjoyment.
3. Other hardy men and women who fish for a living work long hours for low pay at the pier.
4. Tourists, who stroll to the waterfront before dawn, wave to the departing fishing boats.
5. Anglers catch many kinds of fish that swim close to shore.
6. The local waters, which are full of plankton, provide plenty of food for fish.
7. Small fish often consume plankton, which is microscopic plant and animal life.
8. These small fish become food for the larger fish that lurk nearby.

B. Answers may vary. However, commas should be used correctly with the appositives, as shown in the examples below.

1. Scuba diving, a popular form of recreation, involves going underwater while breathing with the aid of air tanks.
2. Navy divers are called frogmen because of one distinctive piece of equipment, their swim fins.
3. One of the devices used by novice divers, a snorkel, allows them to breathe underwater.
4. An important part of the aqualung, the regulator, lets scuba divers control the flow of air from their air tanks.

In the first combined sentence on the previous page, the director's name is essential for understanding which director has made films about social issues, so the name is not set off with commas. In the second combined sentence, the added detail is extra information about Spike Lee. It is set off with commas.

Practice Your Skills

A. Use *who, which,* or *that* to combine each pair of sentences. Add commas if needed. Delete any unnecessary words.

1. The pier on Main Street draws a variety of visitors. The pier extends nearly a block into the ocean.
2. Some people fish mostly for enjoyment. These people spend a relaxing afternoon dangling a hook and line in the water.
3. Other hardy men and women work long hours for low pay at the pier. These people fish for a living.
4. Tourists wave to the departing fishing boats. These tourists stroll to the waterfront before dawn.
5. Anglers catch many kinds of fish. The fish swim close to shore.
6. The local waters provide plenty of food for fish. These waters are full of plankton.
7. Small fish often consume plankton. Plankton is microscopic plant and animal life.
8. These small fish become food for the larger fish. The larger fish lurk nearby.

B. Use appositives to combine the following pairs of sentences. Add commas where they are needed.

1. A popular form of recreation involves going underwater while breathing with the aid of air tanks. The form of recreation is scuba diving.
2. Navy divers are called frogmen because of one distinctive piece of equipment. That piece of equipment is their swim fins.
3. One of the devices used by novice divers allows them to breathe underwater. The device is a snorkel.
4. An important part of the aqualung lets scuba divers control the flow of air from their air tanks. It is the regulator.

5. A potentially fatal condition faced by divers is caused by rising too quickly to the surface. The condition is the bends.

C. Combine the following sentences. Delete the words in italics and follow the directions that are given in parentheses.

1. Behind the library is a pond. *It* is great for skating during the winter. (Use *that.*)
2. Sometimes skaters must watch for thin ice. *These skaters* go out on the pond early in the season. (Use *who.*)
3. The sheriff's office sends a patrol car past the pond. *The office* is several blocks away. (Use commas and *which.*)
4. One watchful deputy has rescued several skaters. *His name is* Jefferson Douglass. (Use an appositive.)
5. In midwinter the pond is covered by a layer of ice. *The ice* is often eight or more inches thick. (Use *that.*)
6. Several teenagers shovel snow from the ice. *These teenagers* also work as lifeguards in the summer. (Use commas and *who.*)
7. Ye Old Woodworks donated two wooden sleds to the town. *Ye Old Woodworks is* a well-known local carpentry shop. (Use an appositive.)

D. Revise the following passage, using what you know about combining sentences. Some sentences can remain the same.

[1]People often need patience. [2]These people are learning a new sport. [3]Not everyone has the physical strength of a natural athlete. [4]Not everyone has the ability of a natural athlete. [5]A natural athlete masters any sport. [6]A natural athlete does it easily. [7]Soccer may take years to master. [8]Soccer requires precise footwork. [9]Tennis is another difficult sport to learn. [10]Tennis requires speed and stamina. [11]Bowlers must have good eye-hand coordination. [12]These athletes try to knock over ten wooden pins. [13]The pins are at the end of a wooden lane. [14]In all sports, practice and persistence are important factors. [15]These factors lead to improved skills and winning scores.

5. The bends, a potentially fatal condition faced by divers, is caused by rising too quickly to the surface.

C. Answers may vary. Students should use *who, that, which* and appositives properly. Possible answers are shown below.

1. Behind the library is a pond that is great for skating during the winter.
2. Sometimes skaters who go out on the pond early in the season must watch for thin ice.
3. The sheriff's office, which is several blocks away, sends a patrol car past the pond.
4. One watchful deputy, Jefferson Douglass, has rescued several skaters.
5. In midwinter the pond is covered by a layer of ice that is often eight or more inches thick.
6. Several teenagers, who also work as lifeguards in the summer, shovel snow from the ice.
7. Ye Old Woodworks, a well-known local carpentry shop, donated two wooden sleds to the town.

D. Revised passages may vary. Possible answers are shown below.

People who are learning a new sport often need patience. Not everyone has the physical strength and ability of a natural athlete, who masters any sport easily. Soccer, which requires precise footwork, may take years to master. Tennis, which requires speed and stamina, is another difficult sport to learn. Bowlers, who try to knock over ten wooden pins at the end of a wooden lane, must have good eye-hand coordination. In all sports, practice and persistence are important factors that lead to improved skills and winning scores.

Meaning and Word Choice

Objectives

- To identify the denotation and connotation of words
- To consider the audience when choosing words
- To distinguish between formal and informal English

Related Mini-Lessons

For information on topics related to meaning and word choice, see the following mini-lessons.

- **General Purpose and Personal Goals, pp. 232–233**
- **Audience, pp. 234–235**
- **Revising, pp. 287–289**

Teaching Strategies

for DENOTATION AND CONNOTATION

STUMBLING BLOCK If students have difficulty distinguishing between the denotative and connotative meanings of words, write this word pair on the chalkboard: *young/childish.* Ask "What are the dictionary definitions of these words? Which would you rather be called? How does each make you feel?" To provide students with additional practice, read the following words with positive connotations and ask students to suggest synonyms with negative connotations: *witty (sarcastic, snide); bold (reckless); firm (stubborn).*

WRITING HANDBOOK 25

What's the Best Word for Me to Use?

Meaning and Word Choice

Does a character in your story like to *talk,* or is *gossip* a better word? What about *chat* or *blab?* How can you decide which word to use? How you choose words depends on your purpose for writing and on your audience.

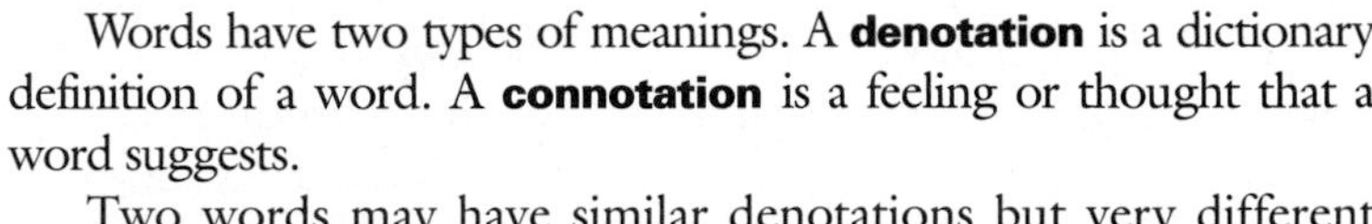

DENOTATION AND CONNOTATION

Fat or *plump?*

Words have two types of meanings. A **denotation** is a dictionary definition of a word. A **connotation** is a feeling or thought that a word suggests.

Two words may have similar denotations but very different connotations. Here are some examples.

Positive Connotation	slender	curious	thrifty
Negative Connotation	skinny	nosy	stingy

AUDIENCE

When you choose words, consider your **audience**—your readers or listeners. Ask yourself questions like the following:

- Who is my audience?
- What are their ages and backgrounds?
- What do they already know about the subject?
- What do they need to know?

These questions help you focus on your audience. For example, to a friend you might describe a computer game as *awesome.* However, you might describe the same game to your grandmother as *exciting.* (For more information about audience, see Writing Handbooks 4 and 5.)

FORMAL AND INFORMAL ENGLISH

Choose words that are suited to the occasion, or situation. If you were writing a letter to a friend about litter around your school, you would use words from everyday speech and possibly some slang to express your feelings. However, if you were writing to the school board about the same problem, you would choose words that made your letter sound more dignified.

Standard English includes both formal and informal English. Business letters, legal documents, and technical articles are written in formal English. **Formal English** has a serious tone, longer sentences, and sometimes includes technical vocabulary. Friendly letters, advertisements, and magazine and newspaper articles are written in informal English. **Informal English** has a casual tone, shorter sentences, and simpler vocabulary than formal English. Slang is sometimes a part of informal English. **Slang** consists of popular, faddish words and phrases spoken by members of a particular group. Note these examples of different language styles.

Formal Exposure to rock music at high decibel levels can cause auditory damage.
Informal Listening to loud rock music can hurt your hearing.
Slang Blasting hip-hop from a boom box can kill your ears.

Practice Your Skills

A. Rewrite this formal invitation to make it informal.

The graduating class of Kennedy Middle School cordially invites you to attend commencement exercises on the evening of June 14, 19— at seven o'clock. The Honorable Jorge Ruiz, mayor of Springfield, will deliver a congratulatory address to the students. Principal Cynthia Davis will distribute the diplomas. In celebration of the graduates, a reception will be held in the school's gymnasium immediately following the ceremony.

B. Find an advertisement in a magazine. List the words that are used to make the product seem appealing. For each word, list another with a similar denotation but a different connotation.

Writing **TIP**

A thesaurus can help you find the right word to say exactly what you mean. Be sure to choose words carefully, however. Remember that the synonyms listed in a thesaurus can have very different connotations.

COMPUTER TIP

Some word processing programs have built-in thesauruses that you can use to find the right word for your purpose, audience, and occasion.

for FORMAL AND INFORMAL ENGLISH

CRITICAL THINKING: COMPARING AND CONTRASTING Ask students to suggest occasions for which they might dress up to show respect or to make a good impression (weddings, funerals, job interviews, special events, and so on). Point out that in many of these situations, they might also tend to use formal, or dignified, language for the same reasons. Next, have them list situations for which they would dress informally. Point out that their language might also be informal at these times.

for FORMAL AND INFORMAL ENGLISH

HELPFUL HINT After discussing the definitions of formal and informal English in the text, point out that formal English also avoids contractions and clipped words such as *vet* for *veteran* or *prof* for *professor.*

for FORMAL AND INFORMAL ENGLISH

ASSESSMENT: SPOT CHECK Ask students to create a chart comparing formal and informal English based on the following characteristics: (1) tone, (2) sentence length, (3) vocabulary, and (4) the use of slang.

Additional Resource

Writing Resource Book, p. 99

Answers to Practice Your Skills

A. Answers will vary. A possible revision is shown.

Please come to the eighth-grade graduation at Kennedy Middle School on June 14, 19—, 7:00 p.m. Mayor Ruiz will give a speech, and Principal Davis will hand out the diplomas. After the graduation ceremony, there will be a party in the school gym for the grads and their guests.

B. Answers will vary. Students should demonstrate an understanding of the difference between denotation and connotation by choosing appropriate examples.

SPICE BOX

Read aloud these "superformal" versions of familiar proverbs and have students identify their informal versions.

- The members of an avian species with identical plumage congregate. (Birds of a feather flock together.)
- It is fruitless to attempt to indoctrinate a superannuated canine with innovative maneuvers. (You can't teach an old dog new tricks.)

Then challenge students to write other familiar proverbs or colloquial expressions in very formal language.

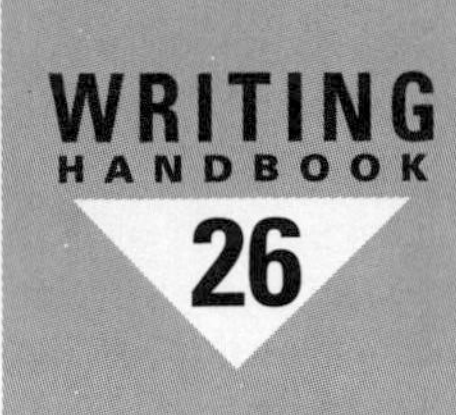

Developing a Personal Voice

Objectives

- To develop a natural-sounding personal voice when writing
- To express feelings and opinions honestly in writing

Related Mini-Lessons

For information on topics related to developing a personal voice, see the following mini-lessons.

- **General Purpose and Personal Goals, pp. 232–233**
- **Revising, pp. 287–289**
- **Meaning and Word Choice, pp. 314–315**

Motivate

Read aloud short samples of selected students' writing without identifying the writer. As students listen to each piece, ask them to try to identify the classmate who wrote it. When students have identified a writer correctly, ask them to state what characteristics of the writing helped them do so. Point out how, as in speaking, each person has a distinctive writing voice.

Teaching Strategies

for STUDENT MODEL

USING THE MODELS Invite students to read and contrast the two models. Ask them to cite examples of overly formal vocabulary in the first model *(strenuous objection; obnoxious trend; affront; barrage).* Ask them to note aspects of the second model that make it more personal. (The writer provides the name of the movie; she mentions a specific commercial.)

WRITING HANDBOOK 26

How Can I Make My Writing Sound Like Me?

Developing a Personal Voice

Your writing has a distinctive sound, or voice. Of course, an entry you write in your journal will read very differently than a geography report on tropical rain forests. However, if you are expressing what you really think or know in words that come naturally to you, your personal voice will come through.

KEEP IT NATURAL

Young writers often don't trust their natural voices. They think they have to use complex words and long, complicated sentences to make their writing seem impressive. One student began the first draft of an article for the school newspaper this way.

> I'd like to raise a strenuous objection to the presentation of commercials before feature films. This obnoxious trend is an affront to the movie viewer who has paid to see a film, not to be subjected to a barrage of advertising.

In reading her draft aloud, she realized that the vocabulary was probably too difficult for most of her audience to understand. More importantly, it didn't sound like her at all. She decided to revise her draft to make it more informal.

> When I went to see *Star Trek VI* recently, I got more than I bargained for. As the lights dimmed, instead of the *Starship Enterprise,* a commercial for a candy bar appeared on the screen. I felt used. I go to the movies to see a feature film, not commercials. Yet I'm part of a captive audience and can't fast-forward through these ads. I believe that theater operators are taking unfair advantage of moviegoers by showing commercials before films.

Social Studies Connection

Primary Sources Ask students to look through their social studies texts to find examples of primary sources—journal entries, speeches, and letters of people who experienced historic events firsthand. Ask them to choose one of these passages to study for details that reveal the writer's personal voice. What, for example, can they tell about Martin Luther King, Jr., from reading the "I Have a Dream" speech? Call on volunteers to read passages aloud, and have the class discuss their conclusions about the writer's voice.

BE TRUE TO YOURSELF

Another way to develop a personal voice is to write about the things you feel, think, and believe—not what you think others want to hear. Does this letter really sound like a student's opinion?

> A recent study showed that U.S. students spend too much time watching television and not enough time reading and doing homework. As a result, their scores on reading tests continue to decline. Parents must put strict limits on the amount of time their children spend watching television.

When the student revised this draft to express her real feelings, her writing became more authentic and thus more powerful.

> Many people blame television for students' low reading test scores. Kids may spend more time watching television than they do reading or doing their homework. However, there are other problems—schools are often overcrowded and funds for education have been cut back. If kids today are having trouble reading, it's not just television's fault.

Student MODEL

How to Develop Your Writing Voice

- WRITE in your journal regularly.
- FREEWRITE before you begin drafting.
- TALK out your ideas before writing them down.
- READ your work aloud.

Practice Your Skills

Rewrite the following paragraph using your personal voice.

It is absolutely essential for each individual person to develop his or her unique potential. A person must never allow himself or herself to be limited by other people's expectations of what he or she is capable of achieving in his or her life. An individual's future is in his or her own hands.

for STUDENT MODEL

USING THE MODELS Have students read the first model and state its main idea. (Parents must limit children's TV watching to improve reading skills.) Have students express why they think the student writer was not being true to her feelings. (It is unlikely that a young person would want her parents to limit her TV watching.) Have students read the second model and state its main idea. (It is unfair to blame TV alone for poor reading scores, when shortcomings in schools also contribute to the problem.) Have students express their opinions on why the second paragraph seems authentic. (The writer seems to draw on her own experiences in school.)

for BE TRUE TO YOURSELF

SPEAKING AND LISTENING Call on volunteers to read aloud from their writing portfolios paragraphs that they feel express their opinions in an authentic way. Direct student peers to listen carefully and then discuss which words or sentences in each passage make it natural and convincing.

for HOW TO DEVELOP . . .

ASSESSMENT: SPOT CHECK Have students look over the four tips. Then ask them to explain how each suggestion might help them bring out a distinct, personal voice in their writing. Encourage students to copy the four tips, add any further thoughts they have on establishing a personal voice, and keep them together in their writing folders.

Additional Resources

Writing Resource Book, p. 100
Spelling and Vocabulary Booklet

Answers to Practice Your Skills

Revisions will vary. Students should express themselves honestly and use natural, informal vocabulary.

PROFESSIONAL NOTEBOOK

Share this advice from critic Theodore Solotaroff for developing a personal style and voice: ". . . young writers should try as much as possible to write to their strengths. If you have a good sense of humor, let it come into your prose. If you have a good ear for spoken language, for the idioms and rhythms of a region or group, try to incorporate them into your style. If you pride yourself on being clear and direct, then make your prose as explicit as possible."

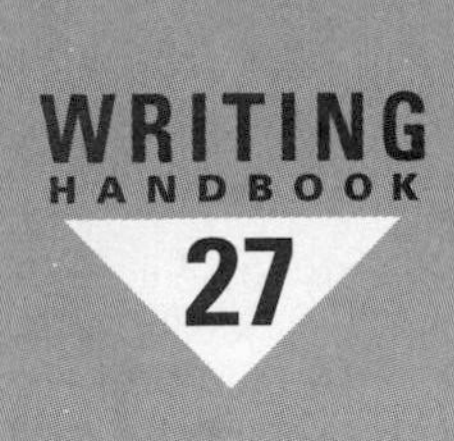

Using Poetic Devices

Objectives

- To distinguish among similes, metaphors, personification, onomatopoeia, alliteration, and assonance
- To use figurative language and sound devices to improve writing
- To avoid using clichés in writing

Related Mini-Lessons

For information on topics related to the use of poetic devices in writing, see the following mini-lessons:

- **Methods of Elaboration, pp. 255–261**
- **Show, Don't Tell, pp. 262–267**
- **Meaning and Word Choice, pp. 314–315**

Teaching Strategies

for LITERARY MODEL

USING THE MODEL Help students rewrite sentences 3, 4, and 6 without figurative language. (Sample: Our orange cats looked on from the fence, with their tails up.) Ask students why Soto's figurative language makes the writing more effective. (It produces mental images that show, as well as tell, what is happening.)

for TYPES OF FIGURATIVE LANGUAGE

COOPERATIVE LEARNING To reinforce your teaching of similes, list on the board persons and objects, such as *toddler, basketball,* and so on. Arrange students into groups, to create similes for each item. Tell them first to ask themselves, "What is this person or object in some way like?" (Sample: The toddler, like a tightrope walker, waved his arms to keep his balance.) Have the groups share and discuss their similes.

WRITING HANDBOOK 27

How Can I Make My Language Richer?

Using Poetic Devices

My first bike got me nowhere, though the shadow I cast as I pedaled raced along my side. The leaves of bird-filled trees stirred a warm breeze and litter scuttled out of the way. Our orange cats looked on from the fence, their tails up like antennas. I opened my mouth, and wind tickled the back of my throat. When I squinted, I could see past the end of the block. My hair flicked like black fire, and I thought I was pretty cool riding up and down the block, age five, in my brother's hand-me-down shirt.

Gary Soto, *A Summer Life*

What images came to mind as you read Gary Soto's paragraph? Did you see the cats' tails sticking up like antennas? Could you feel the wind tickling the back of your throat? Perhaps you imagined the boy's black hair flicking like flames in the wind.

Figurative language enables you to show one thing by comparing it to something else. When you use figurative language, you present your readers with vivid pictures they can see and with sensations they can feel. You make your poems, song lyrics, short stories, and other pieces of writing come to life.

TYPES OF FIGURATIVE LANGUAGE

Some types of figurative language help your readers to compare persons or things that are basically different. Three common figurative devices are **similes, metaphors,** and **personification.**

Simile

What might a baseball mitt and a mousetrap have in common? A **simile** uses the word *like* or *as* to compare two different persons or things. Notice how Annie Dillard's simile on the next page compares the feeling of catching a baseball in a mitt to snaring a mouse in a trap.

Literary MODEL

> On the catch—the grounder, the fly, the line drive—you could snag a baseball in your mitt, where it stayed, snap, like a mouse locked in its trap.
>
> **Annie Dillard, *An American Childhood***

When Dillard wrote this simile, she first identified what she wanted to describe: catching a baseball. Then she zeroed in on a specific feeling she wanted to highlight: the sensation of catching a baseball in a mitt. She thought of something else to compare that sensation to: the snapping of a trap as it snares a mouse. Dillard used *like* to compare the first thing to the second. Follow the same pattern to write your own similes.

Metaphor

When you compare one thing to another without using the word *like* or *as,* you are writing a **metaphor.** What is the airplane compared to in the metaphor that follows?

> The plane is your planet and you are its sole inhabitant.
>
> **Beryl Markham, *West with the Night***

Markham needed a metaphor that described the lonely feeling she experienced when she flew solo. Then she thought of something that might create that same feeling: being the only person on a planet. Finally, she compared the plane to a planet and the passenger in the plane to the only person on a planet. The reader must think about how it might feel to be the only person on a planet in order to understand the loneliness Markham felt when she flew.

Personification

When you give human qualities to nonhuman things, such as plants, animals, places, and objects, you are using **personification.** Gary Soto used personification when he wrote that "wind tickled the back of my throat." In the example on the next page, what human qualities does F. Scott Fitzgerald give to the moon?

for SIMILE

USING THE MODEL Have a volunteer read the quotation from Annie Dillard; discuss the explanatory text. Then invite students to think of other similes that could be used to describe a baseball going into a mitt.

GENERAL NOTE

CRITICAL THINKING: SYNTHESIZING After students have discussed both Literary Models, have them express Dillard's simile as a metaphor (". . . it stayed, snap, a mouse locked in its trap") and Markham's metaphor as a simile ("The plane is like [a] planet, and you are its sole inhabitant"). Invite students to comment on the results.

SPICE BOX

Point out that writers and speakers often run two inconsistent metaphors together. Explain that these "mixed metaphors" are blunders that create incongruous images: *Changing horses in midstream left us out on a limb.*

Then ask students to think of other of mixed metaphors that create a humorous effect.

Literature Connection

Read from "The Grass" by Emily Dickinson.

The Grass so little has to do—
A Sphere of simple Green—
With only Butterflies to brood
And Bees to entertain—

Ask what poetic device the poet is using to describe the grass (personification).

for AVOIDING CLICHÉS

KEY TO UNDERSTANDING Ask students what kind of expression *sly as a fox* is, besides being a cliché (a simile). Point out that many clichés began as fresh metaphors or similes. Encourage students to state as many clichés as they can. Which are similes? Which are metaphors?

for ONOMATOPOEIA

INDIVIDUALIZING INSTRUCTION: ESL STUDENTS Ask students who are fluent in languages other than English to suggest an onomatopoeic word from their first language. (To help students get started, you might create sounds by ripping a piece of paper or tapping a desk.) The class can guess the foreign word's meaning from its sound and from any context clues the ESL student can offer. Once students have guessed the meaning, write the word in English on the chalkboard.

> [Dexter] . . . watched the even overlap of the waters in the little wind. . . . Then the moon held a finger to her lips and the lake became a clear pool, pale and quiet.
>
> **F. Scott Fitzgerald, *Winter Dreams***

To use personification, identify which human quality you want to give to a nonhuman subject. Then let your subject take on that quality, as Fitzgerald did when he wrote that "the moon held a finger to her lips."

Avoiding Clichés

When you write, try to create original expressions instead of using clichés. **Clichés** are expressions, such as *time is money* and *sly as a fox,* that are not effective because they have been overused.

cliché	spread like wildfire
alternative	spread quicker than a rumor in a small town

Cool as a cucumber

SOUND DEVICES

In addition to figurative language, you can use sound devices to create images. Devices such as **onomatopoeia, alliteration,** and **assonance** create pleasing patterns of sound in your writing.

Onomatopoeia

Do you think of the actual sounds when you hear the words *screech, fizz, clang,* and *murmur?* Words such as these are examples of **onomatopoeia.**

Literary MODEL

> The sounds were coming from just across the river, to the north, and they were a weird medley of *whines, whimpers,* and small *howls.*
>
> **Farley Mowat, *Never Cry Wolf***

Alliteration

In **alliteration** the words you use repeat a beginning consonant sound to create a mood in your writing.

> *D*rum on your *d*rums, *b*atter on your *b*anjoes,
> *s*ob on the long cool winding *s*axophones.
>
> **Carl Sandburg, "Jazz Fantasia"**

Assonance

Another sound device, **assonance,** uses the repetition of vowel sounds to give special emphasis to words.

Literary MODEL

> Asl*ee*p h*e* wh*ee*zes at his *ea*se.
> H*e* only wakes to scratch his fl*ea*s.
>
> **Ted Hughes, "Roger the Dog"**

Practice Your Skills

A. Rewrite the sentences below, following the directions given.

1. His hair stood up straight and stiff. (Use a simile.)
2. The house had been recently painted. (Use personification.)
3. Her hands moved quickly across the piano keys. (Use a metaphor.)
4. The basketball dropped through the net. (Use onomatopoeia.)
5. The noisy river flowed through the canyon. (Use alliteration or assonance.)

B. Replace the underlined clichés in the paragraph below with more original language.

[1]The howling of the wind was clear as a bell. [2]My room grew dark as night. [3]No one had to hit me over the head to make me understand. [4]I ran quick as a wink to shut my window. [5]Outside I saw my bike being bounced around like a basketball.

GENERAL NOTE

COOPERATIVE LEARNING Divide students into small groups of three or four students each. Ask each group to select a topic and work together to write a brief poem using as many sound devices as possible. Encourage students to choose topics about school or from current news events. Have them read their poems aloud. As a class, discuss the sound devices'effectiveness in conveying meaning.

Additional Resource

Writing Resource Book, pp. 101–102

Answers to Practice Your Skills

A. Answers will vary. See typical revised sentences below.

1. His hair stood up straight and stiff as the bristles on a brush.
2. The house wore a new coat of paint.
3. Her hands were butterflies, fluttering across the piano keys.
4. The basketball swished through the net.
5. *Alliteration:* The roaring river raced through the canyon.
   Assonance: The river hissed and fizzed as it twisted through the canyon.

B. Answers will vary. See typical revision below.

The howling of the wind was as loud as a train's screeching horn in a tunnel. My room grew dark as the deepest recesses of an underground cavern. No news broadcast was needed for me to understand this storm. I ran with the speed of an Olympic skater to shut my window. Outside I saw my bike flipping around like a porpoise in a pool.

for FURTHER READING

Stories to Read Encourage students to look for poetic devices whenever they read either stories or poetry. Suggest that they read Ray Bradbury's stories, such as "Naming of Names," "All Summer in a Day," and "There Will Come Soft Rains," and share examples of poetic devices that they discover.

Using Poetic Devices 321

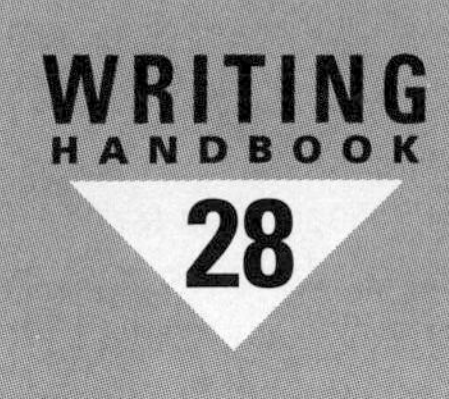

Point of View

Objectives

- To identify the three points of view in writing: first person, second person, and third person
- To write passages from the first- and third-person points of view

Related Mini-Lessons

For more information on topics relating to point of view, see the following mini-lessons:

- **General Purpose and Personal Goals, pp. 232–233**
- **Audience, pp. 234–235**
- **Using Pronouns, p. 436**

Teaching Strategies

for THREE POINTS OF VIEW

INDIVIDUALIZING INSTRUCTION: BASIC STUDENTS These students may have difficulty distinguishing the three points of view. Point out clues in several examples. Tell students to ask themselves these questions:

- What pronouns are used?
- Whose thoughts and feelings are expressed?

for LITERARY MODELS

USING THE MODELS Have volunteers read aloud the two Literary Models on pages 322 and 323. Discuss how the models might sound different if their points of view were switched. (Sample: The Tolkien piece might be just as effective in the first person. In the piece by Myers, the first-person point of view helps the reader sense what the writer is seeing, experiencing. The third-person point of view might distance readers from the characters.)

WRITING HANDBOOK 28

Who Will Narrate My Story?

Point of View

Is the human a zoo visitor or the lion's next meal? That depends on the point of view.

THREE POINTS OF VIEW

In narrative writing, **point of view** refers to who is telling the story. There are three basic points of view: first person, third person, and second person. The point of view you choose depends on who you want to tell your story.

A story narrated by someone who takes part in the action is written from the **first-person point of view.** This point of view reveals the feelings and thoughts of the narrator and uses such first-person pronouns as *I, me, my, we,* and *our.* Letters, journals, opinion essays, and autobiographies are written from the first-person point of view.

Literary MODEL

> I could feel the game. I could feel everything that was going on. It was as if every player had a string on him and the strings were all tied to me. Anytime anybody moved, I could feel it. I saw everything and knew what everybody was doing. We started coming back. The ball felt good in my hands.
>
> **Walter Dean Myers, *Hoops***

A story told by someone who observes and describes the action, but doesn't take part in it, is told from the **third-person point of view.** A third-person narrator will use such third-person pronouns as *he, she, him, her, they,* and *them.* This point of view

Literature Connection

Ask students to identify the point of view of this passage from Toni Cade Bambara's story "Raymond's Run." "Now some people like to act like things come easy to them, won't let on that they practice. Not me. I'll high-prance down 34th Street like a rodeo pony to keep my knees strong even if it does get my mother uptight so that she walks ahead like she's not with me, don't know me, is all by herself on a shopping trip, and I am somebody else's crazy child." (first person) Ask students: What do you find out about the main character that you probably would not find out if the story were told from another point of view? (the character's thoughts about her mother's reaction) is used in many types of writing, but it is especially helpful when the writer wants the narrator to be an objective observer of the action.

Literary **MODEL**

> The stars were coming out behind him in a pale sky barred with black when the hobbit crept through the enchanted door and stole into the Mountain. It was far easier going than he expected. This was no goblin entrance, or rough Wood-elves' cave. **J.R.R. Tolkien, *The Hobbit***

The **second-person point of view,** indicated by the pronoun *you,* is used when the writer wants to address the reader directly. This point of view is most often found in instructions, explanations, advice, or directions.

Practice Your Skills

A. The paragraph below is written from the first-person point of view. Rewrite it as a third-person narrative.

> I went on lathering his face. My hands began to tremble again. The man could not be aware of this, which was lucky for me. But I wished he had not come in. Probably many of our men had seen him enter the shop. And with the enemy in my house I felt a certain responsibility.
>
> I would have to shave his beard just like any other, carefully, neatly, just as though he were a good customer, taking heed that not a single pore should emit a drop of blood. Seeing to it that the blade did not slip in the small whorls. Taking care that the skin was left clean, soft, shining, so that when I passed the back of my hand over it not a single hair should be felt. **Hernando Téllez, *Lather and Nothing Else***

B. Write a paragraph based on one of the topics below, using the first-person point of view. Then write a second paragraph on a different topic using the third-person point of view. In what ways are the paragraphs different?

a childhood memory	an embarrassing moment
an argument	a frightening experience

GENERAL NOTE

ASSESSMENT: SPOT CHECK Ask students what point of view the writer of this handbook used (second person). Challenge students to find a few sentences that exemplify this point of view. (Sample: "The point of view you choose depends on who you want to tell your story," page 322, paragraph 2.)

for PRACTICE YOUR SKILLS

LINKING GRAMMAR AND WRITING Discuss with students the grammatical changes needed to convert a first-person account to a third-person account. Point out that the first-person pronoun *I* must be replaced with a proper noun and a third-person pronoun and that the verb form must be changed to agree with those replacements. Here is an example:

First Person: *I play* on the lacrosse team at *my* school.

Third Person: *John plays* on the lacrosse team at *his* school.

Additional Resource

Writing Resource Book, p. 103

Answers to Practice Your Skills

A. Answers will vary. Students should use third-person pronouns consistently, as in the sample revision below.

The barber went on lathering the man's face. His hands began to tremble again. The customer could not be aware of this, which was lucky for the barber. But he wished this man had not come in. Probably many of the men had seen the customer enter the shop. And with the enemy in his house, the barber felt a certain responsibility.

He would have to shave the man's beard just like any other, carefully, neatly, just as though he were a good customer, taking heed that not a single pore should emit a drop of blood. Seeing to it that the blade did not slip in the small whorls. Taking care that the skin was left clean, soft, shining, so that when the barber passed the back of his hand over it not a single hair should be felt.

B. Answers will vary. Students should use the first person or third person consistently throughout their paragraphs. They should also be able to identify the effect that point of view has on their paragraphs.

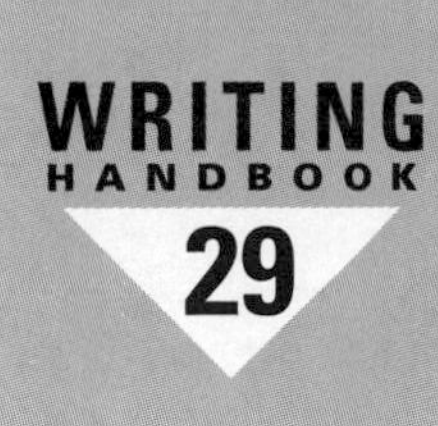

Writing Dialogue

Objectives

- To write dialogue that conveys characterization, action, and setting
- To understand how dialogue and stage directions are used in plays and skits

Related Mini-Lessons

For more information on topics relating to writing dialogue, see the following mini-lessons:

- **Show, Don't Tell, pp. 262–267**
- **Introductions, pp. 278–280**
- **Punctuation, p. 666**

Teaching Strategies

for CHARACTERS

USING THE MODEL Discuss the passage by Richard Wright, helping students see how one character in it is also the narrator. Then ask two students to read the excerpt aloud: a male student for the narrative and the boy's part of the dialogue, and a female student for the mother's lines. Then have students describe the personal characteristics of the mother and son. Lead students to see how dialogue, by revealing their thoughts and feelings, helps the reader get to know the characters.

WRITING HANDBOOK 29

How Do I Create Dialogue?

Writing Dialogue

"What is the use of a book," thought Alice, "without pictures or conversations?"

Lewis Carroll, *Alice in Wonderland*

Of course, Alice is exaggerating. Not every piece of writing has—or needs—pictures and conversations. However, these elements *can* make your writing interesting and exciting to read. In fact, you can use conversation, or **dialogue,** in any kind of writing. Letting people speak for themselves can launch your writing right off the page and into readers' memories.

FICTION AND NONFICTION

In fiction and nonfiction, dialogue can provide important information about the characters, the action, and the setting—the who, what, and where—of your topic.

Characters

In your writing, you can let people reveal who they are by what they say and how they say it. For example, in the following passage from an autobiographical essay, Richard Wright lets readers discover his characters by quoting their own words.

Literary MODEL

My mother met me at the door.

"They b-beat m-me," I gasped. "They t-took the m-money."

I started up the steps, seeking the shelter of the house.

"Don't you come in here," my mother warned me.

I froze in my tracks and stared at her.

"But they're coming after me," I said.

"You just stay right where you are," she said in a deadly tone. "I'm going to teach you this night to stand up and fight for yourself."

Richard Wright, "The Right to the Streets of Memphis"

for **FURTHER READING**

Bring copies of *Alice's Adventures in Wonderland* or *Through the Looking Glass* to class and ask volunteers to present a dramatic reading of some of the dialogue. The Mad Hatter's tea party, the Cheshire Cat scene, the Tweedledee and Tweedledum scene, and the playing-card scenes have especially strong dialogue.

Action

Dialogue can also give readers details about events. The following passage is from a nonfiction account of a near tragedy in an abandoned mine. Notice how readers learn that something has happened to the boy Josh through the comments of the people who were with him.

[Scout leader Terry] Dennis settled by the mine entrance to wait for the others. When [Scoutmaster Kevin] Weaver's group emerged almost an hour later, Josh was not with them.

"Where's Josh?" Dennis shouted, suddenly apprehensive.

"I thought he went with you," Weaver said.

"Have we lost him?" Dennis screamed.

"Maybe Josh came out by himself," Weaver replied. The group fanned out through the underbrush, calling Josh's name. Dennis checked the sleeping bags. *I should have kept him with me. What if he's fallen down a shaft?*

Per Ola and Emily d'Aulaire, "Lost Beneath the Mountain"

Setting

Rather than just describing where events take place, let dialogue do the work for you. In the following passage, the characters are lost in a snowstorm. Their conversation describes the setting.

"I think I know where we are! That old split post just back there's where we made a takedown running coyotes with Dad's hounds this fall. If I'm right, this is Miller's north meadow, and there's a strip of willows down ahead there, off to the right—" . . .

"How far to a house?" she finally asked, her lips frozen.

"There's no house along this fence if it's the Miller's," Chuck had to admit. "It just goes around the meadow, three, four miles long."

"You're sure—" the teacher asked slowly, "—sure there's no cross fence to the ranch? You might get through, find help in time—"

Mari Sandoz, "Winter Thunder"

for ACTION

USING THE MODEL Have a student read aloud the passage from "Lost Beneath the Mountain." Point out that even nonfiction passages can have dramatic action that is shown through dialogue. Have students summarize the action of the passage. (Sample: When the Scout groups meet, Josh's absence is discovered. A search begins.) You also might have students identify some of the emotions revealed in the dialogue. (Samples: worry, panic, hope, self-blame)

for SETTING

INDIVIDUALIZING INSTRUCTION: VISUAL LEARNERS You might encourage these students to sketch the scene described through dialogue in "Winter Thunder." Emphasize that dialogue can give all the information needed about setting. You also might suggest that when doing their own writing, these students reverse the process—making a sketch first and then capturing it in dialogue.

for LITERARY MODEL

MODELING To demonstrate how stage directions are subject to interpretation, model a dramatic reading of the passage by A. A. Milne, using appropriate gestures and tones in accordance with the stage directions. You may wish to have students assist you. Then have one or two groups of students model the passage. Discuss with students how different people will interpret stage directions differently.

for WRITING DIALOGUE

HELPFUL HINT Emphasize to students the importance of reading aloud any dialogue they are writing. Suggest that they read it to a peer who can help them develop natural dialogue, into a tape recorder so that they can critique it themselves, or aloud to themselves.

PLAYS AND SKITS

In plays and skits, dialogue must tell almost everything the audience needs to know about the characters' thoughts and feelings and about events that happen offstage. **Stage directions** provide details about the setting and about characters' appearance and behavior.

In the following passage, notice how A. A. Milne uses the stage directions in parentheses. They describe what the characters look like, how they speak, and what they are doing. The dialogue reveals the characters' personalities and sets the humorous tone of the play. As in many plays, the dialogue is not enclosed in quotation marks.

A Voice (*Announcing*). His Excellency the Chancellor! [The Chancellor, *an elderly man in horn-rimmed spectacles, enters, bowing.* The King *wakes up with a start and removes the handkerchief from his face.*]

King (*With simple dignity*). I was thinking.

Chancellor (*Bowing*). Never, Your Majesty, was greater need for thought than now.

King. That's what I was thinking. (*He struggles into a more dignified position.*) Well, what is it? More trouble?

Chancellor. What we might call the old trouble, Your Majesty.

King. It's what I was saying last night to the Queen. "Uneasy lies the head that wears a crown" was how I put it.

A. A. Milne, *The Ugly Duckling*

WRITING DIALOGUE

No matter how you use dialogue in your writing, the following guidelines can help you make it effective and easy for your audience to follow. Reading your dialogue aloud is a good way to see if it sounds like a conversation real people would have. It can also help you find ways to give each person his or her own special way of speaking.

PROFESSIONAL NOTEBOOK

Author Cynde Gregory shares an overheard discussion in which a student writer complains to her peer readers about the stiltedness of her dialogue:

"My characters don't sound good when they talk. They don't sound like they really are talking. . . ." The [peer readers], one by one, made suggestions . . . but the writer just became more and more frustrated. Nothing helped.

"They just don't sound good enough when they talk," she muttered once again.

A sage voice from an adjacent workshop group said, "Maybe you just aren't listening good enough."

Childmade: Awakening Children To Creative Writing

Guidelines for Writing Dialogue

- Make the dialogue sound like real speech. You can include slang and sentence fragments.

  "Hey, whatcha doin', Silas?" Lucy asked.

- Identify the speaker and tell how the person is speaking by using a speaker's tag.

  "Can I come too?" Lucy begged. "Please, please."

- Set off the speaker's exact words with quotation marks.

  "There's almost nothing I'd rather do than scuba dive," Silas said.

- Begin a new paragraph each time the speaker changes.

  "I'm not afraid," boasted Lucy. "I'm not. I'm not."

  "Well, I can't wait all day," Silas said over his shoulder. "Step on it if you're comin'."

- The first words of quotations are capitalized.
- End marks are usually placed inside quotation marks as you see in these examples.

"I've even seen sharks and stingrays," Silas continued.

Practice Your Skills

The following passage is from an autobiographical essay. Using dialogue, rewrite it as part of a short story.

> The day of the first game some of us met early at Hobo Park to talk about how we were going to whip them and send them home whining to their mothers. Soon others showed up to practice fielding grounders while waiting for the coach to pull up in his pickup. When we spotted him coming down the street, we ran to him, and before the pickup had come to a stop, we were already climbing the sides. The coach stuck his head from the cab to warn us to be careful. He idled the pickup for a few minutes to wait for the others, and when two did come running, he waved for them to get in the front with him. As he drove slowly to the West Side, our hair flicked about in the wind, and we thought we looked neat.
>
> **Gary Soto, "Baseball in April"**

for GUIDELINES FOR WRITING DIALOGUE

INDIVIDUALIZING INSTRUCTION: ESL STUDENTS Initial quotation marks are inverted in some languages, such as Spanish and Russian. Check to see that students understand the correct English form.

Answers to Practice Your Skills

Answers will vary. See typical revision below.

The day of the first game some of us met early at Hobo Park. "We're going to whip them and send them home whining to their mothers," I boasted.

Soon others showed up to practice fielding grounders while waiting for the coach to pull up in his pickup. When we spotted him coming down the street, we ran to him, and before the pickup had come to a stop, we were already climbing the sides.

The coach stuck his head from the cab. "Be careful there!" he yelled. He idled the pickup for a few minutes. "We'll wait for the others," he said.

"There they are now," I called when I spied two players come running up.

"Get in the front," Coach said, waving to them to sit in the cab with him.

As he drove slowly to the West Side, our hair flicked about in the wind, and we thought we looked neat.

Additional Resource

Writing Resource Book, pp. 104–105

Literature Connection

Story to Read You may wish to have students read Gary Soto's short story "Mother and Daughter" on page 443 in *Literature and Language*, Grade 8. Tell students to pay particular attention to Soto's use of dialogue to establish character and tell about action.

Objective

- To use the cartoon and writing prompts as springboards to informal writing

WRITING WARM-UPS

Use this writing warm-up activity as a no-risk journal writing experience. Students should feel free to respond to any of the writing prompts and to keep what they write in their writing folders for possible use in future writing projects.

Tell students who choose to write about the second prompt that they don't need to confine themselves to what they research for school. In fact, they may have more fun writing about how they uncover information outside of school.

Sketch Book

WRITING WARM-UPS

- What do you want to grow up to be? Write about your hopes and your goals.
- How do you find out things you want to know? Tell about some of your strategies.
- Have you ever gotten words mixed up and used the wrong one in a conversation? Tell about the experience.

328

TEACHER'S LOUNGE

Cartoon by Bartholomew/©1984 by Marilyn Barry.

Academic Skills

The Librarian (1556), Giuseppe Arcimboldo.

You won't find any thesaurus bones in the natural history museum. You won't find any synonyms in a tyrannosaurus.

You *can* find ways to think more clearly, study more effectively, and use the information in books more skillfully. In these handbooks you will learn skills that can keep you from becoming extinct as a student.

Academic Skills

INTRODUCING THE HANDBOOKS

Ask students to suggest why the painting is called *The Librarian.* (The subject is literally composed of books, bookmarks, and other book parts.) Remind students that this portrait was painted in the sixteenth century; ask them whether they would include any objects other than books in a painting of a librarian today. Encourage students to suggest other tools librarians currently use, such as card catalogs, computers, and microforms. Explain that the upcoming academic skills handbooks will enable students to make better use of a variety of learning tools.

ART NOTE

Giuseppe Arcimboldo (1530–1593), the painter of *The Librarian,* was an Italian artist who frequently painted portraits composed of objects representing a certain profession or character. Similar works by Arcimboldo include a gardener whose cheeks are apples and whose nose is a pear, and a lady whose face is composed of flowers.

Developing Vocabulary

Objectives

- To explore techniques for learning new words
- To infer meanings of unfamiliar words from context
- To infer the meanings of unfamiliar words by analyzing their prefixes, suffixes, and base words

Related Mini-Lessons

For information on topics related to developing vocabulary, see the following mini-lessons.

- **Revising, pp. 287–289**
- **Meaning and Word Choice, pp. 314–315**
- **Using Poetic Devices, pp. 318–321**

Motivate

Select an unfamiliar word such as *pellucid* ("translucent; transparently clear in style or meaning," as in *pellucid prose)* and write two definitions, one real and one invented. Use the word in a sentence and have students vote on the correct definition. Then discuss the strategies they used to guess the word's meaning.

Teaching Strategies

for GUIDELINES FOR LEARNING NEW WORDS

PERSONAL TOUCH Let your students know the ways in which you regularly improve your own vocabulary, whether by reading, taking classes in unfamiliar subjects, talking with knowledgeable people, or following any of the tips listed on this page.

WRITING HANDBOOK 30

How Do I Strengthen My Vocabulary?

Developing Vocabulary

Consider for a moment how your vocabulary has grown over the years. By the age of eighteen months, you could probably say about fifty words and understand around two hundred. You learned words easily by listening to people around you. As you grew, you stored thousands of words in your memory.

Unfortunately, developing your vocabulary by listening to others becomes less effective as you get older. You must now develop new techniques for learning words.

COMPUTER TIP

Some word-processing programs have built-in spell checkers and thesauruses that you can use to find information about unfamiliar words.

Guidelines for Learning New Words

1. **Read.** One of the best ways of developing a large vocabulary is reading. If you read about a variety of subjects, you will encounter many new and useful words.
2. **Ask about the meanings of unfamiliar words.** When someone uses a word you don't understand, ask what the word means. Besides increasing your vocabulary, inquiring about the meaning shows that you are truly interested in understanding the person's ideas.
3. **Keep vocabulary lists.** Reserve a part of your notebook or learning log to be used as a "vocabulary bank." When you encounter a new word, write it down. Later on, look up the word in a dictionary and jot down its meaning. You might also include a sentence that shows how the word is used. Then make a point of working the word into your writing and conversation. These techniques will help to make the word stick in your mind.
4. **Use context clues.** When you read or listen, be alert for clues to the meanings of unfamiliar words. Later in this handbook, you will read about four types of clues you can use.
5. **Use word parts.** Often you can dissect an unfamiliar word into a base word and other parts to help you determine the meaning of the word. This handbook will explain how. See pages 333–335 for details.

PROFESSIONAL NOTEBOOK

Share this advice from *Writing Well* by poet Donald Hall: "The growing writer finds pleasure in becoming a word collector, picking up, examining, and keeping new words (or familiar words seen suddenly, as if for the first time) like seashells or driftwood. Think of the richness in 'hogwash,' or the exact strength in 'rasp.' English is thick with short, strong words. You can collect words from books, of course, but you can also find them in speech; a sense of lively speech adds energy to the best writing. . . . Patrol the miles of speech looking for words like 'flotsam.'"

INFERRING WORD MEANINGS

Study the picture on this page. Can you guess the meaning of the word *baguette?* If you guessed "a long, thin loaf of bread," you're right. Chances are, the **context**—the pictures and words that surround the word—helped you infer its meaning. When you **infer,** you draw a conclusion based on the facts that are given and on what you know from experience.

Several types of context clues are used by writers. The next few pages describe these clues.

Definition or Restatement Clues

A new or unfamiliar word may be defined directly, or its meaning may be restated in other words. Often a comma, a dash, or parentheses are used to set off the meaning clue. In the example below, notice how the commas help you know that *salutation* means "greeting."

> The *salutation,* or greeting, appears at the beginning of a letter.

Some words that signal definitions or restatements are *in other words, that is, or, this means,* and *to put it another way.*

Example Clues

A writer might choose to use one or more examples to clarify the meaning of a new or unusual word.

> *Primates,* including squirrel monkeys, baboons, chimpanzees, and gorillas, take very good care of their young.

Although the meaning of *primates* is not given, the word *including* signals that the animals named are all types of primates. From these examples, you might infer that primates are such mammals as monkeys and the apes. Example clues commonly use the following words and phrases: *like, especially, for example, for instance, including, such as, to illustrate, this, these,* and *other.*

for INFERRING WORD MEANINGS

CRITICAL THINKING: MAKING INFERENCES Students have many opportunities to make inferences about words from context: for example, when they listen to conversation (gestures, intonation, pauses, and so on, are part of the context); look at pictures that accompany text, such as the one on this page; read books, magazines, or newspapers; or watch television programs or movies. Ask students to share strategies they currently use for inferring meanings of unfamiliar words they see and hear. If students happen to recall specific instances in which they inferred the meanings of new words—perhaps in reading a story—encourage them to share the experiences.

MULTICULTURAL Connection

Bon appétit! From baguettes to pizza, from salsa to chow mein, America offers a rich menu of food items from around the world. In small groups, students might try to list all the dishes they can think of whose names come from other languages. Of course, food does not provide the only source of foreign words in English. Ask your class to name more English words that come from other languages.

for COMPARISON OR CONTRAST CLUES

LINKING GRAMMAR AND WRITING Explain to students that the words *like* and *as* are very useful for defining words in context. However, these words are often used incorrectly. When *like* is used as a preposition, it is followed by a noun or pronoun. (Example: Susan looks *like her sister.*) *As* is a conjunction that introduces a clause. (Example: He did well on the test, *as I expected.*) Remind students that a clause contains a subject and a verb—in this instance *I* and *expected.*

Comparison or Contrast Clues

Sometimes the meaning of a new or unusual word is compared or contrasted with something the reader will understand. Read the sentence below. Notice how the word *like* sets up a comparison that helps you infer that arid land is dry like a desert.

> The new land was *arid,* like the dry, barren desert through which the settlers had come.

In the example that follows, the word *while* is used to introduce a contrast. It helps you infer that an aloof attitude is the opposite of one that is friendly and outgoing.

> Jamal acted *aloof,* while Ed was friendly and outgoing.

Comparisons and contrasts are often signaled by words and phrases such as *but, although, in comparison, in contrast, on the other hand, similarly, like,* and *as.*

Clues from General Context

In some instances, no direct clue to the meaning of a word is given. Instead, the meaning is hinted at in the sentences surrounding the word, as in this example.

> The house was *dilapidated.* Its windows were broken. Its doors were off their hinges. Its paint was peeling. Wind whistled through cracks in the attic walls, and the floorboards creaked.

Writing TIP

Use context clues in your own writing to define words that your readers might not understand.

Although the word *dilapidated* is not directly defined, the broken windows and doors, the peeling paint, and the cracks in the walls help you know that *dilapidated* means "run-down and neglected."

Practice Your Skills

A. Using the context clues given in the sentences, write the meanings of the italicized words and phrases.

1. *Poaching,* the unlawful hunting of protected animals, has put several species on the endangered list.

Literature Connection

The story "The Gift of the Magi" by O. Henry on page 434 of *Literature and Language,* Grade 8, is filled with words that are probably unfamiliar to many students. List the words *bulldozing, imputation,* and *parsimony* on the chalkboard and ask if anyone knows their meaning. Then read aloud the first paragraph of the story. See if students can guess at the meanings of these words after hearing them used within the context of the story.

2. *Fossil fuels,* such as petroleum, coal, and natural gas, are formed from plants that lived long ago and are used as sources of energy.
3. Most of us agreed, but Hector *dissented.*
4. *Stalactites* hung like icicles from the roof of the cave.
5. The Wild Cats are a *formidable* basketball team. Taller than most teams and quick on their feet, the Wild Cats can outplay most opponents. They haven't lost a game all season.

B. Rewrite each of these sentences, adding a context clue to help readers understand the meaning of the italicized word. Use a dictionary if necessary. Be sure to use each type of context clue at least once.

EXAMPLE Martina tried to *rectify* her mistake.
Martina tried to *rectify,* **or correct,** her mistake.

1. The *venue* for the trial has yet to be decided.
2. Please be *frank* in your comments about my report.
3. Pat was not surprised to learn that she had developed *myopia.*
4. Archaeologists uncovered many *artifacts.*
5. Chris *deliberated* for hours about how to begin his speech.

Analyzing Word Parts

Another good way to determine the meaning of an unfamiliar word is to analyze its parts. A complete word to which word parts are added is called a **base word.** If you take word parts that cannot stand alone and add them to a base word, new words are formed. The word *illiterate,* for example, is made by adding the word part *il-,* which means "not," to the base word *literate,* meaning "able to read and write." *Illiterate* means "not able to read and write."

Prefixes

A word part that is added to the beginning of a word is called a **prefix.** The chart on the next page lists some common prefixes.

Answers to Practice Your Skills

A. Answers may vary slightly.

1. the unlawful hunting of protected animals
2. sources of energy, such as petroleum, coal, and natural gas
3. disagreed
4. icicle-shaped deposits that hang from the roofs of caves
5. impressive, hard to overcome

B. Answers will vary. Possible responses are given.

1. The *venue,* or place, for the trial has yet to be decided.
2. Please be *frank* in your comments about my report. I want to know what you honestly think.
3. Because she was having trouble seeing things from a distance, Pat was not surprised to learn that she had developed *myopia.*
4. Archaeologists uncovered many *artifacts,* such as arrowheads, beautifully painted clay pots, and necklaces.
5. Chris *deliberated* for hours about how to begin his speech, but Ellen decided on her introduction after ten minutes.

for ANALYZING WORD PARTS

INDIVIDUALIZING INSTRUCTION: KINESTHETIC LEARNERS Those who learn kinesthetically may enjoy physically putting new words together by mixing and matching prefixes, base words, and suffixes, written on index cards. Be sure to alert these students to some of the common spelling changes that occur, especially when base words acquire suffixes.

SPICE BOX

A book called *Sniglets* by Rich Hall & Friends (Not the Network Company, Inc., 1984) defines a *sniglet* as "any word that doesn't appear in the dictionary, but should." Students may enjoy creating their own sniglets from base words, prefixes, and suffixes. Here are two typical sniglets: *elbonics*—the actions of two people maneuvering for one armrest in a movie theater; and *aquadextrous*—possessing the ability to turn a bathtub faucet on and off with one's toes. For more sniglets, see page 111.

for PREFIXES AND SUFFIXES

COOPERATIVE LEARNING Divide your class into groups of three of four students. Make sure each group has a dictionary, a pencil, and a piece of paper; then assign two or three common prefixes or suffixes to each group, such as *im, re,* and *de* or *-ist, -ize,* and *-ness.* Give each group a short time period, about five or ten minutes, to generate a list of words that begin or end with one of the prefixes or suffixes. Each word must appear in the dictionary; therefore, have one student look up words while another acts as secretary, recording the group's list. Post the lists on a class bulletin board.

Calvin and Hobbes

by Bill Watterson

Prefix	Meaning	Examples
bi-	two	bicycle, biplane
de-, dis-	lower, opposite	devalue, disagree
fore-, pre-	before, ahead of time	forewarn, precook
il-, im-, in-, ir-, non-, un-	not	illegible, improper, incapable, irregular, nonsense, unknown
mid-	middle	midway, midyear
mis-	wrong, badly	misspell, misbehave
re-	back, again	renew, recall
sub-	under, less than	subzero, subdivision
super-	above, more than	superstar, supermarket
trans-	across, to the other side of	transcontinental, transfusion, transplant
tri-	three	tricycle, triangle

Suffixes

A word part added to the end of a word is called a **suffix.** A suffix can change the part of speech of the base word to which it is added. The spelling of the base word may also change. For example, the final letter may be dropped or doubled.

Adding a **noun suffix** to a base word forms a noun.

Noun Suffix	Meaning	Examples
-an, -ant, -eer, -er, -ian, -ier, -ist, -or	one who does or makes something	auctioneer, baker, physician, actor
-ship, -ment, -ness, -hood	the state or condition of, act or process of	kinship, motherhood

Adding a **verb suffix** to a base word forms a verb.

Verb Suffix	Meaning	Examples
-ate	to form, produce	orchestrate
-en	to make, cause	deepen
-ify, -fy, -ise, -ize	to become, cause, make	solidify, legalize

Science Connection

Point out to students that scientific writing often contains a specialized vocabulary of words formed with certain prefixes, such as *bio-* or *eco-.* Have students keep a running list of such words and their meanings and look for other prefixes that are frequently used in a scientific vocabulary.

Adding an **adjective suffix** to a base word forms an adjective.

Suffix	Meaning	Examples
-able, -ible	able to be	manageable, sensible
-al	relating to	natural
-ful, -ous, -ive	full of, having the characteristics of	harmful, poisonous, sportive
-ish	like, similar to, of or belonging to	foolish, yellowish, Spanish
-less	without, not able or likely to	seamless, tireless
-like	relating to	childlike, lifelike

Practice Your Skills

A. Make four columns on your paper. Label them *Base Word, Prefix, Suffix,* and *Meaning.* For each word, write the base word and the prefix or suffix (or both) in the appropriate columns. In the last column, write a definition of the word, based on its parts.

1. brotherhood
2. disrespectful
3. irresistible
4. subtotal
5. finalize
6. awaken

B. Write the new word you form by adding the appropriate prefix or suffix (or both) from the charts to the base word in parentheses in each sentence.

1. Maurice Sendak, a (write) and (illustrate) of children's books, has also been a set designer for operas.
2. If you are tired, a snack or a short nap may (vital) you.
3. Few toys are really (break).
4. The first solo (Atlantic) airplane flight was made by Charles Lindbergh in 1927.
5. The trial lawyer asked for a (play) of the taped conversation.
6. The criminal gave his captors a (murder) look.
7. When you (view) an article, be sure to read the titles, the subtitles, the illustrations, and the captions.
8. Recycling your cans, bottles, and newspapers is an easy way to demonstrate your (commit) to a cleaner environment.

for ADJECTIVE SUFFIX CHART

HELPFUL HINT Magazine and newspaper articles about personalities or fashion usually contain many adjectives. Ask students to find a sample article that contains some of the adjective suffixes in the list on this page.

Additional Resources

Writing Resource Book, pp. 106–108
Spelling and Vocabulary Booklet

Answers to Practice Your Skills

A.

	Base Word	Prefix	Suffix	Meaning
1.	brother		–hood	the state of being like a brother
2.	respect	dis–	–ful	not having or showing respect
3.	resist	ir–	–ible	not able to be resisted
4.	total	sub–		an amount that is less than a complete total
5.	final		–ize	to make final
6.	awake		–en	to make or become awake

B.

1. writer, illustrator
2. revitalize
3. unbreakable
4. transatlantic
5. replay
6. murderous
7. preview
8. commitment

After students have enjoyed this humorous feature, ask them to use the skills they learned in Handbook 30 to figure out the meaning of the word *impenetrability*. You might begin by asking them what they think the word means from its context. Then continue by asking students to analyze the word by determining and defining its base word *(penetrate)*, its prefix *(im-)*, and its suffixes *(-able and -ity)*.

on the LIGHT side

How Words Earn Their Keep

If you are having trouble with your vocabulary, maybe you aren't paying your words enough. Humpty Dumpty gave this advice about how to treat words to Alice when she went *Through the Looking Glass*.

"When *I* use a word," Humpty Dumpty said in rather a scornful tone, "it means just what I choose it to mean—neither more nor less."

"The question is," said Alice, "whether you *can* make words mean so many different things."

"The question is," said Humpty Dumpty, "which is to be master—that's all."

Alice was too much puzzled to say anything, so, after a minute, Humpty Dumpty began again. "They've a temper, some of them—particularly verbs, they're the proudest: adjectives you can do anything with, but not verbs. However, *I* can manage the whole lot of them! Impenetrability! That's what *I* say!"

"Would you tell me, please," said Alice, "what that means?"

"Now you talk like a reasonable child," said Humpty Dumpty, looking very much pleased. "I meant by 'impenetrability' that we've had enough of that subject, and it would be just as well if you'd mention what you mean to do next, as I suppose you don't mean to stop here all the rest of your life."

"That's a great deal to make one word mean," Alice said in a thoughtful tone.

"When I make a word do a lot of work like that," said Humpty Dumpty, "I always pay it extra."

Lewis Carroll

Critical Thinking and Writing

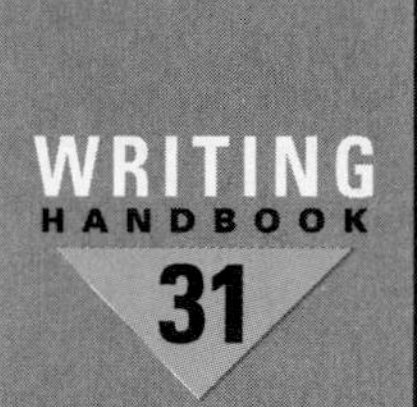

> Our principal and the school board are considering renaming the gymnasium in honor of Coach Harvey. Let our school be the first in this area to honor our town's most famous citizen. Coach Harvey was the finest high school and college coach of this century. Everybody in Norristown admires him.

Suppose that you read this letter to the editor in your school newspaper. Do any of the statements sound exaggerated or misleading? For example, does it seem likely that in one hundred years there hasn't been a better coach than Coach Harvey?

You read and hear statements like these every day—in radio and television commercials, in magazine and newspaper ads, and in casual conversations. How do you know which ones to believe? The ability to think critically will help you judge the truth of statements like these.

Critical thinking is an important skill to bring to your writing too. Carefully examining your ideas and the words you use to express them will help you make your case strongly and clearly.

ERRORS IN REASONING

Detecting errors in thinking can help you avoid problems in your writing. Here are some common errors in reasoning.

Overgeneralization A statement so broad that it cannot be true is an overgeneralization. Words such as *everyone, no one, always, never, best,* and *worst* often signal overgeneralizations.

Everybody in Norristown admires Coach Harvey.

(There must be at least one person in town who doesn't admire the coach—or who hasn't even heard of him.)

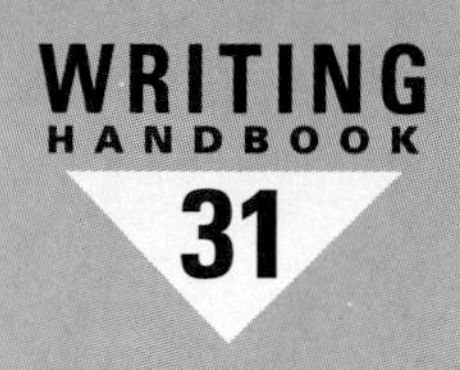

Critical Thinking and Writing

Objectives

- To learn the importance of critical thinking in reading and writing
- To identify errors in reasoning
- To recognize how improper appeals to emotion can weaken rational argument

Related Mini-Lessons

For information on topics related to critical thinking and writing, see the following mini-lessons:

- **Types of Organization, pp. 239–243**
- **Coherence, pp. 273–277**
- **Meaning and Word Choice, pp. 314–315**

Motivate

Ask students whether they ever were lured by an appealing ad on TV and then found the product disappointing. Explain that advertisers often try to influence people by appealing to emotions, rather than to reason. Tell students that this handbook will help them detect faulty reasoning and appeals to emotion.

Teaching Strategies

for ERRORS IN REASONING

INDIVIDUALIZING INSTRUCTION: BASIC STUDENTS Make sure these students understand what it means to overgeneralize. Remind them that many statements are true sometimes for some people, but that very few are true all the time for everybody. Ask students to identify ads or slogans that are examples of overgeneralization.

for ERRORS IN REASONING

COOPERATIVE LEARNING Suggest that students work in pairs or small groups to collect and display newspaper and magazine ads that demonstrate errors in reasoning. Some students may want to create a bulletin board display on being a careful consumer. Others may enjoy rewriting offensive ads to correct the errors in logic.

for IMPROPER APPEALS TO EMOTION

PERSONAL TOUCH Young teenagers are especially prone to emotional appeals made by their peers. You may want to share a personal experience from your youth in which an emotional appeal by a peer influenced you against your better judgment. Ask students for examples of statements that peers sometimes make when they are appealing to emotion rather than to reason. For example, "Everyone's going" is a common phrase that is an example of bandwagon appeal; "Don't be a chicken" is an example of name-calling.

Circular Reasoning Repeating a statement in other words rather than supporting it with good reasons is called circular reasoning.

Baseball is exciting because it is thrilling to the fans.

(We don't know why it's exciting.)

Either/Or Argument Stating that there are only two choices in a situation when other alternatives actually exist is an either/or argument.

Either my parents will have to increase my allowance, or I won't have any social life at all.

(There are other ways to earn money for social activities.)

False Cause-and-Effect Statement A statement wrongly implying that one event caused another is a false cause-and-effect statement.

The neighbor's dog barked all night. The next day I failed a test. I'd get better grades if the dog were quiet.

(Failing a test has more to do with lack of preparation than with lost sleep caused by a barking dog.)

IMPROPER APPEALS TO EMOTION

Be alert for statements that appeal to your emotions—your feelings of pride, insecurity, affection—rather than to your intelligence. Weed these kinds of statements out of your own writing. They weaken your arguments and leave them open to attack.

Bandwagon Appeal A statement that suggests a person should think or act like everyone else is a bandwagon appeal.

Really fashionable teens wear Hiker boots. Get a pair today.

(We don't know anything about the boots themselves.)

Exaggeration A statement that makes something seem larger or better than it actually is involves exaggeration.

ART NOTE

The drawing on this page shows the Pied Piper of Hamelin, a character in the following legend: The German town of Hamelin was overrun with rats. A man wearing a multicolored, or *pied,* coat promised to rid the town of rats—for a price. The mayor agreed to the stranger's fee, and the man pulled out a small flute called a pipe. His haunting melody lured all the rats out of town. When the mayor refused to pay the piper, the piper played again. This time, all the children of Hamelin followed him and were never seen again. Ask students to discuss why this illustration appears beside the text on improper appeals to emotion.

It was the most fantastic concert ever shown on TV.

(There is no way to decide which concert is the "most fantastic . . . ever shown.")

Loaded Language Certain words arouse people's emotions. This kind of loaded language takes advantage of the connotations or emotional associations of words.

The movie *Star People* is action-filled and thrilling.
The movie *Star People* is scary and violent.

(Which sentence makes the movie more appealing?)

Name-calling Criticizing someone's personal qualities is a type of loaded language known as name-calling.

Sue's locker is a mess. Don't elect her class president.

(Sue could still be a good class president.)

Weak Testimonial A testimonial is a statement of support for a product or idea by a famous person. A testimonial is weak if the person has no special knowledge about that product or idea.

Actor Marvin Bosner wears a Rock Mountain jacket.

(Simply wearing it says nothing about the jacket's quality.)

Insufficient Support In your reading, listening, and writing, be alert for strong statements that are not supported by facts.

The candidate's plan to reform health care is worthless.

(We aren't told what the plan is or why it is worthless.)

Practice Your Skills

Identify the errors in reasoning and the emotional appeals in the following ad. Then rewrite it to correct the errors.

Come to Fun 'n Sun theme park to experience the most incredible ride of a lifetime. There's nothing like it on earth; everyone who's in the know realizes that this ride has no equal. The singer Chelsea Nelson says there is nothing more enjoyable. You can't help but enjoy yourself because everything is so much fun.

for IMPROPER APPEALS TO EMOTION

INDIVIDUALIZING INSTRUCTION: ADVANCED STUDENTS These students might enjoy writing two versions of a political ad or a commercial. One version should include improper appeals to emotion; the other version should avoid those tactics.

BASIC STUDENTS These students often unwittingly include unsupported claims in their writing. Explain that unsupported statements leave the reader wondering. To help them revise such errors, suggest that they expand such sentences with a clause beginning with *because*. For example, refer students to "Adding Supporting Details" on page 299 of Handbook 22.

Additional Resource

Writing Resource Book, pp. 109–110

Answers to Practice Your Skills

Sentence 1: exaggeration
Sentence 2: exaggeration; bandwagon
Sentence 3: weak testimonial
Sentence 4: circular reasoning and insufficient support

Revised ads will vary. A sample revision is shown below.

Come to Fun 'n Sun theme park to experience Big Whiz, the fastest roller coaster east of the Mississippi. The only faster roller coaster has fewer large drops and steep turns. Eight out of ten visitors to Fun 'n Sun said that the Big Whiz was the highlight of their visit to the park. If you like roller coasters, you'll love the Big Whiz for its drops, turns, and speed.

for **FURTHER READING**

Story to Read Invite students to read Mona Gardner's short story "The Dinner Party" to find errors in reasoning, and improper appeals to emotion, in the comments the characters make about women.

Study and Research Skills

Objectives

- To identify and apply techniques for organizing assignments
- To take notes efficiently
- To apply methods of studying and reading to improve learning skills

Related Mini-Lessons

For information on topics related to study and research skills, see the following mini-lessons.

- **Critical Thinking and Writing, pp. 337–339**
- **Making Use of the Library, pp. 352–361**

Motivate

Have students in small groups brainstorm a list of problems they have experienced in doing their homework or in preparing for important tests. Ask a spokesperson in each group to read the group's list aloud as you write a composite list on the chalkboard. Then have the same groups brainstorm a list of solutions for these problems. Post the groups' lists where everyone can see them. Tell students that this handbook will offer strategies for solving some of the problems they have identified.

WRITING HANDBOOK 32

How Can I Become a Better Student?

Study and Research Skills

Have you ever imagined a magic spell for doing homework? Even though no such spell exists, there are study skills you can use that will have a powerful effect on your school work. By using proven study methods and learning specific reading skills, you will marvel at your success in school.

UNDERSTANDING YOUR ASSIGNMENTS

One of your most important jobs as a student is keeping track of your assignments. The guidelines below can help.

Organizing Your Assignments

1. **Log your assignments.** List all assignments in a notebook or folder. Your notes should answer these questions: What needs to be done and when? What form will the final product take? What supplies or other materials will you need?
2. **Keep a weekly schedule.** Record your assignments and your study times on a weekly calendar. The calendar allows you to see at a glance what needs to be done every day.
3. **Divide long assignments into parts.** If you're writing a speech, for example, divide your assignment into small tasks. Go to the library one day. Create an outline the next day, and begin your draft on yet another day.

COMPUTER TIP

Weekly schedules and calendars are available for many personal computers. Check with your computer software dealer.

TAKING NOTES

Do you ever look at your notes and find that you don't understand them? You need time and practice to learn how to take notes well. The strategies on the next page will help you become a first-class note taker.

SPICE BOX

Students might enjoy making their own assignment notebooks with illustrated, laminated covers. Ask them to consider what information should go on each page of the notebook. Because assignment notebooks can be neglected as quickly as New Year's resolutions, you might also consider asking students to pair off to encourage each other to continue using the assignment book.

- **Keep a notebook.** Keep all your notes in one place. You might use small notebooks, one for each class or subject area.
- **Identify each set of notes.** Write the subject and date in the upper right-hand corner of the page.
- **Use a modified outline form.** Use phrases to record main ideas in your notes. Then, below the main ideas, indent and write down related ideas.
- **Write key facts and ideas.** Be critical. Don't try to record everything. Look for phrases such as *most important, for these reasons, for example, to review,* and *to summarize.*
- **Use symbols and abbreviations.** Here are some symbols and abbreviations often used in notes. If you wish, you can make up your own symbols and abbreviations.

&	and	w/o	without	=	equals
Amer	American	def	definition	re	regarding
~	approximately	y	why	s/b	should be

- **Review your notes regularly.** Set aside time each day to review your notes.

Notice how one student uses a modified outline form and other guidelines to structure her notes about dinosaurs.

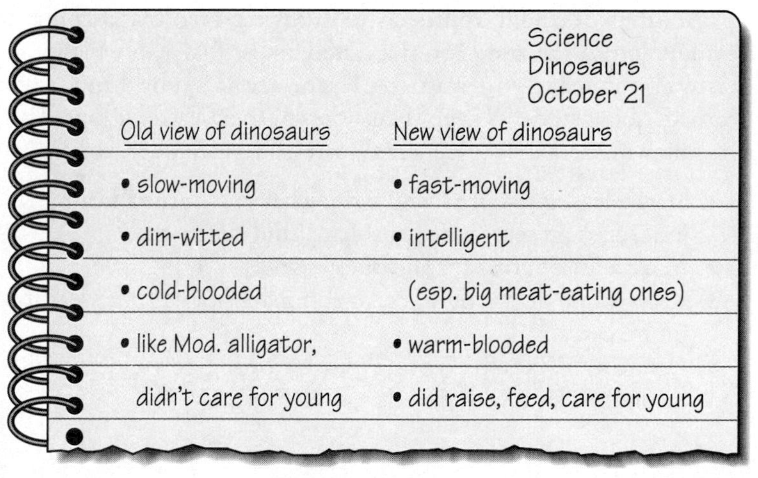
Science
Dinosaurs
October 21

Old view of dinosaurs	New view of dinosaurs
• slow-moving	• fast-moving
• dim-witted	• intelligent
• cold-blooded	(esp. big meat-eating ones)
• like Mod. alligator,	• warm-blooded
didn't care for young	• did raise, feed, care for young

FOX TROT

by Bill Amend

Teaching Strategies

for KEEP A NOTEBOOK

MODELING Model note taking by having a student read a brief nonfiction passage aloud while you take notes on the chalkboard. Demonstrate writing only the most important information in outline form and using symbols and abbreviations.

for USE A MODIFIED OUTLINE FORM

INDIVIDUALIZING INSTRUCTION: VISUAL LEARNERS Students may prefer to take notes on certain subjects in a form that visually suggests relationships among ideas. You might refer them to the cluster diagram or the spider map in the Thinking Skills Worksheets.

for USE SYMBOLS AND ABBREVIATIONS

COLLABORATIVE OPPORTUNITY Have students in small groups brainstorm additional symbols and abbreviations they can use when taking notes. For example, students might suggest using the symbols for greater than (>) and less than (<) that they learned in math class. A few students may enjoy making a poster, showing some of the symbols and abbreviations students have suggested.

Cross-Curricular Connection

Suggest that students use the last page of their notebooks to make a list of the symbols and abbreviations used most often in each subject area. As students learn more technical terms in each field, they can add symbols and abbreviations to the list. Here are some examples.

F°—degrees Fahrenheit (science)
cm^3—cubic centimeters (math, science)
c. 1900—circa (about) 1900 (social studies)

for USING THE KWL STUDY METHOD

LISTENING AND VIEWING Explain to students that the KWL study method can be used not only for reading but also for television viewing. Check local listings or appropriate television programs on subjects students may find interesting. Give students a choice among three or four programs to view during the following week. Tell them to use the KWL method to assess their knowledge before and after watching the program. Ask students to share their discoveries in class after all have had a chance to watch their programs.

for USING THE KWL STUDY METHOD

INDIVIDUALIZING INSTRUCTION: INDEPENDENT LEARNERS The KWL study method may prove to be an effective strategy for independent learners who are likely to be aware of what they already know, have strong opinions about what they want to know, and have the ability to reflect on what they have learned about a particular subject.

for KEEPING A LEARNING LOG

MODELING If you keep a learning log or have followed any of the suggestions on this page, share your work with students.

USING THE KWL STUDY METHOD

One way to study is to use the KWL study method. When you use this method, ask yourself three key questions:

K: What do I already **know?**
W: What do I **want** to know?
L: What did I **learn?**

Answer the first question by listing what you already know about the subject. Then create a list of questions about the subject, ones that show what you want or need to learn. These questions can begin with the question words *who, what, where, when, why,* or *how.* Look for answers to your questions as you study. Finally, answer the third question and make a list of what you have learned.

You can use the KWL method for any kind of studying. Use it to study chapters from a book or notes from a class. Apply the KWL study questions when doing a report or a project. This method will help you whether you are studying alone or with a group.

KEEPING A LEARNING LOG

Another excellent approach to studying involves keeping a learning log. A **learning log** is a notebook or folder in which you write about what you want to learn, are learning, and have learned. Some students keep their notes in their learning logs. Use the following activities to generate material to include in your log:

1. Start a learning journal and write what you learned from projects, class presentations, problems, and successes.
2. Make a list of goals for all your classes.
3. Keep rough drafts, outlines, or summaries of writing ideas for future essays.
4. Create a "Topics for Writing" list by jotting down ideas while reading, talking with friends, or watching TV.

PROFESSIONAL NOTEBOOK

Advice from the Authors A learning log is a kind of writer's journal that can be as formal or as informal as the learner wants it to be. Author Peter Elbow, in *Writing with Power,* says, "Some people find it a treat to write in an elegantly bound journal with fine paper—a sensual event. But for many others this adds the pressure to write nicely, to make it memorable, even to think about readers and this makes writing more of an ordeal. If you make your journal a folder rather than a book, you can write on whatever paper comes to hand at odd moments in the day when a thought strikes you."

5. Freewrite about subjects that interest you.
6. Keep in your log the lists that you make when using the KWL study method.
7. Record questions or comments about homework assignments or class lectures.
8. Formulate a "What I Learned Today" (WILT) list to chart how much you've grown and progressed.
9. On the left side of a two-column page, record notes from books, discussions, or lectures. Reserve the right side for ideas and reactions to your notes.
10. Establish a place in your log to jot down memorable quotes that you read or hear.
11. Set aside a "Reader Response" section for feelings and reactions to your reading.
12. Brainstorm about your dreams and the role that learning plays in fulfilling those dreams.

UNDERSTANDING WHAT YOU READ

One way to improve your understanding of what you read is to **preview** the material first. When previewing a reading selection, follow these steps:

1. Read the title.
2. Read any headings or words printed in special type.
3. Examine any illustrations, maps, diagrams, charts, or other graphics. Read all captions, labels, and headings on the graphics.
4. Read the first and last paragraph closely. Then skim the selection's paragraphs to find the main ideas.
5. Read the summary or conclusion, if the selection has one.
6. List questions that you predict the author will answer about the subject.

Once you have previewed the selection, read it actively. **Reading actively** means responding as you read. Respond aloud or in writing to what the author is saying. Some of the types of responses that you might make are listed on the next page.

for KEEPING A LEARNING LOG

HELPFUL HINT The long list of suggestions for keeping a learning log might be intimidating to some students. Explain that they don't have to do every activity. Ask students to try a few of the suggestions and then report to the class about which ones were the most fun or the most helpful.

for UNDERSTANDING WHAT YOU READ

CRITICAL THINKING: PREDICTING Distribute brief nonfiction pieces appropriate to students' varied reading abilities. Have students cover the reading material with a blank piece of paper and tell them that you will give them a very short period to preview the reading material. After the time is up, have students write three questions they think the reading material will answer when they take time to read more carefully. After they have read more carefully, ask whether they learned what they needed to know to answer their questions.

for UNDERSTANDING WHAT YOU READ

COLLABORATIVE OPPORTUNITY Have students in small groups share how it felt to read actively. Ask them to answer these questions: Did previewing the selection make you more curious about what you were doing to read? Did you learn more about the subject when you read actively? Do you think you will remember what you read longer?

Art Connection

If some students are collecting memorable quotes in their learning logs, ask for volunteers to suggest a "Quote a Day" for a corner of the bulletin board. Visual learners may enjoy inscribing some of their favorite quotes in calligraphy.

for PRACTICE YOUR SKILLS

INDIVIDUALIZING INSTRUCTION: BASIC STUDENTS Before students begin Exercise A, review the various abbreviations for feet (*ft.* or '), meters (*m*), and any other measurement they might need to know.

Additional Resource

Writing Resource Book, pp. 111–112

Answers to Practice Your Skills

A. Answers will vary. A sample answer is shown below.

The Great Pyramid
- Outer structure
  - contains > 2 mil. stone blocks, 2.5 short tons each
  - orig. 481' tall, now 450' tall
- Inner structure
  - Queen's Chamber
  - King's Chamber
  - Grand Gallery
    - corridor 153' long, 28' high

- **Write answers to your preview questions.** Jot down these answers as you read the selection.
- **Ask questions.** Record any additional questions that you think of or that the author raises.
- **Record main ideas and key terms.** Look for main ideas as you read. Note the topic sentences of paragraphs. Write down all key terms and definitions that appear in the selection.
- **Respond critically to the selection.** Record your own ideas and opinions about the author's subject. Do not simply accept everything that the author says. Ask yourself why you agree or disagree.

Once you have finished reading, **review** your notes. Recopy them or organize them if necessary. Then make a list of what the selection has taught you. Write down all questions that remain unanswered.

Practice Your Skills

A. Take notes on the following passage. Use a modified outline form and abbreviations.

> The pyramid of Khufu, called the *Great Pyramid,* contains more than 2 million stone blocks that average 2.5 short tons (2.3 metric tons) each. It was originally 481 feet (147 meters) tall, but some of its upper stones are gone now and it stands about 450 feet (140 meters) high. Its base covers about 13 acres (5 hectares). . . .
>
> The burial chamber is inside the Great Pyramid. A corridor leads from an entrance on the north side to several rooms within the pyramid. One of the rooms is called the *Queen's Chamber,* although the queen is not buried there. The room was planned as the king's burial chamber. But Khufu changed the plan and built another burial chamber, called the *King's Chamber.* The *Grand Gallery,* a corridor 153 feet (47 meters) long and 28 feet (8.5 meters) high, leads to Khufu's chamber. It is considered a marvel of ancient architecture.
>
> ***The World Book Encyclopedia,* 1992**

B. Preview the selection by reading the title, heading, and words in special print. Write down three questions that you predict the author will answer. Then read the passage closely and record its main ideas. Jot down answers to your questions, and write your critical response to the selection.

***Hinamatsuri:* A Japanese Doll Festival**

Japanese children are especially lucky, because there is a holiday just for them! . . . This festival is called *Hinamatsuri,* the Girls' Doll Festival. *Hina,* pronounced hee-na, is the Japanese word for doll, and *matsuri* means festival. . . . Every year this festival is held on March 3. . . .

HISTORY OF THE FESTIVAL

This festival began so long ago that people are not really sure why or how it first started. It may have begun over two thousand years ago, when the third day of the third month was called "the day of the snake" in Japan and China. This was a day of cleansing. Little dolls were used as symbols for human beings—people would "give" all their impurities and bad thoughts to these dolls, which were cast off into streams. . . .

The *Hinamatsuri* dolls are very special. They are ceremonial dolls, often handed down from mother to daughter through the generations. . . . But the dolls are not played with like ordinary dolls—they are for display only.

DESCRIPTION OF THE DOLLS

The *Hinamatsuri* dolls represent the emperor, the empress, and all the figures of the royal court. In Japan there is a long tradition of respect and loyalty for the emperor. . . .

The most important dolls, of course, are the emperor and empress, called the *Dairisama.* They sit on the top shelf of the *hinadan.* . . . The other members of the court sit on the shelves below the emperor and empress. In a full set of dolls, there may be seven ladies-in-waiting, five musicians, two pages, and three guards. . . .

For most of the year the dolls are carefully wrapped up and put away in boxes, so it is always a special treat when March 3 comes and the dolls are displayed.

from *Cricket,* August 1992

An empress doll from a Japanese *Hinamatsuri* doll set. Such dolls reflect the ancient Japanese tradition of honoring royalty.

B. Answers will vary. Students should submit their previewing questions, answers, a list of main ideas, and a critical response. Main ideas may include the following: *Hinamatsuri* is a doll festival that is celebrated by Japanese children each year on March 3. The ceremonial dolls represent the emperor, empress, and other royal figures of the Japanese court.

Writing Paraphrases and Summaries

Objectives

- To recognize the importance of paraphrasing and summarizing as research tools
- To paraphrase and summarize short selections
- To distinguish between paraphrasing and summarizing and to determine when each is appropriate
- To recognize and avoid plagiarism

Related Mini-Lessons

For information on topics related to writing paraphrases and summaries, see the following mini-lessons.

- **Study and Research Skills, pp. 340–345**
- **Making Use of the Library, pp. 352–361**
- **Punctuation, pp. 651–652, and pp. 664–666**

Teaching Strategies

for PARAPHRASING

CRITICAL THINKING: INTERPRETING Put a list of five or six well-known quotations or proverbs on the board. (Examples: Strike while the iron is hot; Don't put all your eggs in one basket.) Ask students to express the meanings in their own words.

WRITING HANDBOOK 33

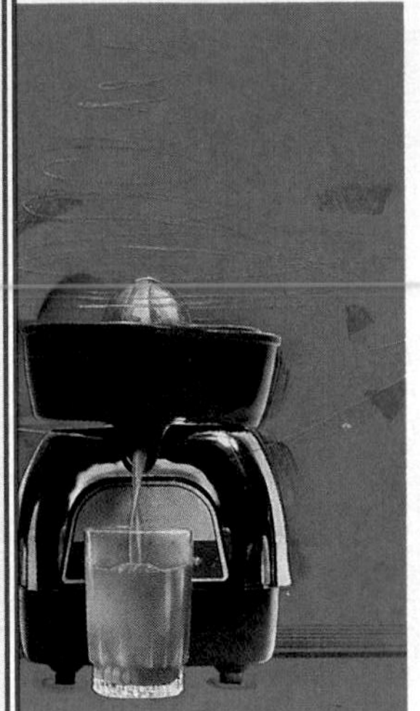

How Do I Put Things in My Own Words?

Writing Paraphrases and Summaries

When you put an orange through a juicer, what do you get? You get the juice and the pulp—in other words, the best parts of the orange. The unimportant part, the rind, is left behind.

When you write a paraphrase or a summary of a piece of writing, you also want to get at the best parts of the writer's work. You restate the writer's most important ideas in your own words, leaving out the unimportant details.

PARAPHRASING

When you **paraphrase** a passage from a book or a magazine, you restate the writer's ideas in your own words. Do not simply use synonyms to replace the writer's original language. Instead, think about the passage and then rewrite it in your own words, using your own voice. Here are some guidelines:

Guidelines for Paraphrasing

1. **Identify the main idea.** Find the main idea and write it in your own words.
2. **List supporting details.** List all the supporting details in the original passage. Include sensory details, examples, facts, and opinions. Write these details in your own words and keep them in their original order.
3. **Simplify the language.** Use familiar words to simplify the way you present the main idea and supporting details. Try not to change the tone of the passage.
4. **Revise your work.** When you've finished paraphrasing, revise your work. Make sure that the final product is in your own words, uses simple vocabulary, has the same content as the original, and is about the same length.

COMPUTER TIP

When writing a paraphrase on a computer, save the different drafts in separate files. This makes it easy to try out changes or keep original material when revising your work.

SPICE BOX

A **lipogram** is a paraphrase of a well-known verse or quotation that replaces any words that contain one of the five vowels. For example, this is a lipogram of the first line of the national anthem, minus words with the letter *a*.

"Oh, tell me, do you see, by the first morning light
The emblem we cheered by evening's closing glimmers?"

Have students choose a favorite poem or quotation to paraphrase as a lipogram. Ask them to decide which vowel they will not use. Then have them paraphrase the work without using words that contain the vowel.

Suppose you are writing a report about the Native American mound builders you learned about in Workshop 8. You read the following passage that discusses a specific type of mound structure:

Some Indians built still another kind of mound. This was the effigy mound in the shape of a living creature, almost always an animal. Most effigy mounds are in southern Wisconsin and in nearby areas of Illinois and Iowa, although Ohio has some, too. All kinds of animals are represented. There are bears, deer, panthers, wolves, turtles, and birds.

Paula Angle Franklin, *Indians of North America*

Here is one way you could paraphrase Paula Franklin's paragraph:

According to Paula Angle Franklin, some Native Americans created mounds that were in the shape of living animals. These mounds can be found within southern Wisconsin, Illinois, Iowa, and Ohio. The animals depicted in these mounds vary: bears, deer, panthers, wolves, turtles, and birds (33).

Main idea

Supporting Ideas

SUMMARIZING

A summary is usually one-third the length of the original. To **summarize** a passage, rephrase the original material in fewer words. Try to capture the original's key ideas. Follow these steps:

Guidelines for Summarizing

1. **List the main idea.** Read the original material closely. Rewrite the main idea in as few words as possible.
2. **Select details.** Select the most important points to support the main idea.
3. **Rewrite ideas.** Rewrite key ideas, using simpler language and combining ideas.
4. **Revise your summary.** Reread your draft and make sure it is in your own words. Remember that the tone of your summary should match the original.

TIP

You can use summarizing to help you write a report, take notes, or study.

for PROFESSIONAL MODEL

STUMBLING BLOCK Many students probably will not know the meaning of the word *effigy.* Explain that an *effigy* is an image or representation of a person or animal.

for SUMMARIZING

INDIVIDUALIZING INSTRUCTION: VISUAL LEARNERS According to an ancient Chinese proverb, "A picture is worth a thousand words." Visual learners might enjoy summarizing a paragraph like the one on effigy mounds by making a chart, a drawing, or a map.

for SUMMARIZING

LISTENING AND VIEWING Summarizing can also be used when students watch television, listen to book tapes, or go to the movies. You might want to ask students to listen to or watch a particular program and summarize its content in a few sentences. Ask them to present their summaries orally to the class.

Additional Resource

Writing Resource Book, p. 113

Answers to Practice Your Skills

Answers may vary. Sample answers are shown below.

Topic Sentence: The rain forests are vanishing.

Supporting details: • Some say that nearly half the rain forests have been cut down in the last one hundred years. • They continue to be destroyed at a rate of 43,000 sq. miles per year—1/2 the size of Pennsylvania. • In fifty years, all of the rain forests may be gone. • The destruction of every sq. mile of rain forest means the deaths of thousands of plants and the loss of animal habitat.

Paraphrase:

The world's rain forests are disappearing. Some people say that nearly half of the rain forests have been cut down in the last one hundred years. They continue to be destroyed at a rate of 43,000 square miles per year. That's an area equal to about half the size of the state of Pennsylvania. In fifty years, all the rain forests may be gone. The destruction of every square mile of rain forest causes the deaths of thousands of plants and the loss of animal habitat.

Summary:

The rain forests are disappearing along with many thousands of native plants and animals. At the current rate of destruction, the world's rain forests may be gone in fifty years.

Here is a summary of the passage on Native American mounds:

Native Americans built effigy mounds in the Midwest. These mounds resembled different animals.

PLAGIARISM

PROBLEM SOLVING

"How can I cite a source correctly?"

To find out the correct form for citing a source, see

• Writer's Workshop 8, page 201

When you paraphrase or summarize an original idea, or quote a passage directly, always give credit to the original source to avoid plagiarism. **Plagiarism** is the dishonest practice of presenting another person's ideas or language as your own.

You can avoid plagiarism by citing your sources as you write. These steps will help you avoid plagiarism:

- **Credit all direct quotations.** Use quotation marks when quoting directly from a source. Do not use quotation marks when you are paraphrasing or summarizing another person's ideas.
- **Credit all ideas that are not your own.** However, you do not need to credit a source if the material you paraphrase or summarize is general knowledge.

Practice Your Skills

Read the following selection carefully. Jot down its topic sentence and supporting ideas. Then paraphrase the paragraph. Finally, use your paraphrase to write a summary.

> The rain forests are vanishing. By some estimates, nearly half of the rain forests that existed a century ago have already been cut down, and more are being destroyed, at a rate of 43,000 square miles (111,000 sq km) per year, an area roughly half the size of Pennsylvania. Within half a century, there may be no rain forests left at all. And for every square mile of rain forest that is removed, untold thousands of plants are killed, and an important animal habitat is lost.
>
> **Christopher Lampton, *Endangered Species***

How Can I Use Charts and Graphs in My Writing?

Creating Graphic Aids

Calvin knows that a visual aid will help make his report interesting and memorable. You too can use visuals, or **graphic aids,** in your writing to help your readers understand and remember information, especially information involving numbers. Some common graphic aids are line graphs, bar graphs, and circle graphs.

Line Graphs

If you were writing a report on world hunger, you might want to show how population increases affect world hunger. A line graph is a good way to show how the world population is growing. Here are the steps for creating the line graph shown below:

- **Research the topic.** Look through an encyclopedia or a reference book to find statistics on world population.
- **Create a grid.** Label your grid. The vertical scale goes up the left side of the grid. It shows population size. The horizontal scale goes across the bottom of the grid. It shows time.
- **Plot the information.** Plot the points on your grid, pairing each year with its matching population number. Use a ruler to draw lines connecting the points.

Projected World Population Growth, 1950–2020

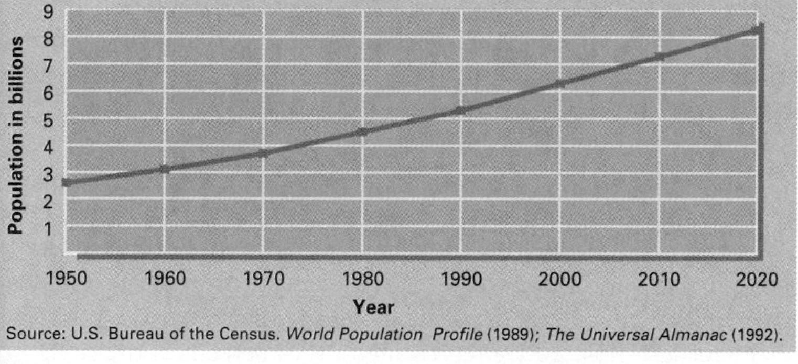

Source: U.S. Bureau of the Census. *World Population Profile* (1989); *The Universal Almanac* (1992).

Calvin and Hobbes
by Bill Watterson

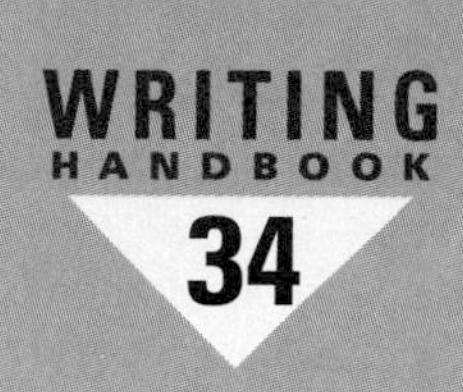

Creating Graphic Aids

Objectives

- To identify and interpret line, bar, and circle graphs
- To determine the most appropriate graph to illustrate information
- To create a graph

Related Mini-Lessons

For information on topics related to graphic aids, see the following mini-lessons.

- **Graphic Devices for Writing, pp. 227–231**
- **Methods of Elaboration, pp. 255–261**

Motivate

Explain that TV-news producers limit the time devoted to "talking heads," or views of persons just sitting and talking. To break up these static shots, they may direct the camera at a graphic device, such as a chart or graph, to help viewers grasp information easily and quickly. Assign several students to watch the nightly news and report any use of graphic devices they note.

Teaching Strategies

for LINE GRAPHS

HELPFUL HINT Tell students that line graphs often show the changes occurring in some characteristic over a period of time. As the line graph on this page shows, time is usually plotted horizontally, and the characteristic under study is plotted vertically. Ask students to think of other possible changes over time that could be charted on a line graph. (Possible response: the mean temperature or rainfall in a particular city during each month of the year)

Science or Social Studies Connection

Line graphs are useful for recording and presenting data and are frequently used in the fields of science and social studies. Students might want to create a line graph to illustrate an aspect of science, history, or geography that they are currently studying. First, suggest that students choose some data they want to graph, then try two different ways of displaying it: in a line graph and in some other visual form. Discuss which form is more effective in each case, and why.

for BAR GRAPHS

CRITICAL THINKING: ANALYZING A BAR GRAPH Ask students whether the same information could have been arranged in a different way on this graph. (Sample: The city names could have been placed at the bottom of the graph, and the population numbers along the side.) Ask students to think of other information about homeless people that could be added to this graph and to decide how this information could be shown. (Sample: The number of homeless people as a proportion of the city's entire population could be indicated by adding another bar in a different color to the information for each city.) Also ask students what information about the same topic could have been shown in a line graph. (Sample: the change in the number of homeless people over a period of time)

for CIRCLE GRAPHS

COOPERATIVE LEARNING Form the class into small groups to create circle graphs. Have each group brainstorm a list of topics and then choose one to research. Have the group discuss and decide on a specific job for each member. For example, one student might collect the information, and another might tabulate it, while a third (and possibly a fourth) student might design and draw the graph.

COMPUTER TIP

Some computer programs can help you produce graphs. Check your computer to see if it has a special graphing program.

TIP

Use colors in your graphs to help make the information easier to compare.

Bar Graphs

Suppose you are writing a report on the problem of homelessness. You want to compare the problem in six cities. A good way to compare numerical information is to create a bar graph.

To make a bar graph, first gather information and create a grid. Write the "name variables," in this case the names of the cities, along one side of the graph. Arrange the "number variables," or the sizes of the homeless populations, along the other. Use these variables to mark the length of each bar on the graph. In this case, the bars are drawn from the left side of the graph and end at the points marked on the grid.

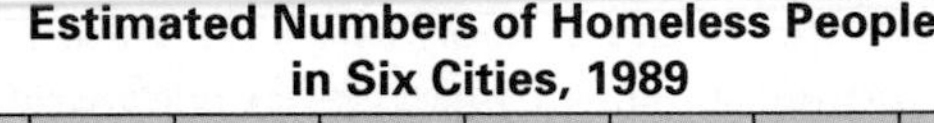

Estimated Numbers of Homeless People
in Six Cities, 1989

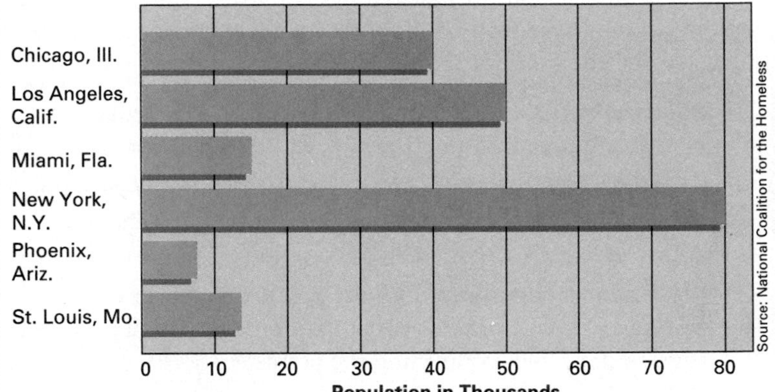

Circle Graphs

If you were writing about teenagers' attitudes toward TV, you might conduct a poll and show the results in a circle graph like the one on the next page. In this example, the circle represents the total number of people polled.

To make a circle graph, list the information you want to represent. Draw a circle and divide it into "pie slices." Label each slice. To determine the size of each slice, you must figure out what percentage, or part of the whole, it represents. For example, if 200 students are polled and 20 of them answer that television has too many reruns, these 20 are represented by 10 percent of the circle.

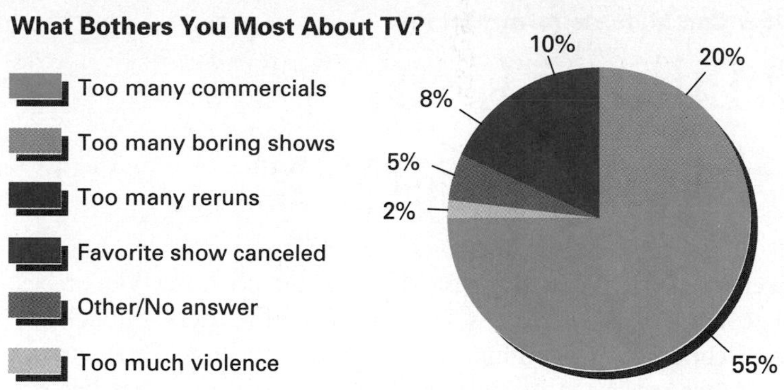

Practice Your Skills

A. Use the graphs in this handbook to answer these questions.

1. Between 1970 and 1990, by approximately how many people did the world population grow?
2. In 1989, what was the difference between the homeless population in New York and in St. Louis?
3. According to the circle graph, what are the two aspects of television that bother students the most? What aspect bothers them the least?

B. Use the information in the table below to draw a line graph. Be sure to include a title and headings in the appropriate places.

Average Attendance at Chicago Bulls Professional Basketball Games, 1966–1990

Year	Attendance in Thousands
1966	4.5
1970	10.0
1974	10.5
1978	9.0
1982	7.0
1986	16.0
1990	18.5

Additional Resource

Writing Resource Book, pp. 114–116

Answers to Practice Your Skills

A. **1.** approximately 1.5 billion
2. approximately 67,000
3. too many commercials and too many boring shows; too much violence

B. Average Attendance at Chicago Bulls Professional Basketball Games, 1966–1990

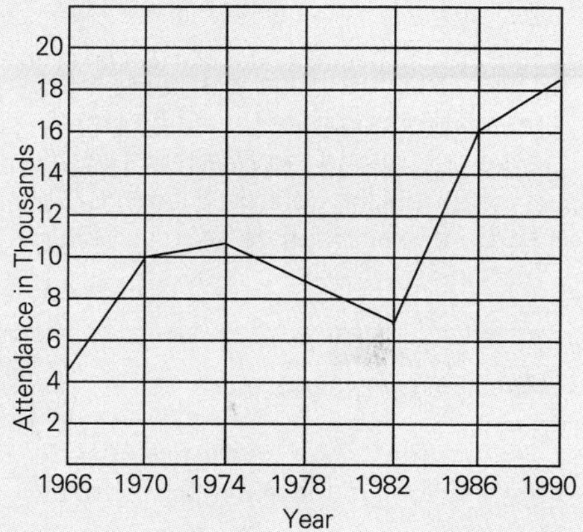

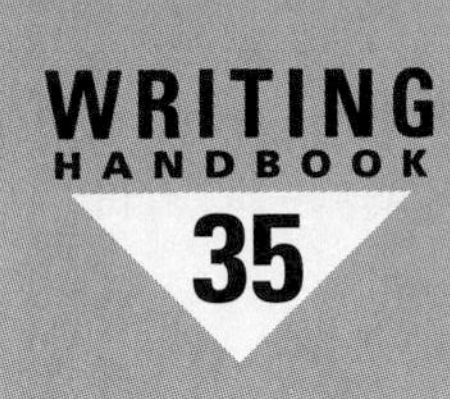

Making Use of the Library

Objectives

- To recognize how libraries are organized and the different resources they contain
- To locate information in a library, using the card or computer catalog, reference books, and the *Readers' Guide* or a computerized periodical index
- To identify appropriate sources of information for different subjects

Related Mini-Lessons

For information on topics related to using the library, see the following mini-lessons.

- **Methods of Elaboration, pp. 255–261**
- **Study and Research Skills, pp. 340–345**
- **Writing Paraphrases and Summaries, pp. 346–348**

Teaching Strategies

for HOW LIBRARIES ARE ORGANIZED

INDIVIDUALIZING INSTRUCTION: VISUAL LEARNERS After a class tour of your school or local library, ask students to draw a diagram showing the library's layout.

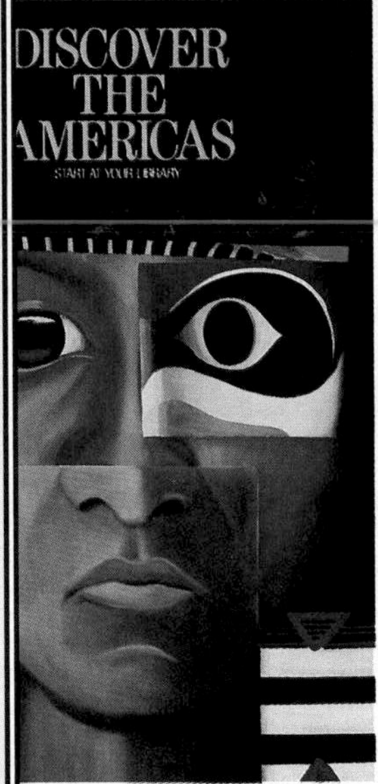

How Can I Locate Information?

Making Use of the Library

A typical modern library is very different from a library of twenty years ago. In the past, libraries did not offer videotapes, artwork, CDs, photographs, laser discs, or computers. Public readings, children's story time, movies, and workshops were among the other services not available. The library of today has become an important community resource center.

HOW LIBRARIES ARE ORGANIZED

With so much to offer, libraries can be confusing places. It's important to learn how libraries organize their materials.

The Sections of the Library

Most libraries are organized into the following sections:

Section	*Contents*
The Stacks	shelves of fiction and nonfiction books
Catalog and Index	card catalogs, computer catalogs, and indexes
Reference	atlases, encyclopedias, and other fact-filled works
Periodicals	magazines, newspapers, and journals
Audiovisual	audiotapes, tape recorders, CDs, films, filmstrips, projectors, laser discs, and records
Children and Young Adult	materials for toddlers, children, and teenagers
Special Services	rooms for story readings, lectures, computer users, job searches, and community services

How the Books Are Arranged

Library books are usually grouped into the following main types: **fiction, nonfiction, biography and autobiography,** and **reference.**

Fiction Novels, short story collections, and mysteries are classified as fiction. You will find these books shelved in alphabetical order according to the author's last name.

Nonfiction Books that contain only factual information are nonfiction. Libraries use one of two systems for classifying these books: the Dewey Decimal System or the Library of Congress System. The **Dewey Decimal System** divides nonfiction books into ten subject categories and into subcategories as shown below.

Dewey Decimal System

000–099	General Works (encyclopedias, bibliographies)
100–199	Philosophy (self-help, psychology)
200–299	Religion (the Bible, mythology, theology)
300–399	Social Science (law, education, economics)
400–499	Language (books on grammar, dictionaries, foreign languages)
500–599	Science (mathematics, biology, chemistry)
600–699	Technology (medicine, inventions, cooking)
700–799	Fine Arts (painting, music, theater, sports)
800–899	Literature (poetry, plays, essays)
900–999	History (biography, geography, travel)

Very large libraries use the **Library of Congress System** to classify nonfiction books into twenty-one subject categories. Each category is assigned a letter of the alphabet. A librarian can provide you with a guide to this system.

Biography and Autobiography A **biography** is a nonfiction book about a person's life. An **autobiography** tells the author's own life story. Biographies may be kept in the 900's section or they may be shelved in a special section. In either case, biographies are shelved alphabetically according to the name of the person the book is about.

for HOW THE BOOKS ARE ARRANGED

INDIVIDUALIZING INSTRUCTION: KINESTHETIC LEARNERS You might bring to class two or three cartons of books you think students will enjoy reading or browsing through. (Cover any call numbers on the books with blank labels that can be easily removed.) Give students shelf space and ask students to organize these books into a classroom library. Have them use the Dewey Decimal System described on the pupil page.

for DEWEY DECIMAL SYSTEM

HELPFUL HINT Assure students that they need not memorize all these numbers and categories. They will be able to refer to a chart posted in the library.

for CATALOG SYSTEMS

HELPFUL HINT Inform students that they may need to think of alternate headings when they look up some subjects in a library. An example might be *genetics* and *heredity*. Suggest that students try every variation they can think of for a given subject, if necessary.

for CATALOG SYSTEMS

INDIVIDUALIZING INSTRUCTION: ESL STUDENTS Some students may have difficulty identifying key words and alternative headings to use when looking up a subject in a catalog. Ask students to list five subjects they would like to explore. Pair them with native English speakers to find books on the subjects in the catalog. Have them keep a list of the alternate subject headings they tried. If other students might benefit, share these lists with the entire class.

Reference Books These sources include almanacs, encyclopedias, dictionaries, and other fact-filled works. Reference books are shelved in the reference section and are labeled with an *R* or *REF*. Usually you cannot check out reference books.

CATALOG SYSTEMS

One of the first steps in using a library or doing research is finding out what materials are available. A **catalog system** lists all the materials a library has to offer.

No matter what catalog system a library uses, you can find a listing for a book by looking it up in one of three ways: by the author's last name, by the first word of the title, or by the subject the book is about. Two common types of library catalog systems are card catalogs and on-line computer catalogs.

Card Catalogs

A card catalog is a file of cards for all the materials in the library. The cards are filed alphabetically and are usually kept in drawers in a cabinet.

Guide Cards These cards are labeled with letters or general headings and extend above the other cards in the catalog. They help you quickly locate the specific entry card you need. To find entry cards on the California gold rush, for example, you would look in the G drawer between the guide cards *Gold Coins* and *Goldberg, Isaac*.

Conditions were primitive in the California gold fields of the 1850s. Here a woman brings lunch to three miners.

Entry Cards There are usually three file cards for each book: an author card, a title card, and a subject card. To find a book about the California gold rush, you could look for a subject card labeled *GOLD RUSH* or for a title card labeled *The Great American Gold Rush*. An author card would be filed under *B* for Rhoda Blumberg. Each type of entry card provides the same information about a source. Study the subject entry card that follows.

MULTICULTURAL Connection

Invite students to list highly respected people from their own cultural backgrounds (for example, Mohandas Gandhi, José Martí, Corazon Aquino, Bishop Desmond Tutu). Students can then look for biographies and autobiographies of these people in the library.

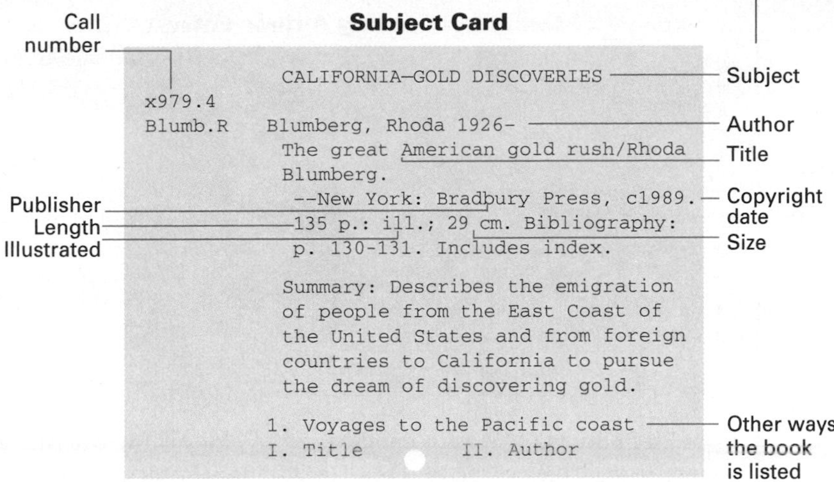

Subject Card
Call number
CALIFORNIA—GOLD DISCOVERIES
x979.4
Blumb.R
Blumberg, Rhoda 1926-
The great American gold rush/Rhoda Blumberg.
--New York: Bradbury Press, c1989.
135 p.: ill.; 29 cm. Bibliography: p. 130-131. Includes index.
Summary: Describes the emigration of people from the East Coast of the United States and from foreign countries to California to pursue the dream of discovering gold.
1. Voyages to the Pacific coast
I. Title II. Author
Subject
Author
Title
Publisher
Length
Illustrated
Copyright date
Size
Other ways the book is listed

Cross-reference Cards Some of the cards between the guide cards may begin with the words *See* or *See also.* These cross-reference cards suggest other related subject, title, or author entries. When researching a topic, you may find cross-reference cards useful for finding additional sources.

Computerized Catalogs

Many libraries list all their materials on a computer. To find a specific source, you use a computer terminal to search for listings. Computerized systems vary, so ask your librarian for help.

Computer Searching Generally, you use a terminal keyboard, and begin a search by typing the subject, the author's last name, or the title. A screen appears with choices for related listings. For example, if you type the words *California gold rush,* the choices *California—Gold discoveries, California—Gold discoveries—Fiction,* and *California—Gold discoveries—Songs and music* may appear. Select a choice and the screen displays a list of book titles on that subject. Choose a title, and the computer provides an entry with information similar to that found on an entry card in the card catalog. Compare the computer entry on the next page with the subject card you studied earlier.

for SUBJECT CARD

KEY TO UNDERSTANDING Review the model subject card in class, making sure students understand each part and its importance. For example, ask what *copyright date* means (the year the book was first published) and why it is important (indicates how up-to-date the book's information is). Point out that the card lists information that students will need to include in a Works Cited list (author, title, place of publication, publisher, copyright date). The summary helps people see if the book contains the information they're looking for.

for COMPUTER SEARCHING

STUMBLING BLOCK Some library computer systems find matches only for the exact heading that is entered, not for related listings. If the system's heading differs from the one entered, the screen may indicate that there are no matching entries. With such systems, users must enter alternate headings until they find one that matches a heading in the computer's index.

for COMPUTER SEARCHING

HELPFUL HINT If students do not know how to use the computerized catalog system in your school or local library, arrange for the librarian to demonstrate its use.

for SPECIAL FEATURES

HELPFUL HINT Tell students that if a source is not on the shelf, they can fill out a reserve slip or postcard at the checkout desk. (In some systems, they can enter the information themselves in an electronic "reserve" file.) When the book is returned, the library will notify them and hold the book.

for UNDERSTANDING CALL NUMBERS

HELPFUL HINT: LETTER CODES Ask a volunteer to prepare a list of the letter codes used at your school or local public library and to share it with the class. Note that some libraries classify and shelve short story collections in a separate category, and that some libraries shelve autobiography and biography together.

for UNDERSTANDING CALL NUMBERS

HELPFUL HINT: LOCATING A BOOK You might point out that because books are often misshelved, students who are trying to find a particular book should look among nearby books and shelves. Note that because library patrons often put books back in an incorrect spot, many libraries request that books removed from shelves be returned to a central location for reshelving by the library staff.

COMPUTER TIP

With some computer catalogs, you direct the search for a topic by touching headings and options on the computer screen instead of by typing key words.

Computer Catalog Author Entry

```
   AUTHOR:   Blumberg, Rhoda
    TITLE:   The great American gold rush
PUBLISHER:   Bradbury Press [1989]
 SUBJECTS:   Voyages to the Pacific coast. Overland journeys
to the Pacific.

## ----Call number ------Volume Material  Location  Status
1      x979.4/Blumb.R          Juv. Book CHILDRNS  Available

Enter: F       to see Full title record.
>>                       Enter ? for HELP.
```

Special Features Most computerized catalogs show whether a source is available or checked out. In addition, some systems can provide a printout of all the sources available on a subject, including sources in neighboring libraries.

LOCATING AND USING MATERIALS

Once you know what sources are available, your next step is to find the materials you need. Libraries use **call numbers,** codes of letters and numbers, that tell you where a book is shelved.

Understanding Call Numbers

To find a book in the stacks, you match the call number on the catalog entry with the call number printed on the spine of the book. Some libraries use a letter code before the Dewey number to tell you the section of the library where the book is kept. A list of commonly used letter codes is shown below.

R, REF = Reference	B, BIO = Biography
C, CHILD = Children's	X, J, JUV = Juvenile
X, Y, YA = Young Adult	AV = Audiovisual
P, PER = Periodicals	SC = Short Story Collection
SF = Science Fiction	MYS = Mystery

Other parts of the call number also help you locate a book. Look at the call number below for *The Great American Gold Rush* by Rhoda Blumberg.

Section letter — **x979.4**
Blumb.R

Subject subdivison (North America—States of the Pacific Area)
Dewey Decimal number (History)
Author designation

In this call number, the letter *x* tells you that this book is in the young adult section. The 979.4 is the Dewey number. The Dewey number tells you to go to the 900 section of the shelves. In the 900s, look for books with the same subcategory number. Then, since books are arranged alphabetically by the author's last name, look for the author designation, *Blumb.R.*

Research Resources

Imagine being able to find the answer to every question you ever had. In the reference section, you are surrounded by the most up-to-date information sources. Such a variety of materials not only allows you to answer questions but also to learn a variety of viewpoints on a topic. The chart below lists some of the most useful resources.

Library References

Reference	Contents	Examples
Encyclopedias	articles on various topics	*Encyclopaedia Britannica*
Almanacs and Yearbooks	current facts and unusual information	*Facts on File, The Information Please Almanac*
Atlases	detailed maps and geographical information	*The National Geographic Atlas of the World*
Vertical File	pamphlets, booklets, and clippings of topics	
Periodicals	newspapers, magazines, and journals	*Chicago Tribune, Time, The Reading Teacher*

If there is a bibliography in a reference source you use, examine it for possible additional research sources.

for LIBRARY REFERENCES

STUMBLING BLOCK Caution students against limiting their research to articles in encyclopedias or other general reference sources when writing research reports. Note that although these sources can be used to answer many factual questions, they may not provide enough in-depth information on a particular aspect of a topic. Encyclopedia articles may, however, include bibliographies that name other sources students can consult.

SPICE BOX

Devise a library scavenger hunt by listing twenty factual questions whose answers can be found in a library's reference books. Students can work together to find the answers. For example, "Who won the Oscar for best actress in 1985?" (Geraldine Page for *The Trip to Bountiful;* almanac) *for* USING PERIODICAL INDEXES

VIEWING AND LISTENING The H. W. Wilson Company, publishers of the *Readers' Guide,* has produced a twenty-minute video called "How to Use the *Readers' Guide.*" You may also obtain fifty free copies of the booklet *How to Use the Readers' Guide to Periodical Literature* by writing the H. W. Wilson Company, 950 University Avenue, Bronx, NY 10452-9978.

for PRINTED INDEXES

INDIVIDUALIZING INSTRUCTION: ESL AND LEP STUDENTS Read aloud the sample entries, helping students decipher the abbreviations, which they are likely to find puzzling. (For example, *Ja/F* means January/February; *F/Mr* means February/March. These abbreviations indicate that the magazines are published once every two months.) You also may need to explain *cross-reference* and *volume number.*

for COMPUTERIZED INDEXES

INDIVIDUALIZING INSTRUCTION: ADVANCED STUDENTS Encourage those students who enjoy research projects and working with computers to become class experts in using the library's computerized indexes. Have them give demonstrations and assist other students who are having difficulty finding the information they need.

for COMPUTERIZED INDEXES

VIEWING AND LISTENING To teach students how to use InfoTrac, call the Information Access Company at 1-800-227-8431. Ask for their free fifteen-minute video or overhead transparencies on how to use InfoTrac. The latest video for middle schools is called "TOM Jr."

TIP

When you need to come up with a writing topic, try browsing in magazines that deal with an area of interest to you.

Using Periodical Indexes

A reference work that lists articles from magazines and newspapers is called a **periodical index.** The two types of periodical indexes—printed and computerized—are valuable tools.

Printed Indexes The *Readers' Guide to Periodical Literature* is a printed index published monthly. Articles are listed by subject and author. At the end of the year, the issues are bound into one volume. Study this excerpt from the *Readers' Guide:*

Excerpt from the *Readers' Guide*

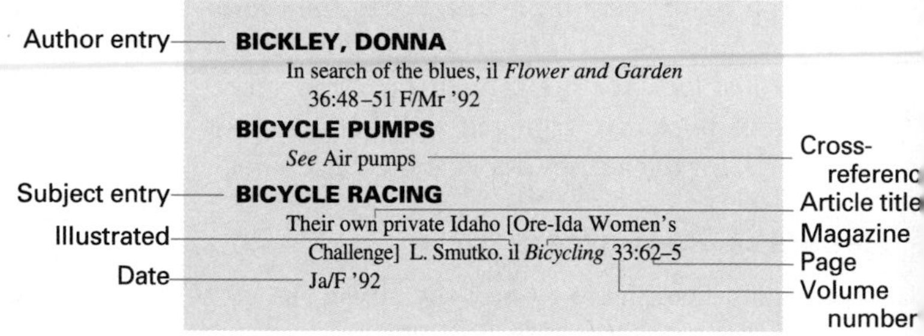
BICKLEY, DONNA
In search of the blues, il *Flower and Garden* 36:48–51 F/Mr '92
BICYCLE PUMPS
See Air pumps
BICYCLE RACING
Their own private Idaho [Ore-Ida Women's Challenge] L. Smutko. il *Bicycling* 33:62–5 Ja/F '92

Computerized Indexes Computerized indexes such as *InfoTrac, ProQuest,* and *Uncover* list periodicals by subject and sometimes by author for the period of years covered by the index. A librarian can help you use the index. Look at this entry from *ProQuest:*

Computerized Periodical Index Entry

```
TITLE:        Bernard Hinault On: Bike Fit
AUTHORS:      Drake, Geoff
JOURNAL:      Bicycling  Vol: 33  Iss: 2  Date: March 1992
              pp: 86-87
Jrnl Code:    GBIK  ISSN: 0006-2073  Jrnl Group: Lifestyles
ABSTRACT:     Five-time Tour de France winner Bernard
              Hinault offers guidelines for proper bike fit,
              including information on saddle setback, frame
              height and saddle/handlebar distance.
              Photograph; Table
SUBJECTS:     Bicycles; Bicycle racing
NAMES:        Hinault, Bernard
TYPE:         Feature
LENGTH:       Medium (10-30 col inches)
```

Microforms Usually, recent periodicals are shelved in the periodical section. However, many libraries save space by using **microforms,** pieces of film that show pages from certain recent and all older periodicals. When the microforms are rolled-up strips of film, they are called **microfilm.** When the microforms are film cards, they are called **microfiche.** Check with a librarian to learn which issues of periodicals are stored on microforms. The library has special machines that you must use to read microforms. A librarian will gladly instruct you on how to use the machines.

Experts

Experts aren't just "talking heads" on TV. Your friends, relatives, teachers, librarians, and school administrators may be experts you can interview. Often you can find experts at local organizations such as businesses, museums, and clubs. A good interview can provide interesting material for a report. For more information about interviewing, see Handbook 36, "Interviewing Skills," page 362.

Government Agencies

Many libraries have special sections that contain government publications. In addition, the government agencies listed in a telephone book can provide information about federal issues. The General Services Administration publishes a catalog that lists free or inexpensive government pamphlets on many subjects. You can receive this free catalog by writing to: Consumer Information Catalog, P.O. Box 100, Pueblo, CO 81002.

For information about local issues, you can contact your town hall or mayor's office. For information on state issues, you might try the office of your state legislator.

Computer Services

Computer information services offer on-line encyclopedias and dictionaries, as well as news, weather, and sports reports. If you have the use of a computer, a modem, and a telephone line, you can access an information service. A librarian may be able to provide you with a listing of available computer services.

COMPUTER TIP

Some libraries also provide on-line computer bulletin boards that display community information and notices of upcoming events.

for EXPERTS

COLLABORATIVE OPPORTUNITY

A group of volunteers might interview classmates and create a resource list of subjects on which fellow students (or their parents or both) are "experts." For example, students might consider themselves experts on a particular hobby or sport.

for GOVERNMENT AGENCIES

HELPFUL HINT Try to have available at least one copy of the GSA-published Consumer Information Catalog for student inspection. (Some libraries have a supply of the free catalogs available.) Point out the various subjects covered (such as "Children," "Exercise and Weight Control," "Housing," and "Money") and some of the pamphlet titles that students would find interesting. Emphasize that all the publications listed are either free or available at low cost.

for AUDIOVISUAL MEDIA

HELPFUL HINT Many students are surprised by the wide array of audiovisual media available from a library. Ask a group of volunteers to report on some titles of available videotapes and audiotapes that they think will interest their classmates.

for EVALUATING MEDIA SOURCES

CRITICAL THINKING: EVALUATING By discussing the questions on the chart in class, you can help students overcome the tendency to believe everything they see in print. Emphasize that information from some sources, such as many supermarket tabloids, tends to be unreliable and sensationalistic, whereas most major newspapers and newsmagazines are considered relatively reliable. Note that in all reporting, however, decisions are made about what information to include and exclude and that such decisions may be biased. You might bring copies of some tabloids, newspapers, and newsmagazines to class to discuss specific examples of sensationalism and bias.

The Media

"The media" refers to all of the communication methods used by people. There are two main kinds of media: audiovisual and print.

Audiovisual Media Audiotapes, CDs, computer programs, films, filmstrips, laser discs, photos and slides, transparencies, and videotapes are examples of audiovisual media. Two types of audiovisual media are broadcast and narrowcast. **Broadcast media** send messages from one point to many points through network TV or radio programs. You can sometimes purchase transcripts of these broadcasts for a slight fee. **Narrowcast media** send messages from one point to one point through cable or telephone wires. You can receive narrowcast messages through computer networks, pay-per-view television, and facsimile machines.

Print Media Any media printed on paper—books, letters, fliers, posters, magazines, newspapers—are considered print media.

Whenever you use media sources, it is important to think critically about the sources and to use the information responsibly. Ask yourself these questions as you evaluate the media sources:

Evaluating Media Sources

- Have my sources presented different views of the topic?
- Are my sources reliable?
- Is the information from each source accurate?
- Are my sources as current as possible?
- Have my sources provided unbiased information or are they trying to persuade me?
- Have I discussed my interpretation of the information with a peer?

Practice Your Skills

A. Find and list the call number of one book in each of the following general categories:

1. mythology
2. foreign languages
3. biology
4. plays

B. Follow the directions for each item. Use your library's card catalog or computer catalog to find the information requested.

1. Find a book about Mexico. List the title, the author, and the call number.
2. Find the title of a book by Virginia Hamilton.
3. Find the title of a biography about any sports hero.
4. Find a collection of short stories or poems. List the title of the collection and its editor or editors.

C. Use reference works in your library to answer the following questions. Write the answer to the question and the name and type of the reference work that you used. (encyclopedia, almanac, atlas, etc.)

1. How many people now live in Brazil?
2. In what part of California is the town of Santa Rosa located? Who is the town named after?
3. Who founded Howard University, and when was it founded?
4. What were the high and low temperatures in your town last Monday?

D. Use the *Readers' Guide* or a computerized periodical index to find two magazine articles, one that is on the shelves and one that is on microfiche, for each of the following subjects:

1. Texas
2. solar energy

E. List all the sources you would use for the following topics. Explain why you would use each source.

1. space shuttle astronauts and scientists
2. early settlers in your town

Additional Resource

Writing Resource Book, pp. 117–122

Answers to Practice Your Skills

A. Titles will vary. Books on mythology, however, will appear in the 200s, foreign languages in the 400s, biology in the 500s, and plays in the 800s.

B. Answers will vary. Sample answers are shown below.

1. *Mexico,* R. Conrad Stein, J917.2
2. *The People Could Fly: American Black Folktales*
3. *Wilma Ruldoph*
4. *The Complete Ghost Stories of Charles Dickens,* edited by Peter Haining

C. Answers will vary. Sample answers are shown below.

1. In 1991 the population was 155,356,073. *The Universal Almanac* (1993); almanac
2. Santa Rosa is in northwestern California at the foot of the Sonoma Mountains. It was probably named after St. Rose of Lima. *Illustrated Dictionary of Place Names;* dictionary or atlas
3. Howard University was founded by the United States Congress in 1867. *Encyclopedia Americana;* encyclopedia
4. High of 76°F, low of 62°F; *The Miami Herald;* newspaper

D. Answers will vary. Sample answers are shown below.

1. "Lone Star State to America: Come On Down!" Janice Castro, *Time,* February 10, 1992; "The Lone Star of Texas," K. Northcott, *Ladies' Home Journal,* March 1991
2. "Sun Power," Graham Dutton, *Forbes,* November 9, 1992; "Solar Energy's New Place in the Sun," W. Konrad, *Business Week,* October 7, 1991

E. Answers may vary. Possible answers are shown below.

1. Sources may include reference materials, biographical books, historical and scientific books, government agencies such as NASA, audiovisual media, computer services, and experts.
2. Sources may include historical books, photos, experts such as local residents whose ancestors settled in the town, local museums and historical societies, and the mayor's office.

Interviewing Skills

Objectives

- To recognize interview techniques
- To write good interview questions

Related Mini-Lessons

For information on topics related to interviewing, see the following mini-lesson:

- **Critical Listening and Observing, pp. 363–366**

Motivate

Have students discuss TV talk-show hosts. Then ask, "How do they get guests to talk in an interesting way?"

Teaching Strategies

for GUIDELINES FOR INTERVIEWERS

MODELING Stage a short interview of a student, parent, or school employee. You might interview them about a sport or a hobby or a certain type of work. Beforehand, write your questions on the board as examples of questions requiring more than yes-or-no answers.

Additional Resource

Writing Resource Book, p. 123

Answers to Practice Your Skills

Questions will vary but must require more than yes-or-no responses. Sample questions:

1. What do you like most about being a jet pilot?
2. What other aircraft can you fly?
3. What hobbies do you have?
4. How did you feel on your first solo flight?
5. How do you feel about having chosen this career?

WRITING HANDBOOK 36

How Can I Become a Good Interviewer?

Interviewing Skills

Have you ever noticed how quotes from interesting people or experts on a subject can make a newspaper or magazine article come alive? For this reason, reporters value interviews as an important way of gathering information. You can use interviewing to add firsthand information and interest to many kinds of writing, such as eyewitness reports, research papers and I-Search papers. These guidelines will help you conduct a successful interview.

Guidelines for Interviewers

Planning the Interview

1. Contact the person you want to interview. Arrange to meet.
2. Learn about the subject and the person before the interview.
3. Make a list of questions that require more than yes-or-no answers. For example "What was it like . . ." or "How do you . . ."

Conducting the Interview

1. Listen carefully and take accurate notes. If necessary, ask the person to slow down or to repeat or explain statements.
2. Ask permission if you want to tape-record or quote the person.
3. Be flexible. Follow your plan, but be willing to ask follow-up questions during the interview.
4. Thank the person, and then review and rewrite your notes while the interview is fresh in your mind.

Practice Your Skills

Rewrite the following questions so that they require more than a yes-or-no answer.

1. Do you like being a jet pilot?
2. Are you trained to fly other types of aircraft?
3. Do you have any hobbies?
4. Were you scared on your first solo flight?
5. Are you glad you chose this career?

TEACHER'S LOUNGE

"Something tells me that we'll see him on 'Geraldo' some day."

How Can I Become a Good Listener?

Critical Listening and Observing

Stop! Close your eyes. Notice what you hear for the next twenty seconds.

You may have heard two classmates whispering or a videotape from another classroom. You have just used your sense of hearing. But were you really listening? When you **listen,** you also try to understand and make use of what you hear.

When and why do you listen? You listen to the news to become informed, to TV or radio to be entertained, to commercials to learn about products, and to conversations to gather the ideas of friends. To make the best use of what you hear, however, you must become a critical listener. As a **critical listener,** you not only hear but also think about and evaluate the messages.

IMPROVING LISTENING SKILLS

Before you can become a critical listener, you need to sharpen your basic listening skills.

Strategies for Effective Listening

Do

- think about why the topic might be important to you
- keep an open mind
- listen for the speaker's purpose and main ideas
- try to anticipate the speaker's next point
- summarize as you listen
- take notes if appropriate

Don't

- tune out the speaker
- become distracted
- let your own thoughts and feelings interfere
- try to remember too many details
- jump to conclusions
- let note taking get in the way of your listening

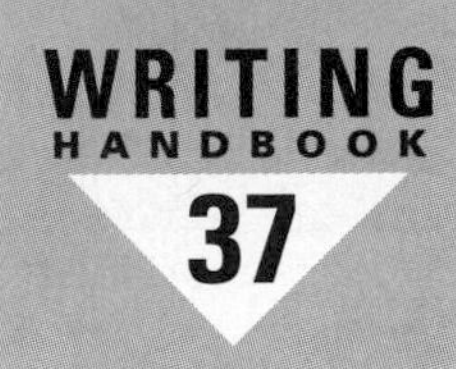

Critical Listening and Observing

Objectives

- To recognize how to listen effectively and critically
- To evaluate spoken arguments and identify a speaker's purpose
- To recognize the effects of nonverbal messages and visual images and symbols

Related Mini-Lessons

For information on topics related to critical listening and observing, see the following mini-lesson:

- **Critical Thinking and Writing, pp. 337–339**

Motivate

Ask students to think about times when they were persuaded by a radio or TV commercial to go to a concert or a movie and then were disappointed by the show. Have them tell where they went and why they were disappointed. Then point out to students that this handbook will help them analyze both verbal and nonverbal messages.

Teaching Strategies

for STRATEGIES FOR EFFECTIVE LISTENING

HELPFUL HINT Have students take turns reading the Strategies for Effective Listening and describing a situation to illustrate each point. (Sample for the first item in the "Do" list: If you're listening to a news report about inflation, you might think about how it will affect the price of athletic shoes and hamburgers.)

for WEIGH THE EVIDENCE

CRITICAL THINKING: EVALUATING Elicit from students definitions of *fact* (a statement that can be proved) and *opinion* (a belief that can be supported but not proved). Read the following statements and ask students to identify them as facts or opinions:

- The electrical workers' union is voting on whether to strike. (fact)
- The electrical workers should not go out on strike. (opinion)

for WEIGH THE EVIDENCE

INDIVIDUALIZING INSTRUCTION: BASIC STUDENTS Ask students how they recognize whether a statement is a fact or an opinion. Help them begin a list of words and phrases that signal an opinion (for example, *should/should not, ought to, I think, I believe, better/best, worse/worst*).

for OPINIONS

STUMBLING BLOCK Tell students that even experts on a particular subject may have different opinions. Therefore, even though a speaker may be qualified, his or her opinions should not be taken for fact unless they can be proved.

EVALUATING WHAT YOU HEAR AND SEE

Today we rely on a variety of sources for information, especially TV. In order to understand what you hear, you must be able to evaluate, or judge the value of, the speaker's ideas. Don't assume that the speaker's ideas are valid or truthful just because he or she is a so-called expert, a newscaster on TV, or even a relative. Be skeptical!

Weigh the Evidence

Often speakers use a mix of facts and opinions to support main ideas. Even a newscaster, whose job is to present only facts, may mix opinions with the facts of a story. As a critical listener, you must be able to tell the difference between fact and opinion and judge the soundness of both. Then you can decide if a speaker has presented his or her conclusions fairly. Ask yourself these questions.

Facts	***Opinions***
• Can I prove the facts by asking an expert or checking resource materials?	• Are the opinions reasonable and based on the facts?
• Are there enough facts to support the main ideas?	• Is the speaker qualified to give knowledgeable opinions?
• Have I heard all the facts? Have I heard facts that support the other side of the issue?	• How does the opinion compare with my own experience? with that of people familiar with the subject?

Some speakers use faulty reasoning when discussing issues. In advertisements, political statements, and other types of persuasive speeches, these errors in reasoning may be deliberate attempts to mislead listeners. Learn to recognize faulty reasoning so that you can judge the value of messages. (See also "Critical Thinking and Writing," pages 337–339.)

Look Beyond the Words

Sometimes the words of a message may be right, but something still doesn't ring true. Don't be afraid to trust your own judgment. You may not be an expert, but you probably know enough about a topic to do some questioning. In addition to the words, consider the speaker's motive and point of view and any nonverbal messages that accompany the speaker's words. Also notice visual images and symbols that may affect your opinion.

Motive and Point of View A citizen presents an editorial on the "sound off" segment of a local news program to complain that skateboarders and Rollerbladers on public sidewalks are safety hazards. How would your evaluation of the complaint be affected if you knew that the citizen was preparing to run for a position on the village board? Is the citizen really concerned about the welfare of villagers, or could the speech be a preview of campaign issues? Always ask yourself what reason a speaker has for taking a certain position.

Nonverbal Messages A political candidate broadcasts a campaign message from his living room. He wears a shirt with the sleeves rolled up, sits casually in a relaxed position, and smiles a great deal. Does his appearance make his ideas seem more believable? Facial expression, posture, gestures, and dress are all ways good speakers get a message across. However, it is important to think about whether these elements have been purposely crafted to create a certain impression.

Visual Images and Symbols One network reports a criminal's parole hearing and shows a police photo of the criminal, while another network reports the same story but shows a family photo of the criminal hugging his elderly mother. How does each photo affect your opinion about the parole issue?

Now imagine a TV commercial for automobile tires that shows toddlers happily sitting in and around tires. Do you associate the safety and happiness of children with that brand of tires? As a critical listener, think about how your judgment is affected by the associations you make. Notice the symbols and pictures that accompany what you hear.

for MOTIVE AND POINT OF VIEW

HELPFUL HINT Provide examples of other cases in which speakers have a particular motive for taking a certain position. For example, expert witnesses in trials are well paid by the side they testify for; tobacco industry spokespeople have a vested interest in the industry's success.

for VISUAL IMAGES AND SYMBOLS

INDIVIDUALIZING INSTRUCTION: VISUAL LEARNERS Call on these students to describe and analyze the images and symbols in a number of current TV commercials, especially those aimed at teenagers. Ask them which commercials they think are most effective in influencing teenagers and why.

Social Studies Connection

From the library obtain a videotape that includes a historic speech or segments of a pre-election debate. Have students view the speech or debate and analyze what they hear and see, including the nonverbal messages.

Additional Resource

Writing Resource Book, pp. 124–125

Answers to Practice Your Skills

A. Answers will vary. You may wish to discuss the photograph with the class before having students read the speech and respond to it in writing. Students might note that the American flag, the eagle emblem, and Schwarzkopf's uniform contribute to Schwarzkopf's patriotic message.

Students should correctly identify the purpose of the speech (to thank United States citizens for loyally supporting the troops during the Persian Gulf War and to stir feelings of patriotism). They should also point out some of the phrases Schwarzkopf uses to drive his message home ("your love . . . gave us strength," "you are . . . the wind beneath our wings," "great American people," "we were in your hearts and you were in our corner"). Schwarzkopf further stirs patriotic emotions by contrasting the war's supporters with the "prophets of doom, the naysayers, the protesters, and the flag burners."

B. Answers will vary. Students should identify both positive and negative qualities and mention verbal and nonverbal aspects of the newscast.

Practice Your Skills

A. Look at the picture below. List any nonverbal messages and visual images you see. Explain what effect they might have on a listener. Then read the excerpt from General Schwarzkopf's speech to Congress after the 1990–91 Persian Gulf War. Write a brief analysis of it. Identify the purpose and any special phrasing used to accomplish the purpose.

. . . We also want to thank our families. It is you who endure the hardships and separations simply because you choose to love a soldier, a sailor, an airman, a marine, or a coast guardsman. But it is your love that gave us strength in our darkest hours. You are truly the wind beneath our wings. Finally, and most importantly, [thanks] to the great American people. The prophets of doom, the naysayers, the protesters, and the flag burners . . . said you would never stick by us. But we knew better. We knew you would never let us down. By golly, you didn't. Since the first hour of Desert Shield until the last minute of Desert Storm, every day in every way all across America, you shouted that you were with us. Millions of . . . students, millions and millions of families, untold numbers of civic organizations, . . . factories, companies and workplaces, millions of senior citizens, and just plain Americans—never let us forget that we were in your hearts and you were in our corner. Because of you, when that terrible first day of the war came, we knew we would not fail; we knew we had the strength of the American people behind us, and with that strength we were able to get the job done, kick the Iraqis out of Kuwait, and get back home. From all of us who proudly served in the Middle East in your armed forces, thank you to the great people of the United States of America.

B. Watch a newscast on television. Write a short evaluation, noting both the positive and the negative qualities of the broadcast.

366 Writing Handbook

Howta Reckanize American Slurvian

In his book *Anguished English,* Richard Lederer describes a familiar style of pronunciation called Slurvian.

Everywhere we turn we are assaulted by a slew of slurrings. We meet people who *hafta, oughta,* or are *gonna* do something or who *shoulda, woulda,* or *coulda* done it. . . . Here's a typically American exchange:

"Jeet jet?"

"No, jew?"

"Sgo."

Translation: "Did you eat yet?" "No, did you?" "Let's go." . . .

To help you translate Slurvian into English . . . I offer [this] glossary.

Bar. To take temporarily. "May I bar your eraser?"

Dense. A tooth expert. "Yuck! I have a dense appointment today."

Forced. A large cluster of trees. "Only you can prevent forced fires."

Less. Contraction of "let us." "Less learn more about Slurvian."

Lining. Electrical flash of light. "We abandoned our picnic when we heard the thunder and saw the lining."

Mere. A reflecting glass. "Mere, mere on the wall, who's the fairest one of all?"

Mill. Between the beginning and the end. "A table stood in the mill of the room."

Mince. Units lasting 60 seconds. "I'll be back in a few mince."

Neck store. Adjacent. "I'm in love with the girl neck store."

Nigh. Opposite of day. "She woke up screaming in the mill of the nigh."

Win. Movement of air. "He was awakened in the mill of the nigh by flashes of lining and gusts of win."

You might have students work in small groups to write a few additional Slurvian entries. Suggest that they follow the format in the text: a Slurvian word in italics, followed by a definition and an example sentence. Have groups share their entries with the entire class.

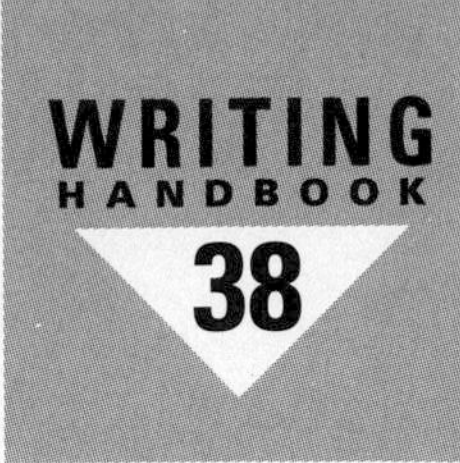

Test-Taking Strategies

Objectives

- To recognize how to prepare for classroom tests
- To recognize the various types of test items on classroom and standardized tests
- To review and apply strategies for taking classroom and standardized tests

Motivate

Write the following headings on the board: *Easiest Type of Test, Hardest Type of Test, Most Worthwhile Type of Test.* Briefly discuss students' ideas on these topics.

Teaching Strategies

GENERAL NOTE

INDIVIDUALIZING INSTRUCTION: ESL STUDENTS The kinds of classroom tests common in schools in the United States may be unfamiliar to some ESL students. In addition, some test directions may be baffling. Spend time familiarizing these students with test formats and directions. You might pair each ESL student with a native English speaker to work through the exercises in this handbook, you may wish to spend extra time discussing the completed exercises.

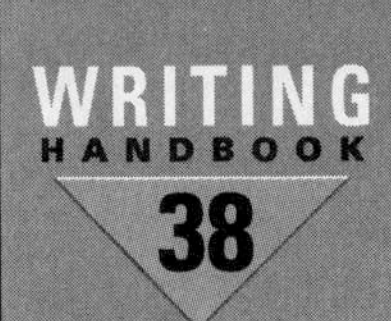

How Can I Perform Better on Tests?

Test-Taking Strategies

"Is this going to be on the test?" That's a question you've probably heard or asked many times. One that is just as important is this: "What type of test will it be?" If you know the kind of test, you can decide how to prepare for it. In this lesson you will learn some helpful strategies for taking classroom and standardized tests.

TAKING CLASSROOM TESTS

Classroom tests cover topics studied in class. In a social studies class, for example, you might be given a test on Spain's conquest of the Inca empire. Here are some ways to prepare for taking a classroom test:

1. **Learn what the test will cover.** Ask your teacher what ideas will be covered and what types of questions will appear on the test.
2. **Plan your study time.** Don't cram for the test at the last minute. Instead, spread out your study times.
3. **Review all written materials and list the key facts.** Quickly reread any notes, textbook chapters, or handouts. Then make a list of key facts and concepts such as names, vocabulary words, dates, events, and math formulas.
4. **Memorize the key facts.** Here are some tips:
   - Read your list of facts aloud.
   - Make and use flash cards.
   - Make up silly sentences to remember groups of facts ("**M**any **v**ery **e**ager **M**artians **j**uggled **s**oft, **un**ripe **p**ears" = **M**ercury, **V**enus, **E**arth, **M**ars, **J**upiter, **S**aturn, **U**ranus, **N**eptune, **P**luto).
5. **Rest and relax.** Go to bed early the night before a test.

In the following sections you will learn how to answer the different types of questions that can appear on classroom tests.

Science Connection

The sentence given as an example of a way to remember the order of the planets is called a *mnemonic device.* Challenge each student to make up one mnemonic device to remember information from the science unit the class is currently studying. Have students share their devices.

Answering Objective Questions

In answering an **objective question,** look for one brief, correct answer. The following information describes four types of objective questions and gives some strategies for answering them.

A **true-false question** is really a statement. Your job is to tell whether the statement is true or false. Use these strategies:

- If even one small part of a statement is false, the whole statement is false.
- Words like *all, always, every, never,* and *only* often but not always appear in false statements.
- Words like *generally, most, often, probably, some, sometimes,* and *usually* often appear in true statements.

(T) F Colorblindness is generally more common among males than among females.

Matching questions ask you to match items in one group with items in a second group. Try these strategies:

- Check to see if you are allowed to match some items more than once or if some items will not be used at all.
- Read all of the items. Then match the ones that you know.
- Cross out items as you match them, unless they can be used more than once.

Write the letter of each poem title next to the correct author's name.

a. "Casey at the Bat"	c	**1.** Lilian Moore
b. "The Raven"	b	**2.** Edgar Allan Poe
c. "The First"	e	**3.** Eloise Greenfield
d. "The Dream Keeper"	d	**4.** Langston Hughes
e. "Way Down in the Music"	a	**5.** Ernest Lawrence Thayer

for ANSWERING OBJECTIVE QUESTIONS

CRITICAL THINKING: GENERALIZING Read aloud the strategies listed under each type of test question. Then ask students whether there is any advice or generalization that can apply to answering most types of objective questions. (Sample: [1] Read the whole item carefully. [2] First complete the items you know. [3] In items that you are unsure of, eliminate the answers that are obviously wrong.)

for MATCHING QUESTIONS

KEY TO UNDERSTANDING The first strategy for matching questions and the Peanuts cartoon suggest a crucial step that you might directly state for students: Read the directions carefully and make sure you understand them before you begin.

for MULTIPLE-CHOICE QUESTIONS

MODELING Use the following question to model the strategies for answering multiple-choice questions:

A word that modifies a noun or pronoun is

a. an infinitive c. an adverb
b. a fragment d. an adjective

Demonstrate for the class how you consider each possible answer, how you decide whether each one is worth further consideration, and how you determine the correct answer. You might say: Answers *a* and *c* don't relate to nouns or pronouns at all, so I will eliminate them. A fragment is an incomplete sentence. Because that doesn't have much to do with nouns or pronouns, I will select *d* as the correct answer.

GENERAL NOTE

HELPFUL HINT Point out that students will inevitably skip certain questions if they first complete the items whose answers they know. If students are recording their answers on a separate sheet of paper or on an answer key, remind them to double-check that the number of the question matches the number of the answer. Otherwise, an entire section of their answers could be wrong!

A **multiple-choice question** asks you to choose the best answer from a group of answers provided. These strategies may help you:

- Read all choices. Ignore the ones that are obviously wrong.
- Choose the best answer from the ones that are left.

1. Which is the most abundant mineral in your body?
A. iron **B.** magnesium **C.** sodium (**D.**) calcium

***Grammar* TIP**

The answer to a fill-in-the-blank or completion question should fit grammatically into the sentence.

A **fill-in-the-blank** or **completion question** asks you to write a brief answer on a blank line. Use these strategies:

- First fill in the answers you are sure of.
- Then go back and reread the questions you left blank.
- If several words are needed, write all of them.

1. The battle that ended the American Revolution happened in 1781 at Yorktown, Virginia.

Answering Short-Answer Questions

Classroom tests also often contain short-answer questions. These questions are especially good for testing both specific knowledge and understanding of a subject area.

A **short-answer question** asks you to give a short, written answer. Give these strategies a try:

- Read the directions completely.
- Answer in complete sentences if asked to do so.
- Make sure that your grammar, spelling, punctuation, and capitalization are correct.

Answer the question below in a complete sentence.

1. Of all the living creatures on earth, which has the largest population?

The beetle has the largest population on earth.

Answering Essay Questions and Writing Prompts

Like a short-answer question, an **essay question** asks for a written answer, but the answer to an essay question is longer and more complex. In science class, for example, you may be asked to explain the process of photosynthesis.

A **writing prompt** asks you to write a short composition. It may tell you the form your composition should take and the audience for whom you should write. Here is an example of a writing prompt:

1. In a letter to your principal, state your opinion about the recent decision to shorten your school's lunch period.

Understanding the Question Try the following strategies:

- **Locate** the topic about which you are to write.
- **Find** key words that tell you what to do, such as *compare, explain, identify,* or *describe.*
- **Identify** the form, such as a letter or an essay.
- **Determine** the audience, such as sports fans.

Writing the Response Be sure to follow these guidelines:

1. **Read** all parts of an essay question. Pay careful attention to the form and audience stated in a writing prompt.
2. **Organize** your ideas on scratch paper before you write.
3. **Proofread** your response. If you left out an important idea, insert it. Correct any mechanical errors.

Practice Your Skills

Write a response to one of the following writing prompts.

1. Write a brief essay for your classmates called "How Not to Take a Test." In your essay, explain four things that a student definitely should not do when he or she takes a test.
2. Choose a music video, television program, or movie and write a review for your school newspaper. Tell students whether or not they should see the production and why.

PROBLEM SOLVING

How can I find out more about essay tests?

For more information about assessment, see Writer's Workshop 6, pages 155–158.

for ANSWERING ESSAY QUESTIONS . . .

STUMBLING BLOCK Some students are so intimidated by time constraints that they "go blank" when facing an essay question. Assure students that they can be successful, as you review the strategies and guidelines in class. Suggest that they make a rough outline before beginning to write. That outline should begin with the main idea stated in a single sentence. Then students should jot down supporting ideas and evidence.

for ANSWERING ESSAY QUESTIONS . . .

COLLABORATIVE OPPORTUNITY

You might duplicate anonymous examples of essay answers from classes of previous years (for example, three answers to the same essay question). Ask students to meet in small groups to evaluate the answers and decide how they would assess each one. Then meet as a class to discuss the groups' evaluations. Encourage students to use this experience to develop their own essay-question answering skills.

Answers to Practice Your Skills

1. Essays will vary. Students should include four main points. (Samples: Don't listen when your teacher tells you what material will be covered on the test. Watch television instead of reviewing your class notes during the week before the test. Stay up really late the night before the test and cram at the last moment. Don't make lists of important facts or formulas.) Students' writing should be coherent and should demonstrate correct spelling, punctuation, capitalization, and grammar.
2. Answers will vary. Students should demonstrate that they have considered audience and form. Look for a clear recommendation and reasons to support it.

Social Studies Connection

Ask a social studies teacher for a sampling of essay questions, writing prompts, or both from old tests. Have students meet in small groups to read and discuss the questions. You might ask each student to choose one and list its topic, key words, form, and audience.

for TAKING STANDARDIZED TESTS

HELPFUL HINT Ask students whether they know what the word *standardized* refers to. (Before they are published, standardized tests are tried out on thousands of students in different regions. The tryout scores are used to set up a standard, or basis, for measuring other students' scores.)

for ANSWERING . . . COMPREHENSION QUESTIONS

HELPFUL HINT Ask students to read the sample question carefully, noting the verb *borrowed.* As they read the sample passage, encourage them to look for this word or a similar word as a clue to the answer. This strategy is useful when the question asks for a detail or main idea that is stated in the passage.

TAKING STANDARDIZED TESTS

COMPUTER TIP

Some on-line services contain special help and question-and-answer departments for students who will be taking standardized tests.

A **standardized test** covers several areas of knowledge. One type of standardized test, an **achievement test,** is designed to find out what you have learned over several years. Subjects covered on an achievement test include math, vocabulary, reading, grammar, usage, science, and social studies. You can't really study for a standardized test. However, you can learn strategies for answering the test questions.

Answering Reading Comprehension Questions

Reading comprehension tests are used to find out how well you understand what you have read. You are asked to read passages that are followed by questions that may ask you to do such things as state the main idea, recall details, or draw a conclusion. In some tests the questions may have more than one correct answer. Read the test directions carefully. Then follow these steps:

- Read the questions before you read the passage.
- Look for answers to the questions as you read.
- Read all of the answer choices. Then choose the best answer. If several answers are allowed, choose all correct answers.

An *oshiya,* or "pusher-in," helps a man into a crowded subway during rush hour in Japan.

Read the following passage. Then answer the question below. The question may have more than one correct answer.

The United States imports many Japanese products, including cars, televisions, and VCRs. At the same time, Japan imports many things from the United States, including English words. Recent Japanese borrowings from the English language include *ice cream*, *taxi*, and *rush hour*. Many teachers in Japan dislike the imported English words, which they think of as slang. Nevertheless, Western popular culture and English words continue to be popular among Japanese teens.

1. Which English words have been borrowed by the Japanese?
   A. boyfriend (**B.**) taxi **C.** airplane (**D.**) ice cream

MULTICULTURAL Connection

Listening and Viewing If they haven't already seen it, students will enjoy watching the video of the prize-winning film *Stand and Deliver* (1988), which is based on a true story. Edward James Olmos stars as a Los Angeles high school math teacher who challenges his Mexican-American students to excel in math. Their record-breaking scores on the standardized Advanced Placement Calculus test caused Educational Testing Service officials to accuse them of having cheated. Seeing how these students learn—and face the challenge of a false accusation—may prove a real inspiration for your students.

Answering Grammar, Usage, and Mechanics Questions

A **grammar, usage, and mechanics question** tests your language skills. You are given a sentence with several parts underlined. Your job is to decide which of the underlined parts contains an error. If no part contains an error, the answer is "No error."

The error occurs in part C. The word *are* should be *is.*

The principal, (A) in addition to (B) the teachers, are (C) here. No error (D).

Use these strategies for answering similar questions:

- Read the entire sentence, not just the underlined parts.
- Look for errors such as word choice, punctuation, capitalization, sentence fragments, improper agreement, and others.

Answering Vocabulary Questions

Standardized tests often contain two types of vocabulary questions. These are synonym questions and antonym questions.

A **synonym question** asks you to find words that are similar in meaning. An **antonym question** asks you to find words that are opposite in meaning. Try these strategies:

- Read all the answers and then choose the best one.
- Choose similar words for synonym questions and opposite words for antonym questions.

Choose the word most similar in meaning to the underlined word.

1. affluence

A. poverty **(B.)** wealth **C.** happiness **D.** freedom

Choose the word most opposite in meaning to the underlined word.

2. affluence

(A.) poverty **B.** wealth **C.** happiness **D.** freedom

for ANSWERING GRAMMAR, USAGE, . . .

HELPFUL HINT Some students may gain confidence if you tell them that they practice these skills whenever they proofread their own or other students' papers.

for ANSWERING VOCABULARY QUESTIONS

HELPFUL HINT The two examples illustrate the crucial importance of reading test directions carefully. Test writers often include both synonyms and antonyms in the answers; if students do not pay attention to which they are to identify, they may get every item wrong.

for ANSWERING ANALOGY QUESTIONS

INDIVIDUALIZING INSTRUCTION: BASIC STUDENTS For many students, analogy questions are the most difficult and intimidating. These questions often include at least one unfamiliar word, besides testing an understanding of two abstract relationships. Review the models and strategies carefully and slowly in class. Note that the incorrect answers are related to the key word, but not in the same exact way as the second word is related to the first in the first pair of words. Make sure that every student can explain *why* the circled answers are correct.

for ANSWERING ANALOGY QUESTIONS

COLLABORATIVE OPPORTUNITY Break the class into small groups; ask each group to write two or three analogy questions. The experience of trying to write these questions will help students understand how the questions work and will help them gain confidence in approaching analogy questions on tests. Have students share their questions with the whole class or exchange questions with another group.

for TAKING TESTS

HELPFUL HINT Point out that most of these guidelines apply to classroom tests as well as to standardized tests. Read the guidelines aloud; then discuss them with the whole class. You might ask students which strategies are new to them and which they already follow.

TIP

Relationships described in analogy questions include cause to effect, member to group, object to use, part to whole, word to antonym or synonym, and worker to product.

Answering Analogy Questions

In an **analogy question,** you must determine how two given words are related. Then you must choose a word that makes the second pair of words relate to each other in the same way as the first pair. Some analogies have fill-in-the-blank lines.

1. Lion is to pride as wolf is to ________.
A. den **B.** cub **(C.)** pack **D.** kin

In the analogy above, you must decide how *lion* and *pride* are related. Follow these steps:

- Make a sentence using the first pair of words that shows their relationship: A group of *lions* is called a *pride.*
- In the sentence, replace the first pair of words with the second pair: A group of wolves is called a ________.
- Complete the sentence: A group of *wolves* is called a *pack.*

Some analogies use symbols instead of the words *is to* and *as.* Follow the same steps as above to help you complete this type of analogy.

1. earthquake → destruction : humor → ________
A. joke **B.** comedy **C.** comedian **(D.)** laughter

In the analogy above, the correct answer is "D. laughter." An earthquake causes destruction, and humor causes laughter.

TAKING TESTS

When taking a test, follow these steps:

1. When you first receive your test, skim over it. Note the types of questions and which sections will require more time to complete, such as a section with essay questions. Plan your time accordingly.
2. Carefully read the questions and all possible answers.

3. Answer all the questions you know. Make a mark next to the questions you can't answer, and go back to them later.
4. On answer sheets, fill in each answer circle darkly and completely. Be sure that you mark each answer in the correct place. If you make a mistake, erase and re-mark neatly.
5. Review your answers, proofreading where appropriate. Correct any confusing answers or illegible handwriting.

Practice Your Skills

A. Reread the passage on page 372. Then answer these questions. There may be more than one correct answer to each question.

1. What conclusions can you draw from the passage?
   (**A.**) People in the United States buy Japanese products.
   (**B.**) Western culture influences people throughout the world.
   C. The United States has imported many words from Japan.
   D. Japan imports ice cream from the United States.
2. According to the passage, what group in Japan opposes the importing of English words from America?
   A. business leaders **B.** politicians **C.** teenagers (**D.**) teachers

B. Choose the word closest in meaning to the underlined word.

1. <u>extravagant</u>
   A. new **B.** outdated (**C.**) excessive **D.** wild
2. <u>distinguished</u>
   A. smothered (**B.**) famous **C.** friendly **D.** right

C. Complete these analogies:

1. slice → pie: foot → ________
   A. sock (**B.**) yard **C.** shoe **D.** inch
2. chick → hen: child → ________
   A. baby (**B.**) adult **C.** person **D.** youngster
3. mathematics → numbers: music → ________
   A. orchestra (**B.**) notes **C.** piano **D.** conductor
4. meat → beef: fruit → ________
   A. bean **B.** peanut (**C.**) peach **D.** cabbage

Additional Resources

Writing Resource Book, pp. 126–128
Spelling and Vocabulary Booklet

Answers to Practice Your Skills

A. Answers are shown on page.
B. Answers are shown on page.
C. Answers are shown on page.

ART NOTE Ask students what they think of the gleeful skeletons on the candelabrum, or candle holder. Then explain that the candelabrum was used in Day of the Dead observances in Mexico. This celebration is ancient indeed, dating from pre-Hispanic times. In those days the first festival of the year was called *Tlaxochimaco,* which means "When the Flowers Bloom." It was also called the Small Celebration of the Dead and occurred in the ninth month of the calendar year (perhaps in our month of August). The festival was solemnly celebrated in temples with harvest offerings in memory of the dead.

The second holiday, occurring a month later, was called *Xocotlhuctzi* ("When the Fruit Falls") and was known as the Big Celebration of the Dead. People celebrated this second festival with much more fervor: worshipers painted their faces with soot and dyed their bodies black as signs of mourning. Originally, they also offered sacrifices and made other offerings in temples, but worshipers gradually began to perform rituals in their homes.

During the Spanish conquest of Mexico, the celebrations of the dead were moved to November 2 to coincide with a Roman Catholic holy day, All Souls' Day, the official day to pray for the souls in purgatory.

Ask students to look closely at the candelabrum and describe what they see. Where do they think the candle(s) would go? Note that a king and other figures are feasting at a table set with cups and dishes—perhaps the offerings of mortals. The skeletons have hair, a crown, and other ornaments. Some carry musical instruments, and all are surrounded by bright flowers and leaves. What mood has the artist suggested? How has he created this mood?

Day of the Dead candelabrum (1992), Oscar Soteno. On November 2, All Souls Day in the Catholic Church, Mexicans and Mexican Americans celebrate *El Dia de los Muertos* (the Day of the Dead). Families honor the dead by visiting cemeteries, where they light candles and decorate graves with flowers. Day of the Dead folk art often features humorous skeletal figures that engage in the customary activities of the living.

MULTICULTURAL Connection

Each culture has its own beliefs and customs regarding the dead. Ask students to describe their own group's customs relating to funerals and memorial observances. (In Jewish tradition, for example, a 24-hour *yahrtseit* candle is lit each year at sundown before the anniversary of a loved one's death.) In some cultures, a day is set aside to honor the dead; in others the dead are remembered daily. Learning about other traditions not only will broaden students' understanding but also will enhance their respect for other cultures.

Grammar and Usage Handbook

MINI-LESSONS

MINI-LESSONS

Grammar and Usage Handbook

Pretest

These tests enable you to assess your students' knowledge of grammar, usage, punctuation, spelling, and capitalization. The format of these tests is similar to that of some standardized tests. Use this assessment as a formal diagnostic tool or as an informal means of deciding which concepts in the Grammar and Usage Handbook you will emphasize.

Answer Key

Corrections for run-ons may vary.

1. **A**—Wow! Some
   C—spout
2. **A**—February
3. **D**—months
4. **D**—country during
5. **A**—Cockroaches
6. **A**—lain
   B—ocean? If
7. **C**—undercoat, which
   D—dog's
8. **A**—I
   D—good
9. **C**—are
   D—sea
10. **B**—its
    C—are
11. **C**—deserts
    D—bigger
12. **B**—any other country
13. **A**—has sat
14. **B**—He
    D—gave
15. **B**—superstition,"
    C—you're

List of Skills Tested

1. **A**—sentence fragment/run-on punctuation: interjection
   B—capitalization: proper noun
   C—subject-verb agreement: intervening words
   D—noun plural
2. **A**—capitalization
   B—noun possessive
   C—spelling
   D—sentence fragment/run-on
3. **A**—capitalization: common noun
   B—capitalization: geographic names
   C—subject-verb agreement: intervening words
   D—noun plural

Directions One or more of the underlined sections in the following sentences may contain an error in grammar, usage, punctuation, spelling, or capitalization. Write the letter of each incorrect section. Then rewrite the section correctly. If there is no error in an item, write *E.*

> ***Example*** The North American [A] continent [B] does not end at the Pacific Ocean [C]. It continues under the Ocean [D] for about forty-five miles. No error [E]
>
> ***Answer*** D—ocean

1. Wow Some [A] of those geysers in Yellowstone National Park [B] spouts [C] water one hundred feet [D] into the air. No error [E]

2. On february [A] 5, 1976, Maude Tull had her driver's [B] license [C] renewed. She [D] was 104 years old at the time. No error [E]

3. The famous pony express system [A], which carried mail from Missouri [B] to California, was [C] in operation for only eighteen monthes [D]. No error [E]

4. King Richard I [A] of England, also [B] known as Richard the Lion-Hearted, spent [C] only about half a year in his own country. During [D] his entire rule. No error [E]

5. Cockroachs [A] are hard to get rid of, and [B] they have been around for a long time. They [C] have existed [D] on the earth for 250 million years. No error [E]

6. Have you ever laid [A] in the ocean, if [B] you have, you know [C] that salt water holds a person up better [D] than fresh water does. No error [E]

378 Skills Assessment

7. A Siberian husky has a thick, oily undercoat. Which keeps water away from the dogs' skin. No error
(A: Siberian; B: thick, oily; C: undercoat. Which; D: dogs'; E: No error)

8. My cousin and me were amazed that frozen yogurt is so healthful and tastes so well. No error
(A: me; B: were; C: healthful and tastes; D: well; E: No error)

9. The lungs and hearts of the natives of the Andean region is larger than those of people who live at Sea level. No error
(A: lungs; B: Andean; C: is; D: Sea; E: No error)

10. Yellowstone National Park has long been famous for it's many active geysers. There is also hot springs, mud volcanoes, fossil forests, and a glass mountain. No error
(A: Yellowstone National Park; B: it's; C: is; D: forests, and; E: No error)

11. The Great Sandy and the Simpson are two of the desserts of Australia. Of the two, the Great Sandy is biggest, covering about 150,000 square miles. No error
(A: Great Sandy; B: are; C: desserts; D: biggest; E: No error)

12. The United States produces more cheese than any country, but the French eat more cheese per person than people in the United States eat. No error
(A: produces; B: any country; C: French; D: eat; E: No error)

13. That letter has set on your desk for several days. To whom is it addressed? No error
(A: has set; B: days. To; C: whom; D: addressed?; E: No error)

14. Robin Hood was a legendary hero. Him and his men robbed from the rich and gived to the poor. No error
(A: legendary; B: Him; C: robbed; D: gived; E: No error)

15. "An old Irish superstition", explained Tim, "says your going to have bad luck if you meet a weasel on the road." No error
(A: "An; B: superstition",; C: your; D: road."; E: No error)

4. A—capitalization: names and titles
B—punctuation: appositive
C—punctuation: appositive
D—sentence fragment/run-on

5. A—noun plural
B—punctuation: compound sentence
C—sentence fragment/run-on
D—spelling

6. A—irregular verb form
B—sentence fragment/run-on punctuation: question mark
C—subject-verb agreement
D—comparative adverb

7. A—capitalization: proper adjective
B—punctuation: comma with multiple adjectives
C—sentence fragment/run-on
D—noun possessive

8. A—pronoun case: compound subject
B—subject-verb agreement: compound subject
C—punctuation: compound verb
D—wrong word: well/good

9. A—noun plural
B—capitalization: proper adjective
C—subject-verb agreement: intervening words/compound subject
D—capitalization: common noun

10. A—capitalization: geographical name
B—possessive pronoun/contraction confusion
C—subject-verb agreement: inverted sentence
D—punctuation: commas in series

11. A—capitalization: geographical name
B—subject-verb agreement: compound subject
C—spelling
D—comparative adjective

12. A—subject-verb agreement
B—illogical comparison
C—capitalization: nationality
D—subject-verb agreement

13. A—wrong word: sit/set
B—sentence fragment/run-on
C—wrong word: who/whom
D—spelling

14. A—spelling
B—pronoun case: subject
C—verb form
D—irregular verb form

15. A—punctuation: quotation
B—punctuation: quotation
C—possessive pronoun/contraction confusion
D—punctuation: quotation

Objective

- To use writing prompts and a passage from literature as springboards to informal writing

WRITING WARM-UPS

Remind students that this assignment will not be graded. The passage and activities are designed to get students thinking, in a broad and imaginative way, about concepts in this handbook, especially regarding the ways in which ideas work together to express meaning. Encourage students to choose one prompt to explore.

For the first writing prompt, ask students to consider what subjects would be likely to interest the animal they choose. What would the animal say about these subjects?

For the second writing prompt, ask students whether each animal would speak in single words or in full sentences. Which aspects of the animal's appearance or behavior give hints about its background and personality?

For the third writing prompt, have students focus on an experience in which their language, rather than their behavior, was misunderstood.

SKETCH BOOK

WRITING WARM-UPS

Animals talk to each other, of course. There can be no question about that; but I suppose there are very few people who can understand them. I never knew but one man who could. I knew he could, however, because he told me so himself. . . . According to Jim Baker, some animals have only a limited education, and use only very simple words, and scarcely ever a comparison or a flowery figure; whereas, certain other animals have a large vocabulary, a fine command of language, and a ready and fluent delivery; consequently these latter talk a great deal; they like it; they are conscious of their talent, and they enjoy "showing off."

MARK TWAIN
"BAKER'S BLUE-JAY YARN"

- What animal would you like to talk to? How would that animal speak? Write the dialogue of your conversation.
- Which animals have limited educations, and which ones like to show off? Write down your speculations.
- Have you ever been misunderstood? How did it happen? Why did it happen? Tell about the experience.

380

Literature Connection

Author Note Mark Twain (1835–1910), whose real name was Samuel Langhorne Clemens, was born in Hannibal, Missouri. He grew up when the frontier was still a vivid part of the American experience, and his books and stories reflect his love of the West. One of his specialties was the tall tale, a story that uses far-fetched events and exaggeration to create humor. "Baker's Blue-Jay Yarn" is one of these. Students who enjoy this excerpt might also like to read "The Celebrated Jumping Frog of Calaveras County," another Twain short story that relies on exaggeration.

The Sentence and Its Parts

GRAMMAR HANDBOOK 39

- Sentences and Sentence Fragments
- Subjects and Predicates
- Simple Subjects and Predicates
- The Verb Phrase
- Sentences Beginning with *Here* and *There*
- Other Sentences with Unusual Word Order
- Objects of Verbs
- Predicate Words and Linking Verbs
- Compound Sentence Parts
- Avoiding Run-on Sentences

No matter whom you talk to, you want to be understood. The way you put your words together—the sentences that you make—can determine how well you succeed.

In this handbook you will learn what makes up sentences and how you can structure sentences to get your message across—to any audience.

The Sentence and Its Parts

Objectives

- To distinguish between sentences and sentence fragments
- To identify the complete subject and predicate of a sentence
- To identify the simple subject and verb in a sentence
- To identify main verbs, helping verbs, and verb phrases
- To identify the subject and verb in sentences beginning with *here* and *there* and in other sentences with unusual word order
- To identify direct and indirect objects and transitive and intransitive verbs
- To identify predicate words and linking verbs
- To identify and use compound sentence parts
- To identify and correct run-on sentences

Writing

- To identify and correct sentence fragments and run-ons
- To use sentences correctly in writing

INTRODUCING THE HANDBOOK

Explain that the photo is from the film *Dr. Doolittle,* in which the title character talks with animals.

Discuss with students some reasons why language is misunderstood. (Samples: People use incorrect terms; they do not connect their ideas clearly.) Explain that by understanding the sentence and its parts, students can avoid some of these problems.

SENTENCES AND SENTENCE FRAGMENTS

Objectives

- To distinguish between complete sentences and sentence fragments

Writing

- To expand fragments into complete sentences

Teaching Strategies

SPEAKING AND LISTENING Point out that sentence fragments are often used in spoken English. Explain that spoken fragments are acceptable because a speaker's tone, expression, and gestures contribute to communication. Also, if something is not understood, the listener can ask questions. The reader has none of these advantages.

LINKING GRAMMAR AND WRITING Point out that writers often use fragments in dialogue. Explain that fragments help reproduce the natural sound of speech. Emphasize that as writers, students must write dialogue very carefully so that readers will understand what the subject is and what is going on.

Additional Resources

Tests and Writing Assessment Prompts, Pretest, pp. 7–8
Grammar and Usage Practice Book, p. 1

Grammar Test Generator

Writing Theme: Whales

Suggest that students use these exercises as a springboard to writing. Other related areas that they might explore include the following:

- nineteenth-century whaling
- why whales are endangered
- communicating with dolphins
- training whales and dolphins

SENTENCES AND SENTENCE FRAGMENTS

A **sentence** is a group of words that expresses a complete thought; a **sentence fragment** does not express a complete thought.

A complete thought is clear. Which of the following groups of words expresses a complete thought?

1. Close by the whale
2. The whale jumped clear of the water
3. Suddenly, a great splash

The second group of words expresses a complete thought. It is a complete sentence.

Sentence fragments do not express complete thoughts. The reader cannot be sure of what is missing or of the author's meaning.

A sentence fragment may be missing a subject, a verb, or both. You may wonder *What is this about?* or *What happened?*

Fragment The huge whale (*What happened?*)
Sentence The huge whale jumped high into the air.

Fragment Eagerly watched for whales (*Who watched for whales?*)
Sentence On the boat, tourists eagerly watched for whales.

Writing TIP

Always express yourself in complete thoughts to avoid confusing your reader.

You can correct a sentence fragment by supplying the missing information. Sometimes a fragment can be corrected by joining it to a complete sentence.

Writing Theme Whales

Practice Your Skills

A. CONCEPT CHECK

Sentences and Sentence Fragments Write *S* for each complete sentence and *F* for each sentence fragment.

1. I saw a TV show yesterday S
2. The show was about dolphins S
3. Actually a kind of small whale F

Answers to Practice Your Skills

A. Concept Check

Sentences and Sentence Fragments

Answers are shown on page.

4. Dolphins are quite intelligent S
5. Playful animals that seem to enjoy games F
6. Under the water in the big tank F
7. The dolphins can be very entertaining S
8. Just for the fun of swimming in front of an audience F
9. Dolphins have a well-developed sense of hearing S
10. They communicate complex messages S
11. A variety of chirps, whistles, and squeaks F
12. Can be heard for great distances under water F
13. Dolphins live in groups, or pods S
14. Swim in oceans around the world and even in some rivers F
15. Because dolphins breathe air and are warm-blooded F

B. REVISION SKILL

Correcting Sentence Fragments Rewrite the following letter. Make the ten fragments into sentences.

Dear Elena,

Yesterday I had a thrilling adventure. My parents and I sailed far out to sea. On a large boat. The passengers boarded the boat. Early in the morning on Cape Cod in Massachusetts. We were at sea for several hours, looking for whales. Almost gave up. Finally, one of the passengers sighted whales. At least twenty or thirty of them. Our boat got very close. A few of the whales leaped into the air. Splashed everyone. When they landed. No one complained! The whales seemed playful. They even seemed to enjoy our company. Got especially close. It pushed its head out of the water right next to the boat. Almost touched it! Time passed so quickly. Soon we had to leave. And return to port. Was sad. I hated leaving the whales. I'll always remember that trip.

Christine

C. APPLICATION IN WRITING

Writing Complete Sentences Write a letter to a friend describing your vacation experience with dolphins in a small cove. Change the five sentence fragments from the following list into complete sentences, and use the sentences in your letter.

the large rubber raft
swimming nearby all afternoon
wanted me to play too
rubbed against the raft
played tag with each other

FOR MORE PRACTICE
See page 408.

B. Revision Skill
Correcting Sentence Fragments

Answers will vary. See typical revision below.

Dear Elena,

Yesterday I had a thrilling adventure. My parents and I sailed far out to sea on a large boat. The passengers boarded the boat early in the morning on Cape Cod in Massachusetts. We were at sea for several hours, looking for whales. We almost gave up. Finally, one of the passengers sighted whales. There were at least twenty or thirty of them. Our boat got very close. A few of the whales leaped into the air. They splashed everyone when they landed. No one complained! The whales seemed playful. They even seemed to enjoy our company. One of them got especially close. It pushed its head out of the water right next to the boat. I almost touched it! Time passed so quickly. Soon we had to leave and return to port. I was sad. I hated leaving the whales. I'll always remember that trip.

Christine

C. Application in Writing
Writing Complete Sentences

Answers will vary. One possible answer is shown below.

Dear Juana,

Yesterday I had the most remarkable encounter with dolphins in a small cove. I was floating on the large rubber raft my father bought last year. Some dolphins were swimming nearby all afternoon; they played tag with each other. One of them rubbed against the raft. Apparently it wanted me to play too. It was quite an interesting experience. All in all, my vacation is going swimmingly!

Anna

Objectives

- To identify subjects and predicates in sentences and in original writing

Writing

- To form complete sentences by adding subjects or predicates to fragments

Teaching Strategies

HELPFUL HINT: WORD ORDER
Point out that in a typical English sentence, the subject precedes the predicate. Inform students that there are exceptions they will learn about later in this handbook.

INDIVIDUALIZING INSTRUCTION: BASIC STUDENTS To help students identify subjects and predicates, encourage them to ask themselves these questions when examining a sentence:

Whom or *what* is the sentence about?

What is said about the subject?"

Additional Resource

Grammar and Usage Practice Book, p. 2

Writing Theme: Animal Behavior

Suggest that students use these exercises as a springboard to writing. Other related areas that they might explore include the following:

- the life cycle of a butterfly
- endangered species
- the reintroduction of wolves into Yellowstone National Park
- hibernation

Answers to Practice Your Skills

A. Concept Check
Subjects and Predicates
Answers are shown on page.

SUBJECTS AND PREDICATES

The **subject** of a sentence tells *whom* or *what* the sentence is about. The **predicate** tells what the subject *does* or *is*.

Every sentence has two basic parts: the subject and the predicate. The **subject** tells *whom* or *what* the sentence is about. The **predicate** tells something about the subject.

Subject (Who or what)	Predicate (What is said about the subject)
Playful puppies	chew on everything.
Lion cubs	sleep about twenty hours a day.

Each sentence expresses a complete thought. Think of the sentence as telling who did something or what happened. The subject tells *who* or *what.* The predicate tells what was *done* or what *happened.*

Who or What	Did or Happened
The deer	leaped over the high fence.
The opossum	curled into a ball.
The horse	galloped gracefully across the field.

Writing Theme
Animal Behavior

Practice Your Skills

A. CONCEPT CHECK

Subjects and Predicates Make two columns on your paper. Label them *Subject* and *Predicate*. Write the proper words from each sentence in the columns.

1. Monarch butterflies are beautiful and interesting animals.
2. We saw several in our yard.
3. Monarchs have black bodies and orange wings with black borders.

4. These butterflies spend the summer in the United States.
5. Fall weather sends them south.
6. They fly about eleven miles per hour.
7. Thousands of these insects may gather together in huge flocks.
8. Some of them will travel as many as three thousand miles.
9. The flocks spend the winter in a remote valley in Mexico.
10. The butterflies head back north in the spring.

B. DRAFTING SKILL

Sentence Completion Use each group of words below to form complete sentences. You may wish to add a subject or predicate, or both where necessary. Tell which part you added.

11. wolves
12. are feared unnecessarily
13. have been the subject of many folk tales
14. their piercing eyes and sharp teeth
15. a German shepherd
16. have a bushy tail
17. the pups, or young wolves
18. live in a den dug into the ground
19. are related to the jackal and the dog
20. the color of their fur
21. the gray wolf, the red wolf, and the prairie wolf
22. sometimes called timber wolf and coyote
23. because wolves roam prairies and pasture land
24. can be dangerous to livestock
25. now an endangered species as a result of overhunting

C. APPLICATION IN WRITING

Describing an Animal Brainstorm a list of experiences you have had with animals. Think about household pets, animals you have seen at the zoo, or animals that live in the wild. Choose one experience and write a description of that experience. When you have finished, underline the subject once and the predicate twice in each sentence.

FOR MORE PRACTICE
See page 408.

B. Drafting Skill
Sentence Completion

Answers will vary. See possible answers below.

11. Wolves are misunderstood animals. Predicate
12. These creatures are feared unnecessarily. Subject
13. They have been the subject of many folk tales. Subject
14. Their piercing eyes and sharp teeth can be frightening. Predicate
15. A German shepherd resembles a wolf. Predicate
16. However, wolves have a bushy tail. Subject
17. The pups, or young wolves, form a litter. Predicate
18. For many weeks, the pups live in a den dug into the ground. Subject
19. Wolves are related to the jackal and the dog. Subject
20. The color of their fur gives some wolves their names. Predicate
21. The gray wolf, the red wolf, and the prairie wolf are three common kinds. Predicate
22. These kinds are sometimes called timber wolf and coyote. Subject and part of predicate
23. Because wolves roam prairies and pasture land, farmers dislike them. Subject and predicate
24. Hungry wolves can be dangerous to livestock. Subject
25. Wolves are now an endangered species as a result of overhunting. Subject and part of predicate

C. Application in Writing
Describing an Animal

Answers will vary. An effective description will contain vivid details organized into complete sentences. Check that students have correctly underlined subjects and predicates.

SIMPLE SUBJECTS AND PREDICATES

Objectives

- To identify simple subjects and simple predicates, or verbs, in sentences

Writing

- To revise sentences by using precise subjects and verbs

Teaching Strategies

LINKING GRAMMAR AND WRITING Point out that interruptions sometimes occur between the simple subject and verb in a sentence: *The young musician in the red coat played skillfully.* Explain that long interruptions make sentences confusing; therefore students should consider whether such information is really necessary and how else they might include it. Offer an example:

Confusing: The young man holding the baton at the front of the orchestra is extremely talented.

Better: The conductor of the orchestra is extremely talented.

SIMPLE SUBJECTS AND PREDICATES

A **verb** is a word that tells about action or that tells what someone or something is. The **subject of the verb** is the most important part of the complete subject.

In every sentence, a few words are more important than the rest. These key words make the basic framework of the sentence.

The young **musician**	**played** skillfully.
His **hands**	**moved** rapidly across the strings.

The subject of the first sentence is *The young musician.* The key word in this subject is *musician.* The predicate in the sentence is *played skillfully.* The key word is *played.* Without this word you would not have a sentence.

The key word in the subject of a sentence is called the **simple subject.** It is the subject of the verb.

The key word in the predicate is called the **simple predicate.** The simple predicate is also called the **verb.**

Finding the Verb and Its Subject

The verb and its simple subject are the basic framework of every sentence. The rest of the sentence is built around them. To find this framework, first find the verb. Then ask *who* or *what* before the verb. The answer identifies the subject.

That musician plays the zither. *Verb:* plays
Who or what plays? musician
Simple subject: musician

You can tell a fragment from a sentence easily by carefully identifying the subject and verb. A fragment will be missing a subject or verb or both.

Fragment	Lively music (*What about it? What happened?*)
Sentence	Lively music *poured from the unusual instrument.*
Fragment	From the unusual instrument.

Looking at the Sentence as a Whole

You have learned how to identify a simple subject, or key word in the subject. The **complete subject** is the simple subject plus any words that modify or describe it.

EXAMPLE The young musician played skillfully.

The young musician is the complete subject. It is made up of the simple subject plus the modifiers *the* and *young*.

Similarly, the **complete predicate** is the verb plus any words that modify or complete the verb's meaning. What is the complete predicate in the example sentence above? What is the simple predicate, or verb?

Sentence Diagraming For information on diagraming subjects and predicates, see page 692.

Practice Your Skills

A. CONCEPT CHECK

Simple Subjects and Predicates Label two columns *Verb* and *Simple Subject.* In the correct column, write the verb and its simple subject for each of the following sentences.

1. The kazoo is a musical instrument about six inches in length.
2. It resembles a tube in appearance.
3. In the early 1900s, people called the kazoo a Sonophone.
4. Alabama Vest invented this popular musical instrument.
5. Even nonmusical people play the kazoo.
6. Perhaps this fact explains the instrument's popularity.
7. Stores sell more than one million kazoos every year.
8. Some musicians view this instrument as more than a toy.
9. Those kazooists play metal kazoos.
10. Recently, four professional kazooists formed a very unusual quartet.
11. They call this quartet Kazoophony.
12. During concerts they wear tuxedos and no shoes.
13. Kazoophony performs silly songs such as "The 1813 Overture" and "Swine Lake."
14. On a more serious side, the University of Chicago formed an informal kazoo marching band.
15. Leonard Bernstein even wrote a part for kazoo in *Mass.*

Writing Theme
Unusual Musical Instruments

INDIVIDUALIZING INSTRUCTION: ESL STUDENTS In some languages, such as Spanish, Vietnamese, and Korean, all verbs have special inflected endings to distinguish them from other parts of speech. In some languages, verbs have consistent positions; for example, in Japanese they are placed at the ends of sentences. The inconsistent forms and positions of English verbs may confuse ESL students whose first language is consistent in this regard. Encourage students to identify English verbs by focusing on their function—expressing action or being—not on their form or placement.

Additional Resource

Grammar and Usage Practice Book, pp. 3–4

Writing Theme: Unusual Musical Instruments

Other related areas students might wish to explore as writing topics include the following:

- steel drums of the Caribbean
- "talking drums" of Africa
- "washtub" bands
- hand organs and calliopes

Answers to Practice Your Skills

A. Concept Check
Simple Subjects and Predicates

Answers are shown on page. Student answers should be in columns.

B. Revision Skill
Precise Word Choice

Replacement subjects and verbs will vary. A typical answer is shown below.

16. Benjamin Franklin (S), made (V); invented
17. Franklin (S), called (V); named
18. thing (S), consisted (V); instrument
19. mechanism (S), moved (V); spun
20. person (S), placed (V); musician
21. bowl (S), vibrated (V)
22. bowl (S), made (V); produced
23. People (S), loved (V); Musicians
24. vibrations (S), damaged (V)
25. no one (S), used (V); played

CHECK POINT

Writing Theme: Orson Welles

Other related areas that students might wish to explore as writing topics include the following:

- William Randolph Hearst's estate, San Simeon
- great Hollywood directors

MIXED REVIEW • PAGES 382–388

You may wish to use this activity to check students' mastery of the following concepts:

- sentences and sentence fragments
- subjects and predicates
- simple subjects and predicates

1. S
2. F; Verb or Subject and Verb
3. F; Verb
4. S
5. F; Subject
6. F; Verb
7. S
8. F; Verb
9. F; Subject
10. S
11. F; Subject
12. S
13. F; Subject and Verb
14. F; Subject
15. F; Verb or Subject and Verb

B. REVISION SKILL

Precise Word Choice Act as a peer reader for the author of the passage below. First, write and label the subject and verb from each sentence. Then suggest words that are more precise as replacements for the underlined subjects or verbs.

[16]Besides all his other accomplishments, Benjamin Franklin made a most unusual musical instrument. [17]Franklin called his invention the armonica. [18]The thing consisted of thirty-seven glass bowls on a long rod. [19]A mechanism moved the bowls rapidly. [20]The person placed a finger on a spinning bowl. [21]The bowl vibrated from the pressure of the finger. [22]Each glass bowl made a different tone.

[23]People throughout Europe and the United States loved the armonica. [24]Unfortunately, the vibrations of the bowls damaged the nerves of the player's fingers. [25]Soon, no one used the armonica anymore.

MIXED REVIEW • PAGES 382–388

Writing Theme
Orson Welles

Write *S* for each complete sentence, *F* for each sentence fragment. Then identify and label the missing element needed to form a complete sentence: *Subject, Verb,* or *Subject and Verb.*

1. Orson Welles was one of Hollywood's most creative actors and directors.
2. First great success as a radio broadcaster.
3. In the radio broadcast *The War of the Worlds,* Welles.
4. Many listeners believed Martians had landed on Earth.
5. Began a long and distinguished career.
6. The remarkable movie *Citizen Kane.*
7. The character of Kane was based on William Randolph Hearst.
8. This colorful ruler of a newspaper publishing empire.
9. Portrayed a publishing tycoon's ambition and ruthlessness.
10. The brilliant director, Orson Welles, also played the lead.
11. First appeared in movie theaters in 1941.
12. Hearst tried to stop its release.
13. Because of inventive filmmaking techniques.
14. Still consider it one of the greatest American films of all time.
15. Viewers for years to come.

FOR MORE PRACTICE
See page 408.

388 Grammar Handbook

THE VERB PHRASE

A **verb** may consist of one word or of several words.

Sometimes the **main verb** in a sentence is used with one or more **helping verbs.** A main verb and one or more helping verbs make up a **verb phrase.**

Helping Verbs	+	Main Verb	=	Verb Phrase
might have		gone		might have gone
will		see		will see
are		driving		are driving
could		go		could go
could be		riding		could be riding

Sometimes the parts of a verb are separated from each other by words that are not verbs. In each of the following sentences, the parts of the verb phrase are printed in bold type. The word in between is not part of the verb phrase.

The old cowpoke **could** always **tell** a good story.
He **is** finally **buying** a new horse.
The trail boss **has** often **made** camp here.
Longhorn cattle **would** sometimes **stampede** unexpectedly.
Cowhands **must** occasionally **ride** great distances.

Some verbs are joined with other words to make contractions. When naming verbs that appear in contractions, name only the verb. The word *not* and the contraction *n't* are adverbs. They are never part of a verb or a verb phrase.

Contraction	Verb
hasn't *(has not)*	*has*
couldn't *(could not)*	*could*
we're *(we are)*	*are*
I've *(I have)*	*have*
we'd *(we had* or *would)*	*had* or *would*

THE VERB PHRASE

Objective

- To identify main verbs, helping verbs, and verb phrases

Teaching Strategies

COOPERATIVE LEARNING Have a group of students work together to create a chart or other visual display of common helping verbs. Point out that there are other helping verbs besides those given on the pupil page. (Examples include *am, was, were, do, did, can, may, should,* and *shall.)* Have the group post the chart for classroom use.

CRITICAL THINKING: DRAWING CONCLUSIONS Have students brainstorm a list of common contractions. (Samples: *didn't, doesn't, isn't, wouldn't, can't, shouldn't, I'm, I'll, I'd, she's, he's, we've, you're,* and *they're)* Then ask students to determine the two kinds of words that are most commonly used in forming a contraction. (helping verbs and the adverb *not)*

INDIVIDUALIZING INSTRUCTION: ESL STUDENTS Helping verbs are used in English and in other languages such as Hindi, French, Italian, Spanish, and German. Some languages, however, use inflectional endings to indicate tense and voice. For ESL students unfamiliar with the concept, helping verbs may be difficult to recognize and use. Encourage these students to make an add-on chart of helping verbs. Pair students with English-proficient partners to help them classify each helping verb according to time of action.

Additional Resource

Grammar and Usage Practice Book, p. 5

Writing Theme: The Wild West

Other related areas students might wish to explore as writing topics include the following:

- the transcontinental railroad
- African-American cowboys
- cowboy songs
- Native Americans of the Great Plains

Answers to Practice Your Skills

A. Concept Check
Verb Phrases

Answers are shown on page.

B. Application in Literature
Verbs and Verb Phrases

Answers are shown on page.

Writing Theme
The Wild West

Practice Your Skills

A. CONCEPT CHECK

Verb Phrases Write the verb or verb phrase in each sentence.

1. In the late 1800s, vast herds of cattle were raised in Texas.
2. The cattle owners couldn't easily get their beef to market.
3. This problem may have contributed to the growth of the West.
4. Before long, in response to the need for a transportation system, railroads slowly advanced westward.
5. Cowhands would drive the cattle to the railheads, or end of the existing rail lines.
6. Railheads would eventually grow into cow towns.
7. Cow towns moved west with the railroads.
8. Cattle arrived in Sedalia, Missouri, for the first time in 1866.
9. By 1867, Abilene, Kansas, had become a main railhead.
10. A few years later, railroads reached Dodge City, Kansas.
11. Cow towns did not always have good reputations.
12. After cattle drives, cowhands were often seeking some fun.
13. The celebrations should have been happy.
14. However, fights and shootings would often occur.
15. Dodge City is still remembered as the roughest cow town of all.

Two young rough-and-ready cowboys scrape off the trail dust and don clean duds for the camera.

B. APPLICATION IN LITERATURE

Verbs and Verb Phrases Write and label each *Main Verb* and *Helping Verb* in the numbered sentences below.

[16]During a trail drive, cowboys would move thousands of cattle across the range to railroad stations. [17]From there the cattle were shipped to markets for sale in the East.

[18]A cowboy's work could be difficult and dangerous. [19]There were hardships involved in tending cattle. . . .

[20]Commonly, cowboys didn't call one another by their real names. [21]Within his first week at the bunkhouse, a new man was generally given a nickname. [22]Often the name described something about him. [23]For example, a redhead might be called "Red" or "Sunset," and a sorrowful-looking man "Gloomy." . . .

[24]After sunset at a roundup, the cowhands would spend some time together. [25]A cowboy might bring an accordion, a fiddle, or a banjo to a roundup. [26]As in the early West, a cowhand today will often enjoy a song after work.

Elaine Landau, *Cowboys*

FOR MORE PRACTICE
See page 409.

SENTENCES BEGINNING WITH *HERE* AND *THERE*

When *here* or *there* is the first word in a sentence, the word can be an adverb or merely an introductory word.

Sentences Beginning with *There*

Many sentences begin with the word *there*. Sometimes *there* is used as an adverb modifying the verb to tell where something is or happens.

There is the cave entrance. (The cave entrance is *there*.)
There stands the guide. (The guide stands *there*.)
There are some unusual cave fish. (Some unusual cave fish are *there*.)

In other sentences, *there* is only an introductory word that helps get the sentence started. It is not necessary to the meaning of a sentence.

There are many large caves in the United States. (Many large caves are in the United States.)

In most sentences beginning with *there,* the subject follows the verb. To find the subject, first find the verb. Then ask *who* or *what*.

There is a deep pool in this cave.
Verb: is
Who or what is? pool.

Sentences Beginning with *Here*

In sentences beginning with *here,* the word *here* is always an adverb telling where about the verb.

Here is another cave opening. (Another cave opening is *here*.)
Here are some very long stalactites. (Some very long stalactites are *here*.)

TIP

Sentences that begin with *here* and *there* can be helpful when you are explaining a process, or how to do something.

SENTENCES BEGINNING WITH *HERE* AND *THERE*

Objectives

- To identify the subject and verb in sentences beginning with *here* or *there*

Writing

- To revise a paragraph, eliminating excessive use of *here* and *there.*

Teaching Strategies

HELPFUL HINT: *THERE* After examining the sample sentences on the pupil page, students should use the "move it" principle in their approach to other sentences. If they can move *there* to the end of the sentence and keep the same meaning, they have an adverb. If they cannot move *there*—if they only can drop it—they have an introductory word.

INDIVIDUALIZING INSTRUCTION: BASIC STUDENTS Students who are easily baffled by unexpected structures may have trouble finding the subject in sentences beginning with *there* and *here.* Remind them that an adverb cannot be the subject of a sentence. The subject must answer the question *Who?* or *What?*, not *Where?*

Additional Resource

Grammar and Usage Practice Book, p. 6

Writing Theme: Caves

Other related areas students might wish to explore as writing topics include the following:

- how caves are formed
- Mammoth Cave
- Carlsbad Caverns
- cave-dwelling bats
- spelunking

Answers to Practice Your Skills

A. Concept Check

Sentences Beginning with *Here* and *There*

Answers are shown on page.

B. Revision Skill

Sentence Variety

Sentences will vary slightly. See typical answers below.

11 There can be many animals in caves. 12 Part of the time, certain animals live here, near the cave entrance. 13 Bears, rats, porcupines, and various birds and insects may be in this part of the cave. 14 Here the animals leave the cave for part of the day. 15 Other animals are somewhat farther back in caves. 16 Bats, crickets, spiders, cockroaches, certain kinds of owls, and other animals live in this sort of twilight zone area. 17 Many animals in the deepest reaches of the cave never leave the darkness.

18 There are blind animals, such as fish and salamanders, as well as many insects. 19 You will also find here animals with no skin color at all.

20 In total darkness, skin color would not be visible.

Writing Theme
Caves

Practice Your Skills

A. CONCEPT CHECK

Sentences Beginning with *Here* and *There* Write the simple subject and the verb in each sentence.

1. There are three experienced cavers in your group.
2. Here at this point you can go down into the cave.
3. There is only one way down.
4. Here the path becomes very steep and slippery.
5. There are no lights of course.
6. Here you will need a flashlight.
7. There, just a little beyond the opening, the cave ceiling gets extremely low.
8. There you must crawl on your hands and knees.
9. There goes a bat!
10. Here are hundreds of bats hanging from the ceiling.

B. REVISION SKILL

Sentence Variety The overuse of *here* or *there* at the beginning of sentences can create dull, repetitive writing. Rewrite the following paragraph. Revise sentences **12, 13, 15, 16, 19,** and **20** so that they do not begin with *here* or *there.* You may want to drop *here* or *there,* or you may want to reposition the words. Underline the subject once and the verb twice in the sentences of your revised paragraph.

EXAMPLE There are unusual animals in caves.
Unusual animals live in caves.

[11]There can be many animals in caves. [12]Here, near the cave entrance, certain animals live part of the time. [13]There may be bears, rats, porcupines, and various birds and insects in this part of the cave. [14]Here the animals leave the cave for part of the day. [15]There are other animals somewhat farther back in caves. [16]There are bats, crickets, spiders, cockroaches, certain kinds of owls, and other animals in this sort of twilight zone area. [17]Many animals in the deepest reaches of the cave never leave the darkness. [18]There are blind animals, such as fish and salamanders, as well as many insects. [19]Here you will also find animals with no skin color at all. [20]There, in total darkness, skin color would not be visible.

FOR MORE PRACTICE
See page 409.

Other Sentences with Unusual Word Order

The subject does not always come at the beginning of the sentence.

The usual order of words in a sentence is *subject-verb.* Writers and speakers often vary the order to make more interesting sentences. You have seen examples of a varied pattern in sentences beginning with *here* and *there.* In questions, too, sentence order is often *verb-subject:*

Is that the space shuttle? (That is the space shuttle?)
Would you travel in space? (You would travel in space?)

Other sentences begin with phrases or adverbs:

Finally the countdown began. (The countdown finally began.)
Into the darkness zoomed the space shuttle. (The space shuttle zoomed into the darkness.)
At the beginning the flight was rough. (The flight was rough at the beginning.)

To find the subject in a sentence that has an unusual word order, first find the verb. Then ask *who* or *what.*

Did the space colonists worry? *Verb:* did worry
Who or *what did worry?* colonists
Subject: colonists

In **imperative sentences,** which state commands or requests, the subject is usually not given. Since commands and requests are always directed to the person spoken to, the subject is *you.* Because the *you* is not given, we say that it is understood.

(You) Check all the gauges and instruments carefully.
(You) Watch out for that asteroid!

Sentence Diagraming For information on diagraming imperative sentences, see page 692.

Other Sentences with Unusual Word Order

Objectives

- To identify the subject and verb in sentences with unusual word order

Writing

- To add variety to writing by using sentences with unusual word order

Teaching Strategies

KEY TO UNDERSTANDING: QUESTIONS Point out that in a question containing a helping verb, the subject usually comes after the helping verb, but before the main verb: *Would you travel in space?* In a question with more than one helping verb, the subject usually follows the first helping verb: *Will you be traveling in space?* Similarly, an adverb might also separate two helping verbs: *Will you ever be traveling in space?*

Additional Resource

Grammar and Usage Practice Book, p. 7

Literature Connection

Note that the *verb-subject* order adds variety and emphasis to sentences. Explain that poets often use this technique. To illustrate, read aloud or write on the board these lines from "Paul Revere's Ride" by Henry Wadsworth Longfellow.

Have volunteers identify the subjects and verbs.
Beneath, in the churchyard, lay the dead,
On the opposite shore walked Paul Revere.

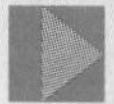

Writing Theme: Space Travel

Other related areas students might wish to explore as writing topics include the following:

- the Apollo program
- NASA's current projects
- Dr. Sally Ride
- how astronauts train
- science fiction about space travel

Answers to Practice Your Skills

A. Concept Check

Unusual Word Order

Answers are shown on page. Student answers should be in columns.

B. Revision Skill

Sentence Variety

Some answers may vary slightly. See typical answers below.

11 In the future, humans might be living in colonies on Mars. 12 Imagine what that might be like. 13 Underground lie people's homes. 14 Can you guess why? 15 Near the equator, colonists enjoy 50 degree weather on hot days. 16 Elsewhere, frigid temperatures of about 100 degrees below zero Fahrenheit exist. 17 However, residents are quite comfortable inside their underground homes. 18 Advanced equipment controls temperature and humidity constantly. 19 On the surface, a spacesuit is a necessity at all times. 20 Throughout the atmosphere lurks the danger of harmful radiation.

21 Clearly, one drawback of each colony is size. 22 Wander through the entire area very quickly. 23 What will you do to amuse yourself? 24 Perhaps you will get bored.

Writing Theme
Space Travel

Practice Your Skills

A. CONCEPT CHECK

Unusual Word Order Label two columns *Subject* and *Verb.* Write the subject and verb for each sentence below.

1. Picture yourself as a crew member of the European Space Agency's Spacelab. (you)
2. In November 1983 you and three other scientists journeyed into space.
3. Within the roomy lab, you monitor many instruments.
4. Past the window in the ceiling streaks a meteoroid.
5. Frequently, such events interrupt the team's work.
6. From this mission may come answers to many questions.
7. In zero gravity, do roots grow down?
8. Will trees grow horizontally rather than vertically?
9. Apparently, gravity limits a plant's growth on earth.
10. Can a plant grow forever in space?

B. REVISION SKILL

Sentence Variety Revise the following passage to improve the sentence variety. Follow the directions in parentheses.

11 Humans might be living in colonies on Mars *in the future.* (Move the italicized phrase.) 12 You can imagine what that might be like. (Use an imperative.) 13 People's homes lie underground. (Use verb-subject order.) 14 You can guess why. (Use a question.) 15 Colonists enjoy 50 degree weather on hot days *near the equator.* (Move the italicized phrase.) 16 Frigid temperatures of about 100 degrees below zero Fahrenheit exist *elsewhere.* (Move the italicized adverb.) 17 Residents are quite comfortable inside their underground homes, *however.* (Move the italicized adverb.) 18 Advanced equipment *constantly* controls temperature and humidity. (Move the italicized adverb.) 19 A spacesuit is a necessity at all times *on the surface.* (Move the italicized phrase.) 20 The danger of harmful radiation lurks throughout the atmosphere. (Use verb-subject order.)

21 One drawback of each colony is *clearly* size. (Move italicized adverb.) 22 You can wander through the entire area very quickly. (Use an imperative.) 23 You will do what to amuse yourself? (Use verb-subject order.) 24 You will *perhaps* get bored. (Move italicized adverb.)

394 Grammar Handbook

C. APPLICATION IN WRITING

Writing a Letter Imagine that a year ago you participated in settling the first space colony on Mars. Now you are writing a letter home to a friend. In your letter, describe the space settlement or your experiences there. Use your imagination. Write at least five sentences with the verb coming before the subject.

MIXED REVIEW • PAGES 389–395

Write each of the following sentences on your paper. Underline the subject once and the verb or verb phrase twice.

1. Watch out! (you)
2. That flying monster is getting much too close!
3. Suddenly, behind you appears another one.
4. Out of the darkness comes yet a third.
5. Whew! You're only dreaming.
6. Every night your mind will spin new dreams—possibly five or six times.
7. What is the reason for dreams?
8. There is no certain answer.
9. Scientists have learned a little about dreams, though.
10. Your dream may have been triggered by an anchovy pizza at dinner or a scary movie later in the evening.
11. Was your day very busy?
12. During the night your brain may reshape the day's happenings.
13. There is often little similarity between real events and the dream version of those events.
14. However, out of the dreams may come important solutions to problems or questions.
15. Here in your dreams may also lie the idea for a new invention or a great artistic creation.

FOR MORE PRACTICE
See pages 409–410.

Writing Theme
Dreams

C. Application in Writing
Writing a Letter

Answers will vary. Letters should contain at least five sentences in which the verb precedes the subject.

CHECKPOINT

Writing Theme: Dreams

Other related areas that students might wish to explore as writing topics include the following:

- the health benefits of dreaming
- the meaning of dreams
- recent discoveries about dreaming
- how to remember your dreams

MIXED REVIEW • PAGES 389–395

You may wish to use this activity to check students' mastery of the following concepts:

- the verb phrase
- sentences beginning with *here* and *there*
- other sentences with unusual word order

Answers are shown on page.

Objectives

- To identify direct and indirect objects of verbs
- To distinguish between transitive and intransitive verbs

Writing

- To expand sentences by adding direct objects

Teaching Strategies

MODELING Remind students that the subject tells *who* or *what performs* the action of the verb; the direct object tells *who* or *what receives* the action. To clarify, write some of the sample sentences on the board, using arrows to show the progress of the action. For example:

Sara won the race.

We cheered the winner.

KEY TO UNDERSTANDING: DIRECT OBJECTS Explain that because a direct object receives the action of a verb, only a verb that expresses action can have a direct object. Point out that the action expressed may be mental rather than physical:

Sara *loved* the race.

Gertrude *pondered* a swim across the English Channel.

OBJECTS OF VERBS

Objects of verbs are words that complete the meaning of a sentence.

Some verbs complete the meaning of spoken or written sentences without the help of other words. The action that they describe is complete.

The waves *rose.* Yoko *is swimming.*

Some verbs do not express a complete meaning by themselves. They need to be combined with other words to complete the meaning of a sentence.

Chris saw ______. (Saw who or what? Chris saw *Mike.*)
Rosa wears ______. (Wears what? Rosa wears *goggles.*)

Direct Objects

The word that receives the action of a verb is called the **direct object** of the verb. In the sentences above, *Mike* receives the action of *saw. Goggles* receives the action of *wears.*

Sometimes the direct object tells the *result* of an action.

Sara won the *race.* She received a *trophy.*

To find the direct object, first find the verb. Then ask *whom* or *what* after the verb.

We cheered the winner.	The swimmers left the water.
Verb: cheered	*Verb:* left
Cheered whom? winner	*Left what?* water
Direct object: winner	*Direct object:* water

A verb that has a direct object is called a **transitive verb.** A verb that does not have an object is an **intransitive verb.** A verb may be intransitive in one sentence and transitive in another.

Intransitive They were swimming.
Transitive They were swimming the English Channel.

Direct Object or Adverb?

Many verbs used without objects are followed by adverbs that tell *how, where, when,* or *to what extent.* These words are adverbs that go with or modify the verb. Do not confuse them with direct objects. The direct object tells *what* or *whom.*

To decide whether a word is a direct object or a modifier of the verb, decide first what it tells about the verb. If it tells *how, where, when,* or *to what extent,* it is an adverb. If it tells *what* or *whom,* it is a direct object.

Brian swam *slowly.* (*Slowly* is an adverb telling *how.*)
Kathy swam a tough *race.* (*Race* is a direct object telling *what.*)

Verbs can also be followed by a phrase that tells *how, when,* or *where.* A direct object is never found in such a phrase.

Cara swam *across the pool.* (*Across the pool* tells *where* Cara swam.)

Practice Your Skills

A. CONCEPT CHECK

Direct Objects Write the verb or verb phrase from each of the following sentences. Then write the direct object. If a sentence does not have a direct object, write *None.*

1. Some competitive swimmers will attempt almost any long-distance course.
2. The English Channel has challenged the best of them.
3. These remarkable athletes must swim tirelessly for at least twenty-one miles.
4. Cold water, rough seas, and strong currents persist.
5. The first crossing of the Channel occurred in 1875.
6. Captain Matthew Webb achieved this milestone.
7. He swam doggedly for almost twenty-two hours.
8. No one else successfully swam the Channel for the next thirty-six years.
9. Now people swim it almost every year.
10. The best swimmers now cross the English Channel in less than ten hours.

Writing Theme
Long-Distance Swimming

INDIVIDUALIZING INSTRUCTION: ESL STUDENTS In some languages—Spanish, for example—direct and indirect objects often precede the verb. Students whose first language often has objects before the verb may have difficulty with identifying direct and indirect objects in English. You might pair these students with native English speakers to complete the Concept Check and to check the Application in Literature.

Additional Resource

Grammar and Usage Practice Book, p. 8

Writing Theme: Long-Distance Swimming

Other related areas students might wish to explore as writing topics include the following:

- Gertrude Ederle
- training for a long-distance swim
- Olympic swimming

Answers to Practice Your Skills

A. Concept Check
Direct Objects

1. will attempt; course
2. has challenged; best
3. must swim; None
4. persist; None
5. occurred; None
6. achieved; milestone
7. swam; None
8. swam; Channel
9. swim; it
10. cross; English Channel

B. Application in Literature
Direct Objects
11. Intransitive
12. Intransitive
13. Transitive; body
14. Intransitive
15. Intransitive
16. Transitive; (first) list
17. Transitive; places
18. Intransitive
19. Intransitive
20. Transitive; hours

LINKING GRAMMAR AND WRITING Explain that in English an indirect object can usually be replaced by a prepositional phrase. Students can interchange the two as a check of their usage or as yet another way to add variety to their writing. For example:

He gave *her* a gift.

He gave a gift *to her.*

KEY TO UNDERSTANDING: INDIRECT OBJECTS Point out that a sentence cannot have an indirect object without also having a direct object, and that the indirect object precedes the direct object.

MODELING To help students distinguish among subject, direct object, and indirect object, write some of the sample sentences on the board, using arrows to show the progress of the action. For example:

He gave her a gift.

Additional Resource

Grammar and Usage Practice Book, p. 9

B. APPLICATION IN LITERATURE

Direct Objects Identify the italicized verbs in the following selection as *Transitive* or *Intransitive.* If the verb is transitive, write the direct object.

> **11**Diana Nyad *sat* back on her heels. . . **12**For three weeks Diana's living room floor *had been covered* with maps. **13**They *showed* every major body of water in the world. **14**The champion swimmer *was searching* for a route. . . .
>
> **15**For days on end, Diana *bent* over the maps and charts in her New York apartment. **16**She *made* list after list of water temperatures, wind speeds, and currents. **17**Each day she *crossed* out certain places and added new ones. **18**Finally, in April 1977 her goal *came* into view.
>
> **19**She *would swim* nonstop from Cuba to Florida—130 miles through shark-filled waters. **20**The crossing *would take* . . . sixty hours, maybe sixty-five.
>
> **Valjean McLenighan, *Diana: Alone Against the Sea***

Indirect Objects

Some words tell *to whom* or *for whom* something is done. Other words tell *to what* or *for what* something is done. These words are called the **indirect objects** of the verb.

King Kong showed **Fay Wray** deep *affection.* (showed *for* Fay Wray)
He gave **her** a *gift.* (gave *to* her)

In the sentences above, the words in bold type are indirect objects. The words in italics are direct objects.

The words *to* and *for* are never used with indirect objects. The words *to* and *for* are prepositions. Any noun or pronoun following *to* or *for* is actually the object of the preposition.

The mad scientist gave the *monster* a brain. (*Monster* is the indirect object of *gave.*)
The mad scientist gave a brain to the *monster.* (*Monster* is the object of the preposition *to.*)

Sentence Diagraming For information on diagraming direct objects and indirect objects, see page 692.

Writing TIP

Objects of verbs help you express complete thoughts in your writing. Notice the difference:
Joe cooked.
Joe cooked me dinner.

Practice Your Skills

A. CONCEPT CHECK

Indirect Objects Label three columns *Verb, Indirect Object,* and *Direct Object.* In the columns, list whichever of these parts of speech you find in each sentence.

1. Many moviegoers love monster movies.
2. Fans will gladly tell you their favorites.
3. However, monster movies often do not receive good reviews.
4. Critics assign them poor marks for production and writing.
5. Sometimes these movies depend on low-budget special effects.
6. Dull writing can give monster movies predictable endings.
7. In spite of such flaws, fans show these movies great loyalty.
8. The 1931 Academy Award for best picture went to *Cimarron.*
9. Few people in recent generations have even heard of that movie.
10. However, another 1931 movie, *Frankenstein,* would still fill a theater.

B. REVISION SKILL

Sentence Expansion Identify the verb in each sentence as either *T,* transitive, or *I,* intransitive. Then rewrite each sentence that contains an intransitive verb. Use one of the choices from the word bank as a direct object in your revised sentence.

EXAMPLE Monsters chase through dark streets. *I*
Monsters chase their prey through dark streets. *T*

WORD BANK		
	his terrified victims	spellbinding scripts
	audiences	a variety of roles
	the world	

11. Monster movies can entertain by using special effects.
12. Screenwriters have written for countless horror films.
13. You have no doubt seen Count Dracula.
14. This favorite has been stalking through movies since silent films.
15. King Kong, Wolf Man, and Mr. Hyde awakened us to other horrors.
16. A weird collection of monsters performs in the *Star Wars* movies.
17. However, these odd creatures generate smiles instead of fear.
18. Other movies have brought viewers dangers of a different sort.
19. Germs from outer space attack Earth in *The Andromeda Strain.*
20. In *The Invasion of the Body Snatchers,* plant monsters take over.

Writing Theme
Monster Movies

FOR MORE PRACTICE
See page 410.

Writing Theme: Monster Movies

Other related areas students might wish to explore as writing topics include the following:

- Boris Karloff, the first movie actor to portray Frankenstein's monster
- special effects and monster makeup
- Japanese monster movies
- folk-legend monsters

Answers to Practice Your Skills

A. Concept Check
Indirect Objects

Student answers should be in columns.

1. love, Verb; movies, Direct Object
2. will tell, Verb; you, Indirect Object; favorites, Direct Object
3. do receive, Verb; reviews, Direct Object
4. assign, Verb; them, Indirect Object; marks, Direct Object
5. depend, Verb
6. can give, Verb; movies, Indirect Object; endings, Direct Object
7. show, Verb; movies, Indirect Object; loyalty, Direct Object
8. went, Verb
9. have heard, Verb
10. would fill, Verb; theater, Direct Object

B. Revision Skill
Sentence Expansion

11. I; Monster movies can entertain audiences by using special effects.
12. I; Screenwriters have written spellbinding scripts for countless horror films.
13. T
14. I; This favorite has been stalking his terrified victims through movies since silent films.
15. T
16. I; A weird collection of monsters performs a variety of roles in the *Star Wars* movies.
17. T
18. T
19. T
20. I; In *The Invasion of the Body Snatchers,* plant monsters take over the world.

PREDICATE WORDS AND LINKING VERBS

Objectives

- To identify linking verbs and predicate words in sentences
- To distinguish among predicate nouns, predicate pronouns, and predicate adjectives

Writing

- To improve writing by making predicate words and direct objects more specific

Teaching Strategies

STUMBLING BLOCK: PREDICATE WORDS Some students may have difficulty in distinguishing predicate words from adverbs or from objects of prepositions that follow linking verbs. Explain that a predicate word is never an adverb, which tells *where, when, how,* or *to what extent:*

Mustangs were once common. (*Once* is an adverb that tells when; *common* is a predicate adjective.)

In addition, a predicate word is never the object of a preposition, which is the noun or pronoun that a preposition joins to the rest of the sentence:

Mustangs are horses of the Southwest. (*Southwest* is the object of the preposition *of; horses* is a predicate noun.)

INDIVIDUALIZING INSTRUCTION: ESL STUDENTS Some languages have more than one verb that means "be." For example, in Spanish both *estar* and *ser* are translated to English as *be.* Point out to students whose first language is Spanish that English does not distinguish between the more temporary "being" of *estar* and the more permanent "being" of *ser.*

PREDICATE WORDS AND LINKING VERBS

Linking verbs connect the subject with a word or group of words in the predicate.

Not all verbs express action. A verb may simply say that the subject exists. Such a verb may also link the subject of a sentence with a word or group of words in the predicate. A verb that links the subject with words in the predicate is called a **linking verb.**

Mustangs *are* wild horses.
Mustangs *were* once a common sight in the Southwest.
Bronco *is* another name for a wild horse.

The most common linking verb is the verb *be.* This verb has many forms. Study these forms of *be* to make sure that you can easily recognize them:

be	been	is	was
being	am	are	were

The verbs *be, being,* and *been* can also be used with helping verbs. Here are some examples:

might be	is being	have been
could be	are being	might have been
will be	was being	would have been

The words linked to the subject by a linking verb like *be* are called **predicate words.** There are **predicate nouns, predicate pronouns,** and **predicate adjectives.**

The mare is a *thoroughbred.* (predicate noun)
That pony is *mine.* (predicate pronoun)
The colt was *frisky.* (predicate adjective)

Notice how the subjects and the predicate words in the above sentences are linked by *is* or *was.*

400 Grammar Handbook

Here are some other common linking verbs:

seem	feel	become	look	remain
appear	taste	grow	sound	

Like *be,* these verbs can have various forms (*seems, appears, felt*), or they can be used with helping verbs (*will appear, could feel, might have become*).

The *story* seems *believable.* (predicate adjective)
You sound *excited.* (predicate adjective)
My *brother* has become an *expert.* (predicate noun)

Sentence Diagraming For information on diagraming predicate words following linking verbs, see page 692.

Practice Your Skills

A. CONCEPT CHECK

Predicate Words Write the predicate words in the following sentences.

1. Horses are central figures in many stories of fact and fiction.
2. Pegasus is a winged horse in Greek mythology.
3. Bellerophon was the owner of this special creature.
4. With the help of Pegasus, Bellerophon became the slayer of a fire-breathing monster.
5. The hero grew famous after this deed.
6. He felt very proud of his accomplishment.
7. According to the myth, Pegasus eventually became a constellation.
8. Sleipnir was the horse of Odin, a god in Norse mythology.
9. This animal must have looked very odd indeed.
10. His eight legs were no doubt his strangest feature.
11. Another of Sleipnir's characteristics, the capability of running on both land and water, seems quite unusual too.
12. Comanche, a cavalry horse, became a part of United States history.
13. He was the only survivor of Lieutenant Colonel George Custer's "last stand."
14. A horse from Roman history, Incitatus, must have appeared quite grand in his ivory manger.
15. Did his oats taste especially good in such elegant surroundings?

Writing **TIP**

Using linking verbs with predicate adjectives is one way to create vivid sensory description.
The lemonade tasted *cool* and *tart.*

Writing Theme
Horses

HELPFUL HINT: LINKING VERBS
Point out that although forms of *be* are always linking verbs, many of the verbs listed on the pupil page may be action verbs as well, depending on their use in a given sentence. Tell students that when a form of *be* can be substituted for one of these verbs without substantially changing a sentence's meaning, the verb is a linking verb.

The horse *looked* wild.

The horse *was* wild.

In this instance, *looked* is a linking verb.

INDIVIDUALIZING INSTRUCTION: SOCIAL LEARNERS Have students work in small groups to expand the list of linking verbs given on the page. They should write an example sentence for each linking verb. Have groups exchange lists and compile a master list of linking verbs; the list can be used as a reference.

ADVANCED STUDENTS As students complete the Concept Check, have them label each predicate word as a *Predicate Noun, Predicate Pronoun,* or *Predicate Adjective.*

Additional Resource

Grammar and Usage Practice Book, p. 10

Writing Theme: Horses

Other related areas that students might wish to explore as writing topics include the following:
- the Trojan horse
- the Royal Lipizzaner stallions
- horseback riding and dressage
- mustangs of the American West
- novels or films about horses

Answers to Practice Your Skills

A. Concept Check
Predicate Words

Answers are shown on page.

B. Application in Literature
Predicate Words

Student answers should be in columns.

16. She, Subject; was, Verb; mare, Predicate Word
17. she, Subject; was, Verb; beautiful, Predicate Word
18. Colonel Carter, Subject; had bred, (had) reared, Verb; her, Direct Object
19. She, Subject; was, Verb; cross, Predicate Word
20. she, Subject; had, Verb; sense, Direct Object
21. She, Subject; flung, Verb; head, Direct Object
22. She, Subject; tucked, Verb; nose, Direct Object
23. I, he, Subject; have handled, said, Verb; her, Direct Object
24. She, Subject; is, Verb; kind, Predicate Word
25. You, Subject; can spoil, Verb; her, Direct Object
26. she, Subject; is, Verb; unbroken, Predicate Word

C. Application in Writing
Writing a Letter

Answers will vary. Student letters should use precise predicate words and direct objects.

B. APPLICATION IN LITERATURE

Predicate Words Draw four columns on your paper. Label them *Subject, Verb, Direct Object,* and *Predicate Word.* Write in the columns the parts you find in each sentence in the passage below. Notice how the writer has used these structures to include vivid details.

> [16]She was a cream-colored mare with a black forelock, mane, and tail and a black stripe along the middle of her back. [17]Tall, slender, and high-spirited, . . . she was the most beautiful of horses. [18]Colonel Carter had bred and reared her with me and my uses in mind. [19]She was a careful cross of a mustang mare and a thoroughbred stallion. . . . [20]And she had a sense of fun. . . . [21]She . . . flung her head high in the air . . . [22][She] tucked her nose affectionately under his [Carter's] arm.
>
> [23]"I have handled her a lot," he said. [24]"She is as kind as a kitten. . . . [25]You can spoil her by one mistake. . . . [26]And she is unbroken."

Lincoln Steffens, *Boy on Horseback*

C. APPLICATION IN WRITING

Writing a Letter Imagine that you have just been given the pet horse you have always longed for. Write a letter to a friend, describing the experience and your horse. After completing your letter, review it yourself or ask a classmate to read it. Look for predicate words and direct objects that could be changed to make your letter more specific. Here are some examples.

My colt is nice. (*affectionate*)
I gave him some food. (*oats*)

FOR MORE PRACTICE
See page 410.

Literature Connection

Author Note Despite the simple charm of his work *Boy on Horseback,* Lincoln Steffens (1866–1936) is best known, not as a novelist but as a leader of the muckrakers, a group of journalists who exposed corrupt business and government practices around the turn of the century. Steffens, who was born in California, moved to New York City, where he worked as an editor for *McClure's* and other magazines. His series of magazine exposés were later compiled in essay collections, such as *The Shame of the Cities* (1904).

COMPOUND SENTENCE PARTS

A **compound subject** has two or more parts. A **compound predicate** has two or more parts. Many parts of a sentence may be compound.

Every part of the sentence you have studied in this handbook can be compound—subjects, verbs, direct objects, indirect objects, and predicate words.

If the compound form has only two parts, there is usually a conjunction (*and, or, but*) between them. If there are three or more parts, the conjunction usually comes between the last two of these parts. Use a comma after every part but the last.

Compound Subjects

Anne and *Marc* are building a time machine.
The *future* and the *past* will be within their reach.

Compound Verbs

The time machine *thundered, crackled,* and *spewed* smoke.
People *laughed* and *jeered.*

Compound Objects of Verbs

Direct Objects:
They tried new *theories* and *strategies* for time travel.
They will visit tenth-century *London* and third-century *Egypt.*

Indirect Objects:
We wish *Anne* and *Marc* luck.
They will bring *Cathy* and *me* a souvenir from the future.

Compound Predicate Words

The time machine was *small* and *round.*
It looks *fragile* and *unsafe.*

Sentence Diagraming For information on diagraming compound sentence parts, see page 693.

Writing **TIP**

Using compound sentence parts is a way to streamline your writing. Compound sentence parts also show a close relationship between ideas.

Objectives

- To identify compound subjects, verbs, objects of verbs, and predicate words in sentences

Writing

- To combine sentences by using compound sentence parts

Teaching Strategies

KEY TO UNDERSTANDING: CONJUNCTIONS Explain that *and* is used to show addition; *or,* to show an alternative; and *but,* to show contrast. *And* and *or* can be used to link all compound sentence parts. *But* cannot be used alone to link subjects, objects, or predicate nouns; however, it can link other sentence parts: *Time travel interests but worries me. It is fascinating but impossible.*

MODELING Reinforce the Writing Tip by showing students some of the original sentences that were joined to create the more streamlined sentences on the page. For example:

They will visit tenth-century London. + They will visit third-century Egypt. = They will visit tenth-century London and third-century Egypt.

LINKING GRAMMAR AND WRITING Point out that when students join two sentences to form a streamlined sentence with a compound subject, they may have to make some other words plural. For example:

Anne is a daydreamer. + Marc is a daydreamer. = Anne and Marc *are daydreamers.*

Additional Resource

Grammar and Usage Practice Book, p. 11

Writing Theme: Time Travel

Other related areas students might wish to explore as writing topics include the following:

- the career of H. G. Wells
- Mark Twain's *A Connecticut Yankee at King Arthur's Court*
- time capsules
- Einstein's theories and time travel

Answers to Practice Your Skills

A. Concept Check
Compound Sentence Parts

Answers are shown on page.

B. Revision Skill
Sentence Combining

Student answers may vary slightly. See typical answers below.

11 Time travel is popular and exciting. 12 Several good books and movie scripts have been written about time travel. 13 "The Time Machine," a short story by H. G. Wells, and the movie *Back to the Future* take us on trips through time. 14 In Wells's short story, we meet the Morlocks and the Eloi in the year 802,701. 15 The Morlocks are technologically more advanced, more cruel, and more inhumane than the Eloi. 16 Wells's story shows you and me a possible future for humans.

17 People may laugh or worry about the consequences of time travel in *Back to the Future*. 18 The hero, Marty McFly, travels back in time to 1955 and meets his parents. 19 Marty almost gives his parents and himself different futures. 20 The audience sees the complications and the dangers of time travel.

Writing Theme
Time Travel

Practice Your Skills

A. CONCEPT CHECK

Compound Sentence Parts Write the compound parts in each of the following sentences. Then write whether each is a *Compound Subject, Verb, Object,* or *Predicate Word.*

1. Many people talk and dream about time travel. V
2. Movie scripts and books have been written about it. S
3. Yet, time travel remains a mystery and a scientific puzzle. PW
4. To some people, time travel seems impossible and ridiculous. PW
5. No one has ever seen objects or travelers from the future. O
6. Therefore, people don't travel and will never travel in time. V
7. On the other hand, physicists and other scientists agree on the possibility of time travel. S
8. Time travelers and time machines must go faster than light. S
9. Traveling at light's speed may sound fantastic and absurd. PW
10. Nevertheless, a hundred years ago you couldn't have convinced critics and disbelievers of the future existence of jet planes. O

B. REVISION SKILL

Sentence Combining Make the following paragraphs more precise and interesting by combining each numbered pair of sentences into a single sentence with a compound part.

[11]Time travel is popular. It is also exciting. [12]Several good books have been written about it. Movie scripts have also been written about time travel. [13]"The Time Machine," a short story by H. G. Wells, takes us on a trip through time. The movie *Back to the Future* takes us on a trip through time too. [14]In Wells's short story, we meet the Morlocks in the year 802,701. Wells also introduces the Eloi at this same time. [15]The Morlocks are technologically more advanced than the Eloi. They are more cruel and inhumane as well. [16]Wells's story shows you a possible future for humans. It shows me a possible future too.

[17]People may laugh about the consequences of time travel in *Back to the Future.* They also may worry about its consequences. [18]The hero, Marty McFly, travels back in time to 1955. He meets his parents then. [19]Marty almost gives his parents a different future. He almost gives himself a different future too. [20]The audience sees the complications of time travel. They see its dangers too.

C. APPLICATION IN WRITING

Writing a Travel Journal Imagine that you have been given the opportunity to take a trip through time. Choose a time and place to visit. Think about what you might see and experience. Then write a brief journal entry describing your first day. Use compound parts in at least half of your sentences.

FOR MORE PRACTICE
See page 411.

MIXED REVIEW • PAGES 396–405

Writing Theme
Hannibal's Elephants

Write each of the sentences below on your paper. Underline any compound parts. Then write *D.O.* over all direct objects, *I.O.* over all indirect objects, and *P.W.* over all predicate words.

EXAMPLE Hannibal's army threatened
D.O. D.O.
Rome and its cities.

1. Rome and Carthage both had mighty empires 2,200 years ago.
2. For several centuries, these cities fought bloody battles and very long wars.
3. A general by the name of Hannibal led the army of Carthage in one of the most famous wars.
4. Hannibal was a great soldier and leader.
5. Hannibal often used elephants in battle.
6. They frightened and pushed aside enemy soldiers.
7. Hannibal brought thirty-eight elephants and fifty thousand troops to Italy.
8. The elephants were a problem for Hannibal.
9. With great difficulty he brought them to Italy from Spain across high mountains.
10. Deep snow and narrow mountain trails were dangerous for the elephants.
11. Food and water were not always available in large enough quantities.
12. The elephants weren't really effective or successful in Italy.
13. Their appearance in Italy must have given soldiers and peasants a surprise, though.
14. For about fifteen years, Hannibal's army gave the city of Rome considerable trouble.
15. Hannibal fought well but never conquered Rome.

C. Application in Writing
Writing a Travel Journal

Answers will vary. Make sure students have used compound sentence parts in at least half their sentences. Also check for errors in agreement.

CHECK POINT

Writing Theme: Hannibal's Elephants

Other related areas students might wish to explore as writing topics include the following:
- the history of domesticated elephants
- great Roman generals
- Carthage today

MIXED REVIEW • PAGES 396–405

You may wish to use this activity to check student's mastery of the following concepts:
- objects of verbs
- predicate words and linking verbs
- compound sentence parts

Student answers should use full sentences and should underline compounds.

1. Rome, Carthage: empires, D.O.
2. battles, wars, D.O.
3. army, D.O.
4. soldier, leader, P.W.
5. elephants, D.O.
6. frightened, pushed; soldiers, D.O.
7. elephants, troops, D.O.
8. problem, P.W.
9. them, D.O.
10. snow, trails; dangerous, P.W.
11. Food, water; available, P.W.
12. effective, successful, P.W.
13. soldiers, peasants, I.O.; surprise, D.O.
14. city, I.O.; trouble, D.O.
15. fought, conquered, Rome, D.O.

AVOIDING RUN-ON SENTENCES

Objectives
- To identify run-on sentences

Writing
- To correct run-on sentences in writing

Teaching Strategies

HELPFUL HINT: PUNCTUATION You might explain that students can also correct closely related run-on sentences by using a conjunction or a semicolon:

Folk tales are old, and their origin is unknown. Folk tales are old; their origin is unknown.

SPEAKING AND LISTENING Point out that speakers sometimes link too many sentences with the conjunction *and:*

"She gave me directions, and I followed them, and I got lost, and that's why I'm late."

Although this usage is not grammatically incorrect and does not result in a run-on sentence, it is likely to seem tiresome and juvenile to listeners. For more information, see "Revising Stringy Sentences," page 298.

Writing Theme: Folk Tales

Other related areas students might wish to explore as writing topics include the following:
- Charles Perrault, first publisher of Mother Goose tales
- Hans Christian Andersen
- Paul Bunyan stories or other American folk tales

Answers to Practice Your Skills

A. Concept Check
Run-on Sentences

1. Run-on
2. Run-on
3. Correct
4. Correct
5. Run-on
6. Correct
7. Run-on
8. Run-on
9. Run-on
10. Correct

AVOIDING RUN-ON SENTENCES

A **run-on sentence** is two or more sentences written incorrectly as one.

When two sentences are incorrectly written as one, the result is a **run-on sentence.** Sometimes no punctuation mark is used between run-on sentences. At other times, a comma is incorrectly used.

Incorrect	Folk tales are old their origin is unknown.
Incorrect	Folk tales are old, their origin is unknown.
Correct	Folk tales are old. Their origin is unknown.

As you can see, a run-on sentence confuses readers. You can avoid run-on sentences by using a period or other end mark to show the reader where each complete thought ends. For other ways to correct run-on sentences, see Handbook 22, page 297 and Handbook 45, pages 556–559.

Writing Theme
Folk Tales

Practice Your Skills

A. CONCEPT CHECK

Run-on Sentences Identify and label each of the following sentences as *Run-on* or *Correct.*

1. Almost everyone has heard of Mother Goose the tales and rhymes have been told for generations.
2. Most Mother Goose tales are older than the first Mother Goose books the tales were told orally before they were published.
3. These entertaining tales have been told in many languages.
4. For example, the stories and rhymes were popular in France in the 1600s.
5. Many of the Mother Goose tales come from England they were written for adults as a form of political criticism.
6. In the United States, Mother Goose tales first appeared in 1786.
7. People argue about whether there really was a Mother Goose no one is sure.
8. Some people think she was real others insist she was fictional.
9. Mother Goose may have been Elizabeth Goose, she was a grandmother living in Boston during the colonial period.
10. Others think the real Mother Goose lived in an earlier time.

Additional Resource
Grammar and Usage Practice Book, p. 12

B. REVISION SKILL

Correcting Run-On Sentences Rewrite the run-on sentences, correcting the mistakes. Write *Correct* if the item does not contain a run-on.

11. Jakob and Wilhelm Grimm collected folk tales.
12. "Little Red Riding Hood" is one of their most famous tales, "Snow White" is another.
13. The brothers worried about the loss of the oral German folk tales, the young men preserved them on paper.
14. The tales recorded by the Grimms had been told for centuries, they were passed on from one generation to the next.
15. The Grimms collected tales between 1807 and 1814, they collected them from farmers in villages.
16. Nineteen of the tales were told by an elderly woman.
17. All tales were recorded faithfully and exactly.
18. The first printed volume of the brothers' tales appeared in 1812, it held eighty-six tales.
19. The second contained seventy tales, it appeared in 1815.
20. The Grimms were influenced by German history, they also wrote about German myths.

FOR MORE PRACTICE
See page 411.

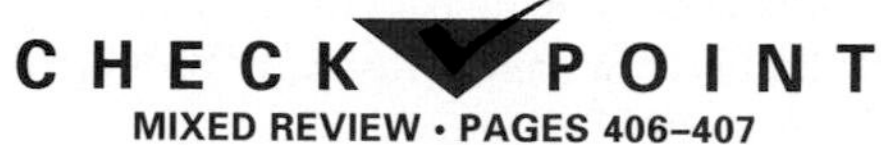

MIXED REVIEW • PAGES 406–407

Writing Theme
Toothpaste

Write each of the sentences, correcting all run-on sentences. If a sentence contains no run-ons, write *Correct.*

1. A tube of toothpaste looks innocent inside are some weird ingredients, though.
2. White toothpaste is made partly of chalk.
3. Chalk comes from shellfish it scrubs your teeth clean.
4. Gel toothpastes use silica for scrubbing silica is found in sand.
5. There are other ingredients, too, such as mouthwash and fluoride.
6. These ingredients are held together by a substance this special substance comes from seaweed.
7. Today our toothpaste seems plain, the first toothpastes were made from coral, fish bone, burnt eggshells, and porcelain.
8. Those early toothpastes may also have included insect bodies.
9. The insects were used for coloring the toothpaste.
10. What is used for color today, could it still be insect bodies?

TEACHER'S LOUNGE

DEPARTMENT OF & ADMINISTRATION OF, NOT TO MENTION THE ENTIRE STAFF, ALL OF WHOM MONITOR AND ATTEMPT TO REGULATE RUN-ON SENTENCES AND EXCESS VERBIAGE
S. Harris

B. Revision Skill
Correcting Run-on Sentences

Corrections may vary slightly. Sentences 11, 16, and 17 are correct as written.

12. "Little Red Riding Hood" is one of their most famous tales. "Snow White" is another.
13. The brothers worried about the loss of the oral German folk tales. The young men preserved them on paper.
14. The tales recorded by the Grimms had been told for centuries. They were passed on from one generation to the next.
15. The Grimms collected tales between 1807 and 1814. They collected them from farmers in villages.
18. The first printed volume of the brothers' tales appeared in 1812. It held eighty-six tales.
19. The second contained seventy tales. It appeared in 1815.
20. The Grimms were influenced by German history. They also wrote about German myths.

CHECK POINT

Writing Theme: Toothpaste

Other related areas students might wish to explore as writing topics include the following:
- why teeth decay
- how teeth grow
- the first dentures

MIXED REVIEW • PAGES 406–407

You may wish to use this activity to check students' mastery of the following concept:
- avoiding run-on sentences

Corrections may vary slightly. Sentences 2, 5, 8, and 9 are correct as written.

1. A tube of toothpaste looks innocent. Inside are some weird ingredients, though.
3. Chalk comes from shellfish. It scrubs your teeth clean.
4. Gel toothpastes use silica for scrubbing. Silica is found in sand.
6. These ingredients are held together by a substance. This special substance comes from seaweed.
7. Today our toothpaste seems plain. The first toothpastes were made from coral, fish bone, burnt eggshells, and porcelain.
10. What is used for color today? Could it still be insect bodies?

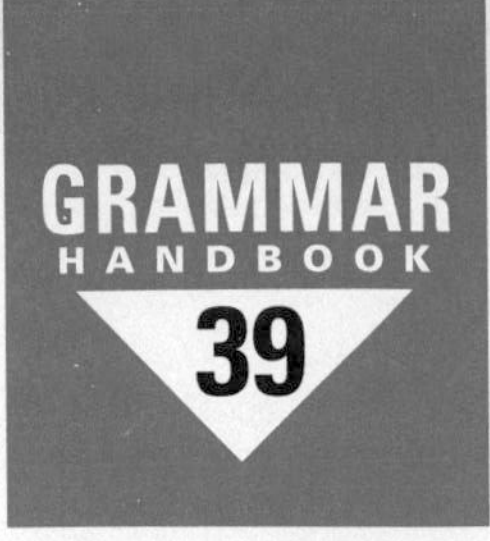

ADDITIONAL PRACTICE

Each of these exercises correlates with a section of handbook 39, "The Sentence and Its Parts." The exercises may be used for more practice, for reteaching, or for review of the concepts presented.

Additional Resource

Grammar and Usage Practice Book, p. 14

Writing Theme: Adventures

Other related areas students might wish to explore as writing topics include the following:

- Thor Heyerdahl's other adventures
- Diane Fossey and mountain gorillas
- famous polar expeditions
- The Appalachian Trail
- underwater treasure hunts

A. Identifying Sentences and Sentence Fragments
Answers are shown on page.

B. Complete Subjects and Predicates
Answers are shown on page.

C. Finding Verbs and Simple Subjects
Answers are shown on page. Student answers should be in columns.

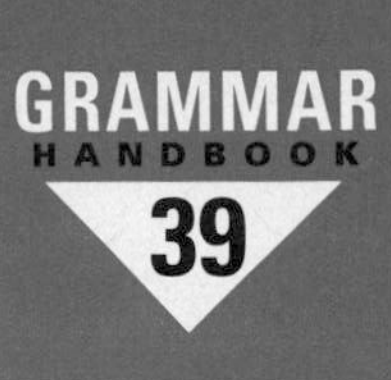

Writing Theme
Adventures

A. Identifying Sentences and Sentence Fragments Write *S* for each sentence and *F* for each sentence fragment.

1. All schools and classrooms are not alike S
2. Outward Bound is one of the oldest wilderness schools S
3. Held on sheer cliff walls or violent rivers F
4. Teaches self-confidence and cooperation with others F
5. You may feel a rush of fear S
6. Leaping from the side of a cliff F
7. Your companions' strong arms and legs help support you S
8. Sometimes the fear and uncertainty F
9. At the end of the course F
10. You'll have new courage and greater self-confidence S

B. Complete Subjects and Predicates Write each sentence. Draw a line between the complete subject and complete predicate.

11. The study of ancient people | can often lead to real adventure.
12. Thor Heyerdahl | wrote a book, *The Ra Expedition,* about his experiences in 1970 as an explorer.
13. Heyerdahl | sailed a boat, the *Ra,* from Africa to the West Indies.
14. The boat | was made of papyrus reed, a kind of plant.
15. Some of the earliest boats | were made from papyrus.
16. Ancient Egyptians | also made paper from papyrus.
17. Heyerdahl and his crew | sailed this paper boat across the entire width of the Atlantic.
18. They | provided support for a theory about the ancient Egyptians, a people of North Africa.
19. These people | may have reached America long before the Vikings.
20. Heyerdahl's voyage on the *Ra* | took about two months.

C. Finding Verbs and Simple Subjects Draw two columns and label them *Simple Subject* and *Verb.* Write the verb and its simple subject for each of the following sentences.

21. Some people find great excitement and adventure in wild places.
22. Sometimes they turn their interest into a profession.
23. Jane Goodall chose her profession as a zoologist that way.
24. Her research on chimpanzees made her famous.
25. She devoted her efforts to wild animals in their native habitat.
26. She stalked wild animals as part of her job.

27. Goodall's work took her to the wildest forests and jungles.
28. Dangerous and unpredictable animals were a constant threat.
29. She patiently observed her subjects for days and even years.
30. Precise field notes described all of the animals' activities.

D. Finding Main Verbs and Helping Verbs Label two columns *Main Verb* and *Helping Verb.* Write the appropriate words from each sentence in the columns.

31. The fifteen-year-old commander is speaking to Mission Control.
32. Something has suddenly gone wrong with the main fuel tank.
33. It couldn't have happened at a worse time in the mission.
34. The astronauts can't find a solution.
35. Tension is quickly building in the shuttle.
36. The crew members aren't worried, though.
37. The shuttle crew is only working in a simulator, or model.
38. They'll get another chance at the mission.
39. They're attending the U.S. Space Camp in Huntsville, Alabama.
40. Since 1982, thousands of boys and girls have gone to this camp.

E. Sentences with *Here* and *There* Write the simple subject and the verb in each sentence. Tell whether *there* or *here* is used as an adverb or as an introductory word.

41. There are many kinds of adventure available to you.
42. Here in Antarctica many people seek adventure.
43. There were mainly scientific expeditions in the past.
44. There are now many recreational adventurers as well.
45. There may be many reasons for the increased interest.
46. Here is a frozen wonderland of almost untouched wilderness.
47. Here are giant glaciers, huge icebergs, and active volcanoes.
48. There are penguins, whales, seals, and many birds in Antarctica.
49. Here you will find many places for skiing, hiking, and exploring.
50. There are tours traveling regularly to Antarctica.

F. Sentences with Unusual Word Order Write the following sentences. Underline each subject once and each verb twice.

51. Do archaeologists live quiet, uneventful lives?
52. "Not always," might have responded Louis Leakey.
53. Remarkable were the adventures of this famous scientist in Africa.

D. Finding Main Verbs and Helping Verbs
Answers are shown on page. Student answers should be in columns.

E. Sentences with *Here* and *There*
Simple subjects and verbs are shown on page.

41. kinds; are; There, Introductory Word
42. people; seek; Here, Adverb
43. expeditions; were; There, Introductory Word
44. adventurers; are; There, Introductory Word
45. reasons; may be; There, Introductory Word
46. wonderland; is; Here, Adverb
47. glaciers, icebergs, volcanoes; are; Here, Adverb
48. penguins, whales, seals, birds; are; There, Introductory Word
49. you; will find; Here, Adverb
50. tours, are traveling; There, Introductory Word

F. Sentences with Unusual Word Order
Answers are shown on page.

G. Recognizing Transitive and Intransitive Verbs

Transitive and intransitive verbs are also shown on page.

61. can give, Transitive; you, I.O.; adventure, D.O.
62. load, Transitive; bike, D.O.
63. take, Intransitive
64. promises, Transitive; you, I.O.; challenges, D.O.
65. offers, Transitive; riders, I.O.; freedom, D.O.
66. are, Intransitive
67. can take, Transitive; you, D.O.
68. have enjoyed, Transitive; trips, D.O.
69. go, Intransitive
70. has been, Intransitive

H. Objects and Predicate Words

Student answers should be in columns.

71. is, Verb; restless, Predicate Word
72. was, Verb; teenager, Predicate Word
73. had, wanted, Verb; dream, adventure, Direct Object
74. seemed, Verb; fantastic, Predicate Word
75. had, Verb; experience, Direct Object
76. had taught, Verb; him, Indirect Object; much, Direct Object
77. gave, Verb; Dan, Indirect Object; confidence, Direct Object
78. felt, Verb; ready, Predicate Word
79. began, Verb; journey, Direct Object
80. became, Verb; reality, Predicate Word

54. Can you picture Leakey in an open truck on a sunny African veldt?
55. Calmly lounging on the road are twelve lions.
56. Suddenly after him charge all of them!
57. Watch out! (you)
58. Barely does he escape in time.
59. Quite an adventure, don't you think?
60. Around every corner may be wild adventure for an archaeologist.

G. Recognizing Transitive and Intransitive Verbs Write the verb in each numbered sentence. Label the verb *Transitive* or *Intransitive.* If the verb is transitive, write the objects of the verb and identify each as *D.O.,* direct object, or *I.O.,* indirect object.

61A little imagination and planning can give you an adventure anytime. **62**Load your bike with a tent, sleeping bag, water bottles, extra clothes, and a little food. **63**Now, take off! **64**A bicycle trip promises you great challenges. **65**It offers riders almost unlimited freedom. **66**The route, destination, and schedule are entirely up to you. **67**A train or plane can even take you to unusual starting points. **68**Europeans have enjoyed bicycle trips for decades. **69**In the United States, some people go on long trips every year. **70**Bicycle travel has never been as popular here as in some other places, though.

H. Objects and Predicate Words Label four columns on your paper *Verb, Direct Object, Indirect Object,* and *Predicate Word.* Write these parts from each sentence in the columns.

71. Everyone is occasionally restless for a new experience.
72. Dan Jelsema was an average teenager living in Michigan.
73. Dan had a dream; he wanted adventure.
74. His dream seemed fantastic: a sea voyage around the world.
75. However this young man had experience.
76. His father had taught him much about sailing.
77. This training gave Dan confidence.
78. The eager sailor felt ready for the test.
79. With a boat full of provisions, Dan began his journey.
80. The dream became a reality.

I. Finding Compound Parts of a Sentence Write the compound parts in the following sentences. Tell whether they are *Compound Subjects, Verbs, Objects,* or *Predicate Words.*

81. French astronomer Serge Brunier and seven other amateur astronomers wanted to establish the world's highest observatory. CS
82. They researched and chose as a site Ojos del Salado, a mountain in South America. V
83. Ojos del Salado is 22,572 feet high and icy. PW
84. It also has a dry atmosphere and low pollution. O
85. In this clear, thin air the stars appear clearer and brighter. PW
86. On maps, Ojos del Salado looked accessible and climbable. PW
87. The determined astronomers drove as far as possible and then began their hike. V
88. They took observations at 19,000 feet but never climbed to the mountain's top. V
89. The effects of the altitude gave Brunier and his friends great problems. O
90. Thin air and waist-deep snow forced them to stop 1,000 feet short of the summit. CS

J. Avoiding Run-on Sentences Rewrite correctly the run-on sentences in the paragraph. If a sentence does not need to be rewritten, write *Correct.*

[91]Jacques Cousteau was one of the first ocean explorers, he made many contributions to the field of oceanography. [92]He made one especially important contribution it was the development of oxygen tanks for diving. [93]Previously, divers could not go far under water they wore heavy diving suits. [94]These had metal helmets air was pumped down a tube from a boat. [95]These diving suits were dangerous and clumsy Cousteau's invention was a big step forward. [96]It made possible the exploration of the world's oceans. [97]Cousteau studied all kinds of ocean life people had almost no knowledge of these plants and animals before. [98]He explored shipwrecks he searched for the lost civilization of Atlantis. [99]Cousteau also studied pollution in the ocean, plants and animals were being killed. [100]Cousteau made people aware of the ocean now people think more about keeping it healthy.

I. Finding Compound Parts of a Sentence
Answers are shown on page.

J. Avoiding Run-on Sentences
Corrections may vary slightly. See typical answers below.

91 Jacques Cousteau was one of the first ocean explorers. He made many contributions to the field of oceanography. **92** He made one especially important contribution. It was the development of oxygen tanks for diving. **93** Previously, divers could not go far under water. They wore heavy diving suits. **94** These had metal helmets. Air was pumped down a tube from a boat. **95** These diving suits were dangerous and clumsy. Cousteau's invention was a big step forward. **96** Correct. **97** Cousteau studied all kinds of ocean life. People had almost no knowledge of these plants and animals before. **98** He explored shipwrecks. He searched for the lost civilization of Atlantis. **99** Cousteau also studied pollution in the ocean. Plants and animals were being killed. **100** Cousteau made people aware of the ocean. Now people think more about keeping it healthy.

GRAMMAR HANDBOOK 39

REVIEW

These exercises may be used as mixed review or as an informal evaluation of the skills presented in Handbook 39, "The Sentence and Its Parts."

Writing Theme: Australia

Other related subjects students might wish to explore as writing topics include the following:

- kangaroos
- Australian aborigine civilization
- European explorers of Australia

A. Identifying Subjects and Verbs

Subjects and verbs are also shown on page.

1. continent, Simple Subject; is, Main Verb
2. trip, Simple Subject; is, Main Verb
3. you, Simple Subject; can, Helping Verb; go, Main Verb
4. you, Simple Subject; may, Helping Verb; notice, Main Verb
5. cities, Simple Subject; may, Helping Verb; look, Main Verb
6. cities, Simple Subject; lie, Main Verb
7. people, Simple Subject; speak, Main Verb
8. stores, Simple Subject; have, Main Verb
9. You, Simple Subject; will, Helping Verb; recognize, Main Verb
10. you, Simple Subject; may, Helping Verb; see, Main Verb

B. Identifying Verbs, Objects, and Predicate Words

11. seems, Verb; unpopulated, Predicate Word
12. is, Verb; outback, Predicate Word
13. raise, Verb; livestock, Direct Object
14. are called, Verb; "stations," Direct Object

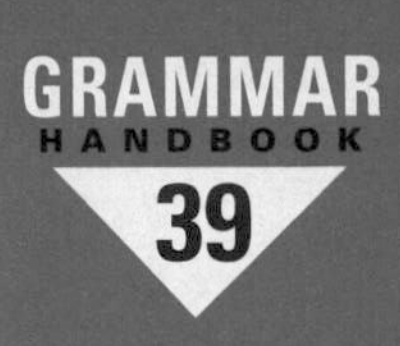

REVIEW

Writing Theme
Australia

A. Identifying Subjects and Verbs Write the simple subject and the verb or verb phrase from each sentence. Identify each *Main Verb* and *Helping Verb.*

1. The continent of Australia is halfway around the world.
2. Even by plane, a trip there is a long journey.
3. In your imagination, you can easily go there in a second.
4. At first, you may notice very little difference between Australia and your home in the United States.
5. The cities, especially, may look similar to those here.
6. The cities lie mainly along the east coast of Australia.
7. The people speak English.
8. Their stores have many of the same items as ours.
9. You'll even recognize the name of their currency—dollars.
10. Before long, though, you may see a great many differences.

B. Identifying Verbs, Objects, and Predicate Words Write the verbs, direct objects, and predicate words in the following sentences. Label each *Verb, Direct Object,* or *Predicate Word.*

11. The great interior of Australia seems unpopulated.
12. This vast area is the outback.
13. Most Australians of the outback raise livestock.
14. Their ranches are called "stations."
15. These stations are usually huge.
16. One of medium size might cover two hundred square miles.
17. You could build three cities the size of Washington, D.C., on such a station.
18. Most of the outback is extremely dry.
19. In some sparsely vegetated places, fourteen acres of pasture land will feed only one sheep.
20. Despite the harsh land and the isolation, the lonely outback has been the home of a few hardy Australian families for generations.

C. Identifying Compound Sentence Parts Write the compound parts in each of the following sentences. Then write whether each is a *Compound Subject, Verb, Object,* or *Predicate Word.*

21. Two interesting Australian animals are the wombat and platypus.
22. The grass-eating wombat is large and powerful. PW

Additional Resources

Grammar and Usage Practice Book, p. 15
Tests and Writing Assessment Prompts, Mastery Test, pp. 9–12
Elaboration, Revision, and Proofreading Practice, p. 25

23. It weighs up to eighty-eight pounds and lives in burrows deep in the ground. V
24. The platypus has the tail and fur of a beaver. O
25. However, the snout and feet are like those of a duck. S

D. Identifying Fragments and Run-ons Identify each of the following sentences as *Fragment, Run-on,* or *Correct.*

26. For tens of thousands of years
27. Australia was rich in plants and animals no people lived there
28. About 40,000 years ago, the first people arrived
29. These people, the Aborigines, probably came to Australia on rafts they came from Southeast Asia
30. Great forests and many rivers, swamps, and lakes
31. People must have had easy lives they spread across the continent
32. Then the land began to dry out
33. Many of the large animals became extinct life got difficult
34. Adapted to the changes in their land
35. Life again became good for the Aborigines

E. Correcting Fragments and Run-ons Rewrite the following sentences to correct fragments and run-ons.

36. Great Britain once shipped convicts to the American colonies the practice ended during the American Revolution
37. Overcrowded prisons in Britain
38. Looked for another place for its convicts
39. In 1788, eleven British ships landed in Australia they brought settlers and about seven hundred convicts
40. The settlers and convicts suffered greatly the first year food shortages, cold weather, and lack of shelter made life difficult
41. Worked together to build the new Australian colonies
42. Improved after two or three years
43. Spent only a little time behind bars
44. The convicts worked as laborers many were soon pardoned
45. In the first 80 years, more than 160,000 convicts were sent to Australia the settlements grew rapidly

15. are, Verb; huge, Predicate Word
16. might cover, Verb; miles, Direct Object
17. could build, Verb; cities, Direct Object
18. is, Verb; dry, Predicate Word
19. will feed, Verb; sheep, Direct Object
20. has been, Verb; home, Predicate Word

C. Identifying Compound Sentence Parts
Answers are shown on page.

D. Identifying Fragments and Run-ons
26. Fragment
27. Run-on
28. Correct
29. Run-on
30. Fragment
31. Run-on
32. Correct
33. Run-on
34. Fragment
35. Correct

E. Correcting Fragments and Run-ons
Student answers will vary. See typical answers below.
36. Great Britain once shipped convicts to the American colonies. The practice ended during the American Revolution.
37. Overcrowded prisons in Britain created a need for prison colonies.
38. Great Britain looked for another place for its convicts.
39. In 1788, eleven British ships landed in Australia. They brought settlers and about seven hundred convicts.
40. The settlers and convicts suffered greatly the first year. Food shortages, cold weather, and lack of shelter made life difficult.
41. The settlers and convicts worked together to build the new Australian colonies.
42. Life in the colonies improved after two or three years.
43. The convicts spent only a little time behind bars.
44. The convicts worked as laborers. Many were soon pardoned.
45. In the first 80 years, more than 160,000 convicts were sent to Australia. The settlements grew rapidly.

WRITING CONNECTIONS

Elaboration, Revision, and Proofreading

This activity will allow your students to see some of the concepts presented in this Handbook at work in a piece of descriptive writing. By revising and proofreading this passage, students will have the chance to identify and correct sentence fragments and run-on sentences. They will also improve sentence variety by combining strings of sentences into fewer sentences, with compound sentence parts, and by changing the usual word order of sentences.

Ask students to proofread and revise the passage independently. Then place them in groups of three or four to compare their revisions.

Revisions may vary slightly. See typical revision below. Elements involving change are shown in boldface.

Supporters of Lisa Vogel, **the candidate for state senator,** gathered in the ballroom of the Grant Hotel. People jammed every corner of the vast room. They seemed ready for a big celebration. They carried campaign **posters, balloons, and noisemakers. Anxiously,** they waited for the votes to be counted. The results were finally announced after what seemed like hours. **The results showed that Vogel was the winner.** The people **roared, threw confetti, released their balloons, and chanted the candidate's name.** Then Vogel walked onto the stage of the ballroom **with a broad grin on her face.** She stepped to the microphone and thanked all the people for their support. She promised to be the best senator the people had ever elected. As she left the stage, the crowd responded with thunderous applause.

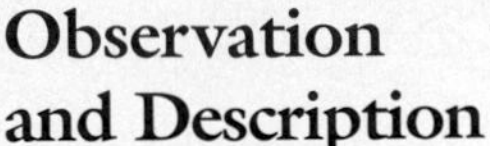

WRITING CONNECTIONS

Elaboration, Revision, and Proofreading

Observation and Description

An eyewitness report lets readers experience an event as if they were actually there. (See Workshop 2.) When you revise an eyewitness report, make your descriptions as vivid as possible. Use compound sentence parts to help your readers understand relationships more clearly. Also look for ways to add interest to your writing by varying sentence openers.

Revise and proofread the following draft of an eyewitness account. Begin by following the directions at the bottom of the page. Then proofread the passage, paying particular attention to correcting sentence fragments and run-ons. Also look for other errors in grammar, capitalization, punctuation, and spelling.

[1]Supporters of Lisa Vogel gathered in the ballroom of the Grant Hotel. [2]People jammed every corner of the vast room, they seemed ready for a big celebration. [3]They carried Campaign Posters. [4]They also had ballons and noisemakers. [5]They waited anxiously for the votes to be counted. [6]The result's were finally announced. [7]After what seemed like hours. [8]The people roared. [9]They threw confetti. [10]They released thier balloons. [11]They chanted the candidates name. [12]Then Vogel walked onto the stage of the ballroom, looking happy. [13]She stepped to the microphone and thanked all the people for there support. [14]She promised to be the best sentor the People had ever elected. [15]As she left the stage. [16]The crowd responded with thunderous applause.

1. In sentence 1, explain who Lisa Vogel is by adding the phrase "the candidate for state senator." Set off the phrase with commas.
2. Combine sentences 3 and 4 to make a sentence with compound objects of the verb.
3. Improve sentence variety by changing sentence 5. Begin with the word "anxiously."
4. Add this detail in an appropriate place: "The results showed that Vogel was the winner."
5. Combine sentences 8, 9, 10, and 11 to form a sentence with a compound verb.
6. Make sentence 12 more descriptive by replacing the phrase "looking happy" with the phrase "with a broad grin on her face."

on the LIGHT side

Poetic License

License plates can say a lot with just a few letters or numbers. C if U can figure out these license pl8s.

(Answer: His excellency; Why are you mad?; Excuse me; Anyone for tennis?; I'm a cutie; See you later; Boy wonder; Be great; Water skier; Wait for me too; Tooth fairy; Too quick for you; Sore tooth; Wonderful; Great day to you)

on the LIGHT side

When discussing this feature, have students tell about amusing license plates that they have seen on the road. You might mention that people usually pay extra for these plates, which are sometimes called vanity plates. Encourage students to decipher the license plates on the page without looking at the answers. Then ask students to create their own clever license plates, using letters and numbers.

Objective

- To use results of a survey and writing prompts as springboards to informal writing

WRITING WARM-UPS

Begin by reminding students that they will not be graded for this assignment. The illustration and activities are intended as springboards to get them to think imaginatively about the concepts of this handbook. Unless students volunteer to explore more than one prompt, allow them to work on one activity.

SKETCH BOOK

WRITING WARM-UPS

- What would be the perfect meal? Describe it in detail.

Kids' Favorite Foods

Source: Gallup Poll of 1,034 parents of 3 to 11-year-olds. Respondents could choose more than one.

- What would be a good name for a rock band? a football team? a town in the desert? a newly discovered planet? Think up as many creative names as you can.
- What's on your top-ten list? Choose a category, such as food, athletes, or video games, and make out your top-ten list.

Using Nouns

- What Is a Noun?
- Singular and Plural Nouns
- Possessive Nouns

Cheese, sausage, tomatoes, mushrooms, green peppers, olives. . . . You need nouns to order a pizza with everything on it. Nouns name what you want—pizza and toppings of your choice.

Without nouns, writers couldn't name the people, places, things, and ideas they write about. By choosing precise nouns, you can make your writing clear and expressive.

Using Nouns

Objectives

- To recognize nouns and distinguish between common and proper nouns
- To form the plurals of nouns
- To form the possessives of nouns

Writing

- To correct errors in the capitalization of proper nouns and in the use of plural and possessive nouns
- To add clarity to writing by replacing common nouns with proper nouns
- To spell plural nouns correctly

INTRODUCING THE HANDBOOK

Write the following sentences on the board:

Victor's favorite pizza has anchovies and onions.

Julia's favorite subject is home economics.

Toshio's father makes delicious sushi.

Shana's favorite restaurant is in New York City.

Ask students to identify all the words in these sentences that name people, places, things, or ideas. Tell them they have just identified the nouns in the sentences.

Now ask for volunteers to use different colored chalk to underline the nouns that (1) name a particular person or place, (2) name more than one thing, and (3) show that something belongs to someone. Tell students that they have just identified the proper nouns, plural nouns, and possessive nouns in these sentences. As they work through Handbook 40, students will learn more about how these naming words function in writing.

Objectives

- To identify nouns
- To distinguish between common and proper nouns

Writing

- To recognize and correct errors in the capitalization of proper nouns
- To replace common nouns with proper nouns in writing

Teaching Strategies

HELPFUL HINT The nouns in the columns labeled *Person, Place,* and *Thing* are sometimes called concrete nouns. In addition to naming things people can see, these nouns also name things people can hear, smell, taste, or touch. The nouns in the columns labeled *Idea, Feeling,* and *Characteristic* are called abstract nouns. They name things people can think about but cannot perceive with their senses.

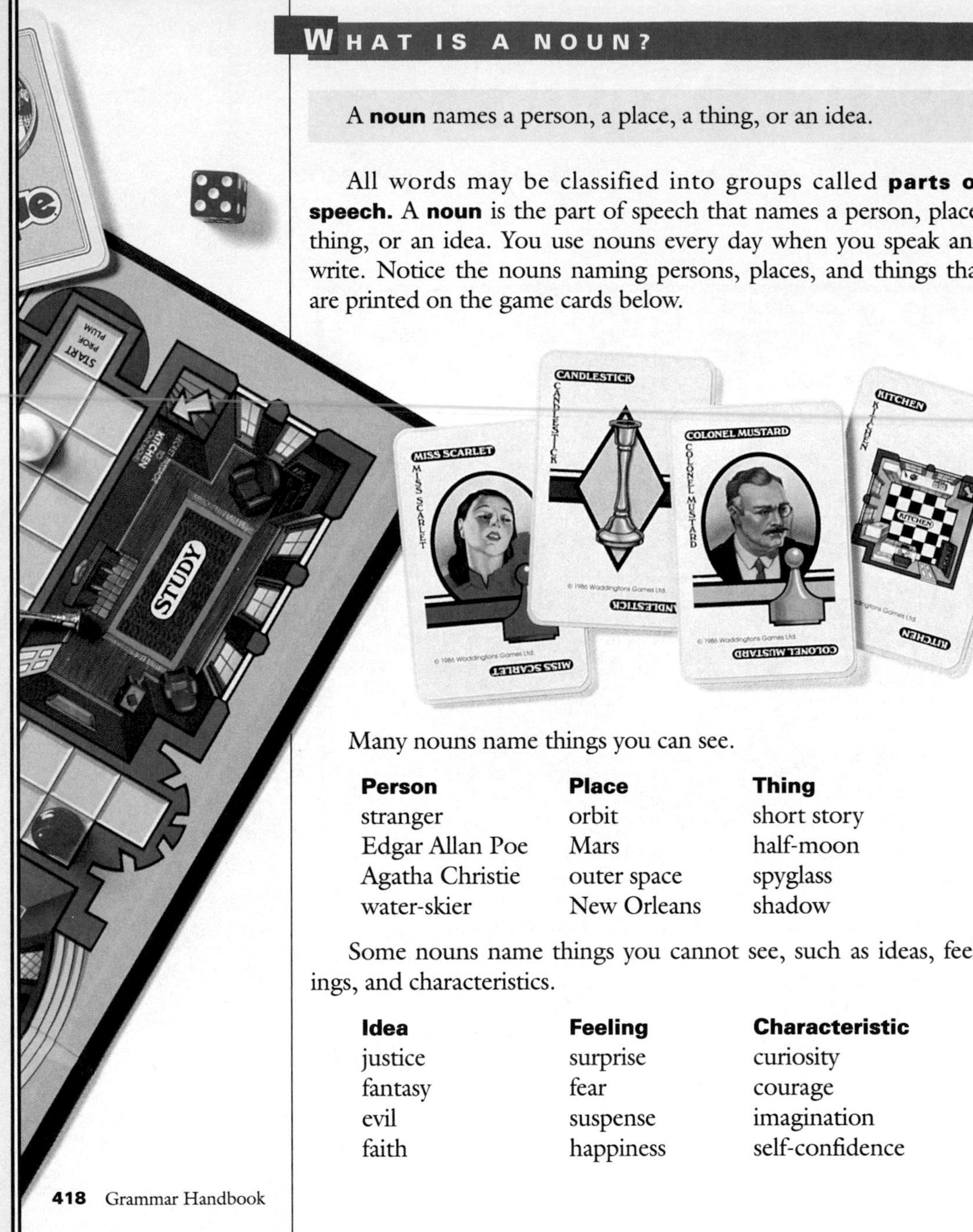

WHAT IS A NOUN?

A **noun** names a person, a place, a thing, or an idea.

All words may be classified into groups called **parts of speech.** A **noun** is the part of speech that names a person, place, thing, or an idea. You use nouns every day when you speak and write. Notice the nouns naming persons, places, and things that are printed on the game cards below.

Many nouns name things you can see.

Person	Place	Thing
stranger	orbit	short story
Edgar Allan Poe	Mars	half-moon
Agatha Christie	outer space	spyglass
water-skier	New Orleans	shadow

Some nouns name things you cannot see, such as ideas, feelings, and characteristics.

Idea	Feeling	Characteristic
justice	surprise	curiosity
fantasy	fear	courage
evil	suspense	imagination
faith	happiness	self-confidence

418 Grammar Handbook

Literature Connection

Nouns naming things that cannot be perceived with the senses sometimes have, because of their associations, a powerful effect on the emotions. There are two such nouns in Langston Hughes's "Refugee in America":

There are words like ***Freedom***
Sweet and wonderful to say.
On my heart-strings freedom sings
All day everyday.

There are words like ***Liberty***
That almost make me cry.
If you had known what I knew
You would know why.

As you can see in the charts on the previous page, some nouns are compound (more than one word), and some of these compound nouns are hyphenated. In this handbook you will learn to recognize different kinds of nouns and to use specific nouns to make your writing more precise.

Common Nouns and Proper Nouns

All nouns can be described as either common or proper. A **common noun** is the general name of a person, a place, a thing, or an idea. A **proper noun** is the name of a particular person, place, thing, or idea. Proper nouns always begin with capital letters.

Common Nouns	Proper Nouns
author	Sir Arthur Conan Doyle
detective	Sherlock Holmes
assistant	Dr. Watson
villain	Professor Moriarty
country	England
city	London
street	Baker Street

Proper nouns are important to good writing. They make your writing more specific, and therefore clearer.

Practice Your Skills

A. APPLICATION IN LITERATURE

Common Nouns and Proper Nouns Write the italicized nouns in the following sentences. Identify each one as a Common Noun or a Proper Noun. Be sure to capitalize the proper nouns.

[1]"Many noble *russians* lost everything. [2]I, luckily, had invested heavily in [foreign] *securities*, so I shall never have to open a *tearoom* in *monte carlo* or drive a *taxi* in *paris*. [3]Naturally, I continued to hunt—*grizzlies* in your *rockies*, *crocodiles* in the *ganges*, *rhinoceroses* in *east africa*. . . . [4]Hunting was beginning to bore me! [5]And hunting, remember, had been my *life*. [6]I have heard that in *america*, *businessmen* often go to pieces when they give up the *business* that has been their *life*."

[7]"Yes, that's so," said *rainsford*.

Richard Connell, "The Most Dangerous Game"

Writing TIP

Using specific common nouns and proper nouns makes your writing more vivid and colorful. For example, the common noun *giant* creates a clearer picture than the common noun *creature*. The proper noun *Cyclops* names a more specific being than the common noun *giant*.

Writing Theme Science Fiction and Suspense

INDIVIDUALIZING INSTRUCTION: ESL STUDENTS Point out to students that, in English, one way to distinguish a common noun from a proper noun in writing is to check to see whether it is capitalized.

BASIC STUDENTS To reinforce their learning, suggest that students copy the lists of nouns on page 418 and then color-code the common and proper words. You might check their coding to be sure they are on the right track.

Additional Resources

Tests and Writing Assessment Prompts, Pretest, pp. 13–14
Grammar and Usage Practice Book, p. 16

Writing Theme: Science Fiction and Suspense

Suggest to students that they use these exercises as a springboard to writing. Other related areas they might explore include the following:

- favorite science fiction or suspense writer, such as Isaac Asimov, Agatha Christie, H. G. Wells, John Christopher, or Jay Bennett
- the opening paragraph of a suspense or science fiction story
- a suspenseful scene in a movie

Answers to Practice Your Skills

A. Application in Literature
Common Nouns and Proper Nouns

Common and proper nouns are also shown on page.

1. Russians, Proper Noun
2. securities, Common Noun; tearoom, Common Noun; Monte Carlo, Proper Noun; taxi, Common Noun; Paris, Proper Noun
3. grizzlies, Common Noun; Rockies, Proper Noun; crocodiles, Common Noun; Ganges, Proper Noun; rhinoceroses, Common Noun; East Africa, Proper Noun
4. None
5. life, Common Noun
6. America, Proper Noun; businessmen, Common Noun; business, Common Noun; life, Common Noun
7. Rainsford, Proper Noun

B. Proofreading Skill
Capitalizing Proper Nouns

Errors in proofreading exercises are counted as follows: (a) Each word is counted as one error. For example, a misspelled word is one error; two initials and a last name not capitalized are counted as three errors. (b) Run-on sentences and sentence fragments are each counted as one error even though the correction involves both punctuation and capitalization corrections. Errors are underlined on page. Answers may vary. See typical revisions below.

Ray Bradbury is an author of science fiction and suspense stories. Whether set on Mars or in the midwestern United States, his stories are full of excitement and suspense. Bradbury has followed in the tradition of such well-known writers as Jules Verne and Edgar Allan Poe. Jules Verne, a native of France, was the first writer to specialize in science fiction stories. In some of his adventure tales, the characters take unusual trips. For example, Phileas Fogg travels around the world, and Captain Nemo journeys under the sea. The details and explanations in the stories make Verne's science fiction believable.

Edgar Allan Poe, on the other hand, wrote frightening suspense stories. They take place in such locations as Spain, Paris, and the United States. One of his tales is a chilling murder mystery set on a street called the Rue Morgue. Poe is considered the creator of the modern detective story. In three stories a private detective named C. Auguste Dupin investigates a crime. All three authors—Bradbury, Verne, and Poe—capture the reader's attention through well-told tales.

C. Application in Writing
Using Common and Proper Nouns

Paragraphs and word choices will vary. Good paragraphs will contain appropriate and specific proper nouns.

B. PROOFREADING SKILL

Capitalizing Proper Nouns Rewrite the following paragraphs, correcting errors in grammar, capitalization, punctuation, and spelling. Pay special attention to the capitalization of proper nouns. (15 errors)

Ray bradbury is an author of science fiction and suspense stories. Whether set on mars or in the midwestern united states, his stories are full of excitement and suspense. Bradbury has followed in the tradition of such well-known writers as jules verne and Edgar Allan Poe Jules Verne, a native of france, was the first writer to specialize in science fiction stories. In some of his adventure tales, the characters take unusual trips. For example, Phileas fogg travels around the world, and captain nemo journeys under the sea. The details and explanations in the stories make Verne's science fiction beleivable.

Edgar Allan Poe, on the other hand, wrote frightening suspense stories. They take place in such locations as spain, paris, and the United States. One of his tales is a chilling murder mystery. Set on a street called the Rue Morgue. Poe is considered the creater of the modern detective story. In three stories a private detective named C Auguste dupin investigates a crime. All three authors—Bradbury, Verne, and Poe—capture the reader's attention through well-told tales.

C. APPLICATION IN WRITING

Using Common and Proper Nouns Ray Bradbury, Jules Verne, and Edgar Allan Poe have all written stories filled with suspense. Write a paragraph about one of your own favorite suspense stories.

Before you begin writing, study the following list of common nouns. Choose five that relate to your topic. Then substitute proper nouns for the common nouns. Include the proper nouns in your paragraph.

detective	villain	organization
city	country	crime
heroine	hero	planet
book	movie	robot
author	actor	alien

FOR MORE PRACTICE
See page 428.

420 Grammar Handbook

MIXED REVIEW • PAGES 418–420

A. Write the italicized nouns in the following sentences. Identify each one as a Common Noun or a Proper Noun. Capitalize the proper nouns.

1. Have you read about *mary hays* in a *class?*
2. She worked as a *nurse* during the *american revolution*.
3. During the war her *husband, john,* joined the *continental army*.
4. Like many *wives* of colonial *soldiers,* Mary traveled with her husband.
5. One bitter *winter* they camped at *valley forge, pennsylvania*.
6. Despite the weather, they did not give up the *cause* for *freedom*.
7. During the *summer* of 1778, Mary earned her *nickname, molly pitcher.*
8. At the *battle of monmouth, men* were dropping from fatigue.
9. Mary heard the soldiers' *cries*.
10. She grabbed a *pitcher* and brought them *water.*
11. After the *battle george washington* made her an army *sergeant*.
12. Molly Pitcher became a *symbol* of colonial women's *devotion* to the *united states of america*.

B. Make three columns on your paper. Label the columns *Person, Place,* and *Thing or Idea*. Write each of the nouns in the following sentences in the correct column.

13. One afternoon, headlines stunned people throughout the world.
14. The *Challenger,* a space shuttle, had exploded above Cape Canaveral.
15. Viewers watched in horror as television showed the explosion.
16. Newscasters with teary eyes reported the tragedy.
17. It was the worst accident in the history of NASA.
18. All the astronauts aboard the shuttle lost their lives.
19. One of those astronauts, Christa McAuliffe, taught at a high school in New Hampshire.
20. She was the first teacher selected by the government of the United States to travel into space.
21. Her goal was to educate students all over the world.
22. She had planned to broadcast lessons from the *Challenger.*

Writing Theme
Newsmakers

CHECK POINT

Writing Theme: Newsmakers

Suggest that students use these exercises as a springboard to writing. Other related areas they might explore include the following:

- the Battle of Monmouth
- another war hero
- a heroic person in your community
- a newsmaker from today's headlines

MIXED REVIEW • PAGES 418–420

You may wish to use this activity to check students' mastery of the following concept:

- common nouns and proper nouns

A. Common nouns (CN) and proper nouns (PN) are also shown on page.

1. Mary Hays, PN; class, CN
2. nurse, CN; American Revolution, PN
3. husband, CN; John, PN; Continental Army, PN
4. wives, CN; soldiers, CN
5. winter, CN; Valley Forge, Pennsylvania, PN
6. cause, CN; freedom, CN
7. summer, CN; nickname, CN; Molly Pitcher, PN
8. Battle of Monmouth, PN; men, CN
9. cries, CN
10. pitcher, CN; water, CN
11. battle, CN; George Washington, PN; sergeant, CN
12. symbol, CN; devotion, CN; United States of America, PN

B. Student answers should be in columns.

13. afternoon, Thing or Idea; headlines, Thing or Idea; people, Person; world, Place
14. *Challenger,* Thing or Idea; space shuttle, Thing or Idea; Cape Canaveral, Place
15. Viewers, Person; horror, Thing or Idea; television, Thing or Idea; explosion, Thing or Idea
16. Newscasters, Person; eyes, Thing or Idea; tragedy, Thing or Idea
17. accident, Thing or Idea; history, Thing or Idea; NASA, Thing or Idea
18. astronauts, Person; shuttle, Thing or Idea; lives, Thing or Idea
19. astronauts, Person; Christa McAuliffe, Person; high school, Place; New Hampshire, Place
20. teacher, Person; government, Thing or Idea; United States, Place; space, Place
21. goal, Thing or Idea; students, Person; world, Place
22. lessons, Thing or Idea; *Challenger,* Thing or Idea

SINGULAR AND PLURAL NOUNS

Objectives

- To differentiate between singular and plural nouns
- To form plurals correctly

Writing

- To write a paragraph, using correctly spelled plural nouns

Teaching Strategies

INDIVIDUALIZING INSTRUCTION: ESL STUDENTS In many languages rules regarding plurals differ from those of English. Spanish, for example, has no irregular plural nouns and requires plural forms of articles, adjectives, and possessives. Some ESL students may not recognize irregular plurals in English and may incorrectly make articles, adjectives, and possessives plural. Discuss with them the differences between plurals in English and their native language, and point out irregular plurals and correct usage when appropriate.

for RULE 2

KEY TO UNDERSTANDING There is an exception to this rule: If the final *ch* is pronounced like a *k,* you just add *-s: monarchs.* Point out that Rule 2 also applies to proper nouns: *the Davises, the Rodriguezes, the Mosses.*

for RULE 3

KEY TO UNDERSTANDING Students might be confused by the rules for forming the plurals of nouns ending in *o.* Point out that when the *o* follows a vowel, always add *-s,* rather than *-es: cameos, patios, folios, radios, rodeos, studios, tattoos.* When the *o* follows a consonant, usually add *-es.* Here's an exception that's easy to remember. If the noun is a musical term, add *-s: concertos, pianos, solos, sopranos, banjos.*

for RULE 4

KEY TO UNDERSTANDING Do not change a final *y* to *i* in forming the plural of proper nouns: *the McCarthys.*

SINGULAR AND PLURAL NOUNS

A **singular noun** names one person, place, thing, or idea. A **plural noun** names more than one person, place, thing, or idea.

A noun may be either singular or plural. The singular noun *teacher* refers to only one teacher. The plural noun *teachers* refers to more than one teacher. Here are guidelines for forming plurals.

Forming Plurals

1. To form the plural of most singular nouns, add *-s.*

painters museums shelters events attitudes

2. When a singular noun ends in *s, sh, ch, x,* or *z,* add *-es.*

dresses brushes coaches boxes waltzes

3. When a singular noun ends in *o,* add *-s* to make it plural.

concertos cameos pianos solos patios

For some nouns ending in an *o* preceded by a consonant, add *-es.*

heroes potatoes echoes tomatoes vetoes

4. When a singular noun ends in a *y* preceded by a consonant, change the *y* to *i* and add *-es.*

story—stories activity—activities library—libraries

When the *y* is preceded by a vowel (*a, e, i, o, u*), just add *-s.*

alley—alleys essay—essays survey—surveys

5. To form the plural of many nouns ending in *f* or *fe,* change the *f* to *v* and add *-es* or *-s.*

leaf—leaves self—selves scarf—scarves
half—halves life—lives shelf—shelves
loaf—loaves wife—wives thief—thieves

For some nouns ending in *f*, add *-s* to form the plural.

motif—motifs   proof—proofs   belief—beliefs

6. Some nouns have the same spelling in both the singular and the plural.

series   species   trout   sheep   moose

7. The plurals of some nouns are formed in special ways.

child—children	tooth—teeth	ox—oxen
woman—women	mouse—mice	man—men

If you can't figure out the correct spelling of a plural noun, a dictionary can help. Look at the dictionary entry for the word *elf,* below. Notice that the entry includes the plural form, *elves.* Most dictionaries show the plural of a noun if the plural is formed in an irregular way.

elf (elf) ***n.***, *pl.* **elves** (elvz) ⟦ ME < OE *ælf,* akin to OHG *alb* (Ger, nightmare), prob. < IE base **albho-*, white > L *albus,* white: prob. basic sense "whitish figure" (in the mist) ⟧ **1** *Folklore* a tiny, often prankish imaginary being in human form, supposedly exercising magic powers and haunting woods and hills; sprite **2** a small child or being, esp. a mischievous one — **elf'like'** ***adj.***

Practice Your Skills

A. CONCEPT CHECK

Plural Nouns Write the plurals of the italicized nouns.

1. Many *child* and *adult* think that they cannot write *poem.*
2. The poet Kenneth Koch tried to change *opinion* about poetry by teaching poetry *class* to young *student* in New York City.
3. Koch published their work in his book about *wish, lie,* and *dream.*
4. He encouraged his *student* to make unusual *comparison* about *thing* in their *life.*
5. One young poet compared bumpy *mattress* to the *back* of *camel.*

Writing TIP

Use a thesaurus to help improve your writing. A thesaurus lists synonyms for words. For example, the noun *writer* has many noun synonyms, such as *author, novelist, poet, journalist, playwright,* and *screenwriter.* A thesaurus can help you choose the most precise noun to say exactly what you mean.

Writing Theme
Inspirations

SPEAKING AND LISTENING Ask students to practice saying aloud the plurals of nouns ending in *f.* Notice that in *motifs, proofs,* and *beliefs,* the final *f* sound is heard in the plural form. In the words at the bottom of page 422, a *v* sound is heard in the plural form.

for DICTIONARY ENTRY

INDIVIDUALIZING INSTRUCTION: BASIC STUDENTS Point out that the letters *pl.* in a dictionary entry stand for the word *plural.* To check their understanding, ask students to use their dictionaries to find the plural form of these nouns: *ellipsis, swine, sheep.*

Additional Resource

Grammar and Usage Practice Book, pp. 17–18

Writing Theme: Inspirations

Other related areas students might wish to explore as writing topics include the following:

- student volunteer opportunities in school or the community
- inspirational speeches, such as Martin Luther King's "I Have a Dream"
- someone who has inspired them to aim higher or work harder

Answers to Practice Your Skills

A. Concept Check

Plural Nouns

1. children, adults, poems
2. opinions, classes, students
3. wishes, lies, dreams
4. students, comparisons, things, lives
5. mattresses, backs, camels

6. pianos, radios, mice, babies
7. Youngsters, skies, volcanoes *or* volcanos, sheep, goldfish
8. beaches, waterfalls, leaves
9. heroes
10. pupils, fantasies, beliefs
11. holidays, books, stereos
12. activities, authors, senses
13. concertos, symphonies, compositions
14. eyes, students
15. stories, scenes

B. Proofreading Skill
Plural Nouns

Errors are shown on page. Answers will vary. Typical revisions are shown below.

In the winter of 1983, eleven-year-old Trevor Ferrell saw individuals and families living on the streets. They warmed their hands over ashes and huddled in doorways. Trevor decided to help these people by offering them blankets. Soon his family and friends were giving away coats, scarves, and sweaters. They bought loaves of bread and made sandwiches to give away. Then they decided to open a home for some people from the streets. They called it Trevor's Place. Volunteers—children, men, and women—from nearby communities and churches donated time and money. Trevor inspired many people, including the President of the United States, by showing that kindness can turn ordinary individuals into heroes.

C. Application in Writing
Using Plural Nouns

Paragraphs and word choices will vary.

6. Some described the sounds of *piano, radio, mouse,* and crying *baby.*
7. *Youngster* described the colors of *sky, volcano, sheep,* and *goldfish.*
8. Others wrote about *beach, waterfall,* and *leaf.*
9. Writing as a group, one class created a poem about comic-book *hero.*
10. Koch's *pupil* learned to explore their *fantasy* and *belief.*
11. They wrote about what they saw during their *holiday,* read in *book,* or heard on their *stereo.*
12. Koch used creative *activity* to help young *author* sharpen their *sense.*
13. To inspire them, he played records of *concerto, symphony,* and jazz *composition.*
14. With their *eye* closed, *student* listened to the music.
15. The music helped them imagine strange *story* and *scene.*

As part of his campaign to help the homeless, eleven-year-old Trevor Ferrell offers a hot beverage to a homeless woman.

B. PROOFREADING SKILL

Plural Nouns Write the following paragraph, correcting errors in grammar, capitalization, punctuation, and spelling. Pay special attention to the plural spellings of plural nouns. (15 errors)

In the winter of 1983, eleven-year-old Trevor Ferrell saw individuals and families. Living on the streets. They warmed there hands over ashs and huddled in doorwayes. Trevor decided to help these people by offering them blankets. Soon his family, and friends were giving away coats, scarfs, and sweaters. They bought loafs of bread and made sandwichs to give away. Then they decided to open a home for some people from the streets, they called it trevor's Place. Volunteers—childrens, men, and women—from nearby communitys and churchs donated time and money. Trevor inspired many people, including the president of the united states, by showing that kindness can turn ordinary individuals into heros.

C. APPLICATION IN WRITING

Using Plural Nouns People, places, things, and ideas can be sources of inspiration. Write a paragraph about something or someone you find inspiring. Include the plural forms of nouns. Check a dictionary if you are unsure of the correct plural spellings.

FOR MORE PRACTICE
See page 428.

POSSESSIVE NOUNS

A **possessive noun** shows who or what owns something.

The noun following a **possessive noun** may name a thing or a quality.

Thing	Yoki's raincoat	Bianca's umbrella
Quality	storm's fury	Bob's courage

Forming Possessives of Nouns

Type of Noun	Rule	Examples
Singular noun	Add an apostrophe and *s.*	Mr. Ross's plight tornado's path
Plural noun ending in *s*	Add an apostrophe.	the Rosses' home victims' losses
Plural noun not ending in *s*	Add an apostrophe and *s.*	children's fears women's boots

Practice Your Skills

A. CONCEPT CHECK

Possessive Nouns In each sentence find the noun that should be possessive. Write the correct possessive form of that noun.

1. For years scientists gave hurricanes women names.
2. In 1978, however, scientists began giving hurricanes men names as well.
3. For example, the hurricane that slammed into South Carolina coast in 1989 was called Hugo.
4. The Caribbean islands were the first to feel Hugo fury.
5. This storm winds, waves, and rains caused widespread destruction.
6. The hurricane damaged homes, businesses, and merchants stores.
7. The destruction affected the islands tourist industry.
8. Worst of all, though, people lives were lost.
9. The Red Cross began relief efforts after the hurricane end.
10. Victims of the decade most costly storm also received aid from the government.

Writing TIP

Use the possessive forms to make phrases more concise.

Hurricane Andrew destroyed *homes of people.*
Hurricane Andrew destroyed *people's homes.*

Writing Theme
Storms

POSSESSIVE NOUNS

Objectives

- To recognize the possessive form of nouns
- To form possessives correctly

Writing

- To recognize and correct errors in the use of possessive nouns

Teaching Strategies

INDIVIDUALIZING INSTRUCTION: ESL STUDENTS The apostrophe does not occur in many foreign languages. ESL students often form possessives by using the "of" construction. Have students practice forming possessives by rewriting simple phrases:

the coat of my sister (my sister's coat)
the cat of my family (my family's cat)
the house of my neighbors (my neighbors' house)

Additional Resource

Grammar and Usage Practice Book, p. 19

Writing Theme: Storms

Other related areas students might wish to explore as writing topics include the following:

- the naming of hurricanes
- preparing for a storm
- worst storm you have experienced
- causes of hurricanes or tornadoes

Answers to Practice Your Skills

A. Concept Check
Possessive Nouns

1. women's
2. men's
3. South Carolina's
4. Hugo's
5. storm's
6. merchants'
7. islands'
8. people's
9. hurricane's
10. decade's

B. Drafting Skill
Sentence Completion

11. Jacobs's
12. city's
13. family's
14. twister's
15. children's
16. mother's
17. homes'
18. families'
19. neighbors'
20. season's

C. Proofreading Skill
Possessive Nouns

Errors are shown on page. Answers will vary. A typical revision is shown below.

Midwesterners fear the sight of a tornado's funnel cloud. They know that a twister's powerful force can level a town in minutes. One Illinois man's memory of a tornado that struck his town in 1965 has never faded. John Boden vividly recalls the storm's devastation. The tornado tore families' homes from their foundations, turned a plane upside down, and uprooted trees. One family's pool table sat undisturbed in the basement, but the rest of the house was blown away. The twister damaged the town's businesses and totally destroyed one building. Boden still remembers the residents' fear and shock after the tornado. Yet the community's citizens and businesspeople began at once to rebuild their town.

B. DRAFTING SKILL

Sentence Completion You are a newspaper reporter writing about one family's experience during a tornado. Write each sentence, using the correct possessive form of the word in parentheses.

11. Kris __________ two children were playing outside. (Jacobs)
12. Suddenly, the __________ siren warned citizens of a nearby tornado. (city)
13. Kris took her children and the __________ dog to the basement. (family)
14. The __________ loud noise sounded like a speeding train. (twister)
15. The __________ tearful eyes grew wide with fear. (children)
16. Their __________ soothing voice seemed to calm them. (mother)
17. After the siren blew the all-clear notice, the Jacobses and other families inspected their __________ condition. (homes)
18. Fortunately, the tornado did not severely damage many _______ homes. (families)
19. However, some __________ houses were destroyed. (neighbors)
20. Men, women, and children were frightened, but everyone in the community survived the __________ worst tornado. (season)

C. PROOFREADING SKILL

Possessive Nouns Write the following paragraph, correcting errors in grammar, capitalization, punctuation, and spelling. Pay special attention to the possessive forms of words. (15 errors)

Midwesterners fear the sight of a tornadoes' funnel cloud. They know that a twisters powerfull force can level a town in minutes. One illinois mans' memory of a tornado. That struck his town in 1965 has never faded. John Boden vividly recalls the storms devastation. The tornado tore families homes from their foundations. Turned a plane upside down, and uprooted trees. One families pool table sat undisturbed in the basement, but the rest of the house was blown away. The twister damaged the towns businesses and totaly destroyed one building. Boden still remembers the residents fear and shock after the tornado. Yet the communitys' citizens and businesspeople began at once to rebuild there town.

FOR MORE PRACTICE
See pages 428–429.

MIXED REVIEW • PAGES 422–426

A. Write the sentences, changing each singular noun in parentheses to either its plural or its possessive form. Some nouns need to be both plural and possessive.

1. (Fairy), ghosts, and (witch) appear in many legends.
2. Some legends are about strange (species) such as sea serpents.
3. Other legends praise (hero) remarkable achievements.
4. For example, John (Henry) life is celebrated in ballads, stories, and songs.
5. Like many folk (hero), John Henry was probably a real person.
6. He was an African American who worked for railroad (company) during the 1870s.
7. One day, John Henry met his (foreman) challenge.
8. Which could dig a tunnel faster, John Henry's hammer or his (boss) powerful steam drill?
9. John Henry hammered faster than the (company) drill.
10. This contest symbolizes (worker) struggles against being replaced by (machine).
11. (Artist) have also featured John Henry in their paintings.
12. Palmer C. (Hayden) painting *His Hammer in His Hand* shows John Henry walking proudly down a railroad track.

B. Correct each incorrect plural or possessive italicized noun in the following sentences. If a word is correct, write *Correct.*

13. *Sailors* tall tales are amazing *storys.*
14. They portray folk *heroes lifes* and incredible adventures.
15. New England *sailors* invented fantastic *seamen,* such as Alfred Bulltop Stormalong, or Stormy.
16. Few could match this *superheros* enormous size or *abilitys.*
17. *Stormys* height was measured in fathoms, not *foots* and *inchs.*
18. *Ships* cooks were always busy preparing special *dishs* for Stormy.
19. He once helped a cook steam *salmons* in pots full of the *seas* fog.
20. Stormy drank *whales* milk through a fire hose and enjoyed eating *ostriches* eggs.
21. After his *feasts* Stormy picked his huge *tooths* with a marlinespike, a pointed iron tool.
22. These tall tales still capture the *readers* attention.

Writing Theme
Legends

CHECK  POINT

Writing Theme: Legends

Other related areas students might wish to explore as writing topics include the following:

- a legendary frontier hero, such as Davy Crockett, Annie Oakley, or Johnny Appleseed
- an animal hero from world folklore, such as Coyote, Anansi the Spider, Reynard the Fox
- a parody, or humorous imitation, of a tall tale, set in the 1990s

MIXED REVIEW • PAGES 422–426

You may wish to use this activity to check students' mastery of the following concepts:

- singular and plural nouns
- possessive nouns

A.
1. Fairies, witches
2. species
3. heroes'
4. Henry's
5. heroes
6. companies
7. foreman's
8. boss's
9. company's
10. workers', machines
11. Artists
12. Hayden's

B.
13. Sailors', stories
14. heroes', lives
15. Correct, Correct
16. superhero's, abilities
17. Stormy's, feet, inches
18. Ships', dishes
19. salmon, sea's
20. whale's or whales', ostriches'
21. Correct, teeth
22. reader's

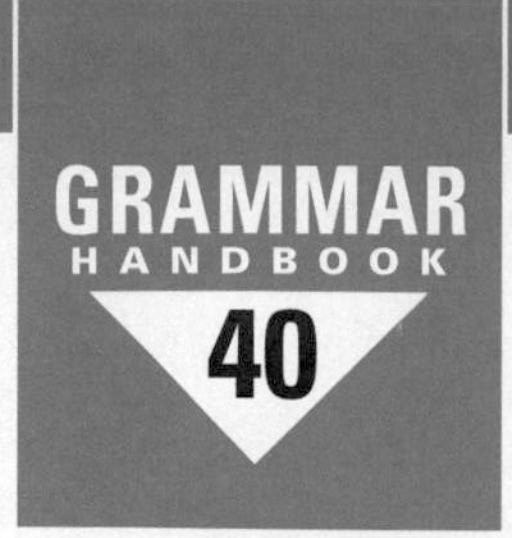

ADDITIONAL PRACTICE

Each of these exercises correlates to a section of Handbook 40, "Using Nouns." The exercises may be used for more practice, for reteaching, or for review of the concepts presented.

Writing Theme: Sports Standouts

Other related areas students might wish to explore as writing topics include the following:

- basketball stars such as Michael Jordan, Larry Bird
- tennis champions such as Chris Evert, Arthur Ashe
- Baseball Hall of Famers Roberto Clemente and Reggie Jackson

A. Identifying Common and Proper Nouns

Common and proper nouns are also shown on page.

1. Gertrude Ederle, Proper Noun; swimmer, Common Noun
2. records, Common Noun; afternoon, Common Noun; Brighton Beach, Proper Noun
3. Olympic Games, Proper Noun; team, Common Noun; medal, Common Noun
4. achievement, Common Noun
5. year, Common Noun; English Channel, Proper Noun
6. woman, Common Noun
7. Calais, Proper Noun; France, Proper Noun; Dover, Proper Noun; England, Proper Noun; swim, Common Noun; time, Common Noun
8. Ederle, Proper Noun; heroine, Common Noun
9. parade, Common Noun; New York City, Proper Noun
10. United States, Proper Noun; champion, Common Noun

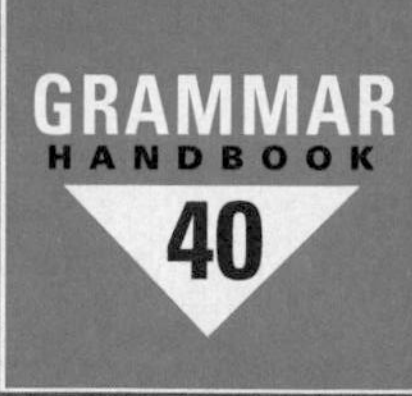

Writing Theme
Sports Standouts

A. Identifying Common and Proper Nouns Write the italicized nouns in the following paragraph. Identify each one as *Common Noun* or *Proper Noun*. Capitalize the proper nouns.

[1]*gertrude ederle* was an excellent *swimmer*. [2]In 1922, she broke seven amateur swimming *records* in one *afternoon* at *brighton beach*, New York. [3]In the 1924 *olympic games*, she helped the U.S. relay *team* win a gold *medal*. [4]However, many believe her greatest *achievement* occurred in 1926. [5]In that *year* she swam the *english channel*. [6]She was the first *woman* to swim across this body of water. [7]She swam from *calais, france*, to *dover, england*, and finished the *swim* in record *time*. [8]*ederle* returned home a *heroine*. [9]A *parade* in *new york city* welcomed her. [10]The citizens of the *united states* were proud of their amazing *champion*.

B. Forming Plurals of Nouns Write the correct plural form of each italicized noun in the following sentences.

11. Nancy Lopez started playing golf when she was eight *year* old.
12. She competed in *match* with other *child*.
13. Lopez's *coach* quickly recognized her talent.
14. She was the first girl to play with *boy* on a high school golf team.
15. In 1977, she competed in professional *tournament* for *woman*.
16. Soon afterward, she became one of the greatest *rookie* in the history of the *Lady* Professional Golf Association (LPGA).
17. *Photo* of Lopez appeared in many sports *magazine*.
18. Over the years Lopez has received many *trophy* for her *victory*.
19. Many people admire Lopez's *series* of *success*.
20. Lopez has strong *belief* about the role of hard work in the *life* of successful *athlete*.

C. Forming the Possessives of Nouns Find the nouns that should be possessive. Write the correct possessive form.

21. Tennis history is filled with athletes amazing achievements.
22. In the 1970s and 1980s, Sweden Bjorn Borg was one of the sport finest players.
23. During his successful career, he earned his opponents admiration.
24. Reporters stories also praised Borg for his accomplishments.
25. Borg helped win his country first Davis Cup.

Additional Resource

Grammar and Usage Practice Book, p. 21

26. The tennis star triumphs included becoming a Wimbledon champion five times in a row.
27. Another triumph was winning the men championship six times at the French Open.
28. In 1978, Borg won three nations major tournaments.
29. However, Borg never won tennis grand slam.
30. He also failed to win two other countries national championships.

D. Forming the Plurals and Possessives of Nouns Write the correct plural or possessive form of each italicized noun in these sentences.

31. *Jackie Robinson* professional baseball career began in 1945.
32. Robinson played for the *Monarch,* an all-African-American team.
33. At that time no African *American* were playing in the *nation* major leagues.
34. In the late 1940s, the Brooklyn *Dodgers* president, Branch Rickey, hired Robinson to play on his team.
35. *Rickeys* decision was a bold step and helped to end prejudice in professional baseball.
36. At first Robinson faced *bias* against African Americans.
37. He had to contend with *players* cruel remarks and *fans* insults.
38. Eventually, they showed their respect for his outstanding *abilityes.*
39. For many years he was his *team* most valuable player.
40. In 1962, Robinson was elected to *baseballs* hall of fame.

E. Using Plural and Possessive Forms Correctly Write the following sentences, correcting the errors in plural and possessive forms.

41. Jim Thorpes great-grandfather was Black Hawk, one of the famous Native American chieves of the 1800s.
42. As a young man, Thorpe attended class at the Carlisle Indian Industrial School, where he played on the schools football team.
43. From 1915 to 1930, Thorpe achieved fame as one of professional footballs' heros.
44. He could kick the football eighty yard and outrun his opponentes.
45. Such displayes of strength and speed earned him peoples' praise.
46. Many authoritys consider Thorpe to be the most talented football player who ever lived.
47. In 1950, a journalists association selected Thorpe as the centuries greatest male athlete.

B. Forming Plurals of Nouns

11. years
12. matches, children
13. coaches
14. boys
15. tournaments, women
16. rookies, Ladies
17. Photos, magazines
18. trophies, victories
19. series, successes
20. beliefs, lives, athletes

C. Forming the Possessives of Nouns

21. athletes'
22. Sweden's, sport's
23. opponents'
24. Reporters'
25. country's
26. star's
27. men's
28. nations'
29. tennis's
30. countries'

D. Forming the Plurals and Possessives of Nouns

31. Jackie Robinson's
32. Monarchs
33. Americans, nation's
34. Dodgers'
35. Rickey's
36. biases
37. players', fans'
38. abilities
39. team's
40. baseball's

E. Using Plural and Possessive Forms Correctly

Errors are shown on page.

41. Jim Thorpe's great-grandfather was Black Hawk, one of the famous Native American chiefs of the 1800s.
42. As a young man, Thorpe attended classes at the Carlisle Indian Industrial School, where he played on the school's football team.
43. From 1915 to 1930, Thorpe achieved fame as one of professional football's heroes.
44. He could kick the football eighty yards and outrun his opponents.
45. Such displays of strength and speed earned him people's praise.
46. Many authorities consider Thorpe to be the most talented football player who ever lived.
47. In 1950, a journalists' association selected Thorpe as the century's greatest male athlete.

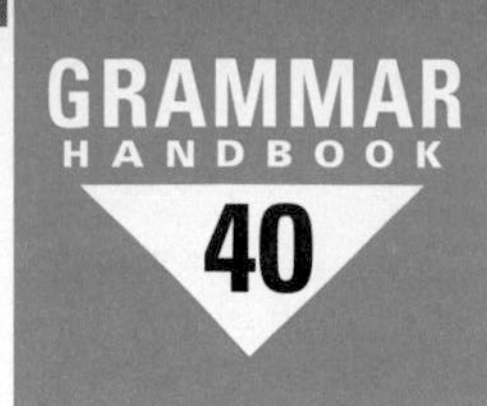

REVIEW

These exercises may be used as a mixed review or as an informal evaluation of the skills presented in Handbook 40, "Using Nouns."

Writing Theme: Miniature Worlds

Other related areas that students might wish to explore as writing topics include the following:

- the electron microscope
- penicillin
- Persian miniatures
- miniature dog breeds

A. Identifying Nouns

Common nouns (CN) and proper nouns (PN) are also shown on page.

1. Bacteria, CN; organisms, CN
2. environment, CN; earth, CN
3. Antarctica, PN; springs, CN; Yellowstone National Park, PN
4. microscope, CN; Anton, PN
5. scientist, CN; Holland, PN
6. chemist, CN; physician, CN
7. France, PN; Louis Pasteur, PN
8. changes, CN
9. Germany, PN; Robert Koch, PN; diseases, CN
10. techniques, CN

B. Forming Plurals

11. doll houses
12. women
13. couches
14. curios
15. models
16. eyelashes
17. roofs
18. draperies
19. glasses
20. knives
21. shadow boxes
22. miniatures
23. pianos
24. scarves
25. displays
26. inches
27. hobbies
28. feet
29. elk *or* elks
30. geese

C. Forming Possessives

31. city's
32. museum's
33. rooms'
34. people's

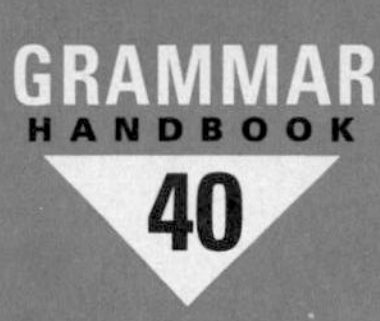

Writing Theme
Miniature Worlds

A. Identifying Nouns Write the italicized nouns in the following sentences. Label each one *Common Noun* or *Proper Noun*. Capitalize the proper nouns.

1. *Bacteria* are tiny one-celled *organisms*.
2. They are able to thrive in almost any *environment* on *earth*.
3. Scientists have discovered bacteria in icy regions of *antarctica* and in the hot *springs* of *yellowstone national park*.
4. Using a simple *microscope*, *anton* van Leeuwenhoek first observed bacteria around 1675.
5. He was an amateur *scientist* in *holland*.
6. During the late 1800s, a French *chemist* and a German *physician* made important contributions to the study of bacteria.
7. In *france*, *louis pasteur* showed that bacteria cause milk to sour and change wine to vinegar.
8. He identified the kinds of bacteria that cause different chemical *changes*.
9. In *germany*, *robert koch* discovered that specific bacteria cause certain *diseases*.
10. Koch also developed *techniques* for isolating and growing bacteria.

B. Forming Plurals Write the plural of each of the following nouns.

11. doll house
12. woman
13. couch
14. curio
15. model
16. eyelash
17. roof
18. drapery
19. glass
20. knife
21. shadow box
22. miniature
23. piano
24. scarf
25. display
26. inch
27. hobby
28. foot
29. elk
30. goose

C. Forming Possessives Write the possessive form of each italicized noun. If the italicized noun is plural, be sure to use the plural possessive form.

31. The Thorne Miniature Rooms, displayed at the Art Institute of Chicago, are one of the *city* popular attractions.
32. The lifelike settings have fascinated the *museum* visitors since the exhibit opened in 1954.
33. Narcissa Niblack Thorne, the *rooms* creator, began collecting miniatures during her childhood.
34. Later, with several *people* help, Thorne began making shadow-box displays of her miniatures.

Additional Resources

Tests and Writing Assessment Prompts, Mastery Test, pp. 15–16
Grammar and Usage Practice Book, p. 22
Elaboration, Revision, and Proofreading Practice, p. 26

35. She used *architects* drawings to design some of the rooms.
36. Thorne decorated the rooms with *weavers* colorful rugs and tapestries.
37. This *designer* attention to detail made her rooms seem magical.
38. The *shadow boxes* charm enchanted viewers of all ages.
39. In 1932, Thorne's first set of rooms was displayed at a benefit for the Architectural *Students* League.
40. The same rooms were then shown at *Chicago* Century of Progress Exposition in 1933.
41. Other rooms were on exhibit at a *World* Fair in 1939.
42. Some of *Thorne* shadow boxes were donated to charities for sale.
43. Thorne also created two rooms for a *children* hospital.

D. Using Plural and Possessive Forms Write the following sentences, correcting errors in plural and possessive forms.

44. Did you know that some full-grown horses are shorter than ponys?
45. Miniature horses stand less than three foot tall.
46. Miniatures, however, are not natures smallest horses.
47. Horses earliest ancestor's lived millions of years ago.
48. They stood between ten and twenty inches' tall.
49. In contrast, todays miniature horses are much larger.
50. The first modern miniatures were probably the pets of Europes' royal familys.
51. Later, in the 1700s, some miniatures performed tricks in circus.
52. Monkies often rode on small horses to entertain the audience.
53. Sometimes miniatures played comic roles in clowns acts.
54. Other miniatures spent their lifes hauling coal in underground mines.
55. They obeyed their masters commands and became coal miners reliable companions.
56. Today some miniatures are raised as childrens' pets.
57. Others are bred to perform at rodeoes.
58. The miniatures compete in different class of events.
59. Some shows feature the miniatures jumping abilities.
60. Before the shows the miniatures are groomed, and sometimes their hoofs are painted.
61. The best horses earn winners prizes.
62. Whether or not they win blue ribbons, miniature horses always receive an audiences' applause.

35. architects'
36. weavers'
37. designer's
38. shadow boxes'
39. Students'
40. Chicago's
41. World's
42. Thorne's
43. children's

D. Using Plural and Possessive Forms
Errors are shown on page.

44. Did you know that some full-grown horses are shorter than ponies?
45. Miniature horses stand less than three feet tall.
46. Miniatures, however, are not nature's smallest horses.
47. Horses' earliest ancestors lived millions of years ago.
48. They stood between ten and twenty inches tall.
49. In contrast, today's miniature horses are much larger.
50. The first modern miniatures were probably the pets of Europe's royal families.
51. Later, in the 1700s, some miniatures performed tricks in circuses.
52. Monkeys often rode on small horses to entertain the audience.
53. Sometimes miniatures played comic roles in clowns' acts.
54. Other miniatures spent their lives hauling coal in underground mines.
55. They obeyed their masters' commands and became coal miners' reliable companions.
56. Today some miniatures are raised as children's pets.
57. Others are bred to perform at rodeos.
58. The miniatures compete in different classes of events.
59. Some shows feature the miniatures' jumping abilities.
60. Before the shows the miniatures are groomed, and sometimes their hooves are painted.
61. The best horses earn winners' prizes.
62. Whether or not they win blue ribbons, miniature horses always receive an audience's applause.

WRITING CONNECTIONS

Elaboration, Revision, and Proofreading

This activity will show students some concepts in this handbook that are at work in informative writing. By revising and proofreading this passage, students will gain practice in using plural, possessive, and proper nouns and in using and organizing information.

You may want students to work in pairs or groups. Revisions may vary slightly. See a typical revision below. Elements with changes are shown in boldface.

In the late 1970s, **Akio Morita** convinced his company to design a tiny portable tape player with **lightweight** headphones. **Morita's idea** became a commercial success. Today, several **companies** in **the United States** and Japan market little portable stereos. ~~Many corporations also make large stereo systems and big-screen televisions.~~ Many different models are now available to **consumers** who enjoy music. Some models have radios, cassette players**, or** combinations of **both. Some** even play compact discs.

What kind of portable stereo to buy depends on **your** needs. Consider the cost, the size, the quality, and the features. Portable **stereos** with only radios are the smallest, lightest, and least expensive. Models with only tape players are **ideal if** you listen just to cassette recordings. **More expensive tape players have Dolby, a noise-reduction system.** Portable **compact** disc players are the largest and most expensive, but they are a worthwhile investment for true music lovers. A recording of a piece of music on a compact disc most closely resembles a live performance.

WRITING CONNECTIONS

Elaboration, Revision, and Proofreading

Informative Writing: Explaining *What*

Writing a consumer report is an effective way to analyze information about a product or service. (See Workshop 5.) When you revise a consumer report you have written, make sure you present accurate information in a logical order. Use precise nouns to make details and examples more specific.

On your paper revise the draft of a consumer report below. Follow the directions at the bottom of the page. Proofread your revision, paying special attention to errors in the use of nouns. Also look for other errors in grammar, capitalization, punctuation, and spelling.

[1]In the late 1970s, akio morita convinced his company to design a tiny portable tape player with lightwieght headphones. [2]The idea of Morita became a commercial success. [3]Today, several companys in our country and japan market little portable stereos. [4]Many corporations also make large stereo systems and big-screen televisions. [5]Many different models are now available to consumers' who enjoy music. [6]Some models have radios, cassette players or combinations of both [7]Some even play compact discs. [8]What kind of portable stereo to buy depends on you're needs. [9]Consider the cost, the size, the quality, and the features. [10]Portable stereoes with only radios are the smallest, lightest, and least expensive. [11]Models with only tape players are ideal. [12]If you listen just to cassette recordings. [13]Portable Compact disc players are the largest and most expensive, but they are a worthwhile investment for true music lovers. [14]A recording of a piece of music on a compact disc most closely resembles a live performance. [15]More expensive tape players have Dolby, a noise-reduction system.

1. Delete the sentence that does not support the main idea of the report.
2. Make sentence 2 more concise by changing the phrase "the idea of Morita" to a phrase containing a possessive form.
3. Make the phrase "our country" in sentence 3 more precise by changing it to a proper noun.
4. Move sentence 15 to a more logical position.
5. Divide the passage into two paragraphs.

on the LIGHT side

A Collection of Nouns

Speakers of English have had a great deal of fun making up words for groups of things. You're already familiar with some of these—a *school* of fish, a *herd* of cattle, a *flock* of sheep or birds. If you hear of a *swarm,* you probably think of bees. But do you know what a *clutch* is? It's a bunch of eggs—a *clutch* of eggs in a nest. Then there's the word *brood,* which is related to *breed* and means a family of young animals—such as newly-hatched birds.

Some of these words have an interesting connection to the animals they name. For example, a *pride* of lions seems quite fitting for the king of beasts. Was it the quality of wisdom that led to a *parliament* of owls? How about a *leap* of leopards, a *plague* of locusts, a *gaggle* of geese, and a *shrewdness* of apes? What does an *exaltation* of larks make you picture?

Most of these words have been around for almost six hundred years. However, some are newcomers. In a book titled *An Exaltation of Larks,* James Lipton put together a collection of these group terms and even added some new ones. Playfully making a connection to the thing named, he suggested a *piddle* of puppies. How about a *wince* of dentists, an *intrusion* of cockroaches, or a *shush* of librarians? Lipton also suggests a *stand* of flamingoes, a *dash* of commuters, and a *wobble* of bicycles.

If this all seems confusing, why not send your questions to a *wrangle* of philosophers, or better yet, add some collective nouns of your own. Can you think of any?

a Leap of Leopards

on the LIGHT side

You might ask artistically inclined students to draw images inspired by these collective nouns: for example, "a parliament of owls" dressed as legislators or "a shrewdness of apes" dressed as college professors. Students could model their work after the leopard picture on this page or create cartoons that use the collective terms. You might "publish" a book of these drawings or display them on a class bulletin board. Have students think of a good title for their book, such as *A Collection of Collectives* or *A Giggle of Cartoons.*

Finally, you might want to connect this page to Sketchbook page 416 by asking students whether any of these collective expressions would make a good name for a rock band. Do any of the band names that students listed include collective nouns?

Objective

- To use writing prompts and mementos as springboards to informal writing

WRITING WARM-UPS

Begin by reminding students that they will not be graded for the assignment. The activities are intended as springboards to get them thinking about the ways in which they use pronouns whenever they speak or write. Unless students volunteer to explore more than one prompt, have them work on one activity.

For students who choose the first prompt, you may want to provide some facts about Niagara Falls. (There are two falls on the Niagara River. The river forms the border between New York State and Ontario, Canada. On the American side, the falls are about 176 feet high and 1,000 feet wide; the more spectacular Horseshoe Falls in Canada are about 167 feet high and 2,600 feet wide. *Maid of the Mist* is the name of several boats that take tourists close to the falls.)

Sketch Book

WRITING WARM-UPS

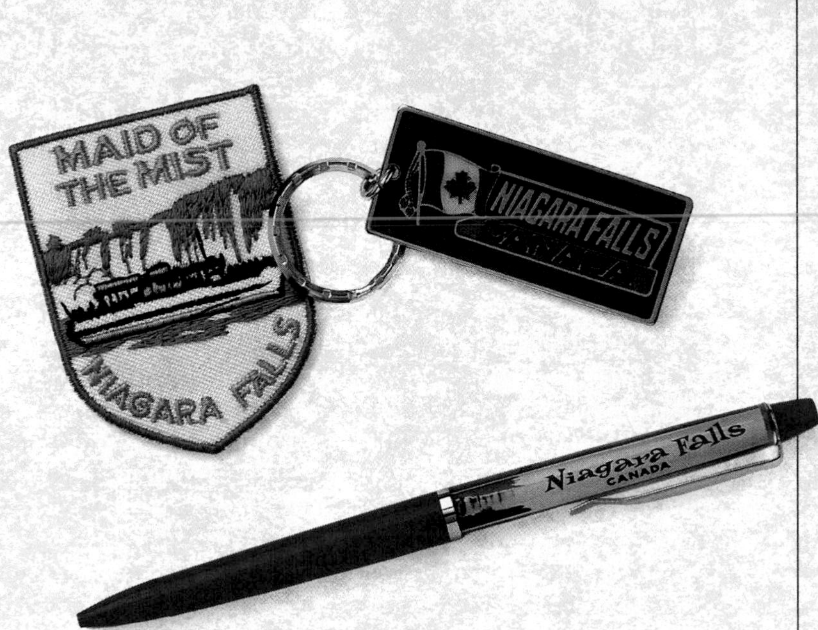

- Imagine that you and your family were at Niagara Falls. Write a postcard to a friend telling about your experiences.
- Tell the story of an adventure you and your friends had.
- What is your most prized possession? Describe something that is special to you, and tell why it is special.

Using Pronouns

Can you imagine telling what you did on your summer vacation without using such words as *I, we, he, she,* and *they?* If a person tries to write without using pronouns, a person quickly discovers that a person's writing sounds very awkward and wordy.

The sentence you just read certainly shows that problem! Pronouns take the place of nouns. By using pronouns effectively, you can make your writing flow smoothly.

- Writing with Pronouns
- The Forms of Pronouns
- Pronouns in Compound Subjects and Objects
- Possessive Pronouns and Contractions
- Indefinite Pronouns
- Demonstrative and Interrogative Pronouns
- Using *Who, Whom,* and *Whose*
- Reflexive and Intensive Pronouns
- Pronouns and Their Antecedents
- Special Pronoun Problems

Using Pronouns

Objectives

- To identify personal pronouns and the referents for pronouns and the gender of pronouns
- To identify subject, object, and possessive forms of personal pronouns and to use those forms correctly in sentences
- To use pronouns correctly in compound subjects and objects
- To distinguish between possessive pronouns and contractions
- To identify singular and plural indefinite pronouns and to use possessive pronouns and verbs that agree in number with indefinite pronouns
- To identify and use demonstrative and interrogative pronouns
- To use *who, whom,* and *whose; we* and *us; them* and *those* correctly in sentences
- To identify and use intensive and reflexive pronouns correctly
- To make pronouns agree with their antecedents

Writing

- To revise writing, correcting errors in pronoun usage
- To use personal pronouns to avoid repetition of nouns
- To use pronouns correctly in various kinds of writing

INTRODUCING THE HANDBOOK

After discussing the introductory text on the pupil pages, ask students to take their Sketchbook writing (page 434) and cross out the words *I, me, you, he, him, she, her, it, we, us, they,* and *them* wherever they appear. Have students work for a few minutes to reword sentences with crossed-out pronouns. They will soon see how awkward writing is without these personal pronouns.

Objectives

- To recognize and identify personal pronouns

Writing

- To revise a draft, using personal pronouns to avoid repetition

Teaching Strategies

KEY TO UNDERSTANDING Point out that personal pronouns are classified by number, as well as person and gender. The number of a pronoun depends on whether it refers to one person or thing (singular) or many (plural). To help students grasp this concept, write the following chart on the chalkboard.

PERSON	SINGULAR	PLURAL
first	I, me	we, us
	my, mine	our, ours
SECOND	you	you
	your, yours	your, yours
THIRD	he, him, his	they, them
	she, her, hers	their, theirs
	it, its	

INDIVIDUALIZING INSTRUCTION: ESL STUDENTS English encourages the use of personal pronouns to avoid repeating the same noun. This stylistic practice, however, does not hold in Japanese. Therefore, ESL students whose first language is Japanese may construct English sentences that seem awkward. (Mike's friend walks to school with Mike.) These students may need individual help and encouragement in the use of personal pronouns for concise writing.

WRITING WITH PRONOUNS

A **personal pronoun** is a word that is used in place of a noun or another pronoun.

Personal pronouns are used to refer to nouns that name persons or things. Study the following examples.

Awkward Jane put on Jane's boots. Then Jane went hiking.
Improved Jane put on her boots. Then she went hiking.

Note how the personal pronoun *her* helps the writer avoid repeating the same noun. Also notice how the pronoun *she* acts as a bridge to connect the two sentences.

To use personal pronouns to make your writing concise, you should understand how they are classified. First, pronouns are classified by **person:**

1. Pronouns in the **first person**—*I, my, me, we, our,* and *us*—refer to the person(s) speaking.
2. Pronouns in the **second person**—*you, your, yours*—refer to the person(s) spoken to.
3. Pronouns in the **third person**—*he, his, him, she, hers, her, it, its, they, their, them*—refer to some other person(s) or thing(s) that is being spoken of.

The personal pronoun *it* usually replaces a noun that stands for a thing or an animal. *It* is never used in place of a person.

Second, personal pronouns are classified by **gender.** Pronouns in the **masculine gender** refer to male people. Pronouns in the **feminine gender** refer to female people. Pronouns in the **neuter gender** refer to animals or things.

Lewis studied *his* map. (*His* is in the third person, masculine gender.)
Ilsa said the compass was *hers.* (*Hers* is in the third person, feminine gender.)
The parrot flapped *its* wings. (*Its* is in the third person, neuter gender.)

Writing TIP

Pronouns can help you express your ideas smoothly when you are writing about literature. Notice how Annie Maxwell uses pronouns in her analysis of "Dancing for Poppa" on pages 168–169.

Literature Connection

Students may know the concept of "person" from discussing point of view in short stories. Read aloud this paragraph from "The Circuit" by Francisco Jiménez.

"As we drove home Papá did not say a word. With both hands on the wheel, he stared at the dirt road. My older brother, Roberto, was also silent. He leaned his head back and closed his eyes."

Point out the narrator's use of the first-person pronouns, *we* and *my*. Explain that the use of first-person pronouns identifies the narrator as a character in the story and the point of view of the story as first person.

Practice Your Skills

A. APPLICATION IN LITERATURE

Personal Pronouns Write the personal pronoun(s) in each sentence. Then identify each as *First Person, Second Person,* or *Third Person.*

[1]During my stay in the Kelabit highlands, I looked across the wide, green valley to study the mountains that marked the border of Kalimantan. [2]They were only a few miles away, and I knew that this time I would reach them. [3]A few nights before I left, Pedera Ulan gave me some travel advice for the land beyond the mountains. [4]"You must obtain a *surat jalan* (walking letter). . . . [5]It is your letter of introduction. [6]For your safety always travel from one headman to another. [7]Each headman will write you a new letter. . . ."

[8]I was warned to take only guides who had been arranged by the headman. [9]This was because a guide who is answerable to the head of his village will take care of you. [10]He is responsible for your safety and well-being. . . . [11]Any local who violates the code of village hospitality can expect his family and their descendants to bear the guilt of his actions.

Eric Hansen, *Stranger in the Forest*

Eric Hansen rides an express cargo boat up the Baram River, Sarawak, Borneo.

B. REVISION SKILL

Using Pronouns to Avoid Repetition Revise the following draft by writing pronouns to replace the words in italics.

[12]Borneo is very densely forested in *Borneo's* interior. [13]Eric Hansen managed to penetrate *Borneo.* [14]*Eric Hansen* walked through *Borneo's* dense jungles to find the Penan people. [15]The Penans spend *the Penans'* lives as nomads. [16]Hansen's Penan guides taught *Hansen* survival skills in the rain forest. [17]Most important to *Hansen* was *Hansen's* sense of humor. [18]At night the guides told *Hansen* stories of *the guides'* people. [19]Hansen adapted "Cinderella" for *the guides.* [20]Cinderella worked for *Cinderella's* ugly sisters, and *Cinderella* fell in love with the son of a headman of a Penan village. [21]The guides enjoyed *Hansen's* story, and *the guides* asked *Hansen* to tell *the story* often.

Writing Theme
Travels in Borneo

Additional Resources

Test and Writing Assessment Prompts, Pretest, pp. 17–18
Grammar and Usage Practice Book, p. 23

Grammar
Test Generator

Writing Theme: Travels in Borneo

Suggest that students use these exercises as a springboard to writing. Other related areas that they might explore include the following:

- the countries that make up Borneo
- the Dyaks of Borneo
- the rain forests of Borneo
- orangutans of Borneo and Sumatra

Answers to Practice Your Skills

A. Application in Literature
Personal Pronouns

1. my, First Person; I, First Person
2. They, Third Person; I, First Person; I, First Person; them, Third Person
3. I, First Person; me, First Person
4. You, Second Person
5. It, Third Person; your, Second Person
6. your, Second Person
7. you, Second Person
8. I, First Person
9. his, Third Person; you, Second Person
10. He, Third Person; your, Second Person
11. his, Third Person; their, Third Person; his, Third Person

B. Revision Skill
Using Pronouns to Avoid Repetition

12 Borneo is very densely forested in its interior. 13 Eric Hansen managed to penetrate it. 14 He walked through its dense jungles to find the Penan people. 15 The Penans spend their lives as nomads. 16 Hansen's Penan guides taught him survival skills in the rain forest. 17 Most important to him was his sense of humor. 18 At night the guides told him stories of their people. 19 Hansen adapted "Cinderella" for them. 20 Cinderella worked for her ugly sisters, and she fell in love with the son of a headman of a Penan village. 21 The guides enjoyed his story, and they asked him to tell it often.

Objectives

- To identify the subject, object, and possessive forms of personal pronouns

Writing

- To use proofreading skills to correct errors in pronoun usage
- To use personal pronouns correctly in writing

Teaching Strategies

CRITICAL THINKING: ANALYZING Before proceeding with the lesson, you may wish to have students generate their own definition of the grammatical terms *subject, object,* and *possessive.* Have them use their definitions to explain the roles of the italicized pronouns in the first set of model sentences.

SPEAKING AND LISTENING Using the subject form for predicate pronouns will sound strange to many students who are used to hearing the object form used (incorrectly). Encourage students to create and read aloud additional examples based on the models on the pupil page; use their sentences to lead into the Writing Tip on page 439.

THE FORMS OF THE PRONOUN

A personal pronoun has three forms: the **subject form,** the **object form,** and the **possessive form.**

In English, personal pronouns have three special forms. Like nouns, they have a **possessive form.** In addition, they have a **subject form** and an **object form.**

She is a writer. (subject form)
A lyric poet is *she.* (subject form as predicate pronoun)
This poem was written by *her.* (object form)
It is *her* best one. (possessive form modifying a noun)
The idea was *hers.* (possessive form as a predicate pronoun)

Notice that the subject form of a pronoun may be used as the subject of the sentence or as a predicate pronoun. You may recall that predicate pronouns follow linking verbs and rename the subject of the sentence. The object form may be used as the direct or indirect object or as the object of a preposition. The possessive form is used to show ownership.

The Subject Form of Pronouns

A personal pronoun is used in the subject form (1) when it is the subject of a sentence or (2) when it follows a linking verb as a predicate pronoun. Here are the subject forms of personal pronouns:

The Subject Form of Pronouns

Singular	I	you	he, she, it
Plural	we	you	they

I love to write. (subject of a sentence)
He is also a writer. (subject of a sentence)
The illustrator is *she.* (predicate pronoun)
The playwrights were *they.* (predicate pronoun)

The Object Form of Pronouns

A personal pronoun is used in the object form (1) when it is the direct or indirect object of a verb or (2) when it is the object of a preposition. A preposition is a connecting word such as *of, for, to, with,* or *by*.

The Object Form of Pronouns

Singular	me	you	him, her, it
Plural	us	you	them

The critics praised *her.* (direct object)
The screenwriter thanked *us.* (direct object)
The audience asked *him* many questions. (indirect object)
The autograph is for *me.* (object of a preposition)

The Possessive Form of Pronouns

The possessive form of a pronoun is used to show ownership. There are two groups of personal pronouns in the possessive form: (1) those used like adjectives to modify nouns and (2) those used like nouns as subjects, predicate words, objects of verbs, or objects of prepositions.

Pronouns Used to Modify Nouns

Singular	my	your	his, her, its
Plural	our	your	their

Pronouns Used Alone

Singular	mine	yours	his, hers, its
Plural	ours	yours	theirs

Your story is in the folder. (modifying a noun)
This editorial on sports eligibility in the school newspaper is *mine.* (used alone)
Our deadline is today. (modifying a noun)
Are these notes *yours?* (used alone)

Writing TIP

You may often hear sentences such as the following: "Yes, this is her." "Hi! It's me."

The object forms are sometimes used in casual conversation. Writing is more formal; be sure to use the subject form as the predicate pronoun.

INDIVIDUALIZING INSTRUCTION: ESL STUDENTS Unlike pronoun forms in many other languages, the English *you* and *it* retain the same spelling for both subject and object forms. Therefore, students need to learn only the changing forms for *I/me, he/him, she/her, we/us,* and *they/them.* Have ESL students make a pronoun chart to keep in their notebooks for permanent reference.

COLLABORATIVE OPPORTUNITY
Even if students memorize the charts of pronoun forms in this lesson, they still will not be able to choose a correct pronoun form unless they can identify how a pronoun functions in its sentence. Review definitions for *subject, predicate pronoun, direct object, indirect object,* and *object of a preposition.* Then form the class into groups of four or five; assign each group one of the functions. Have each group create five sentences illustrating pronouns being used in the assigned function. Students may write their sentences on the board or read them aloud. Have the rest of the class check to see (1) that the correct pronoun form has been used and (2) that the pronoun functions correctly.

Additional Resource

Grammar and Usage Practice Book, pp. 24–25

Writing Theme: Writers' Other Jobs

Suggest that students use these exercises as a springboard to writing. Other related areas that they might explore include the following:

- the life and work of Lewis Carroll (Charles Lutwidge Dodgson)
- Mark Twain's many business ventures
- the life and work of O. Henry (William Sydney Porter)

Answers to Practice Your Skills

A. Concept Check

Pronoun Forms

The correct pronouns are underlined on page. The form of each pronoun is shown below.

1. my, Possessive Form; I, Subject Form
2. me, Object Form
3. They, Subject Form
4. them, Object Form
5. my, Possessive Form; he, Subject Form
6. his, Possessive Form
7. He, Subject Form
8. hers, Possessive Form
9. She, Subject Form
10. her, Object Form
11. hers, Possessive Form
12. their, Possessive Form
13. their, Possessive Form; them, Object Form; their, Possessive Form
14. We, Subject Form; his, Possessive Form
15. he, Subject Form
16. him, Object Form
17. his, Possessive Form; he, Subject Form; them, Object Form; his, Possessive Form
18. their, Possessive Form; ours, Possessive Form
19. our, Possessive Form; your, Possessive Form
20. yours, Possessive Form; you, Subject Form

Writing Theme
Writers' Other Jobs

Practice Your Skills

A. CONCEPT CHECK

Pronoun Forms Write the correct pronouns from those given in parentheses. Then label each as *Subject Form, Object Form,* or *Possessive Form.*

1. Because of (me, my, mine) strong curiosity, (I, me, my) often wonder how people get started in their careers.
2. How certain writers got their start has fascinated (I, me, my).
3. (They, Them, Their) often had surprising beginnings.
4. Many of (they, them, their) wrote, but they worked at other jobs too.
5. Much to (I, me, my) surprise, Robert Frost worked as a chicken farmer, but (he, him, his) wasn't very successful.
6. In later years, Frost explained (he, him, his) failure.
7. (He, Him, His) was just too lazy for farming!
8. Doris Lessing also had to work at other jobs; (she, her, hers) was a rocky beginning.
9. (She, Her, Hers) left school at the age of fifteen.
10. Jobs such as nursemaid, typist, and telephone operator gave (she, her, hers) a steady income.
11. Eventually, recognition as a writer was (she, her, hers).
12. Anton Chekhov, Arthur Conan Doyle, and William Carlos Williams earned (they, them, their) living as physicians.
13. Sometimes (they, them, their) medical experiences provided (they, them, their) with material for (they, them, their) writing.
14. (We, Us, Our) have to admire a writer like Kenneth Grahame who worked full time at a bank and wrote in (he, him, his) spare time.
15. It was (he, him, his) who created Toad, Rat, Mole, and all the other lovable characters in *The Wind in the Willows.*
16. Perhaps the dreary bank work gave (he, him, his) the urge to create an imaginary world.
17. However, it was never (he, his, him) intention to have the tales published; (he, him, his) wrote (they, them, their) as entertainment for (he, him, his) son.
18. Because these writers survived (they, their, theirs) hardships, adventure and entertainment can be (we, us, ours).
19. In (we, us, our) world today, it's still very hard to start as a beginning author and work (you, your, yours) way up.
20. However, a writer's life can be (you, your, yours) if (you, your, yours) are willing to work at something else too.

440 Grammar Handbook

B. PROOFREADING SKILL

Using Pronoun Forms Correctly The writer of the following paragraph has made some errors. Rewrite the passage, correcting all errors, especially those of pronoun forms. (10 errors)

For you and I, fans of westrens and Pioneer novels, it's a good thing that Louis L'Amour wrote so many stories. However, for he, just as for many other writers, a number of unusual jobs were a necesity. He worked as a caretaker of a mine a boxer, and a lumberjack. Was even a hobo and a merchant sailor. Truly, the life of a wanderer was him. Many of L'Amour's experiences are described in his book *Education of a Wandering Man.* Its pages are filled with fascinating storys. In later years he wrote, "A wanderer I had been through most of mine early years, and now that I had my own home, my wandering continued, but among books."

C. APPLICATION IN WRITING

Describing a Process Carefully study the picture below. Write a brief explanation of the process that is shown. Be sure to use subject, object, and possessive pronouns correctly.

FOR MORE PRACTICE
See page 463.

B. Proofreading Skill
Using Pronoun Forms Correctly

Errors in proofreading exercises are counted as follows: (a) Each word is counted as one error. For example, a misspelled word is one error; two initials and a last name not capitalized are counted as three errors. (b) Run-on sentences and sentence fragments are each counted as one error, even though the correction involves both punctuation and capitalization corrections.

Corrections are shown below.

For you and me, fans of westerns and pioneer novels, it's a good thing that Louis L'Amour wrote so many stories. However, for him, just as for many other writers, a number of unusual jobs were a necessity. He worked as a caretaker of a mine, a boxer, and a lumberjack. L'Amour was even a hobo and a merchant sailor. Truly, the life of a wanderer was his. Many of L'Amour's experiences are described in his book *Education of a Wandering Man.* Its pages are filled with fascinating stories. In later years he wrote, "A wanderer I had been through most of my early years, and now that I had my own home, my wandering continued, but among books."

C. Application in Writing
Describing a Process

Answers will vary. A sample explanation is shown below. Subject pronouns, object pronouns, and possessive pronouns are italicized.

As the final step in making a puppet, an artist paints *its* face. Using tubes of paint, *he* or *she* squeezes a variety of colors onto a plate. Using brushes of different sizes, the artist paints eyes, eyebrows, lips, and other features on the puppet. With these brush strokes, the artist brings *it* to life.

CHECKPOINT

Writing Theme: Superstitious Customs

Other related areas students might wish to explore as writing topics include the following:

- four-leaf clovers and other supposed good-luck signs
- New Year's Day customs
- spilled salt, cracked mirrors, and other supposed bad-luck signs

MIXED REVIEW • PAGES 436–441

You may wish to use this activity to check students' mastery of the following concepts:

- writing with pronouns
- the forms of the personal pronouns

1. My, Possessive
2. them, Object
3. His, Possessive
4. It, Subject
5. Its, Possessive
6. her, Possessive
7. she, Subject
8. her, Object
9. they, Subject
10. their, Possessive
11. he, Subject; they, Subject
12. His, Possessive
13. them, Object
14. them, Object
15. it, Object
16. she, Subject
17. They, Subject; it, Subject; them, Object
18. her, Possessive
19. hers, Possessive
20. hers, Possessive
21. him, Object
22. You, Subject
23. Yours, Possessive; she, Subject
24. he, Subject
25. he, Subject; her, Object; their, Possessive

CHECKPOINT
MIXED REVIEW • PAGES 436–441

Writing Theme
Superstitious Customs

Write the italicized pronouns in the following sentences. Label each pronoun *Subject, Object,* or *Possessive.*

1. *My* friend Mike belongs to a superstitious family.
2. Strange practices come naturally to *them.*
3. *His* grandfather always carries a rabbit's foot.
4. *It* is the left hind foot of a rabbit that was caught in a graveyard.
5. *Its* power is supposed to be great.
6. Mike's grandmother was an actress in *her* youth.
7. Once *she* accidentally whistled in a dressing room.
8. The other actors made *her* leave the room, turn around three times, and spit to remove the bad luck.
9. Those actors—a very superstitious group were *they.*
10. A list of *their* practices would fill several pages!
11. Mike's father, on the other hand, collects horseshoes; *he* says that even the Romans thought *they* were lucky.
12. *His* always hang over the back door.
13. Long ago, people carried *them* to ward off the "evil eye."
14. The belief is that the iron gives *them* special powers.
15. Mike's mom, however, does not believe in *it.*
16. Instead, *she* collects Pennsylvania Dutch hex symbols.
17. *They* do not have a farm; therefore, *it* is impossible to follow the custom of putting *them* on a barn.
18. A brightly colored hex symbol hangs above *her* desk.
19. Anyone can quickly tell which desk is *hers.*
20. Mike's aunt Matilda is different; *hers* are really outdated superstitions.
21. Matilda once scolded *him* for sweeping dirt out the door.
22. "*You* just swept away the luck of this house.
23. *Yours* is a thoughtless generation!" *she* shouted.
24. Apparently, *he* was supposed to sweep the dirt into the fireplace.
25. However, *he* explained to *her* that *their* modern home is not equipped with an open hearth!

A tourist surveys hex sign artist Johnny Ott's collection of signs decorated with a sunburst motif, an ancient symbol meaning "welcome."

PRONOUNS IN COMPOUND SUBJECTS AND OBJECTS

In a compound subject or a compound object, use the same pronoun that you would use if the pronoun stood alone.

Speakers and writers seldom make mistakes when they use one personal pronoun in a sentence. However, they may have to pause to think when two pronouns, or a pronoun and a noun, are used together in compound sentence parts. For example, would you say *between you and I* or *between you and me?* Study the following examples and read the pointers below.

Mario and she went to the theater. (compound subject)
I joined *Sue and them.* (compound direct object)
Mario gave *Sue and me* a program. (compound indirect object)
It was very helpful to *Sue and me.* (compound object of a preposition)

Read the sentences above a second time. This time, drop out the noun in each compound part. For example, read "*She* went to the theater." Each sentence should sound complete and sensible when the pronoun is used alone.

Whenever you are in doubt about which form of the pronoun to use in a compound sentence part, drop out the noun or the other pronoun and read the sentence with just one pronoun.

The conductor smiled at (he, him) and (I, me).
The conductor smiled at *him.*
The conductor smiled at *me.*

Remember to use only *I, we, he, she,* or *they* as predicate pronouns after forms of the verb *be.*

The narrator is *she.* The stage manager will be *I.*

PRONOUNS IN COMPOUND SUBJECTS AND OBJECTS

Objectives

- To use pronouns correctly in compound subjects and objects

Writing

- To rewrite a paragraph, correcting errors in pronoun usage

Teaching Strategies

STUMBLING BLOCK Assure students that many people make mistakes in pronoun usage when the subject or object is compound. They may be under the impression that the subject form always sounds "more educated." Therefore, they fall into the error of saying "between you and I." Remind students that the form of a pronoun must reflect its use in the sentence:

- subject pronouns for subjects and predicate pronouns
- object forms for direct objects, indirect objects, and objects of prepositions

Additional Resource

Grammar and Usage Practice Book, p. 26

Writing Theme: Opera Stories

Other related areas that students might wish to explore as writing topics include the following:

- *Madama Butterfly* by Giacomo Puccini
- *Faust* by Charles Gounod
- *William Tell* by Gioacchino Rossini
- *Porgy and Bess* by George Gershwin

Answers to Practice Your Skills

A. Concept Check

Pronouns in Compound Subjects and Objects

Answers are shown on page.

B. Revision Skill

Using Pronouns in Compound Subjects and Objects

Errors are underlined on page. Corrections are shown below.

13 My brother and I had heard of an opera called *The Barber of Seville.* 14 The story, though, was a new one for him and me. 15 It has a lot of romance and intrigue, which are important for me and for many people. 16 The composer, Gioacchino Rossini, put humor into this opera too. He and his music have lasted for almost 180 years; perhaps humor is the reason. 17 The two lovers in the story are Count Almaviva and Rosina, but he and she are kept apart by her guardian.

18 Figaro, the barber, likes Almaviva and her, so he figures out how to bring the count and her together. 19 Figaro and the count provide a variety of clever plans and disguises that keep all of us in the audience happy. 20 One night, for example, Rosina and Almaviva plan to elope, but they and their plans run into trouble. 21 In the end, he and she really do get married. 22 So love always triumphs, as you and I know.

Writing Theme
Opera Stories

Practice Your Skills

A. CONCEPT CHECK

Pronouns in Compound Subjects and Objects Write the correct pronouns from those given in parentheses.

1. Between you and (I, me), I used to not like opera at all!
2. However, Ryan and (I, me) went to see *Carmen.*
3. It was the first opera for both (he, him) and (I, me).
4. The playbill gave other members of the audience and (we, us) a summary of the story.
5. Carmen and a band of gypsies are in Seville, Spain; (she, her) and (they, them) are camped outside the city.
6. A young soldier, Don José, sees the gypsies and (she, her).
7. José must choose between (she, her) and Micaela, his sweetheart from home.
8. Carmen was two-timing (he, him) and Escamillo the toreador.
9. Escamillo and (he, him) fight for Carmen's love.
10. José feels he must stop Escamillo and Carmen; he must prevent (he, him) and (she, her) from being together.
11. His solution, stabbing the fickle Carmen, surprised my friend and (I, me).
12. After the show, the audience and (we, us) clapped loudly.

B. REVISION SKILL

Using Pronouns in Compound Subjects and Objects Rewrite the following paragraph, correcting errors in pronoun use.

13 My brother and me had heard of an opera called *The Barber of Seville.* 14 The story, though, was a new one for him and I. 15 It has a lot of romance and intrigue, which are important for I and for many people. 16 The composer, Gioacchino Rossini, put humor into this opera too. Him and his music have lasted for almost 180 years; perhaps humor is the reason. 17 The two lovers in the story are Count Almaviva and Rosina, but him and her are kept apart by her guardian. 18 Figaro, the barber, likes Almaviva and she, so he figures out how to bring the count and she together. 19 Figaro and the count provide a variety of clever plans and disguises that keep all of we in the audience happy. 20 One night, for example, Rosina and Almaviva plan to elope, but them and their plans run into trouble. 21 In the end, him and her really do get married. 22 So love always triumphs, as you and me know.

FOR MORE PRACTICE
See page 463.

Possessive Pronouns and Contractions

> A **possessive pronoun** never has an apostrophe; a **contraction** always has an apostrophe.

A **contraction** of a pronoun and a verb is formed by omitting one or more letters from the verb and inserting an apostrophe in place of the letters that have been left out. Note that *who* is a pronoun that is used to ask a question. As an interrogative pronoun, it is in the subject form. You will learn more about interrogative pronouns later in this handbook.

it + is *or* has = it's	they + are = they're
you + are = you're	who + is *or* has = who's

Some **possessive pronouns** sound like contractions. Because the words sound alike, they are sometimes confused. Note that *whose* is the possessive form of the pronoun *who*. It is used to ask a question and to modify nouns.

Possessive Pronouns	***Contractions***
its	it's
your	you're
their	they're
whose	who's

Incorrect The school celebrated it's victory.
Correct The school celebrated its victory.

Correct You're (You are) late for the test.
Correct Who's (Who is) the debater whose notes you have?

Follow these two simple rules for using possessive pronouns and contractions correctly:

1. If the word you want to use stands for two words, it is a contraction and needs an apostrophe.
2. Never use an apostrophe in a possessive pronoun.

Writing TIP

Avoid contractions in certain types of writing, such as reports and business letters. Contractions are more appropriate for written dialogue and informal writing.

Possessive Pronouns and Contractions

Objectives

- To identify the correct uses of possessive pronouns and contractions

Writing

- To revise writing, correcting errors in the use of pronouns and contractions

Teaching Strategies

HELPFUL HINT Explain that the contractions and possessive pronouns in the chart are called *homophones*—words that sound alike but have different spellings and meanings. Assure students that confusing possessive pronouns and contractions is not a problem in speaking; it is a spelling problem in writing. If students need work on specific homophones, such as *whose* and *who's,* refer them to "Using the Right Word," page 688.

INDIVIDUALIZING INSTRUCTION: BASIC STUDENTS Students' confusion over the use of apostrophes is aggravated by the fact that possessive nouns contain apostrophes (Elena's, Ted's) and that pronouns take the place of nouns. Emphasize that possessive pronouns *never* have apostrophes.

Additional Resource

Grammar and Usage Practice Book, p. 27

Writing Theme: Education

Other related areas students might wish to explore as writing topics include the following:

- proposals for year-round schools
- Japanese schools
- British schools
- bilingual education

Answers to Practice Your Skills

A. Concept Check

Possessive Pronouns and Contractions

1. their
2. They're; They are
3. you're; you are
4. its
5. Your
6. they're; they are
7. Who's; Who is
8. whose
9. It's; It is
10. their

B. Revision Skill

Using Possessive Pronouns and Contractions Correctly

11. You're (in second sentence)
12. who's
13. their
14. Correct
15. You're
16. You're
17. your
18. Who's
19. They're
20. It's

Writing Theme
Education

Practice Your Skills

A. CONCEPT CHECK

Possessive Pronouns and Contractions Write the correct word given in parentheses in the following sentences. If the word is a contraction, also write the words the contraction represents.

1. The South Koreans have worked hard to improve (their, they're) educational system.
2. (Their, They're) now rightfully proud of the schools.
3. No doubt, (your, you're) probably used to beginning school in the fall.
4. The South Korean school year begins (its, it's) term in March.
5. (Your, You're) school year usually has 180 days.
6. In South Korea (their, they're) used to 210 days in a school year.
7. (Whose, Who's) eligible to go to college in South Korea?
8. Only students (whose, who's) scores are excellent on the entrance examination may go.
9. (Its, It's) a very competitive test.
10. Only half of the high-school graduates may continue (their, they're) education in colleges or universities.

B. REVISION SKILL

Using Possessive Pronouns and Contractions Correctly Revise the following dialogue, correcting errors in the use of pronouns and contractions. If a sentence is correct, write *Correct.*

11. LUIS: Your face looks familiar. Your one of the new exchange students, right?
12. RITA: Yes, I am the one whose from South America.
13. LUIS: Do the other exchange students like they're classes here?
14. RITA: Oh, yes, they're so much more relaxed here.
15. LUIS: Relaxed! Your not saying that it's easier here!
16. RITA: Your always complaining about tests and quizzes.
17. In my school, you're grade depends on one final examination.
18. LUIS: Whose in your classes there? Are they coed?
19. RITA: Oh no! Most schools aren't mixed. Their separate.
20. Its strange for me to be in a class with boys.

FOR MORE PRACTICE
See page 464.

CHECK POINT

MIXED REVIEW • PAGES 443–446

Write the correct pronoun or contraction given in parentheses.

1. (Its, It's) said that English is the world's lingua franca.
2. (Your, You're) probably wondering what a lingua franca is.
3. Recently a Japanese girl, a Brazilian boy, and (I, me) represented our schools at a conference in Saudi Arabia.
4. English was quite useful to (she, her) and (he, him).
5. No one else could speak (their, they're) languages.
6. So the other people and (we, us) spoke English.
7. When a language is used between groups that have no other language in common, (its, it's) called a lingua franca.
8. We learned that the Chinese, (whose, who's) language is difficult for Westerners, are also learning English.
9. "(Their, They're) all learning English," one visitor said.
10. We learned that the British Broadcasting Corporation produced a television series; (its, it's) title was *Follow Me.*
11. It was shown to the Chinese; (their, they're) response was good.
12. English gives the British and (they, them) a lingua franca.
13. Communication exists between the British and (we, us).
14. Yet (they, them) and (we, us) speak our own kinds of English.
15. So if the Chinese learn British English, (we, us) and (they, them) should be able to communicate too.
16. One problem occurred to other students and (I, me).
17. (Whose, Who's) going to decide which variety of English will be the lingua franca?
18. Native speakers of English include, among others, the British, the Australians, the New Zealanders, and (we, us).
19. If you are from Britain, American English is different from (your, you're) English.
20. For example, (your, you're) probably not familiar with the word *flashlight,* but you know *torch.*
21. (Whose, Who's) English will be used?
22. Dictionaries and phrase books can help you and (I, me).
23. (Its, It's) been estimated that about 130 million students are learning English as a second language.
24. Perhaps you and (I, me) should feel a little embarrassed.
25. (Their, They're) learning another language, but not many of us have learned anything except English!

Writing Theme
A World Language

THE FAR SIDE By GARY LARSON

The Far Side cartoon by Gary Larson is reprinted by permission of Chronicle Features, San Francisco, CA.

CHECK POINT

Writing Theme: A World Language

Other related areas that students might wish to explore as writing topics include the following:

- Esperanto
- British vocabulary (e.g., *lorry* for *truck, lift* for *elevator)*
- words that American English has borrowed from other languages
- music, art, and math as international "languages"

MIXED REVIEW • PAGES 443–446

You may wish to use this activity to check students' mastery of the following concepts:

- pronouns in compound subjects and objects
- possessive pronouns and contractions

Answers are shown on page.

Objectives

- To identify singular and plural indefinite pronouns
- To use verbs that agree in number with indefinite pronouns used as subjects

Teaching Strategies

LINKING GRAMMAR AND WRITING To avoid the awkward *his or her* construction, suggest that students reword a sentence to make the subject plural, when possible. Write this example on the board:

Everyone walked *his or her* dog.

The students walked *their* dogs.

HELPFUL HINT When *all, some, any* or *none* is the subject of a sentence, there is an easy way to determine whether the pronoun should be considered singular or plural. Tell students to look at the object of the preposition that follows the subject. If the object is singular (as in *story* and *lake* in the example sentences), the pronoun is singular and takes a singular verb. If the object is plural (as in *reporters* and *photos),* the pronoun is plural and takes a plural verb. Let students find other examples in Concept Check B on page 449 (sentences 17, 18, and 24).

Additional Resource

Grammar and Usage Practice Book, p. 28

INDEFINITE PRONOUNS

An **indefinite pronoun** is a pronoun that does not refer to a specific person or a specific thing.

Pronouns like *everyone* and *somebody* do not refer to any definite person or thing. They are called **indefinite pronouns.**

Singular Indefinite Pronouns

another	anything	everybody	neither	one
anybody	each	everyone	nobody	somebody
anyone	either	everything	no one	someone

Possessive pronouns that refer to indefinite pronouns should agree in number with the indefinite pronoun.

Neither believed *his* eyes. (Not *their* eyes)
Each strained *his or her* neck to see. (Use *his or her* if the person being referred to can be either male or female.)

An indefinite pronoun used as a subject must agree in number with its verb. Do not be confused by phrases that come between a singular indefinite pronoun and the verb.

Each of these men has a boat. (The subject is *each,* not *men.*)

Plural Indefinite Pronouns

both	many	few	several

Several reported *their* findings. Many *are* verifiable.

The pronouns *all, some, any,* and *none* may be singular or plural, depending on their meaning in the sentence.

All of my story is true. All of the reporters are here.
None of the lake is foggy. None of the photos are sharp.

448 Grammar Handbook

Practice Your Skills

A. CONCEPT CHECK

Indefinite Pronouns Write the indefinite pronoun from each sentence. Then write whether it is *Singular* or *Plural.*

1. Anything is possible if you keep an open mind.
2. Everyone has heard about the lake monster in Scotland.
3. However, few know about other lake monsters.
4. Some of the supposed monsters are said to live in North America.
5. No one has photographed the Ogopogo monster in Canada.
6. Many suggest that these monsters are plesiosaurs.
7. None of the evidence confirms the existence of prehistoric large water reptiles.
8. Anyone can tell you that even thirty years ago, such creatures were spotted in Canada.
9. One of the observers claimed to have seen a "creature resembling a large snake."
10. Another reported a "reptile-like beast."
11. Neither had solid proof of the creature.
12. Both, though, stood by what they described.
13. None of their claims have been verified.
14. Perhaps somebody has evidence but is afraid to show it.
15. Everything about the monster remains a mystery.

B. CONCEPT CHECK

Verbs and Indefinite Pronouns For each sentence, write the indefinite pronoun and then write the correct form of the verb.

16. Nobody (know, knows) much about the Loch Ness monster.
17. Some of the Loch Ness visitors (have, has) photographed it.
18. All of the photographs of the monster (is, are) unclear.
19. (Does, Do) everybody know that Loch Ness is in Scotland?
20. Many of the observers (has, have) given their descriptions of the monster.
21. (Has, Have) anybody here seen the famous film of the monster?
22. Many (believes, believe) some animal does live in the lake.
23. Some (call, calls) it "Nessie, the Loch Ness Monster."
24. All of the evidence (indicates, indicate) a creature with a small head and a long neck.
25. Each of the photographs (make, makes) people want more.

Writing Theme
Lake Monsters

FOR MORE PRACTICE
See page 464.

Writing Theme: Lake Monsters

Other related areas students might wish to explore as writing topics include the following:

- large aquatic animals
- dinosaurs that lived in water
- the "Abominable Snowman," or Yeti
- Sasquatch or Bigfoot

Answers to Practice Your Skills

A. Concept Check
Indefinite Pronouns

1. Anything, Singular
2. Everyone, Singular
3. few, Plural
4. Some, Plural
5. No one, Singular
6. Many, Plural
7. None, Singular
8. Anyone, Singular
9. One, Singular
10. Another, Singular
11. Neither, Singular
12. Both, Plural
13. None, Plural
14. somebody, Singular
15. Everything, Singular

B. Concept Check
Verbs and Indefinite Pronouns

16. Nobody, knows
17. Some, have photographed
18. All, are
19. everybody, Does know
20. Many, have given
21. anybody, Has seen
22. Many, believe
23. Some, call
24. All, indicates
25. Each, makes

Literature Connection

Ask students to identify the pronouns (underlined here) in this last stanza of Dorothy Parker's "The Choice."

"He'd have given me laces rare,
Dresses that glimmered with frosty sheen.
Shining ribbons to wrap my hair,
Horses to draw me, as fine as a queen.
You—you'd only to whistle low.
Gayly I followed wherever you led.
I took you, and I let him go—
Somebody ought to examine my head!"

DEMONSTRATIVE AND INTERROGATIVE PRONOUNS

Objectives

- To identify and use demonstrative and interrogative pronouns

Writing

- To use demonstrative and interrogative pronouns correctly in writing

Teaching Strategies

HELPFUL HINT Remind students that a word's part of speech depends on what the word does in a sentence. *This, that, these,* and *those* function as adjectives when they precede a noun *(this* horse, *that* exam). When these words stand alone, however, they are demonstrative pronouns. (What is *this?)* (For more about demonstrative adjectives, see the bottom of page 460.)

STUMBLING BLOCK Students may find their greatest difficulty with interrogative pronouns in *who/whom* dilemmas. You may want to teach the lesson on page 452 before students complete the exercises on pages 450 and 451.

Writing Theme: Small Towns

Other related areas students might wish to explore as writing topics include the following:

- life today in nearby small towns
- town meetings
- small towns of historical importance, such as a presidential birthplace
- Thornton Wilder's classic play *Our Town*

Answers to Practice Your Skills

A. Concept Check

Demonstrative and Interrogative Pronouns

Answers are shown on page.

Writing **TIP**

You can use demonstrative pronouns to connect your ideas in a paragraph. Demonstrative pronouns used in this way are called **transitions.**

The puppy in the middle had white paws.
I chose the puppy in the middle.

The puppy in the middle had white paws.
That's the one I chose.

Writing Theme
Small Towns

DEMONSTRATIVE AND INTERROGATIVE PRONOUNS

A **demonstrative pronoun** is used to single out one or more persons or things referred to in the sentence. An **interrogative pronoun** is used to ask a question.

Demonstrative pronouns help you point out certain persons and things. Interrogative pronouns help you ask questions.

The **demonstrative pronouns** are *this, that, these,* and *those. This* and *these* point to persons or things that are near. *That* and *those* point to persons or things that are farther away.

This is a gazebo.	*These* are the local stores.
That is the town square.	*Those* are the restaurants.

The **interrogative pronouns** are *who, whose, whom, which,* and *what.* You use them to ask questions.

Who is the mayor?	*Which* is her house?
Whose is the blue house?	*What* did you ask me?

Whom should I see to learn about the local history?

Practice Your Skills

A. CONCEPT CHECK

Demonstrative and Interrogative Pronouns Write the correct demonstrative or interrogative pronouns given in parentheses.

1. (This, That) is the general store we are entering now.
2. (Who, Whom) owns the store?
3. Let me see! (Who, Whom) can we ask?
4. I remember! (This, That) is the Kellers' store.
5. (This, That) is their diner across the street too.
6. (Whose, Whom) are the other stores?
7. (Which, What) is the one you want to know about?
8. Well, to (who, whom) does the clothing store belong?
9. I'm sorry! (Which, What) did you ask me?
10. Never mind! (These, Those) are beautiful quilts on the counter over there.

450 Grammar Handbook

11. (These, Those) right in front of you were made by Grandma Keller's quilting group.
12. Look! Are (these, those) old-fashioned candies on the far counter?
13. (This, That) in my hand used to be called penny candy.
14. (Which, What) are the ones on the strips of paper called?
15. I think (these, those) are called buttons.

B. DRAFTING SKILL

Using Demonstrative and Interrogative Pronouns Write the following sentences, adding the correct demonstrative and interrogative pronouns.

16. ________ could resist a town called Nameless?
17. ________ is one of the places mentioned in the book *Blue Highways*.
18. By ________ was the book written?
19. William Least Heat Moon was the author. ________ is one of the places he visited, right here on the map.
20. ________ are some of the other places he visited?
21. Dime Box, Hungry Horse, and Salt Wells— ________ are all places in his book.
22. ________ did he like better, Nameless or Wolf Point?
23. I don't know. ________ can I ask to find out?
24. May I use those travel books? ________ are they?
25. ________ on this shelf are all mine, but ________ over there are my mother's.

Portrait of Orleans (1950), Edward Hopper.

C. APPLICATION IN WRITING

Dialogue Imagine that you are giving someone a tour of your favorite small town. Write a brief dialogue between you and your friend in which you point out attractions of the town and your friend asks you questions. Be sure to include at least four demonstrative and interrogative pronouns in your dialogue.

FOR MORE PRACTICE
See page 465.

B. Drafting Skill
Using Demonstrative and Interrogative Pronouns

Answers may vary. Suggested responses are given below.

16. Who
17. That
18. whom
19. This
20. What
21. those
22. Which
23. Whom
24. Whose
25. These, those

C. Application in Writing
Dialogue

Answers will vary. Dialogues should be realistic and include at least four demonstrative and interrogative pronouns. You might have students underline the demonstrative and interrogative pronouns in their dialogues.

ART NOTE

Edward Hopper (1882–1967), an American painter and realist in style, was fascinated with the play of light. Like many of his paintings, this one shows a solitary figure under the red awning on a deserted street. The setting is Orleans, a small town on Cape Cod in Massachusetts, where Hopper spent his summers.

Ask students to notice the effect of light and shadow on the facades of the buildings. What emotions does this play of light arouse?

USING *WHO, WHOM,* AND *WHOSE*

Objective

- To use *who, whom,* and *whose* correctly in sentences

Teaching Strategies

SPEAKING AND LISTENING

Students may avoid using *whom* because it is practically never used in spoken and informal English. Accustom them to the sound of *whom* by reading aloud the examples in the text and additional examples, such as these:

Whom did you meet?

For *whom* is this valentine?

Additional Resource

Grammar and Usage Practice Book, pp. 29–30

Writing Theme: Origami

Other related areas students might wish to explore as writing topics include the following:

- paper cut art
- Japanese wood block prints
- Mexican folk art
- African masks

Answers to Practice Your Skills

Concept Check

Who, Whom,* and *Whose

1. Who
2. Whom
3. who
4. whom
5. Whose
6. whose
7. Who
8. Whose
9. Whose
10. whom

USING *WHO, WHOM,* AND *WHOSE*

The words *who, whom,* and *whose* may be used as **interrogative pronouns** to ask questions.

Who, whom, and *whose* are often used to ask questions. When that is their function, they are called **interrogative pronouns.** *Who* is the subject form. It is used as the subject of a verb. *Whom* is the object form. It is used as the direct object of a verb or as the object of a preposition.

Who taught you how to do origami? (*Who* is the subject of *taught.*)
Whom did you ask? (*Whom* is the object of *did ask.*)
For *whom* is this gift? (*Whom* is the object of *for.*)

Whose is the possessive form. It can modify a noun: *Whose work* is this? Alone, it can be the subject or object of a verb.

Whose paper sculptures did you see? (*Whose* modifies *sculptures.*)
Whose did you like? (*Whose* is the object of *did like.*)
Whose are those paper dragons? (*Whose* is the subject of *are.*)

Writing Theme
Origami

Practice Your Skills

CONCEPT CHECK

Who, Whom,* and *Whose Complete these sentences with *who, whom,* or *whose.*

1. ________ knows the origin of origami?
2. ________ did you ask about it?
3. Well, ________ is the expert here?
4. Let me see. To ________ should I direct you?
5. ________ skill in paper folding is best?
6. That is, ________ is the most delicate work?
7. ________ is likely to receive the blue ribbon?
8. ________ are those wonderful origami figures that move?
9. I don't know. ________ are you looking at?
10. For ________ did you buy this paper rose?

CHECK POINT

MIXED REVIEW • PAGES 448–452

A. Write the correct verb from those in parentheses.

1. Believe it or not, everything about tugboats (is, are) interesting.
2. Each (has, have) its own history of adventure and work.
3. Any of the stories (is, are) worth telling.
4. People are aware of some jobs tugs do, and many (knows, know) that tugs help huge ships into harbor.
5. Few, however, (is, are) aware of their rescue work.
6. (Has, Have) anybody read *Tugboat: The Moran Story?*
7. Some of the book (describes, describe) daring rescues.
8. One of the saddest (was, were) the story of the *Saale* and the *Main*.
9. Both (was, were) destroyed by fire, despite the valiant efforts of fireboats and tugboats.
10. All of Hoboken (was, were) seen from a great distance; the blaze was so enormous.
11. Some of the crew members (was, were) saved.
12. (Does, Do) anything compare with such a frightening fire?

B. Complete the following sentences by adding the correct demonstrative and interrogative pronouns.

13. Welcome aboard! ________ is a tugboat, the *Seaworthy*.
14. Careful! Pieces of equipment are everywhere, and ________ at your feet are hawsers.
15. ________ is a hawser? Well, it is a heavy rope used for mooring the boat or for pulling cargo.
16. For ________ of the crew do you have questions?
17. ________ is the question about the posts? Is it yours?
18. ________ over there are called bitts. Deckhands connect the hawsers to the bitts on the tug.
19. ________ connects them to the barge? We deckhands do!
20. ________ is the most interesting job of all the crew members?
21. ________ is the captain in the distance. His is the best job.
22. ________ seems harder, the deckhand's job or the captain's? The deckhand's job is harder physically, but the captain's is more difficult.

Writing Theme
Tugboats

CHECK  POINT

Writing Theme Tugboats

Other related areas students might wish to explore as writing topics include the following:

- how steam engines and diesel engines work
- garbage barges
- work of the U.S. Coast Guard
- cargo ships

MIXED REVIEW • PAGES 448–452

You may wish to use this activity to check students' mastery of the following concepts:

- indefinite pronouns
- demonstrative and interrogative pronouns
- using *who, whom,* and *whose*

A. Answers are shown on page.

B. Answers may vary. Suggested answers are shown below.

13. This
14. these (or those)
15. What
16. whom
17. Whose
18. Those
19. Who
20. Whose
21. That
22. Which

REFLEXIVE AND INTENSIVE PRONOUNS

Objectives
- To identify reflexive and intensive pronouns

Writing
- To use reflexive and intensive pronouns correctly in writing

Teaching Strategies

INDIVIDUALIZING INSTRUCTION: ESL STUDENTS Because reflexive and intensive pronoun forms are identical, distinguishing between these forms may be difficult. You may wish to have these students focus instead on Exercises B and C.

SPEAKING AND LISTENING
Caution students to avoid using *theirselves* and *hisself,* forms often used by mistake in speaking. Read aloud the Writing Tip and ask students to correct additional examples:

First prize was awarded to Treneice and *myself.* (me)

The winners were Lon and *myself.* (I)

Additional Resource

Grammar and Usage Practice Book, p. 31

Writing Theme: Unusual Pastimes

Other related areas students might wish to explore as writing topics include the following:
- hang gliding
- indoor rock climbing
- Outward Bound programs
- one-of-a-kind collections

Answers to Practice Your Skills

A. Concept Check
Reflexive and Intensive Pronouns
1. myself, Intensive
2. himself, Intensive
3. yourself, Reflexive
4. themselves, Intensive
5. themselves, Reflexive
6. itself, Intensive

REFLEXIVE AND INTENSIVE PRONOUNS

Pronouns that end in *-self* or *-selves* are called either **intensive** or **reflexive pronouns.**

The reflexive and intensive pronouns are *myself, yourself, herself, himself, itself, ourselves,* and *themselves.*

A **reflexive pronoun** refers to an action performed by the subject of the sentence. The meaning of the sentence is incomplete without the reflexive pronoun.

We pride *ourselves* on our creativity. (If you remove *ourselves,* the meaning of the sentence is incomplete.)
Erika bought *herself* a needlepoint kit.

An **intensive pronoun** is used to emphasize a noun or a pronoun. It does not add information to a sentence, and it may be removed without changing the meaning of the sentence.

I *myself* have an unusual hobby. (If you remove *myself,* the meaning of the sentence does not change.)
Zeke made this paper *himself.*

Writing TIP

When you use a reflexive pronoun, recall that it must refer to a noun or a pronoun that comes before it.
Incorrect: Bob and myself attended the meeting.
Correct: Bob and I attended the meeting.

Practice Your Skills

A. CONCEPT CHECK

Reflexive and Intensive Pronouns Write the reflexive and intensive pronouns in the sentences. Then label them *Reflexive* or *Intensive.*

Writing Theme Unusual Pastimes

1. I myself have never tried mud walking.
2. Willem, a Dutch visitor, has done it many times himself.
3. "If you want to give yourself a treat," he says, "you should try it!"
4. The Dutch themselves call the activity *Wadlopen.*
5. Each year about 30,000 people revitalize themselves by walking through the mud off the coast of the Netherlands.
6. The Netherlands itself is not particularly muddy, but the West Frisian Islands are, especially at low tide.

7. "I have to buy myself a new pair of tennis shoes after a trip from the mainland to a nearby island," says Willem.
8. The monks in the Middle Ages made the trip themselves.
9. However, such a monk was not enjoying himself.
10. He himself was taking cattle to pasture on an island.
11. You may ask yourself about the sanity of mud walking.
12. People on the islands wonder about it themselves.
13. My sister Celia said she would be willing to try it herself.
14. She often challenges herself by doing strenuous activities.
15. Willem invited us to find out for ourselves that walking knee-deep in mud is, indeed, strenuous.

FOR MORE PRACTICE
See page 465.

B. DRAFTING SKILL

Using Reflexive and Intensive Pronouns Write the correct reflexive or intensive pronoun to complete each sentence.

16. Have you ever prepared ________ for a competition?
17. The Jamaicans ________ were in a quandary.
18. They wanted to train ________ for bobsled competitions.
19. However, even one snowflake by ________ is unheard of on their island, not to mention a snow storm.
20. Preparation ________ presents some challenges.
21. "We ________ practice sledding on the beach!" said one aspiring bobsledder.
22. "I made ________ a dummy sled with wheels."
23. He also times ________ on how fast he can push the sled.
24. Enthusiasts on Jamaica and other islands in the Caribbean have formed ________ into a group.
25. "We pride ________ on being goodwill ambassadors first, and bobsledders second," added another sand sledder.

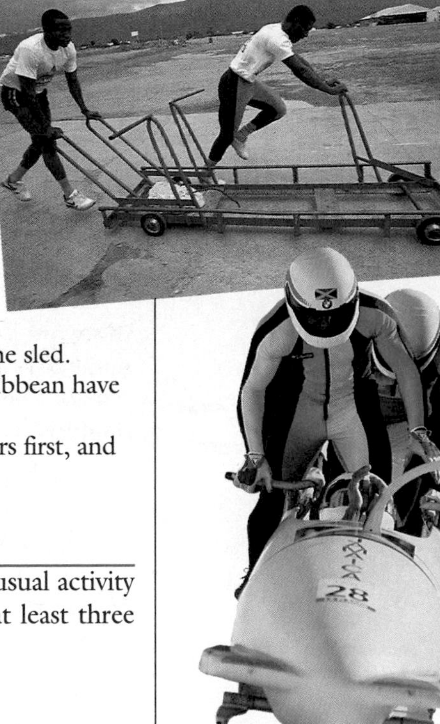

The Jamaican bobsled team trained on sleds with wheels to prepare for the 1992 Winter Olympics in Albertville, France.

C. APPLICATION IN WRITING

Personal Narrative Write a paragraph about an unusual activity you have done with your friends or classmates. Use at least three of the following reflexive and intensive pronouns.

myself	yourselves	herself
ourselves	himself	themselves

7. myself, Reflexive
8. themselves, Intensive
9. himself, Reflexive
10. himself, Intensive
11. yourself, Reflexive
12. themselves, Intensive
13. herself, Intensive
14. herself, Reflexive
15. ourselves, Intensive (*for ourselves* does not change meaning of sentence.)

B. Drafting Skill
Using Reflexive and Intensive Pronouns

16. yourself
17. themselves
18. themselves
19. itself
20. itself
21. ourselves
22. myself
23. himself
24. themselves
25. ourselves

C. Application in Writing
Personal Narrative

Paragraphs will vary but should demonstrate correct usage of reflexive and intensive pronouns.

Pronouns and Their Antecedents

Objectives

- To identify pronouns and their antecedents
- To use pronouns that agree with their antecedents

Writing

- To use proofreading skills to correct errors in pronoun-antecedent agreement

Teaching Strategies

INDIVIDUALIZING INSTRUCTION: LEP STUDENTS Encourage students to work in pairs to write three example sentences and to draw an arrow from each pronoun to its antecedent. If students have made a chart of pronouns in their notebooks, have them use those charts to check that each pronoun agrees in number with its antecedent.

Additional Resource

Grammar and Usage Practice Book, p. 32

Pronouns and Their Antecedents

The **antecedent** of a pronoun is a noun or another pronoun for which the pronoun stands.

A personal pronoun, you remember, is used in place of a noun. This noun is the word to which the pronoun refers and is called its **antecedent.** The noun usually comes first, either in the same sentence or in the sentence before it.

We talked to *Greg. He* is the computer expert.
(*He* stands for *Greg. Greg* is the antecedent.)
The *students* had turned on *their* personal computers.
(*Their* stands for *students. Students* is the antecedent.)

Pronouns may be the antecedents of other pronouns.

Does *everybody* have *her* manual? (*Everybody,* which is singular, is the antecedent of *her.*)
All of the students have brought *theirs.* (*All* is plural here and is the antecedent of *theirs.*)

Pronoun and Antecedent Agreement

A pronoun must agree with its antecedent in number. Here, the word *agree* means that the pronoun must be the same in number as its antecedent. The word *number* means *singular* or *plural.* The pronoun must be singular if the word it stands for is singular, and it must be plural if the word it stands for is plural.

The programmers tested *their* new software.
(*Programmers* is plural; *their* is plural.)
Mr. Johnson turned on *his* terminal.
(*Mr. Johnson* is singular; *his* is singular.)
Nobody left *his* or *her* workstation.
(*Nobody* is singular; *his* and *her* are singular.)

When the antecedent refers to both males and females, many people prefer to use the phrase *his or her.*

Writing TIP

To avoid *his or her* phrases, try using plural subjects.
Each student turned on his or her computer.
Better:
All the students turned on their computers.

Literature Connection

The following paragraph from *The Day Lincoln Was Shot* by Jim Bishop describes what happened at Ford's Theatre in Washington, D.C., right after John Wilkes Booth shot President Lincoln. Have students identify the antecedent (underlined here) of each italicized pronoun.

"The audience did not understand. *They* watched the running actor, and *he* fell again. *He* stood and, as *he* got offstage, *he* was limping on the outside of *his* left foot; in effect, walking on *his* ankle."

Practice Your Skills

A. CONCEPT CHECK

Pronoun-Antecedent Agreement Write the pronouns and their antecedents from the following sentences. Note how the pronouns can link sentences together and avoid awkward repetition.

1. Engineers can now fit computer circuitry into a tiny square. They call the square a chip.
2. Mr. Saez held up a chip. It was quite small.
3. Ms. Estes held up a quartz rock. She explained that silicon comes from quartz.
4. Silicon is important because it is used to make chips.
5. Because of this technology, many people now own their own personal computers.
6. Anyone can buy his or her own PC at a relatively low price.
7. Computer chips are used in many things. They can be found in watches, cars, games, and telephones.
8. Have you ever seen a computer chip with your own eyes?
9. Daryll says that he saw a chip under a microscope. He thought it looked like the view of a city from an airplane.
10. Tricia said she once saw an interesting picture. It showed an ant carrying a computer chip.
11. When the chip was first developed, scientists called it the integrated circuit.
12. The first completely electronic digital computer was built in 1946. It was huge compared to the computers of today.
13. Less than fifty years ago, only top-level scientists used computers. They were an elite group.
14. Now, even children use computers in their classrooms for both games and lessons.
15. We have come to rely on the tiny chip in almost every part of our lives. It helps us do everything from telling time to balancing our budgets.

Writing Theme
Computers

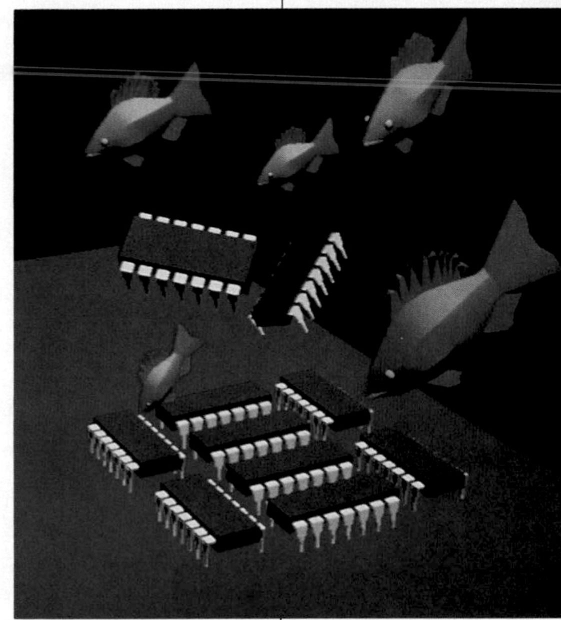

Fish and Chips © 1985 Vibeke Sorensen. Produced at the Caltech CSCGG.

Writing Theme: Computers

Other related areas students might wish to explore as writing topics include the following:

- latest computer games
- computers in medical research
- computer-generated art
- magazines for computer users

Answers to Practice Your Skills

A. Concept Check
Pronoun-Antecedent Agreement

1. They, Engineers
2. It, chip
3. She, Ms. Estes
4. it, Silicon
5. their, people (*This* is used as a demonstrative adjective.)
6. his, her; Anyone
7. They, chips
8. your, you
9. he, Daryll; He, Daryll; it, chip
10. she, Tricia; It, picture
11. it, chip
12. It, computer
13. They, scientists
14. their, children
15. our, We; It, chip; us, We; our, We

ART NOTE

Tell students that *French fries* are called *chips* in Great Britain and that fish and chips is an extremely popular dish there. Students will then understand the artist's pun in *Fish and Chips.* Sorensen used a computer to produce this three-dimensional image of goldfish and computer chips. You might ask students to compare her computer art with Hopper's painting on page 451. Encourage them to explain which piece of art they prefer, and why.

B. Drafting Skill
Using Pronoun-Antecedent Agreement

16. her
17. her
18. He
19. them
20. his or her
21. their
22. his or her
23. its
24. his
25. their

C. Proofreading Skill
Correcting Errors in Agreement

Errors are underlined on page. Corrections are shown below.

"Someone may spend his or her life joining groups, but that's not for me," said Millie. "Then I bought myself a computer and didn't know what to do next!" Millie and others have found answers to their questions by joining computer user groups. One of the oldest groups got its start in 1977. Today the group has 32,000 people on its membership list. Anyone who owns a computer can increase his or her knowledge by sharing information in a group. "We talk about programs, PCs, and problems in our group. A software company even asked us to test a brand-new computer game. The company actually used one of our suggestions to improve the game." All of the members enjoyed giving their opinions of the game.

B. DRAFTING SKILL

Using Pronoun-Antecedent Agreement Write the following sentences, adding pronouns that agree with the antecedents.

16. Juanita Lewis says computers changed ________ life.
17. Blind since birth, Lewis runs ________ own company.
18. Ira Gold, a paraplegic, agrees. ________ uses a computer to write a weekly advice column.
19. People with disabilities have discovered that computers can open many doors for ________.
20. Not everybody must use ________ fingers and type on a keyboard to input information.
21. Because of voice-activation technology, Juanita and Ira can now dictate ________ letters and reports to the computer.
22. Thanks to some very clever software programs, anybody can add voice activation to ________ computer.
23. One of the software packages has 30,000 words in ________ program.
24. Interestingly, Shakespeare used about 30,000 words in ________ writing.
25. The creators of the software designed ________ program to recognize this large number of words.

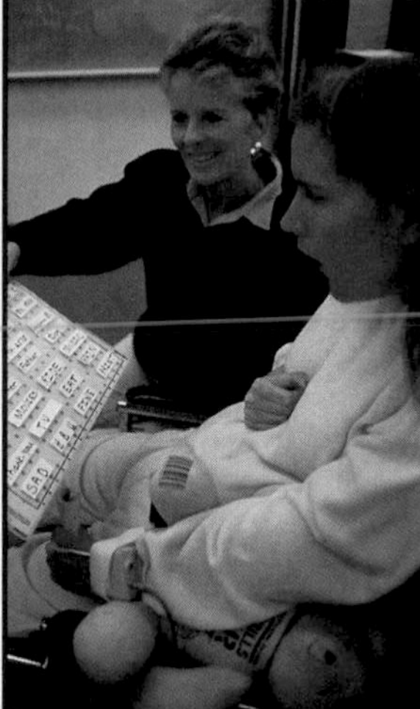

A computerized voice synthesizer allows a disabled person to communicate without speaking.

C. PROOFREADING SKILL

Correcting Errors in Agreement Rewrite the following passage, correcting all errors, especially errors in pronoun-antecedent agreement. (15 errors)

"Someone may spend their life joining groups, but that's not for me," said Millie. "Then I bought myself a computer and didn't know what to do next! Millie and others have found ansers to his or her questions by joining computer user groups one of the oldest groups got their start in 1977. Today the group has 32,000 people on it's membership list. Anyone who owns a computer can increase their knowlege by sharing information in a group. "We talk about programs, PCs, and problems in their group. A software company even asked us to test a brand-new computer game. The Company actually used one of their suggestions to improve the game." All of the members' enjoyed. Giving his or her opinions of the game.

FOR MORE PRACTICE
See page 466.

458 Grammar Handbook

CHECKPOINT
MIXED REVIEW • PAGES 454–458

Write the correct pronoun to complete each sentence. Be sure that each pronoun agrees with its antecedent.

1. Some people must be born with adventure in ________ heart.
2. Why else would they subject ________ to all kinds of danger?
3. Anyone with an ounce of common sense would not leave the safety of ________ home.
4. I ________ can't understand what makes them do it.
5. Sir Francis Chichester often challenged ________.
6. When Sir Francis was sixty-five, ________ sailed alone around the world.
7. More recently, a woman proved ________ equal to the same challenge.
8. Naomi James undertook this adventure in 1977. ________ sailing companion was a kitten named Boris.
9. The voyage lasted about 272 days, and ________ was filled with beautiful sights, dangerous storms, and countless problems.
10. Would you be able to spend that much time all by ________?
11. The ship's rudder gave Naomi problems. ________ tried to repair ________ herself.
12. Five days before Christmas, a powerful storm pounded the ship. ________ howling winds created massive waves.
13. Fortunately, Naomi kept a log of ________ journey.
14. We can read parts of her journal ________ in *Alone Around the World.*
15. By reading Naomi's book, we can take ________ on a thrilling adventure without leaving ________ chairs!
16. Neither Sir Francis nor Naomi can be blamed if ________ was frightened. Both ________ and ________ faced fierce dangers alone.
17. Naomi wrote: "I know that the . . . hours and days of this voyage have enriched ________ life immeasurably."
18. Sir Francis was knighted after ________ voyage.
19. After ________ voyage, Naomi was named Dame Commander of the Order of the British Empire.
20. Sadly, Boris the kitten received no honors. ________ trip ended when a wave swept ________ overboard.

Writing Theme
Solo Adventures

CHECK  POINT

Writing Theme: Solo Adventures

Other related areas students might wish to explore as writing topics include the following:

- solo aviators
- flights of the Mercury program astronauts
- the "adventure" of being a "solo" naturalist, such as Dian Fossey or Farley Mowat
- a fictional or real-life "castaway" tale

MIXED REVIEW • PAGES 454–458

You may wish to use this activity to check students' mastery of the following concepts:

- reflexive and intensive pronouns
- pronouns and their antecedents

1. their
2. themselves
3. his or her
4. myself
5. himself
6. he
7. herself
8. Her
9. it
10. yourself
11. She; it
12. Its
13. her
14. ourselves
15. ourselves; our
16. he or she; he; she
17. my
18. his
19. her
20. His; him

SPECIAL PRONOUN PROBLEMS

Objectives

- To use *we* and *us* correctly with nouns
- To use the pronouns *them* and *those* correctly

Writing

- To revise writing, correcting errors in pronoun usage

Teaching Strategies

INDIVIDUALIZING INSTRUCTION: ESL STUDENTS Because they are not yet familiar enough with subject and object pronouns to "hear" the correct choice, these students may not be able to determine whether *we* or *us* is correct just by testing the pronoun alone. Work with these students to do Exercise A on page 461 as an oral drill.

HELPFUL HINT Point out that what is said about *those* also applies to *this, that,* and *these.* Ask volunteers to make up two sentences that illustrate the use of each of these words, first as a pronoun and then as an adjective.

Additional Resource

Grammar and Usage Practice Book, p. 33

SPECIAL PRONOUN PROBLEMS

When using phrases like *we girls* and *us boys,* choose the correct pronoun by dropping the noun and saying the sentence with only the pronoun.

You may need to decide which of two similar pronouns is the correct choice. The following are some useful suggestions.

We and *Us* Used with Nouns

When you use phrases such as *we students* and *us workers,* be sure that you use the correct pronoun. To tell which pronoun to use, drop the noun and say the sentence without it:

Problem (We, Us) boys study hard.
Solution We study hard. = We boys study hard.

Problem The mayor thanked (we, us) girls.
Solution The mayor thanked us. = The mayor thanked us girls.

Writing TIP

Remember that careful writers never use *them* as an adjective. For example, "them pictures" is incorrect. "Those pictures" is correct.

Using the Pronoun *Them*

The word *them* is always a pronoun. It is always used as the object of a verb or a preposition.

The speaker greeted *them.* (direct object of a verb)
She gave *them* a booklet. (indirect object of a verb)
The data was useful to *them.* (object of the preposition *to*)

Using *Those*

You have already learned that *those* can be used as a demonstrative pronoun (page 450). Sometimes, however, *those* is used as an adjective. An adjective is a word that modifies a noun or a pronoun. If a noun appears immediately after it, *those* is probably an adjective. Used without a noun, *those* is a pronoun.

Those are the new career posters I ordered. (pronoun: subject of a verb)
Those posters are outdated. (adjective modifying *posters*)

Practice Your Skills

A. CONCEPT CHECK

Problem Pronouns Write the correct pronoun in parentheses from each sentence.

1. (We, Us) students started a newsletter about careers.
2. Finding unusual jobs was important to (we, us) writers.
3. Many careers sound dull. (Them, Those) are ones to avoid.
4. An employment agency invited (we, us) reporters to a career fair.
5. "(Them, Those) are interesting exhibits," I said.
6. One of (them, those) career speakers was especially interesting.
7. A bill collector told (we, us) students about his work.
8. "(We, Us) collectors perform an important service," he said.
9. "Some people truly want to pay their bills. (Them, Those) are the ones I try to help."
10. "I help (them, those) find ways to pay their debts."
11. "In fact, (we, us) callers need to be understanding."
12. "However, when people lie, it is hard to make (them, those) tell us the truth."

Writing Theme
Unusual Careers

FOR MORE PRACTICE
See page 466.

B. REVISION SKILL

Correcting Pronoun Errors Write the paragraph below, correcting errors in the use of *we, us, them,* and *those.* If a sentence is correct, write *Correct.*

[13]Many of we inventors have long lists of inventions that failed. [14]We try to forget them inventions. [15]Often it is not enough for us inventors to create a successful product. [16]Often us creators also have to design and make the machines that produce the products. [17]Those are usually the hardest to invent. [18]When people have problems, I simply try to solve those. [19]Most of we inventors are just creative problem solvers. [20]Them problems spark ideas in our minds, and we search for solutions. [21]The solutions sometimes present us inventors with other problems. [22]Them answers lead us to other questions until we creators find the final solution.

The prone bicycle shown here was demonstrated at the Human Powered Vehicle Festival in England. It puts the rider in a more powerful, if less comfortable, position than does a conventional bike.

Writing Theme: Unusual Careers

Other related areas students might wish to explore as writing topics include the following:

- professional magicians
- circus performers
- toy designers
- umpires and referees

Answers to Practice Your Skills

A. Concept Check
Pronoun Problems

Answers are shown on page.

B. Revision Skill
Correcting Pronoun Errors

Errors are underlined on page. Corrections are shown below.

13. us
14. those
15. Correct
16. we
17. Correct
18. them
19. us
20. Those
21. Correct
22. Those

CHECKPOINT

Writing Theme: Stories in Dance

Other related areas students might wish to explore as writing topics include the following:

- classical ballets, such as *The Nutcracker* and *Swan Lake*
- Native American dances, such as the Corn Dance and Buffalo Dance
- folk dances of South America
- choreography

MIXED REVIEW • PAGES 460–461

You may wish to use this activity to check students' mastery of the following concept:

- special pronoun problems

Answers are shown on page.

Writing Theme
Stories in Dance

CHECKPOINT

MIXED REVIEW • PAGES 460–461

Write the correct pronoun or adjective given in parentheses for each sentence. Some items covered earlier in this handbook are included.

1. Folk dances can be a mystery to (we, us) uninformed people.
2. (Them, Those) dances are often used for storytelling.
3. For example, Hawaiians use (them, their) hula dances to tell stories or describe places.
4. We can picture the places as dancers portray (them, those) with graceful movements.
5. The meaning of the dances is sometimes not clear because most of (them, those) have ancient origins.
6. (We, Us) dance fans enjoy watching dance dramas from India.
7. (Them, Those) are especially intricate dances.
8. All parts of the body are used in (them, those) to tell a story—even the eyes.
9. One of the dance styles, *Kathakali,* tells a complete story in (its, their) movements.
10. In some ways it seems like ballet to (we, us) observers.
11. *Manipuri* is one of (them, those) styles of dance that mimic nature.
12. A dancer portrays animals or weather in (his or her, their) movements.
13. Some dances from Balkan countries give (we, us) students of the dance some insight into history.
14. (Them, Those) dances reenact historic battles.
15. Male dancers usually portray Christians, Moors, or Turks in (them, those).
16. I could almost picture (me, myself) as a participant in a folk dance I saw while on vacation in Mexico.
17. The dancers wore traditional costumes, and (they, them) performed a battle between winter and summer.
18. During the dance, devils and death figures move in and out among (them, those) brightly clothed dancers.
19. Of course, it did not surprise (we, us) spectators that summer was victorious.
20. We thoroughly enjoyed (us, ourselves) even if we did not understand all the details of the dance.

ADDITIONAL PRACTICE

A. Using Personal Pronouns Write the correct pronoun from those given in parentheses. Then write whether the pronoun is in *Subject, Object,* or *Possessive* form.

1. Frontier settlers who lived along rivers had almost no entertainment in (they, them, their) lives.
2. William Chapman changed that. (He, Him, His) built the first showboat in 1831 in Pittsburgh with the intention of taking her south.
3. (She, Her, Hers) was named the *Floating Theatre.*
4. Chapman and (he, him, his) family headed for New Orleans.
5. (They, Them, Their) gave shows from landing to landing.
6. Talented people were (they, them, their).
7. At first the program was limited, but he expanded (it, its) by adding plays, songs, and dances.
8. Edna Ferber described showboats in (she, her, hers) novel.
9. (She, Her, Hers) was a lively and accurate account.
10. Lucky are (we, us, our) that Ferber wrote *Show Boat.*
11. Showboats are no longer available to (we, us, our).
12. (We, Us, Our) could have had such great fun!
13. The entertainment provided by motion pictures and the transportation cars offered finished (they, them, their) off.
14. In 1943, the showboat *Golden Rod* made (she, her, hers) last trip.
15. (She, Her, Hers) was the last of the great showboats.

B. Using Pronouns in Compound Subjects and Objects Write the correct pronoun from those given in parentheses.

16. You and (I, me) have heard of the Ringling brothers.
17. John Ringling is the most familiar to (we, us) and others.
18. (He, Him) and his brothers began in a small way.
19. The arts were important to (they, them) and their mother.
20. Their father and (she, her) often disagreed.
21. Performing seemed a waste of time to (he, him) and others of his age.
22. Thus, he never gave (she, her) or his sons any encouragement.
23. A stubborn group were (they, them) and John.
24. Their first show took John and (they, them) far from home.
25. Throughout the Midwest, (he, him) and (they, them) performed plays, music, acrobatics, juggling, and clowning.

GRAMMAR HANDBOOK 41

ADDITIONAL PRACTICE

Each of these exercises correlates to a section of Handbook 41, "Using Pronouns." The exercises may be used for more practice, for reteaching, or for review of the concepts presented.

Additional Resource

Grammar and Usage Practice Book, p. 35

Writing Theme: Traveling Entertainment

Other related areas students might wish to explore as writing topics include the following:

- traveling musical groups
- Ice Capades and other ice shows
- the Lipizzaner horse show
- road companies of Broadway shows

A. Using Personal Pronouns

1. their, Possessive
2. He, Subject
3. She, Subject
4. his, Possessive
5. They, Subject
6. they, Subject
7. it, Object
8. her, Possessive
9. Hers, Possessive
10. we, Subject
11. us, Object
12. We, Subject
13. them, Object
14. her, Possessive
15. She, Subject

B. Using Pronouns in Compound Subjects and Objects

Answers are shown on page.

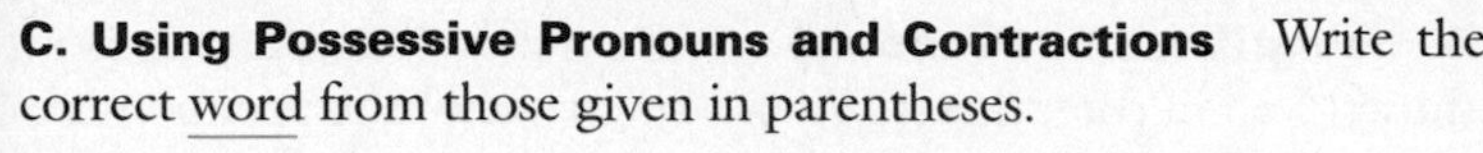

C. Using Possessive Pronouns and Contractions

Answers are shown on page.

D. Finding Indefinite Pronouns

36. all, have
37. Many, think
38. none, were
39. Each, was
40. Someone, remember
41. No one, was
42. Some, has
43. some, perform
44. Everything, is
45. Few, want; no one, is
46. Another, is
47. nobody, goes
48. everyone, enjoys
49. All, are
50. none, make

C. Using Possessive Pronouns and Contractions Write the correct word from those given in parentheses.

26. LIZ: (Whose, Who's) books are on the table?
27. TOM: (Their, They're) mine.
28. LIZ: (Your, You're) reading about equestrian shows?
29. TOM: (Its, It's) sad that (their, they're) not more popular.
30. LIZ: (Whose, Who's) this book about?
31. TOM: George Washington. The shows owe (their, they're) popularity partly to him.
32. He attended John Bill Ricketts's show of daring horsemanship and was (its, it's) greatest fan.
33. LIZ: (Your, You're) example surprises me. I didn't know horse shows went back that far.
34. TOM: Well, Liz, (your, you're) lack of knowledge is not unusual.
35. Unfortunately, (their, they're) part in our history is unknown to many.

D. Finding Indefinite Pronouns Write the indefinite pronoun from each sentence. Then choose the correct verb for the pronoun from those given in parentheses.

36. Probably all of us (has, have) seen puppet shows.
37. Many (thinks, think) of puppets as children's entertainment.
38. However, none of the early shows (was, were) just for children.
39. Each (was, were) entertainment for adults as well.
40. Someone may still (remembers, remember) *Uncle Tom's Cabin* being presented by a traveling marionette company.
41. No one in the audience (was, were) ever disappointed.
42. Some of this kind of entertainment (has, have) changed in recent years.
43. Today, some of the puppeteers (performs, perform) in malls.
44. Everything (is, are) uncertain about the future of puppetry.
45. Few (wants, want) to see puppets disappear, but no one (is, are) able to revive interest in traveling puppet theaters.
46. Another of the problems (is, are) television.
47. With puppets on the screen, nobody (goes, go) to real shows.
48. In China everyone still (enjoys, enjoy) puppet shows.
49. All of the expenses (is, are) paid by the government.
50. Otherwise, none of the shows (makes, make) enough money.

464 Grammar Handbook

E. Finding Demonstrative and Interrogative Pronouns Write and label each *Demonstrative* and *Interrogative* pronoun.

51. Which of the exhibits do you want to see?
52. What can I tell you?
53. This is the greatest traveling menagerie in the world.
54. These before you are exotic South American talking birds.
55. Whom are you addressing, sir?
56. Of course, those are purebred macaws and cockatoos.
57. Who thinks my animals are not authentic?
58. That, over there, is Madame Zazu, a trained cockatoo.
59. Whose is the brand new straw hat with the blue band?
60. Well, this is the rest of it. Madame Zazu was hungry!

F. Using Interrogative Pronouns Write the following sentences, adding the correct interrogative pronouns, *who, whom,* or *whose.*

61. ________ name is linked with the great circus managers?
62. To ________ are you referring?
63. ________ called himself the "Prince of Humbugs"?
64. ________ is the man known for labeling the exit the "exhibit of the egress" and tricking spectators into thinking they were seeing another exhibit like the tigress or the lioness?
65. ________ is this nickname? It's P. T. Barnum's, of course.

G. Using Reflexive and Intensive Pronouns Write the correct reflexive or intensive pronoun to complete each sentence.

66. At the circus we laugh (pronoun) silly over the antics of clowns.
67. Shakespeare (pronoun) wrote about clowns.
68. I found out for (pronoun) how clowns learn their craft.
69. Circus clowns do not train (pronoun); they go to college.
70. Irvin Feld (pronoun) started Clown College in 1968.
71. The college has distinguished (pronoun) as the only professional clown school.
72. Students throw (pronoun) into their studies and into the ring.
73. Peggy Williams is proud of (pronoun) as one of the first women to graduate from the college.
74. The art of clowning is (pronoun) kept a secret.
75. Three of the greatest clowns—Lou Jacobs, Otto Griebling, and Bobby Kay—taught the first classes (pronoun).

E. Finding Demonstrative and Interrogative Pronouns
51. Which, Interrogative
52. What, Interrogative
53. This, Demonstrative
54. These, Demonstrative
55. Whom, Interrogative
56. those, Demonstrative
57. Who, Interrogative
58. That, Demonstrative
59. Whose, Interrogative
60. this, Demonstrative

F. Using Interrogative Pronouns
61. Whose
62. whom
63. Who
64. Who
65. Whose

G. Using Reflexive and Intensive Pronouns
66. ourselves
67. himself
68. myself
69. themselves
70. himself
71. itself
72. themselves
73. herself
74. itself
75. themselves

H. Finding the Antecedents of Pronouns

76. circus
77. acts, stars
78. Irvin Feld; you
79. Gunther Gebel-Williams
80. model
81. Sigrid
82. son
83. Tina
84. No one
85. Many
86. John Culhane
87. horses
88. Gunther; elephants
89. We; Gunther
90. I; I

I. Using Pronouns

Answers are shown on page.

H. Finding the Antecedents of Pronouns Write the antecedents of the pronouns in italics in the following sentences.

76. After World War II, the circus in the United States seemed on *its* way out.
77. Circus acts and circus stars were losing *their* appeal.
78. At the time, Irvin Feld, the owner of Ringling Bros. and Barnum & Bailey Circus, was in Italy, and *he* saw "an act so spectacular that you get shivers up *your* spine."
79. The act was Gunther Gebel-Williams and *his* family.
80. Gunther married a lovely model, and *she* entered the circus.
81. Sigrid started in 1969. Everything scared *her* at first.
82. Gunther's son made *his* debut by riding a giraffe.
83. Stepdaughter Tina developed *her* own act with horses.
84. No one in *his or her* act outshone the great Gebel-Williams.
85. Many have showered *their* praises on this unique trainer.
86. "Gunther was the greatest all-around circus performer of his time," wrote John Culhane in *his* book *The American Circus.*
87. Gunther trained horses first. *They* are the most difficult.
88. Then Gunther advanced to elephants. *He* considers *them* to be highly intelligent animals.
89. We have held *our* breath as Gunther trains *his* tigers.
90. "I thank the animals who have done well . . . . All of *my* animals have come to expect *me* after the show."

I. Using Pronouns Write the correct words given in parentheses in the following sentences.

91. Traveling comes naturally to (we, us) balloonists.
92. Balloons are exciting, and people love to see (those, them).
93. (Those, Them) are the comments of fans of commercial ballooning.
94. (We, Us) pilots take our special balloons on the road.
95. (Those, Them) are the ones with faces or special shapes.
96. Flying at shows is dangerous for (we, us) performers.
97. I often refuse to perform at (those, them).
98. Mid-afternoons are the worst; (those, them) are the windiest times of day.
99. (We, Us) commercial balloonists try hard to please our clients.
100. However, if the weather is bad, we must sometimes disappoint (those, them).

466 Grammar Handbook

A. Personal Pronouns Write the correct pronoun from those given in parentheses for each sentence.

1. Music is the bond between Ivan and (I, me).
2. (Our, Ours) is a special relationship.
3. (He, him) and (I, me) are interested in electronic music.
4. A dedicated pair are (we, us).
5. Electronic music got (it, its) start around 1950.
6. Musicians in Paris developed (them, their) own style.
7. (They, Them) and (them, their) followers called (it, its) *musique concrete,* or concrete music.
8. Musical, natural, and electronic sounds were mixed by (they, them) and altered electronically to suit the music.
9. Ivan writes (him, his) own music and gives it to (I, me).
10. It is (I, me) who can be called the electronic whiz.

Writing Theme
Music

B. Pronouns and Contractions Label each italicized word as *Possessive, Demonstrative, Interrogative,* or *Contraction.*

11. *Who* started jazz in the United States?
12. *It's* largely attributed to former slaves from West Africa.
13. Later, gospel singers added *their* influence.
14. For *whom* did early jazz musicians play?
15. *They're* known to have played at weddings, funerals, and other community events in New Orleans.
16. *Those* were the times when people first heard jazz.
17. *What* are the songs they sang?
18. *That* is a good question. Much of *their* music was improvised.
19. Composer W. C. Handy helped jazz in *its* development.
20. *Whose* is the song "Memphis Blues"?
21. *This* is one of his.
22. *You're* sure it's Handy's song?
23. *Who's* known as "Satchmo"?
24. Louis Armstrong, the trumpeter, is, to answer *your* question.
25. *These* are some of his recordings; you may borrow them.

C. Indefinite, Reflexive, and Intensive Pronouns Identify each italicized pronoun as *Indefinite, Reflexive,* or *Intensive.* For indefinite pronouns, identify each as *Singular* or *Plural.*

26. I consider *myself* a purist about music.
27. *All* of today's computer music is not bad, I will admit.

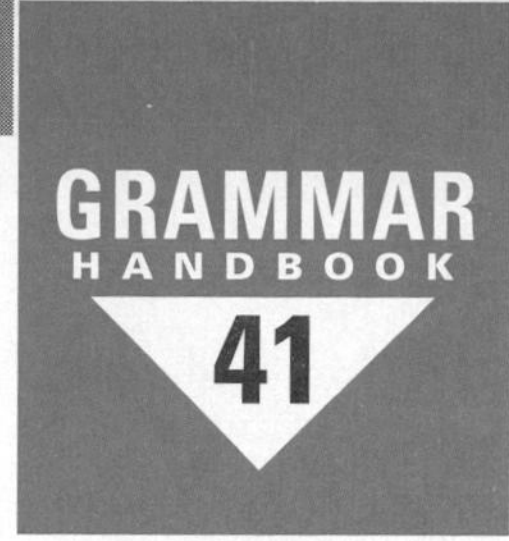

REVIEW

These exercises may be used as mixed review or as an informal evaluation of the skills presented in Handbook 41, "Using Pronouns."

Additional Resources

Grammar and Usage Practice Book, p. 36
Tests and Writing Assessment Prompts, Mastery Test, pp. 19–20
Elaboration, Revision, and Proofreading Practice, p. 28

Writing Theme: Music

Other related areas students might wish to explore as writing topics include the following:

- synthesizers and digital sampling
- unusual instruments
- various kinds of vocal or choral music
- Quincy Jones, music producer
- how to write a song

A. Personal Pronouns

Answers are shown on page.

B. Pronouns and Contractions

11. Who, Interrogative
12. It's, Contraction
13. their, Possessive
14. whom, Interrogative
15. They're, Contraction
16. Those, Demonstrative
17. What, Interrogative
18. That, Demonstrative; their, Possessive
19. its, Possessive
20. Whose, Interrogative
21. This, Demonstrative
22. You're, Contraction
23. Who's, Contraction and Interrogative
24. your, Possessive
25. These, Demonstrative

C. Indefinite, Reflexive, and Intensive Pronouns

26. myself, Reflexive
27. All, Indefinite, Singular
28. everything, Indefinite, Singular
29. anyone, Indefinite, Singular
30. someone, Indefinite, Singular
31. Some, Indefinite, Plural
32. themselves, Intensive
33. yourself, Reflexive
34. many, Indefinite, Plural
35. themselves, Reflexive
36. No one, Indefinite, Singular
37. ourselves, Reflexive
38. Few, Indefinite, Plural
39. myself, Intensive
40. anything, Indefinite, Singular

D. Agreement and Other Problems

41. We kids are forming our own band and will play homemade instruments.
42. None of us have played a light-bulb rattle before.
43. Correct
44. Joe's mother would not let us creators use her good crystal glasses as instruments.
45. Of course everyone knows that crystal makes the best sound.
46. Those glasses, filled with water, make a singing tone.
47. Correct
48. Those are the bumps you have to rub with a stick in order to make sound.
49. All of us budding musicians have also made panpipes out of plastic tubing.
50. Correct

28. Personally, I find that *everything* about computerized music makes me shudder!
29. How can *anyone* enjoy mathematical music?
30. Imagine, *someone* must convert sounds into numbers to produce music.
31. *Some* of my best friends think I am crazy.
32. They *themselves* listen only to those awful sounds.
33. However, how can you call *yourself* an expert if you do not also listen to music made from instruments?
34. It is true that *many* of the great musicians were spontaneous.
35. Musicians must train *themselves* how to interpret music and how to be creative.
36. *No one* can interpret emotions with fake, computer instruments!
37. With artificial sounds are we depriving *ourselves* of the clear notes produced by real instruments?
38. *Few* think computers are more exciting than musicians that perform live.
39. I *myself* have seen many great, exciting performers.
40. I still think *anything,* including piano lessons, is more exciting than music from a computer!

D. Agreement and Other Problems Some sentences below contain errors in pronoun use or pronoun-antecedent agreement. Write the sentences correctly. If a sentence does not contain an error, write *Correct.*

41. Us kids are forming our own band and will play homemade instruments.
42. None of us has played a light-bulb rattle before.
43. We are willing to try our hand at it, though.
44. Joe's mother would not let we creators use her good crystal glasses as instruments.
45. Of course everyone know that crystal makes the best sound.
46. Them glasses, filled with water, make a singing tone.
47. Leon's father let him use a saw to make rasps.
48. Them are the bumps you have to rub with a stick in order to make sound.
49. All of we budding musicians has also made panpipes out of plastic tubing.
50. Those are the instruments we are most proud of!

WRITING CONNECTIONS

Elaboration, Revision, and Proofreading

Revise the following autobiographical incident by using the directions at the bottom of the page. Then proofread the passage, looking especially for errors in the use of pronouns. Also check for other grammatical errors and errors in capitalization, punctuation, and spelling.

[1]I'll never forget the first time I saw a rattlesnake. [2]People have many mistaken ideas about snakes. [3]Jim and Willie and me was camping in the mountains, and Jim and Willie and me decided to go for a hike. [4]Each of my friends had their own idea about where we should go, but we finally settled on a trail. [5]Jim and myself lead the way, and Willie followed. [6]I started to step over a rock and noticed something in the way. [7]Its funny now as I think about all the things that went through my mind so quickly. [8]I realized that the thing in the way was a snake. [9]I noticed that it was a big snake. [10]I heard the hiss and the awful Rattles. [11]All at once I yelped. [12]I leapt into the air. [13]I jumped backward. [14]Jim and Willie looked frozen; neither could move their legs. [15]The snake slithered into the bushes, and us hikers watched more carefuly where we stepped after that.

1. Delete the sentence that doesn't belong.
2. Use a pronoun to avoid repeating the names in sentence 3.
3. After sentence 4, add these details to set the scene: "We headed up the rocky side of a hill, winding back and forth between the boulders."
4. Make the order of events clear by adding introductory words ("first," "then," and "finally") to sentences 8, 9, and 10.
5. Combine sentences 11, 12, and 13 to make one sentence.

Personal and Expressive Writing

Writing about autobiographical incidents is a good way to record your experiences and to share them with others. (See Workshop 1.) When you write about personal experiences, you can use pronouns to avoid repeating names and to make your writing flow smoothly. Make sure, however, that you use the proper forms of pronouns and that each pronoun agrees with its antecedent in number.

WRITING CONNECTIONS

Elaboration, Revision, and Proofreading

This activity will allow your students to see some of the concepts presented in this Handbook at work in a piece of personal and expressive writing. By revising and proofreading this passage, students will practice using the proper forms of pronouns and making pronouns agree with their antecedents.

Have students work with a partner or in small groups to find the errors and revise the passage.

Revisions may vary slightly. Typical changes are shown below. Elements involving change are shown in boldface.

I'll never forget the first time I saw a rattlesnake. ~~People have many mistaken ideas about snakes.~~ Jim and Willie and I were camping in the mountains, and **we** decided to go for a hike. Each of my friends had his own idea about where we should go, but we finally settled on a trail. **We headed up the rocky side of a hill, winding back and forth between the boulders.** Jim and I led the way, and Willie followed. I started to step over a rock and noticed something in the way. It's funny now as I think about all the things that went through my mind so quickly. **First,** I realized that the thing in the way was a snake. **Then,** I noticed that it was a big snake. **Finally,** I heard the hiss and the awful rattles. **All at once I yelped, leapt into the air, and jumped backward.** Jim and Willie looked frozen; neither could move his legs. The snake slithered into the bushes, and we hikers watched more carefully where we stepped after that.

Test 1

This test enables you to evaluate student mastery of the concepts taught in Handbooks 39–41.

Additional Resource

Grammar and Usage Practice Book, pp. 37–38

Answer Key

Corrections for run-ons may vary.

1. A—cousin
   C—me
2. A—monkeys
3. B—America, they
4. A—planets'
   C—sun. Jupiter *or* sun; Jupiter
5. B—She
6. A—trout
7. C—supports
8. A—I
9. B—hump; it *or* hump. It
10. E
11. B—his or her
    D—fits
12. A—We
    D—radios
13. B—activities, each
    C—himself or herself
14. D—Its
15. E

List of Skills Tested

1. A—capitalization: family relationship
   B—capitalization: family relationship
   C—reflexive pronoun
   D—capitalization: common noun
2. A—noun plural
   B—capitalization: geographical name
   C—subject-verb agreement: intervening words
   D—pronoun-antecedent agreement
3. A—noun possessive
   B—sentence fragment/run-on
   C—subject-verb agreement: intervening words
   D—capitalization: geographical name
4. A—noun possessive
   B—noun plural
   C—sentence fragment/run-on
   D—spelling

Skills

ASSESSMENT TEST 1 Grammar Handbooks *39–41*

Directions One or more of the underlined sections in the following sentences may contain an error in grammar, usage, punctuation, spelling, or capitalization. Write the letter of each incorrect section. Then rewrite the section correctly. If there is no error in an item, write *E.*

Example As they get older, humans (A) get taller; mountains get shorter. Old (B) mountains such as the Appalachians (C) have been gradually wearing down for centurys (D). No error (E)

Answer D—centuries

1. My Cousin (A) Juan is visiting Grandpa (B) in Milwaukee. They will meet Grandma and myself (C) at the zoo (D). No error (E)
2. The woolly monkies (A) of the Amazon River (B) basin have (C) fingerprints—or fingerprint-like ridges—on their (D) tails. No error (E)
3. Although Columbus's (A) ships landed in America. They (B) did not land in what is now the United States. His crews' first contact with the New World was (C) in the Bahamas (D). No error (E)
4. The nine planet's (A) orbits take them varying distances (B) from the sun, Jupiter (C), for example, is 507 million miles (D) away at one point and 460 million miles away at another. No error (E)
5. The wife of John Adams, one of the signers of the Declaration of Independence (A), was named Abigail. Her (B) and her husband argued because women's (C) rights were (D) not mentioned. No error (E)
6. Both trouts (A) and salmon (B) migrate (C) to fresh water to spawn (D). No error (E)

7. Ocean oases are created when warm water spurts up from inside the earth's [A] crust to warm the cold ocean floor. Each [B] of these oases support [C] hundreds of underwater creatures [D]. No error [E]

8. "I think; therefore, i [A] am," said [B] the French [C] philosopher René Descartes [D]. No error [E]

9. It's [A] not true that a camel survives without water by storing moisture in its hump, it [B] is the camel's [C] efficient kidneys [D] that help it conserve water. No error [E]

10. The circle of huge pillars called Stonehenge puzzles many of us [A] astronomers. It [B] may have been used as a reference [C] point in the study of stars and planets [D]. No error [E]

11. Somebody has [A] left their [B] keys [C] on the table, but neither of the keys fit [D] the lock. No error [E]

12. Us [A] Americans often hear [B] the 1930s referred [C] to as "the golden age of radio," but the number of radioes [D] sold in 1971 was more than twice the number sold in 1937. No error [E]

13. Before signing [A] up for craft activities. Each [B] of the campers should make themselves [C] a sandwich [D] and tidy up the cabin. No error [E]

14. A neutron star [A] can be smaller [B] than an average-sized island [C]. It's [D] diameter may be no more than ten miles. No error [E]

15. You may not be familiar with the name Dr. G. W. A. [A] Bonwill, but [B] you no doubt know his invention. It [C] was he [D] who gave us the safety pin. No error [E]

5. A—capitalization: document
B—pronoun case: compound subject
C—noun possessive
D—subject-verb agreement

6. A—noun plural
B—noun plural
C—subject-verb agreement: compound subject
D—spelling

7. A—noun possessive
B—sentence fragment/run-on
C—subject-verb agreement: indefinite pronoun
D—noun plural

8. A—capitalization: *I*
B—punctuation: quotation
C—capitalization: nationality
D—capitalization: name

9. A—possessive pronoun/contraction confusion
B—sentence fragment/run-on
C—noun possessive
D—noun plural

10. A—pronoun case: object
B—pronoun-antecedent agreement
C—spelling
D—noun plural

11. A—subject-verb agreement: indefinite pronoun
B—pronoun-antecedent agreement
C—noun plural
D—subject-verb agreement: indefinite pronoun

12. A—pronoun case: subject
B—subject-verb agreement
C—spelling
D—noun plural

13. A—spelling
B—sentence fragment/run-on
C—pronoun antecedent agreement: indefinite pronoun
D—punctuation: compound verb

14. A—capitalization: common noun
B—comparative adjective
C—spelling
D—possessive pronoun/contraction confusion

15. A—punctuation: abbreviation and initials
B—punctuation: compound sentence
C—sentence fragment/run-on
D—pronoun case: predicate pronoun

Objective

- To use writing prompts and a photograph as springboards to informal writing

WRITING WARM-UPS

Remind students that their writing will not be graded. These activities are intended as springboards to the concepts in Handbook 42. Suggest that students choose at least one of the prompts to explore.

Remind students who choose the first prompt to write two descriptions—the first, about the place filled with people; the second, about the place without people. Suggest that students focus on actions they might observe.

For the second prompt, ask students to tell their anecdote with as much drama as possible. They should try to build suspense if it is a scary story, and humor if it is funny. As time permits, ask volunteers to read their stories to the class.

Sports fans will enjoy the third prompt. Encourage students to choose a sport they know well, so that they can use the proper jargon. Suggest that they make up names for players on the team.

Sketch Book

WRITING WARM-UPS

- Write a description of what a place such as a beach or an amusement park is like when it is filled with people. Then write a description of what this same place is like when no one is around.
- What is the funniest or scariest thing that has happened to you lately? Tell the story of what happened.
- You're the coach, and you've just called timeout. Give a pep talk to your team. Tell them what you want them to do.

Using Verbs

- What Is a Verb?
- Verb Phrases
- Principal Parts of the Verb
- Verb Tenses
- Progressive Verb Forms
- Active and Passive Verb Forms
- Troublesome Pairs of Verbs

Untitled painting (1987), Keith Haring.

There is a verb to describe everything you do. There are even verbs to describe doing nothing at all. No sentence is complete without a verb. Verbs tell what action is going on, state that something exists, or link ideas.

In this handbook, you will learn ways you can use verbs to make your writing more precise, interesting, and vivid.

GRAMMAR HANDBOOK 42

Using Verbs

Objectives

- To identify action and linking verbs
- To recognize helping verbs and main verbs in verb phrases
- To form the principal parts of regular and irregular verbs
- To identify and use verb tenses
- To recognize and use the progressive forms of verbs
- To identify and use active and passive verb forms
- To use correctly verbs from pairs that are often confused

Writing

- To choose interesting and specific verbs and use them correctly in writing
- To replace passive verbs with active verbs to strengthen writing
- To correct errors in verb usage

INTRODUCING THE HANDBOOK

Ask students to describe what is happening in the painting. What words might describe the movements of the figures? (Samples: hop, dance, shake)

Explain that, as action can bring a painting to life, verbs can enliven writing—indeed, it can be said that verbs can be called the life of writing. Point out that in this handbook, students will learn how verbs can enliven their own writing.

ART NOTE

When he was very young, American artist Keith Haring (1958–1990) drew cartoons at the kitchen table with his father. He studied art in New York City and developed a style using cartoonlike human figures that usually have no age, race, or gender.

In the 1980s Haring did more than 5,000 subway drawings in New York ". . . purely for the love of doing it and for the love of drawing and for the love of the people that were seeing it. . . ," he said. He is famous for his image of the "Radiant Child," a crawling baby that symbolizes hope and possibility.

Objectives

- To identify and distinguish between action verbs and linking verbs

Writing

- To use action verbs and linking verbs in writing

Teaching Strategies

CRITICAL THINKING: CLASSIFYING

You might write three column headings on the board: (1) *Action You Can See,* (2) *Action You Can't See,* (3) *State of Being/ Linking.* Ask volunteers to put into a bag slips of paper on which they have written a verb. (A verb should be used only once.) Have each student choose one slip from the bag and then write the verb in the appropriate column(s) on the board. Remind students that some verbs may appear in more than one column.

Writing TIP

Lively action verbs can add energy and interest to your writing. Notice the verbs Robert Francis uses in "The Base Stealer" on page 73 to show the ball player's teasing actions.

WHAT IS A VERB?

A **verb** expresses an action, states that something exists, or links the subject with a word that describes or renames it.

When you speak or write, you use two kinds of verbs. These are **action verbs** and **linking verbs.**

Action Verbs

Some verbs express actions: They *crowned* their new queen. The action may be one that you cannot see: She *wanted* power.

Whether you can see the action or not, an action verb says that something is happening, has happened, or will happen.

Linking Verbs

A few verbs do not tell about an action. They may express a state of being, or they may link the subject with a word or words that describe or rename the subject.

She *is* here. (expresses state of being)
The country *seems* prosperous. (links subject with description)

These verbs are called **linking verbs** because they can be used to connect, or link, the subject with some other word or words that describe it.

Linking Verbs

be (am, are, is, was, were, been, being)	look	smell	appear
	seem	taste	sound
became	feel	grow	remain

Some linking verbs can also be used as action verbs.

Linking Verbs	**Action Verbs**
The feast looked delicious.	The king looked at his meal.
The food smelled wonderful.	The king smelled the food.

Practice Your Skills

A. CONCEPT CHECK

Linking Verbs and Action Verbs Write each verb from the following sentences. Then label each verb *Action* or *Linking*.

Writing Theme
Royalty

1. Queen Christina of Sweden seems an interesting historical figure.
2. She became a queen-elect in 1632, at the age of only six.
3. As a girl she appeared wild and tomboyish, with a great love for her studies.
4. She usually studied for about twelve hours a day.
5. As an adult, she often wore men's wigs, coats, and shoes.
6. Her masculine clothes and manners shocked people.
7. However, she was an able queen.
8. She brought an end to the costly Thirty Years' War.
9. She also supported foreign study, school reforms, and the arts.
10. Yet, Christina remained queen only until 1654.

B. APPLICATION IN LITERATURE

Recognizing Verbs Write the italicized verbs from the following selection. Label each verb *Action* or *Linking*.

> [11]Guinevere *became* Arthur's queen. [12]The splendor of Arthur's kingdom *overwhelmed* her. [13]She quickly *established* herself in his court, and King Arthur's knights *were* devoted to her. [14]She *seemed* happy and confident as queen.
>
> [15]In the meantime, Merlin, the magician, also *fell* in love. [16]The lake where Arthur *received* his famous sword also *had* a great rock. [17]Underneath the great rock *was* a palace. [18]The Lady of the Lake *lived* there. [19]One day she *cast* a spell on Merlin. [20]Under the influence of her spell, Merlin *joined* her. [21]No one ever *saw* Merlin again.

Thomas Malory, *The Legend of King Arthur*, based on a retelling of *Le Morte Darthur*

C. APPLICATION IN WRITING

Description Imagine that you have just been named king or queen. Write a paragraph describing the day of your coronation. Include each of the following verbs. Use one of these verbs twice, once as an action verb and once as a linking verb.

tasted smelled felt looked

FOR MORE PRACTICE
See page 496.

INDIVIDUALIZING INSTRUCTION: ESL STUDENTS Explain that Practice Your Skills A and B will be exercises in classification and identification. Reassure students that when they write and speak, they will not have to classify each verb they use. Yet they should include a variety of strong action verbs, not just rely on the limited number of linking verbs available.

Additional Resources

Tests and Writing Assessment Prompts, Pretest, pp. 21–22

Grammar and Usage Practice Book, p. 39

Grammar Test Generator

Writing Theme: Royalty

Suggest that students use these exercises as a springboard to writing. Other related areas that they might explore include the following:

- Queen Elizabeth I of England
- royal dynasties of ancient Egypt or China
- Queen Liliuokalani of Hawaii
- symbols of royalty

Answers to Practice Your Skills

A. Concept Check
Linking Verbs and Action Verbs

Answers are shown on page.

B. Application in Literature
Recognizing Verbs

Answers are shown on page.

C. Application in Writing
Description

Answers will vary. You might ask students to underline the verbs in their paragraphs.

Objectives

- To distinguish between main verbs and helping verbs in verb phrases

Writing

- To complete sentences by adding appropriate helping verbs
- To use interesting and specific verb phrases in writing

Teaching Strategies

KEY TO UNDERSTANDING Point out to students that the function of most helping verbs is to enable a speaker or writer to express the relationship of various actions in time.

She *had been talking* for hours before she *became* hoarse.

However, the helping verbs *could, may, might,* and *would* express possibility or a condition.

I *may go* to school if I feel better.

INDIVIDUALIZING INSTRUCTION: KINESTHETIC LEARNERS Students can create a game of verb phrases. Have them write verb phrases on small pieces of cardboard, then cut them apart so that each "tile" contains only one verb. Students should place each tile face down in a *Helping Verb* or *Main Verb* pile. To play the game, students take turns at drawing one tile from each pile. Students should then arrange their tiles into a verb phrase and make up a sentence using that verb phrase.

Additional Resource

Grammar and Usage Practice Book, p. 40

VERB PHRASES

A **verb phrase** consists of a main verb and one or more helping verbs.

A **verb phrase** consists of more than one verb. It is made up of a **main verb** and one or more **helping verbs.**

Helping Verbs	Main Verb	Verb Phrases
had	taken	had taken
might have	taken	might have taken
must have been	taken	must have been taken

Some verbs, such as *do, have,* and *be,* can be used either as main verbs or as helping verbs. Here are their forms:

do	have	be	is	were
does	has	am	was	been
did	had	are		

The examples below show how they can be used.

Used as Main Verbs	Used as Helping Verbs
Will you *do* the job?	I *do ride* the bus every day.
Who *has* bus fare?	He *has seen* the monorail.
Where *were* they?	The girls *were bicycling*.

Helping Verbs

can	shall	will
could	should	would
may	might	must

Sometimes helping verbs and main verbs are separated by words that are not verbs.

I *did* not *ride* the subway today.
You *must*n't *waste* gasoline.
Can we *solve* the air pollution problem?
We *should* certainly *improve* public transportation.

476 Grammar Handbook

Practice Your Skills

A. CONCEPT CHECK

Verb Phrases Make two columns on your paper. Label them *Helping Verbs* and *Main Verbs.* Write the parts of the verb phrases from the following sentences in the correct column.

1. Automobile companies have stopped development of steam-powered cars.
2. These cars just can't travel very fast.
3. Other types of zero-emission cars will soon be on the roads, however.
4. Zero-emission cars do not produce any pollutants.
5. Your first car could be powered by electricity from batteries.
6. Electric coils in the roads themselves also may provide the power for tomorrow's cars.
7. Future automobiles will probably have small engines.
8. So these cars should look much more streamlined than today's models.
9. Of course, at first these cars will cost more money.
10. However, wouldn't you spend a little more for the sake of our environment?

B. DRAFTING SKILL

Using Helping Verbs Complete the following sentences by adding one or more helping verbs that fit the meaning. (For some sentences, suggestions are given in parentheses.)

EXAMPLE Transportation problems ______ ______ addressed. (Show necessity.)
Transportation problems must be addressed.

[11]Transportation______ become a major problem for our country. [12]Gasoline use and automobile exhaust fumes ______ ______ reduced greatly. (Show necessity.) [13]As a result, planners ______ looking into new forms of transportation. [14]Some cities ______ already created special ways to help workers. [15]Thanks to these services, public car pools and special buses ______ carrying thousands of people to and from work each day. [16]Some manufacturers ______ developed electric people-mover systems. [17]Someday, these electric "trains" ______ carry workers, shoppers, and other travelers from place to place.

Writing Theme
Transportation

Writing Theme: Transportation

Suggest that students use these exercises as a springboard to writing. Other related areas that they might explore include the following:

- visiting an auto show
- solar-powered transportation
- traffic-monitoring systems
- unusual forms of transportation (such as hot-air balloons or kayaks)

Answers to Practice Your Skills

A. Concept Check
Verb Phrases

Answers are shown on page.

B. Drafting Skill
Using Helping Verbs

Answers may vary. Possible answers are shown below.

11. has
12. must be
13. are
14. have
15. have been
16. have
17. will

18. Do
19. may (*or* might)
20. can (*or* do)
21. may (*or* might)
22. will (*or* would)

C. Application in Writing
Writing for a Newspaper
Descriptions will vary.

CHECK POINT

Writing Theme: J. R. R. Tolkien

Other related areas students might wish to explore as writing topics include the following:

- Tolkien's friendship with C. S. Lewis
- other characters from *The Hobbit*
- American novelist Ursula Le Guin's *Earthsea* novels
- American novelist Lloyd Alexander's fantasy novels

MIXED REVIEW • PAGES 474–478

You may wish to use this activity to check students' mastery of the following concepts:

- What is a verb?
- verb phrases

Answers are shown on page.

[18] _______ you know about these systems from amusement parks or airports? [19]Better rail systems _______ also help. (Show possibility.) [20]In France and Japan, trains already _______ reach two hundred miles per hour. [21]Future travelers _______ also ride on magnetic levitation vehicles or maglevs. (Show possibility.) [22]Powerful electric motors _______ move these vehicles along, several inches above the ground, at speeds up to three hundred miles per hour.

FOR MORE PRACTICE
See pages 496–497.

C. APPLICATION IN WRITING

Writing for a Newspaper Imagine that you have invented a time machine that allows you to visit your community in the year 2013. Write a description of your experiences for your local newspaper, comparing how people travel today with how they might get from place to place in 2013. As you write, remember that verb phrases can make your descriptions more interesting and more specific.

MIXED REVIEW • PAGES 474–478

Writing Theme
J.R.R. Tolkien

Write the verbs and verb phrases from the following sentences. Label each *Action* or *Linking*.

1. What reader doesn't enjoy the works of J.R.R. Tolkien?
2. Tolkien spent most of his years at England's Oxford University.
3. Tolkien was a professor of medieval languages.
4. He didn't seem like a person with strange worlds in his head.
5. Tolkien probably would have remained an unknown Oxford professor for the rest of his life.
6. However, during the 1930s he became a novelist.
7. He wrote strange and wonderful fantasies.
8. Tolkien created a new race of fictional beings—the hobbits.
9. Hobbits looked like small people with furry feet.
10. They lived in comfortable holes in the sides of hills.
11. Tolkien's first fantasy novel, *The Hobbit,* appeared in 1937.
12. Later, he published *The Lord of the Rings,* a trilogy.
13. The three novels in the series tell the heroic tale of the hobbits.
14. The trilogy begins with the discovery, by the hobbit Bilbo Baggins, of an evil, magic ring.
15. This is truly a classic story of adventure and excitement.

Principal Parts of the Verb

The many forms of the verb are based on its three **principal parts:** the **present,** the **past,** and the **past participle.**

Verb forms change to show when an action occurred. These forms, called *tenses,* are based on the three **principal parts** of the verb: the *present,* the *past,* and the *past participle.*

Regular Verbs

For all **regular verbs,** the past and the past participle are spelled alike. They are made by adding *-d* or *-ed* to the present form. The past participle is used with a helping verb.

Present	Past	Past Participle
help	helped	(has) helped
rescue	rescued	(has) rescued
rush	rushed	(have) rushed
support	supported	(have) supported

The spelling of many regular verbs changes when *-d* or *-ed* is added. (See page 686 for a review of spelling rules.)

knit + -ed = knitted	pay + -d = paid
carry + -ed = carried	lay + -d = laid
cry + -ed = cried	say + -d = said

Practice Your Skills

CONCEPT CHECK

Regular Verbs Make three columns on your paper labeled *Present, Past,* and *Past Participle.* Write the principal parts of the following regular verbs in the correct column.

1. save	**6.** assist	**11.** prevent	**16.** donate
2. provide	**7.** relieve	**12.** carry	**17.** hurry
3. sob	**8.** aid	**13.** train	**18.** travel
4. share	**9.** worry	**14.** try	**19.** tug
5. use	**10.** pay	**15.** nap	**20.** enroll

Principal Parts of the Verb

Objectives

- To identify the three principal parts of the verb
- To form the principal parts of regular verbs
- To identify the correct forms of irregular verbs

Writing

- To proofread a paragraph, correcting errors in the use of verb forms

Teaching Strategies

KEY TO UNDERSTANDING Stress that the past participle form is used with a helping verb and therefore is shown with the helping verb *has* or *have* in parentheses.

INDIVIDUALIZING INSTRUCTION: ESL STUDENTS The concept of principal parts is common to many languages; thus, the main issue for most ESL students is how the parts are formed in English. You might write examples on the board to show how the last letter is doubled in many one-syllable verbs that contain a short vowel and end in a consonant:

hop—hopped vs. *hope—hoped*
tap—tapped vs. *tape—taped*

Answers to Practice Your Skills

Concept Check
Regular Verbs

Have is also acceptable as the helping verbs in the answers below.

PRESENT	PAST	PAST PARTICIPLE
1. save	saved	(has) saved
2. provide	provided	(has) provided
3. sob	sobbed	(has) sobbed
4. share	shared	(has) shared
5. use	used	(has) used
6. assist	assisted	(has) assisted
7. relieve	relieved	(has) relieved
8. aid	aided	(has) aided
9. worry	worried	(has) worried
10. pay	paid	(has) paid
11. prevent	prevented	(has) prevented
12. carry	carried	(has) carried
13. train	trained	(has) trained
14. try	tried	(has) tried
15. nap	napped	(has) napped
16. donate	donated	(has) donated
17. hurry	hurried	(has) hurried
18. travel	traveled	(has) traveled
19. tug	tugged	(has) tugged
20. enroll	enrolled	(has) enrolled

Using Verbs 479

HELPFUL HINT The verbs in the chart are presented alphabetically, rather than by pattern. Have students identify the verb for which the past and past participle forms are spelled the same (bring). Then help students identify the verbs whose past participle is identical to its present form (come, run) and whose three forms differ by only a change in a vowel (begin, drink, sing, swim). Other patterns are possible, as well.

This activity should help students understand that even though they might want to memorize the forms or check a particular verb form in a dictionary, there is some logic to the patterns of these verbs.

INDIVIDUALIZING INSTRUCTION: ESL STUDENTS Spelling irregularities make some verb forms difficult for ESL students to recognize when reading or to use correctly when writing. Model the process of using a dictionary to locate the principal parts of irregular verbs. Then encourage volunteers to create games designed to help students recall the principal parts of common irregular verbs. Suggest possible approaches (card games, TV quiz shows, board games), but allow students to pursue their own game ideas if they wish.

Additional Resource

Grammar and Usage Practice Book, pp. 41–47

Irregular Verbs

Hundreds of verbs follow the regular pattern of adding *-d* or *-ed* to form the past and the past participle. Verbs that do not follow this pattern are called **irregular verbs.** There are only about sixty frequently used irregular verbs. For many of these, the past and the past participle are spelled the same. The past participle is used with a helping verb.

fight fought (have) fought
make made (has) made

For a few irregular verbs, like *hit* and *cut,* the three principal parts are spelled the same. They offer no problems. Most verb problems come from irregular verbs with three different forms. For example, the irregular verbs *throw* and *ring* have three different forms:

throw threw (had) thrown
ring rang (have) rung

If you are not sure about a verb form, look it up in the dictionary. If the verb is regular, only one form will be listed. If the verb is irregular, the irregular form or forms will be listed.

Common Irregular Verbs

Present	Past	Past Participle	Present	Past	Past Participle
begin	began	(have) begun	know	knew	(have) known
break	broke	(have) broken	lie	lay	(have) lain
bring	brought	(have) brought	ride	rode	(have) ridden
choose	chose	(have) chosen	ring	rang	(have) rung
come	came	(have) come	run	ran	(have) run
do	did	(have) done	see	saw	(have) seen
drink	drank	(have) drunk	sing	sang	(have) sung
eat	ate	(have) eaten	speak	spoke	(have) spoken
fall	fell	(have) fallen	steal	stole	(have) stolen
freeze	froze	(have) frozen	swim	swam	(have) swum
give	gave	(have) given	take	took	(have) taken
go	went	(have) gone	throw	threw	(have) thrown
grow	grew	(have) grown	write	wrote	(have) written

Practice Your Skills

A. CONCEPT CHECK

Irregular Verbs Write the correct form of the irregular verb given in parentheses.

1. The idea for the Red Cross (arose, arisen) in the 1860s.
2. War had (broke, broken) out in Italy in 1859.
3. During a tour of the country, Jean Henry Dunant had (rode, ridden) across a battlefield at Solferino.
4. He (saw, seen) great misery all around him.
5. More than forty thousand soldiers (lay, lain) dead or wounded.
6. By the end of his tour, he had (brought, brung) together volunteers to help the wounded.
7. After three years, Dunant's ideas had (grew, grown).
8. In 1862 he (wrote, written) "Recollections of Solferino."
9. In this pamphlet, Dunant (spoke, spoken) passionately about assistance for the victims of war and natural disasters.
10. Many people soon (knew, known) of Dunant's plans.
11. People from sixteen nations (go, went) to a series of meetings in Geneva, Switzerland.
12. By 1863, a new organization had (laid, lay) out its basic plan.
13. It had also (chose, chosen) its symbol, a red cross on a white background, and its name, the Red Cross.
14. Twelve nations (came, come) to sign the charter in 1864.
15. Eighteen years later, the United States still had not (make, made) the decision to sign this charter.
16. The American Red Cross finally (began, begun) in 1882.
17. Some branches have (took, taken) other symbols, such as a red crescent in Muslim countries, and a red Star of David in Israel.
18. The Red Cross has (wrote, written) rules for the treatment of wartime prisoners.
19. We (known, know) these rules as the Geneva Convention.
20. The Red Cross has always (done, did) much for people in need.
21. For example, if you have ever (fell, fallen), you may have used first-aid skills that you learned from the Red Cross.
22. The Red Cross also (takes, taken) in blood during blood drives.
23. It (freezes, frozen) the blood and uses it in an emergency.
24. Victims of earthquakes and other natural disasters have (sang, sung) the praises of the Red Cross for years.
25. Volunteers from all over the world have (given, gave) their time and money to this worthy cause.

Writing Theme
Humanitarians

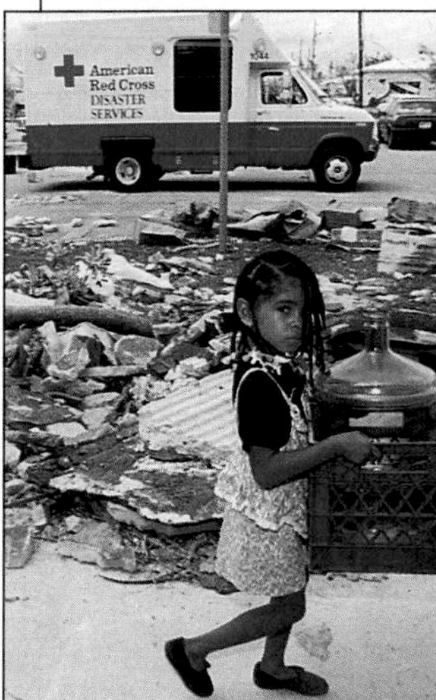

After Hurricane Andrew struck southern Florida in August 1992, residents had great difficulty getting safe drinking water.

Writing Theme: Humanitarians

Other related areas students might wish to explore as writing topics include the following:

- the work of Florence Nightingale, British nurse
- the humanitarian career of Albert Schweitzer or Mother Teresa
- local humanitarian efforts, such as shelters for the homeless or child-abuse prevention
- Care, Oxfam, and other food aid agencies

Answers to Practice Your Skills

A. Concept Check
Irregular Verbs

Answers are shown on page. To give students additional practice in hearing irregular verbs used correctly, do the exercise orally in class.

For help with the troublesome verbs *lie* and *lay* (in numbers 5 and 12), refer students to "Using *Lie* and *Lay*" on page 492.

B. Drafting Skill
Using Correct Verb Forms

26. grew
27. broke
28. gone
29. fallen
30. lay
31. brought
32. ate, drank
33. begun
34. done
35. spoken
36. gave
37. chose
38. rang, sang
39. ran
40. come

C. Proofreading Skill
Checking Verb Forms

Errors in proofreading exercises are counted as follows: (a) Each word is counted as one error. For example, a misspelled word is one error; two initials and a last name not capitalized are counted as three errors. (b) Run-on sentences and sentence fragments are each counted as one error, even though the correction involves both punctuation and capitalization corrections.

Errors are underlined on page.

By the end of the Civil War, Clara Barton had grown very tired. In 1869 she went to Switzerland for a long-overdue rest. The International Red Cross had already begun to operate there. Barton soon knew all about it. She spoke to its organizers and quickly saw how she could help them. Once again she chose to be in a dangerous situation. This time she went to the front lines of the Franco-Prussian War and gave aid to the soldiers. By 1873, she had returned to America, where she began the American branch of the Red Cross. She also wrote several books about her ideas. Clara Barton ran the United States Red Cross from 1882 to 1904. Under her direction, the Red Cross helped the victims of natural disasters as well as victims of warfare.

Clara Barton (1937), Mathilde M. Leisenring. The founder of the American Red Cross, Clara Barton, was called "the angel of the battlefield" for her tireless efforts helping wounded soldiers during the Civil War.

B. DRAFTING SKILL

Using Correct Verb Forms Write the past or past participle form of each verb in parentheses.

26. In 1861, tensions (grow) between the North and South in the United States.
27. Soon the Civil War (break) out.
28. Clara Barton, a clerk in the U.S. Patent Office, had (go) to the battlefields as a nurse.
29. Thousands of soldiers had (fall) in battle.
30. They (lie) in makeshift hospitals.
31. Barton (bring) valuable supplies of food, drink, and medicine.
32. Wounded men gratefully (eat) and (drink) Barton's provisions.
33. By 1864 her humanitarian activities had (begin) to be famous.
34. She had (do) wonders for the sick and wounded.
35. People had (speak) of her as the "Angel of the Battlefield."
36. At first, the government (give) her no encouragement.
37. Later, it (choose) a different path, one of support for her work.
38. In 1865, church bells (ring) and people (sing) in celebration of the end of the war.
39. Then Barton (run) a bureau that tried to locate men missing in action.
40. She had (come) up with another form of help for those in need.

C. PROOFREADING SKILL

Checking Verb Forms Write the following paragraph, correcting all the errors in grammar, capitalization, punctuation, and spelling. Pay particular attention to the verb forms. (15 errors)

By the end of the Civil War, Clara Barton had grew very tired in 1869 she went to switzerland for a long-overdue rest. The international Red Cross had already begun to operate their. Barton soon known all about it. She spoke to it's organizers and quickly seen how she could help them. Once again she choose to be in a dangerous situation. This time she went to the front lines of the Franco-Prussian War and give aid to the soldiers. By 1873, she had returned to america, where she begun the American branch of the Red Cross she also wrote several books about her ideas. Clara Barton run the United States Red Cross from 1882 to 1904. Under her direction, the Red Cross helped the victims of natural disastors as well as victims of warfare.

FOR MORE PRACTICE
See page 497.

ART NOTE

Mathilde M. Leisenring was an American painter and sculptor who won prizes for her watercolors in the early 1900s. She studied in New York City at the Art Students League and in France with the sculptor and engraver Henri Laurens. After her marriage to the successful architect Luther Morris, Leisenring settled in Washington, D.C., where she taught painting at the Corcoran Gallery of Art.

Ask students what they can guess about Clara Barton's personality from this portrait and have them suggest adjectives to describe her appearance.

Different forms of the verb are used to show the time of an action or the time of a state of being. These forms are called the **tenses** of the verb.

A verb has different forms, called **tenses,** to indicate whether an action takes place or a condition exists in the present, past, or future. Verbs change in the ways shown below to indicate time differences.

Verb Forms To Indicate Time Differences

The spelling of the present form of the verb may change:

invent	invented
see	saw

A helping verb may be used:

will grow	has grown	had grown
will protect	has protected	had protected

A verb has three simple tenses and three perfect tenses.

The Simple Tenses

The most common tenses of the verb are the **simple tenses:** present, past, and future. You use these tenses most often in your speaking and writing. Correctly using the tenses helps you convey clearly what you mean.

The **present tense** places the action or condition in the present time. The present form of the verb is used for the present tense: *find, make, play.*

The **past tense** places the action or condition in the past. The past tense of a regular verb is formed by adding *-d* or *-ed* to the present form: *replaced, looked.* The past tense of an irregular verb is shown by changing the spelling within the word: *grow, grew; begin, began.*

The **future tense** places the action or condition in the future. The future tense is formed by using the word *shall* or *will* before the present form: *shall need, will eat.*

TIP

A story that is told or written in many different tenses can confuse the listener or reader. The sequence of events is hard to understand if the tenses change too often.

VERB TENSES

Objectives

- To identify the simple and perfect tenses of verbs
- To form verb tenses correctly

Writing

- To present a sequence of events through the correct use of verb tenses

Teaching Strategies

LINKING GRAMMAR AND WRITING Read the Writing Tip at the bottom of the page. Then ask students to try to follow the sequence of events as you read this paragraph aloud:

> Yesterday our lights will go out when the lightning hits the tree next door. The tree falls and will hit the power line, which had cut the power to all the houses on the block. The power is off for two hours, and we had been sitting around in the dark with a flashlight. We talk and laugh. This must be what it will be like before TV and radios will be invented.

Have volunteers rewrite the paragraph to clarify the sequence of events.

ASSESSMENT: SPOT CHECK Have students work in pairs to make up sentences illustrating each tense. They should label the tense of each sentence and then exchange papers to check whether tenses have been correctly identified.

Using Verbs 483

INDIVIDUALIZING INSTRUCTION: ESL STUDENTS To give ESL students a chance to practice and to hear the present perfect tense, ask native English speakers to interview each ESL student, using variations on "Have you ever ____ [played soccer, eaten a bagel, and so forth]?" Advise the native English speakers to help ESL students respond in the present perfect tense.

Additional Resource

Grammar and Usage Practice Book, pp. 48–49

Writing Theme: Elephants

Other related areas students might wish to explore as writing topics include the following:

- circus elephants
- differences between Indian (Asiatic) and African elephants
- the life cycle and family life of elephants in the wild
- the mammoth, the elephants' prehistoric ancestor

Answers to Practice Your Skills

A. Concept Check
Verb Tenses

1. comes, Present
2. had made, Past Perfect
3. had dwindled, Past Perfect
4. offered, Past
5. won, Past
6. had acquired, Past Perfect
7. has been replaced, Present Perfect
8. has dropped, Present Perfect
9. will perish, Future
10. will have contributed, Future Perfect

B. Drafting Skill
Using Different Tenses

11. has
12. possesses
13. will consume

The Perfect Tenses

Sometimes you want to show that an action was completed or that a condition existed before a given time. In that case, use one of the perfect tenses.

The **perfect tenses** are formed by using *has, have,* or *had* before the past participle. They are formed as follows:

Present Perfect	have gone, has gone, has been gone
Past Perfect	had gone
Future Perfect	shall have gone, will have gone, had been gone

Practice Your Skills

Writing Theme
Elephants

A. CONCEPT CHECK

Verb Tenses Write the verbs from the following sentences. Beside each verb, write its tense.

1. Most ivory comes from the tusks of elephants.
2. Until the late 1800s, people had made jewelry, piano keys, and billiard balls from ivory.
3. By the 1860s, however, the supply of ivory had dwindled.
4. A New England maker of billiard balls offered $10,000 for a good substitute for ivory.
5. John Wesley Hyatt won the prize with celluloid, a form of plastic.
6. He had acquired the patent for celluloid from a British professor.
7. Celluloid has now been replaced by newer plastics.
8. Because of the invention of plastic, the demand for ivory has dropped.
9. With any luck, the elephant population will not perish.
10. Inventors will have contributed to the elephant's survival.

B. DRAFTING SKILL

Using Different Tenses Complete each of the following sentences with the form of the verb given in parentheses.

11. An elephant (present of *have*) the largest ears of any animal.
12. It also (present of *possess*) the keenest sense of smell.
13. If given an unlimited supply of food, an elephant (future of *consume*) as much as five hundred pounds.

484 Grammar Handbook

14. In some parts of Africa, elephants (present perfect of *eat*) all the available foliage.
15. By the time it is an adult, a typical elephant (future perfect of *grow*) to a weight of ten thousand pounds.
16. One of the largest known elephants (past of *weigh*) over two hundred pounds at birth.
17. By the time they die, most elephants (future perfect of *live*) only fifty or sixty years.
18. At one point, elephants (past perfect of *become*) an endangered species.
19. People (past perfect of *hunt*) them for years.
20. Hunters (past of *be*) eager to sell the elephants' ivory.

C. APPLICATION IN WRITING

Problem and Solution Write two brief paragraphs. In the first paragraph, describe one of the endangered species in our world. In the second paragraph, explain the history of the species. Be sure your verb tenses show a logical sequence of events.

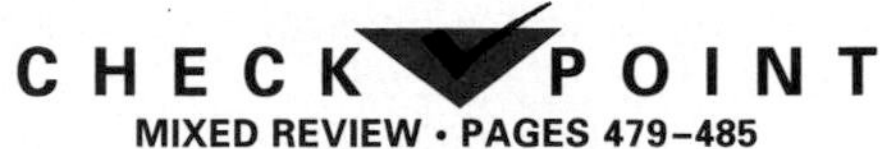

MIXED REVIEW • PAGES 479–485

A. Write the correct form of the verbs given in parentheses.

1. As of this year, the ballet will have (exist, existed) for more than three hundred years.
2. Over the years, audiences have (went, gone) to performances in formal halls as well as in school auditoriums.
3. This year alone, millions of people will (see, seen) a ballet.
4. The dancers especially will (entertain, entertained) them.
5. Ballet (develop, developed) from the parties of Italian nobles.
6. For years the nobles had (gave, given) fancy entertainments.
7. In the 1500s, they had (begin, begun) dance contests among themselves.
8. In 1547 an Italian noblewoman, Catherine de Medici, (came, come) to Paris as France's new queen.
9. She (introduce, introduced) Italy's dance entertainments to France.
10. She also (bring, brought) a gifted musician, Balthazar de Beaujoyeulx.

FOR MORE PRACTICE
See pages 497–498.

Writing Theme
Ballet

14. have eaten
15. will have grown
16. weighed
17. will have lived
18. had become
19. had hunted
20. were

C. Application in Writing

Problem and Solution

Paragraphs will vary, but should demonstrate correct usage of verb tenses.

CHECK POINT

Writing Theme: Ballet

Other related areas students might wish to explore as writing topics include the following:

- modern dance groups, such as the Dance Theater of Harlem
- American choreographers George Balanchine and Martha Graham
- ballet stars, such as Maria Tallchief, Rudolf Nureyev, Isadora Duncan, and Mikhail Baryshnikov
- movies about dancers or dancing, such as *The Red Shoes, A Chorus Line, All That Jazz, The Turning Point,* and *White Nights*

MIXED REVIEW • PAGES 479–485

You may wish to use this activity to check students' mastery of the following concepts:

- principal parts of the verb
- verb tenses

A. Answers are shown on page.

B.
16. has captured, Present Perfect
17. painted, Past
18. focused, Past
19. show, Present
20. had been, Past Perfect
21. created, Past
22. are, Present; extend, Present
23. seem, Present
24. have captivated, Present Perfect
25. will be, Future

11. In honor of Catherine's wedding, he (organize, <u>organized</u>) a magnificent spectacle of dancers.
12. Beaujoyeulx had (wrote, <u>written</u>) music and dance compositions that took over five hours to perform.
13. Actors (<u>recited</u>, recite) poems and (sing, <u>sang</u>) songs for the show.
14. By the 1600s, French ballet had (became, <u>become</u>) very important to the French people.
15. Finally, in 1661, King Louis XIV (<u>established</u>, establish) the Royal Academy as a school for professional dancers.

B. Write the verbs from the following sentences. Beside each, label its tense.

16. Probably no other painter has ever captured scenes from the ballet as well as Edgar Degas.
17. From 1854 to 1859, Degas painted scenes from history such as battles and portraits of famous people.
18. However, he eventually focused on scenes from his life in Paris, such as scenes from ballet classes.
19. These paintings show ballerinas' movements in casual or even awkward positions.
20. Such moments had never been the subject of paintings before.
21. Degas also created daring new compositions.
22. For instance, in some of his pictures, parts of his subjects are not visible; the figures extend beyond the edge of the painting.
23. These pictures seem like snapshots of fleeting moments.
24. No wonder they have captivated viewers for years.
25. Surely they will be popular for many more years.

Ballet Rehearsal (1885), Edgar Degas.

ART NOTE

Edgar Degas (Hilaire Germain) (1834–1917) was one of the great French Impressionist painters and a sculptor as well. Degas, a perfectionist, called himself "the classical painter of modern life." His subjects include dancers, race-track scenes, café scenes, laundry women, and milliners. In his paintings and pastel drawings, Degas freely combines his technical mastery with a fascination with light, color, and line. He also created a series of bronze sculptures of ballet dancers and of racehorses.

PROGRESSIVE VERB FORMS

The **progressive form** of the verb shows continuing action.

Sometimes we tell the time of an action like this:

I *am* playing. (instead of I *play*)
I *was* playing. (instead of I *played*)

In situations like these, we use a form of the verb *be* plus the **present participle,** a verb form that ends in *-ing.* A verb phrase made up of one of the forms of *be* and a present participle is called a **progressive form.**

The progressive form of a verb shows continuing action. For instance, "I am playing" shows that my playing is going on right now, whereas "I play" shows that I can or do play. Here are the progressive forms of *play* that are used with *I:*

I am playing.	I have been playing.
I was playing.	I had been playing.
I will (shall) be playing.	I will (shall) have been playing.

Sports announcers often use the present progressive to convey the excitement of the action as it occurs:

"The ball is *heading* deep into center field.
It's *going.* It's *going.* It's gone!"

Practice Your Skills

A. CONCEPT CHECK

Progressive Verb Forms Write each verb phrase from the following sentences.

Writing Theme
Sports Action

1. In another minute we will have been broadcasting this tense tennis match for four hours.
2. We will be continuing, though, until the very end of the match.
3. The crowd has been standing on its feet for much of the action.
4. Our current champion has been serving well all day.
5. Earlier in the tournament, he had been faulting often.

PROGRESSIVE VERB FORMS

Objectives

- To identify and use the progressive forms of verbs

Writing

- To rewrite sentences, changing the verbs to the progressive form
- To use the progressive forms of verbs in original writing

Teaching Strategies

HELPFUL HINT Point out that the six model sentences at the middle of the page illustrate the progressive forms of the six verb tenses that students studied on pages 483–484. The simple tenses are shown in the left column; the perfect tenses, in the right. Ask students which two helping verbs are needed to create a progressive form in the perfect tenses (have, be). Point out as well that other helping verbs, such as *could* and *would,* can be combined with a form of *be* and a present participle to create a progressive verb:

I *should be trying* harder.

Additional Resource

Grammar and Usage Practice Book, p. 50

Writing Theme: Sports Action

Other related areas students might wish to explore as writing topics include the following:

- history of tennis
- American tennis stars past and present, such as Arthur Ashe, Chris Evert, Michael Chang
- a student's favorite sport and team or individual player
- jargon of a particular sport (such as terms for equipment, action, or scoring)

Answers to Practice Your Skills

A. Concept Check
Progressive Verb Forms

Answers are shown on page.

B. Revision Skill
Using Progressive Forms

11. am broadcasting
12. have been gathering
13. have been practicing
14. are facing
15. will be getting
16. are filing
17. are arriving
18. will be staying
19. are hoping
20. will have been preparing; will be coming

C. Application in Writing
Writing a Script

Scripts will vary but should demonstrate correct use of the present tense and progressive forms of verbs.

6. This afternoon, though, he is concentrating on his serves.
7. From now on he should be delivering each serve flawlessly.
8. His opponent, however, is returning those serves consistently.
9. Earlier, his opponent was hitting a lot of ground strokes.
10. Now he is smashing one overhead shot after another.

B. REVISION SKILL

Using Progressive Forms Rewrite each of the following sentences. Change the verbs to the progressive form.

11. Today I broadcast from the site of the U.S. Open.
12. For several days the greatest names in tennis have gathered here.
13. They have practiced for hours each day.
14. Now, however, they face the real test.
15. This morning the first matches of the tournament will get underway.
16. Already, spectators file into the stands.
17. Players arrive for their first matches.
18. Some will stay for only the first rounds.
19. Others, though, hope for a longer run in the tournament.
20. In the end, of all the players who will have prepared for the thrill of victory, only two—one man and one woman—will come home singles champions.

C. APPLICATION IN WRITING

Writing a Script Imagine that you are auditioning for a job as a sports announcer. Write the script you would use for your tryout. Select an appropriate sports event and describe the quickly changing action. Mix present tense and progressive forms to make your description as exciting as possible.

FOR MORE PRACTICE
See page 498.

488 Grammar Handbook

ACTIVE AND PASSIVE VERB FORMS

When the subject of the sentence performs the action, the verb is **active.** When the subject of the sentence receives the action or expresses the result of the action, the verb is **passive.**

In addition to showing the time of an action, you can use verbs in still another way to express exactly what you mean.

Suppose oil has been leaked into the harbor. If you know who or what did it, you can say something like this:

Our motorboat leaked oil into the harbor.

Suppose that you do not know who or what leaked the oil or that you do not want to say who or what did it. You can say this:

Oil was leaked into the harbor.

In the first sentence, the subject says who or what performed the action. The verb of this sentence is **active.** In the second sentence, the subject says who or what received the action. The verb of this sentence is **passive.** The word *passive* means "acted upon."

The passive form of a verb consists of some form of *be* plus the past participle. Only transitive verbs, those that take objects, can be changed from active to passive:

Active	**Passive**
Beebe explored the sea.	The sea was explored by Beebe.
The bathysphere helped him.	He was helped by the bathysphere.

Practice Your Skills

A. CONCEPT CHECK

Active and Passive Verb Forms Write the verbs from the following sentences. Label each one *Active* or *Passive.*

1. The sea's depths were first explored by an American naturalist.
2. His name was Dr. William Beebe.
3. Beebe built the first bathysphere during the 1920s.
4. This small chamber carried two scientists down into the sea.

Writing Theme
Oceanography

ACTIVE AND PASSIVE VERB FORMS

Objectives

- To identify active and passive verb forms

Writing

- To use the passive form to avoid *you* constructions
- To change passive verbs to active verbs to strengthen writing

Teaching Strategies

LINKING GRAMMAR AND WRITING Tell students that in writing active verb forms are considered stronger and more straightforward than passive forms. Model some additional examples:

These tomatoes *were grown* by Sue.

Sue *grew* these tomatoes.

Explain that the passive form is appropriate, however, when the person who performed the action is unknown or is unimportant to the meaning of the sentence.

These tomatoes *were imported* from Mexico.

HELPFUL HINT Explain that a passive verb form is always a verb phrase containing some form of the helping verb *be* *(am, is, are, was, were, been).*

Additional Resource

Grammar and Usage Practice Book, p. 51

Writing Theme: Oceanography

Other related areas students might wish to explore as writing topics include the following:

- French oceanographer Jacques Cousteau
- the ecosystem of a coral reef
- snorkeling and scuba diving
- the Woods Hole Oceanographic Institution

Answers to Practice Your Skills

A. Concept Check
Active and Passive Verb Forms

Answers are shown on page.

B. Revision Skill
Avoiding the Use of *You*

Answers may vary. A possible revision is shown below.

The bathysphere with the two scientists descends slowly into the depths of the sea. 11 A gentle tug is felt. The cable has neared its end, and the bathysphere floats in an undersea world. 12 At first, the scientists can see only blackness. 13 This darkness might be described as "perpetual night." However, the black world is not completely without light. 14 Hundreds of fish can be observed. Each glows with its own colored lights. 15 For instance, nearby a deep-sea shrimp discharges a bright liquid. 16 Soon the scientists can enjoy a spectacular display of living fireworks.

C. Revision Skill
Using Active Verbs

The italicized verbs in sentences 19, 22, and 23 are passive. All other italicized verbs are active. Revisions may vary. A possible revision is shown below.

17 Undersea exploration has come a long way. 18 Years ago, people could dive only about two hundred feet underwater. 19 They used diving suits with air hoses. 20 Then William Beebe went half a mile down in his bathysphere. 21 However, cables always connected it to the surface. 22 A newer invention, the bathyscaph, does not need cables. 23 Instead, when the craft must return to the surface, it releases ballast to make it lighter. 24 The bathyscaph has reached depths of over six miles. 25 Still, it only can go down or up.

5. In 1930 the bathysphere was lowered for the very first time.
6. Beebe traveled three thousand feet into the inky deep.
7. At two thousand feet below the surface, Beebe was overwhelmed by the unexpected sight of bright lights and colors.
8. The sea was illuminated by bioluminescent fish.
9. Chemicals within the fish gave them a glow, like fireworks.
10. Sights like these had never been seen before by human eyes.

B. REVISION SKILL

Avoiding the Use of *You* In formal writing, the pronoun *you* should be used only to mean "you, the reader." In some cases, changing a verb from the active to the passive will eliminate awkward *you* constructions. Rewrite the following paragraph, using passive verbs in sentences 11, 13, and 14. In sentences 12, 15, and 16, supply a new subject.

> The bathysphere with the two scientists descends slowly into the depths of the sea. **11**You feel a gentle tug. The cable has neared its end, and the bathysphere floats in an undersea world. **12**At first, you can see only blackness. **13**You might describe this darkness as "perpetual night." However, the black world is not completely without light. **14**You can observe hundreds of fish. Each glows with its own colored lights. **15**For instance, nearby you notice a bright liquid discharge from a deep-sea shrimp. **16**Soon you can enjoy a spectacular display of living fireworks.

C. REVISION SKILL

Using Active Verbs In the following paragraph, identify each of the italicized verbs as *Active* or *Passive*. Also make the writing stronger and more straightforward by changing passive verbs to active verbs.

> **17**Undersea exploration *has come* a long way. **18**Years ago, people *could dive* only about two hundred feet underwater. **19**Diving suits with air hoses *were used* by them. **20**Then William Beebe *went* half a mile down in his bathysphere. **21**However, cables always *connected* it to the surface. **22**Cables *are* not *needed* by a newer invention, the bathyscaph. **23**Instead, when the craft must return to the surface, ballast *is released* by the craft to make it lighter. **24**The bathyscaph *has reached* depths of over six miles. **25**Still, it only *can go* down or up.

FOR MORE PRACTICE
See pages 498–499.

490 Grammar Handbook

MIXED REVIEW • PAGES 487–490

A. Write each verb from the following sentences and identify the tense. Also state if the verb is in the progressive form.

1. Early automobiles used steam, gas, and electricity for power.
2. By 1924, however, gasoline had become the major power source.
3. Unfortunately, gasoline adds to air pollution problems.
4. So, for decades U.S. inventors have had an important goal.
5. They have been developing an inexpensive, pollution-free car.
6. Electric cars returned for a short while in the 1960s.
7. Recently, General Motors has been working on a new car.
8. The inside of this car will eventually contain a complex system of batteries and motors.
9. General Motors engineers are still working on the design for the electrical storage systems.
10. New car owners will be facing different issues in the future.
11. By the year 2000, inventors will have been working on electric vehicles for more than a century.
12. Their hard work will have paved the way for future designers.

B. APPLICATION IN LITERATURE

Write the italicized verbs from the following passage. Label each verb as *Active* or *Passive*.

> [13]As we approach the Cape, we *see* again the rocket and its launching tower from far off over the lagoon. [14]It *is illumined* with searchlights, the newest and most perfected creation of a scientific age—hard, weighty metal.
>
> [15]We *watch* the launching with some of the astronauts and their families, from a site near the Vehicle Assembly Building. [16]Our cars *are parked* on a slight rise of ground. . . . [17]A jet of steam *shoots* from the pad below the rocket. [18]"Ahhhh!" The crowd *gasps,* almost in unison. [19]Now great flames *spurt, leap, belch* out across the horizon. [20]Clouds of smoke *billow* up on either side of the rocket, completely hiding its base. [21]From the midst of this holocaust, the rocket *begins* to rise. . . . [22]as if the giant weight *is pulled* by an invisible hand out of the atmosphere.

Anne Morrow Lindbergh,
"Morning—The Bird Perched for Flight"

Writing Theme
Transportation of the Future

CHECK POINT

Writing Theme: Transportation of the Future

Other related areas students might wish to explore as writing topics include the following:

- superfast trains
- the future "family car"
- aircraft of the future
- space stations and space travel

MIXED REVIEW • PAGES 487–490

You may wish to use this activity to check students' mastery of the following concepts:

- verb tenses
- progressive verb forms
- active and passive verb forms

A.

1. used, Past
2. had become, Past Perfect
3. adds, Present
4. have had, Present Perfect
5. have been developing, Present Perfect Progressive
6. returned, Past
7. has been working, Present Perfect Progressive
8. will contain, Future
9. are working, Present Progressive
10. will be facing, Present Progressive
11. will have been working, Future Perfect Progressive
12. will have paved, Future Perfect

B. Application in Literature
Answers are shown on page.

Using Verbs 491

TROUBLESOME PAIRS OF VERBS

Objectives

- To recognize the differences in meaning in the verb pairs *sit, set; lie, lay; rise, raise; let, leave;* and *learn, teach*

Writing

- To revise sentences that contain errors in verb choice
- To proofread a paragraph, correcting errors in verb choice

Teaching Strategies

HELPFUL HINT You may wish to create a chart, such as the one below, showing the present tense, the present participle, the past form, and the past participle for *sit/set* and *rise/raise.*

	lie		**lay**
	lie		lay
	lying		laying
	lay		laid
(have)	lain	(have)	laid

Ask which word appears on both lists *(lay).* Point out that *lay* is the present tense of *lay* and the past tense of *lie.*

INDIVIDUALIZING INSTRUCTION: LEP STUDENTS Because many dialects of English use these verbs in nonstandard ways, oral drill will be useful to accustom students to standard English usage of these verb pairs. You also might complete exercises A and B of Practice Your Skills orally with the class.

TROUBLESOME PAIRS OF VERBS

Many writers find several pairs of verbs confusing. These verbs include *sit* and *set, lie* and *lay, rise* and *raise, let* and *leave,* and *learn* and *teach.*

These pairs of verbs cause trouble because they are similar in meaning and often similar in appearance.

Using *Sit* and *Set*

Sit means "to be in a seated position." The principal parts of the verb *sit* are *sit, sat,* and *sat.* Example: *Sit* on the chair.

Set means "to put or place." The principal parts of the verb *set* are *set, set,* and *set.* Example: *Set* the cage down.

Using *Lie* and *Lay*

Lie means "to rest in a flat position." The principal parts of the verb *lie* are *lie, lay,* and *lain.* Example: It *lies* on the table.

Lay means "to put or place." The principal parts of the verb *lay* are *lay, laid,* and *laid.* Example: *Lay* the slides on the counter.

Using *Rise* and *Raise*

Rise means "to move upward." The principal parts of the verb rise are *rise, rose,* and *risen.* Example: The moths *rise* quickly in the air.

Raise means "to move something upward" or "to lift." The principal parts of the verb *raise* are *raise, raised,* and *raised.* Example: *Raise* the window.

Using *Let* and *Leave*

Let means "to allow or permit." The principal parts of the verb *let* are *let, let,* and *let.* Example: *Let* the spider go free.

Leave means "to depart" or "to allow something to remain where it is." The principal parts of the verb *leave* are *leave, left,* and *left.* Example: *Leave* the window closed.

Using *Learn* and *Teach*

Learn means "to gain knowledge or skill." The principal parts of the verb *learn* are *learn, learned,* and *learned.* Example: I *learned* a lot about those insects.

Teach means "to help someone learn" or "to show how or explain." The principal parts of the verb *teach* are *teach, taught,* and *taught.* Example: That book *taught* me a lot about insects.

Practice Your Skills

A. CONCEPT CHECK

Verb Pairs Write the <u>correct verb</u> from the ones given in parentheses.

Writing Theme
Attack and Defense in Nature

1. Studying insects closely can (learn, <u>teach</u>) us much about how they protect themselves.
2. An insect that (lays, <u>lies</u>) motionless on a leaf can become food for some other animal.
3. If other species (<u>leave</u>, let) this creature alone, however, it can be a predator, or hunter.
4. It will (lay, <u>lie</u>) there waiting for its prey.
5. Many species will not (<u>let</u>, leave) the slightest chance for a meal go by.
6. For example, a spider (lies, <u>lays</u>) a trap with its web.
7. Then the spider (<u>sits</u>, sets) patiently near its web.
8. It will (lay, <u>lie</u>) there motionless for hours.
9. Experience seems to have (learned, <u>taught</u>) moths how to escape from sticky spider webs.
10. Detachable scales on the moth's wings (leave, <u>let</u>) the moth get away from a hungry spider.
11. When the moth (<u>sits</u>, sets) on the spider's web, its wings don't stick.

STUMBLING BLOCK Some of the exercise items require students to choose between *let* and *leave* in the expression "to leave someone or something alone," Point out that *let* and *leave* both mean "allow." However, *leave* means "to allow something or someone to remain as it is," while *let* implies "allowing someone or something to act." Provide additional examples, such as the following:

Please *leave* me alone.

Let my people go.

Let the dog run free.

Additional Resource

Grammar and Usage Practice Book, pp. 52–53

Writing Theme: Attack and Defense in Nature

Other related areas students might wish to explore as writing topics include the following:

- how various animal mothers protect their young
- animals that cooperate for common defense (such as ants or prairie dogs)
- camouflage or mimicry as defenses

Answers to Practice Your Skills

A. Concept Check

Verb Pairs

Answers are shown on page.

Using Verbs 493

B. Revision Skill
Using the Right Verbs

16. Correct
17. However, nature has taught spiders new tricks as well.
18. Correct
19. The spider instantly rises up to attack any moth.
20. Other clever spiders set traps for male moths.
21. An odor exactly like that of a female moth rises from the body of the spider.
22. Some spiders also have laid special traps for moths.
23. Correct
24. A smaller web might let a moth escape.
25. Correct

C. Proofreading Skill
Using Verbs Correctly

Errors are shown on page.

Learning about self-defense in the animal world might teach us something about our own defenses. Animals' defense systems include shells and spines. Some creatures, like armadillos, have hard, protective shells. Others, like porcupines and hedgehogs, have sharp spines. Under attack, these animals lie safely inside their "armor."

Some insects and mammals roll themselves up into a ball. This protects soft body parts. When attacked, a hedgehog quickly rolls up in this way. Then it sits on the ground, without raising its head and with only its needle-sharp spines exposed. Enemies often will leave a hedgehog alone rather than risk an injury to themselves.

12. Soon it (rises, raises) its body and flies to safety.
13. The moth (leaves, lets) some of its wing scales behind, stuck to the web.
14. This (raises, rises) another question.
15. What other insects can (set, sit) on a spider web and then escape?

B. REVISION SKILL

Using the Right Verbs Revise the sentences that contain errors in verb choice. Write *Correct* if a sentence contains no errors.

16. Nature's moths usually leave scales on spiders' webs.
17. However, nature has learned spiders new tricks as well.
18. The orb weaver, for example, is a spider that has learned the difference between moths and other types of prey.
19. The spider instantly raises up to attack any moth.
20. Other clever spiders sit traps for male moths.
21. An odor exactly like that of a female moth raises from the body of the spider.
22. Some spiders also have lain special traps for moths.
23. These spiders raise vertical "skyscraper webs" more than two hundred times their own size.
24. A smaller web might leave a moth escape.
25. In a skyscraper web, however, a moth leaves so many scales on the web that the moth cannot fly.

C. PROOFREADING SKILL

Using Verbs Correctly Write the following paragraphs, correcting any errors in grammar, capitalization, punctuation, and spelling. Watch especially for errors in verb choice. (10 errors)

Learning about self-defense in the animal world might learn us something about our own defenses. Animals' defense systems include shells and spines some creatures, like armadillos, have hard, protective shells. Others, like porcupine's and hedgehogs, have sharp spines. Under attack, these animals lie safely inside their "armer."

Some insects and mammals roll themselves up into a ball. this protects soft body parts. When attacked, a hedgehog quickly rolls up in this way. Then it sets on the ground, without rising its head and with only it's needle-sharp spines exposed. Enemys often will let a hedgehog alone rather than risk an injury to themselves.

FOR MORE PRACTICE
See page 499.

CHECK POINT

MIXED REVIEW • PAGES 492–494

The following sentences are part of an imaginary interview between a reporter and Donald McKay, builder of the renowned clipper ships of the 1800s. Write the correct verb from the pair in parentheses.

1. REPORTER: We are (setting, sitting) here today with shipbuilder Donald McKay. How fast were your sailing ships?
2. McKAY: Well, *The Champion of the Seas* (taught, learned) the steamboats a lesson. Her record was unbeaten for twenty-five years.
3. REPORTER: How did you (set, sit) such a record?
4. McKAY: We simply (raised, rose) as much canvas as possible.
5. Sometimes, five rows of sails were (raised, risen) on each mast.
6. REPORTER: Who (learned, taught) you to sail this way?
7. McKAY: Experience has (learned, taught) me everything.
8. REPORTER: What cargo did the ships carry to (raise, rise) money?
9. McKAY: In the early days, we (laid, lay) bags of tea in most holds. Later, ships carried gold, silver, or passengers.
10. Passengers would (set, sit) on deck as often as possible.
11. They didn't like to (lay, lie) below deck.
12. REPORTER: (Teach, Learn) me about a typical voyage. Tell me, please, what was a day aboard ship like?
13. McKAY: Well, we often sailed before the sun (raised, rose).
14. We hoped the weather would (leave, let) us alone to sail freely.
15. My ship has often (laid, lain) still in the water on windless days and my hopes would (raise, rise) at any hint of breeze.
16. REPORTER: Did you (leave, let) the crew relax at any time?
17. McKAY: No skipper has ever (left, let) a crew become too relaxed. The sea is too dangerous for that.
18. REPORTER: As you (set, sit) here today, which would you say is your favorite among your ships?
19. McKAY: If you (let, leave) me choose a favorite, it would be the *Great Republic,* the biggest wooden ship ever built.
20. REPORTER: Thank you, Donald McKay. We'll (let, leave) you to your work.

Writing Theme
Clipper Ships

Clipper Ship "Dreadnought" off Tuskar Light, (1856), Nathaniel Currier. Lithograph.

CHECK POINT

Writing Theme: Clipper Ships

Other related areas students might wish to explore as writing topics include the following:

- the sport of sailing
- the America's Cup sailboat race
- the history of whaling ships out of New Bedford, Massachusetts
- the tea trade with China

MIXED REVIEW • PAGES 492–494

You may wish to use this activity to check students' mastery of the following concept:

- troublesome pairs of verbs

Answers are shown on page.

ART NOTE

At the age of fifteen, Nathaniel Currier (1813–1888) became apprenticed to a Boston lithographer. (Explain that a *lithograph* is a type of art print.) Currier opened a lithography shop in New York City around 1835; he made James Ives, his bookkeeper, a partner in 1857. The extremely successful firm of Currier and Ives produced more than 7,000 hand-colored, detailed lithographs of the American scene.

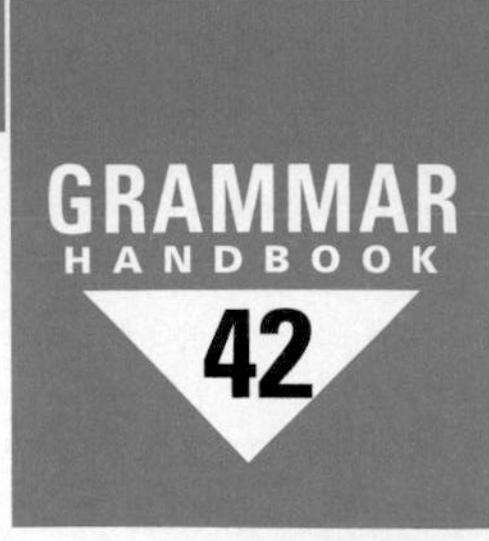

ADDITIONAL PRACTICE

Each of these exercises correlates to a section of Handbook 42, "Using Verbs." The exercises may be used for more practice, for reteaching, or for review of the concepts presented:

Additional Resource

Grammar and Usage Practice Book, p. 55

Writing Theme: Toys

Other related areas students might wish to explore as writing topics include the following:

- the history of the game of marbles
- best-selling board games in the United States today
- popular computer games

A. Identifying Verbs

Answers are shown on page. Students' answers should be in columns.

B. Identifying Verb Phrases

Answers are shown on page. Tell students that a sentence may have more than one verb phrase.

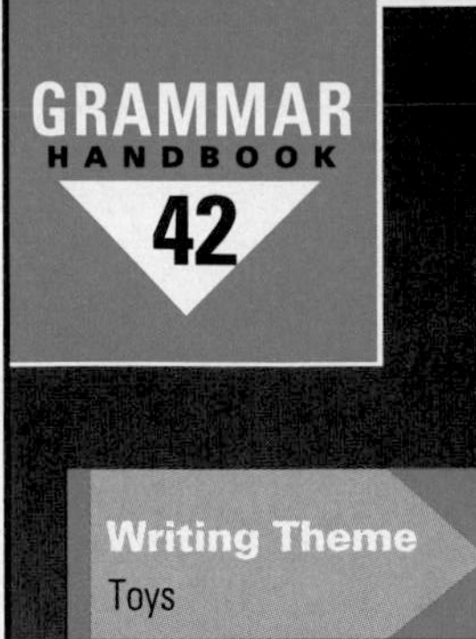

Writing Theme
Toys

A. Identifying Verbs Make two columns on your paper. Label them *Action Verbs* and *Linking Verbs.* Write the verbs from the following sentences in the correct columns.

1. Toys often have interesting histories.
2. Yo-yos, for example, first became popular in the United States during the 1930s.
3. However, they were not a new invention at the time.
4. People in the Philippines used yo-yos for many years.
5. Their yo-yos worked as weapons as well as toys.
6. In Europe, people made toys like yo-yos almost three thousand years ago.
7. Some toys, though, are even older than the yo-yo.
8. In ancient Egypt, children pulled and rolled toys from place to place.
9. Egyptian children played ball too.
10. They also enjoyed toy animals of various kinds.
11. In ancient Greece and Rome, children often pushed hoops.
12. They floated toy boats in local lakes and ponds.
13. Greek and Roman children also rode hobbyhorses.
14. Toys like these remain popular today.
15. Some good ideas last forever.

B. Identifying Verb Phrases Write the verb phrases from the following sentences. Underline the helping verbs once and the main verbs twice.

16. Did you ever spin a toy top?
17. You can find these wonderful toys almost all over the world.
18. In China and Japan, children have played with tops and spinners for thousands of years.
19. Historians have uncovered evidence of tops in ancient Egypt.
20. Some tops might have appeared more than five thousand years ago.
21. Can you picture ancient-Egyptian children and their tops with the great pyramids in the background?
22. Archaeologists have discovered wonderful tops at the sites of ancient Native American communities.
23. People must have made them by hand from hollow nuts and gourds.
24. Further north, Inuit children have always used ivory tops.

25. Their tops might have been carved from walrus tusks.
26. In Europe, children have had tops and spinners since Roman times.
27. Over the years, tops have come in all shapes and sizes.
28. A twist of the wrist will start some tops.
29. Others are spun with the help of a string.
30. Once a top has been started, it will turn for a long time.

C. Using Irregular Verbs For each sentence write the correct form of the verb given in parentheses.

31. Do you ever (took, take) a kite out on a breezy day?
32. Not much has been (written, wrote) about the very first kites.
33. Kites probably (begin, began) in China about three thousand years ago.
34. By 200 B.C. kites had even (went, gone) into battle.
35. Bamboo pipes (rode, ridden) up into the air on the kites.
36. The sound of these whistles usually (frozen, froze) the enemy in its tracks.
37. Over the years kites have (did, done) other useful things.
38. During the construction of a bridge in the 1840s, kites (bring, brought) equipment across the Niagara River.
39. Airplane designers have also (chose, chosen) kites as models.
40. For example, the Wright brothers had (saw, seen) kites in action before they built their first airplane.

D. Recognizing Verb Tenses Make two columns: *Verbs* and *Verb Tenses.* In the first column, write the verbs from the following sentences; in the second, write the tenses of those verbs.

41. Dolls are among the world's most popular toys.
42. They will probably remain popular for years to come.
43. People have not always used dolls as toys, however.
44. In ancient Egypt, people buried special dolls with the dead.
45. According to Egyptian religious beliefs, these dolls became servants in the afterlife.
46. In ancient Greece, young girls gave their dolls away shortly before marriage.
47. For centuries this had been a sign of the girls' adulthood.
48. In most parts of Europe, dolls became popular children's toys in the 1700s.

C. Using Irregular Verbs
Answers are shown on page.

D. Recognizing Verb Tenses
Students' answers should be in columns.

41. are, Present
42. will remain, Future
43. have used, Present Perfect
44. buried, Past
45. became, Past
46. gave, Past
47. had been, Past Perfect
48. became, Past

49. do have, Present
50. had become, Past Perfect
51. have survived, Present Perfect
52. had been made, Past Perfect
53. Have, Present
54. will use, Future
55. will have become, Future Perfect

E. Using Progressive Forms

56. Surfers will always be riding the big waves.
57. However, during the 1950s, surfers had been searching for alternatives to waves.
58. These surfers were looking for a new approach to the sport.
59. For years they had been noticing youngsters on roller skates.
60. This everyday sight was giving some surfers an idea.
61. Soon surfers were attaching roller skates to their surfboards.
62. Thanks to these inventive surfers, people have been enjoying skateboards for years.
63. Since the 1950s, fun-seekers have been riding skateboards.
64. Today, people are skateboarding more than ever before.
65. They still are finding excitement in the speed of the ride.
66. In the past, skateboarders were practicing on local streets.
67. Now they are using elaborate ramps too.
68. Some cities have been building parks with skateboard ramps.
69. Without a doubt, skateboarders will be developing new ways of practicing their skills.
70. Maybe even more people will be taking up the sport in the future.

F. Identifying Active and Passive Forms

Answers are shown on page.

49. Dolls from that era do not have the sophisticated appearance of dolls today.
50. Back then, woodcarvers had become doll makers.
51. Many of their dolls have survived to this day as puppets.
52. By the 1800s, many dolls had been made from papier-mâché.
53. Today, doll collectors still have china dolls, with china faces and heads.
54. In the future, doll makers will probably use high-tech materials for dolls.
55. By then, dolls will have become more lifelike than ever.

E. Using Progressive Forms Rewrite the following sentences, using the progressive forms of the verbs.

56. Surfers will always ride the big waves.
57. However, during the 1950s, surfers had searched for alternatives to waves.
58. These surfers looked for a new approach to the sport.
59. For years they had noticed youngsters on roller skates.
60. This everyday sight gave some surfers an idea.
61. Soon surfers attached roller skates to their surfboards.
62. Thanks to these inventive surfers, people have enjoyed skateboards for years.
63. Since the 1950s, fun-seekers have ridden skateboards.
64. Today, people skateboard more than ever before.
65. They still find excitement in the speed of the ride.
66. In the past, skateboarders practiced on local streets.
67. Now they use elaborate ramps too.
68. Some cities have built parks with skateboard ramps.
69. Without a doubt, skateboarders will develop new ways of practicing their skills.
70. Maybe even more people will take up the sport in the future.

F. Identifying Active and Passive Forms Write each verb from the following sentences. Label each *Active* or *Passive.*

71. Puppets have been around for thousands of years.
72. Today the simplest puppets are finger puppets.
73. The puppeteer's own hands and fingers form the puppets.
74. The puppet's face is usually drawn on the person's hands or fingers.

75. Hand puppets are used by both professional and amateur puppeteers.
76. Hand, or glove, puppets usually are topped by a hollow head.
77. Puppeteers place their hands inside this hollow head.
78. A glove or piece of cloth forms the puppet's body.
79. The puppet's arm movements are controlled by the puppeteer's fingers.
80. During the 1950s and 1960s, hand puppets were revolutionized.
81. Jim Henson, for example, developed the Muppets, highly flexible puppets.
82. Rods and strings were used for the control of arms and legs.
83. Recently, computers have been added to the puppeteer's bag of tricks.
84. Puppets' movements and voices are created by complicated hardware and computer programs.
85. Computers make these electronic puppets incredibly lifelike.

G. Choosing the Correct Verb Write the correct verb given in parentheses.

86. People who enjoy model trains love to (learn, teach) the hobby to others.
87. First the experts (let, leave) the person run the train.
88. Then they (learn, teach) the person to build a setting.
89. Other experts (leave, let) newcomers learn on their own.
90. No matter what their age, though, model railroaders (lay, lie) out tracks in intricate patterns.
91. They (set, sit) houses, barns, and crossings all around the landscape.
92. Model mountains (rise, raise) dramatically into the air.
93. Valleys and rivers (lie, lay) between the mountains.
94. Typical hobbyists (set, sit) for hours with their rigs.
95. Some people never (let, leave) their work alone.
96. These people are always (sitting, setting) new equipment in place.
97. Their excitement (raises, rises) with each new addition.
98. Many young people (learn, teach) about another kind of model building from kits.
99. They (set, sit) patiently with tiny pieces of plastic or wood and a small tube of glue.
100. These hobbyists (raise, rise) entire model cities.

G. Choosing the Correct Verb
Answers are shown on page.

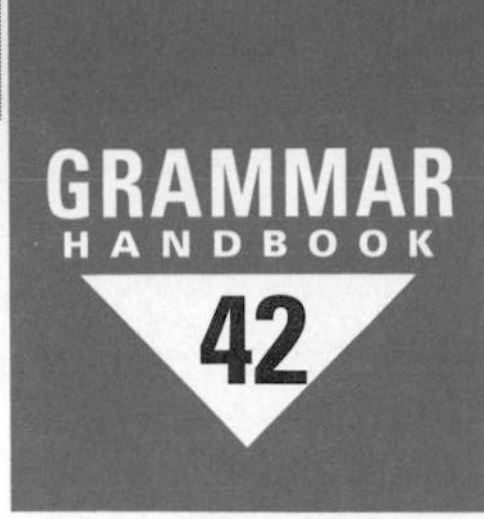

REVIEW

These exercises may be used as mixed review or as an informal evaluation of the skills presented in Handbook 42, "Using Verbs."

Additional Resources

Grammar and Usage Practice Book, p. 56
Tests and Writing Assessment Prompts, Mastery Tests, pp. 23–24
Elaboration, Revision, and Proofreading Practice, p. 28

Writing Theme: Amusement Parks

Other related areas students might wish to explore as writing topics include the following:

- George W. Gale Ferris and the largest ferris wheel
- Tivoli Gardens in Copenhagen, Denmark
- famous roller-coaster rides
- nearby county fairs and state fairs

A. Identifying Verbs

1. had meant, Linking Verb
2. had been enjoying, Action Verb
3. were, Linking Verb
4. sprang, Action Verb
5. would come, Action Verb
6. had become, Linking Verb
7. built, Action Verb
8. connected, Action Verb
9. would be coming, Action Verb
10. were, Linking Verb

B. Verb Tenses and Progressive Forms

11. opened
12. is
13. lived
14. watched

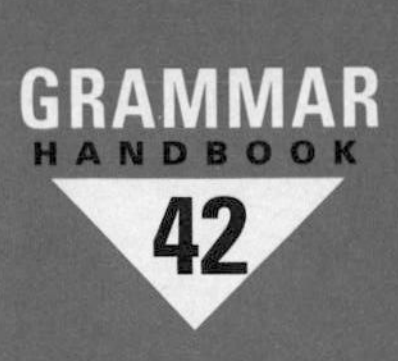

REVIEW

Writing Theme
Amusement Parks

A. Identifying Verbs List the verbs and verb phrases in the following sentences. Identify each main verb as an *Action Verb* or *Linking Verb*. Underline all helping verbs.

1. For over seventy-five years, Coney Island had meant thrills, excitement, and fun.
2. However, people had been enjoying Coney Island long before the arrival of its amusement parks.
3. Sun and sand were the main attractions in the early days.
4. In the 1850s, hotels sprang up along the beach.
5. Hundreds of visitors would come for a weekend by the sea.
6. By 1860, Coney Island had become a major resort area.
7. Then, in 1875, New York City built a new railroad line.
8. It connected Coney Island with central Brooklyn.
9. Soon people would be coming to Coney Island just for the afternoon or evening instead of for a weekend or summer.
10. The brand-new amusement parks were exciting for the tens of thousands of visitors.

B. Verb Tenses and Progressive Forms Complete the following sentences with the verb forms in parentheses.

11. In 1897, Steeplechase Park (past tense of *open*).
12. That park (present of *be*) probably the greatest symbol of Coney Island in its prime.
13. As a child, George Tilyou, the founder of Steeplechase, (past of *live*) in his parents' Coney Island hotel.
14. In the 1890s, he (past of *watch*) the construction of Coney Island's first real amusement park, Sea Lion Park.
15. He quickly (past perfect of *realize*) the appeal of the parks.
16. In fact, few people ever (present perfect of *understand*) fun, thrills, and entertainment as well as Tilyou.
17. People (future of *pay*) good money for a thrill.
18. The thrills and rides (present of *chase*) away their worries.
19. From the beginning, Tilyou (past progressive of *call*) Steeplechase "the Funny Place."
20. Soon visitors even (past progressive of *travel*) on a fantasy trip to the moon.
21. By 1980, though, everything (past perfect of *change*).
22. Steeplechase Park and Coney Island itself (past perfect progressive of *decline*) rapidly since the 1960s.
23. Today few traditional amusement parks (present of *remain*).

24. Yet people (future progressive of *look*) for relief from tension for years to come.
25. The legends of the old amusement parks, too, probably (future of *live*) forever.

C. Using Irregular Verbs Write the verb in parentheses that correctly completes each of the following sentences.

26. Most people (have ridden, rode) a carousel.
27. Surprisingly, the word carousel (begin, began) as a name for a serious war game.
28. In the original version of the game, Arab soldiers on horseback had (threw, thrown) clay balls at one another.
29. The game (gave, given) the riders practice in the arts of war.
30. This activity (grown, grew) into a sport for Europe's nobles.
31. For training, young men on human-powered carousels (take, took) stabs at targets with swords and lances.
32. By 1900, mechanical carousels had (come, came) along.
33. The horses, camels, elephants, and other fanciful creatures on these new carousels (run, ran) smoothly for hour after hour.
34. Over the years, these carousels have (bring, brought) endless enjoyment to amusement park visitors.
35. People still can (see, seen) horses and other figures from these antique carousels in parks and museums.

D. Choosing the Right Verb Write the correct verb given in parentheses.

36. In this article I will (teach, learn) you a little about Clarkson's Carnival.
37. This is the headline for my article: Mayor (Leaves, Lets) Carnival Come to Town.
38. Right now I am (setting, sitting) at the site of the carnival.
39. Off in the distance, a group of workers (lies, lays) railroad ties around the perimeter of the park.
40. The owners (leave, let) the crews alone so they can work.
41. Close by, several crews are (setting, sitting) rides in place.
42. Yesterday's crews (rose, raised) tents in the park.
43. Inside those tents, lions and tigers (lie, lay) quietly now.
44. Nearby a worker (leaves, lets) visitors feed the elephants.
45. Tomorrow, the elephant trainer will (teach, learn) the animals a new trick.

15. had realized
16. have understood
17. will pay
18. chase
19. was calling
20. were traveling
21. had changed
22. had been declining
23. remain
24. will be looking
25. will live

C. Using Irregular Verbs
Answers are shown on page.

D. Choosing the Right Verb
Answers are shown on page.

Using Verbs **501**

Writing Theme: World Records

Other related areas students might wish to explore as writing topics include the following:

- longest tennis match
- largest building in the world
- the fastest running animal's speed

E. Using Active Verb Forms

Rewritten sentences may vary. Possible answers are shown below.

46. Unusual world records surprise most people.
47. For example, two Clydesdales in Michigan pulled the heaviest load for horses—ninety-six thousand pounds.
48. Scientists have estimated the number of nematode sea worms, the commonest animal on earth, at 4 x 1025 (four followed by twenty-five zeros).
49. Sailors in the South Atlantic Ocean caught a whale measuring 110 feet, 2-1/2 inches.
50. Stan Barrett drove a rocket-propelled car 739 mph in 1979.
51. A Chicago woman endured a ninety-six hour surgical operation.
52. Shridhar Chillal of India grew a fingernail 34 1/2 inches long.
53. Generations of irrigation workers in Egypt have sung the world's oldest song, the shadoof chant, since the beginning of recorded time.
54. The Cambodian alphabet contains seventy-two letters.
55. Engineers in Konstantynow, Poland, built the tallest structure in the world, a radio tower more than four-tenths of a mile high.

F. Using Passive Verb Forms

Rewritten sentences may vary. Possible answers are shown below.

56. Many surprising records can be found in the history of sports and games.
57. The largest game of musical chairs on record was attended by a total of 8,238 people.
58. Ten balls were juggled at one time by Enrico Rastelli of Italy.
59. A 2,664-pound white shark once was caught by an Australian fisherman.
60. The longest recorded chess game—165 hours and nine minutes—was played by two university students in England.

Writing Theme
World Records

E. Using Active Verb Forms Rewrite the following sentences, changing the verbs from the passive to the active form.

46. Most people are surprised by unusual world records.
47. For example, the heaviest load for horses—ninety-six thousand pounds—was pulled by two Clydesdales in Michigan.
48. The number of nematode sea worms, the commonest animal on earth, has been estimated by scientists at 4 x 10^{25} (four followed by twenty-five zeros).
49. A whale measuring 110 feet, 2½ inches was caught by sailors in the South Atlantic Ocean.
50. A speed of 739 mph was attained by a rocket-propelled car driven by Stan Barrett in 1979.
51. A ninety-six-hour surgical operation was endured by a Chicago woman.
52. A fingernail 34½ inches long was grown by Shridhar Chillal of India.
53. The world's oldest song, the shadoof chant, has been sung since the beginning of recorded time by generations of irrigation workers in Egypt.
54. Seventy-two letters are contained in the Cambodian alphabet.
55. The tallest structure in the world, a radio tower more than four-tenths of a mile high, was built by engineers in Konstantynow, Poland.

F. Using Passive Verb Forms Rewrite the following sentences, changing the verbs from the active to the passive form.

56. You can find many surprising records in the history of sports and games.
57. A total of 8,238 people attended the largest game of musical chairs on record.
58. Enrico Rastelli of Italy juggled ten balls at one time.
59. An Australian fisherman once caught a 2,664-pound white shark.
60. Two university students in England played the longest recorded chess game—165 hours and nine minutes.
61. Skateboarder Richard K. Brown reached a record speed of 71.79 miles per hour in a prone position on a course at Mt. Baldy, California.
62. Louis Scripa, Jr., did more than sixty thousand sit-ups in twenty-four hours in Sacramento, California.

61. A record speed of 71.79 miles per hour was reached by skateboarder Richard K. Brown in a prone position on a course at Mt. Baldy, California.
62. More than sixty thousand sit-ups were done in twenty-four hours by Louis Scripa, Jr., in Sacramento, California.

WRITING CONNECTIONS

Elaboration, Revision, and Proofreading

Revise the following draft of a cause-and-effect paper by using the directions at the bottom of the page. Then proofread the passage, paying close attention to correcting errors in the use of verbs. Also look for other errors in grammar, capitalization, punctuation, and spelling.

[1]A new way of cooking food was discovered accidently in 1946 by Dr. Percy Spencer, an Engineer for Raytheon Corporation. [2]Spencer was testing a magnetron tube. [3]A magnetron tube is an electronic tube that produces microwave energy. [4]Spencer reaches into his pocket for a candy bar he had brung along for a snack. [5]And found the candy bar had melted. [6]It was determined by Spencer that microwaves had heated the candy. [7]In a microwave oven, radio waves from a magnetron penetrates the food and make the water molecules in the food vibrate. [8]The vibration caused friction, which heats the food from the inside out. [9]Conventional ovens cook food in the oposite way. [10]They heated the outside of the food first and then the heat had went to the inside. [11]If you have ate food cooked by microwaves, you know it doesn't taste no diffrent from food cooked in other ways.

1. Add the information in sentence 3 to sentence 2 as an appositive.
2. Change sentence 6 to the active voice.
3. After sentence 6, add this information: His discovery led to the development of the microwave oven.
4. In sentence 10 replace the verb phrase "had went" with the precise verb "penetrates."
5. Divide the passage into two paragraphs.

Informative Writing: Explaining *How*

Cause-and-effect writing answers the questions "What happened?" and "Why did it happen?" (See Workshop 4.) When you revise this type of writing, check to see if you have used precise verbs and consistent verb tenses to explain the relationship between causes and effects.

WRITING CONNECTIONS

Elaboration, Revision, and Proofreading

This activity will allow your students to see some of the concepts presented in this handbook in a piece of cause-and-effect writing. By revising and proofreading this passage, students will practice using precise verbs and consistent verb tenses.

You might have students complete this revision with a partner or in a small group.

Revisions may vary slightly. See a typical revision below. Elements involving change are shown in boldface.

A new way of cooking food was discovered accidentally in 1946 by Dr. Percy Spencer, an engineer for Raytheon Corporation. Spencer was testing a magnetron tube, **an electronic tube that produces microwave energy.** Spencer reached into his pocket for a candy bar he had brought along for a snack. He found the candy bar had melted. (*or* Spencer reached into his pocket for a candy bar he had brought along for a snack and found the candy bar had melted.) **Spencer determined that microwaves had heated the candy. His discovery led to the development of the microwave oven.**

In a microwave oven, radio waves from a magnetron penetrate the food and make the water molecules in the food vibrate. The vibration causes friction, which heats the food from the inside out. Conventional ovens cook food in the opposite way. They heat the outside of the food first and then the heat **penetrates** to the inside. If you have eaten food cooked by microwaves, you know it doesn't taste different from food cooked in other ways.

Objective

- To use an illustration and writing prompts as springboards to informal writing

WRITING WARM-UPS

Begin by reminding students that they will not be graded for this assignment. The illustration and the activities are intended as springboards to get them to think imaginatively about the concepts presented in this handbook. Unless students volunteer to explore more than one prompt, have them work on a single activity.

For the first prompt, you might have on hand old magazines from which students can cut material to illustrate their movie ads.

For the second prompt, encourage students to brainstorm a list of ten or fifteen terms from which to choose the five that describe the book or program most vividly.

For the third prompt, consider telling students that their description may take the form of either a prose paragraph or a brief poem. Urge them to include "showing" details that appeal to as many of the five senses as possible.

Sketch Book

WRITING WARM-UPS

- "Fantastic!" "Hilarious!" "Suspenseful!" "Outrageously Funny!" You've seen movie advertisements with glowing quotes from the critics. Create an ad for your favorite movie. Be sure to include some made-up quotes.

- Think of a book and a television program you've seen that you especially liked or disliked. Write a list of five terms that describe the book or program.
- Write a brief description of a scene you remember vividly. It could be something you saw yourself or something from a movie or television program.

Using Modifiers

- What Are Modifiers?
- Adjectives
- Articles
- Adverbs
- Adjective or Adverb?
- Adjectives in Comparisons
- Adverbs in Comparisons
- Special Problems with Modifiers

When was the last time you saw a movie? How good was the movie? How does it compare to others you've seen? To answer questions like these, you need to use modifiers—adjectives and adverbs. Modifiers help you clarify, describe, and qualify your thoughts.

This handbook can help you choose *precise* (adjective) modifiers that you can use to express yourself *clearly* (adverb).

Using Modifiers

Objectives

- To identify adjectives, adverbs, articles, and pronouns used as modifiers
- To distinguish between adjectives and adverbs
- To form and use adjectives and adverbs in comparisons
- To avoid common errors in the use of modifiers

Writing

- To use modifiers for elaboration and clarity
- To use comparative and superlative forms correctly to indicate comparisons and contrasts

INTRODUCING THE HANDBOOK

With students, read the text. Then ask volunteers to write on the board answers to the three questions that open the paragraph. Underline the modifiers in each student sentence. Then block out the modifiers and ask students how the sentences have changed. (Stripped of modifiers, sentences can lose precision; some become so vague that they make no sense.)

WHAT ARE MODIFIERS?

Objective

- To recognize the functions of modifiers in sentences

Teaching Strategies

HELPFUL HINT: MODIFIERS

Students may be more familiar with the terms *adjectives* and *adverbs* than with the term *modifiers*. Explain that *modifiers* is a general term; both adjectives and adverbs are types of modifiers.

This handbook focuses on one-word modifiers. For information about phrases and clauses used as modifiers, see the following parts of the text:

Prepositional Phrases as Modifiers, pp. 540–542

Types of Subordinate Clauses, pp. 564–569

Participles, pp. 599–603

Additional Resources

Tests and Writing Assessment Prompts, Pretest, pp. 25–26

 Grammar Test Generator

WHAT ARE MODIFIERS?

Modifiers are words that make other words more precise.

Nouns and pronouns help us name and identify things and people in the world around us. Verbs help us express action. **Modifiers** provide additional information about nouns, pronouns, and verbs. Modifiers help us describe what we have seen and heard.

Vincent van Gogh loved *bright* colors.
He painted *quickly* and *forcefully*.
He sold *only one* painting during his life.

Modifiers can also help describe feelings about things and people.

Van Gogh was *happiest* when he painted outdoors.
Bright, yellow sunflowers were a *favorite* subject.
He felt *especially content* when painting *ordinary* people.

Remember, to change something slightly is to *modify* it. An artist can modify a painting by adding details that make the picture more interesting. Writers and speakers modify an idea or image by choosing certain describing words—modifiers.

Notice how modifiers both describe and point out the differences in the two paintings below. Behind the *yellow* sunflowers in the *copper* vase is a *roughly textured blue* background. The *blue* irises in the *gold* vase sit in front of a *bright yellow* wall.

Writing TIP

Writers can use modifiers to bring a reader into a scene. Notice how modifiers add accuracy and detail to *Last Chance to See*, pages 62–63.

Left, *Crown Imperial Fritillaria in a Copper Vase* (1887), Vincent van Gogh.
Right, *Vase with Irises* (1890), Vincent van Gogh.

ART NOTE

Vincent van Gogh (1853–1890), Dutch postimpressionist artist, painted his most famous works after moving to France in 1883. In many of his still lifes with flowers he was experimenting with unusual color combinations, trying to achieve especially vivid effects. An artist friend once criticized some of van Gogh's flower paintings as "flat" and complained, "of that I cannot convince him. He always answers me: 'But I was trying to introduce this and that colour contrast!'"

ADJECTIVES

An **adjective** is a word that modifies a noun or pronoun.

What is the difference between these sentences?

Van Gogh painted scenes of life.
Van Gogh painted simple scenes of rural life.

The difference is in the descriptive words that tell what kind of scenes and what kind of life. These words are called **adjectives.** They modify nouns or pronouns.

Some adjectives tell *how many* or *what kind* about the words they modify.

There were *many* painters. He tried *new* techniques.
He had *few* friends. The *older* painters disapproved.

Some adjectives tell *which one* or *which ones.*

This painting is famous. *Those* peasants are in the field.
His paintings did not sell. *These* fields are colorful.

Self-portrait with Felt Hat (1887), Vincent van Gogh.

Proper Adjectives

Proper adjectives are adjectives formed from proper nouns. They are always capitalized.

a Flemish painter a French artist
a Renaissance painting a Belgian village
the Dutch countryside the Japanese watercolor

Predicate Adjectives

Sometimes a **linking verb** separates an adjective from the word it modifies. An adjective that follows a linking verb and that modifies the subject is called a **predicate adjective.** (See page 474 for information about linking verbs.)

Van Gogh seemed *lonely.* He became *enthusiastic.*
His brother was *upset.* The painting is *priceless.*

ART NOTE

Van Gogh began painting portraits because, at the time, portraits were selling better than landscapes and still lifes, which were his main interests. For practice, he paid models to sit for him when he could afford them. More often, however, he painted friends or, as in the portrait above, himself. Altogether, van Gogh painted about forty self-portraits. Some critics maintain that in this self-portrait, his choice of a soft, light felt hat and a shirt with no tie shows that he wanted to look artistic and sophisticated.

ADJECTIVES

Objectives

- To recognize the functions of adjectives in sentences
- To identify proper adjectives, predicate adjectives, and pronouns used as adjectives

Writing

- To use adjectives to write vivid descriptions

Teaching Strategies

HELPFUL HINT: NOUNS AS ADJECTIVES Explain that common nouns, as well as proper nouns, can sometimes function as adjectives—they can modify other nouns. Give examples, such as *raisin* bread, *attic* room, *copper* kettle, or *brake* pedal.

INDIVIDUALIZING INSTRUCTION: ESL STUDENTS In Spanish and other Romance languages, adjectives often follow the words they modify. Remind students who speak these languages that in English, adjectives usually come directly before the words they modify.

KEY TO UNDERSTANDING Remind students that a proper noun is a noun naming a specific person, place, or thing. Offer more examples of proper adjectives made from proper nouns, such as *Korean, Shakespearean, Grecian,* and *Islamic.*

INDIVIDUALIZING INSTRUCTION: LEP STUDENTS Some students speak dialects in which forms of *be* used as linking verbs are regularly omitted from sentences. Emphasize that there must be a linking verb between a subject and a predicate adjective. For example:

Incorrect: I tired tonight.

Correct: I am tired tonight.

COLLABORATIVE OPPORTUNITY

Have students work together to decide which underlined words in the following sentences function as pronouns and which function as adjectives.

That museum has three works by van Gogh. (adjective)

This is an oil painting, not a watercolor. (pronoun)

I think *these* portraits show van Gogh's feelings toward his friends. (adjective)

Van Gogh may have intended *those* as gifts. (pronoun)

Writing Theme: Vincent van Gogh

Suggest that students use these exercises as a springboard to writing. Other related areas that they might explore include the following:

- impressionism and postimpressionism
- Dutch artists
- Mary Cassatt, American impressionist
- Berthe Morisot, French impressionist

Answers to Practice Your Skills

A. Concept Check

Adjectives

1. Dutch, painter; extraordinary, Vincent van Gogh
2. his, lifetime; this, artist; numerous, paintings
3. financial, failure
4. Many, galleries; fine, galleries; major, cities; his, works; colorful, works
5. His, pictures; early, pictures; quiet, pictures; serious, pictures
6. that, time; dark, colors; heavy, brushstrokes
7. Later, paintings; intense, color; unusual, energy
8. Those, works; later, works; various, shades; special, paint; blue, paint; French, painters
9. One, work; that, paint; remarkable, paint; famous, work
10. that, painting; *Starry, Night;* dark, sky; brilliant, stars
11. night, sky; stormy, sea
12. dark, city; calm, city; peaceful, city
13. Asian, painting
14. Japanese, art; his, painting; some, women; peasant, women
15. simple, tasks; everyday, life; that, picture

Pronouns Used as Adjectives

As you learned on page 450, the words *this, that, these,* and *those* can be used as demonstrative pronouns. When used alone, they are pronouns. When followed by a noun, they are adjectives telling *which one* or *which ones.*

Those drawings are very old. (adjective modifying *drawings*)
These are by van Gogh. (pronoun)
That one was painted in Paris. (adjective modifying *one*)

The words *my, her, his, its, our,* and *their* are possessive pronouns, but they can also be classified as adjectives. These modifiers tell *which one* or *which ones.*

My mother likes van Gogh's work; *her* sister does not.
Of *his* works, *Sunflowers* is *her* favorite.
Our museum collects watercolors; *its* collection is large.

Practice Your Skills

Writing Theme
Vincent van Gogh

A. CONCEPT CHECK

Adjectives Write the adjectives from the following sentences. After each adjective, write the word it modifies.

1. The Dutch painter Vincent van Gogh was extraordinary.
2. In his lifetime, this artist completed numerous paintings.
3. He was a financial failure however.
4. Many fine galleries in major cities exhibit his colorful works.
5. His early pictures were often quiet and serious.
6. At that time he favored dark colors and heavy brushstrokes.
7. Later paintings feature intense color and unusual energy.
8. Those later works often contain various shades of a special blue paint—a favorite of French painters of the time.
9. One work with that remarkable paint is very famous.
10. In that painting, *The Starry Night,* the dark sky is filled with brilliant stars.
11. The night sky moves like a stormy sea.
12. The dark city below the sky seems calm and peaceful.
13. Van Gogh studied Asian painting.
14. Japanese art influenced his painting of some peasant women washing clothes in a river.
15. He showed the simple tasks of everyday life in that picture.

508 Grammar Handbook

Additional Resource

Grammar and Usage Practice Book, p. 57

The Starry Night (1889), Vincent van Gogh.

B. APPLICATION IN LITERATURE

Recognizing Adjectives Notice how the writer of the passage below uses adjectives to add detail and to set the tone of the passage. Read the passage, and list the adjectives.

> [16]Well over a hundred years ago a small boy ran through the moist fields and woods of Brabant in the southern Netherlands. [17]He loved the fresh, clean wind on his face; he loved to watch . . . the hidden joys of nature, the peasants at work and at rest—all the wonders of the natural world were, to him, remarkable beyond words. [18][His] name was Vincent van Gogh. He was born March 30, 1853. . . .
>
> [19]He was a quiet child but a stubborn and willful one. [20]He suffered long, dark moods that suddenly gave way to bright moments of great happiness.

Arnold Dobrin, *I Am a Stranger on the Earth: The Story of Vincent van Gogh*

C. APPLICATION IN WRITING

Description Look carefully at the painting above. Then write a brief paragraph that describes your reactions to the painting. Use at least five adjectives in your description. Include one predicate adjective.

TIP

Think carefully about the image you want to convey. Then choose specific adjectives that describe that particular image.

FOR MORE PRACTICE

See page 529.

B. Application in Literature
Recognizing Adjectives

Answers are shown on page.

C. Application in Writing
Description

Answers will vary.

ART NOTE

Van Gogh's dramatic effects were achieved through meticulous, painstaking artistic methods. In *The Starry Night,* he is employing expressionist techniques—that is, using colors and shapes to convey mood and feelings. Critics have described the sky as "whirling" and "exploding" and the village as "huddle[d] in anticipation of cosmic disaster."

ARTICLES

Objectives

- To identify articles
- To recognize the correct use of definite and indefinite articles

Teaching Strategies

INDIVIDUALIZING INSTRUCTION: ESL STUDENTS In many languages, such as French, articles indicate gender. Therefore, some ESL students have trouble grasping that the choice between *a* and *an* is based solely on sound. Have these students practice orally inserting *a* and *an* before nouns.

Some other languages, like Russian and Vietnamese, have no articles. You may wish to pair students with these language backgrounds with native English speakers for proofreading of writing assignments.

LEP STUDENTS In some American dialects, the indefinite article *an* is not used. Provide a list of nouns beginning with vowel and consonant sounds. Pair students and have them take turns orally inserting the correct article before each noun.

Additional Resource

Grammar and Usage Practice Book, p. 58

Writing Theme: Mountain Rescue

Suggest that students use these exercises as a springboard to writing. Other related areas that students might explore include the following:

- rock climbing
- guidelines for safe hiking
- Edmund Hillary and Tenzing Norkey, conquerors of Everest
- exploring glaciers

Answers to Practice Your Skills

A. Concept Check
Choosing Articles

Answers are shown on page.

ARTICLES

A, an, and *the* are special adjectives called **articles.**

The is a special kind of adjective known as the **definite article.** It is used to refer to a particular thing.

The climber was stranded. (a particular climber)

A and *an* are also special adjectives called **indefinite articles.** They are used when the noun does not refer to any particular thing.

A guide explained the danger. (no specific guide)
An avalanche may threaten climbers. (no particular avalanche)

Use *a* before a word that begins with a consonant sound (*a* hiker). Use *an* before a vowel sound (*an* accident). The first sound of a word, not the spelling, makes the difference. This means that a speaker would say *an hour* but *a hallway.*

All articles are adjectives. Use *the* with both singular and plural nouns, but use *a* and *an* only with singular nouns.

the skier	the skiers	a skier
the adventure	the adventures	an adventure

Practice Your Skills

Writing Theme
Mountain Rescue

CONCEPT CHECK

Choosing Articles Write the correct article from those given in parentheses.

1. (A, An) hiker slipped on a sheet of ice.
2. She slid down a cliff and was stranded on (a, an) rock ledge.
3. No one knew (a, the) route she had taken.
4. (The, An) hiker's friend called the local mountain rescue team.
5. The team began the search within (a, an) hour.
6. A specially trained dog followed (a, the) hiker's scent.
7. A helicopter began (a, an) air search of the mountains.
8. The dog followed the trail to (a, the) edge of the cliff.
9. A climber from (a, the) same rescue team descended to the ledge.
10. (A, An) rope was attached and the hiker was pulled to safety.

ADVERBS

An **adverb** modifies a verb, an adjective, or another adverb.

Adverbs help make meaning clear by telling *how, when, where,* or *to what extent* something is true.

Adverbs Used with Verbs

Adverbs that modify verbs tell *how, when, where,* or *to what extent* an action happened. Study the following list of adverbs.

How?	When?	Where?	To What Extent?
carefully	sometimes	inside	fully
quickly	once	underground	very
sorrowfully	now	here	quite
hurriedly	finally	there	extremely

Notice how adverbs make the following sentence clearer:

The door of the tomb opened.
Finally, the door of the tomb *slowly* opened.

Adverbs make the meaning of the verb *opened* clearer.

Adverbs Used with Adjectives or Other Adverbs

Adverbs that tell *to what extent* can also modify adjectives and other adverbs.

Frequently Used Adverbs

very	not	somewhat	more
just	nearly	so	most

Notice how the adverbs in the following sentences make the adjective and adverb more understandable and more precise.

The tomb was dark.	The guide spoke softly.
The tomb was *nearly* dark.	The guide spoke *very* softly.

Writing TIP

Adverbs are useful in persuasive writing. By using qualifiers such as *quite, nearly,* and *somewhat,* you can avoid overgeneralization.

ADVERBS

Objectives

- To identify adverbs and to recognize their functions in sentences
- To form adverbs correctly

Writing

- To vary word choice by replacing certain adverbs with adverbs of similar meaning

Teaching Strategies

STUMBLING BLOCK Some words that tell *where,* such as *inside, around, out, up,* and so on, can function either as adverbs or as prepositions. To minimize confusion, explain that if a word telling *where* has an object, it is a preposition; if it has no object, it is an adverb. Examples:

Dee looked *around.* (adverb)

The dog ran *around* the yard. (preposition)

For more information and practice, refer students to Preposition or Adverb? on page 538.

LINKING GRAMMAR AND WRITING You might explain that overuse of adverbs such as *very, extremely,* and *tremendously* can weaken writing. For example, rather than describing a noise as *very loud,* an experienced writer will choose a more precise "showing" adjective, such as *roaring, thunderous, deafening,* or *echoing.* Challenge students to write more precise modifiers to replace the underlined terms:

an <u>extremely dark</u> night

a <u>very frightening</u> movie

a <u>tremendously old</u> mummy

CRITICAL THINKING: CLASSIFYING Point out that not all words ending in *-ly* are adverbs. Remind students that words telling *what kind, which one,* or *how many* are adjectives; words telling *how, when, where,* or *to what extent* are adverbs. Have students use the above criteria to classify each of the following *-ly* words as an adjective or an adverb: *friendly* (adjective), *quietly* (adverb), *silly* (adjective), *recently* (adverb), *motherly* (adjective), *boldly* (adverb), *homely* (adjective), *really* (adverb). (You also might note that *only* can function either as an adjective or as an adverb, depending upon the context.)

Additional Resource

Grammar and Usage Practice Book, p. 89

Writing Theme: Mummies

Other related areas students might wish to explore as writing topics include the following:

- King Tutankhamen
- gods and goddesses of ancient Egypt
- pyramids—ancient Egyptian tombs
- the classic horror movie character, the Mummy

Answers to Practice Your Skills

A. Concept Check

Adverbs

1. highly, successful
2. very, carefully; carefully, preserved
3. First, removed; painstakingly, removed
4. often, were stored
5. generally, remained
6. still, needed
7. then, dried; very, gradually; gradually, dried
8. Finally, rubbed; intricately, wrapped
9. extremely, dry
10. very, elaborate; sometimes, took

Forming Adverbs

Many adverbs are made by adding *-ly* to an adjective.

careful + *-ly* = carefully   slow + *-ly* = slowly

Sometimes the addition of *-ly* involves a spelling change in the adjective.

easy + -ly = easily (*y* changed to *i*)
full + -ly = fully (*ll* changed to *l*)

Some modifiers, like *soon* and *quite,* can be used only as adverbs.

The coffin was *soon* open. The mummy was *quite* well preserved.

Some other modifiers, like *late* or *first,* can be used either as adverbs or as adjectives.

The archaeologist arrived *late*. (adverb)
The *late* arrival delayed the discovery. (adjective)
Grave robbers had gotten there *first*. (adverb)
The *first* tomb was already open. (adjective)

Practice Your Skills

A. CONCEPT CHECK

Writing Theme
Mummies

Adverbs Write the adverbs from the following sentences. Beside each adverb write the word it modifies.

1. Egyptians were highly successful with mummification.
2. The bodies, or mummies, were very carefully preserved.
3. First, Egyptian embalmers painstakingly removed the brain.
4. The intestines were often stored in jars.
5. The heart and kidneys generally remained in the body.
6. The dead person still needed these organs in the afterlife.
7. Workers covered the body with a special substance, and then they dried the body very gradually.
8. Finally, the embalmers rubbed the body with oils and spices and intricately wrapped it in fine linen.
9. The extremely dry climate aided the process of preservation.
10. This very elaborate process sometimes took seventy days.

B. REVISION SKILL

Using Adverbs There are many adverbs available for writers to use. Write the following paragraph, replacing the italicized adverbs with other adverbs that convey a similar meaning.

> [11]When you think of mummies, do you think of the *very* old mummies of the ancient Egyptian Pharaohs? [12]It was *once* thought that the Egyptian embalmers used mysterious methods and secret formulas to preserve the bodies *totally.* [13]*Today* scientists know that it was the climate, which is *extremely* dry, that prevented the bodies from decaying *horribly.* [14]Archaeologists have found bodies of poor Egyptians *also.* [15]These bodies are as ancient as those of the Pharaohs and *likewise* well preserved. [16]Yet, *surprisingly,* archaeologists have learned that these bodies were *never* embalmed.

MIXED REVIEW • PAGES 506–513

Write the italicized modifiers and identify them as *Adjectives* or *Adverbs.* Then write the word that each adjective or adverb modifies.

1. You *probably* know about *the* nine planets of our *solar* system.
2. Do you know that *some* scientists think there may *actually* be *more* planets?
3. *Several* astronomers *now* think there are hundreds or even thousands more in *our* solar system.
4. Scientists suspect that these planets may be *completely* covered with ice.
5. The *great* majority of these *undiscovered* planets could be a thousand times *farther* away than Pluto.
6. A few, however, may be *somewhat* closer.
7. Scientists have not *yet* found any of *these* planets.
8. The planets are probably *very* small, and so of course they are *quite* difficult to see.
9. However, a few may be *barely* visible through our *most* sensitive telescopes.
10. Astronomers are *systematically* searching for these *distant* neighbors.

FOR MORE PRACTICE
See page 529.

Writing Theme
Discovering New Planets

B. Revision Skill
Using Adverbs

Answers will vary. Possible replacements are the adverbs shown in italics below.

11 When you think of mummies, do you think of the *extremely* old mummies of the ancient Egyptian Pharaohs? 12 It was *originally* thought that the Egyptian embalmers used mysterious methods and secret formulas to preserve the bodies *completely.* 13 *Now* scientists know that it was the climate, which is *quite* dry, that prevented the bodies from decaying *terribly.* 14 Archaeologists have found bodies of poor Egyptians *too.* 15 These bodies are as ancient as those of the Pharaohs and *equally* well preserved. 16 Yet, *amazingly,* archaeologists have learned that these bodies were not embalmed.

CHECK POINT

Writing Theme: Discovering New Planets

Other related areas students might wish to explore as writing topics include the following:

- *Voyager I* and *II* or other space probes
- the life cycle of a star
- black holes

MIXED REVIEW • PAGES 506–513

You may wish to use this activity to check students' mastery of the following concepts:

- What are modifiers?
- adjectives
- articles
- adverbs

1. probably, Adverb, know; the, Adjective, planets; solar, Adjective, system
2. some, Adjective, scientists; actually, Adverb, may be; more, Adjective, planets
3. Several, Adjective, astronomers; now, Adverb, think; our, Adjective, system
4. completely, Adverb, may be covered
5. great, Adjective, majority; undiscovered, Adjective, planets; farther, Adverb, away
6. somewhat, Adverb, closer
7. yet, Adverb, have found; these, Adjective, planets
8. very, Adverb, small; quite, Adverb, difficult
9. barely, Adverb, visible; most, Adverb, sensitive
10. systematically, Adverb, are searching; distant, Adjective, neighbors

ADJECTIVE OR ADVERB?

Objectives

- To distinguish between adjectives and adverbs by identifying words modified

Writing

- To correct errors in modifier use

Teaching Strategies

SPEAKING AND LISTENING To give students more practice in recognizing the sound of correctly used modifiers, ask them to choose the correct sentence in each pair as you read aloud.

1. Our team won easy.
   Our team won easily. (c)
2. Tina always arrived promptly. (c)
   Tina always arrived prompt.
3. Marie thought deeply. (c)
   Marie thought deep.

Writing Theme: Native American Literature

Other related areas students might wish to explore as writing topics include the following:

- modern Native American authors such as Leslie Marmon Silko, Paula Gunn Allen, and Louise Erdrich
- Native American oral histories such as *Waheenee: An Indian Girl's Story,* and *Black Elk Speaks*
- tales of Coyote the trickster

Answers to Practice Your Skills

A. Application in Literature
Adjectives and Adverbs

1. hot, Adjective, day
2. marvelous, Adjective, Horse; very, Adverb, far; far, Adverb, had ridden; friendly, Adjective, village
3. on, Adverb, traveled; his, Adjective, people
4. Finally, Adverb, came
5. listlessly, Adverb, sat
6. out, Adverb, had gone
7. suddenly, Adverb, awakened; elegant, Adjective, warrior; magic, Adjective, animal

ADJECTIVE OR ADVERB?

A Hopi storyteller

An **adjective** modifies a noun or pronoun. An **adverb** modifies a verb, an adjective, or another adverb.

Study the following sentences. Which sentence sounds right?

The Hopi storyteller spoke *quiet.*
The Hopi storyteller spoke *quietly.*

The second sentence is the correct one. An adverb (*quietly*) should be used, not an adjective (*quiet*).

When you are not sure whether an adjective or an adverb should be used, ask yourself these questions:

1. *Which word does the modifier go with?* If it goes with an action verb (like *spoke* in the sentences above), it is an adverb. It is also an adverb if it goes with an adjective or another adverb. If it goes with a noun or pronoun, it is an adjective.
2. *What does the modifier tell about the word it goes with?* If the modifier tells *when, where, how,* or *to what extent,* it is an adverb. If it tells *which one, what kind,* or *how many,* it is an adjective. In the sentences above, the modifier tells *how* the storyteller spoke; it must therefore be an adverb.

Practice Your Skills

A. APPLICATION IN LITERATURE

Writing Theme Native American Literature

Adjectives and Adverbs Write each italicized word. Identify it as an *Adjective* or an *Adverb.* Then write the word it modifies.

[1]It was a *hot* day. [2]Anpao had ridden his *marvelous* Horse *very far,* hoping he might find a *friendly* village where he could make camp and get something to eat. [3]He traveled *on* and on but he saw no sign of *his* people. [4]*Finally* at midday he came upon a cluster of lodges. [5]The people sat *listlessly* in the shade sleeping. [6]All the lodge skins were raised to let the air in, and all the cooking fires had gone *out.* [7]No one heard Anpao ride into camp until a chief *suddenly* awakened and shouted in surprise to see such an *elegant* warrior astride a *magic* animal.

[8]Anpao greeted the people *warmly,* but they were *selfish* and *unfriendly.* [9]They stared *enviously* at Anpao's possessions, and they peered at his horse. . . . [10]All they could think about were *devious* ways of getting his belongings and *his magic* animal.

Jamake Highwater, *Anpao: An American Indian Odyssey*

This Hopi pottery tile depicts a kachina, a Hopi deity. These deities may be drawn as human, plant, or animal forms.

B. CONCEPT CHECK

Adjectives and Adverbs Make four columns. In the first column, write each adjective and adverb. In the second column, identify its part of speech. In the third, write the word modified. In the fourth, write what the modifier tells, such as *which one, what kind, how,* or *when* and so on. List no articles.

11. Native American cultures have a very old and remarkably rich literature.
12. Their songs and tales are quite colorful.
13. Originally, these stories were not written down.
14. They were passed along orally to each new generation.
15. Usually men were the storytellers. Women were not.
16. Myths and legends strongly reinforced important values and beliefs of the community.
17. Often, stories reflected the close relationship of a people to other creatures, land, sky, and water.
18. In fact some cultures viewed the natural elements as their ancestors.
19. Sometimes the literature served a dual purpose.
20. It might provide a historical record of an important event and honor the deeds of past heroes.

Adverbs and Predicate Adjectives

Recall that a predicate adjective appears after a linking verb and modifies the subject. Notice the predicate adjectives below.

The music sounds delightful. (*delightful* modifies *music*)
The people are friendly. (*friendly* modifies *people*)
The crawfish taste delicious. (*delicious* modifies *crawfish*)

You should also remember that in addition to the forms of *be,* the following words can be used as linking verbs: *become, seem, appear, look, sound, feel, taste, grow,* and *smell.*

8. warmly, Adverb, greeted; selfish, Adjective, they; unfriendly, Adjective, they
9. enviously, Adverb, stared
10. devious, Adjective, ways; his, Adjective, animal; magic, Adjective, animal

B. Concept Check
Adjectives and Adverbs

Student answers should be in columns.

11. Native American, Adjective, cultures, what kind; very, Adverb, old, to what extent; old, Adjective, literature, what kind; remarkably, Adverb, rich, to what extent; rich, Adjective, literature, what kind
12. Their, Adjective, songs and tales, which one; quite, Adverb, colorful, to what extent; colorful, Adjective, songs *and* tales, what kind
13. Originally, Adverb, were written, when; these, Adjective, stories, which one; not, Adverb, were written, how *or* to what extent; down, Adverb, were written, where
14. along, Adverb, were passed, where; orally, Adverb, were passed, how; each, Adjective, generation, which one or how many; new, Adjective, generation, what kind
15. Usually, Adverb, were, when; not, Adverb, were, to what extent
16. strongly, Adverb, reinforced, how *or* to what extent; important, Adjective, values *and* beliefs, what kind
17. Often, Adverb, reflected, when; close, Adjective, relationship, what kind; other, Adjective, creatures, which one
18. some, Adjective, cultures, which one *or* how many; natural, Adjective, elements, what kind *or* which one; their, Adjective, ancestors, which one
19. Sometimes, Adverb, served, when; dual, Adjective, purpose, what kind
20. historical, Adjective, record, what kind; important, Adjective, event, what kind; past, Adjective, heroes, what kind

COLLABORATIVE OPPORTUNITY

Group students and ask them to use each verb listed in the last two lines on page 515 in two sentences, first as an action verb and then as a linking verb. (Sample: a. Uncle Kenji grew strawberries. b. The tree grew taller.)

SPEAKING AND LISTENING

Because most students will benefit from additional drill on the correct use of *good* and *well,* read the following sentences aloud and have students repeat them after you.

The football players performed well.

Do you feel well enough to play?

These pears look good.

Do pears grow well in this climate?

Additional Resource

Grammar and Usage Practice Book, pp. 60–61

Sometimes these verbs are used as action verbs. When they are used as action verbs, they are followed by adverbs, not adjectives. The adverbs modify the verbs and tell *how, when, where,* or *to what extent.* The problem of choosing an adjective or an adverb form is often difficult when these verbs are used.

Look at the following sentences to see when adjectives are used and when adverbs are used.

Linking Verb with Adjectives	Action Verbs with Adverbs
The *performer* looked *happy.*	The performer *looked up.*
The *pie* tasted *good.*	We *tasted* the pie *eagerly.*
The *audience* appears *pleased.*	A soloist *appears suddenly.*

If you are uncertain whether to use an adverb or adjective after verbs such as *sound, smell,* or *look,* ask yourself these questions:

1. Can you substitute *is* or *was* for the verb? If you can, the verb is probably a linking verb, and the modifier is probably an adjective.
2. Does the modifier tell *how, when, where* or *to what extent?* If it does, the modifier is probably an adverb.

Good and *Well*

Good and *well* have similar meanings, but they differ in their use in a sentence. Study the following sentences.

Incorrect He tells the story *good.*
Correct He tells the story *well.*

Good is always an adjective and modifies nouns or pronouns. Never use *good* to modify a verb; use *well.*

Well can be used as either an adjective or an adverb, depending on the situation. When used as an adjective, *well* usually refers to a person's health. For example, "I feel *well*" means "I feel healthy." Remember that "feeling good" refers to being happy or pleased.

Literature Connection

Have students identify adverbs and predicate adjectives in the following excerpt from Jack London's "To Build a Fire."

He worked slowly and carefully, keenly aware of his danger. Gradually, as the flame grew stronger, he increased the size of the twigs with which he fed it. . . . When it is seventy-five below zero, a man must not fail in his first attempt to build a fire—that is, if his feet are wet. If his feet are dry, and he fails, he can run. . . .

Practice Your Skills

A. CONCEPT CHECK

Correct Forms of Modifiers Write the correct form of the modifiers given in parentheses.

1. Cajuns tell you (quick, quickly) that their heritage is French.
2. Over the years the French *Acadian* (gradual, gradually) became *Cadien* and (final, finally) *Cajun*.
3. These Louisiana residents will also say that their rice tastes especially (good, well) with boudin, a local sausage.
4. The popularity of spicy Cajun dishes has grown (rapid, rapidly).
5. The name of one favorite food, mudbugs, may sound (strange, strangely) to some.
6. Also known as crawfish, these shrimplike creatures look a little (odd, oddly) too.
7. The idea of popping their heads off before eating them doesn't sound too (reasonable, reasonably) either.
8. Yet natives and visitors alike will put away steaming platters of these tasty crustaceans very (rapid, rapidly).
9. If crawfish have been prepared (good, well), they taste even better than shrimp.
10. Since they are high in protein and low in fat, they are bound to keep you (good, well).

B. PROOFREADING SKILL

Correcting Adjectives and Adverbs Write the following paragraph, correcting all errors. Pay special attention to errors in the use of modifiers. (15 errors)

Early in the seventeenth century, settlers from Western France migrated to Nova scotia. The change did not go smooth, however. Very quick, they were caught up in the French and english rivalry for control of north America. England demanded loyalty the Acadian's declared themselves neutral. The english felt certainly that the Acadians were comiting treason. And ordered them deported. For thirty years the Acadians lived in exile, a few in Louisiana, many back in France. In 1762 spanish control of Louisiana made it possible for Acadians to be reunited with thier family members in Louisiana. Today many Cajuns point proud to their family tree and tell of this long, hard journey.

Writing Theme
Cajuns

FOR MORE PRACTICE
See page 529.

Writing Theme: Cajuns

Other related areas students might wish to explore as writing topics include the following:

- zydeco and other Cajun music
- Cajun food: gumbos, creoles, and jambalaya
- Louisiana bayou wildfire
- Longfellow's poem *Evangeline*

Answers to Practice Your Skills

A. Concept Check
Correct Forms of Modifiers

Answers are shown on page.

B. Proofreading Skill
Correcting Adjectives and Adverbs

Errors in proofreading exercises are counted as follows: (a) Each word is counted as one error. For example, a misspelled word is one error; two initials and a last name not capitalized are counted as three errors. (b) Run-on sentences and sentence fragments are each counted as one error even though the correction involves both punctuation and capitalization corrections.

Errors are shown on page.

Early in the seventeenth century, settlers from western France migrated to Nova Scotia. The change did not go smoothly, however. Very quickly, they were caught up in the French and English rivalry for control of North America. England demanded loyalty. The Acadians declared themselves neutral. The English felt certain that the Acadians were committing treason and ordered them deported. For thirty years the Acadians lived in exile, a few in Louisiana, many back in France. In 1762 Spanish control of Louisiana made it possible for Acadians to be reunited with their family members in Louisiana. Today many Cajuns point proudly to their family tree and tell of this long, hard journey.

Adjectives in Comparisons

Objectives

- To recognize and form comparative and superlative forms of adjectives

Writing

- To correct errors in the use of comparisons in writing

Teaching Strategies

LINKING GRAMMAR AND WRITING Point out that comparative forms of adjectives can help clarify ideas in comparison-and-contrast writing. For example, a writer comparing and contrasting apatosaurus and diplodocus might explain that both dinosaurs were plant eaters, but that apatosaurus was *longer* and *heavier* than diplodocus.

HELPFUL HINT Tell students that people usually decide "by ear" whether to use *-er* and *-est,* or *more* and *most.* Suggest that when students are in doubt, they should look up the correct form in the dictionary. You might use a dictionary and an opaque projector to demonstrate how to locate the part of an entry that shows correct comparative and superlative forms.

Adjectives in Comparisons

Use the **comparative form** of an adjective to compare two things. Use the **superlative form** of an adjective to compare more than two.

Comparing people and things is one way of learning about the world. Someone could say, "The dinosaurs were like modern-day lizards. Many were *larger* and *more common* than modern lizards."

The Comparative

Use the **comparative form** of the adjective to compare one thing or person with another thing or group. The comparative is formed in two ways:

1. For short adjectives, such as *great* or *fierce,* add *-er.*

   great + er = greater   fierce + er = fiercer

2. For longer adjectives, such as *unusual* or *remarkable,* use *more.*

   more unusual   more remarkable

Most adjectives ending in *-ful* and *-ous* also form the comparative with *more.*

more successful   more curious   more ferocious

The Superlative

To compare a thing or a person with more than one other of its kind, use the **superlative form** of the adjective.

Dinosaurs were the *largest* land animals ever to live.
However, they are not the *most ancient* animals.

The superlative of an adjective is formed by adding *-est* or by using *most.* The ending *-er* in the comparative becomes *-est* in the superlative, and *more* becomes *most.*

Notice how the adjectives in the chart on the next page change forms according to these rules.

Literature Connection

Ask students to identify comparative and superlative forms (underlined) in this excerpt from the play *The Diary of Anne Frank,* by Frances Goodrich and Albert Hackett.

"I was horrible, wasn't I? And the worst of it is, I . . . can't stop. . . . Every night I think back over all the things I did that day that were wrong . . . and this thing now with Mother. . . . I'm never going to do that again. Never! Of course I may do something worse . . . but at least I'll never do *that* again! . . . I have a nicer side, Father . . . a sweeter, nicer side. But I'm scared to show it. . . "

Adjective	Comparative	Superlative
strong	stronger	strongest
fast	faster	fastest
mysterious	more mysterious	most mysterious
awkward	more awkward	most awkward

Remember these four things when using adjectives for comparison:

1. Use the comparative to compare two persons or things or two groups of things. Also use the comparative to compare a person or a thing to a group.

   Comparative A brontosaurus was *larger* than a mammoth.
   Comparative Lizards are *smaller* than their prehistoric ancestors.
   Comparative A mammoth probably moved *faster* than most dinosaurs.

2. Use the superlative to compare a thing or person to more than one other of its kind.

   Superlative Sauropods were the *largest* of all dinosaurs.
   Superlative Brachiosaurus, brontosaurus, and diplodocus were giants; brachiosaurus was the *largest.*

3. Do not leave out the word *other* when you are comparing something with everything else of its kind.

   Incorrect Tyrannosaurus rex was more ferocious than any dinosaur. (This sentence says that tyrannosaurus rex was not a dinosaur.)
   Correct Tyrannosaurus rex was more ferocious than any *other* dinosaur.

4. Do not use both *-er* and *more* or *-est* and *most.*

   Incorrect The plant-eaters began to die out more sooner than the meat-eaters did.
   Correct The plant-eaters began to die out *sooner* than the meat-eaters did.
   Incorrect Dinosaurs are not the most oldest of all reptiles.
   Correct Dinosaurs are not the *oldest* of all reptiles.

INDIVIDUALIZING INSTRUCTION: LD STUDENTS Students with poor long-term memories may benefit from use of this mnemonic device for forming regular comparisons: Use two letters *(-er)* when comparing two things; use three letters *(-est)* when comparing three things.

ASSESSMENT: SPOT CHECK You might use this activity as a spot check. Hold up a pencil or other object and have the class brainstorm a list of adjectives that describe it. Choose five adjectives from the list; then have students supply the comparative and superlative forms of each adjective. (Samples: stubby [stubbier, stubbiest]; pointed [more pointed, most pointed])

KEY TO UNDERSTANDING You might tell students that each of the four rules for using comparative and superlative form is based on common sense. For example, we need the word *other* in some comparisons to prevent confusion, as shown in the examples given for the third rule. You might encourage students to look for the logic behind the rules, rather than to just try to memorize them.

STUMBLING BLOCK Caution students against the use of forms such as *more unique* or *most complete.* Explain that modifiers such as *unique* and *complete* are considered "absolute"; thus, it makes no sense for them to have comparative or superlative forms.

Additional Resource

Grammar and Usage Practice Book, pp. 62–63

Writing Theme: Dinosaurs

Other related areas students might wish to explore as writing topics include the following:

- Dinosaur National Monument, Colorado
- the Jurassic era of the dinosaurs
- the discovery of the world's first complete tyrannosaurus rex skeletons, 1990, in Montana and South Dakota
- stories about dinosaurs

Answers to Practice Your Skills

A. Concept Check

Comparative Forms of Adjectives

1. most fascinating
2. less
3. more difficult
4. more
5. longer
6. briefer
7. most successful
8. more
9. more massive
10. most fearful
11. swifter
12. better; most important

Irregular Comparisons

We form the comparative and superlative of some adjectives by changing the words, as shown in the chart below.

Adjective	Comparative	Superlative
good	better	best
well	better	best
bad	worse	worst
ill	worse	worst
little	less *or* lesser	least
much	more	most
many	more	most
far	farther	farthest

Practice Your Skills

A. CONCEPT CHECK

Comparative Forms of Adjectives Write the correct form of each adjective given in parentheses.

1. Dinosaurs are perhaps the (fascinating) of all animals.
2. We have (little) information about them than we would like.
3. It is (difficult) to learn about dinosaurs than about some other animals, because dinosaurs are extinct.
4. However, we have (much) knowledge now than ever before.
5. Dinosaurs dominated the earth for 150 million years, a (long) period than humans have inhabited earth.
6. The period of 3 million or 4 million years of human influence is indeed (brief) than the dinosaur period.
7. These mammoth reptiles were among the (successful) survivors of all creatures.
8. There were (many) plant eaters than meat eaters among the dinosaurs.
9. The brontosaurus, which was (massive) than six of today's elephants grouped together, was a plant-eater.
10. One of the (fearful) of the dinosaurs was tyrannosaurus rex.
11. It had huge teeth for tearing flesh and massive rear legs that probably made it (swift) than most other dinosaurs.
12. We have (good) methods of gathering scientific information than ever before, but the (important) question remains unanswered: Why did they disappear?

B. PROOFREADING SKILL

Errors in Comparisons Write the following paragraph, correcting errors in grammar, capitalization, punctuation, and spelling. Pay special attention to the use of comparisons. (10 errors)

No one knows what happened to the dinosaurs. During their reign, dinosaurs were more dominant than any creature, yet they suddenly died out. One of the popularist and better supported explanations suggests that a meteor crashed into the earth the crash raised a huge cloud of dust that blocked out the sun. Without sunlight, plants died and tempratures got more colder. The suporting evidence for this theory is more concrete than the evidence for any theory. Scientists have found a likely meteor crater in mexico. About 180 kilometers in diameter.

MIXED REVIEW • PAGES 514–521

Write the correct form of the modifiers in parentheses. Then identify each as an *Adjective* or *Adverb.* If an adjective is used for comparison, identify it as *Comparative* or *Superlative.*

1. Wilma Rudolph was one of the (most great, greatest) runners in field and track history.
2. In the 1960 Olympics, she was (faster, more fast) than every other woman runner and won both the 100- and 200-meter dashes.
3. Her 400-meter relay team ran extremely (good, well) and won a gold medal.
4. Rudolph's achievements are even (incredibler, more incredible) because she had serious health problems as a child.
5. She was born (premature, prematurely) and almost didn't live.
6. Due to a bout with polio, she walked (awkward, awkwardly).
7. Doctors said her left leg would never grow (strong, strongly).
8. Few polio victims have been (more determined, most determined) to recover.
9. Slowly the leg grew (better, more good).
10. Finally, when she was twelve, she was (well, good) again.
11. At sixteen, she ran so (well, good) that she qualified for the 1956 Olympic team.
12. She made the team again in 1960, when she had the (better, best) results of all her Olympic performances.

FOR MORE PRACTICE
See page 530.

Writing Theme
Wilma Rudolph

B. Proofreading Skill
Errors in Comparisons

Errors are underlined on page.

No one knows what happened to the dinosaurs. During their reign, dinosaurs were more dominant than any other creature, yet they suddenly died out. One of the most popular and best supported explanations suggests that a meteor crashed into the earth. The crash raised a huge cloud of dust that blocked out the sun. Without sunlight, plants died and temperatures got colder. The supporting evidence for this theory is more concrete than the evidence for any other theory. Scientists have found a likely meteor crater in Mexico. It is about 180 kilometers in diameter.

CHECK POINT

Writing Theme: Wilma Rudolph

Other related areas students might wish to explore as writing topics include the following:

- American women in track and field, such as Evelyn Ashford and Jackie Joyner-Kersee
- other athletes who overcame physical disabilities or other health problems
- sports medicine

MIXED REVIEW • PAGES 514–521

You may wish to use this activity to check students' mastery of the following concepts:

- adjective or adverb?
- adjectives in comparisons

Correct forms are underlined on page.

1. greatest, Adjective, Superlative
2. faster, Adjective, Comparative
3. well, Adverb
4. more incredible, Adjective, Comparative
5. prematurely, Adverb
6. awkwardly, Adverb
7. strong, Adjective
8. more determined, Adjective, Comparative
9. better, Adjective, Comparative
10. well, Adjective
11. well, Adverb
12. best, Adjective, Superlative

ADVERBS IN COMPARISONS

Objectives

- To identify comparative and superlative forms of adverbs

Writing

- To use adverbs correctly in comparisons

Teaching Strategies

KEY TO UNDERSTANDING

Students may be relieved to learn that English includes few irregular adverbs. The three most common are:

well (better, best)

badly (worse, worst)

far (farther, farthest)

HELPFUL HINT: ACCURATE COMPARISONS Remind students that since adverbs are used in making comparisons between two or more actions, sentences should make the relationship clear. To illustrate, write this sentence on the board: *The car's engine started more quickly.* Ask students what is wrong with it. (The sentence does not state what the timing of the action—starting—is being compared to.) A corrected sentence might read: *The car's engine started more quickly in summer than in winter.*

ADVERBS IN COMPARISONS

Use the **comparative form** of an adverb to compare two actions. Use the **superlative form** of an adverb to compare more than two actions.

Adverbs are used to compare one action with another. We say, "This clown dresses oddly, but that one dresses *more oddly.*" We also say, "That trapeze artist swings *more daringly* than any other trapeze artist I've seen." Adverbs have special forms or spellings for use in making comparisons, just as adjectives do.

The Comparative

Use the **comparative** form of the adverb to compare one action with another. The comparative is formed in two ways:

1. For short adverbs, such as *soon* or *high,* add *-er.*

   The parade entered the big top *sooner* than we expected.
   The lion leaped *higher* than the tiger.

2. For most adverbs ending in *-ly,* use *more* to make the comparative.

   Sara laughed *more frequently* than Andrew.
   The horse ran *more rapidly* around the ring this time than it had earlier.

The Superlative

Use the **superlative** form of the adverb to compare one action with two or more others of the same kind.

Of the three horses, that one runs *fastest.*
The lion roared the *most ferociously* of all the big cats.

The superlative of adverbs is formed by adding *-est* or by using *most.* Adverbs that form the comparative with *-er* form the superlative with *-est.* Those that use *more* for the comparative use *most* for the superlative.

522 Grammar Handbook

Notice how the following adverbs change forms.

Adverb	Comparative	Superlative
long	longer	longest
daringly	more daringly	most daringly
carefully	more carefully	most carefully

Keep these three things in mind:

1. Use the comparative to compare two actions and the superlative to compare more than two.

   Comparative The acrobat jumped *higher* today than yesterday.
   Superlative Of all the acrobats, that one jumped *highest.*

2. Do not leave out the word *other* when you are comparing one action with every other action of the same kind.

   Incorrect Jumbo trumpeted louder than any elephant.
   Correct Jumbo trumpeted louder than any *other* elephant.

3. Do not use both *-er* and *more* or *-est* and *most.*

   Incorrect The performer juggled more faster than before.
   Correct The performer juggled *faster* than before.

Practice Your Skills

A. CONCEPT CHECK

Comparisons Write the correct form of each adverb.

1. The Romans celebrated holidays (frequently) than we do.
2. They invented the circus as a form of celebration, and they clapped (loud) of all for the most spectacular performances.
3. Chariot races were (bitterly) contested than any modern auto race.
4. The best driver was not the one who raced (fast).
5. He was the one who (quickly) forced other drivers to crash.
6. Gladiators trained (hard) than any of today's performers.
7. Those who fought (fiercely) of all lived.
8. Each circus event was staged (elaborately) than the last.
9. Crowds cheered (long) for land battles than for races.
10. The (heavily) attended of all was Circus Maximus.

Writing Theme Circuses

STUMBLING BLOCK Stress that the comparative form, not the superlative, is used when only two things are being compared. Example: *Of the two boys, Jesse lives nearer* (not *nearest*). Have students orally correct the sentences below.

1. Which do you like *best,* plain chocolate or rocky road? (better)
2. Kayla and Tran both run fast, but Tran runs *fastest.* (faster)
3. When Dan and Carlos had a pie-eating contest, who quit *soonest?* (sooner)

Additional Resource

Grammar and Usage Practice Book, pp. 64–65

Writing Theme: Circuses

Other related areas students might wish to explore as writing topics include the following:

- P. T. Barnum
- the Flying Wallendas
- clown colleges
- training animals to perform
- how to juggle

Answers to Practice Your Skills

A. Concept Check

Comparisons

1. more frequently
2. loudest
3. more bitterly
4. fastest
5. most quickly
6. harder
7. most fiercely
8. more elaborately
9. longer
10. most heavily

B. Drafting Skill
Using Adverbs Correctly

11. No other circus entertainers capture audience attention more completely than these tiny creatures.
12. Fleas are more naturally talented than people know.
13. Fleas can jump the farthest of all circus performers.
14. If a flea were the size of a human, it could leap over Grant's Tomb more easily than a human can leap a five-foot wall.
15. In the flea circuses of eighteenth-century France and Italy, fleas wore the most cleverly made collars imaginable.
16. Fleas performed under a magnifying glass so they could be seen better.
17. They learned tricks more quickly than horses did.
18. Fleas pulled loads the most effortlessly of all circus animals.
19. One of the most exceptionally trained fleas pulled a miniature cannon many times its own weight.
20. Records show that fleas were once the most richly rewarded of circus performers.

C. Proofreading Skill
Correct Comparisons of Adverbs

Errors are shown on page.

Do you make people laugh harder than they have ever laughed? Among your friends, are you the most daring? Do you jump your bike the highest? Perhaps you should consider a circus career. The National Center for Circus Arts in France offers college training for the circus. Students specialize in the skill they do best of all. One group, clearly the braver, tries the trapeze. The other group, whose hearts are pounding louder than a drum, stays on the ground. Don't think that they are necessarily less adventuresome, however. They may end up learning how to train lions!

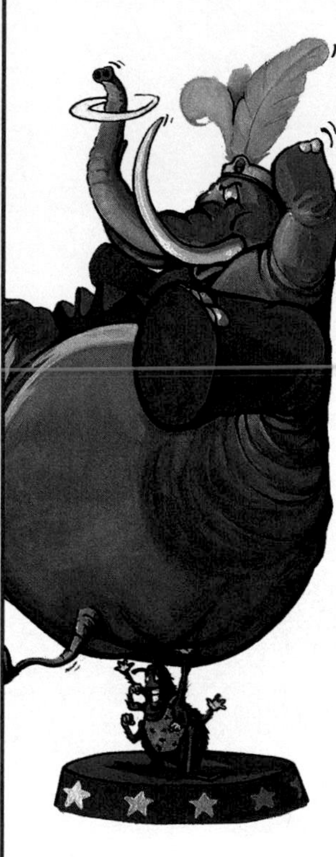

B. DRAFTING SKILL

Using Adverbs Correctly Write the following sentences, completing each with the correct form of the adverb given in parentheses.

EXAMPLE Considering their size, fleas perform (dramatic—comparative) than other circus performers.
Considering their size, fleas perform more dramatically than other circus performers.

11. No other circus entertainers capture audience attention (complete—comparative) than these tiny creatures.
12. Fleas are (natural—comparative) talented than people know.
13. Fleas can jump the (far—superlative) of all circus performers.
14. If a flea were the size of a human, it could leap over Grant's Tomb (easy—comparative) than a human can leap a five-foot wall.
15. In the flea circuses of eighteenth-century France and Italy, fleas wore the (clever—superlative) made collars imaginable.
16. Fleas performed under a magnifying glass so they could be seen (good—comparative).
17. They learned tricks (quick—comparative) than horses did.
18. Fleas pulled loads the (effortless—superlative) of all circus animals.
19. One of the (exceptional—superlative) trained fleas pulled a miniature cannon many times its own weight.
20. Records show that fleas were once the (rich—superlative) rewarded of circus performers.

C. PROOFREADING SKILL

Correct Comparisons of Adverbs Write the following paragraph, correcting all errors. Pay special attention to comparisons of adverbs. (15 errors)

Do you make people laugh more harder than they have ever laughed? Among your friends are you the more daring. Do you jump your bike the higher? Perhaps you should consider a circus career? The National Center for Circus Arts in france offers college training for the Circus. Students specialise in the skill they do better of all. One group, clearly the bravest, tries the trapeze. The other group, who's hearts are pounding more louder than a drum, stays on the ground. Dont think that they are necessarilly least adventuresome, however. They may end up learning how to train lions!

FOR MORE PRACTICE
See page 530.

524 Grammar Handbook

SPECIAL PROBLEMS WITH MODIFIERS

Use **modifiers** according to rules for their use, not according to the way you hear them used in everyday conversation.

People sometimes write things the way they hear them. Doing so may cause mistakes in writing because spoken English is sometimes less precise than written English. Here are some common adjective and adverb problems to watch for.

Them and *Those*

Them is always a pronoun. It is used only as the object of a verb or as the object of a preposition. *Them* is never used as an adjective.

Those is an adjective if it is followed by a noun. It is a pronoun if it is used alone.

We heard *them robots* whirring down the hall. (incorrect)
We followed *them*. (object of a verb)

Those robots can talk! (adjective modifying *robots*)
Those are the new robots. (pronoun)

The Extra *Here* and *There*

How often have you heard someone say "this here job" or "that there movie"? The word *this* includes the meaning of *here*. The word *that* includes the meaning of *there*.

Saying *this here* is like repeating your name every time you say *I* or *me*: "Please show me, Pat Smith, your robot."

Kind and *Sort*

Kind and *sort* are singular. Use *this* or *that* with *kind* and *sort*. *Kinds* and *sorts* are plural. Use *these* or *those* with *kinds* and *sorts*.

I like *this kind* of story.   *Those sorts* of movies scare me.

SPECIAL PROBLEMS WITH MODIFIERS

Objectives

- To avoid common usage problems with modifiers

Writing

- To revise and proofread writing to correct errors in comparisons

Teaching Strategies

INDIVIDUALIZING INSTRUCTION: ESL STUDENTS Remind ESL students that unlike most adjectives in English, the adjectives *this, that, these,* and *those* must agree in number with the nouns they modify.

HELPFUL HINT: AGREEMENT Explain that matching the adjectives *this, that, these,* and *those* with nouns like *kind* and *sort* can be especially tricky when there are no other nouns in the sentence for reference. Put the following examples on the board; have students decide which are correct.

Rosa likes *that kind.* (c)

Rosa likes *those kinds.* (c)

Rosa likes *those kind.*

Literature Connection

Explain that writers sometimes choose to use spoken forms that are considered incorrect in standard written English. For example, in "Raymond's Run," by Toni Cade Bambara, the main character says, "And I have a big rep as the baddest thing around." Ask students why a writer might have a character use an adjective form like *baddest.* (Sample: to show the character's personality) Point out that in order to make effective choices, writers need to know the correct forms.

INDIVIDUALIZING INSTRUCTION: ESL STUDENTS In Spanish, the double negative is grammatically correct. Therefore sentences such as "He didn't do nothing" are common errors for students who learned Spanish before English. Remind Spanish-speaking students that the double negative is not standard English. Explain that although they may hear double negatives in oral English, double negatives are still incorrect in standard written English.

Additional Resource

Grammar and Usage Practice Book, p. 66

Writing Theme: Robots

Other related areas students might wish to explore as writing topics include the following:

- robotics in medicine or space exploration
- Isaac Asimov's "Laws of Robotics"
- ideas for a personal robot
- famous film or literary robots

Answers to Practice Your Skills

A. Concept Check
Using Modifiers

Answers are shown on page.

The Double Negative

Negative words are such words as *no, none, not, nothing,* and *never.* A **double negative** is the use of two negative words together when only one is needed. Good speakers and writers take care to avoid the double negative.

Incorrect We do*n't* need *no* more problems.
Correct We do*n't* need *any* more problems.

Incorrect That robot ca*n't* do *nothing* right.
Correct That robot ca*n't* do *anything* right.

In the sentences above, the first negative is a contraction for *not.* When you use contractions like *don't* and *can't,* do not use negative words after them. Instead, use words such as *any, anything,* and *ever.*

It *won't ever* respond to a command.
We *haven't any* idea what is wrong.
We *couldn't* see *anything* to reconnect.

Hardly, barely, and *scarcely* are most often used as negative words. Do not use them after contractions like *haven't* and *didn't.*

Incorrect We could*n't hardly* continue working.
Correct We *could hardly* continue working.

Incorrect The robot ca*n't barely* operate.
Correct The robot *can barely* operate.

Practice Your Skills

A. CONCEPT CHECK

Writing Theme
Robots

Using Modifiers Write the correct modifier given in parentheses.

1. You know that a robot is one of (those, them) machines that looks and acts human.
2. (These, This) sorts of machines are popular in movies and on TV.
3. You probably don't have (any, no) idea where the word *robot* comes from.
4. (This, This here) name was coined in 1921 by Karel Čapek, a Czechoslovakian who wrote a play called *R.U.R.* about mechanical people.

5. (Them, Those) machines were produced to serve people tirelessly.
6. Čapek needed a name for (them, those) machines; since *robot* means "work" in Czech, he chose this name for (them, those).
7. Eventually, people in the story couldn't control the robots (any, no) longer.
8. (Them, Those) robots took over the world.
9. (That, That there) play was so popular, the name *robot* stuck.
10. People now call (these, this) kinds of machines robots.

B. REVISION SKILL

Modifiers Write the following sentences, correcting all errors in the use of modifiers. If a sentence is correct, write *Correct.*

11. Robots can't hardly be described as newcomers to entertainment.
12. In 1893, Ambrose Bierce wrote about them in a short story.
13. This here story is called "Moxon's Master."
14. A robot plays chess, but the robot isn't never a good loser.
15. After a human defeats that there robot, the robot strangles the human.
16. Ever since Bierce's chess-playing robot, books, movies, and TV haven't hardly ever missed a chance to include robots as characters.
17. Maybe you saw these sort of machines in the *Star Wars* movies.
18. Artoo Detoo and See Threepio were robot stars in them films.
19. *Star Trek* also had many of them humanlike machines.
20. Humans have a fascination with those kind of machine.

C. PROOFREADING SKILL

Correct Use of Modifiers Write the following paragraph, correcting all errors. Pay special attention to modifiers. (15 errors)

Wouldn't you love to have a robot? That there idea isn't so far-fetched. Allready there are robots that can cut the grass vacuum the carpet and patroll for burglars. Even more advanced ones in industry and science. They do those kinds of jobs that people wouldn't hardly want to do, such as handeling explosives and cleaning up Radiation leaks. As yet, however, there aren't none quite like them you see in the movies. Experts say them advances are not far off. In fact, many Scientists feel it won't be scarcely any time at all before many homes have a robot

FOR MORE PRACTICE
See page 530.

B. Revision Skill
Modifiers

Answers may vary slightly. Possible answers are shown below.

11. Robots can hardly be (*or* can't be) described as newcomers to entertainment.
12. Correct
13. This story is called "Moxon's Master."
14. A robot plays chess, but the robot isn't ever (*or* is never) a good loser.
15. After a human defeats that robot, the robot strangles the human.
16. Ever since Bierce's chess-playing robot, books, movies, and TV have hardly ever (*or* haven't ever) missed a chance to include robots as characters.
17. Maybe you saw these sorts of machines in the *Star Wars* movies.
18. Artoo Detoo and See Threepio were robot stars in those films.
19. *Star Trek* also had many of those humanlike machines.
20. Humans have a fascination with this kind of machine.

C. Proofreading Skill
Correct Use of Modifiers

Errors are shown on page. Revisions may vary. See typical revision below.

Wouldn't you love to have a robot? That idea isn't so far-fetched. Already there are robots that can cut the grass, vacuum the carpet, and patrol for burglars. There are even more advanced ones in industry and science. They do those kinds of jobs that people wouldn't want to do, such as handling explosives and cleaning up radiation leaks. As yet, however, there aren't any quite like those you see in the movies. Experts say those advances are not far off. In fact, many scientists feel it will be scarcely any time at all before many homes have a robot.

CHECKPOINT

Writing Theme: Women Journalists

Other related areas students might wish to explore as writing topics include the following:

- Ida B. Wells, African-American journalist and activist
- Connie Chung, Asian-American broadcast journalist
- Dorothea Lange, American photojournalist
- Jovita Idar, Hispanic-American journalist and humanitarian

MIXED REVIEW • PAGES 522–527

You may wish to use these activities to check students' mastery of the following concepts:

- adverbs in comparisons
- special problems with modifiers

A. Revisions may vary. Possible revisions are shown below.

1. Of all the reporters in her day, Nellie Bly tracked stories most fiercely.
2. She didn't ever give up on a story. *or* She never gave up on a story.
3. Correct
4. These sorts of stories were unusual in the nineteenth century.
5. Bly got those stories by becoming part of the event she was covering.
6. Her first story for the New York *World* was one of this kind.
7. Bly pretended to be insane, trying the strangest behavior she could imagine.
8. She was put in a hospital for the insane that provided the worst care imaginable.
9. Correct
10. Thanks to Bly's courage, this hospital improved its care.
11. Of her many accomplishments, Bly is probably best known for her trip around the world.
12. She modeled that trip on the journey in Jules Verne's novel *Around the World in Eighty Days.*
13. It was hardly a trip for a woman to take alone in those days.
14. Others had circled the earth, but she did it the fastest.
15. She traveled even more rapidly than did the hero of the novel.

B. Answers are shown on page.

Writing Theme
Women Journalists

Nellie Bly, January 25, 1890, the day she completed her record-breaking 72-day trip around the world.

CHECKPOINT
MIXED REVIEW • PAGES 522–527

A. Write each sentence, correcting the error in the use of modifiers. If a sentence is correct, write *Correct.*

1. Of all the reporters in her day, Nellie Bly tracked stories more fiercely.
2. She didn't never give up on a story.
3. Her reports took a more personal slant than most news stories of her time.
4. These sort of stories were unusual in the nineteenth century.
5. Bly got them stories by becoming part of the event she was covering.
6. Her first story for the New York *World* was one of these kind.
7. Bly pretended to be insane, trying the most strangely behavior she could imagine.
8. She was put in a hospital for the insane that provided the worse care imaginable.
9. Some of her best stories came out of those hospital experiences.
10. Thanks to Bly's courage, this here hospital improved its care.
11. Of her many accomplishments, Bly is probably better known for her trip around the world.
12. She modeled that there trip on the journey in Jules Verne's novel *Around the World in Eighty Days.*
13. It wasn't hardly a trip for a woman to take alone in those days.
14. Others had circled the earth, but she did it the more fast.
15. She traveled even most rapidly than did the hero of the novel.

B. Write the word or phrase that correctly completes each sentence.

16. Charlayne Hunter-Gault (isn't, is) hardly an ordinary journalist.
17. As an African-American teen, she (couldn't, could) barely get into the university of her choice.
18. There weren't (no, any) African-American students there then.
19. Hunter-Gault became the first African-American woman to attend (that, that there) university.
20. (Them, Those) were difficult times for her.
21. There were riots; she heard (them, those) outside her dormitory.
22. She stayed in school, despite (this kinds, these kinds) of problems.
23. It didn't (ever, never) occur to her to leave.
24. When (them, those) days were past, she became a reporter.
25. (That, That there) beginning set the stage for an amazing career.

A. Finding Adjectives Write the adjectives. After each adjective, write the word it modifies. Do not write the articles.

1. Alaska was the forty-ninth state to join the Union.
2. It is our largest state, and everything about it is big.
3. It has 5,000 glaciers, 3,000 rivers, and 3 million lakes.
4. One Alaskan glacier, Malaspina, is larger than Rhode Island.
5. Mt. McKinley, in Alaska, is the tallest mountain on the continent.
6. Because Alaska is huge, many of its areas are remote and isolated.
7. Its tiny population numbers about one-half million.
8. That is less than the population of Memphis, Tennessee.
9. Most of those people live in a few cities along the coast.
10. The rest of Alaska is empty except for small, scattered towns.
11. You cannot even visit these towns by car.
12. There are no roads through vast sections of the Alaskan interior.
13. To visit many places, you must fly, walk, or take a boat.
14. Your trip will take you across vast wilderness.
15. There are huge forests and treeless prairies called tundra.

Writing Theme
Alaska

B. Finding Adverbs Write and label the *Adverbs* and *Predicate Adjectives* from the following sentences. Then write the word each adverb or predicate adjective modifies.

16. Alaskan travelers always tell stories about the mosquitoes.
17. In some tales the mosquitoes seem much larger than life.
18. One Alaskan mosquito could never carry away a person.
19. Can two drag off a small animal?
20. Of course, such feats are not possible.
21. However, the great number of mosquitoes has not been exaggerated.
22. Water can be found everywhere, and the forty species of mosquitoes are plentiful.
23. The ground grows hard in the winter, trapping the water.
24. In spring the ground melts slowly and becomes a mosquito nursery.
25. Mosquitoes are worst in the months of May through July.

C. Choosing Modifiers Write the correct form of the modifier.

26. In Alaska, the aurora borealis looks (fantastic, fantastically).
27. The northern lights, as this phenomenon is also called, may seem (real, really) close.

Additional Resource

Grammar and Usage Practice Book, p. 68

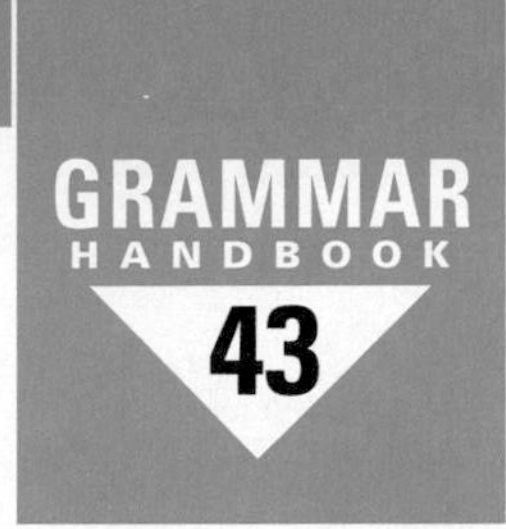

ADDITIONAL PRACTICE

Each of these exercises correlates to a section of Handbook 43, "Using Modifiers." The exercises may be used for more practice, for reteaching, or for review of the concepts presented.

Writing Theme: Alaska

Other related areas students might wish to explore as writing topics include the following:
- Inuit culture
- the Yukon gold rush
- the Brooks range, endangered Alaskan wilderness

A. Finding Adjectives
1. forty-ninth, state
2. our, state; largest, state; big, everything
3. 5,000, glaciers; 3,000, rivers; 3 million, lakes
4. One, glacier; Alaskan, glacier; larger, glacier
5. tallest, mountain
6. huge, Alaska; its, areas; remote, areas; isolated, areas
7. Its, population; tiny, population; one-half, million
8. less, That
9. those, people; few, cities
10. empty, rest; small, towns; scattered, towns
11. these, towns
12. no, roads; vast, sections; Alaskan, interior
13. many, places
14. Your, trip; vast, wilderness
15. huge, forests; treeless, prairies

B. Finding Adverbs
16. always, Adverb, tell
17. much, Adverb, larger; larger, Predicate Adjective, mosquitoes
18. never, Adverb, could carry; away, Adverb, could carry
19. off, Adverb, can drag

20. not, Adverb, possible; possible, Predicate Adjective, feats
21. not, Adverb, has been exaggerated
22. everywhere, Adverb, can be found; plentiful, Predicate Adjective, species
23. hard, Predicate Adjective, ground
24. slowly, Adverb, melts
25. worst, Predicate Adjective, Mosquitoes

C. Choosing Modifiers

Answers are shown on page.

D. Using Modifiers in Comparisons

36. Imagine a day more tiring than any other day of your entire life.
37. You're on Kodiak Island, home of the largest bear in the world.
38. You hiked harder than you ever have before to get back to camp by sundown.
39. You fell asleep more quickly than at any other time on this trip.
40. Suddenly, you awaken—your heart is pounding more rapidly than it did when you were hiking.
41. You hear something growling more loudly than a jet taking off.
42. You peer outside and see the most monstrous bear imaginable.
43. You've always wanted to see a Kodiak bear in the worst way.
44. You couldn't have a better view, but you'd rather be anywhere but here.
45. The Kodiak stares directly at you and then turns and ambles into the night more slowly than ice melts during an Alaskan winter.

E. Avoiding Problems with Modifiers

Answers may vary slightly. See typical answers below.

46. Can you imagine living where there isn't any sunlight for months?
47. You'll find that kind of situation in one-third of Alaska.
48. That part of Alaska is north of the Arctic Circle.
49. Those places can be dark and dreary.
50. Each fall, the sun in those areas sets farther south every day.
51. By November, in some places the sun hardly rises at all.
52. Soon, those places don't have any sunlight.
53. Correct
54. This darkness lasts two months in northernmost Alaska.
55. What would your life be like in this sort of place?

28. The borealis is (actual, actually) about 100 miles above ground.
29. The curtain of light can (easy, easily) be 150 miles high.
30. The lights may dance (crazy, crazily) over hundreds of miles.
31. They move (erratic, erratically) in amazing patterns.
32. The pale green and pinkish rose lights shine (bright, brightly).
33. People tell many (good, well) stories about the lights.
34. They say that if you whistle (good, well), the lights approach.
35. Listen (careful, carefully), and you may hear the lights sing.

D. Using Modifiers in Comparisons Write the following sentences, correcting all errors in the use of comparative forms.

36. Imagine a day more tiring than any day of your entire life.
37. You're on Kodiak Island, home of the larger bear in the world.
38. You hiked hardest than you ever have before to get back to camp by sundown.
39. You fell asleep more quick than at any other time on this trip.
40. Suddenly you awaken—your heart is pounding rapider than it did when you were hiking.
41. You hear something growling more louder than a jet taking off.
42. You peer outside and see the monstrousest bear imaginable.
43. You've always wanted to see a Kodiak bear in the worse way.
44. You couldn't have a gooder view, but you'd rather be anywhere but here.
45. The Kodiak stares directly at you and then turns and ambles into the night more slow than ice melts during an Alaskan winter.

E. Avoiding Problems with Modifiers Write the following sentences, correcting the errors in the use of modifiers. If a sentence is correct, write *Correct.*

46. Can you imagine living where there isn't no sunlight for months?
47. You'll find that kind of situations in one-third of Alaska.
48. That there part of Alaska is north of the Arctic Circle.
49. Them places can be dark and dreary.
50. Each fall, the sun in them areas sets farther south every day.
51. By November, in some places the sun doesn't hardly rise at all.
52. Soon, those places don't have no sunlight.
53. The darkness lasts longest in those places that are farthest north.
54. This here darkness lasts two months in northernmost Alaska.
55. What would your life be like in these sort of place?

530 Grammar Handbook

GRAMMAR HANDBOOK 43

Writing Theme Walls

A. Choosing the Correct Modifier Write the correct form of the modifiers given in parentheses. Identify the correct form as an *Adjective* or *Adverb* and tell what word it modifies.

1. Thousands of years ago, everyday life must have been (hazardous, hazardously).
2. Survival depended on thinking and acting (quick, quickly).
3. Every day, people faced some (dreadful, dreadfully) new threat.
4. Hunting wild animals was a (real, really) important part of survival.
5. Wild animals in turn (continual, continually) stalked people.
6. At any moment, a saber-toothed tiger might decide that a wandering hunter would taste (wonderful, wonderfully).
7. At times, warlike neighbors may have pounded drums quite (loud, loudly).
8. No doubt, that pounding sounded (dangerous, dangerously).
9. Mere survival must often have seemed (uncertain, uncertainly).
10. The construction of walls seemed (logical, logically).
11. Some of the first walls were (actual, actually) made of bones from such prehistoric animals as the elephantlike mammoth.
12. That may have been because large trees were (rare, rarely).
13. Mammoth tusks and bones worked (good, well).
14. The tusks grew (gigantic, gigantically)—up to ten feet long.
15. Would those bone walls have made you feel (safe, safely)?

B. Modifiers in Comparisons Some of the following sentences contain errors in comparisons. Write each sentence correctly. If a sentence contains no errors, write *Correct.*

16. The Middle Ages were perhaps more warlike than any period.
17. People thought they would be most safest behind strong walls.
18. The walls were most thickest at the bottom.
19. People prepared the best they could for the worse siege.
20. Even the most strong armies failed to capture well-defended cities.
21. Cities with the greater advantages over invaders were those with walls.
22. Defenders could shoot arrows more accurate from on top of the walls than from below.
23. Defenders up above poured the most hottest oil on attackers.
24. Sometimes, however, the invaders were better equipped than the defenders within the walls.
25. They had the greatest number of soldiers between the two groups.

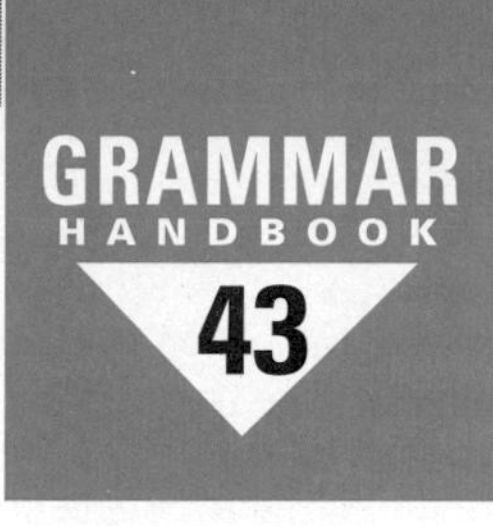

REVIEW

These exercises may be used as a mixed review or as an informal evaluation of the skills presented in Handbook 43, "Using Modifiers."

Additional Resources

Grammar and Usage Practice Book, p. 69

Tests and Writing Assessment Prompts, Mastery Test, pp. 27–28

Elaboration, Revision, and Proofreading Practice, p. 29

Writing Theme: Walls

Other related areas students might wish to explore as writing topics include the following:

- famous walls, such as Hadrian's Wall in England and the Berlin Wall
- the poem "Mending Wall," by Robert Frost
- murals and muralists, such as Diego Rivera
- Carcasonne, walled city of France

A. Choosing the Correct Modifier

Correct forms are underlined on page.

1. hazardous, Adjective, life
2. quickly, Adverb, thinking *and* acting
3. dreadful, Adjective, threat
4. really, Adverb, important
5. continually, Adverb, stalked
6. wonderful, Adjective, hunter
7. loudly, Adverb, may have pounded
8. dangerous, Adjective, pounding
9. uncertain, Adjective, survival
10. logical, Adjective, construction
11. actually, Adverb, were made
12. rare, Adjective, trees
13. well, Adverb, worked
14. gigantic, Adjective, tusks
15. safe, Adjective, you

B. Modifiers in Comparisons

16. The Middle Ages were perhaps more warlike than any other period.
17. People thought they would be safest behind strong walls.
18. The walls were thickest at the bottom.
19. People prepared the best they could for the worst siege.
20. Even the strongest armies failed to capture well-defended cities.
21. Cities with the greatest advantages over invaders were those with walls.
22. Defenders could shoot arrows more accurately from on top of the walls than from below.
23. Defenders up above poured the hottest oil on attackers.
24. Correct
25. Between the two groups, they had the greater number of soldiers.
26. The *mangonel,* one of an attacking army's most powerful weapons, hurled huge rocks into the city.
27. Frequently, the attackers used battering rams that they hoped would break through the most fortified walls or gates.
28. Sometimes the invaders were more secretive in their attack than at other times.
29. The most clever tactic of all was to dig a tunnel under the wall, hoping to surprise the defenders or to cause the wall to collapse.
30. Some of the most famous walled cities stood for hundreds of years and withstood many assaults.

C. Special Problems

Answers are shown on page.

26. The *mangonel,* one of an attacking army's powerfullest weapons, hurled huge rocks into the city.
27. Frequently the attackers used battering rams that they hoped would break through the most fortifiedest walls or gates.
28. Sometimes the invaders were most secretive in their attack than at other times.
29. The more clever tactic of all was to dig a tunnel under the wall, hoping to surprise the defenders or to cause the wall to collapse.
30. Some of the famousest walled cities stood for hundreds of years and withstood many assaults.

C. Special Problems Write the correct modifier.

31. Of all (them, those) walls that have been built in many parts of the world, perhaps the most incredible is the Great Wall of China.
32. Like (them, those) other walls, it was built for protection.
33. The Chinese (were, weren't) scarcely ever safe from invaders.
34. (Those, Them) enemies swept down from the north and attacked.
35. The builders of the Great Wall (were, weren't) hardly slowed down by anything.
36. (These, This) kind of wall was built from stones and earth.
37. (This, This here) wall was more than 3,600 miles long.
38. It was built over deserts, rivers, mountains, and other natural land features of (this, these) kind.
39. (That, That there) wall was first built in small sections.
40. Most of (them, those) sections were built from 224 to 214 B.C.
41. (Them, Those) first sections averaged twenty-five to thirty feet high and twenty-five feet wide.
42. A million people worked on the wall during (them, those) years.
43. About 400,000 of (them, those) laborers died.
44. Those laborers (were, weren't) hardly there from choice.
45. (That, Those) sort of laborer was actually a political prisoner.
46. China's first great emperor ordered that the individual sections of (this here, this) wall be linked together.
47. From the sixth century to the fourteenth century, the Great Wall wasn't (no, an) effective barrier against invaders.
48. The Ming emperors in the fourteenth century reinforced the wall with cement and other material of (this, these) sort.
49. Of the world's structures, there isn't (none, any) as large.
50. It is said that the Great Wall is the only one of (them, those) structures that can be seen with the naked eye from space.

532 Grammar Handbook

WRITING CONNECTIONS

Elaboration, Revision, and Proofreading

Revise the following draft of a report for a computer club. Follow the directions at the bottom of the page, and then proofread the draft, looking for errors in grammar, capitalization, punctuation, and spelling. Pay special attention to the use of adjectives and adverbs.

[1]To stay up-to-date on whats happening in the world of computers, you need to know about laptop computers and how they compare with desktop models. [2]Both types offer a lot, but each have their own strengths and weaknesses. [3]For years the desktop type have been the most popular of the two. [4]Desktops generally have screens that are larger and clearer than those on laptops. [5]They also have the largest keyboards. [6]Some desktops have more memory capcity and can do jobs more quicker. [7]On the other hand, they are more bulkier. [8]Some laptops way as little as five pounds and are no bigger than a notebook. [9]Desktops can't be moved easy from one place to another. [10]Portibility is the main attracation of laptop models. [11]As their name implies, they are small enough to be used on a persons lap. [12]However, because of their smaller size, their screens are often more fuzzier and their keyboards more cramped.

1. Replace the vague expression "a lot" in sentence 2 with the more precise phrase "a variety of features."
2. Move sentence 8 to a more appropriate position.
3. Add the following information about laptops in an appropriate position: "Laptops generally can run on batteries and come with adapters for household current, so you can take them anywhere."
4. Add a concluding sentence that sums up the pros and cons of desktop and laptop computers.
5. Divide the passage into three paragraphs.

Informative Writing: Explaining *What*

When you compare and contrast items, you examine their similarities and differences. (See Workshop 5.) As you revise writing about comparisions and contrasts, make sure you have given specific examples to show how the items are similar and how they differ. Also look to see if you have used adjectives and adverbs effectively to draw attention to the points of comparison and contrast.

WRITING CONNECTIONS

Elaboration, Revision, and Proofreading

This activity will let students see concepts in this handbook at work in informative writing. They will have the chance to use modifiers to elaborate on writing and make it precise, and to make comparisons more accurate by using correct comparative and superlative forms.

Revisions may vary slightly. See typical revisions below. Elements involving change are shown in boldface.

To stay up-to-date on what's happening in the world of computers, you need to know about laptop computers and how they compare with desktop models. Both types offer **a variety of features,** but each has its own strengths and weaknesses.

For years the desktop type has been the more popular of the two. Desktops generally have screens that are larger and clearer than those on laptops. They also have larger keyboards. Some desktops have more memory capacity and can do jobs more quickly. On the other hand, they are bulkier. Desktops can't be moved easily from one place to another.

Portability is the main attraction of laptop models. As their name implies, they are small enough to be used on a person's lap. **Some laptops weigh as little as five pounds and are no bigger than a notebook. Laptops generally can run on batteries and come with adapters for household current, so you can take them anywhere.** However, because of their smaller size, their screens are often fuzzier and their keyboards more cramped. **Clearly, laptops have become very popular, but people who need memory and speed still like using desktops.**

Objective

- To use writing prompts and a picture as springboards to informal writing

WRITING WARM-UPS

Begin by reminding students that they will not be graded for this assignment. The picture and the activities are intended as springboards to get students to think imaginatively about the concepts taught in this handbook. Unless students volunteer to explore more than one prompt, have them work on a single activity.

For the first writing prompt, invite students to sketch a map of the holes of a miniature golf course. Suggest that they note hazards and important landmarks. Then they can use the map as a guide as they imagine themselves as golf balls traveling around the course.

Sketch Book

WRITING WARM-UPS

- Miniature golf is sometimes called goofy golf because the holes can be, well, goofy. What if you could design a hole for a miniature-golf course? Describe what it would be like. Make it as outrageous as you please.

- Imagine you are a golf ball being putted around a miniature-golf course. Describe your journey.
- Imagine you are a tour guide taking visitors to some of your favorite spots. Point out to your visitors where things are and what is interesting about them.

Using Prepositions, Conjunctions, and Interjections

- Prepositions
- Prepositional Phrases as Modifiers
- Conjunctions and Interjections

To describe miniature golf, you would probably need to use some miniature words—words like *in, on, over, under, and, or,* and *but.* If you play miniature golf, you might find yourself using some words like *wow, oh,* and *oops.*

These words—prepositions, conjunctions, and interjections—may be small, but they play a big role in showing relationships and linking ideas. In this workshop you will learn how to use them to explain connections and add details in your writing.

GRAMMAR HANDBOOK 44

Using Prepositions, Conjunctions, and Interjections

Objectives

- To identify prepositions and their objects
- To distinguish between prepositions and adverbs
- To identify adjective and adverb phrases
- To identify coordinating and correlative conjunctions
- To identify interjections

Writing

- To use appropriate prepositions to show clear relationships between words in a sentence
- To use conjunctions to combine ideas in sentences

INTRODUCING THE HANDBOOK

Point out that these three parts of speech—prepositions, conjunctions, and interjections—are important in writing. Prepositions such as *in, on, under,* and *over* show the relationship of things in space. The words *and, or,* and *but* connect concepts and ideas. On the other hand, interjections such as *wow* express emotions. Encourage students to read this handbook to learn how to use these words effectively.

PREPOSITIONS

Objectives

- To identify prepositions and objects of prepositions
- To distinguish between prepositions and adverbs

Writing

- To choose prepositions that clearly show the relationship between words in a sentence

Teaching Strategies

INDIVIDUALIZING INSTRUCTION: ESL STUDENTS Students whose first language is Urdu, Hindi, or another South Asian language may have difficulty in understanding the concept of prepositions. These languages use connectives, called *postpositions,* that *follow* their objects. As you work through the examples, stress how this connective in English, the preposition, precedes its object.

COLLABORATIVE OPPORTUNITY To help students work with prepositions, have them form small groups; then give each group a list of four prepositions. Have group members generate four sentences: one sentence with one preposition, one sentence with two prepositions, and so on. Have them check that the prepositions function as connectives by circling each object.

PREPOSITIONS

A **preposition** is a word that links another word or word group to the rest of a sentence. The noun or pronoun after the preposition is called the **object of the preposition.**

When you write or speak, you use certain kinds of words to show ideas and you use other kinds of words to show the relationships between those ideas. **Connectives** are words that show the relationships between ideas. They join together two or more words or groups of words. **Prepositions** are one kind of connective. Notice the italicized prepositions in the sentences below.

The plane flew *through* the cloud.
The plane flew *over* the cloud.

The pilot hung *from* the plane.

The prepositions *through* and *over* join parts of each sentence. In the first sentence, *through* connects the verb *flew* with *cloud. Cloud* is the noun following the preposition and is the **object of the preposition.** *Through* points out the relationship between *flew* and *cloud.*

In the second sentence, the preposition *over* connects its object, *cloud,* with the verb *flew.* It points out a different relationship between *flew* and *cloud.*

Now look at the prepositions in the following sentences:

The pilot stood *on* the wing.
The pilot stood *under* the wing.

You can see that *on* and *under* join sentence parts. These words show the relationship between *pilot* and *wing* in each sentence. Changing the preposition from *on* to *under* changes the meaning of the sentence. Someone standing *on* a wing is above the ground. Someone standing *under* a wing is on the ground.

Below is a list of words often used as prepositions. Some of these prepositions tell *where.* Others indicate *time.* Still others show such special relationships as *reference* or *separation.* Study the prepositions in this chart and see if you can figure out the relationship that each of them shows.

Words Often Used as Prepositions

aboard	before	during	off	to
about	behind	except	on	toward
above	below	for	onto	under
across	beneath	from	out	underneath
after	beside	in	outside	until
against	between	inside	over	up
along	beyond	into	past	upon
among	by	like	since	with
around	concerning	near	through	within
at	down	of	throughout	without

Practice Your Skills

A. APPLICATION IN LITERATURE

Prepositions Write the prepositions in the following passage. A sentence may contain more than one preposition. Write *None* if a sentence does not contain a preposition. Notice how the writer uses prepositions to clearly show the relationship between words and ideas in each sentence.

[1]Robin took her place before the left propeller with her hands resting on the blade. [2]I took my place beside the right propeller. [3]Father himself lay . . . on the bottom wing. [4]With his left hand he grabbed hold of the frame. [5]With his right, he took the front rudder controls. [6]He pulled back on the controls and the front rudders tilted upward. [7]He pushed forward and they tilted downward. [8]Then Father shifted his hips to the left. The rear vertical rudders twisted to the left and the wings curled slightly, as if they were alive. . . . [9]The wind drummed at the canvas over the wings. [10]The sky seemed alive and waiting.

Laurence Yep, *Dragonwings*

Writing Theme Aviation

INDIVIDUALIZING INSTRUCTION: ESL STUDENTS Certain African and Asian languages contain very few prepositions. In these languages verbs and adverbs are used like prepositions. Students with this kind of linguistic background may find it helpful to categorize the prepositions on the chart, using the headings *Time, Place,* and *Special Relationship.* Pair these students with native English speakers to check their charts before they begin the exercises.

LEP STUDENTS If LEP students experience difficulty learning how to use prepositions, help them by pairing prepositions that have opposite or contrasting meanings; for example: *off/on; under/over.* Also, group prepositions with similar meanings, in order to distinguish the subtleties of usage; for example: *among/between; over/above.* In addition, be sure to provide concrete objects for students to manipulate as they compose original sentences, using various prepositions.

Additional Resources

Tests and Writing Assessment Prompts, Pretest, pp. 29–30
Grammar and Usage Practice Book, p. 70

Grammar Test Generator

Writing Theme: Aviation

Suggest that students use these exercises as a springboard to writing. Other related areas that they might explore include the following:

- the disappearance of Amelia Earhart
- transoceanic balloon flights
- blimps as modes of transportation
- the supersonic transport (SST)

Answers to Practice Your Skills

A. Application in Literature

Prepositions

Answers are shown on page.

Using Prepositions, Conjunctions, and Interjections **537**

B. Drafting Skill
Using Precise Prepositions

Answers may vary. Possible answers are given.

11. for
12. Before; through
13. In
14. above; for; to; on; below
15. During or In; for
16. to
17. off
18. during
19. of; until
20. by; in

Additional Resource

Grammar and Usage Practice Book, p. 71

Answers to Practice Your Skills

A. Concept Check
Preposition or Adverb

Answers are shown on page. Prepositions are underscored once; adverbs are underscored twice.

B. DRAFTING SKILL

Using Precise Prepositions Write prepositions to complete the sentences below. Choose the prepositions that make clear the relationships between the words in the sentences.

11. Flying has been a dream _______ centuries.
12. _______ 1783, no one had successfully flown _______ the air.
13. _______ that year the first hot-air balloon flight was made.
14. Two Frenchmen floated _______ the ground _______ more than five miles, and they waved _______ the people standing _______ the ground _______ them.
15. _______ the 1800s, gliders were flown _______ short distances.
16. Inventors soon added engines _______ their gliders.
17. A few of these early planes could lift _______ the ground, but they could not fly very far.
18. None of these planes could be controlled _______ their flights.
19. The great dream _______ controlled, engine-powered flight was not achieved _______ 1903.
20. In that year, the *Flyer,* built _______ Wilbur and Orville Wright, made four short but successful flights _______ a single day.

Preposition or Adverb?

A word can be used as a preposition in one sentence and as an adverb in another. How can you tell the difference between a preposition and an adverb? A preposition never stands alone. It is always followed by its object, a noun or a pronoun. If the word is not followed by a noun or pronoun, it is probably an adverb.

The plane flew *past* the watchtower. (preposition)
The plane flew *past.* (adverb)

The aircraft is parked *inside* the hangar. (preposition)
The aircraft is parked *inside.* (adverb)

Writing **TIP**

Your sentences may be clearer and more specific if you use a preposition and its objects instead of adverbs. Notice the difference between "There's a bird *outside*" and "There's a bird *outside my window.*"

Practice Your Skills

A. CONCEPT CHECK

Preposition or Adverb Write the preposition or adverb in the following sentences. Label each *Preposition* or *Adverb.*

1. Orville and Wilbur Wright were fascinated by aviation.
2. They used gliders in their first experiments.

538 Grammar Handbook

3. The brothers attached a gasoline engine to their first plane.
4. This two-winged airplane, the *Flyer,* could carry one person along.
5. The pilot lay between the top and bottom wings.
6. He could look over and see the engine.
7. Behind the wings, two wooden propellers whirled around.
8. In place of wheels, there were thin, wooden runners attached below.
9. One chilly December morning, Orville Wright climbed on.
10. Moments later, the plane flew through the air.

B. REVISION SKILL

Using Prepositions for Clarity Complete each of the following sentences with a group of words from the list below.

of the wings	of the plane	to that question
for flight	above it	off the ground
of lift and thrust	on earth	in a forward direction

11. How does an airplane stay _________ during a flight?
12. The answer _________ is lift.
13. Before takeoff, planes, like all objects, are held _________ by gravity.
14. However, lift pushes a plane upward and gets it _________.
15. Lift is created by the wings _________.
16. The curved shape _________ lowers the air pressure above them.
17. With less air pressure _________, the plane can take off.
18. Another force, called thrust, is necessary _________.
19. Thrust from the plane's engines keeps a plane moving _________.
20. As long as the forces _________ are strong enough, a plane can remain in flight.

C. APPLICATION IN WRITING

Description of an Activity Write a paragraph or two, describing one of your favorite activities. You might describe a ride on a roller coaster, a game you play with friends, or something else that you really enjoy. Try to include prepositions as you write. When you have finished, revise your description. To make your writing clearer or more specific, check to see if you should use a preposition and an object instead of an adverb.

FOR MORE PRACTICE
See page 547.

B. Revision Skill
Using Prepositions for Clarity

11. off the ground
12. to that question
13. on earth
14. off the ground
15. of the plane
16. of the wings
17. above it
18. for flight
19. in a forward direction
20. of lift and thrust

C. Application in Writing
Description of an Activity

Answers will vary. Paragraphs should reflect accurate use of prepositions and adverbs.

PREPOSITIONAL PHRASES AS MODIFIERS

Objectives

- To identify prepositional phrases
- To distinguish between adjective and adverb phrases

Teaching Strategies

KEY TO UNDERSTANDING An adjective phrase is like an adjective because it modifies, describes, or limits a noun. In addition, a prepositional phrase, like other adjectives, can act as a predicate adjective:

Perrault was in a hurry.

An adverb phrase is like an adverb because the phrase modifies a verb, an adjective, or another adverb.

v.
He ran with great speed to the store.

adj.
Hope was impossible in that situation.

Students can identify an adverb phrase by remembering that it often tells *how, when, where,* or *to what extent* an action takes place.

HELPFUL HINT Tell students that prepositional phrases that begin with the word *of* are almost always adjective phrases. *Of* phrases frequently answer the question *what* about the noun or pronoun they modify. Use the following examples as illustrations:

The scrapbook is filled with memories *of childhood.* (memories of *what?*—childhood)

I live in the southern part *of the city.* (part of *what?*—the city)

Additional Resource

Grammar and Usage Practice Book, p. 72

PREPOSITIONAL PHRASES AS MODIFIERS

A **prepositional phrase** consists of a preposition, its object, and any words that modify the object. A prepositional phrase can modify a noun, a pronoun, or a verb.

A **phrase** is a group of related words that lacks a subject and a verb. A **prepositional phrase** consists of a preposition, its object, and any modifiers, or words that describe the object. Look at the italicized prepositional phrase in the first example below. The preposition is *for,* its object is *light,* and the modifier, or adjective, is *green.* The entire prepositional phrase modifies the verb *watched.* Find the preposition, object, and modifier in the second example. What noun does the prepositional phrase modify?

The gentle guide dog watched *for the green light.*
The man *with the gentle guide dog* crossed the busy intersection.

Sometimes two or more nouns or pronouns are used as objects in a prepositional phrase.

He needs a dog *with intelligence and a good disposition.*

Prepositional phrases can be **adjective phrases** or **adverb phrases.** Adjective prepositional phrases modify nouns and pronouns. Adverb prepositional phrases modify verbs, adjectives, or other adverbs.

A guide dog wears a harness *with a stiff handle.* (adjective phrase modifying the noun *harness*)
Guide dogs train *for many months.* (adverb phrase modifying the verb *train*)

Sometimes one prepositional phrase immediately follows another. Read the example at the top of the next page. The first prepositional phrase is an adverb phrase. The second phrase is an adjective phrase, modifying the object of the first phrase.

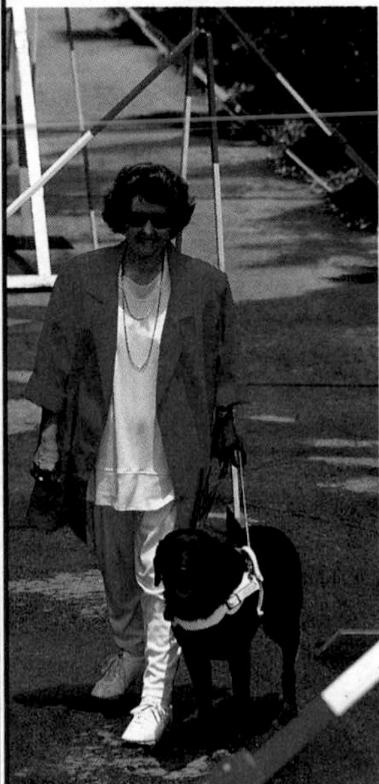

A visually impaired woman practices with her guide dog in a training maze at the International Guiding Eyes Center in Sylmar, California.

PROFESSIONAL NOTEBOOK

Advice from the Authors Students sometimes have difficulty understanding why grammar is important in writing. You might want to share with them Peter Elbow's view: "Grammar is writing's surface. When you meet strangers, you can hardly keep from noticing their clothing before you notice their personality. The only way to keep someone from noticing a surface is to make it 'disappear,' as when someone wears the clothes you most expect her to wear. The only way to make grammar disappear—to keep the surface of your writing from distracting readers away from your message—is to make it right."

Writing With Power

The dog led him *through the door on the left.* (*Through the door* modifies *led* and tells *where. On the left* modifies *door* and tells *which one.*)

Sentence Diagraming For information on diagraming sentences with prepositional phrases, see page 693.

Practice Your Skills

A. CONCEPT CHECK

Prepositional Phrases Write the prepositional phrase from each sentence. Underline the preposition once and its object or objects twice.

1. Dogs throughout the world help people in many ways.
2. Guide dogs assist people without sight.
3. On farms and ranches, dogs herd livestock into corrals.
4. Watchdogs protect people from crime and danger.
5. Dogs also work with the police.
6. They help police search for missing people.
7. In large cities, police dogs help with crowd control.
8. Dogs can even find illegal drugs in packages at airports.
9. Although some people are allergic to dogs, they keep them for companionship anyway.
10. Dogs bring happiness to the people around them.

B. APPLICATION IN LITERATURE

Adjective and Adverb Phrases Write each italicized phrase from this passage. Label each *Adjective Phrase* or *Adverb Phrase.* Then write the word or words modified by each phrase.

> [11]As a rule, Perrault traveled ahead of the team, packing the snow *with webbed shoes* to make it easier for [the dogs]. [12]François, guiding the sled at the gee pole, sometimes exchanged places *with him* but not often. [13]Perrault was *in a hurry*. . . . [14]Always, they broke camp *in the dark,* and the first gray *of dawn* found them hitting the trail with fresh miles reeled off *behind them.* [15]And always they pitched camp *after dark,* eating their bit *of fish,* and crawling to sleep *into the snow.* [16]The pound and a half *of sun-dried salmon,* which was [Buck's] ration *for each day,* seemed to go nowhere. [17]He never had enough, and suffered *from perpetual hunger pangs.*
>
> **Jack London, *The Call of the Wild***

Writing Theme
Dogs

FOR MORE PRACTICE
See pages 547–548.

Writing Theme: Dogs

Suggest that students use these exercises as a springboard to writing. Other related areas that they might explore include the following:

- dogs in the movie industry
- a special dog or breed of dog
- the role of dogs in the lives of elderly persons or people with disabilities
- methods of training dogs

Answers to Practice Your Skills

A. Concept Check
Prepositional Phrases

Answers are shown on page. Prepositions are underlined once; objects of prepositions are underlined twice.

B. Application in Literature
Adjective and Adverb Phrases

11. with webbed shoes: Adverb Phrase, packing
12. with him: Adverb Phrase, exchanged
13. in a hurry: Adjective Phrase, Perrault
14. in the dark: Adverb Phrase, broke; of dawn: Adjective Phrase, gray; behind them: Adverb Phrase, reeled
15. after dark: Adverb Phrase, pitched; of fish: Adjective Phrase, bit; into the snow: Adverb Phrase, crawling
16. of sun-dried salmon: Adjective Phrase, pound and a half; for each day: Adjective Phrase, ration
17. from perpetual hunger pangs: Adverb Phrase, suffered

CHECK POINT

MIXED REVIEW • PAGES 536–541

You may wish to use this activity to check students' mastery of the following concepts:

- prepositions
- objects of prepositions
- adjective phrases
- adverb phrases

A.

1. by: Prep; people: O of P; over: Prep; years: O of P
2. around: Adv; in: Prep; search: O of P; of: Prep; food: O of P
3. ways: O of P
4. of: Prep; about: Prep; strangers: O of P; animals: O of P
5. from: Prep; meals: O of P; by: Prep; dogs: O of P
6. at: Prep
7. of: Prep
8. near: Adv
9. down: Adv
10. for: Prep; masters: O of P
11. from: Prep; camp: O of P; to: Prep; camp: O of P
12. on: Prep; along: Adv; carts: O of P
13. with: Prep
14. for: Prep
15. of: Prep; breeds: O of P

B. Prepositions and their objects are underlined on the page.

16. of dogs: Adjective Phrase, breeds; in our society: Adjective Phrase, work
17. for example: Adjective Phrase, Dalmatians; in fire stations: Adverb Phrase, can be found
18. over horse stables: Adverb Phrase, stood
19. In 1870: Adverb Phrase, was given; to a New York City fire company: Adverb Phrase, was given
20. around the country: Adjective Phrase, companies
21. in the fire station: Adjective Phrase, equipment; from danger, Adverb Phrase, protect
22. from New York: Adjective Phrase, Dalmatian; of one urban legend: Adjective Phrase, hero
23. in front: Adverb Phrase, dashed; of a fire engine: Adjective Phrase, front; *or* in front of a fire engine (idiomatic *in front of*): Adverb Phrase, dashed
24. to the rescue: Adverb Phrase, leaped; to safety: Adverb Phrase, pulled
25. to the dog: Adverb Phrase, gave

MIXED REVIEW • PAGES 536–541

A. Write the italicized words in the sentences below. Then label each word *Preposition, Object of Preposition,* or *Adverb.*

1. Dogs were trained *by* nomadic *people over* 12,000 *years* ago.
2. These people traveled *around in search of food.*
3. Dogs helped these hunter-gatherers in many *ways.*
4. The barking *of* people's dogs warned them *about strangers* or dangerous *animals.*
5. The leftovers *from* people's *meals* were eaten *by* the *dogs.*
6. There was no waste *at* the nomads' camps.
7. The dogs' keen sense *of* smell also helped hunters.
8. The dogs followed their noses and knew when game was *near.*
9. Small animals were brought *down* by hunters' spears and arrows.
10. Dogs retrieved this game *for* their *masters.*
11. The nomads' dogs carried goods *from camp to camp.*
12. Goods were put *on* dogs' backs or pulled *along* in small *carts.*
13. Eventually, people began breeding dogs *with* specific traits.
14. Some of these dogs were bred *for* hard work.
15. Today, many *of* these *breeds* are popular house pets.

B. Write the prepositional phrases in the following sentences. Underline the preposition once and its object twice. Label each phrase *Adjective Phrase* or *Adverb Phrase.* Then write the word or words each phrase modifies.

16. Some breeds of dogs still do important work in our society.
17. Dalmatians, for example, can often be found in fire stations.
18. Originally, these spotted dogs stood guard over horse stables.
19. In 1870, a Dalmatian was given to a New York City fire company.
20. Soon, fire companies around the country had similar pets.
21. The dogs guard the equipment in the fire station and help protect firefighters from danger.
22. A Dalmatian from New York is the hero of one urban legend.
23. One day a small boy supposedly dashed in front of a fire engine.
24. The Dalmatian leaped to the rescue and pulled the child to safety—or so the story goes.
25. It sounds preposterous, but if it's true, perhaps someone gave an award to the dog.

Conjunctions and Interjections

A **conjunction** is a word that connects words or groups of words. An **interjection** is a word or short group of words that expresses a strong feeling.

A **conjunction** is another type of connecting word you can use to link words and ideas. Like prepositions, conjunctions show a relationship between the words they connect. Unlike prepositions, however, conjunctions do not have objects.

Coordinating Conjunctions

Coordinating conjunctions connect related words, groups of words, or sentences. The most common coordinating conjunctions are *and, but,* and *or.*

Wagons *and* livestock moved slowly in a wagon train. (connects subjects)
The wagons carried pioneers *and* their belongings. (connects direct objects)
The journey west was hard *and* dangerous. (connects predicate adjectives)
Each night, wagons gathered in a circle *or* near some natural barricade. (connects prepositional phrases)
Some wagons were lost during a trip, *but* most completed their journeys successfully. (connects sentences)

Correlative Conjunctions

A few conjunctions are used in pairs to connect sentence parts. Such pairs are called **correlative conjunctions.**

Correlative Conjunctions

either . . . or	not only . . . but also	both . . . and
neither . . . nor	whether . . . or	

Grammar **TIP**

When you use a coordinating conjunction to combine two complete sentences, remember to use a comma before the conjunction. See Handbook 24, "Sentence Combining," pages 304–313, for more information on using conjunctions to combine sentences.

Conjunctions and Interjections

Objectives

- To identify coordinating conjunctions
- To identify correlative conjunctions
- To identify interjections

Writing

- To use coordinating and correlative conjunctions to combine sentences

Teaching Strategies

INDIVIDUALIZING INSTRUCTION: ADVANCED STUDENTS The word *but* is often used as a conjunction. However, it can also be used as another part of speech. Challenge students to find an example of a sentence in which *but* is not used as a conjunction, or provide them with the following model:

We did all the chores but one.

Then ask students to make a generalization about the function of *but,* based on this instance. (Sample: *But* can be a preposition when it means *except* and is followed by a noun or pronoun.)

LINKING GRAMMAR AND WRITING
Point out to students that interjections can often be used as dialogue, to make writing more vivid. Discuss which of these two sentences is livelier, and why:

Jody felt relieved.

"Whew!" gasped Jody as she wiped the perspiration from her brow.

Additional Resource

Grammar and Usage Practice Book, p. 73

Writing Theme: Pioneers

Other related areas students might wish to explore as writing topics include the following:

- modern-day pioneers
- government help for pioneers
- frontier schools
- pioneers in space

Answers to Practice Your Skills

A. Concept Check
Conjunctions and Interjections

1. both . . . and: Correlative Conjunction
2. Whether . . . or: Correlative Conjunction
3. and: Coordinating Conjunction
4. and: Coordinating Conjunction
5. not only . . . but also: Correlative Conjunction

Notice how correlative conjunctions are used in the following examples:

Both men *and* women moved west on wagon trains.
People brought *not only* household belongings *but also* their pets and livestock.
People *either* rode on horseback *or* in wagons.
When times were tough, people had to decide *whether* to push on *or* head back.
Neither storms *nor* other natural disasters stopped people from moving west.

Interjections

An **interjection** is a single word or short group of words that is used to express a feeling or emotion. Interjections can express such feelings as urgency, surprise, relief, joy, or pain.

An interjection that expresses strong emotion is often followed by an exclamation point. An interjection that expresses mild emotion is usually followed by a comma.

Let's go! We can't rest until we reach the river.
Whew! I was afraid we'd never make it.
Oh, look at that beautiful valley.
Well, I've never seen so many wildflowers.

Practice Your Skills

A. CONCEPT CHECK

Writing Theme
Pioneers

Conjunctions and Interjections Write the interjections and conjunctions in these sentences. Label them *Interjection, Coordinating Conjunction,* or *Correlative Conjunction.*

1. Pioneers traveled west via both water and land routes.
2. Whether they went by boat or by wagon, the pioneers had a long, difficult journey.
3. Sometimes the terrain was flat and sometimes it was mountainous.
4. More than a hundred families at a time might move their belongings and livestock in a wagon train.
5. Wagon trains often had not only an experienced scout but also a leader chosen by the pioneers.

Literature Connection

Story to Read Edgar Allan Poe's story "The Tell-Tale Heart," on page 129 of Grade 8 *Literature and Language,* contains many interjections. Read this sentence from page 129 aloud, and challenge a volunteer to find an interjection, a preposition, and a conjunction in it: "*And* every night, *about* midnight, I turned the latch *of* his door and opened it—*oh,* so gently!" Encourage students to read the whole story and to observe Poe's use of interjections.

6. Say, have you heard about Jim Bridger and Kit Carson—the famous pioneer scouts who led many wagon trains?
7. Trains not only went northwest along the famous Oregon Trail but also southwest along the Santa Fe and Old Spanish trails.
8. The pioneers took the southern route into areas that are now New Mexico and Arizona and southern California.
9. Neither the northern nor southern route was easy for the pioneers.
10. Yes, many people and animals perished along the way.

B. REVISION SKILL

Using Conjunctions Use the coordinating or correlative conjunctions in parentheses to combine the following sentences.

EXAMPLE Men wanted to settle in the West. Women also wanted to settle in the West. (both . . . and)
Both men and women wanted to settle in the West.

11. The pioneers traveled across the plains. Their livestock also traveled across the plains. (and)
12. Wagon trains stopped for repairs. Wagon trains stopped for supplies. (either . . . or)
13. This constant movement was hard on people and animals. It saved many lives. (but)
14. The pioneers knew they had to travel more than fifteen miles each day. If they did not travel more than fifteen miles, they would have to endure harsh winter storms. (either . . . or)
15. Those who reached their destination felt triumphant. They still faced many hardships. (but)
16. Pioneer families built their own homes. Pioneer families grew their own food. (not only . . . but also)
17. Individual families worked alone to set up their homesteads. Families worked with the help of their neighbors to set up their homesteads. (or)
18. Work was done by hand. Some work was done with the help of mules or oxen. (or)

6. Say: Interjection; and: Coordinating Conjunction
7. not only . . . but also: Correlative Conjunction; and: Coordinating Conjunction
8. and: Coordinating Conjunction; and: Coordinating Conjunction
9. Neither . . . nor: Correlative Conjunction
10. Yes: Interjection; and: Coordinating Conjunction

B. Revision Skill
Using Conjunctions

Answers may vary. Possible answers are given.

11. The pioneers and their livestock traveled across the plains.
12. Wagon trains stopped either for repairs or for supplies.
13. This constant movement was hard on people and animals, but it saved many lives.
14. The pioneers knew they either had to travel more than fifteen miles each day or endure harsh winter storms.
15. Those who reached their destination felt triumphant, but they still faced many hardships.
16. Pioneer families not only built their own homes but also grew their own food.
17. Individual families worked alone or with the help of their neighbors to set up their homesteads.
18. Work was done by hand or with the help of mules or oxen.

19. Both corn and meat were important parts of the pioneers' diet.
20. Corn was both easy to grow and easy to store for long periods of time.

CHECK POINT

MIXED REVIEW • PAGES 543–546

You may wish to use this activity to check students' mastery of the following concepts:

- coordinating conjunctions
- correlative conjunctions
- interjections

1. Look: Interjection
2. and: Coordinating Conjunction
3. Hey: Interjection; and: Coordinating Conjunction; and: Coordinating Conjunction; Neither . . . nor: Correlative Conjunction
4. whether . . . or: Correlative Conjunction; either . . . or: Correlative Conjunction
5. neither . . . nor: Correlative Conjunction
6. and: Coordinating Conjunction
7. Oh: Interjection; both . . . and: Correlative Conjunction
8. and: Coordinating Conjunction
9. or: Coordinating Conjunction
10. Both . . . and: Correlative Conjunction; but: Coordinating Conjunction
11. Wow: Interjection
12. or: Coordinating Conjunction; and: Coordinating Conjunction; whether . . . or: Correlative Conjunction
13. not only . . . but also: Correlative Conjunction
14. and: Coordinating Conjunction; Ouch: Interjection
15. Sorry: Interjection; Well: Interjection; and: Coordinating Conjunction

FOR MORE PRACTICE
See page 550.

19. Corn was an important part of the pioneers' diet. Meat was important too. (both . . . and)
20. Corn was easy to grow. Corn was easy to store for long periods of time. (both . . . and)

MIXED REVIEW • PAGES 543–546

Write the interjections and conjunctions in these sentences. Label them *Interjection, Coordinating Conjunction,* or *Correlative Conjunction.*

1. MARTHA: Look! The Johnsons' wagon is ready to go.
2. JOSH: Help me get the pots and pans back into our wagon.
3. MARTHA: Hey! Sam and Megan are riding up front with their father and mother. Neither you nor I ever get a chance to do that.
4. JOSH: I don't care whether we do or we don't. I'd rather ride either inside the wagon or on horseback.
5. MARTHA: I suppose neither you nor I would survive if we had to walk.
6. JOSH: Do you really think Oregon will be perfect and wonderful?
7. MARTHA: Oh, I've heard both Ma and Pa say so about a hundred times.
8. JOSH: I've heard people say the rivers are made of milk, and they say the mountains are made of flapjacks.
9. MARTHA: Who told you that? Was it Sam Johnson or his sister Megan?
10. JOSH: Both Sam and Megan said it, but I don't believe it.
11. MARTHA: Wow! Wouldn't it be great if it were true?
12. JOSH: Pa said our cabin will be in a valley or near a river, and I believe it whether you do or not.
13. MARTHA: Ma says it will have not only real windows but also a wooden floor some day.
14. JOSH: Let's finish packing, and then we can go. Ouch! You dropped that pan on my toe!
15. MARTHA: Sorry! I didn't mean to drop it. Well, everything's in the wagon and fastened down.

A. Identifying Prepositions Write the prepositions in the following sentences.

1. In the past, people sometimes did business without money.
2. They simply exchanged goods with each other.
3. A farmer might trade some wheat for cloth or a new plow.
4. *Barter* is the name of this trading system.
5. The barter system is still used in many places today, but trading one thing for another can be inconvenient.
6. Many historians believe that money was developed thousands of years ago by the people of ancient China and India.
7. Over three thousand years ago, these people traded knives and other metal tools for the things they needed.
8. By 1100 B.C., they had begun trading with miniature bronze tools in place of real tools.
9. These small tools eventually developed into coins, and people bought and sold things among themselves.
10. Coins were used elsewhere around the ancient world as well.
11. In the 600s B.C., Lydia, a region that is now part of Turkey, had a money system based on small, bean-shaped coins.
12. The coins were made under the king's supervision and had a special design stamped on them.
13. The Chinese developed paper money during the A.D. 600s, but it was not used in Europe for another one thousand years.
14. The use of money spread through Europe when banks issued paper bills called bank notes to their depositors and borrowers.
15. Today, people buy things with coins, paper money, checks, and credit cards, and they can even buy things electronically through computer programs.

B. Using Prepositional Phrases Write the prepositional phrase in each of the following sentences. Label each phrase *Adjective Phrase* or *Adverb Phrase*. Then write the word each phrase modifies.

16. Over the years, the people of North America have used many kinds of money.
17. The native peoples of the continent bartered among themselves.
18. Playing cards were used as paper money during the 1600s and 1700s when Canada was a French colony.
19. Initially, coins and paper money were scarce in the American colonies.

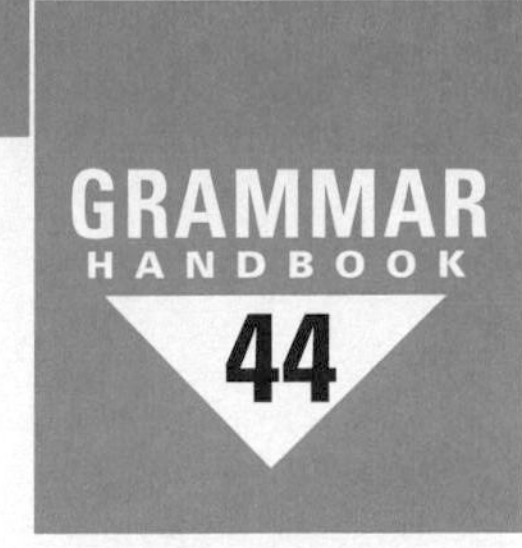

ADDITIONAL PRACTICE

Each of these exercises correlates to a section of Handbook 44, "Using Prepositions, Conjunctions, and Interjections." The exercises may be used for more practice, for reteaching, or for review of the concepts presented.

Additional Resource

Grammar and Usage Practice Book, p. 75

Writing Theme: Money

Other related areas students might wish to explore as writing topics include the following:

- silver in U.S. coins
- 1943 pennies
- modern-day bartering

A. Identifying Prepositions

Answers are shown on page.

B. Using Prepositional Phrases

16. Over the years: Adverb Phrase, have used; of North America: Adjective Phrase, people; of money: Adjective Phrase, kinds
17. of the continent: Adjective Phrase, peoples; among themselves: Adverb Phrase, bartered
18. as paper money: Adverb Phrase, were used; during the 1600s and 1700s: Adverb Phrase, were used
19. in the American colonies: Adverb Phrase, scarce

20. The English government hoped that their colonies would trade only with England, so they limited the supply of money.
21. Without money, colonists could not trade with countries that wanted payment in cash.
22. As a result, coins from many nations circulated in the colonies.
23. The most common coins of all were Spanish silver dollars called pieces of eight.
24. These coins were accepted everywhere, and people often broke them into smaller pie-shaped pieces for change.
25. Making money was illegal in the colonies until 1652.
26. The Massachusetts Bay Colony first minted coins in that year.
27. The coins were silver shillings stamped with tree designs.
28. England later declared the coins illegal, but colonists used the oak tree shillings for many years anyway.
29. In 1783, independence led to a new system of money for the young nation.
30. Since that time, citizens of the United States have used both coins and paper money for their financial transactions.

C. Recognizing Interjections and Conjunctions Write the interjections and conjunctions in these sentences. Label them *Interjection, Correlative Conjunction,* or *Coordinating Conjunction.*

31. Our class visited Washington, D.C., last week and saw many historic monuments and museums.
32. My favorite place was the Bureau of Engraving and Printing.
33. Wow! Seeing money being made was exciting!
34. I found both the giant machines and the printing process fascinating.
35. “All right!” I yelled to my friends. “This is what I call a cash machine!”
36. We examined not only the paper but also the plates that print the designs on the money.
37. Different plates print the fronts and backs of the bills.
38. Inspectors check each bill for both mistakes and imperfections.
39. Did you know that bills with mistakes are destroyed, and new bills with the same serial number are marked with a star and used in their place?
40. No, the bureau gives out neither free samples nor any of the imperfect “seconds” from its work.

20. with England: Adverb Phrase, would trade; of money: Adjective Phrase, supply
21. Without money: Adverb Phrase, could trade; with countries: Adverb Phrase, could trade; in cash: Adjective Phrase, payment
22. As a result: Adverb Phrase, circulated; from many nations: Adjective Phrase, coins; in the colonies: Adverb Phrase, circulated
23. of all: Adjective Phrase, coins; of eight: Adjective Phrase, pieces
24. into smaller pie-shaped pieces: Adverb Phrase, broke; for change: Adjective Phrase, pieces
25. in the colonies: Adverb Phrase, illegal; until 1652: Adverb Phrase, illegal
26. in that year: Adverb Phrase, minted
27. with tree designs: Adverb Phrase, stamped
28. for many years: Adverb Phrase, used
29. In 1783: Adverb Phrase, led; to a new system: Adverb Phrase, led; of money: Adjective Phrase, system; for the young nation: Adjective Phrase, system
30. Since that time: Adverb Phrase, have used; of the United States: Adjective Phrase, citizens; for their financial transactions: Adverb Phrase, have used

C. Recognizing Interjections and Conjunctions

31. and, and: Coordinating Conjunctions
32. and: Coordinating Conjunction
33. Wow: Interjection
34. both . . . and: Correlative Conjunction
35. All right: Interjection
36. not only . . . but also: Correlative Conjunction
37. and: Coordinating Conjunction
38. both . . . and: Correlative Conjunction
39. and, and: Coordinating Conjunctions
40. No, Interjection; neither . . . nor: Correlative Conjunction

548 Grammar Handbook

A. Identifying Prepositional Phrases Write the prepositional phrases in the following sentences. Underline the prepositions once and the objects of those prepositions twice.

1. Whales travel more than any other mammal on earth.
2. Whales migrate across vast distances to and from their breeding grounds.
3. They swim effortlessly in seawater.
4. Finback whales may make winter journeys of five thousand miles.
5. Their voyage begins deep within the Bering Sea and the Arctic Ocean and ends at their breeding grounds in the Indian Ocean.
6. It may take a month or more for the entire trip.
7. Interestingly, whales do not swim across the zone near the equator.
8. So, nearly all species of whales are divided into two groups, the northern and the southern.
9. The streamlined shape of whales helps them survive.
10. A whale's nostril, or blowhole, lies on top of its head.
11. When the whale needs a breath of air, it comes to the surface of the water.
12. The top of the whale's head breaks the sea's surface so the whale can breathe, while the rest of its body lies underwater.
13. As whales have evolved, their bones have become lighter in weight.
14. Their skeletons are now too weak for the survival of these creatures on land.
15. The weight of whales' bodies on land is too much for their light bone structures.

B. Prepositional Phrases as Modifiers Write the prepositional phrases in these sentences. Label each one *Adjective Phrase* or *Adverb Phrase.* Then write the word each phrase modifies.

16. For centuries, European whalers traveled to the Arctic.
17. The narwhal is among the sea creatures in that region.
18. Narwhals are members of the whale family.
19. These creatures once roamed throughout the northern seas.
20. One of the whalers' favorite trophies was a narwhal's tusk.
21. This tusk grows from the narwhal's jaw, like a giant tooth.
22. Tusks are found only on adult male narwhals.
23. Many narwhals reach about fifteen feet in length.
24. Their tusks, however, may reach a length of eight feet.

GRAMMAR HANDBOOK 44

Writing Theme
Whales

GRAMMAR HANDBOOK 44

REVIEW

These exercises may be used as a mixed review or as an informal evaluation of the skills presented in Handbook 44, "Using Prepositions, Conjunctions, and Interjections."

Writing Theme: Whales

Other related areas students might wish to explore as writing topics include the following:

- the whaling industry in nineteenth-century New England
- international efforts to protect whales
- whale watching excursions

A. Identifying Prepositional Phrases

Answers are shown on page. Prepositions are underlined once and their objects twice.

B. Prepositional Phrases as Modifiers

16. For centuries: Adverb Phrase, traveled; to the Arctic: Adverb Phrase, traveled
17. among the sea creatures: Adjective Phrase, narwhal; in that region: Adjective Phrase, creatures
18. of the whale family: Adjective Phrase, members
19. throughout the northern seas: Adverb Phrase, roamed
20. of the whalers' favorite trophies: Adjective Phrase, One
21. from the narwhal's jaw: Adverb Phrase, grows; like a giant tooth: Adverb Phrase, grows
22. on adult male narwhals: Adverb Phrase, are found
23. about fifteen feet: Adverb Phrase, reach; in length: Adjective Phrase, feet
24. of eight feet: Adjective Phrase, length

Additional Resources

Grammar and Usage Practice Book, p. 76

Tests and Writing Assessment Prompts, Mastery Test, pp. 31–32

Elaboration, Revision, and Proofreading Practice, p. 30

25. of the narwhal's tusk: Adjective Phrase, function
26. in the search: Adverb Phrase, might use; for food: Adjective Phrase, search
27. on the ocean floor: Adverb Phrase, uncover
28. in combat: Adverb Phrase, might be used; between narwhals: Adjective Phrase, combat
29. over females: Adverb Phrase, fight; at mating time: Adverb Phrase, fight
30. During such fights: Adverb Phrase, could be
31. in another way: Adverb Phrase, might help
32. like these: Adjective Phrase, tusks; through ice: Adverb Phrase, can break
33. for breathing: Adjective Phrase, holes
34. To this day: Adverb Phrase, do know; about these creatures: Adjective Phrase, much
35. about them: Adjective Phrase, theory
36. Through the years: Adverb Phrase, told; about unicorns: Adjective Phrase, tales
37. of these gentle, horselike creatures: Adjective Phrase, each; in the middle: Adverb Phrase, had; of its forehead: Adjective Phrase, middle
38. about the magical powers: Adverb Phrase, tell; of these horns: Adjective Phrase, powers
39. with sailors' tales: Adverb Phrase, originated; of narwhals: Adjective Phrase, tales
40. of the sea: Adjective Phrase, unicorn

C. Recognizing Interjections and Conjunctions

41. and: Coordinating Conjunction
42. and: Coordinating Conjunction
43. Wow: Interjection
44. not only . . . but also: Correlative Conjunction
45. but: Coordinating Conjunction
46. and, and: Coordinating Conjunctions
47. and: Coordinating Conjunction
48. whether . . . or: Correlative Conjunction
49. Boy: Interjection; but: Coordinating Conjunction
50. Both . . . and: Correlative Conjunction; but: Coordinating Conjunction
51. Oh: Interjection; and: Coordinating Conjunction
52. Either . . . or: Correlative Conjunction
53. Thank goodness: Interjection; and: Coordinating Conjunction
54. Whale ho: Interjection; and: Coordinating Conjunction
55. Neither . . . nor: Correlative Conjunction

25. The function of the narwhal's tusk remains a mystery.
26. Narwhals might use their tusks in the search for food.
27. Tusks uncover shrimps and crabs on the ocean floor.
28. Tusks also might be used in combat between narwhals.
29. Perhaps adult males fight over females at mating time.
30. During such fights, a tusk could be an effective weapon.
31. The tusks might also help narwhals in another way.
32. Tusks like these can break through ice.
33. Narwhals could make holes for breathing.
34. To this day, people do not know much about these creatures.
35. Scientists have one interesting theory about them, though.
36. Through the years, people often told tales about unicorns.
37. Supposedly, each of these gentle, horselike creatures had, in the middle of its forehead, a single horn.
38. Many legends tell about the magical powers of these horns.
39. The stories possibly originated with sailors' tales of narwhals.
40. Perhaps the strange narwhal is really the unicorn of the sea.

C. Recognizing Interjections and Conjunctions Write the interjections and conjunctions in the following sentences. Label them *Interjection, Correlative Conjunction,* or *Coordinating Conjunction.*

41. Three friends and I went on a whale watch last weekend.
42. None of us had been on a boat before, and we were excited.
43. Wow! Was it something!
44. It was not only fun but also educational.
45. We started very early, but it was worth the loss of sleep.
46. I arrived at the boat about five in the morning and met my friends, ten other whale watchers, and our crew.
47. Within moments, we cast off and headed into the ocean.
48. Whether tired or energetic, you caught the excitement in the air.
49. Boy! Some people felt wonderful being out on the open water, but I just felt queasy.
50. Both the wind and the ocean smelled great, but the water was incredibly rough!
51. Oh, did that boat rock back and forth for a while.
52. I kept crying, "Either we stop moving or I die!"
53. Thank goodness, the water calmed, and I felt better.
54. Whale ho! Suddenly a humpback whale surfaced and spouted!
55. Neither my friends nor I will forget our first view of a whale.

WRITING CONNECTIONS

Elaboration, Revision, and Proofreading

Revise and proofread this scene adapted from the short story "The Lady, or the Tiger?" Begin by using the directions at the bottom of the page. Then look for errors in grammar, capitalization, punctuation, and spelling. Pay special attention to the use of prepositions, conjunctions, and interjections.

[Scene: 1The PRINCESS, a beautiful young woman, is alone. 2She is pacing back and forth talking to herself.]

PRINCESS: 3What can I do. 4Either I must send my lover to the Lady. 5Or to the tiger. 6I cant bear either idea. 7how could I stand to watch him open the door? 8How could I stand to watch him face the cruel fangs of the tiger? 9No, I cant think of that.

[10The PRINCESS lies down on her bed.]

11Yet how will I feel if I send him to the lady. 12The thought of my love in the arms of the lady makes me crazy with jeolosy. 13At least he would still be alive. 14Oh, I wish someone could tell me what to do.

[15Sitting up in her bed and starting to cry again, the PRINCESS faces the audience.]

1. Add to sentence 1 these prepositional phrases describing the princess: "in her room" and "with a look of distress on her face."
2. Add more feeling to sentence 3 by beginning with an interjection.
3. Combine sentences 7 and 8 to form one sentence by using a compound verb. Choose a conjunction that correctly reflects the relationship of ideas. Delete words as necessary.
4. Combine this sentence with the stage directions in line 10: "She covers her face and cries for a moment."
5. Combine sentences 12 and 13 by using the conjunction *but.*

Narrative and Literary Writing

A script tells a story by presenting both the description needed to set the scene and the words the actors speak. (See Workshop 3.) When you revise a script, look for ways you can use prepositional phrases, conjunctions, and interjections to make your stage directions clear and your dialogue believable.

WRITING CONNECTIONS

Elaboration, Revision, and Proofreading

This activity will allow your students to see some of the concepts presented in this handbook at work in a scene from a script. By revising and proofreading this passage, students will have the chance to add information through the use of prepositional phrases, combine sentences with appropriate conjunctions, and add life to the dialogue through the use of interjections.

You may wish to have students work independently on the exercise and then meet in small groups to decide on the strongest revisions.

Answers may vary slightly. Typical changes are shown.

[Scene: The Princess, a beautiful young woman **with a look of distress on her face, is alone in her room.** She is pacing back and forth, talking to herself.]

Princess: **Oh,** what can I do? I must send my lover either to the lady or to the tiger. I can't bear either idea. How could I stand to watch him open the door and face the cruel fangs of the tiger? No, I can't think of that.

[The Princess lies down on her bed, **covers her face, and cries for a moment.**]

Yet how will I feel if I send him to the lady? The thought of my love in the arms of the lady makes me crazy with jealousy, but at least he would still be alive. Oh, I wish someone could tell me what to do.

[Sitting up in her bed and starting to cry again, the princess faces the audience.]

Test 2

This test enables you to evaluate student mastery of the concepts taught in Handbooks 42–44.

Additional Resource

Grammar and Usage Practice Book, pp. 77–78

Answer Key

Corrections for run-ons may vary.

1. A—grew
   B—Asia
2. B—mother
   D—bad
3. A—sits
4. D—any other insect
5. D—better
6. A—won
   D—well
7. A—knights
   B—wore
8. B—rise
9. D—cheaper
10. D—lie
11. A—camel's
    D—annoyed. Many *or* annoyed; many
12. C—ever
13. A—did
    B—really
14. E
15. C—this

List of Skills Tested

1. A—irregular verb form
   B—capitalization: geographical name
   C—capitalization: nationality
   D—possessive pronoun/contraction confusion
2. A—capitalization: geographical name
   B—capitalization: family relationship
   C—capitalization: day
   D—adjective/adverb confusion
3. A—wrong word: sit/set
   B—adjective/adverb confusion
   C—wrong word: lie/lay
   D—wrong word: rise/raise
4. A—noun plural
   B—possessive pronoun/contraction confusion
   C—comparative adverb
   D—illogical comparison

Skills

ASSESSMENT TEST 2 Grammar Handbooks *42–44*

Directions One or more of the underlined sections in the following sentences may contain an error in grammar, usage, punctuation, spelling, or capitalization. Write the letter of each incorrect section. Then rewrite the section correctly. If there is no error in an item, write *E.*

Example Not many writer's (A) have (B) mastered both poetry and fiction. Alice (C) Walker is a striking exception (D). No error (E)

Answer A—writers

1. People growed (A) soybeans in eastern asia (B) at least five thousand years ago, and the ancient Chinese (C) considered soybeans their (D) most important crop. No error (E)
2. In colonial Connecticut (A), it was against the law for a Mother (B) to kiss her child on Sunday (C). Both of them probably felt badly (D) about that. No error (E)
3. Yeast is a living substance that sets (A) quietly (B) on the shelf until warm water is added. Without it bread dough would just lie (C) there and would not rise (D). No error (E)
4. Swallowtail butterflies (A) beat their (B) wings more slowly (C) than any insect (D), only about five times per second. No error (E)
5. Some van Gogh paintings (A) have been sold for more money than any painting by Rembrandt. That (B) does not mean, however, that they're (C) best (D). No error (E)
6. Warren Spahn winned (A) more games during his career (B) than any other left-handed pitcher. In fact (C), few right-handed pitchers have pitched as good (D). No error (E)
7. Medieval nights (A) weared (B) armor that protected them well (C) from weapons. However, horsemen who fell (D) into the mud might drown. No error (E)

8. In some swamps gases [A] raise [B] up from rotting [C] plants and catch fire, causing [D] a ghostly light. No error [E]

9. Why is a little red schoolhouse red? In the Northeast, [A] where the custom of painting schoolhouses [B] red began, [C] red paint was more cheaper [D] than any other color. No error [E]

10. Someone who [A] doesn't sweat at all "sweats [B] like a pig," because pigs don't sweat. In [C] fact they have to lay [D] around in mud to keep their skin moist and to stay cool. No error [E]

11. A camels' [A] split lip helps it pick leaves [B] and also spit with amazing accuracy when it's [C] annoyed, many [D] surprised zoo visitors have suddenly discovered that the animal has this talent. No error [E]

12. How can you tell a duck from a goose? [A] Geese [B] don't never [C] dive, and ducks can't walk very well. [D] No error [E]

13. In his books Mark Twain done [A] a real [B] good job of showing how Americans live. He [C] was funny too. [D] No error [E]

14. When the moon is bright after a rain, you might see something similar to a rainbow; however, [A] you can see rainbows [B] in daylight more easily [C] because the sun is brighter [D] than the moon. No error [E]

15. All sturgeon are large, but [A] the largest [B] of these [C] kind of fish is the beluga, which can weigh [D] more than 2,500 pounds. No error [E]

5. A—noun plural
B—sentence fragment/run-on
C—possessive pronoun/contraction confusion
D—comparative adjective

6. A—irregular verb form
B—spelling
C—sentence fragment/run-on
D—wrong word: well/good

7. A—spelling
B—irregular verb form
C—wrong word: well/good
D—irregular verb form

8. A—noun plural
B—wrong word: rise/raise
C—spelling
D—spelling

9. A—capitalization: geographical name
B—noun plural
C—irregular verb form
D—comparative adjective

10. A—pronoun case: subject
B—subject-verb agreement: intervening words
C—sentence fragment/run-on
D—wrong word: lie/lay

11. A—noun possessive
B—noun plural
C—possessive pronoun/contraction confusion
D—sentence fragment/run-on

12. A—punctuation: question mark
B—noun plural
C—double negative
D—wrong word: well/good

13. A—irregular verb form
B—adjective/adverb confusion
C—sentence fragment/run-on
D—spelling

14. A—run-on sentence
B—noun plural
C—comparative adverb
D—comparative adjective

15. A—punctuation: compound sentence
B—superlative adjective
C—wrong word: this/these
D—spelling

Objective

- To use writing prompts and proverbs as springboards to informal writing

WRITING WARM-UPS

Begin by reminding students that they will not be graded for this assignment. The proverbs and the activities are intended as springboards to get students to think imaginatively about the concepts presented in this handbook. Unless students volunteer to explore more than one prompt, have them work on a single activity.

For the first writing prompt, note that a proverb is a brief, memorable statement that makes an observation about human experience. Most proverbs use figurative language, so their broader meanings must be inferred.

For the second writing prompt, note that some well-known sayings contradict each other; for example, "Birds of a feather flock together" contradicts "Opposites attract." You might have students argue the validity of several proverbs before reacting to one in writing.

SKETCH BOOK

WRITING WARM-UPS

A teacher can open the door, but the pupil must go through by himself.
CHINESE PROVERB

Whoever lies down with a dog will get up with fleas.
HEBREW PROVERB

Three may keep a secret if two of them are dead.
BENJAMIN FRANKLIN

When the mouse laughs at the cat, there is a hole nearby.
AFRICAN PROVERB

If you want the hen's eggs, you must put up with her cackling.
ENGLISH PROVERB

If you don't like worms, don't be an early bird.
JUNIOR-HIGH STUDENT'S PROVERB

- You have probably heard many sayings like these. Now it's your turn to think up some proverbs of your own. They can be serious or silly.
- Do you think proverbs always speak the truth? Choose a proverb you agree with or one you disagree with. Then explain why you feel the way you do.
- What advice do you have for students just entering junior high school? Give some suggestions for how to avoid the pitfalls of junior-high life.

554

Literature Connection

Author Note Explain that Benjamin Franklin (1706–1790), best known as a colonial patriot, is also famous as a writer, printer, scientist, and inventor. In *Poor Richard's Almanack*, a yearly publication that he began in 1733, Franklin included proverbs that he wrote himself or collected from other sources. Among Franklin's many other achievements were the Franklin stove, bifocal lenses, important experiments with electricity and lightning, and an unfinished autobiography.

Using Compound and Complex Sentences

GRAMMAR HANDBOOK 45

- Compound Sentences
- Complex Sentences
- Types of Subordinate Clauses

People who live in glass houses shouldn't throw stones.
ENGLISH PROVERB

A proverb is a saying that packs a great deal of meaning into one sentence. There may be times when you want to pack a lot of meaning into your sentences too. The way you structure your sentences can help you combine ideas or expand on them.

In this workshop you will learn to express yourself more completely and to add variety and richness to your writing by using compound and complex sentences.

Using Compound and Complex Sentences

Objectives

- To understand the form and function of compound and complex sentences
- To distinguish compound sentences and sentences with compound verbs
- To distinguish between main and subordinate clauses
- To identify and avoid fragments
- To identify subordinate clauses as adjective, adverb, or noun clauses
- To identify and use relative pronouns correctly in adjective clauses

Writing

- To improve sentence variety by using compound and complex sentences
- To use subordinate clauses correctly

INTRODUCING THE HANDBOOK

Have a volunteer explain the meaning of the English proverb on this page. (People with faults of their own shouldn't be so quick to criticize others.) Point out that this proverb, like those in the Sketchbook, is clear and succinct and conveys a definite meaning. Help students understand that much of this meaning is conveyed by the use of figurative language and by the combining of two separate ideas into one sentence. Have students restate the proverb using just one idea per sentence. (Some people live in glass houses. Those people shouldn't throw stones.) Explain that in combining the ideas, the writer has shown the relationship between them. Point out that in this handbook, students will learn more about how to combine ideas in compound and complex sentences.

COMPOUND SENTENCES

Objectives

- To understand the form and function of compound sentences
- To distinguish compound sentences from simple sentences with compound verbs and from run-on sentences

Writing

- To combine sentences to form compound sentences
- To punctuate compound sentences correctly

Teaching Strategies

KEY TO UNDERSTANDING: SIMPLE AND COMPOUND SENTENCES Explain that a simple sentence has just one subject and one verb and expresses a complete thought: The *site* (subject) *is* (verb) prehistoric. *Bradley* (subject) *likes* (verb) archaeology. Elicit that in a compound sentence, each part has a subject and a verb.

SPEAKING AND LISTENING Note that by using too many *and*s, speakers often link more sentences than they should:

> The alarm didn't go off, and I got up late, and I ran to catch the school bus, and I forgot my homework, and I missed the bus anyway.

Point out that such speaking is monotonous. Good speakers—and writers—avoid the excessive use of *and.*

INDIVIDUALIZING INSTRUCTION: ESL STUDENTS The use of coordinating conjunctions to join sentences is not always easy for ESL students. In Japanese there are at least eleven different equivalents for *and,* with different usage rules for each. Arabic is much freer than English in its use of periods and commas and commonly begins sentences with *and.* Look for error patterns in ESL students' use of coordinating conjunctions and punctuation in compound sentences. Work individually with these students to correct misunderstandings.

COMPOUND SENTENCES

A **compound sentence** consists of two or more simple sentences joined together.

Sometimes two simple sentences are so closely related in thought that you can join them together. You can join them by using a coordinating conjunction—*and, but,* or *or.* Two or more simple sentences joined together are called a **compound sentence.**

> The site is prehistoric. Archaeologists are studying it.
> The site is prehistoric**, and** archaeologists are studying it.

Compound sentences are useful, but they must be written carefully. Two sentences should be combined to form one sentence only if the ideas they express are closely related. If the ideas are not closely related, the resulting sentence may not make sense.

Incorrect The mound is old, and Bradley likes archaeology.
Correct The mound is old, and it contains ancient pottery.

Punctuating Compound Sentences

When you write a compound sentence, use a comma before the conjunction. The comma tells your reader where to pause. Without a comma, compound sentences can be quite confusing.

Confusing Jan studies the fragment and her assistant takes notes. (Did Jan study her assistant?)
Better Jan studies the fragment**, and** her assistant takes notes.

The first sentence might cause someone reading quickly to think that Jan studies both the fragment and her assistant. The comma prevents this confusion.

Sometimes you can join the parts of a compound sentence with a semicolon (;) rather than with a comma and a conjunction.

> The dwelling had partly collapsed**;** many stones had tumbled from the walls.
> The site had been abandoned**;** no one knows why.

TIP

Compound sentences can give your writing variety and interest. Notice the compound sentences Margaret Poynter uses in "Krakatoa: The Greatest of Them All," pages 94–95 to describe the volcano's eruption.

556 Grammar Handbook

Never join simple sentences with a comma alone or a run-on sentence will result. A comma is not powerful enough to hold the sentences together. Inserting a semicolon will correct the run-on error.

Incorrect	The stone tool was ancient**,** we did not know its use.
Correct	The stone tool was ancient**, and** we did not know its use.
Correct	The stone tool was ancient**;** we did not know its use.

Two Ways to Join Simple Sentences

1. Join them with a comma and the conjunction *and, but,* or *or.* Place the comma before the conjunction.
2. Join them with a semicolon without using a conjunction. Place the semicolon at the end of the first sentence.

Compound Sentences and Compound Verbs

A simple sentence with a compound verb looks and sounds like a compound sentence. Here are two reasons to learn to tell them apart:

1. Compound verbs are not separated by commas.
2. Sometimes you can improve your writing by changing a compound sentence to a simple sentence with a compound verb.

Notice that the compound sentence below has two subjects and two verbs. The simple sentence has one subject and two verbs.

Compound Sentence	Prehistoric *people* (S) *built* (V) forts, and *they* (S) *created* (V) burial mounds.
Simple Sentence	Prehistoric *people* (S) *built* (V) forts and *created* (V) burial mounds.

Often both subjects of a compound sentence refer to the same person or thing. Then you can make your writing more concise by changing the sentence to a simple sentence with a compound verb.

Sentence Diagraming For information on diagraming compound sentences, see page 693.

LINKING GRAMMAR AND WRITING Point out that the conjunctions *and, but,* and *or* show specific relationships between ideas. *And* shows the addition of a similar idea; *but* shows a contrast between ideas; *or* shows a choice between ideas:

Our town has an archaeology museum, *and* the state university offers archaeology courses. The museum is excellent, *but* I have never been there. Shall we visit the museum, *or* is it closed today?

COOPERATIVE LEARNING Challenge students to write a story in groups of four. Begin by asking one student to write a simple sentence on the board. Then have another student add a related idea to the sentence, changing it to a compound sentence. Have a third student write another simple sentence, one that builds on the idea of the first sentence. A fourth student will add to the last sentence, converting it to a compound sentence. Have students continue to write the story in compound sentences.

INDIVIDUALIZING INSTRUCTION: KINESTHETIC LEARNERS Using the two related sentences below, create note cards with one word from the sentences per card. Make one comma card as well. Have students arrange the cards to form the two sentences. Point out that the compound sentence requires more cards than the simple sentence because the subject is repeated.

Compound: A good tennis player serves, and then he charges the net.

Simple: A good tennis player serves and then charges the net.

Additional Resources

Tests and Writing Assessment Prompts, Pretest, pp. 33–34

Grammar and Usage Practice Book, pp. 79–80

 Grammar Test Generator

Writing Theme: Ancient Structures

Suggest that students use these exercises as a springboard to writing. Other related areas that they might explore include the following:

- the giant statues of Easter Island
- Heinrich Schliemann and ancient Troy
- the Mayan ruins of Central America

Answers to Practice Your Skills

A. Concept Check

Compound Sentences

1. Compound
2. Run-on Sentence
3. Simple Sentence with Compound Verb
4. Run-on Sentence
5. Compound Sentence
6. Compound Sentence
7. Compound Sentence
8. Simple Sentence with Compound Verb
9. Run-on Sentence
10. Simple Sentence with Compound Verb

B. Revision Skill

Sentence Combining

Answers will vary. Suggested answers are shown. Alternative answers are in parentheses.

11. There are many mysterious monuments in the world, and some of the most mysterious are in the deserts of Peru in South America. (world; some)
12. Vast figures have been drawn on the ground; they are known as the Nazca Lines. (ground, and)
13. Many are geometric shapes, but others are shaped like animals. (shapes; others)
14. From ground level, the shapes cannot be seen; in fact, their existence was unknown for centuries. (seen, and, in fact,)
15. The lines were not easily noticeable; perhaps they were natural lines on the ground and nothing more.
16. Should not be joined
17. Should not be joined
18. Some people see a calendar in the lines, but other people disagree. (lines; other)
19. The calendar theory could explain some of the drawings, but it cannot explain all of them. (drawings; it)
20. No theory seems adequate, and the drawings remain a mystery. (adequate; the)

Writing Theme
Ancient Structures

Practice Your Skills

A. CONCEPT CHECK

Compound Sentences Identify each of the following sentences as a *Compound Sentence,* a *Simple Sentence with Compound Verb,* or a *Run-on Sentence.*

1. You can pass an ancient mound, and you may not even notice it.
2. Mounds look natural, they often seem like enormous hills.
3. One covers many acres and is bigger than an Egyptian pyramid.
4. Mounds were built by Native Americans, some are well known.
5. Once thousands of mounds existed; now many are gone.
6. Some of these earthworks were built thousands of years ago, but others were constructed less than three hundred years ago.
7. Ancient people built them for burial purposes, or they used them as fortresses.
8. One mound covers fifteen acres and is one hundred feet high.
9. People call it Monk's Mound, it is near Cahokia, Illinois.
10. Great Serpent Mound in Ohio is curved and is 1,254 feet long.

This Nazca drawing of a spider can be recognized only from the air.

B. REVISION SKILL

Sentence Combining Join the following sentence pairs to make compound sentences. Two of the pairs are not related and should not be joined. Use correct punctuation and appropriate conjunctions. Use semicolons at least two times.

11. There are many mysterious monuments in the world. Some of the most mysterious are in the deserts of Peru in South America.
12. Vast figures have been drawn on the ground. They are known as the Nazca Lines.
13. Many are geometric shapes. Others are shaped like animals.
14. From ground level, the shapes cannot be seen. In fact, their existence was unknown for centuries.
15. The lines were not easily noticeable. Perhaps they were natural lines on the ground and nothing more.
16. The figures can be recognized only from an airplane. Native Americans created the drawings centuries ago.
17. Why were the drawings made? There are many theories.
18. Some people see a calendar in the lines other people disagree.
19. The calendar theory could explain some of the drawings. It cannot explain all of them.
20. No theory seems adequate. The drawings remain a mystery.

558 Grammar Handbook

C. PROOFREADING SKILL

Correcting Errors in Compound Sentences Proofread the following paragraph, correcting errors in grammar, capitalization, punctuation, and spelling. Pay particular attention to improperly punctuated compound sentences. (10 errors)

On a remote mountain in the Big horn Mountains of wyoming is a mysterious rock circle. Is called the Big Horn Medicine Wheel. The circle is eighty feet in diameter, it has twenty-eight spokes. The spokes start at the center of the circle and they extend to the outer ring. In the middle is a pile of rocks it is called a *cairn*. The circle could be 200 years old. It could be 2,000 years old. No one knows how old it is and no one is sure about its purpose, either. Perhaps it was the sight of a religious ceramony. It may have been an astronomical calender.

FOR MORE PRACTICE

See page 571.

CHECK POINT

MIXED REVIEW • PAGES 556–559

Writing Theme Team Mascots

Some of the following sentences are compound sentences, and others are simple sentences with compound verbs. Identify each as a *Compound Sentence* or a *Simple Sentence.*

1. Baseball, basketball, and football games are great fun, and part of the fun is watching the crazy antics of the mascots. C
2. You know the kind; all the professional sports teams have them. C
3. The San Diego Padres' Chicken was not the first mascot, but it was the first totally crazy one. C
4. The Chicken appeared in 1974 and was an instant hit. S
5. Soon fans everywhere enjoyed and applauded these crazy mascots. S
6. A mascot is not just a comic; he or she is also a cheerleader. C
7. Fans can get bored, but they always laugh at the mascot. C
8. A mascot's job can be fun, but it requires a strong person. C
9. A costume can weigh forty pounds and can be tight and heavy. S
10. The mascot wears it on the hottest days, and that takes stamina. C
11. A baseball mascot slides into bases and jumps into the stands. S
12. Some basketball mascots jump on trampolines and do wild dunks. S
13. Fans love the action, but the mascot suffers from the heat. C
14. A mascot can lose four or five pounds during a game and may not be able to wear the costume more than twenty minutes at a time. S
15. The work is hard, but few mascots would give up the applause. C

C. Proofreading Skill
Correcting Errors in Compound Sentences

Errors in proofreading exercises are counted as follows: (a) Each word is counted as one error. For example, a misspelled word is one error; two initials and a last name not capitalized are counted as three errors. (b) Run-on sentences and sentence fragments are each counted as one error, even though the correction involves both punctuation and capitalization corrections.

Errors are shown on page. Answers may vary slightly.

On a remote mountain in the Big Horn Mountains of Wyoming is a mysterious rock circle. It is called the Big Horn Medicine Wheel. The circle is eighty feet in diameter, and it has twenty-eight spokes. The spokes start at the center of the circle, and they extend to the outer ring. In the middle is a pile of rocks; it is called a *cairn*. The circle could be 200 years old. It could be 2,000 years old. No one knows how old it is, and no one is sure about its purpose, either. Perhaps it was the site of a religious ceremony. It may have been an astronomical calendar.

CHECK POINT

Writing Theme: Team Mascots

Suggest that students use this exercise as a springboard to writing. Other related areas that they might explore include the following:

- animal mascots
- sports marketing

MIXED REVIEW • PAGES 556–559

You may wish to use this activity to check students' mastery of the following concept:

- compound sentences

Answers are shown on page.

COMPLEX SENTENCES

Objectives

- To identify simple, compound, and complex sentences
- To distinguish between main clauses and subordinate clauses

Writing

- To use subordinate clauses to combine sentences

KEY TO UNDERSTANDING: NAMING CONJUNCTIONS You might explain that the conjunctions *and, but,* and *or,* which can be used to link clauses in compound sentences or to link compound elements in any kind of sentence, are called coordinating conjunctions. Instead of making one clause *subordinate* to another, they keep clauses equal, or *coordinate.*

COMPLEX SENTENCES

A **complex sentence** is a sentence that contains one *main clause* and one or more *subordinate clauses.*

To understand what a complex sentence is, you need to know about clauses. A **clause** is a group of words that contains a verb and its subject. There are two types of clauses—main clauses and subordinate clauses.

Main Clauses

A clause that can stand as a sentence by itself is a **main clause.** A compound sentence contains two or more main clauses, because it contains two or more simple sentences. Each of these simple sentences is a main clause.

Computers store information, and they solve math problems.

In the example above, *Computers store information* and *they solve math problems* are both main clauses. They are also simple sentences. Main clauses are sometimes called **independent clauses.**

Subordinate Clauses

Some clauses do not express a complete thought, so they cannot stand by themselves. These clauses are called **subordinate clauses.** Read these examples:

If technology (S) will improve (V)	When robots (S) can do (V) the work
While electronics (S) will work (V)	After the system (S) is (V) complete

None of these clauses express a complete thought. Each one is a sentence fragment that leaves you wondering *then what?* Now cover the first word in each of these clauses. What happens? Each clause now expresses a complete thought.

The words *if, when, while,* and *after* are important. They *subordinate* the groups of words they introduce and are called **subordinating conjunctions.** They introduce subordinate clauses.

560 Grammar Handbook

Words frequently used as subordinating conjunctions are listed in the box below.

Words Often Used as Subordinating Conjunctions

after	because	so that	whatever
although	before	than	when
as	if	though	whenever
as if	in order that	till	where
as long as	provided	unless	wherever
as though	since	until	while

Now you have the information you need to understand complex sentences. A **complex sentence** is a sentence that contains one main clause and one or more subordinate clauses.

Main Clause	Subordinate Clause
The robot began operating	before we were out of bed.
Its battery needs recharging	so that it can work tonight.

Avoiding Sentence Fragments

When a subordinate clause is used by itself, as if it were a sentence, it is a **sentence fragment.** A subordinate clause must be joined to a main clause to form a sentence.

Fragment When the power failed.
Complex Sentence When the power failed, the computer stopped.

Practice Your Skills

A. CONCEPT CHECK

Subordinate Clauses Write the subordinate clauses from the following sentences. Underline the subject of each subordinate clause once and the verb twice.

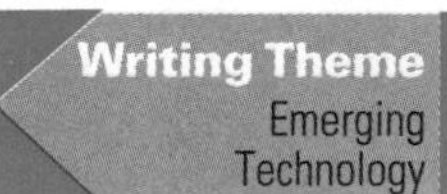

1. Before you know it, your flat television picture may be gone.
2. The image looks flat because it is two-dimensional.
3. The image would look more realistic if it were three-dimensional.

STUMBLING BLOCK Students sometimes have difficulty identifying subordinating conjunctions because some subordinating conjunctions are also used as prepositions. Explain that a subordinating conjunction must introduce a clause, which must contain a verb and its subject; a preposition introduces a phrase that ends with the object of the preposition and does not contain a verb. Discuss the use of *since* in these sentences:

We put your name on the project *since* you helped. (subordinating conjunction followed by subject and verb)

We have been working *since* Monday. (preposition, followed by an object)

INDIVIDUALIZING INSTRUCTION: BASIC STUDENTS These students may avoid using compound and complex sentences; their writing therefore, displays little sentence variety. Emphasize Exercise C on pages 562–563, which provides practice in sentence combining. You then may wish to have students bring current writing assignments to class. Pair students and have them collaborate to improve sentence variety in their compositions.

Additional Resource

Grammar and Usage Practice Book, pp. 81–83

Writing Theme: Emerging Technology

Other related areas students might wish to explore as writing topics include the following:
- high-definition television
- digital audio equipment
- advances in fiber optics
- advances in biotechnology
- advances in aerospace

Answers to Practice Your Skills

A. Concept Check
Subordinate Clauses

Subjects and verbs are underlined on page.
1. Before you know it
2. because it is two-dimensional
3. if it were three-dimensional

4. since technology is changing
5. so that the images look real
6. although they are not very common
7. If you have ever seen a bank card
8. when you look closely
9. Unless problems develop
10. Until it is

B. Concept Check
Kinds of Sentences

Answers are shown on page.

4. That 3-D image is not far off, since technology is changing.
5. Televisions will use holograms so that the images look real.
6. Holograms are available today, although they are not very common.
7. If you have ever seen a bank card, perhaps you have seen a hologram.
8. You can see a 3-D picture on the card when you look closely.
9. Unless problems develop, holographic television should be available in the near future.
10. Until it is, we will have to depend on today's technology.

B. CONCEPT CHECK

Kinds of Sentences Read each sentence and identify as *Simple, Compound,* or *Complex.*

11. Most people associate robots with science fiction, but today robots are found in everyday life. C
12. A robot is programmed like a computer. S
13. A robot can move and do work, and some robots can even sense changes in their environment. C
14. When it senses a change, the robot will respond. CX
15. Room thermostats are actually a kind of robot. S
16. Whenever the temperature in a room falls below a certain point, the thermostat responds by turning on the heat. CX
17. The automatic-pilot system of an airplane is a robot and can control the plane from takeoff to landing. S
18. Industrial robots are used wherever the work required is too hazardous for a person. CX
19. They can pick up very hot pieces of metal or work in a room that is filled with harmful gases. S
20. Robots have not been in existence for very long, but they will become more and more common. C

C. APPLICATION IN WRITING

Combining Sentences Writers use subordinate clauses to avoid the monotony and choppiness that is created by writing too many simple sentences. Subordinate clauses also help make relationships among ideas clearer. Combine each pair of sentences on the next page into one complex sentence by changing one of the simple sentences into a subordinate clause.

562 Grammar Handbook

EXAMPLE Cars will have guidance systems. They can travel faster and be safer. (Use *so that.*)
Cars will have guidance systems so that they can travel faster and be safer.

21. Imagine your daily routine in 2001. You drive to work. (Use *as.*)
22. You reach a new thoroughfare. You push a button on the dashboard of your car. (Use *when.*)
23. Then you take your hands off the steering wheel. You lean back and relax. (Use *as.*)
24. The car accelerates on its own. It angles into the traffic. (Use *while.*)
25. Six closely bunched cars approach at one hundred miles per hour on your left. They are going to pass. (Use *as though.*)
26. A gap opens in the line of traffic. Your car smoothly slips into line. (Use *when.*)
27. You have experienced this before. You do not pay attention to the car's maneuvering. (Use *since.*)
28. This scenario seems fantastic. It is not far from reality. (Use *although.*)
29. Car manufacturers and highway departments are developing smart cars and highways. Travel can be faster and safer. (Use *so that.*)
30. Research is proceeding quickly. Actual implementation of such a smart system is still a few years away. (Use *though.*)
31. A few systems are already being tested. The most useful systems can be identified. (Use *in order that.*)
32. The system is in place. Automobiles will drive themselves. (Use *after.*)
33. They will travel at high speeds. Cars will be bunched closely together in convoys. (Use *although.*)
34. Traffic congestion and accidents will be reduced. Human error will be removed from driving. (Use *since.*)
35. The systems work well. Roadways will be able to carry much more traffic. (Use *as long as.*)

Powerful dashboard computers and holographic displays may enable "smart cars" of the future to whisk you to your destination with little or no effort from you.

FOR MORE PRACTICE
See pages 571–572.

Using Compound and Complex Sentences **563**

C. Application in Writing
Combining Sentences

21. Imagine your daily routine in 2001 as you drive to work.
22. When you reach a new thoroughfare, you push a button on the dashboard of your car.
23. Then you take your hands off the steering wheel as you lean back and relax.
24. The car accelerates on its own while it angles into the traffic. *or* While the car accelerates on its own, it angles into the traffic.
25. Six closely bunched cars approach at one hundred miles per hour on your left as though they are going to pass.
26. When a gap opens in the line of traffic, your car smoothly slips into line.
27. Since you have experienced this before, you do not pay attention to the car's maneuvering.
28. Although this scenario seems fantastic, it is not far from reality.
29. Car manufacturers and highway departments are developing smart cars and highways so that travel can be faster and safer.
30. Research is proceeding quickly, though actual implementation of such a smart system is still a few years away. *or* Though research is proceeding quickly, actual implementation of such a smart system is still a few years away.
31. A few systems are already being tested in order that the most useful systems can be identified.
32. After the system is in place, automobiles will drive themselves.
33. Although they will travel at high speeds, cars will be bunched closely together in convoys.
34. Traffic congestion and accidents will be reduced since human error will be removed from driving.
35. As long as the systems work well, roadways will be able to carry much more traffic.

TYPES OF SUBORDINATE CLAUSES

Objectives

- To identify subordinate clauses as adjective clauses, adverb clauses, and noun clauses
- To identify the functions of words that introduce subordinate clauses
- To identify words modified by adjective and adverb clauses

Writing

- To combine sentences, using subordinate clauses
- To use subordinate clauses in original writing

Teaching Strategies

CRITICAL THINKING: EVALUATING

Point out that the three model sentences labeled *Adjective, Adjective Phrase,* and *Adjective Clause* say basically the same thing. Have students discuss which sentence seems clearest to them, and why. (The middle one is clearer than the first, which could refer to a legend told *by* pirates rather than *about* pirates; it also is briefer than the last, thus avoiding wordiness.)

TYPES OF SUBORDINATE CLAUSES

Subordinate clauses may be used in sentences as adjectives, adverbs, and nouns. Such clauses are called **adjective clauses, adverb clauses,** and **noun clauses.**

Complex sentences can be used to add variety to your writing. They can also make your writing more interesting by adding details.

Original The old sailor told us about a hidden treasure.

Revised The old sailor**, who knew many legends,** told us about a hidden treasure.

A subordinate clause can act as an adjective, an adverb, or a noun in a complex sentence.

Adjective Clauses

An **adjective** is a word that modifies a noun or a pronoun. An **adjective phrase** is a phrase that acts as an adjective. An **adjective clause** is a subordinate clause that acts as an adjective. Remember, a clause has a subject and a verb; a phrase has neither.

Adjective	The sailor told a *pirate* legend.
Adjective Phrase	The sailor told a legend *about pirates.*
Adjective Clause	The sailor told a legend *that involved pirates.*

An adjective clause usually comes immediately after the word it modifies, as in the following examples:

People still search for the treasure *that the pirate hid.*

Blackbeard was the pirate *who stole the treasure.*

The treasure, *which was buried,* has never been found.

Literature Connection

To show how good writing uses subordinate clauses, write the following passage from O. Henry's "The Gift of the Magi" on the board. Ask students to identify the subordinate clauses (underlined here).

"Now, there were two possessions of the James Dillingham Youngs <u>in which they both took a mighty pride.</u> One was Jim's gold watch <u>that had been his father's and his grandfather's.</u> The other was Della's hair."

Point out how the complex sentences help set off the final simple sentence.

Relative Pronouns and Adjective Clauses

Adjective clauses may begin with a subordinating conjunction or with the word *who, whom, whose, that,* or *which.* These words relate the subordinate clause to the word it modifies in the main clause. When used this way, *who, whom, whose, that,* and *which* are called **relative pronouns.**

Relative Pronouns				
who	whom	whose	that	which

A relative pronoun relates the adjective clause to a noun or pronoun in the main clause. It may also act as the subject, object, predicate pronoun, or object of a preposition in the clause.

This is the island *that has the secret cave.*
(*That* is the subject of *has.*)
The map, *which you saw,* shows the way.
(*Which* is the object of *saw.*)
The map leads to the treasure *of which we spoke.*
(*Which* is the object of the preposition *of.*)
Jon is the one *who found the pirate's cave.*
(*Who* is the subject of *found.*)

Put commas around adjective clauses only if they merely add additional information to a sentence.

Sentence Diagraming For information on diagraming sentences with adjective clauses, see page 695.

Practice Your Skill

A. CONCEPT CHECK

Adjective Clauses Write each adjective clause and underline the subject of the clause once and the verb twice. Write the word or words modified by the clause.

1. Have you read *Treasure Island,* which was written by Robert Louis Stevenson?
2. The island that he wrote about was based on a real place.

Writing Theme
Hidden Treasure

KEY TO UNDERSTANDING: RELATIVE PRONOUNS Review with students the uses of *who, whom,* and *whose,* which (like *he, him,* and *his)* express the same general idea but serve different functions: *who* is used as a subject or predicate pronoun; *whom* is used as the object of a verb or preposition; *whose* shows possession.

KEY TO UNDERSTANDING: *THAT* AND *WHICH* As you discuss the matter of using commas to set off nonessential (nonrestrictive) adjective clauses, you may want to point out that *that* is generally used to introduce an essential (necessary) adjective clause and therefore should not be set off by commas, whereas *which* generally introduces a nonessential clause and should be set off by commas. *Who, whom,* and *whose* may be used in either type of clause.

Writing Theme: Hidden Treasure

Other related areas students might wish to explore as writing topics include the following:
- salvaging sunken ships, such as the *Atocha*
- legendary pirates, such as William Kidd and Edward Teach (Blackbeard)
- legends of El Dorado
- the Comstock Lode
- the Klondike and California gold rushes

Answers to Practice Your Skills

A. Concept Check
Adjective Clauses

Subjects and verbs are underlined on page.
1. which was written by Robert Louis Stevenson; *Treasure Island*
2. that he wrote about; island

3. which is off the coast of Costa Rica; Cocos Island
4. who buried their gold there; pirates
5. who hid treasure on the island; two
6. that was hidden by Captain Thompson; one
7. that Spain was trying to capture; cathedral
8. who guarded it on his ship, the *Mary Dear;* priests
9. whose greed overcame his duty; Thompson
10. for whom people have little pity; Thompson

B. Revision Skill
Sentence Combining

Punctuation of subordinate clauses may vary.

11. The Lost Dutchman gold mine is said to lie somewhere in the Superstition Mountains, which are in Arizona.
12. This mine was discovered by Don Miguel Peralta, who led several expeditions to mine the gold.
13. On an expedition in 1864, Peralta and his crew were killed by Apaches, whose lands were overrun by gold hunters.
14. The legend of a hidden treasure was believed by two German prospectors, Jacob Waltz and Jacob Wiser, who heard of the mine from Peralta's son.
15. The two Germans went into the mountains with Peralta's son, who shared the secret of the mine's location with them.
16. The three came safely away with $70,000 in gold, which was a great deal of money in those days.
17. Waltz and Wiser could not resist going back to the mine that had brought them such easy wealth.
18. This time, however, the sole survivor was Waltz, who fled with more gold.

3. It is Cocos Island, which is off the coast of Costa Rica.
4. The island was known to pirates, who buried their gold there.
5. Captain Edward Davis and Bonito of the Bloody Sword are only two who hid treasure on the island.
6. The richest treasure is one that was hidden by Captain Thompson.
7. It was from a cathedral that Spain was trying to capture.
8. The English captain Thompson was supposed to protect the treasure and the priests who guarded it on his ship, the *Mary Dear.*
9. Instead, Thompson, whose greed overcame his duty, threw the priests overboard and hid the treasure in a cave on Cocos Island.
10. Thompson, for whom people have little pity, died without recovering the treasure.

B. REVISION SKILL

Sentence Combining Combine each of the following sentence pairs into one complex sentence by changing one of the sentences into an adjective clause. Use the relative pronoun provided.

EXAMPLE The Lost Dutchman gold mine was named for Jacob Waltz. He was from Holland. (Use *who.*)

The Lost Dutchman gold mine was named for Jacob Waltz, who was from Holland.

11. The Lost Dutchman gold mine is said to lie somewhere in the Superstition Mountains. They are in Arizona. (Use *which.*)
12. This mine was discovered by Don Miguel Peralta. He led several expeditions to mine the gold. (Use *who.*)
13. On an expedition in 1864, Peralta and his crew were killed by Apaches. Their lands were overrun by gold hunters. (Use *whose.*)
14. The legend of a hidden treasure was believed by two German prospectors, Jacob Waltz and Jacob Wiser. They heard of the mine from Peralta's son. (Use *who.*)
15. The two Germans went into the mountains with Peralta's son. He shared the secret of the mine's location with them. (Use *who.*)
16. The three came safely away with $70,000 in gold. That was a great deal of money in those days. (Use *which.*)
17. Waltz and Wiser could not resist going back to the mine. It had brought them such easy wealth. (Use *that.*)
18. This time, however, the sole survivor was Waltz. He fled with more gold. (Use *who.*)

19. The Apaches then filled in the mine. It had brought so many invaders into their lands. (Use *that.*)
20. Later an earthquake finished hiding the mine. It has remained the object of treasure hunters ever since. (Use *which.*)

Adverb Clauses

An **adverb** is a word that modifies a verb, an adjective, or another adverb. An **adverb phrase** is a prepositional phrase used as an adverb. An **adverb clause** is a subordinate clause used as an adverb. Adverbs, adverb phrases, and adverb clauses all modify words by telling *where, when, how,* or *to what extent.* In addition, an adverb clause may tell *why.*

Adverb We rode the train *once.*

Adverb Phrase We rode the train *to the Japanese fishing village.*

Adverb Clause We rode the train *until we reached the Japanese fishing village.*

An adverb clause contains a subject and a verb, like any other clause. It is always introduced by a subordinating conjunction. (See the list of subordinating conjunctions on page 561.

Sentence Diagraming For information on diagraming sentences with adverb clauses, see page 695.

Practice Your Skills

CONCEPT CHECK

Adverb Clauses Write the adverb clauses from the following sentences. Underline the subject of each adverb clause once and the verb twice. Label the subordinating conjunction *SC.*

1. When we arrived in Tokyo, we were exhausted.
2. All we wanted was a hotel room, because we had been traveling all day.
3. We did not know what would happen, since this was our first trip.
4. Until the rest of the tour group arrived, we waited in the airport.
5. While we were waiting, we tried to spot our guide.
6. Since we were on a group tour, we would depend on our guide.

Writing Theme Traveling

19. The Apaches then filled in the mine that had brought so many invaders into their lands.
20. Later an earthquake finished hiding the mine, which has remained the object of treasure hunters ever since.

HELPFUL HINT: ADVERB CLAUSES
Point out to students that an adverb clause, like an adverb, often can be shifted to a different position in a sentence without changing the sentence's meaning: *Until we left,* the children were quiet. The children, *until we left,* were quiet. The children were quiet *until we left.*

HELPFUL HINT: PUNCTUATION
Explain to students that when an adverb clause begins a sentence, or when it falls between the subject and the verb of the main clause, it is usually set off with commas; when it concludes a sentence, it often is not preceded by a comma.

Writing Theme: Traveling

Other related areas students might wish to explore as writing topics include the following:

- travel writers
- tourist attractions in Tokyo
- how to prepare for foreign travel
- guided tours versus exploring on one's own

Answers to Practice Your Skills

Concept Check

Adverb Clauses

Subjects and verbs are underlined on page.

1. When we arrived in Tokyo; When, SC
2. because we had been traveling all day; because, SC
3. since this was our first trip; since, SC
4. Until the rest of the tour group arrived; Until, SC
5. While we were waiting; While, SC
6. Since we were on a group tour; Since, SC

7. After the entire group arrived; After, SC
8. before we left the airport; before, SC
9. As soon as we had our baggage; As soon as, SC
10. so that we could absorb the sights around us; so that, SC

INDIVIDUALIZING INSTRUCTION: BASIC STUDENTS Have students work in small groups to write sentences with noun clauses that are introduced by each word listed on the chart and each word used to introduce a subordinate clause in the sample sentences. Students might share their sentences orally or post them for class reference and discussion.

CRITICAL THINKING: ANALYZING Ask whether students can identify noun clauses, adjective clauses, and adverb clauses by their introductory words (generally, no). Elicit that some of the words that introduce noun clauses can also be used as relative pronouns to introduce adjective clauses; others are also used as subordinating conjunctions to introduce adverb clauses. Ask students what they must examine to identify a type of clause (the clause's function in the sentence).

LINKING GRAMMAR AND WRITING Point out that it is grammatically acceptable to drop the word *that* used to introduce some noun and adjective clauses. In such cases, *that* is understood: She knows (that) wilderness life is challenging. The first winter (that) she spent in the wilderness was predictable.

Additional Resource

Grammar and Usage Practice Book, pp. 84–87

7. After the entire group arrived, our guide introduced herself.
8. She helped us change dollars for yen before we left the airport.
9. As soon as we had our baggage, we set off for the hotel.
10. The tour guide did not speak much on the bus so that we could absorb the sights around us.

Noun Clauses

A **noun clause** is a clause used as a noun. It can be used in any way that a noun is used. The following sentences show different ways of using noun clauses.

Subject	*Why she lives in the wilderness* is a mystery.
Object	She knows *that wilderness life is challenging.*
Object of Preposition	Wilderness is available to *whoever enjoys it.* (The clause is the object of the preposition *to.* Notice, however, that *whoever* functions as a subject within the clause.)
Predicate Noun	Her first winter in the wilderness was *what she expected.*

Words Often Used to Introduce Noun Clauses

that	where	who, whom
what	when	whose
how	whatever	whoever, whomever

You cannot tell the kind of clause from the word that introduces it. You can tell the kind of clause only by the way it is used in a sentence. If the clause is used as a noun, it is a noun clause. If the clause is used as a modifier, it is an adjective clause or an adverb clause.

Whoever built the cabin was not home. (noun clause as subject)
No one knew *where he went.* (noun clause as object)
He climbed the mountain *whenever he wished.* (adverb clause)
This is the lake *where he lives.* (adjective clause)

Sentence Diagraming For information on diagraming sentences with noun clauses, see page 695.

Practice Your Skills

A. CONCEPT CHECK

Noun Clauses Write the noun clauses from the following sentences. Underline the subject of each noun clause once and the verb twice. Label the clause *Subject, Object, Predicate Noun,* or *Object of Preposition.*

1. What Anne LaBastille wanted was a home in the wilderness.
2. She knew that the place should be far from civilization.
3. She found what she was after on a remote mountain lake.
4. Her Black Bear Lake cabin was what she had dreamed of.
5. There were no roads to where the cabin was located.
6. Whatever neighbors she had were miles away across the lake.
7. She kept a small boat for when a trip to town was necessary.
8. LaBastille became what she called a woodswoman.
9. How LaBastille lived is the subject of her book *Woodswoman.*
10. In it, she also explains why a wilderness home appealed to her.

B. APPLICATION IN LITERATURE

Subordinate Clauses Write the italicized clauses and underline the subject of each once and the verb twice. Then identify the clause as an *Adjective Clause,* an *Adverb Clause,* or a *Noun Clause.*

> [11]This June morning is hot and humid with a haze so dense I can barely see the huge hemlock tree *in which I live. . . .*
>
> [12]*As a hot dry wind clears the air,* I can see Frightful, my peregrine falcon, sitting in front of the six-foot-in-diameter hemlock tree *that I hollowed out for a home. . . .* Sticks snap in the distance. Someone is coming. . . . I smell the musky scent of warning from my friend Baron Weasel. [13]The Baron, *who was living here when I arrived,* considers himself the real owner of the mountaintop, but *because he finds me interesting,* he lets me stay.
>
> **Jean Craighead George, *On the Far Side of the Mountain***

C. APPLICATION IN WRITING

Writing an Explanation Imagine that you are going to live in the wilderness. You must take everything you will need with you. Other than food, what will you take? Write a paragraph explaining what you will take and why. Use at least five subordinate clauses.

Writing Theme Wilderness Experiences

Anne LaBastille at her cabin in the Adirondack Mountains of New York.

FOR MORE PRACTICE

See page 572.

Writing Theme: Wilderness Experiences

Other related areas students might wish to explore as writing topics include the following:

- Daniel Defoe's *Robinson Crusoe*
- Henry David Thoreau's *Walden*
- Barry Lopez's Arctic experiences
- newspaper accounts of wilderness survival

Answers to Practice Your Skills

A. Concept Check

Noun Clauses

Subjects and verbs are underlined on page.

1. What Anne LaBastille wanted; Subject
2. that the place should be far from civilization; Object
3. what she was after; Object
4. what she had dreamed of; Predicate Noun
5. where the cabin was located; Object of Preposition
6. Whatever neighbors she had; Subject
7. when a trip to town was necessary; Object of Preposition
8. what she called a woodswoman; Predicate Noun
9. How LaBastille lived; Subject
10. why a wilderness home appealed to her; Object

B. Application in Literature

Subordinate Clauses

11. in which I live; Adjective Clause
12. As a hot dry wind clears the air; Adverb Clause
    that I hollowed out for a home; Adjective Clause
13. who was living here; Adjective Clause
    when I arrived; Adverb Clause
    because he finds me interesting; Adverb Clause

C. Application in Writing

Writing an Explanation

Answers will vary. Paragraphs should contain at least five subordinate clauses.

Literature Connection

Author Note Born in 1919, Jean Craighead George has written many books of fiction and nonfiction about nature, sometimes collaborating with her husband John L. George. Her best-known books are *Julie of the Wolves,* which won the Newbery Medal in 1972, and *My Side of the Mountain,* the tale of a city boy who lives for a year in the woods of upstate New York. *On the Far Side of the Mountain* is a sequel to that book.

CHECK POINT

Writing Theme: Unusual Sports

Other related areas students might wish to explore as writing topics include the following:

- lacrosse
- jai-alai
- curling
- Sumo wrestling

MIXED REVIEW • PAGES 560–569

You may wish to use this activity to check students' mastery of the following concepts:

- complex sentences
- types of subordinate clauses

A. Answers are shown on page.

B.

11. While the skier plodded wearily up the mountain; Adverb Clause
12. What looked like a parachute; Noun Clause
13. that was designed for skiing; Adjective Clause
14. when she reached the mountaintop; Adverb Clause
15. After the sail was put away; Adverb Clause
16. who was tired of slow trips up snow-covered mountains; Adjective Clause
17. that the skier must have complete control of the sail; Noun Clause
18. that he or she pulls to change directions; Adjective Clause
19. who wants to slow down or stop; Adjective Clause
20. what was a problem in skiing; Noun Clause
21. Until the sail was invented; Adverb Clause
22. that lack chairlifts; Adjective Clause
23. what was a major difficulty; Noun Clause
24. how a skier can travel rapidly across frozen lakes or vast snow-covered flatlands; Noun Clause
25. when they travel to the South Pole; Adverb Clause

Writing Theme
Unusual Sports

CHECK POINT

MIXED REVIEW • PAGES 560–569

A. Identify each of the following sentences as *Simple, Compound,* or *Complex.*

1. Have you heard of wallyball? S
2. The game is not very old; it was invented in 1979. C
3. It has a strange name, but the game might look familiar. C
4. Wallyball is similar to volleyball, although it is played on a racquetball or handball court. CX
5. In fact, the name *wallyball* comes from *walls* and *volleyball.* S
6. The net is like a volleyball net that is attached to the walls. CX
7. Players can bounce the ball off the walls and over the net. S
8. The action is fast, because the walls keep the ball in play. CX
9. Since a team has fewer than four players, everyone is busy. CX
10. It is good exercise, and you do not have to be a great athlete. C

B. Write the subordinate clause in each sentence and identify it as an *Adjective Clause,* an *Adverb Clause,* or a *Noun Clause.*

11. While the skier plodded wearily up the mountain, another skier practically flew past him up the hill!
12. What looked like a parachute pulled the skier up the mountain.
13. The parachute was really a sail that was designed for skiing.
14. The skier packed the sail away when she reached the mountaintop.
15. After the sail was put away, the skier began skiing back down.
16. This sail was invented by a man who was tired of slow trips up snow-covered mountains.
17. He knew that the skier must have complete control of the sail.
18. The skier holds lines that he or she pulls to change direction.
19. A skier who wants to slow down or stop pulls another line to open a hole in the sail.
20. The sail is a solution to what was a problem in skiing.
21. Until the sail was invented, it could take skiers many hours to reach the upper slopes of back-country mountains.
22. Now skiers can easily climb mountains that lack chairlifts.
23. In fact, what was a major difficulty has become a popular sport.
24. The sail also answers the question of how a skier can travel rapidly across frozen lakes or vast snow-covered flatlands.
25. Some adventuresome Antarctic explorers plan to use the sails when they travel to the South Pole.

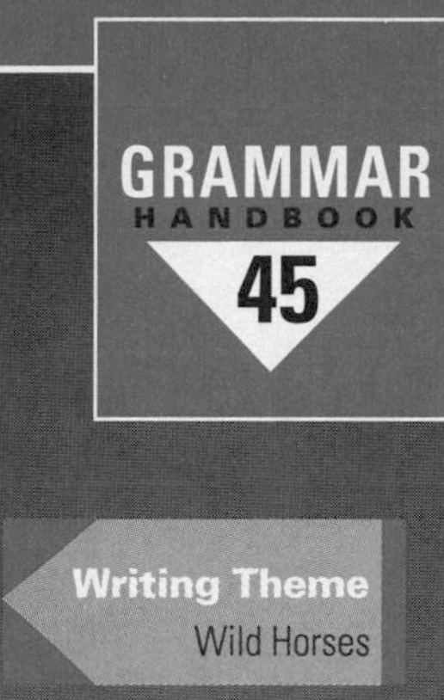

A. Recognizing Compound Sentences Write the following sentences. Underline each subject once and each verb twice. Then label each sentence *Simple* or *Compound.*

1. The ancestor of the horse probably originated in North America. S
2. One early horse was *Eohippus,* and it lived 55 million years ago. C
3. *Eohippus,* or "dawn horse," was about 15 inches tall and looked somewhat like a greyhound. S
4. Horses changed over time and gradually got bigger. S
5. The modern horse developed about 3 million years ago, but it was still small. C
6. Early in its history, the horse lived on every continent except Australia. S
7. That was fortunate, or the horse might have become extinct. C
8. We do not know why, but the horse died out in America about ten thousand years ago. C
9. Humans on other continents eventually tamed horses and trained them for riding. S
10. People began riding horses at least five thousand years ago. S

B. Recognizing Complex Sentences Write the following sentences. Underline each subject once and each verb twice. Then label each sentence *Simple, Compound,* or *Complex.*

11. The horse first developed in North America, but it became extinct here about ten thousand years ago. C
12. Then Christopher Columbus brought horses to the New World on his second voyage. S
13. The population of horses increased when Spanish conquerors brought them to Mexico in the 1500s. CX
14. In 1519, Hernán Cortés brought sixteen horses from Cuba so that he could use them in his invasion of the Aztec Empire. CX
15. Later Spanish explorers brought more horses to America, where they were useful in battle and on long expeditions. CX
16. Because Native Americans did not have horses, the Spanish had a great advantage in war. CX
17. The Spanish soldiers defeated the Native Americans and took possession of their lands. S
18. Without land, many Native Americans had no means of livelihood, and they were forced to work for the Spanish. C

Writing Theme
Wild Horses

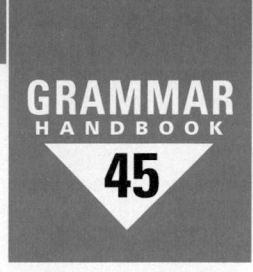

GRAMMAR
HANDBOOK
45

ADDITIONAL PRACTICE

Each of these exercises correlates to a section of Handbook 45, "Using Compound and Complex Sentences." The exercises may be used for more practice, for reteaching, or for review of the concepts presented.

Additional Resource

Grammar and Usage Practice Book, p. 89–90

Writing Theme: Wild Horses

Other related areas students might wish to explore as writing topics include the following:

- Przewalski's horse
- Arabian horses
- appaloosas
- taming wild horses

A. Recognizing Compound Sentences
Answers are shown on page.

B. Recognizing Complex Sentences
Answers are shown on page.

C. Recognizing Clauses
Answers are shown on page.

19. Although these workers cared for horses, they were not allowed to ride the horses. CX
20. However, the Native Americans watched the Spanish landowners and soldiers, and by 1600, they had learned to train and ride horses. C
21. Some of the native peoples stole horses from the Spanish and then traded the horses among their different groups. S
22. Before many years had passed, Native Americans were riding and breeding horses throughout the West. CX
23. Some horses escaped from the Spanish and the Native Americans; they thrived on the vast grasslands. C
24. Wild horses in America are most likely descendants of these Spanish horses. S
25. In fact, the word *mustang* probably comes from the Spanish word *mesteño;* it means "stray animal." C

C. Recognizing Clauses Write the subordinate clauses from the following sentences. Then label each clause *Adjective Clause, Adverb Clause,* or *Noun Clause* to show what kind of clause it is.

26. When you think of wild horses, do you think about the herds in the western states? ADV
27. Some of the most interesting wild horses that live in the United States roam the island of Assateague off the coast of Virginia. ADJ
28. Where these horses came from is a mystery. N
29. Many people think that they survived the wreck of a Spanish ship several hundred years ago. N
30. Part of the island, Chincoteague National Wildlife Refuge, is for the horses and other animals that live there. ADJ
31. Although the refuge is protected, the horses must still struggle for survival in a rugged land. ADV
32. Mighty storms from the Atlantic Ocean lash the small, flat, island, whose highest point is only forty-seven feet above sea level. ADJ
33. The grazing land is what you might expect. N
34. The poor land produces scraggly vegetation that is adapted to salty environments. ADJ
35. In spite of the extremely harsh conditions, the rugged horses survive because they have adapted so well to the environment. ADV

572 Grammar Handbook

GRAMMAR HANDBOOK 45

Writing Theme
The Moon

A. Recognizing Compound Sentences Write the subjects and verbs in these sentences. Label each sentence *Simple* or *Compound.*

1. The moon orbits the earth every 29½ days. S
2. Early people used this cycle as a type of calendar, and they based certain decisions on it. C
3. Usually, months began with the first crescent of the new moon. S
4. Over the course of many days, the visible part of the moon changed shape, but it eventually returned to its starting point. C
5. People identified and named four particular phases of the moon. S
6. The moon calendar helped people to predict the beginning of spring and fall and, therefore, good planting and harvesting times. S
7. To this day we still use the expression "harvest moon." S
8. Early people established festivals based on the moon calendar, and these became the basis for some later religious holidays. C
9. Moon calendars were useful, but they became inaccurate. C
10. On these calendars, spring would arrive earlier and earlier every year, and spring holidays might end up in midwinter. C

B. Complex Sentences Write the subordinate clause from each sentence. Underline the subject once and the verb twice.

11. Wherever people live, there are superstitions about the moon.
12. Some people watch the moon as though it affects their lives.
13. Perhaps these beliefs developed because the moon changes.
14. A crescent moon gets larger every day, as if it were growing.
15. According to folklore, living things grow as the moon grows.
16. When the moon becomes smaller, living things cease growing.
17. Therefore, if you plant a tree, plant it during the new moon.
18. Even if you do not plant trees, you should be aware of other superstitions.
19. For example, do not look at a new moon through a window, because you will have bad luck.
20. When you do that, the glass comes between you and good luck.
21. Also, never look at the moon over your left shoulder unless you are prepared for bad luck.
22. Some superstitions developed when people felt helpless about the world around them.
23. Farmers used weather signs so that they could plan their work.
24. When they saw a ring around the moon, they planned for rain.
25. Finally, do not believe any moon lore until you test it.

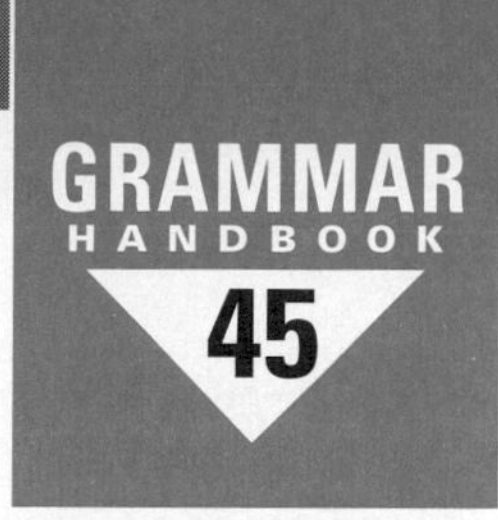

REVIEW

These exercises may be used as mixed review or as an informal evaluation of the skills presented in Handbook 45, "Using Compound and Complex Sentences."

Additional Resources

Grammar and Usage Practice Book, p. 91

Tests and Writing Assessment Prompts, Mastery Test, pp. 35–36

Elaboration, Revision, and Proofreading Practice, p. 31

Writing Theme: The Moon

Other related areas students might wish to explore as writing topics include the following:

- the Apollo space project
- stories about lunar exploration
- the Chinese or Jewish calendar
- *Old Farmer's Almanac*

A. Recognizing Compound Sentences

Answers are shown on page.

B. Complex Sentences

Subjects and verbs are underlined on page.

11. Wherever people live
12. as though it affects their lives
13. because the moon changes
14. as if it were growing
15. as the moon grows
16. When the moon becomes smaller
17. if you plant a tree
18. Even if you do not plant trees
19. because you will have bad luck
20. When you do that
21. unless you are prepared for bad luck
22. when people felt helpless about the world around them

23. so that they could plan their work
24. when they saw a ring around the moon
25. until you test it

C. Identifying Sentence Structure
Answers are shown on page.

D. Types of Subordinate Clauses
Answers are shown on page.

C. Identifying Sentence Structure Label each of the following sentences *Simple, Compound,* or *Complex.*

26. Although the moon is relatively close to the earth, we did not know much about it until very recently. CX
27. As astronomy advances, our knowledge of the moon increases. CX
28. However, scientific observations have not always been accurate, and some early scientific conclusions are amusing. C
29. Galileo was the first to look at the moon through a telescope. S
30. He called the dark areas seas since they looked like oceans. CX
31. Other scientists have also drawn incorrect conclusions. S
32. In 1822, F. P. Gruithuisen saw a city on the moon. S
33. Although people finally gave up the idea of people on the moon, W. H. Pickering saw "insects" there as recently as 1922. CX
34. A reputable U.S. astronomer, Pickering saw shadows, and they seemed to move about. C
35. Pickering's shadows were "insects," and they were migrating! C

D. Types of Subordinate Clauses Write the subordinate clause in each sentence. Then identify the clause as an *Adjective Clause,* an *Adverb Clause,* or a *Noun Clause.*

36. One of history's great hoaxes, which are practical jokes, occurred in 1835. ADJ
37. In that year, the English astronomer Sir John Herschel was in South Africa so that he could make observations of the stars. ADV
38. Richard Adam Locke, a journalist, wrote a series of fictitious stories about what Herschel supposedly discovered. N
39. The hoax was effective because accurate news traveled slowly. ADV
40. Locke's stories circulated before true sources disproved them. ADV
41. His stories told about a huge telescope that could magnify the surface of the moon to an astonishing degree. ADJ
42. According to the hoax, when Herschel focused this telescope on the moon, he saw flowering plants and living beings! ADV
43. The people, who were about four feet tall, had wings. ADJ
44. The story said that they were intelligent beings. N
45. What supposedly convinced Herschel were their buildings. N
46. They had what seemed to be temples with gold roofs. N
47. The stories, which were widely reprinted, were very convincing. A
48. The hoax ended when the newspaper confessed to the joke. ADV
49. Herschel, who heard about the hoax much later, was amused. AD
50. The publicity was not what he had expected from his trip. N

WRITING CONNECTIONS

Elaboration, Revision, and Proofreading

Revise the following analysis of a story by using the directions at the bottom of the page. Then proofread your revision, paying special attention to your use of compound and complex sentences. Also check for errors in grammar, capitalization, punctuation, and spelling.

[1]Guy de Maupassant's short story The Necklace tells of a young woman. [2]Who suffers many years for one evening of glory. [3]It is a memorable story. [4]O. Henry is often called the master of the surprise ending. [5]The story tells of a woman. [6]She borrows a necklace from a friend. [7]Unfortuately, she loses the necklace. [8]She believes the necklace is very expensive. [9]She is afraid to tell her friend about the loss. [10]Instead she buys her friend a new one. [11]She spends the next ten year's paying for it. [12]The story is written in such a way. [13]That the reader beleives the necklace is very valuable. [14]In the surprise ending, the reader learns the original necklace was fake. [15]It changes the reader's feelings about the suffering of the young woman. [16]It also changes the message of the story.

1. Delete the sentence that does not belong.
2. Rewrite sentence 3 to say that the story is memorable because it has a surprise ending.
3. Combine sentences 5 and 6, making one of them into a subordinate clause.
4. Add sentence 8 to the beginning of sentence 9 as a subordinate clause beginning with *since.*
5. Combine sentences 10 and 11 to make a compound sentence.
6. Replace the vague pronoun *it* in sentence 15 with a more precise phrase.
7. Combine sentences 15 and 16 to make a compound sentence.

Responding to Literature

Analyzing a story helps you understand the story's meaning and the techniques of the writer. (See Workshop 7.) When you revise an analysis, look to see that your reasoning is clear and that you have given enough details to support your points. Using compound and complex sentences can add clarity as well as variety to your analysis.

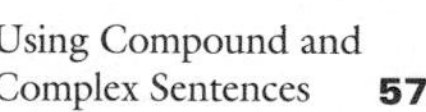

WRITING CONNECTIONS

Elaboration, Revision, and Proofreading

This activity will allow your students to see some of the concepts presented in this handbook at work in writing that responds to literature. By revising and proofreading this passage, students will see how they can use clauses to eliminate sentence fragments, to elaborate, to show relationships between ideas, and to create sentence variety.

After students complete their revisions, have them exchange papers and check each other's work. Then discuss the activity as a class.

Errors are underlined on page. Revisions may vary slightly. See typical revision below.

Guy de Maupassant's short story "The Necklace" tells of a young woman who suffers many years for one evening of glory. **It is a memorable story because of** its surprise ending. **The story tells of a woman who borrows a necklace from a friend.** Unfortunately, she loses the necklace. **Since she believes the necklace is very expensive, she is afraid to tell her friend about the loss. Instead, she buys her friend a new one, and she spends the next ten years paying for it.** The story is written in such a way that the reader believes the necklace is very valuable. In the surprise ending, the reader learns the original necklace was fake. **This unexpected twist** changes the reader's feelings about the suffering of the young woman, and it also changes the message of the story.

Objective

- To use an illustration and writing prompts as springboards to informal writing

WRITING WARM-UPS

In these motivational activities, students begin using the concepts they will explore further in Handbook 46, "Understanding Subject and Verb Agreement." Encourage them to choose whichever prompt or prompts they like best. Reassure them that these activities are ungraded; urge them to explore new ideas and try new techniques.

For the first prompt, invite students to look carefully at *Green Sliding* for a few moments. Then suggest that they close the book and freewrite everything they recall about the art. If their freewriting leads them into memories or other ideas, encourage them to follow these leads.

For the second prompt, you might let students form groups and brainstorm aloud to generate their lists of synonyms, with a volunteer acting as recorder. Have students work individually to match nouns to verbs; then have students compare the results.

For the third prompt, have students consider using their letters to start a correspondence with a real pen pal. They can write Pen Pals International, 166 East 61st Street, New York, NY 10021.

Sketch Book

WRITING WARM-UPS

- What's going on in this piece of art? Describe what you see here.

Green Sliding (1980), Kim MacConnel.

- Play a form of word association by first listing all the synonyms of *run* that you can think of. Then match each synonym with a person, a group, an animal, or a thing that fits that word. For example, batters slide—a horse gallops.
- Write a letter to a pen pal in another country, explaining some family tradition. Help your friend experience the event by describing what each person or group does and how each person acts.

ART NOTE

In *Green Sliding,* American artist Kim MacConnel (1946–) uses bold black lines to show the excitement generated as a runner slides into home plate. MacConnel works on collated paper (paper crumpled and folded back on itself) to show the action in relief, making it even more vivid. MacConnel, a leading figure in the Pattern and Decoration movement of the 1970s, has a studio in Encinitas, California, and is a professor of visual arts at the University of California, San Diego.

Understanding Subject and Verb Agreement

- Making Subjects and Verbs Agree in Number
- Compound Subjects
- Indefinite Pronouns
- Other Problems of Agreement

Beckett and Baseball (1986), Harvey Breverman.

In baseball and in life, disagreements are sometimes inevitable. In writing, however, some disagreements can be avoided—disagreements between subjects and verbs. You can reach agreement in your sentences by making sure that singular subjects are matched with singular verbs and plural subjects with plural verbs.

In this workshop you will learn ways subject-verb agreement keeps the meaning of your sentences clear.

Understanding Subject and Verb Agreement

Objectives

- To recognize subject-verb agreement in sentences
- To select verbs that agree in number with compound subjects
- To select verbs that agree in number with indefinite pronoun subjects
- To avoid other common agreement errors

Writing

- To use correct subject-verb agreement

INTRODUCING THE HANDBOOK

Read the first sentence on page 577 with students. Ask them to share examples of sports disagreements they have witnessed or experienced. Next, tell students how the art involves "disagreement." On the right is Samuel Beckett (1906–1989), a winner of the Nobel Prize for literature. He lived in France, his only sport was tennis, and he probably never stood nose-to-nose with an umpire. The art humorously shows two people and also two extremes of culture in "disagreement."

Point out that in writing, as in art, images that "disagree" can create interesting contrasts and convey complex messages. However, in writing, disagreement between subject and verb confuses readers and can make them lose interest. Explain that in this handbook, students will learn how to keep subjects and verbs in agreement and make their sentences clear.

ART NOTE

Beckett and Baseball, a color pastel, shows an imaginary standoff between the uncompromising Samuel Beckett (Nobel laureate and author of the plays *Waiting for Godot, Molloy,* and *Malone Dies,* among other works) and an anonymous, apparently equally uncompromising, baseball umpire. Harvey Breverman (1934–) is best known for his paintings and prints. He was born in Pittsburgh and lives and teaches in western New York. Breverman's works can be seen at New York's Museum of Modern Art as well as at the Whitney Museum of American Art; they have also appeared in numerous American and European exhibitions.

MAKING SUBJECTS AND VERBS AGREE IN NUMBER

Objectives

- To identify subjects and verbs that agree in number

Writing

- To revise sentences to make subject and verb in each sentence agree in number

Teaching Strategies

INDIVIDUALIZING INSTRUCTION: ESL STUDENTS Subject-verb agreement in English is difficult for many ESL students because in many languages, the verb form does *not* have to agree in number with the subject. In Korean and Japanese, the subject and verb agree in politeness or degree of honorific. In Vietnamese, there is only one verb form; it does not change. Students who have been speaking these languages will need much practice to master subject-verb agreement. Pair them with native English speakers or let them work in groups, to complete the exercises in this handbook.

HELPFUL HINT Stress that verbs in the present tense change only for the third person singular. Examples:

I *pour;* you *pour*

(he, she, it, the waiter) *pours*

For more about singular and plural verb forms, see Handbook 42, "Using Verbs," pages 483–502.

Additional Resources

Tests and Writing Assessment Prompts, Pretest, pp. 37–38

Grammar and Usage Practice Book, p. 92

Grammar Test Generator

MAKING SUBJECTS AND VERBS AGREE IN NUMBER

The subject and the verb in a sentence must agree in **number.**

When a word refers to one thing, it is **singular.** When it refers to more than one thing, it is **plural. Number** refers to whether a word is singular or plural.

A verb must agree in number with its subject. A singular subject takes a singular verb. A plural subject takes a plural verb.

To find the subject of a sentence, first find the verb. Then ask *who* or *what* performs the action of the verb. By asking this question, you will have no trouble with agreement, even when words come between the subject and its verb.

The tea burned my mouth. (*Burned* is the verb. What burned? Tea burned. *Tea* is the subject.)

Notice in the examples below that the third person singular form of the verbs *pour* and *sip* ends in *s.* Plural verbs, however, do not end in *s.*

Singular	The waiter *pours.*	One guest *sips.*
Plural	The waiters *pour.*	Two guests *sip.*

Amitie (1991), Mara Superior. Plural teapots are much more difficult to use than plural nouns and verbs.

Interrupting Words and Phrases

Watch for phrases that occur between the verb and its subject.

Tables by the door *are* empty. *Ned,* one of the hosts, *greets* us.

The subject of the verb is never found in a prepositional phrase or an appositive. In the two sentences above, the nouns *door, one,* and *hosts* cannot be subjects.

Other phrases, such as those beginning with *with, together with, including, as well as, along with,* and *in addition to,* can also separate the subject and the verb.

The *owner,* as well as the waiters, *is* friendly.

ART NOTE

American artist Mara Superior (1951–) enjoys working with watercolors and etchings as well as ceramics. Her designs reveal her fascination with classic forms and her love for primitive and folk art. She says, "I feel like a kindred spirit to the ancient Greek vase painters as I turn (and I hope elevate) daily events into archetypal messages." *Amitié* ("friendship"), sculpted in porcelain and handpainted with underglaze colors, typifies the playfulness of many of her creations.

Practice Your Skills

A. CONCEPT CHECK

Agreement in Number Write the subject of each sentence. Then choose and write the correct verb.

1. Some old customs still (lives, live) on today.
2. In Britain four o'clock in the afternoon (marks, mark) more than just the time.
3. Daily at this time, many British people (stops, stop) work.
4. This break in the day (has, have) been a tradition for many years.
5. The average worker, as well as people from other walks of life, (enjoys, enjoy) the ritual of teatime.
6. A tea in some areas of England (tends, tend) to be a meal.
7. For example, workers in the country (eats, eat) hearty food.
8. Tea with hard-boiled eggs, ham, and tomatoes (satisfies, satisfy) their appetites.
9. Well-to-do persons, as well as an occasional tourist, (goes, go) to fancy London tearooms.
10. Elegant waiters in formal attire (serves, serve) tea and goodies.
11. Exotic tea, along with finger sandwiches of cucumbers, salmon, or ham, (makes, make) up a typical feast.
12. Other food, including sweet cakes, (tempts, tempt) diners.

B. REVISION SKILL

Making Subjects and Verbs Agree Write the following sentences, correcting errors in subject-verb agreement. If a sentence has no error, write *Correct.*

13. What game does British people play with a bat?
14. Their traditional sport, cricket, share some characteristics with baseball and field hockey.
15. However, cricket's many rules, as well as unfamiliar terms and equipment, makes it difficult to understand.
16. Two goals, or wickets, marks the central playing area.
17. Eleven players are on a team.
18. A fielder on one team bowl the ball to a batsman on the other.
19. Using a long, flat bat, the batsman try to hit the ball.
20. The batsman, together with a teammate, try to score runs by dashing from wicket to wicket.
21. The fans, along with team members, cheers for a run.
22. Cricket matches sometimes are five days long.

Writing Theme
British Traditions

FOR MORE PRACTICE
See page 587.

Writing Theme: British Traditions

Suggest that students use these exercises as a springboard to writing. Other related areas that they might explore include the following:

- Boxing Day
- Scottish, Irish, or Welsh traditions
- English rugby

Answers to Practice Your Skills

A. Concept Check
Agreement in Number

Answers are shown on page.

B. Revision Skill
Making Subjects and Verbs Agree

13. What game do British people play with a bat?
14. Their traditional sport, cricket, shares some characteristics with baseball and field hockey.
15. However, cricket's many rules, as well as unfamiliar terms and equipment, make it difficult to understand.
16. Two goals, or wickets, mark the central playing area.
17. Correct
18. A fielder on one team bowls the ball to a batsman on the other.
19. Using a long, flat bat, the batsman tries to hit the ball.
20. The batsman, together with a teammate, tries to score runs by dashing from wicket to wicket.
21. The fans, along with team members, cheer for a run.
22. Correct

COMPOUND SUBJECTS

Objectives

- To recognize and choose verbs that agree with compound subjects

Writing

- To revise writing to correct errors in subject-verb agreement

Teaching Strategies

LINKING GRAMMAR AND WRITING Remind students that they can use compound subjects to add information and to avoid repetition. A compound subject can consist of nouns, pronouns, or both. To help students recognize subject-verb agreement when compound subjects include pronouns, write the following examples on the board:

Vinh, Meg, and I *are* members of the French Club.

Either she or he *is* leaving for France this summer.

Neither they nor the French teacher *has* visited the Rhone Valley before.

For more about compound subjects, see Handbook 24, "Sentence Combining," pages 304–313, and Compound Sentence Parts in Handbook 39, "The Sentence and Its Parts," pages 403–405.

Additional Resource

Grammar and Usage Practice Book, p. 93

Writing Theme: Advertisements

Suggest that students use these exercises as a springboard to writing. Other related areas that they might explore include the following:

- the process of writing and producing a commercial
- award-winning commercials
- how to get a job acting in commercials

Answers to Practice Your Skills

A. Concept Check
Compound Subjects

Answers are shown on page.

COMPOUND SUBJECTS

Compound subjects joined by *and* take a plural verb. When the parts of a subject are joined by *or* or *nor,* the verb agrees with the part of the subject nearer to it.

Compound subjects joined by *and* take a plural verb regardless of the number of each part. Consider these examples:

The actor and the director *are* on the set.
Good actors and directors *are* important in making commercials.

When the parts of a compound subject are joined by *or* or *nor,* the verb agrees with the part nearer to it. Read the following sentences:

Either the camera or the lenses *have* broken.
Neither the lenses nor the camera *has* been fixed.
Either the actors or the director *has* the final script.

Practice Your Skills

Writing Theme
Advertisements

A. CONCEPT CHECK

Compound Subjects Write the compound subject in each sentence. Then write the correct form of the verb in parentheses.

1. The cast and the crew members (arrives, arrive) at 5:00 a.m.
2. Actors and musicians (is, are) on the beach set within an hour.
3. Neither the director nor her assistants (has, have) arrived.
4. Time and patience (is, are) required for filming ads.
5. Often either the cameras or the weather (creates, create) problems.
6. Glare and blowing sand (stops, stop) the filming.
7. The actors and the crew (waits, wait) impatiently.
8. Neither the actors nor the actress (leaves, leave) the set.
9. Scenes and lines (is, are) rehearsed several times before the camera begins to roll.
10. Either the director or the sponsors (approves, approve) finished commercials.

B. PROOFREADING SKILL

Agreement with Compound Subjects Rewrite this paragraph, correcting errors in grammar, capitalization, punctuation, and spelling. Pay special attention to errors in agreement. (10 errors)

According to recent polls. Videocassette recorders (VCRs) are in more than 70 percent of all homes in the united states. Advertisors are successfully taking advantage of this market. Auto makers, stores, and even a cosmetic company has ads on videocassettes. Neither the advertisers nor the viewers thinks this kind of advertising will fail, consumers at home see them with no interferance from other commercials. Depending on your point of view, either the consumer or the advertiser benefits more from advertising on videocassettes. The possibilitys and future of this new type of advertising is unlimited. Progress marches on!

MIXED REVIEW • PAGES 578–581

Write the correct form of each verb in parentheses.

1. A rider (ropes, rope) the largest steer in the herd.
2. Other cowhands, near the fire, (grabs, grab) a branding iron.
3. Neither the steer nor the cowhands (is, are) in the Old West.
4. This scene, along with similar ones, (occurs, occur) in Hawaii.
5. These cowhands (is, are) called *paniolos.*
6. People from Mexico (was, were) among the first to work on Hawaiian cattle ranches.
7. Either the skills or the excitement (was, were) appealing to Hawaiians, who quickly learned from the Mexicans.
8. Today many *paniolos* (works, work) on the Parker Ranch.
9. A straw hat, together with chaps and spurs, (serves, serve) as the *paniolos'* work clothes.
10. Parker Ranch, along with more than two hundred other ranches, (is, are) part of the Hawaiian cattle industry.
11. On the smaller Hawaiian islands, neither the cattle nor the industry (has, have) survived.
12. Herds on Molokai (was, were) wiped out by tuberculosis.
13. However, the *paniolos* on Hawaii still (rides, ride).
14. February and March (marks, mark) the time for rodeos.
15. Races and rodeo events (tests, test) the *paniolos'* skills.

FOR MORE PRACTICE

See pages 587–588.

Writing Theme
Modern Cowhands

B. Proofreading Skill
Agreement with Compound Subjects

Errors in proofreading exercises are counted as follows: (a) Each word is counted as one error. For example, a misspelled word is one error; two initials and a last name not capitalized are counted as three errors. (b) Run-on sentences and sentence fragments are each counted as one error, even though the correction involves both punctuation and capitalization corrections.

Errors are shown on page.

According to recent polls, videocassette recorders (VCRs) are in more than 70 percent of all homes in the United States. Advertisers are successfully taking advantage of this market. Auto makers, stores, and even a cosmetics company have ads on videocassettes. Neither the advertisers nor the viewers think this kind of advertising will fail. Consumers at home see them with no interference from other commercials. Depending on your point of view, either the consumer or the advertiser benefits more from advertising on videocassettes. The possibilities and future of this new type of advertising are unlimited. Progress marches on!

Writing Theme: Modern Cowhands

Other related areas students might wish to explore as writing topics include the following:

- Argentine gauchos
- rodeos and rodeo riders
- country music
- ranching in the Southwest

MIXED REVIEW • PAGES 578–581

You may wish to use this activity to check students' mastery of the following concepts:

- making subjects and verbs agree in number
- compound subjects

Answers are shown on page.

Understanding Subject and Verb Agreement 581

INDEFINITE PRONOUNS

Objectives

- To recognize subject-verb agreement in sentences with indefinite pronoun subjects

Writing

- To use verbs that agree in number with indefinite pronoun subjects

Teaching Strategies

STUMBLING BLOCK Point out that agreement with the pronouns *some, all, any, none,* and *most* can be tricky when the word referred to is not part of the sentence. Example:

Did Doug drop the eggs? *None* are broken.

Advise students to check the antecedent of the indefinite pronoun to choose the correct form of the verb.

COOPERATIVE LEARNING Before students go on to Practice Your Skills, have them quiz each other—in pairs or small groups—by creating sample sentences for each pronoun on the chart and challenging the other(s) to verify or correct the number of the verb.

Additional Resource

Grammar and Usage Practice Book, p. 94

Writing Theme: Nicknames

Other related areas students might wish to explore as writing topics include the following:

- nicknames of famous athletes
- the story behind a nickname
- feelings about personal nicknames
- meanings of first or last names

Answers to Practice Your Skills

A. Concept Check

Indefinite Pronouns

Answers are shown on page.

INDEFINITE PRONOUNS

Some **indefinite pronouns** are singular and some are plural. A few can be either singular or plural.

Study the chart of indefinite pronouns below. Then study the examples that follow. Notice that interrupting words do not change the agreement of subject and verb in number.

Indefinite Pronouns

Singular			Plural
another	either	nobody	both
anybody	everybody	no one	few
anyone	everyone	one	many
anything	everything	somebody	several
each	neither	someone	

Singular	Plural
Everybody *has* a name.	Many *have* nicknames.
Neither of us *is* satisfied.	Both of our names *are* silly.

The words *some, all, any, none,* and *most* may be either singular or plural. They are singular when they refer to a singular word and plural when they refer to a plural word or words.

Singular	Plural
All of the *book* is factual.	All of the *facts* are new.
Most of the *chapter* is done.	Most of the *names* are real.

Writing Theme
Nicknames

Practice Your Skills

A. CONCEPT CHECK

Indefinite Pronouns Write the correct form of each verb in parentheses.

1. Anything that has a nickname (has, have) a given name.
2. Some of the cities in the United States (is, are) nicknamed.
3. Most of the nicknames (has, have) a long history.

582 Grammar Handbook

4. Today, however, nobody (knows, know) for sure how the cities got their names.
5. Several even (shares, share) a nickname.
6. Few of us (recognizes, recognize) Waco as the Athens of Texas.
7. However, everyone in Massachusetts probably (knows, know) Boston as the Athens of America.
8. Some of its citizens (connects, connect) this nickname with Boston's history of culture, education, and literature.
9. Another of Boston's nicknames (is, are) the Cradle of Liberty.
10. Either of these nicknames (applies, apply) to Boston today.
11. (Does, Do) many of Utah's residents know that Springfield, Utah, is the Cradle of Industry?
12. Today nobody (calls, call) Cincinnati the Paris of America.
13. Neither of Chicago's old nicknames (has, have) endured.
14. Both of these names, Phoenix City and New York of the West, (is, are) forgotten.
15. Each of the nicknames (lives, live) only as long as the people who use it.

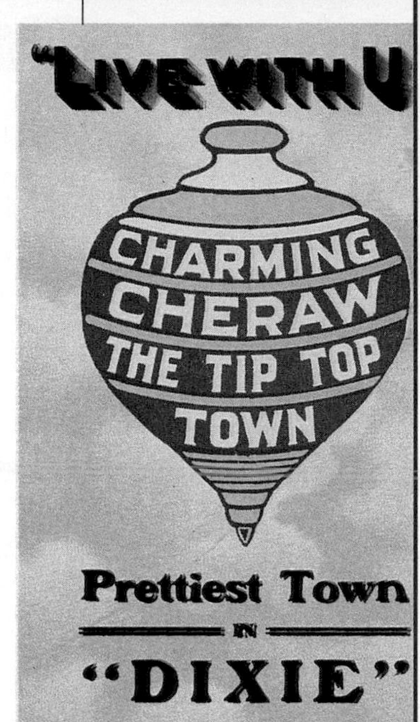

"LIVE WITH U
CHARMING
CHERAW
THE TIP TOP
TOWN
Prettiest Town
IN
"DIXIE"

B. DRAFTING SKILL

Using Indefinite Pronouns Write these sentences, using the correct present-tense form of each verb in parentheses.

16. All of the computer industry (be) expanding.
17. Undoubtedly, everybody (have) heard of Silicon Valley.
18. However, (do) anybody know about Silicon Prairie?
19. Probably no one (know) about Silicon Glen either.
20. Each of these places (be) known for its computer industry.
21. Many of the computer businesses in Texas (be) in an area near Dallas, nicknamed Silicon Prairie.
22. Some of the companies located between Glasgow and Edinburgh in Scotland (produce) silicon chips that are used in computers.
23. All of the area between these cities (be) called Silicon Glen.
24. Each of these places (remind) us that silicon is the second most abundant element in the earth's crust.
25. (Have) anyone thought to call Earth the Silicon Planet?

FOR MORE PRACTICE
See page 588.

B. Drafting Skill
Using Indefinite Pronouns

16. All of the computer industry is expanding.
17. Undoubtedly, everybody has heard of Silicon Valley.
18. However, does anyone know about Silicon Prairie?
19. Probably no one knows about Silicon Glen either.
20. Each of these places is known for its computer industry.
21. Many of the computer businesses in Texas are in an area near Dallas, nicknamed Silicon Prairie.
22. Some of the companies located between Glasgow and Edinburgh in Scotland produce silicon chips that are used in computers.
23. All of the area between these cities is called Silicon Glen.
24. Each of these places reminds us that silicon is the second most abundant element in the earth's crust.
25. Has anyone thought to call Earth the Silicon Planet?

OTHER PROBLEMS OF AGREEMENT

Objectives
- To recognize common subject-verb agreement problems

Writing
- To revise sentences to eliminate common problems in subject-verb agreement

Teaching Strategies

LINKING GRAMMAR AND WRITING Remind students that inverting the order of subject and verb can add emphasis to a sentence or help achieve sentence variety. Urge them to check for subject-verb agreement when they use inverted constructions. For more about subjects and verbs in inverted order, see Sentences Beginning with *Here* and *There* and Other Sentences with Unusual Word Order, pages 391–394 of Handbook 39, "The Sentence and Its Parts."

CRITICAL THINKING: ANALYZING The forms *do, does, don't,* and *doesn't* are italicized on the pupil page for emphasis. Ask students if these are the complete verbs in the model sentences (no); then have them identify the complete verb phrases. (In order, they are as follows: *does[n't] use, does[n't] appeal, does use, does like, does[n't] wear, do like, do[n't] wear, do think, do[n't] need,* and *do come.*)

Additional Resource

Grammar and Usage Practice Book, p. 95

OTHER PROBLEMS OF AGREEMENT

In sentences beginning with *here, there,* and *where,* the subject often comes after the verb. The order of words in inverted sentences does not affect the agreement of subject and verb.

With the pronouns *he, she,* and *it,* the verb *does* is used. With all other personal pronouns, *do* is used.

Agreement in Inverted Sentences

A sentence is **inverted** when the subject comes after the verb. Questions are usually in inverted order. Sometimes writers achieve a special tone by inverting the order of a sentence.

Across the room drifts the scent of roses.
Are roses really used to make perfume?

Here, There, Where In sentences beginning with *here, there,* and *where,* the subject often comes after the verb. First find the subject to be sure the verb agrees with it in number.

Here is the laboratory.
There is the secret formula.
Where are the ingredients?

Agreement with Forms of *Do*

Does and *doesn't* are used with singular nouns and the singular pronouns *he, she,* and *it. Do* and *don't* are used with plural nouns and with the personal pronouns *I, you, we,* and *they.*

Sam *doesn't* use cologne.
It *doesn't* appeal to him.
He *does* use after shave.
Erin *does* like the smell of musk.
She *doesn't* wear perfume herself.

I *do* like to wear perfume.
I *don't* wear it everyday, though.
We *do* think you'll like this scent.
You *don't* need more than a drop.
Many perfumes *do* come from France.

584 Grammar Handbook

Literature Connection

Show these sentences from parts of *The Black Cauldron* by Lloyd Alexander. Ask students to identify subjects and verbs in inverted order.

"In the northernmost realms of Prydain many trees were already leafless, and among the branches clung the ragged shapes of empty nests. . . ."

"Shortly before dusk, the trail led downward toward a shallow basin set with scrub and pines. There, Gwydion halted. Ahead rose the baleful crags of Dark Gate. . . ."

"From a distance came a long, wavering cry. Another voice answered it, then another. . . ."

Practice Your Skills

A. CONCEPT CHECK

Problems of Agreement Write the correct form of each verb.

1. Most of us probably (doesn't, don't) know what making perfume was like in ancient Rome.
2. Here (is, are) one perfume maker's description of a typical day.
3. Into the shop (comes, come) my first customer, a soldier.
4. Like all soldiers, he (does, do) need to anoint himself with perfume.
5. However, he (doesn't, don't) know much about scents.
6. He asks, "Where (is, are) the oils of tangerine and lemon made?"
7. "From my Greek friends (comes, come) those fine oils," I reply.
8. "What ingredients (does, do) the other scents contain?"
9. "Into one concoction (goes, go) jasmine and hyacinth oils."
10. "For your feet, here (is, are) a lotion called *aegyptium."*
11. "(Does, Do) you have any ginger?" he inquires.
12. "None of the scents (smells, smell) more exquisite," he adds.
13. "Here (is, are) the best place to find ginger," I boast.
14. "Out of my own experimenting (comes, come) a new formula."
15. "Only for special clients (is, are) this scent reserved."

B. DRAFTING SKILL

Making Subjects and Verbs Agree Complete each sentence, using a present-tense verb.

16. _______ you wear perfume or some other kind of scent?
17. There _______ great secrecy in the perfume business.
18. Where _______ the perfume makers create new scents?
19. In guarded laboratories _______ the scientists.
20. Here _______ equipment for distilling essential oils.
21. There _______ one of the scientists.
22. She _______ the extraction procedure.
23. In one perfume there _______ often one hundred ingredients.
24. From all over the world _______ exotic herbs and roots.
25. _______ one of the main ingredients flower petals?
26. Here _______ alcohols for extracting the scents.
27. What substances _______ the fragrance last?
28. One substance, ambergris, _______ as a preservative.
29. From the sperm whale _______ ambergris.
30. There _______ laws against using it, though, because the sperm whale is an endangered species.

Writing Theme
Perfume

The cartoon character Pepe Le Pew, star of the 1949 animated film *For Scent-imental Reasons.* ©1949 Warner Bros.

Writing Theme: Perfume

Other related areas students might wish to explore as writing topics include the following:

- perfume advertising
- animal testing of cosmetics
- perfume allergies

Answers to Practice Your Skills

A. Concept Check
Problems of Agreement

Answers are shown on page.

B. Drafting Skill
Making Subjects and Verbs Agree

Answers will vary. Typical answers are given below.

16. Do you wear perfume or some other kind of scent?
17. There exists great secrecy in the perfume business.
18. Where do the perfume makers create new scents?
19. In guarded laboratories work the scientists.
20. Here sits equipment for distilling essential oils.
21. There is one of the scientists.
22. She does the extraction procedure.
23. In one perfume there are often one hundred ingredients.
24. From all over the world come exotic herbs and roots.
25. Is one of the main ingredients flower petals?
26. Here are alcohols for extracting the scents.
27. What substances make the fragrance last?
28. One substance, ambergris, acts as a preservative.
29. From the sperm whale comes ambergris.
30. There are laws against using it, though, because the sperm whale is an endangered species.

C. Proofreading Skill
Agreement Errors

Errors are shown on page.

You have probably heard of Cleopatra. There have been many stories written about her beauty. Around the Johnson farmyards, though, romps another Cleopatra. Here are the facts about this unusual creature. Ms. Johnson named her favorite dog after the Egyptian ruler. Where's the connection? Well, the Egyptian Cleopatra was fond of fragrance. Oils of roses, crocuses, and violets were always on her hands. Another lotion, with almonds, cinnamon, and honey, was used for her feet. The Johnsons' Cleopatra is also fond of fragrance. On her head are the scents of stinkweeds and mud. There are also skunks around the farm. Cleo doesn't ever leave them alone. So throughout the rooms wafts the horrible scent of skunk! Cleo needs to take a lesson in "scent-sibility" from her Egyptian namesake.

CHECK POINT

Writing Theme: Dinosaur Mania

Other related areas students might wish to explore as writing topics include the following:

- the Loch Ness monster—last of the dinosaurs?
- recent theories about the disappearance of dinosaurs

MIXED REVIEW • PAGES 582–586

You may wish to use this activity to check students' mastery of the following concepts:

- indefinite pronouns
- other problems of agreement

Answers are shown on page.

C. PROOFREADING SKILL

Agreement Errors Write the following paragraph, correcting errors in grammar, capitalization, punctuation, and spelling. Pay special attention to errors in agreement. (10 errors)

You have probaly heard of Cleopatra. There has been many stories written about her beauty. Around the Johnson farmyards, though, romp another Cleopatra. Here's the facts about this unusual creature Ms. Johnson named her favorite dog after the Egyptian ruler. Where's the connection? Well, the Egyptian Cleopatra was fond of fragrence. Oils of roses, crocuses, and violets were always on her hands. Another lotion, with almonds, cinnimin, and honey, was used for her feet. The Johnsons' Cleopatra is also fond of fragrance. On her head are the scents of stinkweeds and mud. There's also skunks around the farm. Cleo don't ever leave them alone. So throughout the rooms waft the horrible scent of skunk! Cleo needs to take a lesson in "scent-sibility" from her Egyptian namesake.

FOR MORE PRACTICE
See page 588.

MIXED REVIEW • PAGES 582–586

Writing Theme
Dinosaur Mania

Write the correct form of each verb in parentheses.

1. (Is, Are) dinosaurs really extinct?
2. I, for one, (doesn't, don't) think so.
3. In the human imagination still (roams, roam) the "terrible lizards."
4. There (has, have) actually been an outbreak of dinosaur mania!
5. Here (is, are) some of the evidence.
6. Everybody (has, have) probably seen a television show or a movie about dinosaurs.
7. Well, there also (exists, exist) more than two hundred books about them in print today.
8. One of the books (is, are) *Jurassic Park* by Michael Crichton.
9. (Doesn't, Don't) it keep you on the edge of your seat?
10. "Dinomania," however, (does, do) not stop there.
11. (Has, Have) any of you eaten dinosaur macaroni?
12. In the stores (is, are) T-shirts, stickers, and all kinds of other dinosaur merchandise.
13. Where (has, have) all of the dinosaur action figures gone?
14. Because of their popularity, few (remains, remain) in stores long.
15. No one (doubts, doubt) the never-ending popularity of dinosaurs.

A. Making Verbs Agree with Their Subjects Write the correct form of each verb in parentheses.

1. This letter, along with others like it, (pleads, plead) for change.
2. An injustice to my friends the Guillotins (continues, continue).
3. Citizens of the land (uses, use) their name unjustly.
4. A new machine for beheading convicts (has, have) been created.
5. The inventor of this device (is, are) Dr. Antoine Louis.
6. The name Louisette (suits, suit) the device well.
7. However, people in France (calls, call) it the guillotine.
8. The crowds in the plaza (chants, chant) that name.
9. Dr. Guillotin, as well as his colleagues, (is, are) upset.
10. Members of Guillotin's family (feels, feel) outrage.
11. A belief in humane executions (was, were) Dr. Guillotin's reason for supporting the use of the device.
12. Speed, along with mercy, (is, are) its main feature.
13. Dr. Guillotin, with his family, (argues, argue) that the name *guillotine* is inappropriate.
14. However, calls for *la guillotine* still (rings, ring) out.
15. Supporters, including me, (wants, want) to protest this undeserved fame.

B. Using Verbs with Compound Subjects Write the correct form of each verb in parentheses.

16. The lives and experiences of famous people (sounds, sound) glamorous and satisfying.
17. Yet neither fame nor status (creates, create) happiness.
18. Therefore, many entertainers and other celebrities (chooses, choose) to share their success with others.
19. Either their talents or their money (is, are) donated to worthy causes.
20. Neither politicians nor businesspeople (has, have) more opportunities than entertainers to help the needy.
21. For example, the actor Paul Newman's food-product sales and humanitarian work (has, have) benefited many charities.
22. Newman's salad dressing and popcorn (is, are) gourmet treats that also provide food, housing, and medical care for needy people.
23. The actress Liv Ullmann (has, have) worked hard for the United Nations Children's Fund.
24. Both the rock group U2 and the singer Willie Nelson (is, are) still famous for their participation in the Farm Aid concerts.

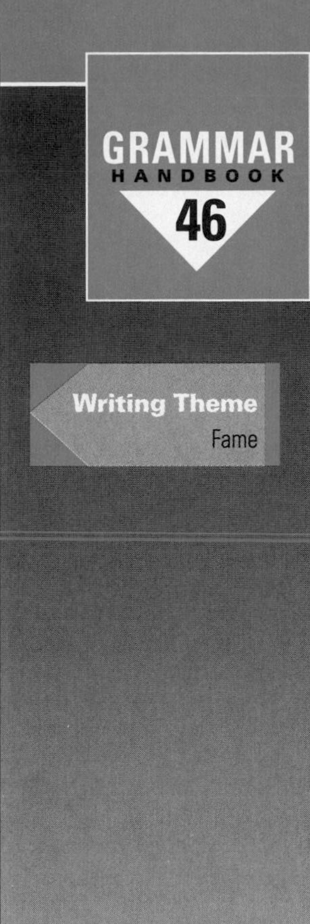

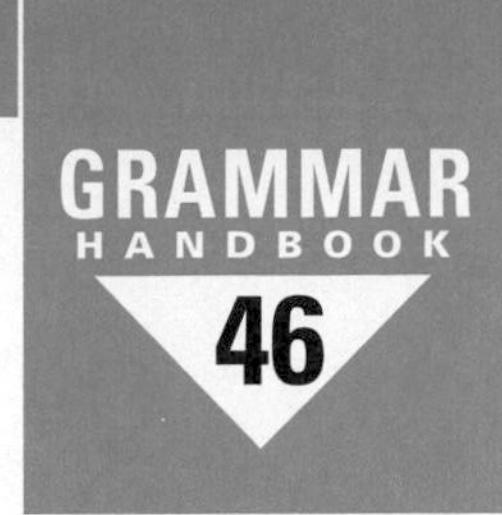

ADDITIONAL PRACTICE

Each of these exercises correlates to a section of Handbook 46, "Understanding Subject and Verb Agreement." The exercises may be used for more practice, for reteaching, or for review of the concepts presented.

Additional Resource

Grammar and Usage Practice Book, p. 97

Writing Theme: Fame

Other related areas students might wish to explore as writing topics include the following:

- awards that recognize—or create—fame
- science terms from names of famous scientists, such as *pasteurize* and *volt*
- famous sports or entertainment figures
- the disadvantages of fame

A. Making Verbs Agree with Their Subjects
Answers are shown on page.

B. Using Verbs with Compound Subjects
Answers are shown on page.

C. Using Verbs with Indefinite Pronouns
Answers are shown on page.

D. Avoiding Problems of Agreement

41. Here is a story from the memoirs of conductor André Previn.
42. He does remember it with a smile.
43. On a certain day there is an important meeting of film people.
44. Down the hall comes the dog Lassie, along with her trainer.
45. So where are the funny parts?
46. On command, Lassie does her trick of shaking hands with Fred Astaire, Cyd Charisse, and all the other celebrities.
47. However, she does not shake hands with André Previn.
48. There stands the famous conductor, snubbed by a dog!
49. Here is proof that fame does not ensure good manners.
50. Somewhere in the back of Previn's mind gnaws this memory.

25. Apartheid and other injustices in South Africa (was, were) fought with money earned by Paul Simon's *Graceland* album.
26. Neither the success of this album nor his fame (has, have) been as important to Simon as achieving this humanitarian goal.
27. The comedians Robin Williams and Whoopi Goldberg (was, were) important participants in the telethon "Comic Relief."
28. Health care and other services (has, have) been made available to thousands of homeless people thanks to their efforts.
29. Our enjoyment and appreciation of these performers (grows, grow) because of their generosity.
30. For these celebrities, sharing and caring (goes, go) hand in hand.

C. Using Verbs with Indefinite Pronouns Write the sentences, using the correct form of each verb in parentheses.

31. One of the benefits of fame (is, are) money from endorsements.
32. Some of the stars (collects, collect) millions of dollars.
33. All of the ads (sounds, sound) sincere.
34. Each (attempts, attempt) to influence people to buy a product.
35. Most of this advertising (has, have) been aimed at teenagers.
36. (Does, Do) anyone really pay attention to these ads?
37. Someone (is, are) taking celebrity endorsements seriously.
38. Most television viewers (remembers, remember) seeing them.
39. Many (claims, claim) to enjoy watching the stars.
40. Few, however, (admits, admit) that the celebrities influence their purchases.

D. Avoiding Problems of Agreement Write the sentences, using the correct present-tense forms of the verbs in parentheses.

41. Here (be) a story from the memoirs of conductor André Previn.
42. He (do) remember it with a smile.
43. On a certain day there (be) an important meeting of film people.
44. Down the hall (come) the dog Lassie, along with her trainer.
45. So where (be) the funny parts?
46. On command, Lassie (do) her trick of shaking hands with Fred Astaire, Cyd Charisse, and all the other celebrities.
47. However, she (do) not shake hands with André Previn.
48. There (stand) the famous conductor, snubbed by a dog!
49. Here (be) proof that fame (do) not ensure good manners.
50. Somewhere in the back of Previn's mind (gnaw) this memory.

588 Grammar Handbook

REVIEW

A. Agreement in Number Write the form of the verb in parentheses that agrees with the subject in number.

1. Two reporters in China (has, have) written a book.
2. The book, *Chinese Lives,* (contains, contain) interviews.
3. Both authors, as well as many people they interviewed, (was, were) born in Beijing, the capital of China.
4. In one interview, a boy thirteen years of age (tells, tell) how he left home to earn a living.
5. The young boy, together with others, (works, work) as a popcorn vendor in Beijing.
6. The popcorn machines, because of their noise, (is, are) called land mines.
7. The noisy popping, as well as the boy's loud cries, (draws, draw) crowds.
8. Customers on the street (brings, bring) their own popcorn kernals to the boy.
9. The young boy with the land mine (pops, pop) them.
10. Another vendor on the street (sells, sell) tea broth.
11. His recipe, including tea and sorghum flour, (is, are) ancient.
12. A young man, but not his companions, (tries, try) the broth.
13. Most young people, unlike the older generation, (prefers, prefer) more modern beverages.
14. However, the street vendor's wares (appeals, appeal) to foreign visitors.
15. Many photographers from abroad (has, have) taken his picture.
16. These photos, as well as the vendor's memories, (fills, fill) him with great pride.
17. In another interview, a young girl, among her other remarks, (talks, talk) about going to college.
18. Only one student in twenty (passes, pass) the examination.
19. The parents of the girl (is, are) worried about her chances.
20. Her dream, more than anything else, (is, are) to write.
21. The authors of the book (gives, give) readers a look at the Chinese people in the mid-1980s.
22. The interviews in the book (precedes, precede) the events of 1989 in Tiananmen Square.
23. The leaders of China still (prohibits, prohibit) democracy.
24. The people, however, (has, have) endured hard times before.
25. This collection of interviews (lets, let) readers appreciate their difficulties and triumphs.

GRAMMAR HANDBOOK 46

Writing Theme
Asian Cultures

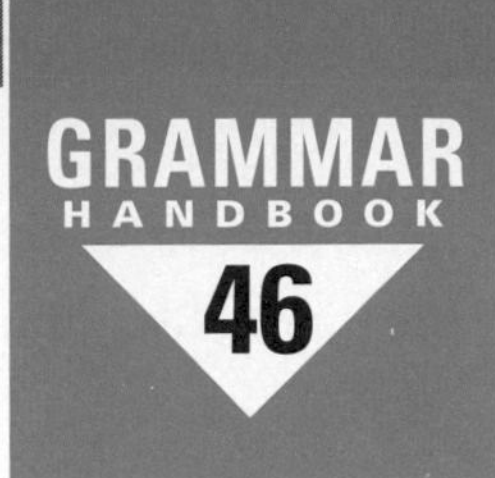

REVIEW

These exercises may be used as a mixed review or as an informal evaluation of the skills presented in Handbook 46, "Understanding Subject and Verb Agreement."

Additional Resources

Grammar and Usage Practice Book, p. 98

Tests and Writing Assessment Prompts, Mastery Test, pp. 39–40

Elaboration, Revision, and Proofreading Practice, p. 32

Writing Theme: Asian Cultures

Other related areas students might wish to explore as writing topics include the following:

- Japanese haiku
- the Hmong of Southeast Asia
- studying a martial art
- Genghis Khan
- a Vietnamese holiday

A. Agreement in Number
Answers are shown on page.

B. Agreement with Compound Subjects

26. Social customs and behavior are different in every culture.
27. Of course, change and progress affect all cultures.
28. In Korea, for example, neither "Good morning" nor "Good evening" is a common greeting.
29. Correct
30. Joy, anger, and sadness are never expressed openly.
31. Either a gentle smile or a touch expresses emotion.
32. Correct
33. Their behavior and speech are well-mannered.
34. Winks between friends or a walk with a boyfriend or girlfriend has been frowned on in the past.
35. In the past neither chairs nor a bed was found in a Korean home.
36. Correct
37. In Korea, customs and rules about naming a child are also changing.
38. A childhood name and a lifelong name are given to each boy.
39. In the past, a girl or a woman was able to live her life without a name.
40. Correct

C. Agreement with Indefinite Pronouns

Answers are shown on page.

B. Agreement with Compound Subjects Write the sentences, correcting any errors of agreement. If a sentence has no error, write *Correct.*

26. Social customs and behavior is different in every culture.
27. Of course, change and progress affects all cultures.
28. In Korea, for example, neither "Good morning" nor "Good evening" are a common greeting.
29. Instead, friends and acquaintances ask about each other's health.
30. Joy, anger, and sadness is never expressed openly.
31. Either a gentle smile or a touch express emotion.
32. Young men and women still respect their elders.
33. Their behavior and speech is well-mannered.
34. Winks between friends or a walk with a boyfriend or girlfriend have been frowned on in the past.
35. In the past neither chairs nor a bed were found in a Korean home.
36. In recent years some homes have added them.
37. In Korea, customs and rules about naming a child is also changing.
38. A childhood name and a lifelong name is given to each boy.
39. In the past, a girl or a woman were able to live her life without a name.
40. In modern Korea neither women nor men support this old custom, however.

C. Agreement with Indefinite Pronouns Write the form of the verb in parentheses that agrees with the subject in number.

41. One of the most interesting Asian countries (is, are) Thailand.
42. Many of us (doesn't, don't) know that its name means "land of the free."
43. Most of the Thai people (makes, make) their living by farming.
44. In riverside villages almost everybody (lives, live) in houses built on stilts.
45. Many of the city workers (has, have) jobs in factories.
46. One of the scenic features of the capital city, Bangkok, (is, are) its canals.
47. Everything the people need (floats, float) down the river in colorful market boats.
48. Few of the favorite Thai pastimes (exists, exist) anywhere else in the world.
49. For example, (has, have) anyone ever heard of *takraw?*

590 Grammar Handbook

50. Everyone in Thailand (knows, know) about this popular sport.
51. Each of the players (tries, try) to keep a ball in the air.
52. No one (touches, touch) the ball with his hands.
53. All of the parts of a person's body (is, are) used in Thai-style boxing, however.
54. Many people in Thailand also (plays, play) *mak ruk,* a game that is similar to chess.
55. One of the more popular activities (features, feature) ferocious fighting fish.
56. Few of the world's spectacles (dazzles, dazzle) viewers more than Thai classical dancing.
57. All of the movements, expressions, and costumes (tells, tell) a traditional story.
58. Each of the Thai meals (includes, include) rice or vegetables.
59. Several of the hot and cold salads (is, are) popular.
60. Many of the things in this country (offers, offer) visitors a special experience.

D. Other Problems of Agreement Write the following sentences, correcting errors of agreement. If a sentence has no errors, write *Correct.*

61. There is quite a few islands in Japan.
62. South of the main island of Honshu are the island of Kyushu.
63. On this island there exist a respect for the old ways.
64. Here is an example of an old tradition.
65. People still goes to the public baths, called *onsen.*
66. Into the mineral water steps the bathers to relax.
67. At the beach of Ibusuki is found the thermal sands.
68. Here is one tourist who bathed in the hot sand.
69. She don't recommend it for everybody.
70. Don't they bury you in the black lava sand?
71. Above the sand appear only your face.
72. It don't matter if you have never tried it.
73. There is friendly people to help you.
74. Here on Kyushu is the city of Nagasaki.
75. Reminders of World War II still does exist.
76. From the top of Mount Inasa is seen the city's lights.
77. The city does look beautiful since its rebuilding.
78. Despite progress and modern developments, there are some of the old way of life still in evidence on Kyushu.

D. Other Problems of Agreement

61. There are quite a few islands in Japan.
62. South of the main island of Honshu is the island of Kyushu.
63. On this island there exists a respect for the old ways.
64. Correct
65. People still go to the public baths, called *onsen.*
66. Into the mineral water step the bathers to relax.
67. At the beach of Ibusuki are found the thermal sands.
68. Correct
69. She doesn't recommend it for everybody.
70. Correct
71. Above the sand appears only your face.
72. It doesn't matter if you have never tried it.
73. There are friendly people to help you.
74. Correct
75. Reminders of World War II still do exist.
76. From the top of Mount Inasa are seen the city's lights.
77. Correct
78. Despite progress and modern developments, there is some of the old way of life still in evidence on Kyushu.

Understanding Subject and Verb Agreement 591

WRITING CONNECTIONS

Elaboration, Revision, and Proofreading

This activity will allow your students to see concepts presented in this handbook at work in a piece of persuasive writing. By revising and proofreading this passage, students can identify and correct errors in subject-verb agreement and gain practice in providing supporting evidence and in organizing paragraphs.

You may wish to discuss the first direction with students before allowing them to work through the remaining directions independently. After students have finished, discuss the revisions and corrections with the class.

Errors are underlined on page. Revisions may vary. See a typical revision below. Elements involving change are shown in boldface.

Many people think Americans watch too much television. They point to studies showing that Americans spend more time watching television than doing anything else except sleeping and working. Others claim that television takes time from other worthwhile activities, **such as reading, conversation, cultural events, and exercise.**

However, there are benefits to television as well. One of the benefits is its ability to give people new experiences. Important governmental activities **and political events** are shown on television. News about real-life tragedies is also presented. Television exposes people to a wide range of cultural events, **such as operas, plays, concerts, and classic films. Even popular entertainment programs can be worthwhile.** A soap opera or a situation comedy gives people a chance to escape for a while from the problems and pressures of the world.

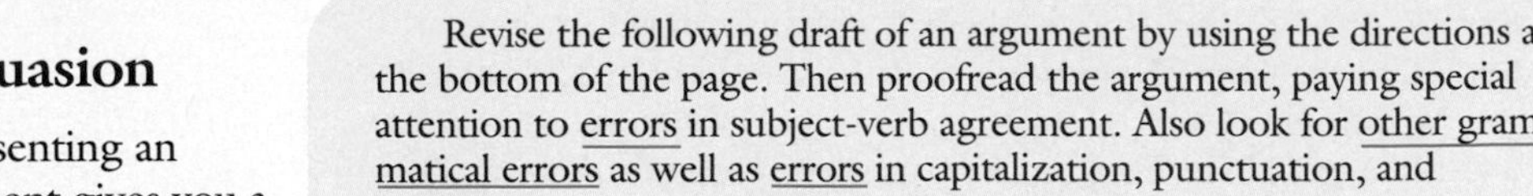

WRITING CONNECTIONS

Elaboration, Revision, and Proofreading

Persuasion

Presenting an argument gives you a chance to persuade others to agree with you. (See Workshop 6.) When you revise persuasive writing, make sure you support your opinions with specific details and respond to opposing viewpoints. Correct errors in subject-verb agreement that might detract from your message.

Revise the following draft of an argument by using the directions at the bottom of the page. Then proofread the argument, paying special attention to errors in subject-verb agreement. Also look for other grammatical errors as well as errors in capitalization, punctuation, and spelling.

[1]Many people thinks Americans watch to much television. [2]They points to studies showing that Americans spend more time watching television than doing anything else. [3]Except sleeping and working. [4]Others claims that television takes time from other worthwhile activities. [5]However, there is benifits to television as well. [6]One of the benefits are its ability to give people new experiences. [7]Important govermental activities are showed on television. [8]Important political events are showed on television. [9]News about real-life tragedies are also presented. [10]Television exposes people to a wide range of cultural events. [11]A Soap Opera or a Situation Comedy give people a chance to escape for a while from the problems and pressures of the world.

1. In sentence 4, explain "other worthwhile activities" by adding the phrase "such as reading, conversation, cultural events, and exercise."
2. Combine sentences 7 and 8 to make a sentence with a compound subject.
3. Add to sentence 10 some examples of cultural events presented on television.
4. Add this information after sentence 10: "Even popular entertainment programs can be worthwhile."
5. Divide the passage into two paragraphs.

Mother Tongue

Oh, to be in England
  If only 'arf a mo',
Where, when they speak of wireless,
  They mean a radio,

Where private schools are public
  And public schools are snobby
And insurance is assurance
  And a cop is called a bobby,

Where a traffic hub's a circus
  And up is down the street
And a sweater is a jumper
  And candy is a sweet,

Where a cracker is a biscuit
  And a trifle is dessert
And bloody is a cuss word
  And an ad is an advert,

Where gasoline is petrol
  And a stone is fourteen pound
And motorcars have bonnets
  And you take the Underground,

Where, holding up your trousers,
  It's braces that you use
And a truck is called a lorry
  And boots are really shoes,

Where a druggist is a chemist
  And the movies are the flicks
And you queue up on the pavement
  For a stall at three and six. . . .

There is no language barrier
  The tourist needs to dread
As long as he knows English
  From A to Z (no, zed).

Richard Armour

When discussing this feature, you might ask students to brainstorm other aspects of English (both American and British) that they find surprising, confusing, or illogical. For example, why do we pronounce *cough* as "coff," *rough* as "ruff," *though* as "tho," and *through* as "threw"? Why is a *driveway* for parking, and a *parkway* for driving? How do people manage to *sit down* and *sit up* at the same time? Help students realize that language is full of quirks and contradictions that, though they can be confusing, are also a source of richness and interest.

Objective

- To use a brochure and writing prompts as springboards to informal writing

WRITING WARM-UPS

Have students focus on at least one of the prompts and write an informal response. Remind them that the purpose of their writing is to get them to think imaginatively about the concepts in this handbook; assure them that their responses will not be graded.

Invite students selecting the first prompt to discuss the video-game camp brochure. Have students brainstorm ideas and humorous names for other unusual kinds of camps.

Sketch Book

WRITING WARM-UPS

THE COUCH POTATO VIDEO GAME CAMP
Learn to play video games better than ever before. At the Couch Potato Video Game Camp, you are guaranteed
• to improve your hand-eye coordination
• to increase finger speed and endurance
You will learn strategies for
• outwitting sorcerers, wizards, and demons
• conquering alien invaders
We provide classes in
• understanding video game fundamentals
• mastering advanced skills
SIGN UP TODAY!

- What kind of camp would you like to run? Make up a brochure, telling what activities your camp would have.
- What are your hobbies? Describe one of your hobbies, telling what it is and why you like it.
- What are your goals for the next year? Make a list of things you would like to accomplish.

Using Verbals

- Infinitives
- Participles
- Gerunds

Is *playing* video games your favorite activity? Perhaps you prefer *collecting* stamps? Perhaps *swimming* is what you like best. The key words in these sentences are usually verbs, but here they are something else. When is a verb not a verb? When it is a verbal. Using verbals—infinitives, gerunds, and participles—gives you more flexibility in writing about actions.

In this handbook you will learn how to use verbals to add variety to your writing.

Using Verbals

Objectives

- To identify the uses of infinitives and infinitive phrases
- To recognize split infinitives
- To identify the uses of participles and participial phrases
- To identify gerunds and gerund phrases
- To distinguish between gerunds and participles

Writing

- To use verbals to add information to sentences
- To use verbals to combine sentences
- To proofread sentences for errors in grammar, capitalization, punctuation, and spelling

INTRODUCING THE HANDBOOK

To introduce the concept of verbals, ask students to name as many forms of the verb *play* as they can. As they answer, list the responses on the board. Then circle *to play, playing,* and *played.* Tell students that this handbook is going to focus on these verb forms. Then have students read the introduction to find out what these forms of the verb are called.

INFINITIVES

Objectives

- To identify infinitives and infinitive phrases
- To recognize split infinitives

Writing

- To use infinitives to add information to sentences

Teaching Strategies

HELPFUL HINT Alert or curious students might question why the definition states that an infinitive usually—rather than always—appears with the word *to.* Tell these students that when an infinitive follows certain verbs, such as *let, hear, help* or *make,* the *to* is often dropped.

The florist *let* the contest winner *pick* a bouquet from the display.

or

The florist *allowed* the contest winner *to pick* a bouquet from the display.

INDIVIDUALIZING INSTRUCTION: BASIC STUDENTS These students may have a difficult time distinguishing an infinitive form from a prepositional phrase starting with *to.* If the word following *to* is a proper noun or is preceded by the article *a, an,* or *the,* the phrase is a prepositional phrase. If the word following *to* conveys an action, it is a verb and the phrase is an infinitive.

To the victor belong the spoils. (prepositional phrase—*victor* is a noun)

Jenna invited Gwen *to the play.* (prepositional phrase—here, *play* is a noun)

Jenna invited Gwen *to play.* (infinitive form—*play* here is a verb)

INFINITIVES

An **infinitive** is a verbal that usually appears with the word *to* before it. *To* is called the **sign of the infinitive.**

You have learned that there are eight parts of speech: nouns, pronouns, verbs, adverbs, adjectives, prepositions, conjunctions, and interjections. In addition, the English language contains three other kinds of words: infinitives, participles, and gerunds. These words are called verbals.

A **verbal** is a word that is formed from a verb but acts as another part of speech. In this handbook section, you will study all three kinds of verbals. You will learn how they can add interest and variety to spoken and written sentences.

The infinitive is the easiest verbal to recognize. An **infinitive** is a form of a verb that usually appears after the word *to.*

to lift   to travel   to orbit   to launch

The word *to* is also used as a preposition. It is a preposition if it is followed by a noun or pronoun that is its object. It is the sign of the infinitive if a verb follows it.

People dreamed of flights *to the moon.* (prepositional phrase)
Not until the 1960s were people able *to succeed.* (infinitive)

Because infinitives are formed from verbs, they are like verbs in several ways. Infinitives can, for example, have objects. They can also be modified by adverbs. An infinitive and its objects and modifiers form an **infinitive phrase.** The italicized groups of words in the sentences below are infinitive phrases.

Astronauts tried *to master space.*
(*Space* is the direct object of the infinitive *to master.*)

Weightlessness began *to give astronauts several problems.*
(*Astronauts* is the indirect object and *problems* is the direct object of *to give.*)

Astronauts eventually learned *to maneuver successfully.*
(*Successfully* is an adverb modifying *to maneuver.*)

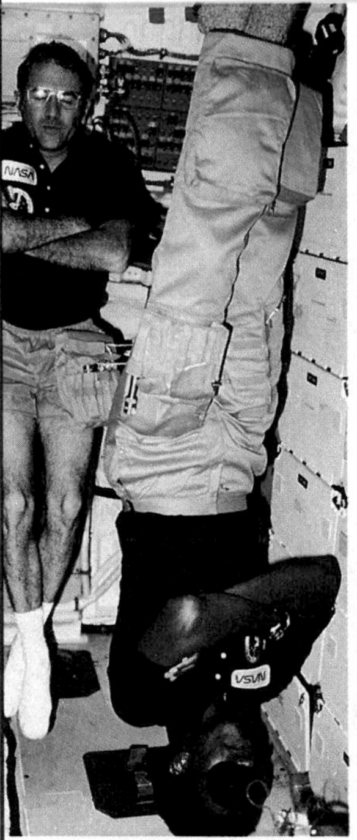

Astronauts Richard H. Truly, crew commander, and Guion S. Bluford, mission specialist, stretch out for a rest session as their space shuttle orbits Earth.

596 Grammar Handbook

The Split Infinitive

When a modifier is placed between the word *to* and the verb in an infinitive, it is said to split the infinitive. A split infinitive sometimes sounds awkward and should usually be avoided.

Awkward Astronauts learn to *quickly* adjust to weightlessness.
Better Astronauts learn to adjust *quickly* to weightlessness.

Uses of Infinitives

Infinitives and infinitive phrases can be used in three ways: as nouns, as adjectives, and as adverbs. Recall that nouns are used as subjects and objects of verbs. Infinitives and infinitive phrases can be used as subjects, as direct objects, and in other ways that nouns are used.

Subject *To move in zero gravity* is not easy. (*To move in zero gravity* is the subject of *is*.)
Direct Object Astronauts learn *to adapt to zero gravity*. (*To adapt to zero gravity* is the object of *learn*.)

Infinitives and infinitive phrases can also be used as modifiers. If the infinitive or infinitive phrase modifies a noun or a pronoun, it is being used as an adjective. If it modifies a verb, an adjective, or an adverb, it is being used as an adverb.

Adjective The landing on the moon was an event *to watch*. (*To watch* modifies the predicate noun *event*.)
Adverb Pictures of the moonwalk were incredible *to see*. (*To see* modifies the predicate adjective *incredible*.)
Adverb Millions gathered *to watch the event*. (*To watch the event* modifies the verb *gathered*.)

Practice Your Skills

A. CONCEPT CHECK

Identifying Infinitives Write the infinitive phrases in the following sentences.

1. To travel into space was the dream of Robert Goddard.
2. This U.S. scientist began to experiment with rockets around 1908.
3. He was one of the first to take these devices seriously.

Writing TIP

Begin some of your sentences with infinitives and infinitive phrases instead of nouns and pronouns. Varying your sentence beginnings makes your writing livelier.

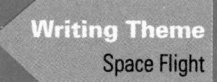

Writing Theme
Space Flight

LINKING GRAMMAR AND WRITING Students once were told never to split infinitives—never to place an adverb between the two parts of the infinitive (as in *to barely escape*). Today, split infinitives are generally accepted in speech. In writing, students should try to place an adverb either before or after the complete infinitive, unless this order would be awkward or stilted.

HELPFUL HINT Sometimes students have difficulty identifying infinitives that function as adverbs. Remind them that when an infinitive functions as an adverb, it tells one of these things: *how, when, where,* or *why*. Have students identify what the infinitives in the two "adverb" sample sentences on the pupil page tell. (*To see* tells *how* or *in what way; to watch the event* tells *why*.)

INDIVIDUALIZING INSTRUCTION: ADVANCED STUDENTS If students need more of a challenge than simply identifying infinitives, encourage them to indicate how each infinitive phrase in the Concept Check is being used: as a subject, a direct object, an adjective, or an adverb.

Additional Resources

Tests and Writing Assessment Prompts, Pretest, pp. 41–42
Grammar and Usage Practice Book, pp. 99–100
 Grammar Test Generator

Writing Theme: Space Flight

Suggest that students use these exercises as a springboard to writing. Other related areas that they might explore include the following:

- the accomplishments of Sally Ride
- lunar landings
- docking in space

Science Connection

Interested students might enjoy interviewing some adults who watched the first lunar landing on television on July 20, 1969. Students can work together to devise questions such as the following: How did you feel as you saw Neil Armstrong take the first steps on the moon? What did you see as the purpose of the lunar landing at that time? What do you think the moon landing accomplished? What should be the goals of our space program today? Have students write up their interviews, share them with classmates, and discuss the subjects' use of infinitive forms.

Answers to Practice Your Skills

A. Concept Check
Identifying Infinitives

Answers are shown on page.

B. Drafting Skill
Using Infinitives

Answers will vary. Possible answers are given.

11. to travel
12. To prepare
13. to conduct
14. to teach
15. to learn
16. to survive
17. to solve
18. to pilot
19. to handle
20. to land

C. Proofreading Skill
Using Infinitives and Infinitive Phrases

Errors in proofreading exercises are counted as follows: (a) Each word is counted as one error. For example, a misspelled word is one error; two initials and a last name not capitalized are counted as three errors. (b) Run-on sentences and sentence fragments are each counted as one error, even though the correction involves both punctuation and capitalization corrections.

Errors are shown on page.

For over twenty-five years, the Vertical Assembly Building (VAB) has stood at the John F. Kennedy Space Center. Here, people work carefully to prepare the giant rockets of the United States space program. Everything from the first spacecraft to the moon to today's space shuttle has used this facility. Over seven hundred feet long and five hundred feet high, the VAB is one of the world's largest buildings.

---

4. His discoveries helped to make rapid progress in rocket science.
5. Goddard was able to launch rockets on high-altitude flights.
6. To send a rocket to the moon was Goddard's ultimate goal.
7. At first few other scientists bothered to listen to Goddard.
8. He was even forced to finance much of his research himself.
9. Goddard worked hard to share his vision of space flight.
10. His work made it easier for scientists to study space today.

B. DRAFTING SKILL

Using Infinitives Write an infinitive to complete each sentence.

11. Rigorous training prepares astronauts _______ into space.
12. _______ for space missions is their chief goal.
13. Astronauts are trained to pilot a spacecraft and _______ scientific experiments in space.
14. As part of the training program, NASA invites instructors from universities _______ the astronauts various skills.
15. Space crews take classes _______ about astronomy and other subjects.
16. Astronauts also learn _______ in the harsh conditions of space.
17. Their ability _______ problems is always being tested.
18. They must know how _______ a spacecraft after it returns to the earth's atmosphere.
19. Special training prepares them _______ difficult situations and emergency landings.
20. Astronauts practice ways _______ their spacecraft in the ocean and to survive in the jungle.

C. PROOFREADING SKILL

Using Infinitives and Infinitive Phrases Proofread the following paragraph. Then write it, correcting errors in grammar, capitalization, punctuation, and spelling. Pay particular attention to split infinitives. (7 errors)

For over twenty-five years, the Vertical Asembly Building (VAB) has stood at the John F Kennedy Space Center. Hear, people work to carefully prepare the giant rockets of the United States space program. everything from the first spacecraft to the moon to today's space shuttle has used this facility. Over seven hundred feet long and five hundred feet high. The VAB is one of the worlds' largest buildings.

FOR MORE PRACTICE
See page 606.

TEACHER'S LOUNGE

I'm going to never split infinitives
S. Harris

598 Grammar Handbook

A **participle** is a verbal that always acts as an adjective.

One of the principal parts of a verb is the past participle. The **past participle** is usually formed by adding *-d* or *-ed* to the present tense: *walk, walked.* The past participles of irregular verbs, however, do not follow this rule: *run, run; throw, thrown.*

Another kind of participle is called the present participle. A **present participle** is formed by adding *-ing* to the present tense of any verb: *walk, walking; hit, hitting.*

Participles may be used as parts of verb phrases: *had tossed, am throwing.* When used as verbals, however, both past and present participles always function as adjectives, modifying either nouns or pronouns. Using participles is a simple way to add information to sentences or to vary sentence beginnings.

Smiling, the batter stepped up to the plate.
(*Smiling* is a present participle modifying the noun *batter.*)

Fooled, he swung at the curve ball.
(*Fooled* is a past participle modifying *he.*)

Because participles are formed from verbs, they can have objects and be modified by adverbs. A participle and its objects and modifiers form a **participial phrase.**

Rounding third base, the runner charged toward home plate.
(*Rounding third base* is a participial phrase modifying *runner; base* is the object of the participle *rounding.*)

Especially pleased, the crowd cheered loudly.
(*Especially pleased* is a participial phrase modifying *crowd; especially* is an adverb modifying the participle *pleased.*)

A participle or participial phrase is not always at the beginning of a sentence. It should be near the noun or pronoun it modifies.

The *skilled* catcher trapped the wild pitch in his mitt.

The pitcher, *losing control,* had overthrown the ball.

Writing TIP

Vary your sentence structure by using participial phrases in different positions. Remember to place a participial phrase near the noun or pronoun it modifies.

The fans watched the ball *sailing into the stands.*

Known as a slugger, the batter hit another home run.

PARTICIPLES

Objectives

- To identify participles and participial phrases
- To identify the noun or pronoun that the participle or participial phrase modifies

Writing

- To use a participle or a participial phrase to combine sentences
- To use participles or participial phrases correctly in writing

Teaching Strategies

INDIVIDUALIZING INSTRUCTION: BASIC STUDENTS Make sure that students understand that a participle is a verb when it is combined with a helping verb such as *have* or *is:*

V
I have been listening to the radio.

However, when a present participle or past participle has no helping verb, it acts as an adjective.

ADJ
Listening to the radio, I fell asleep.

HELPFUL HINT Students sometimes have difficulty in identifying the word that a participle modifies. Share these hints with students:

- A participle or a participial phrase at the beginning of a sentence modifies the subject, which usually appears near the beginning of a sentence, assuming the sentence is not an inverted one.
- A participle or participial phrase at the end of a sentence usually modifies the subject when the participle is preceded by a comma; otherwise, it modifies a noun or pronoun in the predicate.

The player ran down the court, turning around once to eye his opponent.

The masterpiece was a mixture of red and orange paint splashed across the canvas.

Additional Resource

Grammar and Usage Practice Book, pp. 101–102

Writing Theme: Sports

Suggest that students use these exercises as a springboard to writing. Other related areas that they might explore include the following:

- Jackie Robinson, first African-American major leaguer
- organized sports in middle school
- Super Bowl mania

Answers to Practice Your Skills

A. Concept Check

Identifying Participles

1. tiring; job
2. Hired by the best teams; they
3. Playing other positions on their off days; players
4. struggling; teams
5. Unprepared; team
6. faced with the rest of the season; team
7. Sent to the mound nearly every day; pitcher
8. Worried; fans
9. Asked to do the work of two pitchers; Hoss
10. Determined; Hoss
11. seeing no alternative; Manager Frank Bancroft
12. Pitching thirty-eight games in a row; Hoss
13. showing remarkable talent; Hoss
14. Continuing this streak; he
15. honored; place

Writing Theme
Sports

Practice Your Skills

A. CONCEPT CHECK

Identifying Participles Write the participles and participial phrases in the following sentences. Then write the word each one modifies.

1. In the early days of baseball, star pitchers had a tiring job.
2. Hired by the best teams, they played almost every day.
3. Playing other positions on their off days, these players earned their pay.
4. Some pitchers truly "went the distance" for struggling teams.
5. Unprepared, the Providence, Rhode Island, team suddenly lost one of its best pitchers in the middle of the 1884 season.
6. The team, faced with the rest of the season, was in trouble.
7. Sent to the mound nearly every day, the team's other star pitcher might bow to the pressure.
8. Worried, the fans hoped that "Hoss" Radbourn would succeed.
9. Asked to do the work of two pitchers, Hoss thought he could lead the team to victory.
10. Determined, Hoss was ready for the challenge.
11. Manager Frank Bancroft, seeing no alternative, played Hoss in every game.
12. Pitching thirty-eight games in a row, Hoss beat his opponents.
13. Hoss, showing remarkable talent, won the last eighteen games of the season.
14. Continuing this streak, he won every game against the original New York Mets in the World Series.
15. Hoss's excellent record earned him an honored place in baseball's Hall of Fame.

B. DRAFTING SKILL

Sentence Combining Combine each pair of sentences to make a sentence with a participle or participial phrase. Insert the italicized word or phrase from the second sentence into the first sentence at the place indicated by a caret.

EXAMPLE There are many ^ stories about the origins of team names. The stories are *interesting.*

There are many *interesting* stories about the origins of team names.

600 Grammar Handbook

16. An old tradition ^ is to give sports teams colorful names. The tradition is *still followed today.*
17. The San Francisco 49ers football team chose a nickname ^ . The nickname was *associated with California's history.*
18. A historical event ^ occurred in 1849. The event was *called the Gold Rush.*
19. ^ Treasure hunters flocked to California. They were *searching for gold.*
20. The ^ prospectors were called the forty-niners. The prospectors were *daring.*
21. ^ The Giants baseball team got its name by accident. The team has been *playing in San Francisco since 1957.*
22. The team ^ was first called the Gothams. The team was *formed in New York City.*
23. In 1885, the manager ^ proclaimed, "My big fellows! My Giants!" The manager was *impressed by a spectacular victory.*
24. The name ^ remains. It was *based on the manager's remark.*

C. APPLICATION IN WRITING

Directions Have you ever taught someone how to use a piece of sports equipment? Have you ever tried to explain the rules of a sport? Using sports as your topic, describe how to use or do something. Use at least two participles or participial phrases in your explanation.

FOR MORE PRACTICE
See pages 606–607.

MIXED REVIEW • PAGES 596–601

A. APPLICATION IN LITERATURE

Identify each underlined verbal in this passage by writing *Infinitive, Infinitive Phrase, Participle,* or *Participial Phrase.* If a sentence has no verbals, write *None.*

[1]NASA simply calls it "Voyager: The Grandest Tour."
[2]Indeed, there has been nothing like it before, nor will there ever again be anything to match it. . . . [3]Using the gravitational pull of each planet to increase their speed, the [two] spacecraft swooped from one marvelous world to the next. . . . [4]One by one, the mysterious objects came into view. [5]There was

B. Drafting Skill
Sentence Combining
16. An old tradition, still followed today, is to give sports teams colorful names.
17. The San Francisco 49ers football team chose a nickname associated with California's history.
18. A historical event called the Gold Rush occurred in 1849.
19. Searching for gold, treasure hunters flocked to California.
20. The daring prospectors were called the forty-niners.
21. Playing in San Francisco since 1957, the Giants baseball team got its name by accident.
22. The team, formed in New York City, was first called the Gothams.
23. In 1885, the manager, impressed by a spectacular victory, proclaimed, "My big fellows! My Giants!"
24. The name based on the manager's remark remains.

C. Application in Writing
Directions
Answers will vary.

CHECK POINT

Writing Theme: Exploration
Other related areas students might wish to explore as writing topics include the following:
- early Scandinavians in North America
- expeditions to Antarctica
- Jacques Cousteau, explorer of the sea
- the travels of Marco Polo

MIXED REVIEW • PAGES 596–601
You may wish to use this activity to check students' mastery of the following concepts:
- infinitives and infinitive phrases
- participles and participial phrases

A. Application in Literature
1. None
2. to match it, Infinitive Phrase
3. Using the gravitational pull of each planet, Participial Phrase; to increase their speed, Infinitive Phrase
4. None

Using Verbals 601

5. guarded by a fiery moon, Participial Phrase; harboring a place where life could start up, Participial Phrase; tilted, Participle; lashed by 1,200-mile-an-hour winds, Participial Phrase
6. launched from Cape Canaveral on August 20, 1977, Participial Phrase; speeding along at a rate of 290 million miles a year, Participial Phrase
7. launched less than a month later, Participial Phrase; traveling at 320 million miles a year, Participial Phrase

B.

8. to reach the Far East, Infinitive Phrase
9. bound for the East, Participial Phrase, ships
10. made by earlier explorers, Participial Phrase, maps
11. fabled, Participle, riches
12. Convinced, Participle, Magellan
13. to complete, Infinitive
14. to reach the Pacific Ocean, Infinitive Phrase
15. Crossing the Pacific, Participial Phrase, crews
16. To die at sea, Infinitive Phrase
17. to arrive in the Philippines, Infinitive Phrase
18. aiding Filipinos in a battle, Participial Phrase, Magellan
19. Reorganizing the expedition, Participial Phrase, survivors
20. carrying fewer than twenty men, Participial Phrase, ship
21. to finish, Infinitive
22. to sail completely around the world, Infinitive Phrase

spectacular Jupiter, guarded by a fiery moon; beautiful Saturn, harboring a place where life could start up; tilted Uranus, which might have been smacked by a planet-sized object; and blue Neptune, lashed by 1,200-mile-an-hour winds. . . .

[6]Voyager 2, launched from Cape Canaveral on August 20, 1977, is 3.3 billion miles from Earth, speeding along at a rate of 290 million miles a year. [7]Voyager 1, launched less than a month later, is 4.3 billion miles away, traveling at 320 million miles a year.

Ronald Kotulak, "Voyager," ***The Chicago Tribune Magazine***

B. Write the verbals in the following sentences. Label each one *Infinitive, Infinitive Phrase, Participle,* or *Participial Phrase.* Write the word that each participle or participial phrase modifies.

The *Victoria,* the only ship in Ferdinand Magellan's five-ship fleet to complete the voyage around the world. Detail of a map, 1590, by Abraham Ortelius.

8. In the fall of 1519, five ships set out to reach the Far East.
9. Before that time, most ships bound for the East had sailed around Africa.
10. However, Ferdinand Magellan had studied the maps made by earlier explorers.
11. He believed that a brief voyage beyond the Americas would lead to the fabled riches of the East.
12. Convinced, Magellan set sail from Spain on a westward course.
13. This westward voyage was difficult for the ships to complete.
14. Magellan's five ships took more than a year to reach the Pacific Ocean.
15. Crossing the Pacific, the ships' crews faced starvation and disease.
16. To die at sea was a fear of many sailors.
17. In the spring of 1521, three ships finally managed to arrive in the Philippines.
18. Magellan, aiding Filipinos in a battle, was killed.
19. Reorganizing the expedition, the survivors then started their journey home.
20. One ship, carrying fewer than twenty men, returned to Spain.
21. The expedition had taken almost three years to finish.
22. It was the first expedition to sail completely around the world.

GERUNDS

A **gerund** is a verbal that is used as a noun.

A **gerund** is a verb form used as a noun. Adding *-ing* to the present tense of a verb creates a gerund. Gerunds can be used in all the ways nouns are used—as subjects, direct objects, objects of prepositions, and predicate words.

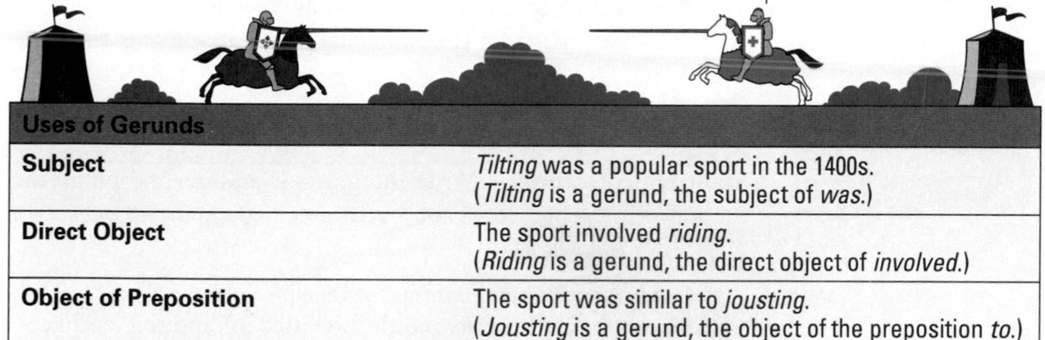

Uses of Gerunds	
Subject	*Tilting* was a popular sport in the 1400s. (*Tilting* is a gerund, the subject of *was.*)
Direct Object	The sport involved *riding.* (*Riding* is a gerund, the direct object of *involved.*)
Object of Preposition	The sport was similar to *jousting.* (*Jousting* is a gerund, the object of the preposition *to.*)

Because gerunds are formed from verbs, they can have objects and can be modified by adverbs. Because they are used as nouns, they can also be modified by adjectives and by prepositional phrases. A **gerund phrase** consists of a gerund with its objects and modifiers. Look at the following examples of gerund phrases:

Unseating a rider was the object of the sport.
(*Unseating* is a gerund; *rider* is the object of *unseating.*)

Successfully overpowering a knight was a challenge.
(*Overpowering* is a gerund; *successfully* is an adverb modifying *overpowering.*)

Accurate aiming contributed to the safety of the sport.
(*Aiming* is a gerund; *accurate* is an adjective modifying *aiming.*)

A barrier, or tilt, was used for *separating contestants.*
(*Separating* is a gerund; *contestants* is its object.)

GERUNDS

Objectives

- To identify gerunds and gerund phrases
- To distinguish between a gerund and a participle

Teaching Strategies

INDIVIDUALIZING INSTRUCTION: ESL STUDENTS Because Spanish often uses the infinitive as a subject *(To smoke is bad for your health.)* whereas English more often uses a gerund *(Smoking is bad . . .),* Spanish-speaking ESL students may have difficulty using *-ing* forms as subjects. Point out this usage difference between Spanish and English, and pair these students with English-proficient classmates who can help them use gerunds correctly in their writing.

CRITICAL THINKING: ANALYZING Have students analyze the italicized gerund phrases to determine how they are used in each sentence. *(Unseating a rider:* subject; *Successfully overpowering a knight:* subject; *accurate aiming:* subject; *separating contestants:* object of the preposition *for.)*

INDIVIDUALIZING INSTRUCTION: ESL STUDENTS Many verbs in English can be followed by either a gerund or an infinitive.

He likes <u>fishing</u>. (gerund)

He likes <u>to fish</u>. (infinitive)

However, some verbs in English can be followed only by a gerund, not by an infinitive. Native English speakers are accustomed to using the correct form, but nonnative speakers are not. Below is a list of some of the verbs that must be followed by a gerund. Go over these words with your ESL students. Have them create sentences, using these verbs with a gerund.

dislike	finish
enjoy	miss
practice	suggest

MULTICULTURAL Connection

When thinking of the Middle Ages, many people picture life during feudal times in Europe: for example, the jousting and the quests of chivalrous knights. Suggest that students find out how people in other parts of the world were living during that time period. Some students might like to research life in the Far East or in the Middle East; others might like to add to their knowledge of pre-Columbian America. Have students share their information in oral reports or by creating posters, highlighting their use of gerunds.

LINKING GRAMMAR AND WRITING Students are often told to "show," not "tell," when they write. One way to "show" when writing is by using verbals, particularly participles and gerunds. Because these words are verb forms, they often create a lively, active effect that helps readers imagine what is going on.

Additional Resource

Grammar and Usage Practice Book, pp. 103–105

Writing Theme: Medieval Times

Other related areas students might wish to explore as writing topics include the following:

- the knights of the Round Table
- the concept of courtly love
- the Crusades
- the architecture of a Norman castle

Answers to Practice Your Skills

A. Concept Check
Identifying Gerunds

1. fighting, Subject
2. capturing enemies, Object of Preposition
3. Killing an enemy in battle, Subject
4. preparing for battle, Object of Preposition
5. training, Object of Preposition
6. caring for horses, Object of Preposition
7. handling smaller versions of weapons, Direct Object
8. acting as a servant to a knight, Direct Object
9. training as a mounted soldier, Direct Object
10. Going into battle, Subject

B. Concept Check
Gerund or Participle?

11. fighting, Participle
12. Splitting up into two sides, Participial Phrase
13. Lasting all day, Participial Phrase
14. Losing, Gerund
15. causing destruction and rebellions, Gerund Phrase

Gerund or Participle?

Both the gerund and the present participle are created by adding *-ing* to the present tense of a verb. How can you tell whether a word is a gerund or a participle? It depends on how the word is used in a sentence. When it is used as a modifier, it is a participle. When it is used as a noun, it is a gerund.

Wearing armor shielded a knight's body.
(*Wearing armor* is a gerund phrase, the subject of *shielded.*)

Wearing armor, a knight felt safer and bolder.
(*Wearing armor* is a participial phrase modifying *knight.*)

Practice Your Skills

A. CONCEPT CHECK

Identifying Gerunds Write the gerunds and gerund phrases in the following sentences. Label each one *Subject, Direct Object,* or *Object of Preposition.*

1. In the Middle Ages, fighting was the profession of knights.
2. However, knights were mostly interested in capturing enemies.
3. Killing an enemy in battle would mean that the knight could collect no ransom.
4. Much of a knight's life was devoted to preparing for battle.
5. A young boy in training spent his first years at home.
6. There he learned about caring for horses.
7. Later, as a page, he started handling smaller versions of weapons.
8. At fifteen or sixteen, he began acting as a servant to a knight.
9. Now called a squire, he received training as a mounted soldier.
10. Going into battle was part of a squire's duty.

B. CONCEPT CHECK

Gerund or Participle? Write the verbals in the following sentences. Label each one *Gerund, Gerund Phrase, Participle,* or *Participial Phrase.*

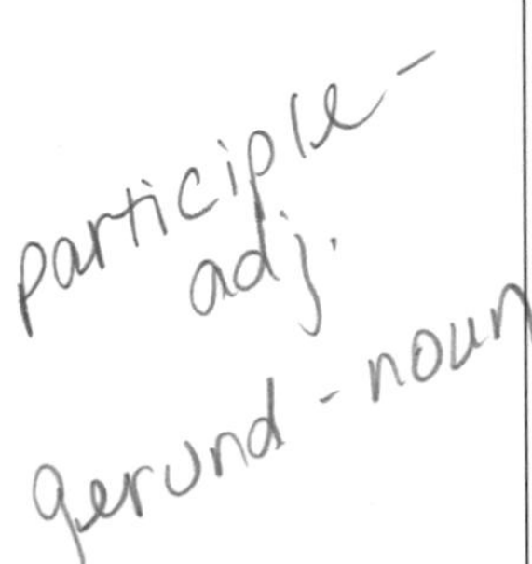

11. In the 1100s, knights practiced their fighting skills in tournaments.
12. Splitting up into two sides, large numbers of knights fought mock battles.
13. Lasting all day, the battles ranged all over the countryside.

604 Grammar Handbook

14. Losing meant that the knight either paid a ransom or lost his possessions.
15. These tournaments were famous for causing destruction and rebellions.
16. As a result, holding tournaments required the king's permission.
17. Hoping to save lives, the government and the church discouraged these events.
18. In the 1200s, jousting, or combat between two people, was introduced as an alternative to tournaments.
19. Using blunt weapons, two knights fought in an enclosed field.
20. The joust became a means of entertaining the public.

CHECK POINT

MIXED REVIEW • PAGES 602–605

Write the verbals in the following sentences. Label each one *Gerund, Gerund Phrase, Participle,* or *Participial Phrase.* Write the word that each participle or participial phrase modifies.

1. Coasting through the air in a glider is a wonderful experience.
2. Airplanes stay aloft by using their engines for power.
3. Having no engines at all, gliders rely only on the air.
4. Airplanes tow the gliders before launching them in the air.
5. The airplanes then release the floating gliders.
6. The gliders are on their own, remaining in the air for anywhere from one to five hours.
7. Some gliders have succeeded in staying aloft for seventy hours.
8. The fascinating story of gliders began in the 1800s.
9. By the 1890s, Otto Lilienthal, a German engineer, had succeeded in making almost 2,500 glider flights.
10. Intrigued, the Wright brothers also tried gliders between 1900 and 1902.
11. Aircraft with engines soon arrived, lessening interest in gliders.
12. During World War II, developing gliders was again important.
13. Moving silently, gliders carried soldiers on surprise attacks.
14. Making a glider was also relatively easy and inexpensive.
15. To the countries fighting the war, expense was a crucial issue.
16. After the war soaring became a recreational sport.
17. By the 1970s, individuals began gliding on large kites.
18. These "hang gliders" were capable of making long flights.
19. Taking off from hillsides, their pilots floated gracefully in the air.
20. Flying like a bird has finally become a reality for people.

FOR MORE PRACTICE
See pages 606–607.

Writing Theme
Gliding

16. holding tournaments, Gerund Phrase
17. Hoping to save lives, Participial Phrase
18. jousting, Gerund
19. Using blunt weapons, Participial Phrase; enclosed, Participle
20. entertaining the public, Gerund Phrase

CHECK POINT

Writing Theme: Gliding

Other related areas students might wish to explore as writing topics include the following:

- parts of a glider
- the Wright brothers' experiment with gliders
- ultralight flying

MIXED REVIEW • PAGES 602–605

You may wish to use this activity to check students' mastery of the following concepts:

- gerunds and gerund phrases
- the use of gerunds and gerund phrases in sentences
- the difference between gerunds and participles

1. Coasting through the air in a glider, Gerund Phrase
2. using their engines for power, Gerund Phrase
3. Having no engines at all, Participial Phrase, gliders
4. launching them in the air, Gerund Phrase
5. floating, Participle, gliders
6. remaining in the air for anywhere from one to five hours, Participial Phrase, gliders
7. staying aloft for seventy hours, Gerund Phrase
8. fascinating, Participle, story
9. making almost 2,500 glider flights, Gerund Phrase
10. Intrigued, Participle, brothers
11. lessening interest in gliders, Participial Phrase, aircraft
12. developing gliders, Gerund Phrase
13. Moving silently, Participial Phrase, gliders
14. Making a glider, Gerund Phrase
15. fighting the war, Participial Phrase, countries
16. soaring, Gerund
17. gliding on large kites, Gerund Phrase
18. making long flights, Gerund Phrase
19. Taking off from hillsides, Participial Phrase, pilots
20. Flying like a bird, Gerund Phrase

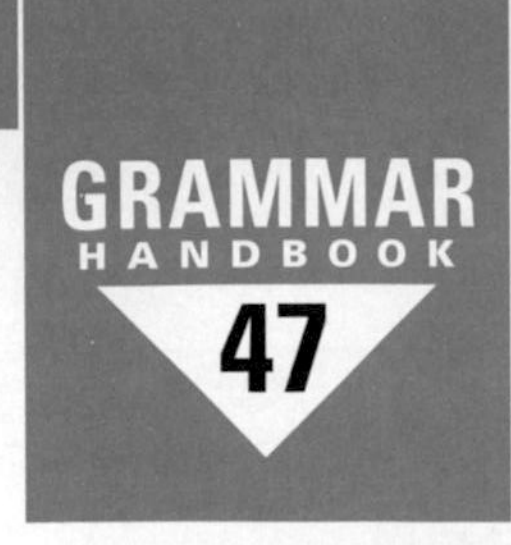

ADDITIONAL PRACTICE

Each of these exercises correlates to a section of Handbook 47, "Using Verbals." The exercises may be used for more practice, for reteaching, or for review of the concepts presented.

Additional Resource

Grammar and Usage Practice Book, p. 107

Writing Theme: Mountain Climbing

Other related areas students might wish to explore as writing topics include the following:

- trekking and rock scrambling
- safety precautions for mountain climbers
- the scaling of Annapurna in the Himalayas

A. Identifying Verbals: Infinitives and Infinitive Phrases

Answers are shown on page.

B. Identifying Verbals: Participles and Participial Phrases

16. fabled, Participle, conquest
17. led by Edward Whymper, Participial Phrase, group
18. Defying many climbers over the years, Participial Phrase, Matterhorn
19. failing each time, Participial Phrase, Whymper
20. experienced, Participle, guide
21. Meeting another group by chance, Participial Phrase, Whymper

GRAMMAR HANDBOOK 47

Writing Theme
Mountain Climbing

A. Identifying Verbals: Infinitives and Infinitive Phrases
Write the infinitives and the infinitive phrases in the following sentences.

1. To find adventure, some people climb mountains.
2. Mountain climbers are not afraid to take risks.
3. The first person to make a major climb was a French aristocrat.
4. In 1492, Antoine de Ville managed to scale Mont Aiguille near Grenoble, France.
5. To accomplish this feat took courage and skill.
6. After that climb enthusiasm for the sport began to build.
7. Among the many people to take up climbing was Leonardo da Vinci.
8. To climb in the Pennine Alps was a joy for the famous painter, sculptor, and inventor.
9. The spirit of adventure led people to try more daring climbs.
10. In time climbers strove to conquer the very highest mountains.
11. Climbers were able to reach more and more of the tallest mountain peaks.
12. Not until 1953, though, did climbers manage to conquer Mount Everest.
13. Today, there are few firsts to achieve.
14. Yet mountains still continue to lure climbers to their heights.
15. To scale mountains has become a sport for thousands of people.

B. Identifying Verbals: Participles and Participial Phrases
Write the participles and participial phrases in the following sentences. Label each one *Participle* or *Participial Phrase* and write the word it modifies.

16. The fabled conquest of the Matterhorn is one of mountain climbing's most famous tales.
17. In 1865, a group led by Edward Whymper braved this deadly peak.
18. Defying many climbers over the years, the Matterhorn had never been scaled.
19. Whymper himself had made seven attempts, failing each time.
20. Originally, Whymper had planned to climb with an experienced guide.
21. Meeting another group by chance, Whymper included them in his effort at the last minute.

22. The seven climbers ascended quickly, making steady progress.
23. Pleased with their progress, the group camped at eleven thousand feet.
24. The next day, the determined Whymper and his party reached the top.
25. Two hours later the daring group began their descent.
26. Problems developed because of an inexperienced climber, Douglas Hadow.
27. Slipping, young Hadow fell against one of the guides.
28. A rope worn from too many climbs then broke.
29. Four of the climbers fell, sliding to their death thousands of feet below.
30. Whymper's victorious climb left him haunted by its tragic results.

C. Identifying Verbals: Gerunds and Gerund Phrases Write the gerunds and gerund phrases in the following sentences. Label each one *Subject, Direct Object,* or *Object of Preposition.*

31. For years conquering Mount Everest was every climber's goal.
32. All great climbers dreamed of reaching its peak.
33. In the end a British group got credit for being the first to the top.
34. Assembling the giant expedition was Colonel John Hunt's job.
35. He started by recruiting some of the best climbers in the world.
36. Planning the climb took months of work.
37. Finally, in 1953, the moment for leaving arrived.
38. Carrying the equipment required a crew of more than three hundred porters.
39. Thirty-four local mountaineers began guiding the dangerous expedition.
40. Toward the top, teams of climbers started taking turns.
41. Getting ready for the final climb was a difficult and tense task.
42. Tom Bourdillon and R. C. Evans started climbing first.
43. They were forced back, however, after coming within three hundred feet of the summit.
44. After waiting out a heavy storm, Edmund Hillary and Tenzing Norgay then started for the top.
45. Hours later, after a risky climb, they began photographing themselves at "the top of the world."

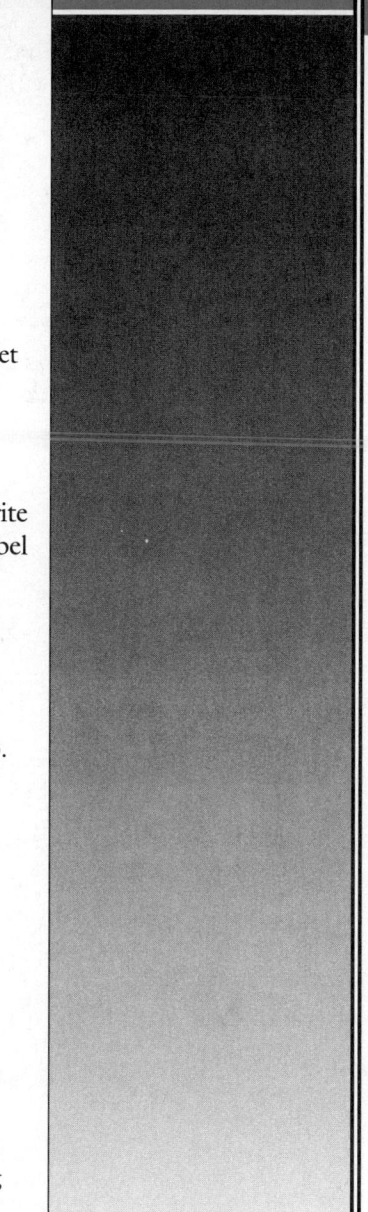

22. making steady progress, Participial Phrase, climbers
23. Pleased with their progress, Participial Phrase, group
24. determined, Participle, Whymper
25. daring, Participle, group
26. inexperienced, Participle, climber
27. Slipping, Participle, Hadow
28. worn from too many climbs, Participial Phrase, rope
29. sliding to their death thousands of feet below, Participial Phrase, Four
30. haunted by its tragic results, Participial Phrase, him

C. Identifying Verbals: Gerunds and Gerund Phrases

31. conquering Mount Everest, Subject
32. reaching its peak, Object of Preposition
33. being the first to the top, Object of Preposition
34. Assembling the giant expedition, Subject
35. recruiting some of the best climbers in the world, Object of Preposition
36. Planning the climb, Subject
37. leaving, Object of Preposition
38. Carrying the equipment, Subject
39. guiding the dangerous expedition, Direct Object
40. taking turns, Direct Object
41. Getting ready for the final climb, Subject
42. climbing, Direct Object
43. coming within three hundred feet of the summit, Object of Preposition
44. waiting out a heavy storm, Object of Preposition
45. photographing themselves at "the top of the world," Direct Object

Using Verbals **607**

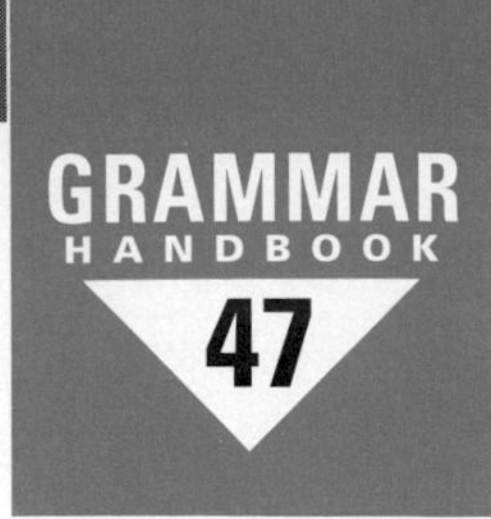

REVIEW

These exercises may be used as a mixed review or as an informal evaluation of the skills presented in Handbook 47, "Using Verbals."

Additional Resources

Grammar and Usage Practice Book, p. 108
Tests and Writing Assessment Prompts, Mastery Test, pp. 43–44
Elaboration, Revision, and Proofreading Practice, p. 33

Writing Theme: Treasures from the Sea

Other related areas students might wish to explore as writing topics include the following:

- salvaging the *Titanic*
- the expeditions of Mel Fisher
- coral reefs, a natural treasure
- pros and cons of offshore oil drilling

A. Infinitives
Answers are shown on page.

B. Participles
16. carrying priceless treasures; ships
17. collected in the Americas; gold, silver, and jewels
18. scheduled; trips
19. waiting for shipment to Spain; worth
20. valued at 14 million dollars; treasure
21. Traveling in the hurricane season; fleet

Writing Theme Treasures from the Sea

REVIEW

A. Infinitives Write the infinitives and infinitive phrases in the following sentences.

1. To find sunken treasure is a magical dream.
2. In the 1600s, William Phips, a ship's carpenter from Boston, asked the king of England to pay for his treasure hunts.
3. Phips's arguments were strong enough to win the support of two kings.
4. To find the wreck of a well-known Spanish ship was Phips's main goal.
5. There was no reason to doubt the ship's location.
6. Everyone wanted to believe the story of its sinking in 1643.
7. According to stories, the ship continued to lie on a reef off the coast of Hispaniola.
8. Phips hoped to find a fortune in treasure.
9. After a long search, he was able to locate the ship.
10. In 1686, Phips began to bring the treasure to the surface.
11. To the delight of everyone, Phips managed to recover a fortune in gold, jewels, and silver.
12. To reward him, King James II presented Phips with seventy-five thousand dollars.
13. Later, Phips was chosen to serve as governor of the Massachusetts colony.
14. To be wealthy and powerful, however, was not in Phips's future.
15. He was unable to buy happiness and died a poor man.

B. Participles Write the participles and participial phrases in the following sentences. Then write the word or words that each one modifies.

16. The silver fleet was an armada of Spanish ships carrying priceless treasures.
17. Each year the silver fleet brought back gold, silver, and jewels collected in the Americas.
18. Between 1713 and 1715, however, warfare interrupted the scheduled trips.
19. As a result, two years' worth of treasure accumulated, waiting for shipment to Spain.
20. The silver fleet finally sailed in July 1715, with a treasure valued at 14 million dollars.
21. Traveling in the hurricane season, the fleet ran into trouble.

22. A violent storm, striking the fleet, sank every one of the ships.
23. For centuries, tales of the destroyed fleet spread around Florida.
24. Then, in 1955, Kip Wagner, a Florida beachcomber, found a coin marked with the royal seal of Spain.
25. Wagner hunted for the missing fleet for more than three years.
26. Wagner's next find was a gold ring containing a giant diamond.
27. Searching the area by plane, Wagner found signs of the fleet.
28. Heavy equipment, removing the sand, helped in the search.
29. Divers found thousands of gold coins scattered on the ocean floor.
30. In time Wagner's group, discovering all eleven ships, uncovered more than a million dollars in treasure.

C. Gerunds Write the verbals in the following sentences. Label each one *Gerund Phrase, Participle,* or *Participial Phrase.*

31. Gold and silver are not the only treasures found in the sea.
32. Getting energy from the sea has become even more important than extracting these precious metals.
33. Over the years people have used much of the oil found under land.
34. Now oil companies have begun taking their "black gold" from under the sea.
35. Exploring for oil takes time and money.
36. Searching for this undersea resource costs companies millions of dollars.
37. After finding oil, the companies establish giant platforms on the sea.
38. Pumping the oil to the surface, these rigs make available a natural resource with hundreds of uses.
39. Oil, of course, is not the only energy source provided by the sea.
40. Hundreds of years ago, people used water power from ocean tides for grinding wheat into flour.
41. Today, this tidal power can produce clean energy, keeping the environment safe.
42. A tidal power plant operating on France's Rance River is an example of this clean energy.
43. There, giant turbines capture the energy of the flowing water.
44. Water rushing through the turbines generates electricity.
45. In the future this electricity may prove more valuable than the gold and silver sought by treasure hunters.

22. striking the fleet; storm
23. destroyed; fleet
24. marked with the royal seal of Spain; coin
25. missing; fleet
26. containing a giant diamond; ring
27. Searching the area by plane; Wagner
28. removing the sand; equipment
29. scattered on the ocean floor; coins
30. discovering all eleven ships; group

C. Gerunds

31. found in the sea, Participial Phrase
32. Getting energy from the sea, Gerund Phrase
33. found under land, Participial Phrase
34. taking their "black gold" from under the sea, Gerund Phrase
35. Exploring for oil, Gerund Phrase
36. Searching for this undersea resource, Gerund Phrase
37. finding oil, Gerund Phrase
38. Pumping the oil to the surface, Participial Phrase
39. provided by the sea, Participial Phrase
40. grinding wheat into flour, Gerund Phrase
41. keeping the environment safe, Participial Phrase
42. operating on France's Rance River, Participial Phrase
43. flowing, Participle
44. rushing through the turbines, Participial Phrase
45. sought by treasure hunters, Participial Phrase

WRITING CONNECTIONS

Elaboration, Revision, and Proofreading

This activity will allow your students to see some of the concepts presented in this handbook at work in a piece of poetry. By revising and proofreading this passage, students will have the opportunity to replace vague language with more precise verbals, to combine sentences by using participles, and to maintain parallel structure by using an appropriate verbal form.

Since this passage is a poem, you might want to read it aloud before students begin working on it. By hearing the poem, students will more readily recognize what needs to be changed.

Answers may vary slightly. Typical changes are shown. Elements involving change are shown in boldface.

Listening for the sound of a car in the distance,
Looking for headlights to appear,
Hoping for them to come,
Waiting . . .

The night is **gloomy.**
The shadows are my only friends.
Not a sound disturbs the quiet.

Soon they will arrive.
Do I hear them **now, coming** around the corner?
No, just the **whispering** of the wind.

To wait is **to be lonely.**

WRITING CONNECTIONS

Elaboration, Revision, and Proofreading

Narrative and Literary Writing

Writing poetry enables you to use language to express your ideas and feelings in a uniquely personal way. (See Workshop 3.) When you revise a poem you have written, experiment with the sounds as well as the meanings of words. Try different ways of creating rhythm. For example, you can repeat a pattern of verbals.

On your paper revise the draft of a poem below. Follow the directions at the bottom of the page. Proofread your revision, paying special attention to the use of verbals. Also look for other errors in grammar, as well as errors in capitalization, punctuation, and spelling.

Listening for the sound of a car in the distance,
Looking for headlights to appear,
To hope for them to come,
Waiting . . .

The night is dark.
the shadows are my only friends.
Not a sound disturbs the quite.

Soon they will arrive.
Do I hear them now?
Will they come around the corner?
no, just the sound of the wind.

To wait is being lonely.

1. Make the words beginning the first four lines the same form by changing the infinitive in line 3 to a participle.
2. Replace the weak adjective "dark" in line 5 with a word or phrase that is more descriptive.
3. Combine the information in lines 9 and 10. Put a participial phrase beginning with "coming" into line 9.
4. Replace the vague noun "sound" in line 11 with a gerund that more precisely suggests or names a sound.
5. Make the verbals the same form in line 12 by changing the gerund phrase to an infinitive phrase.

All in the Family

You've probably never heard the term *grubbled water.* Or *train trails.* Both are expressions created by a six-year-old on a Colorado vacation. To her, the foaming mountain rapids were grubbled. Gleaming railroad tracks stretching westward to the horizon were train trails.

"Trains," Smedley said, "and by the look of the trails, big trains."

Every family creates words, and many are both funny and useful. The following are from a collection, *Family Words,* by Paul Dickson. He loves them, he says, because they are "family traditions wrapped up in words." What words from your family can you add to his list?

Chizzly *Chilly* plus *drizzly.* A particular kind of day.

Eardo Condition of a dog's floppy ear when it is flipped backwards.

F.H.B. Family Hold Back, used to let the family know that an article of food is in short supply and to hold back so that the guests will have enough.

Foiling Peeling after sunburn.

Gummatajuma To ride over the railroad tracks in the car, from the noise made.

Lapkin A cloth napkin.

Musgos Leftovers and other food that "must go."

Odoralls Toddler's overalls.

One! Do it now, or else. Comes from a father's "counting to three."

Pass the potatoes Family code phrase to change the subject at the table.

Pididdle A car with one headlight burnt out.

Show towel One family's term for a guest towel. "Show towel" is more accurate, since guest towels are never used, even by guests.

Toad Cloth Any dishrag that has gotten too wet and clammy to dry dishes.

When discussing this feature, you might want to make a distinction between puns and these family words. Although some of the family words listed can be considered puns—for example, *odoralls*—many cannot.

To encourage students to share family words, you might want to model a few of your own or suggest that they think of some apt phrases that a younger sibling uses.

Test 3

This test enables you to evaluate student mastery of the concepts taught in Handbooks 45–47.

Additional Resource

Grammar and Usage Practice Book, pp. 109–110

Answer Key

Corrections for run-ons may vary.

1. E
2. A—Wow!
3. B—mountains, and
   C—opportunities to
4. A—done, the
   B—Heyerdahl and
5. C—temperatures, a
   D—results.
6. C—are. Pewees *or* are; pewees
7. A—includes
   C—those or these
8. B—life, the Roman
   D—were
9. A—There are
10. B—.518 and
    D—him
11. D—is
12. A—bird and
13. A—seems
14. C—contain
15. B—is

List of Skills Tested

1. A—capitalization: abbreviations
   B—adjective/adverb confusion
   C—possessive pronoun/contraction confusion
   D—pronoun case: object
2. A—punctuation: interjection
   B—subject-verb agreement: inverted sentence
   C—spelling
   D—punctuation: exclamation point
3. A—subject-verb agreement
   B—punctuation: compound sentence
   C—sentence fragment/run-on
   D—spelling
4. A—punctuation: comma with introductory phrase
   B—punctuation: compound subject
   C—spelling
   D—punctuation: end mark

Skills

ASSESSMENT **TEST 3 Grammar Handbooks *45–47***

Directions One or more of the underlined sections in the following sentences may contain an error in grammar, usage, punctuation, spelling, or capitalization. Write the letter of each incorrect section. Then rewrite the section correctly. If there is no error in an item, write *E*.

Example The Pulitzer Prize(A)–winning writer N. Scott Momaday grew up on a Kiowa(B) reservation and(C) his books show(D) his interest in the culture of Native Americans. No error(E)

Answer C—reservation, and

1. In the second century B.C.,(A) Hipparchus was almost exactly(B) correct in his estimation of the circumference of the earth. It's(C) too bad there couldn't have been a little conversation between Columbus and him(D). No error(E)
2. Wow.(A) There are(B) some squids that are not quite(C) an inch long and some that are fifty-two feet long!(D) No error(E)
3. Highways are(A) often cut through hills or mountains and(B) the resulting cross sections are wonderful opportunities. To(C) view rock layers(D). No error(E)
4. To show that it could be done the(A) writer Thor Heyerdahl, and(B) a five-person crew sailed(C) a wood raft named *Kon-Tiki* across 4,300 miles of ocean.(D) No error(E)
5. When light passes(A) through two(B) layers of air with different temperatures. A(C) mirage results(D) No error(E)
6. Some birds are difficult to identify, but(A) other birds say who(B) they are, pewees(C) and whippoorwills call out their(D) own names over and over. No error(E)

7. Every colony of penguins include(A) a great number of members. Sometimes(B) millions of them(C) large birds live(D) in one rookery. No error(E)

8. Although some people believe(A) that someone with epilepsy cannot live a normal life the Roman(B) emperor Julius Caesar and the world conqueror Alexander the Great(C) was(D) both epileptics. No error(E)

9. There's(A) perfectly(B) preserved insects in pieces(C) of amber, which is fossilized tree sap. Some amber pins and necklaces have flies(D) in them. No error(E)

10. In 1869, George Wright batted(A) .518, and(B) earned a salary of $1,400(C). One could make some interesting comparisons between Cubs player Ryne Sandberg and he(D). No error(E)

11. Each of the two(A) most serious(B) cat illnesses(C) are(D) preventable with a vaccine. No error(E)

12. A supposedly crippled bird, and(A) a motionless(B) opossum are(C) both using the common defense(D) of trickery. No error(E)

13. The row of buttons on a coat sleeve seem(A) useless to us, but(B) those buttons once kept soldiers from wiping(C) their noses on their sleeves. Ouch!(D) No error(E)

14. Leaves(A) in spring and summer actually(B) contains(C) all the fall colors, but(D) green chlorophyll masks the orange and red. No error(E)

15. Neither(A) the liger nor the tigon are(B) imaginary; both(C) are(D) the children of rare matings between lions and tigers. No error(E)

5. **A**—spelling
B—spelling
C—sentence fragment/run-on
D—punctuation: end mark

6. **A**—punctuation: compound sentence
B—wrong word: who/whom
C—sentence fragment/run-on
D—pronoun-antecedent agreement

7. **A**—subject-verb agreement: intervening words
B—sentence fragment/run-on
C—wrong word: them/these
D—subject-verb agreement: intervening words

8. **A**—spelling
B—punctuation: complex sentence
C—capitalization: nationality
D—subject-verb agreement: compound subject

9. **A**—subject-verb agreement: inverted sentence
B—adjective/adverb confusion
C—spelling
D—noun plural

10. **A**—spelling
B—punctuation: compound verb
C—punctuation: end mark
D—pronoun case: object

11. **A**—spelling
B—superlative adjective
C—noun plural
D—subject-verb agreement: indefinite pronoun

12. **A**—punctuation: compound subject
B—spelling
C—subject-verb agreement: compound subject
D—spelling

13. **A**—subject-verb agreement: intervening words
B—punctuation: compound sentence
C—spelling
D—punctuation: interjection

14. **A**—noun plural
B—adjective/adverb confusion
C—subject-verb agreement: intervening words
D—punctuation: compound sentence

15. **A**—spelling
B—subject-verb agreement: indefinite pronoun
C—punctuation: compound sentence
D—subject-verb agreement: indefinite pronoun

Skills Assessment 613

Objective

- To use writing prompts and team logos as springboards to informal writing

WRITING WARM-UPS

Remind students that this assignment will not be graded. The logos and activities aim to get students thinking, in a broad and imaginative way, about concepts in the upcoming handbook. Unless students wish to explore more than one prompt, have them develop just one activity.

For the first writing prompt, ask volunteers to name their favorite sports teams. Then have students offer opinions about the names of those teams. Elicit the qualities that a good team name should have. (Samples: It should be catchy, relevant to the sport, regionally appropriate.) Tell students to keep these qualities in mind in responding to this writing prompt.

For the second writing prompt, encourage students to list a few brands of clothing before they begin writing. After students have completed their descriptions, have them compare responses.

For the third writing prompt, point out that students might write about their first names, their family names, or both. Encourage students to research their names in books about names or in other reference sources, before they begin writing.

SKETCHBOOK

WRITING WARM-UPS

- If you had your own sports team, what would you name it? Play around with some interesting names.
- What is your favorite brand of clothing? Write a description of your favorite clothing and compare it to other brands.
- What do you know about your name? Where does it come from? What does it mean?

Capitalization

GRAMMAR HANDBOOK 48

- Proper Nouns and Proper Adjectives
- Geographical Names
- Organizations, History, and Time
- Languages, Peoples, Courses, Transportation, and Abbreviations
- First Words

What's the difference between a bear and a Bear? Besides fur and shoulder pads, an important difference is capitalization. Capitalization helps readers tell these "beasts" apart in print.

In this handbook you will study the ways capitalization affects the meanings of words and sentences.

Capitalization

Objectives

- To recognize and capitalize proper nouns and proper adjectives
- To capitalize personal titles, family relationships, and religious terms correctly
- To capitalize the pronoun *I*
- To capitalize correctly the names of geographical locations, organizations and institutions, documents, historical events, periods of time, months, days, holidays, languages, peoples, school subjects, and transportation vehicles
- To capitalize the abbreviations *B.C.*, *A.D.*, *A.M.*, and *P.M.*
- To capitalize the first words of sentences, of lines of most poetry, of direct quotations, and of outline entries
- To capitalize correctly the greetings and closings of letters
- To capitalize correctly the titles of literary works, motion pictures, works of art, and other such works

INTRODUCING THE HANDBOOK

Write *famous bear* on the board and tell students to imagine that they are doing a crossword puzzle with this phrase as one of the clues. Ask what students think the answer might be. (Samples: Yogi, Smokey, Paddington) Then write *famous Bear,* and ask what the answer now might be. (Samples: Chicago Bears players Brad Muster and William Perry) Stress how the mere difference of a capital letter changes the meaning. Point out that in Handbook 48 students will learn more about capital letters and how to use them correctly.

PROPER NOUNS AND PROPER ADJECTIVES

Objectives

- To recognize and capitalize proper nouns and proper adjectives
- To capitalize correctly personal titles, family terms, and certain religious terms
- To capitalize the pronoun *I*

Writing

- To correct capitalization errors in writing

Teaching Strategies

INDIVIDUALIZING INSTRUCTION: ESL STUDENTS In Chinese, Japanese, Korean, Hindi, and many other languages not written with the Roman alphabet, there are no lowercase and capital letters. The capitalization rules in this handbook may be new concepts for native speakers of those languages.

In German, all nouns are capitalized; German-speaking students will have to learn to distinguish proper nouns from common nouns.

In French and Spanish, adjectives showing nationality—such as *French*—are not capitalized. Remind students to capitalize them in English.

Allow adequate time for all these students to complete the handbook exercises; you also might encourage them to work in groups.

STUMBLING BLOCK Point out that when a proper noun consists of more than one word, its important words are capitalized:

New Orleans
Prince of Wales
District of Columbia

Writing TIP

Using proper nouns and adjectives helps make your meaning clear and your writing specific.

PROPER NOUNS AND PROPER ADJECTIVES

Capitalize proper nouns and proper adjectives.

A **common noun** is the name of a whole class of persons, places, things, or ideas. A **proper noun** is the name of an individual person, place, thing, or idea. A **proper adjective** is an adjective formed from a proper noun. All proper nouns and proper adjectives are capitalized.

Common Noun	Proper Noun	Proper Adjective
person	William Shakespeare	Shakespearean
country	France	French
city	Rome	Roman

There are many different types of proper nouns. The following rules and examples will help you solve problems in capitalizing proper nouns and proper adjectives.

Names and Titles of Persons

Capitalize the names of persons and also the initials or abbreviations that stand for those names.

J. M. W. Turner	**J**oseph **M**allord **W**illiam **T**urner
E. B. White	**E**lwyn **B**rooks **W**hite
Ida **B. W**ells-**B**arnett	**I**da **B**ell **W**ells-**B**arnett

Capitalize titles used with names of persons and capitalize the initials or abbreviations that stand for those titles. Capitalize the titles *Mr., Mrs., Ms.,* and *Miss.*

Mayor Diane Adare	**M**r. David Chang
Dr. T. George Bellini	**M**rs. G. H. Nelson
Lt. C. E. Morro	**M**s. Angela Ruiz

Do not capitalize titles used as common nouns.

Yesterday the **m**ayor addressed the city council.
One of the **d**octors on call is Dr. Ramirez.

Capitalize the following titles when used alone if they refer to the current holders of the positions.

the **P**resident (of the U. S.)	the **Q**ueen (of England)
the **V**ice-**P**resident (of the U. S.)	the **P**ope

Family Relationships

Capitalize words such as *mother, father, aunt,* and *uncle* when these words are used as names.

Uncle **B**en gave **M**other a vase for her birthday.

Note that when the noun is modified by a personal pronoun, the noun is not capitalized.

My **m**other helped me make my costume for the party.

The Pronoun *I*

Capitalize the pronoun *I*. Will **I** see you later?

Religious Names and Terms

Capitalize words referring to the Deity and to religious scriptures.

God **A**llah **J**esus the **B**ible the **K**oran

Do not capitalize the words *god* and *goddess* when they refer to mythological deities.

In Greek myths, Athena is the goddess of wisdom.

Practice Your Skills

A. CONCEPT CHECK

Proper Nouns and Proper Adjectives Write the words that should be capitalized in each sentence.

1. My uncle, dr. carlos p. montoya, is an expert on the major religions of the world.
2. According to uncle carlos, these religions include judaism, hinduism, buddhism, confucianism, taoism, shinto, christianity, and islam.

Writing Theme
Heritage

INDIVIDUALIZING INSTRUCTION: ESL STUDENTS Even among languages that distinguish between lowercase and uppercase (capital) letters, the rules of capitalization differ. In German and in the Romance languages, among others, the words for *I* are not capitalized. This latter rule should cause little difficulty; but it is helpful to be aware of differences in students' first languages.

Additional Resources

Tests and Writing Assessment Prompts, Pretest, pp. 45–46
Grammar and Usage Practice Book, pp. 111–112

Grammar
Test Generator

Writing Theme: Heritage

Suggest that students use these exercises as a springboard to writing. Other related areas that they might explore include the following:

- ethnic folk traditions
- holiday foods in different cultures
- why people immigrated to the United States
- lives of first-generation Americans

Answers to Practice Your Skills

A. Concept Check

Proper Nouns and Proper Adjectives

Answers are shown on page.

B. Application in Literature
Correcting Proper Nouns and Adjectives

Words to be capitalized and words incorrectly capitalized are underlined on page.

11 "Thanksgiving is an important American holiday," Poppa would say. 12 "You kids are Americans, and you ought to celebrate important American holidays. 13 On Thanksgiving, you eat turkey. 14 Would you want people to think you were ungrateful?" 15 Poppa came from Poland, and he was very big on holidays, and being an American. There was no arguing with him. 16 They had turkey every year.

17 Most of the kids in the neighborhood had the same scene at home. 18 Some of them liked turkey, some of them didn't—but they all had it on Thanksgiving. 19 They all had fathers like Arthur Bobowicz's father—they came from Italy, and the Ukraine, and Puerto Rico, and Hong Kong. 20 The kids were all being raised to be Americans, and everyone's father knew that Americans eat turkey on Thanksgiving.

3. jewish tradition teaches that judaism began with abraham in the Middle East.
4. The jewish religion is based on the torah, the first five books of the bible.
5. hinduism and buddhism are two religions that developed in india.
6. buddhism is based on the teachings of a prince named siddhartha gautama.
7. Two religions that developed in china are taoism, which emphasizes individual freedom, and confucianism, which is based on the teachings of confucius.
8. The oldest surviving religion of japan is shinto.
9. The christian religion derives from the teachings of jesus christ in palestine, and the islamic religion was founded in arabia by muhammad.
10. Thanks to uncle carlos, i appreciate the role of religion in the heritage of many countries.

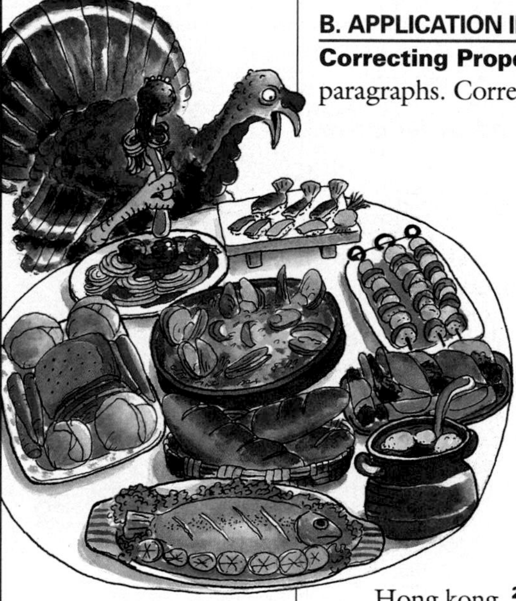

B. APPLICATION IN LITERATURE

Correcting Proper Nouns and Adjectives Write the following paragraphs. Correct errors in capitalization. (20 errors)

[11]"Thanksgiving is an important american holiday," poppa would say. [12]"You kids are americans, and you ought to celebrate important American holidays. [13]On thanksgiving, you eat turkey. [14]Would you want People to think you were ungrateful?" [15]Poppa came from poland, and he was very big on Holidays, and being an American. There was no arguing with him. [16]They had Turkey every year.

[17]Most of the kids in the Neighborhood had the same scene at home. [18]Some of them liked turkey, some of them didn't—but they all had it on thanksgiving. [19]They all had fathers like arthur bobowicz's Father—they came from italy, and the ukraine, and Puerto rico, and Hong kong. [20]The kids were all being raised to be americans, and everyone's Father knew that Americans eat turkey on thanksgiving.

D. Manus Pinkwater, *The Hoboken Chicken Emergency*

FOR MORE PRACTICE
See page 631.

Literature Connection

Author Note D. Manus Pinkwater, also known as Daniel Pinkwater and Manus Pinkwater, is the author of more than twenty books for children and young adults. A world traveler, Pinkwater was born in Tennessee and lived for many years in Hoboken, New Jersey. Humor and fantasy are characteristic of his works, which include *Blue Moose* (1975), *Lizard Music* (1976), *Fat Men from Space* (1977), and *The Magic Moscow* (1980). *The Hoboken Chicken Emergency* (1977) blends fantasy and realism in a comical Thanksgiving tale of a six-foot pet chicken that wreaks havoc in the New Jersey city.

GEOGRAPHICAL NAMES

Capitalize major words in geographical names. Also capitalize names of sections of the United States but not compass directions.

The following are examples of geographical names:

Continents	**N**orth **A**merica, **A**sia, **E**urope
Bodies of Water	the **A**tlantic **O**cean, the **N**ile **R**iver, the **B**lack **S**ea, the **B**ay of **F**undy, the **S**uez **C**anal, **L**ake **O**ntario
Landforms	the **R**ocky **M**ountains, the **N**ullarbor **P**lain, the **K**alahari, **A**concagua, **T**ierra del **F**uego, the **V**ermilion **R**ange
Political Units	**N**ew **Y**ork **C**ity, **W**est **V**irginia, **T**hailand, the **P**rovince of **B**ritish **C**olumbia
Public Areas	**D**inosaur **N**ational **M**onument, **C**entral **P**ark, **C**herokee **N**ational **F**orest, **F**ort **M**cHenry, **P**oint **L**obo **S**tate **R**eserve
Roads and Highways	**I**nterstate 80, **R**oute 41, **S**tate **S**treet, **F**ifth **A**venue, **B**lue **S**tar **H**ighway

Directions and Sections

Capitalize the names of sections of the United States and proper adjectives derived from them.

Many large cities are located in the **N**ortheast.
The **S**outhwest is known for its hot, dry weather.
The **W**est has many mountain resorts.
Tornadoes sometimes sweep across the **M**idwestern prairies.

Do not capitalize directions of the compass or adjectives derived from them.

The flight **e**ast was smooth.
I drove **s**outh along the coast.
He likes **n**orthern winters.
The **w**estern route is scenic.

GEOGRAPHICAL NAMES

Objectives

- To correctly capitalize geographical names and adjectives derived from those names
- To use lowercase letters for compass directions and for adjectives derived from those directions

Writing

- To correct capitalization errors in writing

Teaching Strategies

STUMBLING BLOCK Remind students to use lowercase letters when referring to a geographical place, but not when using its proper name:

When we arrived at Dinosaur National Monument, the monument was closed.

Many ships have used the Panama Canal since the canal was built.

HELPFUL HINT: GEOGRAPHICAL NAMES Note that major words in the names of buildings, bridges, and other structures are also capitalized:

the Taj Mahal
the Golden Gate Bridge
Hoover Dam
the Holland Tunnel
the Leaning Tower of Pisa
the Statue of Liberty

Additional Resource

Grammar and Usage Practice Book, p. 113

Social Studies Connection

You might discuss with students the major landmarks and geography of your community or state. As students name a place or describe its location, have them write the name and relevant directions on the board. Discuss the correct capitalization with students.

Writing Theme: Adventurers

Suggest that students use these exercises as a springboard to writing. Other related areas that they might explore include the following:

- mountain-climbing gear
- Arctic or Antarctic explorers
- Charles A. Lindbergh's adventures
- Beryl Markham's adventures

Answers to Practice Your Skills

A. Concept Check

Geographical Names

Answers are shown on page.

B. Proofreading Skill

Correct Capitalization

Errors in proofreading exercises are counted as follows: (1) Each word is counted as one error. For example, a misspelled word is one error; two initials and a last name not capitalized are counted as three errors. (b) Run-on sentences and sentence fragments are each counted as one error, even though the correction involves both punctuation and capitalization corrections.

Errors on shown on page. See revision below.

As a child in the Midwest, Amelia Earhart lived in Kansas, Iowa, Minnesota, Missouri, and Illinois. However, it was in California that she first flew an airplane. In 1928 she became the first woman passenger to fly across the Atlantic Ocean. Four years later she became the first woman pilot to fly solo across the Atlantic. She was also the first woman to make a solo flight from New York to Los Angeles and back. In 1935 she became the first person to fly from Hawaii to California. She was also the first to fly solo from Los Angeles to Mexico City, then across the Gulf of Mexico and on to Newark, New Jersey. Two years later Amelia and her navigator, Fred Noonan, began a round-the-world flight, flying from west to east. Leaving Lae, New Guinea, they headed for Howland Island in the Pacific. They disappeared without a trace.

Writing Theme
Adventurers

Practice Your Skills

A. CONCEPT CHECK

Geographical Names Write the words that should be capitalized in each sentence.

1. On May 29, 1953, an explorer from new zealand made history.
2. The explorer was Edmund Hillary, a mountain climber already well-known in europe and north america.
3. Hillary succeeded in reaching the top of mount everest, the highest mountain in the world.
4. According to a survey by the government of india, this mountain towers 29,028 feet.
5. It is part of the himalayas, a great mountain system that separates northern india from tibet, an area in china.
6. This system extends across southern asia, west of the great bend of the indus river and eastward to the brahmaputra river.
7. Many asian legends, including that of the Abominable Snowman, are associated with this mountain system.
8. For his climb, Hillary was knighted by the Queen of england.
9. Besides climbing mount everest, Hillary had other adventures.
10. He crossed antarctica from the pacific ocean to the South Pole.
11. In 1977, Hillary took a jet boat up the ganges river in india.
12. This river flows into the bay of bengal, in the indian ocean.
13. Hillary built schools and a hospital for the Sherpas of nepal.
14. He also established sagarmatha national park.
15. This park helped to preserve the himalayan wilderness.

B. PROOFREADING SKILL

Correct Capitalization Write the paragraph, correcting all errors in capitalization, spelling, punctuation, and grammar. (30 errors)

As a child in the midwest, Amelia Earhart lived in Kansas, Iowa, minnesota, Missouri, and illinois. However, it was in California that she first flue an airplane. In 1928 she became the first women passanger to fly across the Atlantic ocean. Four years later she became the First Woman pilet to fly solo across the atlantic. She was also the first women to make a solo flight from new york to los angeles and back. In 1935 she became the first person. To fly from hawaii to California. She was also the first to fly solo from Los Angeles to Mexico city, then across the gulf of mexico and on to Newark, New jersey.

Two years later Amelia and her navigator, Fred Noonan, began a round-the-world Flight, flying from West to East. Leaving Lae, new guinea, they heeded for Howland island in the Pacific they disappeared without a trace.

MIXED REVIEW • PAGES 616–621

Write the following sentences, adding capital letters where necessary. If a sentence requires no added capitalization, write *Correct.*

1. Myths are traditional stories, usually about superhuman beings. C
2. These stories were passed down from one generation to the next in north america, africa, asia, and europe.
3. An american writer, t. bulfinch, became famous for his popular retelling of these stories.
4. His books introduced generations of readers to greek, roman, celtic, scandinavian, and oriental mythologies.
5. The greeks and romans used myths to help explain the world.
6. According to greek myths, thunder occurred because Zeus hurled thunderbolts from mount olympus.
7. Zeus, the supreme god, was worshiped in elevated places, including Mount Lycaeus in arcadia, mount apesas in Argolis, Mount olympus in macedonia, and mount Ida in crete.
8. Zeus was the father of heracles, one of the greatest heroes of greek mythology.
9. To complete one of his twelve labors, this son of zeus had to journey to the western edge of the ancient world.
10. poseidon ruled the waters, sometimes causing mighty storms to ravage the aegean, the ionian, or the mediterranean sea.
11. The greeks believed that winter came whenever demeter, the mother of persephone, grieved for her absent daughter.
12. Aphrodite, the goddess of love, was worshiped in greece and at mount eryx in sicily, an island off the southern tip of italy.
13. The romans, who adopted much of greek mythology, worshiped their chief god, jupiter, in a temple that graced the capitoline hill in rome.
14. Venus took the place of aphrodite, the goddess who inspired love in humans.
15. A famous statue of venus is displayed at the louvre, a french museum in paris.

FOR MORE PRACTICE
See page 631.

Writing Theme
Myths

CHECK POINT

Writing Theme: Myths

Other related areas students might wish to explore as writing topics include the following:

- words derived from classical mythology, such as *jovial* and *January*
- Scandinavian (Norse) mythology
- creation myths of Africa or North America
- famous art depicting mythological characters

MIXED REVIEW • PAGES 616–621

You may wish to use this activity to check students' mastery of the following concepts:

- proper nouns and proper adjectives
- geographical names

Words to be capitalized are shown on page. Sentence 1 is correct.

ORGANIZATIONS, HISTORY, AND TIME

Objectives

- To capitalize correctly the names of organizations and institutions, historical events, documents, periods of time, months, days, and holidays
- To use lowercase letters for common nouns referring to organization and institutions and for the names of the seasons

Writing

- To correct capitalization errors in writing

Teaching Strategies

ASSESSMENT: SPOT CHECK As you read aloud the following sentences, ask students to identify whether the italicized words are common nouns that should not be capitalized or proper nouns that should be capitalized.

We attend *Barton Junior High School.*

The *school* is across the street from the *state university.*

It is the oldest *junior high school* in the *city,* having opened in the *fall* of 1949.

The *Heywood Construction Company* is building our *football stadium.*

My *mother* has worked for the *company* since last *June.*

STUMBLING BLOCK Note that centuries and decades are not capitalized, although historical terms or nicknames for those time periods are capitalized:

the twentieth century

the twenties

the Roaring Twenties

Additional Resource

Grammar and Usage Practice Book, p. 114

ORGANIZATIONS, HISTORY, AND TIME

Capitalize the names of

- organizations
- institutions
- historical events
- documents
- periods of time
- months
- days
- holidays

Organizations and Institutions

Capitalize all the important words in the names of organizations and institutions, including their abbreviations.

Winston **P**ark **H**igh **S**chool
University of **T**exas
Affordable **R**oofing **C**o.
City of **L**ombard
Prentice **W**omen's **H**ospital
OAS
United **N**ations
Park **M**iddle **S**chool

Do not capitalize such words as *school, college, church,* and *hospital* when they are not used as parts of names.

There will be a pep rally at **s**chool.
My mother is teaching two classes at the **u**niversity.
Turn left at the **c**hurch, then go right at the traffic light.

Events, Documents, and Periods of Time

Capitalize the names of historical events, documents, and periods of time.

Battle of **N**ew **O**rleans
Civil **W**ar
Gettysburg **A**ddress
Treaty of **G**hent
Age of **R**eason
Reconstruction

Months, Days, and Holidays

Capitalize the names of months, days, and holidays but not the names of seasons.

June
Thursday
Independence **D**ay
Memorial **D**ay
Presidents' **D**ay
autumn

Practice Your Skills

A. CONCEPT CHECK

Organizations, History, and Time Write the words that should be capitalized in each sentence.

1. George C. Marshall, who was born on new year's eve, 1880, made history as a soldier and a statesman.
2. After graduating from the virginia military institute, Marshall received a commission as a second lieutenant.
3. In 1918 he helped plan the final battles of world war I.
4. On september 1, 1939, world war II erupted in Europe.
5. As Chief of Staff, George C. Marshall helped make the U.S. army the greatest fighting force in history.
6. On tuesday, january 21, 1947, he was appointed Secretary of State.
7. Marshall gave an address at harvard university in late spring.
8. In this address he proposed the european recovery program.
9. This program, called the marshall plan, provided about $13 billion to help Europe rebuild after world war II.
10. Marshall, who died on october 16, 1959, is buried at arlington national cemetery.

B. REVISION SKILL

Correcting Capitalization Errors Write the following sentences, correcting all errors in capitalization.

11. Who could have predicted that Woodrow Wilson, a former University professor, would lead the u.s. in war and peace?
12. In march 1913, president Woodrow wilson took office.
13. In the Winter of 1913, he signed the federal reserve act, which changed the banking system in the united states.
14. When he signed the declaration of war against Germany in the Spring of 1917, America entered world war I.
15. On monday, november 11, 1918, the war ended.
16. november 11 became armistice day and later veterans' day.
17. After the War, Wilson helped draw up the treaty of versailles.
18. A provision of this treaty established the league of nations, an international association to promote peace.
19. Although the Association was Wilson's idea, the United States never became a member nation.
20. Wilson left office in march 1921, with the world at peace.

Writing Theme
Leaders in War and Peace

FOR MORE PRACTICE
See pages 631–632.

Writing Theme: Leaders in War and Peace

Other related areas students might wish to explore as writing topics include the following:

- recipients of the Nobel Peace Prize
- Winston Churchill and World War II
- the founding of the United Nations

Answers to Practice Your Skills

A. Concept Check
Organizations, History, and Time
Answers are shown on page.

B. Revision Skill
Correcting Capitalization Errors
Words to be capitalized and words incorrectly capitalized are shown on page.

LANGUAGES, PEOPLES, COURSES, TRANSPORTATION, AND ABBREVIATIONS

Objectives

- To capitalize correctly the names of languages, races, ethnic groups, nationalities, religions, and transportation vehicles
- To use capital and lowercase letters appropriately for names of school subjects
- To capitalize the abbreviations *B.C., A.D., A.M.,* and *P.M.*

Writing

- To correct capitalization errors in writing

Teaching Strategies

COOPERATIVE LEARNING This lesson presents several abbreviations that students may take for granted. Have volunteers research and report to the class on the meaning of these abbreviations:

B.C. (before Christ)

A.D. (*Anno Domini*—"in the year of the Lord")

A.M. (*ante meridiem*—"before noon")

P.M. (*post meridiem*—"after noon")

U.S.S. (United States Ship, *or* United States Steamer, *or* United States Steamship)

Students also should be aware of the abbreviations C.E. (Common Era) and B.C.E. (Before the Common Era), which sometimes replace A.D. and B.C.

Additional Resource

Grammar and Usage Practice Book, pp. 115–116

LANGUAGES, PEOPLES, COURSES, TRANSPORTATION, AND ABBREVIATIONS

Capitalize the names of
- languages
- races
- nationalities
- religions
- courses
- transportation

Capitalize abbreviations:
- B.C.
- A.D.
- A.M.
- P.M.

Languages, Races, Nationalities, and Religions

Capitalize the names of languages, races, ethnic groups, nationalities, religions, and the adjectives derived from them.

Korean **C**aucasian **F**rench **C**hristianity
Bantu **H**ispanics **N**igerian **M**uslim

School Subjects

Do not capitalize the names of school subjects unless they are languages or unless a course name is followed by a number.

World **H**istory II **m**athematics **B**iology I

Ships, Trains, Aircraft, Automobiles

Capitalize the names of ships, trains, and aircraft. Capitalize brand names of automobiles.

M*ayflower* ***S****anta* ***F****e* ***C****hief* ***S****pruce* ***G****oose*
U.S.S. M*issouri* ***V****oyager 2* **G**old **R**acer

Abbreviations

Capitalize the abbreviations *B.C., A.D., A.M.,* and *P.M.*

Native Americans used canoes perhaps as early as 3000 **B.C.**
Eric the Red sailed a Viking ship to Greenland in **A.D.** 982.
The plane will arrive at 10:45 **A.M.**, not 11:45 **P.M.**

Writing TIP

Remember to place the abbreviation *A.D.* before the year and the abbreviation *B.C.* after the year.

624 Grammar Handbook

Practice Your Skills

A. CONCEPT CHECK

Languages, Peoples, Courses, Transportation, and Abbreviations Write the words that should be capitalized.

1. For centuries, the legend of Atlantis, an island that supposedly sank into the sea, has fascinated europeans.
2. The ancient greeks believed that the people of a large island named Atlantis once ruled the western parts of the european and african continents.
3. The tale of Atlantis first appeared in two dialogues by Plato, the *Timaeus* and the *Critias,* written in the fourth century b.c.
4. Students in philosophy I might read these dialogues, which recount the destruction of Atlantis as a result of the people's greed.
5. They might also read *The New Atlantis,* an account of an ideal state by Francis Bacon, an english writer.
6. Plato's tale may derive from accounts of volcanic eruptions that destroyed the island of Thira in 1470 b.c.
7. James Mavor, an american, tested this theory in the 1960s.
8. Aboard the research ship *chain,* Mavor sailed to the Aegean Sea to explore the sunken island of Thira.
9. This island once belonged to an ancient cretan civilization named after the legendary King Minos.
10. Mavor concluded this minoan island was the legendary Atlantis.

B. PROOFREADING SKILL

Capitalization Rewrite this paragraph, correcting all errors in capitalization, spelling, punctuation, and grammar. (18 errors)

Late on the night of april 14, 1912, the *titanic* radioed for help. The british luxury liner, the largest Ship ever built up to that time, had struck an iceberg in the Atlantic Ocean? At 2:20 a.m. on April 15, the *titanic*, with more than fifteen hundred people still abroad, sank into the sea, survivors in lifeboats on the icy waters watched in horor. Responding to the destress call, the first rescue ship arived around 4:00 a.m. The *carpathia* picked up more than seven hundred survivors and took them to New York city. At the time of the disaster, another liner, the *californian*, was less than twenty miles away. However, no operator was on duty. To recieve the radio signal.

Writing Theme
Lost at Sea

An artist's representation of *Alvin,* a research submersible, as it explores the stern of the sunken *Titanic.*

FOR MORE PRACTICE
See page 632.

Writing Theme: Lost at Sea

Other related areas students might wish to explcre as writing topics include the following:

- the Bermuda Triangle
- the sinking of the *Andrea Doria*
- hunting for sunken treasure
- the legend of the *Flying Dutchman*

A. Concept Check
Languages, Peoples, Courses, Transportation, and Abbreviations

Answers are shown on page.

B. Proofreading Skill
Capitalization

Errors are shown on page.

Late on the night of April 14, 1912, the *Titanic* radioed for help. The British luxury liner, the largest ship ever built up to that time, had struck an iceberg in the Atlantic Ocean. At 2:20 A.M. on April 15, the *Titanic,* with more than fifteen hundred people still aboard, sank into the sea. Survivors in lifeboats on the icy waters watched in horror. Responding to the distress call, the first rescue ship arrived around 4:00 A.M. The *Carpathia* picked up more than seven hundred survivors and took them to New York City. At the time of the disaster, another liner, the *Californian,* was less than twenty miles away. However, no operator was on duty to receive the radio signal.

ART NOTE

The picture of the *Alvin* and the sunken *Titanic* is by Ken Marschall, an artist who specializes in maritime paintings. An expert on the *Titanic,* Marschall studied thousands of photographs before creating the painting. It is one of several used to illustrate a book about the *Titanic* by scientist Robert D. Ballard, who discovered the sunken ship on the ocean floor.

CHECK POINT

Writing Theme: The Olympic Games

Other related areas students might wish to explore as writing topics include the following:

- Olympic sports of ancient Greece, as compared to modern Olympic sports
- how athletes qualify for Olympic competition
- the Olympic career of Jim Thorpe or Wilma Rudolph
- suggested events for future Olympics

MIXED REVIEW • PAGES 622–625

You may wish to use this activity to check students' mastery of the following capitalization concepts:

- organizations, history, and time
- languages, peoples, courses, transportation, and abbreviations

A. Answers are shown on page.

B. Answers are shown on page. Number 20 is correct.

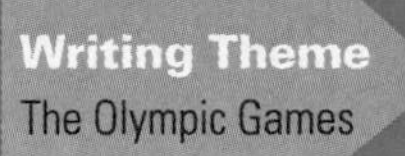

Writing Theme
The Olympic Games

CHECK POINT

MIXED REVIEW • PAGES 622–625

A. Write the words that should be capitalized in each sentence.

1. The ancient greeks originated the olympic games as part of religious festivals honoring Zeus, the ruler of the gods.
2. The first competitions were probably held in 776 b.c.
3. After the romans conquered Greece during the second century b.c., the games gradually lost their religious meaning.
4. Theodosius, a roman emperor, ended the games in a.d. 394.
5. In the 1890s, Baron Pierre de Coubertin, a french educator who was born on new year's day, organized the international olympic committee.
6. The members of this committee all spoke french or english.
7. At 2 p.m. on sunday, april 10, 1896, the marathon began.
8. A young greek shepherd won this race, earning the first gold medal for the homeland of the olympic games.
9. Jesse Owens, an african american who excelled in track and field at ohio state university, won four gold medals in 1936.
10. Because of world war II, the olympic games were canceled in 1940 and 1944.

The Unified Team at the opening ceremonies of the 1992 Summer Olympics in Barcelona, Spain.

B. Write the following sentences, adding capital letters where necessary. If a sentence needs no added capitalization, write *Correct.*

11. The french hosted the XVI olympic winter games.
12. The opening ceremonies took place in Albertville, France, on saturday, february 8, 1992.
13. One of the trains known as the tom george victor, or the tgv, brought many spectators from Paris to Albertville each day.
14. The XVI winter olympics were important for several reasons.
15. The ussr, which had won many gold medals since world war II, was no longer one nation.
16. Athletes from this former nation became the unified team.
17. Also, for the first time since 1964, german athletes marched as members of a single nation.
18. On monday, february 10, Bonnie Blair made history.
19. She became the first american woman to win a gold medal for speed skating in two different winter olympics.
20. The Olympic Games were held during both winter and summer in 1992. C

626 Grammar Handbook

FIRST WORDS

Capitalize the first word in sentences, most lines of poetry, quotations, outline entries, and the closings of letters. Capitalize the first word and all important words in the greetings of letters and in titles.

Sentences

Capitalize the first word of every sentence.

Did you see that movie about baseball?
The main character is a farmer who builds a baseball field.

Poetry

Capitalize the first word in most lines of poetry.

Sometimes in modern poetry, the lines of a poem do not begin with a capital letter. The following poem shows the traditional style for capitalization of poetry.

Gaily bedight,
A gallant knight,
In sunshine and in shadow,
Had journeyed long,
Singing a song,
In search of Eldorado.
Edgar Allan Poe, "Eldorado"

Quotations

Capitalize the first word of a direct quotation.

Jennifer exclaimed, "**T**his book would make a great movie!"

Do not capitalize the first word of the second part of a divided quotation unless it starts a new sentence.

"**I** think," replied Sasha, "**t**hat book was made into a very popular movie."
"**Y**ou are right," said Dan. "**T**he movie was made in 1990."

To add a lively touch to your writing, try using a direct quotation now and then.

FIRST WORDS

Objectives

- To capitalize the first words of sentences, of lines of most poetry, of direct quotations, and of outline entries
- To capitalize all important words in the greeting of a letter, but only the first word of the closing
- To capitalize the first, last, and all other important words in titles

Writing

- To correct capitalization errors in writing

Teaching Strategies

LINKING GRAMMAR AND WRITING Note that the first word of a direct quotation is always capitalized only in conversations. When quoted words are not part of a conversation, a capital letter is used only if the quotation is given as a complete sentence:

According to Thomas Jefferson, "All men are created equal."

According to Thomas Jefferson, all people have a right to "life, liberty, and the pursuit of happiness."

Literature Connection

Author Note Edgar Allan Poe (1809–1849) is one of early America's best-known authors. Famous for such poems as "The Raven" and "The Bells," Poe was also the father of the detective story, a master of the horror story, and one of the first literary critics in the United States. His most popular short stories include "The Tell-Tale Heart," "The Fall of the House of Usher," "The Pit and the Pendulum," and "The Murders in the Rue Morgue."

HELPFUL HINT: GREETINGS OF LETTERS Note that a colon is used after the greeting of a business letter; a comma is used after the greeting of an informal, or friendly, letter.

STUMBLING BLOCK: NEWSPAPER AND MAGAZINE TITLES Note that the words *the* and *magazine* should be capitalized and italicized, or underlined, only if they are part of the newspaper's or magazine's name:

Do you read the *Boston Globe?*

Many nineteenth-century writers contributed to *The Gentleman's Magazine.*

Gardeners often subscribe to *Horticulture* magazine.

Additional Resource

Grammar and Usage Practice Book, pp. 117–118

Outlines

Capitalize the first word in each entry of an outline.

I. **M**otion pictures
  A. **S**tory lines
    1. **O**riginal scripts
    2. **B**ook adaptations
  B. **C**ostume design

Letters

Capitalize all the important words in the greeting of a letter.

Dear **M**s. **H**ardin:	**D**ear **D**r. **M**artinez:	**D**ear **M**rs. **W**ong:
Dear **M**adam:	**D**ear **P**ublisher:	**D**ear **A**nton,

Do not capitalize the word *or* or *and* in a greeting.

Dear **S**ir or **M**adam: **D**ear **M**r. and **M**rs. **C**ortesi:

In the closing of a letter, capitalize only the first word of the phrase.

Sincerely yours, **Y**ours truly,

Titles

Capitalize the first word, the last word, and all important words in the titles of books, poems, short stories, articles, newspapers, magazines, plays, motion pictures, works of art, television programs, and musical compositions.

Articles (the words *a, an,* and *the*), conjunctions, and prepositions with fewer than five letters are not usually considered important words. However, note that an article, a conjunction, or a preposition used as the first or last word of a title must be capitalized.

Book	***T**he **I**sland of the **B**lue **D**olphins*
Poem	"**T**he **D**ream **K**eeper"
Story	"**T**o **B**uild a **F**ire"
Article	"**H**arnessing **N**uclear **F**usion"
Play	***T**he **S**ound of **M**usic*
Magazine	***R**eader's **D**igest*
Movie	***F**ield of **D**reams*

Writing TIP

The titles of books, plays, magazines and newspapers, and movies are underlined when typed or written. The titles of poems, short stories, and articles are enclosed in quotation marks.

Literature Connection

Point out that some poets experiment with capitalization. Emily Dickinson (1830–1886), for example, used capital letters to stress key ideas:

I'm Nobody! Who are you?
Are you — Nobody — Too? . . .
How dreary — to be — Somebody!

E. E. Cummings (1894–1962) experimented with lowercase letters in unusual places, and with words oddly placed on the page.

your little voice
          Over the wires came leaping
and i felt suddenly
dizzy

Practice Your Skills

A. CONCEPT CHECK

First Words and Titles Write the words that should be capitalized in the following letter.

dear cecily,

have you seen any good movies lately? I just saw *white Fang* on videotape. it is based on the novel *White fang* by Jack London. it is about a wolf who is tamed and lives with people. "this movie," one critic said, "is dynamite entertainment." was that critic ever right!

Mom told me that other books by Jack London have also been made into movies. According to Mom, "the movie version of *the call of the wild* is great!" I'm going to see if the movies *adventures of martin eden* and *the sea wolf* are on videotape. mom suggested that I compare the movies with the books for my report. Here is the first part of my outline:

I. the works of Jack London
  A. the stories in his books
  B. movie adaptations

Why don't you rent the videotape *white fang* and let me know what you think of it?

your friend,
angelo

B. PROOFREADING SKILL

Correcting Errors Write the paragraphs, correcting all errors in capitalization, spelling, punctuation, and grammar. (18 errors)

Lewis Carroll's classick tale *alice's adventures in wonderland* was published in 1865. in this imaginative story, Alice tries to recal a poem that she mistakenly thinks begins like this:

how doth the little crocodile
improve his shiny tail,

alice then meets extraordinary characters. As she wanders through Wonderland. Suddenly, she hears her sister exclaim, "wake up, Alice dear!" it had all been a dreem!

In 1951, Walt Disney produced an animated movie titled *alice in wonderland,* which was based on the book. since then, people of all ages have enjoyed the delightfull cartoon characters romping through Wonderland in the movie?

Writing Theme
Books into Movies

Alice, the Mad Hatter, and the White Rabbit from Walt Disney's 1951 animated version of *Alice in Wonderland.*

FOR MORE PRACTICE
See page 632.

Writing Theme: Books into Movies

Other related areas students might wish to explore as writing topics include the following:

- other classic works that have become popular films
- literary agents and the negotiation of movie rights
- a book students think should be made into a film

Answers to Practice Your Skills

A. Concept Check
First Words and Titles

Answers are shown on page.

B. Proofreading Skill
Correcting Errors

Errors are shown on page.

Lewis Carroll's classic tale *Alice's Adventures in Wonderland* was published in 1865. In this imaginative story, Alice tries to recall a poem that she mistakenly thinks begins like this:

How doth the little crocodile
Improve his shining tail. . . .

Alice then meets extraordinary characters as she wanders through Wonderland. Suddenly, she hears her sister exclaim, "Wake up, Alice dear!" It had all been a dream!

In 1951, Walt Disney produced an animated movie titled *Alice in Wonderland,* which was based on the book. Since then, people of all ages have enjoyed the delightful cartoon characters romping through Wonderland in the movie.

CHECK POINT

Writing Theme: On Stage

Other related areas students might wish to explore as writing topics include the following:

- other famous works that became Broadway musicals (for example, the origins of *The King and I; The Secret Garden; West Side Story; Annie;* and *Kiss Me, Kate)*
- the development of a Broadway show, from original idea to opening night
- careers in the performing arts

MIXED REVIEW • PAGES 627–629

You may wish to use this activity to check students' mastery of the following concept:

- first words

Words to be capitalized and words incorrectly capitalized are shown on page.

Writing Theme
On Stage

MIXED REVIEW • PAGES 627–629

Write each sentence, correcting all errors in capitalization.

1. According to the *Information Please almanac,* some of the most popular musicals on Broadway were adapted from other famous works.
2. In 1981 Andrew lloyd Webber set poems to music in *cats*.
3. Webber selected poems from *Old possum's Book of practical cats* by T. s. eliot.
4. Frank Rich of the *New york times* said, "the songs—and *Cats* is all songs—give each cat his or her voice."
5. The most popular song from this Musical was "memory."
6. In the musical *annie*, the most loved Song was "Tomorrow."
7. The first line from this song begins this way:
   the sun will come out tomorrow.
8. *Annie* features popular characters from *Little orphan annie*, a comic strip by harold gray.
9. The strip first appeared in the *new york Daily News* in 1924.
10. The musical *hello, Dolly!* is based on *The matchmaker,* a Play written by thornton Wilder in 1954.
11. This play is a revision of Wilder's earlier play, *the merchant of Yonkers.*
12. the Idea for *The Merchant of yonkers* came from an austrian play by Johann nestroy.
13. in alan lerner and frederick loewe's *My fair lady,* professor Henry Higgins and flower seller eliza Doolittle are the main characters.
14. *"my Fair Lady,"* Brooks atkinson said in the *New York times,* "Is the finest musical play in years."
15. It is based on george bernard Shaw's Comedy *Pygmalion* that mocks the english class system.
16. Shaw adapted the greek myth of pygmalion and galatea.
17. according to this myth, Pygmalion made a Statue of the perfect woman, galatea, which then came to Life.
18. Like *Hello, dolly!* and *my Fair Lady, Oklahoma!* is based on an earlier play, *Green grow the lilacs,* by Lynn Riggs.
19. *Oklahoma!* was the First musical on which richard rodgers and oscar hammerstein II collaborated.
20. they later wrote several more musicals together, including *south Pacific, The King and i,* and *The sound of music.*

A. Capitalizing Proper Nouns and Adjectives Write the words that should be capitalized in each sentence.

1. i admire women who braved the american frontier.
2. narcissa prentiss whitman and her husband, dr. marcus whitman, were missionaries and teachers of the bible.
3. She was the first white woman to follow the oregon trail.
4. She and her husband settled in waiilatpu.
5. henrietta chamberlain king helped her husband, captain richard king, build a cattle ranch near brownsville, texas.
6. mrs. king dealt with mexican settlers and union soldiers.
7. After the captain's death, henrietta ran the king ranch alone.
8. My great-grandmother grew up in what is now wyoming.
9. She told grandpa stories about teaching in south pass city.
10. i would like to write about frontier women like her.

B. Capitalizing Geographical Names Write the words that should be capitalized in each sentence.

11. The colorado river, one of the longest rivers in north america, is a source of fresh water in the american southwest.
12. This river flows across five states—colorado, utah, arizona, nevada, and california—and ninety miles of mexico.
13. The colorado begins at la poudre pass in the rocky mountains.
14. Snows from the tetons and the uintas melt into the river.
15. The green river, the san juan river, and the gunnison river flow into the colorado.
16. Over time, the river formed the walls of the grand canyon.
17. Each year tourists visit grand canyon national park.
18. The hoover dam on the colorado provides electricity for southern california.
19. The city of los angeles gets its water from the colorado.
20. The colorado river mouth empties into the gulf of california.

C. Capitalizing Organizations, History, and Time Write the words that should be capitalized in each sentence.

21. The United States and Spain signed a treaty in february 1819.
22. The adams-onis treaty drew up a western boundary for the U. S.
23. The mexican war resulted from long-standing border disputes.
24. When Texas became a state in december 1845, Mexico broke off diplomatic relations with the United States.

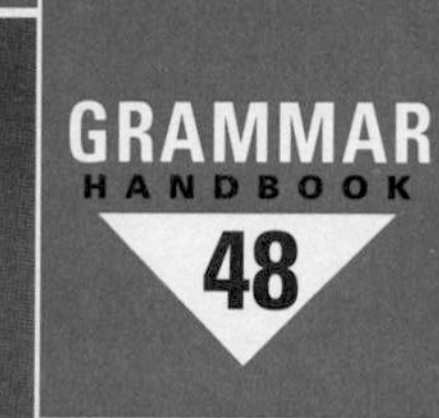

Writing Theme
The American West

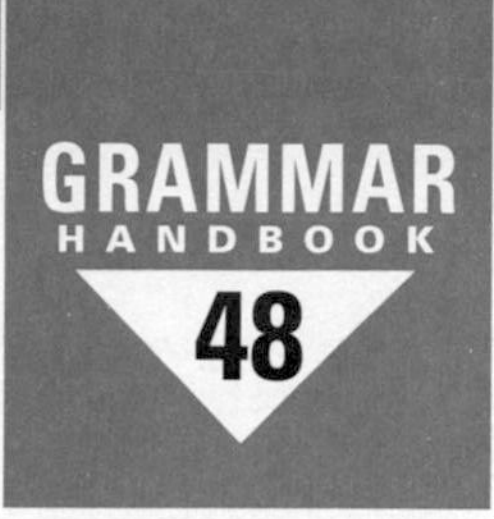

ADDITIONAL PRACTICE

Each of these exercises correlates to a section of Handbook 48, "Capitalization." The exercises may be used for more practice, for reteaching, or for review of the concepts presented.

Additional Resource

Grammar and Usage Practice Book, p. 120

Writing Theme: The American West

Other related areas students might wish to explore as writing topics include the following:

- Sacajawea and the Lewis and Clark expedition
- the Oregon Trail
- the California Gold Rush
- the Rio Grande
- Southwestern design and fashion

A. Capitalizing Proper Nouns and Adjectives

Answers are shown on page.

B. Capitalizing Geographical Names

Answers are shown on page.

C. Capitalizing Organizations, History, and Time

Answers are shown on page.

D. Capitalizing Languages, Peoples, Courses, Transportation, and Abbreviations
Answers are shown on page.

E. Capitalizing First Words and Titles
Answers are shown on page.

25. On may 13, 1846, congress declared war on Mexico.
26. American and Mexican forces had clashed at the battle of palo alto.
27. On christmas day, American troops won at El Brazito.
28. The treaty of guadalupe hidalgo, signed on february 2, 1848, recognized the Rio Grande as the Mexico-Texas border.
29. As a result of the mexican war, the United States gained more than 525,000 square miles.
30. This land is known as the mexican cession.

D. Capitalizing Languages, Peoples, Courses, Transportation, and Abbreviations Write the words that should be capitalized in each sentence.

31. american history I classes study native american cultures.
32. The hohokam were a group of north american indians.
33. They lived between 300 b.c. and a.d. 1400 in what is now Arizona.
34. This was long before Columbus's ships—the *niña,* the *pinta,* and the *santa maría*—reached the West Indies.
35. The hohokam lived together in small farming villages.
36. Sometime between 3000 b.c. and a.d. 500, the hohokam built their first irrigation canal.
37. After a.d. 500, they built ball courts like those of the maya.
38. The hohokam disappeared during the early fifteenth century.
39. The hohokam may have been the ancestors of the pima indians.
40. The name may be a pima term meaning "those who have vanished."

E. Capitalizing First Words and Titles Write the words that should be capitalized in each sentence.

41. Painter georgia O'Keeffe lived in the New Mexico desert.
42. The drawing *the maid of athens* inspired her to try painting.
43. Her high school yearbook was called the *Mortar board yearbook.*
44. it contained a rhyme about her.
45. "o is for O'Keeffe, an artist divine;
her paintings are perfect and her drawings are fine."
46. Her paintings include *summer days* and *Ranchos church.*
47. they capture the stark beauty of the Southwest.
48. O'Keeffe said, "i found my inspirations and painted them."
49. "it's mostly a lot of nerve," she also said, "and a lot of very, very hard work."
50. In 1976 her autobiography, *Georgia o'Keeffe,* was published.

A. Rewrite the following letter, correcting the words that should be capitalized.

dear andy,

You asked me, "what is it like to live in australia?" We live in a state called the northern territory on a large sheep station, or ranch, called clonkilty. it is named after the irish village my great-grandparents came from. Have you heard of a book called *a town like alice?* It's about our nearest town, alice springs, which is one hundred kilometers away, almost in the center of australia. Alice springs began as a station on the telegraph line from adelaide in the south to darwin in the north. When we go to town, we can drive down the stuart highway, but we usually fly in our airplane, *the southern cross*. Living so far away from town, i have to attend alice springs's school of the air. That means I use a two-way radio to talk to my teacher, mrs. abruzzi, and my classmates. Last week i played beethoven's *moonlight sonata* over the radio. The whole class meets in alice springs twice a year. In may we attend the camel cup to watch the camel races, and in august we go to the henley-on-todd regatta to watch the boat races. the todd river is dry, so the boats are carried by people!

My older brother, michael, goes to essex house school in sydney, where he lives with aunt janet, my mom's sister. sydney, australia's largest city, is famous for its beautiful bay, the sydney harbour bridge, and the sydney opera house. Most australians live in cities in the southeast, like sydney and melbourne. But i love clonkilty. I like riding around the station on my horse beau, but dad says, "give me a land rover anytime!" (It's like a jeep.) i wish you could visit the australian outback. Please write and tell me more about florida.

your pal,
jamie

B. Write the words that should be capitalized in each sentence.

1. At 10:00 a.m. on september 23, 1988, michael palin walked down the stairs of the reform club in london, england.
2. palin, a british actor and writer, was about to begin circling the world as Phileas Fogg had done.
3. phileas fogg is a fictional character in a jules verne novel.

GRAMMAR HANDBOOK 48

Writing Theme
International Travel

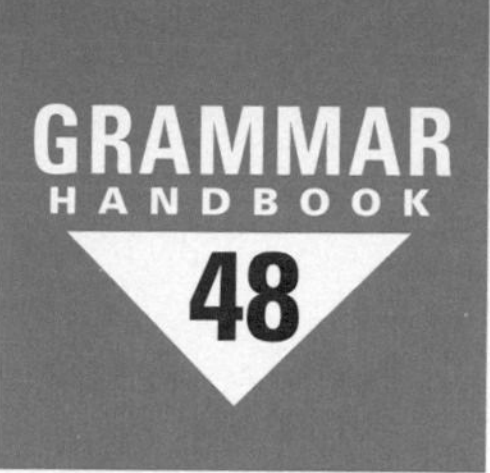

REVIEW

These exercises may be used as a mixed review or as an informal evaluation of the skills presented in Handbook 48, "Capitalization."

Additional Resources

Grammar and Usage Practice Book, p. 21

Tests and Writing Assessment Prompts, Mastery Test, pp. 47–48

Elaboration, Revision, and Proofreading Practice, p. 34

Writing Theme: International Travel

Other related areas students might wish to explore as writing topics include the following:

- a letter of reply from Andy to Jamie about Florida
- Nellie Bly's trip around the world
- Australian geography or history
- one of Thor Heyerdahl's expeditions
- the transatlantic voyage of *Double Eagle II* (a balloon)

A.

Answers are shown on page.

B.

Answers are shown on page.

4. verne published *around the world in eighty days* in 1873 after gaining great popularity in 1870 with his science-fiction adventure, *twenty thousand leagues under the sea.*
5. In the novel, members of the reform club challenge fogg to circle the globe in eighty days.
6. in 1873, this challenge seemed absurd.
7. when palin attempted the journey in 1988, however, people could circle the earth in less than two days by airplane.
8. However, with the support of the british broadcasting company, or BBC, palin tried to re-create phileas fogg's journey.
9. like fogg, palin traveled by boat, train, and other means of transportation available in 1873.
10. unlike fogg, he was accompanied by a television crew from the bbc.
11. The bbc filmed palin's extraordinary journey for a travel documentary.
12. Palin and the film crew sailed across the english channel on the ship *horsa*.
13. Once in paris, france, Palin boarded the *orient express* for a train trip through europe.
14. After a scenic ride through austria, Palin got off the *orient express* in venice, italy.
15. There he boarded the ship *espresso egitto*.
16. The ship crossed the adriatic sea and sailed to greece, crete, and egypt.
17. As the ship approached the coast of egypt, palin thought about alexander the great.
18. Alexander, a mighty greek king, had conquered egypt around 332 b.c.
19. Palin then traveled through arabia, where many people are muslims, worshippers of allah.
20. he visited india, china, singapore, and japan.
21. he crossed the united states by train, dog sled, and balloon.
22. Palin sailed across the atlantic ocean on the ship *leda maersk*.
23. Finally, he arrived back in great britain on december 12, 1988.
24. By 4:55 p.m. of that seventy-ninth day, he once again stood in front of the reform club, just as fogg had.
25. "my journey gave me a sense of global scale," he said, "of the size and variety of this extraordinary planet."

634 Grammar Handbook

WRITING CONNECTIONS

Elaboration, Revision, and Proofreading

Revise this portion of a report by using the directions at the bottom of the page. Then proofread your paper, paying special attention to correcting errors in capitalization. Also look for errors in grammar, punctuation, and spelling.

[1]Alice Walker is an important african-american Novelist, Poet, and Social Activist. [2]She is perhaps best known for her novel The color purple. [3]It won a pulitzer prize and an American Book Award. [4]Walker was born on febuary 9, 1944 in Eatonton, georgia. [5]She was the youngest of eight children in a family of share-croppers. [6]Growing up poor in the south was offen difficult for Walker. [7]When she was eight, she was playing with her Brothers, and a shot from one of there BB guns struck her right eye. [8]She was blinded and scar tissue covered the eye. [9]"I used to pray every night that i would wake up and somehow it would be gone." [10]Finally, when she was 14, she visited her older Brother Bill, who took her to a Hospital. [11]They operated on her eye. [12]"I was a changed person," She said.

1. Add sentence 3 to sentence 2 as a subordinate clause beginning with "which."
2. Add the explanatory words "Walker said" after the quotation in sentence 9.
3. Replace the vague pronoun "they" in sentence 11 with the more precise noun "doctors."
4. Explain the result of the operation by adding the clause "and because the scar was gone, Walker no longer felt ugly and shy" to sentence 11.
5. Divide the passage into paragraphs.

Informative Writing: Reports

Writing a report gives you a chance to explore a topic in depth. (See Workshop 8.) When you revise a report, make sure that you have presented all the information your readers will need. Also check the accuracy of your facts and make sure you have used proper capitalization.

WRITING CONNECTIONS

Elaboration, Revision, and Proofreading

This activity will allow your students to see some of the concepts presented in this handbook at work in part of a research report. By revising and proofreading the passage, students will demonstrate their understanding of capitalization. They also will strengthen their understanding of elaboration techniques.

After students complete their revisions, you may wish to have them exchange papers for an informal peer review. Then bring the class together for a group discussion of the activity.

Revisions may vary slightly. See typical revision below. Elements involving changes are shown in boldface.

Alice Walker is an important African-American novelist, poet, and social activist. She is perhaps best known for her novel *The Color Purple,* **which won a Pulitzer Prize and an American Book Award.**

Walker was born on February 9, 1944, in Eatonton, Georgia. She was the youngest of eight children in a family of sharecroppers.

Growing up poor in the South was often difficult for Walker. When she was eight, she was playing with her brothers, and a shot from one of their BB guns struck her right eye. She was blinded, and scar tissue covered the eye. "I used to pray every night that I would wake up and somehow it would be gone," **Walker said.** Finally, when she was 14, she visited her older brother Bill, who took her to a hospital. **Doctors** operated on her eye, **and because the scar was gone, Walker no longer felt ugly and shy.** "I was a changed person," she said.

Objective

- To use writing prompts and a concrete poem as springboards to informal writing

WRITING WARM-UPS

Remind students that they will not be graded on their responses; rather, the activities are intended as springboards to get students thinking imaginatively about the concepts in this handbook. Encourage students to work on a single activity, unless they express a special interest in exploring more than one.

For the first writing prompt, have students interpret Merriam's poem (intermittent rain; hard rain; intermittent rain; brief sun; more rain; sun and clouds; sun). Suggest that students prewrite by jotting down punctuation marks in different combinations to see what those marks suggest. Students might also check a dictionary or other reference source for other punctuation marks and symbols.

WRITING WARM-UPS

Showers, Clearing Later in the Day

```
 !! !! !!    !  !    !
!!!!!!!!  !!!!  !! !!!
!!!!!!!!!!!!!!!!!!!!!!!!!!!
!!!!!!!!!!!!!!!!!!!!!!!!!!!
!!!!!!!!!!!!!!!!!!!!!!!!!!!!       !!!!!
      !!!!!!!! !!!!!!!!!!!
      **!!!!!!!!!!
          !!  ! !!
          * ! * !

              ..   * ! ! ...
                *..

                    .



                        .


            *


                 .
```

Eve Merriam

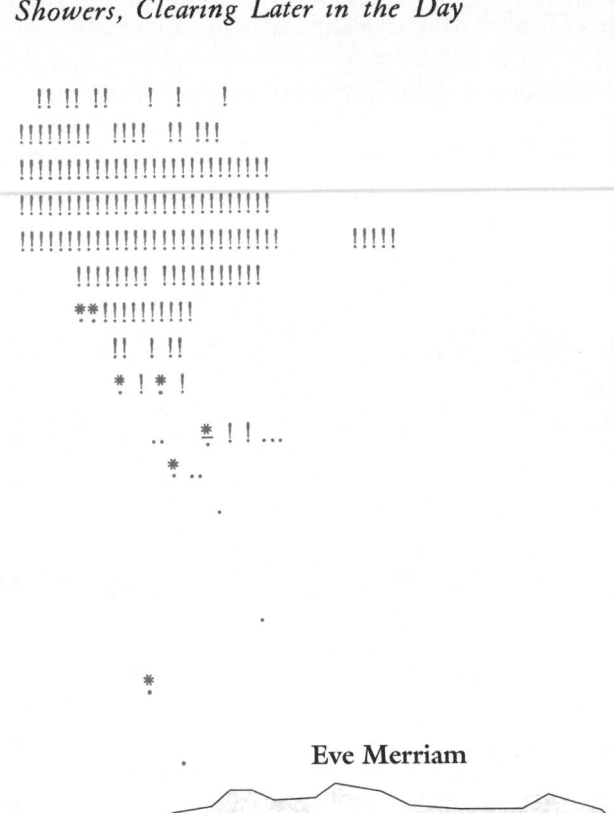

- Make your own poem or drawing using various punctuation marks.
- Write a description of a storm you experienced recently.
- Tell about a time when someone misunderstood something you said or wrote. Use dialogue as you write about this experience.

Punctuation

When do we get to cook Dad?
Lectro
RANGE

Is Dad the cook or the meal? A single mark of punctuation can change the entire meaning of a sentence. Punctuation marks tell you when to pause or to stop completely. They interrupt and add emphasis. They link and they clarify.

In this handbook, you will learn how you can use punctuation to point readers toward your meaning.

Punctuation

Objectives

- To use periods, question marks, and exclamation points correctly
- To use commas correctly to separate ideas and to set off special elements
- To recognize other situations when commas are needed and to use commas correctly in those situations
- To use semicolons and colons correctly
- To use hyphens correctly
- To use apostrophes correctly
- To use quotation marks correctly

Writing

- To use punctuation to make writing clear

INTRODUCING THE HANDBOOK

Write on the board the following sentences:

After eating our dog, Ralph took a nap.

After eating, our dog Ralph took a nap.

Ask how the position of the comma changes the meaning of the sentence. Explain that although the meaning of most sentences does not depend upon a particular mark of punctuation, the purpose of all punctuation is to make sentences clear for the reader.

Have students preview the handbook contents listed in the right column. Point out that by understanding the basic marks of punctuation for writing in English, students will better understand how to clarify words and ideas.

Objectives

- To learn the uses of periods, question marks, and exclamation points as end marks

Writing

- To use end marks correctly in writing

Teaching Strategies

KEY TO UNDERSTANDING: PUNCTUATION AND MEANING

To show how end marks affect the tone of a sentence, write *This is important* on the board; then ask volunteers to read it aloud as if the end punctuation were first a period, then a question mark, and finally, an exclamation point. Point out that the choice of end mark helps determine how the sentence is interpreted.

INDIVIDUALIZING INSTRUCTION: ESL STUDENTS The rules for punctuating sentences vary from language to language. For example, in Hindi and related Indian languages, a vertical bar is used to denote the end of a declarative sentence. In Spanish, in addition to the end mark, there is an inverted exclamation point or question mark at the beginning of an exclamatory or interrogative sentence or phrase. ESL students may try to transfer these rules of punctuation from their native languages to English. Contrast English punctuation rules with the rules from their native languages and allow these students to work in pairs or groups to complete the Practice Your Skills exercises.

LD STUDENTS Students with poor fine-motor skills may have difficulties with this handbook's exercises, due to the amount of writing required. You may wish to limit the number of items these students must answer in each exercise, or allow them to respond orally.

END MARKS

Use a **period,** a **question mark,** or an **exclamation point** to end a sentence.

The tone of voice you use to communicate a message tells a great deal about what you are saying. Your tone may tell that your message is a complete thought, that it is a question, or that it is something about which you are very excited. When you write, punctuation marks called **end marks** do the job your tone of voice does when you speak.

End marks show where sentences end. There are three kinds of end marks: the **period,** the **question mark,** and the **exclamation point.**

The Period

Use a period at the end of a declarative sentence.

A **declarative sentence** is a sentence that makes a statement. You use it to tell something, that is, to give information.

The Statue of Liberty is more than 150 feet tall.
It stands on Liberty Island in New York Harbor.

Use a period at the end of an imperative sentence.

An **imperative sentence** is a sentence that makes a request or tells someone to do something. It is followed by a period except when it expresses a strong emotion. Then it is followed by an exclamation point.

Please board the boat carefully. Watch your step!

Use a period at the end of an indirect question.

An **indirect question** tells what someone asked, without using the person's exact words. If you use the exact words of a person's question, however, the question is a **direct question.** A direct question ends with a question mark. This question mark should always appear within the quotation marks that set off the person's exact words.

638 Grammar Handbook

Indirect Question The tour guide asked if anyone knew who wrote the poem on the statue's base.
Direct Question Dominic asked, "Who wrote the poem?"

The Question Mark

Use a question mark at the end of an interrogative sentence.

An **interrogative sentence** is a sentence that asks a question.

When was the statue erected? Who built the statue?

The Exclamation Point

Use an exclamation point at the end of an exclamatory sentence and after an interjection.

An **exclamatory sentence** is a sentence that expresses strong feeling. An **interjection** is a word or group of words that expresses strong feeling.

Exclamatory Sentence Oh, what a beautiful statue it is!
Interjections Fantastic! Impressive! Great view!

You may also use an exclamation point at the end of an imperative sentence that expresses strong feeling.

Stop! Get back in line!

Exclamation points can be used to add more feeling or emphasis to declarative sentences.

The observation deck of the statue is closed for repairs.
Deck closed! Danger ahead!

Practice Your Skills

CONCEPT CHECK

End Marks In these sentences end marks are used incorrectly or are missing. Rewrite each sentence using the correct end mark.

1. Dad asked if I knew what *Liberty Enlightening the World* is?
2. I replied, "It's the Statue of Liberty, isn't it."
3. The people of France gave Lady Liberty, designed by Frédéric Auguste Bartholdi, to the United States

Writing Theme
Lady Liberty

HELPFUL HINT: EXCLAMATORY SENTENCES You may want to point out that a sentence beginning with *What* or *How* that is not a question is likely to end with an exclamation point; for example, *What a good job you did!* or *How nice you look!* Sentence fragments beginning with *What* or *How* may also be exclamations: *What a guy!*

LINKING GRAMMAR AND WRITING A common writing problem is the overuse of exclamation points. You might explain that if too many sentences end with this mark, the effect of strong feeling is lost. Discuss the kinds of writing that might include exclamatory sentences (personal narratives, short stories, personal letters) and the kinds of writing that use exclamatory sentences only rarely (informational writing, business letters).

Writing Theme: Lady Liberty

Suggest that students use these exercises as a springboard to writing Other related areas that they might explore include the following:

- how the Statue of Liberty was created and brought to America
- Liberty Island today
- Ellis Island as an immigration point of entry
- other national monuments

Answers to Practice Your Skills

Concept Check
End Marks

1. Dad asked if I knew what *Liberty Enlightening the World* is.
2. I replied, "It's the Statue of Liberty, isn't it?"
3. The people of France gave Lady Liberty, designed by Frédéric Auguste Bartholdi, to the United States.

4. Lady Liberty raises a torch in one hand and grasps a tablet with the date of the Declaration of Independence in the other.
5. Do you know why this majestic structure is so important?
6. It symbolizes a new life for immigrants.
7. Could anything other than Lady Liberty have been such a powerful symbol?
8. For more than one hundred years, immigrants have been welcomed by the statue.
9. If you visit it, read Emma Lazarus's poem on its base. The poem is beautiful! *(or* beautiful.)
10. How inspiring! What a magnificent tribute it is to America!

HELPFUL HINT: ABBREVIATIONS
You might explain that an abbreviation that is part of a word, such as *Oct., Wed., Eng.,* and *asst.,* almost always needs a period. However, acronyms and abbreviations that stand for several words in the names of organizations, companies, or government agencies do not usually include periods—for example, NASA, CARE, CORE, CBS, and IBM.

INDIVIDUALIZING INSTRUCTION: BASIC STUDENTS Point out that some dictionaries provide a separate list of abbreviations; others incorporate abbreviations into the body of the dictionary. You may wish to demonstrate how to find abbreviations in the standard school dictionary.

Glorious Lady Freedom (1985–1986), Moneca Calvert. Winner of the Great American Quilt Contest, 1986. The Museum of American Folk Art, The Scotchgard Collection of Contemporary Quilts.

4. Lady Liberty raises a torch in one hand and grasps a tablet with the date of the Declaration of Independence in the other?
5. Do you know why this majestic structure is so important
6. It symbolizes a new life for immigrants?
7. Could anything other than Lady Liberty have been such a powerful symbol!
8. For more than one hundred years, immigrants have been welcomed by the statue!
9. If you visit it, read Emma Lazarus's poem on its base! The poem is beautiful.
10. How inspiring? What a magnificent tribute it is to America.

Other Uses of the Period

Without periods, sentences would run together, and initials and titles would run into names. Abbreviations would look like words. The letters and numbers of outlines and lists would run into the words beside them. Without periods, your writing would be so confusing that no one could understand it.

Use a period after initials and after most abbreviations.

L. L. Corum	Mr. Joe Dawson, Jr.	10:00 A.M.
Sept.	Tues.	4 hr. 16 min.

Some abbreviations do not require periods. When you are not sure whether to use periods following the letters of an abbreviation, look up the abbreviation in a dictionary.

m (*meters*) FM (*frequency modulation*) km (*kilometers*)

Writing **TIP**

Dictionaries vary in their use of periods with abbreviations. Check with your teacher about which dictionary to use.

ART NOTE

When Moneca Calvert of Carmichael, California, visited the Statue of Liberty for the first time, she did not know what to expect. "I was overwhelmed," she said later. "I learned so much about myself and my country." A quilt contest in honor of the statue's hundredth anniversary gave her the chance to express her patriotic feelings.

As Calvert planned her quilt, she thought about the words to "America the Beautiful" and tried to incorporate the song's message into her design. Calvert has been making quilts since 1980 and teaches quiltmaking as well. She worked on this quilt twelve hours a day for more than six months.

Use a period after each number or letter that shows a division of an outline or precedes an item in a list.

Outline	List
I. Automobile racing	1. Formula One racing
A. Racing courses and tracks	2. Sports car racing
1. Road-racing course	3. Indy car racing
2. Oval track	4. Stock car racing
B. Major events	5. Drag racing
1. Le Mans	6. Super Vee racing
2. Indianapolis 500	7. Sprint car racing

Use a period between numerals representing dollars and cents and before a decimal.

$25.95   167.58   66.6%

Practice Your Skills

A. CONCEPT CHECK

Periods Add and delete periods in these sentences.

1. How are A J Foyt, Sr, and Al Unser, Sr, alike?
2. Both have won the Indianapolis 500, or the Indy 500, four times
3. The Indy is held in Indianapolis, Ind, on Memorial Day weekend
4. The race begins promptly at 11:00 AM and lasts between 2 hr 30 min and 4 hr
5. The oval track at the speedway is 2½ (or 25) miles long
6. Drivers race for 500 miles (805 km.), often at speeds greater than 200 m.p.h.
7. Foyt and Unser now have competition from their sons, A J Foyt, Jr, and Al Unser, Jr
8. Other racers include Mario G Andretti and his son Michael
9. In 1990, Al Unser, Jr, was the highest-paid driver of Indy-style cars
10. He earned about $1,936,83300 in that year!

B. DRAFTING SKILL

Periods in an Outline Rewrite this outline, adding and deleting periods and capitalizing the first words of the entries.

I stock car racing.
  A type of cars
    1 late-model sedans
    2 steel bodies.

Writing Theme
Indianapolis 500

FOR MORE PRACTICE
See page 669.

TEACHER'S LOUNGE

"I need the SAT's, ACT's, and GED's—ASAP."

HELPFUL HINT: OUTLINES You may want to point out that the items in a list or an outline do not require end punctuation unless they are complete sentences. The models on the pupil page are phrases—beginning with capital letters but not requiring end punctuation.

Additional Resources

Tests and Writing Assessment Prompts, Pretest, pp. 49–50
Grammar and Usage Practice Book, p. 122–123

Grammar Test Generator

Writing Theme: Indianapolis 500

Suggest that students use these exercises as a springboard to writing. Other related areas that they might explore include the following:
- stock car racing
- road rallying
- Janet Guthrie, auto racing's first woman driver
- the work of a pit crew

Answers to Practice Your Skills

A. Concept Check
Periods

1. How are A. J. Foyt, Jr., and Al Unser, Sr., alike?
2. Both have won the Indianapolis 500, or the Indy 500, four times.
3. The Indy is held in Indianapolis, Ind., on Memorial Day weekend.
4. The race begins promptly at 11:00 A.M. and lasts between 2 hr. 30 min. and 4 hr.
5. The oval track at the speedway is 2 1/2 (or 2.5) miles long.
6. Drivers race for 500 miles (805 km), often at speeds greater than 200 mph.
7. Unser now has competition from his son, Al Unser, Jr.
8. Other racers include Mario G. Andretti and his son Michael.
9. In 1990, Al Unser, Jr., was the highest-paid driver of Indy-style cars.
10. He earned about $1,936,833.00 in that year!

B. Drafting Skill
Periods in an Outline

I. Stock car racing
  A. Types of cars
    1. Late-model sedans
    2. Steel bodies

Objectives

- To recognize the use of commas before conjunctions in compound sentences
- To recognize the use of commas to separate items in a series

Writing

- To use commas to clarify ideas in writing
- To use proofreading skills to correct errors in comma usage

Teaching Strategies

INDIVIDUALIZING INSTRUCTION: BASIC STUDENTS Review with students the definition of a compound sentence: two or more simple sentences joined together by *and, or,* or *but.* For reinforcement, supply a simple sentence, such as *Pete opened the window,* and challenge students to supply a conjunction and a second simple sentence to create a compound sentence. (Sample: *but Nick closed it again)*

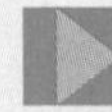

Writing Theme: It's a Snap

Other related areas students might wish to explore as writing topics include the following:

- Ansel Adams
- Dorothea Lange
- George Eastman and the camera
- Louis Daguerre and the history of photography

Answers to Practice Your Skills

A. Concept Check

Commas in Compound Sentences

1. Margaret Bourke-White had always wanted to be a biologist, but she discovered photography in college.

COMMAS THAT SEPARATE IDEAS

Use a **comma** before the conjunction in a compound sentence and to separate items in a series.

When you speak, your pauses and the tone of your voice punctuate what you are saying. However, when you write, commas indicate your pauses and show which words belong together.

Commas in Compound Sentences

Use a comma before the conjunction that joins the clauses of a compound sentence.

Two simple sentences joined by a conjunction become a compound sentence made up of independent clauses.

Matt photographed the event, and he sold his pictures to the newspaper.
Most of his photographs were beautiful, but some were blurry.

A comma is not required in a very short compound sentence in which the parts are joined by *and.* However, always use a comma before the conjunctions *but* and *or.*

Marilena photographed the event and Tony reported it.
Marilena photographed the event, but Tony reported it.

A comma is not required before the conjunction that joins the parts of a compound verb unless there are more than two parts.

Erin entered and won the photography contest.
That camera focuses, flashes, and rewinds automatically.

Writing Theme
It's a Snap

Practice Your Skills

A. CONCEPT CHECK

Commas in Compound Sentences Rewrite the following sentences, adding and deleting commas where necessary.

1. Margaret Bourke-White had always wanted to be a biologist but she discovered photography in college.

642 Grammar Handbook

2. She had to make a decision and it was not an easy one.
3. Would she be a biologist or would she be a photographer?
4. Bourke-White finally decided on a career in photography and she became a pioneer of the photo-essay form of journalism.
5. She organized, and published her photos in books and magazines.
6. During World War II, she became the first U.S. woman war correspondent and she photographed battle scenes.
7. Once she was on a ship that was shot at hit and sunk.
8. She survived the attack, and went on to photograph the war.
9. Her photos stunned shocked and upset many Americans.
10. The war photography helped make Bourke-White famous but it was just a small part of her award-winning work.

B. DRAFTING SKILL

Achieving Clarity with Commas Combine each pair of sentences to form a compound sentence or verb. Add commas and appropriate conjunctions where necessary.

11. Who are *paparazzi*? What do they do?
12. *Paparazzi* are professional photographers. They earn a living by taking and selling their pictures.
13. They may be employees of newspapers. They may be freelancers.
14. Not all professional photographers are *paparazzi.* Some of them are.
15. *Paparazzi* specialize in taking pictures of well-known people. The celebrities do not pose for the pictures.
16. Many people enjoy seeing famous people in candid photos. *Paparazzi* provide such pictures.
17. *Paparazzi* follow celebrities. They photograph celebrities.
18. They take pictures. They do not ask permission to do so.
19. Celebrities may know they're being photographed. They may not.
20. *Paparazzi* stalk the celebrities. They hide near their homes.
21. Many celebrities dislike *paparazzi.* They avoid them.
22. *Paparazzi* followed Elizabeth Taylor. They photographed her.
23. Taylor didn't like the intrusion. She wanted it stopped.
24. She tried to keep her privacy. She wasn't always successful.
25. Should *paparazzi* be able to take candid pictures of celebrities? Should they be stopped?

FOR MORE PRACTICE
See page 669.

2. She had to make a decision, and it was not an easy one.
3. Would she be a biologist, or would she be a photographer?
4. Bourke-White finally decided on a career in photography, and she became a pioneer of the photo-essay form of journalism.
5. She organized and published her photos in books and magazines.
6. During World War II, she became the first U.S. woman war correspondent, and she photographed battle scenes.
7. Once she was on a ship that was shot at, hit, and sunk.
8. She survived the attack and went on to photograph the war.
9. Her photos stunned, shocked, and upset many Americans.
10. The war photography helped make Bourke-White famous, but it was just a small part of her award-winning work.

B. Drafting Skill

Achieving Clarity with Commas

Answers may vary. Possible answers are shown below.

11. Who are *paparazzi,* and what do they do? (or omit comma)
12. *Paparazzi* are professional photographers, and they earn a living by taking and selling their pictures.
13. They may be employees of newspapers, or they may be freelancers.
14. Not all professional photographers are *paparazzi,* but some of them are.
15. *Paparazzi* specialize in taking pictures of well-known people, but the celebrities do not pose for the pictures.
16. Many people enjoy seeing famous people in candid photos, and *paparazzi* provide such pictures.
17. *Paparazzi* follow and photograph celebrities.
18. They take pictures, but they do not ask permission to do so.
19. Celebrities may know they're being photographed, or they may not.
20. *Paparazzi* stalk the celebrities, and they hide near their homes.
21. Many celebrities dislike and avoid *paparazzi.*
22. *Paparazzi* followed and photographed Elizabeth Taylor.
23. Taylor didn't like the intrusion, and she wanted it stopped.
24. She tried to keep her privacy, but she wasn't always successful.
25. Should *paparazzi* be able to take candid pictures of celebrities, or should they be stopped?

Additional Resource

Grammar and Usage Practice Book, pp. 124–125

Writing Theme: On Wheels

Other related areas students might wish to explore as writing topics include the following:

- go-carting
- skateboarding
- roller derbies
- bicycles of the future
- unicycles

Answers to Practice Your Skills

A. Concept Check
Commas in a Series

1. Correct
2. Local businesses sponsored, organized, and monitored the event.

Commas in a Series

Use a comma after every item in a series except the last.

The three or more items in a series can be nouns, verbs, adjectives, adverbs, phrases, independent clauses, or other parts of a sentence.

Kristin**,** Kerry**,** and Tessa ride their bikes to school. (nouns)
Ted located**,** patched**,** and sealed the leak in his tire. (verbs)
I pedaled quickly**,** steadily**,** and calmly. (adverbs)
The racing route wound through the park**,** over the bridge**,** and onto the city streets. (prepositional phrases)
The bicycle race was over**,** the crowd cheered**,** and Terrel accepted the first-place trophy. (independent clauses)

In the examples above, a comma followed by a conjunction precedes the last item in each series. That comma is always used.

If you can use *and* between two or more adjectives that precede a noun and if you can reverse the order of the adjectives without changing the meaning, use a comma after each adjective except the last one.

That crowded**,** narrow path is a long**,** winding**,** bumpy trail.

If two or more adjectives preceding a noun work together to express a single idea, do not use commas between the adjectives.

Luis wants a *big red* bike and *blue racing* skates.

Use commas after the adverbs *first, second, third,* and so on, when these adverbs introduce items in a series.

There are three rules of bicycle safety: first**,** keep your bike repaired; second**,** wear a helmet; third**,** follow the rules of the road.

Practice Your Skills

Writing Theme
On Wheels

A. CONCEPT CHECK

Commas in a Series Write the following sentences, adding commas where needed. If a sentence is correct, write *Correct.*

1. The annual spring bicycle rally was held today.
2. Local businesses sponsored organized and monitored the event.

3. The schools the police department and the recreation center had encouraged riders of all ages to participate in the rally.
4. Riders wove in, out, and in again through the obstacle course.
5. Cyclists sped down the streets over hills and into the park.
6. To join the rally, riders first paid a small fee; second wore helmets; and third demonstrated bicycle safety procedures.
7. You joined the race you pedaled hard and you were in front.
8. You wanted to win, but so did Tanya, Julio, and Jackson.
9. They were strong eager and fast competitors.
10. Your determination, your hard training, and your new bike helped you win.

B. REVISION SKILL

Achieving Clarity Rewrite the following paragraphs, adding commas where necessary to help make the meaning clear. Then write five sentences of your own that contain items in a series.

[11]Did you know that several years ago a popular musical featured performers on roller skates? [12]The dancers in *Starlight Express* skated glided and sped across the stage. [13]They skated up down over and under elaborate stage ramps. [14]Their dynamic athletic and energetic skating dazzled audiences.

[15]This musical health concerns and innovative roller skates have all helped to revive interest in skating. [16]The new skates have wheels down the middle they glide easily and they have an interesting name—Rollerblades. [17]People wear them at rinks on streets and in parks. [18]Rollerblades are fun fast and dangerous. [19]Beginning users should first wear kneepads and elbow pads; second practice in traffic-free areas; and third learn to brake properly. [20]Beginners usually find that Rollerblading is an enjoyable invigorating pastime.

C. PROOFREADING SKILL

Commas in a Series Rewrite the following paragraph, correcting all errors in capitalization, punctuation, and spelling. (15 errors)

As a baby a toddler and a child, you had your "wheals." You rode in strollors, on tricycles, and in little red wagans. Then you got a bicycle you learned to ride it and you could get from place to place on it. In just a few years. You will, first aply for; second test for; and third recieve a learner's permit to drive a car. You are impatiently, and excitedly awating the day when you can drive.

Bicycle race at the 1992 Summer Olympics in Barcelona, Spain.

FOR MORE PRACTICE
See page 669.

3. The schools, the police department, and the recreation center had encouraged riders of all ages to participate in the rally.
4. Correct
5. Cyclists sped down the streets, over hills, and into the park.
6. To join the rally, first riders paid a small fee; second, wore helmets; and third, demonstrated bicycle safety procedures.
7. You joined the race, you pedaled hard, and you were in front.
8. Correct
9. They were strong, eager, and fast competitors.
10. Correct

B. Revision Skill

Achieving Clarity

[11] Did you know that several years ago a popular musical featured performers on roller skates? [12] The dancers in *Starlight Express* skated, glided, and sped across the stage. [13] They skated up, down, over, and under elaborate stage ramps. [14] Their dynamic, athletic, and energetic skating dazzled audiences.

[15] This musical, health concerns, and innovative roller skates have all helped to revive interest in skating. [16] The new skates have wheels down the middle, they glide easily, and they have an interesting name—Rollerblades. [17] People wear them at rinks, on streets, and in parks. [18] Rollerblades are fun, fast, and dangerous. [19] Beginners should observe the following safeguards: first, wear kneepads and elbow pads; second, practice in traffic-free areas; and third, learn to brake properly. [20] Beginners usually find that Rollerblading is an enjoyable, invigorating pastime.

Students' original sentences will vary.

C. Proofreading Skill

Commas in a Series

Errors in proofreading exercises are counted as follows: (1) Each word is counted as one error. For example, a misspelled word is one error; two initials and a last name not capitalized are counted as three errors. (b) Run-on sentences and sentence fragments are each counted as one error, even though the correction involves both punctuation and capitalization corrections.

Errors are shown on page.

As a baby, a toddler, and a child, you had your "wheels." You rode in strollers, on tricycles, and in little red wagons. Then you got a bicycle, you learned to ride it, and you could get from place to place on it. In just a few years, you will, first, apply for; second, test for; and third, receive a learner's permit to drive a car. You are impatiently and excitedly awaiting the day when you can drive.

COMMAS THAT SET OFF SPECIAL ELEMENTS

Objectives

- To use commas to set off introductory elements, interrupters, nouns of direct address, and appositives

Writing

- To combine sentences through the use of introductory elements and interrupters

HELPFUL HINT: INTERRUPTERS
To be sure students understand the concept of interrupters, have them work in pairs to brainstorm examples of common interrupters and compile a class list. Point out that whether or not a word or group of words is an interrupter depends somewhat upon its placement in the sentence. For example, *I think* is an interrupter in the sentence "He is, I think, wrong" but not in the sentence "I think he is wrong."

INDIVIDUALIZING INSTRUCTION: BASIC STUDENTS To help students recognize the pauses that commas indicate in writing, you might wish to have them work in pairs to complete Exercise A. Have students take turns reading the sentences aloud and listening for the natural pauses.

Additional Resource

Grammar and Usage Practice Book, p. 126

COMMAS THAT SET OFF SPECIAL ELEMENTS

Use **commas** to set off introductory elements, interrupters, nouns of direct address, and appositives.

In speaking, you pause to indicate the presence of a special element such as an interruption. In writing, punctuation does the work of these pauses.

Special elements add specific information to a sentence, but they are not essential. Any sentence is complete without its special elements.

Commas After Introductory Elements

Use a comma to separate an introductory word, phrase, or clause from the rest of the sentence.

Nervously, I played a concerto for the audition.
After my last audition, I had practiced the concerto daily.
Because I had practiced for hours, I played the concerto perfectly during the audition.

If the pause after a short introductory element would be very brief, you may omit the comma. Note that it is also correct to use a comma in these instances.

At first I was unsure of my playing ability.
Finally it was my turn.

Commas with Interrupters

Use commas to set off interrupters.

An interrupter is a word or words that break, or interrupt, the flow of thought in a sentence. The commas around an interrupter indicate a pause before and after the interruption.

I didn't expect, however, to get the job.
So many people, I thought, play as well as I do.
I was chosen, nevertheless, as the new orchestra member.

Practice Your Skills

A. CONCEPT CHECK

Commas with Special Elements Rewrite the following dialogue, adding commas where necessary.

1. JOE: Our grandma I suppose is not what you would call a traditional grandmother.
2. KIM: True she doesn't stay home as some grandmothers do.
3. JOE: In fact Grandma is seldom at home.
4. KIM: You can usually find her at the health club however.
5. JOE: Since she manages it you would expect her to be there.
6. KIM: I wouldn't however expect her to teach aerobic dance classes as well.
7. JOE: You do remember I imagine that Grandma was a professional dancer when she was younger.
8. KIM: Yes I have seen pictures of her onstage.
9. JOE: I for one am proud of Grandma and her career.
10. KIM: Indeed she's a great grandmother and manager.

B. DRAFTING SKILL

Sentence Combining Rewrite these sentences to place the words in parentheses at the caret. The new material is either an introductory element or an interrupter.

11. Some dog trainers ^ specialize in teaching dogs to help visually impaired people. (I have learned)
12. ^ A good trainer can teach a dog to guide a sightless person. (in the course of several months)
13. Not just any dog ^ can be a guide dog. (however)
14. ^ A dog must be obedient, good-tempered, and intelligent to qualify for training. (in fact)
15. ^ Trainers like Evan Rogers begin the dogs' special training. (when the future guide dogs are a little over a year old)
16. Rogers ^ helps a dog get used to its harness. (at first)
17. He ^ teaches the dog to obey commands. (of course)
18. ^ Rogers teaches the dog to guide a person safely across streets. (in addition)
19. ^ He works with both the dog and its future owner. (finally)
20. A good guide dog ^ will give its owner greater independence. (according to Rogers)

Writing Theme
America at Work

FOR MORE PRACTICE
See page 670.

Writing Theme: America at Work

Other related areas students might wish to explore as writing topics include the following:

- careers in health care
- sports administration
- outdoor jobs: forestry and conservation
- training for the job's they want

Answers to Practice Your Skills

A. Concept Check
Commas with Special Elements

Words preceding and following commas are shown below.

1. grandma, I suppose, is
2. True, she
3. In fact, Grandma
4. club, however.
5. Since she manages it, you
6. wouldn't, however, expect
7. remember, I imagine, that
8. Yes, I
9. I, for one, am
10. Indeed, she's

B. Drafting Skill
Sentence Combining

Answers may vary. Possible answers are shown below.

11. Some dog trainers, I have learned, specialize in teaching dogs to help visually impaired people.
12. In the course of several months, a good trainer can teach a dog to guide a sightless person.
13. Not just any dog, however, can be a guide dog.
14. In fact, a dog must be obedient, good-tempered, and intelligent to qualify for training.
15. When the future guide dogs are a little over a year old, trainers like Evan Rogers begin the dogs' special training.
16. Rogers, at first, helps a dog get used to its harness.
17. He, of course, teaches the dog to obey commands.
18. In addition, Rogers teaches the dog to guide a person safely across streets.
19. Finally, he works with both the dog and its future owner. (or omit comma)
20. A good guide dog, according to Rogers, will give its owner greater independence.

STUMBLING BLOCK: APPOSITIVES

To help students understand when to use commas to set off an appositive, write these sentences on the board:

Edgar Allan Poe's poem *"The Bells"* is one of his best-known poems.

The painter *Salvador Dali* was a leader of the Surrealist movement.

Do you mean James *the novelist* or James *the philosopher?*

Cover up the appositive in each sentence (italicized above) and have a student read the sentence aloud without it. The sentences become almost meaningless. Emphasize that when an appositive adds information that is essential to understanding the meaning, it is not set off with commas.

Writing Theme: Congresswomen

Other related areas students might wish to explore as writing topics include the following:
- women in the current session of Congress
- qualifications for membership in the House of Representatives
- the role of Congress in the lawmaking process
- the history of women in the Senate

Answers to Practice Your Skills

A. Concept Check

Commas with Direct Address and Appositives

1. Theo and Maria, who was the first woman in Congress?
2. Jeannette Rankin, a Republican from Montana, was.
3. That's right, Maria; she was elected to the House of Representatives, the lower house of Congress, in 1916.

Commas with Nouns of Direct Address

Use commas to set off nouns of direct address.

You often address by name the person to whom you are speaking. When you do this, you are using a **noun of direct address.** Nouns of direct address are the words you use to name the persons you address.

> Yes**,** Sara**,** members of Congress serve two-year terms.
> Sal**,** do you know when Clare Boothe Luce served in Congress?

Commas with Appositives

Use commas to set off most appositives.

An **appositive** is a word or group of words used directly after another word to explain it. Most appositives are nouns. Nouns used as appositives are called **nouns in apposition.** When an appositive adds extra information about the word preceding it, the appositive is set off with commas. Note the italicized phrase in the following sentences:

> Lynn Martin**,** *the secretary of labor***,** had served in Congress.
> The legislative branch of the federal government**,** *or Congress***,** is responsible for lawmaking.

When an appositive is necessary for understanding the meaning of a sentence, it is not set off with commas.

> The New York congresswoman Bella Abzug was known for her support of federal jobs programs.

Writing Theme
Congresswomen

Practice Your Skills

A. CONCEPT CHECK

Commas with Direct Address and Appositives Rewrite the sentences. Add commas where necessary. If a sentence has no errors, write *Correct.*

1. Theo and Maria who was the first woman in Congress?
2. Jeannette Rankin a Republican from Montana was.
3. That's right Maria; she was elected to the House of Representatives the lower house of Congress in 1916.

648 Grammar Handbook

4. That was before women had national voting rights or suffrage.
5. Congresswoman Rankin supported women's voting rights.
6. She encouraged others to support these rights too Maria
7. In 1920, Theo women gained national suffrage.
8. Rankin was a pacifist a person who doesn't believe in war.
9. As a pacifist, she voted against entering the "war to end all wars," World War I.
10. In 1918, she ran for the Senate the upper house of Congress.
11. Rankin lost the election Maria and left Congress in 1919.
12. However, Rankin returned to Congress in 1941, only months before Pearl Harbor Naval Base a U. S. base in Hawaii was attacked.
13. Franklin Roosevelt the President at the time asked Congress to declare war.
14. For a second time, Rankin still a pacifist voted against war.
15. Maria and Theo Rankin's vote reflected her beliefs about war.

B. REVISION SKILL

Commas with Appositives The following paragraph has a choppy, abrupt writing style. Rewrite the paragraph, making the writing style smoother by combining sentences and using the underlined words as appositives. Remember to punctuate all appositives correctly.

Barbara Jordan became a member of Congress in 1973. She was a Texas Democrat. She was the first African-American woman from Texas to be elected to Congress. In 1974, Jordan was serving on the House Judiciary Committee, which was investigating the Watergate scandal. Jordan and the other committee members recommended three articles of impeachment against President Richard M. Nixon for his role in the coverup of the Watergate scandal. Articles of impeachment are charges of wrongdoing. However, Nixon resigned before the vote for impeachment reached the full House of Representatives. In 1976, Jordan was asked to give the keynote address at the Democratic National Convention. It was the opening speech. Jordan received a standing ovation for the address. She was known as a powerful and eloquent speaker. Throughout her years in Congress, Jordan promoted legislation that called for equal rights for all citizens. She continued serving in Congress until 1979.

Barbara Jordan, a former congressional representative from Texas, delivers a keynote speech at the 1992 Democratic Convention.

FOR MORE PRACTICE
See page 670.

4. That was before women had national voting rights, or suffrage.
5. Correct
6. She encouraged others to support these rights too, Maria.
7. In 1920, Theo, women gained national suffrage.
8. Rankin was a pacifist, a person who doesn't believe in war.
9. Correct
10. In 1918, she ran for the Senate, the upper house of Congress.
11. Rankin lost the election, Maria, and left Congress in 1919.
12. However, Rankin returned to Congress in 1941, only months before Pearl Harbor Naval Base, a U.S. base in Hawaii, was attacked.
13. Franklin Roosevelt, the President at the time, asked Congress to declare war.
14. For a second time, Rankin, still a pacifist, voted against war.
15. Maria and Theo, Rankin's vote reflected her beliefs about war.

B. Revision Skill
Commas with Appositives

Answers may vary. Possible answers are shown below.

Barbara Jordan, a Texas Democrat, became a member of Congress in 1973. She was the first African-American woman from Texas to be elected to Congress. In 1974, Jordan was serving on the House Judiciary Committee, which was investigating the Watergate scandal. Jordan and the other committee members recommended three articles of impeachment, or charges of wrongdoing, against President Richard M. Nixon for his role in the coverup of the Watergate scandal. However, Nixon resigned before the vote of impeachment reached the full House of Representatives. In 1976, Jordan was asked to give the keynote address, or opening speech, at the Democratic National Convention. Jordan, a powerful and eloquent speaker, received a standing ovation for the address. Throughout her years in Congress, Jordan promoted legislation that called for equal rights for all citizens. She continued serving in Congress until 1979.

CHECK POINT

Writing Theme: It's a Mystery

Other related areas students might wish to explore as writing topics include the following:

- Agatha Christie's Miss Marple
- the continuing popularity of Sherlock Holmes
- Edgar Allan Poe and detective fiction
- famous unsolved mysteries

MIXED REVIEW • PAGES 638–649

You may wish to use this activity to check students' mastery of the following concepts:

- end marks
- commas that separate ideas
- commas that set off special elements

A.

1. Do you enjoy watching mystery shows on TV?
2. If so, you may have seen the show *Murder, She Wrote* in reruns.
3. It stars Angela Lansbury as J. B. Fletcher, a mystery story writer.
4. In every show, J. B. Fletcher helps the police solve a crime, but the police do not always want her help.
5. Some consider her a nuisance, an obstacle, or even a pest.
6. J. B., however, continues to search for clues, and she sometimes seeks the help of Dr. Seth Hazlitt, one of her friends.
7. She might ask him, "Seth, what do you think it means?"
8. The smallest clue, such as a missing button, smudges on a wall, or a few flower petals, can help her solve a mystery.
9. How, you might ask, is she able to piece together the clues?
10. J. B. Fletcher uses keen, insightful observations and thinking to solve crimes. What a crime solver! What a show!

B. Application in Literature

11 My sister and I, you will recollect, were twins, and you know how subtle are the links which bind two souls so closely allied. 12 It was a wild night. 13 The wind was howling outside, and the rain was beating and splashing against the windows. 14 Suddenly, amid all the hubbub of the gale, there burst forth the wild scream of a terrified woman. 15 I knew that it was my sister's voice. 16 I sprang from my bed, wrapped a shawl around me, and rushed into the corridor. 17 As I opened the door, I seemed to hear a low whistle.

Sir Arthur Conan Doyle, "The Adventure of the Speckled Band"

Writing Theme
It's a Mystery

CHECK POINT

MIXED REVIEW • PAGES 638–649

A. Rewrite the sentences, adding end punctuation, periods, and commas where necessary.

1. Do you enjoy watching mystery shows on TV
2. If so you may have seen the show *Murder, She Wrote* in reruns
3. It stars Angela Lansbury as J B Fletcher a mystery story writer
4. In every show J B Fletcher helps the police solve a crime but the police do not always want her help
5. Some consider her a nuisance an obstacle or even a pest
6. J B however continues to search for clues and she sometimes seeks the help of Dr Seth Hazlitt one of her friends
7. She might ask him, "Seth what do you think it means"
8. The smallest clue such as a missing button smudges on a wall or a few flower petals can help her solve a mystery
9. How you might ask is she able to piece together the clues
10. J B Fletcher uses keen insightful observations and thinking to solve crimes. What a crime solver What a show

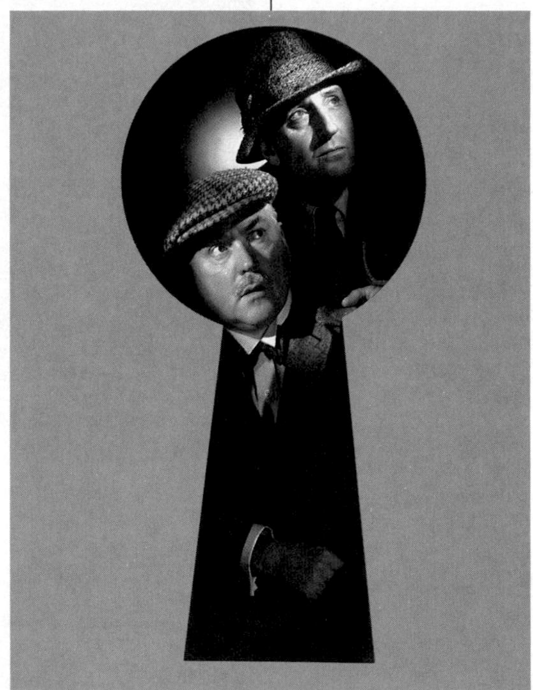

Basil Rathbone and Nigel Bruce starred as Sherlock Holmes and Dr. Watson in the 1945 film *House of Fear*.

B. Application in Literature Rewrite the following paragraph, adding end marks and commas where necessary.

11 My sister and I you will recollect were twins and you know how subtle are the links which bind two souls so closely allied 12 It was a wild night 13 The wind was howling outside and the rain was beating and splashing against the windows 14 Suddenly amid all the hubbub of the gale there burst forth the wild scream of a terrified woman 15 I knew that it was my sister's voice 16 I sprang from my bed wrapped a shawl around me and rushed into the corridor 17 As I opened the door I seemed to hear a low whistle

Sir Arthur Conan Doyle, "The Adventure of the Speckled Band"

Literature Connection

Author Note Sir Arthur Conan Doyle (1859–1930) was educated as a doctor, studying for five years at Edinburgh University in Scotland. He then served for a time as a ship's doctor before setting up his own private practice as an oculist, or ophthalmologist. However, Doyle's medical practice was never successful. In fact, he created Sherlock Holmes out of boredom—and for a source of income—while waiting for his infrequent patients. His Sherlock Holmes stories became so popular that Doyle eventually gave up medicine altogether to devote his time to writing.

Use **commas** to set off quotations, parts of dates, parts of addresses, and parts of a letter.

Certain elements in your writing require commas to separate them from the rest of the sentence. In this section, you will learn when to use such commas.

Commas with Quotations

Use commas to set off the explanatory words of a direct quotation.

When you use the exact words of a speaker or writer, you are using a **direct quotation.**

When you quote directly, you usually include explanatory words such as *Marilena said, Karen asked,* or *Mike answered.* If the explanatory words precede the direct quotation, you place a comma after the last explanatory word. When the explanatory words follow the quotation, place a comma after the last word of the quotation and before the end quotation mark.

Timothy said**,** "After my injury I had to learn to walk again."
"The therapists urged me to keep trying**,**" he continued.

When the explanatory words interrupt the quotation, the quotation is called a **divided quotation.** In a divided quotation, use commas after the last word of the first part of the quotation and after the last word in the explanatory phrase.

"After a while**,**" he noted**,** "I was walking with only a cane."

The quotations you have just looked at are all direct quotations. When you rephrase the words of a speaker or writer, you are using an **indirect quotation.** You need not set these words off with commas. In most cases, however, you should credit the quotation to the original speaker or writer.

Timothy said that *the many hours of therapy had paid off because he was now able to run again.*

OTHER USES OF THE COMMA

Objectives

- To use commas in quotations, parts of dates, parts of addresses, and parts of a letter

Writing

- To use commas correctly in writing

Teaching Strategies

HELPFUL HINT You might help students distinguish between direct and indirect quotations by pointing out that many direct quotations refer to the speaker as "I," and many indirect quotations begin with the word *that.* Provide a few sample sentences, such as the following, and have students identify them as direct or indirect:

Lucia said, "I will be on time." (direct)

Paulo said that he will be late. (indirect)

Additional Resource

Grammar and Usage Practice Book, pp. 127–128

Writing Theme: Facing Life's Challenges

Other related areas students might wish to explore as writing topics include the following:

- physical therapy or rehabilitative medicine
- the Special Olympics
- prosthetics
- the Americans with Disabilities Act

Answers to Practice Your Skills

A. Concept Check

Commas with Quotations

1. I asked, "Mom, do you know anyone who is blind?"
2. "No," Mom replied, "but let me tell you about Tom Sullivan."
3. Mom continued, "Tom, a singer and guitar player who performed on stage and TV, lost his sight soon after birth."
4. "At times," she said, "he would be angry about being blind."
5. "He wanted to be like all other people," explained Mom.
6. "However, he learned to accept his blindness," she noted, "and did not let it stop him from enjoying many activities."
7. Mom told me that he even learned to play golf with help.
8. I asked, "How do you know so much about Tom Sullivan, Mom?"
9. "Years ago, I saw him sing on TV programs," she replied.
10. She then said that she had also read a biography about him.

B. Revision Skill

Sentence Variety

Answers will vary. Possible answers are shown below.

11. "I just finished reading the book *Alesia* by Eloise Greenfield and Alesia Revis," stated Carlos.
12. Elena inquired, "What is it about?"
13. "It's a story about how Alesia recovered from severe injuries after she was hit by a car when she was nine years old," explained Anna.
14. "That's right," said Carlos, "and Alesia tells the story."
15. Anna continued, "At first, Alesia was completely disabled."
16. "She had to learn to crawl first and then to walk," explained Carlos.
17. Anna noted, "She spent years in physical therapy, exercising."
18. Carlos said, "She finally learned to walk with help."
19. "Learning to walk again was hard work," Anna explained, "but Alesia never gave up, and she triumphed!"
20. "It sounds like a great story," responded Elena. "May I borrow the book?"

Writing Theme
Facing Life's Challenges

Practice Your Skills

A. CONCEPT CHECK

Commas with Quotations Write the following sentences, adding and deleting commas where necessary.

1. I asked "Mom, do you know anyone who is blind?"
2. "No" Mom replied "but let me tell you about Tom Sullivan."
3. Mom continued "Tom, a singer and guitar player who performed on stage and TV, lost his sight soon after birth."
4. "At times" she said "he would be angry about being blind."
5. "He wanted to be like all other people" explained Mom.
6. "However, he learned to accept his blindness" she noted "and did not let it stop him from enjoying many activities."
7. Mom told me, that he even learned to play golf with help.
8. I asked "How do you know so much about Tom Sullivan, Mom?"
9. "Years ago, I saw him sing on TV programs" she replied.
10. She then said, that she had also read a biography about him.

B. REVISION SKILL

Sentence Variety Write each of the following sentences as a direct quotation. Place the name of the speaker, identified in parentheses, at the position indicated by a caret. Add appropriate punctuation and explanatory words, such as *said, stated,* or *asked.*

EXAMPLE "Cass, when will you finish the book?" ^ (Jeff)
"Cass, when will you finish the book?" asked Jeff.

11. "I just finished reading the book *Alesia* by Eloise Greenfield and Alesia Revis." ^ (Carlos)
12. ^ "What is it about?" (Elena)
13. "It's a story about how Alesia recovered from severe injuries after she was hit by a car when she was nine years old." ^ (Anna)
14. "That's right, ^ and Alesia tells the story." (Carlos)
15. ^ "At first, Alesia was completely disabled." (Anna)
16. "She had to learn to crawl first and then to walk." ^ (Carlos)
17. ^ "She spent years in physical therapy, exercising." (Anna)
18. ^ "She finally learned to walk with help." (Carlos)
19. "Learning to walk again was hard work, ^ but Alesia never gave up, and she triumphed!" (Anna)
20. "It sounds like a great story. ^ May I borrow the book?" (Elena)

FOR MORE PRACTICE
See page 670.

Commas in Dates, Addresses, and Letters

When you are writing dates, place a comma after the day of the month.

When a date falls in the middle of the sentence, use a comma after the day of the month and another comma after the year. When only a month and year are given, no commas are necessary.

July 4, 1776   November 10, 1992   April 1865

The bill was proposed in November 1988. It wasn't until September 15, 1991, that it became a law, however.

When referring to a geographical location, place a comma between the name of the town or city and the name of the state, district, or country. When a postal address is used in a sentence, place a comma after each part of the address.

Springfield, Illinois   Paris, France

The senator lives at 2395 Saddlebridge Drive, Houston, Texas 77069, when she isn't in Washington.

Note that there is no comma between the name of the state and the ZIP code.

Use a comma after the greeting of a friendly letter and after the closing of a friendly or business letter.

Dear George,   Sincerely,

Practice Your Skills

CONCEPT CHECK

Commas in Dates, Addresses, and Letters Write the following sentences, adding necessary commas and deleting unnecessary commas.

1. Dear Allison
I've finally arrived in Washington D.C.
2. My train left Lexington Kentucky on July 15.
3. I'm staying at 35 Wisconsin Avenue Washington D.C. 10017.
4. I've learned so much about this city. Did you know that the dome on the Capitol wasn't completed until December, 1863?

Writing Theme
Historical Places

INDIVIDUALIZING INSTRUCTION: ADVANCED STUDENTS In addition to the date styles given in the text, you might point out the absence of commas in a style that students occasionally will see:

4 July 1776   10 November 1992

Explain that this style is used by the military but that students also may encounter it in British and other European writing.

Writing Theme: Historical Places

Other related areas students might wish to explore as writing topics include the following:

- James Hoban, architect of the White House
- Pierre Charles L'Enfant, designer of Washington, D.C.
- the British attack on Washington, D.C., during the War of 1812
- state capitals

Answers to Practice Your Skills

Concept Check
Commas in Dates, Addresses, and Letters

1. Dear Allison,
I've finally arrived in Washington, D.C.
2. My train left Lexington, Kentucky, on July 15.
3. I'm staying at 35 Wisconsin Avenue, Washington, D.C. 10017.
4. I've learned so much about this city. Did you know that the dome on the Capitol wasn't completed until December 1863?

MULTICULTURAL Connection

The conventional uses of punctuation vary from culture to culture. For example, in European style, a house number is followed by a comma (400, Drury Street), and commas go outside end quotation marks. Invite students to interview people from outside the United States about differences in punctuation rules and to report their findings to the class.

5. On May 30, 1922, the Lincoln Memorial was dedicated.
6. I visited 1600 Pennsylvania Avenue, Washington, D.C.
7. President Adams and his family became the first residents of the White House in November 1800.
8. Did you know that on August 24, 1814, the White House was burned down?
9. The rebuilt White House was formally opened in January 1818 by President Monroe.
10. Your friend,
Robert

Writing Theme: At the Amusement Park

Other related areas students might wish to explore as writing topics include the following:

- the history of the carousel
- Coney Island and Atlantic City
- planning a new theme park
- Disneyland

Answers to Practice Your Skills

Concept Check
Commas for Clarity

1. The day before, my dad suggested a trip to the local amusement park.
2. I invited Jessica, and Adam invited Tim.
3. Before leaving, my mom packed the car with food.
4. When we walked in, the park was already crowded and noisy.
5. Screaming, Jessica and I rode the roller coaster five times.
6. When the roller coaster zoomed by, my dad waved to us.
7. While turning, the merry-go-round played the same tune over and over.
8. Calling to Tim, Adam climbed on a wooden horse.
9. After riding around and around, the boys wanted to go on the Ferris wheel.
10. By the time we left, the boys were too tired to walk.

FOR MORE PRACTICE
See page 670.

5. On May 30 1922 the Lincoln Memorial was dedicated.
6. I visited 1600 Pennsylvania Avenue Washington D.C.
7. President Adams and his family became the first residents of the White House in November 1800.
8. Did you know that on August 24 1814 the White House was burned down?
9. The rebuilt White House was formally opened in January, 1818 by President Monroe.
10. Your friend
Robert

Commas to Prevent Misreading

When speaking, you sometimes pause in your statements to keep your listeners from misunderstanding what you mean to say. In writing, commas prevent similar misunderstandings. Even when a comma is not strictly required, you may insert one to prevent misreading. Notice how the following sentence is unclear unless a comma is added.

When we finished packing the bags were ready.
When we finished packing**,** the bags were ready.

Practice Your Skills

Writing Theme
At the Amusement Park

CONCEPT CHECK

Commas for Clarity Write the following sentences, adding commas where necessary.

1. The day before my dad suggested a trip to the local amusement park.
2. I invited Jessica and Adam invited Tim.
3. Before leaving my mom packed the car with food.
4. When we walked in the park was already crowded and noisy.
5. Screaming Jessica and I rode the roller coaster five times.
6. When the roller coaster zoomed by my dad waved to us.
7. While turning the merry-go-round played the same tune over and over.
8. Calling to Tim Adam climbed on a wooden horse.
9. After riding around and around the boys wanted to go on the Ferris wheel.
10. By the time we left the boys were too tired to walk.

654 Grammar Handbook

CHECK POINT

MIXED REVIEW • PAGES 651–654

Write the following letter, adding and deleting commas where necessary. As an alternative, you may write only the words before and after commas in each line.

May, 24 1994

Dear Matt

Saturday May 21 1994 will always be an important date for me because that's the day I went rock climbing for the first time. After worrying my cousin Dana invited me to go with her club, the Alpiners. My mom just said "Have a good time and be careful." My brother said "You have trouble climbing the stairs!" "He's just jealous" said Dana "because I've never invited him to go rock climbing!" Before leaving Dana told me to be sure to wear sturdy shoes with rubber soles, comfortable pants, and a long-sleeved T-shirt. We met at 3115, Meadowview Drive for the drive to the cliffs in the state park. At first I was scared, but while climbing Dana showed me what to do. Most importantly, she told me "Take your time; this isn't a race, so concentrate on finding good holds." I was so happy when she said to me "Good job!" The next climb takes place Saturday June 18 1994 at the same site. Not only am I planning on going again, but I'm going to the Alpiners' next meeting on Monday June 6. Also, I think I will get some more information on rock climbing by writing the American Alpine Club 113 East Ninetieth St. New York, New York 10028.

Love

Jenna

Writing Theme

Rock Climbing

CHECK  POINT

Writing Theme: Rock Climbing

Other related areas students might wish to explore as writing topics include the following:

- freestyle climbing
- ice climbing
- indoor climbing
- climbing Yosemite's El Capitan

MIXED REVIEW • PAGES 651–654

You may wish to use this activity to check students' mastery of the following concepts:

- commas with quotations
- commas in dates, addresses, and letters
- commas to prevent misreading

May 24, 1994

Dear Matt,

Saturday, May 21, 1994, will always be an important date for me because that's the day I went rock climbing for the first time. After **worrying, my** cousin Dana invited me to go with her club, the Alpiners. My mom just **said, "Have** a good.time and be careful." My brother **said, "You** have trouble climbing the stairs!" "He's just **jealous," said Dana, "because** I've never invited him to go rock climbing!" Before **leaving, Dana** told me to be sure to wear sturdy shoes with rubber soles, comfortable pants, and a long sleeved T-shirt. We met at **3115 Meadowview** Drive for the drive to the cliffs in the state park. At first I was scared, **but, while climbing, Dana** showed me what to do. Most importantly, she told **me, "Take** your time; this isn't a race, so concentrate on finding good holds." I was so happy when she said to **me, "Good** job!" The next climb takes place **Saturday, June 18, 1994, at** the same site. Not only am I planning on going again, but I'm going to the Alpiners' next meeting on **Monday, June** 6. Also, I think I will get some more information on rock climbing by writing the American Alpine **Club, 113** East Ninetieth **St., New** York, New York 10028.

Love,

Jenna

THE SEMICOLON AND THE COLON

Objectives

- To learn the use of the semicolon and the colon

Writing

- To use semicolons and colons correctly in writing

Teaching Strategies

LINKING GRAMMAR AND WRITING Explain that a semicolon is used to form a compound sentence only if the clauses are very closely related in meaning. A semicolon, unlike the conjunctions *and, or, but, for,* and *nor,* does not show the relationship between the clauses.

HELPFUL HINT: CONJUNCTIVE ADVERBS You might make these points when discussing the conjunctive adverbs on the pupil page:

- The conjunctive adverb need not be the first word after the semicolon:

  The safari takes place in May; I, however, prefer June.

  The safari takes place in May; I prefer June, however.

- *Then* follows a semicolon, not a comma (as a substitute for *and);* if it introduces a short clause, it need not be followed by a comma:

  I finished my work at the library; then I went home.

- Like coordinating conjunctions, conjunctive adverbs suggest a relationship between the ideas they connect.

Have students use conjunctive adverbs in original sentences and explain why they chose a particular one.

Additional Resource

Grammar and Usage Practice Book, pp. 129–130

THE SEMICOLON AND THE COLON

Use a **semicolon** to separate parts of a compound sentence.

Use a **colon** to introduce lists of items, to follow the greeting of a business letter, and to separate hours from minutes in time expressions.

The Semicolon

Semicolons are frequently used to punctuate compound sentences. A compound sentence is made up of two or more independent clauses.

Use a semicolon to separate the parts of a compound sentence when no conjunction is used.

Adventure travel is exciting**,** but it can also be dangerous.
Adventure travel is exciting**;** it can also be dangerous.

Note that the semicolon replaces the comma and the coordinating conjunction *but.* Conjunctions commonly replaced by semicolons are *and, but, or, for,* and *nor.*

Use a semicolon before a conjunctive adverb that joins the clauses of a compound sentence.

Conjunctive adverbs commonly used are *therefore, however, hence, so, then, moreover, nevertheless, yet, consequently,* and *besides.*

The safari takes place in May**;** *however,* I prefer June.

Use semicolons to separate the parts of a series when commas occur within the parts.

Like commas, semicolons are used in sentences to prevent misreading. For example, if you list a series of cities and their countries without semicolons, the list would confuse a reader.

In recent years, I have flown to Beijing, Nanjing, and Shanghai, China**;** Cairo and Alexandria, Egypt**;** Jakarta, Indonesia**;** and Kuala Lumpur, Malaysia.

656 Grammar Handbook

The Colon

Use a colon to introduce a list of items.

In speaking and writing, people often use lists. Someone gives you a list of things to bring on a trip. You tell someone the list of your favorite books. You make lists to remind you to do certain things. You should introduce these lists with a colon.

My flight bag contains the following items**:** my camera, ten rolls of film, batteries, a change of clothes, a guidebook, several maps, and a sweater.

Never place a colon immediately after a preposition or a verb.

Incorrect I made sure I had**:** passport, credit cards, traveler's checks, and driver's license.

Correct I made sure I had the following items**:** my passport, credit cards, traveler's checks, and driver's license.

Place a colon after the greeting of a business letter.

Dear Ms. Albertson**:**
Thank you for sending my ticket so quickly.

Use a colon between numerals that represent hours and minutes and between chapter and verse in a biblical reference.

9**:**00 A.M. 6**:**30 P.M. Genesis 7**:**1–5

Practice Your Skills

A. CONCEPT CHECK

Semicolons and Colons Write the following sentences, adding and deleting semicolons and colons where necessary. If a sentence is already correct, write *Correct.*

1. *Safari* originally meant: "having to do with a journey" in Arabic subsequently the word passed into Swahili.
2. Safaris can be hunting trips often they are sightseeing trips.
3. They are most common in these African countries Zimbabwe, Botswana, Kenya, Tanzania, and South Africa.
4. People on photographic safaris always carry two things: cameras and binoculars.

Writing Theme Adventure Travel

Writing Theme: Adventure Travel

Other related areas students might wish to explore as writing topics include the following:
- rafting on wild and scenic rivers in the United States
- trekking the Himalayas
- a boat trip down the Amazon River
- the animals of Africa

Answers to Practice Your Skills

A. Concept Check
Semicolons and Colons

1. *Safari* originally meant "having to do with a journey" in Arabic; subsequently, the word passed into Swahili.
2. Safaris can be hunting trips; often, they are sightseeing trips.
3. They are most common in these African countries: Zimbabwe, Botswana, Kenya, Tanzania, and South Africa.
4. Correct

5. You go to water holes at 5:00 A.M. to observe animals.
6. Around 9:00 P.M. is another good time to watch for animals.
7. You may see zebras, giraffes, and antelopes early; elephants later; and wild dogs and baboons still later.
8. At night you can hear the animals; they may come to the camp.
9. Correct
10. Antelopes, zebras, and gnus in Tanzania; giraffes in Kenya; and hyenas in Botswana live on protected reserves.

B. Proofreading Skill

Using Semicolons and Colons Correctly

Errors are shown on page. Students' corrections may vary slightly. Typical corrections are shown below.

674 Cleveland Place
Metairie, Louisiana 70003
March 24, 1994

Adventure Travel, Inc.
1197 Powell Street
San Francisco, California 94108

Dear Sir or Madam:

I recently read an article describing your company. It sounded like my kind of travel agency! The article was very informative; however, I would like to know more. I am particularly interested in traveling to the following countries: Malaysia, India, and China. If you have any upcoming trips to those countries, please send me the following information: dates, departures, itineraries, prices, and restrictions. Also, do you arrange trips to Myanmar? Do you have any plans to visit Nepal? Thank you for your help; I look forward to hearing from you soon.

Sincerely yours,
Anna Gonzalez

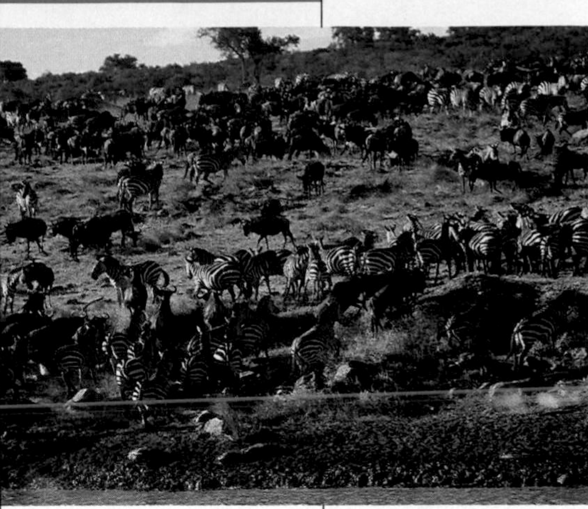

5. You go to water holes at 500 A.M.; to observe animals.
6. Around 900 P.M. is another good time to watch for animals.
7. You may see zebras, giraffes, and antelopes early, elephants later, and wild dogs and baboons still later.
8. At night you can hear the animals they may come to the camp.
9. The guide knows how to look for animals; however, anyone can learn to spot animals in the wild.
10. Antelopes, zebras, and gnus in Tanzania, giraffes in Kenya, and hyenas in Botswana live on protected reserves.

B. PROOFREADING SKILL

Using Semicolons and Colons Correctly Write this letter, correcting all errors in grammar, capitalization, punctuation, and spelling. (25 errors)

674 Cleveland place
Metairie Louisiana, 70003
March 24 1994

Adventure Travel, inc.
1197, Powell Street
San francisco, California, 94108

Dear Sir or madam:

I recently read an article describing your company it sounded like my kind of travel agency! The article was vary informative however, i would like to know more. I am partickularly interested in traveling to the following countries Malaysia, India, and china. If you have any upcoming trips to those countries. Please send me the following information dates, departures, itineraries, preices, and restrictions. Also do you arrange trips to Myanmar. Do you have any plans to visit Nepal? Thank you for your help I look forward to heering from you soon.

Sincerely yours;
Anna Gonzalez

FOR MORE PRACTICE
See page 671.

THE HYPHEN

Use a **hyphen** to mark the division of a word at the end of a line. Use hyphens in compound numbers, nouns, and adjectives.

Use a hyphen to divide a word at the end of a line of writing.

Only words of two or more syllables may be divided at the end of a line. Words should be divided only between syllables.

When tracing my family history, I began with my local library's collection of books on genealogy.

Never divide a word of one syllable. Do not divide words to leave a single letter at the end or at the beginning of a line.

Incorrect a-luminum *Correct* alu-minum

Use hyphens in compound adjectives that precede the words they modify and in certain compound nouns.

Dr. Herbert is a world-famous authority on census records.
But: Dr. Herbert is world famous.

sister-in-law great-grandson self-knowledge

Use hyphens in compound numbers from twenty-one through ninety-nine and in fractions.

seventy-three relatives one-half full

Practice Your Skills

CONCEPT CHECK

Hyphens Write the following sentences, adding hyphens where necessary.

1. My great grandparents came from Poland ninety two years ago.
2. She traveled with twenty one relatives and neighbors.
3. He came with his great uncle, who was seventy five.
4. She carried a much loved quilt made by a great aunt.
5. His prize possession was a well worn family Bible.

Writing **TIP**

Do not use a hyphen between an adverb that ends in *-ly* and a participle acting as a modifier.

My great-grandmother was known for her beautifully stitched embroidery.

Writing Theme Family History

FOR MORE PRACTICE
See page 671.

THE HYPHEN

Objectives

- To learn the use of the hyphen to divide words at the ends of lines
- To learn the use of the hyphen in certain compound adjectives, nouns, and numbers

Writing

- To use hyphens correctly in writing

Teaching Strategies

HELPFUL HINT: COMPOUND ADJECTIVES You may wish to emphasize that compound adjectives are often hyphenated when they precede the nouns they modify, but usually are not hyphenated when they function as predicate adjectives modifying subject nouns:

Annie Dillard is a *well-known* writer.

Many of her books are *well known.*

Additional Resource

Grammar and Usage Practice Book, p. 131

Writing Theme: Family History

Other related areas students might wish to explore as writing topics include the following:

- genealogy, the tracing of one's ancestry
- family heirlooms
- family stories
- an unforgettable family member

Answers to Practice Your Skills

Concept Check

Hyphens

1. My great-grandparents came from Poland ninety-two years ago.
2. She traveled with twenty-one relatives and neighbors.
3. He came with his great-uncle, who was seventy-five.
4. She carried a much-loved quilt made by a great-aunt.
5. His prize possession was a well-worn family Bible.

THE APOSTROPHE

Objectives

- To recognize the uses of apostrophes in certain possessives and plurals and in contractions

Writing

- To use apostrophes correctly in writing

Teaching Strategies

LINKING GRAMMAR AND WRITING Point out that the misuse of apostrophes can make writing unclear. For example, readers can be confused about the meanings of two similar-looking words, such as *well* and *we'll, shell* and *she'll,* and *its* and *it's*. Mixing up *its* and *it's* is an especially common mistake. You might emphasize that since *its* is a possessive pronoun, no apostrophe is needed to show possession.

INDIVIDUALIZING INSTRUCTION: ESL STUDENTS The apostrophe does not exist in most other languages. Therefore, ESL students may confuse the apostrophe with the comma. You may wish to emphasize the difference in form and function between the two punctuation marks and to give extra practice in using apostrophes.

THE APOSTROPHE

Use **apostrophes** to show possession, to form the plurals of letters and words used as words, and to show where letters are omitted in contractions.

The apostrophe is a punctuation mark that is helpful only to a reader. The apostrophe can be used to show possession, to represent the omitted letters in contractions, and to help form some plurals.

Forming Possessives and Plurals

To form the possessive of a singular noun, add an apostrophe and an *s*.

the baby's toy   Charles's coat   Maria's book

To form the possessive of a plural noun that does not end in *s*, add an apostrophe and an *s*.

children's   men's

To form the possessive of a plural noun that ends in *s*, add only an apostrophe.

visitors'   animals'

To form the possessive of an indefinite pronoun, use an apostrophe and an *s*.

everybody's   somebody's   no one's

For a listing of indefinite pronouns, see Handbook 41, "Using Pronouns," page 448.

Never use an apostrophe with a possessive pronoun.

our   yours   hers   theirs

Use an apostrophe and an *s* to form the plural of a letter or a word referred to as a word.

p's and q's   too many *thus*'s

SPICE BOX

The misuse of apostrophes in simple plurals is almost epidemic. Invite students to find examples of signs and public notices in which apostrophes have been used incorrectly. Have students present their findings to the class and discuss what should be done to correct the sign.

In names of organizations and businesses, in hyphenated terms, and in cases of joint ownership, show possession in the last word only.

the chamber of commerce's brochure
my great-aunt's photograph album
Henry and Elizabeth's vacation

Forming Contractions

Use an apostrophe in a contraction.

In contractions, apostrophes replace omitted letters.

she's = she is	aren't = are not	I'm = I am
it's = it is	isn't = is not	we'll = we will
won't = will not	can't = cannot	they've = they have

If you remember the rule that an apostrophe replaces one or more omitted letters, you will be less likely to confuse *it's* with *its*. *It's* is a contraction of *it is*. *Its* is a possessive pronoun. Note that *won't* is the exception to the apostrophe rule.

Use an apostrophe to show that part of a date has been omitted.

Klondike gold rush of '96 (Klondike gold rush of 1896)
the '64 earthquake (the 1964 earthquake)

Practice Your Skills

A. CONCEPT CHECK

Apostrophes Correctly write the words in these sentences that have incorrect or missing apostrophes.

1. Polar bear's live on Canadas and Alaskas northern coasts.
2. They cant see or hear well, but they have a keen sense of smell.
3. Theyll wait at seals dens or breathing holes in the ice.
4. Their white fur helps hide the bears when theyre hunting.
5. The pads of fur on a polar bears feet help it walk on ice.
6. Its a good climber, swimmer, and runner, even though an adult males' weight may be more than a thousand pounds.
7. Peoples fear of being attacked by the bears is unjustified.
8. In fact, the polar bears survival is threatened by hunters.

Writing Theme
In the Far North

HELPFUL HINT: CONTRACTIONS

Students may benefit from keeping a list of contractions in their notebooks, especially if they expand on the list in the text. Additional examples include the following:

that's = that is
I'd = I had (would)
you'd = you had (would)
shouldn't = should not
don't = do not
they're = they are

You also might explore some cases in which students have options:

we will not = we'll not *or* we won't
they have not = they've not *or* they haven't

Additional Resource

Grammar and Usage Practice Book, pp. 132–133

Writing Theme: In the Far North

Other related areas students might wish to explore as writing topics include the following:

- the Inuit people of the Arctic
- exploring the Arctic
- the snowy owl
- plants of the Arctic

Answers to Practice Your Skills

A. Concept Check
Apostrophes

1. bears, Canada's, Alaska's
2. can't
3. They'll, seals'
4. they're
5. polar bear's
6. It's, male's
7. People's
8. bears' (*or* bear's)

9. world's, *The World Book Encyclopedia*'s '91
10. It's, anybody's

B. Revision Skill
Using Apostrophes Correctly

Errors are shown on page.

11. I've
12. They're
13. *z*'s, *s*'s
14. sun's
15. earth's, earth's, earth's
16. *earth's*'s
17. that's
18. I'm
19. snake's, spirits'
20. I'd

C. Application in Writing
Notes

Notes on the North Pole

Geographic North Pole—at northern end of earth's axis
—located near Arctic Ocean's center
—Robert Peary's expedition in 1909
—N. Uemura's solo expedition by dog sled in 1978
Magnetic North Pole—in different location
—compass needle points to this pole's location
Geomagnetic North Pole—in different location
—at northern end of earth's geomagnetic field

9. The worlds polar bear population is estimated to be around twenty-five thousand in *The World Book Encyclopedias'* 91 edition.
10. Its anybodys guess how many polar bears will survive in the future.

B. REVISION SKILL

Using Apostrophes Correctly Write the following paragraph, adding apostrophes where necessary.

[11]Ive been reading about the aurora borealis, commonly called the northern lights. [12]Theyre the lights that can be seen in the night sky, particularly in Alaska. [13]They appear as green, red, and purple arcs and streaks, even shapes like zs and ss, that move and flicker. [14]The lights are one of the suns effects on the atmosphere. [15]When electrically charged particles from the sun reach the earths magnetic field, some are trapped and move toward the earths magnetic poles, releasing energy as they strike atoms and molecules in the earths atmosphere. [16]I think I used too many earth'ss in that sentence! [17]Anyway, thats the current explanation; scientists are still studying the phenomenon. [18]Im interested in less scientific explanations. [19]Some people believed that a radiant snakes dancing caused the lights; others thought the lights were spirits torches. [20]Id like to see the aurora borealis someday.

C. APPLICATION IN WRITING

Notes Imagine that you took the following science notes in a hurry. You notice that you did not make the possessives clear. Write the notes, adding apostrophes where they are needed. Use an encyclopedia to check the facts if necessary.

Notes on the North Pole

Geographic North Pole—at northern end of earths axis
—located near Arctic Oceans center
—Robert Pearys expedition in 1909
—N. Uemuras solo expedition by dog sled in 1978
Magnetic North Pole—in different location
—compass needle points to this poles location
Geomagnetic North Pole—in different location—at northern end of earths geomagnetic field

FOR MORE PRACTICE
See page 672.

MIXED REVIEW • PAGES 656–662

Write these sentences, adding and deleting semicolons, colons, hyphens, and apostrophes where necessary.

1. People learned how to weave thousands of years ago however, no one is exactly sure when.
2. Early weavers materials included: grasses, palm leaves, wood strips, and twigs.
3. People first wove these objects hats, masks, mats, and baskets.
4. Dried grass baskets were used to store and carry peoples food.
5. Every culture has made baskets each has added something to make it's baskets different.
6. Decorating with shells and feathers is the Pomo Indians style.
7. Theyre considered the finest basket makers in the Americas.
8. Basket makers and cloth weavers techniques are the same.
9. Cloth weavers make these things blankets, clothes, and rugs.
10. Cloth is woven from the following materials silk, wool, cotton, and synthetic fibers, such as nylon.
11. Its anybodys guess who were the first people to weave cloth.
12. The Egyptians weaving techniques are shown in ancient paintings.
13. The Chinese first used the silkworms thread four thousand years ago.
14. About two thousand years ago, the Romans traded for wool from Britain, Gaul, and Spain: cotton from Egypt; and silk from China.
15. Seventh century Pueblos knew how to weave cotton.
16. The Navajos learned how to weave from the Pueblos subsequently, the Navajos developed their own unique blanket patterns.
17. Inca weavers fine wool cloth is still-admired today.
18. By the 1400s weaving was a well developed art in Europe too.
19. Weaving on a hand loom is an ancient craft still practiced to day in many of the worlds cultures.
20. Its also a popular handicraft many people weave as a hobby.

Writing Theme
Weaving

Hopi basketweaver Fermina Banyacya continues a family tradition of weaving with yucca leaves.

Writing Theme: Weaving

Other related areas students might wish to explore as writing topics include the following:

- African basketry
- Navajo rug design
- weaving as a hobby

MIXED REVIEW • PAGES 656–662

You may wish to use this activity to check students' mastery of the following concepts:

- the semicolon and the colon
- the hyphen
- the apostrophe

1. People learned how to weave thousands of years ago; however, no one is exactly sure when.
2. Early weavers' materials included grasses, palm leaves, wood strips, and twigs.
3. People first wove these objects: hats, masks, mats, and baskets.
4. Dried-grass baskets were used to store and carry people's food.
5. Every culture has made baskets; each has added something to make its baskets different.
6. Decorating with shells and feathers is the Pomo Indians' style.
7. They're considered the finest basket makers in the Americas.
8. Basket makers' and cloth weavers' techniques are the same.
9. Cloth weavers make these things: blankets, clothes, and rugs.
10. Cloth is woven from the following materials: silk, wool, cotton, and synthetic fibers, such as nylon.
11. It's anybody's guess who were the first people to weave cloth.
12. The Egyptians' weaving techniques are shown in ancient paintings.
13. The Chinese first used the silkworm's thread four thousand years ago.
14. About two thousand years ago, the Romans traded for wool from Britain, Gaul, and Spain; cotton from Egypt; and silk from China.
15. Seventh-century Pueblos knew how to weave cotton.
16. The Navajos learned how to weave from the Pueblos; subsequently, the Navajos developed their own unique blanket patterns.
17. Inca weavers' fine wool cloth is still admired today.
18. By the 1400s weaving was a well-developed art in Europe too.
19. Weaving on a hand loom is an ancient craft still practiced to-day [end-of-line word division] in many of the world's cultures.
20. It's also a popular handicraft; many people weave as a hobby.

Objectives

- To use quotation marks in direct quotations correctly
- To use single quotation marks correctly

Writing

- To use quotation marks, and other punctuation for dialogue, correctly in writing

Teaching Strategies

STUMBLING BLOCK Students may find it difficult to decide whether a question mark or exclamation point belongs inside or outside quotation marks. Suggest that they try mentally moving explanatory words, such as *he said,* to the end of the sentence. If the end mark still makes sense with the quotation, it belongs inside the quotation marks. Otherwise, it belongs outside.

Additional Resource

Grammar and Usage Practice Book, pp. 134–137

QUOTATION MARKS

Use **quotation marks** at the beginning and the end of direct quotations and to set off titles of short works.

When you use another person's exact written or spoken words, you are using a **direct quotation.** On the other hand, when you refer to a person's words but do not quote him or her exactly, you are using an **indirect quotation.**

Use quotation marks to enclose a direct quotation. Indirect quotations need no quotation marks.

Direct Quotation The candidate for the senate said, **"**Creating new jobs will be my first priority.**"**

Indirect Quotation The candidate for the senate said that creating new jobs would be her first priority.

Remember to place the quotation marks before the first word and after the last word of a direct quotation.

Always begin a direct quotation with a capital letter.

Senator Ruiz said, "You must believe that every vote counts."

When a direct quotation is divided by explanatory words, begin the second part of the quotation with a lowercase letter.

If the second part of the quotation is a complete sentence, the first word of this sentence is capitalized.

"Register to vote," said Liz, "**b**efore the end of the day."
"I did," said Carol. "**I**t took only a few minutes."

Place commas and periods inside quotation marks. Place semicolons and colons outside quotation marks.

"Last night**,**" said Liz, "I listened to a debate**.**"
Carol said to Liz, "One candidate was more persuasive than the others"**;** however, Liz did not agree.
These candidates were quoted in the article "Our Country's Future"**:** Senator Ruiz, Governor Henry, and Judge Wong.

Place question marks and exclamation points inside quotation marks if they belong to the quotation. Place them outside if they do not belong to the quotation.

Liz asked, "Whom are you voting for?"
Did Carol say, "I don't know yet"?
I can't believe that she said, "I don't know yet"!
"Don't get excited!" exclaimed Liz.

Use single quotation marks to enclose a title or quotation within a quotation. If the title or quotation within the quotation ends the sentence, use both the single and the double quotation marks after the last word of the sentence.

"Liz heard you say, 'Call Carol,' before you hung up."
"Liz heard you say, 'Call Carol.'"
"Carol told Liz that her favorite song was 'Memory.'"

In a quotation of more than one paragraph, use quotation marks at the beginning of each paragraph and at the end of the final paragraph.

"Being elected the first time is not difficult," said Senator Ruiz, "because voters will give you a chance.

"Being elected the second time is trickier; then you must prove that you used your chance wisely."

Practice Your Skills

CONCEPT CHECK

Quotation Marks Write the following sentences, punctuating quotations correctly. If a sentence is correct, write *Correct.*

1. Being President is like riding a tiger, said Harry S. Truman, A man has to keep on riding or be swallowed.
2. Is it true that Jimmy Carter said, I can get up at nine and be rested, or I can get up at six and be President
3. Dwight Eisenhower said, "Always take the job, but never yourself, seriously"; that was his advice about the presidency.
4. Eisenhower also said There is one thing about being President; nobody can tell you when to sit down!
5. Joan said I read that Truman used to say The buck stops here, to show the difficulties of the President's job.

Writing Theme
Presidents on the Presidency

Writing Theme: Presidents on the Presidency

Other related areas students might wish to explore as writing topics include the following:

- the sayings of Harry S Truman
- sayings of Theodore Roosevelt
- the sayings of Abraham Lincoln
- the sayings of Franklin D. Roosevelt

Answers to Practice Your Skills

Concept Check
Quotation Marks

1. "Being President is like riding a tiger," said Harry S Truman. "A man has to keep on riding or be swallowed."
2. Is it true that Jimmy Carter said, "I can get up at nine and be rested, or I can get up at six and be President"?
3. Correct
4. Eisenhower also said, "There is one thing about being President; nobody can tell you when to sit down!"
5. Joan said, "I read that Truman used to say, 'The buck stops here,' to show the difficulties of the President's job."

6. "A President's hardest task," said Lyndon Johnson, "is not to do what is right, but to know what is right."
7. Correct
8. "No President," said Theodore Roosevelt, "ever enjoyed the presidency as I did"; that sounds like something he would say!
9. "I think the President is the only person," said Jimmy Carter, "who can change the direction or attitude of our nation."
10. "When he was appointed, Gerald Ford said, 'I guess it proves that in America anyone can be President,'" said Joan.

STUMBLING BLOCK Students may fail to paragraph dialogue correctly because it seems to them that all the sentences in a conversation are related to the same main idea, as in a single paragraph. Explain that even though the ideas relate to the same general topic, each quotation is a new thought because it comes from a different person.

6. A President's hardest task, said Lyndon Johnson, is not to do what is right, but to know what is right.
7. Herbert Hoover said that the only two occasions when Americans respected the President's privacy were prayer and fishing.
8. No President, said Theodore Roosevelt, ever enjoyed the presidency as I did; that sounds like something he would say!
9. I think the President is the only person, said Jimmy Carter, Who can change the direction or attitude of our nation.
10. When he was appointed, Gerald Ford said, I guess it proves that in America anyone can be President, said Joan.

FOR MORE PRACTICE
See page 672.

Punctuating Dialogue

There is one simple rule to remember when you write dialogue: begin a new paragraph each time you quote a different speaker.

> **"**Truman often commented on the difficulties of being President,**"** said Alice.
>
> Jake said, **"**He once compared the White House to a prison—a nice prison, of course, but still a prison.**"**
>
> Alice laughed at that. **"**That sounds like something Truman would have said.**"**
>
> **"**Yes, I have always admired his sense of humor.**"**

Punctuating Titles

Use quotation marks to enclose the titles of poems, short stories, songs, reports, articles, and chapters of books.

Poem	**"**Fame**"**
Short Story	**"**Hail and Farewell**"**
Song	**"**Everything's Coming Up Roses**"**

Underline titles of books, plays, magazines, newspapers, television series, works of art, musical compositions, epic poems, and motion pictures. Titles that are underlined are italicized in print.

Book	Max Malone, Superstar
Magazine	People
Television Series	Entertainment Tonight
Motion Picture	The Band Wagon

Literature Connection

Write on the board the following passage from Pearl Buck's "The Big Wave." Do not show paragraph breaks. Then ask students to divide the passage into paragraphs.

After supper that evening, Kino turned to his father. "Why is Jiya afraid of the ocean?" he asked.

"The ocean is very big," Kino's father replied. "We do not understand the ocean."

"I am glad we live on the mountain," Kino went on. "There is nothing to be afraid of on our farm."

"But one can be afraid of the land too," his father replied.

Practice Your Skills

A. CONCEPT CHECK

Using Punctuation Correctly Write these sentences, adding and deleting punctuation and underlining where necessary.

1. All right said Ms. Kehoe, What play do you want to do for this year's Spring Festival
2. Well, last year we did a science fiction play called Return to Planet Oog said Will
3. It was based on the short story Final Frontier said Jo
4. Annie asked How about writing a mystery based on a Sherlock Holmes story, like The Red-Headed League.
5. Susan suggested We could do a musical, like Grease
6. No musicals! groaned Doug. Let's do a play, like Our Town
7. I think we should write our own play said Eric We could dramatize a book, like The Outsiders
8. Did you read the article Making People Laugh asked Will. I think we should write a series of funny skits?
9. How will you choose from so many good ideas asked Ms. Kehoe
10. I'll make a list of the ideas, said Jo and then we should do as Mr. Bell always says, and I quote Let's put it to a vote.

Writing Theme
Show Time!

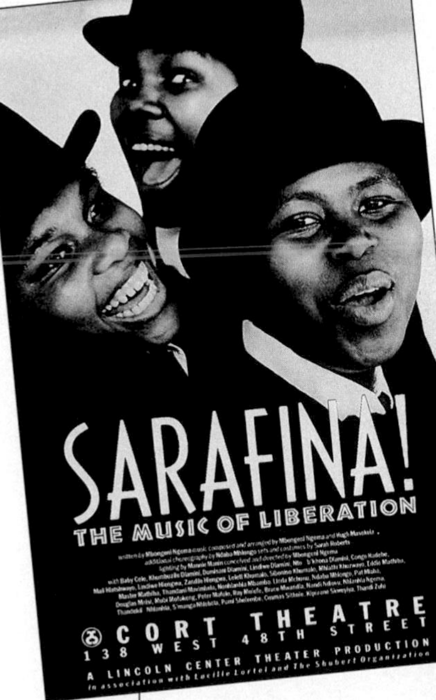

SARAFINA!
THE MUSIC OF LIBERATION
CORT THEATRE
138 WEST 48TH STREET
A LINCOLN CENTER THEATER PRODUCTION

B. APPLICATION IN LITERATURE

Punctuating Dialogue Write this dialogue, adding the correct punctuation and paragraph divisions.

[11]Mrs. Bacon I said trying to think fast remember how you said that the play was really about kids? [12]You know, Juliet thirteen, Romeo a little older? [13]That's true [14]Shakespeare isn't just for all times of the day but for all ages [15]That's the whole point I agreed [16]We thought since it's about kids and we're doing it for kids it's only fair that kids get to do it themselves [17]Right Lucy chimed in nobody knows us more than us [18]Except him I quickly said [19]Who is him said Mrs.Bacon a bit confused [20]The Bard I said edging Lucy toward the door

Avi, *Romeo and Juliet: Together (and Alive!) at Last*

FOR MORE PRACTICE
See page 672.

Writing Theme: Show Time!

Other related areas students might wish to explore as writing topics include the following:
- stage design
- people behind the scenes
- regional theater
- putting on a school play

Answers to Practice Your Skills

A. Concept Check
Using Punctuation Correctly

1. "All right," said Ms. Kehoe. "What play do you want to do for this year's Spring Festival?"
2. "Well, last year we did a science fiction play called *Return to Planet Oog,"* said Will.
3. "It was based on the short story 'Final Frontier,'" said Jo.
4. Annie asked, "How about writing a mystery based on a Sherlock Holmes story, like 'The Red-Headed League'?"
5. Susan suggested, "We could do a musical, like *Grease."*
6. "No musicals!" groaned Doug. "Let's do a play, like *Our Town."*
7. "I think we should write our own play," said Eric. "We could dramatize a book, like *The Outsiders."*
8. "Did you read the article 'Making People Laugh'?" asked Will. "I think we should write a series of funny skits."
9. "How will you choose from so many good ideas?" asked Ms. Kehoe.
10. "I'll make a list of the ideas," said Jo, "and then we should do as Mr. Bell always says, and I quote, 'Let's put it to a vote.'"

B. Application in Literature
Punctuating Dialogue

11 "Mrs. Bacon," I said, trying to think fast, "remember how you said that the play was really about kids? 12 You know, Juliet thirteen, Romeo a little older?"

13 "That's true. 14 Shakespeare isn't just for all times of the day but for all ages."

15 "That's the whole point," I agreed. 16 "We thought, since it's about kids, and we're doing it for kids, it's only fair that kids get to do it themselves." [first two commas optional]

17 "Right," Lucy chimed in. "Nobody knows us more than us."

18 "Except him," I quickly said.

19 "Who is him?" said Mrs. Bacon, a bit confused.

20 "The Bard," I said, edging Lucy toward the door.

Avi, *Romeo and Juliet: Together (and Alive!) at Last*

CHECK POINT

Writing Theme: Eco-Watch Meeting

Other related areas students might wish to explore as writing topics include the following:

- student activism
- ecology watchdog groups
- the Environmental Protection Agency

MIXED REVIEW • PAGES 664–667

You may wish to use this activity to check students' mastery of the following concepts:

- quotation marks
- punctuating dialogue
- punctuating titles

1. Correct
2. "What do we want to talk about today?" he asked.
3. John said, "We still haven't decided what to do for Earth Day."
4. "Did you see the article called 'Beware, Polluters: Little Brother Is Watching' in the *Daily News?"* asked Paul.
5. "It said that kids are really getting involved in environmental issues these days," he continued.
6. "We could write a pamphlet," suggested Emma, "that lists things people can do every day to help the environment."
7. Barbara said, "The book *Fifty Simple Things Kids Can Do to Save the Earth* has lots of good suggestions."
8. "Yes," agreed Cathy, "so does the book called *Save the Earth."*
9. "It says, 'Think globally, act locally.' Our group is trying to do that," she pointed out.
10. Ken asked, "What kinds of suggestions would we make?"
11. "Well," replied Cathy, "Chapter 3, 'Water,' lists things like fixing leaks, taking shorter showers, and saving rainwater."
12. She said, "We need simple, helpful hints like those"; the others nodded in agreement.
13. "Good!" said Emma. "We could all collect ideas from books and articles."
14. She added, "Then we can choose the ideas we think are the best."
15. "It'll be a lot of work," said Paul, "and there's not much time."
16. "We can do it if we all work together," Emma reminded him.
17. She said, "I want to be able to say, as one kid said, 'It makes me feel that I'm doing something for the earth.'"
18. "All right," said Ken. "Let's vote. All those in favor say, 'Aye.'"

CHECK POINT

MIXED REVIEW • PAGES 664–667

Writing Theme
Eco-Watch Meeting

Write these sentences, punctuating each correctly by adding quotation marks and underlining where necessary. If a sentence is correct, write *Correct.*

1. Ken asked that the meeting of the local Eco-Watch group come to order.
2. What do we want to talk about today? he asked.
3. John said, We still haven't decided what to do for Earth Day.
4. Did you see the article called Beware, Polluters: Little Brother Is Watching in the Daily News? asked Paul.
5. It said that kids are really getting involved in environmental issues these days, he continued.
6. We could write a pamphlet, suggested Emma, that lists things people can do every day to help the environment.
7. Barbara said, The book Fifty Simple Things Kids Can Do to Save the Earth has lots of good suggestions.
8. Yes, agreed Cathy, so does the book called Save the Earth.
9. It says, Think globally, act locally. Our group is trying to do that, she pointed out.
10. Ken asked, What kinds of suggestions would we make?
11. Well, replied Cathy, Chapter 3, Water, lists things like fixing leaks, taking shorter showers, and saving rainwater.
12. She said, We need simple, helpful hints like those; the others nodded in agreement.
13. Good! said Emma. We could all collect ideas from books and articles.
14. She added, Then we can choose the ideas we think are the best.
15. It'll be a lot of work, said Paul, and there's not much time.
16. We can do it if we all work together, Emma reminded him.
17. She said, I want to be able to say, as one kid said, It makes me feel that I'm doing something for the earth.
18. All right, said Ken. Let's vote. All those in favor say Aye.
19. Everyone shouted Aye at the same time.
20. Ken said that the vote was unanimous.

19. Everyone shouted, "Aye!" at the same time.
20. Correct

ADDITIONAL PRACTICE

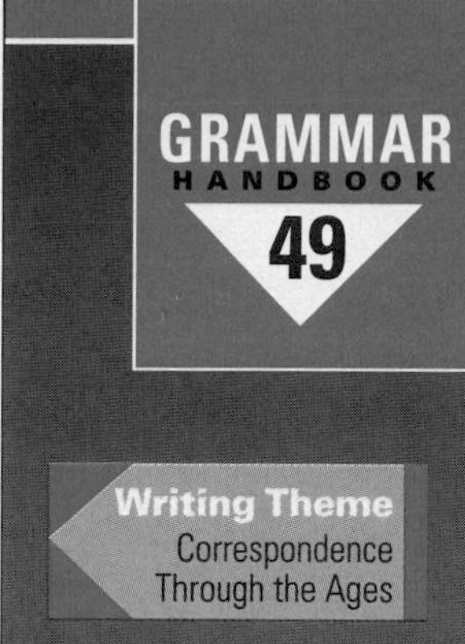

Writing Theme
Correspondence Through the Ages

A. Using End Marks Write the following sentences, adding periods, question marks, and exclamation points where needed.

1. You know who Thomas Jefferson was, don't you
2. He was the writer of the Declaration of Independence, the third President, an inventor, and a founder of the University of Virginia
3. What a wonderful and inspired leader he was
4. He was also a person who corresponded with many people
5. He wrote hundreds of letters in his lifetime
6. About what did he write and to whom did he write
7. He wrote to friends, relatives, political leaders, and government officials
8. In a letter to Mr T J Smith, a friend's son, he wrote:
   "1 Never put off till to-morrow what you can do to-day
   2 Never trouble another for what you can do yourself
   3 Never spend your money before you have it."
9. Did Smith heed the advice We don't know
10. We do know, however, that Jefferson's letters have helped us better understand Jefferson, his times, and the American past

B. Using Commas That Separate Ideas Write the words that should be followed by commas. If a sentence is correct, write *Correct*.

11. Newspapers magazines and news programs receive mail daily.
12. People write them with praise for their work or people write to express their views on issues of interest.
13. Some people write to editors but others write to reporters.
14. Letters to editors are written to express opinions to discuss issues or to ask for corrections.
15. Some of the letters are written by ordinary people and some are written by celebrities and political leaders.
16. Here's how to write to the media: first outline your ideas; second make your statement; and third format the letter properly.
17. Express your opinions, support them with facts, and be polite.
18. Try to write a concise informative and interesting letter.
19. Also make sure that your letter has a heading an inside address a salutation a body a closing and your signature.
20. Good letters are read enjoyed and possibly printed by editors.

ADDITIONAL PRACTICE

Each of these exercises correlates to a section of Handbook 49, "Punctuation." The exercises may be used for more practice, for reteaching, or for review of the concepts presented.

Additional Resource

Grammar and Usage Practice Book, p. 139

Writing Theme: Correspondence Through the Ages

Other related areas students might wish to explore as writing topics include the following:

- electronic mail and voice mail
- secret codes and ciphers
- Lincoln's letters
- Abigail Adams's correspondence

A. Using End Marks

1. You know who Thomas Jefferson was, don't you?
2. He was the writer of the Declaration of Independence, the third President, an inventor, and a founder of the University of Virginia.
3. What a wonderful and inspired leader he was!
4. He was also a person who corresponded with many people.
5. He wrote hundreds of letters in his lifetime.
6. About what did he write and to whom did he write?
7. He wrote to friends, relatives, political leaders, and government officials.
8. In a letter to Mr. T. J. Smith, a friend's son, he wrote:
   "1. Never put off till to-morrow what you can do to-day.
   2. Never trouble another for what you can do yourself.
   3. Never spend your money before you have it."
9. Did Smith heed the advice? We don't know.
10. We do know, however, that Jefferson's letters have helped us better understand Jefferson, his times, and the American past.

B. Using Commas That Separate Ideas

11. Newspapers, magazines
12. work,
13. editors,

14. opinions, issues,
15. people,
16. first, second, third,
17. Correct
18. concise, informative,
19. heading, address, salutation, body, closing
20. read, enjoyed

C. Using Commas That Set Off Special Elements

21. ISAAC: The history of the postal service in the United States is really interesting, Carol. Do you know anything about it?
22. CAROL: Well, I know that Congress issued the first U.S. postage stamps in 1847.
23. ISAAC: True; however, the use of stamps wasn't required until almost ten years later.
24. JERRY: One of the more exciting developments, I believe, was the pony express, a mail delivery system.
25. CAROL: Didn't it operate between Missouri and California, Jerry?
26. JERRY: Right—riders on horses rode day and night in relays, or shifts, to deliver the mail.
27. ISAAC: The service lasted for about a year, Carol.
28. CAROL: It's odd, don't you think, that the service didn't last longer.
29. ISAAC: Well, the transcontinental telegraph began operating in 1861 and, I believe, eliminated the need for the pony express.
30. JERRY: In fact, the pony express service closed just two days after the wire service, or telegraph, opened.

D. Using Commas in Other Ways

31. Dear Carrie,
32. Today is April 5, 1993. I never will forget this date.
33. "We are moving to Libertyville, Illinois," my parents told me this morning.
34. "Where's Libertyville?" I asked. "I've never heard of it."
35. Mom replied, "Libertyville is near Chicago, Illinois."
36. I have lived in Marin County, California, all my life, and I thought that I would always live here.
37. I was really looking forward to starting high school with my friends in San Francisco, California.
38. Dad said, "We will leave San Francisco in August 1993.

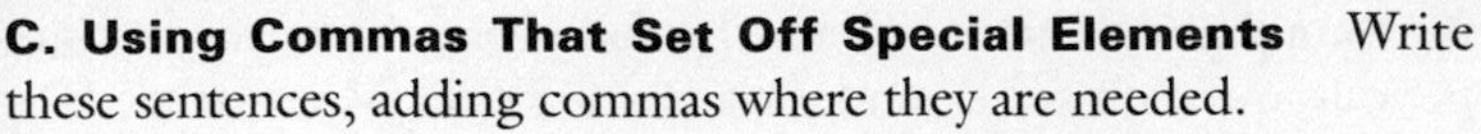

C. Using Commas That Set Off Special Elements

Write these sentences, adding commas where they are needed.

21. ISAAC: The history of the postal service in the United States is really interesting Carol. Do you know anything about it?
22. CAROL: Well I know that Congress issued the first U.S. postage stamps in 1847.
23. ISAAC: True; however the use of stamps wasn't required until almost ten years later.
24. JERRY: One of the more exciting developments I believe was the pony express a mail delivery system.
25. CAROL: Didn't it operate between Missouri and California Jerry?
26. JERRY: Right—riders on horses rode day and night in relays or shifts to deliver the mail.
27. ISAAC: The service lasted for about a year Carol.
28. CAROL: It's odd don't you think that the service didn't last longer.
29. ISAAC: Well the transcontinental telegraph began operating in 1861 and I believe eliminated the need for the pony express.
30. JERRY: In fact the pony express service closed just two days after the wire service or telegraph opened.

D. Using Commas in Other Ways

Write the following letter, adding commas where necessary.

31 Dear Carrie

32 Today is April 5 1993. I never will forget this date.

33 "We are moving to Libertyville Illinois" my parents told me this morning.

34 "Where's Libertyville?" I asked. "I've never heard of it."

35 Mom replied, "Libertyville is near Chicago Illinois."

36 I have lived in Marin County California all my life and I thought that I would always live here. 37 I was really looking forward to starting high school with my friends in San Francisco California.

38 Dad said "We will leave San Francisco in August 1993. 39 After the movers come" he continued "we'll drive east and make a few stops along the way."

40 "We will be stopping in Phoenix Arizona" Mom explained "to visit friends and then in Des Moines Iowa to see Grandma."

39. After the movers come," he continued, "we'll drive east and make a few stops along the way."
40. "We will be stopping in Phoenix, Arizona," Mom explained, "to visit friends and then in Des Moines, Iowa, to see Grandma."

41 Carrie didn't you see two plays an opera and a baseball game when you visited Chicago in June 1991?

42 "In Chicago are the Sears Tower the Field Museum and several sports teams" Dad reminded me "and I think you will love it."

43 Mom told me "After we settle Carrie can visit."

44 Once we move, you can write me at 200 Western Avenue Libertyville Illinois 60048.

45 Your friend always
Elise

E. Using Semicolons and Colons Write the following letter, adding semicolons and colons where necessary.

46 Dear Mr. Samuelson

47 I received your manuscript titled <u>The 820 A.M. Train to Milwaukee</u> however, I am afraid I must return it to you. 48 Davis and Brand, Inc., specializes in publishing the following genres poetry, short stories, essays, and critical reviews. 49 We do not publish novels. 50 Perhaps you could try submitting your work to these publishers Runsom House, Scribblers, and Carter/Hollins in New York Wattleway in Boston and Deal, Inc., in Chicago. 51 They are always looking for new authors they might be interested in reading your novel. 52 Remember, a writing career requires the following traits confidence, perseverance, and a thick skin! 53 Your local library has additional information about publishing for example, <u>Literary Market Place</u> and <u>Writer's Market</u> are valuable sources. 54 I wish you success in your writing career.

55 Sincerely,
Claire Edison

F. Using Hyphens Write these sentences, adding hyphens where necessary.

56. Long ago, people used hand sharpened straws or reeds as pens.
57. Later, people made finer tipped pens by using goose feathers in stead of straws or reeds.
58. Fountain pens were invented in our great grandparents' time.
59. Ballpoint pens became popular after World War II pilots dis covered they wrote well during high altitude flying.
60. Soft tip pens and rolling ball pens were invented about twenty five years ago.

41. Carrie, didn't you see two plays, an opera, and a baseball game when you visited Chicago in June 1991?
42. "In Chicago are the Sears Tower, the Field Museum, and several sports teams," Dad reminded me, "and I think you will love it."
43. Mom told me, "After we settle, Carrie can visit."
44. Once we move, you can write me at 200 Western Avenue, Libertyville, Illinois 60048.
45. Your friend always,
Elise

E. Using Semicolons and Colons

46 Dear Mr. Samuelson:

47 I received your manuscript titled *The 8:20 A.M. Train to Milwaukee;* however, I am afraid I must return it to you. 48 Davis and Brand, Inc., specializes in publishing the following genres: poetry, short stories, essays, and critical reviews. 49 We do not publish novels. 50 Perhaps you could try submitting your work to these publishers: Runsom House, Scribblers, and Carter/Hollins in New York; Wattleway in Boston; and Deal, Inc., in Chicago. 51 They are always looking for new authors; they might be interested in reading your novel.
52 Remember, a writing career requires the following traits: confidence, perseverance, and a thick skin! 53 Your local library has additional information about publishing; for example, *Literary Market Place* and *Writer's Market* are valuable sources. 54 I wish you success in your writing career.

55 Sincerely,
Claire Edison

F. Using Hyphens

56. Long ago, people used hand-sharpened straws or reeds as pens.
57. Later, people made finer-tipped pens by using goose feathers in-stead [end-of-line word division] of straws or reeds.
58. Fountain pens were invented in our great-grandparents' time.
59. Ballpoint pens became popular when World War II pilots dis-covered [end-of-line word division] they wrote well during high-altitude flying.
60. Soft-tip pens and rolling-ball pens were invented about twenty-five years ago.

G. Using Apostrophes

61. couldn't
62. You'd, wouldn't
63. you'd, scribe's
64. people's, letters
65. church's, government's
66. king's, king's, people's
67. church's
68. hadn't, scribes'
69. historians'
70. They're

H. Using Quotation Marks

71. In his book *Biographical Essays,* Lytton Strachey said, "The great letter writer must be an egotist." What do you think he meant by that?
72. "A good letter is an exercise of the ego," agreed Clifton Fadiman.
73. Was it Thoreau who said, "I have received no more than one or two letters in my life that were worth the postage"?
74. But Stephen Spender said, "A letter is like a present." Lena said the same thing when she got a ten-page letter from a friend.
75. Janice said, "I agree with Mark Van Doren, who said, 'The letter that merely answers another letter is no letter at all.'"
76. The lines "Letters of thanks, letters from banks,/Letters of joy from girl and boy" are from W. H. Auden's poem "Night Mail."
77. "Letters are largely written to get things out of your system," said John Dos Passos in his book *The Fourteenth Chronicle.*
78. Dr. Johnson said that a short letter to a friend was an insult.
79. John said, "Voltaire once remarked, 'Letters are the consolation of life.'"
80. "The true use of a letter," said James Russell Lowell, "is to let one know that one is remembered and valued."

G. Using Apostrophes Write the words that need apostrophes and the words that have incorrectly placed apostrophes.

61. What would you do if you couldnt write a letter for yourself?
62. Youd find someone who could write it for you, wouldnt you?
63. If you wanted to write a letter in ancient times, youd have gotten a scribes help.
64. Some scribes made their living writing peoples letter's.
65. The churchs and the governments business also required many written documents.
66. A kings scribe would write out the kings instructions and record peoples tax payments.
67. The churchs sacred books were all written by hand.
68. In the Middle Ages, printing hadnt been developed, so scribes copies were the only books that existed.
69. These copies are important to modern historians research.
70. Theyre one of the main sources historians use to find out about the past.

H. Using Quotation Marks Write these sentences, adding punctuation and underlining where necessary.

71. In his book Biographical Essays, Lytton Strachey said The great letter writer must be an egotist What do you think he meant by that
72. A good letter is an exercise of the ego agreed Clifton Fadiman
73. Was it Thoreau who said I have received no more than one or two letters in my life that were worth the postage
74. But Stephen Spender said A letter is like a present Lena said the same thing when she got a ten-page letter from a friend
75. Janice said I agree with Mark Van Doren, who said The letter that merely answers another letter is no letter at all
76. The lines Letters of thanks, letters from banks, / Letters of joy from girl and boy are from W. H. Auden's poem Night Mail
77. Letters are largely written to get things out of your system said John Dos Passos in his book The Fourteenth Chronicle
78. Dr. Johnson said that a short letter to a friend was an insult
79. John said, Voltaire once remarked Letters are the consolation of life.
80. The true use of a letter said James Russell Lowell is to let one know that one is remembered and valued

A. Using Commas and End Marks Write these sentences, adding commas and end marks where they are needed. If a sentence is correctly punctuated, write *Correct.*

1. Do you know who Esther Pauline Friedman Lederer and Pauline Esther Friedman Phillips are
2. They are better known as Ann Landers and Abigail Van Buren.
3. Did you know that these popular advice columnists are sisters
4. In fact they are twins
5. Since the 1950s the sisters have been writing advice columns
6. Ann began her column in 1955 and Abigail began hers in 1956.
7. Since then both have received thousands of letters
8. The letters ask for advice about problems express readers' concerns and comment on important issues
9. Of course they cannot answer all the letters they receive but they do try to answer ones that deal with common problems.
10. They do not rely only on their own knowledge however when they answer the letters.
11. They consult experts such as lawyers doctors and the clergy.
12. Their advice is usually filled with common sense, good humor, and concern for individuals.
13. At times both urge that writers seek professional help.
14. Thousands have enjoyed their columns and many have benefited from their advice
15. They have been thoughtful realistic problem solvers for years.

B. Using Commas and Semicolons Write these sentences, adding commas and semicolons where necessary.

16. Looking up from her crossword puzzle Mom asked "Jeff do you know a three-letter word for a large African antelope?"
17. I told Mom an avid crossword-puzzle fan that the right answer was probably *gnu.*
18. My parents Ed and Cati Morini enjoy working crossword puzzles they say that doing the puzzles relaxes them.
19. Although they both work puzzles daily Mom always works the puzzles from beginning to end Dad skips around filling in blanks here and there.
20. They work the crossword puzzles in our local newspaper the *Jefferson Times* and in the paper's Sunday magazine and they also buy crossword-puzzle books.

Writing Theme
Puzzles and Problems

REVIEW

These exercises may be used as mixed review or as an informal evaluation of the skills presented in Handbook 49, "Punctuation."

Additional Resources

Grammar and Usage Practice Book, p. 140
Tests and Writing Assessment Prompts, Mastery Test, pp. 51–52
Elaboration, Revision, and Proofreading Practice, p. 35

Writing Theme: Puzzles and Problems

Other related areas students might wish to explore as writing topics include the following:

- riddles and brain teasers
- picture puzzles
- Erno Rubik and the Rubik's cube

A. Using Commas and End Marks

1. Do you know who Esther Pauline Friedman Lederer and Pauline Esther Friedman Phillips are?
2. Correct
3. Did you know that these popular advice columnists are sisters?
4. In fact, they are twins! (or twins.)
5. Since the 1950s, the sisters have been writing advice columns. (or omit comma)
6. Ann began her column in 1955, and Abigail began hers in 1956.
7. Since then, both have received thousands of letters.
8. The letters ask for advice about problems, express readers' concerns, and comment on important issues.
9. Of course, they cannot answer all the letters they receive, but they do try to answer ones that deal with common problems.
10. They do not rely only on their own knowledge, however, when they answer the letters.
11. They consult experts, such as lawyers, doctors, and the clergy.
12. Correct
13. At times, both urge that writers seek professional help.
14. Thousands have enjoyed their columns, and many have benefited from their advice.
15. They have been thoughtful, realistic problem solvers for years.

B. Using Commas and Semicolons

16. Looking up from her crossword puzzle, Mom asked, "Jeff, do you know a three-letter word for a large African antelope?"
17. I told Mom, an avid crossword-puzzle fan, that the right answer was probably *gnu.*
18. My parents, Ed and Cati Morini, enjoy working crossword puzzles; they say that doing the puzzles relaxes them.

19. Although they both work puzzles daily, Mom always works the puzzles from beginning to end; Dad skips around, filling in blanks here and there.
20. They work the crossword puzzles in our local newspaper, the *Jefferson Times,* and in the paper's Sunday magazine, and they also buy crossword-puzzle books.
21. One day as he worked on a puzzle, Dad asked, "Do you know when the first modern crossword puzzle appeared?"
22. "No, Dad, I don't," I replied. "In fact, I never thought about it."
23. I learned that the modern crossword puzzle, now a popular word game, was created by Arthur Wynne.
24. "His first puzzle appeared in a New York paper, the *New York World,* on December 21, 1913," Dad explained.
25. Since then, people in the United States, in Canada, and all over the world have worked crossword puzzles, and some people even compete in crossword-puzzle contests.

C. Using Apostrophes and Quotation Marks

26. The complex patterns of mazes have long tested people's patience and sense of humor.
27. The best-known hedge maze is at England's Hampton Court Palace.
28. The hedge maze at Longleat House is the world's largest.
29. "Finding the center of the maze," said Jill, "is easier than getting out again."
30. "We needed the maze keeper's help to get out," agreed Mary.
31. "People get lost all the time," said the maze keeper. "We've had some in there for three hours."
32. A modern maze builder said, "It's not about getting lost. It's about having fun."
33. At his maze he encourages people to play tag on the paths and forget that they're adults.
34. "It's best to enter a maze with a child's sense of fun," he said.
35. "The turf maze at Saffron Walden is my favorite," Jill said.
36. "Our aunt and uncle's book on tile mazes shows interesting patterns in the floors of churches and houses," said Jill.
37. "The good thing about tile and turf mazes," explained Mary, "is that when you've had enough, you can just walk off."
38. Jill laughed, "Yes, that's not true in hedge mazes."
39. The article "Garden-Variety Puzzles" in the magazine *European Travel & Life* has wonderful pictures of different mazes.
40. You can find more information in books such as *Labyrinth: Solving the Riddle of the Maze* and *The British Maze Guide.*

21. One day as he worked on a puzzle Dad asked "Do you know when the first modern crossword puzzle appeared?"
22. "No Dad I don't" I replied. "In fact I never thought about it."
23. I learned that the modern crossword puzzle now a popular word game was created by Arthur Wynne.
24. "His first puzzle appeared in a New York paper the *New York World* on December 21 1913" Dad explained.
25. Since then people in the United States in Canada and all over the world have worked crossword puzzles and some people even compete in crossword-puzzle contests.

C. Using Apostrophes and Quotation Marks Write the following sentences, adding apostrophes, underlining, quotation marks, and commas where necessary.

26. The complex patterns of mazes have long tested peoples patience and sense of humor.
27. The best-known hedge maze is at Englands Hampton Court Palace.
28. The hedge maze at Longleat House is the worlds largest.
29. Finding the center of the maze said Jill is easier than getting out again.
30. We needed the maze keepers help to get out agreed Mary.
31. People get lost all the time said the maze keeper. Weve had some in there for three hours.
32. A modern maze builder said Its not about getting lost. Its about having fun.
33. At his maze he encourages people to play tag on the paths and forget that theyre adults.
34. Its best to enter a maze with a childs sense of fun he said.
35. The turf maze at Saffron Walden is my favorite Jill said.
36. Our aunt and uncles book on tile mazes shows interesting patterns in the floors of churches and houses said Jill.
37. The good thing about tile and turf mazes explained Mary is that when youve had enough, you can just walk off.
38. Jill laughed Yes, thats not true in hedge mazes.
39. The article Garden-Variety Puzzles in the magazine European Travel & Life has wonderful pictures of different mazes.
40. You can find more information in books such as Labyrinth: Solving the Riddle of the Maze and The British Maze Guide.

674 Grammar Handbook

Elaboration, Revision, and Proofreading

Revise the following draft of a process description, using the directions at the bottom of the page. Then proofread your work, paying particular attention to correcting punctuation errors. Also look for errors in grammar, capitalization, and spelling.

[1]Have you ever wondered how a copy machine works. [2]Electrostatic copying the most common type of copying was invented in 1938 by Chester f Carlson. [3]According to the book "Questions and Answers," Carlsons invention works like this: [4]First a flash of light projects the image of the page being copied onto a drum. [5]The drum has a light-senstive surface. [6]Which takes on an electric charge in the pattern of the image. [7]Then it is dusted with toner. [8]Toner is an inked powder. [9]Toner can be messy. [10]The powder clinged to the part's of the drum with the electric charge. [11]The powder image is transferred to the paper. [12]The paper is heated, to bake on the powder. [13]The result is a exact copy of the orignal image.

1. In sentence 2, identify Carlson by adding the appositive "an American physicist."
2. In sentence 7, replace the pronoun "it" with the more precise "the drum."
3. Add the information in sentence 8 to sentence 7 as a subordinate clause beginning with a comma and "which."
4. Delete the sentence that does not belong.
5. After sentence 10 add this missing step: "Next, a piece of paper is rolled against the drum."
6. Add "finally" to the beginning of sentence 12 to show that heating the paper is the last step of the process.

Informative Writing: Explaining *How*

Describing a process involves giving a step-by-step account of how something works or how something is done. (See Workshop 4.) When you revise this type of writing, make sure you have presented all the steps in the proper order. Using punctuation effectively can help guide your readers through the steps of the process.

WRITING CONNECTIONS

Elaboration, Revision, and Proofreading

This activity will allow students to see some of the concepts presented in this handbook at work in a piece of informative writing, one that explains a process. In revising and proofreading this passage, students will use punctuation to help clarify ideas. They also will become more aware of the importance of including all—and only—the necessary information.

You might want to work through the first direction in the pupil edition with students. Have them work in pairs to complete the exercise; discuss the completed revisions with the class.

Revisions may vary slightly. See a typical revision below. Elements involving change are shown in boldface.

Have you ever wondered how a copy machine works? Electrostatic copying, the most common type of copying, was invented in 1938 by Chester F. Carlson, **an American physicist.** According to the book *Questions and Answers,* Carlson's invention works like this: First, a flash of light projects the image of the page being copied onto a drum. The drum has a light-sensitive surface, which takes on an electric charge in the pattern of the image. Then, **the drum** is dusted with toner, **which is an inked powder.** ~~**Toner can be messy.**~~ The powder clings to the parts of the drum with the electric charge. **Next, a piece of paper is rolled against the drum.** The powder image is transferred to the paper. **Finally,** the paper is heated to bake on the powder. The result is an exact copy of the original image.

Test 4

This test enables you to evaluate student mastery of the concepts taught in Handbooks 48–49.

Additional Resource

Grammar and Usage Practice Book, pp. 141–142

Answer Key

Corrections for run-ons may vary.

1. D—Maine
2. B—writing, "He
   C—often, and
3. E
4. A—growing, a
5. B—said, "They
6. D—"Nuts!"
7. A—Rogers's
   C—"as
8. A—Copenhagen, Denmark,
9. C—as
   D—flute, and
10. D—Fourth of July
11. A—World War II
    C—Navajo
12. B—Rev.
    D—sat
13. E
14. B—English
15. C—wide, but

List of Skills Tested

1. A—subject-verb agreement: inverted sentence
   B—spelling
   C—punctuation: compound sentence
   D—capitalization: geographical name
2. A—irregular verb form
   B—punctuation: quotation
   C—punctuation: comma in a series
   D—punctuation: quotation
3. A—punctuation: comma with appositive
   B—punctuation: end mark
   C—punctuation: period before a decimal
   D—punctuation: hyphen with numbers
4. A—punctuation: comma to avoid confusion
   B—wrong word: lie/lay
   C—punctuation: compound predicate
   D—wrong word: rise/raise

Skills ASSESSMENT

Directions One or more of the underlined sections in the following sentences may contain an error in grammar, usage, punctuation, spelling, or capitalization. Write the letter of each incorrect section. Then rewrite the section correctly. If there is no error in an item, write *E.*

Example Lester nixon (A) may need a wheelchair, but he certainly gets around; he (B) has visited (C) more than one hundred countries (D). No error (E)

Answer A—Lester Nixon

1. There is (A) a church in the Channel Islands that has room for only one priest (B) and two congregation members; a (C) church in maine (D) is even smaller. No error (E)

2. Bessie Anderson won (A) a magazine contest by writing "He (B) has achieved success who has lived well, laughed often and (C) loved much." (D) No error (E)

3. The substance vanillin (A) is really smelly! (B) The odor of just 0.0001 (C) ounce can be detected in a room the size of a football field with a roof forty-five (D) feet high. No error (E)

4. While growing a (A) baby cuckoo may find home a tight squeeze.The mother cuckoo lays (B) an egg in the nest of another, often smaller, bird and (C) leaves her child to be hatched and raised (D) by a "foster parent." No error (E)

5. Explaining (A) why she loved books, Helen Keller said "They (B) talk to me without embarrassment (C) or awkwardness." (D) No error (E)

6. When a pair (A) of German officers demanded the surrender of the 101st Airborne Division (B), Anthony McAuliffe replied simply, (C) "Nuts"! (D) No error (E)

676 Skills Assessment

7. Victims of practical jokes prove Will Rogers' (A) wisdom. "Everything (B) is funny," said Rogers, "As (C) long as it is happening to somebody else." (D) No error (E)

8. The town-hall clock in copenhagen, denmark, (A) took ten years to make and has (B) fourteen thousand parts. It's (C) accurate to within one-half (D) a second in three hundred years. No error (E)

9. Among the earliest (A) musical instruments in history are (B) simple ones such as: (C) the bell, the flute and (D) the mouth bow. No error (E)

10. Observances of Easter (A) and Passover (B) vary from year to year; Independence Day, (C) on the other hand, always falls on the fourth of July (D). No error (E)

11. Some World war II (A) American radio operators (B) used a code no enemy could break. They were navajo (C) Indians, and the code was their (D) language. No error (E)

12. A journalist (A) who dined with the rev. (B) Francis Egerton wrote (C) that a dozen dogs set (D) at the dinner table, each wearing a linen napkin. The dogs were well-behaved. No error (E)

13. At the Bingham Canyon (A) copper mine in Utah, more (B) earth has been taken (C) out than was moved to make the Panama Canal (D). No error (E)

14. Although thirty-eight (A) other english (B) words are pronounced the same as *air*, a (C) frequent (D) reader will probably come across only two or three. No error (E)

15. Some meteors (A) that fell thousands (B) of years ago left craters a mile wide; but (C) most of these "shooting stars" are (D) the size of a grain of sand. No error (E)

5. A—spelling
B—punctuation: quotation
C—spelling
D—punctuation: quotation

6. A—spelling
B—capitalization: organization
C—adjective/adverb confusion
D—punctuation: quotation

7. A—punctuation: apostrophe in possessive
B—punctuation: quotation
C—capitalization: divided quotation
D—punctuation: quotation

8. A—capitalization: geographical name
B—subject-verb agreement: intervening words
C—possessive pronoun/contraction confusion
D—punctuation: hyphen in fraction

9. A—adjective comparison form
B—subject-verb agreement: inverted sentence
C—punctuation: colon introducing series
D—punctuation: commas in series

10. A—capitalization: holiday
B—capitalization: holiday
C—capitalization: holiday
D—capitalization: holiday

11. A—capitalization: event
B—noun plural
C—capitalization: proper adjective
D—possessive pronoun/contraction confusion

12. A—spelling
B—capitalization: title
C—irregular verb form
D—wrong word: sit/set

13. A—capitalization: geographical name
B—punctuation: comma with introductory phrase
C—irregular verb form
D—capitalization: geographical name

14. A—punctuation: hyphen with numbers
B—capitalization: language
C—punctuation: complex sentence
D—spelling

15. A—noun plural
B—noun plural
C—punctuation: complex sentence
D—subject-verb agreement: indefinite pronoun

Post-Test

This test assesses your students' mastery of skills acquired in the Grammar and Usage Handbook.

Answer Key

Correction for run-ons may vary.

1. C—grown
2. A—Angel Falls
   C—fall
3. C—most
4. A—are
   B—hobbies. Each *or* hobbies; each
5. A—inches
   D—heavily
6. B—South
   C—War. four *or* War; four
7. B—speaker. In *or* speaker; in
   C—there are
8. B—slowly
9. A—Whom
   C—"To
10. E
11. C—Esperanto, a
    D—spoken
12. B—appetites. Most *or* appetites; most
    C—their
13. C—he
14. A—summer
    B—scientists
15. C—lies

Lists of Skills Tested

1. A—capitalization: common noun
   B—punctuation: compound sentence
   C—irregular verb form
   D—capitalization: geographical name
2. A—capitalization: geographical name
   B—capitalization: geographical name
   C—subject-verb agreement: intervening words
   D—spelling
3. A—punctuation: question mark
   B—capitalization: first word in sentence
   C—comparative adverb form
   D—capitalization: common noun

Skills

Directions One or more of the underlined sections in the following sentences may contain an error in grammar, usage, punctuation, spelling, or capitalization. Write the letter of each incorrect section. Then rewrite the section correctly. If there is no error in an item, write *E.*

> ***Example*** Centipedes (A) don't really have a hundred legs, they (B) have one pair (C) of legs per body segment and (D) have as few as 5 segments or as many as 170. No error (E)
>
> ***Answer*** B—legs; they *or* legs. They

1. In half the world (A), rice is a major part of the diet, and (B) 90 percent of it is growed (C) in Asia (D). No error (E)
2. At angel falls (A) in Venezuela, (B) thousands of gallons of water falls (C) every second from a height (D) of 3,212 feet. No error (E)
3. Did you put the correct ZIP code on that package? (A) Forgetting (B) to include a ZIP code is the more (C) common error the post office (D) encounters. No error (E)
4. Both photography and stamp collecting is (A) popular hobbies each (B) requires (C) some special knowledge and (D) equipment. No error (E)
5. About ten inchs (A) of snow and (B) one inch of rain contain (C) the same amount of water. Therefore, to wet the earth, it must snow heavy (D). No error (E)
6. Not all slave states fought (A) on the side of the south (B) during the Civil War, four (C) of them supported the Union Army (D). No error (E)

7. Many languages (A) have only one remaining speaker, in (B) fact there is (C) more than twenty such languages in the world. (D) No error (E)

8. The French (A) artist Paul Cezanne painted so slow (B) that he often used wax fruit as models; real (C) fruit would have rotted. (D) No error (E)

9. Who (A) do you think of when (B) you hear, "to (C) be, or not to be"? (D) No error (E)

10. Most people know (A) that the bloodhound is the world's (B) best tracker, but few realize (C) that this dog is capable of following an eight-day-old (D) trail. No error (E)

11. There are (A) no irregular (B) verbs in Esperanto. A (C) language invented in 1887 and spoke (D) by at least a million people. No error (E)

12. Interestingly, birds (A) do not have dainty appetites, most (B) of them eat close to half there (C) weight (D) each day. No error (E)

13. When Langston Hughes was young and unknown, he (A) was helped and encouraged by the famous poet Vachel Lindsay (B). Now him (C) and Lindsay are equally (D) famous. No error (E)

14. During the Summer (A) of 1982, sceintists (B) at the State University of New York (C) recorded 15,000 lightning bolts in just one storm. Amazingly, that's not unusual! (D) No error (E)

15. The site of the Incan (A) city of Machu Picchu (B) lays (C) high in the Andes. (D) No error (E)

4. A—subject-verb agreement: compound subject
B—run-on sentence
C—subject-verb agreement: indefinite pronoun
D—punctuation: comma in series

5. A—noun plural
B—punctuation: compound subject
C—subject-verb agreement: compound subject
D—adjective/adverb confusion

6. A—irregular verb form
B—capitalization: geographical name
C—run-on sentence
D—capitalization: organization

7. A—noun plural
B—run-on sentence
C—subject-verb agreement: inverted sentence
D—capitalization: common noun

8. A—capitalization: nationality
B—adjective/adverb confusion
C—punctuation: compound sentence
D—spelling

9. A—wrong word: who/whom
B—punctuation: clause
C—capitalization: first word in quotation
D—punctuation: question mark outside quotation

10. A—subject-verb agreement
B—punctuation: apostrophe in possessive
C—spelling
D—punctuation: hyphens in compound adjectives

11. A—subject-verb agreement: inverted sentence
B—spelling
C—punctuation: comma with appositive
D—irregular verb form

12. A—punctuation: comma after introductory phrase
B—run-on sentence
C—wrong word: there/they're/their
D—spelling

13. A—punctuation: comma with introductory clause
B—punctuation: comma with appositive
C—pronoun case: subject
D—adjective/adverb confusion

14. A—capitalization: season
B—spelling
C—capitalization: institution
D—punctuation: exclamation point

15. A—capitalization: proper adjective
B—capitalization: geographical name
C—wrong word: lie/lay
D—capitalization: geographical name

Skills Assessment **679**

Appendix

Appendix

Techniques for Peer Response

Sharing your writing with others is an important part of being a writer. The following response techniques can help you give and receive useful feedback as you share your writing and as you read the writing of others.

Sharing

How to Use Read your words aloud to a peer. Your only purpose is to share and to hear how your words sound. Your listeners may ask you to slow down or to read your piece again, but at this stage their only response should be to listen carefully.

When to Use Do this when you are just exploring and you do not want criticism. Reading to a peer is also a good way to celebrate finishing a piece of writing.

Pointing

How to Use Ask readers to tell you what they like best in your writing. Tell them to identify specific words and phrases that they especially like. Encourage readers to say why those particular words are memorable.

When to Use Use this technique when you want to find out what is getting through to your readers or when you want some encouragement and support.

Summarizing

How to Use Ask readers to tell you what they think are your main ideas. The idea is to have readers tell you the points that most stand out for them, not the points that they like or the ones that confuse them. Tell readers that at this stage you are not asking for an evaluation of your writing.

When to Use Use this technique when you want to know if the main ideas or goals of your writing are clear to your readers.

Techniques for Peer Response 681

Telling

How to Use Ask readers to tell you a bit about what happened to them as they read your words. For example, did they feel surprised at any point? Did anything in the writing make them feel happy or sad? As readers describe their reactions, ask them to connect their responses to specific passages in the writing.

When to Use Use this technique when you want to know which words and phrases and ideas are especially effective and which ones are confusing to readers.

Replying

How to Use Discuss with your readers the ideas you used in your writing. Ask readers to give you their own ideas on your topic.

When to Use Use this technique when you want to get some new ideas to use in your writing.

Identifying Problems

How to Use Ask for feedback on specific features of your writing, such as the organization, the development of ideas, or the choice of words. Ask questions that require more than a yes-or-no answer, such as the following: "What parts, if any, were confusing?" "How can I improve the organization?" "Where do you like the wording, and where does it need improvement?"

When to Use Use this technique to identify the strengths and weaknesses of your piece.

Outlining

An outline can help you organize information logically. In a formal outline, the key ideas are the headings of the main parts. The details are the subpoints. A **sentence outline** uses complete sentences; a **topic outline** uses words or phrases, as in this model.

Zoos

Thesis Statement: Zoos serve three main functions: educating the public, promoting research, and conserving wildlife.

I. Educating the public (Key idea)
  A. Displays (Subpoint for I)
  B. Tours
  C. Lectures
  D. Attractions for children
II. Promoting research
  A. Study of animal organisms (Subpoint for II)
  B. Study of animal behavior
III. Conserving wildlife
  A. Breeding of zoo animals (Subpoint for III)
  B. Return of animals to the wild
    1. European bison (Detail for B)
    2. Hawaiian goose
  C. Care of zoo animals
    1. Re-creation of natural habitats (Detail for C)
    2. Feeding
    3. Veterinary aid

Correct Outline Form

1. Write the title at the top of the outline.
2. Arrange Roman numerals, capital letters, and Arabic numerals as shown in the model.
3. Indent each division of the outline.
4. Do not use a single subheading. Subdivide a main heading only if it can be broken down into at least two subpoints.
5. In a topic outline, use the same form for items of the same rank. If A is a noun, then B and C should be nouns.
6. In a topic outline, begin each item with a capital letter but use no end punctuation.

Outlining 683

LETTER FORM

Heading These lines contain your street address; your town or city, state, and ZIP code; and the date of the letter.

Inside Address Include the name of an individual if you know it and the name and address of the organization.

Salutation This begins two lines below the inside address and ends with a colon. If you are writing to a specific person, use the person's name. If you do not know who will receive your letter, use a general greeting.

Body This section should be brief, courteous, and clear. State the purpose of your letter and indicate any items that you are requesting or have enclosed.

Closing This appears two lines below the body and is always formal. "Sincerely" and "Yours truly" are examples.

Signature Skip four spaces below the closing, print or type your name, and write your signature in the space.

Heading 58 Eagle Road
La Crosse, Wisconsin 54601
February 10, 19--

Superintendent of Documents Inside Address
U. S. Government Printing Office
Washington, D.C. 20402

Dear Sir or Madam: Salutation

Body I am writing a report about solar energy. I understand that your agency has several publications on this subject.

Please send me any free pamphlets you have available about solar energy. Also please send me your free catalog <u>Selected List of U. S. Government Documents</u> so that I can learn about inexpensive books you may have about solar energy.

I am also interested in any bills in Congress that deal with solar energy. Can you give me any information about legislation that may be pending? I will appreciate any help you can give me.

Sincerely, Closing
Stella Noyes Signature
Stella Noyes

IMPROVING YOUR SPELLING

Good spelling gives your writing a professional look and impresses your audience. You can improve your spelling by applying the strategies used by successful spellers. The following guidelines and tips should help.

Good Spelling Habits

1. **Conquer your personal spelling demons.** Keep a list of the words you misspell in your writing.

2. **Pronounce words carefully.** Pronouncing words correctly can help you spell them correctly. For example, if you spell *helpfully* as *helpfly,* it might be because you are mispronouncing the word.

3. **Get into the habit of seeing the letters in a word.** Some English spellings are tricky. By looking at new or difficult words letter by letter, you will remember the spellings more easily.

4. **Create memory devices for difficult words.** For example:

a**cq**uaint (cq)	To get a**cq**uainted, I will *seek you.*
princi**pal** (pal)	The princi**pal** is my *pal.*
princi**ple** (ple)	Follow this princi**ple,** *ple*ase.

5. **Proofread everything you write.** Slowly read what you've written, word for word. You might even try reading a line in reverse order. Otherwise, your eyes may play tricks on you and let you skip a misspelled word.

Guidelines for Spelling Difficult Words

1. Look at the word and say it one syllable at a time.
2. Look at the letters and say each one.
3. Write the word without looking at it.
4. Check to see whether you spelled the word correctly. If so, write the word two more times.
5. If you made a mistake, note exactly what the mistake was. Then repeat steps 3 and 4 above.

Improving Your Spelling 685

Words Ending in a Silent *e*

Before adding a suffix beginning with a vowel to a word ending in a silent *e*, drop the *e* (with some exceptions).

amaze + -ing = amazing
create + -ed = created
love + -able = lovable
nerve + -ous = nervous

Exceptions: change + -able = changeable; courage + -ous = courageous

When adding a suffix beginning with a consonant to a word ending in a silent *e*, keep the *e* (with some exceptions).

late + -ly = lately
noise + -less = noiseless
spite + -ful = spiteful
state + -ment = statement

Exceptions: true + -ly = truly; argue + -ment = argument

Words Ending in *y*

Before adding a suffix to a word that ends in *y* preceded by a consonant, change the *y* to *i*.

easy + -est = easiest
crazy + -est = craziest

However, when you add *-ing,* the *y* does not change.

worry + -ed = worried *but* worry + -ing = worrying

When adding a suffix to a word that ends in *y* and is preceded by a vowel, the *y* usually does not change.

play + -er = player
employ + -ed = employed

Words Ending in a Consonant

In one-syllable words that end in *one* consonant preceded by *one* vowel, double the final consonant before adding a suffix beginning with a vowel, such as *-ed* or *-ing.* These are sometimes called 1+1+1 words.

dip + -ed = dipper
hop + -ed = hopped
set + -ing = setting
drug + -ist = druggist

The rule does not apply to words of one syllable that end in a consonant preceded by two vowels.

feel + -ing = feeling
reap + -ed = reaped
peel + -ed = peeled
heat + -ing = heating

In words of more than one syllable, double the final consonant (1) when the word ends with one consonant preceded by one vowel and (2) when the word is accented on the last syllable.

be•gin′ per•mit′ re•fer′

In the following examples, note that in the new words formed with suffixes, the accent remains on the same syllable.

be•gin′ + -ing = be•gin′ ning
per•mit′ + -ed = per•mit′ ted

In the following examples, the accent does not remain on the same syllable; thus, the final consonant is not doubled.

re•fer′ + -ence = ref′ er•ence
con•fer′ + -ence = con′ fer•ence

Prefixes and Suffixes

When adding a prefix to a word, do not change the spelling of the base word.

dis- + approve = disapprove	re- + build = rebuild
ir- + regular = irregular	mis- + spell = misspell

When adding *-ly* to a word ending in *l*, keep both *l's*. When adding *-ness* to a word ending in *n*, keep both *n*'s.

careful + -ly = carefully	sudden + -ness = suddenness
final + -ly = finally	thin + -ness = thinness

Special Spelling Problems

Only one English word ends in *-sede: supersede.* Three words end in *-ceed: exceed, proceed,* and *succeed.* All other verbs ending in the sound *-seed* are spelled with *-cede.*

concede precede recede secede

In words with *ie* and *ei* when the sound is long *e* (ē), the word is spelled *ie* except after *c* (with some exceptions).

i* before *e	thief	relieve	piece	field	grieve	pier
except after *c*	conceit	perceive	ceiling	receive	receipt	
Exceptions:	either	neither	weird	leisure	seize	

Improving Your Spelling 687

Using the Right Word

Good writers master words that are easy to misuse and misspell. Study the following words, noting how their meanings differ.

accept, except *Accept* means "to agree to something" or "to receive something willingly." *Except* usually means "not including."

Did the teacher *accept* your report?
Everyone smiled for the photographer *except* Jody.

all ready, already *All ready* means "all are ready" or "completely prepared." *Already* means "previously."

The students were *all ready* for the field trip.
We had *already* pitched our tent before it started raining.

all right *All right* is the correct spelling. *Alright* is nonstandard and should not be used.

a lot *A lot* may be used in informal writing. *Alot* is incorrect.

borrow, lend *Borrow* means "to receive something on loan." *Lend* means "to give out temporarily."

Please *lend* me your book.
He *borrowed* five dollars from his sister.

bring, take *Bring* refers to movement toward or with. *Take* refers to movement away from.

I'll *bring* you a glass of water.
Please *take* these books back to the library.

capital, capitol, the Capitol *Capital* means "excellent," "most serious," or "most important." It also means "seat of government." *Capitol* is a "building in which a state legislature meets." *The Capitol* is "the building in Washington, D.C., in which the U.S. Congress meets."

Proper nouns begin with *capital* letters.
Is Madison the *capital* of Wisconsin?
Protestors rallied at the state *capitol.*
A subway connects the Senate and the House in *the Capitol.*

choose, chose *Choose* is a verb that means "to decide or prefer." *Chose* is the past tense form of *choose.*

He had to *choose* between taking art or band.
She *chose* to write for the school newspaper.

desert, dessert *Des´ ert* means "a dry, sandy, barren region." *De sert´* means "to abandon." *Des sert´* is a sweet, such as cake.

The Sahara in North Africa is the world's largest *desert.*
The night guard did not *desert* his post.
Alison's favorite *dessert* is chocolate cake.

farther, further *Farther* refers to distance. *Further* refers to something additional.

We traveled two hundred miles *farther* that afternoon.
This idea needs *further* discussion.

fewer, less *Fewer* refers to numbers of things that can be counted. *Less* refers to amount, degree, or value.

Fewer than ten students camped out.
We made *less* money this year on the walkathon than last year.

good, well *Good* is always an adjective. *Well* is usually an adverb that modifies an action verb. *Well* can also be an adjective meaning "in good health."

Dana felt *good* when she finished painting her room.
Angela ran *well* in yesterday's race.
I felt *well* when I left my house.

its, it's *Its* is a possessive pronoun. *It's* is a contraction for *it is* or *it has.*

Sanibel Island is known for *its* beautiful beaches.
It's great weather for a picnic.

lay, lie *Lay* is a verb that means "to place." It takes a direct object. *Lie* is a verb that means "to be in a certain place." *Lie* never takes a direct object.

The carpenter will *lay* the planks on the bench.
My cat likes to *lie* under the bed.

Using the Right Word 689

lead, led *Lead* can be a noun that means "a heavy metal" or a verb that means "to show the way." *Led* is the past tense form of the verb.

> *Lead* is used in nuclear reactors.
> Raul always *leads* his team onto the field.
> She *led* the class as president of the student council.

learn, teach *Learn* means "to gain knowledge." *Teach* means "to instruct."

> Enrique is *learning* about galaxies and black holes in space.
> Marva *teaches* astronomy at a college in the city.

loan, lone *Loan* refers to "something given for temporary use." *Lone* refers to "the condition of being by oneself, alone."

> I gave that shirt to Max as a gift, not a *loan.*
> The *lone* plant in our yard turned out to be a scraggly weed.

lose, loose *Lose* means "to mislay or suffer the loss of something." *Loose* means "free" or "not fastened."

> That tire will *lose* air unless you patch it.
> My little brother has three *loose* teeth.

of Use *have,* not *of,* in phrases such as *could have, should have,* and *must have.*

> He could *have* passed if he had studied for the test.

principal, principle *Principal* means "of chief or central importance" and refers to the head of a school. *Principle* is a "basic truth, standard, or rule of behavior."

> Lack of customers is the *principal* reason for closing the store.
> The *principal* of our school awarded the trophy.
> One of my *principles* is to be honest with others.

quiet, quite *Quiet* refers to "freedom from noise or disturbance." *Quite* means "truly" or "almost completely."

> Observers must be *quiet* during the recording session.
> We were *quite* worried about the results of the test.

690 Appendix

raise, rise *Raise* means "to lift" or "to make something go up." It takes a direct object. *Rise* means "to go upward." It does not take a direct object.

The maintenance workers *raise* the flag each morning.
The city's population is expected to *rise* steadily.

set, sit *Set* means "to place" and takes a direct object. *Sit* means "to occupy a seat or a place" and does not take a direct object.

He *set* the box down outside the shed.
We *sit* in the last row of the upper balcony at every concert.

stationary, stationery *Stationary* means "fixed or unmoving." *Stationery* means "fine paper for writing letters."

The wheel pivots, but the seat is *stationary.*
Rex wrote on special *stationery* imprinted with his name.

than, then *Than* is used to introduce the second part of a comparison. *Then* means "next in order."

Ramon is stronger *than* Mark.
Cut the grass and *then* trim the hedges.

their, there, they're *Their* means "belonging to them." *There* means "in that place." *They're* is the contraction for they are.

All the campers returned to *their* cabins.
I keep my card collection *there* in those folders.
Because Lisa and Beth run daily, *they're* on the track team.

whose, who's *Whose* is the possessive form of who. *Who's* is a contraction for *who is* or *who has.*

Whose parents will drive us to the movies?
Who's going to the recycling center?

your, you're *Your* is the possessive form of you. *You're* is a contraction for *you are.*

What was *your* record in the fifty-yard dash?
You're one of the winners of the essay contest.

Using the Right Word **691**

Sentence Diagraming

A sentence diagram is a drawing that shows how the parts of a sentence are related to each other. Use these models as guides.

Subjects and Verbs

Diagram subjects and verbs as you see here. Capitalize words capitalized in the sentence. Do not use punctuation except for abbreviations.

Spring arrived.

Spring | arrived

Interrogative and Imperative Sentences

In an interrogative sentence, the subject often comes after the verb. In diagraming, place the subject before the verb.

Did Carlos win?

Carlos | Did win

In an imperative sentence, the subject is usually not stated but is understood to be *you.* In diagraming, place the understood subject *you* before the verb. Enclose *you* in parentheses.

Wait. (you) | Wait

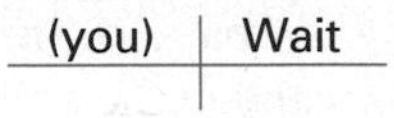

Stop! (you) | Stop

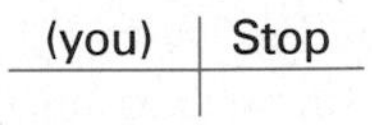

Direct and Indirect Objects

Write a direct object after a verb. Draw a short vertical line between them. Write an indirect object on the horizontal part of an angled line below the verb.

We sent him letters.

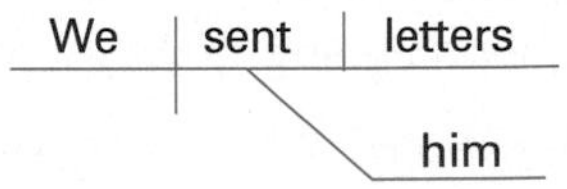

We | sent | letters

him

Predicate Words

Write predicate words—nouns, pronouns, or adjectives—after a slanted line following the verb.

Gary felt lonesome.

Gary | felt \ lonesome

692 Appendix

Modifiers

Write adjectives and adverbs on slanted lines below the words they modify.

The lanky pitcher threw wildly.

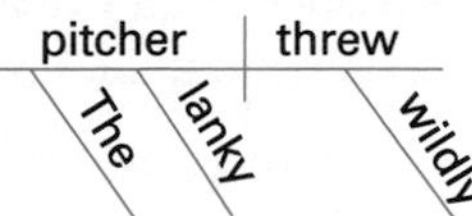

Sentences with Compound Parts

Split the line for the compound part. Draw a broken line for the conjunction.

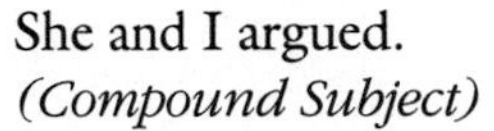

She and I argued.
(Compound Subject)

People clapped and cheered.
(Compound Verb)

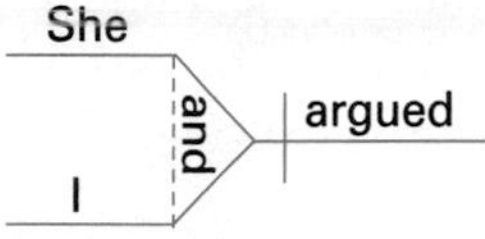

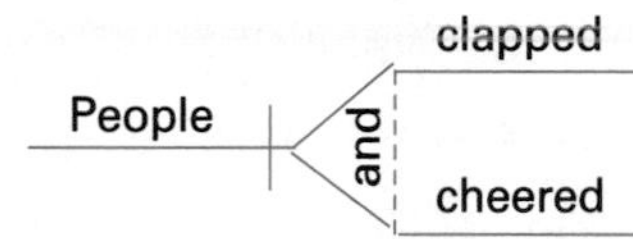

Prepositional Phrases

Draw an angled line below the word modified. Write the preposition on the slanted part and its object on the horizontal part. Put any modifiers on slanted lines below the object.

We heard footsteps
in the attic.

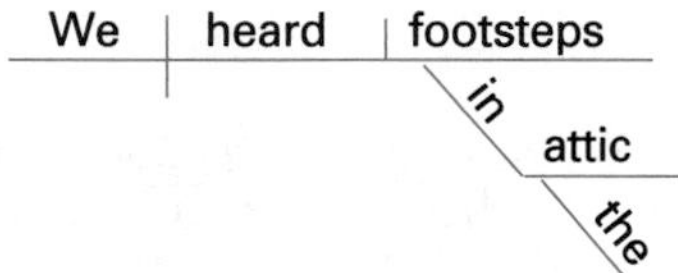

Infinitives and Infinitive Phrases

Draw an angled line. Write the word *to* on the slanted part and the verb on the horizontal part. Put the angled line on a bridge (⅄) at the place where the infinitive is used in the sentence.

To err is human.
(Infinitive used as subject)

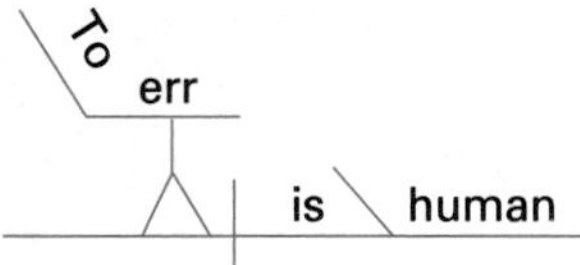

Sentence Diagraming 693

Participles and Participial Phrases

Write a participle on an angled line below the word it modifies. If a participle has a direct object, write the direct object after the participle and draw a vertical line between them. Put modifiers on slanted lines below the words they modify.

Opening the box,
he held his breath.

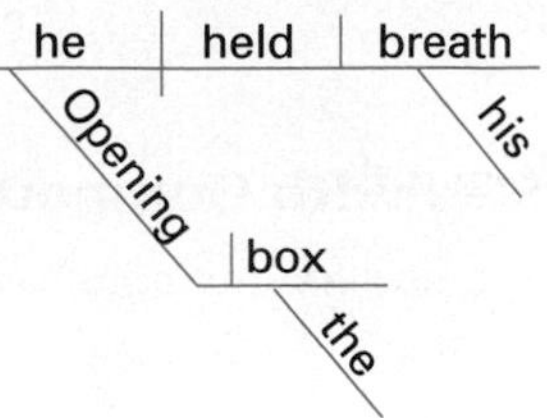

Gerunds and Gerund Phrases

Write a gerund on a step (⅂). Put the step on a bridge and place it where the gerund is used in the sentence. If a gerund has a direct object or modifiers, diagram them as shown.

Kitt enjoys riding a frisky pony.
(Gerund phrase used as direct object)

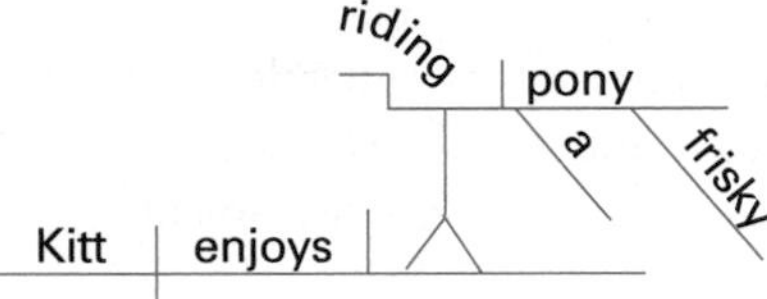

Compound Sentences

Show one simple sentence above another. Join them with a broken line and a step for the conjunction, as shown here.

The boys explored the cave, but they found no treasure.

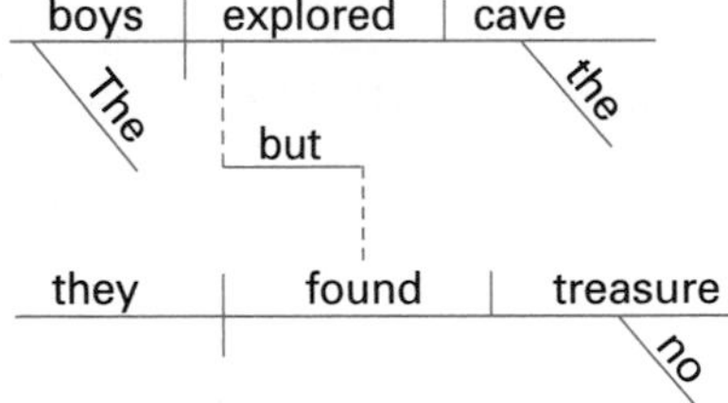

694 Appendix

Complex Sentences

To diagram a complex sentence, determine the function of the subordinate clause.

Diagram an **adjective clause** on a line drawn below the line for the main clause. Draw a broken line from the word that introduces the adjective clause to the word it modified in the main clause.

Kareem is the student who won the contest.

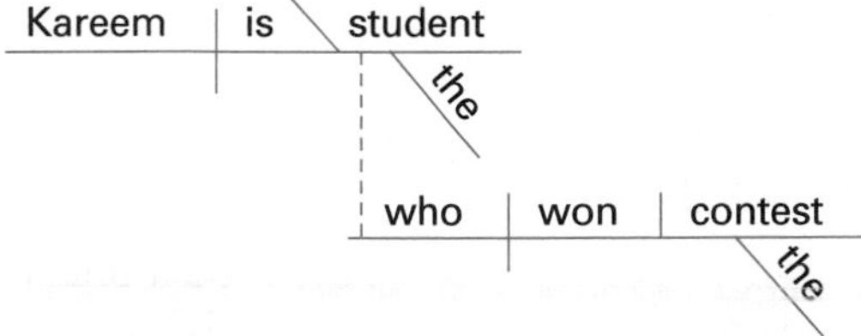

Diagram an **adverb clause** on a line below the line for the main clause. Write the subordinating conjunction on a broken line that connects the adverb clause to the word it modifies.

As we boarded the bus, we noticed a stranger.

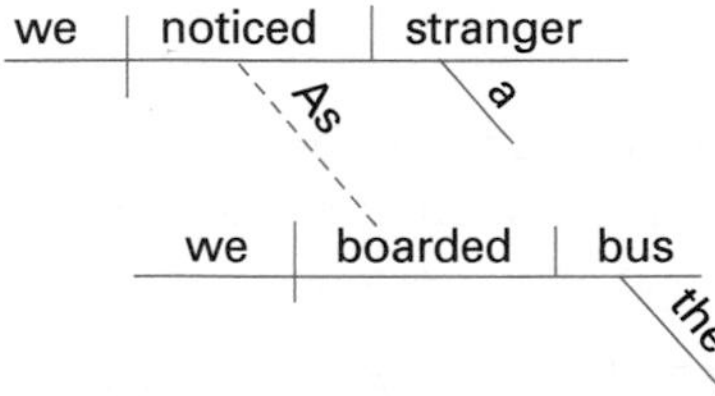

Diagram a **noun clause** on a bridge at the place where the clause is used in the sentence. Write the word that introduces the noun clause on a horizontal line above the clause.

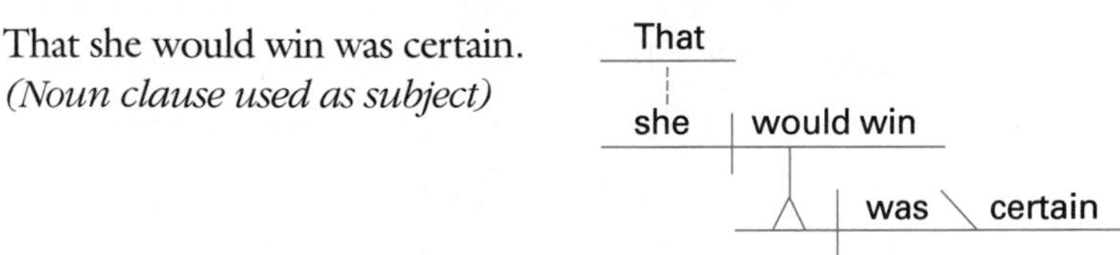
That she would win was certain.
(Noun clause used as subject)

Sentence Diagraming **695**

GLOSSARY FOR WRITERS

ADJECTIVE a word that modifies a noun or pronoun: *old* fence.

ADVERB a word that modifies a verb, an adjective, or another adverb; in "She sang well," *well* is an adverb modifying *sang*.

ARGUMENT speaking or writing that takes a position or states an opinion and gives evidence or reasons to support it; an argument often takes into account other points of view.

AUDIENCE your readers or listeners.

BRAINSTORMING a way of finding ideas that involves listing them without stopping to judge them.

CAUSE AND EFFECT a strategy for analyzing a subject that involves examining the reasons for actions or the results of specific actions.

CLASSIFICATION a way of organizing ideas by grouping them according to certain characteristics.

CLICHÉ an overused expression, such as "quiet as a mouse."

CLUSTER a kind of map made up of circled groupings of related details.

COHERENCE a paragraph has coherence when its sentences flow logically from one to the next; a composition has coherence when its paragraphs are connected logically.

COMPARISON AND CONTRAST a way of grouping ideas or things by showing their similarities and differences.

COMPLEX SENTENCE a sentence that contains one independent clause and one or more subordinate clauses.

CONJUNCTION a word or pair of words that connects other words or groups of words: Maya *and* Amy traveled.

CONNOTATION the ideas and feelings associated with a word as opposed to the dictionary definition of the word.

DENOTATION the dictionary definition of a word.

DIALECT a form of a language that has a distinctive pronunciation, vocabulary, and word order.

DIALOGUE spoken conversation; the conversation in novels, stories, plays, poems, or essays.

ELABORATION the support or development of a main idea with facts, statistics, sensory details, incidents, examples, or quotations.

FIGURATIVE LANGUAGE the imaginative and poetic use of words; writing that contains such figures of speech as similes, metaphors, and personifications.

FREEWRITING a way of exploring ideas, thoughts, or feelings that involves writing freely—without stopping or otherwise limiting the flow of ideas—for a specific length of time.

GRAPHIC DEVICE a visual presentation of details; graphic devices include charts, graphs, outlines, clusters, and idea trees.

IDEA TREE a graphic device in which main ideas are written on "branches" and details related to them are noted on "twigs."

INTERJECTION a word or phrase used to express strong feeling.

LEARNING LOG a kind of journal specifically for recording and reflecting on what you have learned and for noting problems and questions to which you want to find answers.

METAPHOR a figure of speech that makes a comparison without using the word *like* or *as;* "all the world's a stage" is a metaphor.

NONSEXIST LANGUAGE language that includes both men and women when making reference to a role or group that comprises people of both sexes; "A medic uses his or her skills to save lives" and "Medics use their skills to save lives" are two nonsexist ways of expressing the same idea.

NOUN a word that names a person, a place, a thing, or an idea.

PARAPHRASE a restatement in your own words that keeps the ideas, the tone, and the general length of an original passage.

PEER RESPONSE suggestions and comments on a piece of writing provided by peers, or classmates.

Glossary for Writers **697**

PLAGIARISM the dishonest act of presenting someone else's words or ideas as if they were your own.

POINT OF VIEW the angle from which a story is told, such as first-, third-, or second-person point of view.

PORTFOLIO a container (usually a folder) for notes on work in progress, drafts and revisions, finished pieces, and peer responses.

PREPOSITION a word that relates its object to some other word in the sentence; in "Marta moved to Detroit," *to* is a preposition.

PRONOUN a word that is used to replace a noun or another pronoun; in "She called him at home," *she* and *him* are pronouns.

SENSORY DETAILS words that express the way something looks, sounds, smells, tastes, or feels.

SIMILE a figure of speech that uses the word *like* or *as* to make a comparison; "trees like pencil strikes" is a simile.

SPATIAL ORDER organization in which details are arranged in the order that they appear in space, such as from left to right.

SUMMARY a brief restatement in your own words of the main idea of a passage; supporting details are not included in a summary.

THESIS STATEMENT a one-to-two-sentence statement of the main idea or purpose of a piece of writing.

TOPIC SENTENCE a sentence that expresses the main idea of a paragraph.

TRANSITION a connecting word or phrase that clarifies relationships between details, sentences, or paragraphs.

UNITY A paragraph has unity if all its sentences support the same main idea or purpose; a composition has unity if all its paragraphs support the overall goal.

VERB a word that expresses an action, a condition, or a state of being; in "Juan scored a touchdown," *scored* is a verb.

WRITING VOICE the personality of the writer that comes across in the writing through word choice and sentence structure.

698 Appendix

INDEX

Index 699

700 Index

D

Index 701

702 Index

Index 703

704 Index

Index **705**

706 Index

Index 707

Q

R

708 Index

S

Index 709

710 Index

Index 711

W

Y

712 Index

ACKNOWLEDGMENTS

Sources of Quoted Materials

22: Ashley K. Kuhlman and Northwestern University Center for Talent Development Summer Program: For "Dear Omoni" by Ashley Kuhlman; copyright © 1990 by Ashley Kuhlman. Reprinted by permission of the author. **26:** Liveright Publishing Corp.: For "to be nobody-but-yourself" by E. E. Cummings, from "A Poet's Advice to Students," from *A Miscellany* by E. E. Cummings, edited by George C. Firmage with the permission of Liveright Publishing Corporation; copyright 1955 by E. E. Cummings. Copyright © 1965 by Marion Morehouse Cummings. Copyright © 1958, 1965 by George James Firmage. **40:** Warner/Chappell Music, Inc.: For lyrics of "The Circle Game" by Joni Mitchell; copyright 1966 & 1974 Siquomb Publishing Corp. All rights reserved. Used by permission. **51:** The New York Times Company: For excerpts from "The Days of a Scavenger amid the Rubble" by Deborah Sontag, from *The New York Times*, September 1, 1992; copyright © 1992 by The New York Times Company. Reprinted by permission. **70:** Little, Brown & Company: For "Further Reflection on Parsley," from *Verses from 1929 On* by Ogden Nash; copyright 1942 by Ogden Nash. Reprinted by permission of Little, Brown & Company. For "Song to My Mother's Macaroni and Cheese" and "Song Against Broccoli," from *One Fell Soup* by Roy Blount, Jr.; copyright © 1976 by Roy Blount, Jr. By permission of Little, Brown & Company. **72:** T. D. Allen: For "Celebration" by Alonzo Lopez, from *The Whispering Wind*, Doubleday, 1972. Used by permission of the author. **73:** Farrar, Straus & Giroux, Inc.: For "The Drum," from *Spin a Soft Black Song* by Nikki Giovanni; copyright © 1971 by Nikki Giovanni. University Press of New England: For "The Base Stealer" by Robert Francis, from *The Orb Weaver;* copyright 1948 by Robert Francis. Wesleyan University Press by permission of University Press of New England. **84:** Tom Musca/Green Light Productions: For excerpts from the script *Stand and Deliver* by Tom Musca and Ramon Menendez; copyright © 1988 by Tom Musca and Ramon Menendez. **94:** Margaret Poynter: For excerpts from "Krakatoa, the Greatest of Them All" by Margaret Poynter, from *Cricket*, June 1985 issue. By permission of the author. **106:** HarperCollins Publishers: For edited text excerpts from *Mummies Made in Egypt* by Aliki; copyright © 1979 by Aliki Brandenberg. Reprinted by permission of HarperCollins Publishers. **111:** Macmillan Publishing Company: For six sniglets from *Sniglets* by Rich Hall and Friends; copyright © 1984 by Not the Network Company, Inc. Reprinted with the permission of Collier Books, an imprint of Macmillan Publishing Company. For two sniglets from *More Sniglets* by Rich Hall and Friends; copyright © 1985 by Not the Network Company, Inc. Reprinted with the permission of Collier Books, an imprint of Macmillan Publishing Company. **116:** The Time Inc. Magazine Company: For an excerpt from "A Land of Staggering Proportions" by Steve Petranek, Brad Darrach, and Ann Hollister, from *Life Magazine;* copyright © 1991, The Time Inc. Magazine Company. Reprinted with permission. **128:** Consumers Union: For "Why Is Everybody Eating Frozen Yogurt?" published in the August/September 1991 issue of *Zillions;* copyright © 1991 by Consumers Union of United States, Inc., Yonkers, NY 10703. Reprinted by permission from *Zillions*, August/September 1991. **138:** Scholastic, Inc.: For excerpts from "Privacy and Teens" by Lauren Tarshis, from *Update*, September 2l, 1990; copyright © 1990 by Scholastic, Inc. Used with permission. **164:** Pat MacEnulty: For an excerpt from "Dancing for Poppa" by Pat MacEnulty, from *American Way*, November 1991. By permission of the author. **178:** HarperCollins Publishers: For excerpts from "Why Monkeys Live in Trees," from *African Folk Tales* by Jessie Alford Nunn; copyright © 1969 by Jessie Alford Nunn. Reprinted by permission of HarperCollins Publishers. **206:** John Hawkins & Associates, Inc.: For "My Furthest-Back Person" by Alex Haley, published in *The New York Times Magazine*, July 16, 1972; copyright © 1972 by Alex Haley. Reprinted by permission of John Hawkins & Associates, Inc. **272:** Washington Journalism Review: For excerpts from "Take 2" by Carl Sessions Stepp, from *Washington Journalism Review*, issues 12/90, 4/91, 10/9l, and 10/90. Reprinted by permission of Washington Journalism Review. **345:** Deborah Hopkinson: For excerpts from "The Girls' Doll Festival" by Deborah Hopkinson, from *Cricket*, August 1992 issue. Reprinted by permission of the author. **593:** The New Yorker Magazine, Inc.: For "Mother Tongue" by Richard Armour, from *The New Yorker*, May 26, 1956, issue; copyright © 1956, 1974 The New Yorker Magazine, Inc. Reprinted by permission. **611:** Addison-Wesley Publishing Company: For excerpts from *Family Words* by Paul Dickson; copyright © 1988 by Paul Dickson. Reprinted with permission of Addison-Wesley Publishing Company.

The authors and editors have made every effort to trace the ownership of all copyrighted selections found in this book and to make full acknowledgment for their use.

Illustration & Photography Credits

Commissioned Illustrations: Ray Ameijide: **94-95;** Al Brandtner: **206-207;** Rondi Collette: **258;** Eddie Corkery: **164-167;** David Cunningham: **564;** Joe Fournier: **128-129, 233;** Roz Hosier: *graphics* **153;** Mary Jones: **26, 283, 417;** Tim Jonke: **138-139;** Linda Kelen: **220, 618;** Jared D. Lee: **3, 4, 7, 8, 314, 342;** Peg Magovern: **637;** Eric Masi: **92, 119** *l*, **320, 380, 504, 524, 638;** Beth Morrison: *graphics* **294;** Richard Murdock: **147, 324, 336** *t*, **338;** Steve Musgrave: **136,** *graphics* **637;** Lance Paladino: **72-73;** Kevin Pope: **67, 183, 111, 267, 367, 433, 593, 611;** Precision Graphics, Inc.: **45** *t* **;** Ruben Ramos: **40-41;** Jesse Reisch: **178-179;** John Rodgers: **211** *t* ; Richard Shanks: **36, 133** *t* , **142, 149** *t*, **504;** Troy Thomas: **331;** Russell Thurston: **28-29, 116-117;** Robert Voigts: **70, 84-85, 108, 228, 229, 230, 231, 272, 336** *b* **, 341, 349, 350, 351, 415, 416, 423, 483, 554, 594, 603, 614;** Amy Wasserman: **360;** Cheryl Winser (*handcoloring*): **45** b, **133, 292, 300, 381**.

Assignment Photography: John Morrison: **12-13, 22-23, 30-31, 52-53, 62** *t*, **74-75, 77, 81, 83, 96-97, 118-119, 140-141, 149** *b* , **152, 168-169, 188-189, 190-191, 192-193, 376, 418, 434;** Art Wise: **ii**.

Art and Photography: xxii: Photography © Jack Parsons; **13:** Ashley Kuhlman; **24:** From the Collection of Nancy Berliner and Zeng Xiaojun. Copyright Nancy Berliner; **28-29:** Family photographs courtesy of Dr. Leo F. Buscaglia, Ph.D.; **33:** © David Barnes; **39:** © David Barnes; **43:** © G. Kalt/Allstock; **44:** © Obremski/The Image Bank; **45:** UPI/Bettmann; **48:** Illustration from *The Mysteries of Harris Burdick* by Chris Van Allsburg. Copyright © 1985 by Chris Van Allsburg. Reprinted by permission of Houghton Mifflin Company. All rights reserved; **50-51:** © Porter Gifford/Gamma-Liaison; **55:** © Superstock; **58:** © Lawrence Migdale; **61:** © Lawrence Migdale; **62:** *b* Gerry Ellis/The Wildlife Collection; **62-63:** *border* © Gerry Ellis/The Wildlife Collection; **63:** © 1990 Boyd Norton; **65:** © Keiji Terakoshi/The Image Bank; **66:** *t* © John Terence Turner/FPG; *b After the Alaskan Oil Spill*, by Sigrid Holmwood, age 11. Courtesy The National Exhibition of Children's Art, London; **87-88:** © Mitzi Trumbo/Shooting Star; **89:** *t* © James Marsh; *b* © Martha Swope; **97:** ©

Acknowledgments **713**

Peter Miller/Photo Researchers, Inc.; **98:** © Bruce Davidson/Magnum Photos, Inc.; **102:** © David Robinson; **106-107:** Field Museum of Natural History, Chicago, Neg# A111057C; **107:** The Oriental Institute, Chicago; **110:** *t* Field Museum of Natural History, Chicago/Illustration by Carl Kock; *b* © Laurence Hughes/The Image Bank; **114:** © George Rodriguez/Shooting Star; **116-117:** United States Geological Survey, public domain; **117:** ESA/Science Photo Library/Photo Researchers, Inc.; **119:** *r* © Ron Kimball; **121:** © Bob Torrez/TSW; **122:** © Ron Kimball; **124:** © John Terence-Turner/FPG; **127:** Copyright William Wegman, Courtesy Pace/MacGill Gallery, New York; **131:** © 1990 G.A.S./PhotoBank, Inc.; **132:** Photograph from "Why is Everybody Eating Frozen Yogurt?" Copyright 1991 by Consumers Union of U.S., Inc., Yonkers, NY 10703-1057. Reprinted by permission from *Zillions*. August/September 1991; **133:***c* © 1992 The Andy Warhol Foundation for the Visual Arts, Inc.; *b* From the Collections of Henry Ford Museum and Greenfield Village; **149:** *b* Courtesy Thro Dough Studios, Toronto; **150-151:** © Jim Sloane; **152:** T-Shirt Courtesy Citizen Alert; **153:** © Jim Sloane; **159:** *t* © 1988 Middleton/Liittschwager; *c* Illustration by Guy Billout, reprinted with permission of A.C. Nielsen Company; *b* Courtesy The Mill Valley Film Festival; **162:** © Brian Seed/TSW; **170:** © Comstock; **172:** © Superstock; **177:** © Theo Westenberger; **181:** © Peter Kuper; **182:** *t* Photofest, New York; *b* Photography Courtesy Perls Galleries, NY; **186:** © Robert McCall; **188:** *t* Cahokia Mounds State Historic Site; *b* Courtesy Illinois Historic Preservation Agency/Photograph by Terry Farmer; **189:** Courtesy Cahokia Mounds State Historic Site; **193:** © T. Linke/Superstock; **194:** Courtesy National Park Service/ Photography courtesy Detroit Institute of Arts; **195:** Courtesy National Museum of the American Indian/Smithsonian Institution, NEG # 18/9306; **201:** Gilcrease Museum, Tulsa, OK; **203:** Gilcrease Museum, Tulsa, OK; **204:** Ohio State Historical Society; **209:** © Dan Krovatin; **210:** Design and Art: George Tscherny; **211:** *cl* Ralph Brunke; *cr* The "T" ball, manufactured in England and used extensively in America in the 1930s and 1940s is from the Archives of the National Soccer Hall of Fame, Oneonta, NY/ Photograph by Ed Clough; *b* © Alain Choisnet/The Image Bank; **214:** © Faith Ringgold, Collection of Marilyn Lanfear; **217:** The Carson Collection; **219:** The Art Institute of Chicago, Friends of American Art Collection, 1942.51; **223:** © Jill Freedman; **224:** Copyright William Wegman, Courtesy Pace/MacGill Gallery, New York; **227:** © Andrew Shachat; **236:** © Doron Ben-Ami/The Image Bank; **243:** © Chip Simons; **247:** Photography Courtesy United States Geological Survey; **248:** © Lupus; **251:** © Richard Kolar/Animals, Animals; **253:** The Hayden Collection, Courtesy Museum of Fine Arts, Boston; **254:** © Shooting Star; **261:** © Ormond Gigli/The Stock Market; **269:** Courtesy Cirque du Soleil/Photography © Al Seib; **271:** Curt Teich Postcard Archive, Lake County (IL) Museum; **278:** © 1989 Wendell Minor; **285:** © Clayton Fogle/Allstock; **289:** AP/Wide World Photos; **292:** Photograph Courtesy Myrt and John Deambrogio, Queensland, Australia; **294:** © Paul Natkin/ Photo Reserve Inc.; **295:** © 1983 Ron Scherl/The Bettmann Archive; **299:** © 1992 The Andy Warhol Foundation for the Visual Arts, Inc.; **300:** UPI/The Bettmann Archive; **302:** © Paul Natkin/Photo Reserve Inc.; **307:** © Kevin Horan; **311:** © William Caxton/ Archive Photos; **317:** © Chip Simons; **322:** BOUND & GAGGED comic strip series by Dana Summers. Reprinted by permission: Tribune Media Services; **328:** MOTHER GOOSE & GRIMM comic strip series by Mike Peters. Reprinted by permission: Tribune Media Services; **329:** © Erich Lessing/Art Resource, NY; **345:** From the Collection of Charlene Lopez/ Photography Courtesy Pat Smith; **346:** © Jon Conrad; **352:** "Discover the Americas" poster © 1991 American Library Association. Design: Belinoff & Bagley, Albuquerque, NM. Used by permission; **354:** Courtesy California State Library, California Section; **365:** Photograph Courtesy Michelin Tire Corporation; **366:** © Gilles Bussignac/ Gamma-Liaison; **372:** © Andrew Stawicki; **376:** Permanent Collection of the Mexican Fine Arts Center Museum, Chicago, 1992.165, Candelabro, Oscar Soteno, polychrome ceramic and wire, 1992, 19" x 17 3/4 x 7 1/2, Museum Purchase Fund; **381:** © Springer/Bettmann Film Archive; **385:** © Pat Crowe/Animals, Animals; **390:** Montana Historical Society, Helena; **393:** NASA; **395:** Illustration from *Just A Dream* by Chris Van Allsburg. Copyright © 1990 by Chris Van Allsburg. Reprinted by permission of Houghton Mifflin Company. All rights reserved; **399:** The Carson Collection; **402:** © Derek Berwin/The Image Bank; **418:** CLUE ® is a registered trademark of Waddingtons Games Ltd. Used with permission of Parker Brothers, the exclusive licensee; **424:** Photograph from *Trevor's Place: The Story Of The Boy Who Brings Hope To The Homeless* by Frank and Janet Ferrell with Edward Wakin. Copyright © 1985 Frank and Janet Ferrell. Afterword copyright © 1985 by Rebecca J. Laird. Reprinted by permission of HarperCollins Publishers; **435:** © Dilip Mehta/Contact Press Images; **437:** © Eric Hansen; **441:** © Superstock; **442:** © Mel Horst; **447:** The Far Side cartoon by Gary Larson is reprinted by permission of Chronicle Features, San Francisco, CA; **451:** Private Collection, oil on canvas, 26 x 40 inches. Fractional Gift to The Fine Arts Museums of San Francisco, CA; **455:** *t* © 1990 Rob Nelson/Black Star; *b* © David Madison/ Duomo; **458:** © Spencer Grant/ PhotoBank, Inc.; **461:** © Martha Cooper/ Peter Arnold, Inc.; **472:** © Bill Dekay/ Nawrocki Stock Photo, Inc.; **473:** © 1993 The Estate of Keith Haring/Courtesy Fotofolio, New York; **477:** © Ken Biggs/ TSW; **481-482:** American Red Cross; **486:** Photography Courtesy Yale University Art Gallery, Gift of Duncan Phillips, B.A. 1908; **488:** © William R. Sallaz/Duomo; **492:** © Geoffrey Moss; **495:** The Granger Collection, New York; **505:** © Mark W. Richards; **506:** *l* Giraudon/Art Resource, NY; *r* Vincent Van Gogh Foundation/Van Gogh Museum, Amsterdam; **507:** Art Resource, NY/Van Gogh Museum, Amsterdam; **509:** Collection, The Museum of Modern Art, New York. Oil on canvas, 29 x 36 1/4. Acquired through the Lillie P. Bliss Bequest; **514:** © John Running; **515:** Photograph © 1987 Jack Parsons; **519:** © Jane Burton/Bruce Coleman Limited; **528:** The Library of Congress; **534-535:** © John Margolies/Esto. All rights reserved; **536:** © Tom Sanders/Adventure Photo; **540:** © Spencer Grant/Photobank, Inc.; **545:** Photo by Alma Walters Compton, Denver Public Library, Western History Department; **555:** © Eric Meola/The Image Bank; **558:** © Jean-Claude Carton/Bruce Coleman, Inc.; **563:** © George Haling/Photo Researchers, Inc.; **569:** © Anne La Bastille; **576:** Courtesy of the Holly Solomon Gallery, New York; **577:** Collection of Dr. and Mrs. Paul Chapnick/Photography Courtesy of the New York State Museum; **578:** Photography by Geoff O'Connell, Courtesy of Ferrin Gallery, Northampton, MA; **583:** Curt Teich Post Card Archive, Lake County (IL) Museum; **585:** Still Courtesy of Warner Bros.; **595:** © Chip Simons; **596:** NASA; **602:** The Granger Collection, New York; **615:** © Darrell Gulin/Allstock; **625:** © Ken Marschall; **626:** © Steven E. Sutton/Duomo; **629:** © Shooting Star; **640:** Collection of the Museum of American Folk Art, New York, 1986.14.1; **645:** © William D. Adams/FPG; **649:** © Tom Sobolik/Black Star; **650:** Photofest, New York; **655:** © Uli Wiesmeier/Adventure Photo; **658:** © Jeff Foott/Tom Stack & Associates; **663:** © 1987 Jack Parsons; **667:** Poster Courtesy Triton Gallery, NY; **668:** © Richard A. Goldberg/Stockworks.

Cover
Ryan Roessler

714 Acknowledgments